www.ingramcontent.com/pod-product-compliance
Lightning Source LLC
Chambersburg PA
CBHW050400110426
42812CB00006BA/1759

סידור נוסח האר"י ז"ל

MEDITATION LIKE FIRE AND WATER

The Siddur (Shacharit) with Chasidut in English

Praying with Chasidic meditation

Compiled and translated, with a commentary

by

Rabbi David Sterne

Meditation like Fire and Water
The Siddur with Chasidut in English

ISBN 978-1-7321079-1-5

Copyrighted by the author, April 2010
Second edition: 2013
Third edition: 2017

POB 28186
Jerusalem, Israel
jerconn@netvision.net.il

This edition is dedicated to all the students, tourists and new immigrants to Israel whom we encounter and who pass through Jerusalem and its old city, and all those who wish to pray with meaning. May all of us find our true calling and successfully put it into action!

Sponsored in part by the Rothschild family
(Geoffrey and Sylvie and their children) of Melbourne,
Australia

Credits

Mrs. Uriela Sagiv for editing and general advice

R' Ami Meyers for reviewing and checking most of the text for accuracy

Rabbis Avidan Shenhav and Yakov Fauci for proofreading

Rabbi Moshe Kaplan for typesetting

Friends and family for their support

TABLE OF CONTENTS

FOREWORD

"Would that a man pray the whole day long!" — Talmud, Tractate Berachos 21a

"[The Divine Soul of a Beinoni (Intermediate/Regular person)] does not hold constant, undisputed sovereignty over the "small city" (his body), except at special times, such as during [prayer], [because then] is...an auspicious time for every man, for it is then that he binds his intellect upon G-d. It is the time to meditate deeply on the greatness of the blessed Ein Sof (Infinite One), and to arouse the burning love in his heart, (enabling him) to cleave to Him...At that time, the evil that is in his heart is subjected to and nullified in the goodness that is diffused in it from his mind, which is bound to the greatness of the blessed Ein Sof." — Tanya, Chapter 12

"[A Beinoni could have] day and night the passionate craving and longing of a soul yearning for G-d with overwhelming love, such as experienced during [prayer]...As indeed our Sages have said, "Would that a man pray the whole day long!" — Tanya, Chapter 13

"And I AM prayer." — King David, Psalms 109

Prayer is not an act. It is a state of being. The primary experience of prayer, when practiced according to Chabad Chassidic teachings, is not just speaking to G-d. It is a radical encounter with G-d; an intense exposure of the consciousness to G-d; an ascent from the separateness of a created human being to become enveloped into G-d. As spark into bonfire, the approach to prayer is a leap into His Infinite Light. And prayer, as such, remains immeasurably more than a limited activity done during a limited time of the day. It is rather a complete redefinition of self, an opening of the psyche allowing G-d to permeate one's whole being.

For one who has truly prayed, every subsequent moment of the day is lived on hallowed ground. Life is lived in the atmosphere of supernal, spiritual realms. The world and reality experienced transforms from an obstacle on the path to spirituality to become a way that G-d reveals Himself.

An anecdote is told about Rabbi Shlomo Chaim Kesselman, of blessed memory, the famed spiritual guide of the Yeshiva of Kefar Chabad, Israel. One of his students went to visit an aunt in Tel Aviv. Neglecting to keep track of time, he missed the last bus of the evening and had to spend the night at his aunt's house. Upon returning to yeshiva the following day, Reb Shlomo Chaim asked the student where he had slept the night before. The young man explained the situation to his teacher, who inexplicably remained silent. That Shabbat, during the farbrengen (Chassidic gathering), Reb Shlomo Chaim suddenly began scolding the young man. "How dare you go to a movie theater? How could a student of a Chabad yeshiva possibly allow himself to enter the cinema?"

The student was shocked. He had done no such thing, but didn't dare contradict his teacher publicly, even as he continued to berate him terribly. Finally, respite came in the form of a Chassidic melody that the participants began singing. The young man sheepishly approached Reb Shlomo Chaim and respectfully informed him of his mistake. He had not been in a cinema.

Whereupon Reb Shlomo Chaim looked at him, and with a perplexed look said, "Impossible! Of course you went to the cinema! *Du Davenst Duch Nisht!* (You don't pray) Someone that doesn't pray and is in Tel Aviv for the night... it's not possible that he didn't go the cinema!" The words penetrated the student, and from that day on he began praying...

What did Reb Shlomo Chaim mean? Why did he feel it impossible for someone that didn't "pray" to withstand the pull of the movie theater? And what does it mean that the student didn't "pray"? He was after all in a chassidic yeshiva, where all the students attended and participated in the prayer services thrice daily.

As explained in the passages from Tanya quoted above and throughout Chabad Chassidic literature, to truly pray is not just to recite words with the lips. That, of course, the young man did numerous times daily. More, it's not even to do so while having what is usually understood to be "kavanah," intensely concentrating on the words' meaning. Even the general awareness of standing before G-d, while crucial to the prayer act, is not yet what Chassidus teaches the essence of prayer to be. That is only the start.

As indeed conveyed by the very name of the movement, true Chassidic prayer is to firmly affix one's CHaBa"D (Chochma, Bina, Daas; Wisdom, Understanding, and Knowledge) on G-d, to bind the thoughts Above by focusing on and contemplating various aspects of G-d and His Emanations, His Unity with the world and specifically with the worshipper, and many other involved meditations, finally culminating in the deep sensation and awareness of the most profound of all truths, that all of existence is only Him. By attaching the mind to contemplate G-d for a long enough period of time, the Chassidic worshipper is to become completely captured by and eventually lose himself in G-dliness, oblivious to anything other than the Divinity with which he's become enamored.

Initially, before praying, the chassid studies and affixes in his mind (his ChaBa"D) very detailed accounts of the various ways G-d manifests Himself, progressing from His very Essence, until the lowest level of His Light that becomes nothing other than the world we perceive. Then during prayer he dives into these meditations. By closing off his awareness of anything around him and becoming conscious of nothing other than these profound truths, G-d becomes the only reality he's aware of. He reaches a state of intensely feeling only the truth of G-d's Unity, His being the only Existence that there is. His heart begins to beat to the rhythm of the Light that has dominated the mind, feeling that there is nothing to be drawn after with passion except for Him. His whole being has become enveloped in the magnificent grandeur of Divinity that has overcome all senses, that has become the single felt reality. When he then opens his eyes and looks at the world around him, the Chassidic worshipper retains that wondrous feeling, that exalted cognizance, that illuminated perception. Though looking at the world with his physical eyes, his mind's eye perceives only G-dly Light. And that becomes his state of being. He prays all day. He is prayer.

And hence, obviously, he's incapable of going into a movie theater.

This is what Chabad Chassidus is all about. All the hundreds of volumes from seven generations of the Chabad *Rebbeim* (leaders, teachers) maintain this endeavor as their focus: that the mind should become utterly permeated by G-dly ideas, until they overflow and overtake the heart, and through the heart, the rest of the body. It's no wonder that in Chabad yeshivot at least three hours a day are dedicated to the deep study of Chassidus. The ability to train the mind (see Tanya, end of chapter 42) to become so concentrated on G-d is the result of much study and practice. Months and years of serious learning are needed to adequately internalize the ideas conveyed in this vast area of Torah, the innermost essence of Torah.

For many if not most people, however, this is not an option. Lack of time is not the only obstacle. Even in our day when many Chassidic discourses and tracts have been translated, the possibility of culling from them a systematic repertoire of contemplations with which to pray is very faint, as one has to become very familiar with the style and lexicon of the texts in order to know "how to pray with them." And this is why the Jewish people have been truly blessed and enriched by this work of Rabbi David Sterne.

Many commentaries and books have been written about prayer. But for the first time, Rabbi Sterne has given the layman access to Chassidic meditations for each part of prayer, showing us what needs to be thought of at each step, allowing us to bind our thoughts to G-d as we say the words. This siddur guides us by the hand and shows the proper Chassidic meditations for each paragraph and stanza. This siddur has provided us with the ability to truly pray.

And, of course, to truly pray, to become prayer, is not just the antidote against all the many movie theater aspects of the world around us. Truly praying is living with Moshiach. For two thousand years we've been yearning for that time when G-d will remove all the concealments hiding Him, and "Your eyes will see your Master" (Isaiah 30:20). He will be completely revealed, and we will see Him in the world as tangibly as we now see physicality. We can begin that revelation even now by focusing our thoughts on Him throughout the day, the result of Chassidic prayer.

This is not just a preparation for the time of Moshiach. It is a taste of that time, and therefore indeed hastens its arrival. As Moshiach himself said, the spreading of Chassidic teachings will bring about that ultimate revelation. Let us therefore appreciate Rabbi Sterne's superb work, and hope that it will be the final measure necessary to allow Jews to truly pray and to truly see G-d, with the coming of our righteous Moshiach.

Rabbi Shmuel Braun
November, 2011
Jerusalem, Israel

Rosh Chodesh Shevat, 5772

To Whom it May Concern,

I have read several parts of Rabbi David Sterne's excellent rendition of the Siddur with Chassidic insights. I have found his translation and explanations to be both inspiring and thought provoking. One who is striving to achieve a more meaningful "davening," will certainly benefit from this unique *sefer*.

With blessings of *hatzlocho* in *avodas Hashem*,

Aryeh Citron
Miami, Florida

THE ART OF DAVENING

Not so long ago a famous returnee to Judaism boldly announced that, "Prayer is basically boring." His declaration did not seem to generate much controversy at the time.

When a Jew discovers Judaism, and takes on the responsibilities and obligations of the Torah, he often starts off starry-eyed and enthusiastic. But, as the reality of everyday religiosity sinks in, he realizes that Judaism places daily obligations upon him, and his initial enthusiasm gives way to stoic persistence. He continues to fulfill mitzvoth, because he believes that the Torah is from Above. And he continues to learn Torah as well, since he knows that it is necessary and important to learn at least some Torah every day. But prayer? That's just a daily duty to be discharged quickly in the morning, afternoon and night. Once we know how to put on the *talit* and *tefillin* in the morning, and utter the words that are in the *siddur*, prayer becomes something that we do by rote, without experiencing any meaning or spirituality. From there, it is but a short step to proclaim, "Prayer is basically boring."

Nothing could be further from the truth. There is an art to prayer (in Yiddish, *davening*). In fact, the sages referred to prayer as the true "profession" of a Jew (see Rashi, Ex 14:10). It is a craft and a skill, and Jews have honed and cultivated the art of prayer over many generations. The problem is, though, that we are an orphan generation. The colorful figures who could have taught us how to pray were cut down in the Holocaust, and since then, prayer has became a lost art. Seventy and eighty years ago, there was a "second room" in many synagogues, in which the old men and others who wanted to pray slowly would go and pull the *talit* over their eyes for hours on end. Yet now, we don't know how to make the connection on High that could turn our prayers into a meaningful experience. There are clues buried in the voluminous Chassidic literature of the last two hundred years, but who has the time and inclination to go through all of that material? The Chassidim of the turn of the nineteenth century as well as the generations preceding them would pray for hours on end, meditating upon Chassidic concepts, reaching the pinnacles of Jewish spirituality. But where are those people now? Most of us are happy just to make it through the day and fulfill our halachic obligations.

Throughout the Jewish world, there are wonderful people, who aside from making a living and raising a family, strive to fulfill mitzvoth and learn Torah. Their time is limited, but they fill every minute. Much to their credit, they raise wonderful, G-d fearing families, and manage to learn Torah and keep mitzvoth as well. However, they, like the new returnee above, report that their prayers are deficient – that their experience in shul lacks meaning and spirituality. In one sense, this should not be surprising. The sages (in *Pesikta Rabba* 22:12 as well as *Midrash Tehillim* 91:8) ask, "Why do the Jews call upon G-d and fail to receive answers? Because, when they call upon Him, they do not know how to focus properly on His name..." That is, we do not know how to direct our prayers properly in order to make them effective. And if that was true in the time of the Talmudic sages, it must necessarily be true now as well (since our collective level of spirituality has declined over the generations).

But, the truth is that there are enough clues and instructions left, in Chassidic literature and lore, to re-construct the nearly hidden art of davening. Within the discourses of the first Lubavitcher Rebbe (the "Alter Rebbe") and all of the subsequent Lubavitcher rebbeim, are found teachings and descriptions that set out the path of prayer and tell us how to embark on it. These discourses were written and recited over the past two hundred years or more, but since few people have the time and inclination to thoroughly research them, the clues to meditative prayer remain buried.

However, that is only part of the problem. The *mashpi'im*, or spiritual mentors of our day do not teach the art of prayer, and therefore we do not know how to put it into effect. That is the rationale for producing this compilation of Chassidic commentary on the siddur. Few people have the time to comb through the resources of Chassidic literature in order to reproduce the art of prayer. And even fewer have the background and knowledge to make it a useful activity. But, when we do the research, studying the literature of Chassidut (especially the Chassidut of the Rebbe Rashab), we reveal gems of Chassidic thought that provide clues. They enable us to attempt to reconstruct the nearly lost art of prayer. But, before we do so, it will be helpful to understand something about the nature of Chasidut in general, and Chabad Chasidut in particular…

When revolutions occur, they take time to percolate into our daily routines and permeate our consciousness. This is true of all revolutions – be they scientific, political, or (in our case) spiritual. It is well documented, for example, that when a new scientific paradigm is revealed, it takes time for the scientific community to accept it. This is true even when the new paradigm has demonstrably more power to explain, predict and verify empirical information.

The same is true of political revolutions. A political philosophy may change overnight, bringing in its wake a new set of rulers with a novel approach (i.e., democracy in place of dictatorship, or communism in place of elitist royalty). Nevertheless, it takes time to replace the former governors, rulers, and middle-level managers who previously ran the country, with those of the new political/economic outlook. The larger the country or economy, the longer the new political philosophy takes to implement.

If this is true regarding scientific and political revolutions, it is certainly true regarding the greatest and most essential revolutions of all – spiritual revolutions. Revolutions of the spirit – involving man's faith and belief-system – touch the very essence of man's soul. They are, therefore, the most comprehensive of all revolutions. Science affects our intellect, and politics affects the social fabric of our life. But, faith and spirituality affect the very essence of our being. Spiritual revolutions affect the totality of man, including how we think, how we act toward others, and how we relate to that which is beyond us – to God. For that reason, spiritual revolutions take the longest time to implement and to reach full expression.

The "mother" of all spiritual revolutions took place some thirty-four hundred years ago, when the Torah was given on Mt. Sinai. On that day, a wall fell – the wall that separated between the higher spiritual realms and the lower physical world in which we live. Until the giving of the Torah, man could yearn for spiritual fulfillment, but could do nothing to achieve it. Even our forefathers (Abraham, Isaac and Jacob) could do nothing more than bring spirituality temporarily to bear on the physical world. They kept the Torah even before it was given, but the spirituality which they brought to bear on the physical world only lasted as long as they were involved in the deed. As soon as they ceased doing the "mitzvah," the spirituality which it brought down to the world diffused and disappeared – like a nice fragrance that is here and then gone.

That all changed with the giving of the Torah. With that singular event, the wall separating higher spiritual realms from lower physical worlds was eliminated. Man could now approach the Creator. He could now cultivate and develop a relationship with Him. More importantly, he could now infuse the world with spiritual meaning. With the giving of the Torah, the wall separating the physical and spiritual worlds fell – a revolution took place that allowed spirituality to descend to the physical world, and man to ascend to the spiritual worlds above. The creation, which formerly stood in opposition to anything spiritual, now allowed spirituality to "enter" into its midst (though the world does not yet to "encourage" spirituality – which is the end-point of the revolution).

The inner dimensions of the Torah (Kaballistic and Chassidic literature) tell us that spiritual revolutions do not occur in isolation. In fact, spiritual revolutions spawn transformation in all other aspects of life. In this context, a prediction found in the Zohar is relevant. The Zohar (Section 1, 117A) says that "six hundred years into the sixth millennium, the gates of wisdom will open up above, as well as the gates of wisdom below..." The "sixth hundredth year of the sixth millennium" corresponds to the year 5500 on the Jewish calendar, or roughly the year 1740 on the common calendar. The Zohar predicts that at that time, there would occur a new revelation of spirituality, spawning revolutions in realms of secular knowledge as well. And we do find that roughly 270 years ago, the Chassidic movement swept through eastern Europe, wakening Jews to their spiritual heritage. Virtually simultaneously a new spirit of scientific inquiry, and of political awakening also began to sweep through Europe. It became more apparent at the end of the eighteenth century, during the scientific revolution and the French revolution, but the roots were already planted earlier. What is of note is that precisely as a message of spiritual unity began to permeate the world in the time of the Baal Shem Tov, a scientific and political awakening also occurred, confirming the prediction of the Zohar.

The spiritual revolution of the Chassidic movement, led by the Baal Shem Tov (R' Yisrael Baal Shem) revealed the deepest secrets of the Torah and how they could be used to further the connection between man and Creator. The Ba'al Shem Tov demonstrated that the essential foundation of the Jew – from the most educated rabbi to the ignorant peasant Jew – is a divine spark that is intrinsically connected with the One above. His revolutionary message was that "every Jew can connect with the One above." The spiritual impulse is not dependent upon intellect (learning Torah) alone nor upon action (fulfilling mitzvoth) alone but also upon the actualization of the inner infinite core of the person – the soul. The new movement took the form of an inner revolution, that drives every Jew to actualize the essence of the soul within and connect it with the One above.

This process of discovery, with its message that "every Jew may serve G-d" sounds obvious to us. However, it was by no means clear to the generation of the Ba'al Shem Tov. Just prior to his generation, historical events transpired that made it virtually impossible for the Jewish man on the street to acquire a Jewish education. Though he may have yearned for a Godly connection, the "Jew on the street" lacked the confidence and the means for actualizing his innate connection. But, with the advent of the Baal Shem Tov's Chasidic movement, the Jews were galvanized and rejuvenated. In a very short period of time, a full third of the Jews of eastern Europe considered themselves "Chasidim."

However, it fell to a student of a student of the Baal Shem Tov to explain to the Jews exactly how they could get involved. The Baal Shem Tov revealed that every Jew has an intrinsic soul connection, regardless of his social status or level of knowledge. But, it was the Alter Rebbe (R' Shneur Zalman of Liadi), founder of the Chabad Chasidic movement, who explained to the Jews how to make the connection. He concentrated the rules and principles of Jewish *avodat Hashem* ("service of the One above") into a single volume – called Tanya – that at once explained the physiology of the Jewish soul and answered all the practical questions that emerge as one strives to make his personal connection with God. As one of his colleagues, R' Zusia of Anipol said at the time, the Alter Rebbe succeeded in "putting a large God into a small book." Since then, Tanya has been the seminal work of Chabad chasidut and served as a handbook for other Chasidim as well.

This Ba'al Shem Tov's revolution of the spirit is discernible within the history of Chabad as well. The students of the Alter Rebbe were of the highest caliber. Not every Jew could approach the Alter Rebbe and bask in his presence, nor could every Talmud scholar partake of his teachings. Those who wished to do so were divided into "classes" according to their level of knowledge. The "inner circles" of the Alter Rebbe's students and protégés were proficient in all of Torah literature: Talmud, Midrash, Zohar and Kaballah. During the generation of the Alter Rebbe, the intellectual message of the Chassidic movement did not penetrate to the masses, even though the basic message of the Baal Shem Tov remained the same and spoke to every Jew. That is, "every Jew is intrinsically connected on High." Roughly one hundred years later, in 1897, the fifth Lubavitcher Rebbe, R' Shalom Dov Ber (known as the "Rebbe Rashab") founded the yeshiva of Chabad, known as *Tomchei T'mimim*. With the founding of the yeshiva, not only learned Jewish scholars, but also young men and single students in the teens and twenty's, could learn the Torah of the Baal Shem Tov, bask in the Rebbe's teachings, and apply Chassidut to their *avodat Hashem* (service in making the connection with the One above). Not only the learned and refined Chasid, but also those with a relatively "clean slate" (*tmimim*) could absorb the secrets of the Torah as expressed by the Rebbe. Now, even those who were observant, yet unschooled in Torah could throw themselves into the study of Talmud together with Chasidut and aspire to cleave to the One above. In other words, the new path of Chasidut, at first accessible to the select few among those who sought it, became the path of even the uneducated and the youth one hundred years later, during the generation of the Rebbe Rashab.

In this siddur with Chasidic excerpts, we have placed emphasis upon the Chasidut of the Rebbe Rashab. His Chasidic discourses are the most didactic and best suited for teaching purposes (they were often written and recited with the education of the students of *Tomchei Tmimim* in mind). Since we have placed so much emphasis on the chasidut of the Rebbe Rashab in this siddur (the included excerpts include translations of almost all that the Rebbe Rashab wrote about the process of meditative prayer during the years of his leadership, from 1883 to 1920), it is appropriate to understand his generation and the nature of the Chasidut that he brought into the world.

The Rebbe Rashab (born 1860) was the leader of the Chabad movement from the year 1883 until his passing in 1920. Among the movements that impinged upon Judaism during his reign were (*lehavdil*), communism and enlightenment. These two movements had a devastating effect upon the pious Jews of Russia, forcing them out of their homes, both spiritual and physical. In this historical context, the yeshiva, *Tomchei Tmimim* played a vital role. In a world of political and intellectual upheaval, the yeshiva served as a spiritual light and anchor of Russian Jewry. Many graduates of the yeshiva went on to play important roles in the remaining Jewish communities of Russia. Only a yeshiva that advanced the principles of the latest expression of the Torah revolution (based upon the insights of the Baal Shem Tov and involving the secrets of the Torah) could survive the turbulence induced by the Bolshevik revolution and the subsequent anti-Jewish decress that besieged Russian Jewry in its wake.

Simultaneously, the Rebbe Rashab held sway over the Chabad movement at a confluence in history that included some of the most fruitful ideas and culture in all of history. Not only was most of the long and nuanced literature of the Russian novelists (for example, Tolstoy, d. 1910 and Dostoevsky, d. 1881, *lehavdil*) penned during this period, but the Rashab was also the contemporary of Marx (died 1883), of Freud (1856-1939) and of Einstein (1879-1955). His leadership coincided with revolutions that took place in the scientific sphere (Einstein), in the political/economic sphere (Marx) and in the realm of psychology (Freud). Correspondingly, the Chasidut of the time (of the Rebbe Rashab) is long and nuanced, and appeals to the devoted and dedicated mind. Just as the Rambam in his generation provided the Torah (in his *Mishneh Torah* and *Moreh Nevuchim*) that enabled his generation to cope with the intellectual challenges of the time, so the Rashab's Chasidic discourses allowed the dedicated Jew of his generation to cope with the challenges of secular knowledge and dedicate himself to spiritual pursuit alone. That is precisely the nature of the thousands of discourses and letters that the Rebbe Rashab wrote.

Arguably, the Rebbe Rashab's most famous and important work was the series of Chasidic discourses of the year *5666*, or 1905-1906. The series is entitled, *Yom Tov shel Rosh Hashana*, or

"The high holiday of Rosh Hashana," (after the Mishna beginning with the same words in tractate Rosh Hashana of the Talmud). The climax of the series takes place when the Rashab, in an incredibly nuanced series of discourses, discusses levels of spirituality that transcend the *tzimtzum*, or "great contraction" that preceded the creation of the world. In this endeavor, the Rashab tread on spiritual "ground" that no man had ventured before. Kaballah explicitly refuses to discuss such high and ethereal levels.[1] And although previous Lubavitcher rebbeim mentioned the existence of such levels, they did not go into the detail and nuance in discussing them that we find in this series of discourses from the Rashab. In this respect, the Rebbe Rashab pioneered the exploration of new realms of spiritual reality, previously thought to be unfathomable. While lower levels of spirituality could be explained and discussed, it was thought that the Godliness preceding the *tzimtzum* was simply beyond the scope of man. The Rebbe Rashab demonstrated otherwise, in the process mapping out realms of spiritual unity and oneness never before explored by man.

In addition to the above-mentioned prediction of the Zohar, kaballistic lore also provides an interesting calculation regarding when the meshiach (Jewish messiah) is likely to arrive. The calculation is based upon the assumption that every thousand years of Jewish history corresponds to one "day." The seventh millenium, corresponding to the Sabbath (seventh day of the week) will herald the messianic age. This assumption is based upon the verse in Psalms (90:4), "For one thousand years is like yesterday in Your eyes..." However, the meshiach may also arrive earlier, prior to the advent of the seventh millennium. If that does

---

1. The *Emek Hamelech* of R' Yisrael Srug, discusses the *reshimu* which precedes the *tzimtzum*, but R' Chaim Vital says (regarding A"K, the first level after the *tzimtzum*) in the *Otzrot Chaim* (*Shaar ha'igulim drosh A"K*) and elsewhere, "We do not have permission to discuss such high levels..." If this is true regarding A"K, then it is certainly true regarding higher levels such as those preceding the *tzimtzum*.

occur, then he is most likely to arrive "on the hour" – that is, during whatever year corresponds to one of the twenty-four hours of that particular "day" (millennium). We can easily ascertain which years are auspicious for his arrival by dividing the millennium (1000 years) by the twenty-four hours of the day, yielding roughly one "hour" every forty-two years (one thousand divided by twenty-four gives us forty-two). There were three such years ("hours") during the previous century. The first of them occurred during the leadership of the Rebbe Rashab, in the year 1905-6 (5666 on the Jewish calendar). Although the meshiach did not arrive in any of those years, nevertheless major advances occurred in each of those years.

It is fascinating that at precisely the same time that the Rebbe Rashab produced his series of discourses, *Yom Tov shel Rosh Hashana 5666*, Einstein revealed his "special theory of relativity." Einstein's theory challenged the way we look at and understand the physical world. In fact, his theory disrupted conventional notions of time and space, forcing scientists to realize that both are the product of some higher, more united forces that exist in the universe. Einstein's theory transformed accepted notions of the physical world, and postulated that there exists far more unity among the basic physical forces of creation than previously suspected. The Rebbe Rashab did the same in the world of spirituality. His new set of Chasidic discourses totally disrupted previous notions of spirituality, and took the meditative thinker to realms far beyond his previous concepts. By describing Godliness beyond the *tzimtzum*, the Rebbe Rashab revealed concepts of spiritual unity never before revealed. The meshiach may not have arrived in the year 5666 (1906), but the new Chasidic series, *Yom Tov shel Rosh Hashana* certainly raised the level of Godliness in the world.

Einstein published his theory of special relativity on September 26, 1905 (26 of Ellul). The Rebbe Rashab recited the first discourse of his series (*Yom Tov shel Rosh Hashana*) on the second night of Rosh Hashana of that same year, or October 1, 1905 - a mere five days after the special theory of relativity was published. Both were obviously worked upon and developed for a significant period of time before they were published. This is a striking demonstration of the concurrence of spiritual and physical unity, as the "gates of wisdom" are opened, above and below. It is one more confirmation of the prediction of the Zohar, that spiritual revolution corresponds and points to revolution in the sciences and secular wisdom of the world.

The next auspicious date, during which the meshiach was likely to have arrived, was forty-two years later, in 1948. This, of course, was the year in which the state of Israel was established. It occurred during the leadership of the Rebbe Rashab's son, the "Fredike Rebbe," R' Yoseph Yitzhak Schneerson *ztz'l*, who led the Chabad movement from the passing of his father in 1920 until his own passing in 1950. These were desperate days, which included the Bolshevik revolution in Russia, the Holocaust in Europe, and finally the Fredike Rebbe's arrival in the United States in 1940. Yet, throughout these awful times, the Fredike Rebbe maintained his composure, self-confidence and an amazing ability to utterly disregard and disrespect any forces that are opposed to holiness. He did not emerge unscathed – in particular his imprisonment in Russia for the "heinous" crime of "spreading Judaism" left him permanently crippled. Yet, he never yielded in his defense of Jews and Judaism, and eventually emerged "on top," to lead a revival and rejuvenation of Torah Judaism in America. The meshiach did not arrive during his leadership either, but he is famous for saying that in 1948, we "received a piece of candy" in place of the meshiach. We may not have welcomed the meshiach during his leadership, but even with all of its faults and deficiencies, the state of Israel, established in 1948, has offered safe harbor and protection to millions of Jews.

The third and final "auspicious" year for the arrival of the meshiach occurred forty-two years after the establishment of Israel, in the year 1990. It was at this time that the long-standing restrictions on Jewish emigration from the former Soviet Union came to an end. Previously, Jews from Russia and her satellite Communist states were unable to lead Jewish lives in Russia without suffering discrimination and degradation at the hands of an anti semitic people, bureaucracy, and government. Simultaneously, they were prevented from leaving Russia for Israel or elsewhere. Indeed even the request to emigrate resulted in loss of job and status in Communist Russia. Only when the Communist regime finally imploded in 1990 were the Jews allowed full permission to emigrate – and that they did. Within a few years, a full million Jews left Russia – for Israel, for Europe and for the United States. Those who arrived in Israel provided an infusion of much needed talent and manpower, and they have since revitalized and rejuvenated Israeli society. So, although meshiach did not arrive during this auspicious year, it turned out to be a good year for a large segment of world Jewry.

Nevertheless, the average Jew of today is much further away from Judaism than the average Jew of one hundred years ago, during the leadership of the Rebbe Rashab. The lure of Communism, of general enlightenment and of various other philosophies proved to be too powerful for many Jews of the generation following the Rebbe Rashab, and they forsook Judaism in order to lead secular lives. Moreover, many such Jews found their way to America, with its "melting pot" which made it difficult to lead a Jewish life. Consequently, many Jews of our own generation received only a very weak education, if any, regarding anything Jewish. It is not necessary for these Jews to leave the Jewish world in order to enter the secular world – they are born into and feel comfortable in the secular world. The challenge of this generation's spiritual leaders is to reach these estranged but talented Jews and educate them about Jewish spirituality.

The "average" Jew of today is educated and inquisitive. He is intelligent, and unwilling to let anyone make up his mind for him. He is prepared to study and investigate, and arrive at his own conclusions. My daily work with *olim chadashim*, or new immigrants to Israel brings me into contact with Jews who have moved to Israel from all over the world for a combination of idealistic and pragmatic reasons. They are a self-selected group who are inquisitive about their heritage, but who lack familiarity with the Jewish sources. In this sense, they are no different than any other group of largely secular Jews. They differ only in their higher level of attachment to the land of Israel and overall commitment to Judaism. It is a great privilege to meet such people, and guide them to the sources that can quench their spiritual thirst.

The scholarly work of the Lubavitcher Rebbe, R' Menachem Mendel Schneerson (d. 1994) is uniquely suited to such people. The *sichot*, or study sessions involving Rashi on the Torah, for example, are tailored to the Jewish man on the street who, though as yet uneducated in Torah and mitzvoth, is inquisitive and intelligent. The *sichot* ask basic questions – the kind of questions that any thinking person would ask - on the Torah text. However, the Rebbe's explanations are at once both deep and incisive. They answer basic questions that arise from the text, and they also provide the kind of deep and profound outlook that the "Jew on the street" thirsts for.

Additionally, the spiritual journeys of many such Jews have lead them to seek meditative techniques to practice within Judaism. Having experienced meditation and contemplative spiritual practices in various settings throughout the world, they naturally seek such practices within the Judaism that they recognize as their own heritage. The Lubavitcher Rebbe (who was also the son-in-law of the Fredike Rebbe) recognized the need for such meditative techniques as far back as 1979. At the time, he instructed his Chassidim to address the needs of such people, who searched all over the world for spiritual fulfillment, and finally decided to look in their own "backyard," within Jewish spiritual texts. Significantly, nowhere do such techniques exist more explicitly than in the body of work known as Chabad Chasidut. It is for that reason that we translated and published the Rebbe Rashab's *Kuntres Ha'avoda* ("Love like Fire and Water – a tractate on Jewish Meditation") in 2005. Since it explains many different aspects and techniques of Jewish meditation, it was appropriate to make this guide available to the general public.

However, Jewish meditation is inseparable from prayer. The most important techniques of meditation outlined and described in the *Kuntres Ha'avoda* take place prior to and as preparation for the daily morning prayers (*shacharit*). That is why it is important to produce a prayer book (*siddur*) that describes the process of meditation during prayer, as well as before. This process, combining study and meditation with prayer, has always been a strong point of the Chabad movement. Although in recent years (following the second world war), there have been a dearth of Chasidim who are capable of practicing, let alone transmitting this technique (also known as *davenen b'arichut*, or "praying at length," with *hitbonenut*, or "meditation"), it is an integral component of the Chabad tradition. Our generation of Chassidim has shifted emphasis away from the "inner space" of meditative prayer in order to place more emphasis on basic education and involvement with unaffiliated secular Jews. However, in recent years, the process has come full circle – those very Jews are looking for what Chabad chasidut can best provide – a map of inner spiritual space to guide them the process of connection with the One above. That is what we strive to provide with this *siddur* with Chasidic excerpts and commentary. It is meant to teach and guide the process of meditative prayer.

In this manner, the "mother of all revolutions" continues to percolate down and permeate our consciousness. In its inception two hundred years ago, the Chasidut of the Alter Rebbe reached mostly the learned and refined Torah scholars. One hundred years ago, the Chasidut of the Rebbe Rashab reached also the fresh students and young single men of religious Jewish families. In our generation, through the Torah of the Rebbe (R' Menachem Mendel Schneerson), the message of the Baal Shem Tov reaches the secular Jewish man on the street, who is as yet ignorant in Jewish texts, but inquisitive.

This *siddur* is intended to be experiential, rather than formal and intellectual. There are already several *siddurim* available on the market that contain commentary explaining individual words or phrases of prayer. However, none of them purport to actually present and teach a technique of prayer. The purpose of this *siddur* is to guide and teach, while imparting the technique of meditative prayer embodied in Chabad Chasidut. With this siddur, we hope that the person praying will be able to experience both learning and integration of Chasidut into his prayers. Here, we present a technique, called *hitbonenut*, that both precedes and accompanies the process of prayer.

The "insights" appearing above and around the *nusach* are meant to guide us in the process of *hitbonenut* before and during prayer. They let us know "where we are" on the spiritual hierarchy – or at least where we ought to be - as we proceed up the ladder known as prayer. The "insights" are also intended to explain concepts and help us integrate them into our *tefila*.

The "excerpts" appearing underneath the translations (in shaded boxes) were chosen in order to give the English speaker a feel for what it is like to both study and to pray with Chasidut. Chabad Chasidic discourses are generally long tracts, which we pore over in order to prepare our mind and heart for prayers. It would have been possible to simply summarize these long tracts and present the public with the summaries, but then the experience of delving into them and praying with them in mind would be entirely missing. Our hope is that by providing these translated excerpts (from all of the Chabad rebbeim, with emphasis on the Rashab), we can deliver the same experience to the English speaking public as what a Hebrew speaking person experiences as he studies and prays with Chasidut. Of course, no translation does full justice to the original discourse in the "mother tongue," but nevertheless we hope that our translations provide enough of a "feel" for the material that the English speaking person will be able to gain the experience of Chasidut as he or she prays, using these excerpts. The excerpts are drawn from the Chasidut of all of the Lubavitch rebbeim, but especially from the Rebbe Rashab (we have researched the entire Chasidut of the Rashab, from *5643* (1883) to *5680* (1920) and extracted and translated all of the relevant excerpts). At the same time, they are the textual sources of much of the technique of *hitbonenut*, as explained in the "insights." Furthermore, they lay the groundwork for some scholarly investigation that takes place both within the "insights" and also the end-notes. Thus, the purpose of the siddur is to reproduce the experience of praying and meditating utilizing Chasidut. The idea is to not only look at and read the words of prayer, but to experience the process of prayer while delving into and studying Chasidut.

סִידּוּר עִם חֲסִידוּת
שַׁחֲרִית

Siddur with Chasidut
Shacharit

CHASSIDIC INSIGHTS

"We must fold (mark) the pages of the *Siddur*. We have to recite all the prayers, but we have to fold the pages of the *Siddur* [to identify the places where it is important to stop, ponder and absorb. In this, prayer is like a journey.] Once, the chassidim used to travel slowly -- fourth class on the train or even by foot; now the style is to go by plane..."

from *Sefer HaSichot 5706-5710* (1946-1950), p. 98 of the Rebbe Rayatz (Rabbi Yoseph Yitzhak Schneersohn *ztz'l*)

תְּפִלַּת הַשַּׁחַר

בִּרְכוֹת הַשַּׁחַר

מוֹדֶה אֲנִי לְפָנֶיךָ מֶלֶךְ חַי וְקַיָּם, שֶׁהֶחֱזַרְתָּ בִּי נִשְׁמָתִי בְּחֶמְלָה. רַבָּה אֱמוּנָתֶךָ:

סֵדֶר נְטִילַת יָדַיִם

בָּרוּךְ אַתָּה יְיָ אֱלֹהֵינוּ מֶלֶךְ הָעוֹלָם, אֲשֶׁר קִדְּשָׁנוּ בְּמִצְוֹתָיו, וְצִוָּנוּ עַל נְטִילַת יָדָיִם:

בָּרוּךְ אַתָּה יְיָ אֱלֹהֵינוּ מֶלֶךְ הָעוֹלָם, אֲשֶׁר יָצַר אֶת הָאָדָם בְּחָכְמָה, וּבָרָא בוֹ נְקָבִים נְקָבִים, חֲלוּלִים חֲלוּלִים, גָּלוּי וְיָדוּעַ לִפְנֵי כִסֵּא כְבוֹדֶךָ, שֶׁאִם יִפָּתֵחַ אֶחָד מֵהֶם, אוֹ אִם יִסָּתֵם אֶחָד מֵהֶם, אִי אֶפְשַׁר לְהִתְקַיֵּם אֲפִילוּ שָׁעָה אֶחָת. בָּרוּךְ אַתָּה יְיָ רוֹפֵא כָל בָּשָׂר וּמַפְלִיא לַעֲשׂוֹת:

To receive G-dly illumination, it is necessary to work through the blockages presented by the animal soul. This work begins before prayer and continues through the *Shema* – the quintessential declaration of the Oneness of G-d. Only then are we ready for the pinnacle – the silent *shemonah esreh* (*Amida*) – which is what prayer is really all about.

The structure of the prayer service is designed to take us from the lowest to the highest rungs of spirituality. As the sages of the Kabbalah expressed it in the *Zohar*: "The ladder – that is prayer." The famous ladder that Jacob saw while dreaming on the Temple Mount[1] symbolizes the spiritual ascent from the lowest physical realm to cleaving to G-d on the highest spiritual level. But, how do we do it? What is the technique?

The technique is actually embedded in the *nusach hatefilah* ("text of prayer"). The rabbis who arranged the daily prayers knew exactly where they were going spiritually when they formulated the words for us to say. And they placed the words in the prayer-book (called the *Siddur*, from the word *seder*, meaning "order") so that, by praying the correct words with the correct intention, we can also ascend the four rungs of the ladder of prayer, each rung symbolizing a different world.

While on this journey, it is a good idea to have a map. If we know where we are on the map, then we can better recognize what we see and hear, and we also know how to get to the next stage of our trip. The map of prayer and its correspondences looks like this:

CHASSIDIC EXCERPTS

"I am grateful to You..." – **Modeh Ani Lefanecha**[1]

We direct our *tefilla* ("prayer service") from below to Above, as is written (Genesis 28:12), "a ladder placed on the earth with its head reaching into the heavens..." Prayer begins on the lowest levels and reaches the highest possible peaks. For this reason ... we first recite *Modeh Ani lefanecha* (literally, "I acknowledge/give thanks before You"), as a general acknowledgment of G-d's existence.

This takes place on the lowest rung of our prayer service, because we recite *Modeh Ani* immediately upon awakening in the morning, when we are like new-born infants. Although this is only

CHASSIDIC INSIGHTS

Rung	First	Second	Third	Fourth
World	*Asiya* ("Action")	*Yetzira* ("Formation")	*Bria* ("Creation")	*Atzilut* ("Emanation")
Soul Level	*Nefesh* (action-consciousness)	*Ruach* (emotion-consciousness)	*Neshama* (intellect-consciousness)	*Chaya* (transcendence-consciousness)
Element	Mineral	Vegetable	Animal	Human
Fundament	Earth	Water	Fire	Wind
Stage of Prayer	From *Modeh Ani* to *Baruch SheAmar*	From *Baruch Sh'amar* to *Barchu*	From *Barchu* through the *Shema*	*Shemoneh Esreh* (aka *Amida*)

It is good to memorize this map as it will guide us on our journey.

The map helps us determine the places where it is important to slow down, savor our spiritual thoughts, and "mark the page" (meaning, recognize it as a place to linger and return to). One of the *mashpi'im* ("spiritual mentors") of Chabad-Lubavitch once compared prayer to taking a walk in the park. When we take a walk, we do not usually proceed at a constant pace. We pause as we find interesting flowers, plants and wildlife to observe. We spend more time gazing at certain flowers, less at others, and there are many things that we simply note but pass by. The same is true of prayer. The ideas and concepts that come to us, triggered by our learning of Chassidut and our recital of the words of prayer, induce us to spend more or less time at various stages of prayer. So, let us look at a few of the potential "stopping points."

Morning Blessings

J am grateful to You, alive and eternal King, for mercifully returning my soul within me, great is the faith that is due to You.

The Order of Ritual Washing of the Hands

B lessed are You, Lord our G-d, King of the universe, Who has sanctified us with His commandments, and commanded us regarding washing the hands.

After using the facilities and washing our hands ritually, we then say

Blessed are You, Lord our G-d, King of the universe, Who has formed man with wisdom, creating (him) with various openings and orifices, hollows and cavities. It is evident and apparent before the throne of Your glory, that if one of them is clogged, or another one is opened, then it is impossible to exist for even a moment. Blessed are You, G-d, Who heals all flesh and works wonders.

CHASSIDIC EXCERPTS

general acknowledgment,[2] it is *lefanecha* – "before You" – before G-d Himself. Included within it are all the levels of service. Consequently, our self-nullification (*bitul*) takes place from the very essence of our soul, including all of our soul-powers. This occurs only during general acknowledgement, when we are still unaware of how to differentiate between logic and acknowledgment. Therefore, we approach everything with acknowledgement alone. We are entirely permeated with *bitul* ("self-nullification), which infuses all of our soul-powers.

(From *Besha'ah Shehikdimu* 5672 (1912) of the Rebbe Rashab, volume 1, p. 619)

אֱלֹהַי, נְשָׁמָה שֶׁנָּתַתָּ בִּי טְהוֹרָה (בנוסח תהילת ה': הִיא), אַתָּה בְרָאתָהּ, אַתָּה

יְצַרְתָּהּ, אַתָּה נְפַחְתָּהּ בִּי, וְאַתָּה מְשַׁמְּרָהּ בְּקִרְבִּי, וְאַתָּה עָתִיד לִטְּלָהּ מִמֶּנִּי,

וּלְהַחֲזִירָהּ בִּי לֶעָתִיד לָבֹא. כָּל זְמַן שֶׁהַנְּשָׁמָה בְקִרְבִּי מוֹדֶה אֲנִי לְפָנֶיךָ יְיָ אֱלֹהַי

וֵאלֹהֵי אֲבוֹתַי, רִבּוֹן כָּל הַמַּעֲשִׂים, אֲדוֹן כָּל הַנְּשָׁמוֹת:

בָּרוּךְ אַתָּה יְיָ הַמַּחֲזִיר נְשָׁמוֹת לִפְגָרִים מֵתִים:

———⧓———

בָּרוּךְ אַתָּה יְיָ אֱלֹהֵינוּ מֶלֶךְ הָעוֹלָם, הַנּוֹתֵן לַשֶּׂכְוִי בִינָה לְהַבְחִין בֵּין יוֹם

וּבֵין לָיְלָה:

בָּרוּךְ אַתָּה יְיָ אֱלֹהֵינוּ מֶלֶךְ הָעוֹלָם, פּוֹקֵחַ עִוְרִים:

בָּרוּךְ אַתָּה יְיָ אֱלֹהֵינוּ מֶלֶךְ הָעוֹלָם, מַתִּיר אֲסוּרִים:

בָּרוּךְ אַתָּה יְיָ אֱלֹהֵינוּ מֶלֶךְ הָעוֹלָם, זוֹקֵף כְּפוּפִים:

בָּרוּךְ אַתָּה יְיָ אֱלֹהֵינוּ מֶלֶךְ הָעוֹלָם, מַלְבִּישׁ עֲרֻמִּים:

CHASSIDIC EXCERPTS

Two Levels of the soul

Within the soul, we find two facets. The first is the soul as a creation, as an entity that "exists." And the second dimension is the soul prior to its creation, when it is "pre-existent" (ayn). [These two facets] correspond to the statement, "…the soul that You placed within me is pure; You created it, You formed it, and You blew it into me."[3] The word "created" indicates emergence from nothing to something, teaching us that the soul is an entity that "exists" (yesh). The emergence of the soul is not comparable to the creation of other creatures, wherein the Creator and the created are two different entities. No creature is capable of creating, for the creature is not G-dliness (in truth there is nothing other than G-d, but in any case no creature is G-dly). But the soul - even the dimension that "exists" – is true G-dliness. And that is why even a ["low" soul] such as a soul from the worlds of BY"A (Bria, Yetzira, Asiya) may achieve very high spiritual levels. [Moreover], each and every Jew must say, "When will my deeds achieve the status of the deeds of Abraham, Yitzhak and Jacob…" and even of Moshe Rabeinu. [This is because the soul] is G-dliness.

Nevertheless, within G-dliness we find two levels, as known. There is the level of G-dliness that transcends the spiritual hierarchy of creation (seder hishtalshelut), and there is the level that acts within the hierarchy of creation. The difference is that the infinite light that transcends the hierarchy of creation is without limit, as if totally pre-existent

*M*y G-d, the soul that You placed within me is pure; You created it, You formed it, and You blew it into me. And You preserve it within me, and you will remove it from me in the future, returning it within me in the future. The entire duration that the soul is within my innards, I am grateful before You, My G-d and the G-d of my fathers, Master of all deeds, Lord of all souls.

Blessed be You, Who returns souls to lifeless bodies.

*B*lessed are You, Lord our G-d, King of the universe, Who has given the rooster understanding to discern between day and night.

Blessed are You, Lord our G-d, King of the universe, Who opens the eyes of the blind.

Blessed are You, Lord our G-d, King of the universe, Who releases the imprisoned.

Blessed are You, Lord our G-d, King of the universe, Who straightens the bent over.

Blessed are You, Lord our G-d, King of the universe, Who clothes the naked.

CHASSIDIC EXCERPTS

(*ayn*), for it does not exist whatsoever, even as light - to the extent that it is not subject to enclothment in the vessels of the ten *sephirot*. And [the light] that acts within the spiritual hierarchy of creation is limited and measured, and "exists" as light and illumination, to the extent that it is subject to enclothement within the vessels. As a result, "G-dliness" itself, meaning divine illumination – becomes expressed within limitations and boundaries, within created "existence."

And if so, this is especially true of souls, for they are expressions of G-dliness. Although they are truly G-dly, nevertheless they also express elements of creation and existence, to the extent that they become enclothed and grasped within a body and animal soul...

From *Sefer Maamorim 5672-5676* (1912-1016) of the Rebbe Rashab, page 137

The Supernal Rooster...

All creations below possess a spiritual source and counterpart above. For example, when a rooster crows [in the morning], we recite the blessing, "...He Who grants understanding to the rooster..." This is because the spiritual source of the rooster is the angel Gabriel above in the worlds of *yetzira* and *bria*. And his origin is with the *hey gevurot* ("five stringencies") of the world of *Atzilut*, which [are tasked with] arousing the *sephira* of *malchut* to ascend at midnight from the worlds of BY"A to *Atzilut*. And in the [lower] worlds of

CHASSIDIC INSIGHTS

The first stage of prayer – from *Modeh Ani* through *Hodu* until *Baruch She'amar* – is entirely devoted to acknowledgment of G-d. We see it in the very names of these prayers (*Modeh* and *Hodu* are both related to *hoda'a*, meaning ("acknowledgement"), and we see it in their contents. In fact, there are two kinds of acknowledgment. The first happens when we awaken in the morning and say, *Modeh Ani* – "I acknowledge." This we do even before arising from bed and even before washing our hands to rid ourselves of the impurity of death[2] that descended on our bodies while we were asleep. Obviously, it is impossible at this stage to have any real appreciation or feeling for G-dliness. And yet, we immediately acknowledge G-d's presence. This is what the sages call "general acknowledgment," or "acknowledgment of acknowledgment." That is, we don't even know the entirety of what we must acknowledge; we only know that we must acknowledge that G-d exists and that He brought our soul back into our body, and therefore, we "acknowledge that we must acknowledge."

בָּרוּךְ אַתָּה יְיָ אֱלֹהֵינוּ מֶלֶךְ הָעוֹלָם, הַנּוֹתֵן לַיָּעֵף כֹּחַ:

בָּרוּךְ אַתָּה יְיָ אֱלֹהֵינוּ מֶלֶךְ הָעוֹלָם, רוֹקַע הָאָרֶץ עַל הַמָּיִם:

בָּרוּךְ אַתָּה יְיָ אֱלֹהֵינוּ מֶלֶךְ הָעוֹלָם, הַמֵּכִין מִצְעֲדֵי גָבֶר:

The second level of acknowledgment occurs later, toward the end of the first stage of prayer. That is when we begin the series of verses with the words *Hodu laShem, kir'u bishmo* – "Acknowledge/praise G-d, call out His name." This acknowledgement is on a higher level as it has a specific target and direction. We actively acknowledge that there is a Higher Authority and to Him we direct our praises. We are not yet stirred by any emotions of love or fear of G-d, nor do we have any un-

בָּרוּךְ אַתָּה יְיָ אֱלֹהֵינוּ מֶלֶךְ הָעוֹלָם, שֶׁעָשָׂה לִי כָּל צָרְכִּי:

בָּרוּךְ אַתָּה יְיָ אֱלֹהֵינוּ מֶלֶךְ הָעוֹלָם, אוֹזֵר יִשְׂרָאֵל בִּגְבוּרָה:

בָּרוּךְ אַתָּה יְיָ אֱלֹהֵינוּ מֶלֶךְ הָעוֹלָם, עוֹטֵר יִשְׂרָאֵל בְּתִפְאָרָה:

CHASSIDIC EXCERPTS

bria and *yetzira*, the angel Gabriel arouses souls to ascend to *gan eden*, as in the saying of the sages, "at midnight, the Holy One takes delight…"

And down here in the physical world, the rooster arouses man to arise and serve G-d at midnight, as written, "At midnight I arise to acknowledge/thank You…"[4] And similarly, each and every creation below possesses a source and origin Above. When the source and origin illuminates the creature below, it is completely nullified, just as the supernal angels become completely nullified when the Holy One "extends His little finger among them," meaning that He provides a tiny bit more than the divine illumination that was allotted them from *malchut* of *Atzilut*.

**From *Sefer Maamorim* 5672
(in the *Sefer Maamorim* 5672-5676) of the Rebbe Rashab, page 46**

"Blessed are You, Lord…" (the morning blessings)
Among the blessings are some which are intended to illuminate darkness with the power of an essential (G-dly) light…such are the eighteen morning blessings which we say upon awakening from sleep. Now, it is known

CHASSIDIC INSIGHTS

derstanding of Him; we are still only acknowledging G-d's existence but with an informed acknowledgment this time, for we are actively aware of G-d and wish to accede to Him. The sages call this level "specific acknowledgment," since (unlike with "general acknowledgment") we know to Whom we are directing our prayers.[3]

Notice an apparent contradiction. During "general acknowledgment," we say *lefanecha* – "before You." Even though we don't know exactly Whom we are acknowledging, we say *lefanecha*, for we are addressing G-d in His very essence. On the second level of specific acknowledgment though, we theoretically have a target for our acknowledgment. Therefore, we say *Hodu laShem* – "to G-d." Even though specific acknowledgment is on a higher spiritual level, it is *not* an acknowledgment of the very essence of G-d, which cannot be defined or described. But upon waking in the morning – when we lack any awareness or appreciation of His presence – we find ourselves before Him, in His essence. That is because *only* when we lack a defined or limited concept of G-d can we find ourselves "before G-d" – confronting His very essence.[4]

Originally, the morning blessings were intended to be recited as we dress ourselves and prepare to go out to the synagogue. Each of these blessings begins with *Baruch Atah HaShem*, "Blessed are You, G-d..." and is directed to His very essence, even though we have only recently tumbled out of bed and haven't yet had our first cup of coffee.[5] So, how can we possibly direct ourselves to G-d?

Blessed are You, Lord our G-d, King of the universe, Who gives strength to the weary.

Blessed are You, Lord our G-d, King of the universe, Who stretches the land over the waters.

Blessed are You, Lord our G-d, King of the universe, Who guides the steps of man.

On Tisha b'Av and Yom Kippur the following blessing is omitted:

Blessed are You, Lord our G-d, King of the universe, Who has provided all of my needs.

Blessed are You, Lord our G-d, King of the universe, Who girds Israel with strength.

Blessed are You, Lord our G-d, King of the universe, Who crowns Israel with glory.

that night is the time of darkness or concealment. When we sleep, our inner powers of intellect and emotion – as well as our senses of seeing and hearing – depart from us, and a greater emphasis is placed on our connection with our body. During the day, when we are awake and light illuminates our soul, the body is subjugated to the soul and follows in its wake, and the revelation of our soul is predominant. This is especially true among those Jews who place emphasis upon *avodat HaShem* (i.e. prayer), and in whom shines the light of the soul as they pray and study Torah, while the physical substance of their body is hidden, suppressed and subjugated to their G-dly soul.

At night, though, the opposite is the case; the illumination and vitality of our soul is concealed, and our body becomes more evident. It is as if we experience no life in our soul, since sleep is considered one-sixtieth of death. At that time as well, physical substance dominates. It is expressed as the *ruach hatumah* ("spirit of impurity"), which is the aura of death and evil that attaches itself to us, as is known from the verse,[5] "...the life and the good and the death..." This verse equates holiness with the very essence of life and good. Now, the *sitra achra* (the

CHASSIDIC INSIGHTS

The same question was asked regarding the Jews as they left Egypt. Only moments before the exodus, they were still sunk in the "forty-nine gates of impurity," unable to wrest themselves free of their own accord, and yet seven weeks later they were standing in front of G-d to receive the Torah. It was only because the exodus was an event orchestrated by G-d — an act that was executed from Above to below — that it was successful. (Of course, everything is driven from Above. However, sometimes

בָּרוּךְ אַתָּה יְיָ אֱלֹהֵינוּ מֶלֶךְ הָעוֹלָם, שֶׁלֹּא עָשַׂנִי גּוֹי:

בָּרוּךְ אַתָּה יְיָ אֱלֹהֵינוּ מֶלֶךְ הָעוֹלָם, שֶׁלֹּא עָשַׂנִי עָבֶד:

בָּרוּךְ אַתָּה יְיָ אֱלֹהֵינוּ מֶלֶךְ הָעוֹלָם, שֶׁלֹּא עָשַׂנִי אִשָּׁה:

בָּרוּךְ אַתָּה יְיָ אֱלֹהֵינוּ מֶלֶךְ הָעוֹלָם, הַמַּעֲבִיר שֵׁנָה מֵעֵינָי וּתְנוּמָה מֵעַפְעַפָּי:

וִיהִי רָצוֹן מִלְּפָנֶיךָ יְיָ אֱלֹהֵינוּ וֵאלֹהֵי אֲבוֹתֵינוּ, שֶׁתַּרְגִּילֵנוּ בְּתוֹרָתֶךָ, וְתַדְבִּיקֵנוּ בְּמִצְוֹתֶיךָ, וְאַל תְּבִיאֵנוּ לֹא לִידֵי חֵטְא וְלֹא לִידֵי עֲבֵרָה וְעָוֹן וְלֹא לִידֵי נִסָּיוֹן וְלֹא לִידֵי בִזָּיוֹן, וְאַל יִשְׁלוֹט בָּנוּ יֵצֶר הָרָע, וְהַרְחִיקֵנוּ מֵאָדָם רָע, וּמֵחָבֵר רָע, וְדַבְּקֵנוּ בְּיֵצֶר טוֹב וּבְמַעֲשִׂים טוֹבִים, וְכוֹף אֶת יִצְרֵנוּ לְהִשְׁתַּעְבֶּד לָךְ, וּתְנֵנוּ הַיּוֹם וּבְכָל יוֹם לְחֵן וּלְחֶסֶד וּלְרַחֲמִים בְּעֵינֶיךָ וּבְעֵינֵי כָל רוֹאֵינוּ, וְתִגְמְלֵנוּ חֲסָדִים טוֹבִים.

בָּרוּךְ אַתָּה יְיָ הַגּוֹמֵל חֲסָדִים טוֹבִים לְעַמּוֹ יִשְׂרָאֵל:

יְהִי רָצוֹן מִלְּפָנֶיךָ יְיָ אֱלֹהַי וֵאלֹהֵי אֲבוֹתַי שֶׁתַּצִּילֵנִי הַיּוֹם וּבְכָל יוֹם מֵעַזֵּי פָנִים, וּמֵעַזּוּת פָּנִים, מֵאָדָם רָע, וּמֵחָבֵר רָע, וּמִשָּׁכֵן רָע, וּמִפֶּגַע רָע, מֵעַיִן הָרָע, מִלָּשׁוֹן הָרָע, מִמַּלְשִׁינוּת, מֵעֵדוּת שֶׁקֶר מִשִּׂנְאַת הַבְּרִיּוֹת, מֵעֲלִילָה, מִמִּיתָה מְשֻׁנָּה, מֵחֳלָיִם רָעִים, מִמִּקְרִים רָעִים, וּמִשָּׂטָן הַמַּשְׁחִית מִדִּין קָשֶׁה, וּמִבַּעַל דִּין קָשֶׁה, בֵּין שֶׁהוּא בֶן בְּרִית, וּבֵין שֶׁאֵינוֹ בֶן בְּרִית. וּמִדִּינָהּ שֶׁל גֵּיהִנֹּם:

"other side" - opposite of holiness) is the very essence of death and evil, as written elsewhere and soon explained. This refers to the spirit of impurity that dwells upon us, which is the evil and death of the *sitra achra*, which it is liable to cause us to transgress (G-d forbid). Although it is a product of our daytime thoughts - as the sages said regarding

the verse,[6] "And guard yourselves from every evil thing," advising us to be careful of what we think about during the day - nevertheless, it is especially active at night. This is due to the overwhelming dominance of the animal soul at night, when there is greater influence of the death and evil of the *sitra achra*.

Now, when we arise in the morning

CHASSIDIC INSIGHTS

the inspiration from Above triggers effort below, which is then responsible for earthly achievements. But in the case of the exodus from Egypt, there was no active participation from below. On the night of Passover the Jews were merely beneficiaries of G-dly largesse, passive players in an act that sprung them out of their limitations.)

A huge blast of G-dly light lifted the Jews out of Egypt, and something similar happens to us every

Blessed are You, Lord our G-d, King of the universe, Who has not made me a gentile.

Blessed are You, Lord our G-d, King of the universe, Who has not made me a servant.

Blessed are You, Lord our G-d, King of the universe, Who has not made me a woman.

Blessed are You, Lord our G-d, King of the universe, Who wipes away sleep from my eyes, and slumber from my eyelids.

And may it be Your will, Lord, our G-d and G-d of our fathers, to accustom us to Your Torah, and cause us to adhere to Your commandments. And do not bring us to sin, or to transgression or wrongdoing, nor to any test (of our resolve) or disgrace. And deflect the evil inclination from us and distance us from any evil man, as well as from any evil companion. Enable us to cling to the good inclination and to good deeds, and persuade our inclination to be subdued to You. And grant us today and every day, charm and kindness and mercy in Your eyes as well as the eyes of all who see us. And extend positive kindness to us. Blessed are You, Lord, Who grants positive kindnesses to His people, Israel.

And may it be Your will, Lord, our G-d and G-d of our fathers, to rescue us today, and every day from those who are insolent, as well as from insolence, from an evil person and from an evil companion, from a bad neighbor, or bad events, from the evil eye, and from evil speech, from evil reports, from false witness, from the hatred of others, from false accusations, from unnatural demise, from harsh disease, from misfortune, from a destructive opponent, from severe judgment, and from a persistent adversary, whether he is Jewish or not, and from the judgment of *gehinnom*.

CHASSIDIC EXCERPTS

from sleep, our mind and heart are still blunt and dull, and because of the condition of our soul, we are in a state of ultimate spiritual immaturity, like a newborn infant. How can we recite the morning blessings at such a time?

These blessings provide revelation – [contained in the words] of *Baruch Atah HaShem* ("Blessed are You, G-d") –

of the essential influx of the name of G-d [that we are forbidden to pronounce and we render as *HaShem*]. These blessings stimulate a descent of essential G-dliness, as mentioned previously. In truth, prior to all prayers, we say *Modeh Ani* ("I acknowledge"), indicating nothing more than acknowledgment of G-d's existence. But, immediately afterward

בּרכות התורה

בָּרוּךְ אַתָּה יְיָ אֱלֹהֵינוּ מֶלֶךְ הָעוֹלָם, אֲשֶׁר קִדְּשָׁנוּ בְּמִצְוֹתָיו, וְצִוָּנוּ עַל דִּבְרֵי תוֹרָה:

וְהַעֲרֶב נָא יְיָ אֱלֹהֵינוּ אֶת דִּבְרֵי תוֹרָתְךָ בְּפִינוּ, וּבְפִי כָל עַמְּךָ בֵּית יִשְׂרָאֵל. וְנִהְיֶה אֲנַחְנוּ וְצֶאֱצָאֵינוּ, וְצֶאֱצָאֵי כָל עַמְּךָ בֵּית יִשְׂרָאֵל, כֻּלָּנוּ יוֹדְעֵי שְׁמֶךָ וְלוֹמְדֵי תוֹרָתְךָ לִשְׁמָהּ. בָּרוּךְ אַתָּה יְיָ הַמְלַמֵּד תּוֹרָה לְעַמּוֹ יִשְׂרָאֵל:

בָּרוּךְ אַתָּה יְיָ אֱלֹהֵינוּ מֶלֶךְ הָעוֹלָם, אֲשֶׁר בָּחַר בָּנוּ מִכָּל הָעַמִּים, וְנָתַן לָנוּ אֶת תּוֹרָתוֹ. בָּרוּךְ אַתָּה יְיָ נוֹתֵן הַתּוֹרָה:

וַיְדַבֵּר יְיָ אֶל מֹשֶׁה לֵּאמֹר: דַּבֵּר אֶל אַהֲרֹן וְאֶל בָּנָיו לֵאמֹר, כֹּה תְבָרְכוּ אֶת בְּנֵי יִשְׂרָאֵל אָמוֹר לָהֶם:

יְבָרֶכְךָ יְיָ וְיִשְׁמְרֶךָ:

יָאֵר יְיָ, פָּנָיו אֵלֶיךָ, וִיחֻנֶּךָּ:

יִשָּׂא יְיָ, פָּנָיו אֵלֶיךָ, וְיָשֵׂם לְךָ שָׁלוֹם:

וְשָׂמוּ אֶת שְׁמִי עַל בְּנֵי יִשְׂרָאֵל וַאֲנִי אֲבָרְכֵם:

אֵלּוּ דְבָרִים שֶׁאֵין לָהֶם שִׁעוּר, הַפֵּאָה, וְהַבִּכּוּרִים, וְהָרֵאָיוֹן, וּגְמִילוּת חֲסָדִים, וְתַלְמוּד תּוֹרָה:

אֵלּוּ דְבָרִים שֶׁאָדָם אוֹכֵל פֵּרוֹתֵיהֶם בָּעוֹלָם הַזֶּה וְהַקֶּרֶן קַיֶּמֶת לָעוֹלָם הַבָּא, וְאֵלּוּ הֵן: כִּבּוּד אָב וָאֵם, וּגְמִילוּת חֲסָדִים, וְהַשְׁכָּמַת בֵּית הַמִּדְרָשׁ שַׁחֲרִית וְעַרְבִית, וְהַכְנָסַת אוֹרְחִים וּבִקּוּר חוֹלִים, וְהַכְנָסַת כַּלָּה, וּלְוָיַת הַמֵּת, וְעִיּוּן תְּפִלָּה, וַהֲבָאַת שָׁלוֹם שֶׁבֵּין אָדָם לַחֲבֵרוֹ, וּבֵין אִישׁ לְאִשְׁתּוֹ, וְתַלְמוּד תּוֹרָה כְּנֶגֶד כֻּלָּם:

---

we recite the morning blessings, which were established in a particular order. Upon hearing the call of the rooster, we bless "the One Who grants understanding to the rooster..." And upon opening our eyes, we bless, "the One Who opens the eyes of the blind..." etc. The reasoning behind this is that immediately upon rising from sleep – when we are at our most corporeal and when our soul is in a state of ultimate spiritual immaturity – precisely then a high illumination is necessary to give us the power and initiative to recognize the difference between light and darkness, between good and evil. And that is the reason for the blessings containing the words *Baruch Atah HaShem*, which bring down revelation of essential illumination in order to help us discern and recognize G-d. And the in-

Blessings of the Torah

Blessed are You, Lord our G-d, King of the universe, who has sanctified us with His commandments, and commanded us regarding the words of Torah.

Lord, our G-d, please make the words of Torah sweet in our mouths, as well as in the mouths of all your nation, the House of Israel, so that we and our descendents, as well as the descendents of all of your nation, the House of Israel, will all be knowledgeable about Your name and learn Your Torah for its own sake. Blessed are You, Lord, Who teaches Torah to His people, Israel.

Blessed are You, Lord our G-d, King of the universe, Who chose us from among all the nations and granted us His Torah. Blessed are You, Lord, Who gives the Torah.

And the Lord spoke to Moses, saying: Speak to Aaron and to his sons, saying, 'So shall you bless the children of Israel – say to them:

"May the Lord bless you and keep you.

May the Lord shine His countenance upon you, and give you grace.

May the Lord lift up His countenance to you, and grant you peace."

And they shall place my name on the children of Israel, whereupon I will bless them.

These are the laws which have no fixed measure: *peah* ("corners of the fields" – left for the poor), *bikurim* ("first fruits" – for the priests), *reayon* (pilgrimage offering brought during the three festivals), deeds of kindness, and Torah learning.

And these are the deeds from which man "eats interest" in this world, but whose "principal reward" is reserved for the world to come; and these are them: Honoring one's father and mother, doing acts of kindness, rising early to go to the house of study in the morning and evening, providing hospitality for guests, visiting the sick, facilitating marriage of the bride, accompanying the deceased, concentration during prayer, and establishing peace between man and his companion, between husband and wife - and study of Torah is equivalent to all of them.

CHASSIDIC EXCERPTS

tention behind this is that our physical body should also recognize its Creator and liberate itself from its own difficult physical condition...

Now, the power granted to us to recognize this – enabling us to achieve nullification of our physical status and thus to achieve thorough and essential nullification of our very essence – comes from the morning blessings. The sub-stantial benefit imparted by the morning blessings is that with their intense supernal G-dly illumination, they provide a great amount of physical ego-nullification ... as we know from the verse (in Genesis 32:1), "And Lavan arose early in the morning." This verse implies a high illumination, called *luvan haelyon* ("supernal abstraction") in the "morning" in order to awaken and

סדר לבישת טלית קטן

בָּרוּךְ אַתָּה יְיָ אֱלֹהֵינוּ מֶלֶךְ הָעוֹלָם, אֲשֶׁר קִדְּשָׁנוּ בְּמִצְוֹתָיו, וְצִוָּנוּ עַל מִצְוַת צִיצִית:

סדר לבישת טלית גדול

בָּרְכִי נַפְשִׁי אֶת יְיָ, יְיָ אֱלֹהַי גָּדַלְתָּ מְאֹד, הוֹד וְהָדָר לָבָשְׁתָּ: עֹטֶה אוֹר כַּשַּׂלְמָה, נוֹטֶה שָׁמַיִם כַּיְרִיעָה:

בָּרוּךְ אַתָּה יְיָ אֱלֹהֵינוּ מֶלֶךְ הָעוֹלָם, אֲשֶׁר קִדְּשָׁנוּ בְּמִצְוֹתָיו, וְצִוָּנוּ לְהִתְעַטֵּף בְּצִיצִית:

מַה יָּקָר חַסְדְּךָ אֱלֹהִים, וּבְנֵי אָדָם בְּצֵל כְּנָפֶיךָ יֶחֱסָיוּן: יִרְוְיֻן מִדֶּשֶׁן בֵּיתֶךָ וְנַחַל עֲדָנֶיךָ תַשְׁקֵם: כִּי עִמְּךָ מְקוֹר חַיִּים, בְּאוֹרְךָ נִרְאֶה אוֹר: מְשֹׁךְ חַסְדְּךָ לְיֹדְעֶיךָ וְצִדְקָתְךָ לְיִשְׁרֵי לֵב:

סדר הנחת תפילין

בָּרוּךְ אַתָּה יְיָ אֱלֹהֵינוּ מֶלֶךְ הָעוֹלָם, אֲשֶׁר קִדְּשָׁנוּ בְּמִצְוֹתָיו, וְצִוָּנוּ לְהָנִיחַ תְּפִלִּין:

בָּרוּךְ אַתָּה יְיָ אֱלֹהֵינוּ מֶלֶךְ הָעוֹלָם, אֲשֶׁר קִדְּשָׁנוּ בְּמִצְוֹתָיו, וְצִוָּנוּ עַל מִצְוַת תְּפִלִּין:

❧

הֲרֵינִי מְקַבֵּל עָלַי מִצְוַת עֲשֵׂה שֶׁל וְאָהַבְתָּ לְרֵעֲךָ כָּמוֹךָ:

מַה טֹּבוּ אֹהָלֶיךָ יַעֲקֹב, מִשְׁכְּנֹתֶיךָ, יִשְׂרָאֵל:

וַאֲנִי בְּרֹב חַסְדְּךָ אָבֹא בֵיתֶךָ אֶשְׁתַּחֲוֶה אֶל הֵיכַל קָדְשְׁךָ בְּיִרְאָתֶךָ:

וַאֲנִי תְפִלָּתִי לְךָ יְיָ עֵת רָצוֹן, אֱלֹהִים בְּרָב חַסְדֶּךָ, עֲנֵנִי בֶּאֱמֶת יִשְׁעֶךָ:

CHASSIDIC EXCERPTS

arouse the soul, as written elsewhere (regarding the "morning of Avraham" in Genesis 21:14, "Abraham arose early in the morning..." to fulfill G-d's command to offer up Isaac).

Although among the four *tikunim* ("rectifications/tools") of prayer – the bed, the table, the chair and the menorah[7] – the morning blessings represent the bed whose purpose is to clear away impurity [and not to provide revelation], (nonetheless) the bed has a supernal origin...All that descends as light and revelation in the soul and body

The Order of Putting on the Tallit Katan

Blessed are You, Lord our G-d, King of the universe, Who has sanctified us with His mitzvoth, and commanded us regarding *tzitzit*.

The Order of Putting on the Tallit Gadol

Bless the Lord, my soul; Lord my G-d, You are greatly aggrandized, You are garbed in majesty and glory. You envelop Yourself with light as a cloak, Incline the heavens like a curtain.

Blessed are You, Lord our G-d, King of the universe, Who has sanctified us with His mitzvoth, and commanded us to wrap (ourselves) in *tzitzit*.

How precious is Your kindness, G-d, men take refuge in the shadow of Your wings. They are satiated with the sweetness of Your house, and a stream of delight pours over them. For with You is the source of life, in Your illumination, we find light. Draw down Your kindness to those who know You, and Your righteousness upon the pure of heart.

The Order of Donning Tefillin

Blessed are You, Lord our G-d, King of the universe, Who has sanctified us with His mitzvoth, and commanded us to place *tefillin*.

In case of interruption between the tefillin of the hand and of the head, recite the followng blessing:
Blessed be You, Lord our G-d, King of the universe, Who has sanctified us with His mitzvoth, and commanded us regarding *tefillin*.

———✧❈❖❈✧———

Let it be known that I accept upon myself the positive commandment of, "And you shall love your neighbor as yourself."

How goodly are your tents, Jacob, and your dwelling places, Israel! And I, through Your magnanimous kindness, will enter Your House, (and) bow toward Your holy palace, in awe of You. As for me, may my prayer to You be at an auspicious time; G-d in Your abundant kindness, respond to me with Your true salvation.

CHASSIDIC EXCERPTS

throughout the entire order of prayer comes from the power of illumination and revelation (of the morning blessings).

The example that helps us grasp this concept comes from the story of the exodus from Egypt, where the Jews were extremely mired in physicality. It was necessary to remove them from darkness to light, and for this purpose there shone a very high revealed illumination from Above, as written,[8] "I (G-d) will pass through the land of Egypt," and as written,[9] "until the King, King of

אֲדוֹן עוֹלָם אֲשֶׁר מָלַךְ, בְּטֶרֶם כָּל יְצוּר נִבְרָא.

לְעֵת נַעֲשָׂה בְחֶפְצוֹ כֹּל, אֲזַי מֶלֶךְ שְׁמוֹ נִקְרָא.

וְאַחֲרֵי כִּכְלוֹת הַכֹּל. לְבַדּוֹ יִמְלוֹךְ נוֹרָא.

וְהוּא הָיָה וְהוּא הֹוֶה, וְהוּא יִהְיֶה בְּתִפְאָרָה.

וְהוּא אֶחָד וְאֵין שֵׁנִי, לְהַמְשִׁיל לוֹ לְהַחְבִּירָה.

בְּלִי רֵאשִׁית בְּלִי תַכְלִית, וְלוֹ הָעֹז וְהַמִּשְׂרָה.

וְהוּא אֵלִי וְחַי גֹּאֲלִי, וְצוּר חֶבְלִי בְּעֵת צָרָה.

וְהוּא נִסִּי וּמָנוֹס לִי, מְנָת כּוֹסִי בְּיוֹם אֶקְרָא.

בְּיָדוֹ אַפְקִיד רוּחִי, בְּעֵת אִישָׁן וְאָעִירָה.

וְעִם רוּחִי גְּוִיָּתִי, יְיָ לִי וְלֹא אִירָא:

Kings was revealed to them," and as it is written,[10] "With great fear…" The latter refers to revelation of the Divine Presence, the *Shechina* … All this was an introduction leading to the crossing of the Reed Sea, when the Jews walked through on the dry land surrounded by the sea.[11] When they received the Torah, in their physical bodies, G-d spoke with them face-to-face. Similarly, we find that the morning blessings provide an intense illumination and revelation that enables us, in our physical bodies, to recognize and discern between life and death. And it may also enable nullification of our physical nature.

In this manner, the morning blessings progress and continue. To begin with, we say "the One Who grants understanding to the rooster to discern between day and night," meaning between light and darkness, as mentioned previously…And afterward, we say the

blessing, "the One Who opens the eyes of the blind," in order to guarantee [spiritual, but also physical] vision. And then, we say the blessing, "He Who uplifts the bent over," in order to enable us to proceed with an upright posture, not bent over like an animal. This [bent-over posture], representing the *ruach habehema* – the "spirit of the animal" – corellates to physical objects. And, when we straighten out – (that is, separate from physical matters that repel us) – then we should bless "the One Who straightens those who are bent over," since thus we attain an upright posture in order to recognize G-d…

In order to experience revealed illumination from Above, during the morning blessings, we must first achieve a broken heart … This means that we must become "masters of accounting" of ourselves, so that we humble ourselves until we attain a truly broken heart… And

*M*aster of the Universe, Who reigned before formation was created,

When it was done, with His will, then His name as King was coronated.

And after all will cease to be, He alone will awesomely reign,

He was and He is, and He will gloriously be.

He is one and there is no other, without comparison and without peer

He is without beginning, nor with end; His is the strength and the dominion.

He is my G-d and my living Redeemer, Refuge in times of my trouble and distress.

He is my banner and my protection, my drink of salvation on my day of reckoning.

Into His hand I place my spirit, as I slumber and as I awaken.

With my spirit, my body as well, the Lord is mine, I will not fear.

CHASSIDIC EXCERPTS

immediately upon arising from sleep, we say *Modeh Ani*, while putting aside our egos. In this way, we experience revealed illumination internally, as we recite the morning blessings. Now, the influx brought down by the morning blessings is nonetheless unconscious, because all it does is give us the power [to discern between light and dark, good and evil], as mentioned previously, but the eighteen blessings [of the subsequent *Shemonah Esreh*, or *Amida* prayer] provide an influx that is conscious and revealed.

This is because ... we say *Baruch Ata HaShem* ("Blessed are You, G-d") in the *Amida*. And this constitutes a descent and revelation of the very essence of the name of G-d, *HaShem*, as explained elsewhere, and thus the *Shemonah Esreh* (*Amida*) provides a revealed influx into the lower worlds.

(From *Besha'ah Shehikdimu 5672* (1912) of the Rebbe Rashab, vol. 2, pp. 737-8)

"Master of the Universe..." (Adon olam...)

The name of the King that is associated with the worlds *BY"A* [the lower worlds of *Bria*, *Yetzira* and *Asiya*]... is out of range of the very essence of the King, Who is called a King in his own right, in His very essence. On His own, [He is] exalted and removed [from the nation] ...

About this [exalted level], it says *Adon olam asher malach, beterem kol yetzur nivrah* ("Master of the Universe, who reigned before formation was created"). [This line] indicates that [He reigned] even before [it occurred to Him] to become a King over our nation. And when the arousal [to reign] did occur within His will, the creation took place immediately, since His will Above is dissimilar to our will below, as is known. Here in the lower worlds, nothing is created as a

עקדה

אֱלֹהֵינוּ וֵאלֹהֵי אֲבוֹתֵינוּ, זָכְרֵנוּ בְּזִכָּרוֹן טוֹב לְפָנֶיךָ, וּפָקְדֵנוּ בִּפְקֻדַּת יְשׁוּעָה וְרַחֲמִים מִשְּׁמֵי שְׁמֵי קֶדֶם, וּזְכָר לָנוּ יְיָ אֱלֹהֵינוּ אַהֲבַת הַקַּדְמוֹנִים אַבְרָהָם יִצְחָק וְיִשְׂרָאֵל עֲבָדֶיךָ, אֶת הַבְּרִית וְאֶת הַחֶסֶד וְאֶת הַשְּׁבוּעָה שֶׁנִּשְׁבַּעְתָּ לְאַבְרָהָם אָבִינוּ בְּהַר הַמּוֹרִיָּה, וְאֶת הָעֲקֵדָה שֶׁעָקַד אֶת יִצְחָק בְּנוֹ עַל גַּבֵּי הַמִּזְבֵּחַ, כַּכָּתוּב בְּתוֹרָתֶךָ:

וַיְהִי אַחַר הַדְּבָרִים הָאֵלֶּה, וְהָאֱלֹהִים נִסָּה אֶת אַבְרָהָם וַיֹּאמֶר אֵלָיו, אַבְרָהָם, וַיֹּאמֶר הִנֵּנִי: וַיֹּאמֶר קַח נָא אֶת בִּנְךָ אֶת יְחִידְךָ אֲשֶׁר אָהַבְתָּ אֶת יִצְחָק, וְלֶךְ לְךָ אֶל אֶרֶץ הַמּוֹרִיָּה, וְהַעֲלֵהוּ שָׁם לְעֹלָה עַל אַחַד הֶהָרִים, אֲשֶׁר אֹמַר אֵלֶיךָ: וַיַּשְׁכֵּם אַבְרָהָם בַּבֹּקֶר, וַיַּחֲבֹשׁ אֶת חֲמֹרוֹ, וַיִּקַּח אֶת שְׁנֵי נְעָרָיו אִתּוֹ וְאֵת יִצְחָק בְּנוֹ, וַיְבַקַּע עֲצֵי עֹלָה וַיָּקָם וַיֵּלֶךְ אֶל הַמָּקוֹם אֲשֶׁר אָמַר לוֹ הָאֱלֹהִים: בַּיּוֹם הַשְּׁלִישִׁי וַיִּשָּׂא אַבְרָהָם אֶת עֵינָיו וַיַּרְא אֶת הַמָּקוֹם מֵרָחֹק: וַיֹּאמֶר אַבְרָהָם אֶל נְעָרָיו שְׁבוּ לָכֶם פֹּה עִם הַחֲמוֹר, וַאֲנִי וְהַנַּעַר נֵלְכָה עַד כֹּה, וְנִשְׁתַּחֲוֶה וְנָשׁוּבָה אֲלֵיכֶם: וַיִּקַּח אַבְרָהָם אֶת עֲצֵי הָעֹלָה וַיָּשֶׂם עַל יִצְחָק בְּנוֹ וַיִּקַּח בְּיָדוֹ אֶת הָאֵשׁ וְאֶת הַמַּאֲכֶלֶת, וַיֵּלְכוּ שְׁנֵיהֶם יַחְדָּו: וַיֹּאמֶר יִצְחָק אֶל אַבְרָהָם אָבִיו וַיֹּאמֶר אָבִי, וַיֹּאמֶר, הִנֶּנִּי בְנִי, וַיֹּאמֶר, הִנֵּה הָאֵשׁ וְהָעֵצִים וְאַיֵּה הַשֶּׂה לְעֹלָה: וַיֹּאמֶר אַבְרָהָם אֱלֹהִים יִרְאֶה לּוֹ הַשֶּׂה לְעֹלָה בְּנִי, וַיֵּלְכוּ שְׁנֵיהֶם יַחְדָּו: וַיָּבֹאוּ אֶל הַמָּקוֹם אֲשֶׁר אָמַר לוֹ הָאֱלֹהִים, וַיִּבֶן שָׁם אַבְרָהָם אֶת הַמִּזְבֵּחַ, וַיַּעֲרֹךְ אֶת הָעֵצִים, וַיַּעֲקֹד אֶת יִצְחָק בְּנוֹ, וַיָּשֶׂם אֹתוֹ עַל הַמִּזְבֵּחַ מִמַּעַל לָעֵצִים: וַיִּשְׁלַח אַבְרָהָם אֶת יָדוֹ וַיִּקַּח אֶת הַמַּאֲכֶלֶת, לִשְׁחֹט אֶת בְּנוֹ: וַיִּקְרָא אֵלָיו מַלְאַךְ יְיָ מִן הַשָּׁמַיִם וַיֹּאמֶר, אַבְרָהָם, אַבְרָהָם, וַיֹּאמֶר, הִנֵּנִי: וַיֹּאמֶר, אַל תִּשְׁלַח יָדְךָ אֶל הַנַּעַר, וְאַל תַּעַשׂ לוֹ מְאוּמָה, כִּי עַתָּה יָדַעְתִּי, כִּי יְרֵא אֱלֹהִים אַתָּה, וְלֹא חָשַׂכְתָּ אֶת בִּנְךָ

CHASSIDIC EXCERPTS

result of our will, while Above, as soon as it arose within His will, the creation took place immediately. And if so, the statement, "who reigned before formation was created," [indicates a level, so to speak] that arose in His will prior to the decision to become a king over our nation. And the concept of "who reigned" alludes to His state of exalted loftiness and majesty on His own, within Himself.

And the stanza that follows, *le'eit na'aseh becheftzo kol azai melech shmo nikrah* ("when it took place, with His will, then His name as King was coronated") refers to the condition in which He was already called "King" over the nation, since from this [level]

Akeidat Yitzhak

On Shabbat and Festivals, the following paragraph is omitted:
Our G-d and G-d of our fathers, remember us favorably before You, and bring down salvation and mercy upon us from the primordial supernal heavens. And recall on our behalf, Lord our G-d, Your love for our predecessors Avraham, Yitzhak and Yisrael Your servants, and the covenant, the kindness and the oath that You swore to Avraham our forefather on Mt. Moriah, and the binding with which he tied Yitzhak his son on the altar, as written in Your Torah.

And it happened after these events, that G-d tested Abraham, and said to him, "Abraham," and he answered, "I am here." And He said, "Take your son, your only beloved son, Isaac, and go to the land of Moriah, and elevate him there as an offering on one of the mountains, that I will tell you." And Abraham arose early in the morning, saddled his donkey, and took two young lads with him, as well as his son Isaac, and split wood for burning. And he arose and traveled to the place that G-d said to him. On the third day, Abraham raised his eyes, and saw the place from afar. And Abraham said to the young lads, "Remain here with the donkey, and I and the lad will go over there and bow down and return to you." And Abraham took the wood for the offering, and placed it upon Isaac his son, and carried the fire and the knife, and both of them journeyed together. And Isaac spoke to his father, saying, "Father," and he answered him, "Here I am, my son," and he said, "Here is the fire and the wood, and where is the sheep to offer?" And Abraham said, "G-d will show him the sheep to offer, my son," and both of them walked together. And they came to the place that G-d said to him, and there Abraham built the altar, and arranged the wood upon it, and bound his son Isaac, placing him on the altar on top of the wood. And Abraham extended his hand to take the knife in order to ritually slaughter his son. And an angel called out to him from the heavens, saying, "Abraham, Abraham," and he said, "I am here." And he said, "Do not lay your hand upon the lad, and do nothing to him, for now I know that you fear G-d, [so much so] that you would not withhold your son, your only son, from Me." And

CHASSIDIC EXCERPTS

the worlds were created and His Name applies to them, from beyond, transcendent.

The third stanza, *Ve'acharei kichlos hakol levado yimloch norah* ("And after all will cease to be, He alone will awesomely reign") refers to the G-dly revelation of the world to come, which will be filled with illumination of the very essence of His infinite light, as He exists exalted on his own (and the worlds will not "exist" at that time as separate, independent entities. Rather, they will be [so permeated with G-dliness that they will be perceived as] an expression of G-d, as written elsewhere...)[12]

(From *Samech TeSamech* 5657 (1897) of the Rebbe Rashab, p. 11)

אֶת יְחִידְךָ מִמֶּנִּי: וַיִּשָּׂא אַבְרָהָם אֶת עֵינָיו וַיַּרְא וְהִנֵּה אַיִל, אַחַר, נֶאֱחַז בַּסְּבַךְ בְּקַרְנָיו,

וַיֵּלֶךְ אַבְרָהָם וַיִּקַּח אֶת הָאַיִל, וַיַּעֲלֵהוּ לְעֹלָה תַּחַת בְּנוֹ: וַיִּקְרָא אַבְרָהָם שֵׁם הַמָּקוֹם

הַהוּא, יְיָ יִרְאֶה, אֲשֶׁר יֵאָמֵר הַיּוֹם, בְּהַר יְיָ יֵרָאֶה: וַיִּקְרָא מַלְאַךְ יְיָ אֶל אַבְרָהָם שֵׁנִית מִן

הַשָּׁמָיִם: וַיֹּאמֶר, בִּי נִשְׁבַּעְתִּי נְאֻם יְיָ, כִּי יַעַן אֲשֶׁר עָשִׂיתָ אֶת הַדָּבָר הַזֶּה, וְלֹא חָשַׂכְתָּ

אֶת בִּנְךָ אֶת יְחִידֶךָ: כִּי בָרֵךְ אֲבָרֶכְךָ, וְהַרְבָּה אַרְבֶּה אֶת זַרְעֲךָ כְּכוֹכְבֵי הַשָּׁמַיִם וְכַחוֹל

אֲשֶׁר עַל שְׂפַת הַיָּם, וְיִרַשׁ זַרְעֲךָ אֵת שַׁעַר אֹיְבָיו: וְהִתְבָּרְכוּ בְזַרְעֲךָ כֹּל גּוֹיֵי הָאָרֶץ, עֵקֶב

אֲשֶׁר שָׁמַעְתָּ בְּקֹלִי: וַיָּשָׁב אַבְרָהָם אֶל נְעָרָיו, וַיָּקֻמוּ וַיֵּלְכוּ יַחְדָּו אֶל בְּאֵר שָׁבַע, וַיֵּשֶׁב

אַבְרָהָם בִּבְאֵר שָׁבַע:

רִבּוֹנוֹ שֶׁל עוֹלָם, כְּמוֹ שֶׁכָּבַשׁ אַבְרָהָם אָבִינוּ אֶת רַחֲמָיו מֵעַל בֶּן יְחִידוֹ לַעֲשׂוֹת רְצוֹנְךָ בְּלֵבָב

שָׁלֵם, כֵּן יִכְבְּשׁוּ רַחֲמֶיךָ אֶת כַּעַסְךָ מֵעָלֵינוּ וְיָגֹלּוּ רַחֲמֶיךָ עַל מִדּוֹתֶיךָ. וְתִתְנַהֵג עִמָּנוּ יְיָ אֱלֹהֵינוּ

בְּמִדַּת הַחֶסֶד וּבְמִדַּת הָרַחֲמִים, וְתִכָּנֵס לָנוּ לִפְנִים מִשּׁוּרַת הַדִּין, וּבְטוּבְךָ הַגָּדוֹל יָשׁוּב חֲרוֹן

אַפְּךָ מֵעַמְּךָ וּמֵעִירְךָ וּמֵאַרְצְךָ וּמִנַּחֲלָתֶךָ, וְקַיֶּם לָנוּ יְיָ אֱלֹהֵינוּ אֶת הַדָּבָר שֶׁהִבְטַחְתָּנוּ בְּתוֹרָתֶךָ,

עַל יְדֵי מֹשֶׁה עַבְדֶּךָ מִפִּי כְבוֹדֶךָ כָּאָמוּר. וְזָכַרְתִּי אֶת בְּרִיתִי יַעֲקוֹב, וְאַף אֶת בְּרִיתִי יִצְחָק, וְאַף

אֶת בְּרִיתִי אַבְרָהָם אֶזְכֹּר וְהָאָרֶץ אֶזְכֹּר: וְנֶאֱמַר, וְאַף גַּם זֹאת בִּהְיוֹתָם בְּאֶרֶץ אֹיְבֵיהֶם לֹא

מְאַסְתִּים וְלֹא גְעַלְתִּים לְכַלֹּתָם, לְהָפֵר בְּרִיתִי אִתָּם, כִּי אֲנִי יְיָ אֱלֹהֵיהֶם: וְנֶאֱמַר, וְזָכַרְתִּי לָהֶם

בְּרִית רִאשֹׁנִים, אֲשֶׁר הוֹצֵאתִי אֹתָם מֵאֶרֶץ מִצְרַיִם, לְעֵינֵי הַגּוֹיִם, לִהְיוֹת לָהֶם לֵאלֹהִים, אֲנִי

יְיָ: וְנֶאֱמַר, וְשָׁב יְיָ אֱלֹהֶיךָ אֶת שְׁבוּתְךָ וְרִחֲמֶךָ, וְשָׁב, וְקִבֶּצְךָ מִכָּל הָעַמִּים, אֲשֶׁר הֱפִיצְךָ יְיָ

אֱלֹהֶיךָ, שָׁמָּה: אִם יִהְיֶה נִדַּחֲךָ בִּקְצֵה הַשָּׁמָיִם, מִשָּׁם יְקַבֶּצְךָ יְיָ אֱלֹהֶיךָ וּמִשָּׁם יִקָּחֶךָ: וֶהֱבִיאֲךָ

יְיָ אֱלֹהֶיךָ אֶל הָאָרֶץ אֲשֶׁר יָרְשׁוּ אֲבֹתֶיךָ, וִירִשְׁתָּהּ, וְהֵיטִבְךָ וְהִרְבְּךָ מֵאֲבֹתֶיךָ: וְנֶאֱמַר, יְיָ חָנֵּנוּ,

לְךָ קִוִּינוּ הֱיֵה זְרֹעָם לַבְּקָרִים, אַף יְשׁוּעָתֵנוּ בְּעֵת צָרָה: וְנֶאֱמַר, וְעֵת צָרָה הִיא לְיַעֲקֹב, וּמִמֶּנָּה

יִוָּשֵׁעַ: וְנֶאֱמַר, בְּכָל צָרָתָם לוֹ צָר, וּמַלְאַךְ פָּנָיו הוֹשִׁיעָם, בְּאַהֲבָתוֹ וּבְחֶמְלָתוֹ הוּא גְאָלָם, וַיְנַטְּלֵם

CHASSIDIC EXCERPTS

Introductory Meditation

There are people who study the Torah with great effort and unstinting dedication, but who nevertheless fail to receive any G-dly light and illumination. They experience no spiritual excitement, and moreover they fail to achieve any true love and fear of G-d. The reason is that they put no effort into removing the concealments and blockages erected by their animal soul. The work of removing

Abraham raised his eyes and saw, and behold, there was a ram caught in the thicket by its horns, and Abraham went and took the ram, and offered it up as a sacrifice in place of his son. And Abraham called this place, "G-d will see," and about this day will be said, "On the mountain of G-d, He will be seen." And an angel of G-d called a second time from the Heavens, saying, "I myself have sworn, the Lord says, that since you have done this deed, and refrained from withholding your son, your only son. Therefore I will bless, certainly bless you, and increase your seed tremendously, as the stars of the heavens and the sand on the shore of the sea, and your descendents will inherit the gates of their enemies. And through all of your descendents, the nations of the world will bless themselves, since you have listened to my voice. And Abraham returned to the lads, and they arose and traveled together to Beer Sheva, and Abraham dwelt in Beer Sheva.

On Shabbat and Festivals, the following paragraph is omitted:

*M*aster of the universe, just as Avraham our forefather overcame the compassion that he felt for his only son in order to fulfill Your Will with a full heart, so let Your mercy overwhelm Your anger at us, and allow Your mercy to prevail over all of Your attributes. And act with us, Lord our G-d, with a measure of kindness and a measure of mercy, and deal with us within the letter of the law. And in Your great goodness, quash Your wrath from over Your nation and from over Your city and from over Your land and from over Your inheritance. And fulfill for us, Lord our G-d, that which You promised to us in Your Torah, by way of Moshe Your servant in Your very Honor, saying, "And I will recall My covenant with Yakov, and even my covenant with Yitzhak, and even My covenant with Avraham I will remember, and the Land I will remember." And as it says, "Even as they are in the land of their enemies, I will not forsake them, and I will not abhor them in order to destroy them, nor renege upon My covenant with them, since I am the Lord, their G-d." And as it says, "I will remember the covenant of their ancestors, whom I brought out of the land of Egypt in plain sight of the nations in order to be their G-d, I am the Lord." And as it says, "And the Lord Your G-d will return your remnants and have mercy upon you, and return to gather you from all of the nations, where the Lord your G-d has scattered you. If some of you are dispersed to the edge of the heavens, from there He will gather you, the Lord your G-d, and from there He will take you. And the Lord your G-d will bring you to the land that your forefathers inherited and you will inherit it, and He will do well by you and multiply you, more than your forefathers." And it says, "Lord, be gracious to us, in You is our hope, be our strength in the mornings, our salvation at times of trouble." And it says, "It's a time of trouble for Yakov, from which he will be saved." And it says, "In all of their troubles, He is troubled, and an angel of the Lord saves them. In His love and His mercy He redeems them, and He uplifts them and

---

CHASSIDIC EXCERPTS

these...begins during the hour preceding prayer, for the sages advise, "We do not approach prayer except with a contrite mind." Rashi (the 11th century Torah commentator) explains that this involves developing a subdued attitude and humility.

[To achieve this attitude], it is necessary to fix a set hour in which to make a detailed accounting of the negative character traits within ourselves (this is the theme of *tikun hazot* – the midnight

וַיִּנָּשְׂאֵם כָּל יְמֵי עוֹלָם: וְנֶאֱמַר, מִי אֵל כָּמוֹךָ נֹשֵׂא עָוֹן וְעֹבֵר עַל פֶּשַׁע, לִשְׁאֵרִית נַחֲלָתוֹ, לֹא הֶחֱזִיק לָעַד אַפּוֹ, כִּי חָפֵץ חֶסֶד הוּא: יָשׁוּב יְרַחֲמֵנוּ, יִכְבֹּשׁ עֲוֹנֹתֵינוּ, וְתַשְׁלִיךְ בִּמְצֻלוֹת יָם כָּל חַטֹּאתָם: תִּתֵּן אֱמֶת לְיַעֲקֹב, חֶסֶד לְאַבְרָהָם, אֲשֶׁר נִשְׁבַּעְתָּ לַאֲבֹתֵינוּ, מִימֵי קֶדֶם: וְנֶאֱמַר, וַהֲבִיאוֹתִים אֶל הַר קָדְשִׁי, וְשִׂמַּחְתִּים בְּבֵית תְּפִלָּתִי, עוֹלֹתֵיהֶם וְזִבְחֵיהֶם לְרָצוֹן עַל מִזְבְּחִי, כִּי בֵיתִי בֵּית תְּפִלָּה, יִקָּרֵא לְכָל הָעַמִּים:

לְעוֹלָם יְהֵא אָדָם יְרֵא שָׁמַיִם בְּסֵתֶר וּמוֹדֶה עַל הָאֱמֶת, וְדוֹבֵר אֱמֶת בִּלְבָבוֹ וְיַשְׁכֵּם וְיֹאמַר:

רִבּוֹן כָּל הָעוֹלָמִים, לֹא עַל צִדְקוֹתֵינוּ אֲנַחְנוּ מַפִּילִים תַּחֲנוּנֵינוּ לְפָנֶיךָ, כִּי עַל רַחֲמֶיךָ הָרַבִּים. מָה אָנוּ, מֶה חַיֵּינוּ, מֶה חַסְדֵּנוּ, מַה צִּדְקֵנוּ, מַה כֹּחֵנוּ, מַה גְּבוּרָתֵנוּ. מַה נֹּאמַר לְפָנֶיךָ יְיָ אֱלֹהֵינוּ וֵאלֹהֵי אֲבוֹתֵינוּ, הֲלֹא כָּל הַגִּבּוֹרִים כְּאַיִן לְפָנֶיךָ, וְאַנְשֵׁי הַשֵּׁם כְּלֹא הָיוּ, וַחֲכָמִים כִּבְלִי מַדָּע, וּנְבוֹנִים כִּבְלִי הַשְׂכֵּל, כִּי רֹב מַעֲשֵׂיהֶם תֹּהוּ, וִימֵי חַיֵּיהֶם הֶבֶל לְפָנֶיךָ, וּמוֹתַר הָאָדָם מִן הַבְּהֵמָה אָיִן, כִּי הַכֹּל הָבֶל: לְבַד הַנְּשָׁמָה הַטְּהוֹרָה שֶׁהִיא עֲתִידָה לִתֵּן דִּין וְחֶשְׁבּוֹן לִפְנֵי כִסֵּא כְבוֹדֶךָ. וְכָל הַגּוֹיִם כְּאַיִן נֶגְדֶּךָ. שֶׁנֶּאֱמַר הֵן גּוֹיִם כְּמַר מִדְּלִי, וּכְשַׁחַק מֹאזְנַיִם נֶחְשָׁבוּ, הֵן אִיִּים כַּדַּק יִטּוֹל:

אֲבָל אֲנַחְנוּ עַמְּךָ בְּנֵי בְרִיתֶךָ, בְּנֵי אַבְרָהָם אֹהַבְךָ, שֶׁנִּשְׁבַּעְתָּ לּוֹ בְּהַר הַמֹּרִיָּה; זֶרַע יִצְחָק יְחִידוֹ, שֶׁנֶּעֱקַד עַל גַּבֵּי הַמִּזְבֵּחַ; עֲדַת יַעֲקֹב בִּנְךָ בְּכוֹרֶךָ, שֶׁמֵּאַהֲבָתְךָ שֶׁאָהַבְתָּ אוֹתוֹ וּמִשִּׂמְחָתְךָ שֶׁשָּׂמַחְתָּ בּוֹ, קָרָאתָ אֶת שְׁמוֹ יִשְׂרָאֵל וִישֻׁרוּן:

לְפִיכָךְ אֲנַחְנוּ חַיָּבִים לְהוֹדוֹת לָךְ, וּלְשַׁבֵּחֲךָ וּלְפָאֶרְךָ וּלְבָרֵךְ וּלְקַדֵּשׁ וְלִתֵּן שֶׁבַח וְהוֹדָיָה לִשְׁמֶךָ.

prayers). The point is to avoid fooling ourselves, and to acknowledge that, on account of all of our transgressions, we are distant from G-dliness. Indeed, we are extremely far, and we should be very bitter about this, crying from the depths of our soul. In this manner, we subdue our animal soul and begin to radiate G-dly illumination within us (mostly, through the Torah learning that we do afterward). And afterward, our prayers (which will take place in joy), bears them forever." And it says, "Who is a G-d like You, bearing our sins and forgiving the transgression of the remnants of His inheritance, He holds not on to His anger, for he desires kindness. He will return and have mercy upon us, will quash our sins; throw all of our transgression into the sea. Grant truth to Yakov and kindness to Avraham, as You swore to our forefathers in the days of yore." And as it says, "And I will bring them to My holy mountain, and cause them to rejoice in My house of prayers; their constant daily offerings and sacrifices will be accepted with favor upon My altar, for My house will be called a house of prayer, for all of the nations."

Man should always be G-d fearing, even in private, should concede the truth and speak the truth within his heart, arising in the morning to say:

*M*aster of the universe, it is not upon our righteousness that we depend, as we plead before You, but upon Your abundant mercy. What are we, what is our kindness, what is our righteousness, what is our strength and what is our power? What can we say before You, Lord our G-d and G-d of our fathers; for all human heroes are like nothing before You, and men of fame are as if non-existent, and wise men as if without knowledge. And the smart are as if lacking intellect, since most of their deeds are meaningless. The days of their life are like "breath" before You, and the advantage of man over the animals is negligible, for all is vanity - aside from the pure soul, which will make an accounting and judgment in the future before Your glorious throne. And all the nations of the world are like nothing before You, as it says: "The nations are like a drop from a bucket, like dust upon a scale, and the islands are like flying dust."

However, we are Your nation, members of Your covenant, descendents of Abraham Your beloved, to whom You swore on Mt. Moriah; [We are] the seed of Yitzhak his only son, who was tied upon the altar, And we are the congregation of Yakov, Your firstborn, whom out of the love and the happiness that You professed for him, You called his name Yisrael and Yeshuron.

Therefore, we are obligated to acknowledge You, to exalt and to extol You, and to bless and sanctify and give praise and gratitude to Your Name.

CHASSIDIC EXCERPTS

will suppress our animal soul so that it does not obstruct our G-dly soul. [In this manner], we will also develop love of G-dliness, ultimately achieving *ahavah rabba*, the "great love" of the G-dly soul. And then, while learning Torah, we will find G-dly illumination shining through our soul, radiating from Above to below.

(From *Sefer Maamorim 5656* (1896) of the Rebbe Rashab, p. 292)

אַשְׁרֵינוּ, מַה טּוֹב חֶלְקֵנוּ, וּמַה נָּעִים גּוֹרָלֵנוּ, וּמַה יָּפָה יְרֻשָּׁתֵנוּ, אַשְׁרֵינוּ, שֶׁאָנוּ

מַשְׁכִּימִים וּמַעֲרִיבִים עֶרֶב וָבֹקֶר וְאוֹמְרִים פַּעֲמַיִם בְּכָל יוֹם:

שְׁמַע | יִשְׂרָאֵל, יְיָ | אֱלֹהֵינוּ, יְיָ | אֶחָד:

בָּרוּךְ שֵׁם כְּבוֹד מַלְכוּתוֹ לְעוֹלָם וָעֶד:

וְאָהַבְתָּ אֵת יְיָ אֱלֹהֶיךָ, בְּכָל לְבָבְךָ, וּבְכָל נַפְשְׁךָ, וּבְכָל מְאֹדֶךָ:

וְהָיוּ הַדְּבָרִים הָאֵלֶּה אֲשֶׁר אָנֹכִי מְצַוְּךָ הַיּוֹם עַל לְבָבֶךָ:

וְשִׁנַּנְתָּם לְבָנֶיךָ וְדִבַּרְתָּ בָּם, בְּשִׁבְתְּךָ בְּבֵיתֶךָ, וּבְלֶכְתְּךָ בַדֶּרֶךְ, וּבְשָׁכְבְּךָ, וּבְקוּמֶךָ:

וּקְשַׁרְתָּם לְאוֹת עַל יָדֶךָ, וְהָיוּ לְטֹטָפֹת בֵּין עֵינֶיךָ:

וּכְתַבְתָּם עַל מְזֻזוֹת בֵּיתֶךָ וּבִשְׁעָרֶיךָ:

אַתָּה הוּא עַד שֶׁלֹּא נִבְרָא הָעוֹלָם, אַתָּה הוּא מִשֶּׁנִּבְרָא הָעוֹלָם, אַתָּה הוּא

בָּעוֹלָם הַזֶּה, וְאַתָּה הוּא לָעוֹלָם הַבָּא. קַדֵּשׁ אֶת שְׁמֶךָ, וּבִישׁוּעָתְךָ מַלְכֵּנוּ תָּרוּם

וְתַגְבִּיהַּ קַרְנֵנוּ, וְהוֹשִׁיעֵנוּ בְּקָרוֹב לְמַעַן שְׁמֶךָ, בָּרוּךְ הַמְקַדֵּשׁ שְׁמוֹ בָּרַבִּים:

אַתָּה הוּא יְיָ אֱלֹהֵינוּ בַּשָּׁמַיִם וּבָאָרֶץ, וּבִשְׁמֵי הַשָּׁמַיִם הָעֶלְיוֹנִים, אֱמֶת אַתָּה הוּא

רִאשׁוֹן, וְאַתָּה הוּא אַחֲרוֹן, וּמִבַּלְעָדֶיךָ אֵין אֱלֹהִים. קַבֵּץ נְפוּצוֹת קֹוֶיךָ מֵאַרְבַּע

כַּנְפוֹת הָאָרֶץ, יַכִּירוּ וְיֵדְעוּ כָּל בָּאֵי עוֹלָם, כִּי אַתָּה הוּא הָאֱלֹהִים לְבַדְּךָ לְכֹל

מַמְלְכוֹת הָאָרֶץ. אַתָּה עָשִׂיתָ אֶת הַשָּׁמַיִם וְאֶת הָאָרֶץ, אֶת הַיָּם וְאֶת כָּל אֲשֶׁר

בָּם, וּמִי בְּכָל מַעֲשֵׂה יָדֶיךָ בָּעֶלְיוֹנִים וּבַתַּחְתּוֹנִים, שֶׁיֹּאמַר לְךָ מַה תַּעֲשֶׂה, וּמַה

תִּפְעָל, אָבִינוּ שֶׁבַּשָּׁמַיִם, חַי וְקַיָּם, עֲשֵׂה עִמָּנוּ צְדָקָה וָחֶסֶד בַּעֲבוּר שִׁמְךָ הַגָּדוֹל

הַגִּבּוֹר וְהַנּוֹרָא שֶׁנִּקְרָא עָלֵינוּ, וְקַיֶּם לָנוּ יְיָ אֱלֹהֵינוּ אֶת הַדָּבָר שֶׁהִבְטַחְתָּנוּ עַל יְדֵי

צְפַנְיָה חוֹזָךְ כָּאָמוּר: בָּעֵת הַהִיא אָבִיא אֶתְכֶם, וּבָעֵת קַבְּצִי אֶתְכֶם, כִּי אֶתֵּן

אֶתְכֶם לְשֵׁם וְלִתְהִלָּה בְּכֹל עַמֵּי הָאָרֶץ, בְּשׁוּבִי אֶת שְׁבוּתֵיכֶם לְעֵינֵיכֶם, אָמַר יְיָ:

Happy are we, how good is our portion, and how pleasant our lot, and how beautiful is our inheritance. Fortunate are we who early in the morning and early at night, say twice every day:

*H*ear, O Israel, the Lord is our G-d, the Lord is one.

Blessed be the name of His glorious kingdom forever and ever.

And you shall love the Lord your G-d with all your heart, with all your soul, and with all your means.

And these words that I am commanding you today, should be on your heart.

And you shall teach them to your children and speak of them, while sitting in your house and as you travel on the road, when you lie down, and when you arise.

And you shall tie them as a sign on your arm, and they shall be as compartments between your eyes.

And you shall write them on the doorposts of your house and upon your gates.

You were before the universe was created, You are [the same] since the universe was created. You exist in this world, and You exist in the world to come. Sanctify Your Name in Your world through Your nation who sanctify Your name. And in Your salvation, our King, raise and elevate our prestige, and save us soon for the sake of Your Name. Blessed is He Who sanctifies His name in public!

*Y*ou are the Lord, G-d in the heavens and the earth, and in the upper heavens above. It is true that You are the first, and You are the last, and aside from You there is no G-d. Gather together the scattered who long for You from the four corners of the earth, so that all of mankind will know and recognize that You alone are G-d, over all the kingdoms of the earth. You created the heavens and the earth, the sea and all that is in it. And who among all of the works of Your hands, spiritual and physical will tell You what to do, and what to cause to happen. Our Father in the heavens, alive and ever-lasting, perform justice and kindness for the sake of Your great Name, the powerful and awesome Name by which we call You, and fulfill for us, Lord Our G-d, that which You promised via Your prophet and visionary, Zephania, saying, "At that time I will bring you back, and at that time I will gather you, for I will make you renowned and praiseworthy among all of the nations of the earth, as I return your captured remnants before your very eyes, so saith the Lord."

morning. We are not in a spiritual position to appreciate the very high words that we utter, "Blessed are You, G-d, King of the Universe..." But, with those words, we draw down a huge influx of G-dly energy that takes us out of our morning limitations. The word *baruch* ("blessed") is related to the word *berech* ("knee"); it alludes to the bent knee, the posture we take in front of the King (later, during the *Shemonah esreh*, the pinnacle of prayer) as we utter the words, "Blessed are You, G-d" referring to the ineffable four-letter name of G-d. Thus, we bring a very high light down into the world, enabling us to start the day off right.

קרבנות

תרומת הדשן

וַיְדַבֵּר יְיָ אֶל מֹשֶׁה לֵּאמֹר: צַו אֶת אַהֲרֹן וְאֶת בָּנָיו לֵאמֹר, זֹאת תּוֹרַת הָעֹלָה, הִוא הָעֹלָה עַל מוֹקְדָה עַל הַמִּזְבֵּחַ כָּל הַלַּיְלָה עַד הַבֹּקֶר וְאֵשׁ הַמִּזְבֵּחַ, תּוּקַד בּוֹ: וְלָבַשׁ הַכֹּהֵן מִדּוֹ בַד וּמִכְנְסֵי בַד יִלְבַּשׁ עַל בְּשָׂרוֹ וְהֵרִים אֶת הַדֶּשֶׁן אֲשֶׁר תֹּאכַל הָאֵשׁ אֶת הָעֹלָה עַל הַמִּזְבֵּחַ וְשָׂמוֹ אֵצֶל הַמִּזְבֵּחַ: וּפָשַׁט אֶת בְּגָדָיו וְלָבַשׁ בְּגָדִים אֲחֵרִים וְהוֹצִיא אֶת הַדֶּשֶׁן אֶל מִחוּץ לַמַּחֲנֶה אֶל מָקוֹם טָהוֹר: וְהָאֵשׁ עַל הַמִּזְבֵּחַ תּוּקַד בּוֹ לֹא תִכְבֶּה וּבִעֵר עָלֶיהָ הַכֹּהֵן עֵצִים בַּבֹּקֶר בַּבֹּקֶר וְעָרַךְ עָלֶיהָ הָעֹלָה וְהִקְטִיר עָלֶיהָ חֶלְבֵי הַשְּׁלָמִים: אֵשׁ, תָּמִיד תּוּקַד עַל הַמִּזְבֵּחַ לֹא תִכְבֶּה:

But, in truth, the morning prayers – or at least the preparations for them – start at night. King David woke up every night at midnight to say special prayers. According to Kabbalah and Chassidut, the first half of the night (up to *chatzot*, or "midnight") is associated with judgment. But the second half of the night is associated with mercy and sweetness, and King David's prayers accessed that mercy and sweetness. The Talmud tells us that his harp was hung over his bed, and every night at midnight, a north wind would blow through its strings and awaken him to recite the midnight prayers.[6]

The midnight supplications are not a mere adjunct to the rest of prayers, meant only for the extremely pious who are capable of interrupting their sleep in order to pray to G-d.[7] The midnight prayers play an essential role in preparing us to approach G-d in the morning.

According to the great 16th century Kabbalist, the *Ari z'l*, there are two types of *birur* ("refinement") that take place within our animal soul.[8] One type of *birur* involves removing the bad/unwanted elements from the good/desirable elements. The second type involves separating the good from the bad. As we arise to pray at midnight, we transition from the period of judgment into the pre-morning period

Removal of the Ashes (Trumat Hadeshen)

The incineration of the animal offering on the altar is the result of "fire from Above" that descends, appearing as a lion consuming the sacrifice. This initiates a refining process, much as metal goes through a smelting process in order to rid it of waste products. This also corresponds to the excitement of our animal soul as we pray, while the ashes that remain correspond to the nullification of our ego, since the "left side [the side of judgment] repels."[13]

That is why it is a Torah commandment to place the ashes next to the altar,

CHASSIDIC INSIGHTS

of mercy and sweetness. Therefore, our inner work at this time focuses upon refining our negative character traits. Our midnight supplications bring down a high illumination from Above that clarifies the bad within and separates it from the good, and vice versa (this is known as "sweetening the judgment" in Kabbalistic parlance). When that happens, we are left with two kinds of sadness — one is called *merirut* ("bitterness"), and the other *atzvut* ("depression"). The bitterness is the result of our perceived distance from G-d. A realistic assessment informs us that we are still far from Him, causing us to feel bitterness about the distance. This is an uncomfortable but positive trait, for it may motivate us to get closer to Him. But depression is a negative trait that must be eradicated. It is associated with discouragement and laziness, and it cannot be tolerated at all, for it prevents us from trying to get closer to the One Above. So, the midnight prayers are all about removing the bad from the good, so that we will be able to enter the morning prayers with a positive attitude and a light heart.

Entering into prayer with a light heart does not contradict one of the other precepts of prayer, which is that we should only pray with a contrite and respectful mind. This comes as a result of the work that we do on ourselves at the midnight hour. Afterward, having achieved the proper level of respect and ego-nullification, we may approach prayer in a positive frame of mind.

The two by-products of the midnight process of refinement are alluded to in the Torah in the section pertaining to the removal of the ashes from the sacrificial altar. We recite this passage — called *Trumat HaDeshen* — during prayer. The burnt offering of the previous night was still smoldering on the altar when the new morning arrives. So it was necessary to remove the ashes, and clean and prepare the altar for the new morning's burnt offering.

Today, this corresponds to our prayers. The ashes represent what is left once our refinement process

Offerings

Removal of the Ashes

And the Lord spoke to Moshe, saying, 'Command Aharon and his sons, saying, "This is the law of the burnt offering; which is the offering that is placed on the firewood of the altar all night long until the morning, while the fire of the altar is kept burning upon it. And the priest should wear his suit of linen and don pants of linen over his flesh. And he should raise the ashes resulting from the fire that consumed the burnt offering on the altar, and place them next to the altar. He should then remove his clothes and don other clothes, and take the ashes outside the encampment, to a pure location. And the fire on the altar should be kept burning, it should not extinguish; and the priest should burn wood upon it every morning. And he should arrange the offering upon it and smoke the fat of the peace-offerings upon it. It is an eternal fire, kept ignited upon the altar, so as not to extinguish.

CHASSIDIC EXCERPTS

as the verse[14] states, "And he should place it by the altar," where it is spontaneously absorbed [in the earth] ... But, whatever ashes fail to become absorbed near the altar are removed and taken out of the area.[15] They correspond to our sadness and depression which provide no benefit whatsoever in serving G-d. They represent the kind of lowliness that we feel when we give up on ourselves, becoming inanimate like a stone. We then become like one who is tread upon, and then all sorts of negative forces may have an influence on us.

(From the the Alter Rebbe's *Siddur* with *Chasidut*, 31A)

of the previous night is complete. They are the bad/undesirable elements that we still cannot refine, such as depression or laziness. These undesirable elements are removed and placed on the earth next to the altar. Some of the ashes will be swallowed up by the earth – these are the elements that can be absorbed and nullified. But, the rest must be removed from the scene completely – since there is no room for depression and discouragement in the service of G-d. It is the work that we do after the midnight hour that removes the depression and other blockages of our own making, allowing us to begin our spiritual ascent once the morning hour arrives.

Following the *Trumat HaDeshen*, we recite the *Korbanot* ("Sacrifices'). One could legitimately ask, what is the point in spending time reciting passages from the Torah concerning the sacrifices during the prayer service? While it is true that we once offered these sacrifices, we now say prayers in their stead, so what function do they serve now?

Part of the answer, of course, is that reciting the *Korbanot* reminds us of the origins of prayer in the Temple. But in addition, the elements of the sacrifices fit in well with the initial stage of prayer, in the physical World of *Asiya*. That is, the first and lowest rung of prayer lifts up and elevates our physical world.[9] Therefore, we mention physical objects, of which there were plenty in the process of offering the sacrifices. First of all, there were the minerals that are mentioned regarding the incense offering. Then, there were the grains that went into the *mincha*[10] offering as well as the wine of the libations, representing the vegetable world. And then, of course, there were the animals themselves, and the humans who sacrificed them. So, all four elements of the physical world were present during the sacrifices. In reciting them, we attempt to uplift the four "kingdoms" — mineral, vegetable, animal and human — as part of the first rung of prayer.

קָרְבַּן הַתָּמִיד

On Shabbat and Festivals, the following paragraph is omitted:

יְהִי רָצוֹן מִלְּפָנֶיךָ יְיָ אֱלֹהֵינוּ וֵאלֹהֵי אֲבוֹתֵינוּ, שֶׁתְּרַחֵם עָלֵינוּ וְתִמְחָל לָנוּ עַל כָּל חַטֹּאתֵינוּ, וּתְכַפֵּר לָנוּ עַל כָּל עֲוֹנוֹתֵינוּ, וְתִסְלַח לָנוּ עַל כָּל פְּשָׁעֵינוּ, וְשֶׁיִּבָּנֶה בֵּית הַמִּקְדָּשׁ בִּמְהֵרָה בְיָמֵינוּ, וְנַקְרִיב לְפָנֶיךָ קָרְבַּן הַתָּמִיד שֶׁיְּכַפֵּר בַּעֲדֵנוּ כְּמוֹ שֶׁכָּתַבְתָּ עָלֵינוּ בְּתוֹרָתֶךָ עַל יְדֵי מֹשֶׁה עַבְדֶּךָ מִפִּי כְבוֹדֶךָ כָּאָמוּר:

וַיְדַבֵּר יְיָ אֶל מֹשֶׁה לֵּאמֹר: צַו אֶת בְּנֵי יִשְׂרָאֵל וְאָמַרְתָּ אֲלֵהֶם, אֶת קָרְבָּנִי לַחְמִי לְאִשַּׁי, רֵיחַ נִיחֹחִי תִּשְׁמְרוּ לְהַקְרִיב לִי בְּמוֹעֲדוֹ: וְאָמַרְתָּ לָהֶם, זֶה הָאִשֶּׁה אֲשֶׁר תַּקְרִיבוּ לַיְיָ, כְּבָשִׂים בְּנֵי שָׁנָה תְמִימִם, שְׁנַיִם לַיּוֹם, עֹלָה תָמִיד: אֶת הַכֶּבֶשׂ אֶחָד תַּעֲשֶׂה בַבֹּקֶר, וְאֵת הַכֶּבֶשׂ הַשֵּׁנִי תַּעֲשֶׂה בֵּין הָעַרְבָּיִם: וַעֲשִׂירִית הָאֵיפָה סֹלֶת לְמִנְחָה, בְּלוּלָה בְּשֶׁמֶן כָּתִית רְבִיעִת הַהִין: עֹלַת תָּמִיד, הָעֲשֻׂיָה בְּהַר סִינַי לְרֵיחַ נִיחֹחַ אִשֶּׁה לַיְיָ: וְנִסְכּוֹ רְבִיעִת הַהִין

The twice-daily burnt offerings - **Korbanot**

"And G-d spoke to Moses, saying, 'Command the Children of Israel, and tell them, "My sacrifices are sustenance for my servants, a pleasing aroma...'"[16]

In order to understand the nature of sacrifices: In general, they correspond to the four fundamental elements of fire, wind, water and earth. The element of earth corresponds to the inanimate (mineral) world, which is inert like a stone. Water corresponds to the vegetable world, since we see that water germinates all kinds of vegetation; we see clearly that trees, grain and grass all grow near the edge of a river, more so than in other locations. Fire corresponds

CHASSIDIC INSIGHTS

Furthermore, the sacrifices were precursors to prayer. The Torah alludes to this when commanding us to bring the sacrifices. It says, "When you bring *from yourselves* a sacrifice…"[11] hinting that the real sacrifice is of the animal soul inside each and every one of us. Today, our animal soul becomes purified and elevated during prayer. However, originally a Jew would come to the Temple, offer his personal sacrifice, and he would also pray, requesting G-d to fulfill his needs in whatever words emerged from his heart and came to his mouth. But, as the sages observed that Jewish spiritual commitment was lagging, they added to the required prayers. After the sacrifices were discontinued because the Temple was destroyed, formal prayers took the place of sacrifices.[12] The words of prayer eventually became fixed as established by the Sages of the Great Assembly (*Anshei Knesset HaGedolah*).

Possibly the most important sacrifices in the Temple were the two daily offerings (called the Constant Offerings, or *Olat Tamid*) – one was sacrificed in the morning and the other in the evening, as commanded in the Torah. Chassidic literature explains that no less than the very existence of the universe itself was dependent upon the proper offering of these sacrifices.[13] The priest in the Temple had to maintain precise focus in time, in space and in regard to the nature of the offering; if he failed to do so, the sacrifice was considered unfit (*posul*). And if unfit, it meant that the entire life-force that animated creation failed to materialize. Similarly, our prayers demand focus and concentration.[14]

The Hebrew word for "sacrifice" is *korban*, also from the word *kiruv*, meaning "nearness" or "proximity." Our prayers were established in place of the sacrifices, and they bring us closer to G-d, in proximity to His holiness. At the same time, the *olah* sacrifice ("burnt offering") is entirely for G-d – no priest or other human being eats any part

The Continual Tamid Offering

May it be Your Will, Lord our G-d and G-d of our forefathers, to have mercy on us and forgive us for all of our sins, and atone for all of our transgressions, and forgive and pardon all of our iniquity. And may the *Beit Hamikdash* be built speedily in our days, there to sacrifice before You the constant daily offerings in order to atone for us, as You wrote for us in Your Torah by way of Moshe your servant, in Your Honor, saying…"

And the Lord spoke to Moshe, saying, 'Command the children of Israel, and tell them, 'My sacrifices are sustenance for my servants, a pleasing aroma for Me, be careful to offer [them] at the appointed time. And tell them, this is the fire offering that you should sacrifice to the Lord: two one-year old sheep, free of blemishes, every day, for the regular burnt offering. One sheep in the morning, and the second sheep in the afternoon. And a tenth of an *epha* of refined wheat should be offered as a *mincha* offering, mixed with a quarter *hin* of oil, ground from olives. This is a regular burnt offering, as done on Mt. Sinai as a pleasing aroma, fire for the Lord. And the wine libation should be a quarter

CHASSIDIC EXCERPTS

to the animal world, as we see that animals possess natural body heat. Animals – whether domestic or wild – correspond to heat in the soul, as does the intellect in the soul of man. Similarly, fire corresponds to the denizens of the higher spiritual realms as well as to the animal kingdom since the supernal angels are described as "animals" and "wild creatures." In the holy writings of the prophets, we read that the "face of the lion was to the right side and the face of the ox was to the left" (Ezekiel 1:10). And the angels are described as, "His servants who are like a fiery flame" (Psalms 104:4), and their appearance as "fiery coals burning, like flames" (Ezekiel 1:13). And wind corresponds to

CHASSIDIC INSIGHTS

of it. Similarly, true closeness to G-d occurs when we serve Him for no reason whatsoever – solely out of the desire to be close to Him – then, we are "entirely for G-d."

About this closeness and proximity to G-d that occurs during *tefila*, the Ba'al Shem Tov said, "The fact that man remains alive after *tefila* is supernatural, since as a result of the high *kavanot* during prayer, he should have expired. This that man remains alive after *tefila* is not according to the laws of nature, but is rather a great kindness of the One above." By way of explanation, the reason that high and spiritual intentions during prayer may bring us to expiry of the soul is because the elevation of the soul during *tefila* is similar to the burning of the sacrifice on the altar, and its inclusion in the infinite light of the One above.[15]

לְכֶבֶשׂ הָאֶחָד, בְּקֹדֶשׁ הַסֵּךְ נֶסֶךְ שֵׁכָר לַיָי: וְאֵת הַכֶּבֶשׂ הַשֵּׁנִי תַּעֲשֶׂה בֵּין הָעַרְבָּיִם, כְּמִנְחַת הַבֹּקֶר וּכְנִסְכּוֹ תַּעֲשֶׂה, אִשֵּׁה רֵיחַ נִיחֹחַ לַיָי: וְשָׁחַט אֹתוֹ עַל יֶרֶךְ הַמִּזְבֵּחַ צָפֹנָה לִפְנֵי יְיָ, וְזָרְקוּ בְּנֵי אַהֲרֹן הַכֹּהֲנִים אֶת דָּמוֹ עַל הַמִּזְבֵּחַ סָבִיב:

In order to bring down G-dliness to permeate the world at the time of the sacrifices, it was necessary that all three classes of Jews be present. The *Cohanim* were known for their quick and quiet precision. It was they who drew

man, who speaks. About the creation of man, it is said, "and man became a living creature" (Genesis 2:7), which the Aramaic translation[17] renders as "and man became a speaking spirit." So, speech is from the element of wind.

Sacrifices involved the [slaughtering of an animal and] burning it upon the altar. The element of fire that corresponds to the animal kingdom then became subsumed in the supernal element of fire, which is also called the "face of the ox to the left side" and is the source of all animals below. As it was burnt, the sacrifice became included in the supernal element of fire. (This is also what the *Zohar* describes when it speaks of the "lion that consumed sacrifices"...).

Our morning and evening prayers correspond to the regular morning and evening sacrifices in the Temple. The (morning) prayers that we recite prior to the *Shema* - in which we mention the great excitement of the angels - correspond to the animal sacrifices of the morning. The angels express a fiery desire to be included in their source, as we pray, "He who forms ministering an-

gels, and Whose ministering angels stand at the heights of the universe..." Since the "animals and creatures" (i.e. angels) of the upper worlds become included in the fire of Above - which is called a consuming fire, as written,[18] "Because G-d your Lord is a consuming fire" - they correspond to the animal sacrifices on the altar. The time that the fire descends from Above to consume the sacrifice corresponds to the hour during which we pray the *Shemonah Esreh*. Our recital of the blessing, "Blessed are You, G-d, Our Lord..." brings G-dliness down from Above. But, prior to praying the *Shemonah Esreh*, we are obligated to bring our own "ordinary fire" by speaking of the fiery excitement of the angels (which takes place as we recite the prayers prior to the *Shema*). Simultaneously, our animal soul becomes consumed with fiery flames of love, resulting from our meditation and leading to [greater] desire for G-d. Then, during the *Shemonah Esreh*, the fire from Above, about which is written,[19] "And after the fire, a still small voice..." descends...

(From the Alter Rebbe's *Siddur* with *Chasidut*, 33A)

CHASSIDIC INSIGHTS

G-dliness down into the world from Above to below by offering the sacrifices and performing other services in the Temple. The *Leviim* ("Levites," from the tribe of Levi) were assistants to the *Cohanim*, and they had the job of singing and playing instruments as the offerings took place; their role was to elevate and accompany the holy sparks below to their rightful place in the spiritual realms Above. And it was the common Jews (*Yisraelim*) who brought the sacrifices from outside the realm of holiness into the Temple to be offered.[16]

(Perhaps it is because all kinds of Jews had to be present when the sacrifice was offered that we take upon ourselves the *mitzvah* of *Ve'ahavta l'reachecha kamocha* – "Love your fellow as your own self" – before we pray. When a Jew prays in the morning, even if by himself, he must include himself among all other Jews. In that way, even the furthest of all Jews – those who do not yet know anything about Torah and mitzvoth – are included in our prayers.)[17]

The fact that our prayers were established in lieu of the sacrifices leads to another set of ramifica-

of a *hin* for each sheep, poured in holiness, a libation of drink for the Lord. And the second sheep in the afternoon, just as the *mincha* of the morning and its libation it should be done, as a pleasant odor for the Lord.

And it should be slaughtered at the northern side of the altar, before the Lord, and the sons of Aharon, the priests, should sprinkle its blood all around the altar.

CHASSIDIC EXCERPTS

"My sacrifices are sustenance..."

When a man is hungry, not having eaten for three days or so, his energy is sapped, and his soul (*nefesh*) begins to ascend, departing the limbs of his body. He becomes weak intellectually and his eyesight becomes dimmed. Only later when he eats, does his soul return to him from Above to below, permeating his limbs; then his mind becomes strengthened. So, we see that food (i.e. "bread") causes the soul to return to the body.

Similarly, all worlds exist Above in the spiritual image of man, including a body and a soul, as is written,[20] "and on the throne was a form in the image of man." And as the *Zohar* says, "You have provided them with bodies,"[21] since the worlds are called "bodies," and G-dly vitality energizes them, permeates them and enlivens them from nothing to something. This energizing vitality is called *memalleh kol olmin* ("immanent G-dliness") as is known. But, in truth, it is written,[22] "G-d is not man, who changes his mind," and as it is written,[23] "His justice is unknowable ... He is not

associated with any character traits whatsoever." This phrase alludes to the dimension of soul Above, called *sovev kol olmin* ("transcendent G-dliness") as is known. That being the case, in order for the image of man with fully-formed limbs to be expressed in the image of G-d Above, it is necessary to draw the *nefesh* ("enlivening soul") into the (supernal) limbs. This is comparable to the *nefesh* returning to the body as a man eats, [for only by eating does he connect his soul with his body]. In its root, this is the meaning of *korbanot* ("sacrifices"), which are called *lachmi* ("My sustenance") since they cause the soul to return to the body. Similarly, the sacrifices cause G-dly illumination to fill the world, which is also called a "body" overall. This is what was meant by the sages when they said[24] that "Jews sustain their Father in heavens"... And that is the meaning of the phrase,[25] "To my servants," since through the sacrifices, which are called "My sustenance," the Jews cause sustenance to be brought to "My servants."

(From the Alter Rebbe's *Siddur* with Chasidut, Page 33B)

tions, having to do with the timing of prayer. Since the morning "burnt offering" could be offered from sunrise until one third of the day had passed, so we may pray the morning prayers from sunrise until one third of the day. And if for some reason (even purposefully), we fail to pray before a third of the day has passed, we are permitted to pray until midday — just as was the case with the morning sacrifice[18] However, all this does not apply to one who prays at length, accompanied by long meditation.

קטרת

אַתָּה הוּא יְיָ אֱלֹהֵינוּ וֵאלֹהֵי אֲבוֹתֵינוּ, שֶׁהִקְטִירוּ אֲבוֹתֵינוּ לְפָנֶיךָ אֶת קְטֹרֶת הַסַּמִּים, בִּזְמַן שֶׁבֵּית הַמִּקְדָּשׁ קַיָּם, כַּאֲשֶׁר צִוִּיתָ אוֹתָם עַל יַד מֹשֶׁה נְבִיאֶךָ, כַּכָּתוּב בְּתוֹרָתֶךָ:

וַיֹּאמֶר יְיָ אֶל מֹשֶׁה, קַח לְךָ סַמִּים: נָטָף, וּשְׁחֵלֶת, וְחֶלְבְּנָה, סַמִּים, וּלְבֹנָה זַכָּה, בַּד בְּבַד יִהְיֶה: וְעָשִׂיתָ אֹתָהּ קְטֹרֶת, רֹקַח מַעֲשֵׂה רוֹקֵחַ, מְמֻלָּח טָהוֹר קֹדֶשׁ: וְשָׁחַקְתָּ מִמֶּנָּה הָדֵק, וְנָתַתָּה מִמֶּנָּה לִפְנֵי הָעֵדֻת בְּאֹהֶל מוֹעֵד, אֲשֶׁר אִוָּעֵד לְךָ שָׁמָּה, קֹדֶשׁ קָדָשִׁים תִּהְיֶה לָכֶם: וְנֶאֱמַר, וְהִקְטִיר עָלָיו אַהֲרֹן, קְטֹרֶת סַמִּים בַּבֹּקֶר בַּבֹּקֶר, בְּהֵיטִיבוֹ אֶת הַנֵּרֹת יַקְטִירֶנָּה: וּבְהַעֲלֹת אַהֲרֹן אֶת הַנֵּרֹת בֵּין הָעַרְבַּיִם יַקְטִירֶנָּה, קְטֹרֶת תָּמִיד לִפְנֵי יְיָ לְדֹרֹתֵיכֶם:

Since he is involved in preparations for prayer, and in fulfilling the necessity requirements to pray with a contrite attitude, it is better that he pray when he is ready. Otherwise, he may end up praying without a proper attitude, and then his prayers will entirely without merit.[19] Moreover, one who prays at length with meditation is free of the limitations that are imposed by praying with a "minyan" — a prayer quorum of ten Jewish men. However, if he is not praying at length with meditation, then he has no excuse to free himself from public prayers with a minyan.[20] Perhaps the explanation is that since prayer with meditation is d'orayta — Torah ordained — it is not subject to the same limitations as imposed by the rabbis when they established the prayers and their laws.[21]

Our prayers correspond not only to the sacrifices in the holy Temple, but also to the architecture of the Temple itself. The three main features of the holy Temple — the azara (or "plaza," where people prayed and waited for the opportunity to bring offerings), the kodesh (the "holy" area where the sacrifices were offered) and the kodesh hakedoshim ("holy of holies" where the incense was offered and the high priest entered once a year) — are all represented in our prayers. First of all, the pesukei dezimra, or "verses of song" during which we meditate

*"Take for yourselves spices..." – **Ketoret** ("Incense")*

"And G-d said to Moses, 'Take spices for yourself: balsam sap, onycha and galbanum, other spices and pure frankincense...'" (Ex 30:34)

Animal sacrifices took place upon the outer altar, and burning the incense took place upon the inner altar. It is known that the two altars correspond to the external and internal dimensions of the heart. The external dimension corresponds to the love of G-d that develops

in proportion to our understanding and intellect. Such love flows from our meditation upon and grasp of G-dly topics. In general, we are capable of grasping the G-dly illumination that becomes enclothed in creation, since "as the soul permeates the body, so G-d fills the universe..."[26] and therefore, "From my own flesh I grasp G-dliness."[27]

We experience and feel our inner vitality and energy in all of our func-

CHASSIDIC INSIGHTS

and pray regarding the G-dliness that permeates creation correspond to the *azara*. Then, we arrive to the blessings preceding the *shema* and the *shema* itself - during which we pray and meditate regarding G-dliness that transcends the world — correspond to the *kodesh*, where G-dliness from beyond nature was brought down by the sacrifices. And finally, we arrive to the *shemonah esreh*, corresponding to the *kodesh hakedoshim*, where we stand in front of G-d in ultimate self-nullification, like a "servant before his master."[22]

To properly understand the sacrifices, we must know the categories/kingdoms of creation: mineral, vegetable, animal and human. All were present at the time of the sacrifice, and all got a spiritual lift as a result of the offering. The mineral kingdom was present as the salt that was a part of every sacrifice. The vegetable kingdom was represented by the ground wheat offering, as well as the wine libation, both of which were brought along with every animal sacrifice. And, of course, the animal kingdom was represented by the animal that was sacrificed. And the humans that were present at the sacrifice represented the entire human race.[23]

All four categories of creation were uplifted and elevated with the sacrifice. And now it is our prayers that have the potential to elevate the entire world. The mineral within us is our speech. The letters themselves, that comprise the words we speak, have no meaning on their own. But, when arranged into words and sentences, they carry a powerful message from us to G-d. The vegetable within us is our emotions, which grow as we pray, just as plants grow. The animal within us is our intellect, which gives us the ability to objectively assess and improve our situation, potentially moving us to a higher plane of existence. This also corresponds to the unique quality that animals have over plants; they can move.

The animal within us is also the animal soul. Left alone, it gravitates

Incense

*Y*ou are the Lord, our G-d and the G-d of our forefathers, to Whom our forefathers offered incense before You; the incense of spices when the Temple stood, as you commanded them, through Moshe your prophet, as written in Your Torah:

"And the Lord said to Moshe, take for yourself spices, stacte, onycha and galbanum, fragrant spices, and pure frankincense; there should be an equal amount of each. And make it into incense, a pharmaceutical compound, the work of an expert, well mixed, pure and holy. You should take part of it and grind it up thoroughly, and place a portion of it before the Ark in the Tent of meeting, where I will meet with you there, it should be holy of holies for you. And it is said, And Aharon should burn an incense [mixture] of spices upon the altar, every morning as he cleans the lamps [of the menorah], he should burn it. And as Aharon lights the lamps toward the evening, he should burn it, as a constant incense before the Lord, throughout your generations.

CHASSIDIC EXCERPTS

tions, including the power of intellect of our mind, and the emotions of our heart. We are aware of the energy in our external limbs – the ability to move our hands and the ability to walk on our legs. We know and grasp clearly and exactly what they are ... and, in general, we know and feel the primacy of the energy that enlivens us. Similarly, we understand and grasp the il-lumination and G-dly energy within the specific *sephirot*... experiencing the particular level of each *sephira*, as well as the qualities of one over the other. We experience how each particular level illuminates and animates the various worlds Above ... In so doing we grasp the level and quality of each and every world in its own right, and the nature of G-dly service and

CHASSIDIC INSIGHTS

toward all that is physical and coarse. But we can sacrifice and burn it, just as we once offered the sacrifice on the altar, and then it turns its great power and energy toward the service of G-d. And finally, our power of speech is what sets us apart from animals; we have the ability to invent and express ourselves creatively, which is beyond even the power of intellect.[24]

Finally, at this stage of prayer, we also recite the list of minerals that composed the incense offering,

תָּנוּ רַבָּנָן, פִּטוּם הַקְּטֹרֶת כֵּיצַד: שְׁלֹשׁ מֵאוֹת וְשִׁשִּׁים וּשְׁמוֹנָה מָנִים הָיוּ בָהּ.

שְׁלֹשׁ מֵאוֹת וְשִׁשִּׁים וַחֲמִשָּׁה כְּמִנְיַן יְמוֹת הַחַמָּה, מָנֶה לְכָל יוֹם פְּרַס

בְּשַׁחֲרִית, וּפְרַס בֵּין הָעַרְבַּיִם, וּשְׁלֹשָׁה מָנִים יְתֵרִים, שֶׁמֵּהֶם מַכְנִיס כֹּהֵן גָּדוֹל

מְלֹא חָפְנָיו בְּיוֹם הַכִּפּוּרִים, וּמַחֲזִירָן לְמַכְתֶּשֶׁת בְּעֶרֶב יוֹם הַכִּפּוּרִים, וְשׁוֹחֲקָן יָפֶה

יָפֶה כְּדֵי שֶׁתְּהֵא דַקָּה מִן הַדַּקָּה.

וְאַחַד עָשָׂר סַמְמָנִים הָיוּ בָהּ. וְאֵלּוּ הֵן: (א) הַצֳּרִי (ב) וְהַצִּפֹּרֶן (ג) הַחֶלְבְּנָה

(ד) וְהַלְּבוֹנָה מִשְׁקַל שִׁבְעִים שִׁבְעִים מָנֶה, (ה) מוֹר (ו) וּקְצִיעָה (ז) שִׁבֹּלֶת נֵרְדְּ

(ח) וְכַרְכֹּם מִשְׁקַל שִׁשָּׁה עָשָׂר שִׁשָּׁה עָשָׂר מָנֶה, (ט) הַקֹּשְׁטְ שְׁנֵים עָשָׂר,

(י) קִלּוּפָה שְׁלֹשָׁה, (יא) וְקִנָּמוֹן תִּשְׁעָה. בְּרִית כַּרְשִׁינָה תִּשְׁעָה קַבִּין, יֵין קַפְרִיסִין

סְאִין תְּלָתָא וְקַבִּין תְּלָתָא, וְאִם אֵין לוֹ יֵין קַפְרִיסִין מֵבִיא חֲמַר חִוַּרְיָן עַתִּיק. מֶלַח

סְדוֹמִית רוֹבַע, מַעֲלֶה עָשָׁן, כָּל שֶׁהוּא. רַבִּי נָתָן הַבַּבְלִי אוֹמֵר: אַף כִּפַּת הַיַּרְדֵּן

כָּל שֶׁהִיא, וְאִם נָתַן בָּהּ דְּבַשׁ פְּסָלָהּ, וְאִם חִסֵּר אֶחָד מִכָּל סַמְמָנֶיהָ חַיָּב מִיתָה:

ego-nullification associated with that world ... All this corresponds to the external dimension of the heart, which is comparable to the offering of sacrifices on the outer altar.

But, the inner dimension of the heart corresponds to the burning of incense, since the Hebrew word for "incense" (*ketoret*) is associated with the word for "connection" (*hitkashrut*), and specifically with essential connection (with G-d). That is, the love that (corresponds to the incense) does not come as a result of meditation alone. Rather, it is the expression of the essential connection of the soul with the infinite light of the One Above. As Rabbi Shimon bar Yochai said, "With one knot (*ketirna*) I am united (*itkatarna*), with Him. I am

united and consumed..." This expresses unity that transcends intellect ...

Incense symbolizes unity that defies logic and overcomes all limitations. It is the opposite of the love generated by our meditation on our life-force and vitality, which remains proportionate to our own ability to feel and understand it. The unity of incense is one of lasting connection and permanent union, surpassing the intellect. This essential love does not disappear or dissipate.

It emerges then, that the difference between sacrifices and incense is that sacrifices correspond to the immanent light (*ohr penimi*) of our soul, while incense corresponds to the transcendent illumination (*ohr makif*) of the soul.

(From *Beshaah Shehikdimu* 5672 (1912) of the Rebbe Rashab, vol.1, pp. 429-430)

CHASSIDIC INSIGHTS

as well as the recipe for creating the incense. It was offered on the inner (golden) altar, which represented a far higher form of G-dly service than did the outer (earthen) altar. The everyday sacrifices offered on the outer altar correspond to our everyday, thoughtful meditation and step-by-step progress toward understanding G-dliness, and developing fear and love of G-d. This is an orderly process, taking us from one step of intellectual activity to the next, ever higher in the service of G-d, but always

*T*he Rabbis taught, How did the preparation of the incense take place? There were three hundred and sixty-eight portions in it.

Three hundred and sixty-five corresponded to the number of days of the solar year, with one portion for each day, divided into part for the morning and part for the evening. And three portions were left over, from which the High Priest would fill up his hand on Yom Kippur [and take into the Holy of Holies]. On the day before Yom Kippur, these [three portions] were placed back into the grinder and ground very thoroughly to turn it into the finest of the fine.

And there were eleven spices in [the incense]. And these are they: balm, onycha, galanum, frankincense – each of which weighed seventy units; there was myrrh, cassia, spikenard, and saffron, each of which weighed sixteen units. There was costus, weighing twelve units, and aromatic bark weighing three units, and cinnamon, which weighed nine units. There were nine *kavin* of lye from carshina used in the preparation, as well as three *kavin* and three *se'in* of Cypriot wine, and if there was no wine from Cyprus available, strong, white wine could be used instead. A quarter *kab* of sodomite salt went into the preparation, as well as a tiny bit of a herb for smoking. R' Natan the Babylonian said that a small amount of Jordan amber was used as well. If any honey was added, [the mixture] became invalid, and if any one of these spices were missing, the [person making the mixture] was liable for capital punishment.

CHASSIDIC EXCERPTS

The outer altar and the inner altar

The outer altar[28] was placed in the courtyard of the Tent of Meeting (*Ohel Moed*). The service of the outer altar involved sacrifices – offerings of bulls, goats and sheep – which were consumed in a fire that descended from Above ... The act of offering the animal on the altar facilitated its ascent and elevation. When the offering was incinerated in its entirety by the fire from Above, the good [which ascended] separated from the bad [which remained below]. And the sages said that even though a fire came from Above, we have an obligation to bring fire from below, as it is written,[29] "And the sons of Aharon put fire on the altar and arranged wood..." The fire from below was a catalyst for the fire from Above.

And now, since our prayers were established in lieu of the sacrifices, prayer is equivalent to offering up the animal soul, as it is written,[30] "When you bring *from yourselves* a sacrifice..."

רַבָּן שִׁמְעוֹן בֶּן גַּמְלִיאֵל אוֹמֵר: הַצֳּרִי אֵינוֹ אֶלָּא שְׂרָף הַנּוֹטֵף מֵעֲצֵי הַקְּטָף, בְּרִית כַּרְשִׁינָה שֶׁשָּׁפִין בָּהּ אֶת הַצִּפֹּרֶן, כְּדֵי שֶׁתְּהֵא נָאָה; יֵין קַפְרִיסִין שֶׁשּׁוֹרִין בּוֹ אֶת הַצִּפֹּרֶן, כְּדֵי שֶׁתְּהֵא עַזָּה, וַהֲלֹא מֵי רַגְלַיִם יָפִין לָהּ, אֶלָּא שֶׁאֵין מַכְנִיסִין מֵי רַגְלַיִם בַּמִּקְדָּשׁ מִפְּנֵי הַכָּבוֹד:

תַּנְיָא רַבִּי נָתָן אוֹמֵר: כְּשֶׁהוּא שׁוֹחֵק אוֹמֵר: הָדֵק הֵיטֵב, הֵיטֵב הָדֵק, מִפְּנֵי שֶׁהַקּוֹל יָפֶה לַבְּשָׂמִים. פִּטְּמָהּ לַחֲצָאִין כְּשֵׁרָה, לִשְׁלִישׁ וְלִרְבִיעַ, לֹא שָׁמַעְנוּ. אָמַר רַבִּי יְהוּדָה זֶה הַכְּלָל, אִם כְּמִדָּתָהּ כְּשֵׁרָה לַחֲצָאִין. וְאִם חִסַּר אֶחָד מִכָּל סַמְמָנֶיהָ חַיָּב מִיתָה:

תַּנְיָא בַּר קַפָּרָא אוֹמֵר: אַחַת לְשִׁשִּׁים אוֹ לְשִׁבְעִים שָׁנָה הָיְתָה בָאָה שֶׁל שִׁירַיִם לַחֲצָאִין: וְעוֹד תָּנֵי בַּר קַפָּרָא, אִלּוּ הָיָה נוֹתֵן בָּהּ קוֹרְטוֹב שֶׁל דְּבַשׁ, אֵין אָדָם יָכוֹל לַעֲמוֹד מִפְּנֵי רֵיחָהּ, וְלָמָּה אֵין מְעָרְבִין בָּהּ דְּבַשׁ, מִפְּנֵי שֶׁהַתּוֹרָה אָמְרָה, כִּי כָל שְׂאֹר וְכָל דְּבַשׁ לֹא תַקְטִירוּ מִמֶּנּוּ אִשֶּׁה לַיְיָ:

Say three times - יְיָ צְבָאוֹת עִמָּנוּ, מִשְׂגָּב לָנוּ אֱלֹהֵי יַעֲקֹב סֶלָה:

Say three times - יְיָ צְבָאוֹת, אַשְׁרֵי אָדָם בֹּטֵחַ בָּךְ:

Say three times - יְיָ הוֹשִׁיעָה, הַמֶּלֶךְ יַעֲנֵנוּ בְיוֹם קָרְאֵנוּ:

וְעָרְבָה לַיְיָ מִנְחַת יְהוּדָה וִירוּשָׁלָיִם, כִּימֵי עוֹלָם וּכְשָׁנִים קַדְמֹנִיּוֹת:

CHASSIDIC EXCERPTS

But, the inner altar represents the service of the soul itself. On the inner altar, there were no animal sacrifices. Only incense was offered. No fire descended upon it from Above, but whispering coals were brought from the outer altar and placed on the inner altar. Nevertheless, it is known that the incense offering was a far higher service than the sacrifices.

The difference between the outer and the inner altars was similar to the differences between the prayers of the weekdays, and those of Shabbat. The purpose of the weekday prayers is to refine and elevate the mixture of good and bad (*klipat noga*) that characterizes our world, but on Shabbat such refining is forbidden.[31] The prayers of Shabbat are, as stated,[32] "to enjoy G-d," meaning to derive pleasure from G-dliness, about which it is said,[33] "The entire soul praises G-d." This bears no relationship to the physical heart. Rather, it is the service of the essence of the soul...

The service of the inner altar alludes to the very essence of the soul, the aspect of *Ma'h* [the name of G-d of numerical value 45, representing self-nullification] that transcends the flame of G-d ... The fragrance (of the incense) is something that the soul itself enjoys, even before it descends to become enclothed in the body, and this is

Raban Shimon ben Gamliel says, balm is nothing more than sap that exudes from balsam trees. Lye of carshina is used to massage the onycha and make it look nice, and Cypriot wine is used to marinate the onycha and make it stronger. Now, urine would also be good for this job, but we do not bring urine into the Temple out of respect.

It is taught that Rabi Natan said, as the priest would grind the incense, the overseer would recite, *hadak haitaiv, haitaiv hadek* ("grind it well, well it should be ground"), because his voice had a positive impact upon the spices. If only half of the required amount of incense was compounded, it was considered fit for use, but regarding a third or a fourth [of the required amount], we have not heard if it was fit. According to R' Yehuda, the general principle is that if all the spices were ground in the proper proportion, then the incense was fit even if only half the required amount was produced. And if any one of the spices were left out, the cohen was liable for capital punishment.

It is taught that Bar Kapara said, once in sixty or seventy years, half of the yearly quantity of incense came from the left-over portions of incense [from which the High Priest took into the Holy of Holies on Yom Kippur]. Moreover, Bar Kapara also taught that if one would add a bit of honey to the incense, that no-one would be able to resist the fragrance. So, why do we not mix in some honey? Because the Torah says, "No yeast and no honey may be burnt as a fire offering before the Lord."

"The Lord of Hosts is with us, the G-d of Jacob is our fortress forever." *(Say three times).*

"The Lord of hosts, happy is the man who relies upon Him" *(Three times)*

"The Lord saves, the King answers us when we call to Him" *(Three times)*

The gifts of Yehuda and Yerushalayim will be sweet for the Lord, as in the days of yore and in bygone years.

CHASSIDIC EXCERPTS

what is meant by the essence of the power of *Ma'h*.

There was no fire from Above that descended to the inner altar, since the fire from Above was for the purpose of refining and elevating fallen sparks of holiness. This was a process that took place on the outer alter, whose purpose was to elevate the animal soul, but the inner altar corresponded to the G-dly soul, which is not in need of elevation or rectification. It is already refined, since it is associated with the name *Ma'h*, as mentioned previously.

The fire on the inner altar was brought from the whispering coals of the outer altar. This is because the elevation of the G-dly soul took place in proportion to the elevation and refinement of the animal soul on the outer altar. That is, the purpose of the inner altar was to provide reward for the soul on account of its service of G-d in purifying the animal soul on the outer altar ... Its

אַ בַּיִי הֲוָה מְסַדֵּר סֵדֶר הַמַּעֲרָכָה מִשְּׁמָא דִּגְמָרָא, וְאַלִּבָּא דְּאַבָּא שָׁאוּל,
מַעֲרָכָה גְדוֹלָה קוֹדֶמֶת לְמַעֲרָכָה שְׁנִיָּה שֶׁל קְטֹרֶת, וּמַעֲרָכָה שְׁנִיָּה שֶׁל
קְטֹרֶת קוֹדֶמֶת לְסִדּוּר שְׁנֵי גִזְרֵי עֵצִים, וְסִדּוּר שְׁנֵי גִזְרֵי עֵצִים קוֹדֶם לְדִשּׁוּן מִזְבֵּחַ
הַפְּנִימִי, וְדִשּׁוּן מִזְבֵּחַ הַפְּנִימִי קוֹדֶם לַהֲטָבַת חָמֵשׁ נֵרוֹת, וַהֲטָבַת חָמֵשׁ נֵרוֹת
קוֹדֶמֶת לְדַם הַתָּמִיד, וְדַם הַתָּמִיד קוֹדֶם לַהֲטָבַת שְׁתֵּי נֵרוֹת, וַהֲטָבַת שְׁתֵּי נֵרוֹת
קוֹדֶמֶת לִקְטֹרֶת, וּקְטֹרֶת קוֹדֶמֶת לְאֵבָרִים, וְאֵבָרִים לְמִנְחָה וּמִנְחָה לַחֲבִתִּין,
וַחֲבִתִּין לִנְסָכִין, וּנְסָכִין לְמוּסָפִין, וּמוּסָפִין לְבָזִיכִין, וּבָזִיכִין קוֹדְמִין לְתָמִיד שֶׁל בֵּין
הָעַרְבָּיִם. שֶׁנֶּאֱמַר, וְעָרַךְ עָלֶיהָ הָעֹלָה וְהִקְטִיר עָלֶיהָ חֶלְבֵי הַשְּׁלָמִים, עָלֶיהָ הַשְׁלֵם
כָּל הַקָּרְבָּנוֹת כֻּלָּם:

אָ נָא בְּכֹחַ גְּדֻלַּת יְמִינְךָ תַּתִּיר צְרוּרָה   אב"ג ית"ץ

קַבֵּל רִנַּת עַמְּךָ שַׂגְּבֵנוּ טַהֲרֵנוּ נוֹרָא   קר"ע שט"ן

נָא גִבּוֹר, דּוֹרְשֵׁי יִחוּדְךָ, כְּבָבַת שָׁמְרֵם   נג"ד יכ"ש

בָּרְכֵם טַהֲרֵם, רַחֲמֵי צִדְקָתֶךָ, תָּמִיד גָּמְלֵם   בט"ר צת"ג

חֲסִין קָדוֹשׁ, בְּרֹב טוּבְךָ, נַהֵל עֲדָתֶךָ   חק"ב טנ"ע

יָחִיד גֵּאֶה, לְעַמְּךָ פְּנֵה, זוֹכְרֵי קְדֻשָּׁתֶךָ   יג"ל פז"ק

שַׁוְעָתֵנוּ קַבֵּל, וּשְׁמַע צַעֲקָתֵנוּ, יוֹדֵעַ תַּעֲלוּמוֹת   שק"ו צי"ת

בָּרוּךְ שֵׁם כְּבוֹד מַלְכוּתוֹ לְעוֹלָם וָעֶד:

CHASSIDIC EXCERPTS

reward was the subsequent ascent and cleaving (to G-d) from the inner depths of the heart, in proportion to the previous service of G-d.

The coals from the outer altar were brought (to the inner altar) after the flesh of the sacrifice was already consumed and reduced to whispering coals of fire. This alluded to the quality achieved by the soul as man offered his sacrifices on the outer altar. This is why the coals of fire were brought from the outer altar to the inner altar, and it is from them that the burning of the incense took place. The fragrance of the inner altar represented the elevation of the soul and its cleaving to G-d.

(From *Sefer Ma'amorim 5651* (1891) of the Rebbe Rashab, pp. 135, 137-8)

Abbaye systematized the offering of the sacrifices according to the process outlined in the Talmud, according to the opinion of Aba Shaul. First, the main pile of wood was set up before the secondary pile, [from which was lit] the incense offering. The secondary pile for the incense offering was set up prior to placing the two logs of wood on the main pile. The placing of the two logs of wood preceded the removal of ashes from the inner [incense] altar. The removal of ashes preceded the cleaning of the five candelabra [of the menorah]. The cleaning of the five candelabra preceded the sprinkling of the blood of the daily burnt-offering. The sprinkling of the blood of the burnt-offering took place prior to the cleaning of the remaining two candelabra. The cleaning of the two candelabra preceded the lighting of the incense, the lighting of the incense took place before burning the innards of the daily burnt-offering. The burning of the innards took place before the meal offering [of grain], the meal offering [of grain] took place before the pancakes, the pancakes took place before the libations of wine, the libations before the additional offerings (*musaf*) [of Shabbat and Yom tov]. The additional musaf offering took place prior to placing the containers [of frankincense], and the containers prior to the afternoon burnt-offering, as it is said, "And [the Cohen] will arrange for You a daily offering, and burn it upon the altar and smoke the fat of the peace-offering upon it; with this, all of the offerings are concluded."

Ana bekoach

We beseech You, by the power of Your right hand, free the bound. Accept the song of Your nation, grant us strength, purify us, Awesome One.

Please, Mighty One, guard as the "apple of Your eye," those who seek Your unity.

Bless them, purify them, always bestow upon them the mercy of Your goodness and righteousness.

Powerful One, holy One, out of Your bountiful goodness guide Your congregation.

Unique One, lofty One, turn to Your people, who recall Your holiness.

Accept our prayer and heed our cries, You Who knows hidden matters.

Blessed be the Name of the glory of His kingdom forever and ever.

רִבּוֹן הָעוֹלָמִים, אַתָּה צִוִּיתָנוּ, לְהַקְרִיב קָרְבַּן הַתָּמִיד בְּמוֹעֲדוֹ, וּלְהַקְטִיר הַקְּטֹרֶת בִּזְמַנָּהּ, וְלִהְיוֹת כֹּהֲנִים בַּעֲבוֹדָתָם, וּלְוִיִּם בְּדוּכָנָם, וְיִשְׂרָאֵל בְּמַעֲמָדָם, וְעַתָּה בַּעֲוֹנוֹתֵינוּ, חָרַב בֵּית הַמִּקְדָּשׁ וּבֻטַּל הַתָּמִיד וְהַקְּטֹרֶת, וְאֵין לָנוּ לֹא כֹהֵן בַּעֲבוֹדָתוֹ וְלֹא לֵוִי בְּדוּכָנוֹ, וְלֹא יִשְׂרָאֵל בְּמַעֲמָדוֹ: לָכֵן יְהִי רָצוֹן מִלְּפָנֶיךָ יְיָ אֱלֹהֵינוּ וֵאלֹהֵי אֲבוֹתֵינוּ שֶׁיְּהֵא שִׂיחַ שִׂפְתוֹתֵינוּ חָשׁוּב וּמְקֻבָּל לְפָנֶיךָ כְּאִלּוּ הִקְרַבְנוּ קָרְבַּן הַתָּמִיד בְּמוֹעֲדוֹ עַל מַעֲמָדוֹ, וְהִקְטַרְנוּ הַקְּטֹרֶת בִּזְמַנּוֹ, כְּמָה שֶׁנֶּאֱמַר, וּנְשַׁלְּמָה פָרִים שְׂפָתֵינוּ: וְנֶאֱמַר, זֹאת הַתּוֹרָה לָעֹלָה לַמִּנְחָה, וְלַחַטָּאת וְלָאָשָׁם וְלַמִּלּוּאִים וּלְזֶבַח הַשְּׁלָמִים:

אֵ[א] יֵזֶהוּ מְקוֹמָן שֶׁל זְבָחִים, קָדְשֵׁי קָדָשִׁים שְׁחִיטָתָן בַּצָּפוֹן. פַּר וְשָׂעִיר שֶׁל יוֹם הַכִּפּוּרִים שְׁחִיטָתָן בַּצָּפוֹן, וְקִבּוּל דָּמָן בִּכְלִי שָׁרֵת בַּצָּפוֹן, וְדָמָן טָעוּן הַזָּיָה עַל בֵּין הַבַּדִּים, וְעַל הַפָּרֹכֶת, וְעַל מִזְבַּח הַזָּהָב. מַתָּנָה אַחַת מֵהֶן מְעַכָּבֶת. שִׁירֵי הַדָּם הָיָה שׁוֹפֵךְ עַל יְסוֹד מַעֲרָבִי שֶׁל מִזְבֵּחַ הַחִיצוֹן, אִם לֹא נָתַן לֹא עִכֵּב: [ב] פָּרִים הַנִּשְׂרָפִים וּשְׂעִירִים הַנִּשְׂרָפִים שְׁחִיטָתָן בַּצָּפוֹן, וְקִבּוּל דָּמָן בִּכְלִי שָׁרֵת בַּצָּפוֹן, וְדָמָן טָעוּן הַזָּיָה עַל הַפָּרֹכֶת, וְעַל מִזְבַּח הַזָּהָב. מַתָּנָה אַחַת מֵהֶן מְעַכָּבֶת, שִׁירֵי הַדָּם, הָיָה שׁוֹפֵךְ עַל יְסוֹד מַעֲרָבִי שֶׁל מִזְבֵּחַ הַחִיצוֹן, אִם לֹא נָתַן לֹא עִכֵּב, אֵלּוּ וָאֵלּוּ נִשְׂרָפִין בְּבֵית הַדָּשֶׁן:

CHASSIDIC EXCERPTS

Sacrifices consume the animal soul...

The *Zohar* tells us that "the hour of prayer is the hour of battle." Furthermore, on the verse, "I gave you an additional portion...which I took from the Emorites with my sword and my bow,"[34] the *Targum Onkolos* (the Aramaic translation) renders the phrase "sword and bow" – as "prayers and requests." In order to understand the connection between war and prayer and also to understand why we pray every day, [we should recall that] the sages stated "prayers were established in place of the sacrifices."

The Torah says, "My sacrifices are sustenance for my servants..."[35] This verse refers to the sacrifices that were offered in the time of the Temple, elevating the entire animal kingdom [by sacrificing animals] on the altar, while bringing down fire from the heavens to consume the offering. For the vitality of the animal soul is based upon the element of fire. The four categories of creation – mineral, vegetable, animal and human – correspond to the four elements of earth, water, fire and air. The category of fire corresponds to the vital soul of the animal, and air corresponds to the soul of humans. As it is written, "And man was granted a living soul,"[36] which *Targum Onkolos* renders as a "speaking spirit" [since spirit – *ruach* – also means "wind/air"]. And as fire descended from Above, fire from below ascended and become included in the fire from

Aizehu Mekoman

Master of the universe, You have commanded us to offer the constant daily sacrifice at its appointed time, and to burn the incense at its time, with the Cohanim performing their service, and the Levites chanting, and the Israelites standing at attention. And now, because of our sins, the Temple has been destroyed and the constant daily offering and the incense discontinued. We have neither the Cohanim performing their service, nor the Levites chanting, nor the Israelites standing at attention. Therefore, may it by Your Will, Lord our G-d and G-d of our fathers, that the speech of our lips should be considered and accepted before You, as if we offered the constant daily sacrifice at its time and stood at attention and burned the incense at its appropriate time, as said, "[The prayers of] our lips in lieu of the animals [sacrifices]." And as it says, "This is the law of the constant daily sacrifice, the grain offering and the sin offering and the guilt offering, the inauguration offering and the peace offering."

*W*here were the places [in the holy Temple where the offerings were sacrificed]? The holiest sacrifices (*kodshei kodshim*) were slaughtered on the north [side of the altar]. The bull and the goat of Yom Kippur were slaughtered on the north side, and their blood was gathered in a special service vessel. It was necessary to sprinkle their blood between the poles of the ark, and toward the curtain in front of the ark, and on the golden altar. If even one [of these sprinklings] did not take place, the entire sacrifice was invalid. The [priest] poured the remainder of the blood on the western side of the base of the outer altar, but if he failed to do so, the offering remained valid.

[2] Bulls which were meant to be burnt, and goats meant to be burnt were sacrificed on the north side of the altar, and their blood was gathered in a service vessel in the north, and their blood was to be sprinkled on the curtain in front of the ark, and on the golden altar. If either one of these sprinklings did not take place, the offering was invalid. The [priest] poured the remainder of the blood on the western side of the base of the outer altar, but if he failed to do so, the offering remained valid. All of these offerings were burnt at the place where the ashes were deposited.

CHASSIDIC EXCERPTS

Above. Now, the fire from Above was also of an animal (*chaya* and *behama*) nature; both fires came from the high source and spiritual origin known as the *merkava* ("supernal chariot") with its "face of the lion," and "face of the ox." And this was the "lion" that consumed the sacrifices.

And when the Temple was destroyed, the Sages of the Great Assembly (*Anshei Knesset haGedola*) established the prayers, so that everyone could offer up and sacrifice his own animal soul, elevating and binding it to its source.

*

The source of the animal soul is the fundament of fire, and the origin from which it was hewn is the holy pinnacle

CHASSIDIC INSIGHTS

within the boundaries of human thought and emotion.

The incense offered on the inner altar corresponds to our inner self — to our undying desire to connect[25] with G-d. There are times when this desire is conscious, but far more often, it is unconscious. Still, it is always present, and has a way of reminding us to connect with Him just as we are losing that connection. That is also why the incense is considered a more spiritual offering than the

[ג] חַטָּאוֹת הַצִּבּוּר וְהַיָּחִיד, אֵלּוּ הֵן חַטּאוֹת הַצִּבּוּר: שְׂעִירֵי רָאשֵׁי חֳדָשִׁים וְשֶׁל מוֹעֲדוֹת, שְׁחִיטָתָן בַּצָּפוֹן, וְקִבּוּל דָּמָן בִּכְלִי שָׁרֵת בַּצָּפוֹן, וְדָמָן טָעוּן אַרְבַּע מַתָּנוֹת עַל אַרְבַּע קְרָנוֹת, כֵּיצַד: עָלָה בַכֶּבֶשׁ וּפָנָה לַסּוֹבֵב, וּבָא לוֹ לְקֶרֶן דְּרוֹמִית מִזְרָחִית, מִזְרָחִית צְפוֹנִית, צְפוֹנִית מַעֲרָבִית, מַעֲרָבִית דְּרוֹמִית. שְׁיָרֵי הַדָּם הָיָה שׁוֹפֵךְ עַל יְסוֹד דְּרוֹמִי, וְנֶאֱכָלִין לִפְנִים מִן הַקְּלָעִים לְזִכְרֵי כְהֻנָּה בְּכָל מַאֲכָל, לְיוֹם וָלַיְלָה עַד חֲצוֹת:

[ד] הָעוֹלָה, קֹדֶשׁ קָדָשִׁים, שְׁחִיטָתָהּ בַּצָּפוֹן, וְקִבּוּל דָּמָהּ בִּכְלִי שָׁרֵת בַּצָּפוֹן, וְדָמָהּ טָעוּן שְׁתֵּי מַתָּנוֹת שֶׁהֵן אַרְבַּע, וּטְעוּנָה הֶפְשֵׁט וְנִתּוּחַ, וְכָלִיל לָאִשִּׁים:

[ה] זִבְחֵי שַׁלְמֵי צִבּוּר וַאֲשָׁמוֹת, אֵלּוּ הֵן אֲשָׁמוֹת: אֲשַׁם גְּזֵלוֹת, אֲשַׁם מְעִילוֹת, אֲשַׁם שִׁפְחָה חֲרוּפָה, אֲשַׁם נָזִיר, אֲשַׁם מְצוֹרָע, אָשָׁם תָּלוּי. שְׁחִיטָתָן בַּצָּפוֹן, וְקִבּוּל דָּמָן בִּכְלִי שָׁרֵת בַּצָּפוֹן, וְדָמָן טָעוּן שְׁתֵּי מַתָּנוֹת שֶׁהֵן אַרְבַּע, וְנֶאֱכָלִין לִפְנִים מִן הַקְּלָעִים לְזִכְרֵי כְהֻנָּה, בְּכָל מַאֲכָל, לְיוֹם וָלַיְלָה עַד חֲצוֹת:

CHASSIDIC EXCERPTS

known as the *merkava* ("chariot") with its "face of the lion and face of the ox." However, after much descent, leading to the "spiritual hierarchy of creation" (*seder hishtalshelut*) and the enclothement of spirituality in the seventy ministers of the seventy nations (they having been created from the "waste products" of the lower angels called *ofanim*), the physical pleasures of this world also entered into the picture. This includes the power of lust (involving the heat of fire) and the evil inclination (or the "foreign fire" that burns within). As a result, the animal soul must now be uplifted to its source in the fire Above, so as to be included within the holy *merkava*, where "fire consumes fire." [That is, the holy fire of

the *merkava*] burns and incinerates the power of lust and the fire below [i.e. the passion that man feels] for the human pleasures of this world. This prevents us from getting overly involved in these pleasures. Rather, we should approach them with coldness and detachment in order to transform them into a different essence, into the power of lust with flames of fire for the "living G-d."

But, every day, our evil inclination overwhelms us, and therefore we must draw down "fire" from Above. It is written, "Days were formed..."[37] indicating that we have a limited number of measured years to our lives. "The days of man's life are seventy years,"[38] and they were not granted for the G-dly soul

CHASSIDIC INSIGHTS

animal sacrifices, even though it is physical. We cannot touch, feel, hear or see incense, but its fragrance enters directly into the seat of spirituality – the soul itself. Unlike the sacrifices of the outer altar, the incense represents our ability to skip and leap over the limitations of mind and heart, and connect directly to the One Above. We have only limited abilities of intellect and emotion, but the essence of our soul is infinite and unlimited, and that is the type of service of G-d symbolized by the incense offered on the inner altar of the Temple.

[3] Public sin-offerings and individual sin-offerings: these were the public sin offerings: the goats offered on Rosh Chodesh and on the festivals were slaughtered on the north side of the altar, their blood was gathered in a service vessel in the north, and of this blood it was necessary to do four sprinklings, one on each of the four corners of the altar. How? The priest ascended the ramp next to the altar and turned to go around, coming to the southeastern corner, then the northeastern corner, followed by the north western corner and the southwestern corner. He would pour the remainder of the blood on the southern base of the altar. These offerings were eaten within the courtyard of the Temple by male priests, prepared in any fashion, on the day of offering and the subsequent evening, until midnight.

[4] The burnt offering – which is a most holy offering – is sacrificed on the north side of the altar, and its blood is gathered in a service vessel on the north side, and its blood requires two sprinklings that constitute four [because the priest stands at one corner and simultaneously sprinkles the blood on it and on the opposite, diagonal corner]. And it requires the skin to be removed and the body cut up, and it is totally incinerated.

[5] Public peace offerings and guilt offerings: these are the guilt offerings. The guilt-offering for theft, the guilt-offering for misusing sacred objects, the guilt-offering for violating a betrothed maidservant, the guilt-offering of a nazir, and of one who is plague-ridden, and of one who is in doubt whether the act that he committed requires a sin-offering – all of them are slaughtered on the north side of the altar, their blood is gathered in a service vessel, and their blood requires two sprinklings that constitute four [because the priest stands at one corner and sprinkles the blood on that corner and the opposite, diagonal corner simultaneously]. They are eaten within the courtyard of the Temple, by male priests, prepared in any fashion, on the day of offering and the subsequent evening, until midnight.

[ו] הַתּוֹדָה וְאֵיל נָזִיר, קָדָשִׁים קַלִּים, שְׁחִיטָתָן בְּכָל מָקוֹם בָּעֲזָרָה, וְדָמָן טָעוּן שְׁתֵּי מַתָּנוֹת שֶׁהֵן אַרְבַּע, וְנֶאֱכָלִין בְּכָל הָעִיר, לְכָל אָדָם, בְּכָל מַאֲכָל, לְיוֹם וְלַיְלָה עַד חֲצוֹת: הַמּוּרָם מֵהֶם כַּיּוֹצֵא בָהֶם, אֶלָּא שֶׁהַמּוּרָם נֶאֱכָל לַכֹּהֲנִים לִנְשֵׁיהֶם וְלִבְנֵיהֶם וּלְעַבְדֵיהֶם:

[ז] שְׁלָמִים, קָדָשִׁים קַלִּים, שְׁחִיטָתָן בְּכָל מָקוֹם בָּעֲזָרָה, וְדָמָן טָעוּן שְׁתֵּי מַתָּנוֹת שֶׁהֵן אַרְבַּע, וְנֶאֱכָלִין בְּכָל הָעִיר, לְכָל אָדָם, בְּכָל מַאֲכָל, לִשְׁנֵי יָמִים וְלַיְלָה אֶחָד. הַמּוּרָם מֵהֶם, כַּיּוֹצֵא בָהֶם, אֶלָּא, שֶׁהַמּוּרָם נֶאֱכָל לַכֹּהֲנִים לִנְשֵׁיהֶם וְלִבְנֵיהֶם וּלְעַבְדֵיהֶם:

[ח] הַבְּכוֹר וְהַמַּעֲשֵׂר וְהַפֶּסַח, קָדָשִׁים קַלִּים שְׁחִיטָתָן בְּכָל מָקוֹם בָּעֲזָרָה, וְדָמָן טָעוּן מַתָּנָה אֶחָת, וּבִלְבַד שֶׁיִּתֵּן כְּנֶגֶד הַיְסוֹד. שִׁנָּה בַּאֲכִילָתָן, הַבְּכוֹר נֶאֱכָל לַכֹּהֲנִים, וְהַמַּעֲשֵׂר לְכָל אָדָם, וְנֶאֱכָלִין בְּכָל הָעִיר, בְּכָל מַאֲכָל, לִשְׁנֵי יָמִים וְלַיְלָה אֶחָד. הַפֶּסַח אֵינוֹ נֶאֱכָל אֶלָּא בַלַּיְלָה, וְאֵינוֹ נֶאֱכָל אֶלָּא עַד חֲצוֹת, וְאֵינוֹ נֶאֱכָל אֶלָּא לִמְנוּיָו, וְאֵינוֹ נֶאֱכָל אֶלָּא צָלִי:

CHASSIDIC EXCERPTS

within, since the G-dly soul needs no rectification. It is eternal and beyond time. It is united with its source from whence it came, from the infinite light of G-d, as it is written, "it [the soul] sat with the King during His work."[39] It [the soul] does not stem from the "face of lion" or the "face of the ox," like the animal soul of man, but rather from the level described as "the image of the appearance of man."[40] And the "spirit of man ascends Above," while "the animal spirit descends below to the earth,"[41] alluding to the "supernal spiritual earth" Above [that is, *malchut* of *Atzilut*, the source of all creation], as it is written, "The earth is a footstool for My feet."[42]

But, the spirit of man ascends, higher and higher ... so the quantity of life granted to man is for the purpose of [rectifying] his animal soul. And the number of years meted out to us human beings is in accordance with what is measured for us by G-d in His wisdom, so that with our soul we may elevate the many powers and sparks that fell during the shattering of the vessels [in the early stages of creation]...

Now, in order for fire from Above to descend and come down, it is incumbent upon us human beings below to bring our own fire. We do this by meditating on the source from which we were hewn and our origin in the holy *merkava* Above, from where the lust of our animal soul stems. We must meditate upon how our source [the "face of the lion and of the ox"] is nullified and subdued in relation to the "image of man that is above the throne," and therefore they [the "ox" and "lion"] "shake and tremble," and with great ef-

[6] The thanksgiving offering, as well as the ram offering of the nazir, are holy offerings of lesser holiness (*kodshei kalim*). Their slaughtering takes place anywhere in the courtyard, and their blood requires two sprinklings that constitute four [since the Cohen stands at one corner of the altar and sprinkles the blood so that some of it simultaneously falls upon the opposite, diagonal corner as well]. They are eaten anywhere within the city, and anyone may eat them, prepared in any fashion, on the day of offering and the subsequent evening, until midnight.

The portions that are separated from them [for the priests] are treated similar to [the sacrifices themselves], except that the separated portion is eaten by the priests, their wives and their children and their servants.

[7] Peace offerings are holy offerings of lesser holiness. Their slaughtering takes place anywhere in the courtyard, and their blood requires two sprinklings which constitute four [since the Cohen stands at one corner of the altar and sprinkles the blood so that some of it simultaneously falls upon the opposite, diagonal corner as well]. They are eaten anywhere in the city, by anyone, prepared in any fashion, for two days, including the night between them. And the portion that is separated from them [for the priests] is treated similar to [the peace offering itself], except that the separated portion is eaten by the priests, their wives, their children and their servants.

[8] The sacrifice of the first-born animal, as well as the tithe and the Pesach offering are considered holy offerings of lesser holiness. Their slaughtering takes place anywhere within the courtyard, and their blood requires one sprinkling, which must take place above the base [of the altar]. They differ in how they may be eaten: The first born sacrifice is eaten by the priests, and the tithe may be eaten by anyone. They are eaten in the entire city, in any manner of preparation, over the course of two days including the night between them.

The Pesach offering is eaten only at night, and is eaten only up until midnight, and only by those who are appointed to the particular offering, and is eaten only roasted.

CHASSIDIC EXCERPTS

fort and excitement become ignited and engulfed in flame, and nullified and absorbed in the light of G-d that flows down upon them. And then, spontaneously, the light of love from Above will descend upon us [as we meditate] and also subdue the power of lust within our animal soul that comes from there. And this will arouse our heart to become detached from the physical pleasures in which we have sunk, and to be drawn after our spiritual source and be nullified and included in the light of G-d.

(From *Likutei Torah* of the Alter Rebbe, *Parshat Ki Teitzei*, p. 34C)

בְּרַיְתָא - שְׁלֹשׁ עֶשְׂרֵה מִדּוֹת

רַבִּי יִשְׁמָעֵאל אוֹמֵר, בִּשְׁלֹשׁ עֶשְׂרֵה מִדּוֹת הַתּוֹרָה נִדְרֶשֶׁת:

[א] מִקַּל וַחֹמֶר.

[ב] וּמִגְּזֵרָה שָׁוָה.

[ג] מִבִּנְיַן אָב מִכָּתוּב אֶחָד, וּמִבִּנְיַן אָב מִשְּׁנֵי כְתוּבִים.

[ד] מִכְּלָל וּפְרָט.

[ה] וּמִפְּרָט וּכְלָל.

[ו] כְּלָל וּפְרָט וּכְלָל, אִי אַתָּה דָן אֶלָּא כְּעֵין הַפְּרָט.

[ז] מִכְּלָל שֶׁהוּא צָרִיךְ לִפְרָט, וּמִפְּרָט שֶׁהוּא צָרִיךְ לִכְלָל.

[ח] כָּל דָּבָר שֶׁהָיָה בִּכְלָל וְיָצָא מִן הַכְּלָל לְלַמֵּד, לֹא לְלַמֵּד עַל עַצְמוֹ יָצָא, אֶלָּא לְלַמֵּד עַל הַכְּלָל כֻּלּוֹ יָצָא.

CHASSIDIC EXCERPTS

Priests, Levites and Israelites at the sacrifices

The sages said in the Talmud,[43] "[The presence of] *Cohanim* (priests), *Leviyim* (Levites), and *Yisra'elim* (Israelites) was required at the sacrifices." This statement referred to the regular public sacrifice, the *Olat Tamid*, which was offered in the Temple every morning and every evening. Rashi explains that if one of the three groups was not present, the sacrifice was invalid, since the Mishna[44] reads, "During every watch, there was a contingent of *Cohanim*, Levites and Israelites." We find several instances in the Torah that necessitate all three; priests, Levites and Israelites. Among the priests themselves, we find the High Priest, his second in command and the common priests. Among the Levites we find three: the families of Gershon, Kehat and Merari. And among the Israelites, that is the rest of the Jews, we find the three categories of Jacob, Israel and Jeshurun. So, there are three groups of three. In fact, this is a general principal under many circumstances; in order to draw down added G-dly illumination into the world, three are necessary. Similarly, when we extend an invitation to join in the final blessing after a meal, three men are necessary. It doesn't help if there is only one person present. Even if he is the greatest sage of his generation and a Torah scholar, he cannot introduce the blessing (*Birkat HaMazon*) by himself; three are needed. And so it was during the offering of the sacrifices, the three groups of priests, Levites and common Israelites had to be present...

The Talmud tells us that without the three groups present at the sacrifices, the heavens and the earth would not remain in existence. This is because it is due to the sacrifices – and especially to the presence of the three groups of Jews at the sacrifices – that the world remained in existence. The word *korban* ("sacrifice") is related to the word *lekarev* ("to approach/come near"), which indi-

The Thirteen Principles of Interpretation

Rabbi Yishmael said, "The Torah may be interpreted using thirteen different methods:

1) By drawing a conclusion from a lenient premise and applying it to a stricter premise (and vice versa),

2) By applying the same law to two texts that carry identical Biblical expressions (when based upon tradition),

3) By assuming that a law that applies in one or in two Biblical texts applies to all similar texts [in general, but not necessarily in all of their details].

4) When the Torah posits a general principle, followed by specific details, the principle applies only to the specific details.

5) When the Torah lists specific details, followed by a general principle, the principle applies to all details [not only to those listed].

6) When a verse offers a general principle, followed by specific cases, and then returns to the general principle, then the principle applies only to cases which are similar to those listed.

7) When a general principle becomes understood only through specifics cases [then the general principle is not limited to those cases, as in no. 4 above]. But, when specifics become clarified only within the context of the principle, [then the principle applies only to those details, and not to others, as in no. 5 above].

8) Any detail that was included within a general principle, and was then mentioned specifically on its own, was not singled out for the purpose of learning something about the detail, but rather to reflect upon the entire principle,

---

CHASSIDIC EXCERPTS

cates that there is a spark of holiness that approaches, [returning to] its source in the intensely high World of *Tohu* (as the result of the sacrifice). Its return [to its source] results in added illumination of infinite G-dly light coming down into the world ... But now our prayers are in lieu of the *Olat Tamid* sacrifices. It is by and through our prayers that we bring down G-dliness and rectify the world.

(From *Sefer Ma'amorim 5643*, of the Rebbe Rashab, Pp. 105-6)

Priests, Levites and Israelites during prayer…

"Serve G-d in joy, approach Him in song, know that *HaShem* is *Elokim*."[45]

The *Megaleh Amukot* [Rabbi Natan Natah Shapiro, who was the rabbi of Cracow in the late 1500s] explains[46] that the three phrases of the above verse cor- respond to the priests in their service, the Levites in their blessing, and the Is- raelites in their presence [during the of- ferings]. That is, "Serve G-d in joy" cor- responds to the priests and their service in the Temple. And in our service of

[ט] כָּל דָּבָר שֶׁהָיָה בִּכְלָל, וְיָצָא לִטְעוֹן טַעַן אֶחָד שֶׁהוּא כְעִנְיָנוֹ, יָצָא לְהָקֵל וְלֹא לְהַחֲמִיר.

[י] כָּל דָּבָר שֶׁהָיָה בִּכְלָל וְיָצָא לִטְעוֹן טַעַן אַחֵר שֶׁלֹּא כְעִנְיָנוֹ, יָצָא לְהָקֵל וּלְהַחֲמִיר.

[יא] כָּל דָּבָר שֶׁהָיָה בִּכְלָל וְיָצָא לִדּוֹן בַּדָּבָר חָדָשׁ, אִי אַתָּה יָכוֹל לְהַחֲזִירוֹ לִכְלָלוֹ, עַד שֶׁיַּחֲזִירֶנּוּ הַכָּתוּב לִכְלָלוֹ בְּפֵרוּשׁ.

[יב] דָּבָר הַלָּמֵד מֵעִנְיָנוֹ, וְדָבָר הַלָּמֵד מִסּוֹפוֹ.

[יג] וְכֵן (נ"א וְכַאן) שְׁנֵי כְתוּבִים הַמַּכְחִישִׁים זֶה אֶת זֶה, עַד שֶׁיָּבֹא הַכָּתוּב הַשְּׁלִישִׁי וְיַכְרִיעַ בֵּינֵיהֶם:

יְהִי רָצוֹן מִלְּפָנֶיךָ, יְיָ אֱלֹהֵינוּ וֵאלֹהֵי אֲבוֹתֵינוּ, שֶׁיִּבָּנֶה בֵּית הַמִּקְדָּשׁ בִּמְהֵרָה בְיָמֵינוּ, וְתֵן חֶלְקֵנוּ בְּתוֹרָתֶךָ:

CHASSIDIC EXCERPTS

prayer, this alludes to the recital of the sacrifices, up to *Baruch She'amar* (which is the prayer of the World of *Asiya*). "Approach Him in song" refers to the Levites in their blessing, with their singing and music-making, since they would sing and produce music while the sacrifices were offered. In prayers, this refers to the *Pesukei DeZimra* ("Verses of Praise"). And afterward, the *Shema* and its blessings correspond to "Know that *HaShem* is *Elokim*," which refers to the unity mentioned in the first verse of the *Shema*. And [the fact that it begins with the words] *Shema Yisrael* alludes to the presence of the Israelites during the sacrifices.

Now, in order to properly understand all this, we must first explain why the priests, Levites and Israelites were present in the Temple. As the sages said,[47] "Rabbi Yehuda said in the name of Shmuel: '[The presence of] *Cohanim* (priests), *Leviyim* (Levites), and *Yisra'elim* (Israelites) was required at the

sacrifices." This was said regarding the *Olah* offering which came from the public coffers. Since they were all part of the public, they were all part-owners of the sacrifice and therefore representation of all three groups was required during the offering. (This was true of any private sacrifice as well – the one who owned and offered the sacrifice had to be present at the time it was offered.) For, how can a man's sacrifice be offered without him present?[48] This is why the early prophets decreed that there should be twenty-four groups and within each group there be priests, Levites and Israelites..."

...And[49] now that prayer has been established in lieu of the ongoing *Olah* sacrifices, these three groups – priests in their service, Levites in their blessings, and Israelites in their presence – must also be there during our prayers. And their overall presence brings down revelation of the infinite essence of the One Above...

(From *Sefer Ma'amorim 5658* (1898) of the Rebbe Rashab, p. 48, 57)

9) Any case that was part of a general principle, but was singled out to teach a matter related to the principle, was singled out to indicate leniency in the matter and not severity.

10) Any case that was part of a general principle, but was singled out to teach a matter unrelated to the principle, was singled out to indicate leniency in some aspects of the matter and severity in other aspects.

11) Any case that was part of a general principle, but was singled out in order to teach a new case, is not re-included in the general principle unless the Scripture explicitly designates it as such.

12) A scriptural matter may be interpreted according to its context, or it may interpreted based upon the subsequent passage.

13) Similarly, two verses which contradict one another, may be resolved by a third verse that reconciles both of them.

*M*ay it be Your will before You, Lord our G-d and Lord of our fathers, that we build the holy Temple soon in our days, and grant us our portion in Your Torah.

CHASSIDIC EXCERPTS

More on sacrifices...

Even though our prayers these days are in lieu of the sacrifices, nevertheless they are not totally comparable to the aroma of the sacrifices, in that they do not completely awaken our senses. Prayer is called *hiluch* ("progress") as is known. Such progress involves (spiritual) movement from one level to the next, in an orderly progression, which is why we must pray every day. Even though we are elevated through one day's prayers and draw closer to G-dliness, nevertheless we must pray the next day as well, in order to ascend to a yet higher level. And since the elevations take place in an orderly fashion, it is impossible from this perspective to awaken the senses and to remove all the concealments and blockages that hide G-dliness. For this, *teshuva* ("return to God in repentance") is necessary, as will be explained. *Teshuva* involves leaping over limitations and transcending orderly progress, since it comes from the very essence of the soul, and that is where the aroma [of the sacrifices] comes from as well..."

(From *Sefer Ma'amorim 5651* (1891) of the Rebbe Rashab, p. 112)

Remainder of the prayers...

The remainder of the order of prayers [following the morning blessings] progresses through to *Baruch She'amar* in order to separate from evil of the three impure *klipot* as well as *klipat nogah*. And all of this constitutes an exit from evil, termed the "exodus from Egypt," as noted previously. And then, we recite the *Pesukei DeZimra*, incorporating *halicha acharei Havaya* [lit; "walking after Havaya," referring to a path of G-dly service in which we lack direct revelation of G-dliness. Instead, we "walk after G-d," following His "footsteps" which we detect by meditation upon His creation and His divine providence in creation. By detecting evidence of His presence, we increase our appreciation, love and fear of G-d until we can virtually "see Him" in our mind's eye. Nev-

קדיש דרבנן

יִתְגַּדַּל וְיִתְקַדַּשׁ שְׁמֵהּ רַבָּא. (Cong: אָמֵן)

בְּעָלְמָא דִּי בְרָא כִרְעוּתֵהּ וְיַמְלִיךְ מַלְכוּתֵהּ, וְיַצְמַח פֻּרְקָנֵהּ וִיקָרֵב מְשִׁיחֵהּ. (Cong: אָמֵן)

בְּחַיֵּיכוֹן וּבְיוֹמֵיכוֹן וּבְחַיֵּי דְכָל בֵּית יִשְׂרָאֵל, בַּעֲגָלָא וּבִזְמַן קָרִיב. וְאִמְרוּ אָמֵן:

(Cong: אָמֵן. יְהֵא שְׁמֵהּ רַבָּא מְבָרַךְ לְעָלַם וּלְעָלְמֵי עָלְמַיָּא, יִתְבָּרַךְ:)

יְהֵא שְׁמֵהּ רַבָּא מְבָרַךְ לְעָלַם וּלְעָלְמֵי עָלְמַיָּא.

יִתְבָּרַךְ, וְיִשְׁתַּבַּח, וְיִתְפָּאַר, וְיִתְרוֹמָם, וְיִתְנַשֵּׂא, וְיִתְהַדָּר, וְיִתְעַלֶּה, וְיִתְהַלָּל, שְׁמֵהּ דְּקֻדְשָׁא בְּרִיךְ הוּא. (Cong: אָמֵן) לְעֵלָּא מִן כָּל בִּרְכָתָא וְשִׁירָתָא, תֻּשְׁבְּחָתָא וְנֶחֱמָתָא, דַּאֲמִירָן בְּעָלְמָא, וְאִמְרוּ אָמֵן:

עַל יִשְׂרָאֵל וְעַל רַבָּנָן. וְעַל תַּלְמִידֵיהוֹן וְעַל כָּל תַּלְמִידֵי תַלְמִידֵיהוֹן. וְעַל כָּל מָאן דְּעָסְקִין בְּאוֹרַיְתָא דִּי בְּאַתְרָא הָדֵין וְדִי בְכָל אֲתַר וַאֲתַר. יְהֵא לְהוֹן וּלְכוֹן שְׁלָמָא רַבָּא חִנָּא וְחִסְדָּא וְרַחֲמִין וְחַיִּין אֲרִיכִין וּמְזוֹנָא רְוִיחָא וּפוּרְקָנָא מִן קֳדָם אֲבוּהוֹן דְּבִשְׁמַיָּא וְאִמְרוּ אָמֵן:

יְהֵא שְׁלָמָה רַבָּא מִן שְׁמַיָּא וְחַיִּים טוֹבִים עָלֵינוּ וְעַל כָּל יִשְׂרָאֵל, וְאִמְרוּ אָמֵן:

עֹשֶׂה שָׁלוֹם (During the Ten Days of Penitence substitute - הַשָּׁלוֹם) בִּמְרוֹמָיו הוּא יַעֲשֶׂה שָׁלוֹם עָלֵינוּ וְעַל כָּל יִשְׂרָאֵל, וְאִמְרוּ אָמֵן:

CHASSIDIC EXCERPTS

ertheless, this constitutes only "walking after Him," because we lack direct, divine revelation. This is the human condition until the *meshiach* arrives, when the entire world will gain direct apprehension of G-dliness], with meditation on the heavens and the earth and all that is in them, and how "You enliven them all and the legions of the heavens bow down to You..."

And that is followed by the *Yotzer ohr* with meditation on the *bitul* of the angels, the *seraphim* and *chayot hakodesh* ... And then the *Shema*, wherein we give up our life, that is give up our desires/wills over to the service of G-d. And this is *mesirat nefesh* ("self sacrifice"), since *nefesh* means will, as in the phrase, "My will is not with this nation..."[50]

The Rabbis' Kaddish

Yitgadal v'yitkadash sh'mayh raba

B'almah di v'rah chirutay veyamlich malchutay, veyatzmach purkanay vikorave meshichay.

Bechayaychon uveyomaychon uvechayay dekol bayt Yisrael, ba'agoloh u'vizman koriv ve'imru amen.
Yehay shemay rabo mevorach l'olam v'leolmay olmayah.

Yitboraych, vehishtabach, veyitpa'er veyitromom veyitnasay veyithadar, vehitaleh, veyit'halolo, sh'may dekudsha brich hu. L'aylo min kol birchahtah, veshiratah, tush bechatah venechematah, da'amiron b'almah, v'imru amen.

Al Yisrael v'al rabanen, v'al talmidayhon, v'al kol talmiday talmidayhon, v'al kol mahn de'oskin be'roayto. Di be'atrah hadayn, v'di bechol atar ve'atar. Yehay l'hon u'lechon shlamah raba, chinah vechisday v'erachamin vechayin arichin umezonah revichah ufurkanah min kadahm avuhon de'bishmaya ve'imru amen.

Yehay shlahmah raba min shemaya vechayim tovim aleinu ve'al kol Yisrael v'im ru amen.

Take three steps back, and bow to the right when saying "Oseh shalom bimrovov", bow forward when saying "hu", bow to the left when saying "ya'aseh shalom aleinu" and bow forward when saying "ve'al kol Yisrael"

Oseh shalom bimrovov, hu ya'aseh shalom aleinu ve'al kol Yisrael ve'imru amen.

CHASSIDIC EXCERPTS

And this is followed by the *Shemonah Esreh*, in which we achieve *bitul bemetziut*, ["nullification of existence," in which the person is so nullified to G-d that He lacks any conscious experience of his own self] which is the reason that we say, "Lord, please open my lips since there is no word on my tongue..." And then *nefilat apayim*, ["falling on the face," which we perform by putting our head on our arm as we request forgiveness from G-d for our sins] as if we have passed away and are placed on the ground like an inanimate stone, as written elsewhere...

From letters of the *Tzemach Tzedek* in *Meah Shearim*, pp. 90-92

CHASSIDIC INSIGHTS

Hodu is the real beginning of our morning prayers. Essentially, it is a collection of verses from First Book of Chronicles (16) and from the Book of Psalms (105 and 96).[26] Because a section of *Hodu* was recited during the regular morning offering in the Temple, we now recite it after the *Korbanot* and before *Baruch She'Amar*.[27] However, it is apparent that *Hodu* was not part of the original prayers established by the Men of the Great Assembly. According to the *Ari*,[28] one of the verses in *Hodu* (*Kel nekamot hofia...*) was included "in order to elevate sparks of the souls of the ten martyrs" who were executed by the Romans. This terrible event took place several hundred years after the prayers were established, so evidently the entire prayer was not part of the original *Siddur*.[29]

In any case, *Hodu* begins with the words *Hodu L'HaShem*, meaning "Acknowledge/Thank G-d," and this is already the second time that we are doing so, even though the prayers have barely begun. The first time was when we awoke in the morning and, even before arising, we said *Modeh ani lefanecha* – "I am grateful to You..." The difference is that the first acknowledgment is a "general acknowledgment," meaning that

פסוקי דזמרה

הוֹדוּ לַיָי קִרְאוּ בִשְׁמוֹ, הוֹדִיעוּ בָעַמִּים
עֲלִילוֹתָיו:

שִׁירוּ לוֹ זַמְּרוּ לוֹ, שִׂיחוּ בְּכָל נִפְלְאֹתָיו:

הִתְהַלְלוּ בְּשֵׁם קָדְשׁוֹ, יִשְׂמַח לֵב מְבַקְשֵׁי יְיָ:

דִּרְשׁוּ יְיָ וְעֻזּוֹ, בַּקְּשׁוּ פָנָיו תָּמִיד:

CHASSIDIC EXCERPTS

Angelic names
Hodu LaShem ("Acknowledge/ Thank G-d...")

The reason that we recite *Hodu* between the *Korbanot* ("Offerings") and the *Pesukei DeZimra* ("Verses of Song"), rather than during the *Pesukei DeZimra* themselves, is because the *Korbanot* correspond to the World of *Asiya* ("Action"), while the *Pesukei DeZimra* correspond to the World of *Yetzira* ("Formation"). The *Yotzer Ohr* ("Creator/Former of Light") corresponds to the World of *Bria* ("Creation"), and the three correspond to the three types of angels: *ofanim*, *chayot*, and *seraphim*.

The secret of the angelic names is the following: in *Asiya* they are called *ofanim* ("wheels") because they spin like wheels out of holy desire to connect to God ... The angels of *Yetzira* are higher, and their vitality comes from a higher source, which is why they are called *chayot* ("live ones"). And the angels of *Bria* are higher still, with even more desire to connect on high, which is why they are called *seraphim* ("those that burn").

And man, who is a small world, totally lacks fear of G-d when he arises from his bed in the morning. As he recites the *Korbanot*, he whittles down his ego, as is explained in the *Zohar*. This form of G-dly service is associated with the World of *Asiya*, like the *ofanim*, which yearn to connect and roll into unity with G-d. But, how is this achieved? By reciting the *Pesukei DeZimra*, which impart more spiritual excitement than do the *Korbanot*. But before man can achieve such G-dly excitement, he must begin with only minimal stimulation, and that's why the sages began the morning prayers with *Hodu*, which is only a collection of verses and not songs of praise. The idea is that by the time man recites *Pesukei DeZimra*, it should be with great excitement, leading to more G-dly energy, since the energy and the excitement are one. And the blessing of *Yotzar Ohr* is said with even more excitement, corresponding to the level of the *seraphim*.

(From *Tzvat HaRivash* of the Ba'al Shem Tov, no. 43)

CHASSIDIC INSIGHTS

even before we have begun to use our minds or feel anything in our hearts, we already acknowledge G-d's existence. At this point, we do not feel or think about G-d; all we can do is admit that we must acknowledge G-d.

The second acknowledgement, during *Hodu*, comes after we have said the morning blessings, donned the *tallit* and *tefillin*, and already gained some spiritual awareness. At this point – while reciting *Hodu* – we at least know Whom we are acknowledging, even if we haven't yet activated full usage of our mind and heart to understand and feel G-dliness. This is called "specific acknowledgment," and it is a higher spiritual level than "general acknowledgment," though it is still near the bottom of the spiritual hierarchy.[30]

*

There are some basic laws that we must know before launching into our morning prayers. Most of them are derived from the example of Chana, when she prayed at Shilo for a son.[31] Here they are listed in very broad terms:[32]

1) We should only pray with a contrite and humble mind, void of

Verses of Praise

Hodu

*G*ive thanks to the Lord, proclaim His name, inform the nations of His deeds.
Sing to Him, resonate with Him, speak of all His wonders.
Exalt in His holy name, those who seek Him rejoice in their hearts.
Search for the Lord and His might, seek His countenance at all times.

"I am grateful to You..." – **Modeh Ani Lefanecha**[51]

There are two kinds of acknowledgment [of God's existence]. The first takes place when we acknowledge that He exists after having thought about and meditated on the subject. This kind of acknowledgment is comparable to that reached by a man who grasps and understands the tremendous and exalted majesty of a king. He concedes that the king is great since he recognizes and grasps his majesty. Similarly, we might recognize and admit the wisdom of a great sage upon encountering and grasping it.

However, there is another kind of acknowledgment that precedes logic and intellect. [This takes place] when it is totally beyond our ability to grasp and recognize greatness and wisdom for what it is, and all we can do is concede, admit and praise another's greatness. [Then, we're] like a poor man who concedes the greatness of the king, without grasping the king's true essence and elevated status. All we can do is concede, admit and praise his greatness, even

though we don't grasp its true nature.

This kind of acknowledgment occurs in proportion to the great distance between the conceder and the object of concession. The further out of range we are from the object of our praise, the less we are able to apply logic and intellect in order to acknowledge the other's greatness. In such a case, the best we can do is to employ "acknowledgment of acknowledgment." That is, we may only be able to concede that we must acknowledge [without understanding the reason for it]. This is why the sages say, "Multiple acknowledgments [because] He is a G-d of thanksgivings."[52]

From this, we understand that there are myriad levels of acknowledgment (and giving thanks) of G-d. The more we meditate on the greatness of G-d, the more we realize that He is beyond intellectual grasp, and that we are incapable of acknowledging His greatness through the use of logic and understanding. All we can do is concede that we must acknowledge Him, and this may take

CHASSIDIC INSIGHTS

any silly and superfluous intention or anger, but rather in joy and happiness.[33]

2) We should not pray while our mind is pre-occupied with figuring out Jewish law, but rather after we have understood the law.[34]

3) We should wait a bit before beginning to pray in order to prepare our heart. Also, we should wait a bit after praying so that we do not appear to be like one who wants to run out of the synagogue.[35]

זִכְרוּ נִפְלְאֹתָיו אֲשֶׁר עָשָׂה, מֹפְתָיו

וּמִשְׁפְּטֵי פִּיהוּ:

זֶרַע יִשְׂרָאֵל עַבְדּוֹ, בְּנֵי יַעֲקֹב בְּחִירָיו:

הוּא יְיָ אֱלֹהֵינוּ, בְּכָל הָאָרֶץ מִשְׁפָּטָיו:

זִכְרוּ לְעוֹלָם בְּרִיתוֹ, דָּבָר צִוָּה לְאֶלֶף דּוֹר:

אֲשֶׁר כָּרַת אֶת אַבְרָהָם וּשְׁבוּעָתוֹ לְיִצְחָק:

וַיַּעֲמִידֶהָ לְיַעֲקֹב לְחֹק, לְיִשְׂרָאֵל בְּרִית עוֹלָם:
לֵאמֹר:

לְךָ אֶתֵּן אֶרֶץ כְּנָעַן, חֶבֶל נַחֲלַתְכֶם:

4) When we pray, we should have the meaning of the words in our mind as we recite them, we should think that the *Shechina* is with us, and we should remove all troublesome thoughts from our mind so that our thoughts remain pure through prayer. (This is what the early chasidim did; they would isolate themselves and meditate before prayers until they arrived to abstraction of the soul and intensity of the intellect that was on a level close to prophecy.) And if an extraneous thought occurs to us during prayer, we should be still until it passes. And we should think about things that crush the heart and bring us closer to our Father in Heaven, and divorce ourselves from thoughts that are vain and without meaning ... And we should think before prayer about the greatness of G-d and the lowliness of man.[36]

CHASSIDIC EXCERPTS

place on the highest of levels, one level of acknowledgment over the other, corresponding to our intellectual distance from Him.

(From the *Siddur* with *Chasidut* of the Alter Rebbe, p. 606 (303C))

General and Specific Acknowledgment

Our prayers begin with *Hodu LeHashem* ("Give thanks/acknowledgment to the Lord..."), [even though] previously we already said *Modeh Ani Lefanecha* ("I am grateful to You..."). [The latter statement] is a general acknowledgment that takes place when we are lacking spiritual awareness. This is our condition immediately upon arising in the morning from sleep, as we face the new morning like a newborn infant, and that is why it is mere general acknowledgment. Yet, we say *lefanecha* – "before You" – meaning before the essential infinite light of G-d – which includes all spiritual levels. Similarly, the self-nullification associated with this state comes from the essence of our soul, meaning from all of our faculties, and

this occurs only during general acknowledgment. In this condition, we do not yet know how to discern between matters in which the intellect plays a role, and matters that are appropriate to admission and acknowledgment alone. Our entire approach, therefore, is one of acknowledgment alone.

As we [begin, however to] grasp matters with our intellect, we fail to become imbued with [the quality of] self-nullification that infuses all of our faculties. Only our minds are nullified (this takes place regarding particular levels of G-dliness; we become nullified only in relation to the level on which we meditate and understand, according to our soul-level and intellectual grasp). This [nullification of specific faculties]

CHASSIDIC INSIGHTS

These guidelines for meditation before and during prayer are in the realm of *halacha* (Jewish law) and not only in the realm of Kabbalah (Jewish mysticism). They are obligatory for all Jews, and yet they exude spirituality. This is especially true of the final *halacha* cited above, which makes Jewish meditation a virtual requirement.

There is some discussion among the sages about whether the obligation to pray derives from the Torah or from the rabbis. However, one thing is clear. If Jews feel themselves to be in dire need of something, they are required by Torah law to petition G-d to fulfill their needs. This we learn from the example of the Jews during times of stress and calamity (for example, famine or war). The Torah instructed that at such times, we should gather together, blow the *hatzotzrot* ("trumpet") and pray.[37]

Meditation brings us precisely to this position — to the realization how much we need G-d. A little bit of contemplation on the "greatness of G-d and the lowliness of man" leads inescapably to the realization that we are far from G-d, sorely lacking and deficient before Him. And that arouses within us a desire to pray to Him in order to fill our needs — both physical and spiritual —since we are deficient and lacking. Since realistic assessment of our situation, accompanied by meditation, leads us to the stressful conclusion

Recall the wonders that He performed,
His signs and laws from His mouth.

The descendents of Israel are His servants, the sons of Jacob His chosen.
He is the Lord our G-d, His laws apply to all of the earth!

Remember His covenant forever, His command for a thousand generations.
That He established with Abraham, and His oath to Isaac.

He set it up as law with Jacob, and a permanent covenant with Israel.
Saying,

"To you I have given the land of Canaan," as your inheritance.

CHASSIDIC EXCERPTS

filters down to our emotions as well. This is a step by step process, during which [the light filtering down] becomes minimized, as known... The nullification involved is no longer of our very essence, for it emerges only as the result of our use of intellect. The intellect "exists," so to speak [it is not intrinsically nullified to G-d]. And therefore when we know and discern something associated with knowledge and intellect, our level of nullification is not total, [even though] within that framework, we may find it appropriate to admit and concede. We are not imbued with real nullification that permeates all of our faculties, for our element of intellectual grasp implies that there is something that "exists."

And although regarding matters that are beyond our intellect, we may express admission and acknowledgment alone (that is, essential nullification),

nevertheless since we [already] possess knowledge associated with intellect, we fail to achieve a state of total nullification. Our knowledge dilutes and weakens our state of nullification in general, so that it is not real...This is not the case, [though], regarding general nullification in which we do not discern between that which is associated with intellectual grasp and that which is associated with acknowledgment alone. [At that stage], our acknowledgment occurs in relation to the infinite light of G-d and it occurs on all levels. This is essential nullification, in which we "deliver" and give ourselves over entirely to G-dliness from the very essence of our soul and with all of our faculties (this is the beginning of *avoda* of true servants of G-d as they recite *modeh ani*).

Regarding spiritual revelation, [though], this [initial level of nullification] is totally "immature" [lacking any

CHASSIDIC INSIGHTS

that we are far from Him, prayer accompanied by meditation is a Torah obligation.[38]

The subject of meditation before prayer is as unlimited as the Torah itself, but in general it centers on the topic known in the Talmud and in the writings of Maimonides/Rambam as *pardes* ("orchard"), a reference to the inner dimensions of the Torah. Although *pardes* is also an acronym of the words that refer to the various levels of Torah interpretation – *pshat* ("simple/plain" meaning), *drosh* (rabbinic "exegesis"), *remez* ("hints" contained in the letters and numerical values of the Hebrew words) and *sod* ("secrets") – the Talmud[39] uses the term to refer to the mystical dimension of the Torah. Within *pardes* are two main categories of study – *maaseh bereishit* ("workings of creation") and *maaseh merkavah* ("workings of the chariot"). We will elaborate on the latter below.

בִּהְיוֹתְכֶם מְתֵי מִסְפָּר, כִּמְעַט וְגָרִים בָּהּ:

וַיִּתְהַלְּכוּ מִגּוֹי אֶל גּוֹי, וּמִמַּמְלָכָה אֶל עַם אַחֵר:

לֹא הִנִּיחַ לְאִישׁ לְעָשְׁקָם, וַיּוֹכַח עֲלֵיהֶם מְלָכִים:

אַל תִּגְּעוּ בִמְשִׁיחָי וּבִנְבִיאַי אַל תָּרֵעוּ:

שִׁירוּ לַיָי כָּל הָאָרֶץ, בַּשְּׂרוּ מִיּוֹם אֶל יוֹם יְשׁוּעָתוֹ:

סַפְּרוּ בַגּוֹיִם אֶת כְּבוֹדוֹ, בְּכָל הָעַמִּים נִפְלְאוֹתָיו:

כִּי גָדוֹל יְיָ וּמְהֻלָּל מְאֹד, וְנוֹרָא הוּא עַל כָּל אֱלֹהִים:

כִּי כָּל אֱלֹהֵי הָעַמִּים אֱלִילִים (pause) וַיְיָ שָׁמַיִם עָשָׂה:

Rambam, whose *Mishneh Torah* is the first codification of the entire Oral Torah, opens his work with explanation of *pardes*. The first two chapters describe *maaseh merkava*, and the second two describe *maaseh bereishit*. Therefore, it seems contradictory that the Rambam closes this section of his work by saying:

"And I declare that it is inappropriate to stroll in the orchard (*pardes*) unless one's gut is already full of bread and meat. By bread and meat is meant knowledge of what is forbidden and permitted by the commandments..."

What is strange is that just before writing this remark, Rambam himself dedicated four chapters of

---

CHASSIDIC EXCERPTS

development or awareness]. But, after it occurs, we may [begin our prayers by saying] *Hodu leHashem kir'u beshmo* – "Acknowledge *Havaya*, call His Name." This phrase indicates some knowledge of *Havaya*, which is above intellect. At this point, it is only appropriate to acknowledge the name *Havaya* [which remains transcendent]. However, "calling His Name" implies [other names as well] - the names *Adni* and *Elokim* - which indicate the power of the Actor (Hashem) within the acted upon - [G-dly vitality] becoming enclothed within creation. At this point, it is appropriate to

mention *kriah* and *hamshacha* - "calling upon and drawing down." This stage occurs after our preface of the morning blessings, when we say, "He Who grants knowledge to the rooster," and "He Who opens the eyes of the blind." [Recitation of these blessings] "creates the vessels," which enable us to achieve knowledge and grasp. Nevertheless, all of this constitutes mere acknowledgment, following which we recite the *pesukei dezimra*, which involve meditation upon creation from nothing to something...this generally leads to arousal of the emotions...

From *Besha'ah shehikdimu* 5672 (1912) of the Rebbe Rashab, vol. 1, page 619

CHASSIDIC INSIGHTS

his work to *pardes*. In fact, he opened his compendium of Jewish law by describing the inner dimensions of the Torah. And we know that the order in which Rambam wrote his work is just as important as the content itself. Rambam meant for his *Mishneh Torah* to be learned in the same order in which he wrote it. Why, then, did he declare the study of *pardes* to be limited to those who have already learned the rest of the Oral Torah?

Since Rambam began his work with *pardes*, it is evident that he wanted his readers to know something about the inner dimensions of Torah even before learning the rest of the Oral Torah! Furthermore, the first chapters contain the all-important "constant" *mitzvot* of love and fear of G-d. These are the underpinnings of the entire Torah. So we cannot say that Rambam's intention was for people to learn the rest of Torah, and then return to these beginning chapters. Clearly, Rambam's intention was for his readers — whom were likely to be people not yet familiar with the Oral Torah (as he writes in his introduction) — to first learn *maaseh merkava* and *maaseh bereishit*, and then continue to learn the rest of the commandments of the Torah. So, why does he conclude this section with the stipulation that only those who are already "full of bread and meat" (meaning learned in the Oral Torah) may "stroll in the orchard"?

The answer lies in Rambam's choice of words. Unlike the Talmud,

When you were still few in numbers, a minority living there.

Journeying from nation to nation, from a kingdom to a different people.

He permitted no man to bother them, and rebuked kings over them.
"Do not touch my anointed ones, nor harm my prophets!"
Let the entire earth sing to the Lord, announce His salvation daily!

Tell of His honor to the nations, His wonders to all peoples.
For, great is the Lord, and very praiseworthy, awesome over all gods.

For, the gods of the nations are all as naught... but the Lord made the heavens.

CHASSIDIC EXCERPTS

Then all the trees will sing...
Az Yeranenu kol Atzei Ya'ar – ("Then all the trees of the forest will sing") [53]

In order to understand why the World of *Yetzira* is described solely as "vegetation" (*tzomeach*), when in truth the plant world contains no life-energy whatsoever, aside from the natural power of growth, consider the verse, "And then all the trees of the forest will sing..." [54] At first glance, how are we supposed to understand this verse, since trees have no voice whatsoever? Similarly, consider what the sages said regarding the verse, "May the glory of G-d be forever, may G-d be happy with His works" [55] - that this verse was recited by the angel who is called the "grand minister of the universe." At the time of creation, when G-d commanded, "Let the land brings forth vegetation, herbs

which produce seed," [56] the vegetation 'reasoned' [so says the Midrash], "Trees, which do not naturally grow intertwined and mixed together, are commanded to reproduce only among their own species; all the more so we, who naturally grow intertwined together, should be careful to reproduce only among individual species." Here also, it is possible to ask how vegetation can engage in reasoning, since it is not at all in the category of verbal/reasoning creations?

In response, there is a known saying of the sages, "There is no blade of grass down here that is without a spiritual counterpart Above that strikes it, telling it to grow." [57] And similarly, as

CHASSIDIC INSIGHTS

he does not use the word "enter." He does not say that it is inappropriate to "enter" the orchard, but that it is inappropriate to "stroll" in the orchard. A "stroll" implies a long, leisurely walk, in which one ambles through the garden, taking time to stop and examine whatever interesting objects come to one's attention. A "stroll" implies that one is devoting time and devotion to these surroundings, in order to absorb and enjoy them and become intimately familiar with them. This is what Rambam implies is inappropriate for one who has not yet learned the Oral Torah. But, to "enter" and get acquainted with the general principles of the inner dimension (as described in the first four chapters of his *Mishneh Torah*) is the obligation and a duty of every Jew.

הוֹד וְהָדָר לְפָנָיו, עֹז וְחֶדְוָה בִּמְקוֹמוֹ:

הָבוּ לַיָי מִשְׁפְּחוֹת עַמִּים, הָבוּ לַיָי כָּבוֹד וָעֹז:

הָבוּ לַיָי כְּבוֹד שְׁמוֹ, שְׂאוּ מִנְחָה וּבֹאוּ לְפָנָיו, הִשְׁתַּחֲווּ לַיָי בְּהַדְרַת קֹדֶשׁ:

חִילוּ מִלְּפָנָיו כָּל הָאָרֶץ, אַף תִּכּוֹן תֵּבֵל בַּל תִּמּוֹט:

יִשְׂמְחוּ הַשָּׁמַיִם וְתָגֵל הָאָרֶץ, וְיֹאמְרוּ בַגּוֹיִם יְיָ מָלָךְ:

יִרְעַם הַיָּם וּמְלֹאוֹ יַעֲלֹץ הַשָּׂדֶה וְכָל אֲשֶׁר בּוֹ:

אָז יְרַנְּנוּ עֲצֵי הַיָּעַר מִלְּפְנֵי יְיָ, כִּי בָא לִשְׁפּוֹט אֶת הָאָרֶץ:

Even before we have begun to ingest "bread and meat," we must learn the basic underpinnings and foundation of creation and of spirituality. And this is what Rambam delivers in the first four chapters.[40] Although, it is inappropriate to focus intensively on these topics before one has learned much of the Oral Torah, nevertheless, it is vitally important to acquaint oneself with the general principles of creation and spirituality. These are the same topics that are taught and explained in chasidic literature.

In accordance with Rambam's directives at the very beginning of the *Mishneh Torah*, anyone of us who wishes to pray properly and approach the subject of prayer seriously must attain general knowledge

CHASSIDIC EXCERPTS

we ascend higher and higher in the spiritual realms, we find more elevated spiritual beings, each with a sphere of influence that it protects and guides below. Consequently, we may deduce that it was the spiritual origin of the herb as it exists Above that expressed the line of reasoning mentioned earlier. These are angels – messengers of G-dly influence – that operate with logic and with understanding. The same is true regarding the "singing trees" mentioned previously – the singing applies to the spiritual counterparts of the trees as they exist Above. These counterparts are angels, who possess G-dly comprehension. The *Zohar* refers to this when it comments on the verse from Genesis, "Let the land bring forth vegetation, herbs bringing forth seed," noting that "vegetation" alludes

to the angels described in our prayers[58] as "servants," and "herbs" as "those who have served." Specifically, "He forms servants" indicates the angels that are created every day, who sing songs and recite praises and then are subsumed in the infinite light of the One Above. This is also referred to in the verse,[59] "He causes grass to sprout for the animals," since [these angels] are all part of and nullified to the "great animal" (*behama raba*) Above. "And those who have served" indicates the angels who are standing at the peaks of the upper spiritual realms since the six days of creation, namely Michael and Gabriel. They are called only "herbs and grass" since they grow like vegetables, meaning that their service of G-d is mainly emotional. They serve G-d with love

CHASSIDIC INSIGHTS

of "the spiritual hierarchy of creation" (*seder histalshelut*) – from the highest spiritual levels down to the lowest physical world in which we live. This does not require detailed knowledge of the secrets of the Torah, but only general knowledge of the steps leading to creation from nothing to something. Deep study of the secrets of the inner Torah (Kabbalah) is a discipline that is not for everyone. Those who are moved and stirred by this very technical and detailed study (no less detailed than learning the Talmud) may devote their days to doing so after they have learned much Talmud and Jewish law.[41] For the rest of us, the general framework and basic knowledge of *seder hishtalshelut* provided by chasidic literature will suffice. It alone is the basis of Jewish meditation. With it, we may meditate and pray, reaching the pinnacles of Jewish spirituality and G-dliness. Without it, we will have great difficulty starting along any path of Jewish meditation.

Another important point is that mere intellectual knowledge of the higher worlds and *sephirot* is not sufficient. We must actually "be there." We have it within our potential to experience higher spiritual realms that transcend our every day physical existence, and we owe it to ourselves and to our G-dly soul to actualize this potential. To bring the point home, here is a story that was told during a conversation between the Lubavitcher Rebbe and the Rebbe of Toldot Aharon:[42]

"Before he became a disciple of the Baal Shem Tov (*Besht*),

Glory and honor precede Him, might and happiness exist where He is.

Approach the Lord, families of the nations, approach the Lord with honor and might.

Approach the Lord in honor of His name, raise an offering and come before Him, Bow to the Lord in holy splendor.

Tremble before Him, entire earth, even the globe must be firm to avoid faltering.

Be happy, heavens and rejoice, earth, and the nations shall say, "G-d reigns!"

The sea and all that fills it roars, the field and all that is in it exults.

Then, all the trees of the field sing before the Lord, as He comes to judge the earth.

CHASSIDIC EXCERPTS

and fear – Michael with love and Gabriel with fear – and the emotions are described as "vegetable," as explained previously.

(From *Torat Shmuel* of the Rebbe Maharash, 1875, page 338)

Speech enhances our kavana

Just as speech adds to the illumination that we experience in our mind, so it enhances our emotions. As we speak words of love, for example, our speech becomes infused with emotions emerging from the capacity for love within our soul. And then, our speech amplifies our feelings of love. This is because we experience an increased illumination of love as we speak on the subject, which in turn stimulates more excitement of our soul, with love and affection for the object [of our love]. The same applies to stringency and anger as well; our speech has the power to stimulate anger and fits of temper ... and this applies to all of our emotions. When our feelings do not come into verbal expression, the level of [emotional] stimulation is minimized and contracted, and may even become totally suppressed. And the opposite is true as well – when our emotions are expressed in speech, they tend to expand and amplify.

A similar concept applies to prayer, which is why it is important for us to verbalize our words of prayer, even while our words are guided by *kavana* ("concentration on the meaning") alone. And then, in the very act of reciting the

CHASSIDIC INSIGHTS

the Maggid of Mezritch was already a genius in the field of Kabbalah. He would pray with *kavanot* ("intentions") of the Ari, and he had a friend who was also involved in these matters. After he became a disciple of the *Besht*, it happened that he met his friend, and when they stood to pray, the friend concluded his prayers much sooner than did the Maggid. The friend asked the Maggid to explain why it took him so long to pray, saying, "Once upon a time, we would pray together and conclude our prayers at the same time — what has changed in the meantime?"

הוֹדוּ לַיְיָ כִּי טוֹב, כִּי לְעוֹלָם חַסְדּוֹ:

וְאִמְרוּ הוֹשִׁיעֵנוּ אֱלֹהֵי יִשְׁעֵנוּ, וְקַבְּצֵנוּ וְהַצִּילֵנוּ מִן הַגּוֹיִם לְהֹדוֹת לְשֵׁם קָדְשֶׁךָ, לְהִשְׁתַּבֵּחַ בִּתְהִלָּתֶךָ:

בָּרוּךְ יְיָ אֱלֹהֵי יִשְׂרָאֵל מִן הָעוֹלָם וְעַד הָעוֹלָם, וַיֹּאמְרוּ כָל הָעָם אָמֵן וְהַלֵּל לַיְיָ:

רוֹמְמוּ יְיָ אֱלֹהֵינוּ וְהִשְׁתַּחֲווּ לַהֲדֹם רַגְלָיו, קָדוֹשׁ הוּא:

The Maggid's friend was involved in learning Torah most of the year, while his wife ran their business. But, once a year, he would set aside his learning for several weeks and travel to the town of Leipzig, to the country fair there, in order to buy merchandise. And then he would return to his home and continue learning Torah. The Maggid asked him, "Why do interrupt your learning and go to Leipzig? Would it not be better for you to think about the journey, considering that right now you are here and tomorrow you will be there, and then think of actually being in Leipzig, and then think about your return journey to your home? In that way you would have completed the journey in much less time!"

When he heard the

CHASSIDIC EXCERPTS

words of prayer, we experience illumination of the soul that is over and beyond [the meaning that is contained] in the *kavana* itself. For example:

• when we meditate on G-dliness during *Pesukei DeZimra* ("Verses of Song"), contemplating the creation of worlds, the wonders contained in the process of creation, the order in which the worlds are conducted, and considering the praises uttered by all of creation

• when we [ourselves] sing praises while reciting the blessings preceding the *Shema*...

• when we meditate on the unity of G-d – the upper and lower unity (*yichuda ila'ah, yichuda tata'ah*) – during the *Shema*...

Throughout this process of deep meditation, a G-dly light shines in our soul, and we become aroused with love and fear of G-d.

And then, afterward, as we recite the words of prayer containing the same content and meaning as noted previ-

ously, a G-dly light illuminates our very speech, much more-so than when we simply pondered during the preceding meditation. And we become aroused to a greater level of excitement, beyond the level that we experienced during the previous stimulation of intellectual understanding.

This means that an essential, internal G-dly illumination that was not apparent in our intellect and meditation prior to prayers becomes revealed in the speech of our prayers. Nevertheless, [for this to occur], it must be preceded by meditation and intellectual understanding. Failing this, we experience no [spiritual] energy within the letters or within the words that they form [during prayer]. But then, following meditation, an enhanced level of light permeates the very words of our prayers. And as we internalize that light, we experience a higher level of stimulation in our soul.

In truth, even without lengthy meditation, but upon brief contemplation, this same elevated light (which exceeds

CHASSIDIC INSIGHTS

Maggid's suggestion, his friend turned to him in amazement, and said, "How could my thoughts help? I have to be in Leipzig in order to truly bring the merchandise back from there!"

The Maggid responded, "So it is in connection with intentions during prayers. It is not enough to merely think about and have an intention that 'at the moment I am in the World of *Asiya* or the World of *Yetzira...*' We must actually be there in reality, in order to bring back the 'merchandise' – and that takes much more time!"

And since we need to really *be there*, that possibility exists only after learning and knowing about the supernal worlds. We need to internalize that this knowledge is "not in the heavens," and that it is within the reach of each and every person to absorb these matters. These concepts have been discussed by the Baal Shem Tov and his students with long explanations and examples and parables, and have been printed in books, so all that is necessary for us is to read and learn."

Here, then is an outline of the spiritual "chain of creation." It will serve as a map so that we know where we are, spiritually, as we proceed through the prayers. We will start from the lowest spiritual levels and work our way up, following the order of the *Siddur*.

Give thanks to the Lord, for He is good, His kindness is forever!

And let it be said, "Save us, G-d our savior, gather and rescue us from the nations, in order to acknowledge Your holy name, to exult in Your praises.

Blessed is the Lord, G-d of Israel, for all eternity," and then the entire nation will say "Amen" and praise the Lord.

Exalt the Lord our G-d, and bow down at his foot rest, for He is holy.

PRAYER	WORLD	CREATION LEVEL	SOUL LEVEL
Modeh Ani until *Baruch She'amar*	*Asiya* ("Action")	Specific creations	*Nefesh* ("action consciousness")
Baruch She'amar until *Barchu*	*Yetzira* ("Formation")	Forms, templates and archetypes of creation (angels)	*Ruach* ("spirit/emotional awareness")
Barchu and *Shema*	*Bria* ("Creation")	Potential creations (higher angels)	*Neshama* ("intellectual awareness")
Shemoneh Esreh	*Atzilut* ("Emanation")	*Sephirot*, or G-dly emanations	*Chaya* ("transcendent consciousness") and *Yechida* ("unity" – G-d consciousness)

CHASSIDIC EXCERPTS

the illumination of meditation and G-dly intellect in thought alone) may shine within the speech of the words of prayer. This occurs when we pray according to the simple meaning of the words. This is especially true if we understand some of the deeper meanings, including the inner intention [of the words]. But it is still not comparable to reciting the words of prayer after a lengthy meditation, when the essential light of G-d shines with greater intensity ... Moreover, when we place emphasis on our speech – meaning that we utter the words of prayer with greater energy – the illumination of G-dly light intensi-

CHASSIDIC INSIGHTS

First, we live in the physical World of *Asiya* ("Action"). It is the world "where the action is," where by doing a physical act, we can leverage spirituality up to the highest level – the infinite light of G-d above (as explained in the general introduction). *Asiya* is the world of specific creations and, as such, our meditation focuses upon the Hebrew letters that enliven them. It was Adam, the first man, who had the spiritual ability[43] to discern the essence of every created being (whether animal, vegetable or mineral); for the letters of its name actually bring down the spiritual influx that maintains it. By focusing upon the letters, we hope to access the spirituality that enlivens that aspect of creation. For example, the Hebrew word for "stone" is *even*, spelled *aleph-beit-nun*. By focusing on the significance of each letter, we hope to perceive the G-dly essence that creates and maintains the stone. The same is true of all things that inhabit the physical world. For example, "tree" is *etz* (spelled in Hebrew *eyn-tzadik*) and "lion" is *aryeh* (*aleph-resh-yud-hay*). When meditating, it is advisable to choose representatives of the four classes of creation – mineral, vegetable, animal and human – and contemplate the letters that enliven each created thing.[44] In this way, we hope to sense the G-dliness that is at the heart of all creation. This corresponds to the soul level of *nefesh*.

The power of the Hebrew language leads to the following fascinating observation: the same letters that are at the heart of the word *even* (*beit-nun*)[45] are also at the root of the word *boneh* ("build"), and *bina* ("intellectual analysis"), and

רוֹמְמוּ יְיָ אֱלֹהֵינוּ וְהִשְׁתַּחֲווּ לְהַר קָדְשׁוֹ, כִּי קָדוֹשׁ יְיָ אֱלֹהֵינוּ:

וְהוּא רַחוּם יְכַפֵּר עָוֹן וְלֹא יַשְׁחִית, וְהִרְבָּה לְהָשִׁיב אַפּוֹ וְלֹא יָעִיר כָּל חֲמָתוֹ:

אַתָּה יְיָ לֹא תִכְלָא רַחֲמֶיךָ מִמֶּנִּי, חַסְדְּךָ וַאֲמִתְּךָ תָּמִיד יִצְּרוּנִי:

זְכֹר רַחֲמֶיךָ יְיָ וַחֲסָדֶיךָ, כִּי מֵעוֹלָם הֵמָּה:

תְּנוּ עֹז לֵאלֹהִים עַל יִשְׂרָאֵל גַּאֲוָתוֹ, וְעֻזּוֹ בַּשְּׁחָקִים:

נוֹרָא אֱלֹהִים מִמִּקְדָּשֶׁיךָ. אֵל יִשְׂרָאֵל, הוּא נֹתֵן עֹז וְתַעֲצֻמוֹת לָעָם, בָּרוּךְ אֱלֹהִים:

אֵל נְקָמוֹת יְיָ, אֵל נְקָמוֹת הוֹפִיעַ:

fies in our soul. The proof of this comes from the Code of Jewish Law, the *Shulchan Aruch*:[60] "It is permitted to pray on Rosh Hashanah in a loud voice." The entire year we must pray quietly,[61] and one who raises his voice during prayer is described as a person "of minimal faith." But during Rosh Hashanah and Yom Kippur, it is permitted to pray in a loud voice, in order to arouse greater intention. As is known, the voice arouses our intention. And the voice is known to be composed of the same substance as the letters that we recite, as is written in *Igeret Hakodesh* of the *Tanya*, in the discourse starting with the words, "And David made a name..." This is what arouses the intention.

Now, by "intention," we do not mean intellectual grasp of the concepts in our mind, since what connection is there between the voice of the heart and grasp of the mind ... Rather, by "intention" here is meant the feeling in our heart (*reuta deliba*), that transcends the logical concepts underlying intellect. And it is aroused by the voice that comes from our heart, and especially by the substance of the letters that form our speech.

Through the process of speech, the inner depth of our intellect becomes revealed. This cannot take place via thought alone. It is speech that reveals the full breadth, length and manner of our intellect. And our emotions are

CHASSIDIC INSIGHTS

hitbonenut ("meditation"). The Hebrew letters (they are called "stones" in the *Sefer Yetzira*) are the building blocks of creation.[46] As we focus on the letters, and the spiritual vitality that they convey, utilizing our power of "understanding" (*bina*), we "build" (*boneh*) a spiritual structure in our minds. And when we dwell in that structure every day, adding to its girders and beams with greater levels of G-dly understanding, we are practicing the art of *hitbonenut*, as Jewish meditation is called. The art is to think about how the letters combine to form Hebrew words, with the goal being to detect the G-dliness that enlivens every creation. The edifice that we build in our minds corresponds to the spirituality that we bring down by contemplating the letters, as they combine to form words.

In summary, we use our power of *bina* ("analysis") to focus on the concepts underlying *avanim* ("stones") – that is, the letters of the Hebrew alphabet). In this manner, we are *boneh* ("build") a spiritual structure in our mind in which we dwell every day – and this is called *hitbonenut* ("meditation").

*

Our next step is to extrapolate up to the World of *Yetzira* ("Formation"). Here, we focus not on particular creations, but upon the general forms or templates of creation. They are the creatures that "populate" the World of *Yetzira*. They are archetypes and general forms of the specific creatures of the World of *Asiya*. They are spiritual creatures, also known as "angels."

This is the meditation that accompanies us in the World of *Yetzira*, during our prayers from *Ba-*

Exalt the Lord our G-d and bow down at His holy mountain, for the Lord our G-d is holy.

And He, being merciful, atones for our sins and refrains from destroying us, He repeatedly quashes His anger, and avoids arousing all of His wrath.

Lord, may You never withhold Your mercy from me, and may Your kindness and truth always surround me.

Recall Your mercy and Your kindness, for they are eternal.

Ascribe strength to G-d regarding His people, Israel, His pride, and might to the heavens.

G-d, You are awesome from Your sanctuary, the G-d of Israel grants might and power to the nation, blessed is G-d.

The Lord is a vengeful God, God of revenge appear!

CHASSIDIC EXCERPTS

more stimulated by speech as well. The reason behind all of this is the enhanced quality within speech that comes from its source Above, as well as from the source and origin of the intellect...

(From *Sefer Maamorim 5659* (1898-1999) of the Rebbe Rashab, pp. 5-6)

Happiness leads to G-dly revelation

The advice that enables revelation of the emotions within our heart comes from the verse,[62] "Serve G-d happily." This refers to the joy of meditation, based upon intellectual understanding of the greatness of G-d and His wonders, leading us to true happiness of our soul. The meditation itself must take place in joy and with vitality of the soul, rather than be dispensed with dispassionately, as one who does only because he must. In such a case, even though we may grasp the matter, nevertheless, we will experience no excitement or arousal but will remain cold like a corpse. And then, automatically, we will have no interest at all in the concept itself that we have grasped. However, when our intellectual grasp takes place with energy, imbued with the happiness and joy that emerges from our understanding, then we will become excited over it and be aroused with joy of our soul over the wonders and majesty of G-dliness that we have come to understand.

Now, the nature of happiness is that

ruch She'Amar thru *Pesukei DeZimra* til *Yishtabach*. It is associated with the soul-level of *ruach* ("spirit/wind"), which arouses our natural emotions. Yet another clue comes from the Prophet Elijah.[47] As he ran away from Queen Jezebel and arrived at Horeb, G-d spoke to him:

"Go out and stand on the mountain before G-d. And behold, G-d passed before him and there was a great and strong wind, [capable of] disintegrating mountains and shattering rocks before G-d,

הַנֹּשֵׂא שֹׁפֵט הָאָרֶץ הָשֵׁב גְּמוּל עַל גֵּאִים:

לַיָי הַיְשׁוּעָה, עַל עַמְּךָ בִרְכָתֶךָ סֶּלָה:

יְיָ צְבָאוֹת עִמָּנוּ, מִשְׂגָּב לָנוּ אֱלֹהֵי יַעֲקֹב סֶלָה:

יְיָ צְבָאוֹת, אַשְׁרֵי אָדָם בֹּטֵחַ בָּךְ:

יְיָ הוֹשִׁיעָה, הַמֶּלֶךְ יַעֲנֵנוּ בְיוֹם קָרְאֵנוּ:

הוֹשִׁיעָה אֶת עַמֶּךָ וּבָרֵךְ אֶת נַחֲלָתֶךָ, וּרְעֵם וְנַשְּׂאֵם עַד הָעוֹלָם:

נַפְשֵׁנוּ חִכְּתָה לַיָי, עֶזְרֵנוּ וּמָגִנֵּנוּ הוּא:

כִּי בוֹ יִשְׂמַח לִבֵּנוּ, כִּי בְשֵׁם קָדְשׁוֹ בָטָחְנוּ:

יְהִי חַסְדְּךָ יְיָ עָלֵינוּ, כַּאֲשֶׁר יִחַלְנוּ לָךְ:

הַרְאֵנוּ יְיָ חַסְדֶּךָ, וְיֶשְׁעֲךָ תִּתֶּן לָנוּ:

קוּמָה עֶזְרָתָה לָּנוּ, וּפְדֵנוּ לְמַעַן חַסְדֶּךָ:

[but] G-d was not in the wind. And after the wind, there was a noise, but G-d was not in the noise. And after the noise, there was fire, but G-d was not in the fire. And after the fire, there was a still, small voice."

These verses describe the process of prayer, with the "great and strong wind" alluding to the *Pesukei DeZimra*.[48] Just as this section of the prayers alludes to the soul-level of *ruach* meaning "wind," so it refers to wind in the world at large. It is an oblique reference to our natural emotions, which are close to the surface of our soul. All it takes is some meditation on G-dliness in the world to fan the sparks of our natural love of G-d into flames of G-dly revelation. And this is an allusion, as well, to the World of *Yetzira*, in which the emotions dominate.

*

The next higher world is the World of *Bria* ("Creation"). Here, the creation is too close to the World of *Atzilut* (with its G-dly emanations) to contain creatures of the lower worlds of separation or formation. Rather, the creatures of *Bria* are "potential" creations existing as "possible beings," or as Rambam calls them, *sichlim nivdalim* ("detached intellects"). *Bria* is only potential creation and, therefore, our focus during meditation is upon the "possibility of existence" of all of

it draws matters out from a state of concealment to revelation. That is why when we are happy, we experience expression and revelation of our emotions. But, this occurs only when the happiness is conscious in our heart; then and only then do we experience true revelation of our emotions. Otherwise, it is possible that the joy will remain in our mind and fail to stimulate our emotions...

(From *Samech Tesamech* 5657 (1897) of the Rebbe Rashab, p. 47)

Prayer requires kavana and da'at

Prayer, which requires *da'at* (deep, visceral knowledge) supplies the (inner) motivation of the mitzvoth, through which G-dly illumination descends from above into the *kelim* ["vessels" of the *sephirot* of Atzilut] in order to provide revealed infinite light from above in the mitzvoth.

The explanation is as follows. The main point of prayer is to develop *kavanat halev* – "intention of the heart." By "intention," we do not mean mere

CHASSIDIC INSIGHTS

the angels that we already considered in the World of *Yetzira*. Here, the categories would be the "possibility of existence of stones," or the "possibility of existence of trees," or "the possibility of existence of animals," etc. This is a very refined meditation, but if we have properly performed the previous meditation in the World of *Yetzira*, it becomes easier to envision and conceptualize the mere "possibility of creation" of those categories when we arrive to the World of *Bria*.[49]

This meditation accompanies our prayers from *Barchu* until (but not including) the *Shemonah Esreh*. It is associated with the soul-level of *neshama* ("soul/breath"), in which we penetrate to the essence of G-dliness within every creature and identify its source. This level of meditation was described by Elijah the prophet[50] as "a great noise ... but not the noise of G-d," and "a great fire ... but not the fire of G-d." "Noise" refers to the commotion among the angels during the blessings preceding the *Shema*. They are in a state of commotion because they perceive that G-d exists and seek full awareness of His presence. And "fire" refers to the *Shema* itself, during which we develop a strong yearning for G-dliness, such that we burn with desire for His presence. The result is that we ignite inside with a different kind of love of G-d. We ignite with an intellectual love of G-d that is described as "love like fire." We want to cling and cleave to the G-dliness that we detect within, but more importantly, beyond creation.

This is also called "intellectual love" since even though the emotions are present (and they are even stronger than in the World of *Yetzira*), they are contained within the intellect and are infused with intellectual content. At first (during the blessings preceding the *Shema*),

Arise, Judge of the earth, give to the arrogant their just deserts.
To the Lord belongs salvation, let Your blessing be on Your nation forever.
The Lord of Hosts is among us, the God of Jacob is a fortress for us forever.
Oh Lord of Hosts, happy is the man who trusts in You.
The Lord saves, the King answers us on the day that we call.
Rescue Your nation and bless Your inheritance, care for and elevate them forever.
Our soul longs for the Lord, He is our help and our shield.
For, in Him our heart rejoices, and in His holy name we are secure.
May Your kindness, Lord be upon us, as we have placed our hope in You.
Show us Your kindness, Lord, and grant Your salvation to us.
Arise, assist us, and save us for the sake of Your kindness.

CHASSIDIC EXCERPTS

thought. The word *kavana* ("intention") implies direction, as in, "If he directed his heart..."[63] or "until they direct their hearts to HaShem."[64] This means that they were required to direct their hearts to the One above, as in "One who prays should cast his eyes cast down and his heart above."[65] This means that we must focus our intention Above. This is [what creates] the bond and cleaving of the soul with G-dliness, as it detaches from its bodily sheath and we pour our heart out to our Father... And the point is for us to be bound and dedicated to G-d alone. This bond occurs only through [the fac-

ulty of] *daat*. For, it is known that *daat* is not simple knowledge and intellectual grasp, which are equivalent to *chochma* and *bina*. Rather, [*daat* is] recognition and feeling, as King David said to his son, Shlomo, "Know the G-d of your Father."[66] He could have simply informed him about G-dliness. But, the fact is that *daat* is not simple knowledge that can be transmitted [from one person to another]. Rather, *daat* is recognition and feeling, as if one "sees." And this comes as a result of our own power and effort...

(Page 69) This, then is prayer, which is *daat*. By way of *daat*, we focus our this meditation has the effect of transforming and incinerating our animal soul. Afterward, during the *Shema* itself, it carries the potential to impart an experience of the true oneness of creation, as the G-dly soul responds.

*

Finally, we reach the highest world, the World of *Atzilut*, which corresponds to the soul-level of

אָנֹכִי יְיָ אֱלֹהֶיךָ הַמַּעַלְךָ מֵאֶרֶץ מִצְרָיִם, הַרְחֶב פִּיךָ וַאֲמַלְאֵהוּ:

אַשְׁרֵי הָעָם שֶׁכָּכָה-לּוֹ, אַשְׁרֵי הָעָם שֶׁיְיָ אֱלֹהָיו:

וַאֲנִי בְּחַסְדְּךָ בָטַחְתִּי יָגֵל לִבִּי בִּישׁוּעָתֶךָ, אָשִׁירָה לַיְיָ כִּי גָמַל עָלָי:

chaya ("living being"), the pure will of the soul to cling and be one with G-d. It is also the soul-level that accompanies us during the *Shemonah Esreh*, the pinnacle of prayer.

At this stage, our meditation encompasses not only creation, but emanation, for in the World of *Atzilut* shine the ten *sephirot*, which are rays/reflections of G-dliness that emanate directly from the infinite light of the One Above. Here, there are no creations as such, because in *Atzilut*, all creations are nullified to the G-dly light that shines within the *sephirot*. So, in *Atzilut*, there is no ex-

hearts on the One above and form a hermetic bond with G-dliness, that precludes any other bond, rendering it completely impossible. And that is why [*daat*] is the "inner" intention of mitzvoth as well, since by way of our fo-

cus and bonding during prayer, we arouse and draw down the very essence of the infinite light of G-d from Above into the *kelim*, where they shine and illuminate in the vessels of the mitzvoth.

(From *Sefer Maamorim 5668* (1908) of the Rebbe Rashab, Page 68-9)

Prayer is a struggle

There are two types of refinement of the soul. The first occurs with a struggle – similar to a fight between two people who wrestle with one another until one is victorious, [as is described in *Torah Ohr*, in the discourse *Vayeabek ish imo*, "And a man wrestled with him."] The second takes place peacefully, as written regarding King Solomon, who was a "man of rest/peace," [67] since he did not need to fight wars at all. He was so majestic that greatness emanated from him, and the nations of the world were automatically humbled before him. In the days of King Solomon, "the moon was at its fullest," [68] as the illumination of his reign radiated with much strength and intensity. In light of his sovereignty, all of the idol worshippers of his day were spontaneously subjugated to him. [As it is written regarding the Messiah, "and they will flow to him,

all of the nations," [69] in the same way as a spark is spontaneously attracted to a flame and subsumed within it. And these two processes – the way of struggle and the way of peace – are understandable within the context of service of the heart (prayer)].

During prayer, we may become so aroused from illumination of the G-dly soul and so stimulated by meditation on the greatness of G-d that the excitement overcomes us with holy flames of desire for the One G-d. It may even affect our heart physically, inspiring us with conscious zeal ... as it is written, [70] "My heart and my flesh sing..." And yet precisely then, the evil element of the animal soul (*yetzer hara*), which is lodged in the left ventricle of the heart, raises its head and stands in opposition to our G-dly excitement, trying to distract us with various strange thoughts that are completely in-

CHASSIDIC INSIGHTS

citement over the very high spiritual level. Rather, our souls are overwhelmed with revelation of G-dliness, and we cleave to the display before us. That is why we preface the *Shemonah Esreh* (or *Amida*, as it is sometimes called) with "G-d, please open up my lips." We are so nullified before Him that we are unable to make even the conscious effort necessary to speak with Him. Our prayers flow automatically, and this is why Elijah the prophet[51] described this experience as the "still small voice."

The World of *Atzilut* is like a concise summary of infinite G-dliness. Each *sephira* offers a glimpse of infinity that contains all of the details of the infinite light of G-d beyond.[52]

For purposes of meditation, the best way to conceptualize the *sephirot* of the World of *Atzilut* is by using the concepts listed in *Tanya*[53] which give us the psychological corollary for every *sephira*. By meditating upon the psychological corollary (that is, how every *sephira* affects us inside) we are able to "dwell" in the World of *Atzilut*, focused upon the emanations of G-d's infinite light that impart unity with Him.

I am the Lord, Your G-d, Who has raised you up out of the land of Egypt, open your mouth wide [state your requests] and I will fulfill them.
Happy is the nation that so exists, happy is the nation that the Lord is their G-d.

And I will feel secure in Your kindness, my heart rejoices in Your salvation, I sing to the Lord since He has been kind to me.

We begin our analysis with *malchut* ("kingship"), the lowest of the ten *sephirot* of *Atzilut*, which corresponds to the "I" within us — the feeling of self and identity. This is the "I" that needs to be nullified to the One Above, by way of meditation and experience of G-dly revelation. Nullification of the "I" is called *bitul hayesh*, or "nullification of the ego," in chasidic writings. *Malchut* is the experience of accepting upon ourselves the "yoke of Heaven" — that is, the obligations of the Torah and its com-

SEPHIRA	FACULTY OF SOUL	EXPERIENCE
Malchut ("kingship")	Feeling of self and identity, "I"	Accepting yoke of heaven
Yesod ("foundation")	Truth in the soul	Ability to cling to G-d and to the righteous *tzadikim*
Hod ("acknowledgment")	Integrity of the soul	Ability to acknowledge G-d and to proceed without questioning
Netzach ("victory/eternity")	Trust in the soul	Ability to withstand tests and to take a proactive stance in service of G-d
Tiferet ("beauty")	Mercy in the soul	Ability to praise G-d and meditate on His glory
Gevurah ("strength/restraint")	Fear and awe of G-d	Ability to withstand temptation
Chesed ("loving-kindness")	Love of G-d	Motivation to cling to G-d
Daat ("knowledge")	Recognition	Ability to focus and concentrate in meditation
Bina ("understanding")	Happiness in the soul	Ability to break down a concept and analyze it
Chochma ("wisdom")	Self-nullification	Ability to grasp the concept in its organic wholeness in a flash of insight

CHASSIDIC INSIGHTS

mandments. This occurs as we nullify our "I" to G-d.

The next *sephira* from below to above is *yesod* ("foundation), corresponding to "truth" within the soul. It is what gives us our ability to connect and focus on what is above and beyond us. *Yesod* imparts the ability of the soul to cling to G-d with determination and persistence. It also imparts the ability to cling to the advice of *tzadikim* ("righteous"), even though we may not understand the advice that they are giving us.

Above *yesod* is the *sephira* of *hod* ("acknowledgment/thanksgiving"), characterized by the trait of wholesome integrity in the soul. With this attribute, we thank and acknowledge G-d. We acknowledge that all of creation is as naught before Him, and it is His spiritual energy that enlivens and creates everything. At this stage, we do not experience any excitement or understanding of G-dliness, but nevertheless we acknowledge His existence and presence.

Above *hod* is *netzach* ("victory/eternity"), which is characterized as security and trust (*bitachon*) within the soul. It imparts our ability to withstand tests, as for example when we are faced with obstacles in serving G-d. Using the attribute of *netzach*, we fight the necessary battles to enable us to cling to a Torah way of life without being embarrassed by anyone or anything that might want to repel us from the service of G-d. Even when the path is not clear, *netzach* gives us the ability to be proactive in G-dly matters. This is especially important in situations in which we do not feel or understand how to proceed. *Netzach* imparts the ability to act according to the advice of oth-

מִזְמוֹר שִׁיר חֲנֻכַּת הַבַּיִת לְדָוִד:

אֲרוֹמִמְךָ יְיָ כִּי דִלִּיתָנִי, וְלֹא שִׂמַּחְתָּ אֹיְבַי לִי:

יְיָ אֱלֹהָי, שִׁוַּעְתִּי אֵלֶיךָ וַתִּרְפָּאֵנִי:

יְיָ הֶעֱלִיתָ מִן שְׁאוֹל נַפְשִׁי, חִיִּיתַנִי מִיָּרְדִי בוֹר:

זַמְּרוּ לַיְיָ חֲסִידָיו, וְהוֹדוּ לְזֵכֶר קָדְשׁוֹ:

כִּי רֶגַע בְּאַפּוֹ, חַיִּים בִּרְצוֹנוֹ, בָּעֶרֶב יָלִין בֶּכִי, וְלַבֹּקֶר רִנָּה:

וַאֲנִי אָמַרְתִּי בְשַׁלְוִי, בַּל אֶמּוֹט לְעוֹלָם:

יְיָ בִּרְצוֹנְךָ הֶעֱמַדְתָּה לְהַרְרִי עֹז, הִסְתַּרְתָּ פָנֶיךָ הָיִיתִי נִבְהָל:

appropriate at the time of prayer. But these do not occur because there is any trace of evil in our excitement over G-dliness, since that comes from our G-dly soul which is pure and good ... [These occur because of the need of evil to struggle against good.] When the stimulus of the G-dly soul makes contact with the physical heart, wherein dwells the natural enlivening [animal] soul ... precisely then the coarse and negative elements of the animal soul arise to fight against the good [within us]. The portion of the physical heart that is touched by the excitement and illumination of the G-dly soul is the good from within the *noga* of the animal soul. It ascends along with the excitement of the G-dly soul, like a small spark that ascends to become absorbed in a larger flame. Similarly, this limited ray of good from within the animal soul ascends to become subsumed within the divine flame of the G-dly soul ... This is the nature of the purification process, as the G-dly soul purifies and uplifts the good from within the *noga* of the animal soul. And the evil aspect and coarse elements of

CHASSIDIC INSIGHTS

ers or our own gut-level counsel, even when the path before us is not clear.

The next *sephira* from below to above is *tiferet* ("harmony"), corresponding to mercy (*rahamim*) in the soul. *Tiferet* imparts to us the ability to praise and glorify G-d, in all kinds of ways, whether through intellectual meditation, or with our speech, or by embellishing our fulfillment of physical *mitzvot*.

Gevurah ("strength/restraint") is the fear and awe of G-d that we develop after proper meditation on His omniscience and omnipresence. It is what enables us seek punishment for those who deserve it (according to the Torah), as well as to withstand and subdue our own *yetzer hara* ("evil inclination"). Sometimes the "enemy inside" is the strongest, and the attribute of *gevura* gives us the ability to restrain ourselves as well as to create "fences and boundaries" to protect ourselves from it. *Gevurah* also facilitates our fulfillment of the negative commands of the Torah.

Chesed ("loving-kindness") is the love of G-d inside of us that motivates us to cling to Him. Ultimately it is *chesed* that facilitates our fulfillment and performance of the positive *mitzvot* of the Torah. Inside of ourselves, *chesed* translates into love of G-d.

And finally, we have the three intellectual *sephirot*. From below to above, they are *da'at* ("knowledge"), *bina* ("understanding"), and *chochma* ("wisdom"). *Da'at* is the ability to focus and concentrate on a particular subject in order to produce the appropriate feeling or emotion within ourselves. That may be love of G-d or any one of several levels of fear of G-d, but it is produced after meditation, which requires the focus and concentration imparted by *da'at*. The inner dimension of *da'at* is recognition (*hakara*) with

A psalm, a song of dedication of the Temple, by David.

I exalt You, Lord, for You uplifted me, and did not permit my enemies to rejoice over me.

Lord, I cried out to You, and You healed me.

Lord, You have elevated my soul from the grave, enlivened me to keep me from falling to the depths of the pit.

Sing to the Lord, all His pious ones, and acknowledge His holy name.

His wrath lasts but a moment, He wishes long life for us; we fall asleep in tears and awaken with rejoicing.

And I in my self-satisfaction said, "I will never falter."

Lord, by Your will, You established mountains of strength, then You concealed Your countenance, and I was taken aback.

CHASSIDIC EXCERPTS

noga separate and exit like the waste products that exit the body through sweat and other processes. This is similar to the separation of impurities from silver as it undergoes smelting in fire. So, via the divine flame ... of the G-dly soul in the heart, the mixture of good and bad within the animal soul becomes purified. The good elements ascend [elevating the human being together with them], while the negative aspects separate and leave.

And this is the reason for the struggle of the evil within the animal soul as it arises to create confusion [in the mind of the person praying]. Before the divine soul catches on fire with excitement over G-dliness, (as well as when it is aroused over the essence of G-dly illumination, but in such a way that no ray of illumination affects the animal soul whatsoever), the animal soul lies in repose, undergoing no purification at all. At that point, aspects of good and evil within it are still mixed, clinging together as one (more than ever), without undergoing any separation or isolation of the evil. Quite the opposite, the evil is wedged

CHASSIDIC INSIGHTS

which we come to know the subject upon which we are meditating in a deep and intimate fashion.

Bina is our ability to analyze and consider a subject at length, breaking it up into its elements and understanding how they fit together, and how one aspect leads to another. As a result, we experience happiness, because what was previously hidden (the interconnection between the parts, or elements) becomes revealed. Thus, *bina* is associated with happiness in the soul. Additionally, the deep contemplation and analysis of *bina* ultimately gives rise to our emotions, such as love and fear of G-d.

אֵלֶיךָ יְיָ אֶקְרָא, וְאֶל אֲדֹנָי אֶתְחַנָּן:

מַה בֶּצַע בְּדָמִי בְּרִדְתִּי אֶל שָׁחַת, הֲיוֹדְךָ עָפָר הֲיַגִּיד אֲמִתֶּךָ:

שְׁמַע יְיָ וְחָנֵּנִי, יְיָ הֱיֵה עֹזֵר לִי:

הָפַכְתָּ מִסְפְּדִי לְמָחוֹל לִי, פִּתַּחְתָּ שַׂקִּי וַתְּאַזְּרֵנִי שִׂמְחָה:

לְמַעַן יְזַמֶּרְךָ כָבוֹד וְלֹא יִדֹּם, יְיָ אֱלֹהַי לְעוֹלָם אוֹדֶךָּ:

Chochma is the flash of inspiration, the intuitive grasp that exists within us. Our faculty of *chochma* interfaces with the infinite spirituality that is beyond us, and brings it down into thoughts and ideas that we can conceptualize. This only occurs when we nullify ourselves to that which is beyond us, and therefore *chochma* corresponds to self-nullification (*bitul*) in the soul. Our ability to nullify ourselves transforms us into a receptacle to receive G-dly intellect and grasp the fact that G-d is the Master and King over the universe.

In summary:

It is recommended that meditation before and during prayers encompass the entire *seder hishtalshelut* or hierarchy of crea-

CHASSIDIC EXCERPTS

together with the good and united in all respects to the extent that they are one essence. It is from this [unity] that the evil derives its life-force, since the main nourishment of the negative life-force comes only from good. As soon as the bad elements are separated from the good, there is nothing to maintain them, and they expire and cease to exist ... But when the excitement of the G-dly soul illuminates the animal soul so that it also becomes excited over G-dliness, as described previously, then the good within it ascends and separates from the evil of the animal soul. Then, automatically, the evil exits, becoming so coarse that it expires and ceases to exist.

This, then, is the reason that at the time of prayer that aspect which is essentially "waste product" arises to pit itself against us and to confuse us with extraneous, ugly thoughts that are extremely coarse. (It would appear that there are two reasons for this: one, be-

cause the evil resists separation from the good within the animal soul, since it depends upon this life force for its very existence; and two, because it is about to expire and become the worst kind of waste product, as mentioned previously. While it is intermixed with the good, the waste is not so coarse, but as it becomes separated and isolated, it becomes very coarse. And this is when the extraneous and ugly thoughts occur.)

So, from this discussion of the enmeshment of the G-dly soul in the animal soul, we understand clearly how the animal soul is able to torment and distract the G-dly soul. The G-dly soul purifies the animal soul, but nevertheless, the process is called "a time of distress" (*et tzarah*), since it is a result of the exile of the G-dly soul within the animal soul, and that is what causes the torment. However, when the purification takes place in a peaceful/restful fashion and there is so much revelation of G-dliness

CHASSIDIC INSIGHTS

tion, from the lowest to the highest worlds:

The lowest world, the physical world in which we live, is called *Asiya*. Corresponding to our prayers until *Baruch She'amar*, *Asiya* is the world of particular, specific creations.

The next world, corresponding to the *Pesukei DeZimra* (from *Baruch She'amar* until and including *Yishtabach*) is the realm of general templates and archetypes of creation, or angels. It is called the World of *Yetzira*.

The next world up is called *Bria*, and it is the realm of potential or possible creations. It corresponds to the blessings preceding the *Shema* and the *Shema* itself. And finally, the World of *Atzilut* is the realm of emanation, corresponding to the *Shemonah Esreh* or *Amida* during which our souls cleave to the One Above, and we are unable to utter the blessings without support from heaven.

*

The meditation thus far described was culled and distilled from study of thousands of chasidic discourses over many years. It is not to be expected that anyone new to Jewish meditation will master the implicit concepts in a short period of time. However, as the fifth Lubavitcher Rebbe (the Rebbe Rashab) said, "If you are not [in-

To You, Lord, I call, and to the Lord I supplicate.

What profit is there in my blood; in my descent to the grave? Can the dust acknowledge You, can it tell of Your truth?

Listen to me, Lord, and be gracious to me.

You have transformed my eulogy into a dance for me, You loosened my sackcloth and girded me with happiness.

So that I will sing in Your honor and not be silent, Lord, my G-d, I will praise You forever...

CHASSIDIC EXCERPTS

from the G-dly soul that the animal soul is spontaneously subdued, there is no necessity to rise and do battle. The natural soul need not distract [the G-dly soul], since in any case [the evil within it] is nullified. This is comparable to a great and awesome king whom nobody would dare to oppose; rather, all are nullified before him. Similarly, in light of the tremendous revelation of the G-dly soul, the animal soul is spontaneously nullified. In this case, it is not possible for it to distract [the G-dly soul] with its coarseness, since the entire existence of the negative elements is immediately dismissed.

[In this way, we may come to grasp the distinction between *galut* ("exile") and *geula* ("redemption").] Where there is enmeshment [of the G-dly soul in the animal soul], there is *galut* of the *Shechina*, and where there is *geula*, there is no enmeshment, and the *klipa* is spontaneously and automatically nullified.

(From *Sefer Ma'amorim 5655* (1894-1895) of the Rebbe Rashab, pp. 105-107)

Bridge between Heaven and Earth
Hodu Lashem – "Give thanks/acknowledge the Lord..."

The ladder of prayer – which stands on the ground while its head reaches into the heavens – has four rungs; these four rungs correspond to the four worlds of *Atzilut, Bria, Yetzira* and *Asiya*, which connect the physical creation with the essence of the Infinite One. From these four rungs holiness and G-dly revelation descend into all of the worlds. The first/lowest of these four rungs corresponds to the World of *Asiya* and consists of the prayers from *Hodu* through *LaMenatzeach* (Psalm 67), followed by a short declaration beginning, *Leshem yichud* ("For the sake of the unification...") which acts as an intermediary between the World of *Asiya* and the next world, the World of *Yetzira*.

CHASSIDIC INSIGHTS

volved in meditation], what are you doing here?"[54] With practice and time, the study of Jewish meditation and its practice has a refining effect upon the mind, and if we choose to devote ourselves to its study, we will understand and incorporate these concepts into preparation for morning prayers. They will then become the basis for our meditation before and during our morning prayers.

It was already mentioned that the Hebrew word for meditation (*hitbonenut*) includes two words – *bina* ("understanding") and *boneh* ("building"). As we contemplate the G-dly concepts contained in chasidic literature, we achieve greater and more subtle understanding of G-dliness. And as we meditate, we join the concepts together in our mind, and they serve as the girders and beams of a spiritual edifice that we build inside of ourselves. Our meditation allows us to dwell within this spiritual edifice for a certain amount of time every day, adding to it and adjusting it as time goes by to accommodate our ever-growing understanding of G-dly concepts. This, in short, is Jewish meditation.

(For a much more thorough and lengthy treatment, see our translation and commentary on *Kuntres Avoda* – entitled "Love like Fire and Water" – of the Rebbe Rashab.)

יְיָ מֶלֶךְ, יְיָ מָלָךְ, יְיָ יִמְלֹךְ לְעוֹלָם וָעֶד

יְיָ מֶלֶךְ, יְיָ מָלָךְ, יְיָ יִמְלֹךְ לְעוֹלָם וָעֶד

וְהָיָה יְיָ לְמֶלֶךְ עַל כָּל הָאָרֶץ בַּיּוֹם הַהוּא יִהְיֶה
יְיָ אֶחָד וּשְׁמוֹ אֶחָד:

In addition to the above meditation, the sages suggested other, more physical preparations for prayer in the morning. Aside from study of subtle G-dly concepts such as those contained in Chasidut, the sages also recommended immersing in the *mikveh* and giving *tzedaka* ("charity to the poor") as preparations for prayer. Although dipping in the waters of the *mikveh* before prayer was a decree of Ezra (when he returned from Persian exile to build the Second Temple) that was later cancelled; nevertheless, some

CHASSIDIC EXCERPTS

The second rung corresponds to the World of *Yetzira* and begins with *Baruch She'Amar*, ending with *Yishtabach*. In the World of *Yetzira*, one is aware of the G-dly light that enlivens worlds and creations as well as how every aspect of creation, each according to its level, becomes aware of the G-dly life-force that enlivens it. The intermediary between the World of *Yetzira* and the next world, the World of *Bria* begins with *Kaddish* and ends with *Barchu*.

The World of *Bria* begins with the blessings preceding the *Shema*, [includes the *Shema*] and ends with the phrase *goel Yisroel*, [that is, "Blessed are You HaShem, who redeemed Israel."] The intermediary between the World of *Bria* and the next world, the World of *Atzilut*, is the verse that introduces the *Shemonah Esreh*: "HaShem open my lips..." As explained in Chasidic teachings, every intermediary between two subjects or lev-

els is itself composed of two levels – one that is associated with the lower level, and the other is associated with the higher level. So it is with the intermediary between *Bria* and *Atzilut*. The first part of the statement "*HaShem*, open up my lips..." is associated with *Bria*, while the second, "and my mouth will declare Your praise" is associated with *Atzilut*.

The *Shemonah Esreh* is associated with the World of *Atzilut*, and the prayers that follow it allude to and explain the light that is brought down into our every day world...

*

The prayers from *Baruch She'Amar* until the phrase *Chai HaOlamim* ("Life of the Worlds") which concludes *Yishtabach* constitute the second rung of the ladder, which corresponds to the World of *Yetzira*. In the beginning of the World of *Yetzira*, creation appears as an

CHASSIDIC INSIGHTS

Jewish scholars determined that this practice remains helpful and that "according to all opinions, our prayers are more acceptable after immersion."[55] The 17th century Kabbalist known as the *Chesed l'Avraham* (R' Avraham Azulai, grandfather of the *Chida*) explained that negative spiritual forces cling to us as a result of our transgressions. These forces have the nature of "air." But, when we immerse ourselves in the waters of the *mikveh*, these forces are repelled, and we emerge purified.

Another physical preparation that helps before prayers is giving charity – called in Hebrew *tzedaka*, which literally means "justice to the poor." This is based upon the verse,[56] "And in justice (*tzedek*), I perceive Your countenance." The Talmud[57] understands from this verse that those who give *tzedaka* improve the probability that their prayers will be accepted. Though this suggests that the giving should take place before prayers, according to the *Siddur Arizal*, the time to give *tzedaka* is during recital of the *Pesukei DeZimra*. This is because we are all like beneficiaries of charity in relation to G-d. And when we emulate His attribute of giving below, He responds by answering our prayers from above.[58] In addition, the *Tanya*[59] compares giving *tzedaka* to "planting a seed." The seed itself seems insignificant, totally out of proportion to the tall and impressive tree that may grow out of it afterward. Similarly, placing a few coins into the hand of a poor person is like planting a seed – the spiritual and physical rewards that the giver may reap from this simple act go way beyond the act itself.

*

Chasidic masters further elucidated the process leading up to prayers in the morning. They prescribed a three-step progression from pure intellectual activity to emotions of the heart:

Rise and remain standing until "יְהִי כְבוֹד"

The Lord reigns, the Lord reigned, the Lord will reign forever and ever.

The Lord reigns, the Lord reigned, the Lord will reign forever and ever. And the Lord will be King over all the earth; on that day, the Lord will be one and His name one.

independent entity standing on its own. The power of the Creator is hidden and concealed, yet the G-dly light is revealed and shines. This means that creation itself reveals and makes us aware of G-dliness, unlike in the World of *Asiya* which completely hides and conceals G-d...

In man, the ability to act is a power that is detached from the essence of the person. This corresponds to the World of *Asiya* [where appear physical objects which seem to be detached from their spiritual source]. The World of *Yetzira* corresponds to speech, which even as it seems attached to the speaker, nevertheless has enough identity of its own that it can be heard by someone else. It is not equivalent to the power of thought, regarding which someone may know that another person is thinking, but have no idea of what he is thinking. But, after all is said and done, thought speech and action are no more than garments of the soul. The World of *Atzilut*, though, is the world of unity. In man, this world corresponds to the ability to think creatively, and reveal new and deep concepts.

(From *Sefer HaSichot* of the Rebbe Rayatz, 5706-5710, pp. 143-145)

The four rungs of prayer (wind, noise, fire and the still small voice)

Now that we no longer offer sacrifices, the sages decreed that our prayers are in lieu of the sacrifices. Our prayers correspond to offering up our animal soul, so that it becomes refined and as- cends to become included in the fiery flames of the G-dly soul. And these then are the four levels of prayer; *pesukei dezimra*, *bircot kriat shema*, the *shema* and *shemonah esreh*, with which we perform

CHASSIDIC INSIGHTS

First of all, they advised us to learn a chasidic discourse to prepare the mind for prayers. This is a strictly intellectual activity. Even though we must keep in the back of our mind that the subject is G-dly and spiritual,[60] the learning itself is intellectual and does not yet affect our emotions.

Next, we meditate, as described earlier. The process of meditation brings the intellect down from the head to the heart. Thus, it is described as "emotions within intellect." That is, as we think about the concepts that we have just studied, they filter down into our heart. They begin to take on emotional form and have an effect upon our feelings. Though they remain intellectual ideas, within them we begin to feel a direction and a tendency toward love and fear of G-d.

And then, with that nascent feeling in our heart, we begin to recite the prayers, an activity also known as *avoda shebeleiv* – "service of the heart." As we speak the words of prayer, we do not concern ourselves with the discourse we just learned, nor even with the meditation we just performed, but with the simple meaning of the words in front of us. These words serve as vessels for the spiritual light that the One Above wishes to reveal to us this day. Our job is to create the proper vessel by focusing upon the simple meaning of the words of prayer, and then the One Above inserts the light, or spiritual illumination, based upon the learning and meditation that we performed earlier that morning. The prayers are arranged like a "ladder," and as we pray, we hopefully achieve higher and higher levels of G-dly emotion – love and fear of G-d.

הוֹשִׁיעֵנוּ יְיָ אֱלֹהֵינוּ, וְקַבְּצֵנוּ מִן הַגּוֹיִם לְהוֹדוֹת

לְשֵׁם קָדְשֶׁךָ לְהִשְׁתַּבֵּחַ בִּתְהִלָּתֶךָ:

בָּרוּךְ יְיָ אֱלֹהֵי יִשְׂרָאֵל מִן הָעוֹלָם וְעַד הָעוֹלָם

וְאָמַר כָּל הָעָם אָמֵן. הַלְלוּיָהּ:

כֹּל הַנְּשָׁמָה תְּהַלֵּל יָהּ הַלְלוּיָהּ:

*

We will close this introduction to prayer with a passage from the

CHASSIDIC EXCERPTS

the refinement and elevation of the animal soul. For, it is written, "And there was a great and strong wind, [capable of] disintegrating mountains and shattering rocks…[but] *Havaya* was not in the wind. And after the wind there was a noise but *Havaya* was not in the noise, and after the noise, there was fire, but *Havaya* was not in the fire, and after the fire there was a still small voice."[71] And the Zohar comments, "There is found the King."[72]

Now, the "wind" alludes to the *pesukei dezimra*, wherein is explicated the creation of all the higher and lower worlds that were created from nothing to something. For, just as their creation took place with the breath ("wind") of His mouth, as written, "With the word of G-d, the heavens were created, and with the wind of His mouth…"[73] [so]

all of the heavenly hosts as well as creations below were created from the divine utterance and wind of His mouth. This, then is the meditation that takes place during the *pesukei dezimra* regarding the wonderful and amazing nature of creation from nothing to something. [It takes place] as we say, *Baruch She'amar vehaya haolam* ("Blessed be He Who said and the universe came into existence") – with one utterance the universe and all the worlds were created and came into existence. And about this wind the verse says, "a great wind, and strong, disintegrating mountains and shattering rocks," referring to the "greatness of G-d in their throats,"[74] which puts a "double-edged sword in their hands."[75] And this is what is meant by the *pesukei dezimra*, from the phrase *lezamer aritzim* ("to prune away

CHASSIDIC INSIGHTS

Mittler Rebbe of Chabad (son of the Alter Rebbe), who had this to say about the process of prayer:[61]

"I know of several people who are learned in Chasidut, but by nature they are unable to focus deeply and concentrate without speaking, exercising their voice as when learning *Gemara*. And there are many more people who have no readily available storehouse of chasidic knowledge allowing them to dip at will, at length and breadth. And consequently, they have no good way to arouse their soul from its sleep and slumber, aside from their voice that arouses intention and "desire of the heart." And, by my life, their voice ascends and is accepted by the One Above, as long as it is expressed with integrity and humility, since "G-d is close to all who have a broken heart" and to "those who are low and G-d fearing."

And aside from that, anyone who has tasted the secrets of G-dliness knows well that those who delve deeply with knowledge and understanding while meditating still need to recite the *Pesukei DeZimra* in an audible voice, as is written "...and lofty praises of G-d in their throats."[62] What this indicates is that the entire concept of greatness of G-d that enters their intellect at length and depth boils down to a concise summary and synopsis. And it is this form of true grasp that is expressed as the voice of song in their throats, as is written "my heart and my flesh sing to G-d."[63] And also "And Your pious ones sing..."[64] And this singing emerges from the very depths of the flesh of the heart. It occurs as we are aroused by the concise summary of the intellectual concept, whatever it may be, whether about a major topic or something minor. This is true revelation of G-dliness within

Save us, Lord, our G-d and gather us from among the nations, in order to praise Your holy name and to revel in Your praises.

Blessed is the Lord, G-d of Israel, forever and ever. And let the entire nation say "Amen, praise the Lord." Let every soul praise the Lord. Praise the Lord.

CHASSIDIC EXCERPTS

thorns"), because as we pray, we cut away the "thorns and thistles," referring to the physical coarseness of the animal soul, whose very existence is coarse and corporeal.

Yet, "*Havaya* was not in the wind," for it is the wind of *Elokim*, as written, "And *Elokim* caused a wind to pass over the land..." meaning that the creation of the world came from the name *Elokim*, as appears in the verse, "In the begining, *Elokim* created."[76] In regard to the name *Havaya*, this rung of prayer corresponds to the final *hey* of His Name, which is a "light letter without substance," since it represents external breath.

"And after the wind there was a noise," refers to the blessings preceding the *kriat shema*, and especially the *yotzar*, which explicates the nullification of the angels which revere, sanctify and coro-

nate [G-d]. There, the *seraphim* say *kadosh* with great excitement of fiery fire and desire and thirst, and the *ofanim* and *chayot hakodesh* [join in] with great noise...and all of this results from meditation on the infinite light from above that is holy and removed from [the angels]. They are incapable of grasping it with their intellectual faculties, since they only grasp [G-dliness that emanates from] the lower *hey* of G-d's name, about which we say, *vtzidkatecha yeraneinu*[77] - *tzedek malchuta kadisha* - referring to [the lowest *sephira*], *malchut*. There, they do grasp the light and energy that is theirs. Just as man is aware of the vitality of his own soul, so the supernal angels grasp the light and divine energy that is enclothed within them to enliven them. But, what they grasp is a mere reflection, while the essence of the

CHASSIDIC INSIGHTS

that soul, as we recite *Baruch she'amar vehaya haolam* ("Blessed be He who spoke and the universe came into existence"). The concise summary of this entire concept is that via the "word of G-d" the entire universe was created from nothing into something. From this emerges emotion in the physical heart, expressed in song and melody, perhaps accompanied by movement of the hand and foot as well.

And so, as we recite *melech yachid chai haolamim* ("King, the Unique One, life of the universe"), and *malchutecha malchut kol olamim* ("Your reign is the reign over all worlds"), etc., this constitutes the main "sweetening of the judgments," as I heard openly from my father [the Alter Rebbe], not once, and not twice regarding the verse, "...since you failed to serve the Lord your G-d happily ... you will serve your enemies,"[65] referring to everyone's personal accusers who attack us regarding matters of income, family, health and wealth, with various forms of suffering, some small and some big, as is known. And all of this, "because you failed to serve your Lord." This service is the "service of the heart," with G-dly excitement during prayers. The worship must take place in happiness and with a positive heart, meaning with feelings of pleasure and enjoyment within the breath of the physical heart, with song and humming resulting from awareness of the concise summary of G-dliness..."

לַמְנַצֵּחַ בִּנְגִינֹת מִזְמוֹר שִׁיר:

יָאֵר פָּנָיו אִתָּנוּ סֶלָה:

לָדַעַת בְּכָל גּוֹיִם יְשׁוּעָתֶךָ:

יוֹדוּךָ עַמִּים אֱלֹהִים. יוֹדוּךָ עַמִּים כֻּלָּם:

יִשְׂמְחוּ וִירַנְּנוּ לְאֻמִּים, כִּי תִשְׁפֹּט עַמִּים מִישֹׁר,
וּלְאֻמִּים בָּאָרֶץ תַּנְחֵם סֶלָה:

יוֹדוּךָ עַמִּים אֱלֹהִים, יוֹדוּךָ עַמִּים כֻּלָּם:

אֶרֶץ נָתְנָה יְבוּלָהּ, יְבָרְכֵנוּ אֱלֹהִים אֱלֹהֵינוּ:

יְבָרְכֵנוּ אֱלֹהִים, וְיִירְאוּ אוֹתוֹ כָּל אַפְסֵי אָרֶץ:

At least two things are remarkable about this passage. One is that the Mittler Rebbe was known as the most cerebral of the Chabad rebbes, and he was very opposed to extraneous shows of emotion and of false pretense during prayers.[66] And yet, in this passage the Mittler Rebbe instructs us not to shy away from vocal expression when praying. Indeed, he tells us to sing (albeit to ourselves, and not in any way that would disturb other members

infinite light remains removed and holy. And this is what is meant by *kadosh, kadosh, kadosh,* [spelled] with a *vov* that is higher than the *hey,* since this [energy] is holy and removed. And that is the reason for their noise. For, while the divine light that they do grasp does not elicit a reaction from them, the infinite light that is beyond their grasp does excite them. And the *serafim,* which do grasp at least a little of the holiness and the lofty nature [of G-dliness], are in a state of *ratzoh* - running and desiring to be included in the infinite light. But the *ofanim,* which know that there is something holy but do not grasp its amazing nature – because it doesn't illuminate within them at all - say *baruch*

("May He be blessed"), indicating that they wish for it to descend and become revealed to them.

Now, this meditation produces an internal arousal within the animal soul. The *pesukei dezimra* produce only an external "etching" upon the soul, but the above meditation stimulates internal movement within the animal soul, since the source of meditation is the "animals" of the *merkava* and *shmarei haofanim* [mentioned in the prayers]. But even regarding this level, the verse says that "*Havaya* was not in the noise" - meaning that the complete Name *Havaya* was not involved - but only the second two letters *vov-hey* and not the first two letters *yud hey* of His name. And even regard-

CHASSIDIC INSIGHTS

of the congregation) and not to be concerned over involuntary movements that we might make as we spontaneously express our feelings in prayer. In other words, as much as we might meditate and ponder, prayer is still an emotional activity – *avoda shebeleiv*. It is all about bringing the intellect down and experiencing it in the heart.

And the Rebbe, Rabbi Menachem Mendel Schneersohn, himself says the following: [67]

"Song" (spiritual elevation) as an element of worship of G-d, takes place during prayers, when a person ascends from his own spiritual situation and level. As the Alter Rebbe wrote in *Igeret Hakodesh*, our personal redemption occurs while we pray. In practice, this means that we should pray with "song," meaning with the voice, singing happily.

And that brings us to the second interesting item. If we have learned and meditated properly, the concepts that we considered will take on a life of their own. They will distill into a concise summary of intellect that contains all of the details of our meditation. And as they filter down to our heart, they will provide a G-dly backdrop to our prayers.

As elucidated earlier, the preparations for prayer constitute a three-step process:

• First of all, there is the learning, which is a strictly intellectual activity.

• This is followed by meditation, in which the intellect filters down to the heart – this is emotion within intellect.

• And then, we must let go of our meditation and let it distill into a concise summary that forms a backdrop to our prayers. As the Mittler Rebbe describes it, it is a "true revelation of G-dliness in the soul," and it enlivens our prayers, bringing us closer to the One Above.

*F*or the orchestral conductor, a song with instruments, a psalm.

G-d, grant us grace and bless us, shine Your countenance among us forever.

To inform the earth of Your ways, and the nations of Your salvations.

People submit to You, G-d, all peoples submit to You.

The nations will rejoice and sing, for You will judge the people justly and guide the nations of earth forever.

People accede to You, G-d, all peoples accede to You.

The earth gives its grain, may G-d, our G-d bless us.

G-d bless us, and may people from all corners of the globe be in awe of Him.

ing the *vov hey*, only a transcendental light shines upon it.

And after the noise, there was fire, representing the blessing *ahavat olam* as well as the *kriat shema*. [This initiates] the *avoda* of the divine soul, with love like flames of fire. For, following meditation on the unity of G-d, which occurs during the *shema*, we recite *shema Yisrael* with full intellectual grasp and understanding of how G-d is One. This leads us to *veahavta*, wherein we cling to the Oneness of G-d above. And yet even here, where meditation takes place with the first *hay* of *Havaya*, corresponding to

bina, nevertheless the completeness and totality of the name *Havaya* is lacking.

[Only] after the fire, comes the still small voice, and that "is where the King is." The King is the name *Havaya* in its perfect totality. Meaning the voice of Torah, since Torah emerges from *chochma*, from the *yud* of the name *Havaya*…and it also represents the *shemonah esreh*, with a still small voice of elevation from below to Above, as well as descent from Above as we say *Baruch atah Havaya*, bringing down divine influx from the infinite essence above…

(From *Sefer Maamorim 5668* (1908) of the Rebbe Rashab, page 116-17)

CHASSIDIC INSIGHTS

BARUCH SHE'AMAR

Reciting the prayer, *Baruch She'Amar* is a little like jumping out of a plane at high altitude with a spiritual parachute. The chasidic commentaries tells us that *Baruch She'Amar* begins at a very high spiritual level, and that its words bring us down slowly, step-by-step, from one spiritual level to the next, from above to below. From which high level and down to which level? That depends upon the Rebbe you consult, for probably no other prayer is interpreted by so many in such different ways. Moreover, to add to the complication, the spiritual currents of *Baruch She'Amar* do not necessarily take us directly down; sometimes, as we descend, they waft us back up again, like an updraft of air nudging the parachute back up before it continues its unavoidable descent.

לְשֵׁם יִחוּד קֻדְשָׁא בְּרִיךְ הוּא וּשְׁכִינְתֵּהּ לְיַחֲדָא שֵׁם

י"ה בו"ה בְּיִחוּדָא שְׁלִים בְּשֵׁם כָּל יִשְׂרָאֵל:

בָּרוּךְ שֶׁאָמַר וְהָיָה הָעוֹלָם:

But, before launching into specific explanations of the chasidic commentaries, it is important to grasp the spiritual implications of the level of prayer that is initiated by *Baruch She'Amar*.

From the moment we say *Baruch She'Amar*, we activate the soul-level of *ruach* within ourselves, and this is the soul-level we inhabit during *Pesukei DeZimra* until we conclude *Yishtabach*. As noted earlier, *ruach* corresponds to the World of *Yetzira* and to the natural emotions of the soul. These are the natural feelings of love that all Jews have in their heart for G-d, but they remain hidden until we access them by way of meditation and prayer. The key to accessing our natural G-dly emotions is meditation upon creation from nothing to something. Without this meditation, we may experience some emotional response, but it will lack the integrity of emotions informed by the intellect. Moreover, this emotional response may only be a false illusion based upon our imagination alone. Therefore,

CHASSIDIC EXCERPTS

Arousal from Above
Baruch She'Amar – "Blessed be He Who said..."

The general intention of these blessings, expressing spiritual levels from *radl'a* down to *malchut* of *Bria*, is that it is necessary to elicit a spiritual arousal from below (*ha'alat ma'n*) during the following prayers – the *pesukei dezimra* – so that we experience a strong desire to ascend above, as known. Therefore, it is necessary to first draw down stimulation from far above (*ma'ad*, or *mayin* *duchrin*), from the "head" of all levels, which is *radl'a*. And this descends into *malchut* of *bria* in order to instill in it the strength to arouse itself with elevation of *ma'n*, as written in the *Peri eitz Haim*...that even in order to elicit elevation from below, it is necessary to first stimulate it from above...this is the general intention of *Baruch She'amar*...

(From Maamorei Admor Hazaken (the Alter Rebbe) on Maamorei Rz'l ("sayings of the sages"): Tefila, Page 340)

Thirteen blessings of descent
"Blessed be He Who said..."

The sages determined that we must preface the *Pesukei DeZimra* by saying *Baruch She'Amar* ("Blessed is He Who spoke") so that the concept of "He spoke and the universe came into existence" should become "blessed" - meaning evident and revealed - in our hearts, and so that we become conscious of it and excited about it. For, "He spoke and the universe came into existence," means that "He spoke, and it happened automatically"[78] - with one statement the uni-

CHASSIDIC INSIGHTS

meditation is necessary. It is important to realize that the spiritual levels that we meditate upon are real, and that to experience these levels is well within the realm of possibilities for anyone who puts in the effort.

*

To begin with, take note of the reference to God as *Shmo* ("His Name") and as *Shmo Hagadol* ("His great Name"). About half way through *Baruch she'amar*, we find Him mentioned as *Shmo*, and at the end of the prayer, as *Shmo Hagadol*. At first glance this is a curious way of referring to God. Why do our prayers begin to refer to God as "His Name" or "His great Name" just as we launch into *Baruch She'amar?*

A name has two attributes.[68] First of all, it has no identifiable qualities of its own — it is nothing more than a combination of letters, devoid of substance. On the other hand, it has a purpose — to call

Baruch She'Amar

For the sake of unity of the Holy One with His holy presence (the *Shechina*), in order to join the name *yud-kay* with the *vov-kay* [of His name] in total unity in the name of all Israel.

*B*lessed be He Who said, and the universe came into being,

someone. And when we call somebody's name, our call goes right to his essence. The person to whom we call turns to us with his entire being. That is because his name penetrates to the very deepest parts of his personality, accessing his essence, and drawing his attention to us.

The same is true of the names of God. Some of the names that we use in prayer refer to His attributes, such as *El* for *chesed*, *Elokim* for *gevura*, *Tzeva'ot* for *netzach*, etc… But, there is a name that applies to Him as He exists beyond all of His attributes, as He is in His very essence. And that is the name *Havaya* — "is, was, and will be." Here in the prayer, *Baruch She'amar*, God's Name *Havaya* is mentioned, but only after He is referred to as *Shmo* ("His Name"), and *Shmo Hagadol* ("His great Name"). There is a reason for that.

CHASSIDIC EXCERPTS

verse was created! And also in order that *Baruch Hu* ("Blessed be He") - indicating that the level we call *Hu* ("He/Him") - should become a conscious experience in our heart, and our heart should become aware and excited…

[For this reason], the thirteen times that the word *baruch* ("blessed") appears in this prayer correspond to the [kabbalistic level called the] "thirteen strands/hairs of the beard," which … indicate influx that is drawn down from Above via "hairs." By way of illustration, hair is not vitally important to the head itself, nor to the body - rather, it is extraneous. Similarly, the levels of divine influx which descend to us from Above, creating within us awareness [of G-dliness], descend as if they are detached from their essence and from their original source. The essence from which

they originate does not undergo any variation - it undergoes no addition or subtraction as it becomes conscious in our heart. Now, the twelve [initial] times that we say *baruch* correspond to specific levels of influx, while the thirteenth [is a general influx that] includes all of them together. It corresponds to the final blessing, *Baruch Atah HaShem Elokeinu Melech Haolam* ("Blessed are You, Lord, our G-d, King of the Universe") - meaning that G-d should become blessed and revealed as if in front of us and present among us as our divine Sovereign. And this name of G-d [the ineffable four-letter name which outside of prayer we render as *HaShem* or *Havaya*] includes all the particular levels alluded to in the previous times that we said *baruch*, and it is the source and origin of all of them.

(From *Likutei Torah* of the Alter Rebbe, *Parshat Va'etchanan*, p. 2a)

CHASSIDIC INSIGHTS

Sometimes our true qualities are dormant. That is, they are latent, hidden inside until they are called upon and needed. For example, we might be in essence a kind person, but we never had an opportunity to express our kindness. And then, perhaps a situation arises that elicits our potential to demonstrate kindness. Perhaps a loved one needs a favor, or a friend begs for some help. That is likely to elicit our hidden potential for kindness and bring it to fruition, as we actually help out the loved

בָּרוּךְ הוּא,

בָּרוּךְ אוֹמֵר וְעוֹשֶׂה,

person. Similarly, we might possess the wisdom and intellect to solve certain problems. But, since we were never faced with such problems, he may not even know that we possess such skills. When all of a sudden we are confronted with the problem, it is likely to arouse and reveal our latent intellect for solving

problems.[69]

The section of prayer that we are entering, starting with *Baruch she'amar* serves the function of eliciting Godly response from above. At this point in prayers, we have moved beyond the point of being merely grateful and thankful before God, and now we wish to access God and communicate with Him. But, since He is so far beyond, how do we do that? By calling His Name!

This prayer (*Baruch She'amar*) accesses the very essence of Godliness, from a place so far beyond, that we can only refer to Him in the third person, "Blessed be He Who said, and the universe came

CHASSIDIC EXCERPTS

The Tribes in the soul of man

And in the soul of man, the influence of the "tribes" is comparable to the power of germination within the soil, causing all kinds of herbs and grains to grow (as explained elsewhere). And yet, nevertheless, "there is no blade of grass down here that is without a spiritual counterpart above that 'strikes' it and tells it to grow" [implying that the influence comes from above, rather than from the soil...but the explanation is that] although man has the choice to choose good, (as it says, "You shall love..."), this is only in reference to his initiative from below. But, the main ingredient is that which descends from above via an "arousal from above," from the supernal attributes of the ten *sephirot* of the four worlds *ABY"A*. And that descent comes from the tribes, which is why we preface the *pesukei dezimra* by saying the prayer, *Baruch She'amar*. [This prayer] contains the word *baruch* ("blessed be") twelve times, corresponding to the twelve tribes (and the thirteenth time that *baruch* is mentioned corresponds to the tribe of Levi, which includes all of the other tribes). The intention is for G-dliness to descend and become blessed and revealed within the soul, as written in *Likutei Torah*, parshat *Ve'etchanan*. And that is the reason why there were twelve tribes, representing twelve rays of light from *Atzilut*, illuminating within the world of *beriah* - and there are twelve of them corresponding to the twelve tribes. And they represent the entire spectrum of creation, since they are like a "chariot" joining the world of *Atzilut* with *Beriah*. As explained earlier, they include both substance and form, since their origin is from the *sephirot* of *Atzilut* and therefore there are twelve of them, from which diverge and spread myriads of details without measure...)

From *Sefer Maamorim* 5673 (1913 - in the *Sefer maamorim* 5672-5676) of the Rebbe Rashab, Page 80-81

Source of Wisdom
Baruch She'Amar – "Blessed be He Who said..."

The difference between *Atah* ("You") and *Hu* ("He/Him") is as follows: *Atah* indicates a subject that is known and present ... whereas *Hu* indicates a subject that is unknown and obscure, whose essence is veiled...

CHASSIDIC INSIGHTS

into being. Blessed be He."[70] We cannot put a name to this level, because it is beyond names and attributes. However, we can describe His greatness in creating and maintaining the creation from nothing to something, day after day, minute after minute, second after second. When we do that, we actually draw out His latent creative ability and bring it from a state of potential to reality. That is, our prayer does not merely "praise" God; our prayer elicits His latent creative potential and ensures that He does create, and He continues
to maintain the universe from nothing to something. Just as when we praise the wise person in his wisdom, and we praise the kind person for his kindness, so when we praise the One above for His creation, it elicits His attention to His creation.

Blessed be He.
Blessed be He Who says
and accomplishes,

And that is the secret of "His Name" (*Shmo*) and "His great Name" (*Shmo Hagadol*). The kaballists tell us that the potential for creation resides in on the highest levels of His infinite light, prior to the great *tzimtzum*, or contraction, and that He creates the universe with His essential Name, *Havaya* ("is, was and always will be"). However, it is up to us to elicit His Name. Before we praise Him, His Name is there in potential alone. As we praise His creative potential, and His omniscience and omnipotence in the universe, it is we who elicit His Name, bringing it from a state of concealment to revelation. That is why, in this section of the prayers, after praising and describing Him on eleven different levels beginning with the word *Baruch*, we finally utter the words *Baruch Shemo* – "Blessed be His Name."[71]

CHASSIDIC EXCERPTS

Since *chochma* is the origin of revealed spirituality, [when we refer to *chochma*] we use *Atah*. *Keter* is called *ayn* ("divine void") since it is hidden and concealed; [so, when we refer to *Keter*, we use *Hu* which connotes a level that is covert and concealed...

[Nevertheless] the mind has the power to grasp wisdom or illumination in many forms. All intellectual revelation has a source and origin in the level that we call *maskil* ("creative thought") which is the source of intellect and initiates all intellectual activity. The soul-power of *maskil* is [always active, sub-consciously grasping G-dly illumination] ... Its presence may not be experienced at all, since [at the time a concept enters our mind] we experience nothing but its revealed light [and not the concept itself]. Whatever is beyond intellect we don't feel in our soul; it remains beyond our conscious experience. This is one way to illustrate the difference between *chochma* and *keter*; *keter* is generally hidden, while *chochma* emerges from its state of concealment to a state of consciousness.

From this illustration, we can glean yet another fact, and that is even though *keter* is hidden, it is not so concealed that

we are totally unaware of its presence altogether. We are aware of its existence, but since it is not as conscious as the intellectual processes that we experience directly in our minds, we call it "hidden." For the power of *maskil* (intellect in potential) is certainly known to us – we are aware of its existence. That is, we're aware that there must be something that has the potential to be the source of the intellectual illumination that we experience, for if not, where is this illumination coming from? Clearly, there is something that gives rise to intellect and, just as we experience intellectual revelation, we feel this power of *maskil* ... This is like saying about someone that he is not with us, even though we know that he exists. And if so, the word *Hu* indicates the presence of someone/something concealed whose existence is known to us. We are clearly aware of the existence of potential revelation from an origin in the World of *Atzilut*...

However, this is not true of the level we call *radla* ("the unknowable head").[79] This is the innermost point of *keter*, known as *Atik Yomin* ("Ancient of Days"), which receives its spiritual influx from *malchut deAdam Kadmon*

CHASSIDIC INSIGHTS

And toward the end of the prayer, we say *adei ad shemo hagadol* - "until (and including) His great Name forever and ever." Each time, we mention His essential Name *Havaya* only after first praising "His Name," or "His great Name," because we must first elicit His Name above, and only afterward we can call Him by His Name. Throughout this prayer, we only know Him as "the Name," but afterward we know Him as *Havaya*, who "is, was and always will be," Creator of the universe.

בָּרוּךְ גּוֹזֵר וּמְקַיֵּם,

And with this new awareness, we launch the prayers of the *pesukei dezimra*, or "songs of praise" of God. The purpose of these praises is two fold: besides meaning "song," the word *zimra* is also from the root *lezamer*, meaning "to prune," to "remove and cut away."[72] At this point in our prayers, we need to remove the obstacles, whether the last vestiges of tiredness upon awakening, or depression and sadness, or just normal everyday distractions. We need to "prune" and cut them away so that we can concentrate on expressing our prayers to God. This process is also called "engraving from without," since the goal is to remove the external obstacles that otherwise prevent us from ascending the ladder of prayer. Simultaneously, we begin meditation...

*

The student of Chasidut is faced with a dilemma. On the one hand, Chasidut presents general concepts on which to meditate. There are many such concepts, such as creation from nothing to something (*yesh m'ayn*), immanent spirituality (*memalle kol olamim*), transcendent G-dliness (*sovev kol olamim*), the spiritual hierarchy of creation (*seder hishtalshelut*), etc. On the other hand, Chasidut demands that we meditate with attention to details.[73] It is difficult to reconcile these two requirements, because Chasidic literature does not tell us on which details to focus. Instead, it concentrates on the general principles.

One way to resolve this dilemma is to consider the general categories of creation (mineral, vegetable, animal and human categories), and meditate upon specific examples from within each category. By considering specific creations within each category of creation, and then extrapolating to the nature of creation in successively higher worlds, we may develop a technique for applying the general principles of Chasidut to details.[74] We may then meditate upon how the G-dly vitality from above enlivens each creature by examining the letters of its name.

For example, we may have decided to focus on the G-dliness inherent in a specific species of tree – take the cedar (*erez*). And we may have also chosen to meditate upon the spirituality that lies at the basis of creation of an oak (*alon*). Our task at this point in meditation is to discover what creature could possess the traits of both a "cedar tree" and an "oak tree." Obviously, such a creature could not be physical, since a cedar is narrow and tall and an oak is broad and short, and in the physical world, no creature can contain both these shapes simultaneously. However, as the sages said, "there

CHASSIDIC EXCERPTS

("reign of Primordial Man"). We don't even experience awareness of the existence of this level. This is because it is the lowest aspect of the Emanator, and the essence of the Emanator [*Adam Kadmon*] and His emanations [the ten *sephirot* of *Atzilut*] have nothing in common ... and if so, even though it is the lowest and final level of the essence of the Emanator, *radla* is still far from the origin of the emanations. That level [the origin of emanations] is called *keter deArich Anpin* ("crown of the Long Countenance"), and it is only here that we may claim awareness of His existence. And for this reason, we say that *keter deArich Anpin* is the source of emanation in general. And in particular, it is the source of *Abba* ("Father"), which is *chochma* and the source of all revelation. But, regarding *radla*, we have not the slightest awareness of its existence, and it is called "the most covert of all concealments." Not only do the emanations possess no awareness of its existence, but *radla* is unknown in essence, since it is impossible to grasp its essence, as it is absolute *ayn*, [nullified to] the essence of the Emanator Himself...

(From the *Siddur* of the Alter Rebbe)

CHASSIDIC INSIGHTS

is no blade of grass down here which is without a spiritual counterpart above..." meaning that every physical creation has as well a spiritual source. And that spiritual source is not bounded by the limitations of the physical world.

In our case, the source of all species of trees is an archetypal "tree" above in the World of *Yetzira* (we mention it in prayers as we say the verse, *az yeranenu kol atzei ya'ar* – "Then all the trees of the forest will sing")[75]. It is a spiritual creature (which we sometimes call an angel) that serves as the spiritual source for all physical trees. As such, it includes all of the traits and elements that later become manifest in specific creatures in the World of *Asiya*. But, as they exist in the World of *Yetzira*, one world above *Asiya*, all "trees" are part of a spiritual "template" that serves as their source, as well as the conduit for the passing of spiritual influx to the next world. This is what the sages meant when they said that, "There is no blade of grass down here which is without a spiritual source above that strikes it and tells it to grow." The source above is a spiritual creation in the World of *Yetzira* (and higher).

Blessed be He Who decrees and fulfills,

Another clue to the World of *Yetzira* is that it functions like a symbol of reference to the infinite light of G-d. That is, just as a student creates a mnemonic in order to recall intellectual material, so the World of *Yetzira* aids us on our meditative path to revelation of the infinite light of G-d. The mnemonic does not, in itself, tell us what the material is, but it helps us to recall it. So, the World of *Yetzira* does not reveal the infinite light of G-d, but it refers to it and recalls it.[76] With meditation, we will be able to extrapolate from this world to the next, and thus, eventually, to meditate upon higher levels of G-dliness.[77]

*

As noted, our meditation during the *Pesukei DeZimra* focuses upon the G-dly light that is invested in the world, in order to create it.[78] Later, we will see that there is a more advanced meditation that focuses upon the G-dly light that transcends creation. However, from *Baruch She'Amar* through *Yishtabach*, we concentrate upon the holiness that permeates creation. It is the energy that courses through creation in order to enliven it. Normally, we are aware of this energy, since we detect it within ourselves as well, but we are not aware that it is G-dly. The secret of meditation during the *Pesukei DeZimra* is to become aware that this light is G-dly and that it enlivens not only physical creation but also the spiritual creatures of the World of *Yetzira*. As we meditate, we become aware of the spiritual element of this light and how it subtly changes from creature to creature, enlivening each and every one (with the letters of the Hebrew alphabet), and imparting to each one its own unique qualities.

Despite the fact that *Baruch She'Amar* initiates only the second section of our prayers (corresponding to the World of *Yetzira*), it is associated with spiritual levels that far transcend even the World of *Atzilut*. It seems that the sages wanted us to inaugurate the morning prayers with an initial revelation from the highest spiritual levels that would help us proceed through the entire prayer process successfully.[79] Therefore, it makes sense for us to explore the levels of infinite G-liness that transcend *Atzilut*. Although these are levels that the normal human being is unable to reach even upon extensive meditation (in the sense of "being there), nevertheless, we need to have knowledge of their existence.

*

The Creation is out of range of the Creator
Baruch She'Amar – "Blessed be He Who said"

With one utterance, G-d created the entire universe and, in His goodness, He constantly renews the creation at every instant. [The opening words of *Baruch She'Amar* -] "Blessed be He Who said and the universe came into existence," [suggest that] it happened spontaneously, as it is written elsewhere, "...He commanded and they were created." [80] "Were created" also indicates spontaneous creation. And so we find in the phrases used by the sages – such as, "Until the world was created," and "since the world was created," etc.

All these examples come to tell us that there is no comparison between the Creator and His creations. They are completely out of range of one another, since creations are limited and the Creator has no beginning [or end] ... Creation took place after a series of mighty contractions of His holy illumination which

CHASSIDIC INSIGHTS

Let us then begin from the highest level, since that is where chasidic literature begins its discussion of *Baruch She'Amar*. That level is the infinite light of G-d that precedes the *tzimtzum hagadol* ("great contraction"); it is also known as the "general" World of *Atzilut* (as distinct from the "specific" World of *Atzilut*, which we discussed previously). In order to create the universe, it was necessary for G-d to "contract" the infinite illumination of His presence, so that a finite and limited universe could come into being. Where there is infinite G-dly revelation, there is no possibility for anything else to exist. So, G-d caused a contraction of His infinite light. The contraction was only from our perspective; from a Divine perspective it did not occur at all. G-d remained infinite and om-

בָּרוּךְ עוֹשֶׂה בְּרֵאשִׁית,

niscient as before the *tzimtzum*, but afterward, there was "room" for limited and finite creation to exist.

In referring to the infinite light of G-d prior to the *tzimtzum*, it is not appropriate to mention either creation or emanation (*sephirot*) since nothing can maintain an independent separate existence while basking in His infinite light. All that can be said about this level is what the sages said, "before the world was created, there was nothing but He and His name alone." Nothing existed, but His name was embedded in His infinite light, as the potential for creation. There was nothing but G-d and His ability to "make room" for the other to exist – and that is what we call His "name."

Now, between this "general" *Azilut* and the "specific" *Atzilut* and its *sephirot*, there is more spiritual distance than between *Atzilut* and *Asiya* below. The gap between the supernal decision (within His infinite illumination, or "general" *Atzilut*) to create and the subsequent emanation of the ten *sephirot* (of "specific" *Atzilut*) is far greater than the gap between the ten *sephirot* and the physical World of *Asiya*. This great gap is bridged by several intermediate spiritual levels, as follows:

LEVELS BEFORE CREATION	POTENTIAL WORLDS	CREATION PROCESS
Infinite Illumination	"General" *Atzilut*	Decision to create
Tzimtzum ("contraction")		Room for creation
Adam Kadmon ("Primordial Man")	"General" *Bria*	Overall creation plan and potential *sephirot*
Atik Yomin ("Ancient of Days") and internal level of *keter* ("crown")	"General" *Yetzira*	Undifferentiated, essential illumination of G-dliness
Arich Anpin ("Long Face") and external level of *keter* ("crown")		Concentrated *sephirot*, illumination too intense for the *kelim* ("vessels")
"Specific" *Atzilut*	"General" *Asiya*	Emanation of the ten *sephirot*, illumination appropriate for the *kelim*

CHASSIDIC EXCERPTS

greatly obscured and concealed the [infinite spiritual] light until it became possible to create worlds ... and that is why we say, "and they were created," as if spontaneously, to indicate the tremendous gulf between the creations and the Creator, since He is the most hidden of all concealments...

[By way of an analogy, we might erroneously think of] the obvious influence that a mentor has upon his student; theirs is a cause-and-effect relationship since the effect bears some relationship to its cause, as the student has some inkling of who his mentor is. However, this is not true of the ray of illumination that

CHASSIDIC INSIGHTS

The first of those levels is called *Adam Kadmon (A"K)*, meaning "Primordial Man." It is the first spiritual level following the *tzimtzum*, and it contains the overall plan of creation. It encompasses all of time and space in one concentrated spiritual point. Since here even the ten *sephirot* exist only in potential, it is appropriate to call this level the "general" World of *Bria*. That is, just as the lower, "specific" World of *Bria* is described as potential and possible creation, so the level that we call *A"K* (or "general" *Bria*) is the realm of potential emanation of the ten *sephirot* of *Atzilut*.

Below *A"K* is the realm known as the *keter* ("crown") of *Atzilut*. It is composed of an outer external level that corresponds to G-d's *ratzon* ("will") and an inner level that corresponds to His *oneg* ("delight/enjoyment"). The outer

Blessed be He Who accomplishes creation.

level is called *Arich Anpin* ("Long Face"), and the inner level is called *Atik Yomin* ("Ancient of Days"). Within the outer level of *keter*, there are ten *sephirot*, just as in the World of *Atzilut*. However, in *keter*, the *sephirot* exist in an entirely different manner than they do in *Atzilut*. In *keter*, the *sephirot* are much more intense; they are not channeled and limited as they are in *Atzilut*.

By way of description, the soul-powers that correspond to the *sephirot* of *keter* might be termed "adrenalin powers." Under normal circumstances, we use our powers as needed, combining love and fear, mercy and security, integrity and happiness, etc. to achieve our goals. However, there are times when a measured response is not appropriate for the situation. There are times that we must throw

CHASSIDIC EXCERPTS

descends from the transcendent light of the One Above into the worlds. It comes down to us only through a series of concealments and obscurations, so that ultimately, "no thought can grasp Him whatsoever," as mentioned previously. And, therefore, it is appropriate to use the past tense, passive form *nivra'u* ("were created")[81] as if it occurred spontaneously, since within the worlds there is no awareness of the creative power that is continuously flowing through them and creating them from nothing to something ... the Ari tells us that this is the level of *radla* ("unknowable head"). Being unknown, it bears similarity to *chochma*, the first of the ten *sephirot* [of which we have some grasp and knowledge; *keter* is beyond our grasp and intellect], about which we say that it "emerges from nothing" – like one who finds an object and has no idea from where it came. This is equivalent to the concept "and it came into existence" – as if spontaneously and of its own accord.

(From *Likutei Torah* of the Alter Rebbe, *Shir HaShirim*, 41d)

Direct vs Reflected Illumination
"Blessed be He Who has compassion on the earth..."

There are two sets of the ten *sephirot* – the ten *sephirot* of "direct illumination" (*ohr yashar*) and the ten *sephirot* of "reflected illumination" (*ohr chozer*).[82]

The ten *sephirot* of "direct illumination" shine from Above to below, beginning with the highest - *keter* ("crown") - and ending with *malchut* ("kingship"), also known as the "ground level" or the "closing act." This agrees with the Talmud's opinion that in the scheme of creation, the heavens were created before the earth. (As we see from the first verse of the Torah, "In the beginning, G-d created the heavens and the earth"[83] – first the heavens and then the earth...) By way of psychological illustration, this is comparable to our will and intellect, which precede any action we take.

The ten *sephirot* of "reflected illumination" shine from below to Above... beginning from the end result, called "ground level," which arose in His thought [as the ultimate goal] before anything [was actually created]. This provides justification for the opinion that

CHASSIDIC INSIGHTS

ourselves into activity with all we have, from the very essence of our being. For example, when we are running away from danger or protecting a loved one, we do not stop to think if we are using the best combination of soul powers. We do not measure our reaction. The same applies to one who must wage war, for example; this is not the time for measured response. Instead, we react from the very essence to try to escape or to fend off danger. The soul powers that we use under such circumstances are equivalent to the sephirot of keter. They are generalized, archetypal responses that are far more intense and focused than the sephirot of Atzilut. Therefore, it is appropriate to call this combined level (Arich Anpin and Atik Yomin), "general" Yetzira.

בָּרוּךְ מְרַחֵם עַל הָאָרֶץ,

This description of the sephirot of keter applies to Arich Anpin, but not to the higher level of Atik Yomin. In Atik Yomin, we do not find sephirot, but only the infinite light of G-d. Since Atik Yomin is the inner dimension of keter, we find there G-d's infinite light as it is transmuted into the realm of keter. While Arich Anpin is divided into the ten sephirot, Atik Yomin is simple, undifferentiated illumination of G-dliness, as it descends to be expressed after the tzimtzum. This hidden illumination serves as the energy and vitality of keter of Atzilut (or "general" Yetzira).

CHASSIDIC EXCERPTS

the earth was created first, as the verse states, "On the day that the earth and the heavens were created."[84]

Clearly, only when we fulfill our ultimate desire in a concrete manner are we truly satisfied. Consequently, after we achieve satisfaction, and we revisit our original plan to compare it with our final result, we ascend mentally by way of "reflected illumination" to review the initial stages of our desire. And from there, we draw upon the highest most sublime levels of transcendent will ... in order to illuminate the "ground level" or "the 'closing act," the ultimate creation of physical reality, as distant as it might be...[85]

*

And this is what is meant by the phrase within Baruch She'Amar, "Blessed be He Who has mercy on the land" [referring to the "ground level"]. Mercy, in all of its aspects, is associated with the transcendental levels of the soul. [However], in the beginning, the prayer speaks of immanent G-dliness (ohr penimi) [and traces its] descent down to the lowest level of action [the "closing act"] which is [nonetheless] associated with the much higher sephira of chochma as the prayer says, "Blessed is He Who makes creation."

(Here we see the five levels of the soul – nefesh, ruach, neshama, chaya and yechida – descending as immanent illumination. The prayer then follows with the five transcendent levels of the soul [in reverse – that is, ascending – order], corresponding to "Blessed be He Who has mercy on the land" until "Blessed be His name." The latter is a supreme transcendent level that expresses the very essence of His name ... as will be explained).

"Land," or "ground level" symbolizes the potential of action coming to fruition, as in the creative statement, "Let the land give forth vegetation..."[86] Everything emerged from the dust, etc. and so what first originated in the initial stages of Divine thought was [the mineral world]; it was the physical creation that first arose in the Divine thought process. Afterward, the prayer continues, "Blessed be He Who has mercy on the creatures." We see that G-d has mercy on the work of His hands. This was evident after the flood, when G-d expressed remorse over the destruction of His creation. It was also evident at the splitting of the Reed Sea, when G-d expressed sorrow over the drowning of the Egyptians. And so we see as well regarding the town of Ninveh, about

CHASSIDIC INSIGHTS

And finally, we descend to the world of "general" *Asiya*, which corresponds to "specific" *Atzilut* with its ten *sephirot* (described earlier in the introduction to *Hodu*). Although this is the highest level that is associated with prayer, it is not the highest level that we know through meditation. While the highest, most spiritually-accomplished individuals (known as *tzadikim*) may experience the "specific" World of *Atzilut* with its ten *sephirot*, even such individuals do not have real, direct experience of the levels that transcend "specific" *Atzilut*. Through meditation, we may become aware of levels of spirituality beyond that, but even the most actualized human beings are not capable of truly experiencing those levels. The prayer *Baruch She'Amar* begins from the ineffable spiritual

Blessed be He Who has compassion on the earth,

levels that we can only know about and brings us down slowly to the highest level that we can not only know about but also experience (the "specific" World of *Atzilut* with its ten *sephirot*).

*

With this (admittedly insufficient) description, we can now begin to explain the commentaries on *Baruch She'Amar*:

The Alter Rebbe comments upon *Baruch She'Amar* both in his *Siddur* and in *Likutei Torah*. In the

CHASSIDIC EXCERPTS

which G-d asked [Jonah] rhetorically, "Should I not have mercy on them?"[87]

Similarly, man who exerts physical effort with his hands is loath to see the fruit of his labors destroyed after he has sunk into it all of his best and most serious, essential efforts. His concern (mercy) over the work of his hands transcends any enjoyment and desire that he may experience...

Moreover, the lower and more pitiful the creature, the more mercy one feels feel for it. Therefore, the prayer mentions first [in the order of "reflected illumination"], "Blessed be He Who has mercy on the land," since in its inception, the land ("ground level") arose first in G-d's will [and is the lowest creation, eliciting the greatest amount of mercy].

*

The phrase "Blessed is He Who has mercy on the creatures" refers to the transcendent spirit of the World of *Yetzira* (*makif deruach deyetzira*). The sustenance and livelihood of all creatures is derived from this level of *makif*, as we see clearly that every creature, according to its species, possesses a natural means of attaining its own food. However, the [following] phrase, "Blessed be He Who well rewards those who fear Him" refers to souls, who are [far] above

angels in the spiritual hierarchy. For, angels are also called "creatures" and "animals." And here, we find a distinction between *Yetzira* and *Bria*; angels who are born of mere speech are associated with *Yetzira*, as the verse says, "from the breath of His mouth come all of the heavenly hosts"[88]... while souls, rooted in thought, are associated with the World of *Bria*, corresponding to man, who comes from G-d's supernal intellect...

It is man's task to work the ground, to rectify and refine the 288 [sparks of holiness that fell into an impure state]. This is why the Torah says that Adam was placed into the Garden of Eden "to work it and to guard it,"[89] alluding to the 248 positive and the 365 negative commandments. In this way, additional spiritual illumination enters the "garden" every day, day by day. This is what is meant by "He remunerates well those who fear Him," with added illumination in the "garden," specifically for [souls] who fear Him...

*

The phrase, "Blessed be He Who well rewards those who fear Him" applies to souls, as mentioned, but only to the transcendent light of the soul, as associated with the World of *Bria*. How-

CHASSIDIC INSIGHTS

Siddur, the Alter Rebbe emphasizes the difference between referring to G-d as Atah ("You") and Hu ("He/Him"). We begin Baruch She'Amar in the third person – Hu – because the beginning of the prayer alludes to such a high and abstract level that we cannot possibly refer to G-d as if He were in front of us and present among us. That comes only at the end of the prayer when we say Baruch Atah – "Blessed are You." Only at the end of Baruch She'Amar have we descended to the spiritual level where we can allude to G-d in second person – "You" – as if He is truly in our presence, so to speak.

בָּרוּךְ מְרַחֵם עַל הַבְּרִיּוֹת,

The Alter Rebbe then tells us that the opening words of the prayer, in which we refer to G-d in the third person, correspond to the kabbalistic level known as Malchut De'Adam Kadmon ("Reign of Primordial Man"), source of Radla ("Unknowable Head"). In its opacity, this spiritual level is equivalent to the Hu mentioned earlier. In the teachings of the Alter Rebbe, this is the highest spiritual level that is discussed. The Alter Rebbe, unlike the Rebbes who succeeded him, does not discuss spiritual levels that preceded the tzimtzum, or great contraction of G-d's infinite light.[80] But Adam Kadmon is the first spiritual level after the tzimtzum. It is the level on which the entire creation, in both time and space, is launched in one spiritual point. It is from this level that the Alter Rebbe initiates his discussion of Baruch She'Amar. And then he takes us down step-by-step through BY"A, the three lowest worlds of creation.

CHASSIDIC EXCERPTS

ever, the more significant component of the soul consists of the three lower levels [that are clad in the body] – namely, nefesh, ruach and neshama – since they contain and channel spiritual illumination as "light in vessels" (orot bekelim). These vessels include our mind and heart. The transcendent levels of soul – chaya and yechida – remain above and beyond the limited ability of the body to contain illumination, such as in the mind and the heart.

Now, the three levels of "reflected light" mentioned above correspond [to the language of the prayer] as follows: 1) "on the land" alludes to the "reflected light" of nefesh, associated with Asiya; 2) "on the creations" alludes to the "reflected light" of ruach, associated with Yetzira; 3) "those who fear Him" alludes to the "reflected light" of neshama, associated with Bria.

"Blessed be He Who lives forever" alludes to the "reflected light" of chaya, or will of the soul ... This last level surpasses the intellect as it flows into the emotions; it represents the desire of the soul, transcending logic. Yet from it, the internal wisdom (chochma) of the soul receives illumination, as it states, "chochma emerges from nothing..." [Chochma] is

not enclothed in the mind or heart, yet it exists, hidden and concealed... [This inner level of the soul] is called chai ("alive"), meaning alive in essence, as opposed to chai lehachayot ("life that enlivens"), which is an extension of chai b'etzem ("life in essence")[90]...

"Blessed be He Who redeems and saves" alludes to the yechida, which is the loftiest of all transcendent levels of the soul ... In order to understand this better, it will be helpful to analyze why ba'alei tshuva (those who return to the path of Torah and mitzvot after having strayed) are considered greater than tzaddikim (those who have never parted from the path of Torah and mitzvot). The reason is that the source of the ba'al tshuva's soul is from the "will of wills," as it says in the Zohar that ba'alei tshuva are "drawn to G-d with greater strength." The word "greater" (yatir) here refers to the yechida level of the soul, which is the origin of all spiritual aspirations. For, we see an amazing phenomenon regarding ba'alei tshuva. From where within themselves do they find this incredible ability to uproot themselves from the impure transgressions to which they were formerly attached with all of their strength and power? From

CHASSIDIC INSIGHTS

In *Likutei Torah*,[81] the Alter Rebbe discusses what *Baruch She'Amar* means inside of us, in the soul. He tells us that the equivalent of *A"K* in the soul is the unconscious love of G-d that is present in every Jewish heart, and that the purpose of reciting *Baruch She'Amar* is to draw out the latent love and transform it into a conscious emotion. He also says that the thirteen times that the word *Baruch* ("Blessed be") is mentioned in the prayer correspond to the "thirteen strands of the beard" with which G-d brings mercy into the world. Just like a hair contains a very limited amount of vitality (which is why it does not hurt when cut), so the G-dliness coming down to the creation through the "thirteen strands of the beard" is very limited and contracted. The first twelve times the word *baruch* is mentioned correspond to twelve specific spiritual levels, while the thirteenth time includes all of them.

> # Blessed be He Who has compassion on the creatures,

And also in *Likutei Torah*,[82] the Alter Rebbe emphasizes another lesson from *Baruch She'Amar*, which is that the world was created spontaneously. Unlike two entities that bear a direct relation to one another (and therefore impinge directly upon each other), creation occurred only after a tremendous number and amount of contractions and limitations of G-d's infinite light. But because creation is so spiritually distant from G-d, there is no way for us to imagine any step-by-step process which brought the world into being; it was simply "brought into existence" – all at once, spontaneously. This

CHASSIDIC EXCERPTS

where do they get the strength to truly return to G-d with honest regret, to the extent that their souls are embittered to the point of death?[91] We have to conclude that this incredible power exceeds the lust and desire that attached them to all of their former transgressions. Even though the drive [to transgress] surpasses the logic and intellect of the mind and heart, it is only a component of the soul, and it pales in comparison to an arousal from the very essence of the soul. From this very essence of the soul, called the *yechida*, stems every other desire and will. And for that reason, within this extension of the essence of the soul, called the *yechida*, is found the ability to uproot, decisively and forever, whatever strange addiction one might have to transgressions, and return to G-d in true *tshuva*...

This, then, is the meaning of "Blessed be He Who redeems and saves." Among the holy sparks are those that were scattered and rejected, and those who were entrapped in the realm of *noga* (where sparks of holiness intermingle with impure spirituality). [This situation necessitates] new illumination from Above, from the essence of the Emanator, from the Will of all wills, the In-

itiator of all desires. [This new illumination] arouses the *yechida* within all of these sparks and awakens their supreme will to return and ascend from the chambers of spiritual impurity. This is similar to the heavenly voice that emerges every day calling "return, wayward children, return."[92] And this is what is meant by "redeems and saves." It is a daily process, as holy sparks emerge from captivity among the forces that conceal holiness. And it is also a personal process, since we are surrounded by temptation every day, and if it weren't for the help of G-d from Above, we would succumb...

*

"Blessed be His name" refers to the overall transcendent illumination, higher than the five transcendent lights previously described regarding the various levels of *ohr yashar* and *ohr chozer*. This is a revelation of His infinite light...from where originates the beginning of His undifferentiated thought and will [to create the world]. Here, the beginning of His thought (*ohr yashar*) and the final result (*ohr chozer*) exist together. This corresponds to the opinion that the earth and the heavens were created simultaneously. Here, the tran-

CHASSIDIC INSIGHTS

is the meaning of the initial words of *Baruch She'Amar* – "Blessed be He who spoke, and the universe came into existence" spontaneously and immediately.

The Alter Rebbe's son, the Mittler Rebbe (who also wrote the *Siddur* based upon his father's teachings) takes a radically different approach when interpreting *Baruch She'Amar*. The Mittler Rebbe[83] says that not only does the prayer take us from above to below, but it takes us back up again. Elucidating one of his father's themes, he says that all of the spiritual levels of *Baruch She'Amar* are transcendent levels of G-dliness (*makifim*) that we do not grasp or experience. They descend from above to create the universe in two different ways. One is called *ohr yashar*, or "direct light," that comes down from above to below as *orot b'kelim*, or "light within

בָּרוּךְ מְשַׁלֵּם שָׂכָר טוֹב לִירֵאָיו,

CHASSIDIC EXCERPTS

scendent light of the *yechida* of *ohr yashar* and the *yechida* of *ohr chozer* are completely equal, similar to a sphere which possesses neither "up" nor "down."

(From *Sha'ar Hatefila* of the *Mittler Rebbe*, p. 53, sec. 9 (within *Sha'arei Tshuva*))

From overall desire to concrete reality
Baruch She'Amar – "Blessed be He Who said…"

Why, at the beginning of the verses of *Pesukei DeZimra*, which speak of creation and the initial formation of the worlds, do we say *Baruch She'Amar* – "Blessed is He Who spoke, and the universe came into existence"?:

It is known that speech took place in [G-d's] heart, meaning in His thought and will. The goal was to bring into existence something that had the veneer of being "outside of Him" – in other words, the universe. The phrase, "and the universe came into existence" is indicative either of [His plan for] the future (for why would He say (to Himself) something that would not ultimately take place (in a revealed fashion) … or that the universe was [already] created [in the past], immediately, as soon as it arose within His simple will…

Now this [simple] Will was an overall desire, that included no particular details just yet, which is why the text reads *Baruch She'Amar* ("Blessed be He Who spoke"), referring to one statement alone [from which the entire universe was created]. And although we must say that this statement included within itself all that was to be created, [the details

were] totally concealed within the overall desire, and the details were not recognizable at all, even to Himself[93] … This is what is meant by *Baruch Hu* ("Blessed be He"). "Blessed" here indicates drawing something out from a state of concealment into revelation, meaning that that which had been hidden in the supernal Will should become revealed, at least within Himself…

All of this took place within the infinite light of G-d that transcended the great *tzimtzum*, and as yet bore no relation to the creation of the worlds. Even the "estimate" (*hashara*) existed only in potential within the infinite light - it was still totally out of range of the creation … And in order for the creation to take place, it was necessary to contract His infinite light … That is why after *Baruch Hu*, which is the "estimate" that preceded the *tzimtzum*, we say *Baruch omer v'oseh* ("Blessed be He Who says and does") – which is a statement that bears a connection to real action and concrete creation. In fact, this statement corresponds to the will and primordial thought of *Adam Kadmon* [the first level after the *tzimtzum* that contained every-

CHASSIDIC INSIGHTS

vessels." It is channeled through the ten *sephirot* of *Atzilut*, each of which play a specific role during the process of creation. The second manner in which the holy light descends from above is as *ohr chozer*, or "reflected light." Since this is a new concept, it is necessary to add a few words of explanation.

The best way to understand *ohr chozer* is with an analogy to sunlight. As the light of the sun reaches the earth, we might expect it to become colder and colder, as it becomes more and more distant from the sun. However, what actually happens is that the temperature is greater next to the earth than at higher altitudes. This illustrates the concept of "reflected light." When the rays of sunlight strike the earth, they reflect or "bounce" off the ground with great intensity, generating more heat near the earth than higher up.

> Blessed be He Who compensates well those who fear Him.

CHASSIDIC EXCERPTS

thing that was to be created in one spiritual point], which was also the general blueprint of all of creation...

*

As for the phrase, "Blessed be He Who says and does" - to begin with He simply "says" - since [at that point] there was not yet any correlation to concrete action. [That is why] the prayer only indicates that "He said," and the world "happened." But, now the prayer continues, "says and does," indicating a correlation to action. Still, even this remains in thought and will alone, and "says and does" is a statement in the heart. However, [the statement] "Blessed is He Who decrees and fulfills" refers to a decree within speech that something should come to fruition; for example, when a king announces a decree that something should take place in such and such a way, it will certainly take place. This is not so in the case of thought alone, since possibly the thought will not come into expression in reality, or will take a long time to come to fruition. But, when the king makes a verbal announcement, the decree takes effect immediately and with certitude. This is what happens, so to speak Above when we say "Blessed is He Who decrees and fulfills" – it will come to fruition in speech.

This corresponds to the "general"

World of *Yetzira* which emerges into revelation from the level of *Adam Kadmon*...

Afterward we say, "Blessed is He Who makes creation." This phrase corresponds to the "general" World of *Asiya*, which in turn corresponds to "specific" *Atzilut* but is called "general" *Asiya* since it includes vessels possessing, in a refined sense, the quality of existence ... And this is what is meant by, "Blessed is He Who maintains creation (*oseh breishit*)," alluding to the element of *chochma* ("wisdom") which is called *reishit* ("head/beginning"), since it is the source and origin of all *histalshelut* ("chain" of spiritual levels leading to physical creation). [Nevertheless], it is literally like *asiya* in relation to the infinite light of the One Above, as it is written, "You created them all in wisdom," demonstrating that *chochma* bears a relation to *Asiya* or action.

And the explanation of *oseh breishit* is that *chochma* bears a relationship to *Asiya*, and that, via this relationship, *chochma* takes part in creation of the worlds in concrete reality, as *Breishit bara* ("In the beginning, He created...")[94] is translated into Aramaic: *B'chomata bara* ("With wisdom, He created..."), and *Chachamot banta baita...*("Wise women built the house...")[95]

(From *B'shaah Sh'hikdimu 5672* (1912) of the Rebbe Rashab, vol. 1, pp. 129-132)

CHASSIDIC INSIGHTS

In *Baruch She'Amar*, then, as the creative light descends from above to below, there is a corresponding, but opposite illumination of light from below to above – this is "reflected light." But, reflected light, while intense, is also diffuse. It is not as focused and predictable as is the light of direct illumination that shines from above to below. It does not shine as illumination within vessels, but surrounds and envelopes rather than permeates. So, the beginning phrases of the prayer, according to the Mitteler Rebbe, deal with the holy illumination of "direct light," while the subsequent phrases allude to various levels of "reflected light."

בָּרוּךְ חַי לָעַד וְקַיָּם לָנֶצַח,

We are aware of the spiritual levels alluded to in the prayer, even though they are beyond us. That is, we know that they exist, even if we do not directly experience them. The first five levels of *Baruch She'Amar* (called *ohr yashar* or "direct light") bring us down, while the

CHASSIDIC EXCERPTS

Building a house of prayer

When it occurs to man to build a house, there are many details involved in the process, such as how many rooms and attics [to build], one on top of the either. Within the person's [initial] desire for the house, the details are not discernible at all, although they are certainly present. The fact that he desires the house is for a reason and [is motivated by] internal purpose, which is the delight of the soul that he experiences from the house. If so, there is certainly a specific form associated with his desire, [according to the delight that he has in the house]. However, it is not recognizable at all, even though all [of the details] are included there, concealed without any order or organization of what comes first and what follows.

And, when the builders are commanded to actually build the house, of necessity they must reveal each and every independent detail regarding the rooms and the attics and their organization. Everything is included in the overall plan and whatever specific details were unknown become revealed.

Now, the example of this occurring above is when it arose in His mind to emanate and create. In the beginning, it arose as a general will regarding all of the details of the spiritual chain of creation, from the highest levels down to the lowest levels. It all arose in a general manner, as written, "When I said, world..."[96] indicating a statement of the heart, taking place in the mode of thought, as written, *Baruch She'amar* – "Blessed be He Who said and the world came into existence"- within this statement is included everything in a hidden manner, as yet un-recognizable. And this is what is meant by the words *She'amar ve'haya haolam* ("Who uttered and the world came into existence"), which form the Hebrew acrostic, *shaveh*, meaning "equal." This is also equivalent to the spiritual level called the *hashara* ("estimation") within Him, with which G-d "pondered" how to create in potential – after which all the details emerged to become revealed, each detail on its own, via the *kav* ("ray" of spiritual illumination) that descends from the infinite light to emanate and create the entire universe with all of its details. And this is what is meant by *Baruch omar ve'oseh* ("Blessed be He Who says and does...") – including revelation of the details [of creation] from their general principle...

From *Sefer Maamorim 5671* (1911) of the Rebbe Rashab, Page 167

CHASSIDIC INSIGHTS

second five levels (called *ohr chozer* or "reflected light") bring us back up again. Finally, we say *Baruch Shemo* – "Blessed be His name" – and that brings us to the essence of G-dliness that includes all of the previous levels.

The third Lubavitcher Rebbe,[84] the *Tzemach Tzedek* (grandson of the Alter Rebbe) quotes the *Radah* (Rabbi David Abudraham), suggesting that the entirety of the *Baruch She'Amar* prayer corresponds to the first reference to creation in the Torah: "In the beginning, G-d created the heavens and the earth." And the succeeding prayers in the *Siddur* each correspond to one of the subsequent creative statements which brought the world into being: "God said, 'Let there be light,' and there was light," etc. Thus, all of the psalms of *Pesukei DeZimra* correspond to one of the ten creative statements. And if so,

> Blessed be He Who lives
> forever and exists eternally,

CHASSIDIC EXCERPTS

Meditation bridges the gulf
Baruch She'Amar – "Blessed be He Who said..."

By way of meditation on G-dly topics, we achieve ... our ultimate goal – arousal of the heart in conscious love and fear of G-d. This love revealed in the recesses of our heart promotes refinement and purification of the corporeal aspects of our animal soul, as well as rectification of all of our matters. And in this way, we are enabled to fulfill the mitzvot properly, whether by turning away from anything negative or by pursuing the positive, as is written elsewhere at length. And this is the entire purpose of man in the world, and the reason for the descent of his soul into his body.

Now, love and fear [of G-d] emerges only through meditation. In the beginning, the meditation must be focused upon creation from nothing to something in general, meaning on how every object that exists must of necessity have been created from nothing ... meaning from the divine void (*ayn*) ... The meditation must touch upon the details, meaning upon the quality of the G-dly void that creates existence. Although it is true that creation from nothing to something took place "out of range," meaning from a distance (which is why the object can "exist" as a separate entity), nevertheless, we must say

that there is a certain proximity and connection between the G-dly void and created existence that enables the emergence of existence (and this is the difference between the ultimate origin of creation and the very essence of G-d, with Whom alone is the power to create, and *malchut* of *Atzilut*, which is the proximate cause and the will to actually create).[97] And since the G-dly void that preceded creation must stand in proximity to created existence, there must also be a spiritual chain leading from the G-dly void, from level to level, until it becomes the source of created existence. All this constitutes the lengthy meditation that is associated with *Baruch She'Amar*...

*

"Blessed is He Who spoke, and the universe came into existence" is an utterance originating from *Adam Kadmon* ("Primordial Man," the blueprint of creation). And above that, *Baruch She'Amar* corresponds to *malchut* of the infinite light of G-d, and as such it is the utterance of *malchut* of the *Ein Sof* ("Endless One") in order to bring about the creation of *A"K* , the "general" World of *Bria* [just as the first level of created existence lower than *Atzilut* is the "specific" World of *Bria*, so the first world of emanation after the infinite light of G-d is

CHASSIDIC INSIGHTS

they also correspond to the ten *sephirot*, which are associated with the ten statements. Perhaps we could say, then, that the remainder of the *Pesukei DeZimra* corresponds to the final *sephira* of *malchut*. That would be why the final prayers relate the story of the splitting of the Reed Sea. Elsewhere in chasidic literature[85] it is explained that the splitting of the Reed Sea alludes to the "splitting" of the *sephira* of *malchut*, which allowed a huge revelation of G-dly light to penetrate the world. If so, it is appropriate that the final section of *Peshukei DeZimra* should quote the verses of the Torah that narrate the exodus and the splitting of the sea.

בָּרוּך פּוֹדֶה וּמַצִּיל,

The Rebbe Rashab (the fifth Lubavitcher Rebbe and grandson of the *Tzemach Tzedek*) writes that *Baruch She'Amar* alludes to an even

CHASSIDIC EXCERPTS

the "general" World of *Bria*]. And this is what is meant by, "Who spoke and the universe came into existence," referring to *malchut* of *Ein Sof* as it becomes *keter* and *Atik Yomim* of *A"K*...

[Alternatively], "Blessed is He Who spoke" refers to the holy utterance from *A"K*, while "and the universe came into existence" refers to *malchut* of *A"K* as it becomes *keter* and *Atik Yomim* of *Atzilut*, followed by "Blessed be He" as the specific *keter* of *Atzilut*. Then, afterward the prayer alludes to all the specific levels of the ten *sephirot* of *Atzilut*, down to "Blessed be He Who has mercy on the creatures," which is *malchut* of *Atzilut* as it becomes *keter* and *Atik Yomim* of *Bria*, followed by the details of the levels of the worlds of *BY"A*. All of this constitutes the descent of the divine void (*ayn*) as it drops from one level to the next until it becomes the void that is the source of created existence (*yesh*).

Now, all of this involves divine illumination that bears a relationship to the worlds – that is, illumination that is measured and meted out from G-d's infinite light, in order to take on a connection to the worlds. Within this illumination, there are various levels within the order of descent, and because of this there are also variations in the worlds that were created from this *ayn* ("divine void"). This is because in the course of its descent from level to level, the G-dly void created worlds on each level that were in accordance with the G-dliness of that level. This is true whether we are

speaking of the overall perspective of worlds beginning with *A"K* as the "general" World of *Bria*, followed by *A"K* of *Yetzira* and *A"K* of *Asiya*, or whether we are speaking of the lower perspective of the "specific" worlds of *BY"A*. All of this occurs within the G-dly ray of light that follows the *tzimtzum* and bears various different levels, and the difference between them is the amount of revealed illumination. In the higher levels, the *ayn* is more revealed (as in the World of *Bria*, in which there is revelation of the G-dly *ayn*, as written elsewhere), while at the lower levels, there is not so much revealed illumination, which is why it becomes the source of created existence (*yesh*).

Now, even though it is not within the scope of this meditation to produce any particular *midah* ("attribute'), nevertheless, it does produce a certain closeness to G-dliness in general, which is known as the "engraving from without." This means that by way of this meditation and by way sensing the G-dly *ayin* that creates the *yesh*, and in particular regarding the quality of the G-dly *ayin* and the details of the creation that is created from it, we get very close to G-dliness and detach ourselves from physical matters. In this way, we emerge from our previous status and situation and ascend to a higher level.

The "engraving from within" occurs by way of meditation on divine revelation within the worlds, meaning on the G-dly illumination and life-force that

CHASSIDIC INSIGHTS

higher spiritual level than suggested by his great-great grandfather, the Alter Rebbe. As previously stated, the Alter Rebbe mentioned levels preceding the *tzimtzum* only in passing without discussing them in detail. Above the *tzimtzum*, it is not appropriate to speak of worlds at all, since all that exists is the infinite light of G-d, too ethereal and abstract for anything approaching concrete existence.

But, there is something on this level, as the sages said, "Before the world was created, there was only He and His name alone."[86] That is, even before the *tzimtzum* took place (and therefore also before creation), there was "G-d's name." But, one might ask, why would G-d need a name before creation? A name is needed only for an other, so that the other can call or

Blessed be He Who redeems and rescues,

CHASSIDIC EXCERPTS

is enclothed within them in order to enliven them, as is written, "And You enliven all of them."[98] This meditation focuses on how within every creature there is G-dly life that enlivens it, meaning that just as no object creates itself, so no object exists on its own. Rather, it exists only because of the G-dliness that enlivens it. We observe this from our own flesh – we experience within our-selves a soul that enlivens us, and we understand that our soul is the main thing, that every vital movement emerges from our soul, and we see that when the soul exits the body, the body remains like an inert object, a stone. So, too, we understand the same about the world, seeing that it lives, that it possesses life-force that enlivens it, and that the life-force is G-dly...

(From *Besha'ah shehikdimu* 5672 of the Rebbe Rashab, vol. 1, p. 293)

Ten Creative Utterances
Baruch She'Amar – "Blessed be He Who said..."

The *Radah* (R' David Abudrahram) writes that the prayer *Baruch She'Amar* corresponds to the first of the ten creative statements with which the world was created – "In the beginning, G-d created the heavens and the earth." The next prayer, *Mizmor LeTodah,* corresponds to "Let there be light." The prayer after that, *Yehi ch'vod,* corresponds to the utterance, "Let there be a firmament."

It is possible that the reason [so many of] the morning prayers start with the word *Yehi* is that the ten creative utterances also begin with *Yehi* ("Let there be") ... It is explained in the *Zohar* (*Parshat Vayechi*), regarding all of the supernal deeds, that they begin with *Yehi*, unlike facts created down here in the physical world, since *Yehi* represents a drawing down of divine influence from a very high origin...

(From *Ohel Yoseph Yitzhak* on *Tehillim* (*Yahel Ohr*) from the Tzemach Tzedek, p. 652)

What was concealed becomes revealed...

When we cultivate revelation of the faculties of our G-dly soul via meditation, as we contemplate how G-d fills all worlds, transcends all worlds, and how there is no place devoid of His presence, we can no longer allow ourselves to remain under the sway of the darkness and concealment of the animal soul. We become aroused with love like flames of fire for G-dliness, and this overwhelms our animal soul so that it no longer conceals but is rather involved in G-dly matters. In this manner, we draw down revealed G-dliness to illuminate the darkness of the world.

This is the entire purpose of prayer, which involves meditation in order to draw the faculties of the divine soul into conscious revelation. And therefore, in the introduction of *pesukei dezimra*, prior refer to you. And on this level, preceding the *tzimtzum*, there was no other. There was only G-d Himself and His infinite illumination. So, why did He have a name?

The Rebbe Rashab reasons that even in this extremely rarefied spiritual realm preceding the *tzimtzum*, there must also be different levels of G-dliness. First of all, there is G-d Himself (beyond any category or description, even "Light" or "Illuminator"). Then, there is His infinite light. And, within His infinite light and illumination, there was a decision taken (by Himself, so to speak) to relate to an other. And there was a decision taken within His infinite illumination to make room for the other. That is what the sages call G-d's "name." It is the decision within G-d's infinite illumination to minimize (in potential) the illumination and make room for an other. Whatever the other is or what it will be, is unknown as yet, but within G-d's infinite wisdom and illumination, He already made room for it before it was created. This is what the sages meant by, "Before the universe was created, there was only He and His name alone."

בָּרוּךְ שְׁמוֹ.

After the Rebbe Rashab defines this extremely subtle level that preceded the *tzimtzum*, he utilizes the concept of "general" worlds (which we described previously) to fit the new outlook. Since it is possible to discern levels preceding the *tzimtzum*, it is also possible to speak of spiritual realms on a higher plane and fit them into such a spiritual framework. If previously the concept of worlds meant the spiritual process leading to creation of the universe, the new spiritual framework starts with the infinite light of G-d and leads to "emanation" (of the ten *sephirot*). For example, the Rebbe Rashab refers to the levels preceding the *tzimtzum* as "general" *Atzilut*. And the first level following the *tzimtzum* is "general" *Bria*. The next level, called *keter* is "general" *Yetzira*. And the entire world of emanation of the ten *sephirot* (*Atzilut*) is "general" *Asiya*. Previously, this level was only known as the specific world of *Atzilut* – and so it remains. But, now that we have defined four spiritual realms above *Atzilut*, it is also known as the lowest of these "new" worlds, or "general" *Asiya*. The difference is that the four upper or "general" worlds (from before the *tzimtzum* until "specific" *Atzilut*) culminate in the emanation of *sephirot*, while the four lower, or "specific" worlds (*Atzilut* to *Asiya*) lead to the creation of the universe, including the physical world in which we live.

Elsewhere,[87] the Rebbe Rashab concludes that the prayer *Baruch She'Amar* alludes to the four realms just described, as follows:

WORDS OF PRAYER	LEVELS BEFORE CREATION	
Baruch She'Amar vehaya haolam ("Blessed be He who spoke and the universe came into existence")	Essence of G-dliness	
Baruch Hu ("Blessed be He")	Infinite light before *tzimtzum* ("contraction")	"general" *Atzilut*
Baruch omer veoseh ("Blessed be He who says and does")	*Adam Kadmon* "Primordial Man")	"general" *Bria*
Baruch gozer umekayam ("Blessed be He who decrees and fulfill His decrees")	*Keter* ("crown")	"general" *Yetzira*
Baruch oseh breishit ("Blessed be He Who makes creation")	ten *sephirot* of "specific" *Atzilut*	"general" *Asiya*

CHASSIDIC INSIGHTS

The opening phrase, *Baruch She'Amar vehaya haolam* ("Blessed be He who spoke and the universe came into existence") alludes to the very essence of G-dliness that cannot even be described as "light" or "illumination."

The second phrase, *Baruch Hu* ("Blessed be He") alludes to His infinite light before the *tzimtzum* or "general" *Atzilut.*

The third phrase, *Baruch omer v'oseh* ("Blessed be He who says and does") applies to A"K or "general" *Bria.*

Blessed be His name.

CHASSIDIC EXCERPTS

to prayers, we say *Baruch She'amar vehaya haolam* ("Blessed be He Who uttered, and the universe came into existence..."). That is, our meditation on the topic of how He spoke and the universe came into existence, and with one statement all of the worlds were created, should produce revelation within, leading to revelation of our divine soul. In particular, we should meditate on how everything is included in the primordial thought of *Adam Kadmon*, which is what is meant by, "Who uttered and the universe came into existence," wherein the first letters (*shin-vov-hey*) of the final three words (*she'amar vehaya haolam*) form an acrostic meaning "equal" (*shava*), leading to the next phrase, *Baruch hu* ("Blessed be He") – so that *hu* ("He"), previously concealed, becomes *baruch* - "blessed" and revealed within our soul.

From *Sefer Maamorim 5676* (in *Sefer Maamorim 5672-5676*) of the Rebbe Rashab, Page 142

Thirteen descents
Baruch She'Amar – "Blessed be He Who said..."

It is known that the thirteen times that we mention *baruch* in the prayer, *Baruch She'Amar* correspond to the thirteen strands of the beard [kabbalistic terminology for the influx that flows from Above the intellect into the intellect and below]. These are also known as the "thirteen attributes of divine mercy." [In prayer], we call upon the original source of all mercy [after *Barchu*, in the bless- ings preceding the *Shema*] ... And it is known as well that the thirteen times that we mention the word *baruch* in *Baruch She'Amar* all allude to *makifim*, [or transcendent illumination that comes to us from Above]. There are *makifim* of *ohr yashar* (as described earlier) and there are *makifim* of *ohr chozer. Baruch Shemo* is the source that includes all of them, as mentioned elsewhere.

(From *Be'sha'ah Shehikdimu 5672* of the Rebbe Rashab, vol. 1, p. 136)

Creation is but a Name...
Boruch Hu – "Blessed be He..."

From *Baruch Hu* until *Baruch Shemo*, we say the word *baruch* ten times, corresponding to the ten *sephirot*. This corresponds to all of *seder histalshalut* [the spiritual "chain" of levels leading to creation], about which we say, "Blessed be His name." His Name is only a superficial aspect of who He is [yet, with His Name, He created the universe]. Similarly, during *Yishtabach*, which is the conclusion of the prayer *Baruch She'Amar*, we say "May His name be blessed." After our meditation during the *Pesukei DeZimra* on all of the creation of the heavens and the earth, we say, "May Your name be praised," since [we recognize that] all creation comes from His Name alone, although it is only a superficial aspect of who He is.

(From *Torat Menachem* of the Rebbe, HaRav Menachem Mendel Schneerson, ztz'l, vol. 12, p. 166)

CHASSIDIC INSIGHTS

The fourth phrase, *Baruch gozer umekayam* ("Blessed be He who decrees and fulfills His decree") applies to *keter* or "general" *Yetzira*.

And finally, *Baruch oseh breishit* ("Blessed be He Who makes creation") applies to the ten *sephirot* of "specific" *Atzilut* or "general" *Asiya*. This is how the Rebbe Rashab interprets *Baruch She'Amar*, and it is the highest of the interpretations offered by the Rebbes.

בָּרוּךְ אַתָּה יְיָ אֱלֹהֵינוּ מֶלֶךְ הָעוֹלָם, הָאֵל,

אָב הָרַחֲמָן, הַמְהֻלָּל בְּפֶה עַמּוֹ, מְשֻׁבָּח וּמְפֹאָר

בִּלְשׁוֹן חֲסִידָיו וַעֲבָדָיו, וּבְשִׁירֵי דָוִד עַבְדֶּךָ.

Further, the Rebbe Rashab adds[88] that the prayer continues to allude to all of the ten *sephirot* of "specific" *Atzilut*, right down to the lower worlds of BY"A. As for what occurs within us, the Rebbe Rashab explains that it is not within the scope of this meditation to transform our personality traits, since it is too high and cerebral to have an effect upon the animal soul. Nevertheless, it causes us to draw closer

CHASSIDIC EXCERPTS

The King's name rules...

Just as it is the merely the name of the king that rules over the nation [the king rules by issuing edicts and decrees in his name. His actual presence is not required in every corner of his kingdom], and his name is not an expression of his self and essence, but rather an appellation alone, so it is in the divine world above. We say [toward the end of *Baruch She'amar*], *yachid chay haolamim melech* ("The singular One, Life of the universe, King..."), because His infinite light is singular and unique, and the life of the universe comes from the "King" alone. For, *malchut* [the tenth *sephira* – supernal kingship - with which G-d "reigns," so to speak] is only His Name.

And although a man's name is far from his essential life-force, there is nevertheless a ray of the life-force embedded in the letters of his name. For, the name with which the creature is called in the holy tongue is its vivifying force, as written, "And man called out the names of every animal..."[99] [saying, for example] "this one is appropriate to be called *shor* ("ox"), since it is the letters of the word *shor* (*shin-vov-resh*) which enliven [the ox]. However, this [vivifying force] is a mere ray, out of range of the essence. Similarly the aspect of *malchut* that enlivens and creates the worlds is a mere ray, out of range...

From *Sefer Maamorim 5676* (in *Sefer Maamorim 5672-5676*) of the Rebbe Rashab, Page 138

Dynamics of Creation

Yachid Chay HaOlamim Melech ("Unique One, Life of the Worlds, King.")

Sometimes [in *Baruch She'Amar*, at the beginning of prayers] we say *Yachid Chai Haolamim Melech* ("the One and Only, Life of the Worlds, King"), and sometimes [in *Yishtabach*], we say *Melech Yachid, Chai Haolamim* ("King, the One and Only, Life of the Worlds").

The first phrase, *Yachid Chai Haolamim Melech*, [refers to movement] from Above to below, alluding to the descent of G-d's infinite light from *yachid* [simple oneness, devoid of details and particulars] to the level of *melech* [G-d's rule over the universe, composed of details and particulars] ... As is known, there is a distinction between *yachid* ("unique") and *echad* ("one"). *Echad* alludes to oneness composed of various components and details, which nevertheless exist in harmony and unity. And *yachid* implies "one and only," or "singular in essence" – unrelated to details...

CHASSIDIC INSIGHTS

to G-d in general. The Rebbe Rashab calls this effect, "engraving from without." This is a characteristic of the *Pesukei DeZimra*. After we arise in the morning and slowly awaken, the verses of *Pesukei DeZimra* "cut away" and remove the remnants of physicality that cling to us after sleep. However, the *Pesukei DeZimra* do not transform us internally. That takes place later, as we meditate not only upon spiritual levels en-clothed within creation but upon G-dliness that transcends and surpasses creation. Then be-

gins a process known as the "engraving from within" that has the power to alter and transform our animal nature.

The Rebbe Rashab also mentions[89] the concept of *makifim* (in a reference similar to that of the Mittler Rebbe). And he concludes that all thirteen times that the word *baruch* occurs in the prayers refer to these transcendent levels of G-dliness some of which are *ohr yashar* ("direct illumination") and

*B*lessed are you, Lord, our G-d, King of the universe, the [all-powerful] God, merciful Father, extolled in the mouth of His people, praised and glorified by the tongue of those who fear Him and those who serve Him, and in the songs of David, Your servant;

CHASSIDIC EXCERPTS

Yachid Chai Haolamim Melech ("One and Only, Life of the Universe, King") alludes to the descent from *yachid* (where He is "One and Only") into *malchut* via *chai haolamim* ("Life of the universe"). By and large, *chai haolamim* is the life force of the universe, as embodied in the *kav* ("ray") or revelation of holy light, the inner dimension of which comes down to us from the internal essence of the Infinite One, into the *sephirah* of *malchut*.

And *Melech Yachid [Chai Haolamim]* ("King, the One and Only, Life of the Worlds") alludes to the elevation of His kingship (*malchut*) to the very essence of His infinite light, as it is written, "To You, G-d, is the reign,"[100] indicating *malchut* as it ascends to be included within the ten hidden *sephirot*.

(From *Sefer Maamorim* 5680 (1920) of the Rebbe Rashab, p. 134)

Until Forever

Adei Ad Shemo Hagadol... "until (and including) His great Name forever and ever..."

[The end of the prayer *Baruch She'Amar* reads: "... praised and glorified is His great Name forever and ever (*adei ad*)..."]

The phrase *adei ad* can be explained [and translated] in two ways – as "forever" or as "until"... Both are correct [but only one applies here].

G-d's "great name" (*shemo hagadol*) refers to the infinite light of G-d, on whatever spiritual level it may find expression. This may be His infinite light that transcends the upper reaches of the spiritual chain of creation (*seder hishtalshelut*), or even its source in the infinite light preceding the great *tzimtzum*. If the latter, then it refers to the infinite, unlimited illumination that reveals

G-dly essence. On this level, *adei ad* carries the meaning of "forever and ever," since the praise and exultation of His infinite light have no limit whatsoever.

[But] there is a kind of praise and adulation that has a limit or end. This occurs when the object of praise itself is limited, in wisdom and greatness, for example. When we reach the limits of wisdom or greatness of a great or wise person, then our praises cease, since it is not appropriate to praise him beyond his level. However, there is no measure to the heights of G-d's unlimited illumination, so praises and exaltations of G-d also apply without limit and measurement...

(From *Yom Tov shel Rosh Hashana* 5666 (1905-6) of the Rebbe Rashab, p. 17)

others of which are *ohr chozer* ("reflected illumination"). And, as the Mittler Rebbe says, the final *Baruch Shemo* is the origin and source of all of them.

Finally, from the Rebbe, Rabbi Menachem Mendel Shneerson, comes the following radically different interpretation of the prayer. The Rebbe states[90] that from the second time that we say the word *baruch* (*Baruch Hu*) until the final *baruch* (*Baruch Shemo*), we repeat the word *baruch* ten times. These

נְהַלֶּלְךָ יְיָ אֱלֹהֵינוּ בִּשְׁבָחוֹת וּבִזְמִירוֹת. וּנְגַדֶּלְךָ וּנְשַׁבֵּחֲךָ וּנְפָאֶרְךָ, וְנַמְלִיכְךָ וְנַזְכִּיר שִׁמְךָ מַלְכֵּנוּ אֱלֹהֵינוּ,

CHASSIDIC EXCERPTS

Standing, Walking, Jumping

In general, there are three levels; standing, walking and jumping. "Standing" takes place within a framework of order and hierarchy, while "walking" goes beyond order and hierarchy, and "jumping" is beyond "walking," to the extent that "walking" is described as order and hierarchy in comparison to "jumping..."

It is written, "I established you as walkers among these standers,"[101] referring to the angels who are called "standers," as written, "And He stood them up for ever..." and "All of them are standing at the heights of the world..." This is because their creation took place from the letters of speech, as written, "And with the spirit of His mouth, [He created] all the hosts." Now, letters are associated with the category of "inanimate" objects, which do not move or expand. But nevertheless, they do not remain constantly on one level, for it is written regarding the angels that, "With two they fly," implying that there is some sort of hovering and progress among them. For although it is true that the camp of angels associated with the archangel Michael serve G-d with love, and those of Gabriel with fear, nevertheless within their respective frameworks they undergo elevations from one level to the next. However, their elevations are all within a range that are close to one another, and in that sense they are all on one general level.

This is similar to what we know regarding *ad ve'ad b'clal* ("until and including") and *ad ve'lo ad b'clal* ("until and not including"). "Until and including" implies that the lower level is within range of the upper level, and that being the case, there are levels among the lower that overlap with the higher levels. For example, the external aspects of the upper levels become the internal aspects of the lower level, so that among the lower levels we also find some external elements of the upper level. And therefore as we stand on the lower level, we are nonetheless within range of the upper level. And similarly, as we ascend to the upper level, we do not completely exit the lower level, since they are within range of each other.

But, within the framework of "until

CHASSIDIC INSIGHTS

ten repetitions correspond to the ten *sephirot* of the World of *Atzilut*. Thus, according to the Rebbe, the very first *baruch* corresponds to the very essence of G-dliness, including all levels above *Atzilut*. And the final two times that we mention *baruch* correspond to the lower worlds of BY"A.

So, according to this interpretation, there are three general levels of G-dliness and creation: G-d Himself, the World of *Atzilut* as an intermediary, and the lower worlds of creation, BY"A.

We will extol You, Lord our G-d, with praises and psalms, we will adulate You and praise You and glorify You, and we will coronate You and mention Your name, our King our Lord.

CHASSIDIC EXCERPTS

and not including," the levels are not within range of one another. And if so, there is no part of the lower level to be found within the upper level. And as we stand on the lower level, we are totally out of range of the upper level, and similarly as we ascend to a higher level, we completely exit the lower level.

In general, this is the difference between *memalle kol olamim* ("immanent G-dliness") and *sovev kol olamim* ("transcendent G-dliness"). Regarding *memalle*, all levels are within range of each other. But, regarding *sovev*, although there are ten *sephirot* of *igulim* [that is, even among levels that are not measured and hierarchical, there exist *sephirot*, called *igulim*] they are not within range of one another, as explained elsewhere. And that is the difference between "standing" and "walk-ing." "Standing" implies elevations to levels that are within range of one another. This is called "standing" because while ascending, there is no complete exit from the previous level. So, it is as if we are on one level. And the ascent itself is hierarchical, meaning that as we ascend to the higher level, we do not completely separate from the lower level. "Walking," however implies elevations that are completely out of range, so that as we ascend to the next level, we completely detach ourselves from the previous level. And this is *sovev*, wherein the various levels are not within range [of one another]. And this is what is meant by calling the angels "standers." Altough they undergo ascent, it all takes place within *memalle*, meaning within the framework of order and hierarchy.

From *Sefer Maamorim 5671* (1911) of the Rebbe Rashab, Page 69-70

The Glory and the Majesty of the King

Take, by way of example, the king's troops; when they are of one kind, even if they are as numerous as the sand of the sea, they still do not express the "glory" (*hadar*) of the king. But, if there are different kinds of troops – such as cavalry upon horses, and soldiers with various types of weapons, including some with swords and others with bows and arrows, and also infantry, in various uniforms and serving various functions, each serving the king in his own man-

יָחִיד, חֵי הָעוֹלָמִים מֶלֶךְ.

מְשֻׁבָּח וּמְפֹאָר עֲדֵי עַד שְׁמוֹ הַגָּדוֹל:

בָּרוּךְ אַתָּה יְיָ, מֶלֶךְ מְהֻלָּל בַּתִּשְׁבָּחוֹת:

CHASSIDIC EXCERPTS

ner, without switching roles – and if they all come together and gather in honor of the king, each in his own distinct fashion, then this demonstrates the true "glory" of the king. Now, the "majesty" (hod) of the king is internal and essential and does not include divisions and categories at all, but the "glory" (hadar) of the king expresses his expansiveness and the revelation of his reign. Within the expansiveness, there are divisions, and the inter-inclusion of the many distinctions is precisely what expresses the king's "glory."

Now, the counterpart of this Above in the spiritual realm is known as "the honor and glory of His kingship."[102] It is the expansion of His exalted reign over the nation. It comes expressed in many details, causing Him to be known as "the King, exalted by praises"[103] – including many praiseworthy expressions, such as souls and angels. And each and every one [utters praise], according to his category, as it is written, "praised and beautified in the language of His pious ones and His servants"[104] – wherein "pious ones" alludes to souls, and "servants" to angels. Within this are found many groups, such as the camp of angel Michael, serving G-d with love ... while the angel Gabriel serves G-d in fear. And similarly among souls; some serve Him with love and others with fear ... And within this array are many sub-divisions and sub-levels, a great

myriad, without limit. And when all of them gather together – all of the tribes of Israel in the lower world and the angels above in the spiritual realms – to praise their Maker every day at the time of prayers when all people praise and exalt G-d according to their level and essence – this expresses the "glory" of the King.

All of this takes place in the context of expansion of His G-dly illumination. But the very essence of the infinite light of G-d is described as "awesome in praises,"[105] suggesting that the celestial beings are afraid to utter His praises. Furthermore, it is written, "before You, my praises are silenced,"[106] indicating utter self-nullification, leaving no room for divisions or distinctions whatsoever. And since this alludes to His very essence, where there are no specific levels whatsoever, so also, in the self-nullification regarding this level, there are also no distinctions. This is "the majesty of His reign" (hod malchuto) and this is also why the word hod shares its root with hoda'ah ("acknowledgment"), [indicating] prayer which contains no praise or exaltation, but rather acknowledgment of G-d alone. As we say during the Shemonah Esreh – modim anachnu lach ("we acknowledge You") – referring to His very essence, in praise of His glorious name as expressed in the reflection and illumination that comes from Him...

(From Besha'ah Shehikdimu 5672 (1912) of the Rebbe Rashab, p. 238)

The Singular One, life of the worlds, is King.

Praiseworthy and glorious until (and including) His great name forever and ever.

Blessed be You, Lord, King Who is lauded with praises.

Three souls

There are three distinct souls that inhabit the body of every Jew (although in the *Tanya*, only two souls are mentioned, in truth they are three) – the G-dly soul, the animal soul, and the intellectual soul, which is an intermediary between the other two. The three souls are enmeshed within each other [in a hierarchical fashion], so the maintenance of the higher one is dependent upon the lower one that en-clothes it.

Now, we know that the vitality of the soul in the body is dependent upon eating, since food expands the blood supply. The animal soul is ensconced within the refined vapors that emerge from the blood, and within it is en-clothed the intellectual (intermediary) soul, within which is found the G-dly soul.

Because of this, the saying of the sages[107] that "in the World-to-Come, there will be no eating and drinking," is puzzling. For, even in the future, there will be physical bodies with all their attendant details, and they will contain blood. This is implied from the fact that sacrifices will not be eliminated in the future, as it is written,[108] "There, we will perform before You our obligatory sacrifices." And while it is true that the sages said, "All of the sacrifices will be eliminated in the future except for the thanksgiving offering," this statement applies only to sacrifices brought by individuals and not to public sacrifices...

Now, we know that the process of offering the sacrifices involves elevating the blood (within which is the enlivening soul) of the animal upon the altar, which represents the *sephira* ("divine emanation") of *malchut* ("kingship") of the World of *Atzilut* ("Emanation"). Something similar to this process certainly occurs within each and every Jewish soul, especially during the "service of the heart," or prayer, which is called the "altar," since it elevates the blood of our body and the animal soul within it. How will it be possible, then, to live and exist without eating, since according to what is explained above, the very existence of the soul in a body is dependent upon food?

The explanation is as follows: the soul enlivens the body via the process of ingestion, as noted previously. However, that is only now, when our vitality and energy comes from immanent G-dliness (*memalle* – G-dliness that fills and permeates the world). But, the power of transcendent G-dliness (*sovev* – G-dliness that surpasses and transcends creation), which is the real essence of the vitality of living creatures, remains concealed (latent). This is because the light of *memalle* hides the power of *sovev*.[109] We are conscious of *memalle* ("immanent G-dliness") alone. This is because the energy of *memalle* descends in an orderly, step-by-step fashion, as the G-dly soul [comes down to] enliven the animal

מִזְמוֹר לְתוֹדָה: הָרִיעוּ לַיָי, כָּל-הָאָרֶץ:
עִבְדוּ אֶת יְיָ בְּשִׂמְחָה; בֹּאוּ לְפָנָיו בִּרְנָנָה:

CHASSIDIC EXCERPTS

soul, using the intellectual soul as an intermediary. When this happens, the vessel [the intellectual and consequently the animal soul] is illuminated. Of course, the vessel must be capable of receiving the illumination as the G-dly illumination descends towards it. For this purpose, the G-dly soul becomes en-clothed in the intellectual soul, since the intellectual soul is spiritual and capable of accommodating the G-dly soul within it. Of course, only a contracted portion of the lowest level of the G-dly soul descends in this manner to illuminate and enliven that which is below it...

But, in the future, the level known as *memalle* will be subsumed in the infinite light of *sovev*. Its inclusion within *sovev* will occur as it becomes nullified [in the higher light of *sovev*], so that it no longer hides and conceals the infinite light of *sovev*.[110] Quite the opposite, [in the future], the light of *memalle* will reveal the infinite illumination of *sovev*, which will then become the conscious and revealed vitality of all creation. And then, the body will live from the very essence of its own vitality – from the power of *sovev* that is found within it even now (except that presently it is concealed). In the future, it will shine in a revealed and conscious fashion, and will enliven the body. It will be as if the G-dly soul, the intellectual soul and the animal soul will all "live" from the infinite light of *sovev*, which is in truth their very essence.

(From *Sefer Maamorim 5659* (1899) of the Rebbe Rashab)

"Song of gratitude" (Psalm 100)
Mizmor Letoda

The Ari points out that the first letters of the opening words of this psalm, *Hariu LeHaShem Kol Ha'aretz* ("Break out in song to G-d all the earth") spell out the word *halacha* ("Jewish law")... This is what the Ari meant: the word *Hariu* alludes to the verse, "strike with an iron staff,"[111] and *kol ha'aretz* to "all of the coarse earthiness." [When we *hariu leHaShem* – "break physical coarseness for the sake of G-d"], this leads to *halacha* ("Torah law"), which is related to *halicha* ("progress"). That is, progress in serving G-d is dependent upon "breaking" through all of our earthiness.

(From the Baal Shem Tov (*Keter Shem Tov, siman 320; page 196-7 in the Kehot edition, pub. 5764*))

One Hundred Blessings
Mizmor Letoda – "Song of gratitude" (Psalm 100)

This psalm corresponds to the 100 blessings that we recite every day. The first letters of the first four words of the psalm spell the word *halacha*, and since there are four words, they correspond to the four cubits of Torah law. [One who learns Torah is said to be within the perimeter (four cubits) of the *halacha*.] They correspond as well to the four letters of G-d's holy name ... And the remaining verses of the psalm correspond to the worlds.

The first part of the second verse, "serve G-d in joy" corresponds to the

The following Psalm not said on Erev Pesach, Chol HaMoed Pesach, or Erev Yom Kippur

A song of gratitude, lift your voices to the Lord, all the land!

Serve the Lord in joy, come before Him in song.

CHASSIDIC EXCERPTS

Cohanim ("priests") in their service, which extends from the *Korbanot* until *Baruch She'Amar*. The second part of the second verse, "approach Him in song" corresponds to the Levis with their singing, which also alludes to the *Pesukei DeZimra*. The third verse, "know that HaShem is *Elokim*" – corresponds to the *Shema*, in which we say "*HaShem* is *Elokeinu, HaShem* is one," and to the rest of the Jews as they stood in place at the sacrifices in the Temple. Then, the verse continues, "He created us," alluding to our 248 limbs, which correspond to the 248 words of the *Shema*...

(From *Yahel Ohr* of the Tzemach Tzedek)

Nullification leads to Song
Mizmor Letoda – "Song of gratitude" (Psalm 100)

And in the Alter Rebbe's *Siddur* ... it states that *hoda'ah* within *hoda'ah* corresponds to the *sephira* of *hod* within *chochma*, and that this is a more essential level of self-nullification [than *hoda'ah* by itself]. And this is what is meant by *Mizmor Letoda: Hariu leHaShem kol ha'aretz* ("Song of Gratitude: Break out in song to G-d all the earth"). By way of *hoda'ah*, or intense self-nullification and association with G-dliness, we come to "break out in song." This opening phrase of Psalm 100 forms the acrostic *halacha*. This is because it is impossible to come to the truth of Torah except when we are totally nullified. And that is why the *halacha* follows the rulings of the House of Hillel, for its members were modest and self-effacing...

(From *Yom Tov shel Rosh Hashana 5666 (1905-6)* of the Rebbe Rashab, p. 440)

Above to below and back...
Mizmor Letoda – "Song of gratitude" (Psalm 100)

We must understand the *korban toda* ("thanksgiving offering") – what is the connection between *hoda'ah* ("gratitude, acknowledgment") and the faculties of *chochma* and *bina*. We know that the statement, *El dayot HaShem* ("G-d of Divine perspectives")[112] implies that there are two perspectives implicit in the holy name of G-d:

The first is that of the *mashpia* ("Benefactor") who influences us from Above. From this perspective, the universe is as if non-existent. G-d Above truly exists, and He is the source of everything. The creation below is nothing (*ayn*) – but truly nothing. This is what is meant by "before Him all is considered as naught."[113]

The second perspective is from the point of view of the beneficiary. It is the opposite of the one just cited. As beneficiaries, we exist in our own right, seemingly separate, because the G-dly influx that flows into us is like *ayn* ("nothingness") since it is concealed from us. And if so, the point of view of the beneficiary is the opposite of that of the Benefactor; to the beneficiary, what is Above seems non-existent (*ayn*), and only physical creation seems to have real existence. From below, it is impossible to grasp divinity and that it is the real existence, since whatever is Above radiates to below in a transcendent

דְּעוּ כִּי יְיָ הוּא אֱלֹהִים, הוּא עָשָׂנוּ, וְלוֹ אֲנַחְנוּ, עַמּוֹ, וְצֹאן מַרְעִיתוֹ:

בֹּאוּ שְׁעָרָיו בְּתוֹדָה, חֲצֵרֹתָיו בִּתְהִלָּה, הוֹדוּ לוֹ בָּרְכוּ שְׁמוֹ.

כִּי טוֹב יְיָ, לְעוֹלָם חַסְדּוֹ, וְעַד דֹּר וָדֹר, אֱמוּנָתוֹ:

fashion [beyond our grasp].

Although it is impossible for us to grasp the true perspective from Above to below and to internalize it thoroughly, nevertheless, through acknowledgment, we are still capable of conceding its existence. This is because acknowledgment goes beyond knowledge and intellectual understanding. Like one who admits that something is not what he thought it was, acknowledgment takes place precisely regarding that which is way above us and beyond our grasp, and all we can do is concede that it is true. Thus, by way of acknowledgment, we can also arrive to the higher perspective mentioned, albeit without thorough intellectual grasp...

And this is what is meant by *Mizmor Letoda*, which corresponds to the unity of *chochma* and *bina* of the World of *Yetzira*. It is known that these two faculties are called by the *Zohar*, "two partners that never separate." *Chochma* is *ayn* ("nothingness") and *bina* is *yesh* ("existence") from the point of view from below to Above [wherein we perceive our own existence as real]. This occurs only when there is a flow of divinity from *chochma* to *bina*. However, from the perspective of Above to below, from within the light of *chochma* itself, when there is not yet a flow of G-dliness from *chochma* into *bina*, this influx is as if naught and insignificant...

(From the *Siddur* of the Alter Rebbe with Chassidut, p. 44a)

Organizing our praises of G-d

Love (*koseph*) is like silver (*keseph*); the Hebrew word for both "silver" and "love" comes from *nichsepha*[114] ("you yearned, desired") – desire to cleave to our source in the infinite, vital illumination of G-d. This desire is called "concealed love" (*ahava mesuteret*), because it is eternally concealed in the heart of every Jew, as explained elsewhere. And fear is like "gold," as in the verse from Job, "From the north comes gold."[115] [According to Kabbalah, the north is associated with the attribute of *gevura* ("strictness, judgment"), the inner dimension of which is fear.] To achieve this fear demands meditation on the greatness of the Infinite One, on how He permeates all the worlds, and how everything in relation to Him is truly insignificant. Those who meditate on this

subject achieve fear and awe of the light of G-d's infinite greatness. And, therefore, the Men of the Great Assembly included "Verses of Song" (*Pesukei DeZimra*) in our prayers. The Torah does not obligate us to say anything more than *Shema* and a few words of supplication, as was done during the time of the First Temple. In those days, people did not pray [at length] because their minds and intellects were as clear as the heavens, and they were capable of seeing the infinite light of G-d at all times [without praying].

But at the beginning of the Second Temple period, the men of the Great Assembly saw that people's intellects were diminished, and their hearts were attracted to the material world. They were drawn to the corporeal nature of the

Know that the Lord is G-d, He made us; we are His, His nation and the sheep whom He shepherds.

Approach His gates in gratitude, His courts in praise, give thanks to Him, bless His name.

For the Lord is good, His kindness is eternal, and our faith in Him extends from generation to generation.

CHASSIDIC EXCERPTS

world alone. Therefore, [the sages] established the prayers [that we say today], all of which repeatedly narrate praises of G-d. The purpose is to lead us to the fear of G-d. This is what is meant by the verse in the Song of Songs, "He is cushioned as a bed."[116] For just as some arrange their beds, positioning and placing each and every cushion in its proper place, so those who arrange their praises of G-d allocate a role to every aspect of creation, seeing it as an expression of G-d created in His honor so that [man might perceive] His greatness.

(From *Likutei Torah, Beha'alotcha* p. 32d)

Meditation vs. "Gazing upon the glory of the King"

Among Jews, and within the spark of every particular Jewish soul, we find ... an "inner mindfulness" (*mochin penimin*) with which we meditate, using G-dly intellect, upon the topics of upper and lower unity (*yichuda ila'ah* and *yichuda tata'ah*). And as we meditate, we internalize these G-dly concepts in our mind, and in this manner we achieve love and fear of G-d...

However, there is another path and that is the path of "gazing," as described by the Zohar, "to gaze upon the glory of the King."[117] This takes place during the *Pesukei DeZimra* that precede the *Shema*. For the sages said, "We should [first] organize our praises of G-d, and afterward pray." From this, we may surmise that prayer depends on the proper organization of our praises of G-d. That is, in order for our prayers to be considered appropriate, they must take place after we have already organized and recited our praises of G-d.

Now, the matter is as follows: Prayer involves fear and love of G-d, which result from intellectual understanding and meditation. This is called *mochin p'ninim*, or "inner mindfulness." It takes place during the *Shema* and the *Shemonah Esreh*, when occurs the kaballistic unity of *av v'aim* (lit. "father and mother." This is kaballistic terminology for the unity of the first two *sephirot*, *chochma* and *bina*), as well as of *Z'a* and *nukva* (kabalistic terminology for the unity of the lower six emotional attributes and *malchut*) as is known. However, the "organization of praises" of G-d [that takes place] during the *Pesukei DeZimra* involves neither the excitement of love and fear [associated with the unity of *Z'a* and *nukva*] of G-d, nor intellectual arousal[118] [associated with the unity of *av v'aim*]. Rather, [it involves] our speech, as when we praise the king. In the course of our praises, we do not attempt to grasp and understand the nature and the details of the king's reign. Instead, we go out of our way to praise him, mentioning that he is a great king, very majestic, and that everyone is nullified to him, including great ministers and men of honor, and even other kings, and that they are insignificant in comparison to him.

There is no element of intellect within this type of understanding, as there would be, for example, for one who delves deeply into the details of how to conduct the state. For, in the study of "statecraft," there is much wis-

יְהִי כְבוֹד יְיָ לְעוֹלָם, יִשְׂמַח יְיָ בְּמַעֲשָׂיו:
יְהִי שֵׁם יְיָ מְבֹרָךְ, מֵעַתָּה וְעַד עוֹלָם:

CHASSIDIC EXCERPTS

dom, regarding how the state is run. [Administering the state] follows specific principles which, upon close examination, turn out to be the proper way to run a state. And those principles lead to specific results and implications. [Mastery of those principles] demands internal intellectual grasp, and one must be impressed with the depth of the king's intellect and his talent. On the other hand, going out of our way to praise the king demands no special intellectual powers, aside from awareness of the greatness and majesty of the king, whom we then praise.

However, our praises penetrate to and engage the very essence of the king. His greatness and majesty are the source of all revelation that emerges from him. They are what guide him in administering the state in a proper and elevated manner. And all of this emerges because the king [himself] is elevated and exalted. And, with our praises, we engage the very essence of the greatness of the king, which is the source of all of his achievements. The arousal in our soul is clearly evident since, as a result of these praises, we become quite excited to the very depth of our soul, beyond the intellectual excitement that we experience from understanding the principles of [administering] the kingdom. This is because such matters are merely intellectual, while narration of the king's praises elicits essential excitement that is unlimited. This bears similarity to the [process of] "gazing" mentioned previously, during which we are not aware of any revelation of inner light radiating from the king, but, nevertheless, we behold the essence of his glory, along with his beauty and majesty, and we are to-

tally absorbed in the vision ... And this is what occurs as we narrate the [king's] praises with which we comprehend his very essence, greatness and majesty. And in this manner, we become aroused to the very core of our soul.

And so occurs during the *Pesukei DeZimra* as we narrate the praises of G-d, reciting out loud [verses that relate] the greatness and the majesty of the Infinite One: "Great is our Lord, with mighty power..." and "He covers the heavens with clouds..." [We narrate] how G-d creates from nothing to something ... Regarding this, it is not possible for us to understand creation from nothing to something, but we [simply know] that it is within His power and ability to create from nothing to something. And this is what is meant by *Baruch She'Amar vehaya haolam* ("Blessed is He Who spoke and the world came into existence") implying that everything was created with one statement. And, similarly, we speak of the nullification of all the worlds and creations, as we recite the verses from the Psalms – for example, *Hallelu et Hashem min hashamayim* ("Praised G-d from the heavens") – which express the nullification of the four worlds ABY"A. And, as well, we speak of "the waters that are above the heavens" referring to spiritual levels that surpass *Atzilut*, all of which are nullified to G-d. For all [the heavenly] luminaries are dim before G-d, and "before Him, all is as naught." And although we may lack detailed illumination and full grasp of this topic, nevertheless, the theme holds significance for us. It is important to us, for [with this meditation], we grasp the very essence of the greatness and majesty [of G-d, the

Let the honor of the Lord be forever, let the Lord rejoice in His works.

Let the name of the Lord be blessed, from now and forever.

CHASSIDIC EXCERPTS

King] that transcends all revelation [of intellect and feeling] that stem from Him.

And, precisely from this awareness, we derive essential enjoyment over the essence of His greatness and majesty, far beyond the pleasure derived from intellectual grasp, which is confined to the limits of our intellect. Our narration of His praises produces essential enjoyment, with which we derive pleasure from the very essence of His greatness. And this arouses something similar Above as well, bringing down [divine] influx of His essential infinite light, as is known regarding praises that arouse the essence.

For example, when we praise a wise sage regarding the greatness of his wisdom, even when there is no wisdom in his mind, it reveals itself from within, emerging from his faculty of *chochma* as its hidden source. The same occurs, regarding a kind man; when we praise him, describing his kindness, our praise elicits his quality of *chesed* from its essential source and arouses him to bestow much goodness and kindness, over and beyond his normal conduct. This analogy applies Above as well - by narrating G-d's praises, we elicit G-dliness from the ten hidden *sephirot* that are concealed in His essence, as written elsewhere...

*

This, then is what is achieved by first organizing our praises of G-d, and then praying. The only way to properly approach G-d is in prayer. [Our ability to] focus upon divine unity – including intellectual understanding and meditation leading to love and fear of G-d during prayer – depends upon our organization of praises during the *Pesukei DeZimra*. It is the *Pesukei DeZimra* that enable us to gaze upon the essence of the glorious beauty of His greatness. And from Above as well, there emerges a response from the essence of G-dly enjoyment that descends to us.

And, therefore, a far higher light and revelation emerges – whether from below, through intellectual understanding and meditation and desire of the soul ... or from Above through illumination.

And this is what is meant [in the reference in the Song of Songs where] the Jewish people are called, "My dove," as in, "Your eyes are [like] doves."[119] For just as doves gaze upon each other and derive great enjoyment as they prepare to unite, so Jewish souls find immense enjoyment when gazing upon the glory of the King. And this awakens their very essence and constitutes preparation for the supernal unifications that then take place during the recitation of the *Shema* and the *Shemonah Esreh*...

(From *Sefer Maamorim 5662* (1902), of the Rebbe Rashab, pp. 247-8)

The Honor of the King
Yehi kevod – ("Let the honor of the Lord...") - Psalm 113

From the writings of the Ari we see that the previous psalm – *Mizmor Letoda* – is associated with *chochma* and *bina* of *Yetzira*, while this prayer – *Yehi Kevod* – is associated with *Zeir Anpin*, the emo-

tional attributes of *Yetzira*, and the next psalm – *Tehila L'David* – is associated with *malchut* of *Yetzira*.

The sages[120] attribute *Yehi Kevod* to *saro shel olam* (the "grand minister of the

מִמִּזְרַח שֶׁמֶשׁ עַד מְבוֹאוֹ מְהֻלָּל שֵׁם יְיָ:

רָם עַל כָּל גּוֹיִם, יְיָ, עַל הַשָּׁמַיִם כְּבוֹדוֹ:

יְיָ שִׁמְךָ לְעוֹלָם, יְיָ זִכְרְךָ לְדֹר וָדֹר:

יְיָ בַּשָּׁמַיִם הֵכִין כִּסְאוֹ, וּמַלְכוּתוֹ בַּכֹּל מָשָׁלָה:

יִשְׂמְחוּ הַשָּׁמַיִם וְתָגֵל הָאָרֶץ, וְיֹאמְרוּ בַגּוֹיִם יְיָ מָלָךְ:

יְיָ מֶלֶךְ יְיָ מָלָךְ, יְיָ יִמְלֹךְ לְעֹלָם וָעֶד:

יְיָ מֶלֶךְ עוֹלָם וָעֶד, אָבְדוּ גוֹיִם מֵאַרְצוֹ:

יְיָ הֵפִיר עֲצַת גּוֹיִם, הֵנִיא מַחְשְׁבוֹת עַמִּים:

רַבּוֹת מַחֲשָׁבוֹת בְּלֶב אִישׁ, וַעֲצַת יְיָ הִיא תָקוּם:

universe") who is the angel *Metat*, associated with *Zeir Anpin* of *Yetzira* ... and the explanation is as follows:

When the emotional attributes of *Atzilut* are expressed in thought (as distinct from the essential emotions of the heart), they are called *Zeir Anpin* of *Bria*. And when they further descend to verbal expression in speech, they are called *Zeir Anpin* of *Yetzira*. We therefore find both of these levels in the angel *Metat*, who is associated with the external man-ifestation of the vessels of *Zeir Anpin* of *Bria* and *Yetzira* ... and this is why G-d says in the Torah, "Behold I am sending My angel [referring to *Metat* of *Bria*]"[121] ... because the name of G-d [as in *Atzilut*] is within him [in a minor form as thought]. And since there is a preponderance of stringencies (*dinim*) within thought ... which is why the scripture forewarns us, "do not rebel against him,"[122] since his name is like his Master's name.[123]

(From *Pirush Hamilot* of the Mittler Rebbe, Ch. 152 (page 100d))

"Engraving" from without and from within

One of the explanations of the word *behukotai* ("in My decrees") is that it is from the root word *chakika*, meaning "engraving." Since *behukotai* is plural, it implies two different engravings, one an etching from inside and the other from outside. That is, when we carve out something from the inside, it becomes a receptacle. Nevertheless, we must also burnish it from the outside, for if not, it is of no use at all.

Similarly, we may extrapolate to the spiritual realm and infer that there must be two engravings, one from the inside and the other from outside. The engraving from outside corresponds to the *nesira* ("sawing," or "splitting off"). When man was created, the Torah records that "He created them male and female." The sages interpreted this to

From sunrise in the east until sunset, the name of the Lord is praised.

The Lord is exalted over the nations, His honor transcends the heavens.

Lord, Your name is forever, Lord, Your memory for all generations.

The Lord established His throne in the heavens, and His reign in every domain.

The heavens will rejoice and the earth be delighted, and the nations will proclaim, 'The Lord is King.'

The Lord reigns, the Lord reigned, and the Lord will reign forever and ever.

The Lord is King forever, the nations have vanished from His land.

The Lord foils the wiles of nations, annuls the schemes of peoples.

Many are the thoughts in the heart of man, and the plan of G-d is what takes effect.

CHASSIDIC EXCERPTS

mean that man and woman were [originally] created as one being, with two bodily structures, joined to one another back to back. Kaballah explains that otherwise, there would have been room for the negative forces of the universe to attach from behind and siphon away holy energy. The effect of the unity of the two structures [male and female] was to prevent this attachment of negativity from the backside. Now, the "sawing off" or "separation" was a rectification of the hind parts of the body, so that even after the two structures were separated from one another, the negative forces would not be able to attach themselves and siphon away holy energy.

And this is what takes place during the *Pesukei DeZimra* following *Baruch She'Amar*. The very phrase *Pesukei DeZimra* ("Verses of Song") recalls the words *lezamer aritzim* ("to prune the thorns").[124] As the Jews pray, with "lofty praises of G-d in their throats,"[125] they fulfill the second part of the verse - "and a double-edged sword is in their hands." The effect of the sword is to remove and separate the G-dly and animal souls from the negative, extraneous powers and the evil shells (*klipot*) – this is what constitutes the "engraving from outside."

Now, the engraving that takes place from within enables us to attain spiritual progress from below to Above. As it is written, "Let them make for me a sanctuary and I will dwell within them."[126] The verse does not say "within it," but "within them" – that is, within each and every Jew. And if so, an "engraving" must occur within, [transforming us into] vessels that are capable of receiving and accepting the indwelling of the infinite light of G-d. This is the engraving from inside, and by way of it, our soul achieves progress...

(From *Sefer Ma'amorim 5657* (1897) of the Rebbe Rashab, page 122)

עֲצַת יְיָ לְעוֹלָם תַּעֲמוֹד, מַחְשְׁבוֹת לִבּוֹ לְדֹר וָדֹר:

כִּי הוּא אָמַר וַיֶּהִי, הוּא צִוָּה וַיַּעֲמֹד:

כִּי בָחַר יְיָ בְּצִיּוֹן, אִוָּהּ לְמוֹשָׁב לוֹ:

כִּי יַעֲקֹב בָּחַר לוֹ יָהּ, יִשְׂרָאֵל לִסְגֻלָּתוֹ:

כִּי, לֹא יִטֹּשׁ יְיָ עַמּוֹ, וְנַחֲלָתוֹ לֹא יַעֲזֹב:

וְהוּא רַחוּם יְכַפֵּר עָוֹן וְלֹא יַשְׁחִית,

וְהִרְבָּה לְהָשִׁיב אַפּוֹ, וְלֹא יָעִיר כָּל חֲמָתוֹ:

יְיָ הוֹשִׁיעָה, הַמֶּלֶךְ יַעֲנֵנוּ בְיוֹם קָרְאֵנוּ:

❧

CHASSIDIC EXCERPTS

Prayer and the animal soul

The verses of *Pesukei DeZimra* are aimed at the animal soul itself. Their purpose is to cut away the "thorns and the thistles." By way of example, pruning the dry branches of a tree allows the living branches to grow better, and clearing away the thistles from a vine allows it to thrive. Similarly man, who is called a "tree of the field,"[127] finds it necessary to remove the thorns and thistles that prevent and thwart his [spiritual progress]. This allows the "tree" to grow and ascend from height to height. It is called the "engraving from outside," upon the animal soul. Since its nature is material, the animal soul naturally finds its place in the physical strata of the world, just as the G-dly soul, which is in essence holy, is naturally drawn to G-dliness, this being its level. If it weren't en-clothed in the animal soul, [the G-dly soul] of its own nature would be drawn only to G-dly matters, since that is its "place." The animal soul, coming from the *klipa* with its coarse substance, finds its place among the material aspects of the world, and since this is its "locale," so to speak, it is trapped in it – very trapped – and it is impossible for it to ascend. It is necessary to extricate it from its own environment, as one might uproot a plant from one place and transplant it to another place to cultivate it there.

So it is with the animal soul. In its own "location" it is ensnared in physical matters, and the "engraving from outside" is intended to extricate it from its general malaise. This can take place by way of meditation on the "verses of song" (*peshukei dezimra*), on topics that essentially transcend intellect and have

The plan of G-d endures forever, and the thoughts of His heart from one generation to the next.

For, He said and it happened, He commanded and it took place.

For, the Lord chose Zion, desiring it as His place of dwelling.

For, G-d chose Jacob, [and] Israel as his treasure.

For, the Lord will not abandon His people, nor will He forsake His heritage.

And He, being merciful, atones for our sins and refrains from destroying us,

He repeatedly quashes His anger, and avoids arousing all of His wrath.

The Lord saves, the King answers us on the day that we call [Him].

CHASSIDIC EXCERPTS

no basis in logic. Such a topic may be, for example, creation from nothing to something and related concepts that have no intellectual explanation. For, it is impossible to explain how and why a corporeal object may emerge from absolute nothingness. The meditation is simply on the fact that this is the case – the world was created from nothing to something. Our intellect leads us to the inescapable conclusion that this is so, since to create one object from another object is impossible, without a void between them. Also, it is impossible for one object to be created from another, *ad infinitum*, since each object is limited [in time and space]...

And this is what is meant by *Baruch She'Amar vehaya haolam* ("Blessed is He Who spoke and the universe came into existence"). The world is a created entity (*yesh*), emerging from G-d's supernal speech...

In each of the psalms [of *Pesukei DeZimra*] is expounded the subject of creation from nothing to something, as well as meditation upon the nature of creation from nothing to something and all the amazing concepts associated therewith. All of this elicits great excitement in the soul, which provides an added benefit for the animal soul, as it ascends to stand on a higher and more elevated level. Its status is transformed, and it forsakes its natural standpoint. Although inwardly it remains un-refined, and still desirous of physical matters, nevertheless this is the process by which it abandons its essential nature.

(From *BeSha'ah she'hikdimu*, 5672 of the Rebbe Rashab, vol. 2, ch. 392)

אַ‎שְׁרֵי יוֹשְׁבֵי בֵיתֶךָ, עוֹד יְהַלְלוּךָ פֶּלָה:

אַשְׁרֵי הָעָם שֶׁכָּכָה לּוֹ, אַשְׁרֵי הָעָם שֶׁיְיָ אֱלֹהָיו:

תְּהִלָּה לְדָוִד,

אֲרוֹמִמְךָ אֱלֹהַי הַמֶּלֶךְ, וַאֲבָרְכָה שִׁמְךָ לְעוֹלָם וָעֶד:

CHASSIDIC EXCERPTS

Happiness in the house of the Lord
Ashrei yoshvei beitecha ("Happy are those in who dwell in Your house..."),
Ashrei ha'am ("Happy are the people...")[128]

The Men of the Great Assembly established these two verses as preparation and introduction to *Pesukei DeZimra*. They even prefaced these verses to the psalm *Tehila L'David*,[129] which is the foundation of all praises, since it is organized according to the Hebrew alphabet. All of the subsequent praises (which begin with *Halleluyah*) are included within the recital of *Tehila L'David*, which is the *keter* ("crown") that includes the entire alphabet. The overall intention of the *Pesukei DeZimra* is to express praise of G-d via the word *halleluyah*. This praise brings additional light and illumination into the essential name of G-d, the four-letter name, for the word *hallel* comes from the verse, *Bahilu naro alai roshi* ("His candle shone on my head")[130]... It expresses the high praise and exaltation of the *Pesukei DeZimra*. It draws added illumination into the entire four-letter name of G-d, but mainly within the first two letters (*yud-hay*). That is why the psalm concludes with the word *halleluyah* – meaning "praise (*hallelu*) G-d (*Yah*)" – which is the basis and foundation of all praise, as explained elsewhere.

Therefore, these two verses beginning with the word *ashrei* ("happy") were placed before *Tehila L'David* as the source of illumination of *keter*, from which this light is drawn into the essential four-letter name of G-d. This name is associated with the *sephira* of *chochma*, which itself emerges from *ayin* ("nothingness"). This is the explanation of *ashrei*, indicating intense pleasure associated with the will of G-d that illuminates the *kotz* ("point") of the *yud* (first letter of G-d's name). It is the source of the added light that descends when we say *halleluyah*. That is why we say *ashrei yoshvei beitecha od yehallelucha selah*, without any interruption whatsoever...

(From *Pirush Hamilot* of the Mittler Rebbe, ch. 159)

Ashrei three times a day...
Tehila L'David, aromimcha..."I will exalt You..." (Psalm 145)

The Talmud[131] quotes Rabbi Elazar ben Avina: "Everyone who says *Tehila L'David* three times every day is guaranteed to reach the World to Come." Why? Perhaps because the psalm contains the Hebrew alphabet. But if so, why not say Psalm 119 that contains the alphabet eight times over? Perhaps it was because *Tehila L'David* contains the verse "Open Your hand and satisfy the will of every living creature." But if so, why not say the *Hallel* that contains the verse "grant bread to all flesh"? The answer is that both reasons apply ... Armed with these

*H*appy are those who dwell in Your house, they will yet praise You forever.

Happy is the nation for whom this is their lot, happy is the nation whose G-d is the Lord.
A psalm of praise from David;

I will exalt You, my G-d the King, and I will bless Your name forever.

CHASSIDIC EXCERPTS

two – the alphabet, meaning the holiness of the letters of the Torah (which when uttered bring holiness into the world), and awareness of Divine Providence as He prepares and provides sustenance to every living creature – we are guaranteed to reach the World to Come.

This is what is meant by [the advice to recite] *Tehila L'David* three times every day. The three times are the nighttime, morning and afternoon. This means that those who are involved in service of G-d – reading the *Shema* properly before going to sleep, preparing for prayer in the morning, and [finally] praying with real service of the heart – see their daily service accepted.

(From *Sefer Ma'amorim*, 1948, of the Rebbe Rayatz)

Power and strength above
Tehila L'David, Aromimcha - "I will exalt You..." (Psalm 145)

There are two explanations of this verse: 1) that *aromimcha* ("I will exalt You") is about our desire to ascend from below to Above, and 2) that *aromimcha* is about drawing *romemut* ("exalted spirituality") down from Above to below.

Here are the details: The word *Elokai* ("my G-d") is related to the phrase *eili ha'aretz* ("the mighty of the land"),[132] indicating power and strength. This is what King David said [in *Tehila L'David*] on behalf of the entire universe. The power and energy of the universe are drawn from G-d's infinite light, which permeates all spiritual and physical realms, and as such, they express the reign of the King. He rules the entire universe, and as a result of His reign, all beings exist. They are created from nothing to something, from His *malchut* ("reign"). Now, it is known that the reign and the rule of the King are no more than a ray and reflection [of His essence], directed [outward] toward others, unrelated to the King Himself. In this, [His reign] is different than any of His other qualities and attributes, such as His wisdom...

That is why the psalm later says, "His Kingship is the reign of all worlds."[133] The creation of all worlds, spiritual and physical, and the power and energy invested in them, comes from the attribute of *malchut*. This is the essence of G-dly rule, emanating not from the essence of the King Himself, but from His attribute of *malchut*.

Now, for His infinite light to descend and express itself as kingship, many contractions had to take place. As it is written, "In order to inform people of His mighty power (*gevurato*) and the glorious majesty of His reign."[134] *Gevurato* alludes to all the contractions, arriving ultimately to "the glorious majesty of His reign." But, all this is nothing more than a ray, illuminating His glory and majesty. Like we say [as part of the

בְּכָל יוֹם אֲבָרְכֶךָ, וַאֲהַלְלָה שִׁמְךָ לְעוֹלָם וָעֶד:

גָּדוֹל יְיָ וּמְהֻלָּל מְאֹד, וְלִגְדֻלָּתוֹ אֵין חֵקֶר:

דּוֹר לְדוֹר יְשַׁבַּח מַעֲשֶׂיךָ. וּגְבוּרֹתֶיךָ יַגִּידוּ:

הֲדַר כְּבוֹד הוֹדֶךָ, וְדִבְרֵי נִפְלְאֹתֶיךָ אָשִׂיחָה:

וֶעֱזוּז נוֹרְאֹתֶיךָ יֹאמֵרוּ, וּגְדֻלָּתְךָ אֲסַפְּרֶנָּה:

זֵכֶר רַב טוּבְךָ יַבִּיעוּ, וְצִדְקָתְךָ יְרַנֵּנוּ:

CHASSIDIC EXCERPTS

Shema], Baruch shem kevod malchuto leolam vaed – "Blessed be His Name forever" – emphasizing His Name [and not Himself].

And therefore, aromimcha ("I will exalt You") because in so doing I will come to fulfill the commandment veahavta ("you shall love the Lord your G-d"). This refers to the Infinite One [whom we are commanded] to love with all of our "heart(s)" – meaning with both of our inclinations [the yetzer tov or "good inclination" and the yetzer harah, or "evil inclination"]. In so doing we subdue the evil inclination, so that it no longer desires nor wants anything other than G-d ... This is the explanation of aromimcha from below to Above ... and of aromimcha as descent of His exalted presence from Above to below.

(From Torah Ohr of the Alter Rebbe, Parshat Mikeitz (p. 40, col. 3))

With an open hand...
Poteach et yadecha ("Open Your hand...") Psalm 145

Love resulting from meditation and deep contemplation on the creation – ahavat olam – is subject to interruption. For if our heart turns to other topics and we become concerned about worldly matters, then [the love] dissipates and dissolves. This is not true of ahava raba, the great love embedded in the very root of our soul, emerging from the same origin as the soul itself. It knows no interruption. Even if we are drawn to worldly matters, they do not stand in opposition to or contradict our love. Neither do they disturb or interrupt it. Indeed, this love leaves a permanent impression wedged in our heart, as a memory that is immovable and immutable. But, how can we make this great love conscious? How can we ascend to the level [on which we love G-d] with all of our might – a level called bechol me'odecha?

About this, the sages said, "When the wine goes in, the secrets come out."[135] By "secrets" are meant the secrets of the Torah, which are also termed "wine."... When the wine of the Torah goes in, the secrets – that is, the light of hidden love inside – emerges from concealment to consciousness. We become permeated with revelation of this great love, which is embedded in the very source of our soul and which comes from the same place as the soul itself. This condition is called bechol me'odecha and about it we say poteach et yadecha or poteach et yudecha – instead of "Open Your hand" we say "Open your yuds," for the letter yud represents concealment and contraction of light. There are many

Every day, I will bless you, and I will praise Your name forever.

Great is the Lord, and very praiseworthy, there is no limit to His greatness.

One generation to the next praises Your works, and tells of Your might.

Your majesty is glorious, and words of Your wonders I will speak.

They will talk of the boldness of Your awesome acts and of Your greatness I will tell.

Remembrance of Your great goodness will be expressed, and Your righteousness will be sung.

CHASSIDIC EXCERPTS

levels of contraction and tremendous concealment involved in bringing down the infinite light of G-d in order to create the universe as we know it, step by step. His will was the source of all creation, from nothing to something, and via the Torah, which is His will and wisdom, the *yudin* ("contractions") are "opened up" to provide revelation of His supernal will.

*

"And You satisfy the desire of every living creature" with spiritual energy and illumination that expands throughout the worlds, from the highest down to the lowest levels. The purpose is to inspire and reveal the supernal will of G-d within these levels. It is also drawn into the soul of man, to inspire within us a desire for revelation of G-d's will. This revelation is the *ahava raba* ("great love") embedded in the origin of the soul

Above, which enables the soul to tolerate [this great level of illumination, which is otherwise beyond revelation in the soul]. The supernal will Above descends enclothed in the "garments" of the soul – speech and action – the speech of Torah and the action of fulfilling the mitzvot. That is why when the soul departs from the body and returns to G-d, it is asked, "Did you fix times for learning Torah?" In this manner we arouse the sublime love from the source of the soul that is not enclothed within any vessel to hide and conceal it. There is nothing comparable, and nothing to obstruct it. It knows no interruption. Even while we are involved in other matters, this love is wedged in our heart. And this, in turn brings us to [the commandment of the *Shema*]: "you shall speak of them ... [that is, words of Torah]." [136]

(From *Torah Ohr* of the Alter Rebbe, p. 47, col. 2)

From yud to yad ("hand")
Poteach et yadecha ("Open Your hand...") Psalm 145

This verse refers to two "hands" – the right hand which represents kindness (*chesed*) and the left hand which represents strictness (*gevura*). These "hands" also correspond to *ahavat olam* [love resulting from meditation on G-d within nature] and *ahava raba* [love

based upon contemplation of G-d's transcendence of nature]. The latter develops as the Jews ascend spiritually, and G-d's "hands" open up, meaning that they illuminate the Jewish soul, which is called *kol chai* ("every living creature"). The illumination emerges from the di-

חַנּוּן וְרַחוּם יְיָ, אֶרֶךְ אַפַּיִם וּגְדָל חָסֶד:

טוֹב יְיָ לַכֹּל, וְרַחֲמָיו עַל כָּל מַעֲשָׂיו:

יוֹדוּךָ יְיָ כָּל מַעֲשֶׂיךָ, וַחֲסִידֶיךָ יְבָרְכוּכָה:

כְּבוֹד מַלְכוּתְךָ יֹאמֵרוּ, וּגְבוּרָתְךָ יְדַבֵּרוּ:

לְהוֹדִיעַ לִבְנֵי הָאָדָם גְּבוּרֹתָיו, וּכְבוֹד הֲדַר מַלְכוּתוֹ:

מַלְכוּתְךָ, מַלְכוּת כָּל עוֹלָמִים, וּמֶמְשַׁלְתְּךָ בְּכָל דּוֹר וָדֹר:

סוֹמֵךְ יְיָ לְכָל הַנֹּפְלִים, וְזוֹקֵף לְכָל הַכְּפוּפִים:

עֵינֵי כֹל אֵלֶיךָ יְשַׂבֵּרוּ, וְאַתָּה נוֹתֵן לָהֶם אֶת אָכְלָם בְּעִתּוֹ:

פּוֹתֵחַ אֶת יָדֶךָ, וּמַשְׂבִּיעַ לְכָל חַי רָצוֹן:

CHASSIDIC EXCERPTS

vine Will associated with the *ahava raba*. It emerges from concealment to revelation, as we devote ourselves totally to the One Above.

As for the remainder of the verse – "And You satisfy the will of every living creature" – it means that our soul will feel sated and satisfied as a result of *ahava raba*. Our mind and heart will encompass this love with satisfaction, as it is written [in the Shabbat prayers] "And they will be satisfied and joyous." This takes place on Shabbat on account of the ray of G-dly light and absolute enjoyment emanating from the essence of G-dly delight as it illuminates Above...

As for what is written, *yadecha* ("Your hands"), this refers to the Hebrew letters *yud* and *vav*, as is known. The letter *yud* [the smallest letter of the Hebrew alphabet, little more than a point] represents contraction and concealment, similar to the shape of the letter itself. This [contraction] facilitates a descent of spiritual influx to the worlds,

to souls and to angels. The "opening" or expansion of the *yud* to become a *vav* [which has the shape of a vertical line] represents the descent of influx, and its revelation from a state of concealment, emerging from the measured contraction of the letter *yud*. This takes place when there is an arousal from below, from our *ahava raba* and *ahavat olam*, which transform all foreign desires within us into one united will for G-d. This corresponds to the verse, "Whom do I have in heaven [but You]..."[137] In response to the arousal from below, there occurs a revelation from Above as well, causing illumination to emerge from the concealment and contraction of the *yud*. This, then is the "opening of the right hand" alluded to previously, which corresponds to *ahava raba*. From the letter *yud* emerges a *vav*, corresponding to a revelation of G-dly concealment in the lower worlds, in order to "satisfy the desire of every living thing..."

(From the Mittler Rebbe, in *Torah Chaim, Parshat Vayechi* p. 100c (241a in the new version))

The Lord is harmonious and compassionate, He is patient, and of great kindness.

The Lord is good to all, and compassionate over all of His works.

Lord, all of Your works are grateful to You, and they bless You for Your kindness.

They narrate the honor of Your reign, and speak of Your might.

In order to inform men of His might, and the honor of His glorious reign.

Your reign is the Kingship of all worlds, and Your dominion over all generations.

The Lord raises all who have fallen, and straightens all who are stooped.

The eyes of all gaze at You longingly, and You grant them their sustenance at the right time.

You open Your hands, and satisfy the desire of all living creatures.

CHASSIDIC EXCERPTS

Essential illumination
Poteach et yadecha ("Open Your hand...") Psalm 145

This verse is preceded by another verse; "The eyes of everyone look to you expectedly..." The expectation and yearning that is part of the human condition, and for which every man hopes and desires, is G-dly illumination of the heart. Every man wishes to accept the yoke of heaven with love and desire.

The verse states, poteach et yadecha but [we may] read it as poteach et yudecha [meaning two yuds instead of two "hands"]. The letter yud indicates contraction. The G-dly illumination embedded in the creative process is limited, since it is impossible for the creation to absorb the infinite light of revelation of G-d. Therefore, it undergoes contraction, in which the essential G-dly illumination is dimmed and concealed and only a limited ray shines. The verse,

"Open Your hand," refers to illumination of this truly essential light of G-d.

It may also be said that poteach et yadecha refers to the letter yud itself. It is written elsewhere that the contraction of the yud corresponds to the sages' statement, "One should always teach one's students in a concise fashion."[138] But, within this concise synopsis must be found all of the lengthy details and inner depth [of the subject]. Everything should be included in the synopsis, but in a concealed fashion. That is why it is said,[139] "After forty years, one is able to master the essence of his teacher's instructions." That is, after forty years, one is able to plumb the full depths of his teachings, since within the teacher's concise synopsis is to be found everything.

(From Sefer Ma'amorim 5665 (1905), of the Rebbe Rashab, p. 84)

The Hand of generosity
Poteach et yadecha ("Open Your hand...") Psalm 145

Rosh Hashana is the "day of judgment" on which we are judged regarding all the deeds that we did during the past year. For [although we want] addi-

CHASSIDIC INSIGHTS

Something to take note of during the *pesukei dezimra* is the number of times that we say the word "*Halleluyah*." The Alter Rebbe tells us that *Halleluyah* comes from the phrase *behilu narot*, meaning "shining lights."[91] *Halleluyah* is all about making something shine. As we praise God, we bring down a very high light from Above, causing it to shine within the creation. Specifically, the word divides into *Yehallel* and *Yud-Hey*, which together mean "let the two letters *yud-hey* shine."[92] The *yud* and the *hey*

צַדִּיק יְיָ בְּכָל דְּרָכָיו, וְחָסִיד בְּכָל מַעֲשָׂיו:

קָרוֹב יְיָ לְכָל קֹרְאָיו, לְכֹל אֲשֶׁר יִקְרָאֻהוּ בֶאֱמֶת:

are the first two letters of the Name *Havaya*, and they transcend creation. They are not directly involved in the creation process as are the second two letters, the *vov-hey* of His Name. Since they represent a transcendent level of holiness, we seek to draw down their level of spirituality as we pray, in order to further illuminate and reveal Godliness in the creation. That is the

deeper meaning of *Halleluyah* – "let the two first letters of His Name *Havaya* shine into the creation."

As we slow down and meditate during this section of prayers, our focus is on the process of creation, and specifically upon the Godly light that permeates and enlivens the creation.[93] This light is called *memalle kol olamim*, or "immanent, fulfilling light." It is the spirituality that is enclothed in creation in order to enliven it on myriad levels of mineral, vegetable, animal and human.

We can summarize the wondrous process of creation as follows. On the one hand, in order to create, it is necessary for Godly light to penetrate and permeate the creation. But on the other hand, any creative force from God comes from a very high source connected with His essence. In fact, it is so high that it is completely removed from creation, even while it "lowers itself" to relate to creation. So, we are forced to conclude that at one and the same time, a ray of His essential light descends to

CHASSIDIC EXCERPTS

tional vitality to descend from the general vitality measured out for this year, we face many accusers, who weigh in regarding whether we are deserving of that life energy to descend by way of the supernal Will, as revelation of His reign. This may be because of any *prikat ol* ("throwing off of the yoke of heaven") that may have occurred ... but about this it is said, "G-d supports all the fallen ... [for] the eyes of all gaze expectantly upon You..." [140] The expectations to which we are all drawn with desire and will is that G-d should illuminate our hearts in order to help us accept the yoke of heaven in love and desire. And that brings us to request, "Open Your hand and satisfy the will of every living creature," referring to the supernal will for revelation of His kingship ... And after this, we acknowledge that "G-d is just in all of His ways and kind in all His deeds,"[141] meaning that even in all His deeds, referring to physical action, He descends and expresses the kindness from above...

(From *Likutei Torah* of the Alter Rebbe, *Drushim l'Rosh Hashana*, first drasha, sec. 1:)

Supernal examples

All creatures of the lower (physical) world possess a source and origin above, as written in the Zohar, "[God] made the lower world similar to the upper world."[142] Every creature down here in the lower world is a *mashal* ("example") of its corresponding level in the spiritual world. And just as an example bears a similarity to the concept that it represents (*nimshal*) – since as we know, the example and what it portrays are in truth one and the same, even though the example itself is foreign to the concept - so a physical creature is like a mere "example" in regard to its spiritual source. Similarly, the same level in the spiritual realm is an "example" regarding its own source in the next higher spiritual world, and so forth, from world to world.

CHASSIDIC INSIGHTS

enliven and create, while simultaneously it is connected with its source, supremely above and beyond the universe. It is the creative tension formed by these two impossible opposites that lends our meditation its intellectual excitement and power. During the *pesukei dezimra*, our focus during meditation is upon the ray of light enclothed in the creation. Nevertheless, in the background of our mind, we are aware of the transcendent source of this creative ray. The juxtaposition of these polar opposites is what leads to excitement and arousal of love of God during prayer.[94]

> The Lord is righteous in all of His paths, and kind in all His deeds.
>
> The Lord is near to all who call Him, to all who call upon Him in truth.

Looking at the words of the *pesukei dezimra*, we see that they mostly describe physical objects (stars, clouds, the heavens and the earth, mountains and pasture, etc) and the Godly connection with human beings ("He Who renders justice...gives bread...frees the imprisoned...etc"). These are the factors that figure into our physical world below, into which Godly light from Above makes an incursion.[95] The goal during *pesukei dezimra* is to focus on the Godliness filling and permeating the world. The verses of *peshukei dezimra* help us to do this by directing our attention to objects of this world that inspire love and fear of Him (when we meditate upon the Godliness embedded in them). The same is true of the mention of Godly connection with humans – by describing the aid that He extends to us, the *pesukei dezimra* inspire us to feel His Presence, not only in the world at large, but within us as well. As a result, we experience emotional arousal in our soul, based upon the tension and excitement generated by our meditation. This is the emotional arousal of *ruach*, one level of the soul above the gratefulness and acknowledgment of *nefesh*.

Chasidic literature describes the objects of our meditation on this level (natural objects, as well as

CHASSIDIC EXCERPTS

For example, night and day in the lower physical world are equivalent to light and darkness, as written, "And *Elokim* called the light "day" and the darkness He called 'night."[143] And day and night also exist in the spiritual world, as light and darkness. For, light and darkness in the physical world are only a parable to describe the light and darkness in the world above. Similarly, there exist light and darkness within the soul. The conscious faculties of the soul are compared to light and illumination. The revelation of emotions is like light and illumination, and all the more-so the light of the intellect, as *chochma* is called "light," as written, "The fool walks in darkness."[144] For, the illumination of intellect provides total revelation within the soul. It provides spiritual illumination in comparison to the physical light that we are capable of seeing. The proof is that with our power of vision, we grasp physical objects, while the light of intellectual illumination fails to grasp anything visually since it is a spiritual light. There is also such a thing as

"seeing with the mind's eye," which is an especially high form of vision.

And there is also darkness within the soul. This concealment is also spiritual darkness, transcending physical darkness. There is also darkness of the intellect, defined as lack of intellectual grasp. It divides into two categories – it may either be the result of our inability to understand or the result of the depth of the concept. All of this illustrates "examples" that are progressively higher, all of them within the spiritual realm. For, physical light and darkness are out of range [of spiritual light and darkness]...Similarly, in the spiritual realm there exists light that is revealed, and within it are found several levels of revelation. [All this occurs because] the lower light is only a parable regarding the upper spiritual light, and so regarding each level compared to the level above it. And similarly regarding darkness and lack of intellect; this may occur because the creature is unable to grasp the light and illumination, or because this level is in essence beyond revela-

CHASSIDIC INSIGHTS

the discovery of His Presence within ourselves) as the "garments of the King."[96] That is, on the soul-level of *ruach*, we become aware of Godliness en-clothed in nature and in our own souls, but our awareness is bounded and limited by the objects and our perception. Since the objects "en-clothe" the Godliness found in creation, they are called the "garments of the King." And while it makes no difference when embracing the King whether we do so through one garment or more (since it is the

רְצוֹן יְרֵאָיו יַעֲשֶׂה, וְאֶת שַׁוְעָתָם יִשְׁמַע וְיוֹשִׁיעֵם:

שׁוֹמֵר יְיָ אֶת כָּל אֹהֲבָיו, וְאֵת כָּל הָרְשָׁעִים יַשְׁמִיד:

King Himself is within them), nevertheless there is a distinction in our own perception. When meditating upon the Godliness embedded in nature and in our own lives, we become aware of Him only through the "lens" of creation and our own spiritual experience. However, we do not penetrate to the very essence of the Godliness. We are aware of it only as it is refracted through the "handles," the "packaging" and the "garments" that He created in order to conceal His presence as well as to make it possible for us to detect Him.[97] In Chassidic parlance, this is called *hitzoniut hamochin*, or "external mindfulness," and it falls short of awareness of His essential Presence. That awareness awaits a further step in our meditation and prayer, which comes after *Barchu*.

After praying through the section comprised of Psalms (Psalm 113 followed by 145-150), we arrive to the final third of *pesukei dezimra*. Here, the "subject" changes. Instead of considering the nature of creation and Godliness in our soul, we find ourselves reciting an account (from Chronicles 1, 29) of

CHASSIDIC EXCERPTS

tion, as written, *yeshet choshech sitro*...[145]

In the *Yalkut*,[146] it asks, "During the forty days that Moshe was on Mt. Sinai, how did he know when it was daytime and when it was night-time? When [the angels] said *kadosh* he knew that it was daytime and when they said *baruch* he knew that it was night." Now, *kadosh* and *baruch* apply to the angels known as *seraphim* and *ofanim*. The *seraphim* are "standing above him,"[147] since they grasp that the infinite light of God is holy and exalted, above the worlds. In this manner they develop intense desire and impetus to exit from their "sheath" and to become nullified and included in the infinite light above. The *ofanim* as well as the holy *chayot* are in a state of great commotion, stemming from their lack of understanding. They know that there is something above that is beyond their grasp, and that is what causes their excitement. The object of their desire is [as they say and we repeat in our prayers], "Blessed be God from His place"[148] –to receive revealed illumination. That is, because they are in a state of darkness and lack revelation, they strongly desire

Godly illumination. For example, one who sits in darkness pines for light, as written, *nafshi aviticah balailah*[149] ("my soul desires you at night"). Night is the time of darkness, when "my soul desires You" - for revealed illumination.

Both [categories of angels] are totally nullified to God, but the *seraphim* are in a state of spiritual ascent while the *ofanim* are in descent. For, day and night exist in this physical world in a manner that is out of range of the [their spiritual source above], and they exist as mere "examples" [to that which is above them]. Nonetheless, Moshe recognized from their spiritual source when it was day and night. [From the words of the angels, he knew], since they are the source and origin [of day and night], although they are totally out of range of one another.

In the world of Atzilut, this is represented by *orot* ("light," holy illumination) and *kelim* ("vessels" to contain the holy illumination). The *ohr* is G-dly revelation and the *keli* represents concealment. The nature of light is to ascend above, since it is connected and cleaves

CHASSIDIC INSIGHTS

early Jewish history, culminating in the exodus from Egypt. This account is clearly an allusion to the desire of the soul to "free" itself from the constraints of meditation based upon awareness of Godliness in nature. The soul wants more, it desires to know the very essence of Godliness. Meditation on the level of *ruach*, based as it is upon Godliness within nature, does not quench the thirst of our divine soul. On this level, our awareness arrives refracted through the "handles" and "packaging" of the garments of the King. But, the soul wants the King Himself. So, the final third of the *pesukei dezimra* expresses the desire of the soul to free itself of the *chitzoniut hamochin* ("external mindfulness") and penetrate to the very essence and pristine spark of Godliness within. The account of the exodus from Egypt serves as a parable to embody this desire of the soul, to free itself from the bounds of meditation through nature and focus on the pristine spark of Godliness within.

He fulfills the will of those who fear Him, hears their cry and saves them.

The Lord guards over all who love Him, and destroys the wicked.

And then, as the closing "act" of *pesukei dezimra*, we arrive to *Yishtabach*, the prayer that ushers out the *pesukei dezmira* and ushers in a new section of prayer starting with *Barchu*. *Yishtabach* is actually a continuation of the *bracha* that we recited at the beginning of *pesukei dezimra*, during *Baruch she'amar*. It brings to a close what we began with *Baruch She'amar* - the process of meditation upon nature and the garments of the King, corresponding to the soul level of *ruach*. Again, we find reference to God, but this time, rather than *Shmo* ("His Name") and *Shmo Hagadol* ("His great Name"), we find God

CHASSIDIC EXCERPTS

to its source. Therefore its tendency is to ascend above. And the vessel tends to descend and draw [holy influence] down. That is, the vessels draw down the light so that it is in a state of descent and influx, as known that the *kelim* draw down the *orot*. And, the *kelim* also have a tendency to ascend. This occurs on Shabbat, when there is an elevation of the worlds and the vessels. The ascent occurs as the vessels elevate to en-clothe a higher level of illumination. In general the elevation is for the purpose of drawing down that light, so that a higher light will illuminate. This ascent for the purpose of descent takes place mainly within the *kelim*. This explains why the *Yalkut* further tells us that when they learned the written Torah with Moshe, he knew that it was daytime and when they learned the oral Torah with him, he knew that it was night. The oral Torah is compared to night, as we see in the statement of the sages, that the verse, "He has set me in darkness,"[150] refers to the Babylonian Talmud, which is called "darkness." As known, the written Torah and the oral Torah correspond to *chochma* and *bina*.[151] *Chochma* is light,

and *bina* corresponds to the vessels. And in their source, light and darkness come from the *kav*, or ray of Godly light that is drawn down from the infinite light following the great contraction, or *tzimtzum*. And therefore, we say, "He Who rolls the light before the darkness and the darkness before light,"[152] referring to the characteristics of day and night...since day and night below are nothing more than mere "examples," regarding their supernal source above...

And so it is among all creatures. The physical lion, for example, has a spiritual source in the "face of the lion" on the spiritual "chariot" above. And yet, it is incomparable to the lion of the "chariot" – it a mere "example." And as we know, there are several levels of spiritual "chariots," such as the "chariot" of the world of *yetzira* and the "chariot" of *bria*, and there is even a supernal "chariot" in the world of Atzilut, where it represents the attributes of *chesed*, *gevura* and *tiferet* of Atzilut. The "face of the lion" on the chariot of *bria* serves as an "example" regarding the *sephira* of *chesed* of Atzilut, and so *chesed* of Atzilut serves as an "example" regarding the

CHASSIDIC INSIGHTS

addressed as *Shimcha* ("Your Name") and *Shimcha Hagadol* ("Your great Name"). The switch from third person ("He") to second person ("You") is because with our prayers, we have succeeded in bringing down Godliness from the highest, most essential and ineffable levels (therefore referred to as "He," as if not present) to be present among us and therefore possible to reference as "You."[98] This is reflected as well in the fifteen praises that we recite during *Yishtabach*, from *shir u'shvacha* ("songs and praise") through *brachot v'hodaot* ("blessings and acknowledgments").[99] The number fifteen is the *gematria*, or numerical value of *yud-hey*, the first two letters of the Name *Havaya*. As stated previously, they represent the quality of transcendent spirituality that we seek to bring down during the heart of *pesukei dezimra*, as we repeatedly said *haleluyah* ("praised by *Yud-hey*").

תְּהִלַּת יְיָ יְדַבֶּר פִּי, וִיבָרֵךְ כָּל בָּשָׂר שֵׁם קָדְשׁוֹ לְעוֹלָם וָעֶד:

וַאֲנַחְנוּ נְבָרֵךְ יָהּ, מֵעַתָּה וְעַד עוֹלָם, הַלְלוּיָהּ:

Now that we have reached the end of *pesukei dezimra*, the prayer *Yishtabach* with its fifteen praises indicates that we have brought the blessing down further so that the transcendent level of Godliness is now present among us.

There is yet another indication that at this point of prayers, we have drawn upon a transcendent

CHASSIDIC EXCERPTS

sephira of *chochma* of Atzilut, which is also called a "lion." A clue to this is that by reversing the letters of the Hebrew word for "lion" (*aryeh*), we derive the word *reiya*, which means "vision," corresponding to *chochma*, as written, "And he saw its beginning."[153] And so, *chochma* of Atzilut serves as an "example" regarding the lion that is above it, on the level of *keter*, which is also called "lion," as written, "If the lion roars, who is not frightened? When *HaShem Elokim* speaks, who does not prophecy?"[154] The holy books tell us that this applies to the supernal speech of God during the first of the Ten Commandments – "I am the Lord your God"[155] – which is associated with the *sephira* of *keter*. Thus, we establish that every spiritual level above serves as an "example" in relation to the level above it.

Regarding this matter, the holy books say that King Solomon was capable of "stating three thousand examples."[156] That is, he grasped three thousand spiritual levels, each one serving as an "example" in relation to the one above it. In other words, he knew the spiritual source of every physical creature in the supernal realm, each level higher than the previous level, up to three thousand levels, which his intellec-

tual acumen allowed him to detect. And since King Solomon represented the *sephira* of *malchut* of Atzilut, source of the lower worlds of *bria*, *yetzira* and *asiya*, therefore he grasped three thousand levels, corresponding to the three worlds of BY"A.

That is why the Midrash Raba[157] says, "All that God created above, He created correspondingly below. Above, He created *seraphim* standing and below He created cypress trees standing." *Seraphim* are [symbolized by] cypress trees, as written, "Then all the trees of the forest will sing,"[158] alluding to the angels. Similarly, about man, it is written, "For is man like a tree of the field?"[159] [implying that man is comparable to a tree in some sense]. So, both the angels and man are exemplified by trees. The "example" that allows us to grasp this is a tree, which grows from youth to maturity. In the beginning it is a small sapling, and later it grows to become a large tree, similar to man's emotions which grow from youth to full maturity. And so the angel Michael, who embodies love, is nevertheless considered "young" until he expresses his song or until he is sent on a mission. And when he sings his song or as he performs his mission, his love grows in intensity and

CHASSIDIC INSIGHTS

level of Godliness and are now preparing to access it. As we recite *Baruch She'amar* at the beginning of *pesukei dezimra*, we say, *yachid chay haolamim melech* — "The singular One, life of the worlds, is King." With these words we draw down Godliness from the highest, most essential level (so transcendent that we can only refer to it in the third person) prior to the *tzimtzum*, into the level that we call *melech*, or "King." This level corresponds to *malchut* ("sovereignty"), which is the tenth *sephira* of *Atzilut*, from which God creates and maintains the world. However, in *Yishtabach*, the words are inverted, and instead of the word *melech* being at the end of the phrase, it occurs at the beginning (*melech, yachid chay haolamim* — "King, the singular One, life of the worlds"). What this tells us is that now, the Godly light and illumination descends, not from the infinite light of God prior to the *tzimtzum*

> My mouth speaks the praises of the Lord, and all flesh blesses His holy name forever.
>
> And we bless G-d, from now and forever, Halleluyah!

into *malchut*, but from *malchut* of *Atzilut* into the lower worlds.[100] As we began *Baruch She'amar*, we drew down Godliness from above the *tzimtzum* (*Shmo hagadol* — "His great Name"). During *pesukei dezimra* we succeeded in drawing this light down to *malchut* of *Atzilut*, and now as we say the prayer *Yishtabach*, we seek to bring it down yet further, from *malchut* of *Atzilut* into the three lower worlds that we inhabit — *bria, yetzira* and *asiya*.

CHASSIDIC EXCERPTS

strength, because at that point he is able to refer to himself with the name of *Havaya*. As written, "I Myself have sworn, says the Lord."[160] And it is also written, "And she called in the name of the Lord, Who has spoken to her."[161] This is because during the course of the mission, the angel is nullified to such a great extent to God Who sent him, that Godliness permeates his entire essence. This is an especially full expression of spiritual maturity. Similarly, man is compared to a tree, in reference to his character traits (emotions). Prior to meditating upon the greatness of the Creator, man is in a state of spiritual immaturity. Upon meditating and thinking deeply about Godliness, his emotions expand and he experiences love and desire [for Godliness]. So, the physical tree is nothing more than an "example," portraying man's internal emotions as well as that of the angels.

The same is true of the Torah, which is called the "primordial example,"[162] for it as well serves as an example. . This may be understood in two possible ways. The first is that it applies to how the Torah is expressed in the physical world, as it becomes en-clothed

in physical objects, such as *tzitzit* made of wool, or *tefilin* made of physical parchment. The same is true of the oral law which states, "He who exchanges a cow for a donkey..."[163]

The second way that the Torah may be described as an "example" is when the Torah as it exists above in the spiritual realm serves as an "example" in relation to the primordial infinite One above. In this vein, David would "join the Torah of Above" with the Holy One blessed be He," since in this relationship the Torah is like a mere "example" [in relation to God]. However, the "example" of Torah is unlike the previous "examples" that we cited in our physical world. Torah serves as an "example" that allows us to detect and reveal what it represents [in the spiritual realm]. That is, by laboring in Torah, we join the infinite light from above with the Torah itself. This is not true of the examples from this world, which all express concealment and hiddenness. For example, from the lion in this world we have no clue at all about the lion of the supernal chariot, which says *kadosh*, for [this relationship] is completely and totally hidden...

(From *Sefer Maamorim 5679* (1919) of the Rebbe Rashab, pp. 315-317

לְלוּיָהּ, הַלְלִי נַפְשִׁי אֶת יְיָ:
אֲהַלְלָה יְיָ בְּחַיָּי, אֲזַמְּרָה לֵאלֹהַי בְּעוֹדִי:

CHASSIDIC EXCERPTS

Bringing out the best
Halleluyah, halleli nafshi ("Praise G-d, Praise G-d, my soul"), Psalm 146

Here is the explanation of the words *Halleluyah, halleli* that appear throughout the *Pesukei DeZimra*:

Hallelu means "praise" and the suffix *yud-hei* is the first two letters of G-d's essential Name, *Havaya*. The two letters represent the inner dimensions of the intellect as it permeates the emotions. This [that that the first two letters represent intellect and the final letters correspond to the emotions] is the standard interpretation of the name *Havaya* wherever it is used. In order to understand this better, it is first necessary to grasp what is meant by praise of G-d. The overall purpose of the *Pesukei Dezimra* is to praise and extol G-d, but why do we do this? The meaning of *yehallel* ("will praise") is understood from the phrase *behilo naro* ("when his lamp shone"), or *yahil oro* ("let his lamp shine"),[164] both of which indicate illumination [in this case, the illumination of the specific attributes of G-d that we wish to elicit].

By way of explanation, when we praise someone, describing him as wise or kind or the like, he generally responds positively to our praises. The effect that it has upon him corresponds to the praise; he responds by expressing the very trait for which we praise him. If we say that he is a kind and merciful person, this brings out the latent kindness and mercy that is within him at that moment. And if we praise him as wise, it encourages him to display intellect. From this, we understand that praise brings out specific traits from latent potential in the heart to conscious expression. Preceding the praise, the various traits of mercy, kindness or wisdom were latent in the person's heart, but the praise aroused the traits and brought them out from concealment to con-

sciousness, to the extent that now he actually expresses them where, previously, they were hidden within him.

This is the reason that the praise is called *hillul*, as in *yahel oro* ("let his lamp shine") for there is a flash of brilliant illumination as the trait emerges from concealment to revealed light by way of [our] praise.

Above, the essential and infinite light of G-d (*ohr ayn sof*) reflects ultimate simplicity, eschewing categories and divisions. It does not broach the existence of the ten attributes (*sephirot*), such as *chochma* ("wisdom") *bina* ("understanding"), or *chesed* ("kindness"), etc. Only in the most refined sense can we say that *chochma* "exists" potentially in the essential infinite light of G-d, as the sages of the *Zohar* said – that He is "wise with an unknown wisdom, understanding with unknown logic." And, regarding G-d Himself, the *Zohar* says, "Not that You possess justice in any known way ... nor any of these attributes whatsoever." Nevertheless, when we praise and extol Him in the *Pesukei DeZimra*, describing Him as kind and merciful, and great, etc., we arouse these traits within Him, eliciting them from concealment to revealed illumination. At that point, we may describe Him as "kind" on account of the flow of G-dly illumination coming from Him. And to the extent that we praise Him, He is aroused to express and convey that particular trait, from concealment to revelation, as mentioned earlier. This, then, is the explanation of *yehallelu*, from the root word *behilu* ("when it shone"). It serves as the overall origin of the verses of *Pesukei DeZimra*, which are also known as *hillul* ("praise").

However, there is also a specific

*H*alleluyah, my soul praises the Lord. The Lord is my life, I will sing to the Lord from the essence of my being.

CHASSIDIC EXCERPTS

meaning to the word *halleluyah* ... The main purpose of all the praise is to extend the illumination of the *sephirot* of *Atzilut* into the worlds of BY"A (*Bria, Yetzira* and *Asiya*) in order to shine there in a state of concrete revelation. We know that there is a presence of *chitzonim* ("extraneous forces") attached to the *sephirot* of *Atzilut* as they descend into BY"A. (As the *Zohar* states, "The head of Esav was wrapped in the cloak of Isaac," indicating that the cruelty of Esav had its roots in the holy strictness of Isaac, just as the superfluous kindness of Ishmael stemmed from the holy kindness of Abraham, the "man of kindness.") And in order to prevent the extraneous negative forces from siphoning G-dly energy from holiness, we direct our praise of G-d from the intellect (*chochma* and *bina*) into the emotions,

where it is called *Yud-hei*. This is because the catastrophic shattering of the vessels [which allowed "separate" existence to take place] occurred only among the lower seven emotional *sephirot*, while the upper three intellectual *sephirot* [including *chochma* and *bina*] remained intact... Also, because *chochma* and *bina* are closer to the ray of infinite G-dly light, which shines directly into *chochma*, it is where the greatest nullification to G-d exists. For this reason, it is impossible for the extraneous forces to receive G-dly energy from the emotions [once they are imbued with intellect], since "evil will not dwell together with You."[165] This is what is meant by *halleluyah*, referring precisely to the intellect (*chochma* and *bina*) as it is clad in the G-dly emotions (*sephirot* of *Atzilut*).

(From the *Siddur* of the Alter Rebbe with Chasidut, Page 56 (*nun-vov*)

Don't take from strangers
"Do not rely upon gratuitous volunteers, upon man who brings no salvation"

We'll better understand what the psalm means by "volunteers" by looking in the Zohar (*Parshat Terumah*, 128A): "The impure spirit arrives frequently, in a disgraceful and empty manner, and 'sells itself' for free. It coerces man to [allow him] to dwell with him, and seduces him to allow him to remain, utilizing various temptations to allow him to dally among men....the holy spirit is not so – it forces man to pay fully, and demands much effort, and refinement of the self and of one's dwelling place, as well as the will and desire of the heart and the soul. We should only deserve that it should dwell with us..."

From this statement of the Zohar, it is understood that it is not a simple matter for man to draw upon revelation and illumination of the soul from the ten holy *sephirot*. Only with much effort and

self-sacrifice and refinement of his physicality, while eschewing his corporeal nature [does man achieve the goal of revelation]. The opposite is true of the *sitra achra* and *klipa* (the "other side" and "shell," which oppose and conceal holiness) – from them, man is able to attain his needs free of cost and without effort and labor. This is what occurred during the days of the idol worshippers, who succeeded in attaining their needs, in great excitement, as soon as they sacrificed and burnt incense. As they claimed, "And from the time that we ceased to burn incense to the kingdom of the heavens..." This was also the claim of the Jews in Egypt, who said, "We recall the fish that we ate for free in Egypt..." Here, "free" means without effort or labor at all, as written in the saying above, "the impure spirit arrives frequently, disgracefully, and is 'sells it-

אַל תִּבְטְחוּ בִנְדִיבִים, בְּבֶן אָדָם שֶׁאֵין לוֹ תְשׁוּעָה:

תֵּצֵא רוּחוֹ יָשֻׁב לְאַדְמָתוֹ, בַּיּוֹם הַהוּא אָבְדוּ עֶשְׁתֹּנֹתָיו:

אַשְׁרֵי שֶׁאֵל יַעֲקֹב בְּעֶזְרוֹ, שִׂבְרוֹ עַל יְיָ אֱלֹהָיו:

עֹשֶׂה שָׁמַיִם וָאָרֶץ, אֶת הַיָּם וְאֶת כָּל אֲשֶׁר בָּם, הַשֹּׁמֵר אֱמֶת לְעוֹלָם:

עֹשֶׂה מִשְׁפָּט לַעֲשׁוּקִים, נֹתֵן לֶחֶם לָרְעֵבִים, יְיָ מַתִּיר אֲסוּרִים:

יְיָ פֹּקֵחַ עִוְרִים, יְיָ זֹקֵף כְּפוּפִים, יְיָ אֹהֵב צַדִּיקִים:

CHASSIDIC EXCERPTS

self' for free." And so occurred with the impure forces of Egypt – the influx arrived devoid of any refinement, to influence the Jews.

This is actually the claim of all idol worshippers – that it is better for them to receive influx from the stars and constellations, since they do not have to subjugate themselves with self-sacrifice, etc. This indicates that they do not want to subdue themselves with self sacrifice and refinement of the self…to holiness in order to receive their physical needs, since the realm of holiness requires much discipline and self sacrifice in order to achieve anything. Now, there are two levels of klipa, or concealment of G-dliness. The lowest is total evil, such as the three totally impure klipot, as known, while the second, called klipat noga, is mixed good and bad. There is a difference in the manner in which they operate…just as there is a difference in their very essence. One is totally evil, and the other is mixed good and bad. And the difference between them regarding their operation corresponds to the statement of the sages: "The impure spirit arrives frequently, in a disgraceful and empty manner, and coerces man and seduces him" – this is said regarding the totally evil aspects of the "other side," reflecting that which the Jews said in Egypt – "We recall the fish that we ate for free." That is, aside from delivering "for free," it attempts to seduce man. But, klipat noga, which is mixed good and bad, does not attempt to persuade and seduce man. It is true that as soon as man requests [from klipat noga], he receives, without effort or labor, for it is relatively easy to attain whatever one wants from klipat noga. This is comparable to an easy-going person who, although he may be generous in nature, will not give unless he is asked. But, when asked, he responds immediately, since there is no total evil within klipat noga. Rather, it is mixed good and bad – and that is the reason that the ten sephirot of klipat noga are called nedivim – "volunteers." And about them, the prayer here says, "Do not rely upon gratuitous volunteers." That is, do not rely upon [klipat noga] to provide your physical needs – for this will not occur unless you put in effort and self sacrifice from another angle – by subjugating yourself to the klipot noga which is called "volunteers," since then you may receive your needs. For, [as the psalm says], they are "man, who bring no salvation." That is, salvation comes from the chasadim ("kindnesses"), which are called "salvation," as written

Do not rely upon gratuitous volunteers, upon man who brings no salvation.

His spirit departs and returns to its dust, on that day all his plans dissipate.

Happy is he who is aided by the G-d of Jacob, his hope rests upon the Lord, his G-d.

Who creates the heavens and earth, the sea and all within it; Who guards the truth forever.

He renders justice for the wronged, gives bread to the hungry, and frees the imprisoned.

The Lord opens the eyes of the blind, the Lord straightens the stooped over, the Lord loves the righteous.

CHASSIDIC EXCERPTS

elsewhere, in the commentary on, "I will raise a cup of salvation." They correspond to the five "hidden leaves of the rose," as written in the introduction to the Zohar. And although they are sometimes called "salvation" even when they come from the side of *gevurot* ("stringencies") as written elsewhere, nevertheless the source of salvation is associated with *chesed*, from the right side...It may occasionally derive from *chesed* within *gevura* and sometimes from *gevura* within *chesed*, but in any case, there are always *chasadim* involved...

This is not true of the source of sustenance of the *klipot*, which derives solely from *gevura* ("judgment, stringency"), without any of the sweetness of the *chasadim* at all... They have no origins at all from the side of *chesed*, which is called "salvation." And that is why they are called "man in whom there is no salvation." That is, there is nothing in their inception and origin of the kindness that is called "salvation," whatsoever. And if so, it is impossible to rely and trust in these "volunteers," to provide positive kindness, even in the physical needs that they provide in their wake...for this is not true kindness, since it lacks a positive source and origin...

From the siddur of the Alter Rebbe with Chassidut, Page 112 (56B to 57A)

The bent over, the oppressed, and the hungry...
Oseh mishpat la'ashukim, noten lechem lareavim ("He renders justice for the oppressed, He gives bread to the hungry") – Psalm 146

Among *ashukim* ("the oppressed"), there are many levels. There are sparks of holiness that have fallen into the chambers of the *chitzonim* ("extraneous forces") – they are called *noflim* ("the fallen"). About them, it is said, "G-d supports all of the fallen."[166] There are those called *kefufim* ("the bent over"), about which it is said, "He causes the bent over to stand upright." And there are those called *asurim* ("the impris-

oned"), about whom it is said, "He frees the imprisoned." Then, there are the *re'evim* ("hungry"), about whom it is said "He gives bread to the hungry."

In all of these cases, we may gain some understanding by observing our fellow holy Jewish souls, clad in physical bodies. We see people who meditate upon the greatness of the Creator without achieving any excitement at all, lacking even intellectual acknowledgment of

יְיָ שֹׁמֵר אֶת גֵּרִים, יָתוֹם וְאַלְמָנָה יְעוֹדֵד, וְדֶרֶךְ רְשָׁעִים יְעַוֵּת:

יִמְלֹךְ יְיָ לְעוֹלָם, אֱלֹהַיִךְ צִיּוֹן לְדֹר וָדֹר הַלְלוּיָהּ:

CHASSIDIC EXCERPTS

His existence. This condition is called *nefila* ("fallen"). Then, the *asurim* ("imprisoned") are those who manage to achieve some stimulation through intellectual meditation, yet who remain imprisoned by their natural [animal] souls, which are attached to the physical pleasures of this world. They are incarcerated and bound, and unable to achieve any emotional arousal of love and fear, via stimulation of their intellect. They are comparable to one whose two hands are tied, who is unable to move. Beneath them are the *kefufim* ("the bent over"). Their heads are bowed, directed toward the ground like an animal with its head inclined to the earth since its spiritual source lies with the "spirit of the animal," which descends to the earth. So there are sparks that have sunken into the coarse matters of our physical world to such an extent that their minds are very physically oriented. They achieve little or no G-dly perception, being akin to the "spirit of the animal" which grasps nothing aside from those things that matter to it, such as eating grass and the like. This is comparable to the position of the fetus in the womb of the mother – curled with its head between its knees. Its intellectual potential has not yet developed, while its mind remains hidden among its *nehi* [*netzach, hod, yesod*, the lowest three instinctual emotions]. This is known in Kabbalah as "three within three," wherein the person's G-dly intellect is concealed in his "knees," as he understands physical matters alone. Such people are called *kefufim.*

Now, those who are called *re'evim* ("hungry") are above those who are called *asurim* ("imprisoned"). The latter fail to achieve conscious excitement in fear and love of G-d. Rather their excitement is limited to their intellect. But, those who are hungry and thirsty for their Creator manage to achieve excitement of the heart as well. However, they do not achieve the full measure of enjoyment of receiving G-dly light and energy in their souls from this meditation. They merely achieve true thirst and hunger. They experience desire to approach G-d, but His light does not shine within their soul and illuminate them with light and energy, for otherwise they would not be "hungry." This, then, is what is meant by "He gives bread to the hungry"...

Afterward, Psalm 146 continues, "G-d frees the imprisoned," referring to sparks of holiness that fell even further and are called "imprisoned." They are those who achieve excitement in the mind but not in the heart, as mentioned earlier. Then, the psalm continues, "G-d opens the eyes of the blind," since a blind person has the power of spiritual vision, but does not have the capability to express it physically. Similarly, there are people who grasp G-dliness in their souls, "seeing" it with their faculty of *chochma*, as is said, "Who is a wise man? He who envisions the future,"[167] referring to those who see and understand how the universe is created from nothing to something. Still, their spiritual eyesight does not allow them to view this process clearly with full comprehen-

The Lord guards the proselytes, supports orphans and widows, and thwarts the path of the wicked.

May the Lord reign forever, your G-d over Zion, from generation to generation, Halleluyah!

CHASSIDIC EXCERPTS

sion. Instead, they view it from afar, distant from the G-dliness which they grasp in their spiritual mind's eye alone. About this, the verse says, "[G-d] opens their eyes..." meaning that He illuminates their spiritual eyesight so that they achieve total intellectual understanding [like one who sees clearly].

But all of this refers to those who have at least some grasp of G-dliness. Then, the psalm continues and mentions a lower level – "the bent over" – those whose head is between their knees, as explained earlier, and who have no grasp of G-dliness whatsoever. G-d uplifts them, causing them to stand upright. There are many like them, whose souls are like sparks of G-dliness that fell from Above, and about whom the verse says that He "frees the imprisoned."

*

All told, there are four classes of sparks: 1) *re'evim* ("the hungry"), 2) *asurim* ("the imprisoned"), 3) *ivrim* ("the blind"), and 4) *kefufim* ("the bent over"). *Re'evim* correspond to the World of *Atzilut*, *asurim* to *Bria*, *ivrim* to *Yetzira*, and *kefufim* to *Asiya*. All of them join together in *Bria* by way of a supernal unity that takes place in the emotional attributes of *Atzilut* (called *Ze'er Anpin*). That supernal unity is associated with *tzaddikim*, which is why the psalm states, "G-d loves *tzaddikim*," meaning that He causes love and unity among *tzaddikim* ...

In this way, He redeems and rescues all of these sparks, as the One who "frees the imprisoned." By way of revealed G-dliness ... automatically all of the worlds ascend and become refined, including "the blind" and "the bent over."

(From the *Siddur* of the Alter Rebbe, p. 111 (*nun-zayin*))

Tending the sparks
HaShem shomer et gerim ("G-d protects the converts") – Psalm 146

Gerim ("converts") here refers to the sparks of holiness that fell into the realm of the seventy non-Jewish nations of the world, and then entered the world of Judaism, under the wings of the *Shechina* ("Divine Presence"). They are called *gerim*.

By way of example, *ba'alei tshuva* [those who return to the path of Torah and mitzvoth after having strayed] may express a lot of spiritual excitement from the very depths of their heart, yet they need protection so that they do not re-

vert to their former ways. Since they formerly strayed from the path, even though they now act according to the Torah, it could be very easy for them to return to their former ways. So, too, with the sparks called *gerim*. Even though they became attached to the *Shechina*, since their original place was among the nations of the earth, they need serious protection so that they won't be tempted to return to their original place among the non-Jews. This is what is meant by *shomer et gerim*.

(From the *Siddur* of the Alter Rebbe, p. 58b)

מְֽלְוָיָה, כִּי טוֹב זַמְּרָה אֱלֹהֵינוּ, כִּי נָעִים נָאוָה תְהִלָּה:

בּוֹנֵה יְרוּשָׁלַיִם יְיָ, נִדְחֵי יִשְׂרָאֵל יְכַנֵּס:

הָרוֹפֵא לִשְׁבוּרֵי לֵב, וּמְחַבֵּשׁ לְעַצְּבוֹתָם:

מוֹנֶה מִסְפָּר לַכּוֹכָבִים, לְכֻלָּם שֵׁמוֹת יִקְרָא:

גָּדוֹל אֲדוֹנֵינוּ וְרַב כֹּחַ, לִתְבוּנָתוֹ אֵין מִסְפָּר:

מְעוֹדֵד עֲנָוִים יְיָ, מַשְׁפִּיל רְשָׁעִים עֲדֵי אָרֶץ:

עֱנוּ לַיָי בְּתוֹדָה, זַמְּרוּ לֵאלֹהֵינוּ בְכִנּוֹר:

הַמְכַסֶּה שָׁמַיִם בְּעָבִים, הַמֵּכִין לָאָרֶץ מָטָר, הַמַּצְמִיחַ הָרִים חָצִיר:

נוֹתֵן לִבְהֵמָה לַחְמָהּ, לִבְנֵי עֹרֵב אֲשֶׁר יִקְרָאוּ:

CHASSIDIC EXCERPTS

Resonating with joy

Halleluyah ki tov zamra Elokeinu ("Praise G-d for it is good to sing...") – Psalm 147

[Although this phrase is translated as "Praise G-d, for it is good to sing before our G-d," the word "before" is actually missing.]

We need to understand why the verse says *ki tov zamra Elokeinu* ("it is good to sing, our G-d") and not *ki tov zamra lifnei Elokeinu* ("it is good to sing **before** our G-d") – this would be the simple meaning of the psalm, since we sing it before G-d. So, why does the verse leave out this word?

This is understood by way of example. When we sing in front of a bride and groom, we seek to arouse joy and happiness in their heart with our singing. The goal is to awaken emotions of joy and happiness from within, from the source of enjoyment. Singing has the effect of arousing the body, invigorating it with happiness and enjoyment that emerges from a hidden source, called the "origin of all enjoyment," as is known. This par-able will be understood by those who grasp what is going on Above. The songs and melodies of the angels and souls in paradise, where souls receive revelation of G-dliness, [resonate in the] world of Atzilut and there, stimulate joy within *bina* of *malchut* of *Atzilut*. [*Bina* brings understanding of what was previously beyond our grasp, causing us to be happy. This takes place when *bina* descends to *malchut*, the *sephira* that reveals and expresses the higher *sephirot* in the World of *Atzilut*]. *Bina* is called "the mother of the children," as is known, and this is the secret of "the happy mother of the children" [as it is written, "He returns the barren woman to her home, as a happy mother of children."[168] *Bina*, or "intellectual understanding," gives birth to the emotions, which brings happiness when they are born]. This correlates with the name *Elokeinu* – "our G-d" – mentioned here, since

*H*alleluyah, for it is good to sing of our G-d, for He is pleasant and praise is befitting.

The Lord builds Jerusalem, He will gather the dispersed Jews.

He heals the broken-hearted, and treats all of their suffering.

He counts the number of stars, calling them all by name.

Great is our Master, and abundantly powerful, his intellect cannot be quantified.

The Lord supports the humble, lowers the wicked down to the earth.

Respond to the Lord in gratitude, sing to our G-d with a harp.

Who covers the heavens with clouds, prepares rain for the earth, germinates pasture on the mountains.

He provides fodder for the cattle, for the offspring of ravens who call.

CHASSIDIC EXCERPTS

Elokeinu is in *bina* ... And this arousal of joy and happiness within *bina* of *malchut* of *Atzilut* emerges from concealment to revelation from the "source of enjoyment," called *Atik Yomim* [the highest level within *keter*]...

This is why the verse *Halleluyah ki tov zamra Elokeinu* should really be translated as "Praise G-d, for the song of our G-d is good." When the source of enjoyment (*keter*) descends to *bina*, it causes *zamra Elokeinu* – "song of our G-d." That is, in order for *bina*, called *Elokeinu*, to absorb the revelation of *Atik Yomin*, *zamra* is necessary. By accessing joy and revelation within, from the source of all enjoyment Above ... [we resonate with the source of spiritual enjoyment Above, causing G-dly song Above]. And that is why the verse does not say "before our G-d," but rather "song of our G-d," since it is necessary to recite these praises in order to arouse joy within *bina*, which is called *Elokeinu*...

(From the *Siddur* of the Alter Rebbe, bottom of Page 58d)

Influx from Above

Hasholeach imrato aretz - "The One who sends His speech earthward, how fast does His command run!" – Psalm 147

There are two ways in which G-dliness descends – slowly and rapidly. The first part of this verse, "the One who sends His speech" refers to G-dliness which descends slowly. That is, it filters downward via various spiritual levels leading to creation in a step-by-step fashion, from one level to the next, stopping at each level, in every world. For that reason, we ask G-d to fill our needs every day during the *Shemonah Esreh*, in the twelve middle blessings – we say, "Heal us," and "Bless us with sustenance," etc. Yet, at first glance, our sustenance is granted to us on Rosh Hashana, when our health and food for the entire year are meted out. And if so, why are any more requests

לֹא בִגְבוּרַת הַסּוּס יֶחְפָּץ, לֹא בְשׁוֹקֵי הָאִישׁ יִרְצֶה:

רוֹצֶה יְיָ אֶת יְרֵאָיו, אֶת הַמְיַחֲלִים לְחַסְדּוֹ:

שַׁבְּחִי יְרוּשָׁלַיִם אֶת יְיָ, הַלְלִי אֱלֹהַיִךְ צִיּוֹן:

כִּי חִזַּק בְּרִיחֵי שְׁעָרָיִךְ, בֵּרַךְ בָּנַיִךְ בְּקִרְבֵּךְ:

הַשָּׂם גְּבוּלֵךְ שָׁלוֹם, חֵלֶב חִטִּים יַשְׂבִּיעֵךְ:

הַשֹּׁלֵחַ אִמְרָתוֹ אָרֶץ, עַד מְהֵרָה יָרוּץ דְּבָרוֹ:

הַנֹּתֵן שֶׁלֶג כַּצָּמֶר, כְּפוֹר כָּאֵפֶר יְפַזֵּר:

מַשְׁלִיךְ קַרְחוֹ כְפִתִּים, לִפְנֵי קָרָתוֹ מִי יַעֲמֹד:

יִשְׁלַח דְּבָרוֹ וְיַמְסֵם, יַשֵּׁב רוּחוֹ יִזְּלוּ מָיִם:

מַגִּיד דְּבָרָיו לְיַעֲקֹב, חֻקָּיו וּמִשְׁפָּטָיו לְיִשְׂרָאֵל:

לֹא עָשָׂה כֵן לְכָל גּוֹי, וּמִשְׁפָּטִים בַּל יְדָעוּם. הַלְלוּיָהּ:

CHASSIDIC EXCERPTS

necessary? But, the answer is that what is drawn down on Rosh Hashana is the entire influx from its source. But, as it later descends into the world, it may be held up at any step along the way. It may remain Above (in its source) without descending downward, or it may descend from its spiritual level but never arrive to the physical world. For this reason, more requests are necessary.

And this is also what is meant by, "Man is judged every day."[169] And yet we all undergo a judgment on Rosh Hashana, during which our influx of health and sustenance for the new year is established. So what more judgment is necessary? The influx pauses in every world, and therefore there is a further need for judgment – whether it will descend and in what manner. This is the reason for our requests during the Shemonah Esreh, so that the influx is drawn down according to our needs. All this is concerning the influx that descends slowly.

As for the second half of the verse, "how fast does His command run," this applies to influx that that descends rapidly, without pausing in the various worlds. The reason for this is that the source of influx transcends the entire chain of events leading to the creation. For "there is chesed and there is chesed."[170] There is chesed ("kindness") that is subject to the limitations of the chain of creation, and the influx from this level of chesed is the kind that "pauses" as it descends, but there is chesed that is called rav chesed ("great kindness"), which is from beyond the whole chain leading to creation. And when this level descends, it does not pause at all, but rather descends swiftly without any delay.

(From Sefer Maamorim 5659 (1899) of the Rebbe Rashab, p. 114)

He desires not the strength of the horse, nor does he want the legs of man.

The Lord desires those who fear Him, those who yearn for His kindness. Praise the Lord, Jerusalem, praise your G-d, Zion!

For He has strengthened the bolts of Your gates, [and] blessed Your children within.

He establishes peace at your borders, He satiates you with the cream of wheat.

He sends His utterance earthward, His word travels very quickly.

He provides snow [soft] as wool, He scatters frost like ashes.

He hurls His ice like crumbs, who can stand before His cold?

He dispatches His word and [the ice] melts, He makes His wind blow and water flows.

He tells His words to Jacob, His laws and judgments to Israel.

He did not do so for any other nation, [to them His] statutes are unknown. Halleluyah!

CHASSIDIC EXCERPTS

Ice, water and snow
Mashlich karfo k'phitim - "He hurls His ice like crumbs" - Psalm 147

Regarding the Torah, it is written, "He wraps Himself in light like a robe..."[171] That is, G-d wraps the light of the Torah around Himself like a robe, implying that His infinite light is clad in the Torah. And about this it is written, "His garments are like white snow."[172] So, there is such a thing as snow and ice Above, as it is written, "He hurls His ice like crumbs."

Now, ice comes as the result of the strength of the [climate in the] north, which freezes water. Water itself flows, representing a flow from Above to below. But, because of the power of the north, water freezes, creating a lack of descent from Above to below. This is called contraction, as well as concealment, as the illumination is concealed so that it does not descend below. For that reason, it is called "ice," which alludes

to a lack of influx. Now, this "ice" is the "curtain" that separates between *Atzilut* and *Bria*. It conceals so that the infinite light of G-d will not descend to the lower worlds of *BY"A* as it exists in *Atzilut*. This is because, if the infinite light would shine in a revealed fashion as it does in the world of *Atzilut*, the worlds would not be capable of remaining in a state of created existence, as separate and independent entities. Rather, they would be totally nullified, as if non-existent. It is the curtain between *Atzilut* and *Bria* that allows the worlds to take on the veneer of separate entities with an independent existence, permitting the revelation of His kingship...

Torah, however, is "snow." Snow does not undergo the same tremendous contraction that ice undergoes. Even

לְלוּיָהּ, הַלְלוּ אֶת יְיָ מִן הַשָּׁמַיִם, הַלְלוּהוּ בַּמְּרוֹמִים:

הַלְלוּהוּ כָל מַלְאָכָיו, הַלְלוּהוּ כָּל צְבָאָיו:

הַלְלוּהוּ שֶׁמֶשׁ וְיָרֵחַ, הַלְלוּהוּ כָּל כּוֹכְבֵי אוֹר:

הַלְלוּהוּ שְׁמֵי הַשָּׁמָיִם, וְהַמַּיִם אֲשֶׁר מֵעַל הַשָּׁמָיִם:

יְהַלְלוּ אֶת שֵׁם יְיָ, כִּי הוּא צִוָּה וְנִבְרָאוּ:

CHASSIDIC EXCERPTS

though snow is also derived from water, which congeals and becomes snow, nevertheless with a little bit of warmth, it melts, returning to a state of water. This is because snow represents the contraction that leads to *chochma*, since the creation of *chochma* from the infinite light of G-d also comes about by way of contraction. But, still, this is not the total contraction of ice, which becomes the source of the lower worlds of *BY"A*. This is what is meant by "He wraps Himself in light as a robe." Even though the Torah is a garment, within it is clad the infinite light of G-d. Within *chochma* is enclothed the infinite light itself, and Torah stems from *chochma*. This is what is meant by, "His garments are like white snow," since the source of the Torah is from the "garments of white snow" which are the source of *chochma*, the thirteen strands of the beard and the thirteen attributes of mercy. [The latter correspond to] the thirteen attributes with which the Torah is interpreted.

(From *Sefer Maamorim* 5655 (1895), of the Rebbe Rashab, p. 3)

A desirable land

Magid devarav l'Yakov - "He relates His word to Jacob" – Psalm 147

The Jews are called an *eretz chefetz* ("desirable land"), meaning a land that is good for sowing seeds. This is because when Jews fulfill a mitzah, it brings down G-dly illumination. This is not the case with others, who bring down nothing, as it is written, "He relates His word to Jacob, His laws and rules to Israel. He did not do so for any other nation..."

(From *Sefer Maamorim* 5680 (1920) of the Rebbe Rashab, p. 303)

Praise from the heavens

Halleluya, hallelu et Hashem min hashamayim; ("Halleluyah, praised be the Lord from the heavens, praised Him on the heights. Praise Him, all of His angels, praise Him, all of His hosts.") – Psalm 148

"Now, the explanation of "heavens" (*shamayim*), is that it refers to *z'a* (the lower six or seven *sephirot*) of *Atzilut*....The reason is that *z'a*, which is the "emotions" of *Atzilut*, is the core faculty of the *mashpia* ("mentor" or "benefactor") that relates to the lower separate worlds of *BY"A*, as known. And all influx must come through *chesed* [which is the highest *sephira* witin *z'a*], as it is written, *olam chesed yibaneh* ("the world is built upon kindness"...).

*H*alleluyah, praised be the Lord from the heavens, praised Him on the heights.

Praise Him, all of His angels, praise Him, all of His hosts.

Praise Him, sun and the moon, praise Him, all of the shining stars.

Praise Him, heaven's heavens, as well as the waters that transcend the heavens.

Praise be the name of the Lord, for He commanded and they were created.

CHASSIDIC EXCERPTS

...Now, the explanation of *meromim* ("heights") is that it refers to *malchut* of *Atzilut* as it is concealed within *bria*. At that point, it is called *marom*, as written *se'u marom eineichem* – "Raise your eyes to the heights" – for as known, the difference between "heavens" and "heights" is that "heavens" refers to the very essence of the sky...while "heights" refers to what we are able to see. It is what is evident to the one who stands below, to whom the essence of the sky is not visible at all. He is able to detect only what descends as a ray of light, visible to the eye. And since the heavens are extremely elevated... therefore what we are able to see is called *marom*, for His [true] heights are not fathomable or graspable. But, the term *marom* indicates loftiness and elevation alone, meaning to say that He is high, above what we may see – this is why we say "raise your eyes to the heights..."

...the explanation of "His angels" is that it refers to the world of *yetzira*, as written in the siddur [of the Ariz'l] that the four worlds of ABY"A are hinted to in the four praises mentioned here: *shamayim*, *meromim*, angels and hosts... now, the reason that angels are associated with *yetzira* is because an angel –

malach – is an emissary (*shaliach*), and the entire world of *yetzira* functions as an "emissary" to deliver something... it possesses no qualities of its own – so the world of *yetzira* merely enables revelation of what was previously concealed. And therefore, "His angels" are in *yetzira*. And in truth, there is an advantage to *yetzira* over *asiya*, in that the angels [of *yetzira*] are totally nullified within, just as is a proper messenger. Similarly, the angels of are nothing more than emissaries who reveal the divine influx from its state of concealment in *bria*...unlike the angels of *asiya* who possess an existence and identity of their own....

So, "All of His angels praise Him" appears first, after which we say, "All of His hosts..." in reference to the world of *asiya*. This is because a "host" is nothing more than a foot soldier of the king. He is not one who stands before the king, ready to do his bidding, but rather he is one who stands ready to go out to war. And this is similar to the seventy "ministers" of *asiya* and all of the planets and constellations and the nine orbits which accepts their influx from *malchut* of *malchut* of *asiya*, as known..."

(From the Siddur of the Alter Rebbe, on Psalm 148 in the Psukei dezimra, Page Samech-Hey (65 in the Hebrew letters))

וַיַּעֲמִידֵם לָעַד לְעוֹלָם, חָק נָתַן וְלֹא יַעֲבוֹר:

הַלְלוּ אֶת יְיָ מִן הָאָרֶץ, תַּנִּינִים וְכָל תְּהֹמוֹת:

אֵשׁ וּבָרָד, שֶׁלֶג וְקִיטוֹר, רוּחַ סְעָרָה עֹשָׂה דְבָרוֹ:

הֶהָרִים וְכָל גְּבָעוֹת, עֵץ פְּרִי וְכָל אֲרָזִים:

הַחַיָּה וְכָל בְּהֵמָה, רֶמֶשׂ וְצִפּוֹר כָּנָף:

מַלְכֵי אֶרֶץ וְכָל לְאֻמִּים, שָׂרִים וְכָל שֹׁפְטֵי אָרֶץ:

בַּחוּרִים וְגַם בְּתוּלוֹת, זְקֵנִים עִם נְעָרִים:

יְהַלְלוּ אֶת שֵׁם יְיָ כִּי נִשְׂגָּב שְׁמוֹ לְבַדּוֹ, הוֹדוֹ עַל אֶרֶץ וְשָׁמָיִם:

וַיָּרֶם קֶרֶן לְעַמּוֹ, תְּהִלָּה לְכָל חֲסִידָיו, לִבְנֵי יִשְׂרָאֵל עַם קְרֹבוֹ הַלְלוּיָהּ:

CHASSIDIC EXCERPTS

The point of origin

Vayarem keren le'amo - "And He shall raise the prestige of His people" – Psalm 148

Now, the explanation of the word *keren* [literally "horn" but generally translated as "prestige"] is known and explained elsewhere.[173] The basic idea is that *keren* means "point," and [here], it corresponds to the *ayn* ("divine void").

By way of example, the corner between two walls has no surface area of its own whatsoever. Still it joins two opposites, one of which might be a wall to the east and the other a wall to the south, while the corner that is between them is an intermediary joining the two of them together. The same is true regarding a point as an intermediary between two lines; one line could represent length and the other width. From this example, it is clear that *keren* is *ayn*, or a true void that has within its power to join two opposites. Similarly, a point that is the origin of one ray may constitute the conclusion of another and join the two together. Above, in the spiritual realm, this is understood to refer to the very origin of the souls of the Jewish nation. Since we say about them that "G-d's portion is His nation,"[174] Jews are part and parcel of the G-dly light. And since their soul-source is *ayn*, it is as if they are from a point, which we call *keren*...

This is also what is meant by *ayn mazal l'Yisroel*, which can be read as "there is no fortune [in the stars] for the Jews" or "The divine void is the fortune of the Jews." Proof of this is to be found regarding Abraham, to whom G-d said [regarding the number of stars], "Like these (*koh*) will be the number of your offspring."[175] *Koh* refers to *malchut*, the final *sephira*, which is *ayn*, since the beginning is wedged into the end ... Thus, G-d took Abraham outside and told him "Look at the sky and count the stars ... See if you can count them. [*Koh* ("like these") will be the number of your off-

And He established them forever, an immutable law, not to
be transgressed.

Praised be the Lord from the earth, the serpents and all of the depths.

Fire and hail, snow and mist, stormy winds all do His bidding.

The mountains and all of the hills, fruit trees and all the cedars.

The wild beasts and all animals, crawling creatures and winged fowl.
The kings of the earth and all the nations, ministers and all judges of
the earth.

Young men as well as maidens, the elderly with the youth.
Praised be the name of the Lord, for His name is exalted alone, His
majesty over the land and the heavens.
And He raises the status of His people, the praise of all His pious ones,
the Jews, His close people, Halleluyah!

CHASSIDIC EXCERPTS

spring.]" Thus, the verse implies a quantity that defies counting and is indeed beyond numbers, as written elsewhere...

This, then is what is meant by "And He shall raise the prestige of His people," meaning that He elevates the aspect that is called the *keren* of the Jews, as mentioned, and raises it above to the level called *ayn*, meaning to the light of *keter*.

(From the Alter Rebbe's Siddur, p. 67a)

Elevated level of prestige
Vayarem keren le'amo ("And He shall raise the prestige of His people") – Psalm 148

And so it is written,[176] *vayarem keren le'amo* ("And He shall raise the prestige of His people..."). *Keren* ("prestige") indicates descent of essential G-dliness from above. In the previous verse, the psalm said, "Since His name is exalted, alone," meaning that His name is exalted and elevated, and only a ray and reflection [of G-dliness] descends to the earth and the heavens. However, "He raised the prestige of His people," meaning that His people, by way of Torah and mitzvoth draw down the level and aspect called *keren*, which is an expression of essential G-dliness. This ties in [with the conclusion of the verse and the entire psalm] which reads, "for the children of Israel, Your intimate nation," since they are close to the [essential] name of G-d, *Havaya*. [The two names], *Havaya* and *Elokim*, reflect the distinction between essence and mere existence. Regarding the name *Elokim*, the Torah says, *Breishit barah Elokim* ("In the beginning, *Elokim* created"), which is the *tzimtzum* ("contraction") that hides and conceals the essence. And the name *Havaya* represents essence alone, which is why the verse says, "to the children of Israel, Your intimate nation," meaning that they are close to the name *Havaya*...

(From *Sefer Maamorim 5663* (1903), vol. 2 of the Rebbe Rashab, page 169)

הַלְלוּיָהּ, שִׁירוּ לַיָי שִׁיר חָדָשׁ, תְּהִלָּתוֹ בִּקְהַל חֲסִידִים:

יִשְׂמַח יִשְׂרָאֵל בְּעֹשָׂיו, בְּנֵי צִיּוֹן יָגִילוּ בְמַלְכָּם:

יְהַלְלוּ שְׁמוֹ בְמָחוֹל, בְּתֹף וְכִנּוֹר יְזַמְּרוּ לוֹ:

כִּי רוֹצֶה יְיָ בְּעַמּוֹ, יְפָאֵר עֲנָוִים בִּישׁוּעָה:

יַעְלְזוּ חֲסִידִים בְּכָבוֹד, יְרַנְּנוּ עַל מִשְׁכְּבוֹתָם:

רוֹמְמוֹת אֵל בִּגְרוֹנָם, וְחֶרֶב פִּיפִיּוֹת בְּיָדָם:

לַעֲשׂוֹת נְקָמָה בַּגּוֹיִם, תּוֹכֵחוֹת בַּלְאֻמִּים:

לֶאְסֹר מַלְכֵיהֶם בְּזִקִּים, וְנִכְבְּדֵיהֶם בְּכַבְלֵי בַרְזֶל:

לַעֲשׂוֹת בָּהֶם מִשְׁפָּט כָּתוּב, הָדָר הוּא לְכָל חֲסִידָיו, הַלְלוּיָהּ:

CHASSIDIC EXCERPTS

Root of all song

Halleluya, shiru l'HaShem shir hadash - "Praise G-d, sing to G-d a new song" –
Psalm 149

In order to understand what is meant by *shir hadash* ("new song"), first we must grasp why the psalm calls it (a masculine) *shir* and not (the feminine) *shira*.

The root of all song is ascent, from below to Above. Wherever there is spiritual ascent, there is song. This is evident from the Talmud[177] which states, "Go out with song..." [the Mishna tells us that just as we are forbidden to carry on Shabbat, so the animals under our jurisdiction are forbidden to work or carry on Shabbat. The Mishna deals with some specific cases. One is that of an animal carrying a chain, called a *shir* in Hebrew, which it normally carries during the week as well. The Mishna says, "All those animals which have a chain (*shir*) may go out in their chain (*shir*) and may be led by them." This tells us that it is permitted for the animal to wear the chain and to be led by the chain on Shabbat. But, since the word for chain is *shir*, meaning "song"

in Hebrew, the Chasidic commentaries interpreted the Mishna as, "All those who ascend, do so by song, and are led by song." So, in the mishna], carrying refers to going out from a lower level and ascending to a higher world, just like the angels who sing every day ... However, all elevations of the worlds are called *shira* (in the feminine) since all the worlds were created from *malchut* [the final *sephira* which receives G-dly influx from the *sephirot* above it and creates the worlds below it] of the World of *Atzilut* ... This process is described as feminine, since *malchut* receives from the *sephirot* that are above it, namely from the six emotional *sephirot* that precede *malchut*. Similarly, all of the worlds receive from *malchut*, as it is written *malchutecha malchut kol olamim* ("Your reign is the reign over all worlds").

There is a second reason why the elevation of the worlds are described in the feminine, and that is because the cre-

*H*alleluyah, sing a new song to the Lord, His praise among the
pious ones.

The Jews rejoice in their Maker, the sons of Zion delight in their King.

Praise be His name in dance, with drums and harp they will sing to Him.

For, the Lord desires His people, He glorifies the humble with salvation.

The pious ones will revel in honor, they will sing upon their beds.

The greatness of G-d is in their throats, and a double-edged sword in
their hands.

To take revenge among the nations, and rebuke the people.

To imprison their kings in chains, and their notables in iron cables.

To fulfill upon them the written judgment, this will be glory for all of
His pious ones, Halleluyah.

CHASSIDIC EXCERPTS

ation of all three lower worlds BY"A stems from the primordial process known as the "shattering of the vessels." In this process, the *kelim* ("vessels") of the higher World of *Tohu* ("Chaos") shattered and fell below. This is alluded to in the verse from the Torah, "These were the kings who reigned in the land of Edom before any king reigned over Israel..."[178] These Edomite kings "reigned and died," as described there, and they allude to the descent of holy sparks to this physical world where they must be refined, elevated and returned to their spiritual source. The purification process is associated with the "Tree of Knowledge of Good and Bad," and it takes place in the three lower worlds of BY"A, where there is a mixture of good and bad among all of the creations [both physical and spiritual]. The good within them must be separated and elevated ... For this reason, everywhere the elevation of *malchut* is mentioned, it is described as a *shira* (in the feminine)...

Now, all this describes the purification of the 288 fallen sparks which are then called *shira*, alluding to the eleva-

tion of the feminine *sephira* of *malchut*, as mentioned. However, in the future – when "death is banished forever," and the spirit of impurity is totally vanquished and banished from the land – at that time, no purification process will be necessary. It will no longer be appropriate to term the process of elevation by the name *shira*, since all of the *malchiyut* will have been purified already. Rather, the spiritual ascent will then be named *shir*, using the masculine form, since all of the feminine sparks from the "kings of *Tohu*" will have been elevated already. What will remain will be the masculine *sephirot* of *Ze'er Anpin* of the World of *Atzilut* [the six *sephirot* that precede and give to *malchut*], and that world will undergo a further elevation, beyond where it presently exists ... However, this elevation is unlike the purification process which accompanied the elevation of the feminine sparks which was called *shira*. This elevation will come from *Ze'er Anpin* itself [as opposed to from "outside" influence]... [and this is the reason that it is termed *shir* in the masculine form].

הַ‏לְלוּיָהּ, הַלְלוּ אֵל בְּקָדְשׁוֹ, הַלְלוּהוּ בִּרְקִיעַ עֻזּוֹ:

הַלְלוּהוּ בִגְבוּרֹתָיו. הַלְלוּהוּ כְּרֹב גֻּדְלוֹ:

הַלְלוּהוּ בְּתֵקַע שׁוֹפָר, הַלְלוּהוּ בְּנֵבֶל וְכִנּוֹר:

CHASSIDIC EXCERPTS

So, this is what is meant by "Praise G-d, sing to G-d a new song." In the future, spiritual ascent will not come as the result of a purification process [in which good is removed from bad]. Following the present elevations, there will be more spiritual elevations to come, approaching yet higher levels of essential G-dliness, known as *shir chadash* ("a new song"). The reason it is called "new" is because, until now, there has been no G-dly illumination of this sort in the universe, coming from a spiritual origin that transcends the shattering of the vessels and the subsequent rectification. In our world of *tikkun*, there is nothing "new," since everything in this world has its origin in the process called *shivrei kelim* ("shattering of the vessels").

Now, even though there has never been such a spiritual elevation as this *shir chadash*, and it will not occur until the future, nevertheless, every Shabbat something similar to this "new song" illuminates the day, as is known regarding the difference between the days of the week and Shabbat. This is because during the week, we are involved in the *birrur* ("refinement") of the world, while Shabbat is a time for spiritual elevation alone...

(From the Alter Rebbe's *Siddur*, p. 67a)

A celestial orchestra

Halleluhu betekah shofar - "Praise Him with the call of the ram's horn" – Psalm 150

Until now, the *Pesukei DeZimra* alluded to the G-dly light descending from *Atzilut* to *Yetzira*, which is why the phrase *bekadsho* ("His holiness") and *biraki'a uzo* ("in the heaven of His power") are mentioned [in the first verses of this psalm]. They correspond to the highest three *sephirot* (*keter*, *chochma* and *bina*).[179]

Halleluhu kerov gudelo ("Praise Him in His abundant greatness") corresponds to *chesed* of *Atzilut*, followed by *gevura* of *Atzilut*, which when clad in *Yetzira* brings down and creates the *kelim* "vessels") of *Yetzira*. [At that point], they are similar to the *kelim* ("instruments") of song. Even though musical instruments are the main method of expressing music, nevertheless they are separate and distinct from man, and so the creation of spiritual illumination through the medium of *Yetzira* is like a voice, created by man but separate from him. Here, the allusion is to the *chagat* (*chesed*, *gevura* and *tiferet*) of *Atzilut* as it becomes en-clothed in *chagat* of *Yetzira*...

This, then, is what is meant by *halleluhu betekah shofar* ("Praise Him with the call of the ram's horn"). The sound of the *shofar* is not the sound of a typical musical instrument, which produces a sweet and melodious tone; indeed, there is no element of sweetness in the sound of the *shofar*. Quite the opposite; it is a sound that instills trembling in the heart of the one who hears it, as the verse alleluyah, praise G-d in His holiness, praise Him in the firmament of His strength.

Praise Him for His mighty deeds, praise Him for all of His greatness.

Praise Him with blowing of the shofar, praise Him with lyre and harp.

CHASSIDIC EXCERPTS

says, "If the ram's horn is blown in the city, is there anyone who is not frightened?"[180] And during the giving of the Torah, it is recorded that "the sound of the ram's horn was very loud, and the people in the camp trembled."[181] That is, the voice of the *shofar* corresponds to *gevura* of *Yetzira*, which receives illumination from *gevura* of *Atzilut*. From there, the angel Gabriel and his camp derive their song, accompanied by the awesome voice of the *shofar*, which instills fear and trembling, as written regarding the *chayot* [angels of *Yetzira*], who "tremble" before G-d. This is what is meant by "Praise Him with the call of the ram's horn," which applies to the angels ... Their fear is inspired by the holy illumination emerging from *Atzilut*, by way of the sound of the *shofar*.

*

Halleluhu benevel vechinor ("Praise Him with harp and lyre")

Here, the psalm alludes to *tiferet* of *Zeir Anpin* (the lower seven *sephirot* of *Atzilut*), as it becomes clad in *Yetzira*. In so doing, it becomes associated with the camp of the angel Uriel [the angel of light and mercy] ... The *sephira* of *tiferet* includes three different "colors" – green, red and white. When all three appear together, rather than each on its own, then and only then do they produce a nice and pleasant spectacle, which reflects well on their Creator. When this happens, it is termed *tiferet* ("harmony/beauty").

And so it is with the voice that emerges from the breath of the heart – it includes three different facets, corresponding to the three colors mentioned above. The three are fire, wind and water, which correspond to *chagat* (*chesed*, *gevura* and *tiferet*), and they also correspond to the three expressions of joy, bitterness, and of an intermediary that joins the two together. It is not called a sweet voice unless it includes all three of the above together – joy, bitterness and their intermediary. [Together], they comprise a *nigun* ("melody") composed of various voices interspersed in different ways. Some express joy, some express the opposite, and their expressions may reverse, as well ... in this, they are similar to the interaction of the colors, and this is called harmony of the voices...

Similarly, regarding the spiritual worlds it is written, "The voice of G-d in harmony,"[182] alluding to *tiferet* of *Zeir Anpin*. But in this instance, the allusion is to the G-dly attributes of *Atzilut*, where "He and His illumination are one"[183] within the infinite light of G-d Above. But when this illumination descends to *Yetzira*, it becomes enclad in *kelim*. This is similar, by way of example, to the musical instruments, the harp and the lyre. The notes emerging from the harp and from the lyre are balanced and harmonized in various ways, and that is why their music is pleasant, as it is written "a pleasant lyre with harp."[184]

*

הַלְלוּהוּ בְתֹף וּמָחוֹל, הַלְלוּהוּ בְּמִנִּים וְעֻנָב:

הַלְלוּהוּ בְצִלְצְלֵי שָׁמַע, הַלְלוּהוּ בְּצִלְצְלֵי תְרוּעָה:

כֹּל הַנְּשָׁמָה תְּהַלֵּל יָהּ הַלְלוּיָהּ:

כֹּל הַנְּשָׁמָה תְּהַלֵּל יָהּ הַלְלוּיָהּ:

CHASSIDIC EXCERPTS

Halleluhu betof umachol, halleluhu beminim ve'ugav ("Praise Him with drums and dance, praise Him with strings and flute")

After the psalm alluded to the three levels of *chagat* of *Atzilut*, which en-clothe themselves in *chagat* of *Yetzira*, it continues by alluding to *netzach* ("proactivity" or "victory") and *hod* ("reactivity" or "acknowledgment") of *Atzilut* as they become en-clothed in *netzach* and *hod* of *Yetzira*. These correspond to the two musical instruments mentioned here – the *tof* ("drum") and the *ugav* ("flute"). The sound of the drum is noisy and loud, with the sole purpose of providing support and reinforcement of the heart, as is known. The goal is to strengthen the resolve of the heart, so that the people maintain their will-power, without collapsing under any circumstances. Now, even though *netzach* has its origin in the "right side," [the side of kindness], nevertheless it also includes aspects of the "left side," the side of strictness. Therefore, the expression of *netzach* contains some aspects of strength and power, lending reinforcement to the heart.

However, the other musical instruments – *minim* ("strings") and *ugav* ("flute") – correspond to the *sephira* of *hod*. It also includes the "right side," the side of kindness, just as in the World of *Atzilut* there is inter-inclusion of *chesed* and *gevura*, as is known regarding Abraham and Isaac. The two included each other, as there were aspects of love

within Isaac's personality, though it was hidden while the element of fear was conscious and revealed. The opposite was true regarding Abraham – there were elements of fear within his personality, but his love was dominant and conscious while fear was hidden. In any case, each included elements of the other's personality traits and path in serving G-d. Similarly, *chesed* and *gevura* in the World of *Yetzira* display inter-inclusion, and if so, *netzach* and *hod*, which are offshoots of *chesed* and *gevura*, and called their "branches" (*netzach* is a branch of *chesed*, while *hod* is a branch of *gevura*) are also inter-inclusive, just like *chesed* and *gevura*. This is why the psalm says "Praise Him with drums ... and praise Him with strings and flute," indicating all of them together and inter-included, for the reasons explained.

The drum (*tof*) is mentioned after the harp (*nevel*) and lyre (*kinor*), because the harp and lyre correspond to the *sephira* of *tiferet* ("harmony"), which is all-inclusive. And immediately afterward, the psalm mentions drums, strings and flute (as well as dance) ... since dance takes place in a circle, uniting the opposite ends of the spectrum of *chesed* and *gevura* (lyre and drums). This is why in our psalm, drums and dance are mentioned after the harp and lyre.

In general, ten types of musical instruments are mentioned here, corresponding to the ten *sephirot* within the hidden recesses of the Emanator, to

Praise Him with drums and dance, Praise Him with stringed instruments and flute.

Praise Him with resounding cymbals, praise Him with amplifying cymbals.

Let every soul praise Y-H, Halleluyah,

Let every soul praise Y-H, Halleluyah!

CHASSIDIC EXCERPTS

bring them into revelation in the worlds of *ABY'A...*

*

Halleluhu betziltzelei shama, halleluyah betziltzelei teruah ("Praise Him with resounding cymbals, praise Him with clanging cymbals")

The purpose of the instrument called the resounding cymbal is to amplify the tones of the other instruments, and for that purpose, it produces a strong tone that is heard from afar. Above, this is understood to correspond to the spiritual illumination of the *sephira* of *yesod*, which includes G-dly influx from all the other *sephirot*. In the language of the *Zohar*, *yesod* is called the "ingathering of lights," or the "assembly of all illumination," as known, and it is the illumination that shines from the *mashpia* ("mentor/giver") to the *mekabel* ("beneficiary/receiver"). This is not true of [the higher *sephirot* of] *netzach* and *hod*, known as the "advisors," which supply advice but which do not yet put it into practice. However, from *yesod*, the influx becomes directly revealed to the receivers. This is similar to the action in the physical world of the musical instruments known as the *metzaltayim*, which amplify the music for the sake of the listeners. For that reason, they are also called here *tziltzelei shama* ("resounding cymbals"), since they enable people to listen (*shomim*). Thus, everyone who listens receives the music from them.

While the previous verses alluded to *chagat* (the *sephirot* of *chesed, gevura*

and *tiferet*) and to *netzach* and *hod*, this verse alludes to *yesod* of the world of *Atzilut*, as it is enclad in *yesod* of *Yetzira...*

Now, the psalm continues and concludes with *Halleluyah betziltzelei teruah*, corresponding to *malchut*, the final *sephira* of *Atzilut*. These instruments are called *tziltzelei teruah* ("clanging cymbals") because the word *teruah* is related to *tero'em*, as in *tero'em beshevet barzel* ("strike with an iron staff"), indicating that *truah* involves striking or hitting something. It is related as well to the sound of a reverberating ram's horn, [which is cacophonous, like] a scattering and separation of voices, as known. This is because *malchut* is associated with *dina rafyah* ("gentle judgment") being strictness that is mitigated by sweetness, breaking the harshness of *gevura* ...this is why it is called *teruah*.

*

Kol haneshama tehalel Yah ("Let every soul praise G-d")

Until now, the psalms alluded to the ten *sephirot* of *Atzilut* as they descend to the World of *Yetzira* to provide spiritual illumination and energy for the angels. The angels are collectively called a *merkava* ("chariot"), which is a vehicle that is nullified to its driver. In this sense, they correspond to the ten musical instruments mentioned previously (the ram's horn, harp, lyre, drums, dance, strings, flute, resounding cymbals and clanging cymbals). However, all of this is true only regarding the ex-

בָּ֑רוּךְ יְיָ לְעוֹלָם אָמֵן וְאָמֵן:

בָּרוּךְ יְיָ מִצִּיּוֹן שֹׁכֵן יְרוּשָׁלָֽיִם הַלְלוּיָהּ:

בָּרוּךְ יְיָ אֱלֹהִים אֱלֹהֵי יִשְׂרָאֵל, עֹשֵׂה נִפְלָאוֹת לְבַדּוֹ:

וּבָרוּךְ שֵׁם כְּבוֹדוֹ לְעוֹלָם, וְיִמָּלֵא כְבוֹדוֹ אֶת כָּל הָאָֽרֶץ, אָמֵן וְאָמֵן:

CHASSIDIC EXCERPTS

ternal dimensions of the worlds, as expressed by the musical instruments [since they are vessels that express G-dliness outwardly]. Souls, though, come from the inner dimensions, meaning the lights (orot) of the worlds [as opposed to vessels (kelim)]. And souls are all-inclusive, meaning they contain all of the partzufim (structures of sephirot) together ... therefore, the soul is described as inclusive, as we say, "Let every being that has a soul..." "Every" is an inclusive term, since every soul includes everything within it.

So, after the psalm spoke of the descent of the ten sephirot of Atzilut into the external angels of Yetzira, now the psalm tells us that the ten sephirot of every partzuf ("structure" of ten sephirot), from arich and atik [within keter, highest of the sephirot] down to malchut [lowest of the sephirot] are all included within the soul. So, every soul praises G-d with all types of praise and halleluyah, up to the infinite light of G-d en-clothed in av'a (chochma and bina), represented by [the two letters] yud and hey [the first two letters of G-d's name]. And for that reason, the [song of the] souls is not referred to in such detail as that of the angels, since souls are all-inclusive. Therefore, we say simply, "Let every being that has a soul praise Him," since souls are inclusive.

(From the Siddur of the Alter Rebbe, page 70d)

The highest descends to the lowest
Blessed be the Lord, G-d Who is the G-d of Israel, Who alone performs wonders

Here, the words "Lord, G-d..." refer to the kabalistic range called av'a (av v'aim, or "father and mother," corresponding to chochma and bina)...this is the mochin ("mindfulness") that descend to z'a (zeir anpin, or "minor countenance," corresponding to the lower seven sephirot of Atzilut that follow chochma and bina), also known as "Yerushalayim." Thus, the explanation is as follows, Baruch Havaya Elokim (intelligent mindfulness of chochma and bina flows into z'a) to become Elokei Yisrael – "the G-d of Israel." And from z'a,

*B*lessed be the Lord forever, Amen and amen

Blessed be the Lord from Zion, dwelling in Jerusalem, Halleluyah!
Blessed be the Lord, G-d Who is the G-d of Israel, Who alone
performs wonders.
And blessed be His glorious name forever, and let the whole earth be
filled with His glory, Amen and amen.

CHASSIDIC EXCERPTS

malchut is "blessed," from "one world to another..."

And the phrase that follows, "Who alone performs wonders..." is understood according to the general principle that whatever exists on the highest spiritual level is most capable of lowering itself to the lowest level. And whatever is not as high is unable to descend to such a great degree. So, it emerges that from its descent, we are able to deduce the "original" spiritual level above. As we see regarding the wisest of men – he is able to lower himself in order to explain a deep concept even to a toddler, since he is capable of en-clothing a concept so that it may descend many levels. It may descend, for example, by using a multitude of parables, one parable after another, just as in the parables (*Mishlei*) of King Solomon, about whom the sages said that he could provide three thousand parables[185] [in order to explain a concept]. Each parable explained and descended to the next. And this was a result of the tremendous power of his wisdom above – which enabled him to en-clothe his wisdom in three thousand parables. Similarly, the sages said about R' Meir that he was capable of providing three hundred parables,[186] as written elsewhere.

The counterpart is understood above; the descent of the infinite light to become *baruch*, or "blessed," and descend from *av'a* into *zu'n*, all the way down, to such a great extent, indicates that the illumination comes from a very high level, since the amount of descent is in proportion to the original spiritual height.

This is what is meant, then by "Blessed be the Lord, G-d..." The descent of this blessing to the lowest levels, as it says soon, "And blessed be His glory forever..." down to the lowest level, is only possible because "He alone performs miracles." That is, since the light comes from the essence of the Emanator, the inner dimension of *atik* and *arich,* called "wonders," meaning to say, that they are the most hidden and concealed [levels]...

From the *siddur* of the Alter Rebbe with chasidut, page 142 (71B)

‫יְבָרֶךְ דָּוִיד אֶת יְיָ לְעֵינֵי כָּל הַקָּהָל וַיֹּאמֶר דָּוִיד, בָּרוּךְ אַתָּה יְיָ אֱלֹהֵי יִשְׂרָאֵל‬
‫אָבִינוּ, מֵעוֹלָם וְעַד עוֹלָם:‬

‫לְךָ יְיָ הַגְּדֻלָּה, וְהַגְּבוּרָה, וְהַתִּפְאֶרֶת, וְהַנֵּצַח, וְהַהוֹד, כִּי כֹל בַּשָּׁמַיִם וּבָאָרֶץ:‬

‫לְךָ יְיָ הַמַּמְלָכָה וְהַמִּתְנַשֵּׂא, לְכֹל לְרֹאשׁ:‬

‫וְהָעֹשֶׁר וְהַכָּבוֹד מִלְּפָנֶיךָ, וְאַתָּה מוֹשֵׁל בַּכֹּל, וּבְיָדְךָ כֹּחַ וּגְבוּרָה, וּבְיָדְךָ, לְגַדֵּל‬
‫וּלְחַזֵּק לַכֹּל:‬

‫וְעַתָּה אֱלֹהֵינוּ מוֹדִים, אֲנַחְנוּ לָךְ וּמְהַלְלִים לְשֵׁם תִּפְאַרְתֶּךָ:‬

‫וִיבָרְכוּ שֵׁם כְּבוֹדֶךָ וּמְרוֹמַם עַל כָּל בְּרָכָה וּתְהִלָּה:‬

‫אַתָּה הוּא יְיָ לְבַדֶּךָ, אַתָּה עָשִׂיתָ אֶת הַשָּׁמַיִם שְׁמֵי הַשָּׁמַיִם וְכָל צְבָאָם, הָאָרֶץ‬
‫וְכָל אֲשֶׁר עָלֶיהָ, הַיַּמִּים וְכָל אֲשֶׁר בָּהֶם, וְאַתָּה מְחַיֶּה אֶת כֻּלָּם, וּצְבָא הַשָּׁמַיִם‬
‫לְךָ מִשְׁתַּחֲוִים:‬

CHASSIDIC EXCERPTS

Abraham's love for G-d
Atah Hu, HaShem, levadecha. Atah asita et hashamayim…"You are He, G-d, alone Who made the heavens" – (Nechemia 9:5-11)

The word *levadecha* ("alone") alludes to the very essence of G-dliness, beyond the two perspectives [of higher and lower unity (*da'at elyon* and *da'at tachton*)]. G-d alone created the heavens, as well as the earth (which is the *ayn*, or "spiritual void" that precedes the *yesh*, or "physical existence" of the world). And, as the psalm continues to relate, He chose Abram [and renamed him Abraham] having found his heart "trustworthy," meaning capable of *ahava raba* ("great love"), and his ego nullified to what was spiritually above him. And

then, G-d "established a covenant with him." The purpose of the covenant was to further strengthen Abraham's amazing love and absolute attachment to G-d, to attain *yichuda ila'ah* ("supernal unity"), wherein awareness of G-d predominates and the world seems secondary. However, the purpose of the covenant was [also] to connect Abraham's love of G-d based upon reason and logic, with his love that surpassed intellect – thus linking and uniting the two perspectives. Through this process, Abraham purged the seven attributes of

Rise and remain standing until after "בָּרְכוּ"

And David blessed the Lord in the eyes of the entire congregation, and David said, "Blessed are You, Lord, God of Israel our father, in all realms.

To You, Lord belongs the greatness, the might, the harmony, the victory and the majesty, for all that is in the heavens and on the earth [is Yours]. The reign is Yours, Lord, and You are exalted over all other leaders.

The wealth and the honor come from You, and You govern over all, and in Your hand are power and might, and it is in Your hand to aggrandize and to strengthen everyone.

And now, our G-d, we acknowledge You, and we praise Your harmonious name.

And [Israel] will bless Your honorable name, and exalt it over all blessings and praise.

You, Lord, are alone, You made the heavens and the heaven's heavens, and all of their hosts, the earth and all that is upon it, the seas and all that is within them, and You enliven them all, and the hosts of the heavens bow down to You.

CHASSIDIC EXCERPTS

negative love (called here the "Canaanites, Hittites," etc.) from himself and his descendents. This occurs as we recite the words [of the *Shema*]: *bechol levavcha* ("with all of your hearts"), meaning with both inclinations (the evil and the G-dly).

And, therefore, *vatakam et devarecha* ("You fulfilled your words") - G-d uttered the divine words from which the entire chain of creation, from nothing to something, was created. [This chain of creation is so complete that it even includes] life-force for the Canaanite nation ... but since the Jews are linked and joined together with the essence of G-dliness from Above to below, they were purged of the influence and attachment of the seven idol-worshipping nations. The Torah says about them, "Do not leave any soul alive,"[187] that is, "remove whatever G-dly life-force remains hidden in them," in the most convoluted and superfluous places as a result of myriad contractions of G-dly illumination. By dint of revelation of His infinite light from Above to below, even the letters that enliven the [evil] *sitra achra* ("other side") ascend, to become included in G-dliness.

(From *Sefer Maamorim* 5655 (1895-6) of the Rebbe Rashab, pp. 125-126)

אַתָּה הוּא יְיָ הָאֱלֹהִים אֲשֶׁר בָּחַרְתָּ בְּאַבְרָם וְהוֹצֵאתוֹ מֵאוּר כַּשְׂדִּים, וְשַׂמְתָּ שְּׁמוֹ אַבְרָהָם:

וּמָצָאתָ אֶת לְבָבוֹ נֶאֱמָן לְפָנֶיךָ:

וְכָרוֹת עִמּוֹ הַבְּרִית לָתֵת אֶת אֶרֶץ הַכְּנַעֲנִי. הַחִתִּי הָאֱמֹרִי וְהַפְּרִזִּי וְהַיְבוּסִי וְהַגִּרְגָּשִׁי לָתֵת לְזַרְעוֹ, וַתָּקֶם אֶת דְּבָרֶיךָ כִּי צַדִּיק אָתָּה:

וַתֵּרֶא אֶת עֳנִי אֲבוֹתֵינוּ בְּמִצְרָיִם, וְאֶת זַעֲקָתָם שָׁמַעְתָּ עַל יַם סוּף:

CHASSIDIC EXCERPTS

Abraham purified sparks

Vecarot imo habrit – "And You made the covenant with him [Abraham], granting him the land of the Canaanites ... and You fulfilled Your words, since You are righteous..." (Nechemia 9:5-11)

At first glance, why was it necessary to state the reason, "since You are righteous"? Where is the righteousness here, since in any case G-d must keep His word?

In order to clarify this, we must first explain the preceding words, "You are He, Lord, Who alone made the heavens and the heaven's heavens ... You are He, Lord Almighty, Who chose Abram ... and changed his name to Abraham ... and established a covenant with him ... and fulfilled Your words..."

There is logical flow and continuity to these verses. [Earlier in the discourse], it was explained that the soul is capable of achieving comprehension of spiritual levels that transcend *bina* ("intellectual analysis"), all the way up to the essential infinite G-dly light that transcends the *tzimtzum* ("contraction" of His holy light). This occurs because the infinite G-dly light undergoes contraction in order to be graspable within the *sephira* ("divine emanation") of *bina*, while the soul itself is rooted in the essential, infinite G-dly light. This is what is meant by "You are He, Lord, Who alone ..." The verse refers to levels of infinite illumination that transcend the *tzimtzum*. By "alone" here is meant the equivalent of

haya hu ushemo bilvad ("there was He and His name alone"). It also corresponds to the word *Atah*, which elsewhere alludes to the essential infinite One, while *Hu* ("He") alludes to G-dly illumination. And the four-letter name *Havaya* alludes to expression and expansion of His infinite illumination. All of the above is included in the word *levadecha* ("alone") – He and His name are alone.

The phrase "You made the heavens and the heaven's heavens" alludes to *makifim* – which are transcendent levels of supernal G-dliness, such as *tehiru ila'ah* and *tehiru tata'ah* [spiritual levels just prior and just subsequent to the *tzimtzum*]. It also includes the transcendent levels associated with the World of *Tohu* [also known as *keter*, the "crown" or supernal will that supercedes the World of *Atzilut*]. The words, "And the earth and all that is upon it" alludes to the World of *Tikkun* (*Atzilut*), while the "sea" and "land" refer to the "concealed" and "revealed" worlds, respectively, rooted in the *sephirot* of *bina* and *malchut* [of *Atzilut*]...

And from *bina* and *malchut*, more contraction takes place in order to clad the G-dly energy and vitality in the letters of the name *Elokim*, about which we

You, Lord are G-d, Who chose Avram, and took him out of the land of
Ur Chasdim, and changed his name to Avraham.

And You found his heart to be true to You.

And You formed a covenant with him, [promising] to give the land of
the Canaanites, the Chitites, the Emorites, the Perizites and the Jebusites
and the Girgashites to his descendents, and You fulfilled Your word,
since You are just.
And You took note of the poverty of our ancestors in Egypt, and their
cries, and you heard them at the edge of the Reed Sea.

CHASSIDIC EXCERPTS

say, "And You enliven all of them," utilizing the letters from *alef* to *tav* in conjunction with the five modes of oral expression [the tongue, the palate, the
teeth, the throat and the lips]. These are
letters of speech and of thought, including the five *gevurot* ("stringencies") that
divide [the emotions of the heart and intellect of the mind into letters and
words], as is known. And from this
[speech and thought] are created all the
creatures of the lower worlds of *Bria,
Yetzira* and *Asiya*, including the heavenly legions [stars and planets], which
prostrate themselves to G-d [while orbit-
ing] in self-nullification.

Now, all this is quite evident to the
soul, which has a clear grasp of the infinite G-dly illumination that precedes the
tzimtzum, as well as of transcendent and
imminent G-dliness, all the way down to
the lower worlds of *Bria, Yetzira* and
Asiya. Following upon this, [we say],
"You are He, G-d Almighty, who chose
Abram," since after meditation and
grasp of the infinite G-dly illumination,
we receive a spirit of arousal of love of
G-liness. This is expressed in the phrase
"Who chose Abram," since Abram
loved G-d mightily. Abram achieved his
recognition and love of the Creator by
utilizing intellectual grasp and powers
of cognition. And this is what is meant
by, "And He brought him out of Ur
Kasdim." This is an allusion to Abram's

exit from the evil of the *sitra achra* and
subsequent withstanding all of the tests
that G-d put to him. All this was due to
his recognition of G-dliness and the
great arousal [of love] that he experienced.

"And He changed his name to
Abraham," adding the letter *hey*. Abraham became "father to many nations,"
in order to purify and rectify the seven
nations, who represent the seven negative character attributes. And this G-d
did because He "found Abraham's heart
trustworthy," meaning that He found
Abraham capable of purifying and refining [the world]. Consequently, it follows
that, "He established a covenant with
him, granting him and his descendants
the land of Canaan," in order to refine
the seven attributes of the "other side."

[The passage continues: "And You
fulfilled (*va'takem*) Your words" –
va'takem can also be translated as "And
You raised ..."]

Although the Torah commanded
the Jews, "Do not leave any soul [of the
seven Canaanite nations] alive," this
was in order to destroy the evil among
them. Still, it was necessary to elevate
the positive sparks of holiness that were
among them, as well. This is what is
meant by, "And You fulfilled/raised
Your words," referring to supernal, spiritual words – that is, to the holy sparks.
It was necessary to raise and elevate

וַתִּתֵּן אֹתֹת וּמֹפְתִים בְּפַרְעֹה וּבְכָל עֲבָדָיו וּבְכָל עַם אַרְצוֹ, כִּי יָדַעְתָּ כִּי הֵזִידוּ
עֲלֵיהֶם וַתַּעַשׂ לְךָ שֵׁם כְּהַיּוֹם הַזֶּה:

וְהַיָּם בָּקַעְתָּ לִפְנֵיהֶם וַיַּעַבְרוּ בְתוֹךְ הַיָּם בַּיַּבָּשָׁה, וְאֶת רֹדְפֵיהֶם הִשְׁלַכְתָּ בִמְצוֹלֹת
כְּמוֹ אֶבֶן בְּמַיִם עַזִּים:

שירת הים

וַיּוֹשַׁע יְיָ בַּיּוֹם הַהוּא אֶת יִשְׂרָאֵל מִיַּד מִצְרָיִם, וַיַּרְא יִשְׂרָאֵל אֶת מִצְרַיִם מֵת
עַל שְׂפַת הַיָּם:

וַיַּרְא יִשְׂרָאֵל אֶת הַיָּד הַגְּדֹלָה אֲשֶׁר עָשָׂה יְיָ בְּמִצְרַיִם וַיִּירְאוּ הָעָם אֶת יְיָ, וַיַּאֲמִינוּ
בַּיָי וּבְמשֶׁה עַבְדּוֹ:

them, so that they would ascend and become included within the realm of holiness.

About this, it is said "Because You are righteous." Here the word for "righteous" (tzaddik) alludes to the sephira of yesod [the ninth sephira, representing connection and communication in the soul – through this attribute, we connect with the tzadik and he with G-d] in this case yesod of [the very high level known as] Adam Kadmon ("Primordial Man"). The Torah calls this level the "eighth king," whose name was Hadar, and who was a source of the World of Tikkun. [The Torah lists the names of seven kings of Edom, all of whom "reigned and died."[188] But, the Torah mentions the eighth king, Hadar, without saying that he died. Kabbalah interprets this to mean that he was the source of the World of Tikkun, in which the sephirot do not "flame out" and "die" as did the seven lower sephirot of Tohu, but continue to exist in harmony with each other. This harmony is what characterizes the World of Tikkun, or Atzilut.]

It is the nature of one who is good, to do good, and so is the nature of a tzaddik, as the verse says, "Say about the tzaddik that he is good."[189] And the ultimate good is to descend to the lowest spiritual levels in order to gather and elevate the sparks that are present there. [These may be], for example, the souls of converts, which may be very high souls that were caught in the depths of the "shells" (klipot) – [which are so called because just as a shell conceals within itself something edible, so the klipot conceal the good within them] – and ascended from there to the ultimate levels of good, like the souls of Shemaya and Avtalyon[190] and of Rabbi Meir, and others. And, as well, like the true ba'alei teshuva such as Rabbi Eliezer ben Durdaya and Natan Tzutzita, etc.[191]

This, then, is what is meant by "and You fulfilled/raised Your words." The verse refers to the letters and sparks that fell all the way down into the depths. It is necessary to raise them from their low state and elevate them from the dust. And this takes place because "You are righteous," and the nature of good is to do good. And so it is among Jewish souls involved in avodat habirurim ("service of rectification") of the world's physical objects. When we eat physical food with intention to elevate it to its

And You delivered signs and wonders to Pharoah and to all of his servants and all of his land, since You knew that they wronged the Jews, and You made a name for Yourself to this very day.
And You split the sea in front of them, and lead them through the sea to the dry land, and You hurled their pursuers down to the depths, like stones in raging waters.

Song of The Sea

And on that day, the Lord saved Israel from the hand of the Egyptians, and Israel saw the Egyptians dead at the edge of the sea.

And the Jews observed the powerful hand that the Lord deployed against the Egyptians, and the nation was in awe of the Lord, and they believed in the Lord and in Moses, His servant.

CHASSIDIC EXCERPTS

spiritual source, and we learn and pray with the strength given to us from this food, and also when we are involved in business, profiting and teaching our children Torah and giving *tzedaka* ... in all this we refine the good aspects of the world which then ascend to be included within the realm of sublime holiness...

(From *Sefer Maamorim 5680* (~1920) of the Rebbe Rashab, pp. 291-292)

Revealed worlds and hidden universes
Vehayam bakata lifneihem - "And You split the sea before them, and they crossed within the sea on dry land" (Nechemia 9:11)

In spiritual terms, "sea" and "land" are two realms – sea is the "world of hidden objects" and land is the "world of visible objects." For example, consider the ocean and the land here in the physical world; all that exists on land also exists in the ocean.[192] However, while terrestrial creatures are visible to the eye, sea creatures are concealed, submerged and covered in the waters that hide them. In the supernal realm, *malchut* ("kingship"), the final *sephira* of the World of *Atzilut* is sometimes nicknamed "sea" and sometimes nicknamed "land." The extension and expression of *malchut* as it descends to become enclothed in the lower worlds of *Bria*, *Yetzira*, and *Asiya* (which are the "revealed worlds," seeming to exist separate from one another and from G-d) in order to enliven them from nothing into something, is called "land" ... This is as

explained in the *Tanya*[193] which states:
> The main act of creation *ex nihilo*, of a distinct and separate object, takes place from *malchut* of *Atzilut* as it becomes *Atik* of *Bria*, since there is no such thing as a king [*malchut*] without subjects [the creations of the lower three worlds]. This is not true, though of the *midot* [higher *sephirot*] of *Atzilut*...

Now, *malchut* receives illumination and influx from the infinite light of G-d via the *midot* (*sephirot*) of *Atzilut*. Thus, it becomes the sole conduit for divine input into the worlds of *Bria*, *Yetzira* and *Asiya*, since the infinite light as it exists in *Atzilut* cannot possibly come into revelation in the lower worlds ... without first becoming embedded within the *sephira* of *malchut*. From there, the influx descends to the lower worlds. One as-

אָז יָשִׁיר מֹשֶׁה וּבְנֵי יִשְׂרָאֵל אֶת הַשִּׁירָה הַזֹּאת לַיָי וַיֹּאמְרוּ לֵאמֹר, אָשִׁירָה
לַיָי כִּי גָאֹה גָּאָה, סוּס וְרֹכְבוֹ רָמָה בַיָּם:

עָזִּי וְזִמְרָת יָהּ וַיְהִי לִי לִישׁוּעָה, זֶה אֵלִי וְאַנְוֵהוּ אֱלֹהֵי אָבִי וַאֲרֹמְמֶנְהוּ:

יְיָ אִישׁ מִלְחָמָה, יְיָ שְׁמוֹ:

מַרְכְּבֹת פַּרְעֹה וְחֵילוֹ יָרָה בַיָּם, וּמִבְחַר שָׁלִשָׁיו טֻבְּעוּ בְיַם סוּף:

תְּהֹמֹת יְכַסְיֻמוּ, יָרְדוּ בִמְצוֹלֹת כְּמוֹ אָבֶן:

יְמִינְךָ יְיָ נֶאְדָּרִי בַּכֹּחַ, יְמִינְךָ יְיָ תִּרְעַץ אוֹיֵב:

וּבְרֹב גְּאוֹנְךָ תַּהֲרֹס קָמֶיךָ, תְּשַׁלַּח חֲרֹנְךָ יֹאכְלֵמוֹ כַּקַּשׁ:

וּבְרוּחַ אַפֶּיךָ נֶעֶרְמוּ מַיִם נִצְּבוּ כְמוֹ נֵד נֹזְלִים, קָפְאוּ תְהֹמֹת בְּלֶב יָם:

אָמַר אוֹיֵב אֶרְדֹּף אַשִּׂיג אֲחַלֵּק שָׁלָל, תִּמְלָאֵמוֹ נַפְשִׁי, אָרִיק חַרְבִּי, תּוֹרִישֵׁמוֹ יָדִי:

נָשַׁפְתָּ בְרוּחֲךָ כִּסָּמוֹ יָם צָלֲלוּ כַּעוֹפֶרֶת בְּמַיִם אַדִּירִים:

מִי כָמֹכָה בָּאֵלִם יְיָ, מִי כָּמֹכָה נֶאְדָּר בַּקֹּדֶשׁ, נוֹרָא תְהִלֹּת עֹשֵׂה פֶלֶא:

נָטִיתָ יְמִינְךָ תִּבְלָעֵמוֹ אָרֶץ:

pect of *malchut* is its exalted loftiness, about which the verse says, "He Who is exalted above the days of the world,"[194] [wherein "days" refers to the *sephirot* of *Atzilut*]. In general, this exalted loftiness implies aloofness from creation, as if no life-giving creative force could descend to the level of creation. That is why *malchut* is sometimes called "sea," since just as the sea covers and hides what is within it, so *malchut* covers and hides the *midot* (*sephirot*) of *Atzilut*. And that is why in this respect, *malchut* is called the "world of hidden objects."

However, another aspect of *malchut* is that it [lowers itself] to illuminate and extend to the creatures of *Bria*, *Yetzira* and *Asiya*, in order to create the "world of visible objects." In this respect, *malchut* is called "land."

Now, all of the above is true of G-dly light and influx as it descends in an orderly fashion, via various spiritual channels from *Atzilut* to the lower worlds of *Bria*, *Yetzira* and *Asiya*, as an expression of His immanent illumination. Then, it is appropriate to speak of "sea" and "land" - "concealed" and "re-

Then, Moses and the children of Israel sang this song to the Lord, saying,
'I will sing to the Lord, because He is very exalted, He hurled the horse
and its rider into the sea.

The might and vengeance of G-d was my salvation, this is my G-d and
I will glorify Him, the G-d of my father and I will exalt Him.
The Lord is a man of war, Havaya is His name.

He tossed the chariots of Pharoah and his troops into the sea, the best of
his choice warriors He drowned in the Reed Sea.

The deep waters covered them over, they descended into the depths
like stones.

Your right hand, Lord is enhanced with power, Your right hand shatters
the enemy.

In Your immense grandeur, You crush those who rise against You, You
unleash Your fury and it incinerates them like straw.

And with the wind of Your nostrils the waters piled up, the flowing
streams stood erect as a wall, the deep fountains froze in the heart of
the sea.

The enemy said, I will chase and I will overtake them, I will divide the
spoils, they will satiate my lust, I will unsheathe my sword and my hand
will inherit them.

You blew with Your wind and the sea overwhelmed them, they sank like
lead in the mighty waters.

Who is like You Lord, among all divinity, who is comparable to You,
adorned in holiness, too awesome for praises, working wonders?
You extended your right hand, the earth swallowed them.

<hr>

CHASSIDIC EXCERPTS

vealed" (respectively) worlds. The nature of spiritual levels and worlds is that the infinite light and influx of *Atzilut* cannot become revealed to the limited creatures of the lower worlds, unless the illumination first becomes hidden in the "world of concealed objects." In that realm, it remains hidden and concealed. [Subsequently], a mere ray and reflection of the [concealed] light emerges to become the source of all influx into the lower realms of *Bria, Yetzira* and *Asiya,* the "world of revealed objects."

However, on the night of the sev-enth day of Passover (*shevi'i shel Pesach*) – [when we commemorate the splitting of the Reed[195] Sea] – a great light shines from Above, resulting in a tremendous and powerful revelation that transcends all spiritual levels. This revelation comes from the infinite light of G-d Himself, who is the great Equalizer, and in comparison to Whom the worlds of *Atzilut* and *Asiya* are one and the same. Before Him, there is no distinction between light and darkness. The relative concealment and revelation of various levels of spirituality, such as "the world of re-

נָחִיתָ בְחַסְדְּךָ עַם זוּ גָּאָלְתָּ, נֵהַלְתָּ בְעָזְּךָ אֶל נְוֵה קָדְשֶׁךָ:

שָׁמְעוּ עַמִּים יִרְגָּזוּן, חִיל אָחַז יֹשְׁבֵי פְּלָשֶׁת:

אָז נִבְהֲלוּ אַלּוּפֵי אֱדוֹם, אֵילֵי מוֹאָב יֹאחֲזֵמוֹ רָעַד, נָמֹגוּ כֹּל יֹשְׁבֵי כְנָעַן:

תִּפֹּל עֲלֵיהֶם אֵימָתָה וָפַחַד, בִּגְדֹל זְרוֹעֲךָ יִדְּמוּ כָּאָבֶן, עַד יַעֲבֹר עַמְּךָ יְיָ, עַד יַעֲבֹר עַם זוּ קָנִיתָ:

תְּבִאֵמוֹ וְתִטָּעֵמוֹ בְּהַר נַחֲלָתְךָ, מָכוֹן לְשִׁבְתְּךָ פָּעַלְתָּ יְיָ, מִקְּדָשׁ אֲדֹנָי כּוֹנְנוּ יָדֶיךָ:

יְיָ יִמְלֹךְ לְעֹלָם וָעֶד:

יְיָ יִמְלֹךְ לְעֹלָם וָעֶד:

יְיָ מַלְכוּתֵהּ קָאֵם לְעָלַם וּלְעָלְמֵי עָלְמַיָּא:

כִּי בָא סוּס פַּרְעֹה בְּרִכְבּוֹ וּבְפָרָשָׁיו בַּיָּם וַיָּשֶׁב יְיָ עֲלֵיהֶם אֶת מֵי הַיָּם וּבְנֵי יִשְׂרָאֵל הָלְכוּ בַיַּבָּשָׁה בְּתוֹךְ הַיָּם:

כִּי לַיְיָ הַמְּלוּכָה וּמֹשֵׁל בַּגּוֹיִם:

וְעָלוּ מוֹשִׁיעִים בְּהַר צִיּוֹן לִשְׁפֹּט אֶת הַר עֵשָׂו, וְהָיְתָה לַיְיָ הַמְּלוּכָה:

וְהָיָה יְיָ לְמֶלֶךְ עַל כָּל הָאָרֶץ, בַּיּוֹם הַהוּא יִהְיֶה יְיָ אֶחָד וּשְׁמוֹ אֶחָד:

---

vealed objects" and the "world of concealed objects," are meaningless before Him. Since He, in truth, transcends the entire category of "worlds," He can draw upon illumination from the very essence of His being that totally transforms all spiritual levels, so that the "world of concealed objects" is rendered revealed... The general condition of concealment it-self becomes transformed and revealed, not by way of mere reflection and influx alone ... And by dint of this revelation and expression, "the sea became like dry land" – the "world of concealment" became like dry land, totally revealed down here in the physical realm.

This, then, is what is meant by, "splitting the Reed Sea." The *sephira* of

You lead in kindness this nation that You redeemed, in Your strength,
You guided them to Your holy abode.
Nations heard and trembled, waves of fear gripped the dwellers
of Philistia.
Then the leaders of Edom were shocked, the strong men of Moab were
gripped with trembling, all the inhabitants of Canaan melted away.
May fear and terror fall upon them, at the great might of Your arm let
them become still like stones; until Your nation passes, Lord, until this
nation of Yours passes through.
You will bring them and You will plant them upon the mountain of Your
inheritance, the place of Your dwelling that You made, Lord, the
sanctuary of G-d, that You prepared with Your hands.
The Lord will reign forever, eternal,

the Lord will reign forever, eternal.

Lord, Your Kingship lasts forever and ever.

For when the horses of Pharoah, with his chariot and troops [went] into
the sea, and the Lord overcame them with the waters of the sea, and the
children of Israel walked on the dry land in the midst of the sea.

For sovereignty is the Lord's, and He rules the nations.

Redeemers will ascend Mt. Sinai to judge the mountain of Esau, and the
Kingship will belong to the Lord.
And the Lord will be the King over all the land, and on that day, the
Lord will be one and His name one.

CHASSIDIC EXCERPTS

malchut of the World of *Atzilut*, which receives divine influx from the "sea" of *chochma* (the first of the ten *sephirot* of *Atzilut*) is the final *sephira* and the "closing act" of *Atzilut*. Within it is concealed all of the spiritual light and illumination of *Atzilut*, which is why it is called a "sea." But, by way of tremendous reve- lation from Above, from the *Kadmono Shel Olam* ("Primordial One of the Universe") into *malchut*, it becomes illuminated and what was concealed becomes revealed. It truly becomes "dry land," meaning that the essential lights of the World of *Atzilut* become revealed in the lower worlds of *Bria*, *Yetzira* and *Asiya*.

(From *Likutei Torah* of the Alter Rebbe, *Parshat Tzav*, p. 14b)

יִשְׁתַּבַּח שִׁמְךָ לָעַד מַלְכֵּנוּ, הָאֵל הַמֶּלֶךְ הַגָּדוֹל וְהַקָּדוֹשׁ, בַּשָּׁמַיִם

וּבָאָרֶץ, כִּי לְךָ נָאֶה יְיָ אֱלֹהֵינוּ וֵאלֹהֵי אֲבוֹתֵינוּ, שִׁיר וּשְׁבָחָה,

הַלֵּל וְזִמְרָה, עֹז וּמֶמְשָׁלָה, נֶצַח, גְּדֻלָּה וּגְבוּרָה, תְּהִלָּה, וְתִפְאֶרֶת,

קְדֻשָּׁה, וּמַלְכוּת:

בְּרָכוֹת וְהוֹדָאוֹת, לְשִׁמְךָ הַגָּדוֹל וְהַקָּדוֹשׁ, וּמֵעוֹלָם עַד עוֹלָם

אַתָּה אֵל:

CHASSIDIC EXCERPTS

His word is His reign
Yishtabach – "May He be praised..."

The vitality of all worlds stems from "Your reign" (malchutecha). That is, the very fact that G-d is called the King over [the worlds], is what enlivens and sustains them. And that is why we say, "(Yishtabach...) - May His name be blessed forever, our King..." [In this prayer], we extol the expansion of His attribute of Kingship, which is also called "His name." It is "forever," meaning without end or specific goal, since His attribute of sovereignty is also infinite, and it (as well) is an illumination from Him, may He be blessed. And that is why, during the blessings before recit-

ing the shema, we say [about the angels], "and they proclaim together in fear, aloud in unison, the words of the living G-d and King of the universe." They [the angels] grasp no more than the descent [of G-dliness] that comes down from Elokim chaim umelech olam ("the living G-d and King of the universe"), since a "voice" is nothing more than a descent of vitality. But, His essence and real Self is removed and exalted, since "No thought can grasp Him whatsoever," and therefore, "I have not changed..."[196]

(From Torah Ohr of the Alter Rebbe, parshat Vayakhel, page 87a:)

Creation from a mere ray of Divine light
Yishtabach – "May He be praised..."

We recite several verses in the prayers that indicate meditation on the sephira of malchut (His "Kingship" over the universe). [The general theme of these prayers] is acharei Havaya ("after G-d"), [because the prayers demonstrate awareness of His "imprint" - the effect that He has upon the creation - rather than of His Presence]. We say yehalelu et shem Havaya ("praise the name of G-d" - [even though His name is only a way of calling Him, and does not indicate G-d Himself], and also we say, yishtabach shimcha la'ad malcheinu... ("Praised be

Your Name forever, our King...")

These verses indicate a lengthy meditation on how the origin of the creation of the upper and lower spiritual worlds is a mere ray and reflection of light [that is, His "Name"], which is insignificant compared to His essence. Now, the meditation [on these verses] is mainly associated with the second verse of the Shema: Baruch shem kevod malchuto leolam vaed ("Blessed be the name of His Kingdom forever and ever") which refers to a ray and reflection of the sephira of malchut ... And in this way, we fulfill

Yishtabach

*M*ay Your name be praised forever, our King, the almighty G-d, the great and holy Sovereign in the heavens and upon the earth. For to You, Lord our G-d and the G-d of our fathers, it is forever appropriate [to offer];

Song and praise, admiration and melody, power and government, triumph, greatness and strength, adulation and harmony, holiness and reign:

Blessings and acknowledgement of Your great and holy Name, in all of the worlds, You are almighty G-d.

CHASSIDIC EXCERPTS

veahavta et Havaya Elokecha ("You shall love the Lord your G-d") so that we achieve love and desire for the very essence of G-dliness...

(From *Yom Tov shel Rosh Hashana 5666* of the Rebbe Rashab, p. 302)

Praise elicits the reaction
Yishtabach – "May He be praised..."

Just as *Baruch She'amar* (the opening blessing) of *Pesukei DeZimra* mentions praise of G-d's essential name, so does *Yishtabach* (the closing blessing) ... The difference is that in *Baruch She'amar*, the phrase *Baruch shemo* ("Blessed be His name") [indicates movement] from Above to below, after joining together all of the transcendent levels of "direct illumination" and "reflected illumination." However, *Yishtabach* follows the *Pesukei DeZimra*, which is full of songs and praises, and then the mention of His essential name [indicates movement] from below to Above, all the way to His exalted essence ...

This is like praise, which generally elevates the soul of man. If we praise someone for his wisdom, our praise has the potential to elicit from him a greater level of wisdom. And when we praise him for his kindness [it encourages him to perform more acts of kindness]. Similarly, when we praise G-d for His essential illumination, it raises the level of revelation of [His] essential light. Ultimately, the essence of our own soul becomes uplifted and elevated in the grandeur of His essence. With this concept, we may grasp the difference between *Baruch shemo* ("Blessed be His essential name") in which He lowers Himself from Above to below ... and the praises [of *Pesukei DeZimra*] in which we elevate the level of revelation of essential light which is called *shimcha*, "Your name," from below to Above. In this manner [from below to Above], G-d becomes more exalted, like for example one who has become famous and his name is known in faraway places. In a general sense, He is more exalted when the praise comes from a faraway place...

(From *Sha'arei Teshuva – Shaar HaTefila* of the Mitteler Rebbe, p. 61)

Fifteen phrases of praise
Yishtabach... brachot vehodaot - "May He be praised...blessings and thanksgivings

In *Yishtabach* there are fifteen praises ... They correspond to the fifteen words of the verse, "And G-d selected you today..."[197] And they also corre-

בָּרוּךְ אַתָּה יְיָ, אֵל מֶלֶךְ גָּדוֹל וּמְהֻלָּל בַּתִּשְׁבָּחוֹת, אֵל הַהוֹדָאוֹת,
אֲדוֹן הַנִּפְלָאוֹת, בּוֹרֵא כָּל הַנְּשָׁמוֹת, רִבּוֹן כָּל הַמַּעֲשִׂים, הַבּוֹחֵר
בְּשִׁירֵי זִמְרָה, מֶלֶךְ יָחִיד, חֵי הָעוֹלָמִים:

CHASSIDIC EXCERPTS

spond to the fifteen words of the Priestly Blessing. So, we must understand the meaning of the fifteen praises and their connection to the verse, "G-d selected you today," wherein there are also fifteen words...

(From *Sefer Maamorim 5758* (1898) of the Rebbe Rashab, pp. 214)

Solomon's wisdom

Yishtabach...brachot vehodaot – "May He be praised...blessings and thanksgivings"

The reason that King Solomon arrived to the spiritual level that he did, was because he was from the fifteenth generation following Abraham. The subject is as follows; on *Rosh Hodesh* ("beginning of the month") occurs the *molad* ("birth") of the new moon, after which it progresses and grows until the fifteenth of the month when it reaches its zenith. Similarly regarding Abraham, it is written, "Who called attention from the east," and the sages taught us, "Do not say 'called attention,' but rather, 'illuminated,'" since it was Abraham who first began to shine [to illuminate the world with G-dliness]. And since King Solomon was from the fifteenth generation from Abraham, at that time the "moon was at its fullest," shining with its full power of illumination. Now, the specific association with fifteen is because fifteen is the *gematria* ("numerical value") of the *yud-hey*, [the first two letters of G-d's name *Havaya*], corresponding to [the first two *sephirot*] *chochma* and *bina*. And this is what is meant by "the moon was at its fullest," meaning that it received [divine influx] from the *sephirot* of *chochma* and *bina*, just as did *z'a* [the six "emotional *sephirot*," which stand in closer spiritual proximity to *chochma* and *bina*]. And within *chochma* and *bina* dwell the infinite light of G-d, the revelation of "I am G-d, I have not changed..."[198]

This is what is meant by, "And Sol-omon sat on the throne of G-d."[199] The throne represents the *sephira* of *bina* mentioned above, which is the seventh [counting the *sephirot* from below, starting with *yesod*] and *chochma* and *bina* are "two fast friends who never separate," and for that reason *chochma* shines within *bina*. And this is what is meant by *bina* as the "throne of honor" within which dwells the [divine] honor, referring to *chochma*. And within *chochma* shines the infinite light of G-d. And that corresponds as well to the fifteen praises of *yishtabach shimcha* ("may Your name be blessed"), the theme of which is the power of revelation within *shimcha* – "Your name" - and thus we say, "until our King," indicating permanence, "I haven't changed." All this is brought down by the fifteen praises that we [recite], as *yud-hey*, within which dwell the infinite light of G-d. And this corresponds as well to the fifteen words of *Veyevarecha* (the priestly blessing), since the intent of the priestly blessing is to draw down [*chochma* and *bina*] into *malchut* [with its theme of] *coh (cuf-hey)* *tevarachu* ("and so you shall bless them"). [Thus, the intention is to] bless and draw down into *coh* ("as" or "like," indicating revelation of G-dliness that is not clear. Rather, it is somewhat concealed and hidden in proportion to the spiritual level of the lower creation – it is only "like G-dliness," and not *zeh* – "this is G-dliness") and this is the reason

Blessed are You, Lord, the almighty G-d, great Sovereign, extolled in praises, almighty G-d worthy of acknowledgment, Master of wonders, Creator of all the souls, Ruler of all events, Who chooses songs of praise, the one and only King, Life of all the worlds.

CHASSIDIC EXCERPTS

for of fifteen words to bring the "fifteen" [yud and hey, corresponding to chochma and bina] down within malchut.

(From Sefer Maamorim 5762 (1902) of the Rebbe Rashab, p. 354)

Simple unity vs unity of details
Melech yachid chay haolamim - "King, the One and Only, Life of the Worlds"

This is why sometimes [at the end of Baruch She'amar] we say "the Unique One, Life of the Worlds, King", and sometimes [at the end of Yishtabach], we say "King, the Unique One, Life of the Worlds." [The former describes flow] from Above to below, alluding to the descent from yachid [simple oneness, devoid of particulars and details] into malchut [G-d's rule over the universe, composed of details and particulars]...

As is known, there is a distinction between yachid and echad ("one"). Echad alludes to oneness composed of various components and details, which nevertheless exist in harmony and unity. And yachid implies "one and only," or "singular in essence" without particulars ...

This is what is meant by "the Unique One, Life of the Worlds, King." It alludes to the descent from yachid into malchut via chai haolamim. By and large, chai haolamim is the life force of the universe, as embodied in the kav ("ray") and the revelation of holy light, the inner dimension of which comes down from the internal essence of the Infinite One into the sephira of malchut. And "King, the Unique One, Life of the Worlds" alludes to the elevation of malchut to the very essence of His infinite light, as it is written, "To you, G-d, is the reign..."[200] indicating malchut as it ascends to be included within the ten hidden sephirot...

(From Sefer Maamorim 5680 (1920) of the Rebbe Rashab, p. 134)

Simple unity and the ten sephirot
Melech yachid chay haolamim - "King, the One and Only, Life of the Worlds"

Baruch kevod Havaya mimkomo ("Blessed be the glory of G-d from His place") indicates descent of "the glory of G-d" from its source into the "ten hidden sephirot." And malei kol ha'aretz kevodo ("the entire earth is filled with His glory") alludes to what happens after "His glory" has undergone an additional descent from the "ten hidden sephirot."

This corresponds as well to the phrase "the One and Only, Life of the Worlds, King" [which we say during Baruch She'amar], meaning that we draw down the level called yachid – where His

infinite light is unique and united with Him – from within the ten hidden sephirot of the Emanator into Melech ("King"), which alludes to "the entire land is filled with His glory." On the other hand, the phrase "King, the One and Only, Life of the Worlds," [which we say during Yishtabach] alludes to malchut ("Kingship") ... the supernal thought of Ana emloch ("I will reign") as it is still included in the infinite light of G-d, unique and united with Him. And this is what is meant by "the glory of the King."

(From Sefer Maamorim 5643 (1883) of the Rebbe Rashab, p. 90)

From Rosh HaShanah until Yom Kippur, the following is added:

שִׁיר הַמַּעֲלוֹת מִמַּעֲמַקִּים קְרָאתִיךָ יְיָ:

אֲדֹנָי שִׁמְעָה בְקוֹלִי תִּהְיֶינָה אָזְנֶיךָ קַשֻּׁבוֹת לְקוֹל תַּחֲנוּנָי:

אִם עֲוֹנוֹת תִּשְׁמָר יָהּ אֲדֹנָי מִי יַעֲמֹד:

כִּי עִמְּךָ הַסְּלִיחָה לְמַעַן תִּוָּרֵא:

קִוִּיתִי יְיָ קִוְּתָה נַפְשִׁי, וְלִדְבָרוֹ הוֹחָלְתִּי:

נַפְשִׁי לַאדֹנָי, מִשֹּׁמְרִים לַבֹּקֶר שֹׁמְרִים לַבֹּקֶר:

יַחֵל יִשְׂרָאֵל אֶל יְיָ כִּי עִם יְיָ הַחֶסֶד, וְהַרְבֵּה עִמּוֹ פְדוּת:

וְהוּא יִפְדֶּה אֶת יִשְׂרָאֵל, מִכֹּל עֲוֹנוֹתָיו:

יִתְגַּדַּל וְיִתְקַדַּשׁ שְׁמֵהּ רַבָּא. (Cong: אָמֵן)

בְּעָלְמָא דִּי בְרָא כִרְעוּתֵהּ וְיַמְלִיךְ מַלְכוּתֵהּ, וְיַצְמַח פֻּרְקָנֵהּ וִיקָרֵב מְשִׁיחֵהּ.

(Cong: אָמֵן)

בְּחַיֵּיכוֹן וּבְיוֹמֵיכוֹן וּבְחַיֵּי דְכָל בֵּית יִשְׂרָאֵל, בַּעֲגָלָא וּבִזְמַן קָרִיב. וְאִמְרוּ אָמֵן:

(Cong: אָמֵן. יְהֵא שְׁמֵהּ רַבָּא מְבָרַךְ לְעָלַם וּלְעָלְמֵי עָלְמַיָּא, יִתְבָּרַךְ:)

יְהֵא שְׁמֵהּ רַבָּא מְבָרַךְ לְעָלַם וּלְעָלְמֵי עָלְמַיָּא, יִתְבָּרַךְ, וְיִשְׁתַּבַּח, וְיִתְפָּאַר,

וְיִתְרוֹמַם, וְיִתְנַשֵּׂא, וְיִתְהַדָּר, וְיִתְעַלֶּה, וְיִתְהַלָּל, שְׁמֵהּ דְּקֻדְשָׁא בְּרִיךְ הוּא.

(Cong: אָמֵן)

לְעֵלָּא מִן כָּל בִּרְכָתָא וְשִׁירָתָא, תֻּשְׁבְּחָתָא וְנֶחֱמָתָא, דַּאֲמִירָן בְּעָלְמָא, וְאִמְרוּ

(Cong: אָמֵן) אָמֵן

Song of ascents: From the depths, I call to You, Lord.

Master, heed to my voice, lend Your ears to the voice of my pleas.

If You take into account transgressions, G-d, then who can stand [before You]?

It is Your perogative to forgive, in order that You be feared.

I hope for the Lord, my soul hopes, and for His word, I await.

My soul is with the Master, more than the guard waits for the morning, pining for daybreak.

Israel, wait for the Lord, for kindness is with the Lord, and much redemption with Him.

And He will redeem Israel from all of his iniquities.

Chazzan recites the Half Kaddish:
Exalted and sanctified is His great Name. (cong: "Amen")

In the universe that He created according to His Will, May He establish His reign, and sprout forth His redemption, and quickly bring His meshiach. (cong: "Amen")

In your life and during your days and in the life of the entire house of Israel, speedily and soon, and say Amen!
(the congregation here says, "Amen, may His great Name be blessed forever and for eternity")
May His great Name be blessed forever and for eternity. (cong: "Amen")
May He be blessed, may He be extolled, may He be glorified, may He be exalted, may He be elevated, may He be honored, may He be lauded, and may he be praised, the Name of the holy One, blessed be He. (cong: "Amen")
Beyond all the blessings and the hymns, the praises and the consolations that are recited in the world, and let us say Amen.

CHASSIDIC INSIGHTS

BARCHU

The prayer *Yishtabach* signals the end of the *Pesukei DeZimra*. Thereafter begins a new section – *Barchu* – which includes both the blessings preceding the *Shema* and the *Shema* itself. This new section illuminates and uplifts our animal soul, and also activates our G-dly soul. It corresponds to the soul-level of *neshama* and to the World of *Bria*,[101] both of which are characterized by the intense use of intellect to understand G-dliness.

ברכות קריאת שמע

בָּרְכוּ אֶת יְיָ הַמְבֹרָךְ:

בָּרוּךְ יְיָ הַמְבֹרָךְ לְעוֹלָם וָעֶד:

בָּרוּךְ אַתָּה יְיָ אֱלֹהֵינוּ מֶלֶךְ הָעוֹלָם, יוֹצֵר אוֹר וּבוֹרֵא חֹשֶׁךְ, עֹשֶׂה שָׁלוֹם וּבוֹרֵא אֶת הַכֹּל:

הַמֵּאִיר לָאָרֶץ וְלַדָּרִים עָלֶיהָ בְּרַחֲמִים, וּבְטוּבוֹ מְחַדֵּשׁ בְּכָל יוֹם תָּמִיד מַעֲשֵׂה בְרֵאשִׁית.

Our meditation during the *pesukei dezimra* focused upon the Godliness that permeates and penetrates the world. The result of this meditation is a calm and soothing realization that there is Godliness in all that exists. This awareness is called "love like water." As it settles over us, it activates our "natural emotions" – those emotions that are intrinsic to the Jewish soul and that require only a minimum of thought and consideration to activate. These are called the "natural emotions"[102] of the soul level of *ruach*.

However, as we arrive to *barchu*, and the blessings preceding the *shema*, as well as the *shema* it-

CHASSIDIC EXCERPTS

Bria - darkness, Yetzira - light
Yotzar ohr u'borei choshech ("He Who forms light and creates darkness")

The World of *Bria* is described as "dark" since it is not readily apparent and evident. This is due to the large amount of illumination in *Bria* that renders it dark from the perspective of lower spiritual levels [which are blinded by its light] ... This condition is similar to that of a blind person who is unable to see due to the desiccation of the thin layers of tissue covering his eyes. Consequently, the blind person is called a *sagi nahor* ("one who has experienced too much light")... This is also the reason that *bria* is called "darkness," for due to the large amount of illumination present, it is invisible to the spiritual levels that are below it...

*

In the spiritual realms above, revelation of light to "others" is called "speech." By "others," we mean creations that exist as independent objects, separate entities. But, revelation to G-d

Himself, and not to others, is called "thought." Therefore, the world of *Bria* is known as the "world of thought." It is also called "darkness," as it is written *Yotzar ohr u'borei choshech* ("He who forms light and creates darkness...").[201]

And yet, we know that the World of *Bria* is higher than the World of *Yetzira* [so why is it dark]? The darkness of *Bria* is opaque only because it is concealed from others, since the revelation of *Bria* is only to Himself and not to others. It is known that the creatures of *Bria* do not exist as separate entities, but rather as creations that are nullified and united with G-dliness. In this respect, they are similar to creatures of the "hidden worlds" that remain subsumed in their source. This is what is meant by the revelation of *Bria* being closed to others – to those who exist separately unto themselves. To those, He remains hidden.

(From *Yom Tov shel Rosh Hashana 5666* (1905-6) of the Rebbe Rashab, p. 300 and p. 458)

CHASSIDIC INSIGHTS

self, our soul seeks a higher level of meditation. No longer satisfied with detecting the Godliness embedded in and enlivening creation, we now search for its source. The source of this immanent, permeating spirituality is with the transcendent Godliness that is beyond creation. About it, the sages said, *ain kadosh c'Havaya* – "there is no holiness like that of *Havaya*."[103] Meditating on this level, we develop emotions of a different nature altogether. We begin to get a feeling for the Godliness that is beyond

creation. This transcendent level may be outside our purview, but nevertheless it has a transformational effect upon us. We now begin to develop "intellectual emotions." Our love and fear of God become permeated with an intellectual awareness that Godliness not only infuses the creation but also transcends it. The result is a burning desire for Godliness which we call "love like fire." This is the soul level of *neshama*.

As we approach the *shema*, our meditation shifts into "high gear." After we sense (through our medi-

Blessings of the Shema

Barchu: Blessed be the Lord, Who is sanctified!

Bless the Lord, Who is sanctified forever and ever!

Blessed are You, Lord, our G-d and King of the universe, Who forms light and creates darkness, makes peace and creates everything.

He Who illuminates the earth and those who dwell upon it in mercy, and in His goodness constantly renews the act of creation, every day.

CHASSIDIC EXCERPTS

Daily Renewal

Ub'tuvo mechadesh bekol yom... ("And in His goodness He continuously renews creation every day."

Mayim chaim ("live waters") flow constantly without interruption or variation; every day new waters flow. Similarly, the infinite light of G-d is called *makor mayim chaim* ("source of live waters"), since it is renewed constantly, every day, as it is written, "and in His goodness He continuously renews creation every day."[202] [This indicates] that every day, a new vitality descends to renew the old, as it is written, "Renewed every morning, our faith in You is great."[203] And in truth, every day a new life-force descends to renew the old, but the day includes twenty-four hours, corresponding to the twelve combinations of the four letters of the name *Havaya* and the twelve combinations of the four-letter name, *Adni*. In particular, every combination of letters of the name *Havaya* and of the name *Adni* represents a new life-force, and within each combination of letters are to be found several "moments," each of which is comprised

of 1080 "instants," and each instant contains its own new vitality, which is renewed from the One Above. And as it is written, "By each moment you are discerned,"[204] meaning that G-d discerns and examines humanity at every one of the 1080 instants, checking to see if our hearts are complete and recompensing us according to our deeds.

But, it is every day that we become conscious and detect the renewal of vitality. It is written regarding creation, "And there was evening and there was morning"[205] for, as the night descends, nothing is revealed or visible, yet when the day breaks and light begins to shine, we see that renewal occurred as if from nothing to something. And so, every morning upon rising from sleep, we become a new creation, with "new brains," purified and ready to perform our work, of serving our Creator. And so it is for all creations. Therefore, we say in our prayers, "And in His goodness He con-

CHASSIDIC INSIGHTS

tation upon Godliness within nature) the spirituality that pervades creation, we simultaneously seek its source. At this point, our focus shifts from the Godliness that is within creation, to the Godliness that transcends nature. As we know, God does not have to create, and He is not limited to creation. The creative process involves lowering Himself to become invested in creation. But, simultaneously, He remains infinitely above, and creates the universe from "afar," so to speak. It is at his point that

מָה רַבּוּ מַעֲשֶׂיךָ יְיָ, כֻּלָּם בְּחָכְמָה עָשִׂיתָ,

מָלְאָה הָאָרֶץ קִנְיָנֶךָ.

we lift our attention to the level of Godliness that creates from "afar." Since this level is transcendent and beyond, it is associated with His essential name *Havaya*. About it, we say *ain kadosh c'Havaya* – "there is no holiness like that of *Havaya*."[104]

CHASSIDIC EXCERPTS

tinuously renews creation every day." But renewal takes place *at every moment*, and [at first glance] that is an even greater good [than every day] and, therefore, it would have been appropriate to change the words of prayer and say, "and in His goodness He continuously renews creation at every moment." But, since we are not as conscious of renewal at every moment, as we are of daily renewal ... therefore, the sages fixed the prayer to say "every day."

And looking at the bigger picture,

[renewal also] takes place every month, as there is a new combination of the letters of G-d's Name every month, and on Rosh HaShana there is a new life-force for the entire year. And even more generally, it is written, "...New heavens and a new earth I will bring into existence..."[206] And for this reason, He is called the "source of the waters of life (*mayim chaim*)," since His life-force flows at all times, always, and descends without interruption in order to create and enliven the worlds...

(From *Sefer Maamorim 5655* (1895-6) of the Rebbe Rashab, p. 141)

Renewal as return to the source

Uv'tuvo mechadesh bekol yom... ("and in His goodness He continuously renews creation every day")

The process of creation requires constant renewal, since created existence demands constant refreshing [of spiritual input]. And if so, the spiritual void (*ayn*) must act constantly to renew created existence (*yesh*). The moment [the spiritual input] is removed and ceases to act, the created *yesh* will no longer exist. At that point, the renewing power returns to its original source, where it is nothing (*ayn*) whatsoever. This is what is meant by "and in His goodness He continuously renews creation every day." This does not necessarily mean "every day," but in truth at "every instant," since at every instant G-d renews the creation from nothing. This is what is meant by *tamid* – "constantly/continuously" – the creation is ongoing, since it re-occurs at

every instant from the spiritual vacuum (*ayn*) that originates creation. And this is the meaning of the verse, "Forever, G-d, Your word is established in the heavens,"[207] referring to the words of G-d within the creative command, "Let there be a firmament."[208] This command of G-d stands forever in the heavens in order to create and enliven them from nothing to something. And if it should disappear for an instant, the heavens would return to their source as absolutely nothing. The statement, "Let there be a firmament" is an [ongoing] commandment that stands forever, so that the heavens are created [and re-created] from nothing to something. The word [ten utterances of creation] of the King rules, as it creates at every instant from nothing to something. And the root of

CHASSIDIC INSIGHTS

Meditation on this level lifts us beyond the "general creations," archetypes and templates that are associated with the world of *yetzira* and the soul level of *ruach*, to a higher level of "potential creations" that are associated with the world of *bria* and the soul level of *neshama*. Chasidic literature tells us that awareness on this level is "transfixing."[105] Meditation on the nature of the world of *bria* demands intense intellectual concentration, and we lose contact with our physical surroundings as our awareness overwhelms our sense of self. In short, awareness of spirituality is far more interesting than awareness of the physical world. So, we simply shut out the physical world and con-

> How many are Your works, Lord; You made them all in wisdom, the earth is full of Your acquisitions.

CHASSIDIC EXCERPTS

this constant renewal of creation from nothing to something lies in His "goodness," which is why we say "and in His goodness He continuously renews creation every day." This refers to [the kaballistic level of] *Yesod Abba* ("Foundation of Fatherhood"), which is the origin of the World of *Atzilut* [*Atzilut* is the world of G-dly emanations, or *sephirot*, which differ from creations in that they are openly connected with their G-dly source, like a ray emanating from its source. The origin of *sephirot* is in *Adam Kadmon*, which is the first spiritual level after the *tzimtzum*, or great contraction of G-d's infinite light. Hence the reference to *Yesod Abba* within A"K].

Or, we might say that, "and in His goodness" refers to the nature of the

One who is good, and because He is good, it is His nature to do good and to benefit His creation. This, then, is the reason for the existence of creation – so that there will be recipients of His goodness. It results from the fact that "He desires to bestow kindness" – that is, He desires to do good, and this is the good that lies behind His desire to bring about the creation of *chochma*, which is the *ayn* in general [*chochma*, first of the *sephirot*, is the interface between G-d's infinite light and the world. Thus, *chochma* itself has a facet that is *ayn*, or "nothing," like G-d's infinite light. On the other hand, it also directs G-dly influx to the lower *sephirot*, and therefore]...It creates the *yesh* of *bina*, and they are together the source of *ayn* and *yesh*...

(From *Sefer Maamorim 5656* (1896) of the Rebbe Rashab, pp. 293-4)

Fire from Above, fire from below

Uv'tuvo mechadesh bekol yom... ("and in His goodness He continuously renews creation every day")

It is clear that when man apprehends something new, he becomes very excited. Similarly in the meditation described previously, [wherein we meditate upon the constant and instantaneous renewal of every creation at every moment], we see with our own eyes and our heart understands, meaning that we notice the renewal of G-dly energy, both within ourselves and within creation, that takes place every day, at every moment and every instant. Meditation at length on this topic takes place during the *Pesukei DeZimra*, regarding the creation and emergence of worlds and crea-

tures as well as the descent of G-dly energy to each and every one of them, according to the individual need and level of each.

And [we also meditate] on how all creations exalt and praise G-d. As we meditate, our heart ignites and we produce resolutions in our heart and soul. The novelty of this process arouses excitement and arousal in our soul, which is enthralled and attracted to this phenomena. The excitement causes an elevation and exaltation in our soul, extricating it from its physical attachments and drawing it generally closer to

CHASSIDIC INSIGHTS

centrate on the spiritual. At this point, we are seized by love of God that is "like fire," and this fire proceeds to consume and incinerate our animal soul.

As we meditate, our animal soul recedes into the background, and our divine soul begins to "take over." This is especially true as we recite the *shema*, but the process begins with the blessings prior to the *shema*, which have the effect of "softening" and nullifying our animal soul. Unlike the *pesukei dezimra*, which focus on physical creations, the blessings preceding the *shema* direct our attention to spiritual creatures (this is the meaning of *borei kedoshim* – "He creates holy beings"). Of course, focus upon spiritual beings necessitates that we uplift and purify ourselves, which is necessary as we approach holy levels that are associated with the Name *Havaya*. As the verse tells us, not everyone is able to ascend spiritually. It is only those who are *naki kapayim* [106] ("of clean hands" – good deeds, mitzvoth) and *bar levav* ("of pure heart" – holy emotions) who make the grade.

הַמֶּלֶךְ הַמְרוֹמָם לְבַדּוֹ מֵאָז, הַמְשֻׁבָּח וְהַמְפֹּאָר וְהַמִּתְנַשֵּׂא מִימוֹת עוֹלָם.

אֱלֹהֵי עוֹלָם, בְּרַחֲמֶיךָ הָרַבִּים רַחֵם עָלֵינוּ, אֲדוֹן עֻזֵּנוּ צוּר מִשְׂגַּבֵּנוּ, מָגֵן יִשְׁעֵנוּ מִשְׂגָּב בַּעֲדֵנוּ:

CHASSIDIC EXCERPTS

G-dliness. This is the "fire from below," which arouses "fire from Above," relevant to the animal soul in particular. This occurs during the blessings preceding the *Shema*.

And thereafter, during the *Shema* itself, the fire from Above of the G-dly soul descends with its own flames, totally consuming and incinerating the an-imal soul. And yet later in our prayers, we receive the conscious reward – *ahavah rabba* ("great love") from Above – as a result of the labor of our G-dly soul, and the internal meditation of the mind and heart which refine and rectify the animal soul. Thereafter, we merit to receive supernal love from Above...

(From *Sefer Maamorim 5666* (1906) of the Rebbe Rashab, p. 136)

Exalted Above, En-clothed below

Hamelech hameromam levado me'az ("The exalted King, who alone is elevated from aforetime")

The origin of G-dly illumination is the ten *sephirot*, which emerged differentiated and minimized after the *tzimtzum* ("great contraction"). [Only] thus [was the infinite G-dly illumination] enabled to become en-clothed within the vessels of the World of *Atzilut*, which are themselves G-dly. And in the process of becoming enclothed, they took on the characteristics of the vessels.

Now, there are three levels within the illumination: 1) the first is the source of illumination as it remained included within the infinite light of G-d preceding the *tzimtzum* ... 2) the second is the revelation of the illumination from its source, when it emerges from concealment ... 3) [the *orot* ("illumination") as they are en-clothed in the *kelim* ("vessels")]

Regarding the first and second levels, the prayers say, *Hamelech hameromam levado me'az* ("The exalted King, Who alone is elevated from aforetime") and *Hamitnasei miyamot olam* ("He Who is elevated above the days of creation"). The phrase, "The exalted King..." refers to His exalted essence, without reference to the worlds at all. This is what is meant by *Hu levado hu* ("He alone exists"), and *Hu nisgav levad* ("*Havaya* is elevated unto Himself"), both of which allude to *malchut* of the *Ein Sof* ("infinite light") before the *tzimtzum* ... and indicate essential elevation that [is not yet a source of worldly illumination], and therefore automatically remain "essential."

The phrase, "He Who is elevated

CHASSIDIC INSIGHTS

The name *Havaya* is associated with the infinite divine light that surpasses the worlds. Since there are no limits to this light, it penetrates our mind and the heart equally. As a result, our emotions rise to the level of intellect. The holy light from above penetrates our hearts, uplifting and infusing our emotions with intellect.[107]

Having previously grasped well how G-dliness enlivens creation, we no longer need any examples, illustrations, or explanations, and we can now penetrate to the very core of the concept. When we no longer need the intellectual "packaging" that shrouds the spiritual core of creation but are in touch with its very essence, then we have reached the soul level of *neshama*. In chasidic literature, this is also called *p'nimiyut hamochin* ("inner mindfulness"), or *p'nimiyut bina* ("inner understanding"), and it is a transformational experience.

During the *Pesukei DeZimra*, we meditated using *chitzoniut hamochin*

The King Who is exalted, alone from primordial times, praiseworthy and extolled, elevated above the days of creation.

G-d of the universe, in Your great mercy have compassion upon us, Master of our might, Rock of our fortress, Shield of our salvation, Refuge for us.

CHASSIDIC EXCERPTS

above the days of creation," refers to G-dly illumination as it comes to expression via enclothement in the vessels [of *Atzilut*], yet prior to its actual en-clothement. This level is not "exalted and alone," meaning that it is not "essentially exalted," since it has already come into revelation and expression in

order to become a source for the illumination of the ten *sephirot*. Yet, nevertheless, we say about it, "elevated above the days of creation," since these lights are also abstract and ethereal. And, therefore, they are raised and elevated, transcending the "days of creation."

(From *Besha'ah Shehikdimu* 5672 (1912) of the Rebbe Rashab, p. 49)

Mercy on all five levels of the soul

Elokei Olam, berachamecha harabim, rachem aleinu ("G-d of the Universe, in Your great mercy, have mercy upon us")

Elokei Olam ("G-d of the Universe") alludes to "...He Who spoke, and the universe came into existence" [in the prayer *Baruch She'amar*]. "He" is the master of essential divine Will called "Your great mercy," which is the origin of all transcendent illumination (*makifim*). Subsequently, this transcendent illumination descends into the five soul-levels of *nefesh, ruach, neshama, chaya* and *yechida*:

1) The first [descent] is to *yechida*, which is the transcendent light of G-d's undifferentiated Will, about which we say, "He spoke, and the universe came into existence." *Yechida* corresponds to *rachem aleinu* ("have mercy upon us")...

2) The second [descent] is to the transcendent level known as *chaya*. It is

alluded to by the words, *Adon uzeinu* ("Master of our strength"), and corresponds to the will of G-d as it emerges from concealment. It also correlates to *Baruch Hu* ("Blessed be He") [in *Baruch She'amar*], acting as the intermediary [to bring G-d's will from concealment to revelation].

3) Afterward, it contracts to express itself in the details of action and corresponds to the phrase, *Baruch omer v'oseh* ("Blessed is He Who says and does"). This third *makif* ("transcendent light") corresponds to *neshama* and to the phrase *Tzur migaveinu* ("Rock of our stronghold").

4) Afterward, the transcendent Will contracts still further to express itself as a verbal decree, the fulfillment of His

CHASSIDIC INSIGHTS

("external awareness"), which includes the tools of logic and understanding. These are the tools of conventional intellect – examples, illustrations, and reasoning – that enable us to understand and grasp G-dly concepts. They enable us to explain and detect G-dliness in the world. By reasoning as we did in the previous section, during the *Pesukei DeZimra*, we came to realize that there are higher spiritual creations, called angels, which are the templates, or archetypes, for all of creation. Although they are spiritual, they include within themselves all that will be created on a physical level.

אֵל בָּרוּךְ גְּדוֹל דֵּעָה, הֵכִין וּפָעַל זָהֲרֵי חַמָּה,

טוֹב יָצַר כָּבוֹד לִשְׁמוֹ, מְאוֹרוֹת נָתַן סְבִיבוֹת

עֻזּוֹ, פִּנּוֹת צְבָאָיו קְדוֹשִׁים, רוֹמְמֵי שַׁדַּי, תָּמִיד

מְסַפְּרִים, כְּבוֹד אֵל וּקְדֻשָּׁתוֹ:

תִּתְבָּרֵךְ יְיָ אֱלֹהֵינוּ בַּשָּׁמַיִם מִמַּעַל וְעַל הָאָרֶץ

מִתָּחַת, עַל כָּל שֶׁבַח מַעֲשֵׂה יָדֶיךָ, וְעַל מְאוֹרֵי

אוֹר שֶׁיָּצַרְתָּ יְפָאֲרוּךָ סֶּלָה:

תִּתְבָּרֵךְ לָנֶצַח צוּרֵנוּ מַלְכֵּנוּ וְגוֹאֲלֵנוּ בּוֹרֵא

As we followed this line of reasoning and meditation, we began to realize that even this meditation – concluding in awareness of spiritual creation – has its limitations. Since during meditation, we extrapolate to higher spiritual realms based upon our awareness of physical creation, even our spiritual consciousness is based upon the physical world. Even the spiritual properties that we attribute to the angels, or spiritual archetypes, are qualities that are based upon our experience in the physical world. If we wish to reach a higher level of awareness, we need to elevate our meditation to include properties that transcend physical creation altogether. In other words, since our awareness of angels in the World of *Yetzira* is governed by our awareness of G-dliness embedded in the physical

World of *Asiya*, our awareness is finite. It is limited by the details that we recognize and detect here in this physical world. To go beyond this stage, we need to become cognizant of G-dliness that transcends creation.

Seeking a higher level of unity in the creation (since as we ascend spiritually, we encounter greater levels of unity), we want to know not only what "must exist" but what "may exist" because G-d is infinite and may create infinite varieties and categories of creation. We wish to know not only what

CHASSIDIC EXCERPTS

Will, which is commanded in speech and fulfilled. This fourth transcendent light corresponds to *ruach* and to *Magen yisheinu* ("Shield of our salvation").

5) Finally, the divine Will is drawn down into the *chochma* of action [the intellect associated with physical reality], alluded to by *oseh breishit* ("Who makes creation"), which is the fifth *makif*, corresponding to *nefesh*, and to the phrase *Misgav ba'adeinu* ("Refuge for us" – which He actually is).

In any case, the word *baruch* ("blessed") always indicates revelation of something that was previously concealed, such as immanent G-dly light (*ohr p'nimi*) penetrating our intellect, or

transcendent G-dliness (*ohr makif*) of "direct illumination" (*ohr yashar*) operating on the five soul-levels mentioned above. However, when we say *Adon uzeinu*, etc. [in the blessings preceding the *Shema*], the transcendent illumination does not become revealed. It remains beyond us, forming a spiritual shield, a fortress or a source of strength, like an external garment [that we use to protect or shield ourselves], so to speak, just as the words "rock," "fortress," and "shield" imply.

*

The following table summarizes the preceding and succeeding teachings concerning the words of *Baruch She'amar* and the blessings of the *Shema*:

CHASSIDIC INSIGHTS

spiritual "form" (*tzura*) creation "must take" (in order to produce the physical objects of our world), but what form it "may take" just because G-d so wills it. When we pursue this line of reasoning, we conclude that the highest form of creation must be an entity that can take on any form. It is not limited to the details and concepts that we are aware of from our experience in the physical world. Rather, this level of creation may take on any form that the Creator so desires. In other words, it is "potential"

creation, since as of yet, it has no "form." And since it has no form, we cannot apply to it the normal rules of cognition. We cannot reason, for example, that it should include all of the details, however contradictory they might be, of the creations of the physical world. We cannot say that it is an archetypal "tree" or "animal" or "mineral." All we can say about this spiritual level is that it is creation in potential – the ethereal substance of creation that has not yet taken on any form. This spiritual level is the World of *Bria*.

Furthermore, because we cannot ascribe any kind of form to this creation, we cannot apply the normal tools of intellect that we usually have at our disposal. We cannot use any definitions, or any descriptions, or any line of reasoning that leads to a "fixed" concept of creation, even if it is spiritual. We have left behind our own concepts of creation and

Blessed Almighty, of great knowledge, Who prepared and created the illumination of the sun, Who well-formed honor in His name, Who placed the illuminaries around His majesty; the leaders of His holy hosts, exalted beings, constantly narrate the majesty of the Almighty and His holiness.

Be blessed, Lord, our G-d in the heavens above and on the earth below, for all the praiseworthy work of Your hands, and for the radiant illuminaries that You formed, may they glorify You forever. Be blessed forever, our Rock, our King and our Redeemer, Who creates holy

adopted the perspective of what creation "may be," rather than what it "must be." This is what chasidic literature means when it tells us that in order to reach the level of *neshama*, associated with

CHASSIDIC EXCERPTS

Blessings of the *Shema* makifim of ohr yashar	Baruch She'amar makifim of ohr chozer	Baruch She'amar makifim of ohr yashar
Rachem aleinu (**yechida**)	Baruch merachem al ha'aretz (**nefesh**)	Baruch sheamar (**yechida**)
Adon uzeinu (chaya)	Baruch merachem al habriyot (**ruach**)	Baruch Hu (chaya)
Tzur misgabeinu (neshama)	Baruch meshalem ...l'reiav (neshama)	Baruch omer v'oseh (**neshama**)
Magen yisheinu (ruach)	Baruch chai la'ad (chaya)	Baruch gozer umekayam (**ruach**)
Misgav b'adeinu (**nefesh**)	Baruch podeh u'matzil (yechida)	Baruch oseh breishit (**nefesh**)

(From *Sha'arei Teshuva – Shaar HaTefila* of the Mitteler Rebbe, p. 54)

Three levels of angels
Titbarech lanetzach tzureinu ("Be eternally blessed, our Rock")...*borei kedoshim* ("Creator of holy creatures")...

Let us understand why we say, Titbarech lanetzach tzureinu ("Be eternally blessed, our Rock")...*borei kedoshim* ("Creator of holy creatures")...*yotzar*

CHASSIDIC INSIGHTS

the section of prayers that follow *Barchu*, we need *pnimiyut hamochin*. The tools that we employ during *Pesukei DeZimra* (*chitzoniut hamochin*) are no longer sufficient. We can no longer rely on the "conventional" rules of logic and intellect to take us where we want to go. We need *p'nimiyut hamochin* which strips away all of the external casings of definitions, descriptions, and logic and leaves only the kernel of a concept. What's left is a piece of pure intellect – a core idea that can be changed, adapted, and

קְדוֹשִׁים, יִשְׁתַּבַּח שִׁמְךָ לָעַד מַלְכֵּנוּ יוֹצֵר מְשָׁרְתִים, וַאֲשֶׁר מְשָׁרְתָיו, כֻּלָּם עוֹמְדִים בְּרוּם עוֹלָם, וּמַשְׁמִיעִים בְּיִרְאָה יַחַד בְּקוֹל, דִּבְרֵי אֱלֹהִים חַיִּים וּמֶלֶךְ עוֹלָם:

adjusted to fit any kind of form (in short, the potential for creation) before it has taken on any form whatsoever.

At first glance, it may seem counter-intuitive that intense analytic meditation can also lead to spiritual levels that transcend intellect and creation. We use our faculty of *bina* – intellectual analysis during meditation – to understand

CHASSIDIC EXCERPTS

meshartim ("He Who forms servants")... The matter is as follows; here during the blessings [preceding *kriat shema*], we are speaking of angels and creations of the lower three worlds of BY"A, which are called the "supernal army." And that is why first we say, *borei kedoshim*, referring to the *seraphim* of *briah*, and then we say *yotzar meshartim*, referring to the

chayot of *yetzira*, and *asher meshartav omdim* ("and Whose servants stand..."), referring to the *ofanim* of *asiya*. Thus, regarding the angels of *bria* we say *titbarech lanetzach*, blessing them with eternity which is without limit and measure, far more than the angels of *yetzira*...

From *Sefer Maamorim* 5650 (1890-1) of the Rebbe Rashab, p. 297)

A gift vs a find

Borei kedoshim, yishtabach Shimcha... ("He Who creates holy creatures, praised be Your name...")

The creation of *chochma* from *keter* takes place from nothing to something, as it is written, "He Who creates holy creatures, praised be Your name."[209] "Holy creatures" applies to the two *sephirot* of *chochma* and *bina*, about which the prayer says, "He Who creates holy creatures" since they are a creation from nothing to something, as it is written, "and *chochma* emerges from nowhere"[210] like a new find.

Now, the difference between a "gift" and a "find" is that in the former instance, the recipient knows the giver. In spiritual terms, this is equivalent to the process of cause and effect, where one "knows" the other. In fact, there is something of the effect within the cause, since originally the effect was included within the cause before the effect was

born from its cause and emerged to become revealed. The creation of the effect, then, is only a process of emergence from concealment to revelation, and when the effect is revealed, the cause is enclothed within it. All of this takes place because there is proximity between them...

But, when we "find" something, we do not know from where the object came. In spiritual terms, this is equivalent to not knowing or recognizing the source of the object, since it is completely out of range. And, therefore, we cannot say that prior to its creation the object was included in its source. And after it was created, the source is not enclothed [in the creation]. The very essence of creation is that it takes place as a process of constant re-creation and re-

CHASSIDIC INSIGHTS

the G-dly energy that enlivens creation. So, how is it possible that the same power of *bina* can lift us up to transcendent spiritual heights? *Bina* – the intellectual analysis that we employ during meditation – is by definition intellectual, so it is difficult to fathom how it can uplift us to transcendent spiritual levels.

It is for that reason that Chasidut tells us that there are two levels of *bina*, or intellectual analysis. The first functions on the soul level of *ruach* and allows us to grasp and get some feeling for the G-dliness that enlivens creation. Once we realize that there is G-dliness in everything (creating and enlivening it), this produces an "engraving from without" on our animal soul. Since this level of *bina* utilizes the "garments of intellect" (examples, illustrations and reasoning that are not yet involved with the spiritual core of the concept), our meditation influences our animal soul from the

beings: May His name blessed praised forever, our Sovereign, Who forms heavenly servants, and Whose ministering servants all stand at the heights of the universe, letting their voices be heard in awe [and] in unison, reciting the words of the living G-d and King of the universe.

CHASSIDIC EXCERPTS

newal, rather than from concealment to revelation...

*

And in terms of prayer, it is possible that our hidden power of *chochma* is the awareness within the soul that experiences the essence of G-dliness and that, without Him, nothing exists whatsoever. And the faculty of concealed *bina* is the awareness within the soul that G-dliness is in everything, meaning that every object that exists is G-dly ... And, as for the conscious [as opposed to concealed] powers of *chochma* and *bina* within *chochma*, we experience the refinement of the general principle in the details as they are included within the general principle. And [the conscious power of] *bina* is to draw the general principle into its many details. And in this respect, we may describe the power

of *chochma* as "close," while that of *bina* as "distant." And for that reason, precisely within the faculty of *chochma* is where we experience the general principle, since revealed illumination shines there and, therefore, the principle is experienced while the details are merely included in it. And the faculty of *bina*, being "distant" from the essence, is such that the essential light does not shine within it and, therefore, we are more conscious of the details. But, the nature of concealed *chochma* and *bina* is that both are "close," since in both of them we experience the essence of G-dliness. This means that with the faculty of *bina*, we feel that everything is G-dly, because essential G-dliness is also felt there. And from the point of view of essential G-dliness, all is G-dly...

(From *Sefer Maamorim 5665* (1905) of the Rebbe Rashab, p. 261)

Angels occupy space and time

Borei kedoshim, yishtabach Shimcha... ("He Who creates holy creatures, praised be Your name...")

Although the sages said that "[186,000] applies only to how many angels are in one troop, while the quantity of troops are without number," their intention was not that there are an infinite number of troops, but rather than their

number is beyond what we are capable of counting. And this was at the time that the Temple stood; afterward the numbers of the heavenly court diminished until in essence they may be quantified. This implies that they occupy

CHASSIDIC INSIGHTS

"outside," just as garments envelop the exterior of the body. Ultimately though, our goal is to progress beyond the examples and illustrations that shroud the core and arrive at the very essence that shines within. The ability to do so is called *pnimiyut bina*, or *pnimiyut hamochin*, and it is associated with the soul level of *neshama*. When that happens, the very nature of our intellect and of our animal soul is transformed. We come into contact with the "soul" of the concept – the *neshama* – and it rivets our attention and transfixes us, causing us to lose awareness of the outer, physical world.

כֻּלָּם אֲהוּבִים, כֻּלָּם בְּרוּרִים, כֻּלָּם גִּבּוֹרִים, כֻּלָּם קְדוֹשִׁים, וְכֻלָּם עוֹשִׂים בְּאֵימָה וּבְיִרְאָה רְצוֹן קוֹנָם.

וְכֻלָּם פּוֹתְחִים אֶת פִּיהֶם בִּקְדֻשָּׁה וּבְטָהֳרָה, בְּשִׁירָה וּבְזִמְרָה, וּמְבָרְכִים וּמְשַׁבְּחִים, וּמְפָאֲרִים וּמַעֲרִיצִים, וּמַקְדִּישִׁים וּמַמְלִיכִים:

אֶת שֵׁם הָאֵל, הַמֶּלֶךְ הַגָּדוֹל, הַגִּבּוֹר וְהַנּוֹרָא קָדוֹשׁ הוּא:

וְכֻלָּם מְקַבְּלִים עֲלֵיהֶם עֹל מַלְכוּת שָׁמַיִם זֶה מִזֶּה, וְנוֹתְנִים בְּאַהֲבָה רְשׁוּת זֶה לָזֶה, לְהַקְדִּישׁ לְיוֹצְרָם בְּנַחַת רוּחַ בְּשָׂפָה בְרוּרָה וּבִנְעִימָה קְדוֹשָׁה. כֻּלָּם כְּאֶחָד עוֹנִים בְּאֵימָה וְאוֹמְרִים בְּיִרְאָה:

In order to reach this awareness during meditation, we use our faculty of *bina* to arrive at the very essence of creation. And there, we find, not creation, but a G-dly concept. When we succeed in removing all of the shrouds and the "packaging" of creation (using the "inner dimensions" of *bina*) what remains is the pristine kernel of a divine concept, which can later become any form of "tree" (to use our previous example) or any other creation. But, now, in the World of *Bria*, it is a "potential creation." It is so ephemeral that it can later take on the trappings of whatever creature the One Above desires. But, as it exists in the World of *Bria*, it is angel of the highest order – a divine concept.

*

Together with awareness of this potential creation comes another revelation – the process of *hitchadeshut*, or "renewal" of creation. As we refine our conscious-

---

CHASSIDIC EXCERPTS

their own separate physical "place," for it is known that angels are separate from one another both in nature and level – that is, in the range of their intellectual grasp. And that is what is meant by their "place," as we know from the Rambam in *Hilchot Yesodei HaTorah*. And since they are limited in "space," of necessity they are limited in the dimension of time, as well, since time and space are both categories of creation.

(From *Besha'ah Shehikdimu 5672* (1912) of the Rebbe Rashab, vol. 2, p 684)

Angelic "bodies"

Borei kedoshim, yishtabach Shimcha... ("He Who creates holy creatures, praised be Your name...")

Although the angels are also [in the category of] *yesh* ("created beings"), their "bodies" are composed of only two [of the four] basic elements. And those two are the more refined [of the elements] – fire and air[211] – as written, "He creates His angels as spirits, His servants as flaming fire." This refers to the "bodies" of the angels, as stated by the Ramban *z'l*. Moreover, this refers to the primordial spiritual foundations of fire and air above...

(From *Sefer Maamorim 5668* (1908-9) of the Rebbe Rashab, p. 40)

CHASSIDIC INSIGHTS

ness to the point of awareness of potential creations on the highest level, we simultaneously become aware of their ephemeral nature. In the World of *Bria*, we become cognizant not only of "potential creations," but of the fact that they are constantly renewed from their source at every instant. For, the nature of creation is to return to its source, in the infinite light of G-d. It is only with a constant input of G-dly energy from above that the creation manages to remain in existence. This is something that we become especially aware of in the World of *Bria*, for this world is sufficiently close to the infinite light of G-d (shining from *Atzilut*) that we experience *Beria* as *hitchadeshut*, or renewal in the world.[108] We become aware of the source of creation in the infinite light of G-d from where it constantly undergoes renewal in order to maintain its existence. So, inherent in our meditation on the World of *Bria* is the concept of creation constantly being created anew.[109] It is probably for this reason that our prayers following *Barchu* include twice the phrase, "He Who in His goodness continuously renews creation every day."

At this point, not only our intellect, but also our emotions undergo transformation. For, as indicated above, the ability to hone in on the very essence of the spiritual concept also provides access to the infinite light above that is the source of all spirituality. Once we latch on to the spiritual core of the concept, we also become aware of its source in the infinite divine light above – the name *Havaya*, which transcends cre-

All of them are beloved, all are clear, all of them mighty, all of them holy, and all of them fulfill the will of their Creator in fear and in awe.

And all of them open their mouths in holiness and in purity, in song and in melody, and they bless and praise, and extol and laud, and sanctify and coronate: The Name of the Almighty, the great King, the mighty and the awesome – He is holy.

And all of them accept upon themselves the yoke of the Kingship of heaven, each from the other, each granting permission to the other, to pleasantly sanctify their Maker, in a clear language and holy tone. All of them in unison, answer in awe and say in fear,

CHASSIDIC EXCERPTS

Greater and lesser angels

Yotzar mesharatim ("He who forms ministering angels"), and *asher mesharatav* ("He whose ministering angels...")

The ability of the angels to understand G-dliness – within the bounds of their own particular limitations – is a faculty that emerges as if created from nothing to something from the *sephira* of *chesed* of *Atzilut*. And, in general, there are two categories: *yotzar mesharatim* ("He who forms ministering angels"), and *asher mesharatav* ("He whose ministering angels..."). These are the angels who are called standing angels (*seraphim omdim*)[212] and who have been "standing" since the six days of creation. They do not become nullified as a result of their intellectual grasp. That is why they

utter the word *kadosh* ("holy"), since they perceive the infinite holy and exalted light of G-d...

And *yotzar mesharatim* ("He who forms ministering angels") refers to the angels that are created every day from the elevation of holy sparks accomplished by the Jews as they refine [and uplift] the lower world. Those sparks ascend to become included in the *sephira* of *malchut* of *Atzilut*, about which it is written, "He sprouts fodder for the animal,"[213] wherein the word for "animal" (*behama*) has the numerical value of 52 which is associated with *malchut*. And

CHASSIDIC INSIGHTS

ation. And when that happens, the line that demarcates between our emotions and our intellect is erased.[110]

As described earlier, when we pray and meditate during the *Pesukei DeZimra*, we utilize logic and intellect to shed light on the concept. This has the effect of illuminating our natural emotions (love and fear of G-d) and elevating them. In the course of this process, the intellect and emotions function as separate, though interconnected, entities – the intellect illuminates and uplifts the emotions. However, the prayer and meditation that follows *Barchu* not only influences our natural emotions from without, but also transforms them within, so that they function on the level of intellect. There is no longer a dichotomy between our intellect and emotions;

קָדוֹשׁ | קָדוֹשׁ קָדוֹשׁ יְיָ צְבָאוֹת,
מְלֹא כָל הָאָרֶץ כְּבוֹדוֹ:

CHASSIDIC EXCERPTS

"fodder" refers to the angels mentioned earlier, who become included in *malchut* since they are created with a limited tolerance for enlightenment. And when a greater level of G-dly revelation illuminates them, as a result of revelation of G-dliness descending to them from *malchut*, they become nullified and ascend to become included within *malchut*. About this verse ("He sprouts fodder for the animal"), the *Zohar* states that it refers to "the great animal that crouches on a thousand mountains and with one lick absorbs all of them." This is comparable to an animal that drinks by sucking, creating air pressure – as its snout

touches water, the water enters into its mouth along with the air. So it is with these angels; because of the revelation of G-dliness that descends to them from *malchut*, they ascend and become subsumed.

However, the angels who are called "standing angels" are capable of receiving this divine revelation from Above without becoming nullified as a result of their enlightenment. This is because their source and origin is from a much higher level. And, in general, these are the two categories of "animal" and "vegetable" [corresponding to *bria* and *yetzira*].

(From *Besha'ah Shehikdimu* 5672 (1912), of the Rebbe Rashab, vol. 1, p. 288)

Angels 6000 year old
Kadosh, Kadosh, Kadosh... ("Holy, holy, holy...")

[During the *shevirat hakelim* ("shattering of the vessels"), sparks of holiness fell down to the lower worlds of BY"A, thus requiring spiritual elevation and refinement.] But even the good that was refined from the *shevirat hakelim* and became totally separated from the evil is not absolutely good, meaning that it is not yet absolutely nullified to G-d. Rather, it still remains *yesh* (in possession of identity and independence)...

This can be compared to the angels of the World of *Beria* in whom there is no evil whatsoever, and they utter the word *kadosh* ("holy") with tremendous

self-nullification. It is known that there were angels who uttered *kadosh* at the beginning of their creation and then stood totally nullified for two thousand years, whereupon they once more uttered *kadosh* and stood for another two thousand years in a state of total nullification. And now they are in a state of nullification associated with uttering the word *kadosh* for a third time. And yet, they possess their own identity and existence, and, therefore, their level of nullification is *bitul hayesh* ("self-nullification") alone...

(From *Sefer Maamorim* 5655 (1895-6) of the Rebbe Rashab, p. 223)

CHASSIDIC INSIGHTS

the transcendent light of *neshama* shines into our mind and the heart equally. And as a result, we experience intense love and fear of G-d at the very moment that we achieve full intellectual realization. At that point, the emotions on the level of *neshama* are no longer called "natural emotions," as they were during the soul level of *ruach* (during *Pesukei DeZimra*). Now, they are so infused with intellect that they are called "intellectual emotions." That is why the soul level of *neshama* is characterized by transfixion; at that point in meditation, the meditator is unaware of anything else, for both his or her intellect and emotions are singularly devoted to G-dliness.

> "Holy, holy, holy is the Lord of Hosts, the entire earth is filled with His glory."

*

Here are some other clues to the World of *Bria*. It is like a blueprint in relation to the infinite light of G-d. A blueprint of a building is not the building itself, just as a map of a city is not the city itself. Nevertheless, both give a precise description of what the building or the city looks like. Similarly, the World of *Beria* is close enough to the infinite light of G-d to give us a clear idea of what it is.[111] Still, it is outside of the realm of revelation of G-dliness that permeates the World of *Atzilut*, which is why it is called *Beria* – from the word *bar* meaning "outside" in Aramaic.

We also know that *Beria* is associated with *ra'ash*[112] ("noise/commotion") and with *aish* ("fire").[113] For example, the Second Book of Kings says that the Prophet Elijah experienced "noise," but "G-d was not in the noise," and he experienced "fire," but "G-d was not in the fire." "Noise" is an allusion to the tumult and commotion of the angels during the blessings preceding the *Shema*. Since the celestial beings are far from the infinite light of G-d, yet close enough to know that it exists, they make a tumult as they perceive G-d's holiness and strive to become included in their spiritual source. Thus, their commotion relates to the World of *Beria*.

Then, during the *Shema* itself, the soul catches "on fire," so to speak, as it contemplates its source in the name *Havaya* with which Jewish souls are associated. Nevertheless, this is still in the World of *Beria*, and not yet in the World of *Atzilut*, where the name *Havaya* dominates. So, the soul ignites with fire because of its awareness and ascends toward its source, but it has not yet arrived there. That only occurs as we enter the *Shemonah Esreh* and pray with "a still small voice" (*kol demama daka*). But, while still anchored in *Beria*, we experience intense intellectual revelation of G-dliness which transfixes us, but it is not yet the cleaving to G-d that occurs during the *Shemonah Esreh*.

The following chart summarizes the distinctions between what we experience during the *Pesukei DeZimra*, and what we experience during the blessings preceding the *Shema* as well as the *Shema* itself:

CHASSIDIC EXCERPTS

Angels "send their love"
Kadosh, Kadosh, Kadosh ("Holy, holy, holy...")

Each and every one of [the angels] sees and apprehends its own hidden spiritual counterpart as it exists Above. There, his counterpart exists in the *sephira* of *malchut* of *Atzilut* ... as it is written in *Etz Chaim*,[214] all the various templates of mineral, vegetable and animal creatures exist in the World of *Atzilut*. Correspondingly, *malchut* [of *Atzilut*] is sometimes called "rock/stone," and sometimes "dust" or "rose" or "apple." These appellations relate to the ray of G-dly energy that is drawn down to enliven and create all the details of creation. This ray originates from its source, where it contains all the details and levels that emerge

from it and become revealed. Similarly, all the details and levels of angels are included in their source, that is, in the ray that is included within *malchut*.

So, there are myriad levels of descent of illumination within the essential *maor* ("lamp/illuminator") that is the *sephira* of *malchut* of *Atzilut*. Via these channels of illumination, the angels derive tremendous excitement since they possess no independent existence, but must be constantly renewed from their source. Furthermore, their excitement is great since each one is able to detect that his own origin, with all of his qualities, exists within *malchut* of *Atzilut*. [Each is aware that] nothing would be missing if

CHASSIDIC INSIGHTS

PRAYER	SOUL LEVEL	WORLD	G-DLY LIGHT	EFFECT ON INTELLECT	EFFECT ON EMOTIONS	EFFECT ON SOUL
Pesukei DeZimra	Ruach (spirit/wind, but not of Havaya)	Yetzira	Light in the world (immanent spirituality)	External intellect connecting to emotions	Influences the emotions from "without"	Engraving from without
Blessings before the Shema & the Shema	Neshama (noise and fire, but not of Havaya)	Bria	Light beyond world (transcendent spirituality)	Internal intellect transcending emotions	Transforms the emotions from "within"	Engraving from within

CHASSIDIC EXCERPTS

he did not exist [as an angel], nor does his existence add anything to his spiritual counterpart Above – quite the opposite, [he is aware that] his spiritual template exists in a far more praiseworthy manner Above. This is why he and his fellow angels recite: "Holy, holy, holy is the Lord of Legions," since [the name] *Havaya Zevaot*[215] is distant and exalted, out of range of all the angels, and would not be missing anything if the angels did not exist.

Now, this meditation on the arousal of the angels of the supernal *merkava*, draws down revelation and illumination of supernal love from the *merkava* to the animal soul which is derived from there. The animal soul then becomes detached from its physical lusts and its heat becomes subsumed in the supernal [G-dly] fire. That is, it is now aroused with flames of fire, which is like the "fire of the angels." This corresponds to the fire of the sacrificial offering, wherein the animal soul was incinerated by the "lion that consumed sacrifices." It is known that the main element of an offering is the fat and the blood [of the animal]. Within the animal soul, "fat" alludes to physical pleasures that lead to obesity, as alluded to in the verse, "good news expands the bones."[216] And the blood is the "boiling blood" of judgment, such as anger and similar qualities, which come from the fundament of fire within the animal soul in particular ... (Various lusts and physical enjoyment also stem

from the fundament of fire, which is equivalent to the heat of lust ... because in general the animal soul is associated with fire). Also, fat and blood are the source and origin of all lusts and enjoyment, whether of the cold variety or hot, like the flames of fire and boiling blood. And all of this becomes subsumed within the fire Above, since upon in-depth meditation on the service of the angels and their excitement and fiery arousal, illumination descends from Above for the animal soul. This [takes the form of] a ray from the "lamp of love" of the supernal angels, causing [the animal soul] to become detached from all of its lusts and become excited over G-d with a passion like flames of fire.

Within this fiery love are to be found fire from below, and fire from Above. The fire from below is a result of the labor and deeply focused meditation [of man] on the intellectual grasp of the angels and the nature of their spiritual arousal which causes them to become greatly excited. And the fire from Above is an expression of the love of the angels, descending to cause an arousal of love below, in response to the arousal of the fire from below.

(In the Second Temple, the fire from Above no longer descended, as reported in the Talmud.[217] Nevertheless, the sacrifice was kosher, even when accompanied by the fire from below alone. From this, we may derive that even if we fail

CHASSIDIC INSIGHTS

In short, then, the difference between the external dimensions of the intellect (that we experience during *Pesukei DeZimra*) and the internal dimensions of intellect (that we experience during the blessings preceding the *Shema*) is that the former focuses upon the light that is en-clothed within creation, while the latter focuses upon the light that transcends creation.

*

Elsewhere in chasidic teachings,[114] it is explained that meditation on the level of *neshama* may ultimately bring us to the transcendent soul level of *chaya*, as well.[115] This is because our meditation on the level of *neshama*, during which we move beyond the "packaging" of logic and reason, eventually evolves into a much higher form of service.[116] This higher service is described by Rambam as *avodat hashlila* ("service of negation").[117] In this form of service, we grasp all that we are capable of grasping of a G-dly concept – that is, we internalize and absorb it until it is as if we can see it in our mind's eye. This is a much higher level than mere intellectual understanding – even higher than the essential grasp

CHASSIDIC EXCERPTS

to achieve the fire of *yud-hay* [the first two letters of the name *Havaya*], with flames of love of fire from Above, from the "face of the lion," nevertheless [we may achieve fiery love of the animal soul for G-d]. This will occur as long as we work upon ourselves, since at the very least, we are commanded to "bring fire from the common person." That requires meditation on the greatness of G-d within the *Pesukei DeZimra* and on the nullification of the angels, and in this

way we will arouse our animal soul to fiery love and excitement. Or at least, there will be an arousal in the mind, and this itself is the "common fire." It is a separate entity on its own, distinct from the fire that is drawn down from Above from the "face of the lion." However, [the love from Above] descends in response to meditation on the selflessness of the "holy creatures," who are the source of the animal soul.)

(From *Sefer Maamorim 5666* (1906) of the Rebbe Rashab, pp. 141-142)

Divine vitality flows through the angels
Kadosh, kadosh, kadosh ("Holy, holy, holy...")

However, the angels do not utter the word *kadosh* ("holy") regarding themselves, but rather as the result of the vitality that spreads and permeates through them. They pale in significance compared to the G-dly vitality that courses through them. It is the influx and expansion of the vitality inside of them that "speaks" and acts within, of its own accord, with nothing to stop it. That is why the Torah says about Hagar, "And she called in the name of G-d, Who spoke to her,"[218] referring to the angel that spoke with her. Similarly, the angel who came to Avraham said, "I will certainly return to you"[219] - the angel said this as an emissary of G-d, as if G-d Himself were speaking. This is because [angels] are insignificant compared to the G-dly vitality speaking through them. They are nothing but a conduit through whom the speech de-

scends and acts below. This descent and influx flows down through the spiritual order of creation, as written, "and they called one to the other, and said *kadosh*." The Aramaic translation is, "And they received from one another..." The Hebrew original speaks from the perspective of the "benefactor," since each angel conveys the G-dly influx down to the next, while the Aramaic translation was written from the perspective of the beneficiary, using feminine nomenclature.

Now, in regard to this vitality, it is not appropriate to say that G-d is "holy and removed" [from the vitality]. For that would imply that there is something other than Him, separate. [It would imply] that something else exists, but that G-d is holy and removed from it. Rather, we inquire, "Where is His place of honor," and by so doing, we

CHASSIDIC INSIGHTS

of G-dliness that characterizes *neshama*. Here, our meditation brings us to a visceral feeling for the topic, also known as *hakara* ("recognition"). We then "negate" our understanding, as if to say that as high and true as our grasp may be, it is still not the ultimate understanding of G-dliness. In the process, we develop a feeling for G-dliness that is far beyond creation.[118] This is perhaps what the *Zohar* means when it says that, "No thought can grasp Him, but He can be gleaned in the yearning of the heart."

Of course, there is no ultimate comprehension of G-dliness, since the Torah tells us that "No man may see [G-d] and live."[119] However, "negation" propels us to a much higher plane of spirituality. About this new plane we say that G-d is not "this" (the concept upon which we were meditating), but neither is He the "opposite of this." That is, from our new plane of G-dly awareness, we recognize the validity of our previous understanding but at the same time we recognize that it was flawed, and that true G-dly perception is on a yet higher level not grasped by logic and intellect.

According to chasidic teachings, engagement in this form of service of G-d is called "understanding one concept from within a previous concept." The previous concept is one that fulfills the requirements of *ohr pnimi* or *memalle kol olamim*. It is a concept that we understand well, grasp fully, and ultimately feel inside of our minds and hearts. But, by negating it (saying that it still does not accurately describe G-dliness), we extrapolate to a higher plane of spirituality. This is what is meant by understanding a concept from within a previous concept.[120] From a concept of *ohr pnimi* or *memalle kol olamim*, we extrapolate to a higher concept of *ohr makif* or *sovev kol olamim*.[121] In this way, we actually find ourselves meditating upon the *ohr ein sof* ("infinite light of G-d"). This is the type of meditation

CHASSIDIC EXCERPTS

bring the holy vitality down to the Jews, en-clothed in physical bodies, [like] separate entities. The body covers and conceals the holiness of this vitality. And then, via stimulus from below, by nullifying our physical body to G-dliness and to the source of vitality within, with a revelation of G-dly light below as we say, *baruch atah*, etc ("blessed are You…"), [it becomes possible] for the body to say about G-d that He is holy and removed.

And the reason that the angels say *kadosh*, etc, is because this ray and reflection that the Jews bring down passes through the angels. And the three times that they say *kadosh* correspond to the three general contractions that usually occur as the G-dliness descends and spreads down here. At that point it is called "in the name of *Hashem Tzevaot*" ("Lord of Hosts" – the name with which we bring G-dliness down into the lower three worlds of *BY"A* from *Atzilut*). And throughout all of these contractions, G-d remains holy and removed.

Now, the ray and reflection that descends among the Jews in order to nullify the body to G-d has an advantage over the illumination and vitality that spreads among the angels, like the "ad-

vantage of light coming from darkness."[220] [For, this light] contains additional illumination and joy that causes even the body to become a "chariot" for the unity of G-d. And therefore, we say, *HaShem Elokeinu* – "G-d is ours" – really and truly "ours." Man for example, may be proud of his own possessions; even, for example, his foot. But, he cannot be proud of the possessions of others. Even regarding [another person's] hand [for example], which is more important than a [foot], he will not be proud, since it is not "his." Similarly, the reflection and influx, no more than a mere ray and representation that extends downward, [is] like a "foot" in comparison to the G-dly illumination that remains above, unable to permeate the body. Such light is like the "head" in comparison to [the foot]. Nevertheless [the fact is] that He is "our G-d" – truly ours, as it is written, "You are children of the Lord, your G-d."[221] And the "son is the knee [leg] of the father;"[222] like a "foot" in relation to man; they are of one essence. And therefore the sages said, "Nullify your will before His will,"[223] meaning that we must [make ourselves] like a "foot" in relation to G-d. We must be nullified to Him and do His will…

(From *Torah Ohr* of the Alter Rebbe, *parshat Ki Tissa*, P. 86a)

CHASSIDIC INSIGHTS

that characterizes the soul level of *chaya* or "G-d consciousness." On one hand, it demands the deepest and most penetrating use of spiritual intellect, but on the other hand, it accesses the transcendent levels of the soul that are not en-clothed in the body.

Whether meditating on the level of *neshama*, or upon the level of *chaya*, it is imperative that we first undergo the process of *chitzoniyut hamochin* ("external mindfulness"), during which we meditate upon the G-dliness that infuses and permeates the creation. Only after focusing upon and analyzing the G-dliness that fills the creation do we become *kelim* ("vessels") to contain the divine light that transcends the world. We must do our part in meditation, and then if we merit, a corresponding response arrives from above to lift us to higher, transcendent levels of G-dly revelation.[122]

*

As noted, "love like fire" is the result of awareness of and focus upon higher spiritual elememnts — the angels who are the subject of our meditation — who are also the source of our animal soul. According to the Torah, every element of creation has a spiritual counterpart that influences it, and this also applies to our animal soul, which has a source and a spiritual counterpart in the higher worlds.

CHASSIDIC EXCERPTS

Holiness beyond us, holiness within us
Kadosh, kadosh, kadosh...("Holy, holy, holy...")

We need to understand the difference between the word *kodesh* (without a letter *vov*) and the word *kadosh* (with a *vov*) – [both of which mean "holy"] – and why we say *kadosh* three times.

The word *kodesh* (without a *vov*) symbolizes a level of holiness that is completely beyond and detached, as the *Zohar* says, "*kodesh* is a item on its own," meaning that it bears no relationship to the worlds whatsoever. It is above any kind of descent or revelation. And the word *kadosh* (with a *vov*) symbolizes descent and revelation that is drawn down to the worlds in order to enliven them. This is represented by the letter *vov* – [whose form, a straight line, symbolizes a ray (*kav*)] – thus the *vov* symbolizes descent [of the G-dly light] by way of contraction, in order to provide a source for the worlds.

In general, the descending *vov* is comparable to a "hair." Hair contains some energy – that is, individual hairs are hollow and within the hollow there is some energy, though very limited. That is why when we cut our hair, we feel no pain whatsoever, since the [miniscule] energy of the hair has to pass through the skull that totally covers the brain [in order to be felt], and only a minimal and limited energy gets through. This is what occurs with the descent of energy via the *vov* of *kadosh*. A minimal ray descends from the level called *kodesh* (without a *vov*), and is drawn into the *vov* of *kadosh* to become the source from which the worlds are created. And this is symbolized by the form and shape of the *vov*, which is like an elongated *yud*. The *yud* indicates contraction, since only a minimal point of energy is drawn down, while the *vov* indicates descent by way of the ray of light...

We say the word *kadosh* three times, corresponding to the three worlds of *Beria*, *Yetzira* and *Asiya*. This is because three contractions took place, facilitating the creation of the three worlds of BY"A from the world of *Atzilut*. The world of *Atzilut* itself is called *kodesh* (without the *vov*), since it is known that within *Atzilut*, "He and His illuminations are one, He and His effects are one."[224] It is a world of revelation of hidden G-dliness that remains cleaving to its source Above. This is not true of BY"A, which are worlds of separate existence and creation. And in order to create BY"A from *Atzilut*, three contractions took place, corresponding to the three times we say *kadosh*...

(From *Sefer Maamorim 5654* (1894) of the Rebbe Rashab, p. 300)

CHASSIDIC INSIGHTS

And when, through our meditation, we access that spiritual counterpart, it has a transformational effect upon our animal soul. Just as those who have not lived a religious life may discover their spiritual roots, so the animal soul may, through meditation, discover its spiritual source above. When the animal soul becomes aware of its own source in the form of an angel, it is transformed, becoming aware that its source is nullified and subjugated to G-dliness, and this, of course, has the effect of nullifying it as well.

וְהָאוֹפַנִּים וְחַיּוֹת הַקֹּדֶשׁ בְּרַעַשׁ גָּדוֹל מִתְנַשְּׂאִים

לְעֻמַּת הַשְּׂרָפִים, לְעֻמָּתָם מְשַׁבְּחִים וְאוֹמְרִים:

בָּרוּךְ כְּבוֹד יְיָ מִמְּקוֹמוֹ:

לָאֵל בָּרוּךְ נְעִימוֹת יִתֵּנוּ, לְמֶלֶךְ אֵל חַי וְקַיָּם,

זְמִירוֹת יֹאמֵרוּ וְתִשְׁבָּחוֹת יַשְׁמִיעוּ, כִּי הוּא

לְבַדּוֹ מָרוֹם וְקָדוֹשׁ, פּוֹעֵל גְּבוּרוֹת, עֹשֶׂה

חֲדָשׁוֹת, בַּעַל מִלְחָמוֹת, זוֹרֵעַ צְדָקוֹת, מַצְמִיחַ

יְשׁוּעוֹת, בּוֹרֵא רְפוּאוֹת, נוֹרָא תְהִלּוֹת, אֲדוֹן

הַנִּפְלָאוֹת, הַמְחַדֵּשׁ בְּטוּבוֹ בְּכָל יוֹם תָּמִיד

מַעֲשֵׂה בְרֵאשִׁית. כָּאָמוּר, לְעֹשֵׂה אוֹרִים

גְּדֹלִים, כִּי לְעוֹלָם חַסְדּוֹ. (בנוסח הדרכי חיים ושלום

ממונקטש: אוֹר חָדָשׁ עַל צִיּוֹן תָּאִיר וְנִזְכֶּה כֻלָּנוּ

בִּמְהֵרָה לְאוֹרוֹ:

בָּרוּךְ אַתָּה יְיָ יוֹצֵר הַמְּאוֹרוֹת: (Cong: אָמֵן)

But even beyond that, chasidic teachings describe what could only be called a "relationship" that is established via meditation between the animal soul and its source above. The initiative that we show by meditating to find our spiritual source is met with a welcome from the spiritual counterpart above. This is likened to "bringing fire from below" during the sacrifices in the Temple. And just as in the Temple there was a response from above in the form of a divine fire that came down and consumed the sacrifice (at least this was so in the first Temple), the corollary in the soul is divine love ("like fire") that descends from above. The love incinerates the animal soul, leaving room for nothing but the G-dly soul and its true perception of G-dly reality, wherein only G-d is real and the physical world is but a mirage.

All of this is evident in the words of the blessings preceding the *Shema*. There, we describe the higher angels who utter the word *kadosh* ("holy"), while the lower angels utter the word *baruch* ("blessed"). This constitutes a spir-

The nature of angelic excitement
Vehaofanim vechayot hakodesh…("And the *ofanim* and the holy *chayot…*")

And now we may understand the prayers, in which say, "the *ofanim* [angels of *asiya*] and *chayot hakodesh* [angels of *yetzira*], with a great commotion, rise…"

The *avoda* ("service") of the *ofanim* takes place with much commotion. This is not true of the *avoda* of the *seraphim* [angels of *Beria*], who serve without much commotion. This is because the *ofanim* grasp the nature of nullification of the creatures of the lower worlds of BY"A [to G-d]. They grasp that it is precisely within these creatures [of BY"A] that the very essence of G-dliness is re-

vealed, and that there is none other than Him. And this is the difference between them and the *seraphim*; the latter grasp the infinite light of G-d, and how it is holy and lofty, removed from the worlds, and how the worlds bear no significance in comparison to the infinite light of G-d. This is what is meant by the verse, "Of You, HaShem, is the greatness and the *gevura*…" This greatness and *gevura* are subjugated to You…

This implies that the *seraphim* grasp how everything is "as naught" in comparison to G-d. But the *ofanim* grasp how G-d is great and very praiseworthy "in

CHASSIDIC INSIGHTS

itual dialogue between them and G-d which has a beneficial effect upon our animal soul below. In fact, as we meditate, we become aware of divine love being directed to us from above, from the spiritual counterparts (i.e. angels) upon whom we have focused our attention. And as the animal soul becomes aware of the self-nullification of the angels to their source above, the animal soul itself becomes nullified to G-d.

*

Nevertheless, certain aspects of the blessings preceding the *Shema* remain unexplained. Why, for example, do these blessings both begin and end with the words, "and in His goodness He continuously renews creation every day"? This phrase appears almost immediately after the opening blessing (*Yotzar ohr u'borei choshech*, "He who formed light and created darkness"), and again near the closing of the first blessing (*Yotzar hame'orot*, "He who formed the luminaries"). The fact that it is repeated, and both times in close proximity to the mention of G-d's name, suggests that it has special significance. Somehow, the beneficence of G-d in constantly renewing creation is associated with the appearance of transcendent G-dly illumination in the world.

The Alter Rebbe[123] states that there are two kinds of G-dly influence. One category enters the world as cause and effect. It lends strength and harmony to the laws of nature and to the worldly processes that proceed step-by-step in an orderly fashion. Examples of such processes would be the progression from intellect and emotions to

And the *ofanim* and the holy *chayot*, with a great tumult, ascend to the *seraphim*, and facing them, utter praises and say, "Blessed is the glory of the Lord from His place." To the Almighty, they offer pleasant tones; to the almighty King, living and everlasting, they express melodies and utter praises, because He alone is exalted and holy - He performs mighty deeds, does new things, is a master of war, Who sows acts of righteousness, germinates salvation, creates healing, is awesome in praises, Master of wonders, Who in His goodness constantly renews the creation, every day. As is said, [thanks to Him, Who] makes the great luminaries, for His kindness is everlasting. (Nusach Munkatsch adds: A new light will shine over Zion, to which we will all soon merit):

"Blessed be You, Lord, Who forms the luminaries."

the city of G-d." That is, they detect the power of the Infinite one to create from nothing to something, which is rooted in the very essence of G-d – without Whom nothing whatsoever exists. And that is why their [*avoda* and] excitement takes place with "great commotion;" they grasp the truth, which is that ["creation"] is the opposite of what appears to be. For, every created object appears as just that – as something that "exists"- while in truth its very existence is totally nullified [as if naught]. And that is why they react with a "great commotion." This is like man below, who when he grasps a new idea or concept, and realizes that it wasn't like he first thought

and now he sees things with "new eyes," experiences a new-found commotion in his heart.

Similarly, the *ofanim* become excited with a great commotion as they grasp that He is the diametric opposite of what appears to be; that while creatures appear to exist, in truth they are totally nullified, and as if naught... And then they say, *Baruch kevod HaShem mimekomo* ("Blessed be the glory of G-d from His place"). The "place of G-d" is the *sephira* of *malchut* that creates the worlds of *BY"A*. [Its ability to create] comes from its source and origin in the essential infinite light of G-d. And this is what is meant by "*Baruch kavod HaShem*," mean-

CHASSIDIC INSIGHTS

thought, speech and action. Or, the orderly growth of organisms such as plants and animals. The corollary in the spiritual chain of creation (seder hishtalshelut) is the progression of ten sephirot, one leading to another from chochma down to malchut. These processes are characterized by emergence from concealment to open revelation, wherein what was previously hidden emerges into view as if from cause to effect. Indeed, in this type of relationship, the effect is embedded within its cause and only later emerges on its own as something that was hidden and then becomes revealed.

אַהֲבַת עוֹלָם אֲהַבְתָּנוּ יְיָ אֱלֹהֵינוּ, חֶמְלָה גְדוֹלָה וִיתֵרָה חָמַלְתָּ עָלֵינוּ.

אָבִינוּ מַלְכֵּנוּ. בַּעֲבוּר שְׁמְךָ הַגָּדוֹל וּבַעֲבוּר אֲבוֹתֵינוּ שֶׁבָּטְחוּ בְךָ, וַתְּלַמְּדֵם חֻקֵּי חַיִּים, לַעֲשׂוֹת רְצוֹנְךָ בְּלֵבָב שָׁלֵם, כֵּן תְּחָנֵּנוּ וּתְלַמְּדֵנוּ.

אָבִינוּ אָב הָרַחֲמָן, הַמְרַחֵם, רַחֵם (בנוסח תהילת ה': נָא) עָלֵינוּ, וְתֵן בְּלִבֵּנוּ בִּינָה לְהָבִין וּלְהַשְׂכִּיל, לִשְׁמֹעַ לִלְמֹד וּלְלַמֵּד, לִשְׁמֹר וְלַעֲשׂוֹת, וּלְקַיֵּם אֶת כָּל דִּבְרֵי תַלְמוּד תּוֹרָתֶךָ בְּאַהֲבָה:

However, the physical universe was not created and is not maintained based upon this kind of G-dly influence alone, because no amount of step-by-step contraction of spirituality can lead to creation of something physical from something spiritual. For that, there is a second kind of G-dly influence that descends to the creation. And the Alter Rebbe tells us that it is associated with the phrase "and in His goodness He continuously renews creation every day." The operative word here is "His goodness," since it is His goodness – from Him alone, from His very essence – that has the power to create something from nothing. This is the power that constantly refreshes and renews the universe.

The Rebbe Rashab gives us a more nuanced view of the meaning of "renewal."[124] According to him,

CHASSIDIC EXCERPTS

ing that the glory of G-d should be blessed, just as it is in its source and origin. As it exists mimekomo – "from His place (source and origin)" – so should it illuminate and reveal the essence of His infinite light within the creation.
(From Sefer Mamorim 5661 of the Rebbe Rashab, Pp. 198

Meditation on the angels
Ahavat olam ("With an eternal/universal love You have loved us...")

What is the connection between the blessings preceding the *Shema* and the *Shema* itself? (This is a question asked by the *Rishonim*, the medieval commentators on the Torah and Talmud). The main purpose of the *Shema* is to urge us to fulfill the command contained in the first verse, "to love G-d with all your heart(s)," which the sages indicate refers to our animal and G-dly souls. This means that we have to fend off whatever stands in the path of our love of G-d (and this may include wife and children)

... Then, we must love Him with all of our soul (*nafshecha*) and with all of our might (*meodecha*), which in general applies to our health and to our wealth, and we must be prepared to sacrifice them out of love for G-d. How do we achieve such a level?

The answer is contained in the order of the blessings that we recite before the *Shema*. There, we find narrated at length the subject and organization of the angels, who stand at the spiritual pinnacle of the universe and inform us

CHASSIDIC INSIGHTS

renewal of the world is not a constant re-creation from something to nothing, but rather a constant re-creation of what already exists. For example, when man eats, the food and drink that he ingests does not "create" him. However, it does renew his vitality, ensuring that he remains healthy and energetic. Similarly, the daily influx of G-dly energy into the world every day, as described in the phrase, "and in His goodness He continuously renews creation every day" infuses the world with new energy, but does not create the world anew.

From this explanation, it is apparent that the new force coming into the world – to which we refer every morning, praying after *Barchu*, "He who in His goodness constantly renews creation every day" – is not about creating the physical universe anew. Our prayers at this point do not refer to the "basic" influx that maintains the universe as it was created originally; that level we first accessed through our meditation during the *Pesukei DeZimra* when we contemplated the specific nature of divinity within the physical creation. But, once we arrive at *Barchu* and begin reciting the blessings preceding the *Shema*, we begin to focus on a higher level of G-dliness – the *neshama* in the physical world. As the Rebbe Rashab describes it, this is a heightened level of G-dly revelation in the physical world. It is an "enriched" level of G-dliness that emphasizes spirituality within the physical creation – this is *neshama*, and it is associated with the World

*W*ith an everlasting love You have loved us, Lord our G-d, [and] great and extra mercy You have bestowed upon us.

Our Father, our King, for the sake of Your great name and for the sake of our fathers who trusted in You, and to whom you taught living laws regarding how to do Your will with a complete heart, so should You grace us and teach us. Our Father, merciful Father, Who has compassion, have mercy upon us, and place in our heart [the] understanding [necessary] to grasp and to analyze, to perceive, to learn and to teach, to observe and to do, and to fulfill all the words of Your Talmud Torah, with love.

CHASSIDIC EXCERPTS

of the greatness of G-d. These angels are all nullified in light of His holy illumination, and raise their voices in fear, sanctifying Him by saying, "Holy, holy, holy..." That is, they describe how He is removed from them and does not descend to reveal Himself to them. Rather, His glory permeates the universe, through the collective body of Jewish souls Above and the Jews themselves in the physical world below. And so, the *ofanim* and *chayot* exclaim with great fanfare: "Blessed be the glory of G-d from His place"...

This is followed by the second blessing, *Ahavat olam* ("With an eternal/universal love You have loved us)," meaning that He forsook all of the holy heavenly angels and descended with His *Shechina* to dwell among us, the Jewish people, to be our G-d. Because

His love for us "compels the flesh,"[225] it is, therefore, called "eternal love." This loving descent is the result of a great contraction of His unlimited illumination in order to enclothe it within the limitations that we call *olam* ("eternal/universal" – even "eternal" implies time as we know it within the confines of our universe). All this is a result of His great love for the Jewish people, in order to bring them nearer to Him, so that they become included in His unity and oneness.

That is why the prayer continues:

"With a great and abundant mercy," referring to the G-dly closeness that He demonstrates [toward the Jewish people which is greater than that He demonstrates] toward the heavenly legions.

CHASSIDIC INSIGHTS

of *Bria*.[125] Still, though, the worlds were already created and they exist, so why is it necessary for us to pray for their continued renewal?

A clue to the answer can be found elsewhere in the teachings of the Rebbe Rashab.[126] He (like the Alter Rebbe) tells us that there are two categories of G-dliness that descend to the world. There is "basic" G-dliness that is ongoing and dependable, such as the immutable laws of nature that ensure seasons for sowing and harvesting, day and night, etc. Then, there is a second category of G-dliness that descends to the world as "enriched/enhanced" spirituality.

וְהָאֵר עֵינֵינוּ בְּתוֹרָתֶךָ, וְדַבֵּק לִבֵּנוּ בְּמִצְוֹתֶיךָ,

וְיַחֵד לְבָבֵנוּ לְאַהֲבָה וּלְיִרְאָה אֶת שְׁמֶךָ, וְלֹא

נֵבוֹשׁ וְלֹא נִכָּלֵם, וְלֹא נִכָּשֵׁל, לְעוֹלָם וָעֶד:

כִּי בְשֵׁם קָדְשְׁךָ הַגָּדוֹל וְהַנּוֹרָא בָּטָחְנוּ, נָגִילָה

וְנִשְׂמְחָה בִּישׁוּעָתֶךָ:

וְרַחֲמֶיךָ יְיָ אֱלֹהֵינוּ וַחֲסָדֶיךָ הָרַבִּים אַל יַעַזְבוּנוּ

נֶצַח סֶלָה וָעֶד:

Elsewhere, the Rebbe Rashab further clarifies,[127] "It is understood that above there are two types of G-dly influx, stemming from *chochma* and *bina*. The influx from *bina* is what comes down to us as vitality that we feel and experience in the worlds. However, the influx that comes from *chochma* is the opposite; it is the absence of feeling, and its purpose is to introduce nullification in the worlds."[128] That is, the new, "enhanced" G-dliness that descends to the world comes down not to augment the physical nature of the world, but to nullify the physical to the spiritual realm from which it was created. In so doing, it elevates the universe and trans-

CHASSIDIC EXCERPTS

"And He chose us over other nations and languages," referring to our bodies that appear similar in their physical form to non-Jewish bodies.

"And He drew us close ... to acknowledge Him," indicating acknowledgment that is discussed elsewhere.

"And to declare His unity," meaning to be included in the oneness that characterizes Him.

Now, when an intelligent person fo-cuses on these matters and internalizes them in the depth of his heart and mind, then, spontaneously, "like a face peering into water and finding its own reflection," his soul will ignite with excitement and become possessed by a voluntary spirit to give himself up, forsaking and deserting whatever belongs to him that prevents him from cleaving to G-d. And if he does so, he will succeed in cleaving to Him with much desire.

(From *Tanya* of the Alter Rebbe, ch. 49, summary)

Inner heart, outer heart
Veyachad levaveinu...("And unite our hearts...")

In the path of worship of G-d within the soul of man, there are two elements: 1) the external layer of the heart and 2) the internal layer.

The external layer is derived from meditation on the angels – the *seraphim* (angels of *briah*) and the *ofanim* (angels of *asiyah*) and the *chayot hakodesh* (angels of *yetzirah*). This produces the excite-ment that is associated with the *Pesukei DeZimra* and the *Yotzar ohr* (the blessings preceding the *kriat shema*). It includes meditation upon the songs of the angels, such as "Praise G-d from the heavens, praise Him from the heights, praise Him all His angels, praise Him all His hosts..."[226]) And it also includes contemplation during the blessing *Yotzar*

CHASSIDIC INSIGHTS

forms it into a G-dly realm. Thus, the "enhanced" level of G-dliness that we draw down to the universe goes beyond "renewal." It nullifies the creation to G-dliness, producing awareness that the physical world has no intrinsic significance, but is merely an expression of G-dliness.

In yet another discourse,[129] the Rebbe Rashab introduces a third level of G-dliness that descends to the world. The discourse is about the ladder of which Jacob dreamt while leaving the Land of Israel. This ladder, of course, is the archetypal ladder of prayer, anchored on the earth with its top reaching into the heavens. On it, Jacob saw angels ascending and descending. The Rebbe Rashab tells us that Jacob's ladder is specifically associated with the phrase, "and in His goodness He continuously renews creation every day." But, if this is so, then why do we not see any variation in creation from one day to the next? All of nature seems to repeat itself in the same cycles that were established during the six days of creation.[130]

In answer to this, the Rebbe Rashab explains that the phrase of renewal refers to creation through the attribute of *chochma*. The *sephira* of *chochma* is the pinnacle of creation, and through it courses a new creative energy via a ray of G-dliness. *Chochma*, however, is limited, since it follows and is totally

And light up our eyes with Your Torah, and cause our hearts to cleave to Your commandments, and unite our hearts in love and to fear of Your name, without shame, without failure, and without stumbling, forever.

For, in Your great and holy and awesome name we trust, [therefore] will rejoice and be happy in Your deliverance.

And in Your mercy and great kindness, Lord our G-d, do not forsake us, eternally, forever and everlasting.

CHASSIDIC EXCERPTS

ohr, when we meditate upon how the angels stand in fear of G-d and proclaim *kadosh*, together with the *ofanim* and the *chayot hakodesh*. We consider how the angels are standing on the verge of losing their soul, and they are constantly in a state of *ratzoh veshuv* ("running and returning" – "running" to be closer to G-d, then "returning" out of fear of G-d), as it is written, "the *chayot* run and return."[227] In this manner, we draw down upon ourselves the "external unity" of *chochma* and *bina*.

The same is true regarding the love described in the opening paragraph of the *Shema*: "with all of your heart(s) and with all of your soul." With this love, we draw down only the external unity of *chochma* and *bina*, since "with all of your heart(s)" takes place by subduing the animal soul via the meditation described earlier. For, the animal soul originates from the remains of the *ofanim* (the lowest of the angels) and, therefore, medita-

tion upon its nullification to its source and origin produces a response within the animal soul as well. It no longer prevents and obstructs the nullification of the G-dly soul. And when we further meditate on how the external trappings of the universe are like nothing in essence, and the main goal is the G-dly *ayn* that enlivens and re-creates the world, then the animal soul also develops love of G-d. And, as a result, we no longer desire the superficial external matters of the world, but only G-dliness...

However, the internal layers of the heart are activated by the infinite light of His very essence, as it is written, "Who do I have in the heavens [but You]? And besides You, I desire nothing on earth."[228] This means that we do not seek mere revelation of G-d, not even of His *Gan Eden* and the world to come, since all of this is only a ray and reflection [of Him]. Rather, we desire His infinite light, we desire He, Himself in essence...

CHASSIDIC INSIGHTS

out of range of the infinite light of G-d that preceded the *tzimtzum* ("contraction"). Even so, to bring down spiritual light through the *sephira* of *chochma*, our prayers are needed. That is why we recite the blessings before the *Shema* in which we mention various kinds of angels. Our prayers ascend through these angels toward the G-dly light that transcends *chochma*. These are the same angels that the Torah calls "angels of *Elokim*" who ascend and descend on the ladder, all the while "singing" responses to our

מַהֵר וְהָבֵא עָלֵינוּ בְּרָכָה וְשָׁלוֹם מְהֵרָה,

וַהֲבִיאֵנוּ לְשָׁלוֹם מֵאַרְבַּע כַּנְפוֹת הָאָרֶץ, וּשְׁבוֹר

עַל הַגּוֹיִם מֵעַל צַוָּארֵנוּ, וְתוֹלִיכֵנוּ מְהֵרָה

קוֹמְמִיּוּת לְאַרְצֵנוּ, כִּי אֵל פּוֹעֵל יְשׁוּעוֹת אָתָּה,

וּבָנוּ בָחַרְתָּ מִכָּל עַם וְלָשׁוֹן, וְקֵרַבְתָּנוּ מַלְכֵּנוּ

לְשִׁמְךָ הַגָּדוֹל בְּאַהֲבָה לְהוֹדוֹת לְךָ וּלְיַחֶדְךָ

וּלְאַהֲבָה אֶת שְׁמֶךָ:

בָּרוּךְ אַתָּה יְיָ הַבּוֹחֵר בְּעַמּוֹ יִשְׂרָאֵל בְּאַהֲבָה:

prayers and bringing down new G-dly influence into the world. Their song, as well as the song of all of creation — and we know from *Perek Shira* that every creature has its individual song — continues as they descend into the world, renewing creation with a new influx of G-dly light every day. Every creature has its task and its place in the universe, and when it finds its task and performs it, it so resonates with the rest of creation that it "sings."[131] On the physical level, perhaps we observe no change in creation. However, through *chochma*, the nullification of the world is constantly renewed, so that all of creation functions in harmony.

There is, however, a far higher G-dly influx brought down to the world, not by angels and celestial creatures, but by Jewish souls. The new and transcendent light that is accessed by souls is far above that which descends to the universe through the *sephira* of *chochma*. It is a new light that lends creation a transcendent spiritual dimension that goes far beyond the physical. That is why the Torah tells us about Jacob's ladder, that "*Havaya* was standing over it" — that is, *Havaya* transcended nature and creation.

This is the third level of G-dly influx mentioned above.[132] The abject *bitul* ("self-nullification") of the Jewish soul to the One Above brings down a truly new light, far brighter than the ray of G-dliness that is associated with the phrase, "and in His goodness He continuously renews creation every day." This light is not associated with either the *Pesukei DeZimra* or the blessings before the *Shema*, or the *Shema* itself. It is associated with the pinnacle of prayer — the *Shemonah Esreh*.[133]

*

Based on these teachings, we can discern three distinct levels of G-dliness brought into creation by our prayers:

1) During *Pesukei DeZimra*, we meditate upon the G-dliness that enlivens creation, seeking its continued maintenance. This "basic" level of G-dliness is associated in its source with the *sephira* of *malchut* of *Atzilut*, which descends in order to create our physical world. In order to activate this level and bring

CHASSIDIC EXCERPTS

However, what is most important is unity of the inner layer and the outer layer of the heart. And that is why we request, *veyached levaveinu* ("and unite our hearts") in order to unite the inner dimension of the heart with the outer, external heart. This is what is meant by *be'er mayim chayim* ("well of living waters") ...the external layers of the heart become a vessel and receptacle, like a well, to receive the "living waters" of

the inner recesses of the heart. As written elsewhere, digging a well involves two actions. The first is to "make the receptacle" in a place where the spring of water will be revealed. And the second is to actually reveal the flow of water from the spring, water that flows constantly without ceasing. Now, the flow from the spring is comparable to the inner recesses of the heart – it means loving G-d with a great love, with all our

CHASSIDIC INSIGHTS

it down to creation, we use our power of *bina* ("analysis") in *hitbonenut* ("meditation"). Therefore, as the Rebbe Rashab states, this level is associated with *bina*, with which we analyze G-dly concepts and apply them to creation as we know it. During this stage, associated with the *Pesukei DeZimra* and the soul-level of *ruach*, our meditation leads to natural love of G-d, associated with the World of *Yetzira*.

2) When we reach *Barchu*, we ascend to the World of *Bria*, with our focus turning to G-dliness that transcends creation. We seek to bring down this spirituality while reciting, "He who continuously renews the world in His goodness every day." This G-dly energy is not necessary in order to maintain the world, but to renew the world. Every day the creative energy of the previous day departs, and a new energy descends. But, this is not automatic; it is dependent upon our prayers and our arousal from below. When we do bring down the renewal of G-dly energy, it comes from the *sephira* of *chochma*. Obviously, then, this involves an enhanced or enriched spirituality that emanates throughout the *sephirot* in order to re-create the worlds. The energy from *chochma* uplifts and infuses creation with G-dliness from above, and this is what is alluded to in our prayers, when we say, "they were all created with *chochma*."

Hasten and speedily bring upon us blessings and peace, and bring us in peace from the four corners of the earth, and break the yoke of the nations from around our necks, and lead us quickly, upright to our land, because You are an almighty G-d of salvation, and You chose us from among all the nations and tongues, and drew us close to our King for the sake of Your great name, in love and in order to acknowledge You and to unite and to love Your name: Blessed be You, Lord, Who chooses His people, Israel, in love.

This energy comes down not merely to enliven the universe, but to nullify it to the One Above, thereby guaranteeing that even the physical substance of the world will include a transcendent spiritual component. Our prayers, together with the excitement of the angels saying *kadosh* and *baruch*, bring down the higher level of enhanced G-dliness from its ultimate source in *chochma*. This is associated with "great love" (*ahava raba*) of G-d that triggers the "intellectual love" of *neshama* in the World of *Bria*.

3) Finally, there is a third level of G-dly energy – this is the level mentioned previously which the Rebbe Rashab says comes from far beyond the "renewal of the world" – which is brought down by Jewish souls during the *Shemonah Esreh*. This level comes from beyond *chochma*, from *keter*, from the infinite light of G-d Himself. To bring down this infinite light requires total and abject *bitul* to the will of G-d Above. This coincides with cleaving to G-d during the *Shemonah Esreh*. At that point, even the G-dly influx that comes from *chochma* pales in comparison to the infinite light of G-d that we access from *keter*. This light is associated not with creation, but with Jewish souls that far transcend creation.[134]

CHASSIDIC EXCERPTS

might. And the creation of the receptacle for this takes place in the outer layers of the heart. But the main objective is the unity of the external layers of the heart, so that they become a receptacle for the "living waters" of the inner recesses of the heart.

It is possible that this is the unity of *da'at tachton* ("lower consciousness" in which we are mainly aware of the phys-ical world) and *da'at elyon* ("higher consciousness" in which we are mainly aware of G-dliness), which is the unity of *yicuda ila'ah* ("upper or supernal unity," in which we are aware of G-d and creation is secondary) with *yichuda tachta'ah* ("lower or earthly unity," in which we are aware of creation and G-d is in the background), as written elsewhere.

(From *Sefer Maamorim 5656* (1896) of the Rebbe Rashab, pp. 297-298)

SHEMA

The recitation of the *Shema* is one of the pinnacles of the morning prayers. During the *Shema*, we function on the soul-level of *neshama*, but now our G-dly soul becomes fully involved.

During the blessings preceding the *Shema*, a major part of our prayer service concerns getting our animal soul involved in the effort. But, by the time we reach the *Shema*, our animal soul is already

סֵדֶר קְרִיאַת שְׁמַע

שְׁמַע ו יִשְׂרָאֵל, יְיָ ו אֱלֹהֵינוּ, יְיָ ו אֶחָד:

בָּרוּךְ שֵׁם כְּבוֹד מַלְכוּתוֹ לְעוֹלָם וָעֶד:

CHASSIDIC EXCERPTS

Meditations on the words of Shema
Shema Yisrael...("Listen Israel...")

Let us understand a little about the meaning of the words of the *Shema* ... and meditate upon the first verse of the *Shema*.

Yisroel

The Hebrew letters of the word *Yisroel* recombine to form the words *li rosh* ("a head for me"[229]). That is, G-d proclaims about Jewish souls that they are, so to speak, a "head" for Him. Now, the head includes a skull and brains. The skull corresponds to our will, and the brains correspond to the hidden reasoning behind our will. Since ultimately, the purpose of creation is for the sake of the Jewish people (as the sages said, "With whom did G-d consult [regarding creation]? With the souls of the righteous"[230]), it therefore stands to reason that it was they who arose initially in His supernal will, and for them the universe was created. In this sense, the collective souls of the Jewish people are a "head," for they originated from His supernal will as well as from the inner dimensions of His wisdom (*pnimiyut chochma ila'ah*). Thus, they constitute the concealed motivation behind His supernal will.

Furthermore, the sages said that when the Jews recite the third line of *Kaddish – Yehai shmei rabba mevarech* ("May His great name be blessed") – G-d "nods His head." That is, by reciting this line, the Jews draw down revelation of His supernal will together with inner aspects of His wisdom, corresponding to G-d nodding His head. For this reason, the Jews are near to Him and a "head" for Him, so to speak. And because this is so, He admonishes them, "Hear this and meditate on it – on you the world depends to draw down revelation of His infinite light."[231] Since there is none other than Him, and the Jews are like a "head" for Him, [it is the Jews who must bring His holy will and wisdom into expression in the world].

Havaya Elokeinu

These names of G-d (*Havaya* and *Elokeinu*) correspond to the unity of the first two *sephirot* – *chochma* and *bina* – whom the *Zohar* describes as "two fast friends who never part"... The infinite light of G-d shines in *chochma* ... and through *chochma* becomes en-clothed in *bina* [much as a flash of insight comes into the mind, and then filters down to the intellect for analysis and consideration] ... and from there derives the origin of ... both man and the angels.

Now, we can grasp why it is that we do not find this plural possessive language ("our G-d") used in connection with any of the other names of G-d,

CHASSIDIC INSIGHTS

participating, or at least not obstructing the process. So, with the initial line of the *Shema* – *Shema Yisroel, Havaya Elokeinu, Havaya echad* ("Listen, Israel, the Lord is our G-d, the Lord is one,") it is time for the full expression of the G-dly soul.

In Chasidic literature this is called *mesirat nefesh* ("giving oneself over" to G-d). It is total, unquestioning – but very intellectually informed – commitment to G-d and His will, with full acknowledgment of the true reality that only He exists and, therefore, the soul wants to be part of Him and become included in His unity. In the language of Kabbalah, this is called *yichuda ila'ah* ("supernal unity") and it refers to transcendent consciousness of G-d, in which we gain awareness that He is the only true reality, and the physical creation is mere "background noise," so to speak. The second verse (*Baruch shem kevod malchuto leolam vaed* – "Blessed be the name of His glorious kingdom forever and ever") corresponds to *yichuda tata'ah* ("lower unity"), in which we perceive creation as the foreground and G-d as the "background," so to speak. This is our "normal" state of consciousness, which we seek to transcend while reciting the *Shema*.

During the blessings preceding the *Shema*, we meditate upon the transcendent light of G-d that

Kriat Shema

Hear, O Israel, the Lord is our G-d, the Lord is one.

say in an undertone:

Blessed be the name of His glorious kingdom forever and ever.

CHASSIDIC EXCERPTS

aside from *Elokim* as *Elokeinu*, which means that "our G-d" or "G-d is ours"... We don't say this about any of the other names, such as *Havaya* or *Ekeyeh*, etc. The reason is that through this name He becomes "ours," as the infinite light of G-d enclothed within this name becomes revealed and connects with us. This can only take place by way of contraction and limitation of His infinite light, which is hinted at in the name *Elokim*. This is the name of G-d that denotes contraction. The *sephira* of *bina* also corresponds to the name *Elokim*, which is the source of limitation and judgment in the universe ... at any rate, the words *Havaya Elokeinu* connote revelation of the infinite light of the One Above within *chochma*, and from there to *bina* until it descends to us as well, and then *Havaya* becomes *Elokeinu* ("our G-d").

Havaya echad

Here, we need to understand why the verse repeats the name of G-d – *Havaya* – when it could have simply said, *Havaya Elokeinu echad*. In order to understand this, it is important to comprehend what is meant by the word *echad* ("one"). Apparently, it does not indicate the simple oneness of G-d – G-d as the One and only without peer. The word "one" does not indicate this because "one" may also indicate order among members of a group. For example, twelve sons were born to Jacob and nevertheless, Reuben was called "one" since he was the first born. Isaac, however was called *bincha yachidcha* ("your only son") so here (as well) the same term (*yachid*) should have been used.

And the truth is that regarding G-d Himself, as He exists in essence, it is not at all appropriate to use the word "one," since in truth He is unique – *yachid*. But, as the sages said, He is one "in the seven heavens and the earth, and among the four directions of the universe." [232] That is, amidst the heavens and earth and the four directions of the world – which together constitute the six dimensions of creation with all its divisions and separations – His oneness and unity prevails and is revealed ... This is the true explanation of the word "one." It is not intended to merely negate the existence of other deities, since there is no real necessity to repeat the negation every day ... Rather, the intention is to declare that

CHASSIDIC INSIGHTS

surpasses the worlds, bringing it down to bear on our worship during the *Shema* itself. This transcendent light elevates our awareness of G-dliness, and we develop "love like fire," as the divine fire of the G-dly soul descends to devour the animal soul, so all that is left is the G-dly soul itself. During this meditation, we develop deep identification with (and feeling for) the G-dliness that infuses creation and transcends it. This feeling is called *hakara* ("recognition"), and it is accompanied by *pnimiyut hamochin* ("the inner dimensions of intellect") that we achieve after delving deeply into the spiritual reality of creation.[135]

But, when we arrive to the *Shema*, we ascend to an even higher level of spiritual awareness called simply *re'iya* ("vision").[136] At this point, our perception of G-dliness is so clear that it is as if we "see" it in the mind's eye. In fact, this spiritual vision is hinted to in the words and letters of the first line of

CHASSIDIC EXCERPTS

He is one and the universe, and all that is within it, is nullified [to Him] as if it does not exist at all, and only G-d Himself exists. That is not to say there is no world, rather that in truth the world is like a ray of the sun within the sun – that is, as if non-existent – such is the level of nullification of the creation to G-d ...

And this is why the word "one" is used, indicating that He is one and that in truth there is no other. In any case the world was created and exists. It is made of the seven heavens and the earth, but they are subjugated to the One, who is the one and only existence of the world.

(From *Derech Mitzvotecha* of the Tzemach Tzedek, *Shoresh Mitzvat Hatefila*, ch. 18, page 124a)

HaShem echad...("The Lord is One...")

To begin with, we must understand *Havaya echad*. The Talmud explains[233] [that the one who recites the *shema* should have the intention], "I make Him King above and below and in all four directions of the universe." This is all alluded to in [the letters of] the word *echad* as follows:

The *chet* symbolizes the seven heavens and the earth, while the *dalet* represents the four directions of the world. Together, they comprise the six dimensions (up and down, left and right, forward and backward) of *makom* ("space/place"). And the word *echad* [itself also] alludes to the fact that *makom* is nullified to the *Aleph* (One), who is the *Alufo Shel Olam* ("Master/Commander of the Universe"). As it is written, "Behold, space (*makom*) is with Me."[234] Now, even the origin of space in the six spiritual directions, corresponds to the six supernal attributes [of *Atzilut*], listed in the Book of Chronicles – "With You, *Havaya*, is the greatness, the judgment and the harmony, the victory and the majesty, since all is in the heavens and the earth"[235] – all of which are nullified [to G-d] with ultimate devotion. And

this is what is meant by "above and below and to the four directions of the universe," since space is nullified to G-d totally and absolutely.

Now, in the *Zohar*, the explanation of the word *echad* is as follows: The *aleph* is the *Alufo Shel Olam* who is associated with *keter*. And the *chet* alludes to the *sephira* of *chochma*, while the *dalet* alludes to *dibur* ("speech"), associated with the *sephira* of *malchut*, since "With the word of G-d (*Hayava*) the heavens were created."[236] This is a reference to the ten utterances of creation. In truth, this is the same explanation as offered by the Tamud, except that the Talmud interprets the word *echad* as referring to space (the six attributes associated with the six dimensions), while the *Zohar* interprets it as referring to the source of the attributes in the *sephira* of *chochma*, which is the source and origin of the [lower emotional] attributes as well as of supernal speech. And we see that the translation of the Torah's opening verse, "In the beginning created..." according to the *Targum Yerushalmi* reads "With wisdom created..." since *chochma* is the source and origin of the supernal

CHASSIDIC INSIGHTS

the *Shema*. Although the first line of the *Shema* mentions "hearing" ("Hear O Israel…"), the letters hint at something else. Two of the twenty-six letters of the verse are enlarged when written in a Torah scroll – the *eyn* of the first word (*shema*) and the *dalet* of the last word (*echad*). Together, they spell the Hebrew word *eid* ("witness"). According to Torah law, a witness must have seen an event in order to testify about it in front of a *Beit Din* (Jewish court). If the witness has only heard about something, his testimony is not admissible. So, the presence of a witness indicates vision. This hint at vision is embedded in the words and letters of the *Shema* itself.

The command is to "hear," meaning to meditate so deeply and precisely that we achieve "vision" of G-dliness, if not with the naked eye, then in the mind's eye. We are commanded to use the process of "external intellect" (*chitzoniyut hamochin*) – equivalent to hearing[137] – so deeply and accurately that

CHASSIDIC EXCERPTS

emotions, and for that reason, the *Zohar* explains that even the *sephira* of chochma is also nullified completely to G-dliness.

(From *Sefer Maamorim* 5655 (1895) of the Rebbe Rashab, p. 42)

Meditations on the letters of Shema
HaShem echad…("the Lord is one…")

It is possible to further explain the word *echad* ("one") of the *Shema*. The first letter, *aleph* symbolizes the very essence of G-d Himself, the one and only "Being" of the universe Who truly "exists." The second letter, *chet* alludes to *chochma*, G-d's supernal wisdom. And the third letter, the enlarged *dalet*, corresponds to His supernal speech. It is the word of the king that governs [the king remains in his palace, but his word goes out in the form of directives to the kingdom]. And, therefore, speech is associated with *malchut* – G-d's reign and kingship over the universe. [These three letters, then] allude to the entire process of creation, including the emergence of myriad creations from the simple unity of G-d.

This takes place as the infinite light of G-d becomes enclothed in His supernal attribute of *chochma*. The Aramaic translation renders the first verse of the Torah, "In the beginning, G-d created… " as "With wisdom, G-d created…" And from Kabbalah we know that *Aba* ("father" - the *sephira* of *chochma*) established *barta* (the "daughter") – that is, *chochma* established the realm of speech, from which emerge multitudes of creatures. This conforms as well to the verse, "How numerous are your creations, G-d, all of them You made with wisdom; the entire earth is filled with your possessions." [237] The question is asked here: "How numerous are your creations?" How can myriad creatures be formed from G-d's simple unity? And the answer is: all of them were created from *chochma*; all of them emerged from G-d's supernal speech. This is what is meant by, "the entire earth is filled…" indicating the world of speech.

(From *Derech Mitzvotecha* of the Tzemach Tzedek, *Shoresh Mitzvah Hatefila*, ch. 19)

Baruch shem kevod malchuto l'olam va'ed ("Blessed be the Name of the glory of His Kingdom forever and ever")

Baruch shem kevod malchuto l'olam va'ed ("Blessed be the Name of the glory of His Kingdom forever and ever")

This verse alludes to the state of consciousness called *yichuda tata'ah*. The word *va'ed* ("forever") is a permutation of the word *echad* ("one"), by way of interchange of letters.[238] Now here, the prayer alludes to the creation of the lower three worlds of *bria, yetzira* and asiya via His attribute of *malchut*, as it enclothes itself in those worlds. *Shem kevod malchuto* ("the name of the glory of His Kingship") refers to the enclothing of His kingship in the lower three worlds…

Now, the term *bria* ("creation") refers to creation from nothing into something, implying that creation is independent, seemingly in possession of

CHASSIDIC INSIGHTS

we eventually achieve "internal intellect" (pnimiyut hamochin) accompanied by vision of G-dliness in our mind's eye.[138]

The vision that accompanies the Shema transcends the hakara that is associated with the blessings preceding the Shema.[139] While hakara involves intellect, re'iya is beyond logic and intellect, and arrives as a "gift" from Above (after we have meditated deeply, achieving all that we can using our own powers).[140] This level of spiritual "vision" is associated with the sephira and soul faculty of chochma ("wisdom"), as in the statement of the sages, "Who is a chacham ("wise person")? He who sees the future."

וְאָהַבְתָּ אֵת יְיָ אֱלֹהֶיךָ, בְּכָל לְבָבְךָ, וּבְכָל נַפְשְׁךָ, וּבְכָל מְאֹדֶךָ:

Nevertheless, even this vision of chochma is not the ultimate. Since it is only vision within the mind's eye, it leaves us "love-sick," so to speak. That is, it leaves us feeling love for G-d that is unfulfilling because it is not real vision that uses the naked eye. That will only occur in the future messianic era, when we will detect G-dliness not only in the mind's eye, but with the naked eye itself.[141]

*

The intellectual content of the Shema is a vast subject of its own. To begin with, we learn from the Talmudic sages that, "All who lengthen the echad of the Shema will find their days and years length-

CHASSIDIC EXCERPTS

its own separate existence. [In truth], creation is non-existent before G-d, since it is nullified to the illumination and energy flowing into it from its spiritual source in the ten sephirot of ABY"A. The infinite light of G-d illuminates creation as a ray emanating from the sun, even as it remains within the sun, according to the Tanya:

This is only "before G-d," meaning from the point of view of G-d, from Above to below. But, [from our human point of view] from below to Above, creation is a totally independent existence. This corresponds to our knowledge and understanding from below, since we are unaware of the G-dly energy flowing within us. Moreover, the two [creation and its spiritual source] are totally out of range of one another, unlike the typical cause-and-effect relationship, wherein the effect bears a relationship of sorts with its cause. Typically, the effect has some sort of awareness and comprehension of its cause, so that the effect is nullified to the cause. Moreover, in their very essence, cause and effect are not so foreign to one another. One factor happens to be a cause, while the other is an

effect, but this is not at all comparable to the situation regarding the essence of creation in relation to the essence of G-dly light and energy flowing within it to create it from nothing into something. And this is precisely why it is described as from nothing into something.

The Tanya seeks to clarify the difference between the worlds of Atzilut and bria. In Hebrew, the word bria implies the creation of seemingly independent and separate entities. This is not true of ne'etzalim, which are emanations (sephirot) in the World of Atzilut. By definition, they are totally nullified [that is, dependent upon their source], as rays of the sun within the sun. It is inappropriate to describe them as creation, but rather as emanation, as in the verse, vaye'etzal min haruach ("and He emanated from the spirit"[239]), indicating separation of a ray of illumination, as a ray of the sun from within the sun. In addition, the term is related to the word eitzel, meaning "nearby/close." Since such emanations are completely nullified, they are nearby and close to the infinite illumination of the One Above...

(From Derech Mitzvotecha of the Tzemach Tzedek, Shoresh Mitzvat Tefila, ch. 23)

CHASSIDIC INSIGHTS

ened."[142] Though this seems to imply that all those who meditate at length regarding the word *echad* of the *Shema* live longer lives, more likely it is speaking about the spiritual quality of our lives. As we meditate on the oneness of G-d, our outlook on life improves because we are better able to manage our priorities. The only real existence is G-d, while the physical existence of the world is ephemeral and misleading. When we realize this and meditate to find the G-dliness in all of creation, our priorities become more ordered. We are more apt to find the G-dliness and spirituality in creation and see the hand of the Divine Providence in our lives, than to worry about the vicissitudes of life. And that maximizes our quality of life as well as the quantity. However, to achieve this is a demanding intellectual task.

*A*nd you shall love the Lord your G-d with all your heart, with all your soul, and with all your means.

Love as a command from Above
Veahavta...("You shall love...")

Our forefather Abraham, whom G-d called the one "who loves Me,"[240] was the first of the seven "shepherds" who conveyed love of G-d to the Jewish people.

Now, the command *ve'ahavta* ("and you shall love") bears two explanations. One is that it is a commandment, and the other is that it is a promise. And at first glance, this is troublesome, for how is it possible to command someone over an emotion in his heart?

However, the command is to meditate on the greatness of the infinite light of G-d, and in this way to reveal the natural love that exists in each and every Jewish person, as an inheritance from our forefathers. That is why it is appropriate to command us regarding love, since we have it within our power to draw out [the latent love] from concealment to revelation by meditating on the first verse of the *Shema*, that "G-d is one." And in this manner, we come to fulfill the command *ve'ahavta*. This is the level of love that Abraham our forefather conveyed to the Jewish people, fixing it in their very natures from birth. But, it is under the surface and hidden and [only] via meditation are we able to draw it out from concealment to revelation, since it already exists in our genes from birth. For that reason, it is termed "natural love."

But, the second interpretation of *veahavta* is that it is a promise, meaning that ultimately, we will achieve love of G-d. Now, this is the level and quality of love associated with Aharon HaCohen [who conveyed it to the Jewish people in the words and letters of *Birkat Cohanim*]. It is *ahavah rabba* ("great love") that is beyond logic and intellect. It is beyond the power of man to achieve this love through meditation. Instead, it is granted from Above.

[In this respect], it is unlike the natural love of G-d that stems from meditation according to the rules of logic and intellect and is, therefore, limited by them. It is the same kind of love that we describe as, "love Him because He is your life,"[241] meaning that just as we love the very life of our soul, so when we meditate upon the infinite light of G-d and how He is the giver of life to the living ... we achieve love. However, the "great love" that Aharon HaCohen brought down to us is without limit, so much so that we are unable to contain ourselves. This is the opposite of the limitations that are imposed by intellect. As his name Aharon [when permuted] connotes, "we will see" (*nireh*), and as we say [in Psalm 36] "in Your light we will see light."[242]

*

Now, this "great love," although in essence unlimited, is nevertheless granted to us only in proportion to the

CHASSIDIC INSIGHTS

Not surprisingly, the most cerebral book in all of Chabad literature (itself the most intellectual of chasidic literature) was written on the topic of the *Shema*. This is *Imrei Bina* by the Mittler Rebbe, who wrote it for one of his students – Rabbi Yekutiel Lepleker. Rabbi Yekutiel was not a born intellectual and did not naturally tend toward logical analysis; indeed, he had so much trouble learning the discourses of the Mittler Rebbe that he asked for a blessing to be able to understand them. But, he worked very hard on himself in order to grasp the Rebbe's teachings, and the fact that the most intellectually challenging of all chasidic literature was written for him is testament to the extent he succeeded in his efforts. Of course, it is also proof that any of us who put in the effort can also understand this literature, no matter what our limitations are, and no matter the high level of the subject matter.

One thing we may glean from *Imrei Bina* is that meditation during the *Shema* divides into three categories: 1) meditation upon the letters (which generally applies to the first two verses); 2) meditation upon the words (which applies to the entire recitation of the *Shema*); and 3) meditation on the paragraphs including the differences in their respective wordings.

We'll start with meditation upon the letters.

*

The Talmud[143] explains that the initial *aleph* (letter with the numerical value of one) of *echad* (meaning "one") alludes to the *Alupho Shel Olam* ("Master of the World"). The *chet* (with the numerical

CHASSIDIC EXCERPTS

"natural love" that is within our power to achieve and reveal through meditation on G-d's unity. As the sages said, "All who lengthen [their meditation on] *echad* have their days and years lengthened." The explanation of *echad* is that it refers to the content of meditation on how everything is naught before G-d. Although the seven heavens and the earth, as well as the four directions, are all created entities, nevertheless they are totally nullified before the blessed infinite light of G-d, the Master of the Universe ... And similarly it is understood up to the highest spiritual levels, one above the other to the very original source, that there is no real existence aside from Him. And when we lengthen our meditation upon *echad*, meaning that we meditate at length, then in proportion to our meditation, our days and years are lengthened.

Here, "days" implies *chesed* from Above, as it is written, "The day commands the kindness of G-d,"[243] referring to the love that was characteristic of Abraham, the "man of kindness." Then, our "days" are lengthened, meaning that we bring down spiritual influx from *Aarich Anpin* ("Long Countenance"), the source of "great kindness" from above the *sephira* of *chochma*. However, this takes place only when we meditate at length on *echad*, leading to the love associated with Abraham our forefather.

Similarly, the same is true of fear of G-d – the higher form of fear, more properly described as awe of G-d – which is only granted to those who labor to achieve the lower fear of G-d. And then, in proportion to their lower fear, they are granted a higher level of awe from Above ...

(From *Sefer Maamorim 5657* (1897) of the Rebbe Rashab, pp. 101-102)

Veahavta ("You shall love...")

The commandment to love God (*veahavta et Havaya*) implies that, by way of meditation upon the infinite illumination of G-d, we will achieve love of G-d, and this will in turn reveal His infinite light. This is why the word *veahavta* has the same numerical value as *ohr ein sof* ("infinite light"), since the love itself is one with the infinite light, and the love causes the light to become revealed, as

an infinite illumination that shines openly. And since this light is infinite, the love that emanates from it is also infinite.

This is what is meant by *bekol me'odecha* ("with all of your might"), meaning without limitation or interruption whatsoever. This is because the love that results from the meditation on the very essence of the infinite light has the

CHASSIDIC INSIGHTS

value of eight) alludes to the seven heavens and the earth, and the *dalet* (with the numerical value of four) represents the four directions. Taken together, this is a meditation on the spiritual origin of space (*makom*). When all four directions and the seven heavens and earth are dominated by the One Above, then nature is nullified to G-d. This corresponds to the verse, *Hinei makom iti* ("Behold, the place is with Me"), wherein *makom* refers not only to the physical directions, but to their source in the lower seven *sephirot* of *Atzilut*.

The interpretation of the *Zohar* varies slightly from the Talmud's. According to the Zohar,[144] *aleph* alludes to the *Ain sof* ("infinite light"), but the *chet* alludes to the eight *sephirot* starting from *chochma* of *Atzilut* (which is characterized by self-nullification), while the *dalet* alludes to *malchut* of *Atzilut* (which is characterized by its ability to create through the supernal letters of speech).

According to the Rebbe Rashab,[145] the explanation of the Talmud refers to the lower seven *sephirot* in the World of *Atzilut*, while that of the *Zohar* refers to the *sephirot* as they are still included in *chochma* of *Atzilut*.

The Tzemach Tzedek tells us that the three letters of the word *echad* each represent G-dly influence upon the world. The *aleph* represents the *Alupho Shel Olam* – G-d's infinite light that transcends creation. This light descends to become en-clothed in the *chet*, which represents *chochma* as it is revealed in *Atzilut*, or as it is concealed in *keter* of *Atzilut* (*chochma stima*). That is, *chet* represents *chochma*

CHASSIDIC EXCERPTS

quality known as the "advantage of gold over silver."[244]

Gold shines, similar to sparks and glowing embers. This corresponds to "love like flames of fire," which results from the excitement that emerges from the very essence of the soul that can never be silenced. This love will not rest, on account of the great fire raging within. This is because [when we are in this state] we are transformed. In essence, we are unaware of this, nor do we feel any love in our heart, or any particular desire, aside from the great arousal. Yet, we do not know what it is ... At such times, there is no love or desire in our heart, but the excitement itself is a sign of our great connection with the very essence of the object that we are excited about. And, therefore, this love is described as *bekol meodecha*, since there is

no measure or limit to this essential excitement whatsoever. Nor will this excitement ever cease, just as the object of the excitement itself [will never cease] for it is without limit, which is why it is called the infinite light. Similarly, the excitement ... bears no interruption at all, as it is written, "G-d, there is nothing comparable to you, You never cease at all."[245]

This is why the verse says, *veahavta et Havaya*, wherein the superfluous word *et* indicates *bitul* ("nullification") to the infinite illumination of *Havaya*. Regarding this level, love is appropriate, but this love is limitless since the light itself is infinite. So, this love as well is limitless, which is what is meant by *bekol meodecha* ("with all your might") and without interruption whatsoever.

(From *Sefer Maamorim* 5657 (1897) of the Rebbe Rashab, p. 132)

Three kinds of Love
Bekol levavcha, bekol nasfshecha u'bekol meodecha – "with all your heart, with all your soul and with all your might..."

In the verse, "You shall love..." we find three levels; "with all your heart," "with all your soul," and "with all your might." And these are the three levels of love mentioned earlier [in the discourse] – the first is love borne of logic and G-dly intellect, the second is the *ahavah raba* ("great love") that is naturally hidden [inside every Jew] that is beyond

logic and reason (corresponding to "with all your soul"), and the third is "great love" that comes from above, that descends from above to below to arouse the love and desire of the heart within each and every person. This love [descends to us] without our free choice and from beyond our own will within the heart itself. It is what is meant by

CHASSIDIC INSIGHTS

as it exists in potential. This is a bit like our power of intellect before it produces a specific concept or idea; we feel its presence as the potential to understand something although we do not yet comprehend it. The *chet* of *echad* is the potential to understand, which Kabbalah calls *chochma stima* ("concealed wisdom"). This concealed *chochma* descends to the enlarged *dalet*, symbolizing *malchut* of *Atzilut*, which creates from nothing to something. Since *malchut* "has nothing of its own," but only receives

וְהָיוּ הַדְּבָרִים הָאֵלֶּה אֲשֶׁר אָנֹכִי מְצַוְּךָ הַיּוֹם עַל לְבָבֶךָ:

וְשִׁנַּנְתָּם לְבָנֶיךָ וְדִבַּרְתָּ בָּם, בְּשִׁבְתְּךָ בְּבֵיתֶךָ, וּבְלֶכְתְּךָ בַדֶּרֶךְ, וּבְשָׁכְבְּךָ, וּבְקוּמֶךָ:

influx from the *sephirot* above it, it is considered "poor" in kabbalistic terms. And the word *dal* also means "poor" in Hebrew. Thus, as we meditate upon these letters, we contemplate the entire range of G-dliness descending through the World of *Atzilut* while reciting the first verse of the *Shema*. This meditation is associated with the state of consciousness known as *yichuda ila'ah* ("supernal unity") in which we are primarily aware of G-dliness, while the physical creation remains in the background.

CHASSIDIC EXCERPTS

"with all of your might," describing something that is completely beyond the limited faculties of the will of our heart.

From *Torat Chaim* of the Mitteler Rebbe, *parshat Tezaveh*, Page 364, column 3

One love divided into three

Bekol levavcha, bekol nasfshecha u'bekol meodecha – "with all your heart, with all your soul and with all your might..."

For, it is written, "And you shall love the Lord Your G-d,"[246] but in particular this love commanded by "And you shall love..." includes three different levels; "with all your heart," "with all your soul," and "with all your might." They are differentiated from one another in concept and in the nature of the love and in their very essence. For, there are three inclusive categories; *memalle kol olamim* ("immanent G-dliness"), *sovev kol olamim* ("transcendent G-dliness"), and essential, infinite G-dliness that is beyond both immanent and transcendent G-dliness. And they correspond to the three kinds of love; "with all your heart," "with all your soul," and "with all your heart," "with all your soul," and "with all your might." For, regarding the love with "all your heart," the sages said, "with both of your inclinations" – meaning with the good inclination and the evil inclination. That is, the evil inclination as well should achieve love of the Lord. This love is achieved via meditation on how G-d is immanent in the world, permeating all of creation, about which we say that we must "love the Lord your G-d because He is your life." This kind of love results from logic in which we grasp G-dliness from within a "garment" or shroud of intellect. And it is precisely in this manner that the animal soul comes to love *Havaya*.

From *Maamorim Kuntresim Beit*, of the Fredike Rebbe, the Rebbe *Rayatz*, page 776

Love in service of G-d

Bekol levavcha, bekol nasfshecha u'bekol meodecha – "with all your heart, with all your soul and with all your might..."

And so it is regarding the service of love of G-d; there are three levels. They are; "with all your heart," "with all your soul," and "with all your might." As explained in several places, love "with all your heart" is achieved via meditation

CHASSIDIC INSIGHTS

Our meditation continues as we contemplate the word *va'ed*, at the end of the second verse, *Baruch shem kavod malchuto leolam va'ed* ("Blessed be the name of His glorious Kingdom forever and ever"). As the holy influx descends to the lower three worlds, it does so through the three letters of the word *va'ed*. The first letter *vov*, in the form of a straight vertical line, represents the descent of G-d's Will (first expressed in the World of *Atzilut*, but now descending to the lower worlds). His Will does not change, but it does apply differently to various details of creation as it descends through the worlds. In the beginning it is only a general will to create, but as it descends it becomes the will for the World of *Atzilut*, then for *Bria*, then for *Yetzira*, and finally for our world of *Asiya*. But since there is no qualitative change as it descends (it remains at all times G-d's will for creation), it is represented by the straight vertical line of the *vov*.

And these words that I am commanding you today, should be on your heart.

And you shall teach them to your children and speak of them, while sitting in your house and as you travel on the road, when you lie down, and when you arise.

CHASSIDIC EXCERPTS

on the Divinie light that is enclad within creations in order to enliven them. In general, it coincides with *ohr memalle*, or "immanent G-dliness." For, when we contemplate the fact that the energy of every created object is G-dly, and we meditate in a way that enables the intellect of our natural animal soul to grasp as well – in this manner we achieve love of G-d "with all your heart" – with both inclinations (the good inclination and the evil inclination). And we achieve love "with all your soul" as we consider that the divine light that enlivens the worlds is but a ray alone, and that this ray is out of range of the infinite light of G-d above. In general, this is the light of *sovev*, or transcendent light. And in this way, we arrive to love that is "with all your soul." That means that our love of G-d is in a manner of "delivering ourselves to Him," even if He were to "take away" our soul. And the love of "with all your might" comes via revelation of the essential infinite light that is not in the category of worlds at all. And by way of this revelation we achieve love that is beyond any measure or limitation.

From *Torat Menachem, Sefer Maamorim Melukat* of the Lubavitcher Rebbe, R' Menachem Mendel Schneerson, *ztz'l*, volume 1, Page 92

Love from the Depths

At the root of the wells that Yitzhak dug lies the matter of *avoda* (prayer). When one digs a well, the water flows from below to above. This is alluded to in the verse *beyadcha afkid ruchi*[247] ("I place my spirit in Your hands"), which forms an acrostic for the word *be'er*, or "well." This is also related to the verse, *Eilecha HaShem naphsi esah*[248] ("To You, Lord I lift my soul"), which alludes to the concept at the root of the *kriat shema*, wherein we "deliver" our soul while reciting the word *echad* ("one"). And this is similar to the *kriat shema* itself, wherein we med-

itate upon the concept of "the Lord our G-d, the Lord is one," while fulfilling the command of "You shall love the Lord your G-d..."

Now, within this general love of G-d, there are three particular categories; "with all your heart," "with all your soul," and "with all your might." Corresponding to these particular categories, Yitzhak dug three wells; [calling them] *Esek, Sitna* and *Rehovot*.[249] There were quarrels over the first two wells, but over the third, there was no quarrel. And that is why it was called *Rehovot*,

CHASSIDIC INSIGHTS

The second letter of *va'ed* – *ayin* – represents *chochma*, and the third letter *dalet* represents *malchut* as will be explained.

According to Kabbalah, all Hebrew letters are associated with one of five agents of enunciation – the tongue, the teeth, the lips, the throat and the palate. It happens that the second letters of both *echad* and of *va'ed* – the *chet* of *echad* and the *ayin* of *va'ed* – are both associated with the throat. So, the sages tell us that they are interchangeable, and that, therefore, just as the *chet* of *echad* represents *chochma*, so the *ayin* of *va'ed* represents *chochma*. The *chet* of *echad* is concealed *chochma* in *keter* (*chochma* of *keter*, or *chochma stima*) as explained earlier, while the *ayin* of *va'ed* is revealed *chochma* in the World of *Atzilut*. We do not directly experience concealed *chochma*, because it is G-dly illumination that

וּקְשַׁרְתָּם לְאוֹת עַל יָדֶךָ, וְהָיוּ לְטֹטָפֹת בֵּין עֵינֶיךָ:

וּכְתַבְתָּם עַל מְזֻזוֹת בֵּיתֶךָ וּבִשְׁעָרֶיךָ:

has not yet settled into the vessel (*keli*) of our minds. However, the revealed *chochma* of *Atzilut* represents concepts that we can grasp clearly in our minds because the G-dly light has settled into our minds to be understood and internalized. This revealed *chochma* is represented by the *ayin* of *va'ed*. The name of the letter *ayin* also means "eye," and vision is associated with revealed *chochma*. The sages of the Torah in each generation are called *einei ha'eidah* ("the eyes of the congregation") because they are blessed with Torah knowledge that imparts wisdom, descending from the concealed *chochma* associated with the *chet* of *echad*.

And finally, the concluding *dalet* of *va'ed* also represents *malchut*, as does the *dalet* of *echad*. But, while the *dalet* of *echad* is *malchut* in the World of *Atzilut*, the *dalet* of *va'ed* is *malchut* as it descends to enliven and uplift the lower three worlds of *Bria*, *Yetzira* and *Asiya*. The *sephira* of *malchut* operates in two different modes – one in which it receives from the *sephirot* above it, and the other in which it lowers itself to influence and uplift the worlds below it. The *dalet* in *echad* is *malchut* in *Atzilut* as it

CHASSIDIC EXCERPTS

since there was no protest or accusation over this well whatsoever. It came to them *b'rechava* – "openly, freely" – which is why it was called *Rehovot*. And we must understand the difference between [the wells that were accompanied by] discord and [the well that they discovered] without disagreement at all, and how they relate to the three categories of love mentioned in the *kriat shema*.

And within the *kriat shema* itself, we must understand the difference between "love with all your soul and with all your heart," which are associated with *Esek* and *Sitna*, and "love with all your might," which develops in "openness" and "freedom." And also, what is the connection between the positive commandment to love G-d "with all your might" and the topic of *Rehovot*[250].

From *Torat Shmuel* 5634 (1874) of the Rebbe Maharash, Page 61-62

The importance of a contrite approach
Shema Yisrael...("Listen Israel...")

And our teacher, the Alter Rebbe, explained the statement in the *Mishna*, "We do not approach prayer except with a contrite mind"[251]...

In order to understand what is meant by a "contrite mind," it will help to understand why we say *Shema Yisroel* ("Listen Israel"), followed by *ve'ahavta* ("you shall love...") At first glance, it is

difficult to understand how there can be a commandment to love. A commandment is appropriate regarding an action, but how is a commandment appropriate regarding a feeling in the heart?

In order to understand better, it is appropriate to preface with the *Shema*: "Listen Israel, the Lord (*Havaya*) is our G-d, the Lord (*Havaya*) is One." Why do

CHASSIDIC INSIGHTS

receives the influx of the *sephirot* above it. And the *dalet* in *va'ed* is *malchut* as it lowers itself to the worlds below.

Thus, our meditation on the letters of *va'ed* focuses upon the influx of G-dliness from the World of *Atzilut* down to the lower worlds of *BY"A*. It is associated with the state of consciousness known as *yichuda tata'ah* ("lower unity"), in which the physical world occupies our primary awareness, and G-dliness is in the background. And the meditation on both verses covers the entire range of G-dliness as it descends from the infinite light of G-d all the way down to the our physical world. The combination of both meditations together is what the *Zohar* refers to as the *raza d'echad* ("secret of one") wherein the higher unity associated with *yichuda ila'ah* descends to permeate the lower consciousness of *yichuda tata'ah*.

> And you shall tie them as a sign on your arm, and they shall be as compartments between your eyes.
> And you shall write them on the doorposts of your house and upon your gates.

This meditation, outlined in the teachings of the Tzemach Tzedek is also found in the teachings of the Mittler Rebbe (in the *Imrei Bina*). It is repeated in much greater detail in the teachings of the Rebbe Rashab.[146] It is the most detailed and subtle of the meditations upon the letters of the *Shema*. At the same time, it closely fulfills the saying of the sages, that "All who lengthen [in meditation] the *echad* of the *Shema* will find their days and years lengthened."

*

Meditations on the words of the *Shema* are found in the teachings of all the rebbes of Chabad. Among the questions that are asked (and answered) are: "Why does the verse contain the name of G-d twice, after all, would it not be sufficient to say once *Havaya Elokeinu Echad*?" And: "Why does the verse say, *Havaya Echad*, and not *Havaya yachid*?" As we know, *echad* means "one," implying that there are others, while *yachid* means "the only, or the unique one" which seems to more accurately describe the oneness of G-d.

CHASSIDIC EXCERPTS

we mention the name *Havaya* twice, when at first glance it would have been sufficient to say, "*Havaya* our G-d is One?" But, the answer is that the first *Havaya* refers to the souls of the Jews, who arose in His thought. And the creation of souls takes place via the name *Havaya* ... And the second *Havaya* refers to the creation of the universe. The enlarged *dalet* – the final letter of *echad* – is the source of supernal speech, and the universe was created by the supernal speech of G-d. As it is written, "With the word of G-d the heavens were created..."[252] This is why there are two references to *Havaya* in the *Shema* – the first is the source of thought, while the second is the source of speech.

Now, the distinction between speech and thought is that speech becomes something separate from the speaker, while thought is united with the thinker's soul. And so it is Above. The distinction between creation from G-d's speech and from His thought is that creations from His speech are creatures of the "revealed worlds," possessing their own separate existence. However, from His thought are created beings of the "concealed worlds," who are nullified and united with G-dliness ... And the soul as it exists Above unites with G-dliness, as it is written, "As G-d lives, I stood before Him."[253] The soul stands in constant fear and love, cleaving to G-d, and even as it descends below, its image nevertheless remains with G-d. Even though it goes here and there, the image is one with G-d forever. This is what gives rise to the natural love that is present in the soul, which causes the soul to love G-d's essence from its very depths. The soul arose in His thought, and it is always cleaving to its source.

(From *Sefer Maamorim 5680* (1920) of the Rebbe Rashab, p. 266)

CHASSIDIC INSIGHTS

In answer to these questions, the Tzemach Tzedek says that the name *Havaya* appears twice be-cause G-d's special four-letter name operates from above the spiritual chain of creation and also within it. The first *Havaya* unites with the name *Elokeinu* in order to bring G-dliness that is from beyond cre-ation into creation, making it "ours," so to speak, as in the word *Elokeinu* ("our Lord"). In fact, the name *Elokim* – which represents G-dliness within nature (*Elokim* has the same numerical value as *hateva*

וְהָיָה אִם שָׁמֹעַ תִּשְׁמְעוּ אֶל מִצְוֹתַי אֲשֶׁר

אָנֹכִי מְצַוֶּה אֶתְכֶם הַיּוֹם, לְאַהֲבָה אֶת יְיָ

אֱלֹהֵיכֶם וּלְעָבְדוֹ בְּכָל לְבַבְכֶם וּבְכָל נַפְשְׁכֶם:

וְנָתַתִּי מְטַר אַרְצְכֶם בְּעִתּוֹ יוֹרֶה וּמַלְקוֹשׁ,

וְאָסַפְתָּ דְגָנֶךָ, וְתִירֹשְׁךָ וְיִצְהָרֶךָ:

וְנָתַתִּי עֵשֶׂב בְּשָׂדְךָ לִבְהֶמְתֶּךָ, וְאָכַלְתָּ וְשָׂבָעְתָּ:

or "nature") – is the only name of G-d that takes on the suffix of *einu*, meaning "ours." However, the sec-ond *Havaya* refers to G-d as He transcends nature. That is why it is necessary that His holy name ap-pears twice in the verse – to indi-cate that, whether within nature or transcending nature, G-d is one.

As for the second question – why *echad* and not *yachid* – the Tzemach Tzedek explains that, while *yachid* denotes the true singu-larity and uniqueness of G-d, it does not describe our sensory percep-tion of reality. We see many cre-ations of all types and sizes, from minerals and vegetables to animals and man, including everything from

CHASSIDIC EXCERPTS

Veahavta...Vehaya im Shamoah ("And you shall love...And if you will obey...")

Now, in the first paragraph [of the *shema*], there are forty-two words, from *veahavta* ("You shall love...") through *u'bisharecha* ("and in your gates"), allud-ing to *gevura*. And in the second para-graph there are seventy-two words until *vesamtem* ("and you shall put them"), and seventy-two is the gematria of *chesed*. Now, we must understand, for the Zohar explains that among the four paragraphs of the *shema*, [the first and second] refer to *chesed* and *gevura*. And if so, [*veahavta*] should correspond to *chesed*, while *vehaya* [the second para-graph] should correspond to *gevura*, while here, we are saying just the oppo-site!

But, the matter is as follows. The

names of forty-two and seventy-two correspond to the *kelim*, or vessels of the *sephrot*, as written in the *Tikunei Zohar*, "And when You remove Yourself from them, then these names remain like so many bodies without a soul." Now, the division of the *midot* ("attributes") into *chesed* and *gevura* refers to the *sephirot* themselves. However, when an influx of light from the infinite light that is "not of any *midot* at all" shines down upon them, then an inclusion of the *sephirot* occurs, and they "switch places." The light of *chesed* enters the *keli* of *gevura*...and therefore in the first para-graph, wherein the light is of *chesed* and love, nevertheless the *keli* is *gevura*...

(From *Sefer Maamorim 5660* (1900) of the Rebbe Rashab, Page 371)

Grass in the fields

Venatati esev besadecha..."And I will provide grass in your fields for your animals..."

All year long, during the *kriat shema*, we say, "And I will provide grass in your fields for your animals..."[254] "Animals" refers to the animal soul and the intellectual soul. In order to induce

them as well [as the Divine soul] to agree to love G-d, the sages decreed that we should say the *bircot kriat shema*, which consist of two blessings before the *shema*, mentioning the angels called

CHASSIDIC INSIGHTS

sub-atomic particles to planets and stars many light-years away. Therefore, we want our declaration of G-d's oneness to indicate the underlying oneness of these myriad creations, which is why we say *echad* and not *yachid*. Since we see and are aware of myriad details amid creation, we want to declare not the uniqueness of G-d as He transcends creation, but the oneness of G-d within creation. And the word *echad* conveys that better than does *yachid*.

The Rebbe Rashab discusses[147] which of the two names of G-d – the first *Havaya Elokeinu* or the second *Havaya echad* – is higher in the spiritual hierarchy. He says that the first is higher because it is the source of the souls of the Jewish people. Our souls "arose in His thought,"[148] and *Havaya Elokeinu* is associated with His supernal and divine thought. The second *Havaya* is the source of creation. That is, *Havaya echad* is associated with the unity of creation emerging from the "speech" of G-d, associated with *malchut* of *Atzilut*. And since speech is lower than thought on the spiritual hierarchy, the first *Havaya* of the *Shema* takes precedence over the second.

And now, if you will heed My commandments which I am commanding you today, to love the Lord your G-d and to serve Him, with all of your heart and all of your soul.

Then I will provide the rain of your land in its season, in the fall and in the spring, and you will gather your grain and your wine and your oil.

And I will provide grass in your field for your animals, and you will eat and be satisfied.

CHASSIDIC EXCERPTS

ofanim and *chayot*. And they also decreed that we should say the *pesukei dezimra*, which include a lengthy meditation on the greatness of G-d, until the animal soul also agrees that G-d deserves [our praise]…but in order to arouse the love of the G-dly soul itself, meditation is not so necessary since *ner Havaya nishmat Adam* – "the soul of man is a candle of G-d." It is a natural tendency within the soul of every Jew from their birth and from their source to desire and yearn to

be included in the G-dly light and to cling to it.

And this is what is meant by, "And I will provide grass in your field for your animals…" "Grass" refers to the angels who are conduits of G-dly influx, and through them and by them is brought down the influx from above in order to grant power and strength to transform the animal soul, as written in the Zohar…

(From *Likutei Torah* of the Alter Rebbe, parshat *Re'eh*, page 66 (33B))

Raising holy sparks

Venatati esev besadecha…"And I will provide grass in your fields for your animals…"

The level of angels is dependent upon the status of the *sephira* of *malchut*; when *malchut* descends to become en-clothed in the external dimensions of the worlds, called *sadeh* ("field"), then the angels are called "grass of the field" (meaning that at that time our *avoda* is to refine and elevate the sparks called "fodder" (*chatzir*) and "grass" (*esev*…). And when *malchut* ascends to its place in the world of *Atizlut*, then the angels ascend with it and they are then called

"lion" (*aryeh*) and "oxe" (*shor*) (it seems that this is what is meant by *va'asher mesharetav* – "and those who serve Him…" [referring to the angels that were created during the six days of creation, and remain standing]. That is, when *malchut* is in *Atzilut*, then our *avoda* pertains to angels that are called *behamot* ("animals") and *chayot* ("wild animals"), who serve G-d with *mesirat nefesh* ("dedication and self sacrifice")." This is what is meant by, "and the *chayot*

CHASSIDIC INSIGHTS

However, in a different discourse,[149] the Rebbe Rashab says that the first *Havaya* represents the "lower awareness" (*da'at tachton*) of the world in which creation appears real, and G-d seems to be only in the background. The name *Elokeinu* represents contraction of the infinite light of G-d in order to create the world, and our perception of nature takes place through these contracted lenses. Since our perception is that the physical world is real while G-dliness is concealed, we are only partially nullified to the One Above. This state of mind is associated with *bitul hayesh* ("nullification of the ego"). But, the second *Havaya* represents "higher awareness" (*da'at elyon*) in which we are chiefly aware of G-d, and creation is in the background. Our meditation on this name *Havaya* produces *bitul bemetziut* ("nullification of our very being"). According to this interpretation, the second name *Havaya* of the *Shema* is, therefore, higher than the first.

הִשָּׁמְרוּ לָכֶם פֶּן יִפְתֶּה לְבַבְכֶם, וְסַרְתֶּם

וַעֲבַדְתֶּם אֱלֹהִים אֲחֵרִים וְהִשְׁתַּחֲוִיתֶם לָהֶם:

וְחָרָה אַף יְיָ בָּכֶם וְעָצַר אֶת הַשָּׁמַיִם וְלֹא יִהְיֶה

מָטָר וְהָאֲדָמָה לֹא תִתֵּן אֶת יְבוּלָהּ, וַאֲבַדְתֶּם

מְהֵרָה מֵעַל הָאָרֶץ הַטֹּבָה אֲשֶׁר יְיָ נֹתֵן לָכֶם:

וְשַׂמְתֶּם אֶת דְּבָרַי אֵלֶּה עַל לְבַבְכֶם וְעַל

נַפְשְׁכֶם, וּקְשַׁרְתֶּם אֹתָם לְאוֹת עַל יֶדְכֶם

Another word that comes up for interpretation is *ve'ahavta* ("And you shall love"). The question that is asked is — how is it appropriate to issue a command to love? Love is an emotion of the heart, and how can there be a command to activate an emotion? According to the *Tzemach Tzedek* the answer is that the commandment to love G-d is really a command to meditate upon G-dliness, for by meditating we reach a feeling of love in the heart.

In other words, the *Shema* does not legislate love of G-d but it does cultivate love of G-d based upon meditation on His greatness, so that ultimately we develop the emotion. In other words, the command is to cultivate love of G-d by way of meditation, as indicated by its opening words — *Shema Yisroel* ("Listen Israel"). By listening to the voice of our G-dly soul, we arouse the natural love for G-d that is latent in the heart, and this is our inheritance from Abraham our forefather.

However, as the Rebbe Rashab also explains, *veahavta* indicates a promise as well. It is a promise that by meditating, we will eventually achieve much higher love of G-d, called *ahava rabba* ("great love"). This is the love that Aharon, the High Priest, achieved and brought down to the Jewish people. It cannot be achieved via meditation alone. Rather, it is a gift from above to those who have worked hard to cultivate the lower level of love of G-d. Consequently, *ve'ahavata* implies a promise that we may achieve this high level of G-dly love if we put in the effort.

CHASSIDIC EXCERPTS

ascend," as discussed in several places...And this is also the difference between the *pesukei dezimra* and *kriat shema*...

Now, the refining that takes place regarding *esev*, that occurs when we fulfill a mitzvah, takes place only when man does the mitzvah, as in the saying, 'One who fulfills one mitzvah creates one angel.'[255] So, only when man does a mitzvah does he create an angel. And that is what is meant by "and grass for the service of man;" the refinement that takes place through *esev* takes place only

by way of man. And from where does man gain the power [to perform this task]? Jewish souls are associated with the world of *tikun* ("rectification"), containing the name *ma'ah* (spelling of G-d's holy Name *Havaya* in such a way as to attain the number forty-five, which is the gematria of *adam*, or "man") of *Atzilut*, and the angels are associated with the name *ba'n* (gematria fifty-two, or *behama*, "animal") of *malchut* of *Atzilut*. And that is why they are continually renewed every day, created anew from the process of refinement that

CHASSIDIC INSIGHTS

The Maggid of Mezritch points out that the first paragraph of the *Shema* (beginning with *ve'ahavta*) mentions three kinds of love of G-d: *bekol levavcha* ("with all your heart(s)"), *bekol nafshecha* ("with all your soul"), and *bekol me'odecha* ("with all of your might"). Love *bekol me'odecha* corresponds to the highest form of love of G-d, wherein we are ready for spiritual and physical self-sacrifice out of total commitment to G-d and His Torah. While the other forms of love are attainable by way of meditation and arrive in either direct or indirect response to our own service of G-d, love *bekol me'odecha* is an expression of cleaving to G-d because our soul is an essential part of G-dliness. For that reason, the first paragraph of the *Shema* also does not mention the necessity of becoming involved in the physical world in order to elevate it to a more spiritual level. If we achieve love *bekol me'odecha*, we are sustained from above, from our own connection to G-d, and need not worry about making a living or other physical matters.

However, the second paragraph of the *Shema* does not mention love *bekol me'odecha*. It mentions only the first two types of love of G-d – *bekol levavcha* and *bekol nafshecha*. These categories of love arrive as a result of our efforts in the service of G-d – either because our meditation has made us aware of G-dliness in nature (*memalle*), or because our meditation has made us aware of G-dliness that transcends the world (*sovev*). The former enables us to develop love *bekol levavcha* and the latter leads to *bekol nafshecha*. In the latter case, we may be fixated and consumed with love, but it is not guaranteed. This love arrives to us only if we have first achieved all that we can on the first level of love of G-d. Only then, we might be gifted from above with a taste of love *bekol nafshecha*. But, as long as we have not achieved the highest level of *bekol meodecha* – cleaving to G-d because we have actualized the very essence of the soul – we are not clinging to Him with our very essence. And, because of that, we have to work the land, as the second paragraph states. Then, if we do what G-d wants, we are promised to reap a plentiful harvest. When love *bekol meodecha* is lacking, as much as we love G-d and are transfixed by Him, we must still be involved with the physical world, elevating it and making it into a dwelling place for the King.

Take care amongst yourselves lest you be seduced by your hearts, and you turn away and serve foreign deities and bow down to them.

And then the wrath of the Lord will flare up on you and He will close up the heavens, and there will be no rain and the land will fail to provide its produce, and you will be quickly banished from the good earth that the Lord has given you. And you shall place these words of Mine upon your heart and upon your soul, and tie them as a sign upon your hands and as compartments between your eyes.

*

CHASSIDIC EXCERPTS

takes place with the name *ba'n*. For the angels that were created during the six days of creation were created from Above. Just as souls were created, so angels were created (souls were created on a higher level than angels, as known, but nonetheless, the angels were also created from Above). But the angels that are renewed every day are created as a result of the *avoda* of man below, as he performs the divine service of *avodat habirurim* – "refinement of the sparks." Now, the name *ma'h* is what refines the name *ba'n*, and therefore man has the

ability to elevate the "grass of the field" which are the angels that are refined from out of *klipat noga*.

An example of this is the revelation of the *magid* ("teacher") to the Rav Beit Yoseph, *z'l*, from the *mishnayot* that he learned. This *magid* told the Beit Yoseph, "I am the *mishnah* speaking in your mouth." Since the breath of his mouth, coming from his enlivening soul, was completely purified by learning *mishnayot*, the breath itself was totally refined, and from it was created an angel. Similarly, all the learning that man does

CHASSIDIC INSIGHTS

Finally, the Rebbeim describe a compound meditation on the first and second paragraphs of the *Shema*. This meditation requires that we focus simultaneously on two facets of the *Shema*. One is the "meaning" and the other is the "composition" of a given paragraph in terms of numbers of words. The meaning is called the *ohr* ("light") of the paragraph, while the composition is called the *keli* ("vessel") of the paragraph. As we meditate, we must keep both in mind, since both are important elements of focus while reciting the *Shema*. In truth, chasidic literature from the Alter Rebbe and the Mitteler Rebbe on this subject is complicated, and at times contradictory, as pointed out by the Tzemach Tzedek (see the translated excerpts). However, the Rebbe Rashab offers a resolution to the apparent contradictions, and since he is the latest of the Rebbeim to comment, as well as the one who offers a resolution, it is his interpretation that we adopt here.

וְהָיוּ לְטוֹטָפֹת בֵּין עֵינֶיכֶם:

וְלִמַּדְתֶּם אֹתָם אֶת בְּנֵיכֶם לְדַבֵּר בָּם, בְּשִׁבְתְּךָ

בְּבֵיתֶךָ וּבְלֶכְתְּךָ בַדֶּרֶךְ וּבְשָׁכְבְּךָ וּבְקוּמֶךָ:

וּכְתַבְתָּם עַל מְזוּזוֹת בֵּיתֶךָ וּבִשְׁעָרֶיךָ:

לְמַעַן יִרְבּוּ יְמֵיכֶם וִימֵי בְנֵיכֶם עַל הָאֲדָמָה

אֲשֶׁר נִשְׁבַּע יְיָ לַאֲבֹתֵיכֶם לָתֵת לָהֶם, כִּימֵי

הַשָּׁמַיִם עַל הָאָרֶץ:

However, it is appropriate to begin the discussion by mentioning the concept of *orot* ("lights") versus *kelim* ("vessels"). Although we tend to understand these terms intuitively, we can understand them more precisely by examining what seems to be a difference of opinion between two Torah giants, the Rambam and the Maharal of Prague, regarding the descriptions that the Torah applies to G-d.[150] This, in turn, will shed light on the *kavana* ("intention") that we need to develop during the *Shema*. These two (and other) Torah sages seek to explain why the Torah variously describes G-d as "merciful," "vengeful," "loving," "jealous," "patient," etc. If G-d is one and indivisible, as Judaism believes, then how

involves the breath of his mouth as he speaks. This also applies to our knowledge and grasp of Torah as it becomes enclothed in our natural intellect and animal soul. This is particularly true when we coerce ourselves to learn - we refine the animal soul. When we learn one tractate, for example, one angel is created, and so for every mitzvah that we do, we refine *klipat noga*. This is what is meant by *yotzar meshartim* – "He Who forms serving angels..." – referring to the angels that are constantly renewed from the refinement process that we perform every day. Thus, we say "and I will provide grass in your fields" in particular for each and every Jew. For, what we refine of our portion by fulfilling mitzvoth and learning Torah, is called "grass of your fields." And "for your animals" refers to the particular ray of the name *ba'n* of *malchut*...And since man is from the name *ma'h*, he is the one to refine the name *ba'n*, and that is why we say "grass in your fields for your animals..."

(From *Sefer Maamorim 5661* (1901) of the Rebbe Rashab, page 208)

Grass that grows on its own...

Venatati esev besadecha..."And I will provide grass in your fields for your animals..."

And now, we must understand what the verse says, "And I will provide grass in your fields for your animals..." which we say after mentioning human food in the previous verse, "and you will gather your grain and your wine and your oil..." And then, after mentioning "grass for your animals," we go on to say, "and you will eat and be satisfied." From this order of the verses, the

CHASSIDIC INSIGHTS

can all these descriptions, some of which are opposite of one another, apply to G-d simultaneously?

The Rambam distinguishes between wisdom and knowledge, as opposed to other G-dly traits. He says that since G-d created the universe, therefore by knowing Himself, G-d knows all there is to know. And therefore, He, His knowledge and the universe are all one ("He is the Knower, He is the Known, and He is the Knowledge itself – all is one...")[151] However, the Rambam does not apply this solution to other G-dly traits, such as, for example, jealousy, vengeance, patience, etc. These traits describe the various effects that G-d has upon the world, but they do not describe G-d Himself in the same way as intellect and knowledge do.

Writing a few hundred years later, the Maharal of Prague differs from the Rambam. He does not accept the Rambam's distinction between knowledge and the other G-dly attributes. The Maharal says that knowledge is no different from the other "tools" with which G-d affects the world, and we cannot say that G-d is "one" with His knowledge and yet separate from the rest of His attributes. Knowledge is but one of the means with which G-d deals with His world. G-d is far above and beyond the creation, but

> And you should teach them to your children, speaking of them as you sit in your house and as you travel on the road, and when you lie down and when you arise.
> And you should write them on the doorposts of your houses and on your gates.
> In order to prolong your days and the days of your children upon the land that the Lord swore to give to your fathers, for as long as the heavens are over the earth.

He lowers Himself to get involved with man and creation using the "tools" that the Torah mentions. Much the same as a painter paints with a brush and a lumberjack chops wood with an axe, G-d metes out justice with His attribute of *gevura* ("strictness") and administers kindness with His aspect of *chesed*, for example. Similarly, He knows His world using His attribute of "knowledge" and controls it

CHASSIDIC EXCERPTS

sages derived that it is forbidden for man to eat before giving food to his animals.

In order to understand this properly, it is necessary to comprehend what is meant by "grass." The Hebrew word for grass – *esev* – contains three letters; *eyn-sin-beit*. Dissembling the letters, we see that *esev* is composed of *sin* and the letters *eyn-beit*. *Eyn-beit*, with (*gematria*) of seventy-two is one of the ways of spelling G-d's holy name *Havaya*.[256] [Getting back to the scripture], at first glance we have contradictory verses, for elsewhere it states, "And I will germinate fodder for the cattle, and grass for the service of man."[257] And if fodder and grass are two different species, both are nonetheless animal food, so why does the verse say that grass is for the "service of man?"

But, in truth the verse does not say that the grass is "food for man," but rather, "for the service of man." "Service" in this context means "fixing" and "rectifying." It refers to the divine service of man, who was born "in the image of G-d," as he recites the *pesukei dezimra*, singing the praises of G-d. The angels, about whom we say, "I will germinate fodder for the animals..." also serve G-d in this manner [of singing His praises]. The Hebrew word for animal (*behama*) bears the *gematria* of fifty-two, corresponding to the name *ba'n* [associated with G-dly sparks in the physical world which need purifying and uplifting]. And [the service of man] is associated with the name *eyn-bet*...

...this [G-dly service] is comparable to fodder that grows in the field on its own, sprouting from the power of the

CHASSIDIC INSIGHTS

wisely using His "wisdom." All are but "tools" in His repertoire, which He uses or sets aside at His will.

The two sides of the discussion correspond to the two components of the *sephirot*. The early kabbalists (following the Ramban and preceding the Ari) determined that the Rambam was correct regarding the *orot* of the *sephirot*. They are always connected and one with the One Above, like a ray of light to its source. Thus, not only knowledge, but all of G-d's attributes have a source that is infinite, and they are connected with that source just as a ray of light is connected to its source.

וַיֹּאמֶר יְיָ אֶל מֹשֶׁה לֵּאמֹר:

דַּבֵּר אֶל בְּנֵי יִשְׂרָאֵל וְאָמַרְתָּ אֲלֵהֶם וְעָשׂוּ לָהֶם

צִיצִת עַל כַּנְפֵי בִגְדֵיהֶם לְדֹרֹתָם, וְנָתְנוּ עַל

צִיצִת הַכָּנָף פְּתִיל תְּכֵלֶת:

On the other hand, the G-dly attributes also function as tools, with which G-d controls and manipulates His universe. The early kabbalists suggested that this is the aspect of the *sephirot* that we call *kelim*. They are the second component of the *sephirot*, functioning as tools which G-d chooses and discards at will, much as the Maharal of Prague described. Together, the *orot* and the *kelim* comprise the *sephirot*. In this manner, the arguments of the Rambam and the Maharal come together to give us a greater understanding of the *sephirot*.

Now, we may apply our new-found understanding to the *Shema*.

In the first paragraph, it is possible to speak of the *ohr* ("meaning") of the paragraph as love of G-d, as indicated by the first word *ve'ahavta* ("you shall love"). However, the *keli* ("composition") is fear of

CHASSIDIC EXCERPTS

land that was infused by the divine creative utterance, "Let the land give forth pasture..." We cut the fodder, yet it returns and grows back, germinating repeatedly without limit or measure. The elevation of holy sparks that fell into the *klipa* (concealment of spirituality) known as *noga* (which is mixed good and bad) occurs in a similar manner. The sparks emerge on their own, nullified from *yesh* ("ego, existence") to *ayn* ("nothingness, nullification"). Similarly, we find that converts emerge of their own volition from among the holy sparks, from among the nations of the world where they were found, and become included in the *shechina* like a "candle." In this manner, the process of refining the sparks from *noga* takes place every day, and from the sparks are created new angels every day from *yesh* to *ayn*...

Since this elevation takes place daily, the verse uses the word *matzmiach*, or "germinate," regarding the animal food...and the word is in the active form, indicating a force that acts directly upon the vegetation, causing it to germinate...and this is because the power of the land to give forth vegetation of grass and fodder without sowing seeds at all is a power that descends from Above to elicit the ground's innate ability to sprout vegetation on its own, just as in the utterance, "Let the land give forth pasture..." Similarly the verse says, "And I will provide grass in your fields..." meaning that I am the One Who puts this grass in your fields...

And this is why the second paragraph of the *kriat shema* mentions, "And I will provide grass in your fields for your animals..." before [it mentions that man will eat and be satisfied]; this is in order to grant power and strength among the angels and also among the as yet immature G-dly souls [among those who are under the age of bar mitzvah], all the way down to the animal soul of man in this world, to ascend above. That is what the verse means by "I will provide *esev* ('eyn-sin-beit')," alluding to the

CHASSIDIC INSIGHTS

G-d. We deduce this because there are forty-two words in the paragraph. The number forty-two is associated with *Ana Bekoach*, the forty-two letter name of G-d that is recited at moments of spiritual ascent. And spiritual ascent, in turn, is associated with the *sephira* of *gevura*, since it takes discipline and concentration to ascend the spiritual ladder. So, the first paragraph demands focus on two opposites: love, as the *ohr* of the paragraph, and fear (since the inner dimension of *gevura* is fear of G-d) as the *keli* of the paragraph.

The situation is the opposite regarding the second paragraph. The paragraph states that if the Jews turn away from G-d, then He will unleash His fury against them. So, the *ohr* of the second paragraph is *gevura*. However, the *keli* is *chesed*. We deduce the latter because there are seventy-two words from the beginning of the paragraph until the word *vesamtem*, and these seventy-two words represent the "seventy-two bridges of kindness" that come down to us from above. They come from the name *Havaya* as

> And the Lord spoke to Moshe, saying:
>
> Speak to the children of Israel and tell them, 'Make fringes on the corners of your garments throughout their generations, and place a thread of blue-green within the fringes of the corners.'

spelled with the numerical value of seventy-two, which is the highest of the four ways of spelling G-d's holy name. This name serves as a conduit for the descent of kindness to the world, but His kindness is so high, providing so much illumination, that it would overwhelm the world if it weren't broken up into channels. This is comparable to a bridge over a river, standing on several pillars. If the bridge stood on only one pillar, then the water could sweep it away. But, when the flow of water is broken up into

CHASSIDIC EXCERPTS

name *eyn-beit*, associated with the attribute of *chesed*, to descend from on High to below to the lowest point of angels and *ofanim* which are then refined and elevated from *noga*...and then [the verse mentions] "human consumption," alluding to the joining of the G-dly soul in a state of spiritual maturity (*gadlut hamochin*).

(From *Imrei Bina* of the Mittler Rebbe, page *Nun-Zayin* (Ch. 61))

Love with all of our soul

Ubekol nafshecha u'bekol meodecha ("...with all your soul and with all your might")

Now, *ratzoh* ("desire" and "pursuit" of G-dliness) in our *avoda* down here is expressed by the desire to give up our soul while saying the word *echad* [during the *kriat shema*]. It is written in the Zohar in several places that *mesirat nefesh* ("giving up the soul") occurs during the word *echad*, and that this is equivalent to the elevation and expiry of the soul. This is also indicated in what the sages said about R' Akiva,[258] who sought to meditate at length on the word *echad*, until his soul expired. This statement also implies that *mesirat nefesh* occurs while saying the word *echad*.

And at first glance, this is not understood, for regarding the phrase [that we say in the first paragraph of the *kriat*

shema], *ubekol nafshecha* ("with all of your heart"), the sages said [that we must love G-d], "even if He takes away your soul." And if so, the main act of *mesirat nefesh* occurs while saying *ubekol nafshecha*. And similarly regarding R' Akiva, the Talmud records that he used to say to his students, "All of my life I have been troubled about the verse, 'And with all of my soul"[259] - even if He takes away your soul - when will I be enabled to fulfill this mitzvah?" The implication is that *mesirat nefesh* occurs as we say *ubekol nafshecha*, yet nevertheless R' Akiva meditated at length during the word *echad*, until his soul expired?

However, the matter is as follows; there are two types of *mesirat nefesh*. The

CHASSIDIC INSIGHTS

several streams or channels by several different pillars, then the bridge is able to withstand the force of the water. This is what is meant by seventy-two bridges of kindness – each bridge is a channel of kindness that comes down into the world via the seventy-two words of the second paragraph of the *Shema*.

So, here, as in the first paragraph, we see that the meaning (*ohr*) and the composition (*keli*) are opposite of one another. The meaning of the second paragraph (strictness, fear) is about ascent, but the composition (kindness, love) is about descent. The second paragraph is a paragraph of *shuv* ("return") in which the goal is to bring the love down to permeate creation. And for that reason, love with all your might (*bekol meodecha*) is not mentioned. Only love that is *bekol levavcha* and *bekol nafshecha*

וְהָיָה לָכֶם לְצִיצִת וּרְאִיתֶם אֹתוֹ וּזְכַרְתֶּם אֶת

כָּל מִצְוֹת יְיָ וַעֲשִׂיתֶם אֹתָם, וְלֹא תָתוּרוּ אַחֲרֵי

לְבַבְכֶם וְאַחֲרֵי עֵינֵיכֶם אֲשֶׁר אַתֶּם זֹנִים

אַחֲרֵיהֶם:

לְמַעַן תִּזְכְּרוּ וַעֲשִׂיתֶם אֶת כָּל מִצְוֹתָי, וִהְיִיתֶם

קְדֹשִׁים לֵאלֹהֵיכֶם:

אֲנִי יְיָ אֱלֹהֵיכֶם אֲשֶׁר הוֹצֵאתִי אֶתְכֶם מֵאֶרֶץ מִצְרַיִם לִהְיוֹת לָכֶם לֵאלֹהִים, אֲנִי

יְיָ אֱלֹהֵיכֶם

CHASSIDIC EXCERPTS

first is of the G-dly soul, which seeks to become included in its source from where it was hewn, in order to become subsumed and nullified in the infinite light of G-d's simple unity, with expiry of the soul. And the second *mesirat nefesh* is of the body, when we accept upon ourselves any suffering of the body, G-d forbid, with determination not to deny, Heaven forfend, His unity. And this is real *kiddush HaShem* ("sanctification of G-d's Name"). Or it may be sanctification of His Name in potential, as we estimate within ourselves how we may be forced to deny G-d, and made to suffer all types of pain, and yet we make a determined decision within ourselves to undergo all this suffering and to stand up to the test. And this *mesirat nefesh* of the body occurs as we say the phrase, *ubekol nafshecha* – "which all of your soul" – "even if He takes away your soul." It is about this *mesirat nefesh* that R' Akiva said, "all of my life I have been troubled...when will I fulfill..." the

mitzvah of giving up his soul in reality, for *Kiddush HaShem*, regarding the body.

And the meditation that R' Akiva undertook at length during the word *echad* was *mesirat nefesh* of the soul, since the soul seeks to expire, and to be included in G-d's simple unity. (And this that he meditated at length on the word *echad* at the very moment that he was put to death in sanctification of G-d's Name, was certainly *mesirat nefesh* of the soul, even without the meditation – perhaps we can say that the *mesirat nefesh* of his body added intensity and determination to the desire of his soul [to expire], and therefore it took place precisely at that time he meditated at length [on the word *echad*], since he was also in a state of real expiry of the soul).

And in *avoda*, these two aspects of *mesirat nefesh* are *mesirat nefesh* of the G-dly soul, and of the animal soul. For, the *mesirat nefesh* of the animal soul takes place in order to overwhelm its spirit of lust, to prevent it from striving

CHASSIDIC INSIGHTS

are mentioned, because these two kinds of love of G-d are confined to the limitations of our bodies and soul-powers.

The above summary of meditations regarding the *Shema* is limited in scope and fails to do justice to the vastness of chasidic literature on the subject. Obviously, if an entire detailed and nuanced volume (the *Imrei Bina*) was written on the subject – and that is just one composition of one Rebbe – then the amount of material on the *Shema* is voluminous. Hopefully though, this brief summary provides an introduction and starting point to meditation on the *Shema*. Since it is a pinnacle of intellectual activity of our prayers, it is important for us to dedicate a maximum amount of time researching the themes and details of the *Shema* in order that we see our "days and years lengthened."

And they should be fringes for you, and you shall look at them, and remember all the commandments of the Lord, and fulfill them, without straying after your hearts and after your eyes, that you lust after them.

So that you recall and fulfill all of My commandments, and you shall be holy to your G-d.

I am the Lord, your G-d, I am He Who brought you out of the land of Egypt in order to be your G-d, I am the Lord your G-d.

after physical lusts and pleasures. Quite the opposite, [the purpose is] to transform his heart so that it is full of love and desire for G-d – this is the subject of *mesirat nefesh* of the body. And *mesirat nefesh* of the soul occurs within the G-dly soul, for *mesirat nefesh* means to give over the will, since *nefesh* is the will, as in the verse, "I have no desire (*nafshi*) for this people,"[260] wherein the word *nafshi* means "my desire." Here, our goal is to give over our every will and desire to G-d, may He be blessed, in order that there should not be any [other] desire whatsoever...

Sefer Maamorim 5664 of the Rebbe Rashab, Page 191)

HaShem echad…("the Lord is One…")

It is possible that our hidden power of *chochma* is the feeling within our soul that experiences the essence of G-dliness and that, without G-d, nothing exists whatsoever. And the faculty of concealed *bina* is the feeling within our soul that G-dliness is everything, meaning that every object that exists is G-dly. And these are the two perspectives – from below to Above and from Above to below – of the *Shema* as we utter the words *HaShem echad* ("G-d is one"). From below to Above, the seven heavens and the earth, as well as the four di- rections of the universe, are nullified to the infinite illumination of the Master of the Universe, and "before Him, all is as naught." That is, He is the One and Only and there is no other.[261] And the second perspective from Above to below is what the sages said in the Talmud, "When I reign Above and below and in all four directions of the universe, nothing more is necessary."[262] That is, the Infinite One is the Master of the Universe, and this is what is meant when we say that "everything is G-dly."

(From *Sefer Maamorim 5665* (1905) of the Rebbe Rashab, p. 272)

CHASSIDIC INSIGHTS

EMET VEYATZIV

Following the work of refining our animal soul during the blessings preceding the *Shema*, and transforming it during the *Shema* itself, our focus shifts to our G-dly soul. That happens as we arrive near the end of the *Shema*, to the prayer *Emet Veyatziv*.[152] If we have properly labored to refine and ultimately "sacrifice" our animal soul, then the G-dly soul begins to take over as we say *Emet Veyatziv*.[153]

אֱ֒מֶת, וְיַצִּיב, וְנָכוֹן, וְקַיָּם, וְיָשָׁר, וְנֶאֱמָן:

וְאָהוּב וְחָבִיב, וְנֶחְמָד וְנָעִים, וְנוֹרָא וְאַדִּיר,

וּמְתֻקָּן וּמְקֻבָּל, וְטוֹב וְיָפֶה, הַדָּבָר הַזֶּה עָלֵינוּ

לְעוֹלָם וָעֶד:

The Chasidic masters tell us that the G-dly soul is associated with the first two letters of G-d's name – *yud-hey* – because these are the two letters that represent divine intellect (*chochma* and *bina*). And, with meditation, our G-dly soul draws divine intellect into the creation.

These two letters have the *gematria* ("numerical value") of fifteen, and at this time we recite the

CHASSIDIC EXCERPTS

Emet Veyatziv ("True and certain...")

The *Radah* (Rabbi David Abudarham) wrote that in *Emet Veyatziv* are found fifteen *vovin* ("hooks") – one for each of its fifteen words, all of which start with the letter *vov*. These correspond to the fifteen Songs of Ascent (Psalms 120-134) written by King David, and the *Zohar*[263] observes that David sang praises of G-d in order to elevate his level ... saying, "I lift my eyes to the mountains..."[264]

And it is possible that the reason for the fifteen Songs of Ascent is that they correspond to the first two letters (*yud-hey*) of G-d's name, which are called *mima'amakim* ("from the depths") [because they elevate us from the depths], as the *Zohar* says elsewhere ... And it also is explained in *Likutei Torah*[265] – that they correspond to the letters *yud-hey*. And, therefore, the festivals of Passover and Sukkot also fall out on the fifteenth of the month...

And so in the prayer *Emet Veyatziv* [we say] "true and certain, established is this thing," wherein "this thing" refers to *malchut* of *Atzilut*, which is the spiritual level of King David. And about this it is written, "Those who are of strength do His will,"[266] meaning that they rectify "this thing," and that takes place by way of the fifteen words corresponding to the fifteen Songs of Ascent, in order to invoke *yud-hey* from the depths.

(From *Meah Shearim* of the Tzemach Tzedek, p. 99)

Hearing with the heart
Emet Veyatziv ("True and certain...")

There is a statement of the Talmudic sages:[267] "At the time that the Jews said, *naaseh venishmah* ('we will do and we will hear'), the angels descended and crowned them with two crowns, one corresponding to *naaseh* and the other corresponding to *nishmah*."

Now, *nishmah* cannot mean "hearing with the ears," since it was impossible for them to begin fulfilling the commandments before they actually heard [them]. Of necessity, they had to first hear and only then could they could follow the commandments. Rather, *nishmah* refers to "hearing of the heart," meaning that what they heard [the Torah] was acceptable to them. This is similar to the Aramaic rendition (*Targum Onkelos*) of, "And they did not hear Moses" which translates as: "They did not accept what they heard from Moses." That is, they heard with their ears, but what they heard was not acceptable to them.

CHASSIDIC INSIGHTS

fifteen initial words of the prayer, *Emet Veyatziv*, all of which begin with the letter *vov*. As the *Zohar* says regarding this prayer, "with *vovs* you will be connected." The letter *vov* is a connecting letter, since it means "and" (the word *vov* also means "hook" or "connector"), and it serves as the connection between the G-dly soul and the infinite light of the One Above, as well as His creation below.

There are other instances in the Torah in which the number fifteen plays a prominent role. For example, fifteen was the number of steps between the holy area of the Temple where the sacrifices were offered, and the courtyard where people prayed and/or waited to offer their sacrifices. There are fifteen psalms (numbers 120 through 134) called the "songs of ascent," which the Levites recited as they descended to the source of water of the Temple. And in prayer, the first *T*rue; and certain and established and lasting; and straightforward and trustworthy and beloved; and endearing and delightful and pleasant; and awesome and mighty and correct, and acceptable and good and beautiful, is this thing for us forever and ever.

CHASSIDIC EXCERPTS

And if so, this explanation of *venishmah* is as we say in our prayers, *Emet veyatziv ... umekubal vetov veyafe hadavar hazeh* ("true and certain, established ... and acceptable and good and nice is this thing"). We know that *davar hazeh* ("this thing") applies to *echad* ("one") and *veahavta* ("You shall love...") within the recitation of the *Shema*. And "this thing" is acceptable to us, meaning that in our heart we truly desire it, and it is good and pleasant...

(From *Yom Tov shel Rosh Hashana 5666* (1905-6) of the Rebbe Rashab, p. 529)

Letter of connection
Emet Veyatziv ("True and certain...")

All this [*Pesukei DeZimra* and *Kriat Shema*] is intended to transform the physical nature of the body and the animal soul, which become refined only upon arousal of the physical heart, as it says in Psalms, *Libi ubesari yeranenu* ("My heart and my flesh sing out").[268] And then, as we recite the prayer, *Emet Veyatziv*, we begin to serve G-d with the G-dly soul for the purpose of its elevation as the reward for its service. This is what is meant by *bevavin titkatar*[269] ("with *vovin* you will be connected"), referring to the fifteen *vovs* of *Emet Veyayatziv*, which represent descent of spirituality from *tzaddik chai olamin* ("the righteous who is the life of all worlds"), which also corresponds to the theme of the *vov* [for the *tzaddik*, like the *vov*, brings down and joins G-dliness with the world]...

This is what is meant by *emet veyatziv* ("true and certain"), which comes from the phrase, *yetziva milta umetukan umekubal* ("a definite fact, correct and acceptable"),[270] and which confirms the truth of the wholehearted love that is mentioned in the *Shema*. When the love of G-d *bekol levavcha* ("with all your heart(s)") – meaning with both of your inclinations [the good and the evil] – is "true," and the flame of *yud-hay* of the G-dly soul is real, and the animal soul is burned and consumed within it, then a [ray] is drawn down from Above to connect with the G-dly soul, uniting and joining it with Above.

This is supernal love ... which in particular [occurs] during the *Shemonah Esreh*, when we experience the *bitul* of the soul itself as it becomes nullified in existence. This [is also the theme expressed by] the *kol demama daka* ("still small voice"), the "inner voice" mentioned previously. But, all this takes place after the initial labor [of prayer] to purify the animal soul, in proportion to the service of *Pesukei DeZimra* and of the *Shema* which purify the animal soul. Ac-

CHASSIDIC INSIGHTS

fifteen words of *Yishtabach* (immediately preceding *Barchu*), signal the transition from *Pesukei DeZimra* (prayer service on the level of *ruach*) to the blessings before the *Shema* (prayer service on the level of *neshama*). Here, too, a transition takes place as we recite *Emet Veyatziv* and shift from refinement of the animal soul to a focus on the G-dly soul alone. This is because every time that we ascend to a new and higher level of G-dly service, we are in need of illumination from above. This illumination is con-

אֱמֶת, אֱלֹהֵי עוֹלָם מַלְכֵּנוּ צוּר יַעֲקֹב מָגֵן

יִשְׁעֵנוּ, לְדֹר וָדֹר הוּא קַיָּם, וּשְׁמוֹ קַיָּם, וְכִסְאוֹ

נָכוֹן. וּמַלְכוּתוֹ וֶאֱמוּנָתוֹ לָעַד קַיֶּמֶת.

veyed by His holy four-letter name. The first two letters (*yud-hey*) are associated with the *sephirot* of *chochma* and *bina*, which bring down the infinite light of G-d into human intellect while we meditate and pray. The *vovs* continue the task, joining the intellect with the emotions (love and fear of G-d) and uplifting them. The rest takes place as we pray the *Shemonah Esreh*.

Thus the prayer *Emet Veyatziv* transitions us from the *Shema* to the *Shemonah Esreh*. It acts as a reward for our previous work of contemplation, in which we neutralized the animal soul by convincing it that divinity is good for it, and then, we prepared to cleave to G-d by completely eliminating the animal soul. During *Emet Veyatzviv* we confirm the truth and verify all that we have meditated upon during the *Shema* and before. The verification, called *hitamtut* (from the word *emet* or "truth") comes in the form of *reiah d'chochma* ("seeing in the mind's eye"), which is just short of seeing G-dliness with the naked eye (which will only take place during the messianic age, once the third and permanent Temple is built). But, it is enough to assure us that our efforts in meditation had been on the right track. We then launch into the

CHASSIDIC EXCERPTS

cording to that initial labor, do we achieve the nullification of the soul and its unity with G-d during the *Shemonah* *Esreh*, when we experience a revelation of love from Above.

(From *Yom Tov shel Rosh Hashana* 5666 (1906) of the Rebbe Rashab, p. 145)

The Divine soul kicks in
Emet Veyatziv ("True and certain...")

In particular during the weekday prayers, we find the two levels mentioned above. But, as discussed elsewhere, within prayer there are three general levels. The first is from *Baruch She'Amar* until the *kriat shema* (and including the *kriat shema*), *emet veyatzvi* until the *shemonah esreh*, and then the *shemonah esreh* itself.

The subject is as follows; during *Baruch She'amar* and the *pesukei dezimra* we must specifically pray in a loud voice and with excitement that we experience in our heart and mind. Similar to the angels, who sing their "song" with much fanfare and additional excitement, the praise and exultations [uttered by] souls must take place with commotion. The same is true of the *kriat shema* as we say *shema Yisrael*, etc, and *ve'ahavta* – "you shall love with all your heart(s)" – all

this must take place with much noise, as written elsewhere. The reason for this is that we must refine and transform the physicality of the natural soul and turn it into something G-dly. And arousal of our heart of flesh alone does not suffice for this purpose. Just as the sacrifices took place with fire that was ignited from below, so during prayer, the excitement of the fleshly heart takes place with fire from below. Nevertheless, the main objective is the fire from above, which is the excitement of the G-dly soul that is drawn down to refine the animal soul. And since the refiner must enclothe himself within the "garment" of what he wishes to refine, therefore he as well feels the excitement that is experienced, specifically with noise, and in this way the animal soul is refined...and about this, the Torah says, "For the Jews

CHASSIDIC INSIGHTS

Shemonah Esreh, cleaving to the One Above, asking Him to fulfill our specific needs (physical as well as spiritual).

*

In truth, the sages who formulated the prayers gave us many opportunities to prepare for this transition. There are hints of spirituality embedded throughout the prayer service, and these hints become progressively clearer. To begin with, in the opening prayer, *Baruch She'Amar*, we find references to G-d's name without the name itself being mentioned. We see it in the phrase, *Baruch Shemo* ("Blessed be His name"), which includes all of the previous revelations of G-dliness alluded to by the word *baruch* within the prayer.[154] And then we see it again near the end of the prayer, in the phrase, *Meshubach u'mefuar adei ad shemo hagadol*

True, G-d of the universe is our King, the Rock of Jacob is the shield of our salvation, from generation to generation He endures, and His name endures, and His throne is established, and His reign and His faith last forever.

("Praised and glorified is His great name forever and ever"). Why do the sages refer to G-d only as "His name," in this prayer? If the intention was to focus us on a specific name of G-d, then why not specify this name, as most of the prayers do? And if not, why refer obliquely to G-d at all?

At the end of *Pesukei DeZimra*, in the prayer *Yishtabach*, we again refer to the name of G-d. There, we say *Brachot vehoda'ot leshimcha hagadol* ("Blessings and thanks to Your great and holy name"). What is this great and holy name that is apparently so exalted that it cannot be specified or pronounced?

We get some clarification as we recite the blessings preceding the *Shema* when we say, "all of [the

CHASSIDIC EXCERPTS

are Mine like servants," in order to perform the service of refinement, purifying the animal soul. This demands much labor and effort until the animal soul understands and grasps the topic and G-dly light shines within it so that it is excited with love.

And the second level begins from *emet veyatziv*, when we perform the service of the G-dly soul for the purpose of self-elevation – not [merely] to rectify the body, as written, "All souls praise *yud-hey...*" as above. And this is the reward [of the G-dly soul] for all of her service [in this world] – that it should attain elevation for itself (since certainly within this elevation there is additional

illumination over and above the refinement that takes place within the animal soul...).

And the beginning of *emet veyatziv* brings down an influx from above in order to join the souls with G-dliness. This is the matter of the fifteen *vovin* of *emet veyatziv*, which represent fifteen descents from above, as in the [Shabbat nighttime song], *be'vavin titkatar* ("with *vovin* you be connected").

And the third level of the *shemonah esreh* itself, which are the eighteen blessings of prayer, during which we bow at the word *baruch*...represents abject nullification of the self, in total [nullification]

(From *Sefer Maamorim 5663* (1903) of the Rebbe Rashab, Pp. 10-11)

It's all good...more stages of descent
Emet Veyatziv ("True and certain...")

There are many levels of good (*tov*) ... and they correspond to the fifteen levels of the *sephira* of *yesod* within the five *partzufim* ("structures" of ten *sephirot*) of every world. They also correspond to

the fifteen *vovs* of *Emet Veyatziv* as the *Zohar* says, "with *vovin* you will be connected." [The *vov* ("hook/connector") is in the form of a vertical line, joining top and bottom and like *yesod* it joins and

CHASSIDIC INSIGHTS

angels] open their mouths in holiness and purity…and bless and adore, glorify and revere…the name of the Almighty G-d." So, at least we know that not only we but also the angels praise, extol and look for revelation of "His name." Still what is this name, and why do we not specify and describe it?

This name – to which we first refer to obliquely – becomes progressively more defined throughout our prayers. Of course, it is the four-letter name of G-d, the name *Havaya*. It represents G-d in essence, beyond creation, beyond time and space. It is mentioned in a veiled fashion, as "His great name," or just "His name" until we reach the *Shema*, when we recite it openly. (In the first verse, we mention His name twice – once as He is revealed within creation, and once as He transcends the entire spiritual hierarchy of creation). And even though we do mention the name *Havaya* in the psalms that compose the *Pesukei DeZimra*, this is compa-

וּדְבָרָיו חָיִים וְקַיָּמִים, נֶאֱמָנִים וְנֶחֱמָדִים לָעַד

עַל (*kiss and release the tzitzit*) וּלְעוֹלְמֵי עוֹלָמִים

אֲבוֹתֵינוּ וְעָלֵינוּ, עַל בָּנֵינוּ וְעַל דּוֹרוֹתֵינוּ, וְעַל

כָּל דּוֹרוֹת זֶרַע יִשְׂרָאֵל עֲבָדֶיךָ:

rable to how our forefathers mentioned His name before the Torah was given. When G-d said that He would reveal His true name to Moses, the commentaries point out that the forefathers already knew and used this name. However, although Abraham, Isaac and Jacob knew the name *Havaya* and used it, they did so only in conjunction with other G-dly names. It was only to Moses that G-d revealed His name in its full, pristine form.[155] Similarly, when we mention G-d's four-letter name throughout the *Pesukei DeZimra*, it is in relation to how He created and maintains the universe. It is only after *Barchu*, and especially during the *Shema*, that we meditate upon His name in its pristine form, as it transcends creation. (In fact, during the closing prayers of *Pesukei DeZimra*, we recite the story of Moses and the exodus from Egypt, so we see that the historical transition is also embedded in the prayers.)

Since the verses of *Pesukei DeZimra* awaken the natural emotions of love and fear of G-d within us while purifying our animal soul, full-fledged revelation of transcendent G-dliness is not yet appropriate. We are still trapped within the limitations of the animal soul, much as the Jews in Egypt were trapped. (Note that the Hebrew for Egypt, *Mitzrayim*, comes from the word *meitzarim*, meaning "limitations.") The purpose of the *Pesukei DeZimra* is to make us aware of the amazing nature of creation, while "pruning away" the "thorns" or limitations that prevent us from developing full awareness of G-dliness. So, at this stage, it is not appropriate to mention G-d's name in its most pristine state of revelation. However, when we reach the *Shema* and do away with the animal soul, it is time for full revelation of

CHASSIDIC EXCERPTS

unites…] and the connection brings down influx from Above. [This is what is meant by "with *vovin* you will be connected."[271] The fifteen *vovs* represent the fifteen *yesodot* ("levels of connection") within the five *partzufim* of every world. In every *partzuf*, there are three such levels of connection.

The explanation of the three levels of connection (*yesodot*) within every *partzuf* is as follows:

We already know that *yesod* is also called *kol* ("all") [since all influx from Above flows through *yesod* into *malchut*.] The word *kol* has the numerical value of fifty, alluding to the fifty "gates of understanding" (*shaarei bina*). These "gates" are channels of influx flowing

from *bina*, and just as a gate serves as an entrance and exit (in our case spiritual ascent and descent) … everything passes through these gates…

Now, there are "gates" within *bina* ("understanding") itself. And there are gates that lead to the heart, as we say, "the heart understands."[272] That is, what we experience in our heart arrives from the mind via these "gates." In general, they are the emotions of the intellect. Since there are seven such emotions, and each one of them includes the others, there are a total of forty-nine gates. The fiftieth gate [transcends and] includes all of them. This is true whether we are speaking of emotions within the mind or emotions within the heart. This

CHASSIDIC INSIGHTS

G-d's name. And that is why during the *Pesukei DeZimra* and during the blessings before the *Shema*, the prayers refer to G-d in a veiled manner. We are not yet ready for the full revelation of the name *Havaya* because we are still involved in purifying and elevating our animal soul which conceals G-dliness. (Nevertheless, the prayers mention "His Name," and "His great Name" because the G-dly soul is present, though en-clothed in the animal soul, becoming progressively more revealed as we recite the prayers leading to the *Shema*.) But, once we remove the animal soul from the scene and concentrate on the G-dly soul alone, the name *Havaya* comes into full revelation during the recitation of the *Shema*.

And His words live and last, they are dependable and delightful forever and for all eternity, for our forefathers and for us, for our children and for our generations, and upon all generations of the seed of Israel, Your servants.

*

Chasidic literature is not satisfied with merely telling us that our divine soul takes over during *Emet Veyatziv*. It also goes into the details of the process. The Rebbe Rashab[156] explains that each word of *Emet Veyatziv* is a nexus, a basis of connection, conveying G-dly influence from above to below. As mentioned previously, our meditation during the *Shema* focuses upon bringing the infinite light of G-d down in order to elevate us and our portion in the world. The high spirituality that descends from above brings divine influence down to bear on the lower worlds. This is what takes place during the *Shema* as well as during *Emet Veyatziv*. Each of the fifteen words beginning with a *vov* is a basis/foundation (*yesod*) that transfers the G-dly influx from one level to the next. There are five *partzufim* ("structures" of *sephirot*) within every world. In each *partzuf*, there are three *yesodot* ("nexuses" of connection) that serve as gateways, conducting the infinite light of G-d from the higher level to the lower. Thus, there are a total of fifteen, three in each of five *partzufim*, of every world.

Words of the Prayer	*Partzuf* (structure of *sephirot*)
Veyatziv, Venachon, Vekayam ("certain, established, enduring")	*Keter* (*Arich Anpin*)
Veyashar, Vene'eman, Veahuv ("right and faithful and beloved")	*Chochma*
Vechaviv, Venechmad, Venaim ("Cherished, delightful and sweet")	*Bina*
Venorah, Veadir, Umetukan ("Awesome, mighty, correct")	*Zeir Anpin* (six emotional *sephirot* from *chesed* through *yesod*)
Umekubal, Vetov, Veyafeh ("Acceptable, good and beautiful")	*Malchut*

CHASSIDIC EXCERPTS

is what the *Zohar* means when it expounds upon the verse from Proverbs, "Her husband is known in the gates,"[273] by saying: "Each and every person according to his measure," meaning all of us according to the level that we have designated in our own heart. The nature of our "gate" and input from *bina*, as expressed in the intellect and in the emotions of the heart, determines our level of prayer service and attachment to G-d...

*

Bina is the essence of the intellect. It is pure understanding – comprehension of the concept in its most pristine form – before the intellect adopts a direction or inclination in the mind which could lead to a position (in the form of an idea or emotion) either for or against. This is because *bina* transcends the emotions. For example, when we meditate on the essence of a G-dly concept – such as "the greatness of G-d," or the "exaltedness of His infinite light," delving deeply into the essence of the topic – we transcend

CHASSIDIC INSIGHTS

This process involves a number of steps. At the outset, the infinite light from above enters the *sephirot* in a pure, pristine form, known in Kabbalah as *mochin p'nimim* ("pure intellect"). Next, it passes through a "gate/connection" (*yesod*) where the pristine intellect develops an inclination in one direction or another. At this point, the influx is still within the realm of intellect, but it takes on a tendency to lean in a particular emotional direction, even though it remains intellectual in essence. Conse-

עַל הָרִאשׁוֹנִים וְעַל הָאַחֲרוֹנִים דָּבָר טוֹב

וְקַיָּם בֶּאֱמֶת וּבֶאֱמוּנָה חוֹק וְלֹא יַעֲבֹר. אֱמֶת,

שָׁאַתָּה הוּא יְיָ אֱלֹהֵינוּ וֵאלֹהֵי אֲבוֹתֵינוּ, מַלְכֵּנוּ

מֶלֶךְ אֲבוֹתֵינוּ, גּוֹאֲלֵנוּ גּוֹאֵל אֲבוֹתֵינוּ, יוֹצְרֵנוּ

צוּר יְשׁוּעָתֵנוּ, פּוֹדֵנוּ וּמַצִּילֵנוּ מֵעוֹלָם הוּא

שְׁמֶךָ, וְאֵין לָנוּ עוֹד אֱלֹהִים זוּלָתֶךָ סֶלָה:

quently, the pure intellect has become an inclination. It is no longer pristine, objective information. It may not be a full-fledged opinion, but neither is it pure intellect (that is, objective information); it is a tendency in one direction or another that remains in the realm of intellect.

In order to make this process clearer, we may use the example of a teacher and student. When the teacher decides to pass information on to his student, his first step is to contract and limit the information in his own mind. He cannot pass on all the information as it exists in his own mind, because the student is simply unable to absorb all of it. So, the teacher must first select which information to pass on. Prior to doing so, the information exists as

pure, objective information in the teacher's mind. However, once he has decided what information to pass on, it is no longer infinite. Moreover, it is no longer objective, since the decision regarding which information to transfer is a subjective decision; it is the result of an inclination in the teacher's mind to pass on this specific information and not other information. The result is an inclination within the mind, still intellectual in nature, but no longer infinite and objective. At this point, the information has

CHASSIDIC EXCERPTS

the excitement (and even the unconscious arousal) that is associated with love of G-d. We cleave to the essence of the G-dly concept, since our soul clings to it, impelled by its power of intellect as it comprehends G-dliness. The same is true of every intellectual concept. When we delve deeply into its essence, we transcend any inclination toward emotion that might result from it. Even though there is an emotion associated with every concept – since of necessity every intellectual idea gives rise to a feeling (which is why with every intellectual event, there must be an associated specific action in serving G-d) – nevertheless, [at the time of intellectual concentration] we do not experience the emotion whatsoever. At the time that we are wrapped up in the essence of the concept, we transcend the emotions completely...

And when a channel is opened from our mind and intellect – allowing us an opportunity to judge [in accordance with the concept in our mind] – whether positively or negatively – this is called "intellect with a tendency" toward either love of G-d [or fear of G-d]. The opening is called a "gate," and it provides a descent from the essence of the concept, expressed as a tendency toward emotion (as explained earlier, when we are involved in the essence of the concept, we transcend the emotions). Still, the descent remains within the realm of intellect, even as it tends toward expression in a particular direction. This is similar to the thought process leading to a *psak din* ("halachic decision"); [after considering the halachic issue]...the intellect inclines in one direction or another, forming a tendency and a descent of the intellect toward

CHASSIDIC INSIGHTS

passed through one "gate" or "nexus," undergoing transformation from the full gamut of pure and objective information in the teacher's mind to an intellectual tendency within his mind.

In the next stage, the teacher must make the transition from a mere inclination and intellectual tendency into a full-fledged emotion in the mind. As he ponders a concept, for example, the teacher may become excited about it. He may develop love or fear of something, based upon his understanding. This love or fear remains in his mind; it has not yet descended to the heart, but neither is it a mere intellectual tendency; it is a full-fledged feeling in the intellect called "emotion within intellect." The transition from a mere inclination to an informed opinion or emotion in the mind is a second "gate" or "nexus." Finally, the teacher must decide how to transfer the information to the student. He knows what he wants to teach, he has placed his own imprimatur upon it, and now he must decide what words and what method of teaching will best convey the information. The teacher's excitement, or love or fear of the subject, will determine the level of interest of the student.

For the original [generations] and for the recent [generations], [Your] word is good and lasting in truth and in faith, an immutable law that cannot be violated. True, You, Lord, are our G-d and the G-d of our fathers, our King and the King of our forefathers, our Redeemer, the Redeemer of our forefathers, our Fortress and the Fortress of our salvation, our Redeemer and Rescuer You were always named; and we have no other G-d aside from You, forever.

At this point, a third "gate," or "nexus" occurs as the emotion within the mind becomes a full-fledged emotion of the heart. In the example of the teacher and student, this takes place when the teacher successfully transfers his knowledge to the student, and the student himself becomes excited over his new knowledge. When the student becomes capable of not only intellectually repeating the new information, but also of demonstrating his own level of commitment to the concept, then the teacher has succeeded in his job. That

CHASSIDIC EXCERPTS

emotion. This is not yet emotional excitement, which occurs when the emotion itself of *chesed* ("love") or *din* ("fear") is aroused. [The inclination] takes the form of a descent from the essence of intellectual grasp, as described previously, and it constitutes a departure from the intellect through a "gate" leading out of the essence of intellect itself, on the way to emotion, but, nevertheless, no emotional excitement has yet been created that can be considered distinct from the intellect. Rather, this is merely intellect as it begins to incline toward emotion. It is an internal exit, since it hasn't emerged externally in order to create a separate and distinct entity that can be described as emotional excitement ... This is comparable to souls as they reside in *Gan Eden*, grasping G-dliness and basking in the rays of the *Shechina*, each according to its own qual-

ity and level, whether of *chesed* or of *gevura* ... Every soul has a source and unique origin in the supernal *sephirot*, as is known ... and *Gan Eden* corresponds to *bina*...

But what descends from the intellect to become emotional excitement, such as love or fear of G-d, is in essence entirely distinct from the intellect, as explained earlier that the intellect and the emotions are two entities that differ from one another. If so, emergence from the intellect and arousal as an emotion constitutes a departure from the very essence of intellect and logic. This emergence goes beyond the tendency within intellect toward an emotion such as *chesed*. For, [if it were only a tendency, then] the emphasis would be upon the mind within which shines conscious intellectual illumination (even if it is inclined somewhat toward emotion). [In

CHASSIDIC INSIGHTS

means that the student has absorbed not only the concept itself, but also the approach of the teacher, and now the student's appreciation of the knowledge is informed and permeated by the intellect of the teacher. The once infinite and objective information that was in the teacher's mind has been transferred to the student's mind. If the student has a fertile intellect, he will grow and transmit the information to others as well.

עֶזְרַת אֲבוֹתֵינוּ אַתָּה הוּא מֵעוֹלָם, מָגֵן וּמוֹשִׁיעַ לָהֶם וְלִבְנֵיהֶם אַחֲרֵיהֶם בְּכָל דּוֹר וָדוֹר: בְּרוּם עוֹלָם מוֹשָׁבֶךָ, וּמִשְׁפָּטֶיךָ וְצִדְקָתְךָ עַד אַפְסֵי אָרֶץ. אֱמֶת, אַשְׁרֵי אִישׁ שֶׁיִּשְׁמַע לְמִצְוֹתֶיךָ, וְתוֹרָתְךָ וּדְבָרְךָ יָשִׂים עַל לִבּוֹ.

When we meditate, the infinite light must filter through the various stages just mentioned in order to become full-fledged love and fear of G-d within us. The most clear indication of this having taken place is when we enter a state of unity with G-d, and we lose contact with our physical surroundings. When the emotion within the mind becomes an emotion within the heart, we cleave to G-d, oblivious of our surroundings. This is called *gadlut hamochin*, when the infinite light of G-d shines directly into our heart, uplifting the emotions. Even as they remain emotions of the heart, they are filled and permeated with G-dly

CHASSIDIC EXCERPTS

such a case], the emphasis would be upon the intellect and its logical grasp, and not on the essence of the emotion. We are not in a state of emotional excitement based upon the feeling; rather, we are immersed in intellect, which of necessity leads to emotion. But as we become emotionally aroused, our emotion emerges "outside" of the sphere of intellect and enters into the sphere of feelings, and only a ray of intellect remains, permeating the feeling.

Within this [emergence from intellect to emotions], there are two stages: 1) The first is a descent of emotions within the mind, as the logic of the brain stimulates intellectual love or fear, in accordance with the concept [we are thinking about]. And 2) the second is a descent of the emotions to the heart, as we become aroused with conscious love and fear in proportion to [our meditation upon] the concept.

These are what as known as *shaarei bina*, which are channels leading from the essence of the intellect to emotional excitement. The most important point of departure from the intellect is when the emotions become conscious in the heart,

because while the emotions are still in the mind, they are not so clearly defined and experienced. And, as well, the emotions within the mind are the result of excitement over the intrinsic goodness of G-dliness itself, while the emotions of our heart result from excitement over our own personal benefit, since we feel positive about our proximity to G-dliness. If so, then the essence of emotion is about consciousness of ourselves and what is good for us. This takes place in the heart alone and, therefore, the emotions of the heart are the main results that emerge separate from the intellect. Therefore, the most important "gates," which serve as points of departure from the intellect, are those that provide egress to the emotions of the heart.

There are, then, three different *yesodot* (channels of influx) in the *partzuf* of *bina*: 1) The first provides egress from the intrinsic intellectual concept to a tendency or inclination within the mind toward *chesed* [or another emotion]. 2) The second draws the concept down to the realm of emotional excitement, even as it remains included within the mind and

CHASSIDIC INSIGHTS

light that lifts them up to the level of intellect. This is what takes place when the infinite light from above passes through the third "nexus" (*yesod*) in the meditative process. The full-fledged emotion in the mind becomes a full fledged emotion of the heart that is permeated and infused with intellect.

*

This process transmits G-dliness from the realm of the infinite to the world of emotions within us. There are four steps beginning with pure intellect that develops into an inclination in the mind, leading to full-fledged feelings in the mind, and ultimately to full-fledged emotions of the heart (love and fear of G-d, expressed as cleaving to Him). The four stages correspond to the four letters of G-d's holy name, which we use to call upon Him to shine His holiness down to us. Between each step is a *yesod* – a transitional "gate" or "nexus" that connects them – for a total of three *yesodot* in each *partzuf*. Since there are five *partzufim*, each of which goes through this process, there are a total of fifteen connecting transitions

You have always been the help of our fathers, the shield and salvation for them and for their offspring after them, in each and every generation.
In the heights of the universe is Your dwelling plae, and Your laws and Your justice reach the very ends of the earth.
True, happy is the man who heeds Your commandments, and who places Your Torah and Your word upon his heart.

CHASSIDIC EXCERPTS

intellect. 3) The third provides access to the emotions of the heart, about which we say, *bina libah, u'bah halev mavin* ("The heart is *bina* [not only analytic understanding but also intuition], and with it the heart understands").[274]

So it is within every *partzuf* – for every *partzuf* there are three *yesodot*: 1) The first allows flow within the power of intellect itself, which is only a ray of the essential power of intellect and not the power itself, just as intellect inclined toward love is not the essence of intellect, but is included within it. 2) The second allows for the arousal of another quality – emotions – which, nonetheless, remain within the confines of the intellect. 3) The third allows the flow to finally emerge as an independent quality standing on its own. For example, we may wish to learn something, but are not yet aroused [sufficiently] to do so. Then, we may experience the appropriate arousal to master the subject, but the plan to do so remains intellectual and limited to a general will to learn. That is, the power to learn is in place even before we actually start learning. Finally, we actually begin to learn the subject. These are the multiple levels of *tov* that constitute various levels of *yesodot* or channels of connection...

(From *Besha'ah SheHikdimu 5672* (1912) of the Rebbe Rashab, vol. 2, pp. 1031-1033)

Truth and Redemption
Emet Veyatziv ("True and certain...")...*Ezrat Avoteinu* ("You have always been the help of our fathers...")

In [the prayer] *Emet Veyatziv*, we say the word *emet* ("truth") eight times – four times before the paragraph starting with *Ezrat Avoteinu* ("Help of our Fathers"), and four times within that paragraph. In order to understand why the sages placed *emet* four times within the prayer *Emet Veyatziv*, consider the expla- nation of the *Zohar*[275] that the four mentions of *emet* correspond to the four terms of redemption [mentioned in Exodus]: 1) *vehotzeiti* ("and I brought you out"); 2) *vehitzalti* ("and I rescued you"); 3) *vega'alti* ("and I redeemed you"); 4) *velakachti* ("and I took you"). And, [regarding the future redemption], it is

CHASSIDIC INSIGHTS

that bring the influx down from the realm of infinity into the flesh of our hearts. It is to these fifteen steps that the fifteen words of *Emet Veyatziv* correspond, each beginning with a *vov* that indicates connection and transition.

In kabbalistic nomenclature, the teacher-student relationship takes place between the two *sephirot* of *yesod* and *malchut*. The additional, enhanced G-dliness that we draw down into the world through our prayers after *Barchu*, comes down from *chochma*, through the lower nine *sephirot*, to *yesod*. *Yesod* concentrates all of the influx from the previous eight *sephirot* (for this reason, it is also called *kol*, meaning "all") and then channels it to *malchut*. *Malchut* then uses this divine influence to create and maintain the universe. As we pray during the *Pesukei DeZimra*, our focus is upon the creation and its spiritual vitality, which is coming from *malchut*. Our soul-level of *ruach* is involved in these prayers, as we activate our natural emotions. But, as we say *Barchu* and enter into the

אֱמֶת, אַתָּה הוּא אָדוֹן לְעַמֶּךָ, וּמֶלֶךְ גִּבּוֹר לָרִיב רִיבָם, לְאָבוֹת וּבָנִים.

אֱמֶת, אַתָּה הוּא רִאשׁוֹן, וְאַתָּה הוּא אַחֲרוֹן, וּמִבַּלְעָדֶיךָ אֵין לָנוּ מֶלֶךְ גּוֹאֵל וּמוֹשִׁיעַ.

אֱמֶת, מִמִּצְרַיִם גְּאַלְתָּנוּ יְיָ אֱלֹהֵינוּ, וּמִבֵּית עֲבָדִים פְּדִיתָנוּ.

CHASSIDIC EXCERPTS

written, "As in the days that you departed Egypt, I will [in the future redemption] display wonders."[276] Accordingly, the sages determined that *emet* should be mentioned four more times regarding the future redemption.

Emet is associated with *geula*. The Torah states, "I appeared to Abraham ... and my true name *Havaya* I did not make known to them."[277] Rashi explains, "I did not make myself known to them [the forefathers] with my true characteristic." This was because the name *Havaya* was not yet known [in the world]. But, during the exodus from Egypt, G-d said, "Therefore, say to the children of Israel, I am *Havaya*,"[278] and His name *Havaya* became revealed at the time of the giving of the Torah. And the name *Havaya* is called *emet*, as it is written "the *emet* of *Havaya* is forever."[279] This, then, explains the four times *emet* is mentioned, corresponding to the four letters of the name *Havaya*...

And now we can understand the eight times that *emet* is mentioned. Four times it corresponds to the four letters of G-d's essential name *Havaya*. Only His holy name is called *emet*, which in turn corresponds to the higher consciousness

called *da'at elyon*, [that causes us to become aware] of all creation before Him as if non-existent – this is *emet* ("truth"). We cannot say this regarding the lower consciousness called *da'at tachton* [in which we are cognizant of the world as if it has its own independent existence and] of creation as arising from nothingness into something – this is not *emet*. Even though it is also a valid viewpoint, since our lower consciousness has its origin Above ... nevertheless, it is not *emet leamito* ("ultimate truth").

However, the higher name *Havaya*, associated with *da'at elyon* is true and real, as mentioned earlier. This is why Rashi comments that G-d "did not make Himself known with His true attribute," since the name *Shadai* [with which He made Himself known to Abraham] is only *da'at tachton*. However, His name *Havaya* conveys *da'at elyon*. Nevertheless, this is only the truth of G-d manifested in the world. Compared to the infinite light of G-d that transcends the world, it is *da'at tachton*. Thus, the four times that we say *emet* within the prayer (*Ezrat Avoteinu*) correspond to the name *Havaya* Above (transcending the creation), since there are two levels of the

CHASSIDIC INSIGHTS

third stage of prayers – the blessing prior to the *Shema* as well as the *Shema* – our prayers and meditation rise to the level of *yesod*, the source of the G-dly vitality that manifests itself in creation as revealed G-liness. And that is why we begin to see evidence of a higher spiritual influence in our prayers, starting immediately after we say *Barchu*.

The Rebbe Rashab draws several correlations between the *yesodot* and other phenomena that increase our understanding. He points[157] to the connection between *yesod* and *geula* ("redemption") which is associated with revelation of G-dly light. A huge revelation of G-dliness propelled the Jews out of Egypt, and it will be a similarly huge revelation that will herald the future redemption. And G-dly revelation is described as *tov* ("good"), as in the verse from the creation story: "And G-d saw the light, and it was good." Now "good" is associated with the *sephira* of *yesod*. In fact, all good flows down to us through *yesod*, which is why it is also called *kol* ("all"). And that is why the

True, You are the Lord of Your nation, and mighty King, fighting their fights for both fathers and children.

True, You are the original, and Your are the final, and aside from You, we have no King, Redeemer and Savior.

True, You redeemed us from Egypt, Lord our G-d, and from the house of bondage You rescued us.

CHASSIDIC EXCERPTS

name *Havaya*. This is evident from the verse, "And he called *Havaya*, *Havaya*..." which is written in the Torah with an interruption between the two names *Havaya*, symbolizing the *ayn* [that separates between *Havaya* of the infinite transcendent light and] of *Havaya* in *chochma* [first of the ten *sephirot* of *Atzilut*] also known as *eitz chayim* ("tree of life").

And this is why the first four times the word *emet* is mentioned, it corresponds to the redemption from Egypt, since at that time there was a revelation of the name *Havaya*, as it is written, "Therefore so to the children of Israel, I am *Havaya*..."[280] But, all this represents only the revealed dimension of the Torah, while the inner, hidden dimension of the Torah was not revealed at that time. However, in the future, the inner dimension of the Torah will be revealed, since it includes the secrets of secrets which descend from the higher name of *Havaya*. And they constitute the four times *emet* that is mentioned in the prayer (*Ezrat Avoteinu*), which alludes to the future redemption.

Still, it remains to be understood why all this was placed in the order of

prayer between the recitation of the *Shema* and the *Shemonah Esreh*. The answer: the *Shema* is an act of *mesirat nefesh* ("self-sacrifice") [since our ultimate desire during it is for our soul to be included in the oneness of G-d] as it is written, "Who is like our G-d upon whom we call in all things?"[281] ...and the sages have explained that we call to Him and not to His attributes. [We direct our cry and request directly to G-d, in His essence, and not to any of His attributes or *sephirot*]. With the *Shema*, we ascend to His very essence. And even though His attributes are one, since "He and His illumination and His causations are one," nevertheless, the *Shema* must of necessity act as an elevation to His very essence by way of our self-sacrifice [since self-sacrifice is from our very essence, therefore it ascends to the very essence of G-dliness]. And because this is an elevation to His very essence, it allows holy influx to be brought down afterward as G-dly revelation during the eight times that we say *emet*.

Thereafter, the *Shemonah Esreh* constitutes a descent into His particular attributes, as the sages said, "Why do the Jews call upon G-d and fail to receive

CHASSIDIC INSIGHTS

final redemption is associated with yesod, since it is yesod that will bring down all of the G-dly illumination and good that will herald the coming of the Messiah.

Thus we close out the prayer of *Emet Veyatziv* by mentioning *geula* as we approach the *Shemonah Esreh*.

*

כָּל בְּכוֹרֵיהֶם הָרַגְתָּ, וּבְכוֹרְךָ יִשְׂרָאֵל גָּאָלְתָּ, וְיַם

סוּף לָהֶם בָּקַעְתָּ, וְזֵדִים טִבַּעְתָּ, וִידִידִים

הֶעֱבַרְתָּ, וַיְכַסּוּ מַיִם צָרֵיהֶם. אֶחָד מֵהֶם לֹא

נוֹתָר.

עַל זֹאת שִׁבְּחוּ אֲהוּבִים, וְרוֹמְמוּ לָאֵל, וְנָתְנוּ

יְדִידִים זְמִירוֹת שִׁירוֹת וְתִשְׁבָּחוֹת, בְּרָכוֹת

וְהוֹדָאוֹת לְמֶלֶךְ אֵל חַי וְקַיָּם:

Finally, the Rebbe Rashab deals with the paragraphs following *Emet Veyatziv* in which the word *emet* is mentioned eight times. As noted, the final paragraphs joining the *Shema* with the *Shemonah Esreh* serve as confirmation and verification (*hitamtut*, from the word *emet*, or "truth") of the previous service of the soul. In the first paragraphs of the *Shema*, the emphasis is upon our meditation, leading to love of G-d. But, once having achieved love of G-d, we let our G-dly soul take over during the final paragraphs, and the experience of the G-dly soul corroborates and verifies all that we achieved by thinking and conceptu-

CHASSIDIC EXCERPTS

answers? Because, when they call upon Him, they do not know how to focus properly on His Name."[282] The *Shemonah Esreh* involves descent (from the eight times that *emet* is mentioned) into His various names as they apply to His supernal attributes. This is the reason *emet* was placed eight times between the *Shema* and *Shemonah Esreh*, [for during the self-sacrifice and ascent to the essence of G-dliness of the *Shema*, we access the infinite light of G-d, and then] we bring it down through the eight aspects of *emet* into G-d's specific attributes [during the *Shemonah Esreh*]...

(From *Sefer Maamorim 5654* (1894) of the Rebbe Rashab, p. 110, 116)

Once and future redemption

Emet Veyatziv ("True and certain...")...*Ezrat Avoteinu* ("You have always been the help of our fathers...")

Within the verse that begins, "And therefore say to the Children of Israel, 'I am *Havaya*, and I removed you from the oppression of Egypt...'"[283] are quoted four different terms for redemption – "and I removed you (*vehotzeiti*), and I rescued (*vehitzalti*), and I redeemed (*vega'alti*), and I took you out (*velakachti*)." Commenting on this verse, the *Midrash Rabba* says that the four terms correspond to the four decrees that Pharaoh issued against the Jews. And accordingly, the sages decreed that we drink four cups [at the Passover seder]. This is one explanation ... but

there is another explanation (also stated in the *Midrash Rabba*) that the four terms of redemption correspond to the four exiles of the Jews, and the sages decreed four corresponding cups of wine.

Now, in the *Zohar*, it is explained that the four terms of redemption correspond to the four times the word *emet* is mentioned [in *Emet Veyatziv*]. According to this explanation, it emerges that both explanations of the *Midrash Rabba* are correct. For, we say *emet* four times before *Ezrat Avoteinu*, and four time within that section. So, the four times that *emet* is mentioned before *Ezrat Avoteinu* cor-

CHASSIDIC INSIGHTS

alizing during our meditation. That is why the word *emet* is repeated several times during this section of the prayers – to indicate and confirm the truth of what we only hypothesized earlier. Also, after intense meditation, we arrive to confirmation associated with the *rei'ah* ("vision") of *chochma*; this is a high level of achievement during meditation, and as such it arrives late in the prayers, just before the *Shemonah Esreh*.

However, the Rebbe Rashab also asks, why does the word *emet* appear four times immediately following *Emet Veyatziv*, and then another four times in the final paragraph, beginning with *Ezrat Avoteinu*? He answers that the first four times that *emet* appears correspond to redemption from Egypt. There, the Jews first experienced the name *Havaya*, the essential four-letter name of G-d. Previously, as G-d told Moses, He did not reveal this name to the forefathers. However, with this name (associated with a higher G-dly revelation), G-d brought the Jews out of Egypt. So, the first four times that *emet* is mentioned corre-

All of their first-born You slew, and the first-born of the Jews You saved, and You split the Reed Sea for them, and their wicked ones you drowned, You brought Your beloved intimates over and You covering their tormentors with water, leaving not one of them [alive]. For this, the beloved ones praised G-d and exalted G-d, and the dear ones offered songs and melodies and praises, blessings and thanks to the King, the everlasting and living G-d.

CHASSIDIC EXCERPTS

respond to the four redemptions from Egypt, according to which the sages decreed four cups. And the second explanation of the *Midrash Rabba* corresponds to the future, [to the final redemption]...

Accordingly, we may now understand the connection between the four redemptions and the four times that *emet* is mentioned, since the four redemptions correspond to the four letters of the name *Havaya* and *Havaya* is called *emet*, as it is written, *ve'emet Havaya* ("and the truth of G-d endures forever").[284] And the four times that *emet* is mentioned corresponds to the four letters of *Havaya*, since there are four levels of truth. Even though a particular level is true, nevertheless, there are levels of truth that surpass it. And as it is written, "And I appeared to Abraham and to Isaac ... as *Kel Shadai*, but my true name *Havaya* I did not make known to them."[285] Rashi explains that G-d did not make Himself known to our forefathers according to His true attributes. But at first glance, this is not understood ... The explanation is that this name (*Kel Shadai*) is

also "true," but a greater level of truth is associated with the name *Havaya*. Similarly, there are levels within the name *Havaya* itself as well, four levels corresponding to the four letters of the name, which are four distinct levels. And as it is written, "Each higher level guards over [and includes] the lower level,"[286] and there are higher levels as well (although this level is also high. Nevertheless, there are levels beyond it as well), and this is what is meant by the four redemptions of the exodus from Egypt.

And now, we must understand how there could be four redemptions within the exodus from Egypt. In the *Midrash Rabba* it says that when G-d gave the Torah to Moses, He first repeated it four times to Himself and then gave it (and from this the *Midrash Rabba* learns that when man must say over Torah in public, he should review it four times to himself), as it is written, "Then he saw, and told, understood, investigated and then spoke to man."[287] There are four levels mentioned until G-d spoke to man. But, how can we under-

CHASSIDIC INSIGHTS

spond to the four letters of the name *Havaya* that redeemed the Jews from Egypt. In our personal prayer service and connection with G-d, this name *Havaya* corresponds to *da'at tachton* ("lower consciousness" in which we are primarily aware of creation while G-d's existence is only in the background of our awareness).

The Rebbe Rashab points out that there are two levels of the essential name *Havaya*, corresponding to the verse, "And He called, *Havaya, Havaya...*"[158] in which G-d's name appears twice. The second name *Havaya* is a higher level, associated with *da'at elyon* ("higher consciousness" in which we are primarily aware of G-d while creation is only in the background of our awareness). This is the consciousness that will permeate the world when the Messiah arrives. But, for that to happen, a second redemption must occur, and it will require an even higher G-dly revelation than that which brought the Jews out of

רָם וְנִשָּׂא גָּדוֹל וְנוֹרָא, מַשְׁפִּיל גֵּאִים עֲדֵי אָרֶץ,

וּמַגְבִּיהַ שְׁפָלִים עַד מָרוֹם, מוֹצִיא אֲסִירִים,

פּוֹדֶה עֲנָוִים, עוֹזֵר דַּלִּים, הָעוֹנֶה לְעַמּוֹ יִשְׂרָאֵל

בְּעֵת שַׁוְּעָם אֵלָיו.

תְּהִלּוֹת לְאֵל עֶלְיוֹן גּוֹאֲלָם, בָּרוּךְ הוּא

וּמְבֹרָךְ, מֹשֶׁה וּבְנֵי יִשְׂרָאֵל לְךָ עָנוּ שִׁירָה

בְּשִׂמְחָה רַבָּה, וְאָמְרוּ כֻלָּם:

CHASSIDIC EXCERPTS

stand this, for how is it possible to say about G-d that He must repeat the Torah four times to Himself?

The fact is that the origin of the Torah is extremely high, within the inner dimensions of *keter*, and it is necessary to draw it down. If it descended as it exists Above, it would be too high for man to receive it. And, therefore, it was necessary to make a contraction from the beginning. And the name *Havaya* indicates a process of contraction and expansion, descent and once again expansion, because the name *Havaya* is the source of creation. And in order to facilitate the process of creation from G-d's infinite light, there had to be contractions followed by expansion. And so, the descent of the Torah necessitated [a process of] contraction, expansion, descent and once more expansion, a process that could only take place by way of the letters of the name *Havaya*.

So, these are the four levels: 1) "Then He saw" – this corresponds to the *sephira* of *chochma*. In the beginning, the Torah had to descend to *chochma*, and

sight is associated with *chochma*, as it is written, "Who is a wise man? He who sees what will take place."[288] And also the wise men are called the "eyes of the congregation." 2) And then, "He told" – this alludes to the *sephira* of *bina*, since the *sofer* ("scribe" who "tells a story" with his writing) corresponds to *bina*. 3) "Prepared and also investigated" – this corresponds to [the six *sephirot* of] *Zeir Anipin* and [the tenth *sephira* of] *malchut*. 4) And then, "And He said to man," indicating that the Torah came down to the lower worlds of *BY"A*.

This, then, is how we can understand the four redemptions of the exodus from Egypt. Within the exodus itself there were four [stages of] redemption. That is, in order for the infinite light of G-d to descend to redeem the Jews, four stages of redemption took place – contraction, expansion, descent and once more expansion – and, correspondingly, the sages decreed four cups of wine at Passover.

*

And now, it remains for us to un-

CHASSIDIC INSIGHTS

Egypt. The four instances of the word *emet* in the paragraph starting with *Ezrat Avoteinu* correspond to the four letters of this higher name *Havaya*, which will facilitate the final redemption from *galut* to *geula*.

Still, the Rebbe Rashab asks why this higher revelation is alluded to at this point in our prayers, between the *Shema* and the *Shemonah Esreh*? And he answers that as we say the *Shema* with commitment to an ultimate self-sacrifice, we arrive at the very essence of G-dliness. And once that takes place, we are enabled to draw G-dliness down into the specific vessels that we create while uttering the eighteen blessings of the *Shemonah Esreh*. While we recite the *Shemonah Esreh*, we draw down a specific kind of influx that fills our needs. But, in order to do that, we must first experience the self-sacrifice that lifts us to His very essence. Only then can our prayers bring down answers to our needs.

Ultimately, all spiritual influx

He is exalted and transcendent, great and awesome, lowering the proud to the very earth, and raising the low to the heights, He frees the captives, redeems the poor, aids the impoverished, He Who answers His people the Jews when they turn to Him.

Praise to highest G-d Who is their redeemer, Blessed is He and he is blessed, Moshe and the children of Israel answered you in song and in great joy, and all of them proclaimed:

CHASSIDIC EXCERPTS

derstand the four redemptions of the future, which correspond to the four times that the word *emet* is mentioned in the *Ezrat Avoteinu*. It is known that there are two aspects to the name *Havaya*, as the verse says, "*Havaya, Havaya...*" with an interruption placed between them. This is because the lower name *Havaya* is the source of the spiritual chain that leads to creation. There is, as well, a higher name *Havaya* that is not a source of the spiritual process leading to creation at all. Rather [this higher name *Havaya*] arose in G-d's will. We see from our own experience that the will is of highest importance, but from our own will down here in this world nothing is created. As much as we might want something, it will not be created. In fact, the only way something comes into being is when the will descends through the intellect and emotions, and from there to thought, speech and action. This is not the case Above, although, since as [the universe] arose in His will, it was created, as it is written, "All that G-d desired, G-d made."[289] This is what is meant by the higher name *Havaya* within His will,

since that is where are found all of the above-mentioned aspects.

Nevertheless, there is interruption between [the two names *Havaya*] because the higher name *Havaya* is far above the lower name *Havaya* and is not a source of creation at all.

And it is possible that the interruption symbolizes the *tzimtzum*, which is an interruption in the G-dly illumination, for even the light of the ray of G-dly light (*kav*) descends to creation via this great contraction. And in the future, the illumination will shine in a revealed manner from the higher name of *Havaya*, as it is written, "On that day, *Havaya* will be one and His name one."[290] That is, at that time, it will not be as now, with an interruption between [the two names of *Havaya*]. Rather, the higher *Havaya* will shine into the lower *Havaya*, and this is what is meant by "On that day, His name will be one." Automatically, He and His name will be one.

Presently, "not as I am written I am called."[291] That is, G-d is written with the name *Havaya*, but called by the name

CHASSIDIC INSIGHTS

comes from above via the holy four-letter name of G-d. The first two letters of this name are the letters *yud-hey*, which have the numerical value of fifteen. In chasidic terminology, these two letters represent *mochin*, ("intellect"), specifically of *chochma* and *bina*. And the second two letters *vov-hey* represent *midot* ("emotions").

The third letter – *vov* – performs the task of transferring G-dly influence from the first two letters

מִי כָמֹכָה בָּאֵלִם יְיָ, מִי כָּמֹכָה נֶאְדָּר בַּקֹדֶשׁ, נוֹרָא תְהִלֹּת עֹשֵׂה פֶלֶא:

שִׁירָה חֲדָשָׁה שִׁבְּחוּ גְאוּלִים לְשִׁמְךָ הַגָּדוֹל עַל שְׂפַת הַיָּם, יַחַד כֻּלָּם הוֹדוּ וְהִמְלִיכוּ וְאָמְרוּ:

יְיָ יִמְלֹךְ לְעוֹלָם וָעֶד:

וְנֶאֱמַר. גֹּאֲלֵנוּ יְיָ צְבָאוֹת שְׁמוֹ קְדוֹשׁ יִשְׂרָאֵל:

בָּרוּךְ אַתָּה יְיָ, גָּאַל יִשְׂרָאֵל:

of G-d's name (intellect that is not yet associated with the emotions) to the emotions (and from there down to us in this world). That is the connecting function of the letter *vov*. In fact, the Rebbe Rashab alludes[159] to this, saying that the fifteen *vovs* of *Emet Veyatziv* are necessary to connect the first two letters of G-d's name with the second two letters.

During the creation narrative, the Torah hints that the world was created with the letter *hey*. The verse in Genesis states, *Behibaram* ("As they were created"), which the sages interpret as *B'hey baram* ("With the *hey* He created them"). This refers to the second letter of G-d's name, and the Rebbe Rashab

CHASSIDIC EXCERPTS

Ad-ni, since G-dly revelation presently occurs via the name *Ad-ni*. As it is written, "And *Havaya* in His holy palace,"[292] wherein the word *heichal* ("palace") [has the same numerical value as] the name *Ad-ni*. Thus, *Ad-ni* is a "palace" for the name *Havaya*. [That is, the name *Havaya* comes into the world "en-clad" in the name *Ad-ni*.] But, in the future, when the light of the higher name *Havaya* will be revealed, G-dly revelation will descend as *Havaya* alone. It will not descend as *Ad-ni*, for it is written, "And they will no

longer conceal your teachers,"[293] meaning that there will no longer be any concealment at all - not [even] via [spiritual] garments. All will be revealed from the higher name *Havaya*. And this is [what is meant by] the four redemptions of the future. They will correspond to the four letters of *Havaya* within G-d's will. And this is as well the four times that the word *emet* is mentioned in the prayer, *Ezrat Avoteinu*, corresponding to the *emet* within the higher name *Havaya*...

(From *Sefer Ma'amorim 5658* (1898) of the Rebbe Rashab, pp. 87 and 93)

Geula ("redemption") is good...

Tehilot la-kel elyon goalam ("Praises to the almighty G-d, their redeemer...")

It is necessary to understand why four different terms for *geula* ("redemption") are mentioned [in the Torah] regarding the exodus from Egypt...

It is written, "That which was good (*tov*) in your eyes, I did,"[294] and the sages say that means that *tov* refers to *geula*

("redemption"), which is mentioned immediately preceding the *Shemonah Esreh*. Now, the positioning of *geula* (at the end of *Shema*) immediately preceding the *Shemonah Esreh* corresponds to the proximity of the two lowest *sephirot* - *yesod* ("foundation") and *malchut* ("king-

CHASSIDIC INSIGHTS

goes on to say that man (who stands upright and performs the task of spiritual connection by fulfilling G-d's commandments) is himself the *vov*. After all, says the Rebbe Rashab, man is a "tree of the field."[160] Similar to man — and to the letter *vov* — a tree is vertical. Both man (who stands upright) and the tree (the tallest and most vertical of all creations) are compared to the letter *vov*, which connects with the initial *yud-hey* of G-d's name. These two letters transcend the creation, but it is the task of man (as the *vov*) to connect with them and bring down their influence into the creation (via the final *hey* of G-d's name).

The name *Havaya*, transcending all of creation, is associated with the G-dly soul. Our intellect connects with the *yud-hey* of His name, while our emotions as well as the form of our body correspond to the *vov*, which brings G-dliness down to the physical world — represented by the final, receptive *hey* of His name.

Meditation on "there is none as holy as the name *Havaya*" is the theme of the prayers preceding the *Shemonah Esreh*, for during the *Shemonah Esreh* itself, we focus upon specific variations of the name *Havaya* itself.

Who is like You among the deities, Lord, Who is like You, mighty and holy, awesome in praise, performing wonders:

With a new song, those who You redeemed praised Your great name on the edge of the sea, together they all acknowledged and coronated You, saying; The Lord reigns forever and ever. And as is stated, our Savior, the Lord of Hosts is His name, the holy One of Israel. Blessed are You, Lord, who redeemed Israel.

CHASSIDIC EXCERPTS

ship"), [to each other]. *Geula* refers to *yesod* and *yesod* is called *tov* ("good"), as it is written, "the righteous uttered 'it is good'"[295] and "the righteous are the foundation of the universe."[296] This means that all that comes down to us descends via *yesod*, as it is written, "And Joseph [representing the *sephira* of *yesod*] was the supplier,"[297] and "And Joseph supplied,"[298] since all influx and revealed infinite G-dliness descends precisely through the *sephira* of *yesod*. This is why *yesod* is called *tov* in reference to the flow that descends through it.

Now, regarding *geula*, it is written [in the Book of Ruth,[299] "If he will redeem you, good, let him redeem you," which can be read as:] "If he will redeem you, good will redeem you" ... implying that redemption is also related to *tov*. This is because *geula* is associated with revelation of G-d's infinite light. It is known

that exile and redemption are called "pregnancy" and "birth," respectively. Exile is like pregnancy because it implies concealment of G-dly illumination. And redemption is like birth, because it is associated with revelation of infinite light, to the extent that the "King, King of all Kings" becomes revealed.[300]

Now, revelation of G-dly illumination is called *tov*, as it is written, "And *Elokim* saw the light and it was good."[301] And all influx and revelation of light comes about through *yesod*, therefore *yesod* is called *geula*. This is the *geula* that we mention at the end of the prayer *Emet Veyatziv* where it states, "Praises to the Almighty G-d, their redeemer ... the G-d of Legions is our redeemer..."). And in this fashion we bring down revealed illumination from *yesod* of *Atzilut*, as is written in *Pri Eitz Chaim*.

(From *Sefer Maamorim 5654* (1894) of the Rebbe Rashab, p. 124)

SHEMONAH ESREH

The *Shemonah Esreh* — "eighteen benedictions" (which actually contains nineteen blessings) and is also known as the *Amidah* ("the standing prayer") — is, of course, the pinnacle of prayers. Here is where, after the *ruach soarah* ("stormy winds") of the *Pesukei DeZimra* and the *ra'ash gadol* ("great commotion") of the blessings preceding the *Shema* and the *aish mitlakachat* ("consuming fire") of the

שמונה עשרה – עמידה

אֲדֹנָי, שְׂפָתַי תִּפְתָּח וּפִי יַגִּיד תְּהִלָּתֶךָ:

בָּרוּךְ אַתָּה יְיָ אֱלֹהֵינוּ וֵאלֹהֵי אֲבוֹתֵינוּ, אֱלֹהֵי אַבְרָהָם, אֱלֹהֵי יִצְחָק, וֵאלֹהֵי יַעֲקֹב,

Shema itself, we finally find our voice. And that voice turns out to be an inner voice — a *kol demama daka* ("still small voice") — which is inaudible. It is the silent point of the heart that cannot be expressed outwardly. It is so intense that we cannot put it into words. And that is why we begin the *Shemonah Esreh* by saying, "Lord, please open my lips" because we are incapable of opening them ourselves, due to the intensity of feelings inside.

The *Shemonah Esreh* is a time of *devekut* — of "clinging" to G-d. Before we arrived at this point in

Open my lips...
Adny sfaftai tiftach ("Lord, open my lips...")

Regarding our speech during the *Shemonah Esreh* we say, "there are no words upon my tongue..." and "Lord, open my lips..." since this prayer is in the World of *Atzilut*. As is known, there is a difference between reciting the *Shema* and praying the *Shemonah Esreh*. The *Shema* is associated with the World of *Atzilut* within *Bria*,[302] however the *Shemonah Esreh* is associated with *Atzilut* itself. And therefore the service of reciting the *Shema* involves keen intellect and meditation. The person becomes aroused with excitement, yet all intellectual grasp remains external in relation to the essence, [for here, we do not experience] the essence of G-dliness within *Atzilut*, but only as it shines into *bria*. And precisely because of this, the arousal of the *Shema* is associated with commotion. However, during the *Shemonah Esreh*, the service is not of intellect and meditation, but rather of recognition and direct experience. We feel the very essence of G-dliness within our soul, stemming from the verification

and corroboration of the G-dly name *Ma'h* [the Name *Havaya* of gematria forty-five, indicating *bitul*, or self-nullification] in our soul. This is not like comprehending a G-dly concept [intellectually], but rather like verifying and confirming it within ourselves. And this is what is meant by the *pnimiyut hakavana* ("inner intention") of *Ma'h* in the soul. And, therefore, it may only occur quietly, without audible speech or intentional organization of words. Because speech that is expressed intentionally is appropriate only where intellect is in play, since then we organize our thoughts according to our intellectual understanding. But, regarding the "inner intention" of the *Shemonah Esreh*, it is not appropriate to speak of organizing our words with intention. Rather, our speech emerges spontaneously and automatically. Even so, speech does occur, but it is unintentional — it occurs automatically — and it expresses truth, according to the manner of our "inner intention."

(From *Sefer Maamorim* 5659 (1899) of the Rebbe Rashab, p. 200)

CHASSIDIC INSIGHTS

prayer, first our natural emotions were engaged, then our intellectual emotions, and finally our intellect itself. But, during the *Shemonah Esreh*, our very essence is involved. That is why we experience a state of *devekut* - because it is the one time during our prayers that there is no separation between us and the One Above. The previous prayers – the *Korbonot*, the *Pesukei DeZimra* and the *Shema* – were all rungs on the ladder of ascent of the soul. But, the *Shemonah Esreh* is the top rung, the spiritual pinnacle from which we now descend and attempt to bring with us our newly attained spirituality. As it is not possible to remain in a state of cleaving to G-d all day long, the goal of the *Shemonah Esreh* is to bring down the spirituality that we have experienced, so that it will become evident in the world and in the routine of our everyday lives as well.

That is why the *Shemonah Esreh* is a prayer of vital importance. It was formulated by the Sages of the Great Assembly (*Anshei Knesset*

Shemonah Esreh – The Amidah

Lord, open my lips and let my mouth tell Your praise...

Blessed are You, Lord, our G-d and G-d of our forefathers, the G-d of Abraham, the G-d of Isaac, and the G-d of Jacob,

CHASSIDIC EXCERPTS

Eighteen blessings – eighteen vertebrae
Boruch Atah HaShem...("Blessed are You, Lord...")

Now, the service of the heart – the *Shemonah Esreh* – is mandated by the rabbis and is not among the 613 mitzvot of the Torah ... and this must be understood, for the Talmudic sages[303] were much more stringent regarding *kavana* during the *Shemonah Esreh* than they were regarding *kavana* during the *Shema*, though the *Shema* is counted as the foremost of the 613 mitzvot. And this is because the *Shemonah Esreh* is among the items that "stand at the apex of the universe."[304] So we must ask: why is it not counted among the mitzvot of the Torah?

This matter becomes clearer when we understand that the eighteen blessings of the *Shemonah Esreh* correspond to the eighteen vertebrae of the backbone through which is drawn the spinal cord.[305] Now, for example, a man possesses 248 limbs in his body, "thirty of which are in the sole of the foot ... eighteen are the number of vertebrae of the backbone..."[306] But, the spinal cord itself, as drawn through the vertebrae, is not counted among the limbs, even though

it establishes and reinforces all of the limbs. It extends from the head down to the thighs, and by way of it all the vitality of the brain is distributed to the various limbs. And the limbs are connected to the ribcage, and the ribcage to the vertebrae, and the vertebrae to the spinal cord. And yet, the spinal cord is not counted among the limbs, even though it is what connects them ... And similarly in the paradigm described previously, the mitzvot are the 248 limbs of the king. And about them, the sages said that "the mitzvot" demand *kavana* ("intention"),[307] and the *kavana* comes from the *Shemonah Esreh*, which is the inner intention of the mitzvot and the main pillar that establishes and maintains the 248 positive commands. And thus the *Shemonah Esreh* is like the spinal cord that establishes and maintains the limbs, even though it is not counted as part of the 248 limbs.

Now, the main purpose of the *Shemonah Esreh* is to request that the infinite light of G-d from Above become "blessed" and "drawn down" through

CHASSIDIC INSIGHTS

Hagedola) who assumed the reins of Jewish leadership in the 5-4th centuries BCE. They first came together in Babylon following the destruction of the First Temple, when it became apparent that the Jewish people were growing weaker spiritually, and they continued to guide the nation in the Land of Israel during the early days of the Second Temple period. These great and wise men foresaw a time when the Jews would be weaker still, attracted more by the physical world than by the love, fear, and knowledge of G-d. And therefore, they added the *Pesukei DeZimra* to the already-existing prayers, which consisted mainly of the *Shema*. In addition, they added the blessings before the *Shema* and, most importantly, the *Shemonah Esreh*; they did so because it became necessary to pray at length in order to develop the proper connection with the One Above.

הָאֵל הַגָּדוֹל הַגִּבּוֹר וְהַנּוֹרָא אֵל עֶלְיוֹן, גּוֹמֵל חֲסָדִים טוֹבִים, קוֹנֵה הַכֹּל, וְזוֹכֵר חַסְדֵי אָבוֹת, וּמֵבִיא גוֹאֵל לִבְנֵי בְנֵיהֶם לְמַעַן שְׁמוֹ בְּאַהֲבָה:

From Rosh HaShanah to Yom Kippur, the following is added:

זָכְרֵנוּ לְחַיִּים, מֶלֶךְ חָפֵץ בַּחַיִּים, וְכָתְבֵנוּ בְּסֵפֶר הַחַיִּים, לְמַעַנְךָ אֱלֹהִים חַיִּים:

The sages were very strict regarding reciting the *Shemonah Esreh*. They determined that our concentration is even more important during the *Shemonah Esreh* than it is during the recitation of the *Shema*.[161] The question is why, given that the *Shemonah Esreh* is not listed among the 613 commandments of the Torah, while reciting

seder hishtalshelut ("chain of spiritual evolution"). And this is what is meant by *Baruch Atah Havaya* ("Blessed are You, Lord"), meaning that we request the descent of the name *Havaya* from *Atah* ("You"), which is the infinite light of G-d beyond the name *Havaya*, as the name *Havaya* indicates the chain of spiritual descent from one level to the next. The first letter *yud* indicates contraction, the second letter *hey* represents expansion and the third letter *vov* represents the descent ... And this ray that descends through the spiritual chain of levels is a mere contracted reflection in comparison to the infinite light of G-d Above. And this is the reason for our requests during the *Shemonah Esreh* – that there should be a blessing and descent of a greater reflection from Above ... to heal the sick of our people, Israel, and to bless the years, for example. This is the vessel in which His G-dliness is revealed down in the physical world, giving life and health to the sick and a blessing to the earth...

(From *Likutei Torah* of the Alter Rebbe, *Parshat Balak*, p. 140)

Prayer and the Spinal Cord
Boruch Atah HaShem...("Blessed are You, Lord...")

Another possible reason why *tefila* is described as "external," or "behind:" The sages said (in *Berachot*) that the eighteen blessings [of the *amidah*] correspond to the eighteen mentions of G-d's name during the *kriat shema* and to the eighteen vertebrae of the backbone. Now, the subject is as follows; the spinal cord descends from the segment of the brain called *da'at*, which is toward the back of the skull. The segments of *chochma* and *bina* are at the front of the skull, while *da'at* is toward the back. Now, *chochma* and *bina* correspond to

CHASSIDIC INSIGHTS

the *Shema* is among the foremost of them.

The author of *Tanya*[162] answers this question with a parable. He likens the eighteen blessings of the *Shemonah Esreh* to the eighteen vertebrae through which passes the spinal cord. Just as man has 248 limbs, yet the spinal cord is not counted among them, so the *Shemonah Esreh* serves a vital purpose and yet is not included among the mitzvot. The spinal cord stretches from head to foot, establishing and maintaining the entire structure of our body. Moreover, the spinal cord plays the vital role of distributing our bodily vitality from the mind to all of our 248 limbs. So, even though the spinal cord is not counted among the limbs of the body, it joins and connects all of them together. If the spinal cord is severed, then the connection and communication from the mind to the rest of the body is also severed. Similarly, *Shemonah Esreh* gives structure and motivation to our fulfillment of the *mitzvot*, connecting our highest and most sublime intellectual moments with our physical actions. This is why the main *kavana* ("intention") that we must focus upon during the *Shemonah Esreh* is to bring the infinite light of G-d

the great, mighty and awesome G-d, supernal G-d, Who performs good deeds, creates everything, and recalls the good deeds of the forefathers, and brings a redeemer to the offspring of their descendents, for the sake of His name, out of love.

Between Rosh Hashana and Yom Kippur:

Remember us for life, King Who desires life, and inscribe us in the book of life, for Your sake, living G-d.

CHASSIDIC EXCERPTS

Torah, and specifically *chochma* includes the concept of vision, as written, "And he saw the first portion,"[308] wherein 'first' refers to the beginning in *chochma*, about which the verse says "And he saw." And moreover, this is said in regard to Moshe, whose soul root was also from *chochma*, as written, "From the water he was drawn,"[309] which is why the verse says about him, "And he saw the first portion." And this refers to vision of the essence of G-dliness.

And this is what Moshe wished to instill in the Jewish people as they entered the land of Israel. In general, he desired that the Jewish people be capable of seeing the very essence of G-dliness, as written, "Let me please pass through, and I will see the land,"[310] wherein "land" indicates vision from up close. This applies to Jewish souls in general, as written, "For you are a *eretz hefetz* – a desirable land."[311] But, Moshe

was not successful in this endeavor, and he succeeded only in instilling vision from afar, meaning that only special individuals, for whom Torah is their very profession and occupation are capable of seeing the essence, but not every man merits to this level.

But...*da'at* corresponds to *hacara* – recognition and experience of G-dliness. And to this level, every man can aspire, and regarding it there is a commandment in the Torah, as written, "And you shall know the Lord... you shall know today and place it upon your heart,"[312] as well as "Know the G-d of your father"[313]...meaning that the command is for us to feel G-dliness within...

(Page 340) And this [brings us to]...*tefila*, which is solely for the purpose of instilling inner feeling. For although *tefila* demands intention, and one must "focus his heart," nevertheless, the intention is not that we should

CHASSIDIC INSIGHTS

down into the *kelim* ("vessels") that we create when reciting the blessings. In this way, the infinite light of G-d is directed to the appropriate destination, and we receive what we need from the One Above.

As we pray, the main requirement is that we act like a "servant before a master" in relation to G-d. Therefore, our prayers during the *Shemonah Esreh* must take place in a state of ultimate self-nullification. Only in this way can we hope to become a vessel for His blessings. In fact, we must make our requests as if we do not know what we need. For, as we see, there are times that we think something is good for us when in reality it is not, and there are times that we distance ourselves from precisely the things that we should desire. Therefore, the best way to pray is without regard to what is disturbing and bothering us at that particular time, but according to the order decreed by the Sages of the Great Assembly. With their holy insight, they were able to determine the best way to pray for every Jew during their time and until the end of generations.[163]

מֶלֶךְ, עוֹזֵר וּמוֹשִׁיעַ וּמָגֵן.

בָּרוּךְ אַתָּה יְיָ, מָגֵן אַבְרָהָם:

אַתָּה גִבּוֹר לְעוֹלָם אֲדֹנָי, מְחַיֶּה מֵתִים אַתָּה רַב לְהוֹשִׁיעַ:

Summer: מוֹרִיד הַטָּל:

Winter: מַשִּׁיב הָרוּחַ וּמוֹרִיד הַגֶּשֶׁם:

The Sages of the Great Assembly arranged the language of the blessings of the *Shemonah Esreh* in a uniform fashion, called the *matbeah habracha* ("form of the blessing"). Each begins with *Baruch Atah Havaya*

CHASSIDIC EXCERPTS

merely meditate for the sake of intellectual understanding, but rather that we should achieve unity and inner feeling, as written, "Know the G-d of your father and serve Him..." wherein "service" is *tefila*, about which the verse says, "Know your father." Now, knowledge divides into *chesed* and *gevura* ("kindness and strictness"), from which arise the emotions of love and fear of G-d. Now, even though they result from intellect and understanding, nevertheless they are mainly associated with *da'at*, as mentioned in Tanya. If not, the result of our meditation would be mere false illusions [in the heart and imagination], which dissipate and pass away with time. It is only through *da'at* that we experience conscious emotions. And in this manner, we arrive above to the very essence of the infinite One...In *tefila*, by way of *da'at* and via the love and fear that is born from meditation, we bring down the very essence of the Infinite

One. This is reflected in our prayers, as we say *Baruch atah Havaya* ("Blessed are You, Lord...")...indicating descent of G-dliness from *atah* – "You" – essence of the infinite One - into the name *Havaya*, which is part of *seder hishtalshelut* (the "spiritual chain of creation"); the first letter *yud* indicating contraction, the first *hey* indicating expansion, the *vov* indicating descend and the final *hey* also indicating expansion. For these are levels that apply to the spiritual chain of creation, and we say "Blessed are You," meaning that we bring down G-dliness from *Atah* – You – into the name *Havaya*. And although in any case G-dliness descends from above the chain of spiritual creation into the chain, but this is only a ray and mere reflection, while here the intention is that we should bring down the very essence of the Infinite One.

And afterward, as we recite the twelve intermediate blessings, such as "He Who heals the sick," and "He Who

CHASSIDIC INSIGHTS

("Blessed are You, G-d"). The word *baruch* ("blessed") shares its root with the word *berech*, meaning "knee." When we bend our knees and lower our bodies (as we utter the word *baruch* during the first and second blessings, as well as the second to last blessing), we indicate our awe and reverence for G-d. In so doing, we enact "descent" – the principle of bringing G-dly influence down from above to below.

The next word of the blessing is *Atah*, meaning "You," and it implies that G-d is revealed in front of us and present among us. We address Him in this manner because we want the good that He bestows upon us to be obvious and in plain sight. He sometimes bestows His blessings in ways that are not so obvious, but during the *Shemonah Esreh*, we want to be aware of the good that comes down to us from Him, so we refer to Him as "You." Although in essence God is so exalted and removed from us that it would be more appropriate to refer to Him in the third person as "He," here we are asking that He lower Himself to meet our needs and become more obvious and apparent to us – hence, "You."

Finally, the third and most important word of the blessing is

> The King who assists and saves and shields;
> Blessed are You, Lord, the shield of Abraham.
>
> You are forever mighty, Lord, You enliven the dead, very able to save.
>
> During summer: You bring down the dew.
>
> During winter: You cause the wind to blow and the rain to fall.

CHASSIDIC EXCERPTS

blesses the year," – we create the *kelim* ("vessels") to contain His revealed illumination. Even though according to the order of the chain of spiritual creation, it was decreed that this person should be sick, nevertheless by praying for a change in His will, and creating a new will (*Yehi ratzon...*) – this creates the path by which the sick are healed, as we create a vessel for His revealed illumination. Even this, though constitutes mere recognition of G-dliness; although it descends to actually heal the sick nonetheless [we see only the result,] and we do not see revealed G-dliness. [We achieve] only recognition and feeling, as if we see, but [we do not achieve] true vision. And even when we experience a desire for the essence of G-dliness during this *tefila*, still it is only a will and desire to want and yearn for G-dliness to illuminate, and not that it should descend to us as revealed illumination... And therefore, *tefila* is called "external," or "behind," while by way of Torah, true enjoyment descends, which we refer to as "illumination of His countenance." And therefore, Torah is called "internal," (*panim*). And nonetheless we say that [the Ten Commandments – precursors to the Torah] were written *panim v'achor* – "forward and backward," because both levels must be present. For, in order to achieve the true internal vision of the essential G-dliness that is associated with Torah, there must first be *tefila*, which includes recognition and experience. And then afterward we arrive to Torah, which is vision of the essence, as known that *da'at* joins together the inner aspect of *chochma* with *bina*, and the inner aspect of *chochma* is vision within *chochma*, which is triggered by *da'at*, as mentioned above.

From *Sefer Maamorim 5663* (vol. 2) of the Rebbe Rashab, Pp. 339-340

CHASSIDIC INSIGHTS

G-d's name — the special, unique four-letter name which we pronounce outside of prayer as *Havaya* or *HaShem*. Other names of G-d (including the seven names that are forbidden to erase) describe G-d as He lowers Himself to create the world, and as He relates to His creation. However, the four-letter name of G-d describes Him as He exists, alone and exalted, above His creation and above time and space.

מְכַלְכֵּל חַיִּים בְּחֶסֶד, מְחַיֵּה מֵתִים בְּרַחֲמִים רַבִּים, סוֹמֵךְ נוֹפְלִים, וְרוֹפֵא חוֹלִים, וּמַתִּיר אֲסוּרִים, וּמְקַיֵּם אֱמוּנָתוֹ לִישֵׁנֵי עָפָר. מִי כָמוֹךָ בַּעַל גְּבוּרוֹת וּמִי דוֹמֶה לָּךְ, מֶלֶךְ מֵמִית וּמְחַיֶּה וּמַצְמִיחַ יְשׁוּעָה:

From Rosh HaShanah to Yom Kippur, the following is added:

מִי כָמוֹךָ אַב הָרַחֲמָן זוֹכֵר יְצוּרָיו לְחַיִּים בְּרַחֲמִים:

וְנֶאֱמָן אַתָּה לְהַחֲיוֹת מֵתִים. בָּרוּךְ אַתָּה יְיָ, מְחַיֵּה הַמֵּתִים:

With these three words — *Baruch Atah Havaya* — we bring down the infinite light of G-d during the *Shemonah Esreh* prayer, so that it may influence and affect our lives.

*

One could ask, though, why does G-d need a name? Since He is unlimited, undefined, and almighty, why is it necessary to apply a name to Him at all? In fact, the sages say that we should pray "to Him, and not to His attributes," implying that it is to Him in essence (and not any of His names or attributes) that we should pray. Why then, should we apply a name to Him, implying that He is limited by the descriptions and conditions of that name?

The answer is that while G-d does not need a name, we do. We need to call upon G-d, and for that purpose, He gave us a name by which to call Him.

Upon further analysis, it becomes apparent that any name possesses two opposite qualities: 1) a name lacks any substance or physi-

CHASSIDIC EXCERPTS

The pinnacle of prayer
Boruch Atah HaShem...("Blessed are You, Lord...")

The blessings of the *Shemonah Esreh* correspond to the World of *Atzilut*, [which is why] we bow in self-nullification...

The entire purpose of the *Pesukei DeZimra* is to facilitate our spiritual exit from the limitations imposed by our animal soul (*nefesh*) until the concept of "there is no other than G-d" becomes confirmed [in our mind]. Now this cannot take place without a *ratzoh* ("rush") and departure of the soul from the body as a result of our meditation on the concept, "Before Him, all is a naught."

However, during the *Shemonah Esreh*, this matter has already been clearly established and confirmed. With the naked eye, we are aware that there is none other than Him and that enables us to draw down from the World of *Atzilut* into *BY"A*. And when we say the word *baruch* with a bow [from the waist], our

CHASSIDIC INSIGHTS

cal qualities, but 2) a name penetrates to the very essence of the person or object who bears it. When we call someone by name, the person turns to us. And if he happens to be sleeping, it is often enough to call his name in order to wake him up. So, while a name does not add to our physical, emotional or spiritual being, it is necessary for us to have a name so that others may communicate with us. For that, a name is vital.

The same is true of the name of G-d. Even though He does not need a name, He provided us with a way of attracting His attention. And just as with a human name, the name of G-d does not possess any substance, and yet it relates to His very essence. When we call out to Him and make our various requests, He responds by sending down His infinite light to become clad in the appropriate attribute (sephira), from where it descends to our physical world in order to meet our needs.

The Talmudic sages declared, "Before the world was created, there was only He and His name alone."[164] That means that even before G-d created the world, there existed the possibility, the spiritual potential, within the infinite light of G-d, to call to Him, using His name. The sages' statement refers to G-d's name as it existed within His infinite light, but before He decided to create the universe. And after the creation took place, His name became known and eventually fully revealed

He Who in His goodness provides life, in great mercy enlivens the dead, supports the fallen and heals the sick and frees the imprisoned, and fulfills His promise to those [already] sleeping in the dust. Who is like You, master of mighty deeds, and Who is comparable to You, King Who takes away life and Who gives life and germinates salvation...

Between Rosh Hashana and Yom Kippur: Who is like You, merciful

Father, Who recalls His creations for merciful life.

And You are believed to enliven the dead. Blessed are You, Lord, Who enlivens the dead.

———⟩◦⟨———

intention is to draw down spirituality from the source of all emanations (sephirot), beyond vision from *Atik Yomim* and *Arich Anpin* [which are aspects of *keter*, transcending *Atzilut*]. This level is called *Hu* ("He") with terminology that indicates something concealed, since it is in fact beyond eyesight and vision. However, [this level] emerges to become a "head," meaning that it descends to the *sephira* of *chochma* of *Atzilut*, which is called *Atah* ("You") indicating something that is present and revealed in front of us. In general, as creation is revealed to be formed from nothing into something – from a hidden reflection of the concealed worlds called *Hu* – it becomes the level called *Atah*. And as we straighten out from our bow while saying the name *Havaya*, this facilitates the elevation of creation, emerging from darkness to shine in the world of *Atzilut* in order that the darkness will no longer conceal ... And then, time and space become illuminated with the name *Havaya* – "was, is, and will be..."

(From letters of the Tzemach Tzedek in *Meah Shearim, p. 100*)

CHASSIDIC INSIGHTS

when the Torah was given at Mt. Sinai. At that time, G-d became known to us through the four-letter name we call *Havaya* which is spelled in Hebrew *Yud-Hei-Vov-Hei*. This essential name of G-d is a contraction of *haya, hoveh, v'yihiyeh* ("was, is, and will be") and means "existence" (hence the substitution of *Havaya*),

Why these particular letters? What does the *Yud-Hei-Vov-Hei* represent?

קְדוּשָׁה

קְדִישָׁךְ וְנַעֲרִיצָךְ כְּנֹעַם שִׂיחַ סוֹד שַׂרְפֵי קֹדֶשׁ הַמְשַׁלְּשִׁים לְךָ קְדֻשָּׁה, כַּכָּתוּב עַל יַד נְבִיאֶךָ,

Congregation, then chazzan - וְקָרָא זֶה אֶל זֶה וְאָמַר:

קָדוֹשׁ, קָדוֹשׁ, קָדוֹשׁ יְיָ צְבָאוֹת, מְלֹא כָל הָאָרֶץ

Congregation, then chazzan - כְּבוֹדוֹ:

Chazzan - לְעֻמָּתָם מְשַׁבְּחִים וְאוֹמְרִים:

Congregation, then chazzan - בָּרוּךְ כְּבוֹד יְיָ מִמְּקוֹמוֹ:

Chazzan - וּבְדִבְרֵי קָדְשְׁךָ כָּתוּב לֵאמֹר:

יִמְלֹךְ יְיָ לְעוֹלָם, אֱלֹהַיִךְ צִיּוֹן לְדֹר וָדֹר

Congregation, then chazzan - הַלְלוּיָהּ:

Chasidic teachings explain that it is impossible to bring down G-dly influence from above without a four-step process that is represented by precisely these four letters. This can be explained by the following analogy:

When two beings or objects are within range of one another, there are many ways of bringing them together. Generally, the process of bringing them together operates in a "cause-and-effect" manner. Since the two beings or objects are in any case close to one another, all that is necessary is to find the connection. However, when they are out of range of one another, as G-d is from His creation, then the only way to bring His infinite light down is by way of the four-step process associated with His name *Havaya*.

The first letter, *yud*, represents contraction (*tzimtzum*) of His infinite light. In order for it to descend, the infinite G-dly illumination must first contract itself to be within range of the world. Then, the contraction must re-expand on a lower level, in order to reveal the details that are concealed within it. This is associated with the second letter of His name – the *hei* – whose form includes three lines, representing all

CHASSIDIC EXCERPTS

Three Dimensions
Boruch Atah HaShem...("Blessed are You, Lord...")

There are three dimensions: space, time and soul. The entire *Sefer Yetzira* ("Book of Formation") is based upon these three, because they are the foundation of all of *seder hishtalshelut* [the progression of spiritual levels leading to creation]. And they also comprise the triplet of "point, line and surface," which corresponds to the three letters of G-d's name: *yud, vov,* and *hey*. The point corresponds to the *yud* of the name *Havaya*. (The first *hey* is not taken into consideration since it is still

"undeveloped," so to speak, and is considered to be included within the *yud*...)

And the line corresponds to the letter *vov* of the name *Havaya*, while the surface is the final *hey*. The same is true of space, time and soul as well, with the distinction that point, line and surface are the order of the letters of *Havaya* from Above to below [beginning to end], while space, time and soul correspond to the letters from below to Above [from the end to the beginning]. That is, space is alluded to by surface,

CHASSIDIC INSIGHTS

of the dimensions of physical expansion. It represents the next stage of descent, wherein the hidden details of the contracted infinite light come into view. The third stage is for the infinite light, after contraction and re-expansion, to descend. That is represented by the third letter, the *vov*. Since it is in the form of a straight vertical line, it represents descent from above to below. (Note that in other cases the *vov* represents ascent.) And the final *hei* represents the culmination of the journey. After the holy light descends, it culminates its journey as it is absorbed and internalized by the recipient, represented by the final *hei*.

This is the four stage process of bringing the infinite light of G-d from above to below. Since G-dliness is totally out of range of the creation, it can only descend by way of the four-letter name of G-d. And that is why, when we pray, we focus our attention on His infinite light and how it descends, using this name.

Throughout the order of prayer, we find different references to G-d's name. Sometimes, the reference is simply to *Shemo* ("His name"). At other times it appears as *Shemo hagadol* ("His great name"). When His name appears simply as *Shemo*, it refers to *malchut* (the final, tenth, *sephira*, which also descends to create the lower worlds) of the World of *Atzilut*, which is the proximate source of creation. For example, in the middle of the blessings of the *Shema*, we state *et shem HaKel Hamelech* ("the name of G-d, the King"). This is a reference to *malchut* in the World of *Atzilut*. When His name appears as *Shemo hagadol*, it refers to revelation of G-dliness before the *tzimtzum*, above the worlds, before He caused His infinite light to contract and illuminate creation.

*

Kedushah

Congregation, followed by the cantor: We sanctify You and we revere You, as in the pleasant, hidden conversation of the holy seraphim, who thrice-mention You in holiness, as written by Your prophets, 'And they called to one another and said':

Congregation, followed by the cantor: Holy, holy, holy is the Lord of Hosts, the entire earth is full of His glory.

Cantor: And facing them, they praise [G-d] and say...

Congregation, followed by the cantor: Blessed be the glory of the Lord from His place.
Cantor: And in Your holy words, it is written, saying:

Congregation, followed by the cantor: May the Lord reign forever, Your G-d of Zion from one generation to the next, Halleluyah!

CHASSIDIC EXCERPTS

time by the line, and soul by the point. For, space has three dimensions – up and down, east and west, and north and south [and the letter *hey* possesses three lines] ... Now, by space, we do not mean mere physical space, but the spiritual energy that is present in space – this is also included within the category called "space."

From *Sefer Maamorim 5680* (1920) of the Rebbe Rashab, p. 54

Carrying out the verdict

For example, regarding intellect and emotions, the intellect includes the emotions within itself. However, these are not full-fledged emotions, but rather inclinations within the intellect. And although the inclination is toward either *chesed* ("kindness") or *gevura* ("strictness"), nevertheless it has already been

CHASSIDIC INSIGHTS

Since our intention is so important during the recitation of the *Shemonah Esreh*, proper focus is vital. But here, we find what seem to be contradictory directions from the sages. On the one hand, it is written, "Who is like the Lord our G-d (*Havaya Elokeinu*) whenever we call out to Him?"[165] This verse proves, according to the *Sifri* that we must focus upon G-d Himself and not upon His attributes (*sephirot*) as we pray. And yet, the sages also voiced doubt that we can actually cleave to the G-d Himself, implying that it is impossible for man to cling to His Divine Presence on such a high level, and therefore they advised us to "cling to His attributes..."[166]

אַ‌תָּה קָדוֹשׁ וְשִׁמְךָ קָדוֹשׁ, וּקְדוֹשִׁים בְּכָל יוֹם יְהַלְלוּךָ סֶּלָה. בָּרוּךְ אַתָּה יְיָ,

- *During the Ten Days of Repentance substitute)*

הָאֵל הַקָּדוֹשׁ: (הַמֶּלֶךְ הַקָּדוֹשׁ:)

Now, it is possible to resolve this seeming contradiction (as the sages do) by differentiating between "calling upon G-d," and "cleaving to Him." When we call to Him in prayer (as indicated by the verse

CHASSIDIC EXCERPTS

explained elsewhere that the emotions at this stage are not truly either *chesed* or *gevura*. [They are] rather like a judge who delivers a verdict of either "innocent" or "guilty," without getting himself involved in carrying out the decision of exonerating the innocent or punishing the guilty as he delivers the verdict. For, if he himself would get involved in carrying out either verdict, he would not be a true judge. It is only the clerks of the court who put the verdict into action and it is they who get involved in the defendant's guilt or innocence. (This refers to the verdict of *chesed* being declared by by the attribute of kindness and the verdict of *gevura* pronounced by the attribute of judgment.

And beneath this are those who are appointed for the purpose of carrying out the kindess. And we might say that this is what is meant by the importance of "focusing on His Name," even though when we call out to Him, it should be to Him and not to His attributes. For, when one carries out the verdict, he gets involved in it, and for this there are special appointees who are responsible for carrying out the verdict. But, the judge himself does not get involved or become affected by any of these attributes. And this is because the judge remains intellectual at all times, without allowing his emotions to get involved, other than the inclination that takes place within the emotion itself...)

From *Sefer Maamorim 5671* (1911) of the Rebbe Rashab, Page 91

Path of Spiritual Progress

This, then is the spiritual path of the soul down here in this world...And if so, it is not possible for a soul that ascends from our world into Gan Eden to merely "sit and bask in the rays of the *shechina*," without proceeding on a spiritual trajectory, from one level to the next. Without doubt, [the soul above] serves G-d on a trajectory of spiritual progress. That is, there are elevations and steps upon which the soul ascends from one spiritual level to the next, corresponding to the ray of spiritual enjoy-

ment that is a refelction of His infinite light. And the ascent in this manner constitutes progress "out of range." The process of ascent takes place accompanied by nullification from the previous level, followed by inclusinon in the higher level. And this is what is meant by *u'kedoshim bekol yom hehalelucha sela* ("the holy beings praise you daily for all eternity"), and they do this without ceasing, ascent after ascent, without limit...

From *Yom Tov shel Rosh Hashana 5666* (1905-6) of the Rebbe Rashab, p. 16

CHASSIDIC INSIGHTS

quoted above), we call to His very essence. But, by cleaving to Him, we fulfill another commandment: that of emulating His character attributes. That is, we are enjoined to emulate G-d insofar as is possible, by imitating His actions (such as "visiting the sick" – since G-d "visited" Abraham after his circumcision, or by "clothing the naked," since G-d clad Adam). Thus, the mitzvah of cleaving to G-d has to do with character development and proper attitude, rather than meditation and prayer.

Nevertheless, this resolution is insufficient, since elsewhere, the sages ask, "Why do the Jews call upon G-d and fail to receive answers? Because, when they call upon Him, they do not know how to focus properly on His name..."[167] With this question and answer, the sages implied that we must focus not merely upon G-d Himself, but upon His name as well.

*Y*ou are holy, and Your name is holy, and holy creatures praise You everyday, forever. Blessed are You, Lord the holy G-d. (Between Rosh Hashana and Yom Kippur, Blessed are You, Lord, the holy King)

CHASSIDIC EXCERPTS

You and Your Name are Holy

At first glance this is not clear. Since both are holy, the prayer should say, "You and Your Name are holy." Why does it separate them? But the explanation is that "You" refers to G-d in the second person, as if speaking to one who is present. We are addressing G-d's very essence, which is called the essence of the Illuminator ... He is holy and removed altogether, not even close to being the origin of the source of the spiritual evolution of the worlds *ABY'A*. He is not in the category of "worlds" at all, and it is not even appropriate to say about Him that He is transcendent, beyond the spiritual chain of *ABY"A*. He is holy and exalted in His own right, not merely exalted from a particular level, but rather holy and exalted in and of Himself.

However, the aspect that we call His "Name," also referred to as "the in-

finite light," is the light that shines and radiates from the Illuminator, and it is also infinite, as explained previously.[314] And it is also called *kadosh*, even though it is holy and exalted above the spiritual chain of creation since, being light and revelation, it bears a relationship to the chain of creation. Although it bears a relationship, it is nevertheless holy and exalted, being transcendent and beyond it, as is known regarding the *igul hagadol* ("great surrounding light") that precedes the *kav* ("ray") which refers to the infinite light that preceded the great *tzimtzum*. It transcends and remains beyond the spiritual chain of creation that begins with the *kav*, in equal measure from the highest to the lowest levels, since it is holy and removed from all of them. And yet, it is still in the category of *sovev* ("transcendent holy light").

From *Yom Tov shel Rosh Hashana* 5666 (1905-6) of the Rebbe Rashab, p. 182

"The holy King"

As is known, every character trait, from its inception until its readiness for expression, undergoes three stages prior to its revelation. For example, these are the tree stages that the trait of kindness undergoes: 1) The first stage is included and enrooted in the very essence of the soul, before it undergoes any descent whatsoever. At this point, it is not even

a source for what will later emerge as a general arousal of kindness. 2) This is followed by a plan as to what general form this kindness will take. Above, this is known as *ki chafetz chesed hu* ("because He desires to be kind"),[315] and it is characterized by an overall will to bestow good. Thus, we say that the general will of G-d is to "benefit His creations."

CHASSIDIC INSIGHTS

The answer is clarified by considering the nature of a "name" as opposed to an "attribute." An attribute is a character trait that has its own specific quality and nature. It may be part of us, connected to our being, but it is "something," for otherwise we would not call it an attribute. A name, however, has nothing of its own. It has neither form nor substance. On the other hand, as pointed out earlier, a name goes to the very essence of the one who bears it – in this case, G-d.

אַתָּה חוֹנֵן לְאָדָם דַּעַת, וּמְלַמֵּד לֶאֱנוֹשׁ

בִּינָה. חָנֵּנוּ מֵאִתְּךָ חָכְמָה בִּינָה וָדָעַת.

בָּרוּךְ אַתָּה יְיָ (יַהְוֶה :silent kavana), חוֹנֵן הַדָּעַת:

הֲשִׁיבֵנוּ אָבִינוּ לְתוֹרָתֶךָ, וְקָרְבֵנוּ מַלְכֵּנוּ
לַעֲבוֹדָתֶךָ,

וְהַחֲזִירֵנוּ בִּתְשׁוּבָה שְׁלֵמָה לְפָנֶיךָ.

בָּרוּךְ אַתָּה יְיָ (יַהְוֶה :silent kavana), הָרוֹצֶה
בִּתְשׁוּבָה:

In essence, G-d transcends creation and need not have any connection with it. Yet, He chose to create the universe and to be intimately involved in it, even as He remains above and beyond the creation. It is only in the World of *Atzilut* that His infinite light becomes clad in the ten attributes that we speak of: wisdom, understanding and knowledge, kindness, strictness, etc. Therefore, we begin applying names to G-d only in the World of *Atzilut*, since that is where His infinite illumination descends into the ten *sephirot*. Specifically, G-d is called by His four-letter name (*yud-hei-vov-hei*) in the World of *Atzilut* (with which the *Shemonah Esreh* is associated). This is the name which brings G-dly illumination down to bear on our universe from above.

CHASSIDIC EXCERPTS

However, this is an essential and abstract desire. It is an undifferentiated arousal to do good that remains abstract at this stage. 3) Finally, this is followed by an estimate in what specific form and manner to bestow kindness. This is what is meant by *shiar be'atzmo be'koach* ("He estimated within Himself, in potential.")[316]

Similarly, regarding the trait of divine sovereignty, there is [first of all] the essential trait of sovereignty as included within His very essence that does not descend or become revealed whatsoever, as in *hamelech hakadosh* ("the holy [exalted] King").[317] [Then, there is] a general arousal of His will, as it is written, *Ana emloch* ("I will reign").[318] This is followed by a specific estimate in His mind to emanate [the ten *sephirot* of the World of *Atzilut*]. However, in order to proceed from the stage of essential sovereignty as included in His very essence, to the second stage of *Ana emloch*, an intermediate stage, between the stages, is necessary. The intermediary is the Torah...for by way of the Torah, G-d's essential reign over the universe becomes revealed...[319]

From *Besha'ah Shehikdimu*, 5672 (1912) of the Rebbe Rashab, pp. 471-472

Not truly new...

This, then is the difference between prayer and Torah. Prayer takes place from below to Above, while Torah study is from Above to below. And although prayer also involves descent of spirituality (when we say, *Yehi ratzon* - "May it be Your Will" - we draw down a new Divine will from Above), nevertheless, it is new only in comparison to the Divine will that was previously present, en-clad

CHASSIDIC INSIGHTS

*

To grasp this better, it will be helpful to analyze the nature of the ten *sephirot*. Each of the *sephirot* are composed of two components: *ohr* ("light") and *keli* ("vessel"). The *ohr* is the G-dly illumination that remains connected with G-d, even as it descends to the World of *Atzilut* (like a ray of the sun remains connected with the sun). The *keli* is the aspect of each *sephira* that contains and channels the *ohr*.[168] The *keli*, though divine, bears a hidden and indirect connection to the infinite light of G-d. It is the *ohr* (direct illumination from above the World of *Atzilut*) that provides the direct and revealed connection between the infinite light above and our world below.

As we pray during the *Shemonah Esreh*, mentioning the name of G-d, we seek to bring down the *ohr* from above and connect it with its appropriate *keli*. It is our focus upon His name *Havaya*, as we utter the blessings of the *Shemonah Esreh*, that brings the infinite light down to bear upon each *sephira*, as it exists in the World of *Atzilut*.

However, even the above procedure must be insufficient, since, as implied by the sages, we do not receive regular responses to our requests. Even when we "call out" to G-d, concentrating upon His name

*Y*ou grace man with knowledge, and teach man understanding, grace us with wisdom, understanding and knowledge from You. Blessed are You, Lord, Who grants knowledge.

*B*ring us back, our Father to Your Torah, and draw us, our King, to Your service, and return us in total repentance before You. Blessed be You, Lord, Who desires repentance.

CHASSIDIC EXCERPTS

in the attribute of *chochma*. For example, a cure for the sick does not involve anything truly new; before the person fell ill, [his body] was healthy and vital. The cure merely returns the vitality that was previously present, when he was healthy. Therefore, this is not a process of true renewal (nevertheless, it is not comparable to eating, wherein we replenish the vitality and illumination that was already present in the body. The cure draws down the vitality of the soul as it exists prior to enclothment in the body...this is an example of *ohr sovev* ("transcendent light") descending – but in any case, it is not truly anything "new").

Similarly, when we bless the new year, we do not bring down a "new light." Our requests are only in order to renew the previous light... There are

years in which there is a blessing in the produce, and there are years [when the blessing is not evident]. So, here as well, the blessing is for the purpose of renewal of the previous vitality...all this occurs via prayer. After the introduction of the *kriat shema*, when we say *Hashem echad* ("G-d is one"), [concentrating upon how] the seven heavens and the earth and the four directions of the universe are nullified, as well as united...we then proceed to bring down the aforementioned will [of "renewal"] from Above during the twelve middle blessings of the *shemonah esreh*...

However, Torah study, which takes place from Above to below, reveals a truly new light...the words of Torah must seem to us as new words every day, and the influx caused by Torah, is a revelation of an entirely new light.

From *Sefer Maamorim 5680* (1920) of the Rebbe Rashab, Page 145-146

CHASSIDIC INSIGHTS

Havaya, we do not receive a response from above as often or as clearly as we might want or expect. In truth, we should not expect immediate answers to our prayers, and furthermore G-d's answers often arrive in unexpected ways that we do not immediately recognize. Nevertheless, too often our prayers go unanswered. Either, G-d in His infinite wisdom has decided that we do not deserve or need a response, or there is more that we can and should do to assure a response from above. The Midrash indicates there is more that we can do to attain answers from above, including working upon our focus and concentration. Chasidic literature further explains that with our focus, we can direct the infinite light of G-d to the "correct address" in the appropriate sephira during the Shemonah Esreh, thereby increasing the likelihood of receiving answers to our prayers.

סְלַח לָנוּ אָבִינוּ, כִּי חָטָאנוּ, מְחַל לָנוּ מַלְכֵּנוּ, כִּי פָשָׁעְנוּ, כִּי אֵל טוֹב וְסַלָּח אָתָּה.

בָּרוּךְ אַתָּה יְיָ (silent kavana: יְהֹוָה), חַנּוּן הַמַּרְבֶּה לִסְלֹחַ:

In fact, in order for His infinite light and wisdom to filter down through to the appropriate sephira and descend to the physical world, it helps for us to guide its path, so to speak. And, to do that, kabbalistic and Chasidic teachings suggest that we focus on G-d's name as it applies to each sephira. For, not only does every sephira possess its own character and purpose, but every sephira possesses its own association with the essential name of G-d.

רְאֵה נָא בְעָנְיֵנוּ וְרִיבָה רִיבֵנוּ, וּגְאָלֵנוּ מְהֵרָה לְמַעַן שְׁמֶךָ, כִּי אֵל גּוֹאֵל חָזָק אָתָּה. בָּרוּךְ אַתָּה יְיָ (silent kavana: יְהֹוָה), גּוֹאֵל יִשְׂרָאֵל:

Specifically, Chasidic literature recommends that we concentrate upon the proper vowelization

CHASSIDIC EXCERPTS

Forgiveness comes after prayer…
Selach lanu ki chatanu ("Forgive us for we have sinned")

The connection that we establish through our "service of the heart" (prayer) occurs in proportion to the length of our praise [of G-d] and the depth of our knowledge as we meditate, utilizing our faculties of bina and t'vuna (the inner recesses of bina, which lend a hidden emotional dimension to intellect). That is why we recite the blessing Selach lanu ("forgive us") during the Shemonah Esreh. For, at first glance, it would have been appropriate to preface our prayers with this blessing, since there is no lower level than one who has sinned. The word choteh ("sinner") is related to the word chisaron ("lacking") as in the verse, "Myself and my son Shlomo were lacking (chata'im),"[320] indicating that they were lacking everything. So, it would be appropriate to be-

gin our prayers with an expression of what we are lacking, and then request that G-d replenish what we are missing. So, why do we begin with hoda'ah ("acknowledgement" of G-d) as we rise from our sleep saying Modeh Ani, and also as we begin prayer by saying Hodu? And then we follow that up with the Pesukei DeZimra and the blessings preceding the Shema, and the Shema itself, and not until the Shemonah Esreh do we say Selach lanu ("forgive us") That is, only after the entire length of prayer, do we finally mention that we are sinners. At first glance, this does not make sense.

But the truth is that before prayer we tend to be innocent in our own eyes, as if we haven't sinned at all. And if we do a mitzvah, we begin to think that we are already close to G-d, and that we are

CHASSIDIC INSIGHTS

(*nikud*) of the name *Havaya* as we pray the *Shemonah Esreh*. Every blessing of the *Shemonah Esreh* corresponds to a specific *sephira*, and for every *sephira* there is a corresponding method of vowelizing G-d's holy name while reciting the blessing. So, as we mention G-d's name during each blessing, it is recommended that we concentrate not only upon the four-letters of His name, but also on the specific set of vowels that correspond to the *sephira* of that blessing. And those vowels change from one blessing to the next. Since every blessing of the *Shemonah Esreh* is associated with a different *sephira*, in order to cultivate proper intention, we must know to which *sephira* each blessing corresponds. And then, we can apply the proper vowelization. As we recite the blessing, concentrating on the holy name *Havaya* in the prescribed manner, we bring down infinite light from above to bear on the ten *sephirot*.

In essence, by mentioning G-d's name in the appropriate fashion, we join the *ohr* of each *sephira* with its *keli*. We bring down the illumination from above to become en-clothed in its vessel. But, in no case do we pray to the *sephira* itself. We focus on the essential four-letter name of G-d, representing His infinite light. But, when we want to request something in particular, we apply the appropriate vowelization that will direct His infinite light to a particular *sephira* and, from there, down to us. In this manner, we are

*F*orgive us, our Father, for we have sinned, pardon us our King, for we have transgressed, for You are a kind and forgiving G-d.

Blessed are You, Lord, gracious One, Who abundantly forgives.

*S*ee, please, our poverty, and fight our battles, and quickly redeem us for the sake of Your name, for You, G-d are a powerful Redeemer.

Blessed are You, G-d, Redeemer of Israel.

CHASSIDIC EXCERPTS

not sinners. It is only after we meditate a bit, using our powers of analysis to investigate ourselves closely, contemplating such subjects as the nullification of the angels to G-d, [that we begin to get a truer picture of ourselves]. Then we realize that our own nullification does not arrive to even a fraction of that of the angels. And then we follow that up with meditation on the *Shema*, contemplating how G-d is one and His name is one, in both higher unity (*yichuda ila'ah*) and lower unity (*yichuda tata'ah*) with deep knowledge and recognition. Only then, do we arrive at proper recognition of how far away we are from the One G-d. And we gain awareness that all we achieved by fulfilling G-d's mitzvot was only to help ourselves, since we are lacking any proper acceptance of the king-

dom of heaven or of the yoke of the mitzvot. It was for this reason that the sages asked, "Why does the *Shema* precede the paragraph of *vehaya im shamoah*?" And they answered, so that we should first accept the kingdom of heaven and the mitzvot...

And then, when we say *Selach lanu ki chatanu* ("Forgive us for we have sinned") – meaning that we are quite incomplete and that we know and recognize this in ourselves – we become aware of our faults and generally low level. And then we request that forgiveness should be granted to us from the infinite light of G-d, the Master of all wills, source of the will to replenish our shortcomings that we caused by not following His will properly, and this is the root of prayer.

(From *Sefer Ma'amorim 5654* (1894) of the Rebbe Rashab, pp. 186)

CHASSIDIC INSIGHTS

told, we increase the likelihood of receiving answers to our prayers over when we pray without any reference to the vowels.

After all this, we could still ask, "G-d is almighty, without limitations, so why is it necessary to specify our requests with vowelizations that are unique to each *sephira*?" He certainly knows what we need and want, even if we do not specify, and He certainly has the capability of answering, especially when we express it within the context of the *Shemonah Esreh*?" To this, Chasidic literature responds with two parables:

The first comes from the Mittler Rebbe[169] who uses the analogy of a king and his various ministers. It is known that when one wants to make a specific request, he goes to the minister who is appointed over that matter. If it has to do with agriculture, for example, the request must be directed to the minister of agriculture; and if with science, then the request must be made to the minister of science. It will not be helpful to ask the minister of science for permission to cultivate a farm, for example. The king places the administration of the kingdom in the hands of his ministers. And, therefore, it is important to go through the correct channels in order to achieve the appropriate goal.

The second parable comes from the Tzemach Tzedek[170] who uses the analogy of the king himself. When the king is involved in one task, it is difficult, if not impossible, to get Him to turn to another task. It would not be helpful, for example, to approach the king about a matter of defense of the kingdom while he

On a Public Fast Day the following is said by the chazzan during the repetition of the Amidah.

עֲנֵנוּ יְיָ עֲנֵנוּ בְּיוֹם צוֹם תַּעֲנִיתֵנוּ, כִּי בְצָרָה גְדוֹלָה אֲנָחְנוּ, אַל תֵּפֶן אֶל רִשְׁעֵנוּ, וְאַל תַּסְתֵּר פָּנֶיךָ מִמֶּנּוּ, וְאַל תִּתְעַלַּם מִתְּחִנָּתֵנוּ, הֱיֵה נָא קָרוֹב לְשַׁוְעָתֵנוּ, יְהִי נָא חַסְדְּךָ לְנַחֲמֵנוּ, טֶרֶם נִקְרָא אֵלֶיךָ עֲנֵנוּ, כַּדָּבָר שֶׁנֶּאֱמַר: וְהָיָה טֶרֶם יִקְרָאוּ וַאֲנִי אֶעֱנֶה, עוֹד הֵם מְדַבְּרִים וַאֲנִי אֶשְׁמָע, כִּי אַתָּה יְיָ הָעוֹנֶה בְּעֵת צָרָה, פּוֹדֶה וּמַצִּיל בְּכָל עֵת צָרָה וְצוּקָה: בָּרוּךְ אַתָּה יְיָ, הָעוֹנֶה לְעַמּוֹ יִשְׂרָאֵל בְּעֵת צָרָה:

רְפָאֵנוּ יְיָ וְנֵרָפֵא, הוֹשִׁיעֵנוּ וְנִוָּשֵׁעָה כִּי תְהִלָּתֵנוּ אָתָּה, וְהַעֲלֵה אֲרוּכָה וּרְפוּאָה שְׁלֵמָה לְכָל מַכּוֹתֵינוּ. כִּי אֵל מֶלֶךְ רוֹפֵא נֶאֱמָן וְרַחֲמָן אָתָּה.

בָּרוּךְ אַתָּה יְיָ (יהוה :*silent kavana*), רוֹפֵא חוֹלֵי עַמּוֹ יִשְׂרָאֵל:

Focus on His Name
Boruch Atah HaShem...("Blessed are You, Lord...")

In order to improve our understanding of the *Shema* and of the *Shemonah Esreh*, we must add explanation of what should be our thought process during the blessings of this standing prayer known as the *Amida*.

The sages warned us, "Why do the Jews call upon G-d and fail to receive answers? Because when they call upon Him, they do not know how to focus properly on His Name." Now, it is known that the first two letters – *yud* and *hey* – of the name *Havaya* represent contraction and expansion. Afterward, the [third letter] *vov* corresponds to the

descent of G-dly influx from Above to below, while the final *hey* represents the absorption of influx by the receiver. If so, the entire purpose of the name *Havaya* is the transfer of G-dly illumination and influx from Above to below. For this reason, the "name" is called a vessel for light and illumination, as written in the *Zohar* and *Eitz Chayim* regarding the names of G-d as they are written out to their fullest in various ways. The name with the numerical value of seventy-two is written with *yuds*, since it is a vessel for the light of *chochma* [*chochma* represents self-nullification, and the *yud*

CHASSIDIC INSIGHTS

is busy inside of his treasury of precious metals and gems. However, it would make sense at that time to ask the king for financial help, because, while in his treasury, he is capable of giving a handout. Of course, in our situation, G-d the King is unlimited and, no matter what we ask, He is capable of responding. But, it takes a greater amount of personal merit to make a request when it is not an auspicious moment, than when the request is made at a more appropriate time. Similarly, if we pray to G-d,

keeping in mind His infinite light, we will have more success if we focus on the particular vowelization that is associated with that blessing, than if we focus upon another vowelization, or any vowelization at all.

Still, the question may arise, "why the vowels?" There are other elements involved in the writing of the Hebrew language, such as numerical values (*gematria*), various ways of expanding the letters of His name (*miluim*), and decorations (*tagin*) and cantilations (*ta'amim*) associated with all of the letters. So, why do the sages recommend that we focus specifically upon vowels in order to direct G-dly influence down to earth? Why does Chasidic literature tell us to focus on one element alone – the vowels – as the vehicle for bringing G-dliness down to the *sephirot*?

The Rebbe Rashab illuminates this subject in a discourse[171] about the various aspects of the letters of Torah. There, he says that letters (of the Torah and of prayer) are associated with the emotional attributes of *Atzilut*. This is because it is with letters (and the words they make up) that we express our emo-

> *On a Public Fast Day the following is said by the chazzan during the repetition of the Amidah.*
>
> Answer us, Lord, answer us on our fast day, for we are in great distress; Turn not toward our wickedness, do not conceal Your countenance from us, nor hide from our pleas. Be near to our cries, let Your kindness comfort us. Answer us before we call upon You, as in the verse, "And it will be that even before they call, I will answer, even while they speak, I will hear." For, You are the Lord Who answers in times of distress, [Who] redeems and rescues from every season of trouble and crisis.
> Blessed are You, Lord, Who answers His people Israel in times of distress.

Heal us, Lord, and we will be healed, aid us and we will be saved, for You are our Praise, and bring complete cure and healing to all of our wounds, for You G-d are King, a trustworthy and merciful healer. Blessed are You, Lord, Who heals the sick of His people, Israel.

CHASSIDIC EXCERPTS

is a small letter, barely more than a point], and the name of G-d with the numerical value of sixty-three is a vessel for the illumination of *bina*, etc. ...

However, within this, there are two levels. 1) One level occurs after the revelation of illumination and influx, and 2) the other level is the light of the name *Havaya* as it still exists within the essence of the Emanator. At that point, it is called an "essential name," as opposed to a "name of action." As G-d said to Moses, "And by my essential name of *Havaya* I did not make Myself known..."[321] and "I am *Havaya*, dependable under all circumstances," and also "*Havaya* is your G-d,"[322] to quote several

examples in which there is no descent or transfer of influx from Above to below. Therefore, these are examples of *Havaya* as G-d's "essential name." And, there is also "And *Havaya* spoke to Moses saying..."[323] wherein it is *Havaya* Who "speaks" and conveys the words of Torah. Although Torah descends from supernal *chochma*, yet, nevertheless, this name *Havaya* is essential [and does not descend], meaning that it is from the ten *sephirot* that are still hidden within the essence of the Emanator Himself [before they become revealed as *sephirot* in the World of *Atzilut*]. The *yud* is *chochma* within His essence, the *hey* is *bina* within His essence... The *vov* represents the six

CHASSIDIC INSIGHTS

tions. The emotions of our heart are too intense and amorphous to express, and we need to break them down into bite-size pieces that can be expressed in individual words in order to make ourselves understood. This process involves contracting our feelings, breaking them down, and then expressing them in words. It is the letters (and not the vowels, cantilations or other decorations) that facilitate this process. So, the letters are associated with the emotions of our heart (*chesed, gevura* and *tiferet*).[172]

בָּרֵךְ עָלֵינוּ יְיָ אֱלֹהֵינוּ אֶת הַשָּׁנָה הַזֹּאת וְאֶת כָּל מִינֵי תְבוּאָתָהּ לְטוֹבָה, וְתֵן בְּרָכָה (*Summer:* טַל וּמָטָר לִבְרָכָה) (*Winter:* עַל פְּנֵי הָאֲדָמָה, וְשַׂבְּעֵנוּ מִטּוּבֶךָ, וּבָרֵךְ שְׁנָתֵנוּ כַּשָּׁנִים הַטּוֹבוֹת לִבְרָכָה, כִּי אֵל טוֹב וּמֵטִיב אַתָּה וּמְבָרֵךְ הַשָּׁנִים:

בָּרוּךְ אַתָּה יְיָ (*silent kavana:* יֱהֹוִה), מְבָרֵךְ הַשָּׁנִים:

תְּקַע בְּשׁוֹפָר גָּדוֹל לְחֵרוּתֵנוּ, וְשָׂא נֵס לְקַבֵּץ גָּלֻיוֹתֵינוּ, וְקַבְּצֵנוּ יַחַד מֵאַרְבַּע כַּנְפוֹת הָאָרֶץ לְאַרְצֵנוּ:

בָּרוּךְ אַתָּה יְיָ (*silent kavana:* יֱהֹוִה), מְקַבֵּץ נִדְחֵי עַמּוֹ יִשְׂרָאֵל:

However, the letters also need guidance/instruction, just as our emotions need to be guided and instructed by our intellect. And that is the role that the vowels play. The vowels are associated with *chochma* (the first of the ten *sephirot*), which is the intellect that transcends the letters. The meaning of the words changes according to the vowels that are applied to them. For example, the word spelled *aleph-bet*, when vowelized one way (as *av*) means "father," but when vowelized differently (as *ov*) refers to a form of witchcraft (*lehavdil*). This is because the vowels come from *chochma*, which is intellect, and it is the intellect that guides and directs the letters. From this, we understand that it is the vowels which, when applied to the four letters of the name *Havaya*, guide the infinite light of G-d to the correct *sephira*. Just as different vowelizations may change the meaning of the same word, different vowelizations of the name *Havaya* change its meaning and guide the infinite light from above to a particular *sephira*. Thus, it is our intention utilizing the correct vowels that guides the infinite light of each blessing of the *Shemonah Esreh* to the *sephira* with which it is associated.[173]

*

emotional attributes, as in the verse, "With You, *Havaya* are the kindness, the strictness..."[324] And for this reason, His essential name is sometimes described as "light" rather than "vessel," since it alludes to the inner core and essence of G-dliness. And this is the goal of true intention and focus on G-d's name, as it exists within His essence, "holy and removed," as it says, "There is no holiness like *Havaya*..."[325] Similarly, it is what is referred to in most places by the verse, "I am *Havaya* your G-d..." and "You shall

love *Havaya* your G-d,"[326] all of which refer to the inner essence of the name *Havaya*. And it is written, "Your countenance, *Havaya*, I will seek..."[327] [from below to Above, man to G-d]. And from Above to below [this happens] as well, as it is written, "May *Havaya* shine His countenance upon you,"[328] and at the time of the giving of the Torah ["I am *Havaya* your G-d..."[329]]

Therefore, it is understood that our intention within the blessings of the *Amida* – as we say *Baruch Atah Havaya*

CHASSIDIC INSIGHTS

The above discussion overflows beyond the realm of Chasidut and overlaps with the realm of Kabbalah. For that reason, it will be helpful to explore the relationship between the two fields of study. Furthermore, the subject of vowelization will also become clearer when we understand the relationship between Kabbalah and Chasidut. For they are not the same, as some people would like to believe.

Kabbalah in general, but especially Lurianic Kabbalah, is a technical study that involves the use of physical metaphors to refer to spiritual phenomena. Because of the use of physical symbols, some rabbis (by no means all) were nervous about laymen learning Kabbalah. In our day and age, there is not much to worry about because no layman opening a book of Kabbalah on his own will understand it in any case. But, in the days when an educated layman may have thought that he understood Kabbalah while in fact he did not, some rabbis discouraged the learning of the discipline fearing that a student without the proper guidance might confuse the physical terminology with the spiritual meaning. Of course, to attribute anything physical to G-d is anathema in Judaism. So, rather than taking a chance, some rabbis forbid learning Kabbalah except under specific circumstances. For example, the *Shach* (Rabbi Shabtai Cohen) recommended in the 17th century that only those who were fully knowledgeable in Talmud and Jewish law and had reached the age of forty get involved in learning Kabbalah.[174] He felt that only then would they be capable of abstracting the physical symbolism and attributing to it the appropriate spiritual meaning.

Not all rabbis expressed hesitation nor attempted to place limits on who may learn Kabbalah. For example, the Ari himself said that, "It

*O*ur Lord, our G-d, bless this year, as well as all its produce for good, and grant (during the summer) blessing (during the winter) dew and rain for blessing upon the face of the earth, and satisfy us out of Your Goodness, and bless our year like other good years of blessing, since You a good and beneficial G-d and You bless the years.

Bless are you, Lord, Who blesses the years.

*B*low the great shofar for our freedom, and raise a flag to gather our exiles, and gather us together from all four corners of the earth to our land.

Blessed are You, Lord, Who gathers the scattered remnants of His people, Israel.

CHASSIDIC EXCERPTS

bowing on *Baruch*, and then standing upright on *Havaya* – must take place on two levels:

1) One point of focus is on the descent [of G-dliness] that takes place via the four letters of the name *Havaya* as contraction and expansion, etc. This [directs G-dly influx from Above to] the vessel, because in this way [G-dliness] is drawn down and clad in the lowest levels, within the *kelim* of the recipients. For example, during the blessing, *Baruch Atah Havaya chonen hada'at* ("Blessed are

You, Who graciously grants knowledge"), we request that knowledge (*da'at*) as well as understanding (*bina*) and wisdom (*chochma*) descend upon us as a gift. Thus, we say, "And grant us from You insight (*chochma*), ability to analyze (*bina*), and ability to internalize knowledge (*da'at*)" ... These come down to us in a step-by-step process, as "cause and effect" from the illumination of *chochma* and *da'at* Above in the World of *Atzilut*. They come down via a series of intermediaries, through various and

CHASSIDIC INSIGHTS

is a mitzvah to learn this wisdom." And the 19th century leader of Lithuanian Jewry, the Vilna Gaon, declared that, "Without sod ("secrets" of the Torah, as expressed in Kabbalah), it is impossible to understand the pshat ("simple meaning" of the text), and without the pshat, it is impossible to understand the sod."[175]

But, in any case, Chasidic literature, and especially Chabad Chasidut, avoids the pitfall mentioned above because it couches divinity in psychological rather than physical terms. Thus, the "right hand" of G-d became "kindness," while the "left hand" became "judgment/strictness," for example. And as soon as the physical expressions of G-dly topics give way to the symbolism of the soul and of psychology, there is no need to worry about failure to abstract. The symbolism itself is abstract, so the person who studies Chasidic literature is taken directly into the realm of the soul and of spirituality.

This does not mean, however, that chasidim are encouraged to learn Kabbalah.[176] They may be permitted to do so, but that does not mean that it is always a good idea. Without the proper introduction and the proper knowledgeable teachers, Kabbalah is not understood. It is highly technical and complicated, and only those who learn with a teacher who is well versed and who has devoted his life to the study are likely to succeed. Kabbalah is no less difficult and time consuming than Talmud, and proper teachers are far fewer and much harder to find.

Nevertheless, there are occasions when it is useful for the student of Chasidut to reference Kabbalah in order to gain a fuller understanding. The above suggestion from the Mittler Rebbe, the Tzemach Tzedek, and the Rebbe

הָשִׁיבָה שׁוֹפְטֵינוּ כְּבָרִאשׁוֹנָה, וְיוֹעֲצֵינוּ כְּבַתְּחִלָּה,

וְהָסֵר מִמֶּנּוּ יָגוֹן וַאֲנָחָה, וּמְלוֹךְ עָלֵינוּ אַתָּה יְיָ לְבַדְּךָ בְּחֶסֶד וּבְרַחֲמִים, בְּצֶדֶק וּבְמִשְׁפָּט.

בָּרוּךְ אַתָּה יְיָ (silent kavana: יוהווהו), מֶלֶךְ אוֹהֵב צְדָקָה וּמִשְׁפָּט:

- During the Ten Days of Repentance substitute)

הַמֶּלֶךְ הַמִּשְׁפָּט)

וְלַמַּלְשִׁינִים אַל תְּהִי תִקְוָה, וְכָל הַמִּינִים וְכָל הַזֵּדִים כְּרֶגַע יֹאבֵדוּ, וְכָל אֹיְבֵי עַמְּךָ מְהֵרָה יִכָּרֵתוּ, וּמַלְכוּת הָרִשְׁעָה מְהֵרָה תְעַקֵּר וּתְשַׁבֵּר וּתְמַגֵּר, וְתַכְנִיעַ בִּמְהֵרָה בְיָמֵינוּ.

בָּרוּךְ אַתָּה יְיָ (silent kavana: יָהֹוָה), שֹׁבֵר אֹיְבִים וּמַכְנִיעַ זֵדִים:

CHASSIDIC EXCERPTS

sundry vessels, as written regarding King Solomon, "G-d gave chochma to Solomon." This gift descended from exalted levels to the relatively low [compared to essential G-dliness] from chochma of Atzilut into the soul of Solomon, enclad in his body. This would not be possible without the vessel of the sephira of chochma of Atzilut, associated with the four-letter name Havaya ... And via this mechanism, His wisdom descended through many contractions via the World of Atzilut to bria, and all the way down to our physical world.

2) And our second level of focus and intention during the Amida should be upon the light of Havaya as it enters the sephira of chochma. That is, just as chochma and da'at emerge from the essence of His infinite light – about which we say that our thought processes cannot grasp Him at all (even the primordial thought of A"K into which shines the chochma of the infinite light of G-d) – so, too, our focus must be upon the illumination of chochma within His essence.

CHASSIDIC INSIGHTS

Rashab regarding focus on the vowels during the *Shemonah Esreh* is one suggestion that can be elucidated by glancing into the works of Kabbalah.

The source of the vocalization of the name *Havaya* within the *Shemonah Esreh* is the *Sha'ar Hakavanot* ("Gate of Intentions") authored by Rabbi Chaim Vital from the teachings of the Ari.[177] Here are a few excerpts:

• The blessing that begins *Chonen hada'at* ("You grant wisdom to man...") corresponds to the *sephira* of *chochma* ... now it is already known[178] that each and every *sephira* contains a specific name *Havaya* with its own vowelization. And they are as follows: the name *Havaya* with a *kometz* corresponds to *keter*; the name *Havaya* with a *patach* corresponds to *chochma*; *Havyaya* with *tziri* corresponds to *bina*. And, therefore, as you say the words *Baruch Atah Havaya chonen hada'at*, you should focus on this name *Havaya* entirely vowelized with a *patach*, since it is associated with *chochma*, as mentioned.

• The blessing beginning with *Hasheveinu* ("Return us...") corresponds to *bina*, but one must focus on the *chesed* within *bina* ... and therefore one should focus on the name *Havaya* vowelized with a *segol* [and not *tziri*] while reciting *Hasheveinu avinu leToratecha*[179] ... And while reciting the name *Havaya* that concludes this blessing, one should focus on the vowel *tziri*, since it corresponds to *bina* as it descends to *malchut*.

• *Selach lanu avinu* ("Forgive us, our Father...") corresponds to *chesed*, and therefore the name *Havaya* at the conclusion of the blessing takes on the *segol*.

• *Re'eh na be'eineinu* ("See now our poverty...") corresponds to *gevura* and therefore the concluding name

*R*estore our judges to their original status, and our advisors as in the beginning and remove from us all misery and sighing, and reign over us – You alone, Lord – in kindness and mercy, in righteousness and justice. Blessed are You, Lord, King Who loves righteousness and justice.

(*between Rosh Hashana and Yom Kippur -* ...the just King)

*A*nd let the informers have no hope, and all the heretics and the wicked be immediately destroyed, and all the enemies of Your people quickly excised, and may You quickly uproot, break, crush – and subdue the kingdom of evil swiftly in our days. Blessed are You, Lord, Who shatters enemies and subdues the wicked.

CHASSIDIC EXCERPTS

This is what [descends and] shines within the vessel of this name *Havaya* that we focus upon during the blessing, *Baruch Atah Havaya chonen hada'at,* and this is the name *Havaya* vowelized with a *patach* under the first letter *yud*, since the vowel *patach* alludes to *chochma*, while the vowel *kamatz* alludes to *keter*...

From *Imrei Bina* of the Mittler Rebbe, in the Introduction, ch. 17, p. 8a

To Him...and not to His attributes
Boruch Atah HaShem...("Blessed are You, Lord...")

Now, we are able to solve a well-known problem posed by the Midrash in *Sifri*[330] on the verse, "Who...is like our G-d, [Who is near to us] whenever we call Him?"[331] The *Sifri* draws a precise distinction: "that is, to Him and not to His attributes." Yet, elsewhere, the sages say, "Is it possible to cleave to the *Shechina* [Divine Presence]? Rather, one must cleave to G-d's attributes."[332]

CHASSIDIC INSIGHTS

Havaya is vowelized with a sheva.
• Refaeinu ("Heal us...") is associated with tiferet and therefore the concluding Havaya is vocalized with a cholem.[180]
• Barcheinu avinu ("Bless us, our Father...") corresponds to netzach, and therefore the concluding Havaya is vocalized with a chirik.[181]

עַל הַצַּדִּיקִים וְעַל הַחֲסִידִים, וְעַל זִקְנֵי עַמְּךָ בֵּית יִשְׂרָאֵל, וְעַל פְּלֵיטַת בֵּית סוֹפְרֵיהֶם וְעַל גֵּרֵי הַצֶּדֶק וְעָלֵינוּ, יֶהֱמוּ נָא רַחֲמֶיךָ יְיָ אֱלֹהֵינוּ, וְתֵן שָׂכָר טוֹב לְכָל הַבּוֹטְחִים בְּשִׁמְךָ בֶּאֱמֶת, וְשִׂים חֶלְקֵנוּ עִמָּהֶם, וּלְעוֹלָם לֹא נֵבוֹשׁ כִּי בְךָ בָּטָחְנוּ.

בָּרוּךְ אַתָּה יְיָ (יוֹהֱווֹוְהוּ) (silent kavana:), מִשְׁעָן וּמִבְטָח לַצַּדִּיקִים:

וְלִירוּשָׁלַיִם עִירְךָ בְּרַחֲמִים תָּשׁוּב, וְתִשְׁכּוֹן בְּתוֹכָהּ כַּאֲשֶׁר דִּבַּרְתָּ, וְכִסֵּא דָוִד עַבְדְּךָ מְהֵרָה לְתוֹכָהּ תָּכִין, וּבְנֵה אוֹתָהּ בְּקָרוֹב בְּיָמֵינוּ בִּנְיַן עוֹלָם.

בָּרוּךְ אַתָּה יְיָ (יְהֹוָה) (silent kavana:), בּוֹנֵה יְרוּשָׁלָיִם:

• Tekah beshofar ("Sound the great shofar...") corresponds to hod and therefore the concluding Havaya is vocalized with a kibbutz.
• Hashiva shofteinu ("Return our judges...") corresponds to yesod and therefore the concluding Havaya is vocalized with a shurek.
• Velamalshinim ("And regarding the informers...") corresponds to keter ... and therefore the Havaya of the concluding blessing is vocalized with a kamatz.
• Ve'al hatzaddikim ("And regarding the righteous...") and the succeeding blessings follow a different order. Until now, all of the ten sephirot mentioned were those that are emanated and rectified within malchut [of Atzilut]. However, from now on, they are the sephirot that are within the [lower third of Atzilut], in netzach, hod and yesod and the lower two thirds of tiferet of Zeir Anpin [of Atzilut] itself. They illuminate from within Z'A, and now their order is from below to above. The blessing Ve'al hatzadikim is within the yesod of Z"A because the righteous are the foundation of the universe and the tzadik is called yesod. And if so, we must focus on the name Havaya in the conclusion of this blessing with the vowelization of a shurek.
• U'bnei Yerushalayim ("And Your city Jerusalem...") corresponds to

Although it is possible to distinguish between the mitzvah of calling upon G-d (in prayer) and that of clinging to Him (by emulating His good deeds), nevertheless, there is still a difficulty involved. It arises from the statement of the sages, "Why do the Jews call upon G-d and fail to receive answers? Because, when they call upon Him, they do not know how to focus properly on His Name." Here, the difficulty is that we are commanded to call upon Him, that is, upon His very essence, which isn't limited or proscribed by any quality or attribute. If so, why should it matter if we are unable to focus properly on one of His names or another? Each name corresponds to a sephira or attribute of G-d; for example, the name Kel corresponds to chesed, etc., which is very far

CHASSIDIC INSIGHTS

hod and the concluding *Havaya* is vocalized with a *kibutz*. And since this blessing is within *hod*, the left side, therefore mentioned within it is the building of Jerusalem, since Jerusalem is associated with the left [*gevura*], as is known. And as we say the words *Vekisai David avdecha meharah* ("And the throne of David, Your servant, shall be speedily re-established within it"), we should focus upon what Shamaya and Avtalyon explained to my master [the Ari] one day as he walked to Gush Chalav to pray at their graves. And there, they themselves said that we must have in mind that when we pronounce these words three time a day, we should pray to G-d about [the precursor to the Messiah] Mashiach ben Yosef that he will live and not be killed by Armelius the Wicked ... It is known from the *Zohar*[182] that Moses suffered greatly in order to prevent the death of Mashiach ben Yosef ... and about him we should pray that "the throne of David, Your servant, should be speedily re-established."

• *Et Zemach David* ("The salvation of David shall sprout...") corresponds to *netzach*, with the concluding name of *Havaya* vowelized with a *chirik*.

· *Shema koleinu* ("Listen to our prayers...") corresponds to *tiferet* of Z"A, from which *keter* is made ... and the name *Havaya* that concludes this blessing is vowelized with a *chashak* – a *cholem-sheva-kometz* on the first three letters, while the final *hey* is without vowelization. These three vowels are the secret of the three forefathers; the *cholem* is in *tiferet*, the *sheva* in *gevura* and the *kometz* in *chesed* ... and this is the secret meaning of the verse, "Only your forefathers desired (*chashak*) G-d" from all humankind.

*

The following tables summarize the above information:

*R*egarding the righteous and the pious, and regarding the elders of Your people, the house of Israel, and regarding the remnants of their sages, and regarding the righteous proselytes and regarding us, please arouse Your mercy, Lord our G-d, and grant goodly reward to all those who truly trust in Your name, and place our portion among them, and let us never be disgraced, for in You we trust. Blessed are You, Lord, the support and fortress for the righteous.

*A*nd return in compassion to Your city, Jerusalem, and dwell in it as You once spoke, and speedily establish the throne of Your servant, David within it, and build it soon in our days, as an eternal edifice. Blessed are You, Lord, Builder of Jerusalem.

below His essence. And yet, all Jews cry out to Him, to His very essence, as the verse says, *ailov* – "to Him!"

This problem is solved when we realize that there is a big difference between His attributes and His names. Although His attributes are one with Him, and they are G-dly, nevertheless, they are not His very essence. They are but rays emanating from Him, prior to

which there was a void, bereft of revelation. This is not true though of His names, which are indicative of His essence. His names do not describe His very essence as He exists prior to en-clothing within His attributes because, at that point, there is no name that can describe Him; He is understood only in the simple will of the heart and in thought. That is, [at that level] it is

Blessing	*Sephira*	Vowelization
Chonen hada'at	*Chochma*	*Patach*
Hasheveinu	*Bina*	*Tziri*
Selach lanu	*Chesed*	*Segol*
Re'eh na be'eineinu	*Gevura*	*Sheva*
Refaeinu	*Tiferet*	*Cholem*
Barcheinu avinu	*Netzach*	*Chirik*

These are the vowelizations that enable us, according to the sages and Chasidic masters, to more effectively receive answers to our requests during the *Shemonah Esreh*. As during the meditation of the *Shema*, this meditation requires us to maintain focus upon more than one element at a time. While reciting the *Shema*, we must focus on the meaning of the words and the number of words in the paragraph, while during the *Shemonah Esreh*, we must envision both the four-letter name of G-d and the correct vowels. Simultaneously, we must maintain our focus on the infinite light of the One Above, and then our *kavana* will guide the infinite light to its correct address in the corresponding *sephira*. Of course, this is not an easy task; it demands a supple mind and subtle intellect. But like everything else, the practice evolves with time and effort.

אֶת צֶמַח דָּוִד עַבְדְּךָ מְהֵרָה תַצְמִיחַ, וְקַרְנוֹ תָּרוּם בִּישׁוּעָתֶךָ, כִּי לִישׁוּעָתְךָ קִוִּינוּ כָּל הַיּוֹם.

בָּרוּךְ אַתָּה יְיָ (silent kavana: יְהוָה), מַצְמִיחַ קֶרֶן יְשׁוּעָה:

שְׁמַע קוֹלֵנוּ יְיָ אֱלֹהֵינוּ, אָב הָרַחֲמָן, רַחֵם עָלֵינוּ, וְקַבֵּל בְּרַחֲמִים וּבְרָצוֹן אֶת תְּפִלָּתֵנוּ, כִּי אֵל שׁוֹמֵעַ תְּפִלּוֹת וְתַחֲנוּנִים אָתָּה, וּמִלְּפָנֶיךָ מַלְכֵּנוּ רֵיקָם אַל תְּשִׁיבֵנוּ. כִּי אַתָּה שׁוֹמֵעַ תְּפִלַּת כָּל פֶּה.

בָּרוּךְ אַתָּה יְיָ (silent kavana: יְהוָה), שׁוֹמֵעַ תְּפִלָּה:

CHASSIDIC EXCERPTS

possible to know of His existence, but not to know Him directly since "no thought can grasp Him whatsoever." Nevertheless, His names are indicative of His essence, as He chooses to become en-clothed in His attributes, to become known as wise, or kind, or strong, or judgmental, or merciful, etc. ... Yet, after all is said and done, He and His essence are simple and one with ultimate simplicity, and any [apparent] variation is illusory. And since this is the case, the sages said in the *Sifri*, "And not to His attributes," meaning [that we don't

pray] to His attributes, since they are not [essential] G-dliness at all; they are only rays emanating [from Him]. And it is forbidden for us to pray to them, since it is not within their power to benefit us. They are only tools, as written, "Does the axe then become proud...?" [333] Even praying to [G-d's attributes] to arouse mercy before G-d Himself is forbidden, as the Rambam writes in the fifth of his Thirteen Principles of Faith: "It is forbidden for us to establish them as intermediaries and emissaries between ourselves and G-d." Rather, we must direct

CHASSIDIC INSIGHTS

Blessing	*Sephira*	Vowelization
Teka beshofar	*Hod*	*Kibbutz*
Hashiva softeinu	*Yesod*	*Shuruk*
Velamalsinim	*Keter*	*Komatz*
Ve'al hatzadikim	*Yesod of Zeir Anpin*	*Shuruk*
U'bnei Yeruahalayim	*Hod of Zeir Anpin*	*Kibbutz*
Et Zemach David	*Netzach of Zeir Anpin*	*Chirik*
Shema Koleinu	*Tiferet of Zeir Anpin*	*Chashak – cholem-sheva-kometz*

There is saying among the chasidim: "Once upon a time, we had stomachs of leather, and minds like silk. (That is, we could eat almost anything and survive, while meditating upon the highest and most refined topics.) Now, we have stomachs of silk and minds of leather. (We are picky about what we eat and have a tough time meditating.)" Still, we must try. To paraphrase the Rebbe Rashab,[183] if we fail to meditate during our worship of G-d, what are we doing down here? What is the purpose of a life without meditating to bring down G-dliness and refine ourselves and uplift our portion in the world?

*S*peedily grow the sprout of David, Your servant, and raise his profile of Your salvation, for it is Your salvation that we long for all day. Blessed are You, Lord, Who grows the profile of salvation.

*L*isten to our voice, Lord our G-d; merciful Father have mercy upon us, and accept our prayer in compassion and goodwill, for You are G-d Who hears prayers and supplications. From before You, our King, do not turn us away empty-handed, for You hear the prayers of every mouth. Blessed are You, Lord, Who hears prayer.

CHASSIDIC EXCERPTS

all of our thoughts to Him and distance ourselves from everything else..."

What emerges, then, from the saying of our sages, is that we must "focus on His names." [For example], during the blessing in the *Shemonah Esreh* concerning knowledge (*chonen hada'at*) we must think of the name *Havaya* vowelized with a *patach*. The *patach* is from the word *p'tach*, meaning "open/reveal" and *chochma* is the first stage of revelation [of G-d's infinite light]. This is not "calling to His attributes," but to His very essence, which is called *Havaya* with the vowelization of *patach* as it becomes enclothed in the *sephira* of *chochma*. In this way, His infinite light becomes enclothed within [the *sephira* of] *chochma* in order to bring down the influence of *chochma* into the lower worlds of *ABY'A*. We say, "You grant knowledge to man," and how is this possible if not through the vessel and emanation of *chochma* of *Atzilut* into which the infinite light of G-d flows. And through it, the infinite light descends through the entire World of *Atzilut*, from there becoming enclothed

רְ֒צֵה יְיָ אֱלֹהֵינוּ בְּעַמְּךָ יִשְׂרָאֵל וְלִתְפִלָּתָם שְׁעֵה, וְהָשֵׁב הָעֲבוֹדָה לִדְבִיר בֵּיתֶךָ, וְאִשֵּׁי יִשְׂרָאֵל וּתְפִלָּתָם בְּאַהֲבָה תְקַבֵּל בְּרָצוֹן, וּתְהִי לְרָצוֹן תָּמִיד עֲבוֹדַת יִשְׂרָאֵל עַמֶּךָ:

On Rosh Chodesh and Chol haMoed, add the following:

אֱלֹהֵינוּ וֵאלֹהֵי אֲבוֹתֵינוּ, יַעֲלֶה וְיָבֹא וְיַגִּיעַ, וְיֵרָאֶה וְיֵרָצֶה וְיִשָּׁמַע, וְיִפָּקֵד וְיִזָּכֵר זִכְרוֹנֵנוּ וּפִקְדוֹנֵנוּ וְזִכְרוֹן אֲבוֹתֵינוּ, וְזִכְרוֹן מָשִׁיחַ בֶּן דָּוִד עַבְדֶּךָ, וְזִכְרוֹן יְרוּשָׁלַיִם עִיר קָדְשֶׁךָ, וְזִכְרוֹן כָּל עַמְּךָ בֵּית יִשְׂרָאֵל לְפָנֶיךָ, לִפְלֵיטָה לְטוֹבָה, לְחֵן וּלְחֶסֶד וּלְרַחֲמִים לְחַיִּים טוֹבִים וּלְשָׁלוֹם בְּיוֹם

On Rosh Chodesh: רֹאשׁ הַחֹדֶשׁ

On Pesach: חַג הַמַּצּוֹת

On Sukkot: חַג הַסֻּכּוֹת הַזֶּה.

זָכְרֵנוּ יְיָ אֱלֹהֵינוּ בּוֹ לְטוֹבָה וּפָקְדֵנוּ בוֹ לִבְרָכָה וְהוֹשִׁיעֵנוּ בוֹ לְחַיִּים טוֹבִים וּבִדְבַר יְשׁוּעָה וְרַחֲמִים חוּס וְחָנֵּנוּ וְרַחֵם עָלֵינוּ וְהוֹשִׁיעֵנוּ, כִּי אֵלֶיךָ עֵינֵינוּ, כִּי אֵל מֶלֶךְ חַנּוּן וְרַחוּם אָתָּה:

וְתֶחֱזֶינָה עֵינֵינוּ בְּשׁוּבְךָ לְצִיּוֹן בְּרַחֲמִים. בָּרוּךְ אַתָּה יְיָ, הַמַּחֲזִיר שְׁכִינָתוֹ לְצִיּוֹן:

CHASSIDIC EXCERPTS

in *chochma* of BY"A, and down to *Gan Eden* [in which there is revealed G-dly illumination], and all the way down to this physical world in which we live. And yet, the *chochma* in all of these worlds is only an "axe" in the hand of the One Who wields it and Who exercises His influence by way of the *sephira*. And when He exercises His influence, we call Him "wise," in reference to the *chochma* [of each world]. And this is what is meant by the name *Havaya* with the vowelization of *patach*.

It emerges, then, that as we say *Baruch chonen hada'at* ("Blessed be He Who graciously grants knowledge to man") while focusing upon the name *Havaya* vowelized with a *patach*, we are calling out to G-d Himself, as He is enclothed in the vessel of *chochma*. The reason is that it is precisely in this manner that we are

able to exercise influence and receive a response in accordance with our request. This would not be the case if we focused on the name *Havaya* with the vowelization of *segol* during this blessing for the name *Havaya* vowelized with *segol* is indicative of His essence enclothed in the vessel of *chesed* ... In that case, there would be no path to bring our request to fruition, since the infinite light of G-d does not bring down *chochma* by way of the vessel of *chesed*.

Now, in truth, it is within the power of the infinite light of G-d, enclothed in *chesed*, to become enclothed in *chochma* as well, and descend. This, however, requires a huge amount of merit, which is not the case when one requests of G-d to bring down *chochma* through the normal channel when His infinite light is enclothed in the attribute of *chochma*, for

*F*ind favor, Lord our G-d in Your people, Israel, and turn to their prayers, and restore the service to Your glorious house, and lovingly accept the offerings and prayers of Israel, and let the service of Your people Israel always find favor.

On Rosh Hodesh and Chol Hamoed: Our G-d and G-d of our forefathers, may there ascend and come and arrive, be seen and accepted and heard, recalled and remembered before You our remembrances and our recollection, and the remembrance of our forefathers, and the remembrance of Meshiach, son of David Your servant, and the remembrance of Jerusalem, Your holy city, and the remembrance of Your entire people, the house of Israel, before You, for positive deliverance, for grace and kindness and compassion and good life and for peace, on this day of

Rosh Hodesh / Festival of Matzot / Festival of Succot

Remember us, Lord our G-d for the good, and recall us for blessing, and help us for good life. With promise of salvation and mercy, have compassion upon us, and be merciful with us and save us, for our eyes our directed to You, since your G-d are a merciful and compassionate King.

*A*nd may our eyes behold Your return to Zion in mercy. Blessed are You, Lord, Who returns His Divine Presence to Zion.

CHASSIDIC EXCERPTS

then it is much easier.

Take, for example, a man who requests something from the king. If the object of his request is within the king's reach at the time the request is made, it is easier for the person to receive what he is asking for. If he asks for a contribution from the king at the time the king is in His treasury, with unlimited silver and gold in front of him, it is more likely that the request will be granted than if he asks at a time when the king is elsewhere, involved in another task. Even though it is possible for the king to turn his attention away from his present task and make a contribution from his treasury, nonetheless this demands a much greater level of petition. Only if the king

sees the intense level of request and is persuaded of the worthiness of the person's cause [does he accede]...

This is what the sages meant when they said that the Jews do not know how to "properly focus on His name." If they knew how to focus on His name [on His name that indicates His essence as He is enclothed in a particular attribute, by way of which that particular request is meant to arrive], then they would be answered much faster for the aforementioned reasons. From this we understand that when the sages said, "to Him, and not to His attributes," they did not contradict the need for specific intention and focus...

(From *Derech Mitzvotecha* of the Tzemach Tzedek, *Shoresh Mitzvat Tefila*, ch. 7, pp. 117a-b, or 233-4)

מ֓וֹדִים אֲנַחְנוּ לָךְ, שָׁאַתָּה הוּא יְיָ אֱלֹהֵינוּ וֵאלֹהֵי אֲבוֹתֵינוּ לְעוֹלָם וָעֶד צוּר

חַיֵּינוּ, מָגֵן יִשְׁעֵנוּ, אַתָּה הוּא לְדוֹר וָדוֹר נוֹדֶה לְּךָ וּנְסַפֵּר תְּהִלָּתֶךָ, עַל חַיֵּינוּ

הַמְּסוּרִים בְּיָדֶךָ, וְעַל נִשְׁמוֹתֵינוּ הַפְּקוּדוֹת לָךְ, וְעַל נִסֶּיךָ שֶׁבְּכָל יוֹם עִמָּנוּ, וְעַל

נִפְלְאוֹתֶיךָ וְטוֹבוֹתֶיךָ שֶׁבְּכָל עֵת, עֶרֶב וָבֹקֶר וְצָהֳרָיִם, הַטּוֹב, כִּי לֹא כָלוּ רַחֲמֶיךָ,

הַמְרַחֵם, כִּי לֹא תַמּוּ חֲסָדֶיךָ, כִּי מֵעוֹלָם קִוִּינוּ לָךְ:

מודים דרבנן

מוֹדִים אֲנַחְנוּ לָךְ, שָׁאַתָּה הוּא יְיָ אֱלֹהֵינוּ וֵאלֹהֵי אֲבוֹתֵינוּ, אֱלֹהֵי כָל בָּשָׂר, יוֹצְרֵנוּ, יוֹצֵר

בְּרֵאשִׁית, בְּרָכוֹת וְהוֹדָאוֹת לְשִׁמְךָ הַגָּדוֹל וְהַקָּדוֹשׁ, עַל שֶׁהֶחֱיִיתָנוּ וְקִיַּמְתָּנוּ, כֵּן תְּחַיֵּינוּ

וּתְקַיְּמֵנוּ, וְתֶאֱסוֹף גָּלֻיּוֹתֵינוּ לְחַצְרוֹת קָדְשֶׁךָ, וְנָשׁוּב אֵלֶיךָ לִשְׁמוֹר חֻקֶּיךָ, וְלַעֲשׂוֹת רְצוֹנֶךָ,

וּלְעָבְדְּךָ בְּלֵבָב שָׁלֵם, עַל שֶׁאָנוּ מוֹדִים לָךְ, בָּרוּךְ אֵל הַהוֹדָאוֹת:

Holy acknowledgment

Modim anachnu lach ("we acknowledge You") and *sh'atah hu Havaya Elokeinu* ("that You are the Lord our G-d")

The Jews "arose in His supernal thought."[334] This means that the source of their soul and the origin from which they were hewn is from the supernal thought that transcends time.

For example, the thoughts of man in this lower world flow constantly, without interruption, forever. And so, the letters of supernal G-dly thought, about which it is written, "And a river emerged from Eden,"[335] refer to the two *sephirot* of *chochma* and *bina*, which are called "two fast friends who never separate." That means that His holy influx flows at all times from the *ayn* [of *chochma*] to the *yesh* [of *bina*], without interruption, and this is something that occurs beyond time, as explained elsewhere.

And since the Jews arose in His thought, they need no proofs whatsoever of this miracle of constant renewal of thought from *ayn* to *yesh* such as the

constant recycling of the summer and the winter ... since they grasp this instinctively in their souls on account of their source in His supernal thought ... And it is because of this that we say [in *Shemonah Esreh*] *modim anachnu lach* ("we acknowledge You") and *sh'atah hu Havaya Elokeinu* ("that You are the Lord our G-d"), meaning that because You are *Havaya Elokeinu* – alluding to this supernal thought of where the collective souls of the Jews reside in their origin, the source from where they are hewn – we automatically accede to this acknowledgment without any sign or proof whatsoever...

However, this acknowledgment is only from the G-dly soul as it resides Above in G-d's supernal thought. But, as it becomes enclothed in the physical substance of the body, it becomes concealed, so that it is unable to express this acknowledgment of "You are *Havaya*

*W*e give thanks to You, since you are the Lord our G-d and the G-d of our forefathers forever, the rock of our lives, shield of our salvation, in every generation. We acknowledge You and narrate Your praises, for our lives that are placed in Your hands, and for our souls that are entrusted to You, and for Your miracles that occur every day among us, and for the wonders and kindnesses that occur every moment; evening and morning and noon. You are the Good, for Your mercy is unceasing, the compassion One, for Your kindness does not stop, therefore forever we have hope in You.

Modim D'Rabbanan

The cantor says: We give thanks to You, since You are the Lord our G-d and the G-d of our forefathers, the G-d of all flesh, the One Who formed us, and Who formed all creation. We offer blessings and acknowledgement to Your great and holy name, for You have enlivened and sustained us, so may You continue to enliven and sustain us, and gather our exiles to the courts of Your holy Temple. And we will return to You, to keep Your laws and to do Your will, and to serve You whole-heartedly, for which we thank You, blessed is the G-d of acknowledgements.

CHASSIDIC EXCERPTS

Elokeinu," Who constantly renews from nothing to something at all times. The physicality of the body conceals this acknowledgment. And for that reason, the sages decreed that we should say *Modim D'rabanan.* The subject of *Modim D'rabaonen* is *hoda'ah lehoda'ah* ("conceding that we must concede"), meaning that "we acknowledge the necessity to acknowledge You." Or, in other words, we acknowledge that it is appropriate to acknowledge G-d...

(From the *Siddur* of the Alter Rebbe, pp. 303a-303b (606))

Prayer before Torah

We need to understand why the Torah is described as a "garment." We also need to understand what is said regarding [one who learns] Torah but does not pray [properly], that "even his Torah is lacking."

By way of explanation; there are two elements that comprise [the *sephirot*, or emanations of] the world of *Atzilut* – *orot* ("lights") and *kelim* ("vessels"). Furthermore, the *kelim* themselves are composed of two aspects. The *sephira* of *chesed*, for example, possesses both an internal level and an external level, both associated with the vessel itself. Regarding the *ohr*, we cannot speak of *chesed* per se, since the illumination [from above] is simple (undifferentiated). However, the differentiation does apply to the *kelim* ("vessels"), which possess both aspects, an inner and an outer...and that is why there are several names [of G-d] that apply to every *sephira*. There is the name *Kel* in *chesed*, and the name *Havaya* vowellized with a *segol*, also in *chesed*. And there is the name *Elokim* in *gevura* and the name *Havaya* vowellized with a *sheva*, also in *gevura*. They correspond to the external and internal aspects [of the vessel]; the name *Kel* is associated with the external aspect of the vessel of *chesed*, while the name *Havaya* vowellized with a *segol* is also within *chesed* but it reflects the internal aspect of [the vessel of] *chesed*.

On Chanukah and Purim add the following:

וְעַל הַנִּסִּים וְעַל הַפֻּרְקָן וְעַל הַגְּבוּרוֹת וְעַל הַתְּשׁוּעוֹת וְעַל הַנִּפְלָאוֹת שֶׁעָשִׂיתָ
לַאֲבוֹתֵינוּ בַּיָּמִים הָהֵם בִּזְּמַן הַזֶּה:

On Chanukah add:

בִּימֵי מַתִּתְיָהוּ בֶּן יוֹחָנָן כֹּהֵן גָּדוֹל, חַשְׁמוֹנַאי וּבָנָיו, כְּשֶׁעָמְדָה מַלְכוּת יָוָן
הָרְשָׁעָה, עַל עַמְּךָ יִשְׂרָאֵל, לְהַשְׁכִּיחָם תּוֹרָתֶךָ וּלְהַעֲבִירָם מֵחֻקֵּי רְצוֹנֶךָ,
וְאַתָּה בְּרַחֲמֶיךָ הָרַבִּים, עָמַדְתָּ לָהֶם בְּעֵת צָרָתָם. רַבְתָּ אֶת רִיבָם, דַּנְתָּ אֶת
דִּינָם, נָקַמְתָּ אֶת נִקְמָתָם, מָסַרְתָּ גִבּוֹרִים בְּיַד חַלָּשִׁים, וְרַבִּים בְּיַד מְעַטִּים,
וּטְמֵאִים בְּיַד טְהוֹרִים, וּרְשָׁעִים בְּיַד צַדִּיקִים, וְזֵדִים בְּיַד עוֹסְקֵי תוֹרָתֶךָ. וּלְךָ
עָשִׂיתָ שֵׁם גָּדוֹל וְקָדוֹשׁ בְּעוֹלָמֶךָ, וּלְעַמְּךָ יִשְׂרָאֵל עָשִׂיתָ תְּשׁוּעָה גְדוֹלָה וּפֻרְקָן
כְּהַיּוֹם הַזֶּה: וְאַחַר כָּךְ בָּאוּ בָנֶיךָ לִדְבִיר בֵּיתֶךָ, וּפִנּוּ אֶת הֵיכָלֶךָ, וְטִהֲרוּ אֶת
מִקְדָּשֶׁךָ, וְהִדְלִיקוּ נֵרוֹת בְּחַצְרוֹת קָדְשֶׁךָ. וְקָבְעוּ שְׁמוֹנַת יְמֵי חֲנֻכָּה אֵלוּ, לְהוֹדוֹת
וּלְהַלֵּל לְשִׁמְךָ הַגָּדוֹל:

On Purim add:

בִּימֵי מָרְדְּכַי וְאֶסְתֵּר בְּשׁוּשַׁן הַבִּירָה, כְּשֶׁעָמַד עֲלֵיהֶם הָמָן הָרָשָׁע, בִּקֵּשׁ
לְהַשְׁמִיד לַהֲרוֹג וּלְאַבֵּד אֶת כָּל הַיְּהוּדִים, מִנַּעַר וְעַד זָקֵן, טַף וְנָשִׁים,
בְּיוֹם אֶחָד, בִּשְׁלשָׁה עָשָׂר לְחֹדֶשׁ שְׁנֵים עָשָׂר, הוּא חֹדֶשׁ אֲדָר וּשְׁלָלָם לָבוֹז.
וְאַתָּה בְּרַחֲמֶיךָ הָרַבִּים הֵפַרְתָּ אֶת עֲצָתוֹ, וְקִלְקַלְתָּ אֶת מַחֲשַׁבְתּוֹ, וַהֲשֵׁבוֹתָ לוֹ
גְּמוּלוֹ בְּרֹאשׁוֹ. וְתָלוּ אוֹתוֹ וְאֶת בָּנָיו עַל הָעֵץ.

CHASSIDIC EXCERPTS

The name *Havaya* in general applies to the *ohr* that is enclothed in the vessel. This illumination is associated with the name *Havaya* without any vowellization whatsoever, since as explained above, the light is simple and totally undifferentiated. In all places and situations, this *ohr* remains the same – thus it corresponds to the name *Havaya* without any vowellization at all. It is the simple illumination of the vessel without any garment. For, vowellization is a garment. The name *Havaya* vowellized with a *segol* corresponds to the inner dimension of the *kelim*, which unite with the inner aspect and the essence of the *ohr*. And that is why it may take on the name *Havaya* – but in this case, *Havaya*

On Purim and Chanukah:

For the miracles and for the salvation and for the mighty deeds and for the acts of salvation and for the wonders that You did for our forefathers in those days, at this time:

On Chanuka:

In the days of Matitiyahu, son of Yochanan the High Priest, the Hasmonean and his sons, when the wicked kingdom of Greece rose up against Your people, Israel, in order to make them forget Your Torah and to make them forsake the laws that are Your will, and You in Your great mercy stood up for them in the time of their troubles. You fought their fights, judged their judgments, exacted their revenge. You put the strong in the hands of the weak, the many in the hands of the few, and the impure into the hands of the pure, and the wicked into the hands of the righteous, and the iniquitous in the hands of those keeping Your Torah. And as for You, You made and good and holy name for Yourself in Your worlds, and for Your people Israel You provided a great salvation and rescue to this very day. And afterward, Your children entered the shrine of Your holy house, and emptied out Your chambers, and purified Your dwelling place, and kindled candles in Your holy courtyards, and established these eight days of Chanuka, in order to give thanks and to praise Your great Name.

On Purim:

In the days of Mordecai and Esther in Shushan the capital, when Haman the wicked rose up against them, seeking to destroy, to kill and to eradicate all of the Jews, from youth to elders, children and women in one day, the thirteenth day of the twelfth month, which is the month of Adar, and to plunder their property. And You in Your great mercy, foiled his plan and You frustrated his counsel, and repaid his just deserts on his own head, hanging him and his sons on the tree.

CHASSIDIC EXCERPTS

vowellized with a *segol*. And when we say that the name *Elokim* applies to the sephira of *gevura,* we mean that it applies to the external level of *gevura,* meaning to the external dimension of the *keli* of *gevura.* And the name *Havaya* vowellized with a *sheva* applies to the inner dimension of the *keli.*

For that reason, aside from their names, there are several ways of referring to the *sephirot.* We may use, for example, the adjectives of "merciful" and "harmonious" regarding the *sephira* of *chesed.* And we may describe the *sephira* of *gevura* as "forceful" or "capable." These descriptions apply only to the external aspects of the *sephirot,* of which there are several levels. The vessels, then

וְעַל כֻּלָּם יִתְבָּרֵךְ וְיִתְרוֹמֵם וְיִתְנַשֵּׂא שִׁמְךָ מַלְכֵּנוּ תָּמִיד לְעוֹלָם וָעֶד:

From Rosh HaShanah to Yom Kippur add: וּכְתוֹב לְחַיִּים טוֹבִים כָּל בְּנֵי בְרִיתֶךָ:

כָל הַחַיִּים יוֹדוּךָ סֶּלָה וִיהַלְלוּ שִׁמְךָ הַגָּדוֹל לְעוֹלָם כִּי טוֹב, הָאֵל יְשׁוּעָתֵנוּ וְעֶזְרָתֵנוּ סֶלָה. הָאֵל הַטּוֹב. בָּרוּךְ אַתָּה יְיָ, הַטּוֹב שִׁמְךָ וּלְךָ נָאֶה לְהוֹדוֹת:

ברכת כהנים

This blessing is added during the chazzan's repetition of the Amidah, the congregation responds אָמֵן *where indicated:*

אֱלֹהֵינוּ וֵאלֹהֵי אֲבוֹתֵינוּ, בָּרְכֵנוּ בַבְּרָכָה הַמְשֻׁלֶּשֶׁת, בַּתּוֹרָה הַכְּתוּבָה עַל יְדֵי מֹשֶׁה עַבְדֶּךָ, הָאֲמוּרָה מִפִּי אַהֲרֹן וּבָנָיו כֹּהֲנִים עַם קְדוֹשֶׁךָ כָּאָמוּר:

יְבָרֶכְךָ יְיָ וְיִשְׁמְרֶךָ: (אָמֵן) יָאֵר יְיָ פָּנָיו אֵלֶיךָ וִיחֻנֶּךָ: (אָמֵן)

יִשָּׂא יְיָ פָּנָיו אֵלֶיךָ וְיָשֵׂם לְךָ שָׁלוֹם: (אָמֵן)

CHASSIDIC EXCERPTS

include two aspects; one internal and the other external. The Torah emerges from only the external aspects of the *sephirot*, as is evident from the verse, *Torat chesed al leshoncha* [336] – "The Torah of *chesed* is on your tongue" – [and the tongue is only an external aspect of the anatomy]. And that is why the Torah comes enclothed in physical *halachot* ("laws"). And so also it includes explanation and commentary on all of the mitzvoth that are performed in the physical realm. At its source, the Torah "emerges from *chochma*," but only from the external aspects of *chochma*. That is why we compare the Torah to "drops of *chochma* that descend from above," alluding to the external dimensions [of *chochma*]. For that reason as well, the Torah is the source of the laws - kosher vs unkosher, pure vs impure, etc, all of

which follow the decree of His wisdom. The meaning of this is that if G-d, in His wisdom, decreed that something is kosher or pure, it is capable of ascending spiritually to be included in the attribute of *chesed*. And if it is invalid (*posul*), it cannot be refined and spiritually elevated, and it ascends to the attribute of *gevura*, where its refinement takes place merely by dint of its rejection. All this occurs according to the decree of His wisdom, originating from the external dimensions of *chochma*, the source of all of His attributes.

The inner dimensions of His *chochma*, however, do not serve as a source of His attributes...This, then, is the reason why prayer must precede Torah; prayer is the internal illumination that arouses the light of love [of G-d]. It emerges solely from the inner dimen-

And for all of these things, Your name is blessed, exalted and uplifted, our King forever and ever.

Between Rosh Hashana and Yom Kippur: And inscribe all of the members of Your covenant for a good life.

Aーnd all life acknowledges You forever, and praises Your great Name eternally, for You are good. Almighty G-d, You are our salvation and our assistance forever, Almighty G-d. Blessed are You, Lord, Magnanimous is Your name, and to You it is pleasant to give thanks.

Priestly Blessing

This blessing is added during the chazzan's repetition of the Amidah, the congregation responds אָמֵן *where indicated:*

The Cantor says: Our G-d and the G-d of our forefathers, bless us with the three-part blessing written in Your Torah by Moses, Your servant, uttered from the mouths of Aaron and his sons, the priests of Your holy people, as stated:
"May the Lord bless you and keep you. (Amen)
May the Lord shine His countenance to You and grace you. (Amen)
May the Lord turn His countenance to You and grant you peace." (Amen)

CHASSIDIC EXCERPTS

sions [of the *sephirot*], and that is why after [prayer], we may learn Torah in a state of self nullification. And then, regarding "All who read in the Torah - G-d reads and repeats correspondingly."

This means that by uniting the *chochma*, *bina* and *da'at* (intellect) within our own soul with the *chabad* (intellect) of the Torah, we ensure that "both are covered in one talit" [that is, our own intellect is united with the divine intellect of the Torah]. This, then is why it is necessary to pray before learning Torah. Since our prayers are associated with the inner dimension [of the *sephirot*], they stimulate a descent [of G-dliness] from Above. And then afterward, as we learn Torah *lishmah* ("for its own sake") – for the sake of Torah, in-dicating the highest level of Torah learning – both become "covered in one talit."

However, this is not the case regarding one who says, "I have nothing but Torah." Such a person lacks even Torah, since Torah is only a "garment." Without the divine stimulation provided by our prayer, the Torah [that we learn] is like a body without a soul, containing no revealed light. Torah has the quality of *makif*, or "transcendent light," but even this does not descend to [the person who says that he "has only the Torah"]. Only prayer, which provides inner, immanent light – is capable of stimulating and drawing down the transcendent light [so that it becomes conscious and revealed with us...].

From *Sefer Maamorim 5663* (vol. 2) of the Rebbe Rashab, Pp. 232-234

שָׂים שָׁלוֹם, טוֹבָה וּבְרָכָה, חַיִּים חֵן וָחֶסֶד וְרַחֲמִים, עָלֵינוּ וְעַל כָּל יִשְׂרָאֵל

עַמֶּךָ, בָּרְכֵנוּ אָבִינוּ כֻּלָּנוּ כְּאֶחָד בְּאוֹר פָּנֶיךָ, כִּי בְאוֹר פָּנֶיךָ נָתַתָּ לָּנוּ יְיָ

אֱלֹהֵינוּ תּוֹרַת חַיִּים וְאַהֲבַת חֶסֶד, וּצְדָקָה וּבְרָכָה וְרַחֲמִים וְחַיִּים וְשָׁלוֹם, וְטוֹב

בְּעֵינֶיךָ לְבָרֵךְ אֶת עַמְּךָ יִשְׂרָאֵל בְּכָל עֵת וּבְכָל שָׁעָה בִּשְׁלוֹמֶךָ:

From Rosh HaShanah to Yom Kippur, add:

וּבְסֵפֶר חַיִּים בְּרָכָה וְשָׁלוֹם וּפַרְנָסָה טוֹבָה, יְשׁוּעָה וְנֶחָמָה וּגְזֵרוֹת טוֹבוֹת נִזָּכֵר וְנִכָּתֵב

לְפָנֶיךָ, אֲנַחְנוּ וְכָל עַמְּךָ בֵּית יִשְׂרָאֵל, לְחַיִּים טוֹבִים וּלְשָׁלוֹם:

בָּרוּךְ אַתָּה יְיָ, הַמְבָרֵךְ אֶת עַמּוֹ יִשְׂרָאֵל בַּשָּׁלוֹם:

יִהְיוּ לְרָצוֹן אִמְרֵי פִי וְהֶגְיוֹן לִבִּי לְפָנֶיךָ יְיָ צוּרִי וְגוֹאֲלִי:

אֱלֹהַי, נְצוֹר לְשׁוֹנִי מֵרָע וּשְׂפָתַי מִדַּבֵּר מִרְמָה וְלִמְקַלְלַי, נַפְשִׁי תִדּוֹם, וְנַפְשִׁי כֶּעָפָר

לַכֹּל תִּהְיֶה, פְּתַח לִבִּי בְּתוֹרָתֶךָ, וּבְמִצְוֹתֶיךָ תִּרְדּוֹף נַפְשִׁי, וְכָל הַחוֹשְׁבִים עָלַי

רָעָה, מְהֵרָה הָפֵר עֲצָתָם וְקַלְקֵל מַחֲשַׁבְתָּם.

יִהְיוּ כְּמוֹץ לִפְנֵי רוּחַ וּמַלְאַךְ יְיָ דּוֹחֶה. לְמַעַן יֵחָלְצוּן יְדִידֶיךָ, הוֹשִׁיעָה יְמִינְךָ וַעֲנֵנִי.

עֲשֵׂה לְמַעַן שְׁמֶךָ, עֲשֵׂה לְמַעַן יְמִינֶךָ, עֲשֵׂה לְמַעַן תּוֹרָתֶךָ, עֲשֵׂה לְמַעַן קְדֻשָּׁתֶךָ.

יִהְיוּ לְרָצוֹן אִמְרֵי פִי וְהֶגְיוֹן לִבִּי, לְפָנֶיךָ, יְיָ צוּרִי וְגוֹאֲלִי:

עֹשֶׂה שָׁלוֹם (הַשָּׁלוֹם - *During the Ten Days of Repentance substitute*) בִּמְרוֹמָיו,

הוּא יַעֲשֶׂה שָׁלוֹם עָלֵינוּ, וְעַל כָּל יִשְׂרָאֵל, וְאִמְרוּ, אָמֵן:

יְהִי רָצוֹן מִלְּפָנֶיךָ, יְיָ אֱלֹהֵינוּ וֵאלֹהֵי אֲבוֹתֵינוּ, שֶׁיִּבָּנֶה בֵּית הַמִּקְדָּשׁ בִּמְהֵרָה בְיָמֵינוּ,

וְתֵן חֶלְקֵנוּ בְּתוֹרָתֶךָ:

*P*lace peace, good and blessing, life, harmony and kindness and compassion on us and on all of Israel, Your people. Bless us, our Father, all of us as one in the light of Your countenance, for in the light of Your countenance, You gave us, Lord our G-d, the Torah of life and love of kindness, and justice and blessing and mercy and life and peace. Let it be good in Your eyes to bless Your people Israel at all times and all hours, with Your peace.

Between Rosh Hashana and Yom Kipppur:
And recall and inscribe before You, in the book of life, blessing and peace and prosperity, salvation and comfort and good decrees, we and all of Your people, the House of Israel, for good life and for peace. **Blessed are You, our G-d, Who blesses His people in peace.**

May the words of my mouth and the thoughts of my heart find favor before You, Lord, my Rock and my Redeemer

My G-d, guard my tongue from evil, and my lips from speaking deceitfully, and let my soul be still before all those who curse me, and make my soul like dust before all that may occur. Open my heart to Your Torah, and may my soul pursue Your commandments. And all those who plot against me, speedily foil their plans and ruin their thoughts. Let them be as chaff in the wind, let an angel of the Lord deflect them. In order to release your dear ones, let Your right hand save and respond to me. Do this for the sake of Your name, do this for the sake of Your right hand, do this for the sake of Your Torah, do this for the sake of Your Holiness. May the words of my mouth and the meditation of my heart be acceptable before You, Lord, my Rock and my Redeemer. He Who establishes peace (between Rosh Hashana and Yom Kippur, "the peace") in His heavens, may He will establish peace over us and over all of Israel, and let it be said, Amen.

May it be Your will before You, Lord my G-d and the G-d of our fathers, to build the holy Temple speedily in our days, and grant us our portion in Your Torah.

תחנון

ודוי

אֱלֹהֵינוּ וֵאלֹהֵי אֲבוֹתֵינוּ, תָּבֹא לְפָנֶיךָ תְּפִלָּתֵנוּ, וְאַל תִּתְעַלַּם מִתְּחִנָּתֵנוּ, שֶׁאֵין אָנוּ עַזֵּי פָנִים וּקְשֵׁי עֹרֶף, לוֹמַר לְפָנֶיךָ יְיָ אֱלֹהֵינוּ וֵאלֹהֵי אֲבוֹתֵינוּ, צַדִּיקִים אֲנַחְנוּ וְלֹא חָטָאנוּ, אֲבָל אֲנַחְנוּ וַאֲבוֹתֵינוּ חָטָאנוּ:

אָשַׁמְנוּ, בָּגַדְנוּ, גָּזַלְנוּ, דִּבַּרְנוּ דֹפִי. הֶעֱוִינוּ, וְהִרְשַׁעְנוּ, זַדְנוּ, חָמַסְנוּ, טָפַלְנוּ שֶׁקֶר. יָעַצְנוּ רָע, כִּזַּבְנוּ, לַצְנוּ, מָרַדְנוּ, נִאַצְנוּ, סָרַרְנוּ, עָוִינוּ, פָּשַׁעְנוּ, צָרַרְנוּ, קִשִּׁינוּ עֹרֶף. רָשַׁעְנוּ, שִׁחַתְנוּ, תִּעַבְנוּ, תָּעִינוּ, תִּעְתָּעְנוּ:

סַרְנוּ מִמִּצְוֹתֶיךָ וּמִמִּשְׁפָּטֶיךָ הַטּוֹבִים וְלֹא שָׁוָה לָנוּ. וְאַתָּה צַדִּיק עַל כָּל הַבָּא עָלֵינוּ, כִּי אֱמֶת עָשִׂיתָ וַאֲנַחְנוּ הִרְשָׁעְנוּ:

אֵל אֶרֶךְ אַפַּיִם אַתָּה וּבַעַל הָרַחֲמִים נִקְרֵאתָ, וְדֶרֶךְ תְּשׁוּבָה הוֹרֵיתָ. גְּדֻלַּת רַחֲמֶיךָ וַחֲסָדֶיךָ, תִּזְכּוֹר הַיּוֹם וּבְכָל יוֹם לְזֶרַע יְדִידֶיךָ. תֵּפֶן אֵלֵינוּ בְּרַחֲמִים, כִּי אַתָּה הוּא בַּעַל הָרַחֲמִים. בְּתַחֲנוּן וּבִתְפִלָּה פָּנֶיךָ נְקַדֵּם, כְּהוֹדַעְתָּ לֶעָנָו מִקֶּדֶם. מֵחֲרוֹן אַפְּךָ שׁוּב, כְּמוֹ בְּתוֹרָתְךָ כָּתוּב. וּבְצֵל כְּנָפֶיךָ נֶחֱסֶה וְנִתְלוֹנָן, כְּיוֹם וַיֵּרֶד יְיָ בֶּעָנָן. תַּעֲבוֹר עַל פֶּשַׁע וְתִמְחֶה אָשָׁם, כְּיוֹם וַיִּתְיַצֵּב עִמּוֹ שָׁם. תַּאֲזִין שַׁוְעָתֵנוּ וְתַקְשִׁיב מֶנּוּ מַאֲמָר, כְּיוֹם וַיִּקְרָא בְשֵׁם יְיָ וְשָׁם נֶאֱמַר:

CHASSIDIC EXCERPTS

Getting into the details of teshuva
Ashamnu, bagadnu...("We have sinned, we have betrayed...")

Commandment number 364 (in the counting of the *Sefer HaChinuch*) is to confess our sins and to do *teshuva*, as the Torah says, "And you should confess your sins that you committed."[337] According to the Torah, the major component of *teshuva* is forsaking the transgression, as well as confession and requesting of forgiveness.[338] But, we must explain the root and origin of these two matters: 1) forsaking the sin in regard to the future[339] which is called *teshuva*, and

Tachanun

Viduy

Our G-d and the G-d of our forefathers, let our prayer come before You, and hide not from our pleas, for we are not so fold-faced and stubborn as to claim before You, our G-d and the G-d of our forefathers, that we are righteous and have not sinned; rather we and our forefathers have transgressed...

We are guilty, we have betrayed, we have robbed, we have spoken evil: We have acted perversely, we have done wrong, we have purposely sinned, we have acted violently, we have accused falsely: We have given bad advice, we have fooled others, we have scoffed, we have rebelled. We have provoked, we have disobeyed, we have deviated, we have acted criminally, we have oppressed, we have been obstinate: We have been wicked, we have destroyed, we acted abominably, we have strayed, we have forced others astray.

We have turned away from Your commandments and from Your good laws, and it has not been worthwhile. And You are righteous regarding all that has occurred to us, for You act only in truth, and we have acted wickedly.

You are a patient G-d, and You are called the Master of Mercy. And You educate in the path of tshuva ("return to Him"). Great is Your mercy and Your kindness, remember today as well as every day the descendents of Your intimate ones. Turn to us in compassion, for You are the Master of Mercy. We approach Your countenance in pleading and in prayer, as You once informed Your humble one. Retract Your fiery anger, as is written in Your Torah, and in the shade of Your wings we will take cover and lodge, as on the day that "The Lord descended in the cloud." Pass over iniquity and erase guilt, as on the day that we stood with Him there. Take heed of our cry, and listen to our statement, as on the day that he called in the name of the Lord: And there it was said:

CHASSIDIC EXCERPTS

2) the confession, which is called "requesting forgiveness."[340] We must understand how these two acts atone for the blemishes that we have created [with our sins].

Now, the mitzvot are called *mitzvot Havaya* ("commands of the Lord") since they are all about the descent and reve-

lation of G-d's infinite light through the name *Havaya*. The infinite light of G-d [does not descend on its own, because it] is "not associated with any of these attributes whatsoever."[341] However, His infinite light does descend to the attributes of "wise within the *sephira* of *chochma*,"[342] and "understanding within

In the presence of a minyan the following is said together:

וַיַּעֲבֹר יְיָ עַל פָּנָיו וַיִּקְרָא:

יְיָ יְיָ אֵל רַחוּם וְחַנּוּן אֶרֶךְ אַפַּיִם וְרַב חֶסֶד וֶאֱמֶת: נֹצֵר חֶסֶד לָאֲלָפִים נֹשֵׂא עָוֹן וָפֶשַׁע וְחַטָּאָה וְנַקֵּה:

רַחוּם וְחַנּוּן חָטָאתִי לְפָנֶיךָ רַחֵם עָלֵינוּ וְהוֹשִׁיעֵנוּ:

נפילת אפים

לְדָוִד אֵלֶיךָ יְיָ נַפְשִׁי אֶשָּׂא:

אֱלֹהַי בְּךָ בָטַחְתִּי אַל אֵבוֹשָׁה, אַל יַעַלְצוּ אוֹיְבַי לִי:

גַּם כָּל קוֶֹיךָ לֹא יֵבשׁוּ, יֵבשׁוּ הַבּוֹגְדִים רֵיקָם:

דְּרָכֶיךָ יְיָ הוֹדִיעֵנִי, אֹרְחוֹתֶיךָ לַמְּדֵנִי:

הַדְרִיכֵנִי בַאֲמִתֶּךָ וְלַמְּדֵנִי כִּי אַתָּה אֱלֹהֵי יִשְׁעִי, אוֹתְךָ קִוִּיתִי כָּל הַיּוֹם:

זְכֹר רַחֲמֶיךָ יְיָ וַחֲסָדֶיךָ כִּי מֵעוֹלָם הֵמָּה:

חַטֹּאות נְעוּרַי וּפְשָׁעַי אַל תִּזְכֹּר כְּחַסְדְּךָ זְכָר לִי אַתָּה, לְמַעַן טוּבְךָ יְיָ:

טוֹב וְיָשָׁר יְיָ עַל כֵּן יוֹרֶה חַטָּאִים בַּדָּרֶךְ:

יַדְרֵךְ עֲנָוִים בַּמִּשְׁפָּט וִילַמֵּד עֲנָוִים דַּרְכּוֹ:

CHASSIDIC EXCERPTS

the *sephira* of *bina*," which are associated with the first two letters *yud-hey* of G-d's name as well as "kind within *chesed*" or "strong within *gevura*," which are the secrets of the second two letters, *vov* and *Hey* of G-d's name. And all of this takes place through the mitzvot which we fulfill. Our arousal from below to Above [via fulfillment of mitzvot] produces a response from Above to below, because "love compels the flesh,"[343] and impels G-d's infinite light to undergo contraction and descend into these attributes. It does this in order to illuminate and enliven the worlds. There are mitzvot that correspond to the *yud* [of *Havaya*], and there are those that correspond to the *hey*, as written in the *Zohar*, [which describes the mitzvot in relation to G-d's name as] "grapes hanging from a cluster."[344] For the same reason, they are also described as the "limbs of the king," since the ten *sephirot* mentioned are like a body in relation to the G-dly light that flows into them, from the infinite One Above by way of the mitzvot. This, in fact, is the secret of the commandment, *tamim tihiyeh im Havaya* ("Be whole and unquestioning with the Lord"[345]) in order to draw down 248 limbs, forming a complete [spiritual] structure [since man has 248 physical limbs, and the 248 positive mitzvot correspond to his limbs].

However, if a man sinned against

And the Lord passed before him and declared:

Lord, Lord, G-d of mercy and grace, patient and of much kindness and truth. He preserves kindness for thousands of generations, forgiving sin and iniquity and transgression – and He cleanses.

Oh, Merciful and Gracious One, we have sinned before You, have mercy upon us and save us!

Putting Down The Head

For David...To You, Lord, I lift up my soul
My G-d, in You I placed my trust, let me not be embarrassed, let my enemies not gloat over me.
And neither should those who place their hope in You be embarrassed - let the traitors be embarrassed in their emptiness.
Inform me of Your ways, Lord, and teach me Your paths.
Guide me in Your truth and teach me, for You are the G-d of my salvation, it is for You that I yearn all the day.
Recall Your mercy, Lord, for Your kindnesses are eternal.
Remember not the sins of my youth, nor my transgressions; in Your mercy remember me, for the sake of Your goodness, Lord.
Good and straight-forward is the Lord, therefore He informs sinners of the path.
He guides the humble in justice, and teaches the humble His way.

CHASSIDIC EXCERPTS

himself [and G-d] by failing to fulfill one of the positive mitzvot, or by transgressing one of the negative commandments, he created a blemish. [With his misdeed], he diminished the flow of G-dly energy to that particular attribute or *sephira*. Additionally, he drew down spiritual energy from the G-dly attributes [and delivered it] into the depths of the *klipot* [realm of concealment of G-dliness] to a far greater extent than what they were meant to receive. Ordinarily, the *klipot* receive [their energy] from the *kav hamida* ("the conduit" of G-dly energy that metes out the appropriate measure of G-dly energy to each aspect of creation) in a superficial and extraneous manner. But

[with his transgression], he channeled energy to them from a far more intimate level, from the vessels of the ten *sephirot*, so that his transgression is indeed grievous.

It is written[346] that this is the secret of the "king trapped in the troughs,"[347] and that there is no greater disgrace than this. In this context, G-d is called a "disgraced king." This is the secret of the prayer [recited during the *Shema* before retiring for the night], "If I caused a blemish in the letter *yud* ... if I caused a blemish in the letter *hey*," as well as "And he punctured the name *Havaya*,"[348] [referring to one who took G-d's name in vain], because [by transgressing], one "punctures" the vessels of

כָּל אָרְחוֹת יְיָ חֶסֶד וֶאֱמֶת, לְנֹצְרֵי בְרִיתוֹ וְעֵדֹתָיו:

לְמַעַן שִׁמְךָ יְיָ וְסָלַחְתָּ לַעֲוֹנִי כִּי רַב הוּא:

מִי זֶה הָאִישׁ יְרֵא יְיָ יוֹרֶנּוּ בְּדֶרֶךְ יִבְחָר:

נַפְשׁוֹ בְּטוֹב תָּלִין וְזַרְעוֹ יִירַשׁ אָרֶץ:

סוֹד יְיָ לִירֵאָיו, וּבְרִיתוֹ לְהוֹדִיעָם:

עֵינַי תָּמִיד אֶל יְיָ, כִּי הוּא יוֹצִיא מֵרֶשֶׁת רַגְלָי:

פְּנֵה אֵלַי וְחָנֵּנִי, כִּי יָחִיד וְעָנִי אָנִי:

צָרוֹת לְבָבִי הִרְחִיבוּ, מִמְּצוּקוֹתַי הוֹצִיאֵנִי:

רְאֵה עָנְיִי וַעֲמָלִי, וְשָׂא לְכָל חַטֹּאותָי:

רְאֵה אוֹיְבַי כִּי רָבּוּ וְשִׂנְאַת חָמָס שְׂנֵאוּנִי:

שָׁמְרָה נַפְשִׁי וְהַצִּילֵנִי אַל אֵבוֹשׁ כִּי חָסִיתִי בָךְ:

תֹּם וָיֹשֶׁר יִצְּרוּנִי, כִּי קִוִּיתִיךָ:

פְּדֵה אֱלֹהִים אֶת יִשְׂרָאֵל מִכֹּל צָרוֹתָיו:

וְהוּא יִפְדֶּה אֶת יִשְׂרָאֵל מִכֹּל, עֲוֹנֹתָיו:

On all days except for Monday, Thursday and public fast days continue with "אָבִינוּ
מַלְכֵּנוּ". *Between Rosh haShanah and Yom Kippur the extended Avinu Malkeinu is
recited here.*

the ten *sephirot* and siphons off illumination from them, presenting it to the external forces, just as one might puncture a limb and cause it to bleed. And in order to rectify this, G-d presented us, in His great mercy, with the mitzvah of *teshuva*, which brings healing to the world and repairs the blemishes.

Now, replacing what was siphoned off takes place on two fronts: 1) the first is to fill in the blemishes and patch the leaks that caused a diminished flow from the infinite light Above into the ten *sephirot*, and 2) the second is to stanch the bleeding of G-dly energy to the external forces that are opposed to holiness. Regarding stanching the flow of holy energy to the unholy forces, there are two elements: the first is that the external forces should cease to receive more than their required flow, and the second is to eliminate whatever flow already wrongfully arrived.

Now, the first two ["patching the leaks" and "stanching the bleeding"] take place by drawing down a transcendent revelation from the infinite light of G-d Above. This transcendent il-

All the paths of the Lord are kind and true, for those who keep His covenant and testimonies.

For the sake of Your Name, Lord, forgive my iniquities, for they are many.

Who is the man who fears the Lord, show him which way to choose.

His soul will dwell in goodness, and his descendents will inherit the land.

The secret of the Lord is for those who fear Him; they will be informed of His covenant.

My eyes are fastened always upon the Lord, for He who extracts my legs from the net.

Turn to me and grant me grace, for I am alone and poor.

The sorrows of my heart have expanded, extract me from my distress.

See my poverty and my efforts, and put up with all my sins.

See, my enemies have multiplied, and with terrible hatred they detest me.

Guard my soul and save me; do not let me be ashamed for I have taken refuge in You.

Integrity and honesty will guard me, for I have hope in You.

Redeem Yisrael, G-d, from all of its troubles.

And He will redeem Israel from all his iniquities.

CHASSIDIC EXCERPTS

lumination (*makif*) "blinds the eyes of the extraneous forces,"[349] so that they no longer receive energy and nourishment from Above. It also patches the leaks, since G-d [the source of the transcendent revelation] is the most fulfilling and perfect, and all stands as naught in relation to Him like a drop in the ocean. It is only a reflection and ray from Him that creates the earth and heavens ... This all takes place as a result of our *teshuva* and regret over the past. The third aspect, however – elimination of the external forces that were created and subsequently multiplied tremendously – necessitates verbal confession and regret.

The explanation is as follows: It is known that the *klipot* and external forces are also composed of light and vessels (*orot* and *kelim*) [as is the side of holiness and the *sephirot*]. These are comparable to a soul and a body, but they are created when a person transgresses. With his lust, the person creates an evil "soul," and with his actual transgression, the "body" is created. This may take place even in the realm of thought, such as the inappropriate thoughts that we sometimes experience. At such times, the letters of our thoughts create the "body" of the evil forces, while our lust creates the "soul." This may also take place within speech, such as *lashon harah* ("evil speech"), gossip, false oaths and lies and the like. And, obviously, it may take place in action, when the deed

תחנון לשני וחמישי

וְ‏הוּא רַחוּם, יְכַפֵּר עָוֹן וְלֹא יַשְׁחִית, וְהִרְבָּה לְהָשִׁיב אַפּוֹ, וְלֹא יָעִיר כָּל חֲמָתוֹ.

אַתָּה יְיָ לֹא תִכְלָא רַחֲמֶיךָ מִמֶּנִּי, חַסְדְּךָ וַאֲמִתְּךָ תָּמִיד יִצְּרוּנִי.

הוֹשִׁיעֵנוּ יְיָ אֱלֹהֵינוּ, וְקַבְּצֵנוּ מִן הַגּוֹיִם, לְהוֹדוֹת לְשֵׁם קָדְשֶׁךָ, לְהִשְׁתַּבֵּחַ בִּתְהִלָּתֶךָ.

אִם עֲוֹנוֹת תִּשְׁמָר יָהּ, אֲדֹנָי מִי יַעֲמֹד.

כִּי עִמְּךָ הַסְּלִיחָה, לְמַעַן תִּוָּרֵא.

לֹא כַחֲטָאֵינוּ תַּעֲשֶׂה לָּנוּ, וְלֹא כַעֲוֹנֹתֵינוּ תִּגְמֹל עָלֵינוּ.

אִם עֲוֹנֵינוּ עָנוּ בָנוּ, יְיָ, עֲשֵׂה לְמַעַן שְׁמֶךָ.

זְכֹר רַחֲמֶיךָ יְיָ, וַחֲסָדֶיךָ, כִּי מֵעוֹלָם הֵמָּה.

יַעַנְךָ יְיָ בְּיוֹם צָרָה, יְשַׂגֶּבְךָ שֵׁם אֱלֹהֵי יַעֲקֹב:

יְיָ הוֹשִׁיעָה, הַמֶּלֶךְ יַעֲנֵנוּ בְיוֹם קָרְאֵנוּ.

אָבִינוּ מַלְכֵּנוּ חָנֵּנוּ וַעֲנֵנוּ, כִּי אֵין בָּנוּ מַעֲשִׂים, עֲשֵׂה עִמָּנוּ צְדָקָה לְמַעַן שְׁמֶךָ.

וְעַתָּה אֲדֹנָי אֱלֹהֵינוּ, אֲשֶׁר הוֹצֵאתָ אֶת עַמְּךָ מֵאֶרֶץ מִצְרַיִם בְּיָד חֲזָקָה, וַתַּעַשׂ לְךָ שֵׁם כַּיּוֹם הַזֶּה, חָטָאנוּ רָשָׁעְנוּ.

אֲדֹנָי כְּכָל צִדְקֹתֶיךָ, יָשָׁב נָא אַפְּךָ וַחֲמָתְךָ מֵעִירְךָ יְרוּשָׁלַיִם הַר קָדְשֶׁךָ, כִּי בַחֲטָאֵינוּ וּבַעֲוֹנוֹת אֲבֹתֵינוּ, יְרוּשָׁלַיִם וְעַמְּךָ לְחֶרְפָּה לְכָל סְבִיבֹתֵינוּ.

וְעַתָּה, שְׁמַע אֱלֹהֵינוּ אֶל תְּפִלַּת עַבְדְּךָ וְאֶל תַּחֲנוּנָיו וְהָאֵר פָּנֶיךָ עַל מִקְדָּשְׁךָ הַשָּׁמֵם, לְמַעַן אֲדֹנָי:

CHASSIDIC EXCERPTS

creates the "body" of the *klipah* and the illicit desire in our hearts creates the "soul." All this is because man is enrooted Above, in the ten holy *sephirot* [of the World of *Atzilut*], and therefore his illicit desires and deeds bring down a "body" and "soul" that gain nourishment from that source. This is the secret of King David's statement, "My sin stands before me constantly,"[350] referring to the *klipah* that man creates with his sin which remains to torment him, as written, "Your evil will torment you,"[351] and "The acts of man will pay him,"[352] as noted in the *Zohar*.

Now, when the person returns to G-d (in *teshuva*), he must eradicate the *klipa* [that he created] and erase it from

Additional Prayers for Monday and Thursday

And He, being merciful, atones for our sins and refrains from destroying us,

He repeatedly quashes His anger, and avoids arousing all of His wrath.

Lord, do not withhold Your mercy from us, may Your kindness and truth always guard us.

Save us, Lord, our G-d, and gather us from among the nations, in order to acknowledge Your holy Name, and to be extolled in Your praises.

G-d, if You were to preserve sins, my Lord, who could survive?

For, with You resides forgiveness, so You will be feared.

Do not deal with us according to our sins, nor recompense us according to our transgressions.

If our sins speak for us, Lord then deal with us [kindly] for the sake of Your Name.

Remember Your mercy, Lord, and Your kindness, since they are forever.

May the Lord answer us on our day of distress, may the name of the G-d of Jacob protect us.

Lord, help us, may the King answer on the day that we call!

Our Father, our King, grace us and answer us, for we have no [good] deeds, deal with us justly for the sake of Your Name.

And now, Lord our G-d, who took Your people out of the land of Egypt with a strong arm, and made for Yourself a name as of today; we have sinned and we have transgressed.

My Lord, in accordance with all of Your righteousness, hold back Your anger and your wrath, from Your city Jerusalem, Your holy mountain, for through our sins and the sins of our fathers, Jerusalem and Your nation are held in contempt among all who surround us.

And now, our G-d, heed the prayers of Your servant and his pleading, and shine Your countenance on Your devastated Temple, for Your sake, my Lord.

CHASSIDIC EXCERPTS

the world, as it says, "I wiped away your transgression like a cloud."[353] This takes place with regret accompanied by confession. By way of regret, the sinner uproots his desire from the sin and removes the soul from the *klipa*, which was born from the illicit lust in his heart. And now, by uprooting his will and lust, he removes the soul [from the *klipa*]. However, in order to eradicate the body of the *klipa*, he must confess verbally, since the sages made movement of the lips equivalent to action. In this way, he wipes out the body, as if it never existed.

(From *Derech Mitzvotecha* of the Tzemach Tzedek, *Mitzvat Vidui Vetshuva*, p. 75)

הַ**טֵּה** אֱלֹהַי אָזְנְךָ וּשֲׁמָע, פְּקַח עֵינֶיךָ וּרְאֵה שֹׁמְמֹתֵינוּ, וְהָעִיר אֲשֶׁר נִקְרָא שִׁמְךָ עָלֶיהָ, כִּי לֹא עַל צִדְקֹתֵינוּ אֲנַחְנוּ מַפִּילִים תַּחֲנוּנֵינוּ לְפָנֶיךָ, כִּי עַל רַחֲמֶיךָ הָרַבִּים.

אֲדֹנָי שְׁמָעָה, אֲדֹנָי סְלָחָה, אֲדֹנָי הַקְשִׁיבָה, וַעֲשֵׂה אַל תְּאַחַר, לְמַעַנְךָ אֱלֹהַי, כִּי שִׁמְךָ נִקְרָא עַל עִירְךָ וְעַל עַמֶּךָ:

אָבִינוּ אָב הָרַחֲמָן, הַרְאֵנוּ אוֹת לְטוֹבָה וְקַבֵּץ נְפוּצוֹתֵינוּ מֵאַרְבַּע כַּנְפוֹת הָאָרֶץ, יַכִּירוּ וְיֵדְעוּ כָּל הַגּוֹיִם, כִּי אַתָּה יְיָ אֱלֹהֵינוּ.

וְעַתָּה יְיָ אָבִינוּ אָתָּה, אֲנַחְנוּ הַחֹמֶר וְאַתָּה יֹצְרֵנוּ, וּמַעֲשֵׂה יָדְךָ כֻּלָּנוּ.

אָבִינוּ מַלְכֵּנוּ צוּרֵנוּ וְגֹאֲלֵנוּ. חוּסָה יְיָ עַל עַמֶּךָ, וְאַל תִּתֵּן נַחֲלָתְךָ לְחֶרְפָּה לִמְשָׁל בָּם גּוֹיִם, לָמָּה יֹאמְרוּ בָעַמִּים אַיֵּה אֱלֹהֵיהֶם.

יָדַעְנוּ יְיָ כִּי חָטָאנוּ, וְאֵין מִי יַעֲמֹד בַּעֲדֵנוּ, אֶלָּא שִׁמְךָ הַגָּדוֹל יַעֲמָד לָנוּ בְּעֵת צָרָה.

כְּרַחֵם אָב עַל בָּנִים, כֵּן תְּרַחֵם יְיָ עָלֵינוּ וְהוֹשִׁיעֵנוּ לְמַעַן שְׁמֶךָ.

חֲמוֹל עַל עַמֶּךָ, רַחֵם עַל נַחֲלָתֶךָ, חוּסָה נָא כְּרֹב רַחֲמֶיךָ, חָנֵּנוּ וַעֲנֵנוּ, כִּי לְךָ יְיָ הַצְּדָקָה. עֹשֵׂה נִפְלָאוֹת בְּכָל עֵת:

הַ**בֵּט** נָא, וְהוֹשִׁיעָה צֹאן מַרְעִיתֶךָ. וְאַל יִמְשָׁל בָּנוּ קֶצֶף, כִּי לְךָ יְיָ הַיְשׁוּעָה, בְּךָ תוֹחַלְתֵּנוּ, אֱלוֹהַּ סְלִיחוֹת. אָנָּא, סְלַח נָא, כִּי אֵל טוֹב וְסַלָּח אָתָּה:

אָנָּא מֶלֶךְ חַנּוּן וְרַחוּם, זְכוֹר וְהַבֵּט לִבְרִית בֵּין הַבְּתָרִים, וְתֵרָאֶה לְפָנֶיךָ עֲקֵדַת יָחִד וּלְמַעַן יִשְׂרָאֵל אָבִינוּ. אַל תַּעַזְבֵנוּ אָבִינוּ, וְאַל תִּטְּשֵׁנוּ מַלְכֵּנוּ, וְאַל תִּשְׁכָּחֵנוּ יוֹצְרֵנוּ, וְאַל תַּעַשׂ עִמָּנוּ כָּלָה כְּחַטֹּאתֵינוּ, בְּגָלוּתֵנוּ, כִּי אֵל מֶלֶךְ חַנּוּן וְרַחוּם אָתָּה:

Incline Your ear, my G-d and listen, open Your eyes and observe our desolation, and the city upon which Your Name is called, for not on account of our righteousness do we issue our pleas before You, but on account of Your great mercy.
My Lord, hear, My Lord, forgive, my Lord, pay attention and act, do not delay, for Your sake, My G-d, for Your name is declared over Your city and over Your nation.
Our Father, merciful Father, show us a positive sign and gather our scattered remnants for the four corners of the earth, so that the nations will know and recognize, that you are the Lord our G-d. And now, Lord our G-d, You are our Father, we are the raw material and Your are [the Craftsman] Who forms us, and we are all the work of Your hand.
Our Father, our King, our Rock and our Redeemer. Have mercy, Lord upon Your people, refrain from letting Your inheritance become a disgrace that the nations govern over, [for] why should the nations say, 'where is their G-d?'
We know that we sinned, and there is no-one to stand up for us, let Your great Name to stand up for us at the time of distress.
As a father has compassion on his children, so have mercy, Lord, upon us and save us for the sake of Your name.
Have mercy on Your nation, be compassionate over Your inheritance, spare us in Your abundant benevolences, be gracious and answer us, for righteousness is Yours Lord, [He Who] performs wonders at all times.

Gaze [over us], please and save the sheep of Your pastures. Let not anger overwhelm us, for salvation is Yours, it is You we yearn for, G-d of forgiveness. Please, forgive us now, since You are a good and forgiving G-d.

Please, gracious and merciful King, recall and look back upon the covenant [with Abraham] between the pieces, and visualize before Yourself the binding of [Isaac], and for the sake of Israel our father, do not forsake us, our Father, and do not leave us, our King, and do not forget us, our Maker, and do not bring destruction upon us in accordance with our sins in exile, for Your are G-d, King Who is gracious and merciful.

אֵין כָּמוֹךָ חַנּוּן וְרַחוּם יְיָ אֱלֹהֵינוּ, אֵין כָּמוֹךָ אֵל אֶרֶךְ אַפַּיִם וְרַב חֶסֶד וֶאֱמֶת,
הוֹשִׁיעֵנוּ וְרַחֲמֵנוּ, מֵרַעַשׁ וּמֵרֹגֶז הַצִּילֵנוּ. זְכוֹר לַעֲבָדֶיךָ לְאַבְרָהָם לְיִצְחָק
וּלְיַעֲקֹב, אַל תֵּפֶן אֶל קָשְׁיֵנוּ וְאֶל רִשְׁעֵנוּ וְאֶל חַטָּאתֵנוּ. שׁוּב מֵחֲרוֹן אַפֶּךָ וְהִנָּחֵם
עַל הָרָעָה לְעַמֶּךָ.

וְהָסֵר מִמֶּנּוּ מַכַּת הַמָּוֶת כִּי רַחוּם אָתָּה, כִּי כֵן דַּרְכֶּךָ עֹשֶׂה חֶסֶד חִנָּם בְּכָל דּוֹר וָדוֹר.
אָנָּא יְיָ הוֹשִׁיעָה נָּא. אָנָּא יְיָ הַצְלִיחָה נָּא. אָנָּא יְיָ עֲנֵנוּ בְיוֹם קָרְאֵנוּ. לְךָ יְיָ קִוִּינוּ, לְךָ יְיָ
חִכִּינוּ, לְךָ יְיָ נְיַחֵל, אַל תֶּחֱשֶׁה וּתְעַנֵּנוּ, כִּי נֶאֶמוּ גוֹיִם אָבְדָה תִקְוָתָם, כָּל בֶּרֶךְ לְךָ תִכְרַע
וְכָל קוֹמָה לְפָנֶיךָ תִשְׁתַּחֲוֶה:

הַפּוֹתֵחַ יָד בִּתְשׁוּבָה לְקַבֵּל פּוֹשְׁעִים וְחַטָּאִים, נִבְהֲלָה נַפְשֵׁנוּ מֵרֹב עִצְבוֹנֵנוּ,
אַל תִּשְׁכָּחֵנוּ נֶצַח, קוּמָה וְהוֹשִׁיעֵנוּ. וְאַל תִּשְׁפֹּךְ חֲרוֹנְךָ עָלֵינוּ, כִּי
אֲנַחְנוּ עַמְּךָ בְּנֵי בְרִיתֶךָ.

עוֹרְרָה גְבוּרָתְךָ וְהוֹשִׁיעֵנוּ לְמַעַן שְׁמֶךָ, וְאַל יִמְעֲטוּ לְפָנֶיךָ תְּלָאוֹתֵינוּ. מַהֵר
יְקַדְּמוּנוּ רַחֲמֶיךָ בְּעֵת צָרוֹתֵינוּ לֹא לְמַעֲנֵנוּ אֶלָּא לְמַעַנְךָ פְּעַל, וְאַל תַּשְׁחִית אֶת
זֵכֶר שְׁאֵרִיתֵנוּ, כִּי לְךָ מְיַחֲלוֹת עֵינֵינוּ, כִּי אֵל מֶלֶךְ חַנּוּן וְרַחוּם אָתָּה,
וּזְכֹר עֵדוּתֵנוּ בְּכָל יוֹם תָּמִיד אוֹמְרִים פַּעֲמַיִם בְּאַהֲבָה:

שְׁמַע יִשְׂרָאֵל יְיָ אֱלֹהֵינוּ. יְיָ אֶחָד:

יְיָ אֱלֹהֵי יִשְׂרָאֵל, שׁוּב מֵחֲרוֹן אַפֶּךָ, וְהִנָּחֵם עַל הָרָעָה לְעַמֶּךָ:
הַבֵּט מִשָּׁמַיִם וּרְאֵה, כִּי הָיִינוּ לַעַג וָקֶלֶס בַּגּוֹיִם, נֶחְשַׁבְנוּ כַּצֹּאן לַטֶּבַח יוּבָל,
לַהֲרֹג וּלְאַבֵּד וּלְמַכָּה וּלְחֶרְפָּה. וּבְכָל זֹאת שִׁמְךָ לֹא שָׁכָחְנוּ, נָא, אַל
תִּשְׁכָּחֵנוּ:
יְיָ אֱלֹהֵי יִשְׂרָאֵל, שׁוּב מֵחֲרוֹן אַפֶּךָ, וְהִנָּחֵם עַל הָרָעָה לְעַמֶּךָ:

There is none like You, gracious and merciful Lord, our G-d, there is none like You, G-d of patience and abundant kindness and truth, save us and have mercy upon us, rescue us from violence and rage! Recall Your servants, Abraham, Isaac and Jacob, do not turn to our obstinacy and to our wickedness and to our sins. Refrain from Your fiery anger, and retract the evil intended for Your people.

And remove from us the plague of death, since You are merciful, for so is Your way, to perform gratuitous kindness in every generation.
Please, Lord, save us, please Lord grant us success, please Lord answer us on the day that we call. With You, Lord is our hope, for You Lord we are waiting, for You, Lord we yearn, do not be silent and allow us to suffer, for the nations declare, "all their hope is lost." Let every knee bend to You, and every upright person prostrate himself to You.

You Who opens His hand to receive those who return in tshuva - and accepts wrong-doers and sinners - our soul is troubled by deep sorrow; do not forget us forever, rise up and save us.
And do not pour out Your wrath upon us, since we are Your people, members of Your covenant.
Arouse your might and save us for the sake of Your Name, and do not trivialize our suffering before You.
Quickly advance Your clemency at the time of our travails, not for our sake, but for Your sake act, and do not destroy the remembrance of our remnant, for to You our eyes yearn, since Your are G-d, King Who is gracious and merciful. Recall our testimony, lovingly proclaimed twice every day:

Hear of Israel, the Lord is our G-d, the Lord is One.

Lord, G-d of Israel, refrain from Your fiery anger, and retract the evil intended for Your people.
Peer from the heavens and see, that we have become scorned and disdained among the nations, we are thought of as sheep for slaughter and obliteration, to be killed and destroyed, and beaten and disgraced. And nevertheless, we have not forgotten Your Name; please do not forget us! Lord, G-d of Israel, refrain from Your fiery wrath, and retract the evil intended for Your people.

זָרִים אוֹמְרִים אֵין תּוֹחֶלֶת וְתִקְוָה, חוֹן אוֹם לְשִׁמְךָ מְקַוָּה, טָהוֹר, יְשׁוּעָתֵנוּ קָרְבָה, יָגַעְנוּ וְלֹא הוּנַח לָנוּ, רַחֲמֶיךָ יִכְבְּשׁוּ אֶת כַּעַסְךָ מֵעָלֵינוּ: אָנָּא שׁוּב מֵחֲרוֹנְךָ, וְרַחֵם סְגֻלָּה אֲשֶׁר בָּחָרְתָּ:

יְיָ אֱלֹהֵי יִשְׂרָאֵל, שׁוּב מֵחֲרוֹן אַפֶּךָ, וְהִנָּחֵם עַל הָרָעָה לְעַמֶּךָ:

חוּסָה יְיָ עָלֵינוּ בְּרַחֲמֶיךָ, וְאַל תִּתְּנֵנוּ בִּידֵי אַכְזָרִים, לָמָּה יֹאמְרוּ הַגּוֹיִם אַיֵּה נָא אֱלֹהֵיהֶם, לְמַעַנְךָ עֲשֵׂה עִמָּנוּ חֶסֶד וְאַל תְּאַחַר: אָנָּא שׁוּב מֵחֲרוֹנְךָ וְרַחֵם סְגֻלָּה אֲשֶׁר בָּחָרְתָּ:

יְיָ אֱלֹהֵי יִשְׂרָאֵל, שׁוּב מֵחֲרוֹן אַפֶּךָ, וְהִנָּחֵם עַל הָרָעָה לְעַמֶּךָ:

קוֹלֵנוּ תִשְׁמַע וְתָחֹן, וְאַל תִּטְּשֵׁנוּ בְּיַד אוֹיְבֵינוּ לִמְחוֹת אֶת שְׁמֵנוּ, זְכֹר אֲשֶׁר נִשְׁבַּעְתָּ לַאֲבוֹתֵינוּ, כְּכוֹכְבֵי הַשָּׁמַיִם אַרְבֶּה אֶת זַרְעֲכֶם, וְעַתָּה נִשְׁאַרְנוּ מְעַט מֵהַרְבֵּה. וּבְכָל זֹאת שִׁמְךָ לֹא שָׁכָחְנוּ, נָא אַל תִּשְׁכָּחֵנוּ:

יְיָ אֱלֹהֵי יִשְׂרָאֵל, שׁוּב מֵחֲרוֹן אַפֶּךָ, וְהִנָּחֵם עַל הָרָעָה לְעַמֶּךָ:

עָזְרֵנוּ אֱלֹהֵי יִשְׁעֵנוּ עַל דְּבַר כְּבוֹד שְׁמֶךָ, וְהַצִּילֵנוּ וְכַפֵּר עַל חַטֹּאתֵינוּ לְמַעַן שְׁמֶךָ:

יְיָ אֱלֹהֵי יִשְׂרָאֵל, שׁוּב מֵחֲרוֹן אַפֶּךָ, וְהִנָּחֵם עַל הָרָעָה לְעַמֶּךָ:

When the Fast of Gedaliah, which occurs on a Monday or Thursday Selichot for Tzom Gedaliah are recited at this point

שׁוֹמֵר יִשְׂרָאֵל, שְׁמוֹר שְׁאֵרִית יִשְׂרָאֵל, וְאַל יֹאבַד יִשְׂרָאֵל, הָאוֹמְרִים שְׁמַע יִשְׂרָאֵל:

שׁוֹמֵר גּוֹי אֶחָד, שְׁמוֹר שְׁאֵרִית עַם אֶחָד, וְאַל יֹאבַד גּוֹי אֶחָד, הַמְיַחֲדִים שִׁמְךָ יְיָ אֱלֹהֵינוּ יְיָ אֶחָד:

שׁוֹמֵר גּוֹי קָדוֹשׁ, שְׁמוֹר שְׁאֵרִית עַם קָדוֹשׁ. וְאַל יֹאבַד גּוֹי קָדוֹשׁ, הַמְשַׁלְּשִׁים שָׁלוֹשׁ קְדֻשּׁוֹת לְקָדוֹשׁ:

מִתְרַצֶּה בְּרַחֲמִים, וּמִתְפַּיֵּס בְּתַחֲנוּנִים, הִתְרַצֵּה וְהִתְפַּיֵּס לְדוֹר עָנִי כִּי אֵין עוֹזֵר:

Strangers say there is no expectation or hope [for us]. Be gracious to the nation that desires Your Name. Pure One, bring our salvation near; we have became weary and there is no relief for us. Let Your mercy overwhelm Your anger from upon us. Please, back off from Your wrath, have mercy on the
treasured people which You chose.

Lord, G-d of Israel, refrain from Your fiery wrath, and retract any evil
intended for Your people.

In Your compassion, Lord, have mercy upon us, and do not put us in cruel hands, for why should the nations say, 'where is their G-d?' For Your sake, do for us kindness without delay; please refrain from Your wrath, have
mercy upon the treasured people whom Your chose.

Lord, G-d of Israel refrain from Your fiery anger, and retract any evil
intended for Your people.

Hear our voices and be gracious, do not forsake us in the hands of our enemies, to erase our names. Remember what You swore to our forefathers, "I will make your descendents as numerous as the stars of the heavens," and yet now we remain only a few among many. And nevertheless, we have not forgotten Your Name, please, do not forget us.

Lord, G-d of Israel, refrain from Your fiery wrath, and retract the evil
intended for Your people.

Our help, G-d of our salvation, for the sake of the glory of Your Name,
rescue us and atone for our sins, for the sake of Your Name.

Lord, G-d of Israel, refrain from Your fiery wrath, and retract the evil
intended for Your people.

When the Fast of Gedaliah, which occurs on a Monday or Thursday Selichot for Tzom
Gedaliah are recited at this point

Guardian of Israel, guard over the remnants of Israel, do not
destroy Israel, who say 'Hear O Israel.'

Guardian of the one people, guard the remnants of the one people, and refrain from destroying the one people, who unite
Your Name, 'the Lord Our G-d, the Lord is One.'

Guardian of the holy people, guard the remnants of the holy people, and refrain from destroying the holy people, who three
times mention the three-part sanctification of the Holy One.

He Who accepts us in compassion, and is appeased in grace, accept and be conciliated over the this poor generation, for there
is none to help.

Aadditional prayers for Mondays and Thursdays end here
On public fast days selichot are recited at this point

אָבִינוּ מַלְכֵּנוּ אָבִינוּ אָתָּה.

אָבִינוּ מַלְכֵּנוּ אֵין לָנוּ מֶלֶךְ אֶלָּא אָתָּה.

אָבִינוּ מַלְכֵּנוּ רַחֵם עָלֵינוּ.

אָבִינוּ מַלְכֵּנוּ חָנֵּנוּ וַעֲנֵנוּ כִּי אֵין בָּנוּ מַעֲשִׂים עֲשֵׂה עִמָּנוּ צְדָקָה וָחֶסֶד לְמַעַן שִׁמְךָ הַגָּדוֹל וְהוֹשִׁיעֵנוּ:

וַאֲנַחְנוּ לֹא נֵדַע מַה נַּעֲשֶׂה, כִּי עָלֶיךָ עֵינֵינוּ.

זְכֹר רַחֲמֶיךָ יְיָ וַחֲסָדֶיךָ, כִּי מֵעוֹלָם הֵמָּה.

יְהִי חַסְדְּךָ יְיָ עָלֵינוּ, כַּאֲשֶׁר יִחַלְנוּ לָךְ.

אַל תִּזְכָּר לָנוּ עֲוֹנוֹת רִאשֹׁנִים, מַהֵר יְקַדְּמוּנוּ רַחֲמֶיךָ כִּי דַלּוֹנוּ מְאֹד.

חָנֵּנוּ יְיָ חָנֵּנוּ, כִּי רַב שָׂבַעְנוּ בוּז.

בְּרֹגֶז רַחֵם תִּזְכּוֹר, בְּרֹגֶז עֲקֵדָה תִּזְכּוֹר, בְּרֹגֶז תְּמִימוֹת תִּזְכּוֹר, בְּרֹגֶז אַהֲבָה תִּזְכָּר:

יְיָ הוֹשִׁיעָה הַמֶּלֶךְ יַעֲנֵנוּ בְיוֹם קָרְאֵנוּ.

כִּי הוּא יָדַע יִצְרֵנוּ, זָכוּר כִּי עָפָר אֲנָחְנוּ.

עָזְרֵנוּ אֱלֹהֵי יִשְׁעֵנוּ עַל דְּבַר כְּבוֹד שְׁמֶךָ,

וְהַצִּילֵנוּ וְכַפֵּר עַל חַטֹּאתֵינוּ לְמַעַן שְׁמֶךָ.

יִתְגַּדַּל וְיִתְקַדַּשׁ שְׁמֵהּ רַבָּא. (Cong: אָמֵן) בְּעָלְמָא דִּי בְרָא כִרְעוּתֵהּ וְיַמְלִיךְ מַלְכוּתֵהּ, וְיַצְמַח פֻּרְקָנֵהּ וִיקָרֵב מְשִׁיחֵהּ. (Cong: אָמֵן) בְּחַיֵּיכוֹן וּבְיוֹמֵיכוֹן וּבְחַיֵּי דְכָל בֵּית יִשְׂרָאֵל, בַּעֲגָלָא וּבִזְמַן קָרִיב. וְאִמְרוּ אָמֵן: (Cong: אָמֵן. יְהֵא שְׁמֵהּ רַבָּא מְבָרַךְ לְעָלַם וּלְעָלְמֵי עָלְמַיָּא, יִתְבָּרַךְ:) יְהֵא שְׁמֵהּ רַבָּא מְבָרַךְ לְעָלַם וּלְעָלְמֵי עָלְמַיָּא, יִתְבָּרַךְ, וְיִשְׁתַּבַּח, וְיִתְפָּאַר, וְיִתְרוֹמַם, וְיִתְנַשֵּׂא, וְיִתְהַדָּר, וְיִתְעַלֶּה, וְיִתְהַלָּל, שְׁמֵהּ דְּקֻדְשָׁא בְּרִיךְ הוּא. (Cong: אָמֵן) לְעֵלָּא מִן כָּל בִּרְכָתָא וְשִׁירָתָא, תֻּשְׁבְּחָתָא וְנֶחֱמָתָא, דַּאֲמִירָן בְּעָלְמָא, וְאִמְרוּ אָמֵן: (Cong: אָמֵן)

On days when The Torah is not read continue with "אַשְׁרֵי."
The following paragraph is said on Mondays and Thursdays, except when Tachanun is not said:

אֵל אֶרֶךְ אַפַּיִם אַתָּה וְרַב חֶסֶד וֶאֱמֶת, אַל בְּאַפְּךָ תוֹכִיחֵנוּ, חוּסָה יְיָ עַל עַמֶּךָ, וְהוֹשִׁיעֵנוּ

מִכָּל רָע, חָטָאנוּ לְךָ אָדוֹן, סְלַח נָא כְּרֹב רַחֲמֶיךָ אֵל:

Here ends the tachanun prayer for Monday and Thursday, the following is
pertinent to every day of the week:
Our Father, our King, You are our Father.
Our Father our King, we have no King other than You.
Our Father, our King, have mercy upon us.
Our Father, our King, grace us and answer us, for we have no good deeds, perform
with us justice and kindness for the sake of Your great Name, and save us.

And we do not know what we will do, for our eyes are upon You.
Recall Your mercy, Lord, and Your kindness, for they are forever.
May Your kindness, G-d be upon us, as You are our Hope.
Do not recall our former sins, rapidly bring forward Your mercy, since
we are very impoverished.
Be gracious, Lord, be gracious, for we are filled with disgrace.
In anger, recall the mercy [of Abraham], in anger recall the binding [of
Isaac], in anger recall the perfection [of Jacob], in anger remember the
love [of David].
Lord, save us; King, answer us on the day that we call.
For He knows our natural inclination, He well knows that we are
but dust.
Help us, G-d of our salvation, for the sake of the glory of Your Name,
save us and atone for our sins, for the sake of Your Name.

Exalted and sanctified is His great Name. (cong: "Amen") In the universe that He
created according to His Will, May He establish His reign, and sprout forth His
redemption, and quickly bring His meshiach. (cong: "Amen") In your life and
during your days and in the life of the entire house of Israel, speedily and soon,
and say Amen! (the congregation here says, "Amen, may His great Name be
blessed forever and for eternity") May His great Name be blessed forever and for
eternity. (cong: "Amen") May He be blessed, may He be extolled, may He be
glorified, may He be exalted, may He be elevated, may He be honored, may He
be lauded, and may he be praised, the Name of the holy One, blessed be He. (cong:
"Amen") Beyond all the blessings and the hymns, the praises and the consolations
that are recited in the world, and let us say Amen.

*On days when The Torah is not read continue with "*אַשְׁרֵי*."*
The following paragraph is said on Mondays and Thursdays, except when Tachanun
is not said:
Almighty G-d Who is patient, abounding in kindness and truth, do not
rebuke us in anger. Lord, have mercy on Your nation, and save us from
anything bad. We have sinned before You, Master, please forgive us in
Your great mercy, G-d.

סדר קריאת התורה

At this point the Torah is read on Mondays, Thursdays, Rosh Chodesh, Chanukah, public fast days and Chol haMoed.

וַיְהִי בִּנְסֹעַ הָאָרֹן וַיֹּאמֶר מֹשֶׁה, קוּמָה יְיָ וְיָפֻצוּ אֹיְבֶיךָ וְיָנֻסוּ מְשַׂנְאֶיךָ מִפָּנֶיךָ. כִּי מִצִּיּוֹן תֵּצֵא תוֹרָה וּדְבַר יְיָ מִירוּשָׁלָיִם. בָּרוּךְ שֶׁנָּתַן תּוֹרָה לְעַמּוֹ יִשְׂרָאֵל בִּקְדֻשָּׁתוֹ:

בְּרִיךְ שְׁמֵהּ דְּמָרֵא עָלְמָא, בְּרִיךְ כִּתְרָךְ וְאַתְרָךְ, יְהֵא רְעוּתָךְ עִם עַמָּךְ יִשְׂרָאֵל לְעָלַם, וּפֻרְקַן יְמִינָךְ אַחֲזֵי לְעַמָּךְ בְּבֵית מַקְדְּשָׁךְ, וּלְאַמְטוּיֵי לָנָא מִטּוּב נְהוֹרָךְ וּלְקַבֵּל צְלוֹתָנָא בְּרַחֲמִין. יְהֵא רַעֲוָא קֳדָמָךְ דְּתוֹרִיךְ לָן חַיִּין בְּטִיבוּ, וְלֶהֱוֵי אֲנָא פְּקִידָא בְּגוֹ צַדִּיקַיָּא, לְמִרְחַם עֲלַי וּלְמִנְטַר יָתִי וְיָת כָּל דִּי לִי, וְדִי לְעַמָּךְ יִשְׂרָאֵל. אַנְתְּ הוּא זָן לְכֹלָּא וּמְפַרְנֵס לְכֹלָּא, אַנְתְּ הוּא שַׁלִּיט עַל כֹּלָּא. אַנְתְּ הוּא דְּשַׁלִּיט עַל מַלְכַיָּא. וּמַלְכוּתָא דִּילָךְ הִיא. אֲנָא עַבְדָּא דְּקֻדְשָׁא בְּרִיךְ הוּא, דְּסָגִידְנָא קַמֵּהּ וּמִקַּמֵּי דִּיקַר אוֹרַיְתֵהּ. בְּכָל עִדָּן וְעִדָּן לָא עַל אֱנָשׁ רָחִיצְנָא וְלָא עַל בַּר אֱלָהִין סָמִיכְנָא. אֶלָּא בֶּאֱלָהָא דִשְׁמַיָּא, דְּהוּא אֱלָהָא קְשׁוֹט, וְאוֹרַיְתֵהּ קְשׁוֹט, וּנְבִיאוֹהִי קְשׁוֹט, וּמַסְגֵּא לְמֶעְבַּד טַבְוָן וּקְשׁוֹט. בֵּהּ אֲנָא רָחִיץ. וְלִשְׁמֵהּ קַדִּישָׁא יַקִּירָא אֲנָא אֵמַר תֻּשְׁבְּחָן. יְהֵא רַעֲוָא קֳדָמָךְ דְּתִפְתַּח לִבָּאִי בְּאוֹרַיְתָא, וְתַשְׁלִים מִשְׁאֲלִין דְּלִבָּאִי, וְלִבָּא דְכָל עַמָּךְ יִשְׂרָאֵל, לְטַב וּלְחַיִּין וְלִשְׁלָם:

The Torah is taken by the chazzan who lifts it slightly and says:

גַּדְּלוּ לַיְיָ אִתִּי, וּנְרוֹמְמָה שְׁמוֹ יַחְדָּו:

Torah Reading

And when the ark would journey, Moshe would say, "Rise, O Lord, and Your enemies will scatter, and those who hate you will run away from you. For, the Torah goes out from Zion, and the word of G-d from Jerusalem. Blessed be He Who gave Torah to His people, in sanctity.

Blessed is the Name of the Master of the universe. Blessed is Your crown and the place [of Your glory]. May Your will be forever with Your people Israel, and with the deliverance of Your right hand, show [re-build] Your people the holy Temple. And may goodness of Your light should reach us and our prayers be accepted in compassion. May it be Your will before You to lengthen our lives in goodness. May I be considered among Your righteous, so that You will have mercy on me and protect me and all that is mine, and that belongs to Your people, Israel. It is You Who sustains everyone and feeds everyone. You govern over everything. You are the One Who governs over Your Kingdom, and the Kingdom is Yours. I am the servant of the Holy One, may He be blessed before Whom and before Whose holy Torah I bow. At no time do I place my trust in man, nor do I ever rely upon an angel. Rather, I trust in the G-d of the heavens, for He is the true G-d, and His Torah is true and His prophets are true, and He performs multiple deeds of truth and goodness. In Him I trust, and it is His holy and dear Name that I praise. May it be Your will to open our hearts to Torah, and to fulfill the requests of our heart, and the heart of all of Your people, Israel, for the good and for life and for peace.

Exalt the Lord with me, and let us elevate His Name together.

As the Torah is being carried towards the Bimah the following is recited:

לְךָ יְיָ הַגְּדֻלָּה וְהַגְּבוּרָה וְהַתִּפְאֶרֶת וְהַנֵּצַח וְהַהוֹד, כִּי כֹל בַּשָּׁמַיִם

וּבָאָרֶץ. לְךָ יְיָ הַמַּמְלָכָה וְהַמִּתְנַשֵּׂא לְכֹל לְרֹאשׁ. רוֹמְמוּ יְיָ אֱלֹהֵינוּ,

וְהִשְׁתַּחֲווּ לַהֲדֹם רַגְלָיו, קָדוֹשׁ הוּא. רוֹמְמוּ יְיָ אֱלֹהֵינוּ וְהִשְׁתַּחֲווּ

לְהַר קָדְשׁוֹ, כִּי קָדוֹשׁ יְיָ אֱלֹהֵינוּ:

אַב הָרַחֲמִים הוּא יְרַחֵם עַם עֲמוּסִים וְיִזְכּוֹר בְּרִית אֵיתָנִים וְיַצִּיל נַפְשׁוֹתֵינוּ מִן הַשָּׁעוֹת

הָרָעוֹת וְיִגְעַר בְּיֵצֶר הָרָע מִן הַנְּשׂוּאִים וְיָחוֹן עָלֵינוּ לִפְלֵיטַת עוֹלָמִים. וִימַלֵּא מִשְׁאֲלוֹתֵינוּ

בְּמִדָּה טוֹבָה יְשׁוּעָה וְרַחֲמִים:

The Gabbai recites the following to call a Kohen to the Torah. If a Kohen is not present a Levite or Israelite is called up to the Torah instead:

וְתִגָּלֶה וְתֵרָאֶה מַלְכוּתוֹ עָלֵינוּ בִּזְמַן קָרוֹב, וְיָחוֹן פְּלֵיטָתֵנוּ וּפְלֵיטַת עַמּוֹ בֵּית יִשְׂרָאֵל לְחֵן וּלְחֶסֶד וּלְרַחֲמִים

וּלְרָצוֹן וְנֹאמַר אָמֵן. הַכֹּל הָבוּ גֹדֶל לֵאלֹהֵינוּ וּתְנוּ כָבוֹד לַתּוֹרָה, כֹּהֵן קְרַב יַעֲמוֹד (name) בֶּן (father's

name) הַכֹּהֵן, בָּרוּךְ שֶׁנָּתַן תּוֹרָה לְעַמּוֹ יִשְׂרָאֵל בִּקְדֻשָּׁתוֹ:

Congregation, followed by the gabbai responds:

וְאַתֶּם הַדְּבֵקִים בַּיְיָ אֱלֹהֵיכֶם, חַיִּים כֻּלְּכֶם הַיּוֹם:

בִּרְכוֹת קְרִיאַת הַתּוֹרָה

בָּרְכוּ אֶת יְיָ הַמְבֹרָךְ:

The congregation responds:

בָּרוּךְ יְיָ הַמְבֹרָךְ לְעוֹלָם וָעֶד:

The oleh then says:

בָּרוּךְ יְיָ הַמְבֹרָךְ לְעוֹלָם וָעֶד:

בָּרוּךְ אַתָּה יְיָ אֱלֹהֵינוּ מֶלֶךְ הָעוֹלָם, אֲשֶׁר בָּחַר בָּנוּ מִכָּל הָעַמִּים, וְנָתַן לָנוּ אֶת

תּוֹרָתוֹ. בָּרוּךְ אַתָּה יְיָ נוֹתֵן הַתּוֹרָה: (Cong) אָמֵן)

—⸙—

בָּרוּךְ אַתָּה יְיָ אֱלֹהֵינוּ מֶלֶךְ הָעוֹלָם, אֲשֶׁר נָתַן לָנוּ תּוֹרַת אֱמֶת, וְחַיֵּי עוֹלָם נָטַע

בְּתוֹכֵנוּ. בָּרוּךְ אַתָּה יְיָ, נוֹתֵן הַתּוֹרָה: (Cong) אָמֵן)

Yours, Lord, is the greatness, and the might and the glory, and the victory, and the splendor, as all that is in the heavens and on the earth.
Yours, Lord is the sovereignty and You are elevated, over all.
Exalt the Lord our G-d, and bow down to His footrest, for He is holy.
Exalt the Lord our G-d and bow down at His holy mountain, for holy is the Lord, our G-d.
May the merciful Father demonstrate mercy with the nation that is borne [by Him], and recall the ancient covenant and shield our souls from evil times, and repulse the evil inclination from those who are carried [by Him]. May He graciously grant us eternal survival and fulfill our requests in generous measure, with salvation and compassion.

May His reign over us soon be revealed and made visible, and may He deal graciously with our remnant as well as with the remainder of His people, the House of Israel, with harmony and kindness and compassion and goodwill and let us say, Amen. Let us all express the greatness of our G-d and give honor to the Torah. Let a Cohen approach. Stand forth (call the Hebrew name of the person called up to the Torah, together with his father's name), HaCohen. Blessed be He Who in His holiness gave the Torah to His people, the Jews.

And you who cleave to the Lord your G-d, are alive, all of you, today!

Blessings for the Torah Reading

Barchu es adonoy hamevorach.
Blessed be the Lord, Who is blessed

Baruch adonoy hamevorach leolam vo'ed
Bless the Lord, Who is blessed forever and ever

Boruch atah adonoy, elo-heinu melech haolam, asher bachar banu mikol ha'amim ve'nasan lanu es toraso. Boruch atah adonoy, nosayn haTorah.
Blessed are You, Lord, our G-d, King of the universe, Who has chosen us from amongst all the nations and given us His Torah. Blessed are You, Lord, Giver of the Torah.

~𝓯~

Boruch atah adonoy, elo-heinu melech haolam, asher nasan lanu Torat emet, ve'chayei olam natan be'tocheinu. Boruch atah adonoy, nosayn haTorah.
Blessed are You, Lord, our G-d, King of the universe, Who has given us the true Torah, and planted eternal life amongst us. Blessed be You, Lord, Giver of the Torah.

ברכת הגומל

בָּרוּךְ אַתָּה יְיָ אֱלֹהֵינוּ מֶלֶךְ הָעוֹלָם, הַגּוֹמֵל לְחַיָּבִים טוֹבוֹת, שֶׁגְּמָלַנִי טוֹב:

Congregation responds:

אָמֵן. מִי שֶׁגְּמָלְךָ טוֹב, הוּא יִגְמָלְךָ כָּל טוֹב סֶלָה:

ברוך שפטרני

After a bar mitzvah boy's first aliyah his father recites the following blessing (it is our custom to not recite the words in brackets):

בָּרוּךְ (אַתָּה יְיָ אֱלֹהֵינוּ מֶלֶךְ הָעוֹלָם) שֶׁפְּטָרַנִי מֵעָנְשׁוֹ שֶׁלָּזֶה:

חצי קדיש

יִתְגַּדַּל וְיִתְקַדַּשׁ שְׁמֵהּ רַבָּא. (*Cong*) אָמֵן) בְּעָלְמָא דִּי בְרָא כִרְעוּתֵהּ וְיַמְלִיךְ מַלְכוּתֵהּ, וְיַצְמַח פֻּרְקָנֵהּ וִיקָרֵב מְשִׁיחֵהּ. (*Cong*) אָמֵן) בְּחַיֵּיכוֹן וּבְיוֹמֵיכוֹן וּבְחַיֵּי דְכָל בֵּית יִשְׂרָאֵל, בַּעֲגָלָא וּבִזְמַן קָרִיב. וְאִמְרוּ אָמֵן: (*Cong*) אָמֵן. יְהֵא שְׁמֵהּ רַבָּא מְבָרַךְ לְעָלַם וּלְעָלְמֵי עָלְמַיָּא, יִתְבָּרַךְ:) יְהֵא שְׁמֵהּ רַבָּא מְבָרַךְ לְעָלַם וּלְעָלְמֵי עָלְמַיָּא, יִתְבָּרַךְ, וְיִשְׁתַּבַּח, וְיִתְפָּאַר, וְיִתְרוֹמַם, וְיִתְנַשֵּׂא, וְיִתְהַדָּר, וְיִתְעַלֶּה, וְיִתְהַלָּל, שְׁמֵהּ דְּקֻדְשָׁא בְּרִיךְ הוּא. (*Cong*) אָמֵן) לְעֵלָּא מִן כָּל בִּרְכָתָא וְשִׁירָתָא, תֻּשְׁבְּחָתָא וְנֶחֱמָתָא, דַּאֲמִירָן בְּעָלְמָא, וְאִמְרוּ אָמֵן: (*Cong*) אָמֵן)

As the Torah Scroll is raised the congregation should stand, look at the Sefer Torah and say:

וְזֹאת הַתּוֹרָה אֲשֶׁר שָׂם מֹשֶׁה לִפְנֵי בְּנֵי יִשְׂרָאֵל:

עֵץ חַיִּים הִיא לַמַּחֲזִיקִים בָּהּ, וְתֹמְכֶיהָ מְאֻשָּׁר. דְּרָכֶיהָ דַרְכֵי נֹעַם, וְכָל נְתִיבוֹתֶיהָ שָׁלוֹם. אֹרֶךְ יָמִים בִּימִינָהּ, בִּשְׂמֹאלָהּ עֹשֶׁר וְכָבוֹד. יְיָ חָפֵץ לְמַעַן צִדְקוֹ, יַגְדִּיל תּוֹרָה וְיַאְדִּיר:

Thanksgiving Blessing

Blessed be You, Lord our G-d, King of the universe, Who grants goodness to the culpable, Who has granted good to me.

Congregation responds:

Amen. He Who has granted good to you, should grant you all good forever!

Bar Mitzvah Blessing

Blessed be He Who has absolved me from punishment [resulting from] this [boy].

Exalted and sanctified is His great Name. (cong: "Amen") In the universe that He created according to His Will, May He establish His reign, and sprout forth His redemption, and quickly bring His meshiach. (cong: "Amen") In your life and during your days and in the life of the entire house of Israel, speedily and soon, and say Amen! (the congregation here says, "Amen, may His great Name be blessed forever and for eternity") May His great Name be blessed forever and for eternity. (cong: "Amen") May He be blessed, may He be extolled, may He be glorified, may He be exalted, may He be elevated, may He be honored, may He be lauded, and may he be praised, the Name of the holy One, blessed be He. (cong: "Amen") Beyond all the blessings and the hymns, the praises and the consolations that are recited in the world, and let us say Amen.

Upon returning the Torah scroll to the Ark:

And this is the Torah that Moshe placed before the children of Israel.

It is a tree of life for those who grasp it, and its supporters are most happy. Its ways are pleasant, and all of its paths are peace. On its right side is long life, at its left side are wealth and honor. The Lord desires to aggrandize and endear the Torah, for the sake of His people's honor.

אַשְׁרֵי יוֹשְׁבֵי בֵיתֶךָ, עוֹד יְהַלְלוּךָ פֶּלָה:

אַשְׁרֵי הָעָם שֶׁכָּכָה לּוֹ, אַשְׁרֵי הָעָם שֶׁיְיָ אֱלֹהָיו:

תְּהִלָּה לְדָוִד,

אֲרוֹמִמְךָ אֱלוֹהַי הַמֶּלֶךְ, וַאֲבָרְכָה שִׁמְךָ לְעוֹלָם וָעֶד:

בְּכָל יוֹם אֲבָרְכֶךָ, וַאֲהַלְלָה שִׁמְךָ לְעוֹלָם וָעֶד:

גָּדוֹל יְיָ וּמְהֻלָּל מְאֹד, וְלִגְדֻלָּתוֹ אֵין חֵקֶר:

דּוֹר לְדוֹר יְשַׁבַּח מַעֲשֶׂיךָ. וּגְבוּרֹתֶיךָ יַגִּידוּ:

הֲדַר כְּבוֹד הוֹדֶךָ, וְדִבְרֵי נִפְלְאֹתֶיךָ אָשִׂיחָה:

וֶעֱזוּז נוֹרְאֹתֶיךָ יֹאמֵרוּ, וּגְדֻלָּתְךָ אֲסַפְּרֶנָּה:

זֵכֶר רַב טוּבְךָ יַבִּיעוּ, וְצִדְקָתְךָ יְרַנֵּנוּ:

חַנּוּן וְרַחוּם יְיָ, אֶרֶךְ אַפַּיִם וּגְדָל חָסֶד:

טוֹב יְיָ לַכֹּל, וְרַחֲמָיו עַל כָּל מַעֲשָׂיו:

יוֹדוּךָ יְיָ כָּל מַעֲשֶׂיךָ, וַחֲסִידֶיךָ יְבָרְכוּכָה:

כְּבוֹד מַלְכוּתְךָ יֹאמֵרוּ, וּגְבוּרָתְךָ יְדַבֵּרוּ:

לְהוֹדִיעַ לִבְנֵי הָאָדָם גְּבוּרֹתָיו, וּכְבוֹד הֲדַר מַלְכוּתוֹ:

מַלְכוּתְךָ, מַלְכוּת כָּל עוֹלָמִים, וּמֶמְשַׁלְתְּךָ בְּכָל דּוֹר וָדֹר:

סוֹמֵךְ יְיָ לְכָל הַנֹּפְלִים, וְזוֹקֵף לְכָל הַכְּפוּפִים:

עֵינֵי כֹל אֵלֶיךָ יְשַׂבֵּרוּ, וְאַתָּה נוֹתֵן לָהֶם אֶת אָכְלָם בְּעִתּוֹ:

פּוֹתֵחַ אֶת יָדֶךָ, וּמַשְׂבִּיעַ לְכָל חַי רָצוֹן:

צַדִּיק יְיָ בְּכָל דְּרָכָיו, וְחָסִיד בְּכָל מַעֲשָׂיו:

קָרוֹב יְיָ לְכָל קֹרְאָיו, לְכֹל אֲשֶׁר יִקְרָאֻהוּ בֶאֱמֶת:

רְצוֹן יְרֵאָיו יַעֲשֶׂה, וְאֶת שַׁוְעָתָם יִשְׁמַע וְיוֹשִׁיעֵם:

שׁוֹמֵר יְיָ אֶת כָּל אֹהֲבָיו, וְאֵת כָּל הָרְשָׁעִים יַשְׁמִיד:

תְּהִלַּת יְיָ יְדַבֶּר פִּי, וִיבָרֵךְ כָּל בָּשָׂר שֵׁם קָדְשׁוֹ לְעוֹלָם וָעֶד:

וַאֲנַחְנוּ נְבָרֵךְ יָהּ, מֵעַתָּה וְעַד עוֹלָם, הַלְלוּיָהּ:

Ashrei (Psalm 145)

Happy are those who dwell in Your house, they will yet praise You forever.

Happy is the nation for whom this is their lot, happy is the nation whose G-d is the Lord.

A psalm of praise from David;

I will exalt You, my G-d the King, and I will bless Your name forever.

Every day, I will bless you, and I will praise Your name forever.

Great is the Lord, and very praiseworthy, there is no limit to His greatness.

One generation to the next praises Your works, and tells of Your might.

Your majesty is glorious, and words of Your wonders I will speak.

They will talk of the boldness of Your awesome acts and of Your greatness I will tell.

Remembrance of Your great goodness will be expressed, and Your righteousness will be sung.

The Lord is harmonious and compassionate, He is patient, and of great kindness.

The Lord is good to all, and compassionate over all of His works.

Lord, all of Your works are grateful to You, and they bless You for Your kindness.

They narrate the honor of Your reign, and speak of Your might.

In order to inform men of His might, and the honor of His glorious reign.

Your reign is the Kingship of all worlds, and Your dominion over all generations.

The Lord raises all who have fallen, and straightens all who are stooped.

The eyes of all gaze at You longingly, and You grant them their sustenance at the right time.

You open Your hands, and satisfy the desire of all living creatures.

The Lord is righteous in all of His paths, and kind in all His deeds.

The Lord is near to all who call Him, to all who call upon Him in truth.

He fulfills the will of those who fear Him, hears their cry and saves them.

The Lord guards over all who love Him, and destroys the wicked.

My mouth speaks the praises of the Lord, and all flesh blesses His holy name forever.

And we bless G-d, from now and forever, Halleluyah!

CHASSIDIC INSIGHTS

The process of prayer leads us up to the pinnacle of the spiritual ladder, and the implication is that it brings us back down again, as well. The verse from Genesis, "And behold, there was a ladder standing on the ground, with its top reaching into the heavens, and the angels of G-d were ascending and descending on it,"[184] implies that prayer is not merely about elevation, but also about descent. Human nature being what it is, we cannot remain in a state of attachment to G-d all day long. The time to cling to G-d is during the *Shemonah Esreh*, but afterward, we must detach ourselves and pursue our business in the physical world, making best possible use of the spirituality that we accessed during the *Shemonah Esreh*.

On Purim the Megillah is read at this point. On Tisha b'Av the Sefer Torah is returned to the Ark and the Kinot are said. On days when Tachanun is not said the following paragraph is omitted, however it should be recited before the daily reading of Psalms:

לַמְנַצֵּחַ מִזְמוֹר לְדָוִד:

יַעַנְךָ יְיָ בְּיוֹם צָרָה, יְשַׂגֶּבְךָ שֵׁם אֱלֹהֵי יַעֲקֹב:

יִשְׁלַח עֶזְרְךָ מִקֹּדֶשׁ, וּמִצִּיּוֹן יִסְעָדֶךָּ:

יִזְכֹּר כָּל מִנְחֹתֶיךָ, וְעוֹלָתְךָ יְדַשְּׁנֶה סֶלָה:

יִתֶּן לְךָ כִלְבָבֶךָ וְכָל עֲצָתְךָ יְמַלֵּא:

נְרַנְּנָה בִּישׁוּעָתֶךָ וּבְשֵׁם אֱלֹהֵינוּ נִדְגֹּל, יְמַלֵּא יְיָ כָּל מִשְׁאֲלוֹתֶיךָ:

עַתָּה יָדַעְתִּי, כִּי הוֹשִׁיעַ יְיָ מְשִׁיחוֹ, יַעֲנֵהוּ מִשְּׁמֵי קָדְשׁוֹ, בִּגְבוּרוֹת יֵשַׁע יְמִינוֹ:

אֵלֶּה בָרֶכֶב וְאֵלֶּה בַסּוּסִים, וַאֲנַחְנוּ בְּשֵׁם יְיָ אֱלֹהֵינוּ נַזְכִּיר:

הֵמָּה כָּרְעוּ וְנָפָלוּ, וַאֲנַחְנוּ קַמְנוּ וַנִּתְעוֹדָד:

יְיָ הוֹשִׁיעָה הַמֶּלֶךְ יַעֲנֵנוּ בְיוֹם קָרְאֵנוּ:

וּבָא לְצִיּוֹן גּוֹאֵל וּלְשָׁבֵי פֶשַׁע בְּיַעֲקֹב, נְאֻם יְיָ:

וַאֲנִי זֹאת בְּרִיתִי אֹתָם אָמַר יְיָ,

רוּחִי אֲשֶׁר עָלֶיךָ, וּדְבָרַי אֲשֶׁר שַׂמְתִּי בְּפִיךָ, לֹא יָמוּשׁוּ מִפִּיךָ וּמִפִּי זַרְעֲךָ

וּמִפִּי זֶרַע זַרְעֲךָ, אָמַר יְיָ מֵעַתָּה וְעַד עוֹלָם.

The Descent; bringing it down
U'vah letzion ("And a redeemer will come to Zion")
And afterward [after the *Shema* and   the *Shemonah Esreh*], G-dly influence de-

CHASSIDIC INSIGHTS

The descent, like the ascent, is orderly. We go up four rungs, and we come down four rungs. Clinging to G-d takes place in the World of *Atzilut*, and then we bring our new-found spirituality down via the three worlds of *Bria, Yetzira* and finally *Asiya*. Each world corresponds to a section of the prayers following *Tachanun*. *Ashrei* (Psalm 145) and *U'va letzion* correspond to *Bria*. The Song of the Day corresponds to *Yetzira*, and finally *Ein Keloheinu* corresponds to *Ssiya*. (This is the order of prayer according to the Ari, also of the Jews of Sfardi origin, as well as the so-called *Nusach Sfard*, adopted by most chassidim. The *Nusach Ashkenaz* places the Song of the Day and *Ein Keloheinu* after *Aleinu*.)

The prayer *U'va letzion* repeats

For the conductor, a song by David.

The Lord will answer you on your day of distress, the Name of the G-d of Jacob will fortify you.

He will send Your help from His holiness, and from Zion He will support you.

He will recall all of Your offerings, and Your accept Your sacrifices forever.

May He grant you all of your heart's wishes, and fulfill all of your counsel.

We will revel in Your salvation, and be glorified in the Name of Our G-d, may the Lord fulfill all of your desires.

Now I know, that the Lord saved His anointed one, answering him from His holy heavens, with the might of salvation of His right hand.

There are those who arrive in a chariot, and those on horses, our way is to mention the name of the Lord, our G-d.

They stumbled and fell, and we arose reinforced.

The Lord is our salvation, the King will answer us on the day we call out.

U'Va LeTzion

And a redeemer will come to Zion, and to the repentant sinners of Jacob, says the Lord.

And as for Me, this is my covenant with them, says the Lord. My spirit that is upon you, and my words that I have placed in your mouth, will not depart from your mouth, or from the mouths of your descendents, nor from the mouths of your descendents' offspring, says the Lord, from now and forever.

CHASSIDIC EXCERPTS

scends down to the worlds of BY"A, as well. The World of *bria* receives its portion during the prayer beginning with *U'va letzion*; the World of *yetzira* receives during the *Shir shel yom* ("Song of the day"); and the World of *asiya* receives some of the praises of the angels that we already recited before the *Shema*, wherein the angels said, "Holy, holy, holy..." Thus, the service of *U'va letzion* is similar to that of the *Shema* which is associated with the World of *Bria*.

Each Song of the Day is from Psalms and is also preceded by several other psalms, just as the most of the *Pesukei DeZimra* are from the Psalms. They are associated with the World of *Yetzira*.

And finally, the prayer *Ein Keloheinu* is followed by a recital of the physical elements of the *Ketoret* ("incense offering") in the Temple. This corresponds to the World of *Asiya*, similar to what we recite before *Hodu*, which is associated with the World of *Asiya*.

וְאַתָּה קָדוֹשׁ, יוֹשֵׁב תְּהִלּוֹת יִשְׂרָאֵל. וְקָרָא זֶה אֶל זֶה וְאָמַר,

קָדוֹשׁ, קָדוֹשׁ, קָדוֹשׁ, יְיָ צְבָאוֹת, מְלֹא כָל הָאָרֶץ כְּבוֹדוֹ. וּמְקַבְּלִין דֵּין מִן דֵּין וְאָמְרִין: קַדִּישׁ בִּשְׁמֵי מְרוֹמָא עִלָּאָה בֵּית שְׁכִינְתֵּהּ, קַדִּישׁ עַל אַרְעָא עוֹבַד גְּבוּרְתֵּהּ, קַדִּישׁ לְעָלַם וּלְעָלְמֵי עָלְמַיָּא: יְיָ צְבָאוֹת מַלְיָא כָל אַרְעָא זִיו יְקָרֵהּ.

during *pitom haketoret* (the "incense" described in the *siddur* following *Ein Kelokeinu*). It emerges, then, that a new revelation and vitality descends from the infinite light of G-d, from the source of all, every day, until it descends to the worlds of BY"A. And [then, it permeates] every detail of the creations of those worlds, renewing their vitality every day, as it is written, "Every day, they should be in your eyes as if new..."[354] And all this takes place via the *Shema* and *Shemonah Esreh* and the rest of the order of prayer.

(From *Derech Mitzvotecha* of the Tzemach Tzedek, *Shoresh Mitzvat Tefila*, ch. 11, p. 120)

Holy on the way down
Kadosh, kadosh, kadosh...("Holy, holy, holy...")

And this is why the Aramaic translation of the verse, *Kadosh, kadosh, kadosh* ("Holy, holy, holy"), which appears in the prayer *U'va letzion*, reads as follows: "Holy in the Heights of the Heavens Above, the dwelling place of His Divine Presence..." This indicates that the first word *kadosh* represents elevation from below to Above, which in turn facilitates an influx of holiness [from Above to] below.[355] This is what is meant by the words, "in the Heights of the Heavens Above, the dwelling place of His Divine Presence."

The second word *kadosh* symbolizes a descent of influx from Above to below, which is why the Aramaic translation reads "holy on the earth, expression of His might." This is the descent of holiness down to the physical world below.

The third word *kadosh* is translated as "holy forever and ever," and it symbolizes the holiness of the Torah. That is, in order for there to occur the elevation from below to Above, and the subsequent descent from Above to below, there must be a special force applied from Above. For, although it is true that when we "break through" the crust of the earth – meaning the physical body - "living waters" emerge, nevertheless, the catalyst that enables this to take

CHASSIDIC INSIGHTS

Order of Descent after *Shemoneh Esreh*

PRAYER	*Shmoneh Esreh* And *Tachanun*	*Ashrei, U'va Letzion*	*Shir shel* (Song of *Yom* the day)	*Ein Kelokeinu* And *Aleinu*
WORLD	*Atzilut*	*Beriah*	*Yetzira*	*Asiyah*
SOUL-LEVEL	*Chaya-Yechida*	*Neshama*	*Ruach*	*Nefesh*
ELEMENT	*Medaber* (Human)	*Chai* (animal)	*Tzomeach* (vegetable)	*Domam* (mineral)

And You are holy, ensconced upon the praises of Israel. And they [the angels] call to one another, saying:

Holy, holy, holy, is the Lord of hosts, His glory fills the earth.

And they receive each from the other, saying: He is holy in the supernal heights where His Divine Presence dwells, He is holy on the land, his mighty work, He is holy forever and ever, the Lord of Hosts, a ray of His glory fills the entire land.

CHASSIDIC EXCERPTS

place – to penetrate the earthy crust and concealment of the body – must come from Above.

Similarly, the power facilitating the descent of holiness into the world through fulfillment of the mitzvot necessitates energy from Above. This is the special quality and level imparted by the Torah that includes both elevation and descent [of holiness], for the Torah demands both speech and thoughtful investigation. Speech provides the influx and descent, while thought provides the elevation, since it is thoughtful investigation and study that unites our intellect and thought processes with the Torah.

In general, this is implicit in the oral Torah and the written Torah. The written Torah represents speech, as it contains the words, "And G-d spoke, saying..." while the oral Torah is mainly about study and investigation. The thoughtful investigation of the oral Torah is what imparts the power to elevate, while the power to draw down spirituality by doing the mitzvot is imparted by the speech of the Torah. This,

then, is what is meant by "holy forever and ever," meaning that the Torah imparts the power to elevate as well as to bring down spiritual influx for all generations...

And we could possibly say that the three times that the word "holy" is mentioned represent the three paragraphs of the *Shema*. The first paragraph contains forty-two words, alluding to the name of G-d of forty-two letters (*Ana Bekoach*). This name is associated with elevation, as it states in the *Zohar* that the name *Mem-Beit* (42) "ascends, and does not descend." The second paragraph represents descent of influx, symbolized by the seventy-two words of the paragraph, corresponding to the name of G-d of numerical value seventy-two (*shem eyn-beit*). And the third paragraph, discussing the commandment to wear *tzitzit*, corresponds to the "pillar of Torah," which imparts power. As we see, this paragraph contains the sentence, "I am the Lord, your G-d, who has taken you out of the land of Egypt," meaning "I am the one Who gave you power to

וַתִּשָּׂאֵנִי רוּחַ, וָאֶשְׁמַע אַחֲרַי קוֹל רַעַשׁ גָּדוֹל,

בָּרוּךְ כְּבוֹד יְיָ מִמְּקוֹמוֹ:

וּנְטָלַתְנִי רוּחָא וּשְׁמָעִית בַּתְרַי קַל זִיעַ שַׂגִּיא דִמְשַׁבְּחִין וְאָמְרִין

בְּרִיךְ יְקָרָא דַיְיָ מֵאֲתַר בֵּית שְׁכִינְתֵּהּ.

יְיָ יִמְלֹךְ לְעֹלָם וָעֶד.

יְיָ מַלְכוּתֵהּ קָאֵים לְעָלַם וּלְעָלְמֵי עָלְמַיָּא.

יְיָ אֱלֹהֵי אַבְרָהָם יִצְחָק וְיִשְׂרָאֵל אֲבוֹתֵינוּ,

שָׁמְרָה זֹּאת לְעוֹלָם, לְיֵצֶר מַחְשְׁבוֹת לְבַב עַמֶּךָ, וְהָכֵן לְבָבָם אֵלֶיךָ

CHASSIDIC EXCERPTS

enable you to escape from the forty-nine gates of impurity of the land of Egypt." And it says, "And He took us out of Egypt, not by way of an angel..."[356] but by Himself, for His own honor. And so

He gave us afterward the power by accepting the Torah that it should lift us up to the heights of great love of G-d (*bekol meodecha*)...

(From *Sefer Maamorim 5654* (~1894) of the Rebbe Rashab, pp. 251)

Three groups of angels
Kadosh, kadosh, kadosh...("Holy, holy, holy...")

The sages of the Talmud said: "There are three groups of angels. One group says *kadosh*. A second group says *kadosh, kadosh*, while yet a third group says *kadosh, kadosh, kadosh, HaShem Tzevaot*." [357] [What groups of angels are being discussed here?]

We'll preface by analyzing what is meant by *kadosh*. The word means "separate/removed" ... and implies that G-d is removed from all the worlds; that is, even though He enlivens and creates the worlds, He is not like a soul that enlivens the body.

The very essence of the soul is enclothed within the body to enliven it and is trapped within the body. The energy that flows from the soul is distributed throughout the body on three general levels: the head, the torso, and the legs. The energy enclothed in the head is

of a higher form than the energy of the body. It is the "inner dimension" of all energy, since the intellect and the ability to think, as well as the senses of sight and hearing, are all centered in the head. The energy of the torso is lower, since the heart is the epicenter of the emotions, which are inferior to the intellect, and also the power of action within the hands is lower in level than the senses of the face, sight and hearing. And after that come the legs, wherein the energy is lower still...

However, this is not the manner in which G-d enlivens the creation. [The creative energy that enlivens the world] is not divided into variations and levels whatsoever and, therefore, it would not be appropriate to describe Him using the terms "head" and "feet." He is the first, and He is the last. And since He

And a spirit uplifted me, and I heard the sound of a great noise behind me,

"Blessed be the glory of the Lord, from its place."

And the spirit overtook me and I heard a mighty voice moving behind me, praising and saying, "Blessed be the glory of the Lord, from where it dwells."

The Lord reigns forever and ever.

The sovereignty of the Lord is established for all eternity.

Lord, G-d of Abraham, of Isaac and of Israel our fathers; keep this forever, as the desire and the thoughts of the heart of Your people, and incline their hearts toward You.

CHASSIDIC EXCERPTS

does not enclothe Himself within the worlds in the same manner that the soul enclothes itself in the body, it is not appropriate to speak of divisions and levels in the creation of the worlds. These divisions only come about as the result of enclothing ... but when He enlivens the worlds, it is not by way of enclothing Himself and, therefore, there are no divisions whatsoever ... This is what is meant by "holy," meaning that He is removed from the worlds. Even though He enlivens and creates the worlds from nothing, nonetheless He does not enclothe Himself within them...

This explains why the first group of angels says *kadosh*. They are the *seraphim* ("fiery angels"), as explained in the Talmud. They are supernal angels of the World of *bria*, wherein the G-dly intellect is revealed, enabling souls and angels to grasp the infinite light of G-d. As mentioned earlier, the immanent illumination (*memalle kol olamim*) of G-dliness is divided into three general levels: head or the upper *Gan Eden* ("Garden of Eden"), torso or the lower *Gan Eden*, and feet or *olam hazeh* ("this world"). Therefore, the *seraphim*, being of the World of *Beria*, where the upper *Gan Eden* is, com-

prehend the greatness of the infinite light of G-d [beyond themselves]. And the thrust of their intellectual grasp is how He, G-d, is holy and removed, out of their range.

Now, the source of the G-dly energy that comes to us as immanent G-dliness (permeating and filling the creation) can descend only by way of great contraction ... And from this revelation of G-dliness, called *memalle kol olamim*, emerges all of our intellectual perception of G-dliness in the worlds, whether of the upper or lower worlds, or the upper *Gan Eden*. But He, Himself, is holy and removed, and no thought can grasp Him whatsoever. And the energy with which He enlivens the upper worlds, without contraction, is called transcendent illumination (*sovev kol olamim*) and cannot become enclothed at all within them, but rather remains exalted and beyond them. That is why it is written [about G-d], "I have not changed."[358] As well, there is no division within His energy between "upper and lower," as it is written, "I am the first and I am the last."[359]

Their meditation and comprehension of G-dliness leads the *seraphim* to

הוּא רַחוּם יְכַפֵּר עָוֹן וְלֹא יַשְׁחִית, וְהִרְבָּה לְהָשִׁיב אַפּוֹ, וְלֹא יָעִיר כָּל חֲמָתוֹ. כִּי אַתָּה אֲדֹנָי טוֹב וְסַלָּח, וְרַב חֶסֶד לְכָל קֹרְאֶיךָ.

צִדְקָתְךָ צֶדֶק לְעוֹלָם, וְתוֹרָתְךָ אֱמֶת.

תִּתֵּן אֱמֶת לְיַעֲקֹב, חֶסֶד לְאַבְרָהָם, אֲשֶׁר נִשְׁבַּעְתָּ לַאֲבֹתֵינוּ מִימֵי קֶדֶם.

בָּרוּךְ אֲדֹנָי יוֹם יוֹם יַעֲמָס לָנוּ. הָאֵל יְשׁוּעָתֵנוּ סֶלָה.

יְיָ צְבָאוֹת עִמָּנוּ, מִשְׂגָּב לָנוּ אֱלֹהֵי יַעֲקֹב סֶלָה.

יְיָ צְבָאוֹת, אַשְׁרֵי אָדָם בֹּטֵחַ בָּךְ:

יְיָ הוֹשִׁיעָה, הַמֶּלֶךְ יַעֲנֵנוּ בְיוֹם קָרְאֵנוּ:

CHASSIDIC EXCERPTS

great arousal and excitement. With desire and love like flames of fire, they "gaze at the glory of the King," that is, at the transcendent G-dliness of *sovev kol olamim* [transcendent G-dliness]. G-d is holy and removed, and it is on account of their fiery love and tremendous desire for Him that they are called *seraphim*. They say *kadosh* once because they have a singular desire to become included within the transcendent illumination of *sovev kol olamim* ... In this way, they strive to exit their own limitations and contractions, imposed by the immanent illumination that enlivens them from within ... and to cleave to the transcendent light of *sovev kol olamim*.

Now, man is a "small world," and he contains within himself the same elements of the three groups of angels. The first group that says *kadosh* one time, whose great desire is to gaze upon the glory of the King and to become aroused with flames of fire, is present within man as well, in the form of the element of fire within the heart of man. Just as the body of man is composed of four physical elements [fire, water, earth and air], so his animal soul is composed of the four spiritual elements of the world of *noga* (mixed good and bad). And his

G-dly soul also includes these four elements, from a G-dly perspective. The "location" of the element of water is within the mind, and the "location" of the element of fire is in the heart. Now, the relative composition of the four elements is not the same within every person; there are those in whom the element of water is dominant, and there are those in whom the element of fire dominates. By way of analogy, there are different grades of coals; there are coals that burn with flames of fire, and there are coals that smolder like hot embers, exhibiting no signs of fire, even though the spark is present but concealed within. Since the spark is present, although concealed, we can ignite it by blowing forcefully upon the coals and cause it to burst into visible flames. And so it is within the G-dly soul of man; there are those who possess a more forceful and revealed element of G-dly fire in their heart, as in the example of the coals that burn with flames of fire. And there are those whose G-dly spark is hidden inside, as in the example of the hot embers. The spark may be small and concealed within, but in any case, there is some aspect of a spark inside the soul of each and every Jew. It is necessary

And He, being merciful, atones for our sins and refrains from destroying us,

He repeatedly quashes His anger, and avoids arousing all of His wrath.

The Lord saves, the King answers us on the day that we call [Him].

For, You, Lord are good and forgiving, abounding in kindness to all those who call upon You.

Your righteousness is forever just, and your Torah is truth.

Grant truth to Jacob, kindness to Abraham, as you swore to our forefathers in former days.

Blessed is the master, who loads us up [with goodness] from day to day, the almighty G-d is our salvation forever.

The Lord of Hosts is with us, the G-d of Jacob is our fortress forever.

The Lord of hosts, happy is the man who relies upon Him.

The Lord saves, the King answers us when we call to Him."

CHASSIDIC EXCERPTS

only to blow upon it forcefully, and then it bursts into flames of fire and expands to envelop the entire coal, in a visible fashion. And so within the G-dly soul of man, it is necessary only to ignite the spark that is present by "blowing" upon it until it becomes conscious.

The "blowing" takes place during the order of prayer, from the beginning through the recitation of the *Shema*. It starts by meditation upon the greatness of G-d, on how "...He spoke and the universe came into existence." This is the meditation associated with prayer up to the words "with all your heart(s)" during the recitation of the *Shema*, and it constitutes the "blowing" during which we exhale forcefully upon the spark hidden in the element of G-dly fire within the heart so that it ignites to become conscious illumination in the heart. And with the words "all your heart(s)" in the *Shema*, the spark emerges from within the element of fire of the heart and ascends toward G-d, burning with desire and fiery flames.

This, then, is what is meant by, "And I was sanctified within the Jewish people"[360] – meaning within the Jewish psyche – the inner point of spiritual consciousness in the heart of each and every Jew. Within the inner point of the heart is found a place where "I was sanctified," leading the heart to burn like fire with a fierce love [and desire] to "gaze upon the glory of the King," since He is holy and removed and totally out of our range. Therefore, the goal is to ignite within the inner point of the heart our desire for Him by means of meditation on how He is holy. This is what the sages meant when they referred to the first group of angels who say *kadosh* once. Within man, this is love – "with all your heart(s)" – or revelation of the inner dimension of the heart. It means becoming conscious of an overflowing heart, brimming with love of G-d to the point of expiration of the soul, as it is written, "My soul pines and also expires..."[361]

And, afterward, the second group [of angels] says *kadosh, kadosh,* twice. When the word was uttered once by the first group, it corresponded to an elevation from below to Above, since the *seraphim* only wanted to become included in the infinite light and to "gaze upon the glory of the King." This is the spiritual service of the first group. However, the second group, who say *kadosh* twice, seek an influx of G-dliness into this

אָרוּךְ הוּא אֱלֹהֵינוּ שֶׁבְּרָאָנוּ לִכְבוֹדוֹ, וְהִבְדִּילָנוּ מִן הַתּוֹעִים. וְנָתַן לָנוּ תּוֹרַת
אֱמֶת, וְחַיֵּי עוֹלָם נָטַע בְּתוֹכֵנוּ, הוּא יִפְתַּח לִבֵּנוּ בְּתוֹרָתוֹ, וְיָשֵׂם בְּלִבֵּנוּ
אַהֲבָתוֹ וְיִרְאָתוֹ, לַעֲשׂוֹת רְצוֹנוֹ וּלְעָבְדוֹ בְּלֵבָב שָׁלֵם, לֹא נִיגַע לָרִיק וְלֹא נֵלֵד
לַבֶּהָלָה.

וּבְכֵן יְהִי רָצוֹן מִלְּפָנֶיךָ יְיָ אֱלֹהֵינוּ וֵאלֹהֵי אֲבוֹתֵינוּ, שֶׁנִּשְׁמוֹר חֻקֶּיךָ בָּעוֹלָם הַזֶּה,
וְנִזְכֶּה וְנִחְיֶה וְנִרְאֶה, וְנִירַשׁ טוֹבָה וּבְרָכָה, לִשְׁנֵי ,יְמוֹת הַמָּשִׁיחַ וּלְחַיֵּי הָעוֹלָם
הַבָּא.

לְמַעַן יְזַמֶּרְךָ כָבוֹד וְלֹא יִדֹּם, יְיָ אֱלֹהַי לְעוֹלָם אוֹדֶךָ:

בָּרוּךְ הַגֶּבֶר אֲשֶׁר יִבְטַח בַּייָ; וְהָיָה יְיָ, מִבְטַחוֹ.

בִּטְחוּ בַייָ עֲדֵי עַד, כִּי בְּיָהּ יְיָ, צוּר עוֹלָמִים. וְיִבְטְחוּ בְךָ יוֹדְעֵי שְׁמֶךָ, כִּי לֹא
עָזַבְתָּ דֹרְשֶׁיךָ יְיָ.

יְיָ חָפֵץ לְמַעַן צִדְקוֹ, יַגְדִּיל תּוֹרָה וְיַאְדִּיר:

⟡

CHASSIDIC EXCERPTS

world, from Above to below. Now, the desire and yearning of the first group is to cling to the transcendent illumination of the One Above and to be nullified in essence, totally and completely. But, the second group wants and desires to draw His infinite light down into this world...

And the third group says *kadosh* three times. Their service is also part of our service, associated with *bekol*

meodecha ("with all of your might") within the *Shema*. The meaning of *meod* is "without limits," corresponding to the infinite light, beyond the vessels of the *sephirot*, which must always be brought down here. That means that the transcendent illumination needs to descend, and this takes place by way of the mitzvot.

(From *Likutei Torah* of the Alter Rebbe, *Parshat Emor*, p. 31)

Seeing vs. Hearing G-dliness

During our prayers, we place emphasis upon *avoda* ("worship") coming from the essence of our soul, beyond the "vessels" (faculties) of the soul. For, it is written, "The voice (*kol*) is the voice of Yakov,"[362] and the Zohar points out that the first "voice" [of the verse] is written

incompletely, since it is lacking the middle letter *vov*, while the second "voice" is spelled fully, including the letter *vov*. These are the [two voices mentioned in the Zohar, the] "voice that is inaudible" and the "voice that is audible," corresponding to the voices of Torah and of

*B*lessed is He, Our G-d, Who has created in His Honor, and has distinguished us from those who err, and given us His true Torah, and planted everlasting life within us. May He open our hearts to His Torah, and place in our hearts love and fear of Him, [in order] to do His will and to serve Him wholeheartedly, rather than serve Him for naught, nor become confounded.

And so may it be Your will before You, our G-d and G-d of our forefathers, that we fulfill Your laws in this world, and merit to live and observe, and inherit the good and the blessing, of the Messianic years and the life of the world to come.

Therefore, I shall sing to You and not be silent, Lord my G-d, I will forever thank and acknowledge you.

Blessed is the man who trusts in the Lord, and the Lord will be His fortress.

Trust in the Lord forever, for in G-d the Lord is the strength of worlds. And those who know Your name trust You, for You do not forsake those who seek You, Lord.

The Lord desires for the sake of his [Israel's] righteousness, to aggrandize and glorify the Torah.

❧⸸☙

CHASSIDIC EXCERPTS

prayer. The audible voice is heard as it utters the letters of speech. It comes from *chochma*, or intellectual grasp, which results from divine light becoming enclothed within the vessel of the mind, which is why it is expressed in the letters of speech. But, the inaudible voice is an inner voice that expresses the arousal of the soul, beyond enclothement within its conscious faculties, and that is why it cannot be expressed in letters of speech.

Now, the inaudible voice also has two dimensions. The first is inaudible in speech, but is nevertheless expressed in some sort of voice, as when we cry bitterly from the depth of our soul about a matter that is vital to us. [This cry] emerges from beyond our conscious faculties that are enclothed in "vessels,"

meaning that it comes from beyond our faculty of intellect and the like. And so, we cry with a loud voice - at any rate there is the sound of a voice present. This occurs because the matter that troubles us does not touch the very essence of our soul, but rather the illumination the essence, that still bears some sort of relationship with our conscious faculties.

However, when the matter touches the very essence of our soul, it bears no connection whatsoever with our conscious faculties, and then we lack even the power to cry out as well. All that we are capable of doing is standing still like a stone, totally nullified from within. And this is the scream of the heart that is above the cry of the voice described above.

This, in general is the voice of

קַדִּישׁ שָׁלֵם

יִתְגַּדַּל וְיִתְקַדַּשׁ שְׁמֵהּ רַבָּא. (*Cong*: אָמֵן)

בְּעָלְמָא דִּי בְרָא כִרְעוּתֵהּ וְיַמְלִיךְ מַלְכוּתֵהּ, וְיַצְמַח פֻּרְקָנֵהּ וִיקָרֵב מְשִׁיחֵהּ. (*Cong*:
אָמֵן)

בְּחַיֵּיכוֹן וּבְיוֹמֵיכוֹן וּבְחַיֵּי דְכָל בֵּית יִשְׂרָאֵל, בַּעֲגָלָא וּבִזְמַן קָרִיב. וְאִמְרוּ אָמֵן:

(*Cong*: אָמֵן.)

יְהֵא שְׁמֵהּ רַבָּא מְבָרַךְ לְעָלַם וּלְעָלְמֵי עָלְמַיָּא, יִתְבָּרַךְ:)

יְהֵא שְׁמֵהּ רַבָּא מְבָרַךְ לְעָלַם וּלְעָלְמֵי עָלְמַיָּא, יִתְבָּרַךְ, וְיִשְׁתַּבַּח, וְיִתְפָּאַר, וְיִתְרוֹמַם,

וְיִתְנַשֵּׂא, וְיִתְהַדָּר, וְיִתְעַלֶּה, וְיִתְהַלָּל, שְׁמֵהּ דְּקֻדְשָׁא בְּרִיךְ הוּא. (*Cong*: אָמֵן)

לְעֵלָּא מִן כָּל בִּרְכָתָא וְשִׁירָתָא, תֻּשְׁבְּחָתָא וְנֶחֱמָתָא, דַּאֲמִירָן בְּעָלְמָא, וְאִמְרוּ אָמֵן:

(*Cong*: אָמֵן)

תִּתְקַבֵּל צְלוֹתְהוֹן וּבָעוּתְהוֹן דְּכָל בֵּית יִשְׂרָאֵל, קֳדָם אֲבוּהוֹן דִּי בִשְׁמַיָּא, וְאִמְרוּ אָמֵן:

יְהֵא שְׁלָמָה רַבָּא מִן שְׁמַיָּא וְחַיִּים טוֹבִים עָלֵינוּ וְעַל כָּל יִשְׂרָאֵל, וְאִמְרוּ אָמֵן:

עֹשֶׂה שָׁלוֹם (*During the Ten Days of Penitence substitute* - הַשָּׁלוֹם) בִּמְרוֹמָיו, הוּא

יַעֲשֶׂה שָׁלוֹם עָלֵינוּ, וְעַל כָּל יִשְׂרָאֵל, וְאִמְרוּ אָמֵן:

CHASSIDIC EXCERPTS

prayer, which is an inner voice stemming from arousal of the essence of the soul. It is comparable to what is written regarding Chana, "Only her lips moved and her voice was not heard"[363] – it is as if the voice comes from the very walls of the heart, the depth and interior of the heart, which may not be expressed in the voice of speech. Nevertheless, this is the main expression of prayer. The descent and revelation of a new light that, for example, provides a barren woman with a baby and the like, only results from prayers from the very depths and interior of our heart; that is, from arousal of the very interior and essence of the soul.

It is written, "The Lord is close to all who call upon Him, to all who call upon Him in truth."[364] When we call upon Him from the "truth" of our soul, He responds intimately to those who call upon Him. And what is the "truth" of the soul? About the *galut* ("exile"), it is written, "I am sleeping, but my heart is awake."[365] This is said about the collective Jewish nation (*Knesset Yisrael*), which is, so to speak, "sleeping" during the *galut*, as the Zohar embellishes, "I am sleeping in the exile and nevertheless my heart is awake."

By way of analogy, the main mani-

Full Kaddish

Exalted and sanctified is His great Name. (cong: "Amen")

In the universe that He created according to His Will, May He establish His reign, and sprout forth His redemption, and quickly bring His meshiach. (cong: "Amen")

In your life and during your days and in the life of the entire house of Israel, speedily and soon, and say Amen! (the congregation here says, "Amen, may His great Name be blessed forever and for eternity")

May His great Name be blessed forever and for eternity. (cong: "Amen")

May He be blessed, may He be extolled, may He be glorified, may He be exalted, may He be elevated, may He be honored, may He be lauded, and may he be praised, the Name of the holy One, blessed be He. (cong: "Amen")

Beyond all the blessings and the hymns, the praises and the consolations that are recited in the world, and let us say Amen.

May the prayers and requests of all of the house of Israel be accepted before their father in Heaven, and let us say Amen (cong: "Amen").

May there be plentiful peace from Heaven and a good life for all of us and for all of Israel, and let us say, Amen (cong: "Amen").

He Who makes peace (during ten days of repentance – "the peace") on high, may He create peace for us and for all of Israel, and let us say Amen (cong: "Amen").

CHASSIDIC EXCERPTS

festation of sleep is that our eyes are closed, so that automatically, our faculty of vision does not function. Not only our vision but all of our inner powers, such as intellect and feelings – all of them are concealed and unconscious during sleep. And so it is in the realm of spirituality during the *galut*, which is compared to sleep; our power of spiritual vision within the G-dly soul – to "gaze upon the glory of the King" - dissipates.

During the era of the holy Temple, Jewish souls possessed the power of spiritual vision of G-dliness, as written, "...My eyes are constantly upon G-d."[366] And from Above as well, there was rev-

elation of G-dliness on the order of "vision," as written, "the Land which...the eyes of the Lord your G-d are upon..."[367] and "And my eyes and heart were there all day long."[368] Similarly, within Jewish souls we possessed the ability to see G-dliness, corresponding to the concept of "My eyes are constantly upon *Havaya*," which indicates gazing upon the source of the spiritual chain of creation, how it "is, was and will be," all at once. This is illumination of the name *Havaya* as it remains above still, beyond the divisions associated with the name *Elokim*. So automatically, we experience nullification [of the self]

As the Torah is returned to the Ark the following is recited by the chazzan:

הַלְלוּ אֶת שֵׁם יְיָ, כִּי נִשְׂגָּב שְׁמוֹ לְבַדּוֹ:

The congregation then responds:

הוֹדוֹ, עַל אֶרֶץ וְשָׁמָיִם: וַיָּרֶם קֶרֶן לְעַמּוֹ, תְּהִלָּה לְכָל חֲסִידָיו, לִבְנֵי יִשְׂרָאֵל עַם
קְרֹבוֹ, הַלְלוּיָהּ:

On days when Tachanun is not said the following Psalm is omitted. Continue with
"בֵּית יַעֲקֹב":

תְּפִלָּה לְדָוִד: הַטֵּה יְיָ אָזְנְךָ עֲנֵנִי, כִּי עָנִי, וְאֶבְיוֹן אָנִי: שָׁמְרָה נַפְשִׁי כִּי חָסִיד אָנִי,
הוֹשַׁע עַבְדְּךָ אַתָּה אֱלֹהַי, הַבּוֹטֵחַ אֵלֶיךָ: חָנֵּנִי אֲדֹנָי, כִּי אֵלֶיךָ אֶקְרָא כָּל הַיּוֹם: שַׂמֵּחַ
נֶפֶשׁ עַבְדֶּךָ, כִּי אֵלֶיךָ אֲדֹנָי נַפְשִׁי אֶשָּׂא: כִּי אַתָּה אֲדֹנָי טוֹב וְסַלָּח, וְרַב חֶסֶד, לְכָל
קֹרְאֶיךָ: הַאֲזִינָה יְיָ, תְּפִלָּתִי, וְהַקְשִׁיבָה בְּקוֹל תַּחֲנוּנוֹתָי: הַאֲזִינָה יְיָ, תְּפִלָּתִי, וְהַקְשִׁיבָה,
בְּקוֹל תַּחֲנוּנוֹתָי: בְּיוֹם צָרָתִי אֶקְרָאֶךָ כִּי תַעֲנֵנִי: אֵין כָּמוֹךָ בָאֱלֹהִים אֲדֹנָי, וְאֵין
כְּמַעֲשֶׂיךָ: כָּל גּוֹיִם אֲשֶׁר עָשִׂיתָ יָבוֹאוּ וְיִשְׁתַּחֲווּ לְפָנֶיךָ אֲדֹנָי, וִיכַבְּדוּ לִשְׁמֶךָ: כִּי גָדוֹל
אַתָּה וְעֹשֵׂה נִפְלָאוֹת אַתָּה אֱלֹהִים לְבַדֶּךָ: הוֹרֵנִי יְיָ, דַּרְכֶּךָ אֲהַלֵּךְ בַּאֲמִתֶּךָ, יַחֵד לְבָבִי
לְיִרְאָה שְׁמֶךָ: אוֹדְךָ אֲדֹנָי אֱלֹהַי בְּכָל-לְבָבִי, וַאֲכַבְּדָה שִׁמְךָ לְעוֹלָם: כִּי חַסְדְּךָ גָּדוֹל
עָלַי, וְהִצַּלְתָּ נַפְשִׁי מִשְּׁאוֹל תַּחְתִּיָּה: אֱלֹהִים, זֵדִים קָמוּ עָלַי, וַעֲדַת עָרִיצִים בִּקְשׁוּ
נַפְשִׁי, וְלֹא שָׂמוּךָ לְנֶגְדָּם: וְאַתָּה אֲדֹנָי אֵל רַחוּם וְחַנּוּן, אֶרֶךְ אַפַּיִם, וְרַב חֶסֶד וֶאֱמֶת:
פְּנֵה אֵלַי וְחָנֵּנִי, תְּנָה עֻזְּךָ לְעַבְדֶּךָ, וְהוֹשִׁיעָה לְבֶן אֲמָתֶךָ: עֲשֵׂה עִמִּי אוֹת לְטוֹבָה
וְיִרְאוּ שֹׂנְאַי וְיֵבֹשׁוּ, כִּי אַתָּה יְיָ עֲזַרְתַּנִי וְנִחַמְתָּנִי:

CHASSIDIC EXCERPTS

associated with "all is like naught before Him." For, the name *Havaya* is associated with *yichuda ila'ah*, or ("higher unity" – awareness of G-d as the true reality while creation is merely a backdrop). And as written regarding the two states of consciousness, *yichuda ila'ah* and *da'at tachton* ("lower awareness" – in which our primary awareness is of the world and G-d is in the background) - *da'at tachton* is associated with the name

Elokim, which imparts the impression that the world really exists. And therefore, the nullification associated with this awareness is nullification of the ego alone [that is, mere nullification of our ego and not of our actual self].

However, from the perspective of the name *Havaya*, no creature with its own limited identity (within the parameters of "is, was, and will be at once" - implying total lack of limitations within

Let the Name of the Lord be praised, for His Name alone is exalted.

His glory is over the earth and the heavens. He will elevate the prestige of His people, praise to all of His pious ones, to the children of Israel, His intimate nation, Halleluyah.

A psalm for David; Lord, incline Your ear and answer me, for I am a pauper and a poor man. Preserve my soul, for I am pious, deliver Your servant, for You are My G-d, in Whom I place my trust. Be gracious to me, Lord, for to You I call every day. Make the soul of Your servant joyous, for to You, Lord, I lift my soul. For You, Lord are good and forgiving, abundantly kind to all who call to You. Listen, Lord to my prayer, and heed the voice of my pleas. On the day of my distress, I call to You, for You will answer me. There is none like You, G-d, among the celestial creatures, my Lord, and nothing like Your works. All of the nations whom You made will come and bow down before You, Lord, and they will honor Your Name. For Your are Great, and You perform wonders, You alone are G-d. Teach me, Lord, Your ways, that I may walk in Your Truth; unify my heart to fear Your Name. I thank You, Master, my G-d, will all of my heart, and I honor Your Name forever. For Your kindness overwhelms me, and You delivered my soul from the depths of the grave. G-d, wrong-doers rise up against me, and a band of malicious men seeks my soul; and they have not taken You into consideration. And You, Master, are a good and gracious G-d, patient and abounding in kindness and truth. Turn to me and be gracious, give of Your strength to Your servant, and save the son of Your maidservant. Show me a favorable sign, so that those who hate You may see and be ashamed, for You, Lord, have helped me and consoled me.

CHASSIDIC EXCERPTS

time) - can exist. And nevertheless, we do mention "existence," which we experience during *da'at elyon* of *Atzilut*. Moreover, we experience an element of this level of "vision" within ourselves, as explained above. And the associated level of nullification is described "as if naught" – as if non-existent. And this is what occurred during the time of the Temple, as known the Temple provided revelation of the name *Havaya*, as writ-ten, "And there is *Havaya* in this Place..."[369] Moreover, in the Temple, [the priests] would call out His name as it is written.

This is the difference between the Temple and the rest of the world; the name *Havaya* is manifest in the rest of the worlds enclad in the name *Elokim*, for "the sun and a shield are *Havaya* and *Elokim*." That is, the name *Elokim* hides and conceals revelation of *Havaya*, so

בֵּית יַעֲקֹב, לְכוּ וְנֵלְכָה בְּאוֹר יְיָ: כִּי כָּל הָעַמִּים יֵלְכוּ אִישׁ בְּשֵׁם אֱלֹהָיו, וַאֲנַחְנוּ נֵלֵךְ בְּשֵׁם יְיָ אֱלֹהֵינוּ לְעוֹלָם וָעֶד:

יְהִי יְיָ אֱלֹהֵינוּ עִמָּנוּ, כַּאֲשֶׁר הָיָה עִם אֲבֹתֵינוּ, אַל יַעַזְבֵנוּ וְאַל יִטְּשֵׁנוּ:

לְהַטּוֹת לְבָבֵנוּ אֵלָיו, לָלֶכֶת בְּכָל דְּרָכָיו וְלִשְׁמֹר מִצְוֹתָיו וְחֻקָּיו וּמִשְׁפָּטָיו, אֲשֶׁר צִוָּה, אֶת אֲבֹתֵינוּ:

וְיִהְיוּ דְבָרַי אֵלֶּה אֲשֶׁר הִתְחַנַּנְתִּי לִפְנֵי יְיָ, קְרֹבִים אֶל יְיָ אֱלֹהֵינוּ יוֹמָם וָלָיְלָה, לַעֲשׂוֹת מִשְׁפַּט עַבְדּוֹ, וּמִשְׁפַּט עַמּוֹ יִשְׂרָאֵל דְּבַר יוֹם בְּיוֹמוֹ:

לְמַעַן דַּעַת כָּל עַמֵּי הָאָרֶץ כִּי יְיָ, הוּא הָאֱלֹהִים, אֵין עוֹד:

שִׁיר הַמַּעֲלוֹת לְדָוִד: לוּלֵי יְיָ, שֶׁהָיָה לָנוּ, יֹאמַר נָא יִשְׂרָאֵל:

לוּלֵי יְיָ, שֶׁהָיָה לָנוּ, בְּקוּם עָלֵינוּ אָדָם:

אֲזַי חַיִּים בְּלָעוּנוּ, בַּחֲרוֹת אַפָּם בָּנוּ:

אֲזַי, הַמַּיִם שְׁטָפוּנוּ נַחְלָה עָבַר עַל נַפְשֵׁנוּ:

אֲזַי עָבַר עַל נַפְשֵׁנוּ, הַמַּיִם הַזֵּידוֹנִים:

בָּרוּךְ יְיָ, שֶׁלֹּא נְתָנָנוּ טֶרֶף לְשִׁנֵּיהֶם:

נַפְשֵׁנוּ כְּצִפּוֹר נִמְלְטָה מִפַּח יוֹקְשִׁים, הַפַּח נִשְׁבָּר, וַאֲנַחְנוּ נִמְלָטְנוּ:

עֶזְרֵנוּ בְּשֵׁם יְיָ, עֹשֵׂה שָׁמַיִם וָאָרֶץ:

CHASSIDIC EXCERPTS

that there is no revelation of the name *Havaya* in the world. But, in the Temple, there was real revelation of the name *Havaya*, just as had been in the garden of Eden, about which is written the name *Havaya Elokim* in its full spelling. And there was similar revelation in the Temple...and souls received this illumination and the revelation occurred through the holy Temple, as written, "Three times a year, You should see the countenance of the Master, *Havaya* Your G-d..."[370] And this revelation remained with them for the entire year, since they fulfilled the mitzvah of *reiya* ("seeing" and being "seen" in the Temple) during

House of Jacob, let us go and make progress in the light of the Lord.
For, all of the nations walk, each man in the name of his G-d, and we
walk in the name of the Lord, our G-d, for all eternity.
May the Lord, our G-d be with us, as He was with our fathers, may
He not leave us or forsake us.
That He may incline our hearts to Him, to walk in all of His ways and
to keep His commandments and His statutes and laws, that He
commanded our fathers.
And may these words of mine that I have pleaded before the Lord,
be close to the Lord our G-d, day and night, that He may fulfill the
needs of His servant and the needs of His people Israel, according to
their daily requirements.
So that all of the nations of the earth may know that the Lord is our
G-d, there is no other.

A song of ascents for David: Were it not for the Lord Who was with us
– so says Israel -
Were it not for the Lord Who was with us, when man rose up
against us.
Then they would have swallowed us alive, in their burning rage
against us.
Then the waters would have drowned us, the deluge would have
swept us away.
Then, the torrential waters would have inundated our souls.
Blessed is the Lord, Who did not let us become fodder in their teeth.

Our soul is like an escaped bird, from the snare of the trapper; the
snare broke, and we escaped.
Our help is in the Name of the Lord, Creator of heavens and earth.

———◁◦▷———

CHASSIDIC EXCERPTS

the three festivals, as written in *Likutei Torah* in the discourse *mizmor shir chanukat*, in the first of the discourses, "And their *avoda* was to remain constantly in a state of *reiya* of the essence of G-dliness of the name *Havaya*, and in a state of nullification of "all stands before Him as naught."

However, during the *galut*, the power of spiritual vision disappeared and became concealed, together with the ability to "gaze upon the glory of the King" mentioned above, and the general path of worship of souls during the *galut* is called "hearing" alone. That is, [we serve G-d] via intellectual grasp and

שִׁיר שֶׁל יוֹם

Sunday

הַיּוֹם, יוֹם רִאשׁוֹן בְּשַׁבָּת, שֶׁבּוֹ הָיוּ הַלְוִיִּם אוֹמְרִים בְּבֵית הַמִּקְדָּשׁ:

לְדָוִד מִזְמוֹר, לַיְיָ הָאָרֶץ וּמְלוֹאָהּ, תֵּבֵל וְיֹשְׁבֵי בָהּ:

כִּי הוּא עַל יַמִּים יְסָדָהּ, וְעַל נְהָרוֹת יְכוֹנְנֶהָ:

מִי יַעֲלֶה בְהַר יְיָ, וּמִי יָקוּם בִּמְקוֹם קָדְשׁוֹ:

נְקִי כַפַּיִם וּבַר לֵבָב, אֲשֶׁר לֹא נָשָׂא לַשָּׁוְא נַפְשִׁי, וְלֹא נִשְׁבַּע לְמִרְמָה:

יִשָּׂא בְרָכָה מֵאֵת יְיָ, וּצְדָקָה מֵאֱלֹהֵי יִשְׁעוֹ:

זֶה דּוֹר דֹּרְשָׁו, מְבַקְשֵׁי פָנֶיךָ יַעֲקֹב סֶלָה:

שְׂאוּ שְׁעָרִים רָאשֵׁיכֶם, וְהִנָּשְׂאוּ פִּתְחֵי עוֹלָם וְיָבוֹא מֶלֶךְ הַכָּבוֹד:

מִי זֶה מֶלֶךְ הַכָּבוֹד: יְיָ עִזּוּז וְגִבּוֹר, יְיָ גִּבּוֹר מִלְחָמָה:

שְׂאוּ שְׁעָרִים רָאשֵׁיכֶם וּשְׂאוּ פִּתְחֵי עוֹלָם, וְיָבֹא מֶלֶךְ הַכָּבוֹד:

מִי הוּא זֶה מֶלֶךְ הַכָּבוֹד, יְיָ צְבָאוֹת הוּא מֶלֶךְ הַכָּבוֹד סֶלָה:

הוֹשִׁיעֵנוּ יְיָ אֱלֹהֵינוּ וְקַבְּצֵנוּ מִן הַגּוֹיִם לְהֹדוֹת לְשֵׁם קָדְשֶׁךָ, לְהִשְׁתַּבֵּחַ בִּתְהִלָּתֶךָ:

בָּרוּךְ יְיָ אֱלֹהֵי יִשְׂרָאֵל מִן הָעוֹלָם וְעַד הָעוֹלָם וְאָמַר כָּל הָעָם אָמֵן הַלְלוּיָהּ:

בָּרוּךְ יְיָ מִצִּיּוֹן שֹׁכֵן יְרוּשָׁלָיִם הַלְלוּיָהּ:

בָּרוּךְ יְיָ אֱלֹהִים אֱלֹהֵי יִשְׂרָאֵל, עֹשֵׂה נִפְלָאוֹת לְבַדּוֹ:

וּבָרוּךְ שֵׁם כְּבוֹדוֹ לְעוֹלָם, וְיִמָּלֵא כְבוֹדוֹ אֶת כָּל הָאָרֶץ, אָמֵן וְאָמֵן: קדיש יתום

CHASSIDIC EXCERPTS

meditation upon G-dliness, which takes place "from afar." And as known, all intellectual pursuit takes place at an "objective distance" from the essence, and implies mere awareness of the existence [of G-dliness], lacking any apprehension of the essence of [G-dly] illumination whatsoever. And there is a big difference in the love and closeness that results from this. When G-dly light illuminates within us in the form of "vision," it does so from up close and nearby, producing true cleaving to the G-dly light, and total nullification of the self. Hear-

Song of the Day

On Sundays, we recite Psalm 24:

Today is the first day of the week, on which the Levites said the following in the holy Temple:

For David, a Psalm, for the earth and all that fills it is the Lord's, the globe and all who dwell upon it.

For, on the seas, He founded it, and upon the rivers he established it.

Who is allowed to ascend the mountain of the Lord, and who may stand in His holy place?

[He who possesses] clean hands and a pure heart, who has not brought Me up [taken My name] in vain, nor sworn falsely.

He will receive a blessing from the Lord, and justice from the G-d of his salvation.

This is the generation of seekers of Him, who forever search for the countenance of Jacob.

Lift up your heads, gates, and elevate the entrances of the universe, and let the King of honor arrive.

Who is this King of honor, the Lord, strong and heroic, the Lord is a hero of war.

Lift up your heads, gates, and elevate the entrances of the universe, and let the King of honor arrive.

Who is this King of honor, the Lord of Hosts, is the King of honor forever.

After each song of the day, we recite the following:

Save us, Lord our G-d, and gather us from among the nations, to thank Your holy name, and to revel in Your praises.

Blessed is the Lord, G-d of Israel from this world to the next world, and the entire nation said Amen, halleluyah!

Blessed is the Lord from Zion, dwelling in Jerusalem, halleluyah.

Blessed is the Lord, G-d Who is G-d of Israel, Who alone works wonders.

And blessed is His glorious Name forever, and let the entire earth be full of His glory, amen and amen.

CHASSIDIC EXCERPTS

ing, though is not comparable to vision. Although there may be nothing new in what we see, nevertheless, it is clear that with our sense of sight we penetrate to the essence of the object. And then, we cling with all of our power to the very essence of the object, and all of our senses are nullified as we gaze and immerse ourselves in it. This does not occur during the process of "hearing," which occurs ["objectively"], from afar, as it were. Although we may become stimulated from what we hear, nevertheless it is nothing more than an

Monday

הַיּוֹם, יוֹם שֵׁנִי בְּשַׁבָּת, שֶׁבּוֹ הָיוּ הַלְוִיִּים אוֹמְרִים בְּבֵית הַמִּקְדָּשׁ:

שִׁיר מִזְמוֹר לִבְנֵי קֹרַח:

גָּדוֹל יְיָ וּמְהֻלָּל מְאֹד, בְּעִיר אֱלֹהֵינוּ הַר קָדְשׁוֹ:

יְפֵה נוֹף מְשׂוֹשׂ כָּל הָאָרֶץ הַר צִיּוֹן, יַרְכְּתֵי צָפוֹן קִרְיַת מֶלֶךְ רָב:

אֱלֹהִים בְּאַרְמְנוֹתֶיהָ נוֹדַע לְמִשְׂגָּב:

כִּי הִנֵּה הַמְּלָכִים נוֹעֲדוּ, עָבְרוּ יַחְדָּו:

הֵמָּה רָאוּ כֵּן תָּמָהוּ, נִבְהֲלוּ נֶחְפָּזוּ:

רְעָדָה, אֲחָזָתַם שָׁם, חִיל כַּיּוֹלֵדָה:

בְּרוּחַ קָדִים, תְּשַׁבֵּר אֳנִיּוֹת תַּרְשִׁישׁ:

כַּאֲשֶׁר שָׁמַעְנוּ כֵּן רָאִינוּ בְּעִיר יְיָ צְבָאוֹת, בְּעִיר אֱלֹהֵינוּ, אֱלֹהִים יְכוֹנְנֶהָ עַד עוֹלָם סֶלָה:

דִּמִּינוּ אֱלֹהִים חַסְדֶּךָ, בְּקֶרֶב הֵיכָלֶךָ:

כְּשִׁמְךָ אֱלֹהִים כֵּן תְּהִלָּתְךָ עַל קַצְוֵי אֶרֶץ, צֶדֶק מָלְאָה יְמִינֶךָ:

יִשְׂמַח הַר צִיּוֹן תָּגֵלְנָה בְּנוֹת יְהוּדָה, לְמַעַן, מִשְׁפָּטֶיךָ:

סֹבּוּ צִיּוֹן וְהַקִּיפוּהָ, סִפְרוּ מִגְדָּלֶיהָ:

שִׁיתוּ לִבְּכֶם לְחֵילָה פַּסְּגוּ אַרְמְנוֹתֶיהָ, לְמַעַן תְּסַפְּרוּ לְדוֹר אַחֲרוֹן:

כִּי זֶה אֱלֹהִים אֱלֹהֵינוּ עוֹלָם וָעֶד, הוּא יְנַהֲגֵנוּ עַל מוּת:

הוֹשִׁיעֵנוּ וכו' קדיש יתום

CHASSIDIC EXCERPTS

arousal, with no attendent nullification of the self.

And so it is in *avoda*; as a result of "vision" of the essence of G-dliness, we cling and cleave to G-dliness and become nullified in our very essence during the vision and cleaving. We have no connection to either ego or physical substance whatsoever, but only to G-dliness alone. And in this process we find yearning and delight and joy in G-d – it truly becomes our place of fortress. But, from the perspective of "hearing" and intellectual grasp of G-dliness, all that we achieve is apprehension of the existence of G-dliness, while the essence of what G-dliness is remains "afar." And therefore, even when our meditation is real and honest, with depth of *da'at* that allows us to experience the matter and

On Mondays, we recite Psalm 48:

This is the second day of the week, on which the Levites said the following in the holy Temple:

A song, a psalm for the children of Korach.

The Lord is great and very praiseworthy, in the city of our G-d, the mountain of His sanctuary.

Of beautiful scenery, the joy of the whole earth is Mt. Zion, on the northern slopes, the city of the great King.

In its palaces, G-d became known as a tower of strength.

For here, the kings assembled, they joined forces [to attack Jerusalem].

They beheld [the wonders of the Almighty] and were astonished; they were awe-struck and quickly scattered.

They were seized by trembling there, like a woman in the pangs of labor.

[Like] an east wind that shatters the ships of Tarshish.

As we have heard, so we saw in the city of the Lord of Hosts, in the city of our G-d; may G-d establish it for all eternity.

We imagined, G-d, Your kindness [as revealed] within Your Sanctuary.

As Your Name, O G-d [is great], so is Your praise to the ends of the earth; Your right hand is full of righteousness.

Let Mt. Zion rejoice, let the towns of Judah exult, because of Your judgments.

Walk around Zion, encircle her, count her towers.

Consider well her ramparts, behold her lofty citadels, that you may recount it to later generations.

For this G-d is our G-d forever and ever; He will lead us eternally.

Save us...*(found after the song for Sunday)*

CHASSIDIC EXCERPTS

become truly excited with love of G-dliness, it is nothing more than excitement and nullification of our ego alone...

...But, even this power of "hearing" is not manifest during the *galut*. All that remains is the lowest power within it, the "power of imagination" alone, as written, "We were like dreamers..."[371] And as the sages said regarding the par-

able of sleep; when we close our eyes, all of our powers of intellect and emotion fail us, and nothing is left aside from our power of imagination. And therefore we are capable of imagining two things that contradict each other during our dream, since we lack the power of discernment that accompanies the faculty of "hearing" of *bina*, as written, "the ears discern [within] the words."[372] So it is during

Tuesday

הַיּוֹם, יוֹם שְׁלִישִׁי בְּשַׁבָּת, שֶׁבּוֹ הָיוּ הַלְוִיִּם אוֹמְרִים בְּבֵית הַמִּקְדָּשׁ:

מִזְמוֹר לְאָסָף, אֱלֹהִים נִצָּב בַּעֲדַת אֵל, בְּקֶרֶב אֱלֹהִים יִשְׁפֹּט:

עַד מָתַי תִּשְׁפְּטוּ עָוֶל, וּפְנֵי רְשָׁעִים תִּשְׂאוּ סֶלָה:

שִׁפְטוּ דַל וְיָתוֹם, עָנִי וָרָשׁ הַצְדִּיקוּ:

פַּלְּטוּ דַל וְאֶבְיוֹן, מִיַּד רְשָׁעִים הַצִּילוּ:

לֹא יָדְעוּ וְלֹא יָבִינוּ בַּחֲשֵׁכָה יִתְהַלָּכוּ, יִמּוֹטוּ כָּל מוֹסְדֵי אָרֶץ:

אֲנִי אָמַרְתִּי אֱלֹהִים אַתֶּם, וּבְנֵי עֶלְיוֹן כֻּלְּכֶם:

אָכֵן כְּאָדָם תְּמוּתוּן, וּכְאַחַד הַשָּׂרִים תִּפֹּלוּ:

קוּמָה אֱלֹהִים שָׁפְטָה הָאָרֶץ, כִּי אַתָּה תִנְחַל בְּכָל הַגּוֹיִם:

הוֹשִׁיעֵנוּ וכו' קדיש יתום

Wednesday

הַיּוֹם, יוֹם רְבִיעִי בְּשַׁבָּת, שֶׁבּוֹ הָיוּ הַלְוִיִּם אוֹמְרִים בְּבֵית הַמִּקְדָּשׁ:

אֵל נְקָמוֹת יְיָ, אֵל נְקָמוֹת הוֹפִיעַ:

הִנָּשֵׂא שֹׁפֵט הָאָרֶץ, הָשֵׁב גְּמוּל עַל גֵּאִים:

עַד מָתַי רְשָׁעִים יְיָ, עַד מָתַי רְשָׁעִים יַעֲלֹזוּ:

יַבִּיעוּ יְדַבְּרוּ עָתָק, יִתְאַמְּרוּ כָּל פֹּעֲלֵי אָוֶן:

עַמְּךָ יְיָ יְדַכְּאוּ, וְנַחֲלָתְךָ יְעַנּוּ:

אַלְמָנָה וְגֵר יַהֲרֹגוּ, וִיתוֹמִים יְרַצֵּחוּ:

CHASSIDIC EXCERPTS

the *galut*; although all Jews cling to the one G-d and meditate on the oneness of G-d, [meditating upon] how all is nullified and united with Him, and how He creates and enlivens all of creation, and that the main thing is G-dly light and energy, nonetheless, when we later get involved in matters of this world, directing our mind and *da'at* in depth to these matters as if they were the most important...[this is what results] when our meditation is from the power of imagination alone – that is why we can meditate upon "two opposites" as one...

From *Sefer Maamorim* 5669 (1909) of the Rebbe Rashab, Page 99-101

On Tuesdays, we recite Psalm 82:

Today is the third day of the week, on which the Levites said in the holy Temple:

A psalm for Asaf; G-d stands in the assembly of the Almighty, amongst the judges He renders judgment.

How long will you render crooked judgments; and show permanent bias toward the wicked!

Judge the poor and the orphans, justify the impoverished and the destitute.

Rescue the poor and the destitute, save them from the hands of the wicked.

They know not, nor do they understand, they walk in darkness, they stumble, the foundations of the earth all tremble.

I said to them, 'You are angels - all of you – and supernal beings.'

However, like any man you will die, and like a prince you will fall.

Rise, G-d and judge the land, for You will bequeath among all of the nations.

Save us…*(found after the song for Sunday)*

On Wednesdays, we recite Psalm 94, followed by Psalm 95:1-3

Today is the fourth day of the week, on which the Levites said in the holy Temple:

The Lord is a G-d of revenge: G-d of revenge, reveal Yourself!

Judge of the earth, arise, repay the arrogant their just desserts.

How long shall the wicked, Lord, how long shall the wicked exult?

They express, speaking insolently; all of the evildoers boast.

They crush Your people, Lord, and oppress Your heritage.

They kill the widow and the stranger, and murder the orphans.

CHASSIDIC EXCERPTS

Levels of holy angels
Vehaofanim vechayot hakodesh…("And the ofanim and holy chayot…")

Although [bria] is a created world, as opposed to an emanated world [such as Atzilut], nevertheless, it exists in proximity to the Divine void (ayn) of malchut of Atzilut, which creates the World of bria. And therefore, the ayn shines within bria more than it shines in the World of yetzira, where it is more distant spiritually. And, therefore, the seraphim, the angels of the World of bria, say kadosh ("holy"), meaning that they utter the word kadosh because they grasp how G-d is holy and exalted above the category of worlds … And the seraphim, the

וַיֹּאמְרוּ, לֹא יִרְאֶה יָּהּ, וְלֹא יָבִין אֱלֹהֵי יַעֲקֹב:

בִּינוּ, בֹּעֲרִים בָּעָם, וּכְסִילִים, מָתַי תַּשְׂכִּילוּ:

הֲנֹטַע אֹזֶן הֲלֹא יִשְׁמָע, אִם יֹצֵר עַיִן הֲלֹא יַבִּיט:

הֲיֹסֵר גּוֹיִם הֲלֹא יוֹכִיחַ, הַמְלַמֵּד אָדָם דָּעַת:

יְיָ יֹדֵעַ מַחְשְׁבוֹת אָדָם, כִּי הֵמָּה הָבֶל:

אַשְׁרֵי הַגֶּבֶר אֲשֶׁר תְּיַסְּרֶנּוּ יָּהּ, וּמִתּוֹרָתְךָ תְלַמְּדֶנּוּ:

לְהַשְׁקִיט לוֹ מִימֵי רָע, עַד יִכָּרֶה לָרָשָׁע שָׁחַת:

כִּי לֹא יִטֹּשׁ יְיָ עַמּוֹ, וְנַחֲלָתוֹ לֹא יַעֲזֹב:

כִּי עַד צֶדֶק יָשׁוּב מִשְׁפָּט, וְאַחֲרָיו כָּל יִשְׁרֵי לֵב:

מִי יָקוּם לִי עִם מְרֵעִים, מִי יִתְיַצֵּב לִי עִם פֹּעֲלֵי אָוֶן:

לוּלֵי יְיָ עֶזְרָתָה לִּי, כִּמְעַט שָׁכְנָה דוּמָה נַפְשִׁי:

אִם אָמַרְתִּי מָטָה רַגְלִי, חַסְדְּךָ יְיָ יִסְעָדֵנִי:

בְּרֹב שַׂרְעַפַּי בְּקִרְבִּי, תַּנְחוּמֶיךָ יְשַׁעַשְׁעוּ נַפְשִׁי:

הַיְחָבְרְךָ כִּסֵּא הַוּוֹת, יֹצֵר עָמָל עֲלֵי חֹק:

יָגוֹדּוּ עַל נֶפֶשׁ צַדִּיק, וְדָם נָקִי יַרְשִׁיעוּ:

וַיְהִי יְיָ לִי לְמִשְׂגָּב, וֵאלֹהַי לְצוּר מַחְסִי:

וַיָּשֶׁב עֲלֵיהֶם אֶת אוֹנָם, וּבְרָעָתָם יַצְמִיתֵם, יַצְמִיתֵם יְיָ אֱלֹהֵינוּ:

לְכוּ נְרַנְּנָה לַיְיָ, נָרִיעָה לְצוּר יִשְׁעֵנוּ:

נְקַדְּמָה פָנָיו בְּתוֹדָה, בִּזְמִרוֹת נָרִיעַ לוֹ:

כִּי אֵל גָּדוֹל יְיָ, וּמֶלֶךְ גָּדוֹל עַל כָּל אֱלֹהִים:

הוֹשִׁיעֵנוּ וכו' קדיש יתום

CHASSIDIC EXCERPTS

fiery angels who stand in the world of bria – as we know from what is written in the *Tikunei Zohar* that *imah ila'ah* nests in *bria* (that is, the *sephira* of *bina* is dominant in the World of *bria*) – grasp the infinite light of G-d. This is *sovev kol olamim* ("transcendent illumination")

that is holy and exalted, beyond the category of creation and above the name *Adni* that serves as the source of *memalle kol olamim* ("immanent G-dliness")...

We say that the *seraphim* "stand" because – as it is explained elsewhere by the Baal Shem Tov – the will and desire

And they say, 'The Lord does not see, the G-d of Jacob does not grasp.'

Understand, you boors among people; you fools, when will you wise up?

He who implants the ear – does He not hear, He who forms the eye – does He not see?

He who chastises nations – does He not rebuke? - He who imparts knowledge to man - [does He not know]?

The Lord knows the thoughts of man, that they are naught.

Fortunate is the man whom You chastise, Lord, and whom You instruct in Your Torah.

In order to calm him down in times of adversity, until the pit is dug for the wicked.

For the Lord will not abandon His people, nor forsake His heritage.

Until judgment matches [corresponds to] justice, and all the upright of heart pursue it.

Who would rise up for me against the wicked ones, who would stand up for me against the evildoers?

Had the Lord not helped me, my soul would soon have dwelt in the silence [of the grave].

When I thought that my foot was slipping, Your kindness, Lord supported me.

When [worrisome] thoughts multiply within me, Your consolation delights my soul.

Can the seat of evil, which turns iniquity into law, consort with You?

They band together against the life of the righteous, and condemn innocent blood.

The Lord has been my stronghold; my G-d, the Rock of my refuge.

He will turn their violence against them and destroy them through their own wickedness; the Lord our G-d will destroy them.

Come, let us sing to the Lord; let us raise our voices in jubilation to the Rock of our deliverance.

Let us approach Him with thanksgiving; let us raise our voices to Him in song.

For the Lord is a great G-d, and a great King over all supernal beings.

Save us...(*found after the song for Sunday*)

CHASSIDIC EXCERPTS

of the *seraphim* is to receive from what is beyond them, so it is as if they are standing there. That is, although in truth their place is in the World of *bria*, which is a world created from the spiritual void of *malchut* of *Atzilut* and called by the name *Adni* or *Elokim*, and they as well are created from this level, nevertheless, since their will and desire is for the infinite light of G-d that is *sovev kol olamim*, it is considered as if they "stand" there.

And the power within these angels to grasp the infinite light of *sovev kol olamim* comes from *Imma Ila'ah* (or *bina*)

Thursday

הַיּוֹם, יוֹם חֲמִישִׁי בְּשַׁבָּת, שֶׁבּוֹ הָיוּ הַלְוִיִּים אוֹמְרִים בְּבֵית הַמִּקְדָּשׁ:

לַמְנַצֵּחַ עַל הַגִּתִּית לְאָסָף:

הַרְנִינוּ, לֵאלֹהִים עוּזֵּנוּ, הָרִיעוּ לֵאלֹהֵי יַעֲקֹב:

שְׂאוּ זִמְרָה וּתְנוּ תֹף, כִּנּוֹר נָעִים עִם נָבֶל:

תִּקְעוּ בַחֹדֶשׁ שׁוֹפָר, בַּכֶּסֶה לְיוֹם חַגֵּנוּ:

כִּי חֹק לְיִשְׂרָאֵל הוּא, מִשְׁפָּט לֵאלֹהֵי יַעֲקֹב:

עֵדוּת, בִּיהוֹסֵף שָׂמוֹ בְּצֵאתוֹ עַל אֶרֶץ מִצְרָיִם, שְׂפַת לֹא יָדַעְתִּי אֶשְׁמָע:

הֲסִירוֹתִי מִסֵּבֶל שִׁכְמוֹ, כַּפָּיו מִדּוּד תַּעֲבֹרְנָה:

בַּצָּרָה קָרָאתָ וָאֲחַלְּצֶךָּ אֶעֶנְךָ בְּסֵתֶר רַעַם, אֶבְחָנְךָ עַל מֵי מְרִיבָה סֶלָה:

שְׁמַע עַמִּי וְאָעִידָה בָּךְ, יִשְׂרָאֵל אִם תִּשְׁמַע לִי:

לֹא-יִהְיֶה בְךָ, אֵל זָר, וְלֹא תִשְׁתַּחֲוֶה לְאֵל נֵכָר:

אָנֹכִי יְיָ אֱלֹהֶיךָ הַמַּעַלְךָ מֵאֶרֶץ מִצְרָיִם, הַרְחֶב פִּיךָ וַאֲמַלְאֵהוּ:

וְלֹא שָׁמַע עַמִּי לְקוֹלִי, וְיִשְׂרָאֵל לֹא אָבָה לִי:

וָאֲשַׁלְּחֵהוּ בִּשְׁרִירוּת לִבָּם, יֵלְכוּ בְּמוֹעֲצוֹתֵיהֶם:

לוּ עַמִּי שֹׁמֵעַ לִי, יִשְׂרָאֵל בִּדְרָכַי יְהַלֵּכוּ:

כִּמְעַט אוֹיְבֵיהֶם אַכְנִיעַ, וְעַל צָרֵיהֶם, אָשִׁיב יָדִי: מְשַׂנְאֵי יְיָ יְכַחֲשׁוּ לוֹ, וִיהִי עִתָּם לְעוֹלָם:

וַיַּאֲכִילֵהוּ מֵחֵלֶב חִטָּה, וּמִצּוּר דְּבַשׁ אַשְׂבִּיעֶךָ:

הוֹשִׁיעֵנוּ וכו' קדיש יתום

CHASSIDIC EXCERPTS

who nests in *bria*, which is the beginning of created existence as we know it, coming from the *ayn* of *Atzilut* that creates them. And because of the proximity of the *ayn* that creates the *yesh* ("created existence"), the *ayn* itself shines within the *yesh*. This is not true of the World of *yetzira*, which is compared to speech. It is considered to have come into existence *yesh mi-yesh* ("from one created ob-

On Thursdays, we recite Psalm 81:

On the fifth day of the week, the Levites would say in the holy Temple:
For the conductor, a psalm sung on the Gitit [a musical instrument],
for Asaf.

Sing joyously to G-d, our strength; sound the shofar to the G-d of Jacob.

Raise your voice in song: sound the drum, the pleasant harp and the lyre.

Blow the shofar on the new moon, on the designated day of our festival.

For it is a decree for Israel, a ruling of the G-d of Jacob.
He established it as a testimony for Yehoseph when he went forth over
the land of Egypt; I heard a language I did not know.
I relieved his shoulders of their burden; his hands from the cauldron.
In distress you called and I delivered you; [you called] in secret, and I
answered you with thunderous wonders; I tested you at the waters of
Merivah, Selah.
Hear, my people, and I will testify on your behalf; Israel, if you would
only listen to Me!
You shall have no alien god within you, nor shall you bow down to a
foreign deity.
I am the Lord your G-d who brought you up from the land of Egypt;
open your mouth wide [state all of your desires], and I will fill it.
But, My people did not heed My voice; Israel did not want [to listen
to] Me.
So, I sent them away in the stubbornness of their heart, that they
should follow their own [evil] design.
If only My people would listen to Me, if Israel would only walk in
My ways.
I would speedily subdue their enemies, and turn My hand against
their oppressors. Those who hate the Lord would shrivel before Him,
and the time [of the retribution] shall be forever.

And He would feed him [Israel] with the finest of wheat, and satisfy
him with honey from the rock.
Save us...*(found after the song for Sunday)*

CHASSIDIC EXCERPTS

ject to another"). And, therefore, the creations of the World of *yetzira* lack the intellectual grasp of the creations of *bria*. And that is what is meant by the statement in our prayers that the "*ofanim* and *chayot hakodesh*, with a great commotion, arise." [As angels of *Yetzira*], they become aroused with much noise and excitement. Now, their "commotion" is a result of their lack of intellectual grasp.

Friday

הַיּוֹם, יוֹם שִׁשִּׁי בְּשַׁבָּת, שֶׁבּוֹ הָיוּ הַלְוִיִּם אוֹמְרִים בְּבֵית הַמִּקְדָּשׁ:

יְיָ מָלָךְ גֵּאוּת לָבֵשׁ, לָבֵשׁ יְיָ, עֹז הִתְאַזָּר, אַף תִּכּוֹן תֵּבֵל בַּל תִּמּוֹט:

נָכוֹן כִּסְאֲךָ מֵאָז, מֵעוֹלָם אָתָּה:

נָשְׂאוּ נְהָרוֹת יְיָ, נָשְׂאוּ נְהָרוֹת קוֹלָם, יִשְׂאוּ נְהָרוֹת דָּכְיָם:

מִקֹּלוֹת מַיִם רַבִּים אַדִּירִים מִשְׁבְּרֵי יָם, אַדִּיר בַּמָּרוֹם יְיָ:

עֵדֹתֶיךָ נֶאֶמְנוּ מְאֹד, לְבֵיתְךָ נַאֲוָה קֹדֶשׁ, יְיָ, לְאֹרֶךְ יָמִים:

קדיש יתום הוֹשִׁיעֵנוּ וכו'

On Rosh Chodesh, after recital of The Song of the Day, Psalm 104 is recited:

בָּרְכִי נַפְשִׁי אֶת יְיָ, יְיָ אֱלֹהַי גָּדַלְתָּ מְּאֹד, הוֹד וְהָדָר לָבָשְׁתָּ:

עֹטֶה אוֹר כַּשַּׂלְמָה, נוֹטֶה שָׁמַיִם כַּיְרִיעָה:

הַמְקָרֶה בַמַּיִם עֲלִיּוֹתָיו, הַשָּׂם עָבִים רְכוּבוֹ, הַמְהַלֵּךְ, עַל כַּנְפֵי רוּחַ:

עֹשֶׂה מַלְאָכָיו רוּחוֹת, מְשָׁרְתָיו אֵשׁ לֹהֵט:

יָסַד אֶרֶץ עַל מְכוֹנֶיהָ, בַּל תִּמּוֹט עוֹלָם וָעֶד:

תְּהוֹם כַּלְּבוּשׁ כִּסִּיתוֹ, עַל הָרִים יַעַמְדוּ מָיִם:

מִן גַּעֲרָתְךָ יְנוּסוּן, מִן קוֹל רַעַמְךָ יֵחָפֵזוּן:

יַעֲלוּ הָרִים יֵרְדוּ בְקָעוֹת, אֶל מְקוֹם זֶה יָסַדְתָּ לָהֶם:

גְּבוּל שַׂמְתָּ בַּל יַעֲבֹרוּן, בַּל יְשֻׁבוּן, לְכַסּוֹת הָאָרֶץ:

CHASSIDIC EXCERPTS

The *chayot* of *yetzira*, realizing that the matter is beyond their understanding and that they can't grasp it, become aroused with noise and excitement.

And, now we may understand what the sages meant by, "All that the Prophet Ezekiel saw, Isaiah also saw, but Isaiah was like a city-dweller who saw the king, while Ezekiel was like a villager who saw the king."[373] Therefore, Ezekiel was more excited by what he saw, like a villager who is not used to seeing the greatness of the ruler, and therefore gets more excited. But the city-dweller, who regularly sees such displays of majesty, does not become so

On Friday's, we say Psalm 93

On the sixth day of the week, the Levites would say the following in the Holy Temple:

The Lord reigns; He is garbed in majesty, the Lord is en-clothed, He is girded with strength, and He has firmly established the globe so that it will not falter.

Your throne is firmly established from of old, You are from eternity. The rivers raise, Lord, the rivers raise their voices, the rivers uplift their waves.

More than the sound of mighty waters, and the [sound of] ocean breakers, is the might of the Lord above.

Your testimony is very trustworthy, Your house will be magnificent in holiness, Lord, forever.

Save us…*(found after the song for Sunday)*

On Rosh Chodesh (the beginning of the new month, which may be either one or two days), we recite the following after the song of the day:

My soul, bless the Lord; Lord my G-d, You are greatly exalted, You have garbed yourself with majesty and splendor.

You enwrap [Yourself] with light as with a garment: You spread the heavens as a curtain.

He roofs His heavens with water; He makes the clouds His chariot, He causes [them] to move on the wings of the wind.

He makes the wind His messengers, the blazing fire His servants.

He established the earth on its foundations, that it shall never falter.

The depths covered it like a garment; the waters stood above the mountains.

At Your exhortation they fled; at the sound of Your thunder they rushed away.

They ascended mountains, they flowed down valleys, to the place which You assigned to them.

You set a boundary which they may not cross, so that they should not return to engulf the earth.

CHASSIDIC EXCERPTS

excited. That is also the difference between the *seraphim* and the *chayot hakodesh*, since the *seraphim* are in *bria*, where *Imah* (or *bina*) resides, and therefore they do not make as much noise as the *chayot hakodesh*. And for that reason, the [*chayot* and *ofanim*] say *baruch kevod Havaya* ("blessed be the glory of G-d"), since they do not grasp any more than *baruch* (referring to *memalle kol olamim*), but they do not say *kadosh*, which corresponds to *sovev kol olamim*.

(From *Sefer Maamorim 5655* (1895-6) of the Rebbe Rashab, p.142-143)

הַמְשַׁלֵּחַ מַעְיָנִים בַּנְּחָלִים, בֵּין הָרִים יְהַלֵּכוּן:

יַשְׁקוּ כָּל חַיְתוֹ שָׂדָי, יִשְׁבְּרוּ פְרָאִים צְמָאָם:

עֲלֵיהֶם עוֹף הַשָּׁמַיִם יִשְׁכּוֹן, מִבֵּין עֳפָאיִם יִתְּנוּ קוֹל:

מַשְׁקֶה הָרִים מֵעֲלִיּוֹתָיו, מִפְּרִי מַעֲשֶׂיךָ תִּשְׂבַּע הָאָרֶץ:

מַצְמִיחַ חָצִיר לַבְּהֵמָה, וְעֵשֶׂב לַעֲבֹדַת הָאָדָם, לְהוֹצִיא לֶחֶם מִן הָאָרֶץ:

וְיַיִן יְשַׂמַּח לְבַב אֱנוֹשׁ, לְהַצְהִיל פָּנִים מִשָּׁמֶן, וְלֶחֶם, לְבַב אֱנוֹשׁ יִסְעָד:

יִשְׂבְּעוּ עֲצֵי יְיָ, אַרְזֵי לְבָנוֹן אֲשֶׁר נָטָע:

אֲשֶׁר שָׁם צִפֳּרִים יְקַנֵּנוּ, חֲסִידָה בְּרוֹשִׁים בֵּיתָהּ:

הָרִים הַגְּבֹהִים לַיְּעֵלִים, סְלָעִים מַחְסֶה לַשְׁפַנִּים:

עָשָׂה יָרֵחַ לְמוֹעֲדִים, שֶׁמֶשׁ יָדַע מְבוֹאוֹ:

תָּשֶׁת חֹשֶׁךְ וִיהִי לָיְלָה, בּוֹ תִרְמֹשׂ כָּל חַיְתוֹ יָעַר:

הַכְּפִירִים שֹׁאֲגִים לַטָּרֶף, וּלְבַקֵּשׁ מֵאֵל אָכְלָם:

תִּזְרַח הַשֶּׁמֶשׁ יֵאָסֵפוּן, וְאֶל מְעוֹנֹתָם יִרְבָּצוּן:

יֵצֵא אָדָם לְפָעֳלוֹ, וְלַעֲבֹדָתוֹ עֲדֵי עָרֶב:

מָה רַבּוּ מַעֲשֶׂיךָ יְיָ, כֻּלָּם בְּחָכְמָה עָשִׂיתָ, מָלְאָה הָאָרֶץ קִנְיָנֶךָ:

זֶה הַיָּם גָּדוֹל וּרְחַב יָדָיִם, שָׁם רֶמֶשׂ וְאֵין מִסְפָּר, חַיּוֹת קְטַנּוֹת עִם גְּדֹלוֹת:

שָׁם אֳנִיּוֹת יְהַלֵּכוּן, לִוְיָתָן זֶה יָצַרְתָּ לְשַׂחֶק בּוֹ:

כֻּלָּם אֵלֶיךָ יְשַׂבֵּרוּן, לָתֵת אָכְלָם בְּעִתּוֹ:

תִּתֵּן לָהֶם יִלְקֹטוּן, תִּפְתַּח יָדְךָ יִשְׂבְּעוּן טוֹב:

תַּסְתִּיר פָּנֶיךָ יִבָּהֵלוּן, תֹּסֵף רוּחָם יִגְוָעוּן, וְאֶל עֲפָרָם יְשׁוּבוּן:

תְּשַׁלַּח רוּחֲךָ יִבָּרֵאוּן, וּתְחַדֵּשׁ פְּנֵי אֲדָמָה:

יְהִי כְבוֹד יְיָ לְעוֹלָם, יִשְׂמַח יְיָ בְּמַעֲשָׂיו:

He sends forth springs into streams; they flow between the mountains.

They water all the beasts of the field; the wild animals quench their thirst.

Above them dwell the birds of the heaven; they raise their voices from among the foliage.

He irrigates the mountains from His clouds above; the earth is satiated from the fruit of Your works.

He causes grass to grow for the cattle; and vegetation for the labor of man, to bring forth food from the earth.

Wine that gladdens man's heart, oil that makes the face shine, and bread that sustains man's heart.

The trees of the Lord drink their fill, the cedars of Lebanon which He planted.

Wherein birds build their nests; the stork has her home in the cypress.

The high mountains are for the wild goats; the rocks are a refuge for the rabbits.

He made the moon to calculate the festivals; the sun knows its place of setting.

You bring on darkness and it is night, when all the beasts of the forest creep forth.

The young lions roar for prey, and seek their food from G-d.

When the sun rises, they return and lie down in their dens.

Then, man goes out to his work, to his labor until evening. How manifold are Your works, Lord, You have made them all with wisdom, the earth is full of Your possessions.

This sea, vast and wide, where there are countless creeping creatures, living things small and great.

There ships travel, there is the Leviatan that Your created to frolic therein. They all look expectantly to You to give them their food at the proper time.

When You give it to them, they gather it; when You open Your hand, they are satiated with goodness.

When you conceal Your countenance, they are terrified; when you take back their spirit, they perish and return to their dust.

When You send forth Your spirit they are created anew, and you renew the face of the earth.

May the glory of the Lord endure forever; may the Lord find delight in His works.

הַמַּבִּיט לָאָרֶץ וַתִּרְעָד, יִגַּע בֶּהָרִים וְיֶעֱשָׁנוּ:

אָשִׁירָה לַיְיָ בְּחַיָּי, אֲזַמְּרָה לֵאלֹהַי בְּעוֹדִי:

יֶעֱרַב עָלָיו שִׂיחִי, אָנֹכִי אֶשְׂמַח בַּיְיָ:

יִתַּמּוּ חַטָּאִים מִן הָאָרֶץ וּרְשָׁעִים עוֹד אֵינָם,

בָּרְכִי נַפְשִׁי אֶת יְיָ, הַלְלוּיָהּ:

From the first day of Rosh Chodesh Elul through Hosha'ana Rabba, Psalm 27, is recited:

לְדָוִד, יְיָ אוֹרִי וְיִשְׁעִי מִמִּי אִירָא, יְיָ מָעוֹז חַיַּי מִמִּי אֶפְחָד:

בִּקְרֹב עָלַי מְרֵעִים לֶאֱכֹל אֶת בְּשָׂרִי צָרַי וְאֹיְבַי לִי, הֵמָּה כָשְׁלוּ וְנָפָלוּ:

אִם תַּחֲנֶה עָלַי מַחֲנֶה לֹא יִירָא לִבִּי, אִם תָּקוּם עָלַי מִלְחָמָה, בְּזֹאת אֲנִי בוֹטֵחַ:

אַחַת שָׁאַלְתִּי מֵאֵת יְיָ אוֹתָהּ אֲבַקֵּשׁ, שִׁבְתִּי בְּבֵית יְיָ, כָּל יְמֵי חַיַּי, לַחֲזוֹת בְּנֹעַם יְיָ וּלְבַקֵּר בְּהֵיכָלוֹ:

כִּי יִצְפְּנֵנִי בְּסֻכֹּה בְּיוֹם רָעָה יַסְתִּרֵנִי בְּסֵתֶר אָהֳלוֹ, בְּצוּר יְרוֹמְמֵנִי:

וְעַתָּה יָרוּם רֹאשִׁי עַל אֹיְבַי סְבִיבוֹתַי, וְאֶזְבְּחָה בְאָהֳלוֹ זִבְחֵי תְרוּעָה, אָשִׁירָה וַאֲזַמְּרָה לַיְיָ:

שְׁמַע יְיָ קוֹלִי אֶקְרָא, וְחָנֵּנִי וַעֲנֵנִי:

לְךָ אָמַר לִבִּי, בַּקְּשׁוּ פָנָי, אֶת פָּנֶיךָ יְיָ אֲבַקֵּשׁ:

אַל תַּסְתֵּר פָּנֶיךָ מִמֶּנִּי, אַל תַּט בְּאַף עַבְדֶּךָ עֶזְרָתִי הָיִיתָ, אַל תִּטְּשֵׁנִי וְאַל תַּעַזְבֵנִי אֱלֹהֵי יִשְׁעִי:

כִּי אָבִי וְאִמִּי עֲזָבוּנִי, וַיְיָ יַאַסְפֵנִי:

הוֹרֵנִי יְיָ דַּרְכֶּךָ וּנְחֵנִי בְּאֹרַח מִישׁוֹר, לְמַעַן שׁוֹרְרָי:

אַל תִּתְּנֵנִי בְּנֶפֶשׁ צָרָי, כִּי קָמוּ בִי עֵדֵי שֶׁקֶר וִיפֵחַ חָמָס:

לוּלֵא הֶאֱמַנְתִּי לִרְאוֹת בְּטוּב יְיָ בְּאֶרֶץ חַיִּים:

קַוֵּה אֶל יְיָ חֲזַק וְיַאֲמֵץ לִבֶּךָ וְקַוֵּה אֶל יְיָ:

He gazes upon the earth and it trembles; he touches the mountains and they erupt.

I sing to the Lord with my life: I chant praise to my G-d with my [entire] being.

May my prayer be pleasant to Him; I will rejoice in the Lord.

May sin be excised from the earth, and the wicked be no more.

Bless the Lord, my soul, Halleluyah!

From the first day of Rosh Chodesh Elul through Hosha'ana Rabba, Psalm 27, is recited:

For David; the Lord is my light and my salvation – whom shall I fear? The Lord is the strength of my life – whom shall I dread? When evildoers approached me to devour my flesh, my oppressors and my foes, they stumbled and fell.

If an army were to beleaguer me, my heart would not fear; if war were to arise against me, in this I trust.

One thing I have asked of the Lord, this I seek; that I may dwell in the House of the Lord all the days of my life, to behold the pleasantness of the Lord and to meditate in His Sanctuary.

For He will hide me in His tabernacle on the day of adversity; He will conceal me in the nooks of His tent; He will lift me upon a rock.

And now, my head will be raised above my enemies surrounding me, and I will offer sacrifices of jubilation in His tabernacle; I will sing and chant to the Lord.

Lord, hear my voice as I call; be gracious to me and answer me.

On Your behalf my heart says, "Seek My countenance," Your countenance, Lord I will seek.

Do not conceal your countenance from me, nor cast aside Your servant in wrath; You have been my help; do not abandon me nor forsake me, G-d of my deliverance.

Though my father and mother have forsaken me, the Lord has taken me in.

Lord, teach me Your way and lead me in the path of righteousness because of my watchful enemies.

Do not give me over to the will of my oppressors, for there have risen against me false witnesses and they speak evil.

[They would have crushed me] had I not believed that I would see the goodness of the Lord in the land of the living.

Hope in the Lord, be strong, and He will give your heart courage, and hope in the Lord.

קַדִּישׁ יָתוֹם

יִתְגַּדַּל וְיִתְקַדַּשׁ שְׁמֵהּ רַבָּא. (Cong: אָמֵן)

בְּעָלְמָא דִּי בְרָא כִרְעוּתֵהּ וְיַמְלִיךְ מַלְכוּתֵהּ, וְיַצְמַח פֻּרְקָנֵהּ וִיקָרֵב מְשִׁיחֵהּ.
(Cong: אָמֵן)

בְּחַיֵּיכוֹן וּבְיוֹמֵיכוֹן וּבְחַיֵּי דְכָל בֵּית יִשְׂרָאֵל, בַּעֲגָלָא וּבִזְמַן קָרִיב. וְאִמְרוּ אָמֵן.
(Cong: אָמֵן. יְהֵא שְׁמֵהּ רַבָּא מְבָרַךְ לְעָלַם וּלְעָלְמֵי עָלְמַיָּא, יִתְבָּרֵךְ:)

יְהֵא שְׁמֵהּ רַבָּא מְבָרַךְ לְעָלַם וּלְעָלְמֵי עָלְמַיָּא, יִתְבָּרֵךְ, וְיִשְׁתַּבַּח, וְיִתְפָּאַר,
וְיִתְרוֹמַם, וְיִתְנַשֵּׂא, וְיִתְהַדָּר, וְיִתְעַלֶּה, וְיִתְהַלָּל, שְׁמֵהּ דְּקֻדְשָׁא בְּרִיךְ הוּא. (Cong: אָמֵן)

לְעֵלָּא מִן כָּל בִּרְכָתָא וְשִׁירָתָא, תֻּשְׁבְּחָתָא וְנֶחֱמָתָא, דַּאֲמִירָן בְּעָלְמָא, וְאִמְרוּ
אָמֵן (Cong: אָמֵן)

יְהֵא שְׁלָמָה רַבָּא מִן שְׁמַיָּא וְחַיִּים טוֹבִים עָלֵינוּ וְעַל כָּל יִשְׂרָאֵל, וְאִמְרוּ אָמֵן:

עֹשֶׂה שָׁלוֹם (הַשָּׁלוֹם - *During the Ten Days of Repentance substitute*) בִּמְרוֹמָיו הוּא
יַעֲשֶׂה שָׁלוֹם עָלֵינוּ וְעַל כָּל יִשְׂרָאֵל, וְאִמְרוּ אָמֵן:

אֵין כֵּאלֹקֵינוּ

קַוֵּה אֶל יְיָ, חֲזַק וְיַאֲמֵץ לִבֶּךָ וְקַוֵּה אֶל יְיָ: אֵין קָדוֹשׁ כַּיְיָ, כִּי אֵין בִּלְתֶּךָ, וְאֵין צוּר
כֵּאלֹהֵינוּ: כִּי מִי אֱלוֹהַּ מִבַּלְעֲדֵי יְיָ; וּמִי צוּר זוּלָתִי אֱלֹהֵינוּ:

אֵ‏ין כֵּאלֹהֵינוּ, אֵין כַּאדוֹנֵינוּ, אֵין כְּמַלְכֵּנוּ, אֵין כְּמוֹשִׁיעֵנוּ:

מִי כֵאלֹהֵינוּ, מִי כַאדוֹנֵינוּ, מִי כְמַלְכֵּנוּ, מִי כְמוֹשִׁיעֵנוּ:

נוֹדֶה לֵאלֹהֵינוּ, נוֹדֶה לַאדוֹנֵינוּ, נוֹדֶה לְמַלְכֵּנוּ, נוֹדֶה לְמוֹשִׁיעֵנוּ:

בָּרוּךְ אֱלֹהֵינוּ, בָּרוּךְ אֲדוֹנֵינוּ, בָּרוּךְ מַלְכֵּנוּ, בָּרוּךְ מוֹשִׁיעֵנוּ:

אַתָּה הוּא אֱלֹהֵינוּ, אַתָּה הוּא אֲדוֹנֵינוּ, אַתָּה הוּא מַלְכֵּנוּ, אַתָּה הוּא
מוֹשִׁיעֵנוּ, אַתָּה תוֹשִׁיעֵנוּ:

אַתָּה תָקוּם תְּרַחֵם צִיּוֹן כִּי עֵת לְחֶנְנָהּ, כִּי בָא מוֹעֵד:

אַתָּה הוּא יְיָ אֱלֹהֵינוּ וֵאלֹהֵי אֲבוֹתֵינוּ, שֶׁהִקְטִירוּ אֲבוֹתֵינוּ לְפָנֶיךָ אֶת
קְטֹרֶת הַסַּמִּים:

The Mourners Kaddish

Exalted and sanctified is His great Name. (cong: "Amen")

In the universe that He created according to His Will, May He establish His reign, and sprout forth His redemption, and quickly bring His meshiach. (cong: "Amen")

In your life and during your days and in the life of the entire house of Israel, speedily and soon, and say Amen!

(the congregation here says, "Amen, may His great Name be blessed forever and for eternity")

May His great Name be blessed forever and for eternity. May He be blessed, may He be extolled, may He be glorified, may He be exalted, may He be elevated, may He be honored, may He be lauded, and may he be praised, the Name of the holy One, blessed be He. (cong: "Amen")

Beyond all the blessings and the hymns, the praises and the consolations that are recited in the world, and let us say Amen.

May there be plentiful peace from Heaven and a good life for all of us and for all of Israel, and let us say, Amen (cong: "Amen").

He Who makes peace (during ten days of repentance – "the peace") on high, may He create peace for us and for all of Israel, and let us say Amen (cong: "Amen").

Ein Kelokeinu

Hope in the Lord, be strong, and He will give your heart courage, and hope in the Lord. None is holy like the Lord, for there is none other than You, and there is no fortress like our G-d. For, Who is G-d aside from the Lord, and Who is a fortress aside from our G-d.

There is none like our G-d, there is none like our Lord, there is none like our King, there is none like our Deliverer

Who is like our G-d, who is like our Lord, who is like our King, who is like our Deliverer?

We acknowledge our G-d, we acknowledge our Lord, we acknowledge our King, we acknowledge our Deliverer.

Blessed is our G-d, blessed is our Lord, blessed is our King, blessed is our Deliverer!

You are our G-d, You are our Lord, You are our King, Your are our Deliverer!

You will save us!

You will arise, comfort Zion, for the time to be gracious to her has arrived, for the season is upon us!

It is You, Lord, our G-d and the G-d of our fathers, before Whom our fathers burned the smoke of the incense.

פִּטּוּם הַקְּטֹרֶת, הַצֳּרִי, וְהַצִּפֹּרֶן, הַחֶלְבְּנָה, וְהַלְּבוֹנָה, מִשְׁקַל שִׁבְעִים מָנֶה, מוֹר,

וּקְצִיעָה, שִׁבֹּלֶת נֵרְדְּ, וְכַרְכֹּם, מִשְׁקַל שִׁשָּׁה עָשָׂר שִׁשָּׁה עָשָׂר מָנֶה, הַקֹּשְׁטְ

שְׁנֵים עָשָׂר, קִלּוּפָה שְׁלֹשָׁה, קִנָּמוֹן תִּשְׁעָה, בֹּרִית כַּרְשִׁינָה תִּשְׁעָה קַבִּין, יֵין

קַפְרִיסִין סְאִין תְּלָתָא וְקַבִּין תְּלָתָא, וְאִם אֵין לוֹ יֵין קַפְרִיסִין סְאִין תְּלָתָא וְקַבִּין

תְּלָתָא, וְאִם אֵין לוֹ יֵין קַפְרִיסִין מֵבִיא חֲמַר חִוַּרְיָן עַתִּיק, מֶלַח סְדוֹמִית רוֹבַע,

מַעֲלֶה עָשָׁן, כָּל שֶׁהוּא.

רַבִּי נָתָן הַבַּבְלִי אוֹמֵר, אַף כִּפַּת הַיַּרְדֵּן כָּל שֶׁהִיא, וְאִם נָתַן בָּהּ דְּבַשׁ פְּסָלָהּ,

וְאִם חִסַּר אֶחָד מִכָּל סַמְּמָנֶיהָ חַיָּב מִיתָה:

רַבָּן שִׁמְעוֹן בֶּן גַּמְלִיאֵל אוֹמֵר, הַצֳּרִי אֵינוֹ אֶלָּא שְׂרָף הַנּוֹטֵף מֵעֲצֵי הַקְּטָף,

בֹּרִית כַּרְשִׁינָה שֶׁשָּׁפִין בָּהּ אֶת הַצִּפֹּרֶן, כְּדֵי שֶׁתְּהֵא נָאָה; יֵין קַפְרִיסִין שֶׁשּׁוֹרִין

בּוֹ אֶת הַצִּפֹּרֶן, כְּדֵי שֶׁתְּהֵא עַזָּה. וַהֲלֹא מֵי רַגְלַיִם יָפִין לָהּ, אֶלָּא שֶׁאֵין

מַכְנִיסִין מֵי רַגְלַיִם בַּמִּקְדָּשׁ מִפְּנֵי הַכָּבוֹד:

תָּנָא דְּבֵי אֵלִיָּהוּ כָּל הַשּׁוֹנֶה הֲלָכוֹת בְּכָל יוֹם מֻבְטָח לוֹ שֶׁהוּא בֶּן עוֹלָם הַבָּא

שֶׁנֶּאֱמַר הֲלִיכוֹת עוֹלָם לוֹ, אַל תִּקְרֵי הֲלִיכוֹת אֶלָּא הֲלָכוֹת:

אָמַר רַבִּי אֶלְעָזָר אָמַר רַבִּי חֲנִינָא, תַּלְמִידֵי חֲכָמִים מַרְבִּים שָׁלוֹם בָּעוֹלָם,

שֶׁנֶּאֱמַר וְכָל בָּנַיִךְ לִמּוּדֵי יְיָ, וְרַב שְׁלוֹם בָּנָיִךְ: אַל תִּקְרֵי בָּנָיִךְ, אֶלָּא בּוֹנָיִךְ:

שָׁלוֹם רָב לְאֹהֲבֵי תוֹרָתֶךְ, וְאֵין לָמוֹ מִכְשׁוֹל:

From intellect to emotion, with song

Our emotions (even the emotions within our intellect) are distinct from our intellect. Essentially, they are two entities that exist separate from one another. That is, the intellect is a distinct entity that does not exist merely for the purpose of bringing forth emotions ... And, therefore, the content that flows from the intellect and elicits our most es-sential emotions undergoes a process of contraction and interruption. This process is similar to the role played by the throat in the body. The throat is the site of interruption and discontinuity between the mind and the emotions, and the "interruption" is what enables the transformation from intellect-in-essence to emotions-in-essence to take place ...

The composition of the incense includes, balm, onycha, galanum, frankincense – each of which weighed seventy units; there was myrrh, cassia, spikenard, and saffron, each of which weighed sixteen units. There was costus, weighing twelve units, and aromatic bark weighing three units, and cinnamon, which weighed nine units. There were nine kavin of lye from carshina used in the preparation, as well as three kavin and three se'in of Cypriot wine, and if there was no wine from Cyprus available, strong, white wine could be used instead. A quarter kab of sodomite salt went into the preparation, as well as a tiny bit of a herb for smoking.

R' Natan the Babylonian said that a small amount of Jordan amber was used as well. If any honey was added, [the mixture] became invalid, and if any one of these spices were missing, the [person making the mixture] was liable for capital punishment.

Raban Shimon ben Gamliel says, balm is nothing more than sap that exudes from balsam trees. Lye of carshina is used to massage the onycha and make it look nice, and Cypriot wine is used to marinate the onycha and make it stronger. Now, uric acid would also be good for this job, but we do not bring uric acid into the Temple out of respect.

The House of Eliyahu said, "Those who review Jewish law every day, are certain to attain the world to come, as it is said, 'Eternal ways (halichot) are His': Do not say ways (halichot), but rather Torah laws (halachot)."

Rebi Elazar said in the name of Rebi Chanina, "Torah scholars increase peace in the world, as it says, 'And all of your children (banayich) are students of the Lord, and great will be the peace of your children.' Do not say "your children" (banayich), but rather "your builders" (bonayich)."

There is great peace among those who love Your Torah, and they do not stumble:

CHASSIDIC EXCERPTS

This means that the emotions do not emerge spontaneously from the mind, but only after a process wherein the intellect disappears and re-appears in a contracted form, distinct from its previous state. The new state is called a *b'chen* ("sum-total") – the result of the preceding intellectual concept leaving its impression on an emotion in our heart.

To begin with, our intellect grasps the G-dly concept which is the subject of meditation, and a new understanding emerges. This is how the mind works in order to grasp a new idea. And then, after the contraction and interruption mentioned above, the intellect descends to illuminate in a different manner altogether, as something completely new. Our [new awareness] may be described by the phrase, "Closeness to G-d is good

יְהִי שָׁלוֹם בְּחֵילֵךְ, שַׁלְוָה בְּאַרְמְנוֹתָיִךְ:

לְמַעַן אַחַי וְרֵעָי אֲדַבְּרָה נָּא שָׁלוֹם בָּךְ:

לְמַעַן בֵּית יְיָ אֱלֹהֵינוּ, אֲבַקְשָׁה טוֹב לָךְ:

יְיָ עֹז לְעַמּוֹ יִתֵּן, יְיָ יְבָרֵךְ אֶת עַמּוֹ בַשָּׁלוֹם:

קדיש דרבנן

יִתְגַּדַּל וְיִתְקַדַּשׁ שְׁמֵהּ רַבָּא. (Cong: אָמֵן)

בְּעָלְמָא דִּי בְרָא כִרְעוּתֵהּ וְיַמְלִיךְ מַלְכוּתֵהּ, וְיַצְמַח פֻּרְקָנֵהּ וִיקָרֵב מְשִׁיחֵהּ. (Cong: אָמֵן)

בְּחַיֵּיכוֹן וּבְיוֹמֵיכוֹן וּבְחַיֵּי דְכָל בֵּית יִשְׂרָאֵל, בַּעֲגָלָא וּבִזְמַן קָרִיב. וְאִמְרוּ אָמֵן:

(יְהֵא שְׁמֵהּ רַבָּא מְבָרַךְ לְעָלַם וּלְעָלְמֵי עָלְמַיָּא, יִתְבָּרַךְ:)

יְהֵא שְׁמֵהּ רַבָּא מְבָרַךְ לְעָלַם וּלְעָלְמֵי עָלְמַיָּא, יִתְבָּרַךְ, וְיִשְׁתַּבַּח, וְיִתְפָּאַר, וְיִתְרוֹמַם, וְיִתְנַשֵּׂא, וְיִתְהַדָּר, וְיִתְעַלֶּה, וְיִתְהַלָּל, שְׁמֵהּ דְּקֻדְשָׁא בְּרִיךְ הוּא. (Cong: אָמֵן) לְעֵלָּא מִן כָּל בִּרְכָתָא וְשִׁירָתָא, תֻּשְׁבְּחָתָא וְנֶחֱמָתָא, דַּאֲמִירָן בְּעָלְמָא, וְאִמְרוּ אָמֵן: (Cong: אָמֵן)

עַל יִשְׂרָאֵל וְעַל רַבָּנָן. וְעַל תַּלְמִידֵיהוֹן וְעַל כָּל תַּלְמִידֵי תַלְמִידֵיהוֹן. וְעַל כָּל מָאן דְּעָסְקִין בְּאוֹרַיְתָא דִּי בְאַתְרָא הָדֵין וְדִי בְכָל אֲתַר וַאֲתַר. יְהֵא לְהוֹן וּלְכוֹן שְׁלָמָא רַבָּא חִנָּא וְחִסְדָּא וְרַחֲמִין וְחַיִּין אֲרִיכִין וּמְזוֹנָא רְוִיחָא וּפֻרְקָנָא מִן קֳדָם אֲבוּהוֹן דִּבִשְׁמַיָּא וְאִמְרוּ אָמֵן:

יְהֵא שְׁלָמָא רַבָּא מִן שְׁמַיָּא וְחַיִּים טוֹבִים עָלֵינוּ וְעַל כָּל יִשְׂרָאֵל, וְאִמְרוּ אָמֵן:

עֹשֶׂה שָׁלוֹם (הַשָּׁלוֹם - During the Ten Days of Repentance substitute) בִּמְרוֹמָיו הוּא יַעֲשֶׂה שָׁלוֹם עָלֵינוּ וְעַל כָּל יִשְׂרָאֵל, וְאִמְרוּ אָמֵן:

CHASSIDIC EXCERPTS

for me"[374] – this is intellect within emotion which is completely different in nature and essence than intellectual understanding and meditation itself, as will be explained. And [with this new awareness], the emotions come alive and love is aroused in the heart. But, no emotions of the heart can emerge from the mind and intellect alone...

Full-fledged emotions do not emerge spontaneously from our intel-

lect, but rather only after contraction and interruption. And this is why the verse states, "And you should know today and place it upon your heart..."[375] That is, there is a commandment to place the concept [on which we are meditating] on our heart. But why is it not sufficient for it to remain in our knowledge and intellect alone?

Knowledge and logical grasp alone do not have the power to arouse emo-

Let there be peace within your walls, serenity in your palaces.

For the sake of my brothers and my friends, I speak of peace among You.

For the sake of the House of the Lord, our G-d, I seek your welfare.

The Lord shall give strength to His people, the Lord will bless His people with peace.

The Rabbis' Kaddish

Exalted and sanctified is His great Name. (cong: "Amen") In the universe that He created according to His Will, May He establish His reign, and sprout forth His redemption, and quickly bring His meshiach. (cong: "Amen") In your life and during your days and in the life of the entire house of Israel, speedily and soon, and say Amen! (the congregation here says, "Amen, may His great Name be blessed forever and for eternity") May His great Name be blessed forever and for eternity. (cong: "Amen") May He be blessed, may He be extolled, may He be glorified, may He be exalted, may He be elevated, may He be honored, may He be lauded, and may he be praised, the Name of the holy One, blessed be He. (cong: "Amen") Beyond all the blessings and the hymns, the praises and the consolations that are recited in the world, and let us say Amen.

Upon Israel, and upon the rabbis, and upon their students and upon all the students of their students, and upon all those who are involved in Torah, whether in this place or whether in any other place, they and you should experience much peace, harmony and kindness and mercy and long life and plentiful sustenance and salvation from before their King in the heavens, and let us say, Amen.

May there be plentiful peace from Heaven and a good life for all of us and for all of Israel, and let us say, Amen (cong: "Amen").

He Who makes peace (during ten days of repentance – "the peace") on high, may He create peace for us and for all of Israel, and let us say Amen (cong: "Amen").

CHASSIDIC EXCERPTS

tions within our heart. That is why we must undergo "placement upon our heart," so that our heart will become illuminated with the light of the intellect shining within the emotions. There must occur an arousal of the emotions via the contraction and interruption mentioned earlier, so that the *b'chen* will descend. In order to produce the emotions, this contraction and interruption takes place on its own, spontaneously.

Although it is true that the mind and the emotions are two distinct entities, nevertheless, since they exist as cause and effect in relation to each other, and since within the mind there are also emotions, our meditation and logical grasp leads on its own to the straits of the throat, [where it undergoes the process] of interruption and disappearance [of the intellectual concept] before it is revealed, transformed in essence to

CHASSIDIC INSIGHTS

According to tradition, the closing prayer, *Aleinu* was composed by Joshua. When he entered the Land of Israel near Jericho and encountered the idol worship and witchcraft that was widespread among the seven Canaanite nations, he fells on his knees and raised his hands to G-d, proclaiming *Aleinu leshabeach* ("It is incumbent upon us to praise the Master of all"). Others say that it was the Talmud sage known as the Rav who authored this prayer. In either case, it is an ancient prayer, coming from either well before the time

עָלֵינוּ

עָלֵינוּ לְשַׁבֵּחַ לַאֲדוֹן הַכֹּל, לָתֵת גְּדֻלָּה
לְיוֹצֵר בְּרֵאשִׁית,

שֶׁלֹּא עָשָׂנוּ כְּגוֹיֵי הָאֲרָצוֹת, וְלֹא שָׂמָנוּ
כְּמִשְׁפְּחוֹת הָאֲדָמָה, שֶׁלֹּא שָׂם חֶלְקֵנוּ כָּהֶם,
וְגֹרָלֵנוּ כְּכָל הֲמוֹנָם.

שֶׁהֵם מִשְׁתַּחֲוִים לְהֶבֶל וָרִיק.

וַאֲנַחְנוּ כּוֹרְעִים וּמִשְׁתַּחֲוִים וּמוֹדִים, לִפְנֵי
מֶלֶךְ, מַלְכֵי הַמְּלָכִים, הַקָּדוֹשׁ, בָּרוּךְ הוּא:
שֶׁהוּא נוֹטֶה שָׁמַיִם וְיוֹסֵד אָרֶץ, וּמוֹשַׁב
יְקָרוֹ בַּשָּׁמַיִם מִמַּעַל, וּשְׁכִינַת עֻזּוֹ בְּגָבְהֵי
מְרוֹמִים,

הוּא אֱלֹהֵינוּ אֵין עוֹד. אֱמֶת מַלְכֵּנוּ, אֶפֶס
זוּלָתוֹ, כַּכָּתוּב בְּתוֹרָתוֹ:

from either well before the time when the First Temple stood, or from the "Men of the Great Assembly" during the Second Temple period.

In *Aleinu*, we find a hint to the *Shema*, since the first and last letters of both paragraphs of *Aleinu* are *eyn* and *dalet*. These, of course, are the enlarged letters that we find in the first verse of the *Shema*, which together spell *eid* ("witness"). Thus, embedded within *Aleinu* is a hint at the entire purpose of our prayers, which is to ascend the ladder of spirituality until our perception of G-dliness is akin to "seeing," the way a witness sees. The goal is to experience G-dliness, as something that we can see, if not with our naked eye, than in our "mind's eye." That was the goal of Moses, our teacher, when he brought the Jews into Israel. By standing on the mountain ridge overlooking the entire land and peering into the Land of Israel, he managed to instill the potential within every Jew to "see" G-dliness in his/her mind's eye. [185]

Had Moshe actually entered the land, we would now perceive G-dliness as an integral part of creation with our naked eye. But, since G-d did not allow Moses to enter, he stood from afar and instilled in us something akin to vision. He instilled in us the power to meditate

CHASSIDIC EXCERPTS

become emotions within the heart.

However, all this applies [only] when we have prepared ourselves for prayer with the goal of achieving arousal of our heart. Then, the expansion and expression of our intellect, coupled with the depth of knowledge achieved [through meditation], leads the emotion to emerge spontaneously, according to the order described above. That is, the initial illumination of intellect disappears, temporarily interrupted, and then re-appears in a more distant, transcendent form. At this moment, we are neither detached nor separate from the subject of our meditation. Rather, we are pre-occupied with it and absorbed in our excitement over our intellectual grasp of the G-dly concept upon which we meditated and which we came to understand. But, the concept itself only illuminates from afar, not truly permeating our minds as it did before. And then, spontaneously, it

CHASSIDIC INSIGHTS

(especially when we are in the Land of Israel), according to the methods described throughout this *Siddur*, in order to gain spiritual awareness. In so doing, he enabled us to climb the ladder of spirituality and cleave to G-d. Thus, we fulfill the hint embedded in the *Shema* and in *Aleinu*, to become witnesses to His Presence and dominion over the universe.

*

There is one more point to consider in closing. The process of prayer is demanding. It requires discipline and focus over a significant period of time, usually an hour or more. As we conclude our prayers, we may feel a certain agitation or energy that is left over from focusing and concentrating for a long time. It is important that we find a use for that energy, for otherwise it may spill over and be channeled in ways that are not constructive. That is why the best thing to do after prayer is to sit and learn some Torah.

The story is told in the Talmud about Rabbi Shimon bar Yochai, who was a student of the famed Rabbi Akiva and redactor of the *Zohar*. R' Shimon hid in a cave and learned Torah for twelve years together with his son in order to escape the wrath of the Romans who sought to eliminate any vestiges of Torah in the Holy Land. When, after twelve years, he was informed that the danger had passed and he could now emerge from hiding, he did exactly that. He emerged from his cave and found men working in the fields. He was enraged that they were not learning Torah, and everywhere that he glanced, his piercing vision incinerated the field. A voice then emerged from the heavens saying, "Who is destroying my world?"

Aleinu

*I*t is incumbent upon us to praise the Master of all, to glorify the Maker of creation,

For He did not make us like the nations of the earth, nor did He place us among the families of the land; He has not assigned us a portion like theirs, nor placed our lot among all of their masses. For they bow down to vanity and emptiness.

And we bend at the knee, bow down and concede before the King, King of Kings, the Holy One, blessed is He.

For He stretches out the heavens and establishes the earth, and His throne of glory is in the heavens above, and the abode of His mighty presence is in the loftiest heights.

He is our G-d, there is no other; in truth He is our King, and there is none beside Him, as written in His Torah:

CHASSIDIC EXCERPTS

emerges transformed from one essence into another, and we experience the *b'chen* of the meditation, [whereupon it blossoms] into full arousal and revelation in the heart. And this all takes place spontaneously, without effort on our part to transform it from one essence into another.

But, when we have not prepared our soul to arouse the emotions, then we must become consciously involved and aware of the *b'chen* [as it emerges] following intellectual understanding. We must feel it in our heart, so that the emotions of the heart become aroused. And it is understood that, in this case, neither our experience of the *b'chen* nor our conscious arousal of emotions are truly real ... we may become excited in our heart regarding the concept, and we may also receive a bit of illumination, bringing us somewhat closer to G-dliness ... but when we meditate thoroughly upon the details of the concept,

CHASSIDIC INSIGHTS

And G-d told Rabbi Shimon to re-enter the cave and learn for another year, because he wasn't taken out of hiding in order to do harm. Rabbi Shimon learned for one more year, and when he emerged the next year, he lived in peace in the world.

Rabbi Shimon was unique – Torah was his profession. He was free from the obligation of prayer,

וְיָדַעְתָּ הַיּוֹם וַהֲשֵׁבֹתָ אֶל לְבָבֶךָ, כִּי יְיָ הוּא הָאֱלֹהִים בַּשָּׁמַיִם מִמַּעַל, וְעַל הָאָרֶץ מִתָּחַת, אֵין עוֹד:

וְעַל כֵּן נְקַוֶּה לְּךָ יְיָ אֱלֹהֵינוּ, לִרְאוֹת מְהֵרָה בְּתִפְאֶרֶת עֻזֶּךָ, לְהַעֲבִיר גִּלּוּלִים מִן הָאָרֶץ וְהָאֱלִילִים כָּרוֹת יִכָּרֵתוּן, לְתַקֵּן עוֹלָם בְּמַלְכוּת שַׁדַּי;

וְכָל בְּנֵי בָשָׂר יִקְרְאוּ בִשְׁמֶךָ, לְהַפְנוֹת אֵלֶיךָ כָּל רִשְׁעֵי אָרֶץ.

יַכִּירוּ וְיֵדְעוּ כָּל יוֹשְׁבֵי תֵבֵל, כִּי לְךָ תִּכְרַע כָּל בֶּרֶךְ, תִּשָּׁבַע כָּל לָשׁוֹן.

לְפָנֶיךָ יְיָ אֱלֹהֵינוּ יִכְרְעוּ וְיִפּוֹלוּ, וְלִכְבוֹד שִׁמְךָ יְקָר יִתֵּנוּ

וִיקַבְּלוּ כֻלָּם אֶת עוֹל מַלְכוּתֶךָ, וְתִמְלֹךְ עֲלֵיהֶם מְהֵרָה לְעוֹלָם וָעֶד,

כִּי הַמַּלְכוּת שֶׁלְּךָ הִיא, וּלְעוֹלְמֵי עַד תִּמְלוֹךְ בְּכָבוֹד, כַּכָּתוּב בְּתוֹרָתֶךָ:

יְיָ יִמְלֹךְ לְעוֹלָם וָעֶד.

וְנֶאֱמַר: וְהָיָה יְיָ לְמֶלֶךְ עַל כָּל הָאָרֶץ, בַּיּוֹם הַהוּא יִהְיֶה יְיָ אֶחָד וּשְׁמוֹ אֶחָד:

delving deeply with our faculty of da'at, then no active effort is necessary to bring the concept down to our heart and to produce arousal of our emotions. Although it is true that our grasp of the concept is transformed from one essence to another by way of the contraction and interruption mentioned previously, nevertheless it all occurs spontaneously...

All this occurs only when there is proper preparation of the soul for arousal of the heart. But, when there has been no preparation of the soul for an arousal of the heart, it is possible that the excitement will remain in the mind alone. And then, even meditation on the details of the concept in breadth and depth[376] will not cause the [intellectual] illumination to shine into the inner recesses of our heart, and it will remain in

CHASSIDIC INSIGHTS

because his Torah learning was so intense that he achieved far more by learning Torah than we achieve with our prayers. But for the rest of us, learning Torah is the best way to channel our energy after an hour of intense prayer. Lest that un-focused energy be used to destroy some part of our own personal world, it is best to spend some time learning some Torah after prayers.

"And you shall know this today, and place it on your heart, that the Lord is G-d, in the heavens above and on the earth below, there is no other."

A—nd therefore, we place our hope in You, Lord our G-d, to soon behold Your glorious might, to wipe away idols from the earth, and to surely excise false gods, in order to rectify the world for the kingdom of G-d.

And all beings of flesh will invoke Your Name, and all the wicked of the world will turn to You.

All who dwell on the globe will know and recognize You, for every knee will bow to You, and every language swear in Your Name.

Before You, Lord, our G-d, they will bow and they will fall down (prostrate themselves), and in honor of Your Name, they will express respect.

And all of them will accept upon themselves the yoke of Your reign, and You will reign over them soon, forever and ever.

For Kingship is Yours, forever and for all eternity You will reign in glory, as written in your Torah,

"The Lord will reign forever and ever."

And it says, "And the Lord will be the King over all the earth, on that day, the Lord will be one and His Name one."

CHASSIDIC EXCERPTS

the mind alone. And, as well, the excitement [over the illumination] will remain in the mind.

[Therefore, preparation is essential.] The preparation consists of the sadness that we experience before our prayers, as we account for our good and bad deeds [and consequent distance from G-d]. Additionally, our involvement with the inner dimensions of Torah –

that is, learning Chasidut before prayers – opens our heart and draw us closer to G-dliness.

But sometimes, even when there is some preparation in the soul as mentioned earlier, it is still necessary for us to find a way to cause it to illuminate the heart and to produce real emotions. And this takes place by way of the sound of

קדיש יתום

יִתְגַּדַּל וְיִתְקַדַּשׁ שְׁמֵהּ רַבָּא. (Cong: אָמֵן)

בְּעָלְמָא דִּי בְרָא כִרְעוּתֵהּ וְיַמְלִיךְ מַלְכוּתֵהּ, וְיַצְמַח פֻּרְקָנֵהּ וִיקָרֵב מְשִׁיחֵהּ. (Cong: אָמֵן)

בְּחַיֵּיכוֹן וּבְיוֹמֵיכוֹן וּבְחַיֵּי דְכָל בֵּית יִשְׂרָאֵל, בַּעֲגָלָא וּבִזְמַן קָרִיב. וְאִמְרוּ אָמֵן:

(Cong: אָמֵן. יְהֵא שְׁמֵהּ רַבָּא מְבָרַךְ לְעָלַם וּלְעָלְמֵי עָלְמַיָּא, יִתְבָּרַךְ:)

יְהֵא שְׁמֵהּ רַבָּא מְבָרַךְ לְעָלַם וּלְעָלְמֵי עָלְמַיָּא, יִתְבָּרַךְ, וְיִשְׁתַּבַּח, וְיִתְפָּאַר, וְיִתְרוֹמַם,

וְיִתְנַשֵּׂא, וְיִתְהַדָּר, וְיִתְעַלֶּה, וְיִתְהַלָּל, שְׁמֵהּ דְּקֻדְשָׁא בְּרִיךְ הוּא. (Cong: אָמֵן) לְעֵלָּא מִן

כָּל בִּרְכָתָא וְשִׁירָתָא, תֻּשְׁבְּחָתָא וְנֶחֱמָתָא, דַּאֲמִירָן בְּעָלְמָא, וְאִמְרוּ אָמֵן: (Cong: אָמֵן)

יְהֵא שְׁלָמָא רַבָּא מִן שְׁמַיָּא וְחַיִּים טוֹבִים עָלֵינוּ וְעַל כָּל יִשְׂרָאֵל, וְאִמְרוּ אָמֵן:

עֹשֶׂה שָׁלוֹם (During the Ten Days of Penitence substitute - הַשָּׁלוֹם) בִּמְרוֹמָיו הוּא יַעֲשֶׂה

שָׁלוֹם עָלֵינוּ וְעַל כָּל יִשְׂרָאֵל, וְאִמְרוּ אָמֵן:

אַל תִּירָא מִפַּחַד פִּתְאֹם, וּמִשֹּׁאַת רְשָׁעִים כִּי תָבֹא:

עֻצוּ עֵצָה וְתֻפָר, דַּבְּרוּ דָבָר וְלֹא יָקוּם כִּי עִמָּנוּ אֵל:

וְעַד זִקְנָה אֲנִי הוּא, וְעַד שֵׂיבָה אֲנִי אֶסְבֹּל; אֲנִי עָשִׂיתִי וַאֲנִי אֶשָּׂא וַאֲנִי אֶסְבֹּל

וַאֲמַלֵּט:

אַךְ צַדִּיקִים יוֹדוּ לִשְׁמֶךָ יֵשְׁבוּ יְשָׁרִים אֶת פָּנֶיךָ:

CHASSIDIC EXCERPTS

song, as it says, "the voice arouses *kavana*."[377] We see clearly that a melody during prayer has the power to arouse our heart more than quiet meditation ... And this is because the voice arouses *kavana* in the mind and produces revelation in the heart.

From what has been explained here, we may now better understand the command, "And you shall love the Lord, your G-d..." The difficulty with this command is considered elsewhere, regarding the in-appropriateness of issuing a command regarding an emotion in the heart. And the usual answer is that the command is to meditate upon G-dly topics, for then, automatically, the love will emerge. But, according to what was explained here, the emotional arousal occurs only after contraction and inter-

The Mourners Kaddish

Exalted and sanctified is His great Name. (cong: "Amen")

In the universe that He created according to His Will, May He establish His reign, and sprout forth His redemption, and quickly bring His meshiach. (cong: "Amen")
In your life and during your days and in the life of the entire house of Israel, speedily and soon, and say Amen!
(the congregation here says, "Amen, may His great Name be blessed forever and for eternity")
May His great Name be blessed forever and for eternity. May He be blessed, may He be extolled, may He be glorified, may He be exalted, may He be elevated, may He be honored, may He be lauded, and may he be praised, the Name of the holy One, blessed be He. (cong: "Amen") Beyond all the blessings and the hymns, the praises and the consolations that are recited in the world, and let us say Amen.
May there be plentiful peace from Heaven and a good life for all of us and for all of Israel, and let us say, Amen (cong: "Amen").
He Who makes peace (during ten days of repentance – "the peace") on high, may He create peace for us and for all of Israel, and let us say Amen (cong: "Amen").

Have no fear of sudden fright, nor of destruction of the wicked if it occurs.

Come up with a plan, it will be foiled; think of a scheme and it will fail, for G-d is with us.
Until old age, I am [with You]; until you have white hairs, I will accompany you.
I made you, and I will carry you, and I will accompany you, and I will deliver you.

Indeed, the righteous will acknowledge Your Name, the Upright will revel in Your countenance.

CHASSIDIC EXCERPTS

ruption of the intellect; it does not occur automatically, which is why the commandment to "place it upon your heart" is necessary.

And if this is so, the prior question remains in place: How is it possible or appropriate to issue a command regarding an emotion? ... According to the current explanation, the answer is clear. When there is preparation in the soul for this arousal, then everything takes place spontaneously, on its own. And that is why the command to meditate is appropriate, and the emotion follows spontaneously afterward as long as we have performed the proper preparation beforehand.

In any case, it is understood that the descent of the intellect to the emotions ... is a descent from one essence to another.

סדר הנחת תפילין רבינו תם

At the conclusion of Shachrit, it is the custom of some of great piety to lay Rabbenu Tam's Tefillin – however, without pronouncing a blessing over them. One should recite the Shema; some also recite the following biblical portions as well:

וַיְדַבֵּר יְיָ אֶל מֹשֶׁה לֵּאמֹר:

קַדֶּשׁ לִי כָל בְּכוֹר פֶּטֶר כָּל רֶחֶם בִּבְנֵי יִשְׂרָאֵל בָּאָדָם וּבַבְּהֵמָה לִי הוּא:

וַיֹּאמֶר מֹשֶׁה אֶל הָעָם זָכוֹר אֶת הַיּוֹם הַזֶּה אֲשֶׁר יְצָאתֶם מִמִּצְרַיִם מִבֵּית

עֲבָדִים כִּי בְּחֹזֶק יָד הוֹצִיא יְיָ אֶתְכֶם מִזֶּה וְלֹא יֵאָכֵל חָמֵץ: הַיּוֹם אַתֶּם יֹצְאִים

בְּחֹדֶשׁ הָאָבִיב:

וְהָיָה כִי יְבִיאֲךָ יְיָ אֶל אֶרֶץ הַכְּנַעֲנִי וְהַחִתִּי וְהָאֱמֹרִי וְהַחִוִּי וְהַיְבוּסִי אֲשֶׁר

נִשְׁבַּע לַאֲבֹתֶיךָ לָתֶת לָךְ אֶרֶץ זָבַת חָלָב וּדְבָשׁ וְעָבַדְתָּ אֶת הָעֲבֹדָה הַזֹּאת

בַּחֹדֶשׁ הַזֶּה:

שִׁבְעַת יָמִים תֹּאכַל מַצֹּת וּבַיּוֹם הַשְּׁבִיעִי חַג לַייָ:

מַצּוֹת יֵאָכֵל אֶת שִׁבְעַת הַיָּמִים וְלֹא יֵרָאֶה לְךָ חָמֵץ וְלֹא יֵרָאֶה לְךָ שְׂאֹר בְּכָל

גְּבֻלֶךָ:

וְהִגַּדְתָּ לְבִנְךָ בַּיּוֹם הַהוּא לֵאמֹר בַּעֲבוּר זֶה עָשָׂה יְיָ לִי בְּצֵאתִי מִמִּצְרָיִם:

וְהָיָה לְךָ לְאוֹת עַל יָדְךָ וּלְזִכָּרוֹן בֵּין עֵינֶיךָ לְמַעַן תִּהְיֶה תּוֹרַת יְיָ בְּפִיךָ כִּי בְּיָד

חֲזָקָה הוֹצִאֲךָ יְיָ מִמִּצְרָיִם:

וְשָׁמַרְתָּ אֶת הַחֻקָּה הַזֹּאת לְמוֹעֲדָהּ מִיָּמִים יָמִימָה:

Therefore, it can only take place via a process of contraction and interruption and preparation of the soul, combined with the voice of song that arouses *kavana*. And without this it may be impossible for the intellect to descend from the mind to the heart...

From *Sefer Maamorim* 5665 (1905) of the Rebbe Rashab, pp. 247-249)

Rabbeinu Tam's Tefillin

Those who don a second pair of tefillin after the morning prayers (Shacharit) first recite the first three paragraphs of the kriat shema, as it appears in the siddur above, and then say the following (from Ex. 13:1-16), as well as the six remembrances:

And the Lord spoke to Moshe, saying, Sanctify every firstborn to Me, the first to open every womb among the Jews, whether of people or of animals – it is Mine.

And Moshe said to the nation, remember this day on which you went out of Egypt, from the house of slavery, for with a strong arm the Lord brought You out of it, and no leavened bread shall be eaten. Today, you are leaving, during the Spring month.

And it shall be that when the Lord brings you to the land of the Canaanites, the Hittites, the Emorites, the Hivites, the Yebusites, that He swore to your fathers to give you, a land flowing with milk and honey, then you should perform this service, this month.

For seven days, you should eat unleavened bread and the seventh day is a festival for the Lord.
Unleavened bread should be eaten during the seven days, and you should not see any leavened bread, nor should you see any leavening in all of your borders.
And you should tell your son on that day, saying, "this is on account of what the Lord did for me, as I left Egypt."
And it shall be a sign for you upon your hand and a reminder between your eyes, so that the Torah of G-d will constantly be in your mouth, for with a strong arm, the Lord brought you out of Egypt.
And you should observe this law at its appointed season, from year to year.

וְהָיָה כִּי יְבִאֲךָ יְיָ אֶל אֶרֶץ הַכְּנַעֲנִי כַּאֲשֶׁר נִשְׁבַּע לְךָ וְלַאֲבֹתֶיךָ וּנְתָנָהּ לָךְ:

וְהַעֲבַרְתָּ כָל פֶּטֶר רֶחֶם לַיָי וְכָל פֶּטֶר שֶׁגֶר בְּהֵמָה אֲשֶׁר יִהְיֶה לְךָ הַזְּכָרִים לַיָי:

וְכָל פֶּטֶר חֲמֹר תִּפְדֶּה בְשֶׂה וְאִם לֹא תִפְדֶּה וַעֲרַפְתּוֹ וְכֹל בְּכוֹר אָדָם בְּבָנֶיךָ
תִּפְדֶּה:

וְהָיָה כִּי יִשְׁאָלְךָ בִנְךָ מָחָר לֵאמֹר מַה זֹּאת וְאָמַרְתָּ אֵלָיו בְּחֹזֶק יָד הוֹצִיאָנוּ יְיָ
מִמִּצְרַיִם מִבֵּית עֲבָדִים:

וַיְהִי כִּי הִקְשָׁה פַרְעֹה לְשַׁלְּחֵנוּ וַיַּהֲרֹג יְיָ כָּל בְּכוֹר בְּאֶרֶץ מִצְרַיִם מִבְּכֹר אָדָם וְעַד
בְּכוֹר בְּהֵמָה עַל כֵּן אֲנִי זֹבֵחַ לַיָי כָּל פֶּטֶר רֶחֶם הַזְּכָרִים וְכָל בְּכוֹר בָּנַי אֶפְדֶּה:

וְהָיָה לְאוֹת עַל יָדְכָה וּלְטוֹטָפֹת בֵּין עֵינֶיךָ כִּי בְּחֹזֶק יָד הוֹצִיאָנוּ יְיָ מִמִּצְרָיִם:

שֵׁשׁ זְכִירוֹת

(1) לְמַעַן תִּזְכֹּר אֶת יוֹם צֵאתְךָ מֵאֶרֶץ מִצְרַיִם כֹּל יְמֵי חַיֶּיךָ:

(2) רַק הִשָּׁמֶר, לְךָ וּשְׁמֹר נַפְשְׁךָ מְאֹד פֶּן תִּשְׁכַּח אֶת הַדְּבָרִים אֲשֶׁר רָאוּ עֵינֶיךָ
וּפֶן יָסוּרוּ מִלְּבָבְךָ כֹּל יְמֵי חַיֶּיךָ וְהוֹדַעְתָּם לְבָנֶיךָ, וְלִבְנֵי בָנֶיךָ: יוֹם אֲשֶׁר
עָמַדְתָּ לִפְנֵי יְיָ אֱלֹהֶיךָ בְּחֹרֵב:

(3) זָכוֹר אֵת אֲשֶׁר עָשָׂה לְךָ עֲמָלֵק בַּדֶּרֶךְ בְּצֵאתְכֶם מִמִּצְרָיִם: אֲשֶׁר קָרְךָ בַּדֶּרֶךְ
וַיְזַנֵּב בְּךָ כָּל הַנֶּחֱשָׁלִים אַחֲרֶיךָ וְאַתָּה עָיֵף וְיָגֵעַ וְלֹא יָרֵא אֱלֹהִים: וְהָיָה
בְּהָנִיחַ יְיָ אֱלֹהֶיךָ לְךָ מִכָּל אֹיְבֶיךָ מִסָּבִיב בָּאָרֶץ אֲשֶׁר יְיָ אֱלֹהֶיךָ נֹתֵן לְךָ
נַחֲלָה לְרִשְׁתָּהּ תִּמְחֶה אֶת זֵכֶר עֲמָלֵק מִתַּחַת הַשָּׁמָיִם לֹא, תִּשְׁכָּח:

(4) זְכֹר אַל תִּשְׁכַּח אֵת אֲשֶׁר הִקְצַפְתָּ אֶת יְיָ אֱלֹהֶיךָ בַּמִּדְבָּר:

(5) זָכוֹר אֵת אֲשֶׁר עָשָׂה יְיָ אֱלֹהֶיךָ לְמִרְיָם בַּדֶּרֶךְ בְּצֵאתְכֶם מִמִּצְרָיִם:

(6) זָכוֹר אֶת יוֹם הַשַּׁבָּת לְקַדְּשׁוֹ:

And it shall be that when the Lord brings you to the land of the Canaanites as He swore to you and to your fathers, and gives it to you.

You should transfer every [offspring] that first opens the womb to the Lord, and of the cattle, every male that first opens the womb is for the Lord.

Every [male] that first opens the womb among donkeys should be redeemed with a lamb, and if you do not redeem it, then you must break its neck from behind, and every firstborn among men, among your sons, you must redeem.

And if your son shall ask you tomorrow (after time), saying, "what is this?" you should say to him, "With a strong hand, the Lord brought us out of Egypt, from the house of slavery.

And it happened that when Pharoah obstinately refused to send us, the Lord killed every firstborn in the land of Egypt, from the firstborn of man to the firstborn of animals; therefore I slaughter every male animal that opens the womb to the Lord, and every firstborn of my sons, I redeem."

And it should be as a sign on your hand and for compartments between your eyes, for with a strong hand, the Lord brought us out of Egypt.

The Six Remembrances

(1) In order that you remember the day on which you left the land of Egypt, all the days of your life (Deut. 16:3)

(2) But, guard yourself and guard your soul scrupulously, lest you forget the events that your eyes have seen, and lest they turn [empty out] from your heart, all the days of your life, and inform your children and your children's children of these events. Of [what you saw on] the day that you stood before the Lord your G-d on Mt. Horev (Deut. 4:9-10).

(3) Remember what Amalek did to you as you were on the road during your exit from Egypt; how he met you on the way, and attacked all of the weak who straggled behind you, and you were tired and weary, and he was not G-d fearing. And when the Lord your G-d will relieve you of your enemies around you, in the land that the Lord your G-d gives to you as a portion to inherit, erase the memory of Amalek from under the heavens, do not forget! (Deut. 25:17-19)

(4) Remember, do not forget how you provoked the Lord your G-d to anger in the desert. (Deut 9:7)

(5) Remember what the Lord your G-d did to Miriam on the way, as you exited Egypt (Deut. 24:9)

(6) Remember the day of Shabbat, to sanctify it. (Ex. 20:8)

ENDNOTES to INSIGHTS

1. See Genesis 28:12

2. Sleep is described by the sages as "one-sixtieth of death."

3. In *Sefer Maamorim 5677* (Page 174), the Rebbe Rashab says that simple general acknowledgment of G-d (*hod sh'behod*) is associated with the inner dimensions of *keter*, while specific acknowledgment (*hod*) is associated with only the external dimensions of *keter*. For, acknowledgment that is based upon logic and reason ("that we know at least about what we are acknowledging") is limited to our intellect. But, general acknowledgment is beyond intellect, and is not limited by our personal intellectual abilities.

4. See *Kuntres Inyanah shel Torat Hachasidut* ("On the Essence of Chassidut"), published by Kehot Publication Society, for an exposition of *hoda'a* ("acknowledgment") on five different levels.

5. While eating or drinking to the point of satiation is not permitted before morning prayers (*shacharit*), it is permitted to eat or drink enough to remove any discomfort that would otherwise distract us from prayers (*Shulchan Aruch Orach Chayim* 89:4, *Shulchan Aruch HaRav* 89:5). The general rule: It is preferable to eat or drink something in order to pray, rather than pray in order to eat (paraphrased from the *Tzemach Tzedek*, the third Lubavitcher Rebbe, in an instruction given to his daughter).

The "Minchat Elazar," R' Chaim Elazar Shapira (the Munkatcher Rav) would have a cup of coffee before prayer, saying that in this manner he fulfilled the instruction of the Talmud to eat pat shacharit ("breakfast"). See his *sefer, Darchei Chaim ve'Shalom* in the beginning.

6. Talmud, *Berachot* 4

7. See *Sefer Hasichot, Torat Shalom* of the Rebbe Rashab, bottom of page 5, and *Kuntres Hatefila* of the Rebbe Rashab, Ch. 11, page 24 near the bottom.

8. See *Torah Ohr* of the Alter Rebbe on *Bereishit* (Page 10), *Sefer Maamarim 5663* of the Rebbe Rashab, Page 51, *Be'sha'ah shehikdimu 5672* of the Rebbe Rashab, vol. 2, beg Page 1045, *Yom Tov shel Rosh Hashana 5666* of the Rebbe Rashab, beg. Page 393, and many more places

9. See *Sefer Mamaarim 5663* of the Rebbe Rashab, Page 52: "And this is what is meant in the verse regarding the sacrifices, *ishei raiach nichoach* – "my fire, a pleasant aroma" – corresponding to three elevations from the worlds of BY"A (*ishe* corresponds to the ascent from *asiya*, *raiach* from *yetzira*, and *nichoach* from *bria*...)

10. Mincha is the term used for the vegetable aspect of any offering, as well as the term used for specific sacrifices (for example, a poor person who could not afford to buy a even a bird to offer in the Temple was permitted to bring a *mincha* offering of grain) that were composed of grain mixed with oil.

11. Leviticus 1:2

12. To begin with, all prayer in the Temple was voluntary, as the real function in the Temple was to offer sacrifices. Nevertheless, the Jews would recite the *shema* (a Torah obligation) and the *shemonah esreh*, as well as offer their sacrifices. However, as the sages observed that the spiritual level of the average Jew was descending, they added to the required prayers; first, they added the blessings preceding the *kriat shema*, and eventually they added the *pesukei dezimra* as well.

13. See *Tanya, Kuntres Aharon*, Essay 6 (*Dovid zmiros karis hehu*), Page 320: "And if [the priest] deviated and received the blood with his left hand, for example, or without using the appropriate kosher vessel, or there was some kind of obstacle, then the spiritual ascent of the worlds, as well as their vitality and influx from the infinite One above was nullified..."

14. Moreover, the prayers of *tzadikim* (the "righteous") are what bring spiritual energy into creation, ensuring its vitality and spirituality (see Tanya, chapter 1).

15. *Sefer Maamorim Melukat* of the Lubavitcher Rebbe, *z'l* vol. 6, p. 93

16. See *Rav Brachia P'tach* of the Rebbe Rashab in *Sefer Maamorim 5643*.

17. *Derech Mitzvotecha* of the Tzemach Tzedek, *mitzvat Ahavat Yisrael*, Page 28B

18. *Shulchan Aruch, Orech Chaim, siman* 89:1, *Shulchan Aruch Harav, Orech Chaim* 89:2

19. *Igerot Kodesh* of the Lubavitcher Rebbe *ztz'l* , vol. 14, p.407

20. *Heichal Menachem*, vol. 1, p.218

21. The Rebbe Rashab compares the prayers of one who prays alone with "prayer according to logic and intellect," while prayers with a public minyan are comparable to *re'uta deliba*, or the "will of the heart" that transcends logic and intellect. See *Sefer Maamorim 5677*, page 103, at the bottom of the page.

22. *Torat Menachem*, vol. 24, pp. 84 and 95

23. *Tanya,* chapter 34. The mineral and human categories are not expressly mentioned there, but implied.

24. *Likutei Sichot* of the Lubavitcher Rebbe *ztz'l*, Vol. 6, *Parshat Yitro*.

25. The Hebrew word for incense – *ketoret* – is similar to the word *kesher*, meaning "bond" or "connection."

26. We say it after the *Korbanot* ("Offerings") because during the time that the Ark of the Covenant was housed in a temporary location, King David decreed that this is when *Hodu* should be recited (See Samuel 2, 7:12, and *Sefer Yohsin*). Additionally, some among the sages said that when the oxen returned the Ark of the Covenant Ark from captivity among the Philistines, the oxen themselves recited *Hodu*.

27. See *Seder Olam*

28. In *Sha'ar Hakavanot*

29. See *Reshimot* of the Lubavitcher Rebbe, #158

30. See endnote #3.

31. See the First Book of Samuel 2:1-10.

32. As sourced in the Talmud, Tractate *Berachot* 5, and in the *Shulchan Aruch*, the Code of Jewish law

33. *Shulchan Aruch, Orech Haim* 93:2. For detailed explanation of the importance of joyful prayer, see *Sefer Maamorim 5677*, pages 109-112.

34. *Shulchan Aruch, Orech Haim* 93:3

35. *Shulchan Aruch, Orech Haim* 93:1

36. *Shulchan Aruch, Orech Haim* 98:1

37. See *Bamidbar* (Numbers) 14:9, and Rambam, beginning of *Hilchot Ta'aniot* (incl. Halacha 4), as well as Ramban on *Bamidbar* 14:9

38. See *Torat Menachem*, vol. 18, page 240.

39. Talmud, Tractate *Chagiga* 14b

40. From *Siyum HaRambam 5735*, p. 2, in *Hadranim al HaRambam v'Shas*, of the Lubavitcher Rebbe, p. 44

41. The well-known opinion of the *Shach* (Rabbi Shabtai Cohen, 16th century Krakow, Poland) in *Yoreh Deah* 246:6, proposes that in addition to being versant in the oral law, one should be at least forty years old before devoting himself to Kabbalah. Note, however, that his opinion is not universal. The Vilna Gaon (in his commentary to the Book of Proverbs), says nothing regarding age, while writing that it is impossible to understand the

simple level of the text without knowing the secret level, and it is impossible to understand the secret level without understanding the simple level. The obligation to learn the simple level begins from young childhood. Moreover, the Ari claimed that the study of Kabbalah is for all Jews.

42. In the year 5721 (1961) as quoted from *Sha'arei Tefila* pp. 213-4

43. See Ramban on *Bereishit* 2:20, *Ohr Torah* of the Magid 4B, *Sha'ar hayichud v'haemunah* of Tanya

44. In *sefer maamorim 5658* of the Rebbe Rashab, page 139 and onward, there appears a meditation on the letters of *eshel* ("terebinth" tree), involving the letters *aleph-shin-lamed*. Although this is a meditation from the Rebbe, and we cannot be expected to achieve such depth during our own meditation on specific objects of creation, nevertheless the fact that we know the function of letters in general (that they convey the divine vitality of the object), together with some basic knowledge of the functions of specific letters, as described in Chassidut, is more than enough for our purposes.

45. See *Tanya, Shaar Hayichud Vehaemuna*, ch. 7: "…for the word *even*, for example, has a name that indicates that it comes from the name of G-d spelled with the gematria of *B'n*, or fifty-two, with an additional *aleph* from another name, for a reason known to its Creator."

And in *Sefer Maamorim 5668* (p. 16), the Rebbe Rashab adds the following enlightening note: "It is explained in the *Siddur* of the Alter Rebbe (regarding the Ba'al Shem Tov's *kavanot* during blowing the *shofar* on Rosh Hashana) that the letter *aleph* is an intermediary that joins and connects our voice with the letters of speech. Similarly, Above, the *aleph* is an intermediary that joins and connects revealed infinite light of G-d with the *sephira* of *malchut*, in order to produce revealed illumination and vitality in the creation." Although the Rebbe Rashab wrote this regarding the *aleph* missing from another word (*reishit*), perhaps it applies as well to the *aleph* of the word *even* ("stone"). For the second two letters of *even*, *beit-nun*, form the name of G-d (*shem B'n*) that is associated with *malchut* (from which G-d's "speech" emerges to create the universe), to which the *aleph* in the Rashab's explanation draws down infinite light from Above.

Indeed, later in the same *sefer* (*Sefer Maamorim 5668*, page 114), the Rebbe Rashab writes the following: "*Even* ("stone") is spelled *aleph-ba'an*, with the same numerical value as *behama* ("animal"). The *aleph* is a ray of the name *Ma'h* [that descends] in order to refine the animal soul and transform it as well into something good."

The name *Ma'h* is based upon one way of writing the essential four letter name of G-d, carrying the numerical value of 45, or *adam* ("man"). A ray of this name "descends" to refine and uplift the name *Ba'n*, of numerical value *behama*, or "animal." The *aleph* of *even* represents this G-dly ray that descends from Above.

46. It is the *Sefer Yetzira* ("Book of Formation"), the earliest book of Kabbalah, ascribed to Adam the original man, that describes the letters of the Hebrew alphabet as the building blocks of creation – and there they are called "stones" (*avanim*), which are used to build "houses" (*batim*) – for from them words are created and hence the names of all creation. And of course, it was Adam who "called the names of every creature." Later Kabbalah and Chasidut developed this concept and it is emphasized in the works of the Ba'al Shem Tov and his student, the Mezritcher Magid.

47. First Book of Kings 19:11-12.

48. From *Besha'ah shehikdimu, 5672* (1912) of the Rebbe Rashab, vol. 2, p. 822.

49. Other correspondences with the World of *Bria* are the intellect within man, the first *hey* of G-d's Name, *bina* in the World of *Atzilut*, fire among the four physical fundaments, and animals among the four categories of creation.

50. In the First Book of Kings 19:12

51. In the First Book of Kings 19:12

52. See *Sefer Maamorim 5670* (1910) of the Rebbe Rashab, p. 37

53. See *Igeret Hakodesh, no. 15*

54. In *Kuntres Avoda*, ch. 6.

55. See *Tosfos R'Yitzhak* and the *Rif* on *Berachot*, chapter 3

56. In Psalms 17:15

57. Tractate *Baba Batra* 10a

58. *Sichot 11 Nissan*, 5734

59. in *Igeret Hakodesh* 8

60. See *Sefer Maamarim 5610* (1910) of the Rebbe Rashab, page 14, as well as *Kuntres Ha'avoda* of the Rebbe Rashab, Ch. 1, page 2

61. In *Kovetz Meah Shearim*, on p. 22:

62. Psalms 149:6

63. Psalms 84:3

64. Psalms 132:9

65. Deuteronomy 28:47

66. See the Mittler Rebbe's *Kuntres Hahitpaalut* ("Tractate on Ecstasy")

67. In *Sichot Hakodesh* of 5752, II, on p. 594

68. See *Hosafot* to *Torah Ohr*, page 102 (*Kuf-Beit*), first column, *Sefer Maamorim 5679* of the Rebbe Rashab, page 197-8, *Sefer Maamorim* 5662 of the Rebbe Rashab pages 247-8 and many more places...

69. See *Sefer Maamorim 5679* of the Rebbe Rashab, pages 196-201 for a detailed explanation

70. See the Siddur with *Dach* of the Alter Rebbe on *Baruch She'amar*

71. See *Torat Menachem* of the Lubavitcher Rebbe, R' Menachem Mendel Schneerson, *ztz'l* vol. 12, page 166. See also *Likutei Torah* of the Alter Rebbe, parshat *V'etchanan*, page 2a

72. See *Sefer Maamorim 5657* of the Rebbe Rashab, page 122 as well as *Besha'ah shehikdimu 5672* of the Rebbe Rashab, vol. 2 page 392, and many other places

73. See Ch. 6 of "Love like Fire and Water" (translation of *Kuntres Ha'avoda* of the Rebbe Rashab)

74. This seems to be the path set out by the Rebbe (R' Menachem Mendel Schneerson) in a *sicha* published in volume 6 of *Likutei Sichot*, page 107. The entire *sicha* was translated and appears in "Love like Fire and Water" (translation of *Kuntres Ha'avoda* of the Rebbe Rashab), in the commentary to Ch. 6

75. See *Torat Shmuel* of the Rebbe Maharash, 5635 (1875), page 338

76. From *Sefer Maamorim 5670* (1910) of the Rebbe Rashab, p. 37

77. Other correspondences with the World of *Yetzira* are the emotions within man, the letter *vov* of G-d's Name, *Z"A* (the six *sephirot* above *malchut*) in the World of *Atzilut*, water among the four physical fundaments, and vegetables among the four categories of creation.

78. From *Sha'arei Tefila (Heichal Menachem)*, page 299 (quoting a letter of the Lubavitcher Rebbe *ztz'l*): Meditation during the *Pesukei DeZmira* focused upon creation from nothing to something is predicated upon the following intellectual process. We focus on the G-dly ray or reflection of light – called *ohr memaleh* ("immanent light") – that is invested the world in order to create it. And we keep in mind that:

1) No object can create itself. (*Hovot Halevavot, Sha'ar* 1, Ch.5)

2) If an object could create itself, it would not really "exist," nor would it be limited.

3) No object is created directly from another object. There must be a void/vacuum between them – this is the spiritual *ayn* ("nothingness") in which creation takes place, *m'ayn l'yesh* (from "nothing to something").

4) All physical objects are compounded of various elements, which could not have come together on their own accord. They had to be compounded by a higher, external force that is unlimited.

5) After creation, every object begins to wear down and deteriorate. This is an indication that the object was created and did not always exist.

6) Creation is an ongoing process initiated by the ray of G-dliness descending through the ten *sephirot* of the World of *Atzilut*. As it descends, the ray becomes contracted, while remaining "close" to the One Above. Since it descends in a step-by-step fashion through the nine *sephirot* that precede *malchut*, it is never "out of range" of the Creator. Yet, this ray of light must traverse the great gulf that separates the spiritual from the physical.

7) The great gulf or chasm occurs between the tenth/final *sephira* of *malchut* and the lower worlds of *Bria, Yetzira* and *Asiya* (*BY"A*). From *malchut*, the ray of light "jumps" to traverse the chasm below *Atzilut* and create these lower worlds. Thus, the *sephira* of *malchut* acts from afar to create the lower worlds of *BY"A*. The G-dly light within creation continues to maintain *BY"A* in a contracted form.

8) In traversing the chasm between *malchut* and *BY"A*, the G-dly ray of light performs two opposite functions. It creates from "afar," expressing the exalted majesty of the King above, whose power is expressed from a distance. Simultaneously, it is en-clothed in the creation, acting in intimate proximity with it. In its mode of en-clothement in creation, the G-dly light acts as "the power of the Creator within the creation" (*koach hapoel ba-nifal*).

9) Creation is totally unaware of the G-dly light that acts upon it from afar. However, it is aware of the G-dly energy that is en-clothed within it, because this is the energy that courses through it and enlivens it. But, it is not aware that this energy is G-dly.

79. From *Sha'arei Tefila* [*Heichal Menachem*], pp. 14-15:

In *Likutei Torah* [*Bamidbar* 2, col. 3], the Alter Rebbe tells us, "The prayers were established during the destruction of the [first] Temple, since while the Temple was still standing, the powers of evil from the *klipot* and *sitra achra* held no sway or influence, nor could they cling to man that much ... but during the destruction of the Temple ... the evil inclination and the animal soul were strengthened, and we have to separate from them through our prayers, with fire and thirst and crying from the heart..."

Elsewhere in *Likutei Torah* [*Bamidbar* 32, col.4], the Alter Rebbe tells us, "The sages of the Great Assembly decreed that we should pray with the *Pesukei DeZimra* ("Verses of Song"), although from the Torah there is no need for anything other than reciting the *Shema* and a little bit of prayer, just as in the first Temple. At that time, there were no prayers, since people had clear minds and intellects all day long, in order to see and understand the wonder of the Infinite One. But, the Sages of the Great Assembly in the beginning of the second Temple saw that our intellect was minimized, that our hearts were drawn more to the physical, and we were seeing the physical substance alone. And, therefore, they decreed that we should say these prayers and blessings, since all of it consists of the praises of G-d, many times over."

And in *Likutei Torah* [*Bamidbar* 61, col. 4], the Alter Rebbe says that "During the first Temple, there were no prayers at all. And also, during the second Temple, the Sages of the Great Assembly established only a short prayer ... the greater mixture of evil demands a greater and stronger fire to separate from it in order to cleave to the Creator. And, therefore, during the first Temple, when the forces of evil were not so great, there was no necessity to establish prayers in excitement. All that was necessary was to elevate the evil and the *dinim* to their source by way of the sacrifices, and that was enough. But, during the second Temple, the sages began to establish the prayers, and they were short, in proportion to the need to quench the fire and mixture of evil. And we need to pray more and more, with much spiritual arousal. And so, every generation down here needs to pray with greater excitement ... because of the great amount of evil that has become mixed in and maximized within each generation, it must be separated by way of intense prayer...."

In *Likutei Torah* [*Vayikra* 47, col. 4]: "Before reciting the *Shema*, which expresses love ... we must say the *Pesukei DeZimra* ... from the word *lezamer*, meaning 'to cut away thorns.' By way of our meditation on the greatness of the infinite light of G-d, during the *Pesukei DeZimra*, we cut away and remove the bad within, so that love of G-d permeates and expands within ... and, therefore, the obligation to say the *Pesukei DeZimra* does not appear in the *Mishna*, but only the two blessings before the *Shema* – because they did not need to say this every day."

And finally, this, from the *Kuntres Ha'avoda* of the Rebbe Rashab (end of Ch. 7): "The commandment to love G-d does not appear in the Torah until the final book of the Torah. For the generation of the desert [who exited Egypt] were blessed with revelation of G-dliness from above, including spiritual "vision" enabling them to "see" G-dliness ... so, automatically they experienced love ... but the following generation needed a commandment to love G-d ... meaning by way of meditation ... And this is the goal of service of G-d and labor of the heart during prayers, to push ourselves to meditate ... in order to arouse love of G-d."

80. Though he did mention these levels; see *Samach tesamach 5657*, pp. 18-19 for references.

81. In *Parshat Ve'etchanan*, on p. 2 (*beit, amud alef* at the bottom), the idea is discussed in kabalistic terms. Since the *yud-gimmel tikunei dikna* ("thirteen strands of the bears") descend from *malchut* of *A"K*, the implication is that they access the hidden love of G-d that is present in the heart of every Jew, associated with the spiritual level of *A"K*. From there, the prayer enables the Jew to access that hidden love and bring it to a state of revelation in the heart

82. In the section on *Shir Hashirim* ("Song of Songs").

83. In his *Sha'ar Hatefila*.

84. In *Ohel Yoseph Yitzhak* on *Tehillim* (*Yahel Ohr*) from the *Tzemach Tzedek*, p. 652. Translated elsewhere in this work.

85. Likutei Torah of the Alter Rebbe, *Parshat Tzav*.

86. Pirkei d'R'Eliezer, Ch. 3

87. Be'sha'ah Shehikdimu 5672, vol. 1, p. 129.

88. Also in *Besha'ah Shehikdimu 5672*, vol. 1, p. 293.

89. In *Besha'ah Shehikdimu 5672*, vol. 1, p. 136.

90. In *Torat Menachem*, vol. 12, p. 166.

91. See the *Siddur* with *Dach* of the Alter Rebbe, page 56 (nun-vov)

92. See the *Siddur* with *Dach* of the Alter Rebbe, page 56, as well as *Pirush Hamilot* of the Mittler Rebbe, Ch. 159

93. See *Besha'ah shehikdimu 5672* of the Rebbe Rashab, vol. 2, Ch. 392

94. See *Besha'ah shehikdimu 5672*, of the Rebbe Rashab, vol. 2, Ch. 394-6, as well as *Torat Menachem* of the Rebbe, R' Menachem Mendel Schneerson *ztz'l*, vol. 16, Page 4, quoted in *Sha'arei Tefila*, page 295-306

95. See *Sefer Maamorim 5662* of the Rebbe Rashab, page 247-8 as well as *Besha'ah shehikdimu 5672* of the Rebbe Rashab, vol. 2, Ch. 392

96. *Tanya*, *Likutei Amarim* Ch. 42 and elsewhere

97. See *Kuntres Ha'avoda* of the Rebbe Rashab, Ch. 1 and elsewhere

98. See *Sefer Maamorim 5679* of the Rebbe Rashab, page 211 – *Shimcha Hagadol* is *meshutaf banu* ("partnered with us")

99. See *Sefer Maamorim 5658* of the Rebbe Rashab, page 214 as well as *Sefer Maamorim 5662*, page 354

100. See *Ohr HaTorah* of the *Tzemach Tzedek*, *drushim lePesach*, Page 441

101. Here is how the Rebbe Rashab describes the World of *Bria* (in *Sefer Maamorim 5660* (1900), p. 32): "*Bria* is nullified to G-dliness – the creatures of the World of *Bria* are called denizens of the 'concealed worlds' and are nullified to G-dliness. For example, fish of the sea, whose very essence is water, are subsumed in the waters of the sea, unable to detach from them...so it is for the creatures of *Bria* who do not really 'exist' [independently] but are rather nullified and united with their source – they are not disconnected at all. Since the World of *Bria* is the very first *yesh* ('existence') created from the G-dly *ayn* ('nothingness'), there is still a revelation of the G-dly *ayn* shining there, and that is why [its creatures] are not completely *yesh*, but are nullified to G-dliness...The World of *Bria* does not exist unto itself, but nevertheless it is not totally lacking existence...It emerges from 'no existence and absence of existence' to be included in the category of 'possibility of existence.'"

102. Chasidut teaches that they were bequeathed to us from the forefathers, Abraham, Isaac and Jacob and are part of the Jewish "genes."

103. First Book of Samuel 2:2. See *Sha'arei Tefila* (*Heichal Menachem*), p. 305, as well as *Torat Menachem*, vol.6, p. 136

104. Although here, the concept of *Ain kadosh k'Havaya* ("There is no holiness like that of *Havaya*") applies to the "outside world" (the macrocosm), elsewhere, the same concept is used to apply to the "inner world" (the microcosm) – to the *ohr* ("light") and *chayut* ("energy") that enlivens us. In *Sefer Maamorim 5663-5664* of the Rebbe Rashab, p. 128, he writes, "...now, a reflection of the *kav* illuminates and becomes en-clothed in the light of the *neshama* of BY"A, and a ray of a reflection in the *nefesh-ruach*, and a refraction of a ray of a reflection in all of the creations...now this spirituality is not en-clothed in a way that is graspable within the creations. It is en-clothed within them, as inner light and energy that enliven them, about which is said, 'And You enliven all of them'...Nevertheless, it is not grasped within them. Since [this illumination] cleaves to its source [above creation] and it is similar to its [transcendent] origin from, for this reason while it is en-clothed within the creations, nevertheless it is not grasped by them. About this, we say, "There is no holiness like that of *Havaya*," meaning that although this spirituality is en-clothed within the creations, nevertheless it is holy and removed above them. It does not mix in and join with them that much..." This *maamer* discusses the various terminologies on the subject found in *Tanya* (in Ch. 51 and 52 of *Likutei Amarim*, and in Ch. 12 of *Sha'ar Hayichud*).

However, in *Sefer Maamorim 5668* (page 210), the Rebbe Rashab says otherwise: "The energy classified as *ohr* is from a ray of the *kav*, as known, and although we say about it, "there is no holiness like that of *Havaya*," meaning that it is holy and removed, nevertheless it is en-clothed and grasped and experienced as something that is 'felt within.' It is just that in *Atzilut* there is real experience of the essence [of the *ohr*] while in the lower worlds of BY"A, there is only experience of its existence...(and by way of Torah, even the essence shines within, as written in *Tanya*, Ch. 36...).”

In the series of discourses of 5672, vol. 1 (page 489), the Rebbe Rashab lists three levels: *ohr* (“light”), *chayut* (“energy”) and *koach* (“power”), saying that *ohr* corresponds to *ohr makif* (“transcendent illumination”), *chayut* to *ohr pnimi* (“immanent illumination”), and *koach* to *kelim* (“vessels” which contain the illumination). And he adds that even though *chayut* is inner illumination that becomes en-clothed in creation, nevertheless, it is *ayn kadosh k'Havaya* – “There is no holiness like *Havaya*.”

And in *Sefer Maamorim 5680* (1920), page 87, we find the following: ...Regarding the verse (Shmuel 1 2:2), “There is no holiness like that of *Havaya*...” the Zohar (*Tazriah* 44A) says, “There are several [levels of] holiness, but none of them are as holy as *Havaya*...” It is explained that this statement applies [not only to transcendent Godliness – *sovev kol olamim*] but also immanent spirituality (*ohr pnimi*). The nature of immanent spirituality is to become embedded in the *kelim* (“vessels” that hold and channel spirituality) and vitalize them with inner illumination and vitality. This form of en-clothement takes place with true unity, similar to the manner in which the faculties of the soul become united with the limbs of the body. Nevertheless, [the immanent spirituality] does not become integrated [within the *kelim*] and the *kelim* do not produce any variation within the illumination. This is what is meant by, “There is no holiness like that of Havaya.”

Within other holy creations, such as angels, the holy illumination does not become embedded at all. If it does penetrate, the holy light becomes so integrated that it undergoes some sort of variation...Regarding the soul within the body; it is not the entire soul that becomes enclothed in the body, for the body is too small to contain the essence of the soul. [The body] contains only a thin ray and reflection of the soul, [which is all that is capable] of becoming enclothed within the body. These are the lower three levels, or *naran* (*nefesh*, *ruach* and *neshama*) of the soul, while the essence of the soul – the *chaya* and *yechida* - remain beyond. The [higher levels] of the soul are separate from the body, and do not become embedded, while the portion of the soul that is enclothed in the body is totally integrated. It is affected by the events of the body.

However, “there is no holiness like *Havaya*” refers to the *ohr*, or divine illumination. Even though it is enclothed in the vessels and vitalizes them, it nevertheless remains holy and aloof from them. And that is because this light is a revelation from the infinite light of God that precedes the *tzimtzum*, or “great contraction” of His infinite light. As written in *Eitz Haim*, and “afterward He drew down a thin ray from His surrounding light.” That is, [after the *tzimtzum*], He drew down [a thin ray of illumination] from the infinite light, and that is why the illumination of the *kav* itself is infinite in its very essence. However, through the *tzimtzum* it becomes embedded, measured and limited, since it is enclothed within the *kelim*. But in essence, the nature of divine illumination is infinite and simple. And therefore even though it is enclothed within the *kelim* and vitalizes them, nevertheless the illumination remains infinite and simple. It never becomes fully integrated within the *kelim* to the extent that they have influence upon the divine illumination. From *Sefer Maamorim 5680* (1920) of the Rebbe Rashab, page 87.

105. See *Kuntres HaAvoda* of the Rebbe Rashab (translated version entitled “Love like Fire and Water,” published 2005 by Moznaim), Ch. 1, pp. 20-25.

106. Psalms 24:4

107. In *Sefer Maamorim 5677*, the Rebbe Rashab further explores the nature of *Ein kadosh k'Havaya* – “there is no holiness like *Havaya*.” On page 177, “From the beginning of its inception, it is removed, but from it emerges immanent G-dly illumination. It is the source of immanent spirituality (without being its real origin)...the name *Havaya*, although permeating [creation], is also holy and removed – meaning that it is not truly grasped [within creation]..."

And on page 178: "We might say that "there is no holiness like *Havaya*" refers to the inner, immanent illumination; that is, to the "essential illumination that is united and becomes one with the essence and inner aspects of the *kelim*."

And finally on page 179, the Rashab tells us that a reflection of the *kav* illuminates in *Atzilut* and contains within it the essence of the *kav*. And therefore, "There is no holiness like *Havaya*" refers mainly to the *kav* as it exists in *Atzilut*."

However, in *Sefer Maamorim 5680* (1920), the Rebbe Rashab indicates that there is an even higher influence at play:

"Elsewhere, regarding the phrase in Psalms, 'there is no holiness like that of *Havaya*,' about which the *Zohar* (*Tazria* page 44A) says, 'there are many levels of holiness, but none are as holy as *Havaya*,' it is explained that [this level] also applies to immanent light (*ohr pnimi*). Although it is enclothed within the *kelim* ("vessels" of the world of Atzilut) and enlivens them with internal light (*ohr*) and vitality (*chayut*), and this is real enclothement with true unity – similar to the faculties of the soul enclothed in the body - nevertheless it does not "mix in" with them. Nor does this enclothement produce any change in the [immanent] light. This is what is meant by 'there is no holiness like that of *Havaya*.'

Regarding other levels of holiness such as angels, the holiness is not enclothed within them at all. If any enclothing occurs, it so penetrates that it transforms [the object]. For example, when the soul is enclothed in the body, it is not the entire soul that becomes enmeshed in the body. The body is too small to contain the essence of the soul. Only a reflection and small fraction – the *nefesh, ruach* and *neshama* - of the soul is enclothed in the body, while the essence - the *chaya* and *yechida* - remain above. This part of the soul is separate from the body. It is not enclothed in it, but the portion of the soul enclothed within the body is totally enmeshed within it. It is affected by the events that occur to the body.

However, the phrase, 'there is nothing as holy as *Havaya*' refers to the illumination that, while enclothed in the *kelim* and enlivening them is nevertheless separate and removed from them. And this is because the illumination is revelation from the infinite transcendent light that presages the *tzimtzum*, as written in the *Eitz Chaim*, "And afterward He drew down a very thin ray from His transcendent light, that is, from the illumination that is infinite." And therefore, the illumination of this ray (*kav*) is also infinite in its essence. However, it descends via the *tzimtzum* and [becomes expressed] in measured quantities and limitations in order to become enclothed within the *kelim*. But in actual essence, it is infinite and simple. And therefore it does not "mix in" with the *kelim* and they produce no change in the light.

The proof of this is found in the writings of the Ari *z'l* in explanation of the phenomena, *achlifu duchtaihu* – "they switched roles" – the light of *chesed* entered the vessel of *gevura* and the light of *gevura* entered the vessel of *chesed*. [The only way this can occur] is if the illumination (*ohr*) is simple and undifferentiated, while the vessels (*kelim*) take on the characteristic of *chesed* or *gevura*. And therefore even when the light is enclothed in the vessel, it remains unchanged in essence. It is holy and removed even while enclothed [in the vessels]. For example, if light passes through green, or red or clear or darkened glass, the glass has no effect on the light itself. The light remains unchanged, and what does change is the color of the light that shines through to the other side of the glass. [But], there is no real change in the light itself."

108. From *Sefer Maamorim 5668* of the Rebbe Rashab (p. 30), "And this is because in *Bria* shines revealed infinite light, and the reason is explained elsewhere that since *Bria* is the first *yesh* ("existence") that emerged from the *ayn* ("Divine void") that preceded creation, it is close to the *ayn* which illuminates within it in a revealed fashion..."

109. Awareness of *hitchadeshut* is a major factor in triggering "love like fire." See *Kuntres HaAvoda*, Ch. 5.

110. The idea here is not that the emotions "become" intellect and that the difference between them is erased. Rather, the emotions remain intact, and in fact we experience them with even more intensity that during the soul-level of *ruach*. However, the emotions are so infused with intellect that we experience them at one and the same time as we experience the intellect. There is no "break," so to speak, during which the intellect filters down to the heart to activate our emotions; the intensity of G-dly illumination is so great that it immediately uplifts the emotions to the level of intellect.

111. Sefer Mamorim 5670 (1910) of the Rebbe Rashab, p. 37.

112. In *Sefer Maamorim 5663* (1903), vol. 2, (pp. 314-318) the Rebbe Rashab states that the lowest angels, *ofanim* of the World of *Asiya* (*ruchani*) are actually higher in their spiritual root than the *seraphim* (angels of the world of *Bria*). Since, unlike the *seraphim*, the *ofanim* do not grasp G-dliness, even though they are aware of it, they are in a perpetual state of *ra'ash*, or "noise," exiting their *kelim* ("vessels") in order to climb to the spiritual level of the higher *seraphim*, in an effort to attain more understanding. The Rebbe Rashab points out that *ra'ash* has the same Hebrew letters as *sha'ar*, or "gate" of understanding; thus the *ofanim* actually attain understanding that transcends their spiritual level and that of the *seraphim* as well. Therefore, they say, *Baruch kevod Havaya mimkomo* – "Blessed is the Lord from His place" – meaning from the infinite light of G-d (which is beyond the level of the *seraphim* as well).

113. Besha'ah Shehikdimu of the Rebbe Rashab, vol. 2, pp. 822 and 704.

114. Kuntres HaAvoda, Ch. 1 (p. 28 in the translation, entitled "Love like Fire and Water")

115. In *Yom Tov shel Rosh Hashana 5666* (p. 150), the Rebbe Rashab explains that meditation on *memalle kol olamim* ("immanent spirituality") will lead to lead to "true intellectual grasp" that includes *reiya* of *chochma* (this may be said to correspond to the level of *neshama*). But, in order to achieve the level of *reiya* of *ohr eyn sof* – the infinite light of G-d – it is necessary to preface with meditation on *sovev kol olamim* ("transcendent G-dliness") utilizing *avodat hashlila* ("negative meditation") and awareness of the wonderful amazing nature of G-dliness. This may be said to correspond to the soul level of *chaya*.

116. From *Sefer Maamorim 5662* of the Rebbe Rashab, p. 221: "As explained elsewhere, [the soul-level of] *neshama* is the joining together of the soul clad in the body with the source and origin of the soul. For within *bina* [associated with the soul-level of *neshama*], we find two levels. With one, we grasp whatever is possible to grasp, and with the other, we 'understand one thing from within another thing,' meaning that we grasp that there is something lofty and beyond our intellectual understanding..." This demonstrates the two components of *neshama*; the soul as en-clothed in the body, and the ability of the soul even while in the body to grasp spirituality that transcends intellect, using *avodat hashlila* ("service of negation").

117. Interestingly, the Rebbe Rashab seems to contradict himself regarding the process of *pnimiyut hamochin*. In *Kuntres Ha'avoda* (Ch.1, page 22 in the translation, "Love like Fire and Water"), he says, "What is being established here is that intellect – through a process of negation and abstraction – leads us to comprehend the G-dliness at the very core of the concept. We gain an awareness of just what it is and how it exists (it is understood that this is not referring to *yediat hashlila* which is explained elsewhere)." Clearly, here the Rebbe differentiates between the process of abstraction associated with *pnimiyut hamochin*, and the negation and extrapolation associated with *yediat hashlila*. However, in the *Sefer Maamorim 5668* (1908), page 211, the Rebbe Rashab equates *pnimiyut bina* with *yediat hashlila*: "...and as known, *reiya* is more abstract than *yediat hashlila*, for *yediat hashlila* is associated with *pnimiyut bina*, after which we arrive to *hakara*..."

In all likelihood, though, the negation associated with *pnimiyut hamochin* (*neshama* in the soul) refers to negation of the "garments of intellect" with which we grasp a topic and understand it. It is this process which the Rebbe Rashab refers to in *Kuntres Ha'avoda*, saying that it is not *yediat hashlila*. The latter involves negation of the very concept itself (not its mere 'garments'), in order to arrive at a higher understanding that is beyond intellect (associated with *chaya* in the soul). This is the true definition of *yediat hashlila* – negation of our grasp of a concept in order to transport us to an entirely different plane of understanding. So, when the Rebbe apparently equated the two processes (as in *Sefer Maamorim 5668*), he perhaps only meant that "negation" is also a part of the process of *pnimiyut hamochin* – but only in regard to the "garments" of the concept and not the concept itself.

118. For a detailed description of this process, see *Sefer Maamorim 5663* (1903), vol.2 of the Rebbe Rashab, p. 50-52.

119. Exodus 33:20

120. See Ch. 1 of *Kuntres HaAvoda*, (p. 27 in the translation, "Love like Fire and Water")

121. The Rebbe Rashab says the following in *Sefer Maamorim 5619* (1919), page 84: "This is what is meant by *bina*, which is 'understanding one concept from within a previous concept.' From within the concept of creation from "nothing to something," we arrive to the truth that in reality, creation occurs from "something to nothing." Without the concept that creation takes place from "nothing," it is not possible to conclude that it occurs from "something to nothing." For then, the main point is missing, for we do not know or feel that creation in truth is from nothing."

Here, the Rashab is juggling two concepts of divine reality. From our human perspective, the spiritual source of the universe is "nothing," that is, a void from which the creation emerges. It is a void only to us because we are unaware of its nature. We know that it exists, but we don't know what it is, in essence. This is our initial viewpoint, and from it, we extrapolate to a higher perspective. For, although it is true that the spiritual source is "nothing," that is only from our lower point of view. From a higher, God centered point of view, the true reality is not "nothing," but the ultimate "something." Whatever is "higher," closer to Godliness, is more "real." And therefore, it is possible to say that creation takes place from the true reality, called "something" (*yesh*). This is the true nature of creation; it occurs from "something to nothing," but without prior understanding that from our perspective creation is "from nothing to something," we never achieve the higher perspective that in reality it is "from something to nothing."

122. In *Sefer Maamorim 5668* of the Rebbe Rashab, pp. 9-10; "...in order to achieve revelation of *pnimiyut halev*, one must first undergo the process of *hitzoniyut halev*, upon which he arrives to *pnimiyut halev*. For, it was explained above that the process of *pnimiyut halev* is associated with a feeling for the essence of the infinite light of G-d that is beyond intellect. And prior to the process of *chitzoniyut halev*, it is not appropriate at all to experience this. For, this feeling comes from the very inner essence of the soul, and as long as the process of *chitzoniyut halev* has not taken place, one is not at all conscious of the faculties of his G-dly soul, and he will not experience the infinite light of G-d. Rather, there must first occur revelation of the faculties of the G-dly soul as a result of meditation according to logic and intellect, and then he may possibly experience the infinite light in his soul. As the sages said, "Open up to Me the point of a pin, and I will open up to you a vast chamber..."

Although the above quote refers to the external and internal levels of the "heart," it is clear that the same applies to the external and internal levels of the intellect as well, for they are what lead to revelation of the heart.

123. *Likutei Torah* (*Parshat Ve'etchanan*), p. 2, sec. 2.

124. *Sefer Maamorim 5657* (1897) of the Rebbe Rashab, p. 273 (and *Samech Tesamech*, p. 96). In the verse regarding David and Jonathan (Shmuel 1, 20:22), Jonathan says to David, "If I say this to the lad..." The youngster who was an intermediate between David and Jonathan regarding the arrows was called a "lad." [Jonathan, son of King Saul, wished to inform his close friend, David whether he was in danger or not. To do so, he made use of a young boy, who unwittingly passed on the information to David while retrieving three arrows that Jonathan shot]. The arrows are indicative of the influence that descends from above from the Infinite One, to the collective Jewish nation. This is symbolized by the first three letters of the name *Havaya* in Jonathan's Hebrew name (*Yehonatan - yud-hey-vov*), which descend to the lower letter *hey*, symbolizing David. Sometimes, they descend with the "lad"...for sometimes the influx that descends from *z'a* above comes down via an emissary. This is the angel *Metat. Malchut*]the *sephira* associated with David[is concealed within *Metat* and the descent]of influx[takes place through him, as the *Pardess* (Gate 16, Ch 5-7) elaborates. From *Sefer Maamorim 5680* of the Rebbe Rashab, Page 60.

125. The Rebbe Rashab tells us that the relationship between "basic" and "enriched" G-dliness is personified by Yoseph and Yehudah. Yoseph (in the full manifestation of his name, Yehosef), represents "enriched" G-dliness. Yet, his name contains only three (*Yud-hey-vav*) of the four-letters of G-d's name (*Yud-hey-vav-hey*). This is because, as the mentor, or "giving" member, of this partnership, he does not possess a receptive quality. That is represented by the final receptive *hey* of G-d's name, which is found in the name of Yehudah, but not in the name of Yoseph. Yehudah, whose name contains all of the letters of G-d's name, is the recipient of Yoseph's largesse. Therefore, he is able to access the full revelation of "enriched" G-dliness that Yoseph brings into the world.

In a separate discourse (*Sefer Ma'amorim 5658*, p. 183), the Rashab mentions another biblical pair who embodied the same mentor-recipient relationship – Yehonatan and David, who were best of friends. Yehonatan was a son of King Saul, direct descendent of Yoseph's brother Benjamin, and King David was a direct descendent of Yehudah (through Tamar and later through Ruth). And again, we find the first three letters (*Yud-hey-vav*) of the name *Havaya* in the Hebrew name Yehonatan, while the name David represents the receptive *sephira* of *malchut* ("kingship"). Indeed, all of the true kings of Israel are descendents of King David. In one of the interpretations that the Rebbe Rashab offers, the verse "And Yehonatan said to David..." means that King David received and accepted the words of Yehonatan. And then the Rebbe Rashab adds that this is an allusion to one of the seminal events in Jewish history – the splitting of the Reed Sea. Elsewhere (in *Sefer Maamorim* 5663, vol. 2, pp. 309-310), he proceeds to explain that there are two types of G-dliness that come down to the world; one that comes down concealed within nature, such that the G-dly light is hidden. The purpose of the concealment is to allow "room" for physical creation, for without the concealment, there would be no physical world. But, during the splitting of the Reed Sea, a G-dly force penetrated, nature was transformed, and all who were present could detect the G-dliness within nature – this was the second kind of G-dliness that comes down to the world. If so, this is a good example of what the Rebbe Rashab meant when he said that the category of "enriched" G-dliness that is brought into the world by our prayers is open revelation of G-dliness – such as miracles that transform nature, including the splitting of the Reed Sea.

And in *Sefer Ma'amorim 5663*, pp. 59-60, the Rebbe Rashab says the following: "Accordingly, we may understand what is written, 'And Yehonatan said to David...' – [the name] Yehonatan is related to the word *matana*, meaning "gift," , and within his name are three letters from the name *Havaya*, which are the main components of the name, *Yud-Hei-Vov natan*. This indicates that the name *Havaya* is a gift given to the Jewish people...Now, the Torah is called a "gift" [when] it descends to the World of *Bria*, which takes place via David and Yehonatan, since Yehonatan and David personify *Z"A* and *malchut* of *Bria*. For, before he reigned as king, David personified *malchut* of *Bria*, and then, "Yehonatan said to him, tomorrow is Rosh Hodesh," indicating that after minimization and nullification of his former [level of] illumination and after the elevation of an offering, which indicated a general elevation for the Jewish people by way of *malchut*, then, "And you will be visited," indicating a spiritual visitation [revelation] of "new light" from *Havaya*...

(In further support of this idea, we find that *Tanya*, Ch. 2 mentions that the world could not exist if it were created solely through *din* ("judgment"). Only when G-d "partnered" judgment with mercy could the world remain in existence. And mercy is expressed in the miracles and signs of revealed G-dliness that *tzadikim* perform.

126. Sefer Ma'amorim 5658, p. 167. From the context, it seems that the Rebbe Rashab here defines the "enhanced" level of G-dliness as coming from beyond creation (*keter*), since he describes it as "total revelation of light, as written regarding the future, 'and the glory of G-d will be revealed and all flesh will see...' and 'Your teachers will no longer conceal from you,' and 'Your eyes will behold your teachers...' – this is Yoseph." However, this is not necessarily the case, since also the advanced level of *bitul*, or nullification, is associated with *chochma* and "eyesight."

127. In *Sefer Ma'amorim 5663*, p. 111. See also *Imrei Bina* of the Mitteler Rebbe, Ch. 58-59 regarding *yoreh* and *malkosh*

128. The Rebbe Rashab goes on to ask: "If the universe was created from nothing to something, then what did the sages mean when they said (in *Hagiga* 12a), 'At the time that G-d created the universe, it expanded and grew...until G-d stopped it, as it is written, "I am *El Shadai*, who said to the world, *dai*"?

He goes on to explain that the creation of the universe – via the ten statements of Genesis – provided the initial, formless substance of creation. This was the substance that "expanded and grew" without limit, as it emerged from the ten *sephirot* of *Atzilut* en-clothed in *malchut*. However, from above and beyond *Atzilut* descended a higher light, corresponding to the desire and will of G-d to create. This higher light is associated with the form of creation, which it adopts in order to conform to G-d's will. It descends to first become en-clothed in *chochma* (the first of the ten *sephirot*) and from there permeates the rest of creation. This G-dly influx enters the universe through *chochma*, which produces *bitul* ("nullification") in the world, and it corresponds to the statement of the Talmud quoted above, "I am *El Shadai*, who said to the world, *dai*."

From this, we may deduce that the *sephira* of *bina* provides the substance of creation that we feel and experience, while *chochma* is the source of form – that is, the nullification of the creation to its Creator.

129. *Sefer Ma'amorim* 5665, pp. 43-44.

130.   Elsewhere, the Rebbe Rashab indicates that the *avoda* of Yakov Avinu was to draw down this awareness of a higher reality into our mundane worldly consciousness. In fact, this was the process that he performed with the sheep of Lavan, to "draw down awareness of supernal *da'at* into the consciousness of *zerah behama* ("animal offspring" – an oblique reference to the vast majority of Jews who are not *tzadikim*), so that they as well experience supernal *da'at*" – see *Sefer Maamorim* 5678, page 82-84

The influence of the name *Havaya* upon man and creation is described in a parenthetical remark of the Rebbe Rashab: "The effect of 'the name *Havaya* governs' occurs in two ways: [One is that it] produces nullification of created existence (*yesh*) to G-dliness (*ayn*)...and the second is that it produces [the state of awareness known as] 'supernal unity' [in which we are aware of G-liness as true reality while creation recedes into the background]" – And they correspond as well to the two kinds of miracle [those that occur within nature, and those that obviously affect nature from beyond nature].

From *Sefer Maamorim* 5677, Page 197

131. From *Sefer Maamorim* 5662, pp. 267-8, we get the following explanation: "The body of Abraham did not in any way hide or conceal his soul, as written in the *Tanya*, Ch. 23, regarding the forefathers, all of whose limbs were holy and removed from all matters of the world, and they were each a 'chariot for the supernal will alone.' He [Abraham] did not have Torah and its commandments, though, since he was not told to fulfill them. And for that reason, even though his soul descended to become en-clothed in a body, he did not arrive, through his service of G-d, higher than a revelation of the name *Shaddai*, about which the sages said in *Midrash Rabba*, that this name provides 'enough G-dliness for every creature.' This implies that, at this level, miracles may also occur. Even so, these miracles occur within the framework of nature. For, the very name *Shaddai* implies *dai* ('enough'), suggesting limitations. However, here there are two levels: 1) that He said to His world *dai*, referring to borders and limits; and 2) that He supplies sufficient G-dliness to every creature – implying additional revelation of G-dliness, including miracles, as in *dai ma'chsoru*, meaning 'enough to make up what he is lacking.' In this sense, G-d meets the needs of the world, and this includes miracles as well. However, they take place within the bounds of nature."

This quotation demonstrates the second of the three levels, which involves *chochma* (which is the pinnacle of creation and all that is above *chochma* is above creation as well). According to Kabbalah, the name *Shaddai* is associated with the *sephira* of *yesod*, which is the operative *sephira* in the phrase, "In His goodness..." ("good" is associated with *yesod*). So, here we see that on one hand, the name *Shaddai* functions as "enough" for the world, implying limits and boundaries (as in the first, "basic" level of G-dliness), and yet it implies the presence of miracles as well, as G-dliness descends from above the worlds, to become en-clothed within this world, as in the second level (wherein *chochma* descends through *yesod* to *malchut*).

132. In *Sefer Ma'amorim* 5665, p. 43-44

133. Elsewhere, the Rebbe Rashab says that this "new" illumination is none other than the "light" that was set aside from the six days of creation because it was too high for the creation, and it will be fully revealed in the future. It is equivalent to the influx that flows from the hidden *shem Havaya* into the *shem Havaya* of *seder hishtalshelut* (the "spiritual chain of creation"). This is what is meant by the phrase, "And in His goodness He continuously renews creation every day." See *Sefer Maamorim* 5677 page 153, 194.

Yet elsewhere, the Rebbe Rashab appears to follow a different path. He differentiates between the verse, "Forever, *Havaya*, Your speech is established in the heavens" (Psalms 119) – which is the verse quoted by the Ba'al Shem Tov to prove that creation is an ongoing process (and the Alter Rebbe explains in *Sha'ar Hayichud ve'haemunah* that if the letters of creation were to dissipate, the creation would cease to exist) – and our statement (from prayers), "He Who in His goodness, continuously renews creation every day." The Rebbe Rashab writes that the quote from the Ba'al Shem Tov refers to the external (*hitzoni*) aspects of Godly speech, while the main process of renewal of the creation from nothing to something occurs on the internal (*pnimi*) levels of His speech represented by the phrase from *tefila* ("He Who…"). From the internal levels emerge continuous new combinations of letters in order to renew creation. (See Sefer Maamorim 5678, Page 26)

And yet, this influx from the "internal aspects" of Godly speech occurs spontaneously, without any "prompting" or "encouragement" by our performance of Torah and mitzvoth. It originates from the Godly light that is the source of creation. This illumination is associated with the covenant of Noah (when God told Noah that he would never again destroy the world, and provided the rainbow as a sign). It is not nearly as great, for example, as the level of illumination that is associated with the covenant that God made with Abraham. [So, why would it be considered to be the light that was set aside from the six days of creation for the future, as the Rashab indicates above?] – see *Sefer Maamorim 5678*, Page 122

[As if to answer the above question], the Rashab divides the illumination associated with "He Who in His goodness continuously renews the creation" into two levels, "external" and "internal." The external level is that which energizes and enlivens the world from nothing to something (as in the paraphrase above, differentiating between this statement and that of the Baal Shem Tov). The "internal" level is the renewal of the creation not from the source of creation, but from the infinite light of the One above. And that takes place as we fulfill mitzvoth, but especially as we pray. See *Sefer Maamorim 5678*, Page 152.

This "internal" level may be equivalent to that cited at the beginning of this note, (coming from *Sefer Maamorim 5677*), which is the light that was set aside for the righteous in the future. In any case, now that the Rashab has differentiated between an internal level and an external level of "He Who in His goodness continuously renews the creation," we may suggest that the differentiation applies to the two times that we utter this statement during our prayers preceding *kriat shema*. Perhaps the first time that we utter it during prayers (immediately following *Barchu*) is an allusion to the external dimensions of renewal of the creations, which do not demand any effort or input from us. And the second time (just prior to the blessing *yotzar hame'orot*) corresponds to the "internal" dimension, during which we draw upon the infinite light from Above to renew creation, during our prayers.

However, elsewhere in the writings of the Rebbe Rashab, we find a seeming contradiction to the above correspondence. In the *Sefer Maamorim 5679*, the Rashab tells us that there are two ways to leave behind our limitations during prayer. One is by use of our voice. Upon meditating on Godly topics, it helps to sing and say the prayers – this arouses our inner *kavana* or "intention" and aids the concept to filter down to our heart and become a full-fledged emotion. The second path of exit from our spiritual limitations is called *re'uta de'liba*, or the "will of the heart." It is the essential experience of the soul and its innate connection to the One above. The Jewish soul is bound in an essential connection with Godliness, and when we experience the soul directly during prayer, the result is a total and absolute detachment from any personal spiritual limitations we may have experienced previously. This is a transformational experience, totally freeing the soul from its physical bonds, and it is associated with the prayer, *emet ve'yatziv*, about halfway through the *kriat shema*. The first form of exit from our limitations, based upon meditation and logic, is associated with the blessing *ahavat olam* that occurs during bircat kriat shema. This section of prayers is called the *heichal ha'ahava*, or the "hall of love," and it includes the *shema* itself. The second form of, associated with *emet veyatziv*, is called the *hechal haratzon*, or the "hall of will."

Since we see that even the prayer *ahavat olam*, which we say after the second time that we recite, "He Who in His goodness…" is associated with intellectual meditation (which is a lesser level than His essential infinite light), it is difficult to suggest that this stage of prayer is associated with the spiritual light that God set aside for the future. That light seems to be associated with a later stage in prayer…

See *Sefer Maamorim 5679* (1919) of the Rebbe Rashab, page 349

134. In *Sefer Maamorim 5664* (from p. 127 onward), the Rebbe Rashab discusses another level of G-dliness that transcends the spirituality associated with, "And in His goodness, He constantly renews creation every day." This new level is the spirituality that descends to creation on Rosh Hashana, after the blowing of the shofar. It is a "general *chayut*" which then descends to earth on a daily basis, but which comes down as an annual "package" on Rosh Hashana. It is en-clothed in creation, but not grasped by it, and therefore it also is described by the phrase, *ayn kadosh k'Havaya* – "there is no holiness like *Havaya*." Furthermore, it is like a general ability (*koach hapoel haclali*) in relation to the details (*koach hapoel b'nifal*) that emerge from it, comparable to the human power of movement, in relation to the specific movements that we actually make. For although at any particular moment, we may perform a specific bodily movement, that movement is only one of many in the general repertoire of movements that the body possesses. Similarly, the life-force that comes down to us on Rosh Hashana is a general life-force for the year (associated with the verse, "The eyes of the Lord your G-d are upon it, from the beginning of the year until year-end"), which we access specifically every morning in prayer, as we say, "And in His goodness, He constantly renews creation every day." The general annual spirituality that descends on Rosh Hashana is beyond the daily renewal for which we pray every day.

135. In *Sefer Maamorim 5677*, page 93, the Rebbe Rashab states, "It is known that there are two types of intellectual grasp. There is grasp that results from positive intellectual activity, and grasp that is the result of negating our intellect. And *da'at*, which transcends intellectual grasp, also transcends the intellect that results from negating our intellectual grasp. For, by negating whatever intellectual grasp that we achieve, we attain some awareness of the infinite illumination that is beyond and removed from the worlds, as known. However, this awareness is only of the infinite revelation that is concerned with the creation. About this level, we can say that it is beyond the worlds. But regarding that which is totally beyond and out of range of the worlds, we cannot even describe it by saying that it is "beyond worlds"…and this is what is meant by "the ultimate knowledge is 'not to know'" – which refers to *hacara* ('recognition") of the essential infinite illumination, which is not even associated with "negation of grasp." It is equivalent to the essence of the soul that [instinctively] recognizes the essence of the infinite revelation. Just as there is essential unity in the soul, with which the essence of the soul unites with the essence of the infinite One, not via knowledge or grasp at all, but rather through cleaving of the essence with the Essence, similarly, [with] the knowledge and recognition of the

essence of our soul, [we] recognize the essence of the infinite illumination, not via knowledge or grasp, but through essential recognition…

136. See *Besha'ah Shehikdimu 5672* of the Rebbe Rashab, vol. 2, page 1199

137. In *Sefer Maamorim 5651* of the Rebbe Rashab, page 94, "But even the power of hearing is not manifest during the galut, aside from the lowest rung of hearing, which is the power of imagination alone, as is written, 'We were like dreamers…' […Regarding the example of sleeping; when our eyes are closed, all the powers of intellect and emotions disappear and nothing is left but the power of imagination and therefore, we may imagine two opposites in our dream coming together as one, since the ability to distinguish that comes with 'hearing,' associated with *bina*, is missing…this is the situation during the time of galut; although the Jews may cling to the One G-d, nevertheless at the moment that we get involved in worldly matters, with all of our mind and intellect…we are like dreamers…]"

138. This is the spiritual level that was instilled in the Jewish people by Moses as he stood on the east bank of the Jordan river, praying to G-d in *Parshat Ve'etchanan* (in which appears the commandment to recite the *shema*). He sought to enter the Land of Israel, and if he would have been permitted by G-d to enter, it would have constituted the dawn of the messianic age, and with it, vision of G-dliness with the naked eye (as will occur in the future). However, when G-d denied him entry to Israel, by standing on the east bank of the Jordan and gazing over the entire land of Israel, he instilled in the land the ability to impart *re'iya* in the mind's eye; that is, after proper detailed meditation one could reach a spiritual level in which he could detect G-dliness in the mind's eye. (From *Likutei Torah* of the Alter Rebbe on *Parshat Ve'etchanan*, page 3 column 4 of *Devorim*)

139. See *Yom Tov shel Rosh Hashana 5666* of the Rebbe Rashab, page 150 in the parentheses

140. The progression of meditative events is that first, one attains *hakara* (using *pnimiyut hamochin*) of *da'at*, and then while meditating on the *hafla'ah* (amazing transcendent nature) of G-dliness using *avodat hashlilah* ("negative meditation"), achieves *re'iya* (vision in the mind's eye) and *hitamtut* (verification and corroboration of the G-dly experience) of *chochma*. See *Yom Tov shel Rosh Hashana 5666* of the Rebbe Rashab, page 151. Intense focus and concentration is absolutely necessary: "This occurs only after a preface of labor in *avodat hashlilah* and *hakarah*, and one should not lose his focus on the matter [under meditation]; it is an essential requirement that one should not lose his concentration from it and should be constantly focused upon the matter in an ongoing manner and then [the flash of vision and *hitamtut*] will come to him suddenly from Above…"

See also *Sefer Maamorim 5668* (1908) of the Rebbe Rashab, page 211 at the bottom: "…*yediat hashlila* is associated with *pnimiyut bina*, after which we achieve *hakara* which is of the very essence of the object and after *hakara* comes the *hitamatut* associated with *reiya*, which is more abstract. The [high] level of abstraction means that the details are not so recognized, but rather the person graps the overall picture without recognizing anything in particular, since from the experience of *reiya* it is impossible for him to create any form in his soul regarding the quality and essence of the object, just how and what it is. This is unlike the experience of *hakara*, wherein one may create a certain form to himself, just how and what it is, but in *reiya* it is not possible…since he grasps the concept only from the aspect of its simplicity."

141. See *Besha'ah shehikdimu 5672* of the Rebbe Rashab, vol.2, page1199; a summary of which follows: After meditation leading to total grasp of the matter, one achieves *hakara pnimi*, or "inner recognition." That is followed by *reiya b'eyn hasechel*, or "seeing in the eye of the mind." *Hakara* also brings to *hitamtut hainyan* ("corroboration and confirmation" of the matter), which is far higher than confirmation in the mind alone (which itself is beyond mere *hakara*. And that brings to *reiya* and "yearning" which is "love-sickness" for G-dliness, since mere *reiya* cannot satisfy the soul...

142. Talmud *Berachot* 13B

143. Elaboration on saying of R Yirmiya in Talmud *Berachot* 13B

144. Zohar, Raya Mehemna, parshat Pinchas, p. 257A

145. Sefer Maamorim 5655, p. 42.

146. Sefer Maamorim 5678 (1918) of the Rebbe Rashab, p. 383

147. Sefer Maamorim 5655, pp. 124-125.

148. Midrash Raba Bereishit 1:7

149. Sefer Maamorim 5680, p. 256.

150. This discussion occurs in *Derech Mitzvotecha* of the Tzemach Tzedek, *Mitzvat Ha'amanat Elokut*, starting on p. 47B (94)

151. Hilchot Yesodei HaTorah, 2:9-10

152. According to some opinions, the prayer *emet veyatziv* is from the Torah (see *Sha'agat Aryeh, siman* 11)

153. See *Yom Tov shel Rosh Hashana 5666* of the Rebbe Rashab, page 145 and page 296

154. From the interpretation of the Mitteler Rebbe on the prayer *Baruch She'amar*

155. A detailed exposition of this historical process is found in *Sefer Maamorim 5668* of the Rebbe Rashab, page 87-88

156. In *Be'shaah Shehikdimu 5672*, vol. 2, Page 1031

157. In the *Sefer Maamorim 5654* (1894), p. 124.

158. Exodus 34:5.

159. In the *Sefer Maamorim 5665*, (1905) p. 135.

160. Deuteronomy 20:19.

161. See *Mishna, Berachot*, p.16a. See also *Heichal Menachem*, vol. 12, p. 134: *Tefila* specifically must take place with *kavana*, as in the halachic decision of the Rambam who states in *Hilchot Tefila* 4:15: "Any prayer that takes place without *kavana* is not prayer." It must be preceded by an attitude of *koved rosh* ("contriteness"). And for this it is even appropriate to miss the time of prayers in public, and to even miss the proper hour of *tefila*, since the most important thing is that the *tefila* itself should be acceptable.

162. In *Likutei Torah* of the Alter Rebbe, *Parshat Balak*.

163. Sha'arei Tefila, pp. 325-6.

164. Pirkei D' R' Eliezer, Ch. 3

165. Deuteronomy 4:7

166. Talmud *Ketubot* 111B and *Sota* 14A

167. Pesiktai Rabba 22:12, as well as *Midrash Tehilim* 91:8.

168. For more explanation, see our commentary to the section on the *Shema*.

169. Imrei Bina, Petach Sha'ar, end of ch. 17.

170. Derech Mitzvotecha, shoresh mitzvat tefila, ch. 7 (p. 234), and in *Ohr HaTorah, Ve'etchanan*, p. 377, the Tzemach Tzedek uses the parable of a King, who upon receiving the request, refers it to the appropriate "minister."

171. In *Sefer Maamorim 5662*, pp. 247-8. The Rebbe Rashab indicates that 1) the letters themselves correspond to *Zeir Anpin*, 2) the *tagin* to *bina*, 3) the *nekudot* to *chochma*, and 4) the *ta'amim* to *keter*, transcending our intellect.

172. In kabbalistic terms, the letters are associated with *Zeir Anpin*, the seven lower emotional *sephirot* of the World of *Atzilut*.

173. In *Sefer Maamorim 5668* (1908) of the Rashab, page 179 in parentheses, "(And in particular, we might say that there are three aspects of the name *Havaya* in *Atizlut*; the first being that which the name *Havaya* arrives via contraction to be within range of the vessels (*kelim*), meaning that it comes to be limited by the letters of the name *Havaya*. And even more in particular, we might say that this refers to the vowelization of *Havaya*...)." This points to the connection between the name *Havaya* itself and how it connects with the vessels of *Atzilut*, by way of the vowels associated with each *sephira*.

174. In *Shulhan Aruch, Yoreh Deah, siman 246, sif katan 4*

175. In his commentary on *Mishlei* ("Proverbs")

176. In one known case, a Chasidic yeshiva student asked his spiritual mentor if it was permissible for him to study Kabbalah. His mentor replied the "one who has learned a substantial amount of Chasidut may look into Kabbalah." Notice that the reply was not that one may "learn" or "study" Kabbalah, but "look into it." That is, if it is necessary or helpful to clarify a concept by looking into Kabbalah, then an experienced student of Chasidut may reference books of Kabbalah.

177. In the section called *Inyan cavanat ha'amida, drosh vov.*

178. As it is written in the *Tikunim*, no. 70, p. 128a.

179. The Mitteler Rebbe, R' Dov Ber of Lubavitch, says in *Torat Chaim, parshat Noach*, page 64 column 3, that the name *Havaya* of *Hasheveinu* should be a *sheva*, since the subject is *tshuva*, associated with the *sephira* of *gevura*. However, in his *Shaarei Tefila* (within *Shaarei Teshuva*), p. 43 column 4, the Mitteler Rebbe says it should be with a *tzeirei*.

180. The Mitteler Rebbe, R' Dov Ber of Lubavitch, says in *Torat Chaim, parshat Noach*, page 64, column 3, that the name *Havaya* of *Refa'einu* should be a *segol*, since recovering from illness is associated with the *sephira* of *tiferet*.

181. The Mitteler Rebbe, R' Dov Ber of Lubavitch, says in *Torat Chaim, parshat Noach*, page 64 column 3, that the name *Havaya* of *Bareich Aleinu* should be a *tzeirei*, since our *parnasa* is associated with the *sephira* of *chesed*.

182. *Raya Mehemna, Parshat Teitzei*, p. 276b.

183. In *Kuntres Avoda*, ch. 6.

184. Genesis 28:12.

185. *Likutei Torah* of the Alter Rebbe, *Parshat Ve'etchanan.*

ADDITIONAL CHASSIDIC EXCERPTS

"My Lord, the soul that You placed within me..."
RE: *Elokai, neshama shenatati bi* ("My Lord, the soul that You placed within me")
At first glance, this is puzzling ... The body without a soul is like an inanimate stone, incapable of saying anything, and if it is the soul that is expressing this, how can it say, "the soul that you placed within me"?

This is the explanation, as written elsewhere regarding the two souls that every Jew possesses:

The animal soul makes a claim, making this statement regarding the G-dly soul that is enclothed within it. For, just as the animal soul is enclothed within the limbs of the body, the intellect is enclothed in the mind, emotions in the heart, sight in the eyes, etc., so the G-dly soul is enclothed in the animal soul. Its intellect is enclothed in the intellect [of the animal soul], its emotions are enclothed in the emotions [of the animal soul], etc. For, there is no way for G-liness [to descend] without [first] becoming enclothed in human intellect, even though the intellect of the G-dly soul is G-dly and the same is true of the emotions and the remainder of its soul powers.

Thus the phrase, "the soul that You placed within me" refers to the animal soul within the body, since the animal soul in comparison to the G-dly soul is like a body ... However, it is understood that the essence of the G-dly soul – the *yechida* level of the soul – is united with the very essence of G-d like a detail in relation to its general principle. And this is what is meant by *tehora he* ("it is pure") in reference to the soul, wherein the word *tehora* ("pure") is related to the Aramaic word *tihara* ("noon-time sun") or to the Hebrew word, *tohar* ("bright/shining"), indicating bright illumination that descends from its natural level to become spiritual illumination within our *nara'n* (*nefesh, ruach* and *neshama* – the three lower levels of the soul, en-clothed in the body). Or, in the words of the Kabbalists, it descends to illuminate the worlds of *BY"A* (*Bria, Yetzira* and *Asiya*). And thus, the prayer continues: "The soul that You placed within me, You created, You formed, and You blew into me," all for the purpose of en-clothement within the animal soul. For, the G-dly soul itself desires nothing more than to separate from the animal soul and to become included within the very essence of G-dliness. As is written, "The soul of man is like a candle of G-d,"[378] and as described in the *Tanya* that, just as the nature of fire is to ascend of its own volition (meaning the fire that is burning in a wick naturally tends upward as if to separate from the wick), so is the nature of the G-dly soul.

However, "You guard my soul within me" so that I don't sin, as the sages said, "If it weren't for the help of G-d, the person would be unable [to fend off temptation]."[379] For, it is known that the main reason for the descent of the G-dly soul into the animal soul is in order to grant it the power to "embrace the body of the King,"[380] far above [the soul's] present source and origin. [The universe is considered to be a "garment" that both hides and reveals G-dliness. Since it does not directly reveal G-d, it is said to be "concealing Him," but since through meditating upon nature we are able to detect His divine Presence and providence, in a certain sense, the universe also reveals G-dliness. So, whether by meditating to detect G-dliness in nature or by fulfilling His commandments, we don His "garments" so to speak, and ultimately "embrace" the King Himself.]

And that is what is meant by, "And You will take it away from me in the future," referring to G-d as "You," indicating G-d in essence. But all this is "from me," [referring to the animal soul]. And the proof of this is that the main reward of the soul in the future, during the resurrection of the dead, will be received by souls enclothed in bodies and in animal souls. And thus, the prayer continues, "And to return it within me in the future to come" (in accordance with the Ramban and not with the Rambam), and therefore "all the time that the soul is within me, I thank You, master of all deeds..." and it concludes, "He who returns souls to dead bodies," as explained that sleep is one-sixtieth of death...

(From letters of the *Tzemach Tzedek* in *Meah Shearim*, page 90)

Details of the Morning Blessings

RE: *Pokeach ivrim* ("the One Who opens the eyes...")

The main distinction between the realm of holiness and the *sitra achra*, (the "other side" composed of forces opposed to holiness) concerns the spiritual vision of the intellect. The sages are called the "eyes of the congregation"[381] ... but about [those from] the realm of concealment of G-dliness, it is written, "They have eyes but they see not."[382] [It all depends upon] the vision of the intellect, as it is written, "Who is a wise man? He who envisions the future."[383] This spiritual vision involves recognition of the essence of the matter, just as one sees with his eyes. In the language of the *Zohar*,[384] this is called "to gaze upon the glory of the King." And the "the other side" does not possess this vision of the intellect that cuts to the very essence of the matter...

RE: *Matir asirim* ("He who frees the imprisoned")

When man is imprisoned, such that his hands are tied and bound, the hands symbolize the emotions, as the *Zohar* says, "kindness is the right hand..." The animal soul overwhelms the G-dly soul, and then the powers of the G-dly soul are bound and tied like a man who is captured among foreign forces.

RE: *Zokef kefifim* ("He Who uplifts up the bent over")

The main difference between man and animal is that man walks upright, with his head held high and his heart below. And below that are the legs, the locus of action. So, regarding the G-dly soul, the main thing is the intellect that governs the emotions until a decision to act is made. But the feet are the main foundation upon which the body rests. If the person tries to "think with his feet," of course the entire body follows. And the main thing is to conduct ourselves by "refraining from evil" and "pursuing good deeds"[385] in physical terms of action. As it is written, "Keep My laws and My commandments that man should do, and you will live by them..."[386] [That is, when man follows both the rational (with his head) and the supra-rational (without asking questions) commandments of the Torah, he makes spiritual progress in this world and is rewarded in the world to come]. And the opposite as it is written, "the way of the wicked is dark, they know not on what they stumble."[387]

RE: *Malbish arumim* ("He who clothes the naked")

The sages said, "The person who grasps a Torah scroll while naked (holding the parchment with his bare hand, rather than grasping it through a cloth - *Rashi*) will be buried naked,"[388] and they concluded that "naked" means without a particular mitzvah.

Now, we can understand this when we consider what is written: "The snake was naked/clever..."[389] The snake comes from the three totally impure *klipot* (levels of concealment of G-dliness) that possess no good whatsoever – and therefore he was "naked" [lacking holiness or mitzvot]. And in the beginning, when man was born, he was "naked" on account of his animal soul, bereft of any revelation of G-dliness from the fulfillment of mitzvot ... However, when he accepted upon himself the yoke of heaven, he was like one who becomes enclothed in a garment that wraps him from head to foot...

RE: *Hanoten le'yaef koach* ("He who gives strength to the weary")

This is similar to the statement of the sages, "He who answers 'Amen, may His name be great' with all of his strength is rewarded by nullification of any decrees (of up to seventy years[390]) declared against him."[391] The expression, "with all his strength" corresponds to *bekol nafshecha* ("with all of your soul") which we say when reciting the *Shema*. This [power to pray with "all your strength" and thereby to nullify decrees from Above] comes from beyond...our [human] will, intellect and emotions, and the like. And as a result of this [level that is beyond us], we say *Amen yehai shmei rabah* ("Amen, may His Name be great") – [since His great Name] is associated with revelation of infinite G-dliness is beyond all the details of the ten *sephirot* in all the four worlds, etc.

His great Name should be blessed forever, meaning in all four worlds. And this is [also] what is meant by *hanoten le'yaef koach* ("He who gives strength to the weary"), which describes a man who is tired and drained and unable to act with the full strength of his soul-powers in all the limbs of the body. Similarly, when man gets involved in all the activities of this world with all of its vicissitudes, the powers of his G-dly soul fail to shine within his animal soul and within the limbs of his body, unless he strives with overwhelming effort to activate the transcendent element of his G-dly soul. And then, the G-dly soul acts from over and beyond, responding with all of its strength, via his fulfillment of mitzvot...

RE: *Rokah ha'aretz al hamayim* ("He who spreads out the earth upon the waters")

It is among the kindnesses of G-d in the creation that He desires a dwelling place for Himself in the lower worlds. And this is what is intended by this blessing. [G-d's desire for a dwelling place in the "lowest worlds" applies to the] earth, which represents action [since man lives and "acts" on earth. From this perspective, earth] is higher than water, which represents G-dly revelation [Water, since it descends from Above to below, represents G-dly illumination. It is not as significant as G-d Himself 'dwelling' here in the lower physical world of action]. (For this reason, we say that fulfillment of mitzvot does not require our conscious awareness[392]). And that is an example of His kindness [in dwelling among us, even though we are barely aware of Him], which is "forever." And that is what is meant afterward by this blessing...

RE: *Hamachin mitzadei gaver* ("He who directs the steps of man")

It is written, "Man's footsteps are guided by G-d, and it is man's path that G-d desires."[393] [That is, G-d leads us to the path, but it is the steps that we take of our own initiative along that path, that He desires]. And similarly, it is written, "And with You, Lord, is kindness, and You recompense man in accordance with his deeds."[394] At first glance, what is the kindness in repaying someone in accordance with his deeds? But, this matter corresponds to what the sages said, "If it weren't for the help of G-d, man would be unable to withstand temptation,"[395] and as written in the Talmud that "every day a voice emerges [saying, 'Return wayward children, return...]"[396] [All these verses indicate that although man must take the initiative, his initiative from below is ignited and guided from Above. Even when he takes the initiative, man is led to the right path by G-d. Moreover, if it weren't for G-d's guidance and guarding man at every stage along the path, man would not succeed.]

In the language of the Kabbalists, this is called the "power to elevate *ma'n*." [*Ma'n* is *mayin nukvin*, or "feminine waters." It refers to arousal from below to take a spiritual path, or initiative to approach G-d.] And if so, it does not take place purely upon the initiative of man, but rather with support and help from G-d...

This is like by way of example, "The will of those who fear Him, He does" ["those who fear Him" are righteous *tzadikim*, to whom G-d granted the ability to bless and help other human beings, as well as to counter the wicked. Thus, G-d "does the will of those who fear Him," meaning that when they bless others, or curse the wicked, G-d causes their blessing to come to fruition]. ...G-d creates in man a desire and will to serve Him. And nevertheless, "He hears their cry and He rescues them..." [Although man feels that He is acting of his own volition, in truth his desire to act was initiated by G-d. And therefore, when man falters on the path, it is G-d who comes to the rescue]...and this is what is meant by "the steps of man are directed." It refers to the spontaneous power and potential of the G-dly soul to act, that exists within every Jewish person to pursue mitzvot...[Jews, fulfilling mitzvoth, are on the path, doing the will of the One above. They are granted free choice to continue on this path (of *halicha*, meaning progress, corresponding to *halacha*, the laws upon which a Jew bases his life), upon which G-d constantly opens new spiritual horizons. It is man's choice to progress on this path, but G-d led him to the choice and guides and protects him as he progresses].

RE: *Sh'asah li kol tzorki* ("He who provides for my every need")

This we say upon putting on our shoes in the morning, representing the *makif* of the "leg," [Every part of the body needs an inner enlivening vitality, called *ohr penimi*, as well as a transcendent, *makif* force that guides and protects it. Since it encompasses the foot, the shoe represents the transcendent, *makif* force that guides and protects our steps as we progress, spiritually and physically.]

RE: *Ozer Yisroel bigevura* ("He who girds Israel with might")

This we say when donning the belt and surrounding the body with it; the body represents the emotions, for it is known that the emotions are called the "body," as it is written, "*tiferet* is the body,"[397] and this refers to the surrounding light of the emotions themselves.

RE: *Otar Yisroel betiferet* ("He who crowns Israel with glory")

The *atara* ("crown," which is the noun corresponding to the verb, *otar*, the first word of the blessing) is the *makif*, or transcendent illumination of the intellect. It corresponds to the *tefillin* of the head. Thus, the blessing that applies to all of the specific powers of the G-dly soul that shine within the particular powers of the animal soul, whether outside or inside, whether *makif* or *pnimi*.

From letters of the *Tzemach Tzedek* in *Meah Shearim*, pp. 90-92

Salt and meditation

It is written, "There should never cease to be salt, the covenant of the Lord your God (*Havaya Elokecha*)...you should offer salt with all of your sacrifices." Salt contributes taste to whatever it is placed on. For example, when we salt meat, the first result is that it removes the waste (that is, the blood) from the meat. Afterward, the salt contributes flavor to the meat and preserves it. And that is because the spiritual source of salt is from *ta'amim* ("flavors" – a reference to the level of *chochma*, which is *bitul* or self-nullification and therefore imparts the ability to persist. The word *chaich*, embedded in the word *chochma*, means the "palate," the center of our sense of taste). That is why salt is called the "covenant of the Lord your God," since it joins the name *Havaya* with the name *Elokim*.

The name *Elokim* contains one hundred and twenty possible combinations of letters [there are five letters, and the number of possible combinations of those letters is 5!, or 120]. That is, every letter of the name can create twenty-four (one fifth of the total) combinations. So, the final two letters – *yud* and *mem* (yam, or "ocean") - are associated with forty-eight combinations. Since they are the final two letters [and therefore the least important], the negative forces of the universe are able to attach themselves [to them] and siphon off energy. Salt represents *chochma*, about which we say, "with wisdom comes clarity," and this is the "wisdom" that provides the clarity to prevent over-nourishment of the negative forces. This then is what is meant by "salt, the covenant of your God" - alluding to a descent of the Name *Havaya* into the name *Elokim*, so that the negative forces will be unable to siphon away energy [the dark forces can only siphon energy from where there is no revelation of Godliness. But when the essential name *Havaya* shines into *Elokim*, the Godly revelation makes it impossible for the negative forces to siphon energy from the final two letters of *Elokim*].

In *avoda* [our personal worship of God], the verse says, "and *Havaya Elokim* formed the man..." Now, *Havaya* and *Elokim* are the sources of the Godly soul and the animal soul, respectively. The animal soul is formed after many concealments and obscurations of the name *Elokim* as it descends the chain of creation (*seder hishtalshelut*). And the purpose of the divine soul is to refine and rectify the animal soul. It does so using the logic (*ta'am* – "taste") and grasp of the Godly soul. When we meditate on a Godly concept and we understand it with our animal soul as well, while experiencing the good of Godliness, we nullify the animal soul. At that point, it also desires Godliness. As a result, the logic and intellect that grasps Godliness clarifies and refines the waste within the animal soul, so that it emerges from the state of coarse physicality and negative character traits within it and also becomes nullified to Godliness.

This process takes place only while utilizing intellectual grasp and meditation, for this is what performs the refinement of the animal soul. Without the labor of intellectual grasp and meditation, even though we might forcefully subdue our animal soul, thus weakening it, this is not true refinement. That occurs only when we meditate, and only when we meditate utilizing the laws of logic and intellect. For when we meditate upon matters that transcend logic and intellect, it is possible that our meditation will bear no connection with the animal soul. And if it does bear a connection with the animal soul, it is possible that the effect will be to totally nullify it, without refining it at all...in order to perform refinement, it is necessary to meditate using logic and intellect...

...And this is comparable to salt, which refines the waste product from out of the meat and imparts flavor. The animal soul represents the "flesh" of man, and our divine soul imparts "flavor" and logic through meditation, separating out the waste product of the animal soul and imparting logic so that it conducts itself within the boundaries of reason. Although in essence, the animal soul is emotional, nevertheless it may be persuaded to act according to the intellect and logic of the Godly soul. This is the advantage of the sea, in which is salty water, representing the reason of logic and Godly intellect within the soul, with which it performs a refinement and rectification of the animal soul.

From *Sefer Maamorim 5679* (1919) of the Rebbe Rashab, page 390

Spirit of Folly

The spirit of folly *(ruach shtut)* is the spirit of lust that hides and conceals, so that Godly illumination fails to penetrate. The cause of this is lack of *avoda* with effort during prayer. For, if we serve God during prayer with meditation upon Godly concepts, delving into the concepts with our faculty of *da'at* ("knowledge, recognition") so that we feel the concepts within ourselves, we then develop love and fear of God. This in turn weakens the animal soul, since "when one arises, the other falls..." In particular when we meditate in order to have an effect upon our animal soul, it also begins to understand [Godly concepts], using its natural intellect. And this causes it to become aroused with love of God.

However, when *avoda* is lacking, or even when we serve God, but in an inappropriate manner, such as when our meditation lacks depth and honesty, then automatically our love and fear is also superficial. It consists of false images alone, that are temporary and passing. The excitement that we develop is fleeting and temporary, after which the animal soul automatically comes to dominate. At first, this occurs with permitted objects, such as when we are tempted by something and are unable to hold ourselves back since there is no Godly light in our soul. Today, [the animal soul] tells him, "do this," and tomorrow ["do that"]...until he does something that is forbidden. So, it emerges that lack of *avoda* is the cause of the overwhelming domination of the physical side, and the domination of the physical causes us to sin...

From *Sefer Maamorim* 5679 (1919) of the Rebbe Rashab, page 293

Prayer is higher than the sacrifices

Even those who transgressed a command of God, are nevertheless joined with Him throughout the generations by prayer, which is in lieu of the sacrifices. And furthermore, the sages said that prayer is greater than the sacrifices, and we find an advantage to prayer over the sacrifices. For, the sages declared that it is forbidden to eat before praying, because of the verse, "Do not eat over the blood..." which the sages interpret to mean that we should not eat before we pray for our own "blood" (vitality, life-force). Sacrifices on the other hand are described as *achila*, or "eating," as the verse says, "My sacrifices, sustenance for my men..." And since prayer is in lieu of the sacrifices, why is it forbidden to eat before prayers? From this, we conclude that our prayers have a certain advantage over the sacrifices...

From *Sefer Maamorim* 5679 (1919) of the Rebbe Rashab, pp. 535

As a result of eating...

...The spiritual source of food is very high, as written, "There is no blade of physical grass that is without a spiritual source..." and [the source] itself has origins, each higher than the next...all the way up to its origins in the world of *Tohu* that precedes *Tikun*. And therefore when we eat this food with proper intention for the One above, we refine the good from within the food, and elevate it to its source in the world of *Tohu*. [Thus the food] has the effect of elevating him to the level of *Tohu*, and in this manner it adds more holy illumination. Just as physical food enlivens man, so proper purification of the food gives man a spiritual lift, adding Godly illumination. This is additional light, unlike the physical process in which food enlivens us, in a process of mere renewal alone. The vitality that is added by this process of refinement is additional illumination, and whatever God adds to us is over and beyond the basic vitality that we already possess.

And thus, we may offer a new interpretation of the following verse, "Not by bread alone does man live, but by all that emerges from the mouth of God man lives..." We find here two classes; the vitality within the bread, and the vitality that emerges from the mouth of God. For, the verse does not proclaim that man "does not live from bread, but from whatever emerges..." Rather, it says, "Not by bread alone does man live." This implies that the life force of the bread provides mere "renewal of vitality" while the vitality that "emerges from the mouth of God..."

alludes to the holy spark that becomes elevated in the eating process, providing additional illumination.

From *Sefer Maamorim 5679* (1919) of the Rebbe Rashab, pp. 539-540

The proper approach to prayer

re: *Ayn Omdim...* – "We do not approach prayer except with a contrite mind")

"The eyes of the wise man are in his head."[398] This means that a wise man's entire focus and introspection are directed toward the *Shechina* ("Divine Presence"), which is also called the "Head." In this manner, his focus and introspection take place in accordance with the Talmudic directive [in Tractate *Berachot*]: "We do not approach prayer except with a contrite mind." The Maggid of Mezritch [successor to the Ba'al Shem Tov] interprets this as follows:

> When man requests and prays for what he is lacking, he should not pray for his own deficiency, but for the deficiency that exists Above, since there is nothing lacking down here that is not related to a deficiency Above. And as the saying goes, "When man suffers, the *Shechina* says, so to speak, 'My head aches, my arm hurts...'" And when the deficiency Above is rectified, the deficiency below also becomes resolved. This is what is meant by "focus" of the head – that is, praying over whatever is lacking Above...

[How can anything be lacking Above?]

When there is no divine influence shining into [the final *sephira* of] *malchut*, then no influence descends to us. And whatever influence exists Above remains hidden in the "seventy ministers" [of the seventy nations] of *noga* [the fourth level of *klipa*, or concealing "shell," which contains a mixture of good and bad]. And that is why spiritual work is necessary. About this it is said, "We do not approach prayer except with a contrite mind," since it is necessary to pray over the deficiency that exists Above – which is the exile of the *Shechina*. And that is the purpose of *tikun chatzot* [the midnight prayers], when we mourn the destruction of the Temple and the exile of the *Shechina*. And then afterward, we submit our request to fulfill what is lacking. Our request must be submitted in joy, as the sages said,[399] "We do not approach prayer except in happiness," and as it is written, "because you failed to serve the Lord your G-d happily ... you shall serve your enemies..."[400] But, to begin with, we must adopt a contrite attitude, because the deficiency should bother us. And then afterward we may submit our requests in joy ... this is the interpretation of the Maggid of Mezeritch, that prayer must be over the divine deficiency that exists Above...

And the Alter Rebbe further explains that the saying, "We do not approach prayer except with a contrite [literally, "heavy"] mind..." applies to the souls of the Jews. For about the Nation of Israel, G-d says, *li rosh* ("they are a head for Me") [*li rosh* is a permutation of the Hebrew letters of the word *Yisroel*]. And we must pray over the "heaviness" of this head...

This is what is meant by *li rosh*: Jewish souls originate from the thought of G-d. This is the garment most intimately united with Him, and it imparts to the Jews a natural, ingrained love for G-d. Therefore, it is not necessary for the Torah to command this love, because it is naturally present in each and every Jew. However, this love is hidden; the *sephirot* of the World of *Atzilut* (the world of *tikun*, or "rectification") – as well as the emotions of man down here in this world – do not become revealed on their own. They are concealed, and we must arouse them by way of the intellect. And this is why we are commanded [in the *Shema* to "love the Lord Your G-d with all your heart(s), with all your soul and with all your might"]. We must fulfill this commandment by meditating and contemplating how "the Lord is our G-d," and how Jewish souls are absolutely united with G-dliness, and how His infinite holy light arouses our love of G-d...

However, all of this applies only when our love is not diverted in another direction but is simply hidden. Then it is possible to arouse it through meditation. But, when the love becomes diverted to other matters, then it cannot be directed toward G-d ... because the other matters hide and conceal the revelation of love. Then, meditation does not help, for even if our mind meditates, our heart is not affected. And in truth, the meditation itself is compromised, since when we are greatly tempted by material objects, a blockage of our mind (*timtum hamo'ach*) occurs, and we are unable to accurately grasp the subtle refinement of G-dly concepts. Even worse; it affects what we are capable or incapable of absorbing and experiencing in our soul. But, the main thing is that [the temptation of the physical] affects our potential to achieve excitement of the heart, since we experience a blockage. For, it is possible to meditate properly while understanding the topic well and experiencing mental stimulation, and yet the heart remains uninvolved...

And this is what is meant by *koved rosh* – "contriteness," or "heaviness of the head," wherein the "heaviness" is something that occurs in the mind, like a load that is too heavy. And about this it is said, "We do not approach prayer except with a contrite/heavy mind," and Rashi[401] explains that this means, "with a subdued attitude and humility." That is, we should be sad over the lack of G-dly illumination shining [within] and over the weakness of our G-dly soul. In this way, we may eventually achieve a [breakthrough, with] revelation of G-dly love.

Now, this revelation of G-dly light and love arrives through intellectual understanding and meditation while in a state of joy. Love of G-d arrives as the result of revelation of light shining within our intellect, and this is facilitated by happiness, for joy brings revelation. Joy during meditation achieves more than the meditation itself. It provides the energy that facilitates meditation. In this manner, we absorb and integrate the subject matter of the meditation within, arousing excitement of our heart.

But, the happiness must be preceded by contriteness. The contriteness does not cause of revelation of love (which arrives via intellectual grasp and meditation), but rather the bitterness clears away blockages and concealments, allowing revelation of love. But, the love itself is a result of our meditation and intellectual grasp. In any case, we must experience contriteness, because without it, no understanding that we achieve through meditation, with its accompanying energy will be effective. So, first we must undergo bitterness to remove the concealments and blockages, and afterward by way of meditation and understanding, we will achieve revelation of light of love.

This, then, is what is meant by, "When you elevate the heads of the Jewish people..."[402] Sometimes, we experience bouts of "heaviness of the head," and to counter them we must undergo "elevation of the head," referring to the ascent of the G-dly soul to its source and origin and even beyond that...

(From *Sefer Maamorim 5758* (1898) of the Rebbe Rashab, pp.147-151)

Distraction during prayer...

...According to the exalted level of the infinite light above, and its degree of removal from the creation, so the entire existence of the world is called into question (lit: becomes lack of existence). And in the higher worlds, where [spiritual creatures such as angels] feel the lack of their own presence and existence in light of essential Godliness – that is, they are aware of and understand the amazing nature of the infinite light and how the worlds possess no real presence whatsoever – they become nullified in their very essence. This is comparable to a minor sage who becomes nullified in comparison to a great sage – he loses his own sense of existence.

Now, this lack of existence may be understood below, as we observe the ways of one who serves God by fulfilling mitzvoth, and even moreso as he prays. Such a person may at times become distracted by another person, all in accordance with the people and the place and the time. And then, he must struggle within himself so that the other person does not distract him. However, [when his *avoda*] is real and honest, meaning that he performs the mitzvah honestly from his soul, and when his prayer emerges honestly from his heart, or that his prayers lead him to honest, inner conclusions, then nobody distracts or bothers him. He does not nullify the other (who is bothering him), but it is as if the other does not exist. Nothing whatsoever bothers or distracts him. In common language, we say that, "he doesn't think about him." And why not? Because the other carries no significance in his eyes whatsoever. The reason for this is his own spiritual status; he became elevated to a higher level, to which the other bears no connection at all. And then, the other becomes truly nullified...from this we may understand that regarding the essential infinite light that is remove d and out of range from the worlds, the worlds and creations bear no connection whatsoever, and it is if they do not exist.

From *Sefer Maamorim 5679* (1919) of the Rebbe Rashab, page 273-4

Spiritual levels within prayer

Overall, our prayers equate to the excitement and arousal within our soul, which includes a great desire for Godliness. Mainly, the excitement stems from the essential idea that, "If your heart is focused, then your prayers are acceptable; if not, then you have not prayed."

Now, prayer – all of it - is associated with meditation. This applies to the *pesukei dezimra*, and the blessings preceding the *kriat shem* and the *kriat shema* itself, for the entire purpose of prayer is to achieve arousal of the soul with a desire for Godliness. The main point here is the desire that arises from the essence of the soul, about which the Torah says that prayer is a "ladder standing on the ground, with its head reaching into the heavens." The words, "standing on the ground" refers to the soul as it is enclothed in a body. This includes the lower three levels of the soul – the *nephesh, ruach* and *neshama*. Meditation on this level demands logic and intellect, as written, "to love the Lord your God because He is your life." This means that just as man loves the vitality of his own soul, so when he meditates upon the infinite illumination above, which is the "Life of lives," he comes to love Godliness. Now, this love is limited. It occurs in proportion to his intellect and the feelings that he experiences within his soul. In general, when our meditation upon Godliness involves intellectual grasp, our focus is upon Godliness that is en-clothed within the worlds. With this meditation, we feel and experience the elevation and preciousness of Godliness within our soul. In this manner, we approach and cleave our soul to Godliness. All of this is limited according to the manner of our intellectual grasp of Godliness and according to our experience of the Godly elevation.

However, the intense desire that arises from the essence of our soul, inducing us to abandon our *kelim* ("vessels" or faculties of the soul) as well as to leave behind our limitations, [does not occur] according to intellect. The essential, natural will that arises from within our soul, with an essential desire for Godliness is not related to logic and intellect at all. [Rather], it is *mesirat nephesh* ("devotion, self-sacrifice"), which involves nullification of all of our desires. We abandon not only our physical desires, but even our spiritual desires...and this is what is meant by the words, "and its head reaches into the heavens." It is the main goal of prayer – the revelation of transcendent levels (*chaya* and *yechida*) within the soul...

Prayer takes place with utter self sacrifice (*mesirat nephesh*), which grasps the very essence of the Infinite one. Via *avoda* with self sacrifice, we [access and] bring down the very essence of the infinite one, as a revelation of new illumination. This is what is meant by, "And you shall worship the Lord your God" – by worshipping and praying with *mesirat nephesh* from the very essence of our soul, we draw down the essence of the infinite light into the *sephirot* of *chochma* and *bina*. And in order to achieve this revelation of the essence of the soul, our *avoda* must take place in a specific order. The order is that first we must meditate, utilizing logic and intellect. For, in order to arrive to a higher level of grasp, we first need to undergo the *avoda* of logic and intellect. It is impossible to start *avoda* on a level that is beyond intellect. Rather the beginning has to be according to intellect and then afterward our intellect can take us to levels that are beyond the intellect...for our intellect is capable of bringing us to levels that transcend logic, as written (in the *nusach* of prayers), "and place in our heart understanding to grasp one thing from within another." The phrase, "from within another" refers to the immanent spirituality (*memalle kol olamim*) that we daily experience in intellect and feeling, while "to grasp one thing" refers to the transcendent Godliness (*sovev kol olamim*) that is beyond us. From that which we understand and experience, then, we grasp concepts which are beyond us, as well.

Now, this may occur in a number of different ways. We may meditate, for example, on the concept that all that we are capable of grasping is a mere ray and reflection of Godliness alone, from which we conclude that His essence is not really graspable. Or, we may proceed along the path of "negative, or circumscribed" knowledge. As known, this path takes us to the infinite light that is not graspable with any constructive concept or description, but only by negating what we already know and grasp. Nevertheless, this negation brings us to some "recognition" of the infinite, amazing illumination...So, the process begins, first of all from our initial positive intellectual grasp. And then, via our prior knowledge of what is graspable, we develop an ability to know what to negate within the infinite light. And with this negation comes recognition of the infinite, amazing illumination above...That is, via logic and intellect, we transcend our previous level of knowledge and intellect.

Now, it is also true that all levels of revelation of the soul are granted from above. And they arrive after a preface of *avoda* that takes place according to the rules of logic and intellect...moreover, revelation of love from above arrives after we cultivate love of God from below. That is, via true *avoda* predicated upon the laws of logic and intellect, we are granted the ability to serve God in a manner that is beyond logic and intellect as well. Now, this usually took place among "high" souls, whose *avoda* of love and fear of God according to logic and intellect was true, real *avoda*. And their grasp of Godliness was total; their understanding of Godliness led them to true and total spiritual grasp, and they utilized "negative" or circumscribed knowledge, as well. In general, this occurred when the Temple stood, when there was revelation of all of our soul powers, including spiritual vision and hearing. That is, when the Temple still stood, people grasped whatever was possible to understand of Godliness, and they grasped it completely, with *avoda* was true and real. But, in the current time of exile, we are relatively low souls, and our *avoda* of love and fear of God is not fully authentic. Even more-so, our grasp of Godliness is incomplete, and we are incapable of exercising "negation of knowledge" or achieving recognition of the infinite illumination from Above. And so, we are not capable of achieving revelation of the essence of the soul in an orderly manner. And therefore, we resort to *ohr chozer* – "reflected light." This process corresponds to the verse in Psalms, "And they screamed out to *Havaya*," as a result of the concealment and hiddeness [from Godliness] that they experienced. When we meditate upon our distance from God, and even when we succeed in arousing our souls with love and fear of God, our feelings are not authentic at all. In particular, when we recognize that this is because of our utter lack of *avoda* and because we are drawn after physical lusts and the enjoyments of the worlds, we then become embittered within over this state of affairs. This is what compels us to "scream from the heart." And when the essence of our soul becomes revealed with intense desire, that desire is for the very essence of the infinite One. Even though we are not at all within range, and we are nothing in relation to the very essence [of Godliness] and to feeling the infinite One, nevertheless we embody the true concept of what is beyond logic and intellect. We experience an intense desire for His infinite illumination, even though we have no [true] feeling whatsoever for the infinite one Himself. And also, since in essence we are out of range of Him, so this *avoda* for us is a real "jump", beyond anything orderly, and beyond any step by step approach.

From *Sefer Maamorim 5679* (1919) of the Rebbe Rashab, page 231-232

The Four Stages of Prayer

"There are four stages to prayer, corresponding to the four levels of the soul; *nefesh-ruach-neshama* and *neshama d'neshama*, which corresponds to the two *makifim* ("transcendent levels") of *chaya* and *yechida*. Our prayers begin on the level of *nefesh*, meaning "acknowledgment," as written, *Hodu L'HaShem* ("Acknowledge/give thanks to the Lord..."). Now, it is known that acknowledgment is not mere agreement (a "nod of the head"), but rather implies surrendering ourselves (while giving ourselves over). While in this state, we "relinquish ourselves" to G-dliness. For example, one who concedes to his friend, even though he may not understand why, nevertheless admits that his friend is correct. In this sense, he "relinquishes himself" to his friend. And so it is in serving G-d: We deliver ourselves to G-dliness. This means that in the beginning [when we arise in the morning] as we say *modeh ani lefanecha* ("I acknowledge/give thanks to You"), we cede ourselves to G-d in our entirety, even though we do not yet know the details that are involved in this "concession." And afterward [when we start to pray], we say *Hodu LaShem* ("Give thanks/acknowledge the Lord") and we do know the details involved, as known regarding the phrase *Hodu LaShem vekiru b'shmo* ("Give thanks/ acknowledge... proclaim His name")...this is the level of *nefesh*.

And afterward, during the *pesukei dezimra* ("verses of song"), we experience the level of *ruach*, during which we recite praises of the One above; how He enlivens and creates the universe, as we say, *Baruch sheamar vehaya haolam* ("Blessed be He Who uttered and the universe came into existence..."). Or, as we also say, "He Who covers the heavens with clouds, Who prepares rain for the land, Who causes the mountains to sprout fodder, Who gives sustenance to the animals and to the offspring of ravens who call..." In this manner, we arouse within ourselves excitement that goes beyond our mere intellectual grasp. Rather, it develops in proportion to our recital of His praises, [as we consider] how He enlivens the universe and the manner in which [creations] are able to accept Him. And even though it is not understood how all of creation is able to accept Him and His energy, nevertheless they do accept Him. And about this, the psalms say, "He Who covers the heavens with clouds, Who prepares rain for the land, Who causes the mountains to germinate..." [All of these phrases] allude to the hiding and concealment [of G-dliness] that enable us to accept [His divine influx] – for from the perspective of G-dly influence it was not necessary to create the world in this way. Yet, nevertheless He hides and conceals Himself so that we will be able to accept His [goodness]...and from this we become emotionally stimulated. And this is the level of *ruach*, which is devoid of [intellectually infused] love derived from meditation. For, [regarding meditation], the emphasis is upon what we understand of the good and the benefit of G-dliness, which is what induces us to desire and cling to G-dliness. But, this is not the case regarding the *pesukei dezmira*, which are associated with [pure] emotional stimulation.

For, there is such a thing as excitement of the emotions. While the intellect does not become excited in any more than a refined manner, the emotions are receptive to stimulation. This is what occurs during the *pesukei dezimra*, as we recite praises and our emotions are aroused. This is not the love and fear with which we "love the Lord" and fear Him, but this is rather the excitement of the very essence of the emotions themselves. This is a necessary stage of divine service, for it is impossible to achieve the characteristics of [intellectually infused] love and fear without prior stimulation of the emotions during the *peshukei dezimra*. This is a necessary pre-requisite, (which is demanded of us). Without it, it is impossible to fulfill the service of reciting the *kriat shema*, since the order of prayer requires that we first achieve the level of *ruach* during *pesukei dezimra*, only after which we recite the blessings prior to the *kriat shema*, and finally the *kriat shema* [itself], with intellectual grasp.

Now, the blessings preceding *kriat shema* require [that we activate] intellect, in order to grasp the nullification of the angels [to G-d]. [We need to understand] how they say *kadosh*, and how [they grasp] that the infinite light of G-d is holy and removed. [They grasp] that what shines down here to the worlds is a mere ray [of G-dliness], which is why the angels are nullified. The point is for this to be meaningful for us as we pray, for if not, why should the service of the angels be important to us – what have they to do with us? But, here what is significant is what [their service] means to us [which is that we as well should be nullified to G-d]. And then afterward during the phrase *baruch kavod* ["Blessed be His Honor..." – here the angels beseech G-d for divine revelation] we may attain some feeling within ourselves to a greater extent. That is, we may notice that we have a stronger desire for revelation of G-dliness within our soul and within the universe. For, the angels say *baruch* [indicating a desire for G-dliness that is beyond them]...because they are unable to grasp [the G-dly levels that are beyond them]. And we know that we are higher than these angels (the *ofanim*, angels of *asiya*), but nevertheless, there is still no essential divine light shining within us. And even though as we develop understanding, that is as we say the phrase *kadosh*, revealed light shines within, nevertheless this is not revelation of G-d's essential light. For, there are many different varieties of spiritual levels prior to revelation of the essential light of the Infinite One Above, as known regarding the explanation of *baruch kevod Hashem mimkomo* – "Blessed be the Lord from His place" – referring to descent of the essential infinite light below. And the difference is that with this [level of essential revelation], we become like a "*tzadik* who eats to satisfaction."

For, when the essential light does not shine, there may remain extraneous aspects [in his soul]. It is written that during prayer, we experience divine illumination. However, that may cause us to feel good for a short time after the prayers, but soon afterward we find ourselves attracted to the physical realm. That is why it is important to "guard" the feeling for G-dliness that we experience during prayers, for if not, we are drawn to the physical (unless one is naturally spiritual, meaning that he prays for an extended period of time, and after many consecutive days and many prayers, he experiences the divine light and for a long time).

That is, after much devotion during prayer, the G-dly feeling remains with us. Not that this leads us to experience anything new in our feeling for G-dliness (like one who thinks for a long time, and when he stops for a bit, new ideas arise in his mind), but just that we take much time to experience G-dliness (over and over again, like one who is standing for awhile in the air of *gan eden*). That is why one of the explanations of the word *atzeret* [as in the festival of *Shemini Atzeret*] is that it comes from the term *atzara*, meaning "stopping," "absorbing." And so is stated in books (*Bina le'itim*), that when someone is aroused with a good trait, he must remain with it for some time and become immersed in it. But, we cannot really say "immersed," because we do not fully understand [the arousal] to such a great understand. Rather, we are "involved with it," "taken with it." And, as a result, we are not so involved with the physical world.

All of this applies when our feeling for G-dliness is based upon the divine light that is enclothed in the worlds. But, when our meditation and feeling is for the essential infinite light that transcends the worlds, then we are not connected to anything physical whatsoever. This is the condition of a "*tzadik* who eats to the satisfaction of his soul." While meditating upon G-dliness enclothed in the worlds, it is impossible to come to a state of *bitul bemetziut* ("total nullification of the self"). Since this level of G-dliness is enclothed in the world, it is to be expected that it possesses the trait of "existence." Only from meditation upon G-dliness that transcends the worlds is it possible to attain the level of nullification of existence associated with "the *tzadik* who eats to the satisfaction of his soul."

However, we need to know that all this takes place within the "inner dimensions" of *bina* (*pnimiyut bina*), and not within the external manifestations of intellect. The external intellect is the ability to understand and grasp the concept and feel it in our soul...but [the spiritual levels described above] come from *pnimiyut bina*. This occurs as we meditate on G-dliness that is enclothed in the worlds and feel the G-dly illumination in our soul, and then we proceed to meditate afterward on the lofty and amazing nature of the essence of the infinite light which is above our grasp – for the essence of the infinite light is beyond whatever our thoughts are capable of grasping – then automatically we understand from this that whatever we do grasp is not the essence of the infinite One...

And then we meditate upon the nature of this lofty light. For this purpose, we must first return to the original meditation, but with more inner focus and with stronger concentration. And it is understood that this is not yet the essence [of G-dliness], and that the essence is yet more lofty and elevated, and thus this is not the essence. And then, we focus upon the nature of that elevation, which means that [whatever we grasp in the spiritual realm] above, [we postulate that] essence is "not this." One must somehow develop a feeling for this – it is not enough to say down here that "this is not it" – that is understood. Rather, in order to appreciate what is meant above that essence is "not this" – we need to develop a sense of recognition of the nature of "lofty elevation." For example, we may recognize the nature of a great person. We may be able to pinpoint a certain characteristic of his that is lofty and elevated, because his loftiness does not mean that he is removed from all other men. It only means that he himself, of his own nature, is elevated and lofty. And therefore, automatically he possesses certain character traits that lend him a lofty character...[and so the person meditating] must first grasp that the essence of the infinite light is elevated and lofty. [At first], he accepts the existence of loftiness with blind faith, without any intellectual proofs that this is indeed the case. And thereafter, he continues to meditate and comes to recognize the nature of the loftiness and elevation. This process is associated with *pnimiyut bina*, which is [also] the technique known as *yediat hashlila* ("negation of knowledge"). With it, one is able to shine revealed essential G-dly light below. And then, as he experiences the essential infinite light, he is completely removed from anything physical whatsoever. He can "eat a bagel" without relating to it whatsoever.

And then, this is followed by meditation on the [essential] name *Havaya* in two different manners. Either everything is nullified in existence, or everything is

G-dliness, and then there is no connection whatsoever to anything physical. And as is known regarding one who ate a bagel [the intention may be to the *Malach*, son of the Mezritcher Magid. He was oblivious in meditation to the extent that his soul was ready to leave his body, but the Alter Rebbe, who was his study partner, inserted a bagel into the *Malach's* mouth, thereby bringing him "back down to earth." The *Malach* later said that the Alter Rebbe "saved his life," for his soul was about to leave his body], who was on the level of, "everything is G-dly."...

And from this he arrives afterward to *reiyah* – "vision" of the very essence of G-dliness, which occurs during the *shemonah esreh*. And this occurs on the soul level of *yechida*, on which the *neshama* is an intermediary between the soul enclothed in the body and the very essence of the soul. And it is impossible to begin the *shemonah esreh* without first prefacing it with the order of prayer to begin with –

Except during *mincha*, when we begin the prayers with the *shemonah esreh*. For, the prayers of *mincha* is the *shemonah esreh*; one, because it follows the *shacharit* prayer, and moreover because it is an *et ratzon* – and "auspicious time." ...and therefore, we are able to begin with *shemonah esreh*, but otherwise, we are unable to begin with *shemonah resreh* without first reciting the prayers before hand. ..but so is the order of prayer that we must preface with the soul levels of *nefesh ruach neshama* and then afterward we may arrive to the *yechida*. It emerges, then, the *neshama* is the intermediary.

From *Torah Shalom* of the Rebbe Rashab, *Sichat Simchat Torah 5666* (1905-6), Sections 3-5, Page 61 (apparently notes from the Rebbe Rayatz, ztz'l):

The Connection between prayer and joy

This is why service of God must take place in joy. During the service of God during prayer, there are two components; there is spiritual grasp of the intellect, and there is enjoyment, as we enjoy Godliness. The two do not stem from the same source, even though intellectual understanding and enjoyment arrive simultaneously. That is, as we grasp Godliness and meditate upon it well, in great depth, we derive Godly enjoyment. Nevertheless, the two come from separate sources. For, intellectual grasp in its inception, from its origin comes from the external aspects of the vessel of *chochma* of *Atzilut*, similar to the growth of grass which occurs as its *mazal*, or "source," [illuminates it, causing it to grow]....But the enjoyment that we derive within our soul over Godliness, comes from the supernal "vapors" [spiritual energy that exudes from the supernal level of *A"K*]. And that is precisely what arouses the very essence of spiritual enjoyment. From it also comes revelation of the immanent light of *memalle kol olamim*, providing additional high levels of illumination. And that is why *avoda* must take place in joy, for the purpose of *avoda* is to draw down revelation of Godliness. [This revelation] comes from the very essence of the infinite light, descending with additional and exceptionally great strength – and this is what causes revelation in the lower worlds. Such arousal of Godly essence takes place only in joy. For, intellectual grasp in and of itself touches only the source and origin of the outer aspects of the vessels. It is only happiness and enjoyment over Godliness and enjoyment within the soul that arrives to the very essence of the infinite light of God, and in this way alone does revelation descend to the lower worlds. As known, the *Ari z'l* merited to his level of holy spirit only because of the happiness that experienced in performing mitzvoth. That is, not because of the mitzvah alone, but because of the happiness associated with the mitzvah...

From *Sefer Maamorim 5679* (1919) of the Rebbe Rashab, page 84

Organising our praises

The sages said, "Man should first organize his praises of God, and afterward pray..." At first class, what is meant by "organize his praises"? What is intended is that we should [elicit His attributes so that they emerge] from concealment to revelation. For example, when we praise a kind man, who does not always display his kindness, our praise may have the effect of eliciting the trait from concealment to revelation. It is known that this occurs because of our praises, which touch his hidden essence...

From *Sefer Maamorim 5679* (1919) of the Rebbe Rashab, page 560

Prayer is "joining"

Tefila ("prayer") is from the word *tofel*, meaning "joining," as in the phrase, "He who re-joins shards of pottery." This indicates "joining," from below to above, as written, "A ladder stood on the ground and its head reached into the heavens." And the Zohar tells us that this ladder "is prayer." Just as a ladder allows us to ascend from below to above, so prayer joins from below to Above. Now, we say [every morning], "The soul that you placed within me, is pure. You created it, You formed it, and You blew it into me." Here, we find four levels of the soul, corresponding to *nefesh, ruach, neshama* and *neshama* of the *neshama*. This level includes both of the levels known as *chaya* and *yechida*. Within them, we find the main expression of Godliness that is not enclothed in the body. For, what is enclothed in the body is only the *nefesh, ruach* and *neshama*.

The en-clothement [of vitality] and the beginning of revelation within the soul starts with the intellect, which enters us as *ohr pnimi*, or immanent revelation. Now, intellect is not really Godliness. [The true] Godliness of the soul is expressed in our *mesirat nefesh*, or self sacrifice that is beyond logic and intellect. Although there is a verse, "*nishmat shadai tavinam* ("the soul of *Shaddai* understands"), which calls the soul, "the soul of Shaddai," this is not the level of *neshama* which is Godliness. It is only an intermediary which brings us to Godliness, as written, "Place into our hearts *bina* in order to understand." That is, we must "understand one thing from within another thing." "Another thing" refers to immanent Godliness (*ohr pnimi*, or *memalle kol olamim*), while "one thing" refers to "transcendent Godliness," or *sovev kol olamim*. That is, from within immanent Godliness we come to grasp transcendent Godliness. In other words, from within our intellectual grasp we arrive to that which is beyond grasp. For, in true intellectual grasp it is understood that the very essence [of the concept] is not grasped. That is, with our own understanding we know that the deeper that we delve into a Godly concept, we come to realize that it is not graspable within our limited faculty of intellect. With understanding, comes the realization that the essence and the very innermost point [of the concept] is beyond reach.. It is at this point that we practice *yediat hashlila*, ("negative," or "circumscribed knowledge," with which we negate and "go around" whatever we understand or grasp of Godliness. By so doing, we arrive to a higher plane of intellect that is transcendent). This is the point that is called *nishmat Shaddai*, or "the soul of Shaddai," since it is our gate to Godliness.

This, then is prayer. Prayer is based upon meditation. And the ultimate purpose is to arrive to a level of self nullification that is beyond logic and intellect. It is reflected in the four levels of prayer, the first of which is up to *Baruch she'amar*, followed by the *pesukei dezimra*, followed by the blessings of the *kriat shema* as well as the *shema* itself, and then the *shemonah esreh* – these correspond to the four levels of the soul.

The beginning of prayer is *hoda'ah*, or "acknowledgment," as when we say, "I am grateful toYou," or "Give thanks to the Lord..." Such acknowledgment involves neither intellectual grasp, nor excitement of the soul. *Baruch she'amar* and the *pesukei dezimra* correspond to *ruach*, to which applies the saying of the sages, "One should first organize his praises of God, and then pray." "Organization of praises" is what arouses stimulation of the soul, equivalent to arousal of the emotions...This is followed by the blessings preceding the *shema* and the *shema* itself, which demands the meditation on the words *kadosh* and *baruch*, as well as *yichuda ila'ah* and *yichuda tata'ah* ("higher awareness," during which God is at the forefront of our consciousness and the physical world in the background, and "lower awareness," during which the physical creation occupies the forefront of our awareness and God is in the background), which demand nullification of our intellect. And then, we arrive to the *shemonah esreh*, during which we experience the ultimate nullification of the essence of our soul. This is symbolized by the bowing that we do during *shemonah esreh*, which is nullification, beyond logic and intellect.

This, then is the "joining" that takes place during prayers. It joins the soul within the body with the source and origin of the soul [that is beyond the body].

From *Sefer Maamorim 5679* (1919) of the Rebbe Rashab, pp. 596-596

Illumination in the Heart
Baruch She'Amar – "Blessed be He Who said..."

This is [the meaning of] "Blessed be He Who spoke and the universe came into existence":

The goal is that the concept associated with "He Who spoke..." should become "blessed" – that is, conscious and revealed – in the heart of man. And, as well, that meditation on the concept should produce excitement in our heart. And also that we should become conscious of Him in our heart so that we experience excitement and arousal.

All this is the result of added illumination from Above, beginning from *Baruch She'Amar*, since the phrase brings down additional light from its source and origin in the essential infinite light of the One Above. In this way, it provides revelation down here into our G-dly soul as well, in the form of illumination to light up the darkness of the world. It subsequently leads to an influx of essential infinite light of the One Above, and He Himself "hides," so to speak in this darkness, and that the revelation that emerges is an essential revelation of the highest order.

(From *Beha'ah Shehikdimu 5672* of the Rebbe Rashab, vol. 1, pp. 133-134)

Baruch Sheamar and *Yishtabach...*

...the source of *atik* of the world of *bria* is *atik* of *Atzilut*, which itself is *malchut* of the *ein sof* ("infinite illumination"). This corresponds to the concept explained elsewhere , why during the prayer *Baruch Sheamar* we say *yachid chay haolamim melech* ("Singular One, life of the worlds, is King"), while during the prayer *yishtabach*, we say *melech yachid chay haolamim* (The King, the singular One Who is the life of the worlds").

The concept of *melech yachid* refers to the King, *malchut* of *Atzilut* as it becomes *atik* of *bria*. In this case, *atik* corresponds to *yachid*. And it becomes *chay haolamim* – the "life of the worlds" – in order to vitalize the lower worlds of *BY"A*, from nothing to something. At that point, *atik* of *bria* is also called *yachid*. And as explained earlier, *yachid* refers to the very essence of the infinite light that transcends *echad*. For, *echad* refers to *z'a* of *Atzilut*...

This, then is the explanation of *yachid chay haolamim melech* – *yachid* refers to the infinite illumination above as it emerges after the great *tzimtzum* ("contraction") to become *chay haolamim* – the "life of the worlds." From there, it descends to *malchut* of *Atzilut*. But, if so, how can we say, *melech yachid*, [which indicates] that *malchut* of *Atzilut* is called *yachid* as it becomes *atik* of *bria*?

This is because the power within *atik* of *bria* to create from nothing to something is drawn exclusively from the essence of the infinite light above, which alone is unique and singular. For, "the end is wedged in the beginning…"[403]

From *Ohr HaTorah* of the *Tzemach Tzedek*, *drushim lePesach*, Page 441

Rescue from evil
Baruch podeh umatzil - "Blessed be He Who redeems and saves"

[The expression of] the attribute of *hod* within *chesed* occurs when, out of love, [His holy illumination] becomes enlad in a garment of revenge in order to wage war with the enemy and rescue His friends, exacting revenge…in particular, it corresponds to the phrase that we say every day, *Boruch podeh umatzil* ("Blessed is He Who redeems and saves…"), during which we draw down a high level of illumination every day to "save" and rescue the G-dly soul from the wickedness of the animal soul. For, every day man's evil inclination overwhelms him, and if it weren't for help from Above, man would be unable to withstand it. And this high illumination from Above also causes the pulverization and nullification of the animal soul. Similarly, it enables the re-grouping of aspects of man's soul that have become scattered as the result of many foreign thoughts and negative ruminations. This as well is considered "rescue from the enemy." The process is similar to the "exit from evil" that *ba'alei tshuva* ("penitents" who return to the path of Torah) undergo, when the "scattered" holy sparks of their soul, once sunk in the depths of evil, re-emerge as the penitent seeks to do *tshuva*, and exit from the depths of evil. This as well is what occurs when a revelation of light descends from above, as written, "A *bat kol* ("voice") announces every day, return, children…"[404] That is, out of His love for the Jews, G-d determined that "those who were pushed away will no longer be repelled."[405] And for this reason, we bless every day, *Boruch podeh umatzil*, wherein the word *Baruch* indicates added blessings and descent of G-dliness from above. And in this manner a redemption and rescue of holy sparks takes place as the "pieces" of our soul are rescued from evil. And the same is true regarding the "gathering together" from their state of scattering…

Sefer Maamorim 5668 (1908) of the Rebbe Rashab, page 248)

From Essence to Worlds
Yachid Chay HaOlamim Melech ("Unique One, Life of the Worlds, King.")

In the final phrase of *Baruch She'Amar* we address G-d as *Yachid Chay HaOlamim Melech* ("Unique One, Life of the Worlds, King.")

The essence of His infinite illumination – before the *tzimtzum* (contraction of the light of His very essence in order to create the source of all life) – is called *Yachid Levado* ("Alone, the Unique One"). As it is known, there is a difference between *yachid* ("unique") and *rishon* ("first"); "first" implies that there is something following it (a second and a third), but "unique" implies that there is nothing following. There is no second to Him, since He is singular and unique.

However, *Chay HaOlamim* ("Life of the Worlds") represents the spiritual descent that followed the original *tzimtzum*. It originates from the *malchut* ("reign") of the same infinite light that He contracted in order to create a source for the entire chain of creation. [It began as] a *kav* ("ray") and *chut* ("thread") [that emerged to enter the vacated space left after the *tzimtzum*], as it is written, "Your reign is the reign over all worlds"[406] [G-d's reign begins from the very inception of creation, with the essence of His infinite light, and extends down to the lowest of all worlds]. This means that [the infinite light] that was contracted [to allow room for creation] remained "elevated over" [creation]. [This illumination was] outside of His essence, yet beyond the worlds, and about it we say, *hamitnaseh mimot olam*, ("He Who is elevated over matters of the world"). It is [nevertheless] completely out of range of the level on which He reigns exalted, unto Himself. That level is called *Melech meromam levado* ("the King exalted alone") or *Melech HaKadosh* ("the Holy King").

In this way, we may explain the difference between the phrase, *Melech Yachid Chay HaOlamim* ("King, Unique One, Life of the Worlds") [recited at the end of *Yishtabach*], and *Yachid Chay HaOlamim Melech* ("Unique One, Life of the Worlds, King") [recited at the end of *Baruch She'Amar*]. The phrase, "Unique One, Life of the Worlds, King," refers to the reign of the infinite light of G-d after the great contraction. There, it is called the "Source of Life" of the overall chain and hierarchy of creation, starting with the *kav v'chut* [original ray and thread of G-dly energy following the "great contraction"] mentioned earlier.

And *Melech Yachid* ... refers to the reign of the infinite light of G-d before the great contraction, coming from "the Holy King" Himself, as *malchut* of His infinite light prior to the *tzimtzum*. From there, it [descends to become] *Chay HaOlamim Melech*, symbolizing G-d's *malchut* or "reign" over the chain of creation (*seder hishtalshelut*) expressed in the *kav* and *chut*.

As for the words that follow – *meshubach u'mefuar adei ad* ("praiseworthy and glorious without end") – they apply to the first level; that is, to *chay HaOlamim melech* or the *malchut* of His infinite light after the *tzimtzum*.

(From Samech Tesamech 5657 (1897) of the Rebbe Rashab, p. 22)

Baruch She'amar...

Among souls, we find two levels of "great love" (*ahava rabba*). There is love that is the result of meditation upon the ray and revelation within the worlds. Such meditation reflects on how the worlds are out of range in comparison to His essence, as appearing in the prayer, *Baruch she'amar; yachid chay* [with a *tzeiri*] *haolamim melech* ("Singular One, life of the worlds, is King"), *meshubach u'mefuar adei ad shemo hagadol* ("praiseworthy and glorious until (and including) His great name...")

The use of the word *yachid* ("Singular one") indicates a level that surpasses *echad* ("one"). The use of *echad* alludes to the seven heavens and the earth plus the four directions of the world [the second letter *chet* of *echad* carries numerical value of eight, symbolizing the seven heavens and earth, while the third letter *dalet* carries value of four, representing the four directions. All are united as "one"]. That is, *echad* alludes to the infinite light as it comes into range of the worlds. In relation to this level, [it is appropriate to say that] the worlds have no place whatsoever; they are nullified and totally united, since "everything is before Him as naught." They are as non-existent, absent and without any presence whatsoever. They possess no true existence, and therefore they are called *echad*.

Now, all of this is appropriate regarding the infinite light above that bears a relationship with the worlds. In this regard, it is appropriate to say that the worlds "have no place," although we could not say this regarding the Godly vitality that is enclothed in the worlds [because regarding this vitality, the worlds do have status]. But, regarding the infinite light that does bear a connection with the world, [and is moreover] a source of revelation...about which we say "*Havaya* is one" - from the word *mehava*, meaning "to create" - the creation takes place from a mere ray and reflection of *Havaya* that is enclothed within the name *Elokim*. Still, the name *Havaya* acts as a source of creation and origin of vitality, and regarding this level, it is appropriate to say that the worlds "hold no place."

However, in regard to the very essence of the infinite light, which is not within range or category of the worlds at all, it is not appropriate to say even this- that the worlds "hold no place." This is what is known as *yachid*, meaning that He is singular and unique to the utmost. He is not within the category of worlds at all, and the phrase, "life of the worlds" is only in reference [to how He lowers Himself to be a] King. For, the creation of all of the worlds from the highest levels, including their vitality, is only because it "arose in His will, I will reign," and there is no such thing as a king without a nation.

From *Sefer Maamorim 5679* (1919) of the Rebbe Rashab, page 248

Gazing Up on the Glory

And in the Zohar *parshat Teruma* it states that *tiferet* extends from one extreme [of the spiritual spectrum] to the other, meaning from *chochma*. The matter is as follows: *tiferet* implies "gazing upon the glory of the King," and as the *nusach* of the prayer (*Baruch Sheamar*) says, *meshubach u'mefuar b'lashon chasidav* ("praised and glorified by the tongue of those who fear Him..."), which implies "gazing," which is the matter of *reiya*, or vision, which receives from *chochma*...

From *Sefer Maamorim 5677* of the Rebbe Rashab, page 173 (at the bottom)

From Beyond Time into Time

Meshubach umefuar adei ad... "Praiseworthy and glorious until (and including) His great name forever and ever"

...the phrase *meshubach umefuar adei ad* ("praiseworthy and glorious until (and including)") is understood to refer to the eternity of the infinite light of G-d. For, the word *ad* ("until") indicates eternity, as we say *ad olmei ad* ("until and forever"), and also *shochen ad* ("He dwells forever..."[407]), indicating eternity. All the moreso, then that *adei ad* [should connote eternity], as we say *adei ad yimloch* ("He will reign forever"[408]), which connotes eternity. Now, the concept of eternity applies only to something that is in the catgory of "time," meaning in the past, present or future. However, since there occur interruptions and limitations in time, as for example one thousand years and no more, when we say "eternity," we mean without any interruptions or limitations of time. This is similar to saying that one "lives forever" - such is the explanation of *olmei ad*, which connotes a continuum of time without limit or interruption forever.

But, regarding something that is not within the category or concept of time at all, meaning something that is completely beyond time (past, present and future); how is it possible to describe it with the word "eternity"? Since it is not at all within the class of time – if it were, we could say about it that it continues indefinitely, without interruption - but since it is not in the category of time at all, how is it appropriate to say that it that it lasts forever without any interruption? It is not possible to describe any amount of time without mentioning a limit. For any amount of time that we may mention is describable in terms of days or years, which fall under the rubric of time. About them, we might say that much time applies, even an unlimited amount of time. But, we cannot say this about something that is completely above time.

Moreover, we must also understand; we know that time itself is a creation, from nothing to something, as known from the triple concept of space-time-soul, and of necessity we have to say that there is a limit and interruption to time, just as the body of any creation undergoes interruption since it is, after all, a newborn creation and it has a beginning, so automatically it has an end. This is as written in the books of philosophy, that every corporeal object is limited and if so, the spiritual energy enclothed and permeated within it in order to enliven it is also necessarily limited. For, it is impossible for an unlimited power to be enclothed in a limited body or vessel – this is agreed among all of the philophers, as written in the Rambam's *Moreh Nevuchim*, section 2 in the introduction. And therefore it is impossible as well for time to be ongoing without end, since it is in essence limited, and therefore it cannot exist, on its own, without limitation. And how can time itself be eternal, as implied in the phrase *olmei ad* – for, certainly all that is under that category of time is not eternal.

But, the matter is as follows; time itself posseses limitations and is characterized by interruption. But, nevertheless, when a ray or reflection of the infinite light above shines within it, from beyond the whole category of time – past, present, etc – as known regarding the name *Havaya* which means *haya, hoveh* and *yihiyeh* ("was, is and will be") in one – then even time itself becomes illuminated from above time. And this means that the concept of eternity may exist within time as well; that is, also days and years which fall under the rubric of time (past, present...) may know no interruption forever, and this is because of the reflection of infinite light from above time...

(page 184) – And in this manner it is understood that within time itself, there may occur revelation from beyond time. This takes place when the infinite light of G-d unites with His Divine attribute of *malchut*, the source of time, so that "beyond time" shines into time. And from this descends a ray [of G-dly light] to souls as well, as a minor revelation from above time into time, just as G-d showed *Adam Harishon* ("original man") all the details of time of all six thousand years, in one short time span. And similary, we find in the *Pri Eitz Hayim*[409] that in a short interval, the *Ari z'l* grasped secrets of the Torah that if taught would have required eighty consecutive years to present. Similar events occurred to the *Ba'al Shem Tov z'l*, who saw ewvents that took time to occur, as if they already had occurred.[410] And elsewhere it is explained that his vision extended to the world of *yetzira* and there he detected periods of fifteen years from below, at one time. And so in the future there will be revelations involving time and space in which time and space themselves will be completely above time and above space.

(p.185)...In this manner, we may understand the phrase, *meshubach umefuar adei ad*...("Praiseworthy and glorious until"), wherein *adei ad* means "forever," referring to the *ein sof* ("infinite"), which is truly without limit...(p.186) And the ultimate revelation will occur in the furture...when time itself will be above time. And this will concur with revelation of His "great Name," which is the unity of *Havaya* and *Elokim*, and furthermore from revelation of the essence of the infinite light from above the Name *Havaya*, which is the true revelation that will take place in the future...

From *Sefer Maamorim 5668* (1908) of the Rebbe Rashab, page 182-3)

Fire, Wind, Noise and the Still small voice...

Now that we no longer have the holy Temple, our prayers are in lieu of the sacrificial offerings. They represent the offering of the animal soul, which becomes subsumed in the holy fire above, which corresponds to the flames of fire of the divine soul. Now, this takes place during the four rungs of prayer.

It is written, "There was a great and strong wind, [capable of] disintegrating mountains and shattering rocks, but *Havaya* was not in the wind. Following the wind, there was a great noise, but *Havaya* was not in the noise. And after the noise there was fire, but *Havaya* was not in the fire. And following the fire there was a still small voice." The "wind" represents the *pesukei dezimra*, during which we narrate the praises of God as He is evident in the creation and continued existence of the worlds. A multitude of worlds and creatures were created, and all of them praise and extol [God]. The creation emerged from His "mouth," so to speak, as writeen, "With the word of *Havaya* the heavens were made, and with the breath of His mouth all of the heavenly hosts [came into existence]." That is, all of the spiritual beings and the physical creatures came into being from the utterance and breath of His mouth, as written, "He made His angels as *ruchot* ("breaths," or "spirits"). Now, our worship on this level also corresponds to *ruach*, ("wind"), during which we experience arousal of the emotions. For, the themes expressed in the *pesukei dezimra* – creation from nothing to something – are in essence totally beyond intellectual grasp. We have no idea how something may be created from nothing to something. This is only in the scope of the Creator and we creatures cannot grasp the process at all. All we know is that creation from nothing to something does occur. It is on this subject that we focus our meditation; on the greatness of the Creator and the amazing process of creation, and that all is created from His utterance. And this stimulates arousal within the heart and excitement of our emotions, which constitute the soul level of *ruach*.

This is the *ruach* that shatters mountains. The term *pesukei dezimra* (literally, "verses of song," but also alluding to the word *lezamer*, meaning "to prune") comes from the word meaning "to prune thorns." For [during this section of prayers], we "prune" away the "thorns" of the animal soul. That is, we produce an "etching from the outside" upon the animal soul. Just as we see that the effect of praise upon a person is that it uplifts – it lacks any particular inner feeling, but in general it causes him to feel uplifted - so the praises that we recite during the *pesukei dezimra* uplift and elevate our animal soul. It becomes somewhat detached from its formerly physical status, and this is what we mean by an "etching from the outside." [And yet we say about this state that], "*Havaya* was not in the wind" – for this is the "wind of *Elokim*." That is, the creation of the world took place with the name *Elokim*, as well as with the final *hey* of His essential name *Havaya* – for the verse says, *Be'hey – baram* – "with the *hey* they were created." The letter *hey* is a "light letter lacking substance," for it represents a mere external ray alone.

And after the "wind" (*ruach*) comes the "noise." It is associated with the blessings preceding the *shema*, as we recite the section of *yotzar*, during which the *ofanim* (lower angels of the world of *asiya*) and the holy *chayot* (angels of *yetzira*), make much noise as they utter the word, *kadosh*. They grasp the incredibly high level of the infinite light above, which is holy and exalted. And the *ofanim* know that there is something holy and exalted but they do not know what it is – this is what induces them to make "noise," regarding spiritual levels that are beyond their grasp. Now, [within us], this noise occurs as arousal within our soul, stemming from *kadosh* – that which is beyond us. Even though [the excitement that we feel] is the result of lack of intellect, nevertheless we feel the holiness (In Yiddish: "We experience within ourselves how the Infinite is holy..."). But because [the angels] do not grasp the holiness they make noise.

And therefore, this [stage of prayer] is dissimilar to the *pesukei dezimra*, which are also beyond intellectual grasp. [The difference is that] our excitement during the *pesukei dezimra* is over Godliness that is enclothed in nature. That is why our excitement is only superficial in nature. However, the excitement associated with the "noise of holiness" [coming from levels that transcend nature] is accompanied by true inner self-nullification. As is known, the animal soul comes from the "dregs of the *ofanim*," which is why when the *ofanim* themselves are aroused, so the animal soul also becomes stimulated. This is what constitutes the true inner nullification of the animal soul. And yet, [even] within this excitement, the "noise of *Havaya*" is still not present. For, this noise comes from the *vov* of the name *Havaya*. This letter *vov* is the difference between the word *kodesh* (*kuf-dalet-shin*), lacking the *vov*, and the word *kadosh* (*kuf-vov-dalet-shin*), with a *vov*. And thus, all that is involved in this spiritual arousal are the final two letter *vov-hey* of the name *Havaya*. Moreover, even the *vov* of *kadosh* descends to us as *makif* alone; [it is Godly revelation that remains beyond us and fails to penetrate our mind and heart.]

And after the noise, there is fire. This is [associated with] the higher angels, the *seraphim* (angels of *bria*), who grasp the infinite light and how it is holy and exalted. And because of this, they enter a state of excitement, with fiery flames of desire to become included in the infinite illumination above. And that is why they are called *seraphim* (those who "burn"), corresponding to the fiery flames, which consume their very existence.

Within our souls, this corresponds to the prayer *ahavat olam* ("Eternal love") that follows the *yotzar* [during which the angels say *kadosh*, as above]. For, the *seraphim* and the *ofanim* correspond to the Godly soul and the animal soul. The love like fire that we develop within our Godly soul is the result of our divine intellectual grasp. Just as the fiery flames of the *seraphim* come from their grasp of what is holy; that is, since *imma ila'ah* (the "supernal mother" or *bina*) "nestles in the nest" ("resides," so to speak in *bria*) – so the fiery flames of the soul come from the faculty of *bina*. From *bina* (intellectual analysis), we develop love like fiery flames. And that in turn leads to the selfless dedication and *mesirat nephesh* with which we say the *kriat shema*, which also demands intellectual grasp. This is what is meant by *shema Yisrael* ("Listen oh Israel..."), for "hearing" also connotes intellectual grasp. That is, [through our faculty of "hearing," or intellectual analysis], our soul grasps how everything is truly naught before Him, and this instills within us a powerful desire, accompanied by ultimate *mesirat nephesh*. That is, we dedicate all of our various desires so that they become one will for God alone, and they become included and united in the oneness of God...and in this fire, the animal soul is consumed, as written, "And you shall love the Lord your God...with all of your hearts" – with both inclinations [the Godly and the animal]. And thus, the animal soul also develops love for God. But the main point is that it becomes included in the fire of the Godly soul, for the true *mesirat nephesh* occurs as we dedicate all of our other desires, and then the animal soul itself becomes incinerated.

Even though the love that the animal soul develops on its own [from meditation] is *bekol napshecha* ("with all of your soul"), and it also involves nullification of the ego (*bitul ha-yesh*), which is a form of *mesirat nephesh*, nevertheless the fiery flames of the Godly soul incinerates all of the desires of the animal soul. This is the all-inclusive dedication of all of our sundry desires, for this constitutes "consumption of the physical" (*ishtatzei gushma*).

And yet, "*Havaya* was not within the fire..." Even though this level of love is symbolized by the first *hey* of the name *Havaya*, nevertheless it does not encompass the entire name of God, and therefore it is love like fire, with a strong desire [for Godliness, implying that the person is still 'separate' from God]. However, the main revelation of the name *Havaya* is associated with the *yud*, or first letter of His holy Name, which constitutes revelation of the name *Havaya* leading to full and total abnegation of the very self. And this is the "still small voice," about which the Zohar says, "There goes the King." It is revelation of the very essence of the infinite illumination, which absolutely nullifies us from our very existence, in totality. And this is the voice of Torah...

...The "still small voice" is mainly expressed in learning Torah (for prayer implies elevation from below while Torah represents bringing down revelation of the name *Havaya* from Above). But, in order for the revelation of the name *Havaya* to be expressed in the "still small voice," we must first pray. That is, [we must pray] with "wind, noise and fire." And, even though *Havaya* is "not in the wind and not in the noise and not in the fire," nevertheless this process leads to the "still small voice," where we can say, "There goes the King."

This is what takes place: The sages said that, "The angel *Metat* [also described as the "minister of the universe" for his intermediate role in both lifting up the requests of the Jews to God and bringing down answers from Above, this angel has two modes. One is as a *na'ar* ("youngster") in the world of *yetzira*, and the other is as a *zaken* ("elder") in the world of *bria*. Thus, he is described in the verse, "I was a youngster and I also grew old...." He alternates between the two worlds] ties crowns for His Creator from the prayers of the Jews." That is, a crown is made of precious stones, which are mineral in essence, and the category of mineral is the very lowest among the naturally occurring categories of mineral, vegetable, animal and humans. But, their intrinsic light and illumination develops only as they are polished, until they become precious stones that shine. At that point, they are [suitable to be set in] a beautiful crown to be placed on the head. Similarly, the letters of prayer, which are also called "stones" are comparable to the mineral category. When they are recited with intense devotion and desire of the heart, coming from the essential will of the soul, then each and every letter expresses the inner desire for God. They become precious stones, illuminating [the soul]. From them, it becomes possible to make a crown and coronet on the head of the King. And then, He radiates down to us with a revelation of His supernal Will...

From *Sefer Maamorim 5679* (1919) of the Rebbe Rashab, page 253-255

Spiritual food for physical bodies
Mizmor Letoda – "Song of gratitude" (Psalm 100)

[Even at the end of days], in the future, there will be physical bodies with all of the attendant details, containing physical blood, as proven from the fact that sacrifices will not be eliminated in the future (for it is written, "There we will perform before You our obligatory sacrifices."[411]) And while it is true that the sages said, "All of the sacrifices will be eliminated in the future aside from the *korban toda*" [the offering brought by an individual who wishes to express gratitude to G-d for recovering from an illness, being rescued, etc...], this applies only to sacrifices brought by individuals. However, public sacrifices will take place in the future, while among the individual sacrifices [only] the *korban toda* will remain. And as is known, the process of offering the sacrifices involves the elevation of the blood of the animal (which is the physical soul within it) on the altar, representing the *sephira* of *malchut* of *Atzilut*.

From *Sefer Ma'amorim 5659* (1899) of the Rebbe Rashab, pp. 106)

What's in a Name...

Regarding the subject of a "name," we say, "For His Name is greatly exalted..." This means that [not only He, but] even His name is exalted and elevated over the worlds. This is what is meant by the king, whose name is "proclaimed over his people," as a *makif* (overall uniting principle) alone. The name of the king permeates the kingdom, even though it is a mere transcendent factor. It is the laws of the kingdom that govern the real inner workings, but the name of the king remains transcendent over the kingdom. This is equivalent to the name of a person being attached to his house or to his field, as we say, "this is the house or the field of so-and-so." It is merely a name that is attached to us.

Similarly, God's name is a *makif* ("transcendent unifying factor") over the worlds. This is what is meant by, "Let the Name of *Havaya* be praised..." – all of the praise and extolation of all creatures reaches only to the Name of *Havaya* that is "proclaimed" over them. And [His name] is also "exalted and elevated" above them, while only a ray from His name shines upon the earth and the heavens....

From *Sefer Maamorim 5679* (1919) of the Rebbe Rashab, page 327

The hand of G-d
Poteach et yadecha ("Open Your hand...") Psalm 145

The statement here, "Open Your hand" is comparable to that in the verse, "Your hands established a temple for G-d."[412] It is necessary to construct a receptacle – a vessel of *malchut* – that will receive the influx of spiritual energy termed *achlam* ("their food"), which is spiritual revelation that feeds and sustains ...

This is what is meant by "Open Your hand" – G-d opens His upper "hand," so to speak, in order to dig and create a well and receptacle so it may receive food.

This is also what is meant by "Your hands established a temple for G-d." For, it is written, "Make for Me a sanctuary and I will dwell within them..." [413] – not within "it," but within "them." And as the sages said, "After the Temple was destroyed, G-d has nothing but the four cubits of *halacha*," [414] which is the revelation of His will and wisdom. And the influx of spiritual energy described previously is also referred to as a "drop of supernal wisdom." Nevertheless, there has to be a vessel for this, so that we experience what it means "with all my heart I search for You [G-d]." [415] At that point, the seeker is called a *calah* [the term usually means "bride," but here it means one who has fully internalized G-dliness and absorbed it, like a bride after union with the bridegroom].

(From *Likutei Torah* of the Alter Rebbe, *Parshat Matot*, p. 85d 206 (beg with the words, *veshamah aviha*))

"He hurls His ice like crumbs, who can stand before His cold" (from Psalm 147)

The succah provides transcendent illumination (*makif*), while the lulav brings down immanent illumination (*pnimi*)...and about this it is said, 'He hurls His ice like crumbs.' For, in order for illumination to permeate us (about which we say, "in order to know"), so that we truly know and grasp it, the transcendent knowledge must "solidify" and become "ice." And, "He hurls His ice like crumbs to the myriads..."...is in order that they should all grasp on their particular level. However, the verse continues, "...who can stand before His cold?" That is, not every person succeeds in cleaving to the one God above as a result of understanding a concept. For, since the understanding (lit: shuv) occurs at a distance [from the revelation of Godliness], the person may fall into a state of complete "coldness." This is a condition of *klipah* (concealment of Godliness). As the saying goes, "the donkey is cold even during the hot season." That is, even when the sun is at its peak, which is a parable for revelation of Godliness, as in the "sun of *Havaya*", (which represents the supernal unity of *yichuda ila'ah*, about which the verse says, "the sun has tanned me"), nevertheless the person may remain cold. Because of his physical nature, he may fail to achieve spiritual arousal.

And that is why the "ice" must melt. That is, within the "ice," there must be some water as well. "Water" represents the desire to ascend Above, within *chochma*. There must be a mixture (inter-inclusion) of intellectual understanding and yearning to ascend (*shuv v'ratzoh*). And then, even the intellectual understanding will be permeated with yearning to ascend. Even within the intellect there will be elements of revealed illumination. And this occurs on Shemini Atzeret...

From *Sefer Maamorim 5678* (1918) of the Rebbe Rashab, page 45

Physical creation has a spiritual source

We need to understand the connection between the three phrases at the conclusion of the blessing, *yotzar hameorot* (in the *bircot kriat shema*): *Norah tehilot* ("awesome in praises"), *Adon haniflaot* ("master of wonders"), *Hamechadesh b'tuvo bekol yom tamid maaseh bereishit* ("He Who in His goodness constantly renews the creation every day").

Now, the final phrase ("He Who in His goodness constantly renews the creation every day") speaks of "renewal" (*hitchadshut*) of the creation. "Renewal" is not similar to "cause and effect," wherein the effect already exists within the cause [that is, we know that if A happens, it will necessarily cause B to occur] and emerges from concealment to a state of revelation. For that is not "renewal" at all. Prior to creation, the worlds did not exist at all. It is impossible to posit that "existence" (*yesh*) was included within the divine void (*ayn*) that preceded creation.

For example, the physical substance of the body of a lion - whose spiritual source is the "lion" mentioned in the *merkava* ("chariot," referring to a prophecy of Yehezkel), and whose origin is in the *sephira* of *chesed* of *Atzilut* which is also called a 'lion,' as are the *sephirot* of *chochma* and *keter* – is without doubt created in a process of "renewal." It did not previously exist at all, but subsequently materialized from nothing to something. Moreover, the enlivening soul (*nefesh*) of the lion, which descended from spiritual level to spiritual level from its source and origin, the *pnei aryeh* ("countenance of the lion") within the *merkava*, which is *gevura*, alluding to the flames of fire of desire and thirst for Godliness which enable it to carry the "throne of glory" as well as be uplifted by it – comes from these levels. And thus, the soul (*nefesh*) of the physical lion is associated with the *sephira* of *gevura*. The lion is an animal that tears and tramples its prey. Its behavior is very physical, completely out of range of the attribute of *gevura* in its source above.

Although this is because the lion is among the creatures who "fell and shattered" [during the process known as the "shattering of the vessels," during which many high sparks of holiness 'fell' into the *klipa* or concealing forces of the universe because their Godly illumination was too much for the world to contain] and that is why it is considered an "impure animal"…and aside from the fact that the lion is an animal that "tears and tramples its prey," its enlivening soul is quite physical, and totally out of range even of its source in the spiritual world of *asiya*, and even more out of range regarding the "countenance of the lion" within the *merkakva* of *yetzira* and *bria*.

This is true of every creature in the physical world. Even the vitality that descends to them through the spiritual hierarchy of creation is not truly within range, for the vitality that enlivens them below is out of range even of the spiritual aspect of the world of *asiya*. And so regarding the spirituality of the higher worlds of *BY"A*, ascending from one level to the next. The vitality that enlivens the lower physical creation is completely out of range of the higher worlds. And each spiritual level is like an "example" or "parable" to the level above it…which indicates that they are out of range of one another…and so of course they are out of range of their origin in the world of Atzilut, which bears no relation [to all these levels] whatsoever, since the source of their creation is from *malchut* of Atzilut via many stringencies and contractions, creating concealment and hiddenness of the Creator from the creation.

…and all of this occurs because their creation takes place from a state of concealment and obscurity and therefore their grasp is of their existence alone. And for that reason, even within the spiritual hierarchy of creation (*seder histalshelut*), each level is out of range of the next. And that is what is intended by the phrase, "He Who in His goodness constantly renews the creation every day"- the creation of the worlds is a process of constant renewal. This is true not only of the creation of the material substance (*yesh*) but also of the vitality that enlivens the creatures in a process of "renewal."

Generally, the phrase "He Who constantly renews His creation every day" refers to *memalle kol olamim*, or "immanent illumination," that descends to the world after the *tzimtzum*, or "great contraction." It is followed by the *kav*, which [is a thin ray of Godly light], unlike the original illumination…[all of this] this applies to the worlds of *BY"A*, which materialize in a process of "renewal," both regarding their essential substance and also the vitality that enlivens them as "renewal." That is why God's immanent light (*memalle kol olamim*) also arrives as "renewal," for the worlds of immanent light are the "revealed worlds," that are created in the process of "renewal." And about them we say, "He Who in His goodness…" for in truth it reflects the goodness and the kindness of God, for the nature of good is to bestow good, meaning that there should be revealed Godliness among the creations. And if it weren't for the contraction and the descent of Godliness as described, the creation would be unable to accept the illumination. But via the *tzimtzum* the creation is enabled to accept revealed Godliness within the worlds and vessels, and this is what is meant by 'He Who in His goodness constantly renews...'"

From *Sefer Maamorim 5679* (1919) of the Rebbe Rashab, page 372-374

All Encompassing levels...

This is the connection and thread running between the three themes [at the end of the blessing *yotzar hame'orot*, preceding *kriat shema*]: "Awesome in praises" (*norah tehilot*), "Master of wonders" (*adon naniflaot*), "Who in His goodness constantly renews the creation every day" (*hamechadesh betuvo bekol yom tamid maaseh breishit*).

"Who in His goodness..." corresponds to *memalle kol olamim*, or immanent Godliness [that fills and permeates the creation so that we grasp and feel it]. It is expressed in the creation of the universe, in the "revealed worlds" whose emergence into a state of existence is new and novel. And, "Master of wonders" alludes to *sovev kol olamim*, or transcendent Godliness, from which are created the higher spiritual worlds called *peleh* ("wonder"). They are "hidden worlds" which do not become revealed. Even they are called *asiya* ("action") in comparison to the very essence of the infinite One, about Whom we say, "Awesome in praises," out of fear of mentioning His name in praise.

And from Above to below, the process descends from "Awesome in praises" to "Master of wonders" since transcendent Godliness is a revelation from the very essence of the infinite. Everything emerges from the essence, which is what is meant by "Awesome in praises, *oseh peleh* ("Creator of wonders")...(More in detail, the level alluded to by "Awesome" is an intermediary between the essence of Godlines and the revelations emerging from it...*norah* indicates descent and revelation in order to become "awesome." That is, within *malchut* of the *ein sof*, there are two levels. One is still included in the Godly essence and the second is *malchut* of the *eye sof* as it descends, and this is what we call *norah*...) And transcendent illumination (*sovev kol olamim*) is the source and origin of immanent light (*memalle kol olamim*), for the light and illumination of immanent spirituality descends from transcendent Godliness via the *tzimtzum*, or "great contraction."

From *Sefer Maamorim 5679* (1919) of the Rebbe Rashab, page 375

Daily renewal of creation

Uv'tuvo mechadesh bekol yom... ("and in His goodness He continuously renews creation every day")

The prayer "and in His goodness He continuously renews creation every day" speaks of the constant refreshment and renewal of the vitality of the world. This is known to apply to G-d's name *Havaya* which relates to creation – [since] the [first letter] *yud* indicates constant re-creation, creating continuously from nothing to something. And every day and at every hour a new combination of the [letters of the] name *Havaya* appears in order to create the world. Nevertheless, this is not real creation but rather renewal of what was already created. The vitality that is drawn down again acts to renew and maintain the world as it was created and as it already exists. And so it is in all of the worlds; their vitality is drawn down every day to maintain them as they were created ...

This is similar to the sustenance that enlivens man. By way of food, man lives, as food turns into blood and without the food he would die. Nevertheless, this is only for the purpose of renewing him so that he continues to live as he did previously, without truly creating anything new ... so this light and energy that continuously renews creation every day is called renewal (*chidush*) of that which already exists, similar to food ... Although it is true that [this light and energy] enlivens from nothing to something, it does so only in the same manner as was already done, [and thus] it is compared to food ... but no new creation comes from this, since it is only a ray [of G-dliness] and, therefore, no real renewal [of creation] may come from it.

(From *Sefer Maamorim 5657* (1897) of the Rebbe Rashab, p. 273 (and *Samech Tesamech*, p. 96))

Basic vs enriched Divine energy

Uv'tuvo mechadesh bekol yom... ("and in His goodness He continuously renews creation every day")

There are two categories of descent of G-dliness – "basic" and "enriched."

1) There is the category of divine descent that is constant and homogenous, as it is written, "All the remaining days of the land [will include] seasons of sowing and harvesting ... day and night [these cycles] will not cease to function,"[416] meaning that they will be continuously maintained and never found lacking, as "an immutable law, never to vary."[417]

2) However, there is a much different category of divine descent that is "enriched" illumination. And, whatever comes from G-d that is "enriched" or "additional" is far more than the "basic" influx ... this means that the "enriched" G-dly influx descends as totally revealed G-dly revelation, as it is written regarding the future, "And the glory of G-d will be revealed and all people will see, and your teachers will no longer be concealed and your eyes will see your teachers."[418]

Now, this is related to Yoseph [whose Hebrew name Yosef is derived from the word *hosafa*, meaning "additional"]. And, this category of descent of G-dliness is channeled to Yoseph's brother, Yehudah, since Yehudah corresponds to *hoda'ah* or "acknowledgment," as it is written, "This time I will thank G-d."[419] For, it is not possible to create a vessel for this level of G-dly influx, since "no thought can grasp Him whatsoever,"[420] except through self-nullification, or acknowledgment ... And therefore, acknowledgment serves as a vessel for the descent of the infinite light of G-d ... And this is the reason that our prayers start with acknowledgement during *Hodu* and that we say, "And now, *Havaya* our G-d, we acknowledge You." Since it is impossible to completely grasp the essential infinite light of G-d [with the intellect alone, but rather by] admission and acknowledgement...

And for this reason, the complete four-letter name *Havaya* is incorporated into Yehudah's name, while in the name Yoseph, there are only the first three letters of *Havaya* ... this is because the divine influx brought down by Yoseph descends with the first three letters of the name *Havaya*, as in the verse, "I am the Lord (*Havaya*), I have not changed,"[421] and this influx must be drawn down to the final *hey* of *Havaya*. And for this reason, Yoseph and Yehudah must be together. This is what is meant by, "One with the other, together they approach,"[422] meaning that they must be "together with each other" in order to shine the oneness of *yichuda ila'ah* ("upper, supernal unity") into *yichuda tataa'ah* ("lower, earthly unity)..."

(From *Sefer Maamorim 5658* (1898-9) of the Rebbe Rashab, p. 167)

Normal influx vs Additional influx

The following question is mentioned regarding the statement in the *Eitz Haim*, that, "The purpose of prayer is to draw intellectual influx (*mochin*) into the emotional attributes (*z'a*)." [The question is – What is the purpose of this statement?] The entire chain of spiritual evolution leading to the creation of the world descends from *erech anpin* (the external aspects of *keter*) to *ava* (the intellect; *chochma* and *bina*), and from *ava* to *z'a* (the emotional attributes) and from *z'a* to *malchut* (the lowest, receptive attribute), so what is the purpose of a separate statement that prayer is in order to bring intellect down into the emotions? Elsewhere, it is explained that the purpose is to bring down "mature" spiritual influx (*mochin d'gadlut* – which is Godliness from the name *ma'h* of *tikun*, while in *Likutei Torah* it is explained that this is a "gift of illumination," coming from the "new" name *Ma'ah*).

Now, within this intellectual spiritual influx (*mochin*), there are two levels; there is intellect that is related to the emotions, and there is pure, essential intellect. The intellect that is related to the emotions is ("external") intellect that gives "reasons" for and "explains" the emotions, such as why we should love or dislike something. Furthermore, the external dimensions of the intellect serve as the source of the emotions, and within such intellect we can feel the emotions. Within essential, pure intellect, we do not experience the emotions at all, for it is pure intellect. Moreover, such intellect is also not a source for emotions.

For example, while contemplating a *halacha* (Jewish law), we use essential pure intellect to grasp the concept itself. This occurs as we plunge ourselves into the matter to know it well, and not in order to develop an opinion on the matter. That is, at this point we do not consider whether the final decision on that the matter will be that it is forbidden or permitted. Rather, we labor to grasp and know the reasoning behind the intellectual approach. At this point, there is no feeling for what the opinion (emotion) will be.

And in truth, at this point it is impossible to know what halachic decision will ultimately emerge from this process, because from the essential pure concept, any "emotion" or decision may develop. No opinion is yet recognizable and it is impossible to know what will emerge from this intellectual consideration.

The external dimension of intellect is the expansion and expression of the concept. [On this level], we do not deal with intellectual grasp of the concept, but only with how it comes into expression. And this is what is meant when we say that the "external aspects" of the intellect are "related to the emotions." The act of grasping the concept is not involved in this mode of intellect. Rather, at this stage, we form the connection of the concept to the emotions. This mode of intellect serves as the source of the emotions, and at this point, the emotion itself is experienced in a concealed manner.

And so occurs as well as we meditate upon Godly matters. The essence of our intellect is activated as we plunge ourselves into intellectual grasp of the Godly matter. This transcends the emotions, and we experience no excitement of our emotions at all at this stage. Rather, we cleave to the Godly concept, just as a wise man [cleaves to God] in a state of *devekut*. Similarly the inner essential intellectual concept occurs [to us] as we cleave, and we experience no emotional arousal. This is even more true of meditation upon the depth of the concept and the concentrated intellectual them [underlying it], which are beyond excitement of the emotions.

And the external dimensions of the intellect occur as we expand upon the matter and express it within the "garments" of intellect. There, we experience excitement. We become excited over Godliness, and this filters down to our emotions from our heart. This constitutes the intellectual influx that we draw down when serving God in prayer – it is the "mature" form of Godly influx (*mochin degadlut*) – which are the very essence of intellect...

... But the essence of intellect itself is above the emotions. [In the world], it represents "more than what is necessary" [for the purpose of creation]. (Internally, when the inner aspects of intellectual grasp within the mind filter down to the heart, then the emotions within the heart become like the intellect...).

However, the intellect that descends to us as a *matana* ("gift") is even above the intellect that we achieve with our *avoda*. For, prayer in general corresponds to *malchut;* that is, it serves the purpose of bringing down only that which is necessary to meet the needs that we are lacking (*dai m'chsoro*). This is what is meant by, "And I am prayer." Prayer is associated with the attribute of *malchut*, and the theme of "lacking" is also present in *malchut*...and the point of prayer is to meet our deficiencies, by bringing down revelation of spiritual illumination into *malchut*. This is not a "gift." Rather, it descends to us as *tzedoka*, about which is said that we must "meet the needs of he who is lacking." Nonetheless, we are not required to make him wealthy. A gift, though implies wealth. It is a great level of Godly influx, far more than what we need to fulfill our deficiencies.

In spiritual terms, this corresponds to the saying of the sages, "Wealth is specifically tied to *da'at*." More in detail, wealth is associated with "higher *da'at*," or the supernal knowledge (*da'at elyon*) in which we are primarily aware of God in the foreground while the creation is of secondary importance to us, in the background. This awareness stems from the inner dimensions of *keter*...and this is what is meant by the intellect that descends to us as a *matana*. It is completely out of range of *z'a*, the emotional attributes. For, even though the essential [core of] of intellect is beyond the intellect that is related to the emotions, nevertheless they are the same intellect. However, the intellect that descends to us as a *matana* is intellect [of a different nature] – it is completely separate from us. It is also called "intellect that is beyond any concept" (*sechel hane'elam mikol rayon*). And sometimes it is called "amazing intellect" (*sechel muphlah*) associated with *chochma* within *atik*, and this level of intellect is totally novel when expressed in *z'a*...

From *Sefer Maamorim* 5679 (1919) of the Rebbe Rashab, Page 257-259

Beyond renewal
Ub'tuvo mechadesh bekol yom... ("and in His goodness He continuously renews creation every day")

Regarding the top of Jacob's ladder, about which it is written, "*Havaya* stands above it,"[423] we nullify ourselves to G-d Himself [to *Havaya*, and not to His attributes, but to His very self and essence. This does not apply to the ladder itself though, upon which the "angels are ascending and descending." The ladder is associated merely with the phrase, "and in His goodness He continuously renews creation every day." But what is the explanation of this phrase, for at first glance we see no variation in creation whatsoever from one day to the next? The sun, for example, progresses constantly in one cycle – today as yesterday, in the same path that was established for it during the six days of creation. The explanation is as follows:

The statement "and in His goodness He continuously renews creation every day" refers to His attribute of *chochma* ["wisdom," or flash of insight – the first of the ten *sephirot*]. It was mentioned earlier that the pinnacle of the spiritual hierarchy of creation is the *sephira* of *chochma* into which descends each day a new ray that was not present the previous day. Each day the spiritual energy of the previous day departs and returns to its source, and the following day a new ray descends, maintaining creation of the universe. But, this new ray of G-dly energy descends from His holy light after the *tzimtzum* ("great contraction") and the emanation of *chochma*. In order for this to occur, there must also be an arousal/initiative from below. The arousal is expressed in the desire and the service of the angels and in their song. The *seraphim* chant *kadosh* ("holy") while the *ofanim* and *chayot* "with a great commotion ... recite *baruch* ("blessed be..."). And similarly, all of creation sings a song, as it is written in *Perek Shira*, and with their song they draw down the [new] energy of the universe, and then He "in His goodness renews." This is what is meant by "the angels of *Elokim*" who were ascending and descending [the ladder in Jacob's vision]. To begin with they ascended; this was during the stage of song and elevation. And then they descended, since by way of their service they drew spirituality down into the lower worlds.

But, the abject *bitul* ["nullification"] of souls, nullified "to Him and not to His attributes,"[424] draws down a completely new kind of light, as we pray, "Shine a new light over Zion..." This is a totally new influx, descending from above the *sephira* of *chochma*. And whatever G-d adds [to creation] is enhancement of what He originally established. It augments the spiritual basis and foundation of creation. The basis and foundation is in the spiritual chain of creation (*seder hishtalshelut*), but *chochma* in comparison to what is above it is "out of range" completely. And by way of *bitul* to Him, we draw down illumination from Above that far transcends *chochma*, and this additional G-dly illumination far transcends the basis and foundation [of creation].

(From *Sefer Maamorim 5655* of the Rebbe Rashab, pp. 43-44:)

Divine descent demands renewal

Uv'tuvo mechadesh bekol yom... ("and in His goodness He continuously renews creation every day")

The will of G-d also ... comes down to us via contraction, since *ratzon* ("will") contains the same letters as *tzinor* ("pipe/conduit"). And thus, it descends via a process of renewal, in conjunction with the infinite light of G-d. And just as we say "and in His goodness He continuously renews creation every day," indicating that the descent of His will occurs every day, continuously, in order to create and enliven the worlds, so this descent necessitates "renewal" [of the connection of the Divine will with its source]. This is because in comparison to the infinite light of G-d, [the divine will after its descent] is totally out of range whatsoever...

(From *Yom Tov shel Rosh Hashana 5666* (1906) of the Rebbe Rashab, p. 29-30)

Two types of holy influx

Uv'tuvo mechadesh bekol yom... ("and in His goodness He continuously renews creation every day")

It is known that there are two types of holy influx into the world. One is the influx of energy to all of the worlds in order to enliven and maintain them. It is called *mazon* ("sustenance"), and it is for the purpose of renewing the creation alone, rather than for creating something entirely new. And the second is truly a new influx [of energy], as written, "A new light will shine in Zion."

The explanation is as follows: It is written, "and in His goodness, He continuously renews creation every day," implying that every day, the enlivening energy of the universe is renewed. That means that even after the world and all of the creations were created from nothing to something in order to "exist," there is no permanence to their existence without ongoing illumination and energy from above. This is what enlivens them constantly, and without it, they do not exist at all, and they return to be nullified – *ayn* ("nothing") - as they were previously. It is written, "The eyes of all are upon You, and You grant them their sustenance in time," referring to the renewal of energy that descends to each and every creature. At the core of this matter is that the light and energy themselves need to be renewed constantly from the source. And as written elsewhere, this is why the creative energy cleaves to its source; for this is how it renews itself constantly from its origin...but in any case it is not a totally new influx. Rather, the entire creation remains as it was previously and merely undergoes renewal. This is like, by way of example, food here in the lower physical world; when we eat, the food renews our energy by joining the soul with the body in order to enervate it and to maintain it. And without the food, the soul would separate from the body. And if so, the food renews and maintains our energy, attracting the light and energy of the soul into the body...

...Nevertheless, this is not anything new. That is, it is not a new process of creation requiring a different energy than was present previously (although when we refine food [by eating and elevating it], we may bring down a new illumination from its origin in Tohu, causing our intellect may function differently and better, as written elsewhere. But, this is not caused by the eating itself but by the elevation of the spark of holiness that was in the food). Similarly, the sages said that, "Every day man is a new creation," even though he is the same today as he was yesterday...And so it is above. Even though G-d renews the universe constantly from nothing to something, as written, "a river emerges from Eden," meaning that it "emerges" constantly, referring to *chochma* and *bina*, which are in a state of constant unity in order to maintain the worlds. And this alludes to the unity of *ayn* (spiritual void) with *yesh* (created existence) so that the world is constantly recreated from nothing to something...

This is also the process that occurs during a blessing. The blessing brings down added and increased influx from *sovev* (transcendent G-dliness) into *memalle* (immanent G-dliness), in order to produce revelation of *sovev*. But, this only occurs as a process of revelation from a state of concealment.

The matter is as follows; the renewal of creation demands light and energy that descends, but the light itself needs constant renewal. The origin of descent is from *sovev*, or transcendent G-dliness, which is why we say "and in His goodness He constantly renews..." – "In His goodness" alludes to His infinite light of transcendent illumination (*sovev*), which is the "good" that never ceases, as written, "the Good, since Your mercy never ceases." And from there descends the influx of renewal. And this also explains why we say, *Adon haniflaot hamechadesh betuvo* ("Master of wonders, Who in His goodness constantly renews..."). For, "wonders" refers to the light of *sovev kol olamim*, because renewal of "His goodness," originates from the "Master of wonders"...This means that the light and energy of the world, though of the category of *memalle* ("immanent spirituality") nevertheless originates with *sovev* ("transcendent G-dliness"). And that is precisely the reason why the energy of the universe and creations descends constantly without interruption, for "He in His goodness renews the universe every day, constantly." – Although at first glance, since the energy descends in a measured and limited form (corresponding to *memalle*), there should be interruption [in the descent]. And yet, there is no interruption at all. And this is because the source of the influx is *sovev*. In its constant descent to the universe, the influx is revealed as *memalle*, while the infinite light of *sovev* remains hidden. Thus the path of any blessing is to bring down the infinite light of *sovev* so that it illuminates in a revealed fashion.

And that is why we say, during *bircat hamazon* (the "blessing after bread") *hazan et haolam culo betuvo* ("He Who sustains the entire world in His goodness..."). That is, the source of sustenance (*mazon*), which occurs as renewal of what already exists, is also from His Goodness, which is *sovev kol olamim*. However, the light of *sovev* remains concealed (it is the concealed aspect of what comes into revelation). Its revelation occurs only within the light of *memalle*. The purpose of the blessing is for this good to shine in a revealed fashion. As it says in the *Zohar* (*parshat Terumah* page 168B), [during *bircat hamazon*], we must say, "in His Goodness," rather than "From His goodness." And so it says in Talmud *Berachot* as well: "All who say 'from His goodness' are ignorant, while he who says 'in His goodness' is wise. For, 'from His goodness' refers to the illumination of *memalle* descending from *sovev*. But, 'in His goodness' refers to the entire Good as it exists above, descending as revelation of the infinite light of *sovev*.

Nevertheless, this [descent] occurs from a state of concealment to revelation...it is not a completely "new light"...

From *Sefer Maamorim 5669* (1909) of the Rebbe Rashab, Page 92-94

Of wells and underground fountains...

We need to understand the difference between an underground fountain and a well. A well, similar to a fountain, possesses a source of fresh water flowing into it. The difference between a pit and a well is that the pit contains no water...aside from gathered brackish water, while a well contains water flowing into it from a fountain. And if so, what is the difference between a fountain and a pit, such that the water within a well is described as "living waters"...

The difference, though, is that a fountain occurs naturally from above – man is not involved at all. A well, though is created by human activity, since we must dig the well in order to reveal the water within it. And although the water [itself] is a creation from above, nevertheless human assistance is involved...A pit contains gathered water while a well contains a flowing fountain...the fountain occurs spontaneously, while we must manually draw water from the well. Even after we reveal the [location of the] fountain [within a well] , it does not flow on its own. We have to draw the water...

Now, the parallel for this above is known; there are two types of holy influx into the world. One is "basic vitality" and the other is "additional vitality"...the life-force that arrives as "basic vitality" is measured out according to His will, in accordance with the creation of the worlds and the nature of their spiritual evolution on each and every level. For, the worlds that are above Atzilut exist in one way, while the world of Atzilut exist in another way. And also, the worlds of BY"A have a certain character. Similarly all revelation in all worlds, such as how the light should be revealed in Atzilut - whether among the particular ten *sephirot* of Atzilut, so that within *chochma* the revelation should occur in one way and in *bina* in another fashion, and the same within *z'a* and *malchut*. Or regarding Atzilut in general; should revelation of infinite light should take place within Atzilut...and similarly whether within BY"A there should be Godly revelation [whatsoever] – all is measured according to His will. It is in accordance with His will that the descent of vitality into the worlds takes place at all times, without interruption. It is not dependent upon initiative from below, since [this level of vitality] descends down to the world without any arousal from below.

Nothing is ever added or subtracted to this level of vitality. It remains constant, without any variation or interruption...and this is what is meant by "*ava* (*chochma* and *bina*) are constantly together..." in order to sustain the worlds. For, all influx and Godly revelation descends to the world through *chochma* and *bina*, as written, "You made all of them with *chochma*..." and explained, "You made all of them with *chochma* - within *bina*." For, *chochma* and *bina* are the *ayn* (Godly void) and *yesh* (substance, existence) at the beginning of *seder hishtalshelut* (the spiritual chain leading to physical creation)...

And this is what is meant by "*ava* are constantly together...in order to sustain the worlds...." For, elsewhere, it is written, "He Who in His goodness constantly renews creation at all times." That is, the act of creation needs constant renewal from nothing to something, and if not, nothing will exist at all. The creation of the universe is not similar to the act of a craftsman who creates a utensil. At the time that he creates the utensil, we detect his power and influence over it, for without his power, no utensil would be made. So, it is obvious that it comes from his own power. But, after he has already made the vessel, the talent of the craftsman is still recognizable within it, for from its beauty everyone is able to infer the intelligence and the talent of the craftsman...

However, in the spiritual realm, all of creation is renewed as something from nothing, for before it was created, there was nothing whatsoever. And all such renewal occurs in such a fashion that the Renewer must be constantly present in the process in order to renew the creation from nothing to something...Now, what is the source of this renewal? About this it is said, "He Who in His goodness constantly renews the creation at all times." This refers to the kabalistic level called *yesod aba*, or "the foundation of *chochma*"...and "His goodness" refers to the goodness of the essence of the infinite One, for it is the nature of the good, to do good, and to bestow benefit. This is the reason for the creation of the worlds. It is the nature of one who is good, to do good, and therefore there must be creatures on whom to bestow His attribute of good and kindness...and since this descends from the infinite light above, therefore it is constant, without interruption...

However, all of this is only in order to renew that which already existed, for although the worlds are renewed at every moment from nothing to something, this is not anything truly "new." In reality, this is nothing more than renewing what was already present, including the vitality within creation, for "at every season and at every moment," a new vitality descends [from Above]. And this is not truly "new" light. It is similar, for example to a man who eats in order to renew his strength. By eating, he rebuilds his energy, but this is not equivalent to drawing down a new vitality from the soul. As he lived previously, before eating, so he continues to live after he eats. The proof of this is that when it is really necessary do access new vitality, as when we are not healthy, then normal eating has not affect upon us. Rather, it is necessary to find a cure. Similarly, mere renewal of vitality "at every season and every moment" takes place on one general level. It is not a revelation of truly new illumination. That is, although the general influx comes from the infinite light, it is only from the "superficial, external" layers of the infinite One...

However, the "additional vitality" that descends to us as revelation of truly "new light" from the essential infinite light above, about which we say that "whatever God adds is over and above the basis..." is far out of range of the vitality that descends to us a "basic vitality." This influx also comes from *chochma* and *bina*, but it comes from the internal unity of the two of them together. For, within *chochma*, there are thirty two paths – thirty one of which are revealed paths...and about the thirty second path we say that it is the "path unknown to the bird" – that is, it is beyond the entire category of revelation. But this internal unity of *chochma* and *bina* is not constant. It is elicited by our *avoda*, and specifically by our level of self nullification and sacrifice, as will be explained. And therefore it is not constant, since it is based upon our initiative and ability to elevate the world from below.

And this was the service of the forefathers, Abraham and Yitzhak in digging wells. [They did this] in order to draw down the inner unity of *chochma* and *bina*. For, this is the general difference between a well and a fountain. A fountain is from above; it does not require the assistance of man at all. It totally lacks any element of initiative from below. However, its arouses revelation of only the external, superficial aspects of the infinite light Above. The well, though is dug with the assistance of man. That is, it is only our *avoda* [that brings this revelation into the world]. And the influx is a revelation of truly new illumination, from the inner aspects of the essential infinite light...and that is why it is precisely about a well that we say it has within it "living waters." This refers to the descent from the infinite essential light above.

From *Sefer Maamorim 5679* (1919) of the Rebbe Rashab, pp. 405-409

Renewal starts from the head

Uv'tuvo mechadesh bekol yom... ("and in His goodness He continuously renews creation every day")

We say, "and in His goodness, He continuously renews creation every day" – every day, a new life-energy descends, and this occurs every hour and every minute as well. For, the day is divided into day and night, with twelve hours to the day and twelve hours to the night, corresponding to the twelve permutations of His holy name *Havaya* and the twelve combinations of His name *Adni*. Now, we see that night and day are distinct from one another, and their energy is also distinct, for aside from the fact that the twelve hours of the day are bright while the twelve hours of the night are dark, the influence that descends during the day is different than the influence that descends at night. As written, "The sustenance of grain comes from the sun and the sustenance of vegetables from the moon," indicating that there is vegetation that grows under the influence of the day and there is vegetation that grows only at night.

Similarly, man is equally alive during the day as during the night, and yet the energy of the day is not similar to the energy of the night. During the day, man's intellect and emotions illuminate, as well as all of his senses. And in the Talmud, there are opinions as to whether the night is for sleeping or for learning Torah. According to one opinion, there is more influx of wisdom during the night than there is during the day. However that may be, the energy of the day is different from the energy of the night. And so it is during each and every hour; each hour is associated with a specific energy that is unique, and that is why there are various combinations [of G-d's name] that change each hour. There is a new and specific energy that is drawn down, and so it is in general during the day and the night, which reflect the names *Havaya* and *Adni* [respectrively]...

Now, the day is one detail out of thirty days, and Rosh Chodesh includes the entire month. And also Rosh Hashana includes the entire year. For, everything that divides into details, of necessity implies that there is an inclusive unit, from which are derived the many details. And also these details divide into more details, which are general principles relative to the particular details that are derived from them. And this is what is meant when we say that Rosh Hashana includes the entire year, which is divided into twelve months. And every month has its own particular, separate energy by itself. And therefore every month has its own unique combination of letters spelling His name. And every month divides into thirty days that are also each separate and unique. And the days are divided into hours...and a year is also one detail within a thousand years, as we say that six thousand years are associated with the six days, as written, "For a thousand years are like yesterday in Your eyes." And they correspond with the six emotional attributes (in some places it is explained that these are the attributes of *Atzilut*, but here we are saying that they are the attributes of *yetzira* or of *bria*...). Every thousand years corresponds to one unique attribute...and the day Above includes the thousand years that descend from it.

And so it is up to the highest heights, regarding general principles and their details – all of the details are present in the general principle even if they are not recognizable there. And that is why the general principle is called a "head," such as Rosh Hashana ("Head of the year") and Rosh Chodesh ("Head of the month"). For example, man's head contains all of his particular abilities – they all exist in his head, even though they are not recognizable as such there...accordingly, we may understand that every day and every combination [of G-d's name] draws down a new energy. Since they are distinct and separate from one another, the energy associated with each combination is a new energy. Now, this renewal of energy also exists in the general principle, since the detail is included in the principle. And if so, this renewal is also within the general principal all the way up to the highest, all-inclusive "first principle."

Now, in order for this renewal of energy to occur, there must first be an elevation. For, this is a general rule; there is no descent of G-dly energy without a prior elevation occurring...meaning that when energy ascends from the previous combination of letters [of G-d's name] to the highest levels in the "first principle," then a descent occurs. Nevertheless, the main point is the descent, and this occurs via the combinations, or descent of renewal of energy. It is just that for this to occur, there must first be an ascent. And in truth the purpose behind the prior ascent is that in this manner the descent of G-dliness will occur with even more added illumination...via the ascent of the previous combination together with the fulfillment of Torah and mitzvoth that it caused to occur, in this manner descends added illumination in the combination that follows...and this is what is meant by "and in His goodness, He continuously renews creation every day..."

"In His goodness" implies two kinds of good, as written, "G-d is good to all..." and "G-d is good to all who place their hope in Him..." And the Talmud (Sanhedrin) explains that "When He provides rain, it rains on everyone" – thus referring to the "external" energy that enlivens the universe (yichud chitzoni of av'a, which descends constantly even without any ascent of ma'hn). "and when He hoes, He hoes only the good ones among them" – this refers to the work of "tending the garden" which is only for the sake of the "good ones," in order to draw down an inner unity of av'a, which is a descent from the innermost essence of the infinite light above, as explained in Likutei Torah in the biur to venikdashti. And in this way occurs the elevation for the sake of descent of additional illumination. For, since the descent occurs as a result of our service of Torah and mitzvoth, it brings down added illumination...

From Sefer Maamorim 5669 (1909) of the Rebbe Rashab, Page 198-199

Real New Energy

Fulfillment of the commandments - the 613 commandments of the Torah and the seven commandments from the rabbis, totaling 620 "pillars of light" – causes a revelation of keter ("crown" – numerical value 620), which is the transcendent Godliness that surrounds the world. That is, fulfillment of the mitzvoth causes revelation of an entirely new category of divine light into the world. The influence that normally descends is associated with the verse, "The benefit of the land is supreme..." (Kohelet 5:8). It is not truly "new" illumination. It is, rather renewal of the previously existing divine illumination. [On the physical level], it refers to the naturally re-occurring germination of vegetation, based upon the innate potential of the land. This is an expression of renewal alone...it has already been explained that it is the result of sove kol olamim, or transcendent Godliness, which is a function of divine illumination that is associated with creation of the worlds. This is not a "new" divine light in the world. The root of this influence is from the igul hagadol, or "great surrounding light" that precedes the kav ("ray" or "reflection") of divine light that re-entered the void in order to create the worlds). As known, all transcendent divine illumination comes from the igul hagadol that precedes the kav, which is the infinite light that became hidden. In the beginning, this light shone in the void that preceded the creation, but after the tzimtzum, ("great contraction"), the light was removed and hidden. So this descent of illumination is from a condition of concealment to revelation. It is not a revelation of new light. For, since it was already revealed in the "void" that preceded the creation of the world, and it had a connection with creation but later became hidden, therefore when it returned to descend to the world, it was not considered a new light.

However, the mitzvoth draw down a new light, as written, "A new light will illuminate Zion…" This in general is the difference between Torah and *tefila* ("prayer"). Prayer take place from below to Above, while Torah descends from Above to below. Descent also occurs within prayer. This is what occurs when we say *Yehi ratzon* - "May it be Your will…" incurring a new will. However, this occurs as mere renewal of His will as it is embedded in the *sephira* of *chochma*. [For example], when we pray for the complete recovery of a sick person, nothing truly new occurs. Even before he was ill, there was an influx of vitality [in his body] and the healing involved merely re-establishing the previous vitality that was present when he was healthy. So, this is not truly anything new (nevertheless, it is not comparable to eating. In the case of eating, the influx of vitality comes from the illumination and energy that was already enclothed in the body. The vitality that heals, however comes from vitality of the soul that transcends real enclothement…the representative process that occurs above is a descent of Godliness from *sovev kol olamim*, [into the body]. But, it is not truly "new").

Similarly, when we request from God (during *shemonah esreh*) to "bless the year," the resulting influx is not truly new illumination. Rather, it is renewal of what already existed, as written, "He Who in His goodness constantly renews the creation every day…" For, there are years of plentiful produce and years without, so the blessing only renews whatever vitality was already present. The Talmud (end of tractate *Ketubot*) says that "in the future, wheat will be the size of the two kidneys of a large cow." This is the result of a major blessing, but in its source, it comes only from additional illumination that descends to the world from the *sephira* of *malchut*. When the influx coming from *malchut* descends with additional and maximal illumination, then the influx in the physical world is also greater, as written in the blessing that Yakov Avinu gave to the tribe of Asher (Gen 49.20); "From Asher, will come rich food…" There is rich bread, and there is the bread of the poor, for the influx that descends in a contracted manner is what comes down to the bread of the poor. And when the influx multiplies and grows, the result is "rich bread." Now, all of this descends through prayer, when it occurs by prefacing the Godly unity of the *kriat shema* by saying *Hashem echad* – "God is one…" That is, the seven heavens and the earth, as well as the four directions of the world are nullified and unified with an ultimate unity….and then through the twelve middle blessings of the *shemoneh esreh*, His will descends. This is what is meant by "And the benefit of the land is supreme…"

But, via Torah, which brings down influence from Above to below, a revelation of new light descends, as written "The Torah should be new in your eyes every day," for the words of Torah must carry with them new perspectives every day. So, the descent of Torah to the world is revelation of new light. This is similar to the verse (Isaiah 66:22), "Just as the new heavens and the new earth…" for new blessings emerge from only one seed that produces one hundred seeds. This may occur also from the present heavens and earth. But, that there should be a new "heavens and earth" implies that there must be true Godly revelation in the lower physical world as well, as written (Isaiah 52:8), "and the glory of God was revealed and all flesh could see…for with their own eyes they will see." This is a descent of Godliness that takes place through the fulfillment of mitzvoth, which draw down truly new illumination from the infinite light above…

(From *Sefer Maamorim 5680* (1920), page 145-6

Bringing down mercy from Above
Hamelech hameromam levad, ("the King, Who alone is elevated…")
The point is to channel mercy [so that it descends] from the very essence of the infinite illumination of G-d, who is removed and exalted, by Himself. But, at first glance, how is it possible to channel mercy from Him, when in truth there is none other [than Him]? Rather, for that very reason, all that descends and emerges from

the contracted and limited illumination of His essence in order to become a transcendent light ... is as naught in comparison to Him. That is, [all that descends from Him is] very low in comparison to the essence of His infinite light, as He truly exists by Himself, in His intrinsically exalted state. And when He recalls, so to speak, this contraction and descent from His essence ... despite the fact that there is nothing aside from Him, and nothing truly exists aside from Him, and yet this illumination descended [from Him to] to enliven the worlds ... whose existence is truly naught ... About this, it is appropriate to speak of "mercy" that descends upon [creation] ... And this is what is meant by, "In Your great mercy, have mercy upon us."

*

When we say, *Hamelech hamerumam levad*, ("the King who is elevated alone"), we refer to G-d as He exists one and alone, in a state of majesty and loftiness on His own, far beyond His state of elevation above the worlds and creation. About this we say, "In Your great mercy," referring to the essential infinite light, "have mercy upon us." And this is called "great mercy" because mercy coming from the exalted heights of the infinite light of G-d, as He is exalted above worlds and creation, still bears some sort of proximity and connection with the worlds, and they still make some small difference to Him. And if so, this means there must be various different levels (just as the level of mercy bestowed upon plants and minerals is not comparable to that bestowed upon humans). However, the mercy that comes from His very essence, totally out of range of the worlds, is called *rachamim rabim* ("great mercy") and it includes everything.

And there is another explanation of the word *rabim* ... it also means "without limit," since even the overall transcendent illumination is also a flow of influx from His infinite illumination, and automatically it bears a subtle level of limitation regarding which way it will flow. So, the true "unlimitedness," without boundaries, comes from the infinite light which is beyond descent into the world. And, therefore, the mercy that is brought down from His very essence is called *rachamim rabim*, meaning "without any limit."

(From *Sefer Maamorim* 5655 (1895-6) of the Rebbe Rashab, pp. 114-115)

General will, specified desires

Elokei Olam, berachamecha harabim, rachem aleinu ("G-d of the Universe, in Your great mercy, have mercy upon us")

Just as the *keter* ("crown") of *Atzilut* is the specific will and conscious desire for the [creation of the] World of *Atzilut*, so *keter* of *Bria* is the specific will and desire to create the World of *Bria*. In the beginning, all was included in the primordial thought of *Adam Kadmon* – the most ethereal level of created reality, containing within itself all the details of space and time, past, present, and future – where all thought of creation of the worlds with their various spiritual and physical manifestations arose and existed on one level. Afterward, there emerged the particular will associated with each world, such as the *keter* of *Bria* and the *keter* of *Yetzira*, all the way down to the *keter* of *Asiya*, which is the specific will associated with the World of *Asiya*. About this, we say (in the blessings preceding the *Shema*): *Elokei olam berachamecha harabim*, ("G-d of the Universe, in Your great mercy..."), *Rachem aleinu* ("have mercy on us"), *Adon uzeinu* ("Master of our strength"), *Tzur misgaveinu* ("Rock of our stronghold"), *Magen yisheinu* ("Shield of our salvation"), *misgav baadeinu* ("fortify us"). *Adon uzeinu* is the transcendent aspect of *malchut* of *Atzilut* as it exists in *Atzilut*, and *Tzur misgaveinu*, *Magen yisheinu*, etc. are the three general transcendental levels associated with the three worlds of *Bria*, *Yetzira* and *Asiya*.

(From *Be'shaah shehikdimu* 5672 (1912) of the Rebbe Rashab, vol. 1, p. 129)

Two dimensions of His Name

Al kol shevach ma'aseh yadecha...("for all of the praiseworthy work of Your hands")

In general, the source of creation is the *sephira* of *malchut* of *Atzilut*, about which we say, "The kingdom bears the name of the King."[425] Just as the name of a person bears no relationship to his essence, but is useful for others who call him by name, so it is true of *malchut*. Although it is the source of the universe, it is, nevertheless, a mere ray of spirituality, bearing no relationship to G-d in essence...

And about the creation of the worlds, [the prayer says] that G-d should be blessed "for all of the praiseworthy work of Your hands," indicating that the creation is nothing more than the work of His hands. That means that it is nothing more than a superficial reflection, even in relationship to His name.

Now, our name, though having nothing to do with who we are in essence, nevertheless bears a relation to us, since we turn to those who call us by name. However, our actions (the "work of our hands") are not connected to us whatsoever, since we are not "called" by the work of our hands. That is, the work of our hands is a totally superficial expression [of who we are], and meditation on this should bring us to yearning and desire for G-d. It should cause us to want to be not only "with" G-d [as *malchut*, the source of creation is only "with" G-d, meaning secondary and nullified to Him], but to want G-d Himself, in His very [essence].

(From *Yom Tov shel Rosh Hashana 5666* of the Rebbe Rashab, p. 87)

More angels than any other creation

The explanation of *titbarech lanetzach tzureinu malkeinu vegoaleinu borei kedoshim...bekol divrei Elokim chaim u'melech olam* ("Be blessed forever, our Rock, our King and our Redeemer ... reciting the words of the living G-d and King of the universe") is as follows: The Midrash says about the word *shema* ("Listen..." - the first word of the *kriat shema* that we recite twice a day) - *shema* is *shem eyn* [*shema* is the word *shem* plus the letter *eyn*, which bears the numerical value of seventy]: "The Jews are one seventieth of the nations of the world, while the nations are one seventieth of [the number of] domesticated animals, who are one seventieth of wild animals, who are in turn one seventieth of all the fowls of the world. And the fowls of the world are one seventieth of the evil spirits of the world, who are one seventieth of the number of angels..."

From this quote, it emerges that the greatest number of creations occurs among the angels, who are the most spiritual of creatures. They are also called "separate/removed intellects," in the language of the philosophers, as well as in the language of the kaballists. These are, specifically, the angels of *bria*, who receive from the *kelim* ("vessels") of *bria*, and are called *kedoshim* ("holy ones"). That is, they are separate (holy), which is why we say *titbarech lanetzach tzureinu* ("Be blessed forever, our Rock...""), precisely because He is the One Who creates "holy creatures" – and since the angels are the most numerous of all the holy creations, we cannot apply a number or measure to them - that is why we say, "Be blessed forever, our Rock, our King and our Redeemer..." For He creates *kedoshim* ("holy ones" – referring to the "separate intellects" or "angels") without number. This is not true of angels of a lesser spiritual level, which are created in smaller measure and numbers. And that is why we say about them, "In His holy ones, He places no trust and His angels He ridicules." This implies that the "holy ones" mentioned in the verse are closer to Him, and spiritually higher, for whatever descends to a lower level experiences diminished Divine influence. And therefore, angels in general are more numerous than other creations...

This is the reason that there are so many angels, but why should it be that way – this is explained by a subsequent phrase within our prayers: "reciting the words of the living G-d and King of the universe..."

Now, the *sephira* of *malchut* is called *dibur* ("speech"), as written, "the word of the King rules." The voice emerges from the *sephira* of *tiferet* of *z'a*, from where the breath of the heart descends down to *malchut*, which is called *dibur*. From our own flesh we may understand – in man down here in this world, our voice emerges from the breath within our heart. What emerges is a simple voice; even though our breath is compounded of fire, wind and spiritual water, the composition is united in constant equality. There is no recognizable variation in pronunciation, because we do not express the letters at all. It is an ultimately simple spiritual expression, devoid of any divisions whatsoever. This is a simple expression of the voice, since no letters emerge from the breath of our heart, as known. But, this very simple voice is also unlimited; even though limited letters emerge from it. The power that descends into the voice from the breath of the heart is not limited at all. For, this voice can produce unlimited numbers of letters. Even if man were to live a thousand years, his power to produce letters of speech would not cease. Even if the energy and vitality within our blood weakens, it does not prevent us from speaking, nor will advanced age or physical weakness of the body prevent speech. It may affect the body, but not the power of speech. This is because the voice is simple, rather than compounded of various parts of the body that could weaken and dim the illumination of the body. This voice is called *ruach memallela* ("speaking spirit"), and it is spiritual, not physical.

And so, it is understood that above, there is a supernal voice and speech that comes from the breath of the supernal heart, which is *malchut* of *Atzilut*, before it descends to become divided into the elements of speech. And so from the highest heights from the Emanator down to the emanations, meaning from *malchut* of the *ein sof*, which possesses unlimited power...absolutely without end, nevertheless there occur divisions based upon the five enunciations of the mouth, and this division is truly limited.

For, it is evident that even the breath of the heart, from which emerges the voice of man, necessarily becomes divided and interrupted into smaller components, quite distinct from one another, as it comes to expression in speech. For example, when we want to express the letter *aleph* from the throat, we must interrupt the simple voice within in order to express that one letter. And the same is true for the letter *beit*; another limitation [of the simple voice] is specifically required for this pronunciation of the *beit*, and the component of speech necessary to express the *aleph* will not work in order to pronounce the *beit*. For, in the beginning, the voice emerged in order to pronounce the *aleph*, and then afterward another voice emerged to pronounce *beit*, and there was an interruption between them. This is the same thing as dividing something big into many smaller pieces. This is the manner in which first one expression occurs, is interrupted and then another expression begins... and that is why we say the phrase, *bekol divrei Elokim chaim u'melech olam*, meaning "reciting the words of the living G-d and King of the universe..." The recitation begins from the "simple voice (*kol*)" emerging from the heart, and via the *hey gevurot* (five stringencies associated with the *sephira* of *gevura*) of the five enunciations of the mouth, it is divided into the letters of speech. So, the *kol divrei* ("voice of words") is the voice, and from this voice emerges the myriad, uncountable numbers of combinations of letters of speech. And the reason that these *hey gevurot*, associated with the name *Elokim*, are called *Elokim chaim* ("living G-d") is because, every time that the word *chaim* ("life") is used, it represents *chasadim* – "kindness." For, the contraction that was necessary to minimize the G-dly illumination and to divide it into components is really *chesed* and not *gevura* at all. Without the contraction, the worlds would not exist at all, for they would immediately be nullified in the source from whence they came, like the nullification of a ray in the sun. And if so, the contraction is itself the reason for the existence of the world as something that appears to have its own separate identity. And therefore, these *hey gevurot* are called *Elokim Chaim*, and they are the basis for the existence and vitality of all creations..."

From the Alter Rebbe's siddur with *D'ach, Tefilot Rosh Hashana*, P. 472

Angels, trees and honey
Titbarech lanetzach ("be blessed forever") and *borei kedoshim* ("He who creates holy beings")

While reciting the blessing of *yotzar*, preceding the *Shema*, we say *titbarech lanetzach* ("be blessed forever") and *borei kedoshim* ("He who creates holy beings"), since G-d creates myriad angels, without limit and number, as it is written, "...there are a thousand thousands serving Him ..."[426] but can we apply a number to G-d's heavenly hosts? ... And yet all of them praise, glorify, extol and coronate G-d in great noise and excitement... Now, all this is compared to a forest – *ya'ari* ("my forest") – because angels are termed "trees of the forest," as it is written, "Then all the trees of the forest will sing..."[427] This leads us to *divshi* ("my honey") – the sweetness and the enjoyment of the *Shema*.

Although the [date] honey drips from the [palm] trees of the forest, the honey is the main objective while the trees are secondary, since the honey possesses a sweetness and enjoyment that is lacking in the trees. Nevertheless, the honey grows on the tree and drips from [its fruit], so of necessity some small amount of sweetness must also be present in the tree. But, there, the sweetness is far more coarse...

Through this parable, we may come to understand something about the unity and inclusion of souls in the infinite light of G-d. This relationship is called in the *Zohar* "embracing the body of the King." It is achieved via the sweetness and enjoyment of G-dliness, with which we enjoy Him, similar to honey, which also contains sweetness. And this occurs precisely during the recitation of the *Shema*, called *divshi* ("my honey"). The sweetness affects the soul alone, since it is the G-dly soul that enjoys the infinite light of G-d. More specifically, it is associated with the power of spiritual eyesight within the soul, for the main enjoyment comes through vision, as it is written, "Your eyes are [like] doves."[428] And the soul sees the essence of the infinite light of G-d.

This happens only within the soul and does not apply to angels, who do not possess the potential for spiritual eyesight. As the sages said regarding the verse, "No man may see Me and live,"[429] even the angels known as *chayot*, who uplift the "throne," are not capable of seeing His G-dly glory that "sits" upon it. This is because the angels are in the lower three worlds of *Bria, Yetzira* and *Asiya* where there is no revelation of the essence of G-dliness. Even though their origin is in the World of *Atzilut* ... from which all creations have spiritual origin, their actual creation is in the World of *Bria* ... Souls, however, exist mainly in the World of *Atzilut*, and therefore it is precisely within the soul that spiritual vision is found. And this spiritual vision within the soul is part of its own essence, rather than something that it receives from an external source.

Since the soul is associated with the very essence of the World of *Atzilut* ... it contains within it a vision of the infinite light of the Holy One. The creation of souls is really G-dliness of *Atzilut* becoming a soul in the lower worlds of *BY"A*. Therefore, every soul, even as it exits in the lower worlds, possesses the quality of vision of G-dliness, the ability "to gaze upon the glory of the King." This is the great pleasure of the soul, as it enjoys G-dliness and unites to become included within

G-dliness, by way of *ahava beta'anugim* ("love with delight").

Similarly, [the soul] possesses inner intellectual grasp of G-d's infinite light and oneness, and the soul delights in it. That is the reason for the inner quality of love of unity and inclusion [of the soul]. But, what facilitates *ahava beta'anugim* during the *Shema* is the love and fear that we experience in our animal soul during the preceding blessings. And that love comes from the angels. Similarly, as the soul descends below (and adopts the senses of the body), it needs help and support from the beginning, from the angels, which are called "trees of the forest." In this way, the "honey" – the sweetness of the *Shema* – emerges. And, thereafter, the angels enjoy a spiritual elevation via our souls, since the sweetness and love of enjoyment during the *Shema* also gives a lift to the angels, so that they [also] become included "in the body of the King."

To continue the parable, the trees in the forest also become sweet, as a result of the honey that exudes from them and [both] are eaten, [the tree] along with the honey. This is what is meant by, "I consumed my forest with my honey,"[430] meaning that on account of "my honey," I also ate "my forest," referring to the angels. This is similar to what was written regarding the *malachei Elokim* ("angels of G-d") ascending [on Jacob's ladder[431]]. Here as well, the angels underwent elevation on account of the soul [of Jacob]. Since the angels help and support the souls in their service – as is known regarding the saying of the sages, *natati lecha mehalchim bein haomdim* ("I made you walkers amongst the standers") – the angels also arise to the level of "walkers" by way of the souls...

(From *Be'shaah Shehikdimu* 5672 (1912) of the Rebbe Rashab, vol. 3, p. 1453)

Transcendent vs Immanent G-dliness
Borei kedoshim yishtabach shimcha ("He Who creates holy creatures, praised be Your name")

All the elevations of "holy creatures, who praise G-d every day," are merely associated with *shimcha* - "Your Name." For that reason, we say *borei kedoshim*, alluding to the holy creatures/angels, which are a creation from nothing to something. *Chochma* [from where all angels and other holy creatures come] emerges from *ayn*, meaning that the [process leading to] creation of *chochma* as the origin of the spiritual chain of creation from the infinite light of G-d is unlike the spiritual chain of creation as it descends from *chochma* downward. This descent is by way of cause and effect, such as what happens in man, for example, when intellect, emotions, thought, speech and action flow down, each from its previous level ... This is why the verse says, "You created them all in wisdom (*chochma*)," meaning that all creations emerged from concealment in *chochma* to revelation. They were originally included together within *chochma*, equivalent to the original creative statement ("In the beginning, G-d created...") through which G-d formed the universe. This singular original statement included all the subsequent nine statements.

However, the creation of *chochma* from the infinite light of G-d was a creation from nothing to something, since the infinite G-dly light transcends and surpasses the level of *chochma*. And, therefore, the original creation of *chochma* could only take place from nothing to something. This is what we mean when we say *borei kedoshim*. All the levels called *kedoshim* are equivalent to "holy creatures" that praise His name every day. Their source is from *chochma* ... and they are also a creation from nothing to something, and their entire spiritual elevation is only up to *shimcha* ("Your name").

*

There are two aspects of G-dliness: immanent G-dliness (*memalle kol olamim*) and transcendent G-dliness (*sovev kol olamim*). Immanent G-dliness involves the spiritual chain of creation of the worlds (*seder hishtalshelut*) – that is, the ray of G-dliness that descends by way of cause and effect from one level to the next, as it is written, "For the sake of My honor, I created, I formed, I even made,"[432] referring to the three worlds of *Bria*, *Yetzira* and *Asiya* (*BY"A*). They also descend, in tandem with the G-dly energy that comes down from one world to the next...

Now, this descent begins from the four *chayot* of the *merkava* that exist in each [world], and continues from each world to the world beneath it.[433] The *chayot* are the source of all the G-dly life-energy of all creatures of our world. From the "face of the ox" descend the souls of all domesticated animals; from the "face of the lion" come the souls of all wild animals; from the "face of the eagle" emerge the souls of all fowl; and from the "face of man" descend the souls of the righteous gentiles of the world. And there is yet another element, called the "supernal man" who resides above the *merkava* and from this element come all Jewish souls.

Now, these four *chayot* of the *merkava* exist in each and every world of the three worlds – *Bria*, *Yetzira* and *Asiya* – since from *Bria* the energy flows and descends into *Yetzira* and from *Yetzira* to *Asiya*. This is what is called the "spiritual chain of creation," involving the flow and descent of influx from one spiritual level to the next. Even the descent of the soul-levels of *nefesh* and *ruach* to bodies and animals and man in this world is associated with the spiritual chain of creation ... for the animal soul itself is spiritual, and that is why it descends from the "face of the ox" of the *merkava*. And this also applies to the descent of man's soul from the "supernal man" and in particular to the descent of *nefesh* from *Asiya*, of *ruach* from *Yetzira*, and of *neshama* from *Bria*, all occurring within the framework of the spiritual chain of creation. And since the *nefesh*, *ruach* and *neshama* within man are all spiritual levels of the soul, they originate from the very source and origin of the spiritual chain – that is, from *chochma* [of *Atzilut*] ...

But there is no creation of anything new whatsoever from the origin, from *chochma*, for all of this concerns the descent and formation of new spiritual creations, such as the souls of the animals. But the creation of anything physical, such as the bodies of the animals, or of any other mineral or vegetable object, cannot occur within the chain of spiritual creation. That is, it is impossible for the spiritual "face of the ox," for example, to give rise to the creation of a physical body of an ox, since it is impossible to create anything physical from something spiritual, even after infinite levels of descent. Everything is formed within range of its source, meaning that no spiritual level will create anything physical, since that would be out of its range. The only way to facilitate the creation of physical bodies of the human, animal, vegetable and mineral worlds, as well as all that exists, is from beyond the chain of creation, meaning from G-d's very essence and self, since He is without limit. Only with G-d Himself is found the origin of physical creation, since "...He commanded and they were created"[434] ... But, it is impossible for the creation of anything physical to occur from *chochma* ... This occurs only from G-d's supernal will, which transcends *chochma*, from the infinite light of G-d itself, which is called *sovev kol olamim*. From this level it is possible to enable the creation of physicality, as G-d is all-powerful...

(From *Sefer Maamorim 5655* (1895) of the Rebbe Rashab, Pp. 13, 16-17

Two modes of *Bina*

It is known that *bina* is the source of all transcendent Godly influence (*makifim*). At first glance, this is not understood, for *bina* is intellectual grasp and understanding. It requires that we grasp matters with internal knowledge, so how is it possible that it is the source of transcendent awareness?

However, both are correct. For it is clear to us, even with our natural intellect that the nature of intellect is to tolerate that to which it is opposed. We are capable of intellectual investigation and mental imagination of matters that we detest with ultimate disdain, just as much as we are able to tolerate matters that we love. And as we look into and grasp such matters, we are able to hold them in our mind. To the extent that we grasp and consider anything, we do so in our mind and hence the matter becomes "surrounded" with intellect such that it is encircled from all sides. And therefore, even when we grasp matters that we detest, they are grasped and surrounded in our mind and encircled by our intellect, and our mind surrounds the matters from all sides even though we may hate the matter with ultimate detestation.

This is not true of emotions. Emotionally, we are incapable of tolerating that which is hateful to us. When we become aware that something is hateful, we detest it with ultimate disdain and reject it, but in our minds we are still capable of tolerating it. And yet, our emotions stem from our intellect, and since our emotions are not capable of tolerating that which is hateful, why should not the same apply to our minds?

We are forced to conclude that within intellect, there are two modes. One mode occurs as the intellect descends to influence the emotions, and the second mode is as the intellect remains above and removed from the emotions, as a *makif,* aloof from the emotions. On the level of intellect that is aloof from the emotions, we are able to tolerate that which is hateful to us because even that is merely transcendent. Now, that which descends from the intellect to the emotions is no more than a ray and reflection alone. It is merely an offshoot that comes from the intellect into the emotions, but the essence of the intellect does not become involved in the emotions. It remains aloof. We can understand this better from *avodat Hashem*: As we meditate, using our intellect for Godly grasp, when we contemplate the depth of the concept, our contemplation has no influence upon our emotions at all. Even the external aspects of intellect, which bear a connection to the emotions, do not have much influence upon the emotions – they remains aloof. This is similar to one who understands or hears something that has nothing to do with him. Similarly this meditation does not touch him within, even though he understands it.. Only with his faculty of *da'at* ("visceral knowledge") does he feel the concept inwardly, and even then he only feels an offshoot of the intellect. For, what he feels with his faculty of *da'at* is only that closeness to Godliness is "good for him." That is, he merely feels the goodness of Godliness in some way, and this is a good feeling and because of it he desires Godliness. But, he does not feel the concept itself within, since it remains aloof. And this is true nature of intellect itself – we do not feel it within; it remains aloof. That is, even during the service of the mind, the concept remains aloof.

From *Sefer Maamorim 5679* (1919) of the Rebbe Rashab, page 396-7

Yotzer mesharetim va'asher mesharetov...("He who forms ministering angels and whose ministering angels all stand ...")

Externally motivated fear [awe or reverence] is a result of the expression of the greatness of His Kingship. It can be compared to a person who experiences awe of a human king on account of the expansion of the greatness of his reign over the many nations and states of his empire. So it is written [regarding G-d] – "there are a thousand thousands serving Him."[435] And about this, the sages decreed that we should recite the blessing *Yotzar ohr*, in which is described this level of fear: "He who forms ministering angels and whose ministering angels all stand ... and exclaim in fear ... all in unison, responding in awe and declaring in trepidation" ... and the *ofanim* and *chayot hakodesh* with a great commotion rise..." And in this way the Jews as well internalize this level of fear of G-d...

Now, this level of fear precedes love of G-d. After we internalize this level of fear, we experience the level of love mentioned in the next blessing, *ahavat olam ahavtanu* ("With a constant love, we love You ... unite our hearts in love ... He who chooses His people, Israel, with love.") This leads us to the *Shema*, in which we draw down and fulfill the higher level of love commanded in the verse: "You shall love the Lord your G-d..."

Now, regarding these levels of fear and love of G-d, the Torah says, "I consumed my forest with my honey..." The forest contains all types of trees, including the "cypress trees" which symbolize the angels called *seraphim*, who stand upright [in fear of G-d]. This is the meaning of the blessing *Yotzar ohr* in which are mentioned the angels that are standing in awe and making themselves heard, while the lower angels known as *ofanim* create a great commotion. And "my honey" is an allusion to the sweetness and utter enjoyment of *ahava beta'anugim* ("love with delight") that descends during the recital of "You shall love the Lord your G-d with all of your heart(s)." Then, even the hidden recesses of the heart that conceal G-dly love come alive with conscious love. And as we say, "with all your soul," all of our soul powers, including the power to think, [are permeated with love of G-d]. And "with all of your might" means without reservation or interruption, as there is no end or goal to this intense love...

And from this level of love, we make progress and arrive to a level of internally generated awe, associated with total self-nullification, symbolized in our bowing during the *Shemonah Esreh*. This is because the blessing, *Yotzar ohr* is on the level of the angels, whose fear and worship is merely external. But, this is not true of the *Shemonah Esreh*, which represents the nullification and worship of souls that are internal [manifestations of] G-dliness. That is, they are totally nullified from their own existence as a result of the infinite light of G-d whom no thought can reach at all, and this is an aspect of *sovev kol olamim* ("transcendent G-dliness").

From *Likutei Torah* of the Alter Rebbe, *Parshat Re'eh*, p. 38)

Why mention angels before kriat shema?
Kadosh, Kadosh, Kadosh...("Holy, holy, holy...")

The fire from Above that kindles the animal soul descends as a result of our meditation on the selflessness of the angels, who ignite and catch fire in a burst of fiery desire. They become nullified and subsumed in the G-dly illumination that flows down upon them. In this way, the revelation of love [from Above] illuminates the power of physical lust within the animal soul, which stems from [the angels]. [This love] then arouses the heart to detach itself from the physical lusts to which it was formerly attached and rise to its source, becoming nullified and absorbed within the light of G-d.

Accordingly, the "Sages of the Great Assembly" established the two blessings preceding the *Shema*. [Within these prayers] we describe the service of the angels, [including] how they are nullified to G-d. For, at first glance, it is not clear why is it necessary for us to mention the angels who say *kadosh* ("holy"). Are we not familiar with His praises or aware that He is exalted and holy? Why is it necessary to mention this praise in the name of the angels? And why do we describe their excitement, [reciting] how the angels exclaim in fear ... "all in unison, responding in awe and declaring in trepidation"? Need we become aroused with their excitement? After all, our souls are higher than the angels, so what is the point? Either our souls need not get excited over what arouses the angels ... or, if our souls must also become aroused, why do so through the excitement of the angels?

The explanation is that all this takes place on behalf of the animal soul. Since it derives from the *chayot* of the *merkava* [a high class of angels], the meditation on the angels' praises and their excitement of love induces an illumination of love to shine down upon our animal soul, causing it to experience love of G-d. This, then, is the fire from Above that is associated with the animal soul.

Now, the fiery excitement of the angels is produced by meditation on the source from which they were hewn, as well as upon the process of their creation. They were created from a G-dly ray, emanating from the *sephira* of *malchut* [of *Atzilut*; they themselves are in *Bria*]. Their meditation is on their source, which created them, and the manner in which they were created...

(From *Sefer Maamorim 5666* (1906) of the Rebbe Rashab, p. 137-138)

Kadosh, kadosh, kadosh...

The three times that we say the word *kadosh* ["holy," which we say three times during the blessings preceding the *kriat shema*] correspond to the three levels of *nehi* (*netzach, hod, yesod*), *chagat* (*chesed, gevura tiferet*), and *chabad* (*chochma, bina, da'at*)...and as a result of our intellectual grasp of the infinite light and how it is holy and removed, [we achieve] a strong and fiery desire to become included in the infinite light...And the three *vovin* of the three times that we recite the word *kadosh* represent the three *kavin* ("vectors") of the world of *Atzilut* [within *Atzilut* are three tendencies, or "vectors" – the "right side" tends toward kindness, the left side to strictness, and the middle line to a combination of the two], and also three times [the letter] *vov* equals eighteen, which is equivalent to *chai* ("life"), corresponding to the phrase *yachid chay haolamim melech*...

From *Sefer Maamorim 5677* (1917) of the Rebbe Rashab, Page 85

Kadosh, kadosh, kadosh...

It is known that the *sephira* of *tiferet* receives from the *sephira* of *chochma*, as written in the *Pri Eitz Cahim* regarding the *kavanot* during the three times that we say *kadosh*: The first time [that we say *kadosh*], we think about when *tiferet* ascends to receive its ray of light from *chochma*, and the second *kadosh* is when *tiferet* returns to its place with its ray of *chochma*...as written in *Likutei Torah* in the *biur* to *Venikdashti*.

From *Sefer Maamorim 5677* of the Rebbe Rashab, page 173 (at the bottom)

Kadosh, kadosh, kadosh...

The matter is as follows; the spiritual level of souls surpasses that of angels, which is why the song of the souls also precedes the song of the angels. However, in regards to souls en-clothed in bodies, angels have an advantage since they have no body that conceals, while souls are enclothed in bodies that conceal them. And that is why souls in the lower worlds require assistance from the angels.

However, in their source, a preferential light and revelation shines into souls, and the illumination is also far higher [than that which illuminates the angels]. And the order of illumination is as follows: First, the light is drawn down to the soul in its source, and afterward to the angels (possibly, this is a mere ray of light, which is superficial, chitzoni...), and then finally to souls below [as they are enclothed in bodies]. (Possibly, in general, the influx that descends to souls comes from a deep level, while that which descends to angels is superficial...and possibly via the avoda of souls in this world, a deeper level of light descends to the angels as well, as mentioned elsewhere regarding the difference between "walkers" and "standers"...).

And this constitutes the three times that we recite the word *kadosh* in prayers; the first corresponds to the descent of illumination to souls in their source above, while the second *kadosh* corresponds to the descent of illumination to the angels. For the influx descending to them precedes that which comes down to soul en-clothed in a body. They exist in the world of *asiyah*, lower in level then the angels which have no body that conceals, as mentioned above. And for that reason, there must first be a descent to the angels and afterward in the third *kadosh* the descent the descent to souls in bodies takes place...

From *Sefer Maamorim 5678* (1918) of the Rebbe Rashab, page 214-215

Kadosh, kadosh, kadosh...

The angels known as *seraphim* say the word *kadosh* ("holy") three times, following which they declare, "the whole earth is full of His glory..." And at first glance, there is a contradiction here from the beginning to the end. To begin with, they utter *kadosh*, implying that the infinite light of God is holy and removed. And the three times they utter "holy" correspond to the three worlds of *bria, yetzira,* and *asiya*, or to the three letters *yud-hey-vov* of His name *Havaya*, which correspond to the worlds of *Atzilut, bria* and *yetzira*. And then, they say "the whole earth is full of His glory," meaning that the physical earth which is the lowest of levels, is nonetheless full of His glory...

However, the *seraphim* say this for the very reason [that they grasp their true level]. The *seraphim* grasp how the infinite light is holy and removed, even from the world of *Atzilut*. For *Atzilut* is the world of ten *sephirot* and various names of God corresponding to the *sephirot*. And even though the *sephirot* are Godly, nevertheless the infinite light of God, which is "not associated with these *sephirot* whatsoever," is holy and removed. And all the more-so that it is removed from the lower worlds of *bria, yetzira* and *asiya*, which consist of totally limited creations...

And the three times that the *seraphim* say *kadosh* correspond to the letters *yud-hey-vov* of the name *Havaya*, while the name *Havaya Tzeva'ot* refers to the final *hey* of His name *Havaya*. For the letter (*ot*) is part of His army (*tzava*), which is an allusion to His legions of creations, such as the hosts of the heavens...all of whose existence emerged from one letter, which is the letter *hey*, the "light letter that has no substance." And that is why, "the whole earth is full of His glory." Since He is holy and removed, He is also found down here on this earth...as it says, "He is the place of the universe; [but] He is not [limited to] the place of the universe." He grasps all of the worlds, and there are none that grasp Him. These two concepts are co-dependent; since there is nothing that is capable of grasping Him, He grasps all of the worlds equally...

From *Sefer Maamorim 5678* (1918) of the Rebbe Rashab, page 288-289

Three times Kadosh...

...the four letters of the name *Havaya* represent contraction followed by expansion, and then descent followed by another stage of expansion...and the name of *Havaya* is only a ray and reflection of His name, which becomes the source of the worlds. And about that it was said, "For His name is elevated..." This means that even the Name of *Havaya* is exalted and elevated, as a transcendent light over the worlds. And what descends to permeate us is a mere ray and reflection.

And this is also what is meant by the word *kadosh*. The three times that we say *kadosh* correspond to the three first letters, *yud-hey-vov*, and the final *hey* of *Havaya* is the source and origin of the worlds – this is the name *Havaya*.

From *Sefer Maamorim 5679* (1919) of the Rebbe Rashab, page 241

Three levels of kedusha before the Tzimtzum

In general, the infinite illumination of God is described as *kadosh* ("holy"), and within it, there are three levels of *kedusha* ("holiness") corresponding to the three levels within the infinite light...They are, the 1) the very essence of Godly illumination, 2) the infinite light that precedes His will to create the world (*kodem ahlot haratzon*) and 3) the will itself (*ahlot haratzon*). Now, the true aspect of *kodesh* is His essential Name, within His hidden essence...about which we say, "And I sanctified the Great Name," indicating the sanctification of His great name in general within the infinite light that precedes the *tzimtzum*. And thus we bring down *attah kadosh* ("You are holy...") to within *shimcha kadosh* ("Your Name is holy...")

From *Sefer Maamorim 5619* (1919) of the Rebbe Rashab, page 201

Kadosh and *Baruch*

Among angels, there are two levels; there are angels of the "revealed worlds" (*alma d'itgaliya*) and angels of the "hidden worlds" (*alma d'itcasiya*), and they are "benefactors" and "recipients." For, in the realm of cause and effect, the effect cleaves to its "cause" in order to receive influx from it. If it did not do so, it would cease to exist. Now, this cleaving to its cause takes place within the *keter* ("crown," or pinnacle) of the effect; that is, within the very essence of the effect. And from its lower half and downward, the effect influences and becomes a "cause" of that which is below it. That is why there are two levels of angels - *ofanim* and *seraphim*. The *ofanim* exert influence and provide benefit, meaning the through them and by them, divine influx descends. And that is why they say, "blessed be the glory of God from His place." The word *baruch* ("blessed") indicates descent, such as a descent of the glory of God from His place. For, "He is the place of the universe, [but] He is not limited to the place of the universe." And that is what is meant by "Blessed is the Place" [wherein "place" – *makom* – refers to God]. It indicates descent of divine influx into the universe.

And there are angels who are recipients, as implied in our prayers, "they call to one another, saying *kadosh*" – and the Aramaic translation says, "they receive each from the other." This refers to the *seraphim*, which cleave and cling to [what they perceive] above them. They do not issue any influx or influence [toward what is below them] at all, since "while they are striving to absorb, they are incapable of exuding." That is why they utter *kadosh*, which indicates ascent. For, *kadosh* and *baruch* correspond to "running and returning" (wherein "running" is ascent for the purpose of clinging to spirituality above, while "returning" is descent in order to bring the holiness down to the lower worlds and creation). That is why the *seraphim* are above the *ofanim*, for spiritual ascent (*ratzoh*) is associated with the name *ma'ah* and "return" is associated with the name *ba'n*, as written, "the spirit of man ascends above." And "man" (*adam*) has the numerical value of forty-five, while the "spirit of the animal" descends.

And that is what is meant by, "A thousand thousands stand before Him..." The "thousand thousands" that serve Him are the angels through whom the divine influx flows. And the "myriad myriads"...are the angels that receive, for they are in a state of "running" and ascending. And this is what is meant by "standing before him" – before Him means before the very essence of His infinite light. The *ofanim* who say *baruch* are involved in bringing down the divine influx by way of immanent spirituality (*memalle kol olamim*), while those who stand "before Him" are associated with transcendent Godliness (*sovev kol olamim*)....they are the angels who elevate our prayers as well as our love and fear of God, and they are the angels who perform the purification of sparks below. On both of these levels, there are a huge number of angels, as the sages said, "one thousand thousands" is the number of angels within one troop, but there are an unlimited number of troops...

From *Sefer Maamorim 5678* (1918) of the Rebbe Rashab, Page 347-348

Three stages of development

Vehaofanim vechayot hakodesh...("And the *ofanim* and holy *chayot*...")

In general, there are three stages of development; *ibur* ("pregnancy"), *yenikah* ("nursing"), and *mochin* ("intellect," or "maturity"). *Ibur* is the ultimate immaturity, when all of the faculties are concealed and there is no indication of intellect as of yet. For example, the embryo when in the womb of its mother, is doubled over, with its head between its knees, indicating that all that has developed are his instinctual faculties of *nehi* (*netzach, hod* and *yesod*) alone. The intellectual faculties of *chabad* (*chochma, bina* and *da'at*) as well as the emotional faculties of *chagat* (*chesed, gevura* and *tiferet*) are concealed. And therefore, this stage is not yet considered to be in the category of the "form of man." For, "man" implies intellect and emotions, and while in the state of *ibur*, there is no revealed intellect and emotions, and therefore *ibur* is not yet within the category of the "form of man."

Now, it is known that above, this [stage] corresponds to the angels known as *ofanim* (lit; "wheels"), who are in the world of *asiya*, where *nehi* are dominant. Now, the *ofanim* are described as *igulim* ("round or spherical"), as known the difference between *seraphim* and *ofanim*; about *seraphim*, it is written, "With two they cover their face and with two they cover their feet," implying that they are in the form and structure of "man." Man stands with an upright structure, including head, hands, and feet which correspond to *chabad* (intellect) and *chagat* (emotions), and this stance is called *yoshar* (straight, upright). But about *ofanim*, it is written, "As when the *ofan* is within the *ofan*," referring to *igulim*...for they are not yet within the form of man. And yet, this is still considered a stage of development because nevertheless there is some intellect present. In particular, it is known that within *ibur* there is found *chabad, chagat* and *nehi*, and since there exist particular levels we must say that there is some intellect present as well..."

(From *Besha'ah Shehikdimu* 5672 (1912) of the Rebbe Rashab, vol. 1, page 516)

Fire from Above - Fire from Below

The Rebbe Rashab explains this in greater detail: "There are two aspects to the service of sacrifices, corresponding to the two approaches of the G-dly soul in love... above, as well as to the offering of the animal soul which then becomes included in the fire from below and the fire from above. As written, "Adam, when you offer from yourselves a sacrifice, from the animal you should offer it..." The words, "from yourselves a sacrifice" apply to the G-dly soul, since "Adam" refers to the supernal "man" above, representing the fire [that comes down] from above. This process induces the G-dly soul to approach and draw closer to G-dliness.

Subsequently, the verse continues, "from the animal you should offer it." [This part of the verse] refers to the sacrifice of the animal soul, as written in *Likutei Torah* on this verse. And within this are to be found two fires (as mentioned above). There is the fire from below, which symbolizes the love that we develop in proportion to the logic and intellect utilized by the G-dly soul. [This love] produces the fire with which we sacrifice the animal soul. For, the divine soul is enclothed within the animal soul...which hides and conceals it, and when the divine soul becomes aroused with love, it bursts out [of the animal soul] to become revealed. This itself weakens the animal soul...And when in addition, the G-dly soul awakens with excitement, and desires G-dly matters, the same occurs within the animal soul. The animal soul also grasps the wonderful nature of G-dliness within the process of creation. This is what occurs as the natural intellect also comes to terms with G-dly matters, in turn stimulating love within the animal soul as well. This, then is the fire from below.

And the "fire from above" is [produced by] meditation upon the nullification of the angels, as we recite the words of the *bircat kriat shema*, describing how the *seraphim* and the *ofanim* say *kadosh* and *baruch*. For, at first glance, why is it necessary for the angels to say *kadosh*? Souls are also aware of and understand that G-d is holy. But, this process is for the animal soul, whose source is from the "waste products" of the *ofanim*. The meditation regarding how its own source and origin is nullified produces the affect of nullifying the animal soul as well.

In detail, there are two levels within this "fire." The meditation on the nullification of the angels "jars" the animal soul, which then "agrees" to the nullification of the divine soul – but this is a result of its weakness alone. And when its source and origin truly illuminates it from above, it produces an inner nullification of the animal soul (see what is written in the *drosh*, *Yomtov shel Rosh Hashana* of the year *5666)*. This is the "image of a lion that consumes sacrifices," revelation of the source and origin. It is what produces inclusion of the animal soul in the fire from above of the G-dly soul – meaning the "great love" that comes from above, to "turn darkness into light..."

"...And where in prayer do we find allusion to the fire that descends from Above? This we find in the words, *Boruch atah Havaya* ("Blessed are You, Lord...") that we say during the *shemonah esreh...*"

From *Sefer Maamorim 5677* (1917) of the Rebbe Rashab, page 140-1

Seraphim vs ofanim
Vehaofanim vechayot hakodesh...("And the *ofanim* and the holy *chayot...*")

We first need to understand what is meant by, "And the *ofanim* and the holy *chayot*, with great commotion..." [This signifies that] their G-dly service takes place with great noise; while that of the *seraphim* is quiet, [the *avoda*] of the *ofanim* is with noise]. And at first glance, noise is not a praiseworthy quality, for noise implies feeling [oneself and one's ego] and this is a negative trait. Wherever there is less noise, is better. And therefore, silent prayer is equated with the "still small voice," which is on a high spiritual level, while "noise" which is feeling, is a fault. And the entire process of prayer, wherein we organize and recite our praises of the One above, narrating how the creations extol and exalt G-d, is in order to arouse the soul with excitement over love of G-d. The excitement emerges precisely when we grasp the higher qualities of creation – only from this do we achieve excitement of the soul. Whatever is lacking [in the creation] is not a cause for excitement, so why is it necessary to mention that their path of worship takes place with great noise, since this is not a [praiseworthy] quality?

Furthermore, we are forced to conclude that the *ofanim,* with their *avoda* ("path of worship"), reach a higher level than do the *seraphim*, for the [*ofanim*] mention the name of *Havaya* after two words (*Baruch kevod...)...*[while the higher angels – the *seraphim* – mention G-d's name only after three words – they say the word *kadosh* three times]. This implies that [the *ofanim*], who utter G-d's name after only two words, are higher than the *seraphim*. And it is because of their *avoda* that they reach this [higher] level. So, we must conclude that their *avoda* takes place on a higher level, even though it is accompanied by noise. So, why does this *avoda* not exist among the *seraphim*? The *seraphim* exist on a higher spiritual level than the *ofanim*; their abode is in the world of *Bria*, while the *ofanim* are in *asiya*, though the *chayot* are in *Yetzira*, and as known, *bria* is higher than *yetzira* and *asiya* and therefore they are higher than the *ofanim*. And if the *avoda* of noise is higher, why does it not exist among [the *seraphim*] as well?

The matter is as follows; the very reason that the *seraphim* are above the *ofanim*, for their abode is in the world of *Briah*, where "supernal *ima* nests" (meaning that the *sephira* of *bina*, or intellectual analysis "dominates") – [is the reason that the *ofanim* surpass the *seraphim*]. *Ima* is *bina* - intellectual grasp and understanding – intellect that we are capable of integrating with our innate abilities (lit: "vessels"), and the *avoda* of the *seraphim* takes place with intellectual grasp and understanding, for they have tremendous grasp of the G-dliness that they perceive, and [therefore] the concept of "exiting the vessel" (going beyond their innate abilities) does not exist [for them]. Even though they utter the words, *kadosh Havaya* ("G-d is holy"), indicating that He is holy and removed from the worlds, nevertheless their perception comes to them via intellect. And although this level cannot be grasped intellectually, still it comes to them via understanding and meditation, so automatically they know about the nature of G-dly wonder that exists on this spiritual level. And therefore, the [whole concept of] "exiting the vessels" does not exist, for the concept of "exiting the vessels" exists when we know the matter at hand, but cannot grasp it at all, and therefore we "exit" our vessel. But, the *seraphim*, who do know and grasp this spiritual level, and do experience intense arousal, beyond logic and intellect, nevertheless do not undergo complete and total "exiting of the vessels."…

However, the *ofanim* achieve total "exit from the vessels," since they are "located" in *asiya*, yet they come from a much higher source, as known that whatever descends to the lowest level comes from the highest source above. And therefore, on account of their source, the *ofanim* are able to achieve a higher level than the *seraphim*. And furthermore, since the *ofanim* have no intellectual grasp whatsoever, as known that the "six *sephirot* 'nest' in *yetzira*, and the *ofan* in *asiya*," they completely take leave of their "vessel," to the extent that they arrive in this manner to the highest level…and this results from their *avoda* with noise, even though it comes from the grasp and understanding of the *seraphim*, as written that they "raise themselves up facing the *seraphim*,' meaning that they hear how the *seraphim* grasp and say 'holy.' But, for them [the *ofanim*], this matter is not grasped at all, which is why they "exit their vessel." Nevertheless, by "exiting their vessel," they arrive at the highest level above, beyond the *seraphim*, who possess intellectual grasp…so it is understood that although the *ofanim* receive their spiritual level from the *seraphim*, nevertheless their *avoda* takes place with "commotion," – "exiting the vessels" – and in this manner they achieve the highest level, in which they "elevate the throne [of glory], with 'man' upon the throne…"

(From *Sefer Maamorim 5663* (vol. 2) of the Rebbe Rashab, Pp. 314-316)

The angels and our prayers
Baruch kevod HaShem mimkomo ("Blessed be the glory of the Lord from its place")

Now, the *chayot* are also called *chayot hakodesh* ("holy angels"), since they are holy and removed. They clearly comprehend how, "I am G-d, I haven't changed," whether before the world was created or after ... They stand with one desire and motivation – to be included in the transcendent G-dliness that they perceive and to utter "holy." With this power and desire to be included in the source of the transcendent illumination, they bear the "throne."[436] That is, they uplift the "form of man" as he sits on the throne, representing *memalle kol olamim* ("immanent G-dliness") which is divided into categories and divisions [of revealed G-dliness] according to the form of man with a head, a torso and feet. The ten *sephirot* correspond to this form of man. The *chayot* bear this image of immanent G-dliness and elevate and unite it with transcendent G-dliness, so that immanent and transcendent G-dliness come together as one, through the power of their desire and fiery love for G-d. And then, they proclaim, "Blessed be the glory of G-d from His place." By "glory of G-d" is meant immanent G-dliness, as it is written, "The entire earth is filled with His glory (*kevodo*)," which is also translated as "ray of glory." But, "His place" refers to the origin of essential spirituality, that is, transcendent G-dliness.

And so goes the progression of prayer, as well. It begins with the verses of praise (*Pesukei DeZimra*) and moves on to the two blessings preceding the *Shema*. These contain a narrative describing how the angels praise G-d, raise their voices in fear of Him, and say *kadosh*.

By reciting these prayers, we draw into our soul the power to ascend during the *Shema*, inducing within ourselves a strong desire to surrender our soul while saying the word *echad* ("one"). And this is followed by another descent, composed of the acceptance of the yoke of heaven within the first paragraph of the *Shema* (beginning with *veahavta*). Throughout this process, our meditation is focused on self-nullification and elevation to the source that creates and enlivens us, similar to the nullification of the *chayot* ...

This is followed by the *Shemonah Esreh* with its benedictions, each beginning with the words *Baruch Atah* ("Blessed are You"); this indicates drawing down G-dliness so that *Havaya* [essential G-dliness, by way of contraction] becomes "You" or revealed G-dliness. In general, the *Shema* constitutes spiritual ascent, while the prayers of the *Shemonah Esreh* constitute drawing down G-dliness from Above to below...

(From *Sefer Maamorim 5654* (1894) of the Rebbe *Rashab*, p. 53)

The real meaning of mercy...

The *tzedoka* (donation) that we give to a poor person is because we have mercy upon him, and that is why we give him. And in this manner, we arouse mercy from Above so that there will be a descent of *eitan* ("old, long-lasting" – referring to the part of the soul that is always connected with God) within the *vuv-hey*, or second two letters of God's name, *Havaya*. This is why we say, during the blessing *ahavat olam*, "Our Father, merciful Father, have mercy upon us and place understanding in our heart..." We hope that out of His mercy from above, He will enable us to understand in our hearts, and that is the descent of eitan within the emotions and within the oral Torah...

From *Sefer Maamorim 5679* (1919) of the Rebbe Rashab, page 617

Uniting all the levels of the heart
Veyached levaveinu...("Unite our hearts...")

...and so we say during prayers, 'Unite our hearts to love and to fear Your Name.' As is known, there are two aspects; the inner dimension of the heart and the outer. The outer dimension of the heart corresponds to the statement, "*bina* is the heart, and with it the heart understands." This in general corresponds to the level of emotions situated in the heart, which we cultivate via intellect and meditation. And the intellect of which we are speaking here covers matters that are readily grasped and understood. And as written, "to love the Lord your G-d, for He is your life," meaning that just as man loves the life of his very soul, knowing that the main thing is life, similarly when we meditate upon the infinite light of the One above, may He be blessed, how He is the One Who grants life to the living, this arouses within us a fierce and wondrous desire for G-dliness to illuminate the world.. Or, he may meditate in such a way to understand how all the worlds are nothing more than a ray and reflection, out of range of the essence of His *eyn-sof*. This is a concept that is grasped intellectually and logically, and automatically generates a will and desire for revealed G-dly illumination...according to the nature of the spirituality that descends, so we grasp (understand), and according to the level of grasp, so we experience an emotional arousal, as written, "according to his intellect, man is praised" – all this occurs in the outer dimensions of the heart.

And the inner dimensions of the heart is *reuta deliba* – "the will of the heart" – the simple will that is the *yechida* (highest level of the soul, on which a Jew cannot be separated from the One above). For, the sages said, "it [the soul] has five names; *nefesh, ruach, neshama, chaya* and *yechida*. The *Zohar* includes them within four levels; *nefesh, ruach, neshama* and *neshama d'neshama*, which is the *yechida*...[and this is the *avoda*] of desire to be included and nullified within the infinite light of the One above, may He be blessed, which is not commensurate with intellect, but rather comes from the essence of the soul, which stands unfalteringly with a determination to be included and nullified to the infinite One, blessed be He...but this is a matter of simple will which far transcends logic and intellect...

(Page 308-9) And this is what is meant by, "And unite our hearts..." meaning that there should be unity of these two levels; first we should achieve the external levels of the heart, which is *avoda* utilizing our conscious soul powers...and afterward we should achieve the inner levels of the heart, which implies meditation upon our distance, meaning that our meditation must bring us to the realization that all of our *avoda* and enjoyment of G-dliness, as well as what we experience of G-dly matters is out of range in comparison to the essence of the infinite One. Essence is "something else," and all of our [intellectual grasp and love and fear of G-d] occupy no place in regard to essence. And thus, we find ourselves automatically meditating upon our distance from His essence...this is what is meant by "And unite our hearts..." meaning unity of both levels. For this is the entire reason for the descent of the soul, in order to achieve this matter of joining both levels of the heart, as above.

(From *Sefer Maamorim 5663* (vol. 2) of the Rebbe Rashab, Pp. 305-6)

Details leading to the kriat shema
Ahavat olam ahavtanu ("With an everlasting love, You have loved us")

This blessing bears a similarity to the blessings we recite over the Torah, as the Talmud states:[437] "If one has already recited the *Shema*, he need not say the blessings over the Torah, since he already mentioned the great love."

Accordingly, we may now explain the proximity of this blessing to the previous blessing, *Yotzar ohr* ("He Who formed the luminaries"). It was already explained that there is no such thing as *yom* ("day") without *lilah* ("night"), and that the two symbolize revelation and concealment [of G-dliness], as well as the two "unities" – *yichud ila'ah* ("supernal unity," in which we are aware of G-d and the physical world is in the background) and *yichuda tata'ah* ("lower unity," in which we are primarily aware of physical reality, while G-d is in the background)...

This, then, explains the proximity of the blessings of *Ahavat olam* to *Yotzar ohr*, since within the Torah there are also the two themes ... of the daytime luminary (the sun) and the nocturnal luminary (the moon), except that they [the themes in the Torah] are beyond the luminaries, in fact out of their range...

This may also be understood according to the statement of the Talmudic sages that "with the light that was created on the first day of creation, man could see from one end of the universe to the other, and [G-d] concealed it in the Torah, which is why the verse says, 'and He saw that the light was good,' – good to hide and conceal..."[438] And if so, the illumination of the Torah is far higher than the light of the day ...

In more detail, just as there are lights of day and night – meaning the moon and the sun – so, within the Torah, there is the written Torah and the oral Torah ... And this, then, is what is meant by *ahavat olam ahavtanu* where *olam* means "permanent/eternal" ...

In the future, there will be changes to the [impermanent creations like the] sun and the moon ... their present level of illumination will be dimmed until they are like candles in the afternoon sun, compared to their future level of light, but the Torah, which is truly infinite, lives on permanently. And in the future, the luminosity of the Torah will be revealed, and its light will be similar to the light of the sun, which itself is an allusion to His very self and essence, above and beyond any ray or reflection – this is what is meant by *ahavat olam*.

*

RE: *Veyached levaveinu* ("and unite our hearts")

Just as the daily cycle includes night and day, so the heart contains two aspects

... this is what is meant by "and you should know today and establish it in your heart(s)."[439] And, therefore, after we mention the inter-inclusion of day and night in the blessing of *Yotzar ohr*, and in the blessing of *Ahavat olam*, the topic of Torah which also includes these two aspects, we then request that G-d "place within our hearts the ability to understand" ... "and unite our hearts in order to love and fear..." so that in our hearts there will also be this inter-inclusion of the two aspects mentioned previously. As we say, "and all hearts will fear You, and all organs will sing to You..." – all of which is an arousal from below in order to stimulate and draw down revelation of the high spiritual levels...

*

RE: *Vehavieinu leshalom* ("Bring us in peace from the four corners of the earth"
From here through the recitation of the *Shema*, we request the return of the 288 sparks of holiness that fell deep into the *klipot* ("shells" that is, the realms that hide and conceal G-dliness) and were scattered. By way of our request – since "G-d's portion is His nation" – these sparks are gathered. This also occurs during the recitation of the *Shema*, when we gather and elevate them to their source. (This is the process known as *ha'alat mayin nukvin* or "elevation of the feminine waters")...

*

RE: *U'vanu bacharta* ("And You chose us from among all the nations")
The main point of serving G-d is to elevate and gather the sparks from among the nations and to bring them close to G-dliness, including them in the unity of G-d and His great name. And this is what is meant by "G-d is one and His name is one," but none of this occurs without great love.
(From letters of the Tzemach Tzedek in *Meah Shearim* – p. 49)

Divine Will within
Ahavat olam...("Everlasting love...")

We need to understand the difference between the blessings that precede the recital of the *Shema*, and the recital of the *Shema* itself, since both are in the World of *Bria*.

In general, the blessings preceding the *Shema* are associated with the *heichalot* ("palaces") of *Bria*. [This means they are in the World of *Bria* itself as opposed to the *sephirot*, which are the inner sanctum of *Bria*]. Now, the *Shema* is associated with elements of the World of *Atzilut* within *Bria*. As is known, elements of *Atzilut* descend to become united with the worlds of BY"A. They are known as the thirty *kelim* ("vessels") of *malchut* of *Atzilut* which become *naran* (*nephesh, ruach* and *neshama*) of BY"A. And this is the "inner soul" (*neshama*) of BY"A, as written in the *Tanya*[440] ... and even the aspect of *Atzilut* that descends to the lowest world of *Asiya* is higher than *Bria* itself. This is all the more true regarding [elements of] *Atzilut* in the World of *Bria*. And in this we find the difference between the recitation of the *Shema* and the blessings that precede it. The blessings represent the path of worship of the World of *Bria* itself, while the *Shema* is the path of *Atzilut* within *Bria*...

In general, the *bitul* ("nullification") of the World of *Atzilut* is *bitul bemetziut* ("nullification of existence"), which is why the World of *Atzilut* is referred to as the *reshut hayachid* ("region of oneness," or "private arena"), since it is totally integrated with the infinite light of the One Above, in ultimate unity. This is not true of the worlds BY"A, however. There, even what was refined and uplifted after the shattering of the vessels in the World of *Tohu* is still not completely good, since it is not totally nullified to G-dliness. It still possesses a certain amount of *yesh* ("independent existence")...

And, therefore, [the sparks that await elevation] are the source of *klipat noga* in the World of *Bria*. [*Klipat noga*, literally "glowing shell," is kabbalistic terminology for a level of concealment that contains both good and evil elements.] There, good is mixed with bad ... The *heichalot* of holiness in *Bria* are the good within *noga*, devoid of evil, but nevertheless they are called the "good within *noga*," which is *yesh* ("existing," possessing identity and distinct existence, un-nullified to the One Above). And, therefore, the *heichalot* hide and conceal G-dly light ... for the purpose of the *heichalot* is to hide and conceal G-dly illumination in order to limit it in accordance with the needs of creation. The same is true within the soul of man; even the intellect of the G-dly soul comes from the good within *noga*...

*

With the intellect and wisdom of the soul, we attempt to understand the nature of nullification of created beings to their source, from which they were hewn ... And it is possible to say that the nature of nullification that we do comprehend is the *bitul* of the supernal angels, as well as of physical creation, which is comparable to the *bitul* of ministers and servants in relation to a king. They all nullify themselves and follow the king's will, meaning that they do as he desires. In a similar manner, all of creation is nullified to G-dliness. Although they are *yesh* (possessing what seems to them to be their own independent existence), nevertheless, they are nullified to G-dliness and doing His will...

This is clearly evident among the creatures of the lower worlds. We see how all creatures follow a divine plan, according to G-d's will, so that their behavior fulfills some sort of divine intention that they are not aware of at all before it takes place. It is only as a result of divine power and G-dly will that each creature acts, responding spontaneously because of its nullification to G-d's will (and this itself is because of the G-dly energy that enlivens it). And, therefore, each creature acts according to the will of G-d, even though the creature itself does not experience this and thinks that it is acting of its own volition ... But in truth, this is not the case; all of its actions conform with the will of G-d.

It is clear that we progress, without knowing for what purpose and for what intention, until later we become aware that we have fulfilled a particular plan. We cannot say that it is an unconscious, essential will that draws us in a particular direction, since in the majority of cases it is not our own path [alone] that fulfills the divine intention. Rather, it is [together with] the path of another person, who progressed and arrived to the same place that we did, that the divine intention is fulfilled. And who led the other person to this place? Should we say that this as well occurred via our essential, unconscious will?

The Book of Amos[441] states, "Would two people walk together without having planned to meet?" This suggests that it is impossible for two people to do something together without first meeting and uniting for the same purpose. The fact that the two did not meet each other previously proves they both had the same intention only because of a higher power that transcends both of them. And this is a G-dly power, the will of G-d, who creates and enlivens them. He leads both of them and guides them with one purpose that they fulfill without knowing and being aware of at all. And this occurs only as a result of their self-subjugation to the will of G-d.

Now, it is also true that a ray of His will radiates from Above with the desire of the Creator and becomes conscious in our heart. And this is what we experience as our own desire to go somewhere, for example. And [all this] is a result of the divine will that we experience in our heart, of which we are unaware and we think that it is our own will, when in truth it is G-d's will that we feel (and this is why in most cases, our heartfelt emotion is far more accurate than our intellectual grasp).

The will that we feel is higher than our conscious awareness, which is only associated with the soul-power of *chochma* and below. As is known, our conscious powers, being limited, conceal the true spiritual illumination from Above. This is especially true since they are en-clothed in the vessels of our physical body. Both factors [since they are conscious, they are limited to the "vessels" of the body, and since they are limited they conceal true G-dliness] are dependent upon each other. This, however, is not true of the will, which is beyond the conscious soul powers. It is unlimited and un-encumbered by a vessel. And that is why it is precisely within the will that we experience more G-dly power.

All the more so, then, that the angels, who feel and are aware of G-d's will, are nullified to Him, and all of their service and all that they do takes place in accordance with His desire. The angels stand on a much higher spiritual level, since they are aware of and experience G-d's will. Their nullification to G-d, then, takes place on an entirely different plane; it is their total subjugation to Him that brings them to utter *kadosh* and *baruch*.

Now, the nature of the *bitul* of the angels cannot be grasped by the soul down here in this world; only the soul as it exists Above (in *BY"A*) grasps the nature and essence of the *bitul* of the angels, but the soul as it exists down in this world does not grasp the nature of the nullification of the angels (and all the more so that it does not know the essence of this *bitul*). It only knows and understands that they are nullified to G-dliness. Knowledge and understanding of the manner and essence of *bitul* is mainly in the domain of the spiritual creatures.[442] Only the basic concept of subjugation to the One Above is grasped by the soul that has descended to this world.

Now, the nullification known as *he'eder tefisat makom* ("lack of awareness of one's own presence") is also grasped by the soul down here below. The soul realizes that all creations below, as well the supernal spiritual creations in the highest worlds, pale in significance (i.e. "take up no space") in comparison to the infinite light of G-d. And by way of this meditation and comprehension of the nullification of creations, the soul becomes aroused with love and fear of G-dliness.

What emerges from all of this is as follows: The entire intellectual grasp of the soul down here concerns the creation from nothing to something. (But within this, the soul does not grasp the essence and act of creation, since the kernel of the topic of creation from nothing to something is beyond the human intellect, for man has no understanding whatsoever of how from nothing something may emerge. However, the intellect does comprehend that all was created from nothing to something, though it does not have any idea of the nature and essence of the G-dly "nothing" – aside that from it "something" is created.) Now, the soul does grasp the nature of subjugation of created beings to the G-dly source that created them. (Here, its main understanding is of the nullification of beings down in the physical world, while regarding supernal beings, and all the more so regarding the higher spiritual worlds, the soul down here knows only the fact that there is *bitul*, but not the quality of the *bitul*.) So, what emerges is that the love produced from this meditation stems from the creation itself, insofar as it is nullified to G-d. And the creatures that are the subject of the meditation are from *noga*, and if so, the *chochma* that grasps the nature of their *bitul* comes from the good within *noga*, and this is why it is capable of understanding the *bitul* of *noga*.

Now, in general, this love is based upon logic and intellect. It is born of meditation on an intellectual concept, so naturally this kind of love reflects the fact that "there is someone who loves." It is far out of range of the essential spark of G-dliness within the soul, called *ner Havaya nishmat adam* ("The soul of man is like a candle of G-d"), indicating that just as the illumination of a candle flickers upward, constantly and naturally, without any external force moving it, so the essential G-dly spark of the soul constantly ascends of its own volition. It ascends constantly upward with absolute inner self-nullification. (The meditation that produces this is upon the amazing exaltedness of the Infinite One. This is not to be grasped intellectually at all, since "no thought can grasp Him whatsoever." And the meditation is also upon the unity of the worlds, in essence above intellect, as will be explained. All this is in order to arouse the essential inner excitement of the soul. The true arousal of the soul comes from its experience of the infinite light of G-d ... which is a quality beyond logic and intellect.)

But, it is impossible to reveal this G-dly spark so that it shines within the body, without first practicing meditation according to logic and the intellect. This [elevates] the good from within *noga*, and the good causes the revelation of divine will from above the intellect of the G-dly spark. But, without the meditation, the spark will not shine at all. This is why there are two explanations of the word *veahavta* ("And you shall love..."). One explanation is that it is a command, and the other is that it is a promise, that ultimately you will come to love G-d. That is, the command is to use the intellect to engage in meditation, in order to produce *ahavat olam* ("eternal/universal love" derived from meditation upon creation). And this in turn draws down revelation of the divine will from above the intellect...

*

This, then, is the difference between the recitation of the *Shema* and of *Yotzar ohr* (in the blessings preceding the *Shema*). Although *Yotzar ohr* is also within the *heichalot* of *Bria*, where there is no mixture of good with bad whatsoever, nevertheless, this is within the World of *Bria* itself. There, the path of serving G-d is intellectual, based upon understanding the nullification of the created worlds. And from this intellectual activity comes the spiritual excitement mentioned previously. In the *Shema*, however, is revealed the World of *Atzilut* within *Bria* – which is beyond the intellect that man can grasp. In fact, it is similar to the verse mentioned above – *ner Havaya nishmat adam* ("the soul of man is like the candle of G-d") – which alludes to the essential connection of the G-dly spark within the soul, beyond logic and intellect.

This, then, is what is meant by *Shema Yisrael, Havaya Elokeinu*:

[Israel is] like a son born from the mind of the father, united in essence [with the father] without any need to justify or explain [the connection]. And although we must also meditate while reciting the *Shema* on the subject of how *Havaya* is one, this meditation is focused upon the essential infinite light of G-d, and how He is one and united. All meditation upon His essence is of necessity beyond logic and intellect, since the mind is totally incapable of understanding the true nature of G-dly unity. All it knows is that G-d is one, but the exact nature of His oneness, it cannot grasp at all. And for that reason, the meditation on "G-d is one" must be a meditation upon His unity, based upon the worlds...

This indicates that also after the creation, the seven heavens and the earth (as well as the four direction of the universe) are all united from the perspective of creation. And there are intellectual proofs for this – that the worlds even after their creation are nullified and united in ultimate oneness with the infinite illumination from Above, just as before they were created. This is true, for it is inappropriate to say that anything whatsoever exists as something independent and separate. This is the topic [of meditation] of "G-d is one," meaning that even after the worlds were created, they were united, and they continue to express His ultimate singularity, unity and oneness. Thus, they are truly *yachid* ("unique")...

Nevertheless, this is evident only because the intellect proves to us that this is the case. But, exactly what and how [the creation is unique and united] is not within the power of our intellect to grasp at all, since He is totally above intellectual grasp. Quite the opposite, what man is able to detect of these matters seems to indicate that the created worlds exist with their own identity and being. The intellect comprehends spiritual matters as entities possessing independent existence. But at the same time, common sense obligates us to acknowledge that the truth is not that way. Rather, spiritual matters do not have an identity or existence of their own. But, exactly how this is the case is not within the power of intellect to grasp at all. And therefore, the meditation serves to arouse the essential spark of the soul that is beyond logic and the intellect, [upon which the soul] is aroused to become subsumed within the essential infinite light of G-d.

This meditation also serves as an introduction to experiencing the soul as it is in essence and as it experiences the infinite light from Above. The entire topic of feeling and experience of [His infinite illumination] is beyond intellect, as written elsewhere and also explained previously.

It emerges, then, that the worship service of the *Shema* is far beyond that of *Yotzar ohr*. In the recitation of the *Shema*, the service comes from the very essence of the soul, above its enclothement in the body and in the animal soul. What becomes enclothed in the body and within the animal soul is the *naran* – the intellect and emotions alone, which are involved in the service of *Yotzar ohr*. But, in the *Shema*, the service is from the very essence of the soul, beyond its enclothement in the body and within the animal soul. (And this is the difference between *Bria* itself, and *Atzilut* within *Bria*). In any case, the main service involving the essence of the soul takes place during the *Shemonah Esreh*...

And with all this, there is an advantage to the spiritual path of the soul as enclothed in the body, [because then the] service based upon logic and the intellect is involved in refining the animal soul from *klipat noga*. The refinement comes about in a way that is called *bechochma itbariru* ("in wisdom things are purified and refined")...[443]

(From *Sefer Maamorim 5655* (1895) of the Rebbe Rashab, pp. 223-232)

Two Perspectives of Divinity
Shema Yisrael...("Listen Israel...")

Supernal unity pervades the Jewish people as a whole when they recite the *Shema*, since within it are included and intertwined both perspectives of G-dliness. And that is why there are three names of G-d within this verse: *Havaya, Elokeinu, Havaya echad*.

There is a verse in the Torah that begins, "And He proclaimed, "*Havaya, Havaya*,"[444] using the name of G-d twice. The first is the name *Havaya* associated with the hierarchy of spiritual levels leading to creation (*seder hishtalshelut*); it is also the source of creation via the name *Elokim*, as it is written, "great is *Havaya* and very praiseworthy, in the city of *Elokeinu*."[445] And the second is the name *Havaya* as it transcends the origin of creation.

Now, these are the two perspectives of *da'at elyon* ("higher knowledge of G-dliness" in which we are aware of Him as the true reality and of creation as secondary) and *da'at tachton* ("lower knowledge of G-dliness" in which the physical creation seems real and G-dliness is secondary). These are separated by a dividing line between them, for the ray of G-dliness that is responsible for creation is far out of range of G-d's essence. And this is what accounts for the three names of G-d within the opening verse of the *Shema*. The two names *Havaya* are the two perspectives of *da'at tachton* and *da'at elyon*, which correspond to the perspective of the receiver [to whom the world is real and G-d is secondary] and that of the giver [to whom G-d is real and the world secondary], while the name *Elokeinu* corresponds to the dividing line that demarcates between the two names *Havaya*. More specifically, *Havaya Elokeinu* corresponds to *da'at tachton*, and *Havaya echad* corresponds to *da'at elyon*.

This describes the *Shema* as we understand it from below to Above. From this perspective, the word *Shema* connotes gathering together and assembling, as in the verse *vayishma Shaul* ("and Saul gathered"[446]). This is a result of the nullification of the *yesh* ("mortal existence") of all the worlds in comparison to the *ayn* ("divine nothingness") of the name *Havaya*. The nullification takes place when we meditate on the concept that "there is no blade of grass without a spiritual counterpart (*mazal*) that touches it and commands it to grow."[447] This refers to the spiritual beings that convey G-dly influx down to all physical creations. And the source of the spiritual beings are divine angels, each one higher than the next and inclusive of all the levels that are below it, all the way up to *malchut* of *Atzilut*, which enlivens the worlds of *BY'A*.

This is what is meant by "Great is *Havaya*, and very praiseworthy, in the city of *Elokeinu*." Through this meditation, we come to want only G-dliness as we are aroused with desire for G-d and with strong distaste for all the superficial and physical elements of the world. And even in the physical matters in which we must be involved, we remain nullified to the G-dliness within them, seeking to do what we must only for the sake of heaven, while making priority of our Torah learning and relating to our work as transient. In this way, we gather and assemble all physical objects subjugating them to G-dliness ... This is the nullification of *yichuda tata'ah* which results from meditation on the level of *da'at tachton*.

Now, the second *Havaya* (*Havaya echad*) corresponds to the higher perspective from Above to below, as already explained. About it we say, "He forms their hearts all together"[448] ... and ... "all is before Him as naught."[449] This is what is meant by *Havaya echad* – this is the true perspective that He is the one and only, singular existence, and all is as nothing before Him. And by way of this meditation on the essential infinite light of G-d, we arrive to a higher state of nullification – nullification in our very essence. This is true nullification, uniting both perspectives, since both of them are accurate from the perspective of G-d's essence. And this is what is meant by *lemehevei echad b'echad* ("let there be one within one").[450]

*

Elsewhere it is explained that this unity implies that the lower perspective of *yichuda tata'ah* should cause us to be nullified just as much as the higher perspective of *yichuda ila'ah*. This also applies to the future, when all of created existence will be permeated with G-dliness. But, through our service now, we may attain something akin to this state, wherein our physical conduct while eating and drinking, etc. takes place with a heightened level of nullification, and we are nullified in our very essence, devoid of any physical sense whatsoever and completely detached. We are in a state of self-abnegation and cleaving to Him totally, a state which is similar to the love and fear of Him that we develop during prayer.

And we might possibly say that our love and fear and cleaving during prayer also takes place in a different fashion than when it comes from *yichuda ila'ah* on its own. Possibly this is like when the *shuv* ("return" or desire to bring G-dliness down to earth) overwhelms the *ratzoh* ("ascent" or desire to rise Above) at the very moment of greatest desire to ascend ... and the main ingredient is the *shuv* of Torah and mitzvot and subsequent drawing down of G-dliness to the lower realms.

But the unity of *yichuda ila'ah* and *yichuda tata'ah* comes from the very essence of the infinite light of G-d that surpasses both perspectives and includes them together...

(From *Sefer Maamorim 5655* (1895-6) of the Rebbe Rashab, pp.124-125)

Shema Yisrael...Baruch Shem ("Listen Israel...Blessed be His Name")

Possibly, we might say that the unconscious power of *chochma* is the sense in the soul which experiences essential G-dliness and intuits that without G-dliness there is no existence whatsoever, while the unconscious power of *bina* is the sense within the soul that G-dliness is present in every detail. These are the two unities of the *Shema*, when we say that G-d is one from below to Above, or from Above to below. The unity from below to Above occurs when the seven heavens and the earth and the four directions of the world are nullified to the infinite light, the "One" of the world, so that everything exists before Him as naught.[451] And the second unity from Above to below [corresponds to our experience of the oneness of G-d], as in the statement of the sages, "When I [G-d] am crowned Above and below and to the four directions, nothing more is needed."[452]

Now, the conscious experience of *chochma* and *bina* is that within *chochma* we still feel the refined sense of an overall uniting principle, where all of the details are subsumed, while in *bina* we feel that the principle is expressed in the many details. As such, the power of *chochma* is experienced up close, while the power of *bina* is from afar, since we feel the details and are far from the refined consciousness of the overall principle. But the unconscious powers of *chochma* and *bina* within the soul are the two feelings previously described in the soul, and both of them are up close and personal.

(From *Sefer Maamorim 5654* (1894) of the Rebbe Rashab, p. 288)

Faith of the Jew

This is the main faith of the Jew: For, non-Jews also believe in the creation of the universe from nothing to something, and there are those who have investigated [proved] it using signs and wonders. But, the main faith of the Jew is in the name *Havaya* that transcends the spiritual chain of creation. This level is beyond intellectual grasp, which is why we apply "faith." This is the faith that we have in the essential infinite G-dly light and how the worlds are nullified and united with this infinite illumination. It is about this faith that the sages asked, "From where did the Jews merit to the *kriat shema*? From the giving of the Torah, when G-d said, 'I am the Lord your G-d.' This statement caused an influx of the essence of the name *Havaya* into the chain of creation, which in turn caused our exit from limitations and boundaries. That is, it caused the nullification of the chain of creation and all of the worlds were nullified and united with the infinite light above. This itself is the concept of unity contained in the *kriat shema*.

However, all of this applies only to Jewish souls, as the verse says, "For you are a holy people," which is why we merited to this level of revelation...now faith is also intellectual, since it is related to *da'at elyon*, or "supernal knowledge" which expresses itself in knowledge and grasp...but this is not the complete and total grasp that is associated with G-dliness that is enclothed in the world. Of this level, we are capable of achieving total grasp. However, our grasp of the infinite light that transcends the worlds and of the nullification of the worlds, which are "like nothing," is not total grasp. It is for that reason the *Pardess* (in *Erech emunah*) states that faith occurs in two places – *bina* and in *malchut*. At first glance this is not understood; *bina* is all about intellectual grasp, so why is it called "faith?" But, the explanation is that the intellectual grasp that we do attain is not total and complete grasp...it is *pnimiyut bina*, which does not become en-clothed in the garments of logic, and is therefore not totally graspable, except by "feeling and intuition." Yet, it is called "faith" since it is not complete and total grasp. Rather, the intellect obligates us and we recognize that it is correct – this is faith that is based upon knowledge...

From *Sefer Maamorim 5677* (1917) of the Rebbe Rashab, page 155-6

The essential Name *Havaya*

The name *Havaya* is truth. Although the other names of God are also "true," it is only the name *Havaya* which expresses His essence. That is, it expresses revelation of His essence. Although the source of the other names is also from His essence, nonetheless they do not constitute revelation of His essence. For the other names, such as *Kel* and *Elokim*, are associated with the *keilim*, or "vessels" of the *sephirot* of *Atzilut*. And their source is with the "power of limitations" within the infinite light of God, which is the potential for concealment and limitations. This is not revelation of His essence.

And the name *Havaya* is light and illumination, which is revelation of the essence, and this is why it is called truth. For it is like the essence of the unlimited One. And in particular, the name *Havaya* is called truth since it represents *da'at elyon*, which is "supernal awareness" [during which we are primarily aware of God and the creation recedes to the background]. For, the name *Elokim* represents *da'at tachton*, or "lower awareness" [during which we are primarily aware of creation and God is in the background of our awareness], which is the awareness of creations. However, the name *Havaya* is associated with *da'at elyon* and supernal awareness, which is the awareness that Above is *yesh* (truly exists) and what is below is *ayn* (does not exist) – and this is the true perspective. And this is also because the name *Havaya* is associated with the *orot*, or "illumination" of the *sephirot*, which causes *devekut* (cleaving to God). And therefore the essence is experienced within it – that is, that God is the true *yesh*, or existence and that everything is as naught before Him...

From *Sefer Maamorim 5679* (1919) of the Rebbe Rashab, page 405

Two mezuzot and the kriat shema

Now, the entrance [to a building] includes a lintel and two sides (*mezuzot*), alluding to the three paths in which we serve God – Torah, prayer and good deeds (mitzvoth). Prayer and good deeds correspond to the two sides, while Torah, as the "middle path" [which includes both spiritual elevation and descent] corresponds to the lintel. While our main objective should be acceptance of the yoke of heaven, this is a concealed matter [it is known only to the person himself and to God], while the three activities described above are apparent. [However], they must also take place in an atmosphere of *bitul*, or self-nullification.

In greater detail, the lintel and the two sides are alluded to in the statement of the sages, that "one should always enter two entrances and then pray." This is not so clear, for prayer is for the purpose of drawing a new "will" from above the spiritual chain of creation, in order to heal the sick and to bless the year [for example]. That is, even if according to the regular "order" of things, it may already have been decreed, God forbid [that something negative may occur]...we pray that a new "will" be created from above the regular "order" in order to heal, etc...and if so, how can the sages say that we need to enter "two entrances, and then pray?" Moreover, what are these two entrances?

In answer, although the spiritual descent that comes down with our prayers comes from the very essence of the infinite light of God, nevertheless we must make ourselves into vessels to receive it. And that is why we need the two entrances, so that the spirituality will become revealed.

According to kaballah, the two sides of the first entrance represent *netzach* and *hod*, which are the two "kidneys that advise." For the entrance is a gate and segue for the [new] divine influx mentioned above. By way of example of a teacher and student, the teacher must utilize his intellect ("kidneys that advise") to determine exactly how to transfer his knowledge (the divine influx). This process corresponds to *netzach* and *hod*, which are the two sides of the entrance. And the lintel corresponds to *tiferet*. In terms of our actual worship (*avoda*), the first entrance represents *hod*, which is the starting point of prayer, as we declare our thanks and subjugation to God, saying *Modeh ani lefanecha*, followed by *Hodu Lashem*. Now, this is the very foundation of prayers, since with the nullification of *hoda'ah*, we "set our ego aside" in a manner that is completely above the nullification associated with intellect (as written in the *siddur* of the Alter Rebbe regarding *Lag b'Omer*). And therefore, [the first entrance] represents the very foundation of prayer.

However, aside from the fact that prayer begins with *hoda'ah*, it also ends with *hoda'ah* during the *shemonah esreh*, during which we say, *modim anachnu lach* ("we acknowledge/thank You..."). And at first glance, this is not understood. Since the path of prayer includes meditation leading to love and fear of God, and during the *shemonah esreh*, our "heads reach into the heavens" – why do we say that [during the highest point of our prayers], we merely "acknowledge" God alone?

In answer, it is written, "*Havaya* is a God of perspectives" (*El deyot Hashem*). There are two perspectives; "supernal consciousness" (*da'at elyon*) and mundane consciousness" (*da'at tachton*). [From the perspective of *da'at tachton*, the world exists. It is in the foreground, while Godliness is in the background. And this we are capable of understanding thoroughly and completely. However, from the perspective of *da'at elyon*, Godliness is real while the creation is questionable – and this we are incapable of fully grasping with our intellect – aside from very high souls associated with Atzilut]...And therefore, we approach *da'at elyon* with mere acknowledgment. We acknowledge that it is the true perspective, even though we are incapable of understanding it. This is what is meant by *modim anachnu lach* ("we acknowledge You") that we say during the *shemonah esreh* – it refers to the supernal consciousness of *da'at elyon*.

The second side (of the first entrance) is associated with *netzach*, which [in the soul] is the resolve that emerges in our souls after prayers. For, we cannot go through the entire day in a state of meditation or full-blown love and fear of God [All that we can expect] is to remain firm in our resolve, and unshaking in our decision to refrain from evil and to do good...and the lintel represents *tiferet*, which is the trait of mercy This is the personality trait which arouses great mercy over our soul, which once stood above in love and fear of God...and has now descended to become enclothed in a body and animal soul that hides and conceals...and therefore the soul truly deserves mercy. And there is a covenant established regarding the attribute of mercy, such that it does not express itself in vain...

The second entrance includes two sides, representing *chesed* and *gevura*. *Chesed* is revealed Godliness, while *gevura* is Godliness that comes to us in a state of contraction, so that the revelation arrives in a specific manner that allows us to perceive and accept it. And the lintel represents the power of *bina*, the source of the emotions...in *avoda*, these are the three "loves" of the *kriat shema*, "with all your heart" (*bekol levavcha*), "with all your soul" (*bekol naphshecha*) and "with all your might" (*bekol meodecha*). Love with all your heart" (*bekol levavcha*) is associated with *chesed*, which manifests itself in love. And "love with all your soul" (*bekol naphshecha*) occurs "even if He takes away the soul," implying that a great amount of discipline and strength is necessary to achieve this level of love in the soul. And *bina* is associated with "love with all your might" (*bekol meodecha*), as known that *bina* is expressed in *ahava rabba*, or the "great love" that characterizes unlimited feelings of Godly love. And elsewhere it is explained that *bina* is *bekol me'odecha*...

This is what is alluded to by the lintel and the two sides of the entrance. It is not a sign, but rather the formation of a vessel enabling the descent of essential infinite light...

From *Sefer Maamorim 5678* (1918) of the Rebbe Rashab, Page 244-245

Two Levels of Love

In general the two levels that we call "my sister" (*achoti*) and "my lover" (*rayati*)[from *Shir haShirim*] correspond to prayer and to Torah, respectively. Prayer is called "my sister," since during the recital of the *shema*, we "deliver our soul" while saying the word *echad*. And *echad* is compounded of the word *ach* ("sibling, brother") and the letter *dalet*. "Brother" (*ach*) alludes to God...and the letter *dalet* alludes to *malchut*, which is the source of collective Jewish souls. The *dalet* also means "door" or "opening," indicating that it is a source of revelation. And via the self-sacrifice of "my sister" (*achoti*, during *kriat shema*), we achieve revelation of *echad*...

Additionally, during the *shemonah esreh*, we are in a state of total submission, experiencing the "still small voice" (*kol demama daka*), about which the Zohar says, "That's where the King goes." In this manner, the Torah later becomes our "lover," meaning that we become included and united in the very essence of Godliness and bring down revelation of the essence of Godliness from Atzilut to the worlds of BY"A...

From *Sefer Maamorim 5678* (1918) of the Rebbe Rashab, Page 310

More Meditations on the Letters of the Shema
...echad...va'ed ("One...forever")

The word *va'ed* ("forever") is equivalent to *echad* ("one") via an exchange of letters, as explained previously. The word *echad* alludes to the emergence of multiple creations from the simple oneness of G-d.

Now, the first letter *aleph* is the source of *chochma*. It is the conduit (*tzinor*) coming from the supernal kindness of G-d (called *notzar chesed* or "conduit of kindness") into the [two] *alephs* (referring to *chochma* and *bina*), in order to "teach wisdom," meaning to induce wisdom from Above into the *sephirot*. The second letter, *chet*, refers to *chochma* itself. From *chochma*, the letters are combined into the words of the Hebrew language, which is alluded to in the third letter, the enlarged *dalet* symbolizing *dibur* (G-d's creative "speech").

However, there are two levels of *dibur*. The first is *dibur* in the World of *Atzilut*, which is revealed emanation of G-dliness. The entities that are created from it are nullified in essence to His infinite light, as mentioned already regarding *yichuda ila'ah*. This includes the creation of great righteous souls such as Adam (about whom the Torah says that G-d "blew into his nostrils") and the souls of the forefathers and the prophets, who were vehicles for the expression of G-dliness in the world and totally nullified to it. They all come from *dibur* associated with the enlarged *dalet*.

The second level of *dibur* is *malchut* of Atzilut as it descends to become enclothed in *malchut* of the lower worlds of BY"A. There, it brings into existence the souls and angels of BY"A and of our world. This is alluded to in the word *va'ed* wherein the final *dalet* is normally sized, since it acts to create only after contracting, masking and greatly concealing the G-dliness within. Now, the descent of these letters of *malchut* of BY"A also takes place through the intermediary of *chochma*, as mentioned previously regarding *echad*. However, in this case the key word is *va'ed*. The *aleph* [of *echad*] is replaced with a *vav* [in *va'ed*], indicating a vertical descent of G-d's infinite light to the lower worlds, in order to create the souls, angels and worlds of BY"A. The *vav* [in the form of a straight vertical line] indicates a direct descent of light. And the *chet* [of *echad*] becomes an *ayin* [of *va'ed*], since the letter *ayin* also indicates *chochma*. This is why the sages are called *einayim* ("eyes of the congregation"). And our ability to see also comes from the power of *chochma* in our soul, although only from the superficial aspects of *chochma*. Here in the lower worlds, we utilize only what descends to us from G-d's supernal wisdom into

BY"A, enabling the letters of speech from *malchut* of *BY"A* to create. Therefore, we draw down only from the extraneous aspects of His supernal wisdom.

Thereafter, the third and final letter of *va'ed* – *dalet* – gives rise to the letters of speech of *malchut* of the lower worlds of *BY"A*. Thus, the word *va'ed* alludes to nullification just as does the word *echad*. The creatures of *BY"A* are nullified through the letters of speech coming from the *dalet* of *va'ed*, which create them from nothing into something. And the *dalet* is nullified to *chochma*, which is its source and which is associated with the letter *ayin* of *va'ed*. And the *chochma* of the letter *ayin* is nullified to the ray of infinite light enclothed within it and associated with the *vav*, indicating vertical descent from the infinite light Above. And if so, they are all truly as if naught, as mentioned earlier regarding the word *echad*. However, the nullification associated with *echad* is clear and conscious, since it is from the supernal unity of the *sephirot*, which are totally nullified and aware that there is none other than G-d Himself.

This is the real explanation of *echad*. [It is a conscious state of oneness, associated with His supernal unity, wherein all is truly and consciously nullified to G-d, to the extent that nothing else exists.]

This is not the case, however, regarding the lower worlds of *BY"A*, which perceive themselves as independent creations, possessing their own separate awareness and existence. Nevertheless, they know and understand that before G-d all is as if non-existent, and that is why their unity and oneness comes by way of exchange of letters. The exchange indicates a concealed descent of G-dliness so that the created being will be able to experience itself as a separate existence. Then, it may become nullified, losing its ego, which is the ultimate purpose of creation.

(From *Derech Mitzvotecha* of the Tzemach Tzedek, *Shoresh Mitzvat Tefila*, ch. 38, p. 272)

...echad...va'ed ("one...forever")

Now, we need to gain a detailed understanding of the letters of the word *echad*, all of which pertain to the World of *Atzilut*. The *aleph* of *echad* is an intermediary between the Emanator [G-d, but more specifically the kabbalistic level known as *Adam Kadmon*] and His emanations [the *sephirot*] ... This is comparable to the relationship between the voice and speech where there is an intermediary that includes aspects of both. This is the letter *aleph* ... which is the source of all the other letters, acting as the intermediary that expresses the voice and divides it into the letters of speech, each with its particular pronunciation. And so, in the spiritual realm between the infinite light of the Emanator and His emanations, there must be an intermediary that includes elements of both. Now, it is known that the intermediary is *keter* ("crown"), which includes elements of the lowest level of the Emanator, as well as being the head and source of the emanations ... And the main intermediary is *chochma stima* (*chochma* within *keter*) – that is, concealed *chochma* possessing the characteristics of the emanations and which also serves as the source of *chochma* of *Atzilut*. Even though it is the source, it remains separate from [the *sephira* of] *chochma* ... [which emerges from it as] a reflection of a ray, and as a bridge over a chasm, rather than in an orderly step-by-step process of descent...

Now, *aleph* may be rendered as the word *peleh*, meaning "wondrous" or "exalted", or *aleph* may also be rendered as *ulpana*, meaning "teaching" and "learning." In either case, *aleph* alludes to *chochma stima*, which includes both levels. It is both wondrous and exalted, and [at the same time] a source and an origin, as mentioned previously.

The word *aleph* comes from *a'aleph lecha chochma* ("I will teach you wisdom"), indicating activation of the *sephira* of *chochma*, so that it emerges from its source. This is comparable to the potential for intellectual activity that exists within the soul, which transcends intellect. It does not negate the existence of intellect – but rather it serves as the source of intellect ... This is equivalent to *chochma stima* which transcends the real manifestation of *chochma* as a *sephira*. The *sephira* of *chochma* constitutes the true revelation of *chochma* because it exists as *ohr b'keli* [G-dly illumination clad in a G-dly vessel that enables us to detect and channel it]. *Chochma stima* is not a full manifestation of *chochma*, but nevertheless it is still referred to as *chochma*, because in fact, it is the source and origin of manifest *chochma*. Whatever transcends *chochma stima* is not at all within the category of *chochma*. [Above *chochma stima*], there is no emanation of G-dliness that is related to *chochma*, and [it is only in] *chochma stima* that we find the source from whence *chochma* emanates. This corresponds to the letter *aleph*, which alludes to the future, as known regarding the name *Ekeyeh* (*aleph-hei-yud-hei*), which [begins with an *aleph* and] means "I will become revealed in the future." And this is as well the *aleph* of *a'aleph lecha chochma* ("I will teach you *chochma*"), meaning that in the future there will be *chochma*, which is teaching and learning. The *aleph* alludes to the future, since then there will be teaching, originating from *chochma stima*, the source of *chochma*. As such, *chochma stima* is the intermediary channeling the infinite light of G-d into the *sephira* of *chochma*. This is, as well alluded to in the form of the letter *aleph*, which is composed of a small point above, a line in the middle and a point underneath. The upper point is *chochma* within *keter*, the source of *chochma*, and the line is what emerges as the influx into manifest *chochma* from its source (as will be explained). And the lower point, we might possibly say, is *malchut* of *chochma stima*, as the beginning of revelation of the *sephira* of *chochma*.

*

Now, there is another interpretation of the *aleph*, which is that it alludes to *chochma* as we know it – manifest *chochma* of the World of *Atzilut* ... In this case as well, we may explain the form of the *aleph* as we did previously. Although the origin of *chochma* already exists since it came into being by way of the *tzimtzum* ("contraction"), in order for manifest *chochma* to emerge from it, there must be another *tzimtzum*, represented by the *yud* [small point on top of the *aleph*]. This is what brings *chochma* into revelation...

(It might also be explained that the upper point is *chochma* within *chochma*, while the line represents the *midot* within *chochma*, and the lower point is *yesod* or *malchut* within *chochma*...)

*

And now, let us consider the letter *chet* of the word *echad*. The *chet* is *chochma*, since the word *chochma* also begins with a *chet*. However, we must understand; it was already explained in the second interpretation above that the *aleph* represents manifest *chochma* of *Atzilut* ... But that aspect of *chochma* refers to the G-dly illumination and influx that has descended from concealed *chochma* into manifest *chochma*, but which has not yet developed into illumination within a vessel as *chochma* of *Atzilut*. It has already descended and emerged from concealed *chochma* (*chochma stima*), which is the source of *chochma*, as noted in the first interpretation of *aleph*.

By way of further elucidation, there are two facets: 1) *chochma* within *keter*, and 2) *keter* within *chochma*. *Chochma* within *keter* is still considered a part of *keter*, and just as *keter* transcends *chochma* and intellect, so *chochma* within *keter* surpasses intellect. It is only the abstract ability to elicit various forms of intellect and creativity, but it remains apart, removed from all these forms of intellect, as explained. Only in relation to the ethereal power of intellect embedded in the essence of the soul, which is completely separate from the entire realm of intellect, can we say that the potential for intellect possesses any existence of its own. But in truth, it is still *ayn* since it has not yet adopted an intellectual form.

However, *keter* within *chochma* is the intangible predecessor to the manifest existence of *chochma*. That is, it is the intangible "nothingness" that precedes the intellect in its manifest form, as it has already descended from the origin of the intellect in order to become an intellectual concept. It has already emerged and descended from the origin of intellect, and has become intellectual, without yet taking on a definitive form in the vessel of *chochma*.

Let us take, for example, one who is struggling to understand a concept. In the beginning, before he knows anything about it, he comprehends nothing. There is no revelation of light and, quite the opposite, the concept under consideration is opaque in his mind. Afterward, some illumination begins to shine in his mind, but he still does not grasp it. He only experiences the accuracy of his understanding, without yet knowing what it is. This means that the logic of the subject matter has already emerged and descended from its intellectual source, and that's why he experiences the illumination and feels he is correct in his understanding. Previously, his understanding was included within its source (since he has it within his intellectual power to be creative and conceptualize) prior to descending. It remained within him as intellectual potential. It was included in his mind as potential, where it possessed no independent intellectual existence ... and that is why he experienced no intellectual illumination whatsoever. Quite the opposite, he experienced darkness because of his total lack of knowledge. But when the intellect has descended from the *koach hasechel* (potential intellect) and already exists as intellect, he immediately experiences the illumination and confirmation of his understanding of the concept. (And before the idea becomes conscious, he may experience sparks of intellectual illumination in his mind, without yet knowing what they are. And this is, as well, what has already emerged and descended from the source of intellect as an intangible illumination related to the particular topic he would like to understand.)

Nevertheless, all this is only the intangible dimension of manifest *chochma* (which is why it is *keter* within *chochma*). Although it has already descended from its intellectual source and possesses intellectual substance, it is unlike the flash of intellect that characterizes a fully developed concept. At that point, it is actual illumination (*ohr*) of a vessel (*keli*). At that point it is a true intellectual concept, unlike the light that has descended from its intellectual source, which although proportioned to fit a particular intellect, nevertheless has no existence of its own as revealed intellect.

*

Now, the letter *dalet* of *echad* is written large, since it represents *malchut* of *Atzilut* as it exists in the World of *Atzilut*.[453] It is known that *malchut* is the supernal *dibur* ("speech") of G-d, and speech is an expression of the emotions. That is, the feelings of the heart are expressed in the breath underlying our speech. However, [our breath] only conveys the revelation of speech, since letters themselves are not part of the voice, which emerges from the heart. It is just that the voice comes clad in letters, and in this way the emotions are expressed in the letters of our speech. But in essence, their source [of the letters] is in the primordial origins of the intellect (*kadmot hasechel*)[454] ... So, the enlarged letter *dalet* represents the power of speech as it exists in potential...

Now, all of the above is about the word *echad* which refers to the World of *Atzilut* where everything is nullified in the supernal unity of *yichuda ila'ah* [wherein we experience G-dliness and creation is in the background]... But, *yichuda tata'ah* [wherein our main awareness is of creation, and G-dliness in the background] is expressed in the three letters of *va'ed* which exchange with the three letters of *echad*.

This corresponds to the saying of the *Zohar* [and recited in Shabbat night prayers before *Barchu*], "Just as these [the *sephirot* of *Atzilut*] become united Above [in *Atzilut*] as one, so this [*malchut*] becomes united below [in the three worlds BY"A], in the "secret of one." The emphasis is on the "secret of one," as something that is hidden and concealed, referring to the exchange of letters in which the *aleph* of *echad* is exchanged and becomes the *vov* of *va'ed*. It was already explained that the *aleph* is the source of *chochma* of *Atzilut*, while the *vov* is the source of lower *chochma* – that is, *malchut* of *Atzilut* ...

It emerges, then, that just as the *aleph* is the intermediary between the infinite light of the Emanator [*Adam Kadmon*] and His emanations [the *sephirot* of *Atzilut*], so the *vov* is the intermediary between the infinite light of G-d and His creations [which come from *malchut* of *Atzilut*]. And the *vov* is indicative of a long descent to the very lowest levels, since in truth transcendent G-dliness descends to the lowest levels, though it remains aloof without becoming enclothed in any level. For this reason the *aleph* becomes a *vov* [indicating long descent] ... As it is known, there is a distinction between *memalle kol olamim* (immanent G-dliness) and *sovev kol olamimim* (transcendent G-dliness) since *memalle kol olamim* becomes enclothed and embedded in the worlds, internally. And therefore, there are various levels of worlds, such as the World of *Atzilut*, in which there are *orot b'kelim* (G-dly illumination en-clothed in vessels) ... while the worlds of created existence (BY"A) exist in a different manner. That is, they are mere reflections, so that in this lowest of worlds, our physical world, there is also illumination and inner energy, but it comes from a very contracted source of revelation.

However, the element of transcendent G-dliness is not completely concealed from all of the worlds; it is still present. It is found here in this lowly world as much as it is found Above ... It is not merely transcendent and aloof but is found among us and present in creation, just not involved and embedded[455] ... And it is known that the infinite light of G-d, though concealed, has an effect on each and every world.[456] This is because transcendent G-dliness, on whatever level it is found, is the essential G-dly illumination of that level, and not a mere reflection (as is immanent G-dliness). Therefore, although it is concealed, transcendent G-dliness has a G-dly effect on every world...

*

Now, the letter *chet* of *echad* is exchanged and replaced by the letter *ayin* in the word *va'ed* ... But the *dalet* of *echad* does not undergo any exchange with the letters of the word *va'ed*. However the *dalet* of *echad* is a large *dalet*. This is because it represents the very essence of the *sephira* of *malchut*. For there is supernal speech associated with *yichuda ila'ah*, [as well as with *yichuda tat'ah*]. But, *malchut* of *Atzilut* descends to the lower worlds of BY'A, and there it is generally expressed as speech, which reveals to others what was previously hidden [as thought]. Thus, *malchut* in the World of *Atzilut* [which is sometimes compared to supernal thought] is the power or potential for revelation, while the very same level descends and becomes revealed [as speech] in BY"A. So, the two levels are comparable to the potential for speech, and its concrete expression as speech ... for that reason, the *dalet* of *echad* is a *dalet* in the word *va'ed*, as well.

This, then is what is meant by the exchange of letters between *va'ed* and *echad* – [the point is] that *yichuda tata'ah* [in which we are primarily aware of creation, with G-dliness in the background] emerges by way of exchange of letters. Since *yichuda ila'ah* is a [higher] level of nullification and unity, *yichuda tata'ah* descends from *yichuda ila'ah* by way of exchange of letters. This [meditation] is known as "the secret of one," and it demands nullification of the ego alone. This is what is meant by "all who lengthen [their meditation upon] *echad*," meaning that the *echad* of *yichuda ila'ah* should become revealed in *yichuda tata'ah* as well ... And to lengthen *echad* means that nothing should remain hidden or concealed, and the name *Elokim* should be as revealed as the name *Havaya*...

(From *Sefer Mamorim 5678* (1918) of the Rebbe Rashab, pp. 386-395)

Wells of love...

Love "with all your heart" and "with all your soul" are the result of meditation, as written, "to love the Lord your God because He is your life." That is, just as man focuses upon the vitality of his soul, as he meditates upon the infinite light, the "life of all life," and he comes to desire Godliness, so when we meditate on the Godliness enclothed in the worlds, which is something we are able to grasp, with this grasp the Godly concept illuminates within. And at that point we want and desire Godliness.

Within this, there are two levels, "with all your heart," and "with all your soul." Love "with all your heart" occurs when the love is within the heart, as a vessel that contains love. Love "with all your soul" occurs as the love spreads to all of our faculties, even those which are not "vessels" for love. That is, when we meditate on a higher level of Godliness, or when we delve into the depth and the inner meaning of the concept, then Godliness shines with more intensity and in this manner it spreads to all of the faculties of our soul.

But, all this is love that is proportionate to logic and intellect, which does not grasp the very essence [of Godliness]. As written, "My soul desires you at night," during the darkness, when the "nighttime obscures" the essence, for "No thought can grasp You at all." "Thought" refers to the *sephira* of *chochma* (intellect)...and neither *chochma* nor intellect grasps the essence of Godliness. And therefore, all that we grasp and even the love that stems from [our intellectual grasp] actually "obscures" [the essence of Godliness from our perception].

The love "with all your might" is beyond logic and intellect, for it implies forsaking our limitations. Intellect need not imply abandonment of limitations, for the intellect itself is limited. Therefore regarding *mesiras nephesh*, or "giving up our soul" for God, the Torah provides no reason, for this act does not occur according to any kind of intellect or *chochma*. That is why love "with all your might" is without limit and implies forsaking even the limitations of the intellect. And [with this love], we grasp the essence of the infinite One. And therefore fulfillment of mitzvoth accompanied by love "with all your might" is called "doing the will of the One above." It draws upon the inner qualities of His will and reveals them, as immanent Godliness [that can be understood and felt in the world]...

...For this reason, the *HaRav HaMagid* (student of the Baal Shem Tov and mentor of the Alter Rebbe) said regarding the second paragraph of the *kriat shema* that it refers to the state of mind in which we are "not doing the will of the One above." For, love "with all your might" is not mentioned in this paragraph. In order for us to attain the state called "doing the will of the One above," so that revealed Godliness from the inner aspects of His will permeates within us, love "with all of your might" is necessary. And then, our work is done by others. That is, the holy sparks within the *klipa* ["shell," which hides and conceals Godliness] become refined and purified automatically. For, when the infinite light illuminates, the *klipah* and the *sitra achra* [the "other side" - the domain of existence that is opposed to holiness] are nullified. Then, the holy sparks become purified automatically and included in the candle, or the spark becomes included in the flame.

Love "with all your heart," and "with all your soul," are accompanied by a purification and refinement process [to remove good from bad] that involves labor and struggle, as written, "When you go out to war against your enemies." Furthermore, the "hour of prayer is the hour of war," according to the Zohar. For just as the Godly soul contains intellect and emotions, so the animal soul also includes intellect and emotions. The Godly soul understands and grasps the good within Godliness, and on the other hand the intellect of the animal soul understands only the good of worldly matters...but since the animal soul also possesses intellect, it is capable of understanding the opposite as well – that Godliness is good. That is, it is easy to understand that the good of spirituality is better than the good of physicality...

...However, all this takes place within [a context of] labor and effort, because the animal soul does not want to forsake its appetites and lusts, so it struggles against the Godly soul. The Godly soul overwhelms it, but even this is only with reinforcement from Above...and when we nullify the animal soul, refining it, the bad is discarded. That is, the physical lusts dissipate and the good is refined, enabling us to achieve love of Godliness. And in this manner, all o f our physical matters become elevated, since they are not merely to satisfy our lusts but rather for the sake of Heaven...however, all this takes place in a context of "war" and struggle. This is what is meant by "their work is done by themselves," and "you shall gather your grain" – that is, we need to gather the sparks of holiness with labor and effort...

But when "they do the will of the One above," while in a state of love "with all your might," then, "their work is done by others." The refinement and purification [of good from bad] takes place automatically and restfully...for the klipah and "other side" are nullified by the revelation of infinite Godly light of sovev kol olamim ("transcendant Godliness")...and the sparks become automatically included in Godliness just as a spark jumps into a flame. For the spark itself "wants" but does not have the strength to elevate itself and when the flame approaches it, it becomes subsumed in the flame. Similarly, the spark of holiness includes an essential will for elevation, but is unable to elevate. And therefore, when the flame illuminates, that is, when the love "with all your might" shines, the sparks become included automatically within Godliness.

That is why the [third well that Isaac dug] was called Rechovot, because there, the refinement process took place restfully. The first two wells, esek and sitna correspond to love "with all your heart" and "with all your soul," during which the refinement takes place through quarreling and difference of opinion. But, with this [third] well, the refinement took place restfully, which is why it was called Rechovot, as in ki yarchiv Hashem lanu – "When God will expand our borders..." which takes place under conditions of harchava, or "expansiveness."

...In general the subject of the wells is related to elevation from below to above. Within this there are three levels, which correspond to the three levels of kriat shema. Love "with all your heart" and "with all your soul," are associated with intellect and meditation. The refinement process associated with them is accompanied by with disagreement and quarelling. But, love "with all your might" implies "doing the will of the One above," drawing down the essential infinite light in a state of revelation, within the immanent light of God. And in this manner the refinement takes place restfully, which is why the well is called Rechovot..."

From *Sefer Maamorim 5679* (1919) of the Rebbe Rashab, page 104-107

Meditations on the paragraphs of the Shema
Veahavta...Vehaya im Shamoah ("And you shall love...And if you will obey...")

The first paragraph [of the *Shema*] corresponds to the *sephira* of *chesed* ("kindness"), since the command, "You shall love the Lord your G-d" is mentioned. Love is the "vessel" [of the paragraph] but the "light" of the paragraph is *gevura* ("strength/strictness"), associated with the name of G-d of numerical value forty-two. [This is a reference to the forty-two letter name of G-d – *Ana BeKoach* –

with which man attains spiritual ascent since ascent demands discipline and concentration, both of which are associated with *gevura*. There are forty-two words in the first paragraph of the *shema*, corresponding to the forty letters of the name. This is the name designated in the Talmud for spiritual ascent].

From this, we may deduce that the main overall intention of the *Shema* is associated with this name. Since the intention [that we must cultivate during meditation] of the *shema* is the internal element (the *ohr*, or light), therefore it is the real purpose around which the entire prayer is organized, and the rest of it is "external." And therefore, the "body" of the *Shema*, including the words, "And you shall love..." is the "vessel."

All this applies to the first paragraph of the *Shema*, which emphasizes *ratzoh* ("ascent"). However, the second paragraph is all about *shuv* ("return/descent"), bringing *ohr* ("illumination") down into *kelim* ("vessels"). Consequently, the commandment to love G-d "with all your might" is not mentioned at all in this paragraph. In this respect it is the opposite [of the first paragraph], since the vessel, or explicit subject, is *gevura*.

[The second paragraph mentions] *hishamru lachem* ("guard yourselves") and *vecharah af* ("and His anger was kindled") ... However, the inner intention implicit in this paragraph is alluded to by the name of G-d with the numerical value of seventy-two (and seventy-two is also the number of words in the second paragraph, up to *vesamtem*); this name is associated with *chesed* (the word *chesed* which itself bears the numerical value of seventy-two) which is differentiated into seventy-two conduits/channels. The purpose of a conduit, as we see in the case of a canal of water, is to divide the water into locks or compartments, so that not all of the water passes through at any given instant; [rather, there should be a controlled flow of water]. And so, by analogy, there are seventy-two "compartments," providing seventy-two venues of differentiated influx within *chesed*. They differentiate the influx into different types of *chesed*, since there are several sub-categories associated with *chesed*. For example, light is *chesed*, and it was created on the first day of creation. And water is also associated with *chesed*, as is the color white. Similarly, there are many themes down here in this world [that are associated with *chesed*]. And so Above, in the spiritual realms, the songs of the angels and the *tzaddikim*, who "sit and enjoy the rays of the *Shechina*"[457] in the upper and lower *Gan Eden* [are associated with *chesed*]. So, as well are the three-hundred-and-ten worlds inherited by *tzaddikim* and a myriad other details, all of which are included in the seventy-two conduits of *chesed*...

(From *Likutei Torah* of the Alter Rebbe, *Parshat Ve'etchanan*, pp. 13a-b)

Veahavta...Vehaya im Shamoah ("And you shall love...And if you will obey...")

And now, we must understand the name of G-d with numerical value of forty-two – which is called *Shem Mem-Beit*. It corresponds to the first paragraph of the *Shema*, which contains forty-two words from *ve'ahavata* through *u'bisharecha*. And, as well, we must understand why the first paragraph mentions love *bekol meodecha* while the second paragraph doesn't...

The inner intention within the heart – called *re'uta deliba* ("the will of the heart") – is the internal, concealed point that focuses upon spiritual elevation. And this hidden intention is the opposite of the external, conscious quality that is manifested in the physical vessel of the heart. Yet, nevertheless, they unite, and they become like one. For example, "if your heart runs,"[458] meaning that if the [emotion within the] heart seeks to escape, so to speak, from the limitations placed upon it by the [physical] vessel that contains it, then the vessel – which is love that flows like water – places limits on this desire [preventing the soul from escaping from the body]. This is described as light enclothed in a vessel to which it is "opposed." This is what is meant by the 'light of *gevura*' in the 'vessel of *chesed*.' The conscious love that flows like water in the heart is the vessel of *chesed*, while the illumination concealed within it is the inner desire of the heart to escape from the sheath of the body, as noted. And this [internal love], described as *bekol meodecha*, desires to exit from the vessel of *chesed* that enclothes it...

[The love of *bekol meodecha* is associated with the name of G-d containing forty-two letters, which is an expresson of *gevura*]. As known, every inner intention involves contemplation of [some form of] the name of G-d. And this [forty-two letter name] is precisely the one that constitutes our conscious focus of attention, while *reuta deliba* [the unconscious will of the heart] remains as an internal stirring in our heart. It becomes en-clothed within the forty-two letters, [as they are the outer, manifest emotion of which we are conscious in our heart]. It is then expressed as love of G-d when we recite *ve'ahavta*...

*

To understand the second paragraph of the *Shema*, which is the light of *chesed* within the vessel of *gevura*, we need to know that this also follows the metaphor of light and its vessel, wherein the light is the inner [hidden] intention and the vessel is the external meaning.

Now, the name of G-d corresponds to the inner intention that we are calling light, since every intention involves a specific name. (The sages asked,[459] "Why do the Jews call out to G-d and fail to receive answers?" And they answered, "Because when they call upon Him, they do not know how to focus properly on His Name..." ... There must be a specific intention for each name ... and if so, the name is the main component of the intention within the heart...)

So, also here, in the paragraph starting *vehaya*, there are seventy-two words until *vesamtem*, and they correspond to the name of G-d which has the numerical value of seventy-two, and to *chesed*, which also has the numerical value of seventy-two. And these are the seventy-two channels of kindness described previously. The name constitutes the inner focus of our attention, and it is an illumination of kindness, upon which we concentrate while keeping in mind the name of G-d which corresponds to *chesed*.

The vessel is the external dimension [that embodies an internal intention] ... similar to what was described previously [regarding the first paragraph of the *Shema*]. When the escape (*ratzoh*) occurs, as in, "If your heart runs," [this constitutes] escape [of the inner will of the heart] from the vessel, and that is precisely when occurs the return (*shuv*) [the reminder that the soul belongs in a body].

Now, *shuv* is the descent of light and influx from Above to below into all kinds of vessels. And the entire theme of this second paragraph is the light of *chesed* as it descends from Above to below into a vessel, the opposite of light escaping from its vessel...

And this is why *bekol meodecha* is not mentioned in this paragraph, since "love with all your might" implies escape from the vessel that was limiting it. And the main intention of this paragraph is *shuv*, which precisely describes the enclothing and descent of the illumination into a vessel. It is the opposite of the *ratzoh* which was described previously concerning *bekol meodecha*. Yet, the *ratzoh* sets the stage for *shuv*, as a descent of illumination from Above to below in this paragraph of *vehaya im shamoah*...

Now, this illumination of *chesed* that descends from the heights to the depths ... is a descent of revealed G-dliness from Above to below into the seventy-two words of [the second paragraph, from] *vehaya* until *vesamtem*, representing the name of G-d known as *Shem Ayin-Beit* with the numerical value of seventy-two. And this name bears the inner intention of light and illumination. But, the vessel of this light is *gevura* and, therefore, in this paragraph are mentioned words of anger and judgment, such as "the anger of G-d" and "He will halt the rains of the heavens." The beginning [of the paragraph] is mild but the end is severe. Since in the beginning it says *vehaya im* and *venatati metar*, representing the light of kindness, while the end is severe, as it says *hishamru ... vecharah* since this is the light of *chesed* in the vessel of *gevura...*

(From *Imrei Bina* of the Mittler Rebbe, ch. 49-50 (Page 49a-b))

Veahavta...Vehaya im Shamoah ("And you shall love...And if you will obey...")

Now, to understand this matter in more detail, we need to preface with what is written in the *Pri Eitz Hayim*, that in the first paragraph of the *Shema* appears G-d's name *Shem Mem-Beit* of numerical value forty-two, corresponding to the forty-two words from *veahavta* up to *u'bisharecha*. And [the second paragraph], *vehaya im shamoah*, contains G-d's name *Shem Ayin-Beit* with the numerical value of seventy-two, corresponding to the seventy-two words from *vehaya* up to and including *vesamtam*.

At first glance, this is strange, for as we know, the first and the second paragraphs correspond to the *sephirot* of *chesed* and *gevura*, and if the first paragraph is *chesed*, how can it be associated with the name *Shem Mem-Beit* which represents *gevura*? (All spiritual elevations are associated with the name *Shem Mem-Beit*, since *gevura* is the reason for all elevations and ascents, as we see that the nature of fire [which is hot, and associated with *gevura*] is to ascend Above.)

And regarding the second paragraph, associated with *gevura*, which is why in this paragraph we see the words, "And G-d will be angry..." how is it possible for it to contain the name *Shem Ayin-Beit* which represents *chesed*?

The answer that we heard to this question is that the lights of the *sephirot* changed places, so that the lights of *chesed* entered the vessels of *gevura*, and the lights of *gevura* entered the vessels of *chesed* (as written in the *Zohar* and *Eitz Chayim*). Now, the *ohr* of the first paragraph of the *Shema* is from the *sephira* of *gevura*, which is why the name is *Shem Mem-Beit* since the name is associated with light, as written previously at length. However, the vessel is *chesed*, which is why it mentions *veahavta*, for love is associated with *chesed*.

And the light of the second paragraph is *chesed* and, therefore, it is associated with the name *Shem Ayin-Beit*, while the vessel is *gevura*.[460]

(From *Derech Mitzvotecha* of the Tzemach Tzedek, *Shoresh Mitzvat Tefila*, ch. 12, p. 120)

Kriat Shema as personal exodus from Egypt
Ve'asafta deganecha ("And you shall gather your grain...")

This means that we should gather everything together and unite is as "one," alluding to the nullification of the world of separate creations so that all that exists is the realm of spiritual unity.

And then, we mention the exodus from Egypt. Now, we need to understand the connection between the exodus and the recitation of the *Shema*. The matter is as follows:

We should not ask how is it possible to reach the high level of true love of G-dliness, and all the more so of love leading to expiration of the soul, such as we find regarding a "son who strives for his father."[461] [The son is prepared to do whatever his father wants, without asking any questions. He does this out of unstinting devotion to his father, and he feels no need to understand why his father wants this].

After all, this requires overcoming the *yetzer harah* ("evil inclination") so that it has no desire for physical matters ... And, in particular, we all know within ourselves to what extent we are full of transgressions and spiritual blemishes resulting from the sins of our youth which conceal the light of our soul, making it impossible to meditate on G-dliness. As a result – even if we do grasp a G-dly concept, we don't feel it in our soul, and we do not come to love and fear G-d as a result. The transgressions override the revelation of light within our soul, and the love fails to shine through. Since the meditation itself is not fully appropriate, automatically there can be no fear and love. As it is written, "Because your sins separate between you and your G-d Above..."[462]

[In more detail, about the creation of man, we say], "You [G-d] blew into me a living soul." The *Zohar* explains, "One who blows, blows from within himself." [G-d "blew," so to speak, from within Himself to place man's divine soul into his body]. And [since we are using the metaphor of breath], there must be nothing present to block the flow of breath. But, when there is something that blocks it [such as our transgressions], the light of our soul fails to shine. [And in such as case], how is it possible to develop love and fear of G-d?

It is regarding this matter that we mention the exodus from Egypt. In Egypt, the Jews had passed the "forty-nine gates of impurity,"[463] and this was before the giving of the Torah. Nevertheless, on the fiftieth day, they received the Torah, with its revelation of G-dliness. And they communicated face to face with G-d, as it is written, "Face to face, G-d spoke with you."[464] This was a revelation from Above, without any initiative from below (from the Jews), as it is written, "I am *Havaya* your G-d, who took you out of the land of Egypt." With this revelation, G-d, the King of Kings, revealed Himself and redeemed Israel [from Egypt]. As it is written in the Ten Commandments, "*Anochi Havaya Elokecha* - I am the *Havaya* your G-d who took you out of the land of Egypt."[465] So, there was revelation of *Anochi mi she'anochi* ("I, who am whom I am").

And yet, it is written, "Since the nation escaped,"[466] [implying that the Jews did participate of their own volition, aside from the arousal from Above that removed them from Egypt]. And in the *Tanya*, it is explained that they escaped from the evil within themselves. At that time, the evil within them was still at its peak and, nevertheless, they escaped from it, avoiding any further transgressions. This is what is meant by the exodus from Egypt, alluding to their forceful avoidance of sin which took place when they uprooted themselves from [the scene of their] bad deeds. Not that they persuaded themselves not to desire the evil deed, but rather, when their desire was at peak strength, they uprooted themselves from actually doing the deed.

And so occurs every day now as well. There occurs an arousal from Above, as it is written, "And Lavan arose early in the morning,"[467] and the sages say that "the morning" refers to the same morning that was experienced by Abraham [when he arose to take his son Isaac to be sacrificed]. At that hour, there shines a high spiritual level known as *luvan haelyon* ("supernal whiteness") emanating from the very essence of the infinite light of G-d. It descends to us as an arousal from Above.[468] However, this arousal is unconscious, and we do not experience it in our soul. It has no conscious effect on us as far as the "wall that separates us [from G-d]"[469] is concerned. So, we must also do *teshuva*, meaning that we must also regret what we have done and uproot ourselves from all of these evil matters. Prior to prayers, we must strive to be masters of accounting when it comes to ourselves. The best time for this is during the nighttime *Shema*, or during *Tikkun Hatzot* ["Midnight Prayers"], or an hour before morning prayers. At that time, it is necessary to make an accounting in the soul regarding all of our personal details and to be sorry for what we have sullied Above with our transgressions, which now prevent the revelation of the light of our soul. And we must greatly regret all of these matters and uproot ourselves completely from them, [separating ourselves] with great force from all evil.

And, then, there will occur a revelation of spiritual light in the soul. And the arousal from Above during the process of prayer, including meditation on G-dliness, will lead us to love of G-d. This is the reason that we mention the exodus from Egypt, and its relevance to the *Shema*.

*

Now, all of this is preceded by the blessings before the *Shema* – *Yotzar ohr* and *Ahavat olam*.

During the time of Moses, who was part of a generation possessing knowledge of G-d, a minimal amount of meditation on the first verse of the *Shema* was sufficient to arouse people immediately with love and fear [of G-d]. This is because they were high souls who needed no [additional] breadth of explanation or depth of knowledge. But, since then, our hearts have shrunk, and the sages saw that it was no longer sufficient to say the *Shema* alone, since it is so brief. And, therefore, they decreed that we should also say the two blessings that precede it. In general, these [two blessings] constitute explanation and commentary on the verse that begins, *Shema Yisrael*. The blessing, *Yotzar ohr* ("He who forms light") is an explanation and commentary on the words *Havaya echad*, referring to the revealed worlds. This means that the blessing refers to how G-d, "in His goodness continuously renews creation every day," while the *ofanim* in great commotion, and the *seraphim* in great fear and awe praise Him and say *kadosh*. And all of them exalt, glorify, respect, sanctify and crown the name of G-d, since their very source is from His supernal speech. This is then followed by the blessing *Ahavat olam* ("eternal love"), which is an explanation of the words *Havaya Elokeinu*, referring to the "concealed worlds," and how the souls of Jews are beloved to G-d with an essential love.

But, with the passage of time, our hearts shrunk even more, and the sages saw that [these two blessings] were not sufficient, and they further decreed that we need to say the *Pesukei DeZimra*, which contain more explanation. The main theme expressed by the *Pesukei DeZimra* is the nullification of the worlds to G-d. Thus, they constitute a commentary on the words *Havaya echad* since the main goal now is the nullification and elevation of the body and the animal soul, as well as of worldly matters.

In these prayers is also explained the concept of *HaShem Elokeinu* ("the Lord is our G-d") as it applies to the nullification of souls, as it is stated in the prayer *Baruch She'amar* – that the words *Hamehulal bepeh amo* ("He who is praised by the mouth of His people") applies to souls, as do the words, *Hameshubach umefuar b'lashon chasidav* ("He who is praised and glorified by the words of His pious ones"), and as it is written in the *Siddur* of the Alter Rebbe regarding this subject...

And thereafter, we come to the blessing *Emet veyatziv*, which contains the fifteen *vov's*. Now, it is written, "With the *vovin*, You are connected," [470] referring to the connection [with G-d] that takes place by way of the *vovin* [the letter *vov* literally means "hook/connector"], as it is written [concerning the instructions to the Israelites for the making of the portable desert Tabernacle], "Make hooks (*vovin*) for the pillars." [471] [And the instructions also refer to the pegs which were in the shape of *vov's*]; the pegs were to be fastened so as to connect the Tent of the Meeting to the ground, alluding to the verse, "And all that is in the heavens and the earth," [472] which *Targum Onkelos* renders as, "which unites the heavens and the earth."

And, therefore, we say *Emet veyatziv venachon vekayam* ("True and established, correct and existing") all of which corroborate and confirm [our experience] to ourselves. For there is no wise man like he who has experience. It is experience that gives birth to and verifies wisdom, and that is why we meditate to attain love and acquiescence [of the animal soul] to G-dliness.

And this enables us to be united all day long with G-dliness, even while we are involved in business, etc. And this is what is meant by connecting Above, all day long. That is why there are fifteen *vov's*, indicating that they are necessary in order to connect the first two letters of G-d's name, *yud-hey* (possessing the numerical value of fifteen) with the second two letters, *vov-hey*. For, during the creation narrative the Torah tells us that with the letter *hey* G-d created the physical universe.[473] And man himself represents the *vov* [man stands upright in the form of a *vov* and performs the task of spiritual connection] since man is [like a "tree of the field"[474]].[475] And the two [man and creation] must connect with the initial *yud-hey* of G-d's name [which transcends creation].

Now, the *yud-hey* [first two letters of G-d's name] symbolize the first two *sephirot* of *Atzilut* – *chochma* and *bina* – which are called *ayn* ("divine nothingness") and *yesh* ("created existence"). The *Zohar* describes these two as "two fast friends who never part." Yet, at first glance how can they be two fast friends when in truth they are opposite to each other [one is "nothing," while the other is "something"]? But, since in this case, the *yesh* is absolutely nullified to the *ayn*, they can be ["two fast friends who never part"]. And that is why here during the *Shema*, we recite the fifteen *vov's* of *Emet veyatziv*, indicating the descent and drawing down of the first two letters of G-d's name, *yud-hey* into the second two letters *vov-hey*. Together, they correspond to the source of the revealed worlds (also known as the "realm of separation") enabling the nullification of *yesh* to *ayn* in this world.

(From *Sefer Maamorim 5665* (1905) of the Rebbe Rashab, pp. 134-5)

Limitations within the realm of holiness

In the writings of the Ari z'l, (*Likutei Torah* parshat *Vayeishev*), we find a concept called "limitations within holiness." These "limitations within holiness" correspond to the "straits of the throat." What this means is that, as we know, our emotions develop from the mind. When we understand something in a positive light, our minds become stimulated with this knowledge – this produces emotions within our mind, which then filter down to the heart, to become emotions in our heart.

Now, intellect and the emotions are separate from one another and opposites of each other. We feel emotions. Their very foundation is the feeling of self, while the mind is predicated upon nullification of self. Moreover, even the emotions within intellect that occur as our mind is stimulated are not at all similar to the emotions within our heart. With our mind we appreciate the goodness of a concept as we grasp it (as we meditate upon a Godly concept we well grasp the Godliness within it and we are aware of the goodness of Godliness. This leads to stimulation of our intellect, during which we do not experience our 'self.' Rather, we forget about our self. For, the nature of true experience of Godliness is that at such times we forget about ourselves and we become nullified in our very essence) But, as we feel of the emotions of our heart, we experience that "Godliness is good for me." This implies that the stimulation is not over the essential goodness of Godliness but over what is good for "me." This means that our intellect, and even the emotions within our intellect (which result from the stimulation of our mind) are in essence intellectual. Our emotions though, including the 'result' (*bachen*) which is the reason behind our emotion, are associated with feeling our 'self'...the emotions within our mind remain intellect in essence, and only as they descend into our heart do they become emotions in essence.

Since this is the case, (that the holy influx is transformed from essential intellect to emotions), an intermediary is required [to facilitate the transformation from mind to heart]. And that is the purpose of the "straits of the throat." Within the throat is found the esophagus, through which liquid passes from the mind to the heart. Within the straits of the throat, we find neither intellect in essence nor emotions in essence. As the holy influence exists in our mind, it is intellectual in essence and as it descends to the heart it becomes emotions. But in the straits of the throat, there is neither intellect in essence nor emotions in essence. Rather, the "straits of the throat" are similar to a corner of a room. The corner joins two walls, and yet when we search for the precise point of joining, it is not to be found. As far as the eastern wall extends, for example, it remains eastern. And as far as the southern wall extends, it remains the southern wall. And so, the corner itself, where the two walls meet, is non-existent.

So, the "straits of the throat" is neither intellect nor emotions in essence.

Rather, it is like an interval between the mind and the emotions, and it is called the "dividing point" that interrupts...(At first glance, this would seem to be the opposite of a corner, which because it is non-existent, has within it the power to join opposites. As written elsewhere, a higher power is required [in order to join opposites]. For that reason, any intermediary that is above two objects is capable of joining them together. This is similar to what is written elsewhere, for example, regarding midnight. It is also written regarding the *sephira* of *malchut* which [as the final *sephira* of the world of Atzilut] is called a "corner" that joins the world of Atzilut with the lower worlds of BY"A. And so, by way of example, the concept of a "corner" appropriately describes the concept of kingship that joins the king with his people. That is, when the king elevates himself over his people and they accept his reign and are nullified to him, this is what joins them together. Yet, in our case [regarding the intermediary between the mind and the heart] the opposite would seem to be true – there is something [the "straits of the throat"] that we describe as an interruption between the mind and the emotions...but the answer to this will be explained. The "straits of the throat" is really a temporary concealment, which is not truly concealment at all. Rather, it is the result of nullifying its initial presence, as when we are temporarily still and quiet – and this is congruent with the concept of a "corner" [that does not truly exist]).

In truth, there is a moment of stillness that occurs between the mind and the emotions. We experience this clearly during meditative prayer. As we meditate on a Godly concept, which stimulates and arouses the heart, the stimulation descends from the mind to the heart only after a temporary concealment. During that interval, there is "nothing" – neither intellectual grasp nor excitement of the emotions. This stillness is the intermediary that leads from the mind to the heart. The concept of stillness occurs within the intellect as well. We may labor within ourselves to understand a concept. Then after a certain amount of effort, probing the depth of the concept, we become completely still – that is, we experience no illumination of the intellect at all. Initially, we contemplate and examine the concept upon which we wish to meditate, and then a silence [descends upon us] during which there is no illumination whatsoever. It is precisely after this interval that a new thought may occur...in this manner, the stillness mentioned above becomes the intermediary which leads from the mind to the heart.

However, since this is, after all, a vacuum, it can lead to negative by-products. It may lead to the attachment of the "three ministers of Pharoah" – the esophagus, the windpipe and the veins within the neck...which symbolize over-attachment to the physical nature of mundane matters. These matters prevent and block us, interrupting the flow from our mind to our heart so that we are unable to meditate in our mind and understand Godliness well. At any rate, [our thoughts] do not filter down from the mind to the heart to become stimulated by Godliness. That is why we find it much easier to cultivate intellectual meditation than to stimulate excitement of our heart. Even though the intellect functions on a higher level than the emotions, nevertheless it is easier to meditate with our intellect focused on Godly concepts that illuminate our mind. [It is easier to focus upon] Godly matters that we understand well, in which we have a proper foundation. The Godly concepts then illuminate within us, creating an arousal in the mind. But to stimulate the emotions within our heart is much more difficult.

Frequently, those who immerse themselves in prayer, exerting great effort during meditation, achieve solid understanding and intellectual grasp. They develop real excitement in their mind. However, this does not translate into an arousal or excitement within their heart. This is because inside, within the soul, they are fixated upon physical matters. If we were less focused upon physical matters; indeed, if we merely force ourselves to avoid physical temptations (which also causes weakness of our emotions, yet the main goal is to negate our desire for physical objects, aside from that which is necessary, and even that only with intention for the sake of heaven) – then [Godliness] would flow from the mind to the heart in the order mentioned above, via the intermediary of "stillness." In any case, [Godliness] would shine in our heart, for this is what occurs during the step by step process of "cause and effect." It is only because we are attached to physical matters that Godliness fails to descend from the mind to the heart (Yiddish: the connection to physical matters disturbs our prayers).

This then is what is meant by the "three ministers of Pharoah" who prevent and interrupt...they are the *mitzrayim* ("Egypt" – but also "limitations" and "borders") – *meitzar mi* (the "limitations of *mi*" – wherein *mi* alludes to boundaries and concealment). And the "exodus" from these boundaries and limitations also occurs through the throat. That is, a voice emerges from the vapors of our heart, which pass through the throat. For, the voice arouses our intention. We become keenly aware of that as we meditate in our mind on a concept, understanding and grasping it well. And yet, when we repeat the same meditation in a loud voice, describing it in letters of speech, the subject of our meditation becomes part of our prayers [Godliness no longer remains in our minds. It descends to the emotions as well]. The same occurs as we sing a melody in a pleasant voice. It stimulates a strong arousal in our mind, which in turn triggers an arousal of the heart. This is what is meant by a "voice that arouses *kavana*"– the voice has the potential to arouse our "intention." That is, it draws out the inner meaning, latent in the concept, which then causes an arousal of the heart.

During the course of honest meditation, as we achieve real intellectual grasp, we must truly understand the matter upon which we are meditating. Nevertheless, the ultimate goal is to feel the matter within our soul. At that point, the intrinsic kernel of the concept – the Godliness that is inherent within the matter - shines within us. The "voice" that arouses our inner intention, also arouses the inner core of the concept, and then we feel the Godliness of the concept in our mind as well as our heart. That is, the voice that emerges from the vapor of our heart becomes en-clothed in intellectual grasp during the meditation, and then it filters down from the mind to become excitement of the heart...this is the *yetziat mitrayim* ("exodus from limitations" or from "Egypt") that occurs with the throat as intermediary, which is the voice...

Now, there is another way in which the "exodus from Egypt" occurs, and that is without the voice. For, the voice is also a garment, within which the intellect is enclothed, and the intellect itself is a form of concealment. In general, spiritual levels that may be enclothed in a "garment" are within range of the garment and the *kelim* ("vessels")...but there is a higher level of *yetziat metzrayim* ("exodus from Egypt," or from "limitations") that does not occur via the intermediary of a voice. This is the exodus that occurs as we say the prayer, *emet veyatziv* [that follows the first three paragraphs of the *kriat shema* in the morning].

As known, the prayer *emet veyatziv* takes place with cleaving of the soul to the infinite light above. It is an expression of the essential cleaving of the soul, beyond logic and intellect. *Emet veyatziv* is called the *heichal haratzon* ("palace of the will"). The prayer that precedes the *kriat shema* - *ahavat olam* - is called the *heichal ha'ahava* ("palace of love"), and it includes the *kriat shema* as well. It is an expression of love of God that arrives through intellect and meditation. But, *emet veyatziv* is the *heichal haratzon* ("palace of desire"), which is the point of *reuta deliba* ("desire of the heart") that transcends logic and intellect. This is symbolized by the fifteen letter *vov's* within the prayer *emet veyatziv*, for "with *vov's* you are connected." They represent the connection of the essence of the soul with the infinite light above.

Furthermore, in this manner during prayer, we experience the *kol demama daka* – the "still small voice." About Chana, the verse tells us that "her voice was not heard," as she prayed. That is because it was a still small voice that was inaudible, [about which the Zohar says], "there is where the King is." He is the very essence of the infinite One, Who does not come into expression in a voice, since a voice is a garment. As written regarding the future, "Your teachers will no longer conceal (*lo yekanef*) from you," wherein the concealment (*kanaf*) is a garment – in the future, there will be true revelation of His essence. And in this manner, we exit Egypt (limitations) as we overcome all obfuscation and concealment. For, *reuta deliba* causes the transformation of darkness into light. Love "with all your heart" and "with all your soul" produces mere submission [of the animal soul], since both of them are forms of love that are contained within the boundaries of the heart and soul. And for that reason, they cannot produce total transformation of our animal soul. Rather, [this love of God] forces the animal soul to submit [to the will of the divine soul]. But, via love "with all your might," beyond logic and intellect, we totally exit the entire category of limitations, in the process transforming darkness into light...

This then is what is meant by, "burning the *chametz*" [before Pesach]. It is only *reuta deliba* that catalyzes this process. The difference between checking for *chametz* and burning the *chametz* is that "checking" is associated with submission (*itkafia*) within the soul...which is the process of meditation utilizing logic and intellect, which produces submission and nullification of the animal soul. However, "burning the *chametz*" requires that we totally nullify the *chametz*. That entails total transformation, which takes place via *reuta deliba* as mentioned above.

This process has a spiritual counterpart above. Only from the essence of the infinite light is it possible for nullification and total destructions to occur, as written, "And all of Your enemies, destroy," which comes from *keter*. That is, it comes from the inner dimensions of *keter*...which is what is meant by "And I passed over the land Egypt" – Me and not an angel, but God in His self and by Himself. This is what created total nullification, as known that the plague of smiting the firstborn was what finished them off completely, and it took place by God in Himself and by Himself, the very essence of the inifite One above.

And this is what takes place during our personal worship; we seek to eradicate and destroy the *chametz* (symbolizing the *yetzer harah*, or "evil inclination"). [For this], we need *reuta deliba*, which is worship beyond logic and intellect. That is why "checking for *chametz*" takes place on the fourteenth of the month, for *yud-dalet* ("fourteen") also spells *dai* ("enough"), as in *dai meichasoro* ("enough to meet his needs"), which is an allusion to the needs of the chain of spiritual creation (*seder hishtalshelut*). What is required to "meet the needs" of creation comes from its source and origin. That is, via revelation of spiritual intellect (*mochin*) during the exodus from Egypt, there was sufficient illumination to subdue the "other side," the forces opposed to holiness. But, utter "destruction of *chametz*" [eradication of the *yetzer harah*] comes from God alone, from the very inner aspect of the infinite light that transcends the source and origin of creation. This level is called *rishon* ("first"), for the *gematria* of *bayom harishon* ("on the first day") is *keter*, and moreover it refers to the inner dimension of *keter*. And therefore the main manifestation (of destruction of *chametz*) is on the fifteenth – the *hei* –

From *Sefer Maamorim 5679* (1919) of the Rebbe Rashab, pp. 347-350

Four Levels of Emet

This is also why we say *emet* four times. *Emet* is equated with God's name, *Havaya*, as written, "...and by my true name *Havaya*, I did not make Myself known to them" [to the forefathers – Ex. 6:3], and Rashi explains, "I did not make Myself known to them with My true characteristics...as written, 'The Truth of *Havaya* is forever.'"

Now, there are a number of levels of truth. The name *Shaddai* and the name *Elokim* are also "true," although they include several levels, such as *sefat emet* ("boundary of truth"), *emet* and *emet l'amito* ("absolute truth"). The four times that we say *emet* correspond to the four letters of God's name *Havaya*. The final *hey* corresponds to *da'at tachton* ("lower consciousness," in which we are aware of creation in the foreground and God only in the background), which is also "true," since it is a state that is associated with nullification, and which draws down Godliness. And the letter *vov* is higher, as written, "each level is higher than the previous level, shielding them from above..." signifying that each level is high, but the next level is yet higher. Thus, the four times that we say *emet* represent the truth of *da'at tachton* and the truth of *da'at elyone* ("higher awareness," in which God is in the forefront of our consciousness and creations recedes to the background) and the truth that joins them together (*da'at elyon* with *da'at tachton*). And then [as the fourth level], there is the absolute truth of the very essence of infinite Godliness...

...Now, it is written (Ex 34:6), "And he called, *Havaya*, *Havaya*..." indicating that there are two names *Havaya*, with punctuation interrupting between them. And the higher name *Havaya* is associated with the Will of God. The will is of paramount importance because it affects all of our soul-powers. Our will on this planet will not result in the creation of anything; as much as we might want something, nothing will result from it unless our will is expressed in thought, speech and action. But Above, as soon as it rose in His thought, all was created, as written (Psalms 135:6), "All that the Lord desired, He did (made)." If so, all subsequent levels already exist in His will, and thus there is a name *Havaya* embedded in His will. However, there is punctuation separating between the two names *Havaya*, for the supernal name *Havaya* is far higher than the lower name *Havaya*. And in the future, the supernal name *Havaya* will be revealed, as written, "On that day, His Name *Havaya* will be one..." – there will not be two names *Havaya*, but only one. Nothing will obstruct between them, so that automatically they will be one.

Currently, "I am not pronounced as I am written." The name *Havaya* is pronounced as *Ad-ny* [indicating mastery of the universe], meaning that currently *Havaya* is revealed only as *Ad-ny*. And as it is written, "And *Havaya* is in His holy palace (*heichal*)," wherein *heichal* has the same gematria as *Ad-ny*. But, in the future, His name will be pronounced as written, because all revelation will take place via His name *Havaya*, as written, "Your teachers will not longer hide things from you." That is, there will no longer be a "covering" or "garment," as written in Tanya. Since now, the revelation is of the lower name *Havaya*, therefore it is expressed as the name *Ad-ny*. But, in the future, when the revelation will be of the higher name *Havaya*, the revelation will come directly through the name *Havaya*.

Thus, there will be four aspects of redemption in the future, corresponding to the four letters of the name *Havaya* in His will. They are the four times that *emet* is mentioned in the prayer *Ezrat avoteinu*, referring to the future. *Emet* is the revelation of the essential, infinite light...and this is the revelation of the higher name *Havaya*.

All of this refers to the *emet* of the inner dimensions of the Torah. What has been revealed until now is only the external dimensions of the Torah, but the "reasons" underlying the Torah have not been revealed. With the arrival of the meshiach, the inner dimensions of the Torah will be revealed, as written, "He kisses me with kisses of His mouth..." (Song of Songs 1:2). Rashi explains that this refers to the underlying reasons for the Torah which will be revealed in the future. And this is the four times that we say *emet*, referring to the four redemptions of the future...

From *Sefer Maamorim 5678* (1918) of the Rebbe Rashab, pp. 145-146

Why geula before tefila

The reason that "redemption" (*geula*) is placed near to "prayer" (*tefila*) in the order of the morning prayers is to lend strength to the elevation [that occurs during *shemonah esreh* - the end of the *shema* mentions redemption, and that is followed by the *shemonah esreh*, also called *tefila*]]. The sages said that three pairs are to be performed "in proximity" to one another. One; the priest should perform *smicha* (forceful laying of his hands on the head of the animal) immediately before slaughtering it. Two; one should mention redemption immediately prior to praying (the *shemonah esreh*). The implication is that the two pairs - *smicha* prior to slaughtering and redemption prior to prayer - encompass the same concept.

As known, the sacrifices represent the offering of the animal soul. In our days, prayer takes place in lieu of the sacrifices. The main point of prayer in lieu of the sacrifices (referring to the *tamid* constant offering of an *olah* that takes place every morning and every evening) applies to the *shemonah esreh*.

This concept is as described in *Torah Ohr* (of the Alter Rebbe, in the discourse beginning, *Yehuda atah*) regarding Reuven, Shimon and Levi, who correspond to the two first paragraphs of the *kriat shema* and to the following prayer, *emet veyatziv*. Together, they allude to the concept of *mamalle kol olamim*, or inner, immanent light. [This level of illumination] does not induce [the same level of] real nullification to God, as in the *shemonah esreh*. Rather, it elicits love of God, as in "My soul yearns and expires..." At this point in prayers [i.e. during the *kriat shema*], we desire to be included and united with the Emanator, blessed be He. The implication is that currently we are not yet included and united with His infinite light of *sovev kol olamim*...However the *shemonah esreh* elicits full nullification and inclusion within the infinite light above, truly within the category of *sovev kol olamim*. And therefore we recite the *shemonah esreh* quietly, in a whisper. It is not called "love" at all, but rather total and complete abnegation of the self. This is expressed as pouring out our soul into the bosom of our Father...to be like nothing and naught. And that is what is alluded to by our bowing during the *shemonah esreh*.

Now, the point of *kriat shema* is to deliver our [Godly] soul [to God] while saying the word *echad*. This expresses our *bitul*, or nullification to God...(page 155) When we follow that by saying, *Baruch shem kevod malchuto leolam va'ed* ("Blessed be His holy Name forever"), we draw down the power to nullify our animal soul as well (this is a lower level of nullification, called *bitul hayesh* – nullification of the ego). Even so, the animal soul remains a "something" – it retains its existence – but it becomes nullified to a higher authority (this is called *itkafia* – "bending" and "subduing," but not transforming the self).

But, during the *shemonah esreh*, the animal attains true and total nullification and becomes nothing and naught. It is the *shemonah esreh* that facilitates and imparts true nullification to the infinite One above. For as mentioned above, the *shemonah esreh* represents the *korbon*, or sacrifice, which was an animal to be offered up and included in the fire of Above. Similarly, the animal soul becomes included in the divine void as it "delivers itself" to the infinite One above. And then it ascends to its source and origin in the world of *Tohu*...

But in order for the animal soul to gain the power to ascend with true nullification during the *shemonah esreh*, [we must mention] *geula* in proximity to *tefila*. The animal sacrifice required a man to sanctify the animal, after which a priest performed the sacrifice. All of this was facilitated by a descent of influx from Above that enabled the animal to ascend and become included in the divine fire above...

Similarly, the offering and the nullification of the animal soul requires proximity of *geula* to *tefila*. It requires the descent of divine influx from above via the Godly soul which already achieved total self sacrifice during the *kriat shema*. This is what constitutes redemption and exit from limitations in order to become included in the infinite light above, as we say *echad*.

The act of *smicha* ("laying of hands") takes place with both hands. This represents the two kinds of *mesirat nephesh* ("dedication") that are mentioned in the *kriat shema* – during *echad* and during *bekol naphshecha*...The act of *smicha* takes place with all of the power of the priest. It is a forceful act, because it represents revelation of the inner most powers of the soul – the *chaya* and *yechida*. The word for "force" – *koach* – is spelled *caf-chet* – symbolizing the two *sephirot* of *keter* and *chochma*. It corresponds to the *mazal* of the divine soul that joins with the animal soul in order to enlighten all of this divine energy on the animal soul.

And in this manner, the animal soul becomes nullified like a candle before a flame, becoming truly naught. And when the animal soul becomes truly naught, it adds additional illumination to the divine soul. For in general, the purification of the animal soul takes place with nullification of the ego, adding illumination to the divine soul...

(From *Sefer Maamorim 5680* of the Rebbe Rashab, page 153, 155

Reuven, Shimon and Levi – three paragraphs of the shema

The name Reuven is compounded of the words *Reu* ("see") and *ben* ("son"). *Ben* symbolizes love of God, the kind of love that results from visualizing Godliness. Vision occurs as we approach an object with affection, as written (*Hoshea* 9:10), "...like a ripe fig in its beginning, so I saw your forefathers..." This is the affection with which God loved our forefathers. Similarly, the vision that we experienced in the *Beit Hamikidash* (holy Temple) three times a year, as written (Ex 23:17), "All of your males..." is a result of God's love and affection for Jewish souls, as written (*Malachi* 1:2), "I loved you, said God." This [love] is from Above to below and similarly there is love from below to Above, from Jewish souls to God. The Jews also experience love as the result of vision of Godliness. It is a higher level of love, that includes proximity and much cleaving [to Godliness].

Now, [the spiritual] vision [that we experience] from a worldly perspective is what the Zohar describes as "gazing upon the glory of the King." Although such vision is a high spiritual level, which only the prophets experienced, as written (Isaiah 6:1), "And I saw *Adny*...' nevertheless here the intention is not vision with the naked eye, but rather mental vision, as written in the Zohar, "the eye of the mind in your heart sees all..." This as well is a high spiritual level, and yet with meditation it is possible to attain a state similar to vision. This occurs as we meditate, delving in our minds into Godliness until the concept becomes confirmed within, as if we actually see Godliness. Something like this is expressed in the saying of the sages (*Pirkei Avot* 3:1), "Peer upon three items and you will not come to sin: Know from where you come..." The saying says, "Peer..." [which is vision] and also indicates confirmation of the concept. This is what we should experience in *avoda* ("service" of God that includes meditation) – confirmation [of the subject of meditation], as if we actually visualize it.

This is what is meant by (Psalms 37:3), "And cultivate faith." We must cultivate our faith so that it contains *da'at* (visceral knowledge). The Jews are "believers, and offspring of believers" in the creation of the universe from nothing to something as well as in the One God. We espouse simple faith, which is something that the philosophers failed to grasp with all of the investigations. With all of their logic, they failed to grasp the slightest concept; that faith is the basic foundation, fixed and set in the heart of each and every Jew. We have no need for signs or miracles whatsoever. The reason for such faith is that "the *mazal* sees," as the sages said (Tractate *Megila* 3A), "even though they did not see" – referring to the portion of the soul that is enclothed in the body – "their *mazal*..." (referring to the source and origin of the soul) "sees." It sees with true vision, visualizing that which comes into existence from nothing to something, as well as how everything is ultimately nullified and united.

Now, this occurs as real vision, not mere intellect. It is beyond intellect, beyond even the intellect associated with the *mazal* of the soul. It is true Godly vision. And this real vision illuminates from the essence of the soul into the portion of the soul en-clothed in the body, sparking faith within it. This is simple faith, as strong as a wedged peg that will not budge. Within our power is the ability to bring this faith from a state of concealment to revelation within our mind and the recesses of our understanding, so that for us it becomes like confirmation as if we truly see. For, nothing creates itself, and when we see that something "exists," we know with certainty that it came from a divine void that created it. And it is nullified with ultimate nullification to this divine void. We observe the nullification of the physical world to the spiritual world, for the body is nullified to the soul and follows it, and so it is plain and obvious that the physical is nullified to the spiritual. This is the relationship between the body and the soul; even though the body is not created from the soul, still the soul vitalizes the body and the body is totally nullified to it. All the moreso is it true, then, that the substance of existence, which is created from a divine void, is nullified to it, and is as naught in comparison to it.

We observe, for example, how a son is nullified to his father. His nullification comes from the very essence of his being. This is also true of the relationship between a *mashpia* ("mentor") and *mekabel* ("student"). The *mekabel* is nullified from the very essence of his being to the *mashpia*. Even though he has his own mind which does not come from the *mashpia*, nevertheless his intellectual grasp does come from his *mashpia* and therefore he is totally nullified to him. This must be true, then, a priori regarding *yesh* and *ayn* – the creation and existence of *yesh* ("existence") is from the divine void and therefore it must be nullified totally to the divine void. And just as *yesh* is nullified to the divine void, so the void is nullified to spiritual levels that are beyond it.

Now, as we meditate at length upon this concept, plumbing the depths of our knowledge with clarity, while persistently meditating, and not one time alone, we may attain a form of "confirmation" of this concept as if we truly see its truth. This is also what is meant by *emunah*, which [besides meaning "faith"] also indicates regularity, as in "he who trains (*omen*) a child." That is, he slowly trains him how to eat. Similarly, we must apply ourselves regularly to this meditation until we experience "confirmation" within.

That is why during the *kriat shema*, we say, *Havaya echad* ("God is One"), and not *Havaya yachid* ("God is singular"). *Yachid* is indicative of the unity of infinite illumination as it exists above, but the ultimate purpose is to unite Him [down here] in the worlds, where there are seven heavens and the earth, as well as the four directions of the universe. They must become united with the infinite illumination of the Master of the world. Prior to that, we must recite the *pesukei dezimra* and the blessings preceding the *kriat shema*, which tell the story of His praises. The intention is not simply to recite His praises. The goal is that they should creep into our awareness and that based upon this awareness, we should achieve spiritual vision. And the length [of prayers] is to help us achieve confirmation, "as if" we see. And in this manner we will achieve love of God, with yearning and expiry of the soul – "My soul yearned and also expired" to cling to the infinite illumination, with true devotion.

This, then is Reuven – "the son who sees" – who loves his Father and mother even more than himself, his own spirit and his own soul. This process occurs mostly within the Godly soul, when in general the light of the Godly soul illuminates, leading to the confirmation and love described above. But, the command, "And you shall love...with all your heart," applies to both inclinations. That is, the evil inclination should also attain love of God, with the love of a *ba'al tshuva* [one who returns to Torah and mitzvoth after having strayed from the path]. About this matter, we mention Reuven, since [as his mother Leah said], "God saw my poverty," referring his days of poverty and stress. [Within us], this is reflected in bitterness over our distance from God, which leads in turn to *tshuva*. This is not *tshuva* over sins and transgressions, but about return of the soul to its source.

This [process of *tshuva*] occurs as we meditate on how in its inception the soul was included within the Emanator, for "the soul that You placed within me is pure." Its source is in the world of *Atizlut* and above *Atzilut*. It descended from its place of honor to become enclothed in a body and animal soul that hides and conceals Godliness, since it is very far from its source. About this situation, we become bitter within, and we "scream to *Havaya*" from the narrow straits within, from the narrow place within which we exist down here in this world. This, in turn generates a strong love of God within us, that has the advantage of "light over darkness," as written, "Where *ba'alei tshuva* stand, complete *tzadikim* are unable to stand." And this in turn leads to nullification of the animal soul, enabling it to transform its darkness into light. About this, Leah said (Gen 29:32), "My man will love me..." meaning that she will achieve the level known as *ishi* – "my man," as written (*Hoshea* 2:18), "On that day you will call me 'my man' and you will no longer call me 'my husband/master." Now, the difference between "my husband/master" and "my man" is that regarding the husband/master – it is possible for negative forces to siphon off holy energy...while regarding "my man," there is no siphoning by the negative forces, for "my man" is also "my fire" (*ishy* – "my man" is also *aishy* – "my fire") meaning that the fires of Godly desire and the thirst for God is like fire to become included in the holy Godliness above, as written in the *Tikunei Zohar* – "there is fire that is not the fire of *Havaya*, and there is fire that is the fire of *Havaya*." The fire that of *Havaya* elicits total nullification, as written else where, and when "God saw my poverty" (Gen. 31:42, Psalms 9:14, 25:18, 31:8), then the evil within becomes transformed into good, darkness to light and thus we achieve the level of *ishi* – "my man" or "my fire," with fire from within me...

Now, all of the above refers to the first paragraph of the *kriat shema*, which occurs with a desire and "rush" associated with the phrase (Song of Songs 2:6, 3:3) – "And His right arm embraced me..." indicating proximity and cleaving to the infinite light. However, the second paragraph of the *kriat shema* - *vehaya im shamoah tishme'u* – "and if you will listen..." alludes to the spiritual level of Shimon, as Leah said (Gen. 29:33), "Because God heard..." This is a reference to [the spiritual dynamic of] *shuv*, or to spirituality descending to be channeled and utilized. For, vision occurs up close, while hearing occurs from afar. Hearing is not comparable with seeing, since hearing occurs from afar. And that is why it is associated with *shuv*, or spirituality "returning" to within the vessels.

Nonetheless, there is something that we must strive to understand; the sages (tractate *Baba Kama* 85B) said that if one struck his fellow and caused him to go deaf, he must pay him the full amount that he is worth. If he blinded him in one eye he must pay him for that eye, but if he caused him to go deaf he must pay his entire worth. And this does not make sense, for vision is more valuable than hearing. Hearing is not comparable to seeing, so why does he have to pay him all that he is worth if he made him go deaf?

But, the answer is that there is a certain advantage to hearing over seeing. This advantage is understood according to what the sages said (tractate *Baba Batra* 12A); "a wise man is preferable to a prophet." Now, this is not well understood, for prophecy is associated with vision, as written, "I saw *Adni*..." while wisdom and intellect are associated with hearing alone, so without question, prophecy is greater...Moreover, during the second Temple period, prophecy ceased. The sages of that period were very great, but they were not prophets, and why would a wise sage be preferable to a prophet? But, the concept is that prophecy, although associated with vision, arrives through a "lens that is not clear," as written (*Hoshea* 12:11), "And to the prophets I will appear" [the word meaning "appear" – *adameh* – implies an unclear, imprecise image]. And as the saying says, "all of the prophets prophesied with *koh* - "like this" - a mere image appearing through an unclear lens. For, prophecy arrives through *netzach* and *hod* of the world of *bria*, and therefore it does not provide clear vision of the essence, as occurs in the world of *Atzilut*. And even the prophecy of Moshe, which occurred in the world of *Atzilut*, through a "clear lens" nevertheless was described in the Torah (Ex. 33:29), "...you will not be able to see My face, for no man may see Me and live."

But, there are great levels of wisdom, including high levels of intellect that are very exalted, capable of grasping the world of Atzilut and beyond, and also capable of penetrating to the very inner workings of the worlds. There was, for example, the Rashbi, who possessed tremendous intellectual grasp. Similarly in *avoda* (divine worship, including meditation), there is an advantage to hearing. Now, it is true that in the prophets (Habakuk 3:2) it is written, "*Havaya, I heard Your news and I was afraid...*" The first letters of this verse form the acrostic of two times the letters *yud-hey* (the first two letters of God's Name, *Havaya*), which add up to a total of six hundred and twenty, spelling the word *keter*, or "crown," symbolizing the six hundred and thirteen mitzvoth of the Torah and seven mitzvoth from the rabbis (=620). Now the fulfillment of mitzvoth is associated with "hearing," as written (Shmuel 1, 15:22), "listening [obedience in fulfilling mitzvoth] is preferable to a choice offering..."

The sacrifices are associated with vision. [Upon offering sacrifices], people could see the pillar of fire that descended from heaven to consume the sacrifice. Also, the sacrifices elicited revelation of infinite Godliness in the Temple. Nevertheless [the verse above indicates that] a *shamuah* ("hearing" – fulfillment of mitzvah) is preferable. That is, fulfilling the mitzvah with the yoke of heaven upon us enables us to achieve the spiritual level of *keter* - six hundred and twenty. Spiritual vision is associated with *chochma*, as written, "Who is a *chacham* ("wise person") - he who sees..." But, hearing is associated with *keter*. As to the verse above, "*Havaya*, I heard Your news and I was afraid" - it implies that by hearing, we achieve fear of God. For hearing occurs from afar. It is associated with the theme, "His left hand repels." That is, we must discipline and humble ourselves, for (Psalms 24:3), "Who is bold enough to ascend and approach the infinite light...who ascends the mountain of God?" In this manner [via fear of God], fear and terror of

God fall upon us, as written (Ex. 20:15), "and the nation saw and trembled and stood from afar..." This means that they experienced *shuv* ("return" of the Godly illumination to be expressed and channeled in "vessels") in order to remain below and to fulfill the mitzvoth, physically, with acceptance of the yoke of heaven.

This is why fear of God is the basis of the six hundred and thirteen mitzvoth. The negative commandments are based upon fear. Fulfillment of the positive commandments is also based upon accepting the yoke of heaven, which is based upon fear, as above. And this is what it means, "*Havaya*, I heard Your news and I was afraid..." for this fear is the source of all the six hundred and twenty mitzvoth and arrives all the way to *keter*.

And this is why the sages say that if we cause someone to go deaf, we must pay him all that he is worth [even though if we blind him in one eye we need only pay for that eye] – because there is a definite advantage to hearing. For this reason, Leah said (Ex 29:33), "Because God heard that I was hated..." This means that [when we think into our behavior, and come to the conclusion] that we are despicable and low, is precisely when we experience the spiritual dynamic of *shuv* – of chanelling our talents and resources. And the explanation of, "Because God heard.." [in the verse above with Leah] is that acceptance of the yoke of heaven is equivalent to the lower form of fear, which draws down higher fear, because "God heard me..."

Now, after reciting *kriat shema*, we continue with *emet veyatziv, venachon vekayam hadavar hazeh.*" This prayer is associated with Leahs's statement (Gen. 29:34), "...this time my man will accompany me." For "there is the right side and there is the left side and between them is found the *calah*"...the "right side" is the experience of desire and rush for God that occurs during the first paragraph of the shema – "And His right hand embraces me..." And the "left side" is the second paragraph of the *kriat shema* – "His left arm repels".... The two correspond to love and fear of God. And *emet veyatziv* is associated with Levi, which is why we say *venachon vekayam hadavar hazeh* – "this thing is true and correct" – referring to Torah. [This occurs as] we take to heart that on our own, we do not deserve ascent and unity with God, nor do we deserve elevation of our soul from below to above to unite it with the Emanator. For "Who would dare to ascend to the mountain of God"...yet, the infinite light of its own, spontaneously and automatically descends, lowers, and becomes enclothed in the Torah. And there occurs unity of the infinite light down here within the Torah that enables us to draw revelation of Godliness over our soul and to unite our soul with the infinite light. For Israel is connected with Torah, and Torah with the One above. So, via the Torah, Jewish souls become united with Godliness, and this is why we say, *emet veyatziv...venachon vekayam* – "True and established, correct and lasting is this thing" – since we fulfill the Torah – ourselves and our fathers, our children and all of our generations..."upon the early ones and on the later ones this is a good and lasting matter..." meaning that via the Torah we are able to unite with the infinite light. This is what is meant by the fifteen *vovin* of emet veyatziv, for "with *vovin* you are connected..." And this is Levi, who represented "accompanying" and joining. After the love and fear of the first two paragraphs of the *kriat shema*, he joins the infinite light of God via the Torah...

From *Sefer Maamorim 5680* (1920) of the Rebbe Rashab, page 217-220

Total Nullification
...the first two paragraphs of the *kriat shema* and *emet ve'yatziv* are associated with Reuven, Shimon and Levi. But, regarding Yehuda, Leah said, "This time I will thank *Havaya*." This implies that Yehuda was named in recognition of Leah's gratefulness and acknowledgment of God. We express this trait of nullification

while bowing during the *shemonah esreh*. We recite the *shema* while seated, but we pray the *shemonah esreh* while standing. Standing expresses more nullification than does sitting. For example, one who stands before the king demonstrates more humility than one who sits in front of him. And even though reciting the *kriat shema* is a commandment from the Torah, while *shemonah esreh* is from the rabbis, nevertheless the nullification of the *shemonah esreh* is higher than the nullification of the *kriat shema*. For *"Havaya* is a God of perspectives" – higher consciousness (*da'at elyon*) and lower consciousness (*da'at tachton*). Lower consciousness is awareness of creation from nothing to something. It implies awareness of the existence of creation, even though it is nullified to the Godly void (*ayn*) from which it was created. This is "nullification of ego" alone. Higher consciousness (*da'at elyon*) is awareness that what is above truly exists, while what is below is as if naught and insignificant. *Kriat shema* is generally associated with *da'at tachton*, since while we recite the *shema* we are in the world of *bria*. Even though it is written that while saying *Hashem echad*, we are meant to experience higher unity [awareness of God as the true existence while the creation is of questionable reality], nevertheless this is really only lower consciousness since it merely expresses that we wish to become included and united with Godliness. But, currently, we are neither included nor united with God. That is why the command is, "You should love the Lord your God..." [The implication is that] there is one who loves.

But, the *shemonah esreh* implies total nullification of the self (*bitul bemetziut*), as in the description, "All stands before Him as naught." Similarly, the nullification of the *shemonah esreh* is that of one who stands before the King. This is the nullification "like naught," which implies total self abnegation. It is for this reason that the *shemonah esreh* is said in whisper and quietly, without any feeling whatsoever. It does not imply love, but nullification of our existence, expressed in bowing and kneeling. This is called *hoda'ah*. It is not nullification according to intellect, but total self-nullification from the very essence of the soul. And that is why Leah said, "This time I will thank *Havaya.*" Her acknowledgment was beyond Reuven, Shimon and Levi who are associated with the first two paragraphs and *emet veyatziv*. All of them are associated with nullification according to logic and intellect. Yet, the nullification of the *shemonah esreh* surpasses logic and intellect. But in order to achieve this, we must first achieve the nullification associated with logic and intellect, with love and fear of God during the first two paragraphs. Then afterward during the *shemonah esreh* we experience the nullification of existence associated with Yehuda.

(From *Sefer Maamorim 5680* (1920) of the Rebbe Rashab, Page 220

Sublime descent in four stages
Emet Veyatziv ("True and certain...")

In general, there are four *tzimtzumim* ("contractions"). The first produces illumination of the intellect [of the mentor that is then lowered to the] appropriate level for the recipient. That is, from the very essence of mentor's intellectual awareness, there must emerge intellect that is fitting for the recipient. For as is known, the mentor functions on an entirely different intellectual plane than does the recipient. And in order to produce illumination of intellect that is on the level of the recipient, the mentor must totally contract and conceal his own intellect. And when he does so, intellectual illumination that is acceptable to the recipient emerges. But as it emerges, the illumination takes on the form of a concentrated "point" of intellect that is impossible to deliver [as is] to the recipient. For, there is no revelation [to the recipient] at all in this "point." What must be done is to further distinguish among the details of the concentrated intellect and to find ways of packing and enclothing them to enable the recipient to understand them. This constitutes the second contraction, in which the point of concentrated illumination becomes expressed in many distinct details. And in truth, these details have the effect of concealing the light of G-dliness within them. All of this [that is, the first two contractions] takes place within the [conscious awareness of the] mentor himself.

Afterward, when it becomes necessary to reveal and convey the point of intellect to the recipient, another two contractions occur. This is because the process of discerning the details of the concept takes place within thought, before the details become available for speech. And in order to convey them verbally, an organization of words must take place, so that they convey and express the information properly, enabling the concept to be properly accepted by the recipient. And this organization of words is yet a further contraction in relation to the mentor's thought. This contraction is called "speech within thought" – it is still thought but now it relates to speech. And then, finally, the speech that conveys the concept to the recipient is considered "action", which is why the sages said the "the movement of the lips is considered action."

Now, the latter two contractions that reveal and convey the concept, first bring it to light in a general fashion, and then within details and explanations. And so occurs Above, as well, in the process of conveying G-dly illumination from the essence of the Emanator to His emanations [the ten *sephirot*]. A myriad number of contractions take place, from one level [down] to the next, as is known regarding the fifteen *vovin* of *Emet Veyatziv*, which also correspond to the fifteen *yesodot* of *bevavin titkatar* [that is, to the *vov*'s mentioned in the Friday night song]. And they correspond to what is written, "A thousand and ten thousands, and a myriad..."[476] kinds of goodness ... which correspond to the myriad contractions involved in lowering and bringing down the illumination from Above to below...

*

But, in general, there are four contractions, corresponding to the four letters of the name *Havaya*, as known regarding the letters of His holy name. They convey and lower the divine light by way of four contractions, as is written elsewhere regarding the descent of the *kav* ("ray") from the infinite light of G-d. The name of G-d is involved in that process, since the *yud* (first letter of the name *Havaya*) is the beginning and origin of the descent of the *kav* as it exists above or prior to *Adam Kadmon* ("Primordial Man"). And the *hey* [second letter of the name *Havaya*] is A"K itself, including the many details and particulars of creation, for it is said about A"K that "He gazes and observes [all that was, is and will be in all generations], although all of the details are still concealed."[477] And the *vov* [third letter of His name] represents the general World of *Yetzira*, while the final *hey* [of His name] is the "surface area" of the World of *Atzilut*. [This is because one characteristic of *Atzilut* is that the *sephirot* interact in groups of three – *Chabad*, *Chagat*, and *Nehi* – which define neither a point, nor a line, but a surface].

[And there is another even higher scheme corresponding to the name *Havaya*, wherein] the *yud* is the point of the *reshima* ("impression") that preceded the original *tzimtzum*. Within this point is included all that will be revealed in the entire scheme of creation. And the *hey* corresponds to the "231 gates" of the *olam hamalbish* ("realm of enclothement"), and the *vov* is revelation of the *kav* as it emerges after the *tzimtzum* of the *olam hamalbish*. It is the origin of the *kav* as it exists above A"K, and the final *hey* is A"K itself...

(From *Besha'ah Shehikdimu 5672* (1912) of the Rebbe Rashab, vol. 1, p. 161)

All spiritual attainments apply to all Jews

All of the previously mentioned spiritual levels - that is, levels that emerge from the very essence of the Jewish soul - apply to each and every Jew. Every Jew possesses [the trait of] internal self nullification, but for some people it is conscious and for others it is not conscious. But, in any case the essential theme of nullification exists within each and everyone.

Similarly, the state of *hitamtut* ("corroboration," or "verification" – in which we receive spiritual confirmation of our previously intellectual concept of a particular spiritual level) and *reiya* ("vision") in the mind's eye (during which our meditation leads us to perception that is so clear it is if we "see" it in our mind's eye – usually *hitamtut* and *reiya* arrive together) are present in every soul.

Also, *hacara* ("recognition" – internalization that occurs after meditating on a Godly concept and internalizing it to the extent that it becomes "ours" – this level of grasp is visceral and not merely intellectual. It is associated with deep internal knowledge of *da'at*. It is similar but prior to *reiya*) is present in each and every person, including those who have no intellectual grasp of anything Godly. Nevertheless they possess Godly recognition and for this reason they have an innate connection with Godliness. And all Jews have a connection to Torah and mitzvoth. For, even one who has no Torah knowledge, still has an essential connection with the Torah. This applies even to the simplest of simple people who do bear a connection to Torah and mitzvoth, to whom the matter is precious – this is because of the innate recognition of Godliness that is within them. And from this, we may deduce that the soul also possesses the powers of *reiya* and *hitamtut* of Godliness.

Similarly, the potential for *reuta deliba* ("desire of the heart" – when the heart "ignites" with a consuming love of God, generally in the aftermath of intense intellectual meditation upon Godly concepts) is part of the innate makeup of each and every Jew. We may achieve a state of expiry of the soul, as exemplified in the verse, "My soul expires for Havaya..."

Lack of revelation of these levels occurs when our mind and emotions become enmeshed in worldly matters. For the revelation of innate nullification and in particular, revelation on the order of *hitamtut* and *reiya* of Godliness occurs after we first undergo meditation according to logic and intellect. For it is necessary that these levels occur in an organized fashion. First, we must meditate according to logic, and involve our emotions, and [only then] we arrive to revelation of the inner essential soul faculties.

Furthermore, there also must be something [an appropriate 'vessel' within us] on which the essential faculties can dwell. That is why, when we en-clothe our intellect and emotions in coarse physical matters, there is nothing on which the essential soul faculties can dwell. Especially when we enmesh the inner faculties of our soul in matters of this world, upon which such matters touch the very essence of our soul and we become disturbed and worried. This greatly hides and conceals [our essential Godly faculties]. It is for this reason that the tribes chose to be shepherds. They desired to avoid the confusion resulting from worldly matters, so they would be capable of being a *merkava*, or "vehicle" for Godliness. Only Yoseph, being a soul from the world of Atzilut, was not confused by matters of the world. He was King of Egypt and the nations acted only in accordance with his directive, and yet at the same time he was a *merkava* for Godliness. That is, since he was a high soul, he was not affected by the world, and worldly matters did not disturb him.

Similarly, it is possible that among souls of the worlds of BY"A, called *zerah behama* ("animal progeny"), which are affected by matters of the world, there are nevertheless some who are not so troubled by matters of the world. Even as they are involved in mundane matters, they are able to pray with proper intention and fix regular times to learn Torah. And at such times they remove their minds completely from such matters, for they have nothing to do with them, inwardly. But there are also those who, when involved in matters of the world become greatly troubled and worried. As a result, their prayers are inappropriate and they have no time to learn Torah and even when they do learn, their heart is elsewhere, for they are troubled by matters of the world.

From *Sefer Maamorim 5679* (1919) of the Rebbe Rashab, page 339

Emet in the animal soul

...Within the soul, the first two letters of *Havaya* - *yud-hey* - represent the *bitul*, or self nullification of *chochma* and the expansion of intellect within *bina*, as well as strong desire for Godliness, all within the soul. The letter *vov* represents the idea that Godly revelation should permeate the animal soul as well, so that it also becomes nullified to Godliness and desires and yearns for Godliness. This is alluded to by the fifteen letters *vov* that appear in the prayer, *emet veyatziv* that occurs after the *kriat shema*. For, after the *kriat shma*, we say *emet veyatziv venachon ve kayam* ("true and certain, established and lasting..."), all of which confirm and corroborate the soul nullification that we experience during the *kriat shema*. And at first glance, what is the necessity of mentioning this confirmation so many times? If the nullification of *kriat shema* was real ("true"), then we need only mention it once. And if it was not real, then what does it help to "certify" it even one hundred times?

But, the matter is as follows; the nullification that we experience during the *kriat shema* occurs only within our Godly soul. And corroboration of this experience (of nullification during the *kriat shema*) occurs when we also feel it in our animal soul as well. And that is why there are fifteen *vov's*, as in the phrase, "With *vov's* you will connect." The letter *vov* joins [it also means "hook" or "connector"]. It connects the divine soul to the animal soul, so that the nullification of the divine soul penetrates the animal soul as well. This is the *vov* of the name *Havaya*. And in our personal *avoda*, it is the voice of Torah...

From *Sefer Maamorim 5679* (1919) of the Rebbe Rashab, page 639

Two Dynamics

The word *baruch* implies two dynamics; one is from below to above, as written in the Zohar (*Pekudei*, page 261A), which states that the *baruch* at the beginning of *shemonah esreh* is from below to above. It symbolizes the *sephira* of *malchut*, which at this point in our prayers is "blessed" with much spiritual bounty (*ha'alat ma'n*) to be elevated, as the result of the various angels – *chayot*, *seraphim* and *ofanim* – as well as of the prayers of man below. By way of example, when grass grows from seeds, the germination constitutes elevation of the spiritual bounty (*ha'alat ma'n*) that is contained within the seeds. [Nevertheless], there must be a blessing present for the germination to occur in great quantity, as we see regarding the blessing given to Yitzhak ("And Yitzhak sowed...and found one hundred times what he planted, and God blessed him"). Similarly the blessing associated with *malchut* is that it should be full of spiritual bounty (*ha'alat ma'n*) to elevate.

In general, this occurs as a process of arousal from above to incite and elicit an arousal from below. That is, in order for the elevation from below to occur, there must be an arousal from above. An example of this is the statement that "if it weren't for support from above, as reinforcement from above..." as written in Tanya... To enable the Godly soul to refine the animal soul as well as all of its lower physical matters, there must be support from above. Whether regarding the arousal of the divine soul or regarding the refinement of the animal soul, which is the main purpose of elevation of spiritual bounty, there must be a blessing and support from above...

From *Sefer Maamorim 5677* of the Rebbe Rashab

The "fathers" at the beginning of tefila

In order to provide Godly illumination that is within range of the worlds, the *tzimtzum* ("contraction" of God's infinite light) took place. [The resulting] contraction of His infinite light caused it to be hidden. Then, He drew down a thin ray of light, as illumination that is measured and meted in accordance with the level of the worlds, in order to enable the emanation of ten *sephirot*...And that is why we say, *Elokeinu v'Elokei Avoteinu* - "Our God, and God of our fathers..." during the *shemonah esreh*. But, at first glance, why would we first say, "our God" before saying "our fathers?" It would have been more logical to first mention "the God of our fathers" and then "our God."

However, "fathers" in this context refers to the two *sephirot* of *chochma* and *bina*. *Chochma* is completely out of range of God's infinite light, as written, "You created everything with *chochma*..." From the *sephira* of *chochma* and down occurs the spiritual chain of creation (*seder histalshelut*), within which the *sephirot* are in range of one another. But, the *sephira* of *chochma* in relation to God's essential infinite light is totally out of range, as written, "You are One, beyond accounting," implying that there is no comparison whatsoever. In order to enable the emanation of *chochma*, the *tzimtzum* had to take place. That is why we say, *Elokeinu* - "our God," referring to the *tzimtzum*.

For this reason as well, the Torah says (Gen 1:1), *Bereishit bara Elokim* - "In the beginning, *Elokim* created." The "beginning" is *chochma*, as the *targum Yonatan* translated *bereishit* - "with *chochma*." But, *chochma* could only be created from *Elokim*, symbolizing *tzimtzum* or contraction. ...similar to "hairs" which are minimized rays that protrude through the skull, which interrupts the illumination of the mind. The vitality of "hairs" is quite contracted, which is why when we cut them we do not feel any pain. For this reason, it is written (Num 6:5) regarding the *nazir* (one who swears off of wine, for holy purposes), "He should allow the hair of his head to grow." The *nazir* is forbidden to remove the hairs of his head since he is holy, as written (Num 6:8), "he shall be holy..." From a position that is holy and removed, the only descent of Godliness that takes place is via "hairs." This is what is meant by (Daniel 7:9) *Atik yomin yasiv* – "The One of ancient days sat...the hairs of His head are like pure wool." From the level of *Atik yomin*, the influx descends only via "hairs," as written regarding the *nazir* who is on the level of *kadosh* – the influx that he introduces to the world comes through "hairs."

The same is true of the Cohanim, or priests. It is written about them (Yechezkel 44:20), "And they shall not shave their beards, nor shall they let them grow wild..." That is, their heads should be covered with hair because the priests are associated with holiness, as written, "And make them holy..." And it says (Chronicles 1, 23:13), "And separate Aharon and sanctify him, to be holy of holies..." And therefore, the priests had hairs.

But, regarding the Levites, the verse says (Num 8:7), "And pass a razor over their entire bodies," for the Levites were on the level of *tahara* ("purity" as opposed to *kedusha*, or "holiness"). As written (Num. 8:7), "And so should you do in order to purify them..." and therefore it was not necessary for them to possess hairs, since in general the Levites are associated with spiritual levels of *seder histalshelut*, that emerge only after much contraction of His holy light. And on this level of contraction, there is likely to be room for the extraneous powers (opposed to holiness) to gain access [which is why the Levites must be without hair, to prevent this from occurring].

But, the priests, who are on the level of "holiness," must possess hairs, for there is no descent of Godly influx without hairs. Furthermore, the drawing down of holiness that occurs via "hairs" comes from the essence of the infinite Godly light above. They provide a tremendous revelation that prevents the access of the "extraneous forces." However, the illumination that does arrive comes through "hairs" and contraction. This is also what is meant by, *av'a bemazla itcalilu* – "the father and the mother are included in the *mazal*" – implying that the creation of *chochma* takes place only via hairs.

This, then is *Elokeinu v'elokei avoteinu* – "Our God and God of our fathers." "Our God" refers to the *tzimtzum*, while "God of our fathers" refers to the descent of ilumination into the worlds. The influx arrives via "hairs," which are comparable to the letter *vov*, in the shape of a hair, in order to create *chochma* and *bina*, which are *avoteinu* – "our fathers"

In its origin, *Elokeinu* is the original *tzimtzum*, or "contraction" of His infinite light Above. And the following word, *Elokei* ("God of...") represents the descent of the *kav*, which is called *mazal*, as written in the Zohar in the *Idra rabba*, "This precious, holy thread..." And we [add a *vov* to *Elokei*], saying *v'Elokei* - "and the God of..." because there are several contractions that occur during the spiritual descent, before *chochma, bina* and *da'at* are created. There is the contraction of *A"K* and that of the "beard," as written in Tanya...

Now, just as we say *Elokeinu v'Elokei avoteinu* during the *shemonah esreh*, we say *Havaya Elokeinu Havaya...* during the *kriat shema*. The first *Havaya* relates to the saying of the sages, "From before the world was created, there was He and His Name alone." This alludes to the infinite light that preceded the *tzimtzum*. And the second *Havaya* represents the *kav* in general. It contains all four letters of the name *Havaya*. In particular, they are associated with the ten *sephirot* of Atzilut: the *yud* with *chochma*, the *hey* with *bina*, the *vov* with the *midot*, and the final *hey* with *malchut*. And *Elokeinu* alludes to the *tzimtzum* that enabled the emanation of the *kav* and the ten *sephirot* – all this was facilitated by the *tzimtzum*.

(From *Sefer Maamorim 5680* (1920) of the Rebbe Rashab, page 161-162

Refinement of the animal soul

The service of prayer involves refinement of the animal soul, as the verse says, "Man, when you will offer an animal from among yourselves..." This process takes place as we pray, uttering the letters of prayer with arousal of the heart, with love and fear of God, as we are commanded, "And you shall love the Lord your God with all your heart..." This means that we should love Him with both inclinations (the good and the evil)...The Zohar says that an angel "caresses and kisses the letters of prayer in order to polish them..." But, the main act of refinement occurs when we draw down illumination of His holy name (*Ma'ah*), which descends from above as we say [the final paragraph of the shemonah esreh], *Sim shalom* ("Establish peace..."), when the "male drop" descends...

(From *Sefer Maamorim 5680* (1920) of the Rebbe Rashab, Page 229

Prayer and Self Nullification

...prayer is associated with *bitul*, or self nullification. And during the *shemonah esreh*, the self nullification is associated with *chochma*...and for this reason prayer is called *achor* ("after," or "from behind")...as in the verse, "You followed Me from behind..." indicating self-effacement. Another reason why prayer is called "from behind" is that the eighteen blessings of prayer correspond to the eighteen vertebrae of the back bone. And the spinal cord descends down from the faculty of *da'at*, which is at the back of the brain. The faculty of *chochma* is located in front, as written in the verse regarding tefilin, "And they should be for a reminder between your eyes." And the faculty of *da'at* is in back.

The matter is as follows. *Chochma* is equivalent to vision, which apprehends the inner core. It is vision of the essence, but *da'at* is [only] awareness of existence. *Da'at* does include recognition of existence, as known that *da'at* is recognition, But, this recogniztion is only of the intellectual concept. If so, is is only recognition of existence, which is why the faculty of *da'at* is "behind," in the back of the brain.

Now, prayer is associated with *da'at*, as written, "Know the God of your father and serve Him…" implying that service of the heart (prayer) takes place with *da'at*. Prayer takes place with love and fear of God, as in "running and retuning" (*ratzoh veshuv*). Similarly regarding the angels, it is written, "with two they fly," referring to their state of *ratzoh v'shuv*, and the same applies to love and fear of God. And this process takes place in conjunction with the faculty of *da'at*. That is why *da'at* is located between the shoulders, just as the spinal cord descends between the shoulders, meaning between the qualities of love and fear. For, it is known that *da'at* is the "key that includes six" [this is an expression of the Zohar, indicating that *da'at* is the inner vitality that 'unlocks' the emotions, of which there are six].

In order for the Torah to truly illuminate us (*ha'arat panim*), , there must first occur the *avoda* of *achor*. Anyone who says, "I have nothing but Torah," does not really have the Torah either, for prayer, which is the desire and thirst for Godliness must precede it, and then the Torah that descends to him is a revelation of the infinite light. And without this will and desire, how can he draw this down by way of Torah? And therefore, there must be prayer, and then the descendt via Torah may occur…

From *Sefer Maamorim 5678* (1918) of the Rebbe Rashab, Page 202-203S

Ladder of prayer and other ladders
Boruch Atah HaShem…("Blessed are You, Lord…")

"And he [Jacob] dreamt and behold there was a ladder placed on the earth with its head reaching into the heavens, and angels of *Elokim* were ascending and descending upon it."[478]

The Ramban comments[479] that the purpose of a physical ladder is to join and unite what is above with what is below. And so it is Above regarding the task of joining and uniting worlds since there are four worlds (*ABY"A*) as alluded to in the verse, "All that is called in My name [*Atzilut*], and for My honor I created [*Bria*], I formed [*Yetzira*], I even made [*Asiyah*]."[480] The phrase "All that is called in My name" refers to the World of *Atzilut*; "for My honor I created" refers to *Bria*, the world of souls; "I formed" refers to *Yetzira*, the world of angels; and "even made" refers to *Asiya*, the physical world in which we live. Now, the joining of these worlds with one-another is referred to as a "ladder" that connects and unites all of them together. As to the phrase, "And angels of *Elokim* were ascending and descending upon it," this refers to the G-dly influence that comes down into the worlds, descending via the angels of *Elokim* who are "bearers of influence," as in the saying, "There is no blade of grass down here that is without a spiritual counterpart Above that strikes it and tells it to grow."[481]

But, regarding the ladder that Jacob saw in his dream, it is also written, "And *Havaya* stood above it,"[482] meaning above the ladder. This implies that Jewish souls receive their G-dly influence not from the angels, but from G-d's holy name *Havaya*. This is why we say, *Havaya Elokeinu*. *Elokeinu* ("our G-d") connotes ability and potential which translates into influence, and this is why the angels are called "angels of *Elokim*," since they are bearers of influence. However, about Jewish souls, it is written, *Havaya Elokeinu*, since they receive from His holy name *Havaya* itself. Similarly, it is written, "Who…is like our G-d, [Who is near to us] whenever we call Him?" And the *Sifri* remarks, "to Him, and not to His attributes."

*

Now, in the Midrash,[483] there is a story about a wealthy woman who asked Rabbi Yosi ben Halafta, "In how many days did G-d create the world?" He answered, "In six days, as the Torah says, 'In six days G-d created the heavens and the earth.'" She continued, "And what does He do now?" He replied, "He arranges marriage matches." Rabbi Brechia said that he answered differently; "He sits and makes ladders. He brings down this person and elevates that person, he lowers one and uplifts another, in accordance with the verse, 'Elokim judges; this one He lowers and that one He raises.'[484]"

Now, in order to understand what are these "ladders" that G-d makes, let us first understand what is mentioned above: "Who…is like our G-d, [Who is near to us] whenever we call Him?" – that is, to Him and not to His attributes. Yet elsewhere, it states "And to Him you should cling,"[485] and the sages said, "Is it possible to cleave to the Shechina? Rather, cleave to His attributes, meaning that you must conduct yourself in a manner similar to His attributes. Just as He is merciful, so should you be merciful…"[486] However, calling out to G-d must be directly to Him directly and not to His attributes.

But according to this explanation, we still must understand another statement, "Whoever knows My Name, shall call Me and I will answer him."[487] And the Midrash in Tanhuma comments on this verse, "Why do the Jews call upon G-d and fail to receive answers? Because when they call upon Him, they do not know how to focus properly on His Name, but in the future, 'Whoever knows My name shall call Me and I will answer him.'"

Now, names are associated with G-d's supernal attributes. The name Kel is associated with chesed and Elokim with gevura, and the name Havaya with tiferet, etc. The implication is that when we call to G-d, it should be via His attributes. There are those[488] who resolve this apparent contradiction by saying that "to connect with His name" is synonymous with "calling out to Him and not to His attributes." His attributes are what we call kelim ("vessels" to contain His infinite light). For example, the Zohar states that His attribute of chesed ("kindness") corresponds to the "right hand." Accordingly, the right hand is called chesed, meaning that the hand is a keli for chesed, since we do kind deeds using our hands. The hand is only a part of the body, while the soul enclothed in the body is [nonetheless] far above the body. And so it is Above – His attributes are only kelim, while His names are the infinite light about which we say that it "is not associated with any of these attributes whatsoever."[489] But, nevertheless, His names are enclothed in His attributes, the name Kel in chesed etc. … and this is what is meant by "whenever we call out to Him," meaning not to the essence of His attributes but rather to the infinite light of G-d that is enclothed in His attributes…

But, in truth, the simple explanation of what is written, "Whenever we call out to Him," is that it applies to His very essence as He exists even above His names. A name is a mere reflection and ray, as the sages said, "Until the world was created, there was only He and His name alone." "He" and "His name" are two distinct entities, each on its own, and if so, "whenever we call out to Him" means to call out to His very essence, as expressed in the word "He," beyond "His name."

Ultimately, "whenever we call out to Him" applies to our attitude of self-sacrifice during the Shema. [As we recite the] Shema we call out to Him – to His very essence - and not to His attributes. But, "to focus upon His name" applies to the Shemonah Esreh in which we must focus precisely on His name. During the blessing of Ata chonen we must focus on the name Havaya vowelized with a patach, symbolizing a peticha ("opening") leading to chochma and to daat from above chochma … and this is what is meant by "focus properly upon His name."

*

Our self-effacement (bitul) must be directed toward G-d, to His very essence and not toward His attributes. This is not the case, however, regarding the ladder of Elokim, with angels ascending and descending upon it. That ladder is associated only with "the renewal of creation that He, in His goodness, performs every day, at every instant."

And what is the explanation of "the renewal ... in His goodness?" After all, at first glance we see no variation in the creation whatsoever from one day to the next? The sun, for example, progresses constantly in one cycle – today as yesterday, in the same path that was established for it during the six days of creation. The explanation is as follows: "The renewal of creation that He, in His goodness, performs every day, at every instant" refers to creation through His attribute of *chochma*. The pinnacle of the spiritual hierarchy of creation is the *sephira* of *chochma* into which descends a new ray every day that was not present the previous day. Every day the spiritual energy of the previous day departs and returns to its source, and the following day a new ray descends, maintaining the creation of the worlds and the universe. But, this new ray of G-dly energy descends from His holy light after the *tzimtzum* and the emanation of *chochma*. In order for this to occur, there must also be an arousal/initiative from creation below. The arousal is expressed in the desire and the service of the angels, in their "song." The *seraphim* chant *kadosh* ("holy") while the *ofanim* and *chayot* with a great noise ... recite "blessed ("blessed"). And similarly, all of creation sings a song, as is written in *Perek Shira*, and with their song they draw down the [new] energy of the universe, and then "in His goodness He renews..." This is what is meant by "the angels of *Elokim*" who were ascending and descending. To begin with, they ascended, during the stage of song and elevation. And, then, they descended, since by way of their service they draw spirituality down into the lower worlds.

But, the abject *bitul* of souls, nullified "to Him and not to His attributes," draws down a completely new kind of light, as is written, "Establish a new light over Zion."[490] This is a totally new influx, descending from above the *sephira* of *chochma*. And whatever G-d adds [to creation] is enhancement of what He originally established. It augments the spiritual basis and foundation of creation. The basis and foundation, is only an aspect of the natural evolution of creation from *chochma*, and *chochma* – in comparison to what is above it – is "out of range" completely, without any comparison whatsoever. And by way of *bitul* to "Him," we draw down illumination from Above that far transcends *chochma*, and this additional G-dly illumination far transcends the basis and foundation [of creation]...

This, then, is the "ladder" from below to Above, symbolizing ascent, and reaching the heights of the infinite light of G-d. It is a result of absolute *bitul* during the *Shema*, which we utter with total self-nullification, especially during the word *echad*. It comes from the abject nullification of oneself, leaving only desire for G-d Himself and not for His attributes, nor even for His names.

And, now, we must understand why the question and answer of the sages, "Why do the Jews call upon G-d and fail to receive answers? Because, when they call upon Him, they do not know how to focus properly upon His Name." This implies that we are required to focus on His name [not on G-d Himself]. The explanation, though, it that this statement is only in regard to the ladder of descent from Above to below – that may take place only in conjunction with proper intention and focus on His name. That is, [the influx from Above] is brought down by way of the names of G-d, which are associated with His attributes. This takes place during the *Shemonah Esreh*, which constitutes a descent from Above, as we say *Baruch Atah Havaya*...

Now, the *Shemonah Esreh* is also called a "ladder," as written in the Midrash[491] that the "ladder" [of Jacob's dream] alludes to the ramp leading up to the altar [in the Temple]. The ladder was "placed on the earth," just as the altar was filled with earth. And "its head reached into the heavens" just as the aroma of the sacrifices ascended to the heavens. But now, our prayers are in lieu of the sacrifices, and the ladder of prayer consists of the blessings of the *Shemonah Esreh*. Therefore, we must have specific intention and focus on His name while reciting the blessings..

Now, the sages said that the blessings of the *Shemonah Esreh* correspond to the vertebrae of the backbone, and [what did they mean by that?] At first glance, what is the connection between the eighteen blessings and the eighteen vertebrae of the backbone?

For example, man has 248 limbs and 365 connective sinews, all of which are joined together through the eighteen vertebrae of the backbone. The backbone itself stretches all the way from the brain down to the legs and connects them. Similarly, in the spiritual realm, the 248 positive commandments correspond to the 248 limbs of the King,[492] and 365 negative commandments correspond to the 365 sinews. They are joined and connected by way of our prayers, including the eighteen blessings of the *Shemonah Esreh*. It is written, "Keep My laws and my commandments that man should do and you will live by them..."[493] "Live by" alludes to the descent of the infinite light of G-d into the mitzvot through the blessings of the *Shemonah Esreh*. This is what is meant by "and live by," referring to *chai* [which has the numerical value of eighteen and which also means "life"] since in this way infinite illumination from Above permeates the mitzvot with vitality [and intention]. And a mitzvah fulfilled without any intention is like a body without a soul...

Now, prayer provides the connection and coordination between the 248 positive commandments, which correspond to the 248 limbs of "the King." And they in turn are associated with the nine *sephirot* of Z'A, which are His attributes. Since prayer brings influx down into the 248 limbs, we must develop precise focus on His appropriate names. This is the ladder from Above to below, and this is prayer, bringing down influx from Above to below in the form of additional illumination. But, in order for this to occur, it must first be prefaced by the elevation that takes place during the *Shema*, during which we are nullified to G-d, not [just] to His attributes. In this way, afterwards, we bring down additional illumination from G-d into His attributes. This descent occurs during the eighteen blessings of the *Shemonah Esreh*. Therefore, we must focus, using the specific name associated with each attribute, so that, using that name and the blessing that it applies to, we bring down [infinite light] into that attribute, using that specific name [of G-d].

*

Now, just as there is a "ladder" associated with holiness, so is there a ladder associated with the forces of darkness and concealment that are opposed to holiness. As the sages said in Midrash Rabba, the "ladder placed upon the earth" is an allusion to the idols of Nebuchadnezzar (evil king of Babylonia). The word *sulam* ("ladder") is composed of the same letters as the word *semel* ("symbol"), which is the symbol of jealousy. Within the forces opposed to holiness, there is also a "ladder," since the One Above created the universe with a balance between holiness and its opposite, so that whatever exists in the realm of holiness exists on the opposite side as well. That is why, regarding the verse, "And there never arose another prophet among the Jews who was comparable to Moses,"[494] the sages[495] commented that such a prophet did not arise among the Jews, but he did arise among the non-Jews. And who was he? Bilam. Now, Moses prophesied using the word *zeh* ("this"), while all the other Jewish prophets prophesied using the word *koh* ("like this,"). Moses surpassed them. And since Bilam, among the nations, was on the level of prophecy of Moses, we must say that he as well prophesied on the level of *zeh*. But, his *zeh* was from within the realm of darkness, opposed to holiness, as written that G-d created the world *zeh le'umat zeh* ("this corresponding to that"), meaning that He created forces of darkness corresponding to the forces of light and holiness. Thus, there are two aspects to *zeh* – there is the *zeh* of holiness and the *zeh* of *klipah* ("opposition to holiness"). Now, the *zeh* of *klipah* is the ladder of the "other side," opposed to holiness.

Originally upon their creation, the *klipot* were on a very low level, so that only at the bottom of the spiritual pyramid could they receive anything from Above. This is similar to the hair and nails of man, which also receive their life-force from the soul, but only on a very low level, such that we do not experience any physical pain or discomfort when they are cut. This is because the life-force within them is very contracted and limited. And so occurred as well when the *klipot* were created; their life-force came to them in the same way as "hairs" – that is, spiritual energy leftover from a very contracted level of holiness. However, this was prior to the sin of the Tree of Knowledge. But, after the sin of the Tree of Knowledge, they gained strength and received much more energy. And similarly today, after any particular transgression, the *klipot* gain power and leach more energy from the realm of holiness. That is, they bloat themselves up to a very high level, to where "darkness is as light," and each [holiness and its opposite] seems to be equal to each other, and G-d says, "And if you are righteous, so what should I give you?"[496] From this level, the *klipot* are able to receive spiritual influx, [as the illumination is so blinding], the presence of *klipot* goes unnoticed, as it were...

This is what is meant by, "If you raise yourself like an eagle, from there I will bring you down, says G-d."[497] This is the "ladder" of *klipah* which raises itself high in order to receive from a very high level, where "darkness and light are one and the same." This is also the aspect of *zeh* of Bilam, who prophesied with *zeh*. That means that he raised himself to receive from this very high place, and that is why Rabbi Yossi ben Halafta answered the wealthy woman, "G-d makes ladders. He takes down this person..." That is, He lowers the *klipah* and raises the level of holiness. This is what is meant by "He makes ladders," since these two aspects of *zeh* are both ladders...

And ladders (*sulamot*) is in the plural, referring to each and everyone, since each and every one of us has a "ladder" inside. This is what is meant by "He takes down this one, and elevates that one," for He takes down the *zeh* of *klipah* and elevates the ladder of holiness...

(From *Sefer Maamorim 5655* (~1895) of the Rebbe Rashab, pp. 40-49)

More on the Ladder of Prayer

Regarding the command in the *kriat shema*, "You shall love the Lord your God...", we must ask, how is this appropriate as a command? Love only occurs between those who are similar to one another, such as between people. But, how is it appropriate to speak of love of God, Who is totally out of our range?

The semantic root of the word "love" (*ahava*) is from the word *ava*, meaning "will," or "desire"; specifically here, it refers to desire for the essential infinite One above. When we mediate upon how "You are one, and all is as naught before You," and therefore, "I am the Lord, I have not changed," this implies that God has not changed one iota from before the universe was created until after it was created. [Furthermore], the entire creation stems from a mere ray and reflection of Godliness. Meditation on this concept leads us to experience an intense desire for the essence of the Infinite One. Now, this desire surpasses the *kelim*, or mental vessels which would otherwise contain it, since at this point what we desire is beyond revelation of Godliness. Godliness is expressed as revealed illumination within the *kelim*, but in this instance we do not seek revelation. We seek, rather, to completely transcend the *kelim* [which otherwise limit Godly revelation]. And in so doing, we draw down additional illumination to descend into the spiritual hierarchy of creation (*seder hishtalshelut*) from the very essence of Godliness. And the "additional illumination" from God is over and above the principal illumination [that is always present].

The basic vitality of the spiritual hierarchy of creation comes from a mere ray [of Godliness that enlivens the creation] from out of our range. However, via our intense desire, mentioned above, we draw down a truly new level of illumination, as written [in the prayers of the siddur, in *birchot kriat shema*], "a new light will illuminate over *tzion*." We describe the process as "calling out to Him" – to the very essence of the infinite One, accompanied by utter self sacrifice during the *kriat shema*...and in this manner we may say that [we draw down] a truly new illumination.

Now, regarding the power within Jewish souls to call out directly to God and thus to draw down the new illumination – the Ari z'l writes that although the *tanaim* [sages of the Mishna, who lived during and after the second temple period] were souls from the world of *bria*, and the *amoraim* [sages of the gemora, who lived after the destruction of the second Temple] from the world of *yetzira*, current souls are mostly from the world of *asiya* – so, how can we hope to achieve this ability to "call to Him" and draw down such new light?

But the truth is, [their lowly spiritual status] is precisely what confers upon them their ability. For, it is the lowly souls of *asiya* who have it within their power, because of their nullified status, to reach the very essence of Godliness. For, "the end is wedged in the beginning" – the high level of their origin remains an integral part of such souls even as they descend to this world. That is, the souls of *asiya*, with their nullified status, reach further. And for this very reason they experience a greater rush and desire [for Godliness]. Their desire leads them to more easily "give themselves up" for the sake of Godliness. The advantage found in higher souls such as the *tanaim* and the *amoriaim* lay in their knowledge and grasp [of Godliness], which was on a much higher level. But, as known, intellect actually obscures the Godly essence. Although the *tanaim* and *amoraim* certainly experienced *reuta deliba*, the "will of the heart" that transcends intellect and logic, even this desire, within such higher souls, develops as the result of meditation on the transcendent nature of the infinite One. That is, cognizance of the wonderful nature of the infinite One, is the result of the technique known as *yediat hashlila* ("negative," or circumscribed knowledge, during which we negate whatever knowledge and understanding we do attain, saying that 'God is not this, He is beyond this'). The "will of the heart" that results from such meditation is truly on a very high level, appropriate to one is nullified within. But, nevertheless, the intellect has an influence, and because of the influence of the intellect, the soul also experiences enjoyment, and if so, this is not real "self-sacrifice." Even though their desire [was intense to the point of] expiry of the soul, nevertheless it was not sufficient to cause true and total exit from their *kelim*, or faculties of their soul ("vessels"), since enjoyment [of Godliness] was also mixed in with the experience..

However, the "will of the heart" (*reuta deliba*) experienced by souls from the world of *asiya* is not the result of meditation, for such souls do not undertake "negative knowledge" (*yediat hashlila*). Nor do they perceive awareness of the lofty nature (*yediat hahafla'ah*) of Godliness. The most they are aware of is that Godliness is "out of range." And therefore, their desire for Godliness leads to [true] self-sacrifice (*mesirat nephesh*). That is, it leads to true exit from their *kelim*, or faculties of their soul (even though their true level of *mesirat nephesh* is far less than that of higher level souls). Furthermore, it is easier for such souls to achieve the self sacrifice of *mesirat nephesh*, because their path to direct revelation of the essence is more direct [they need not utilize and involve their intellect to such a great degree].

Furthermore, the souls who currently inhabit the world of *asiya* are souls enclothed in a body. The *tanaim* and *amoraim*, who were souls of *bria* and *yetzira* were also enclothed in bodies that were from *bria* and *yetzira*. They may have been present in the world of *asiya*, but they existed in *asiya* only in transition – their [Godly awareness] was not minimized, nor did they adopt any of the characteristics of the world of *asiya*. For example, the Rashbi (redactor of the Zohar) and the Rosh Mesivta, who were souls from the world of *Atzilut*, also had to pass through the worlds of BY"A, but they were merely "in transit." Our souls, however, are truly enclothed in the world of *asiya* [the difference between "in transit" and "enclothed" has to do with whether or not the lower worlds exert influence upon the soul. Higher souls that are only "in transit" in the world of *asiya* are not affected by this world, while lower souls that are "enclothed" in *asiya* are affected and influenced by this world].

Nevertheless, each and every soul has a source and origin in the world of *Atzilut*. We all arise in the morning and say, "The soul that You have placed within me is pure, You created it..." And the word "pure" (*tehora*) refers to the source of the soul as it exists in the world of *Atzilut* and above. And when we stimulate this source of the soul from below, even though the lower component of the soul is on the level of *nephesh* (instinct) alone, nevertheless, the *ruach* [second, emotional level of the soul], located in the world of *yetzira* also becomes aroused. (It is possible that all levels of the soul - the *naranchai* (*nephesh, ruach, neshama, chaya* and *yechida*) - are included within one another. [And if so, this stimulation] continues up to the highest level of the soul, the *yechida* in the world of *Atzilut*, which is equivalent to praying "to He Himself" [*eilav*, and not to His attributes alone].

This, then is what constitutes [love of God] "with all your might" – meaning, "with all that You are." When the soul below is ignited with the "will of the heart," unrestrained by any limitations, this creates a stimulus on all of the levels of the soul above. And all of them respond "with all their might," without limitations (because this elevation that occurs within the source of the soul, is initiated by the component of the soul that is enclothed within the body...).

A similar and corresponding elevation takes place in the higher spiritual worlds. This is similar to what occurs, by way of example when one places a lever underneath the lowest beam of a wall. He is then able to lift up the entire wall. Similarly, elevation of the soul in the physical world leads to elevation in all of the higher worlds. This then is what occurs as the result of meditation according to logic and intellect (in the service of God) - by refinement below, we affect refinement above. As written elsewhere, every act of refinement that man performs below within his own realm of existence (*yesh*) creates impetus for refinement above, even within the *kelim*, or "vessels" of the world of *Atzilut*. Similarly, the "will of the heart" within stimulates arousal in all of the worlds, producing an intense desire, which penetrates all the way up to the very essence of the infinite light. And this in turn stimulates a descent from above, bringing down addition illumination, over and beyond the principal illumination [that is always present]. This occurs during the *shemonah esreh*, during the twelve intermediate blessings during which we submit our own individual requests [to God].

As known, [all that occurs down here in the physical world] has a spiritual counterpart above. When we request a *refuah shleimah* ("a full and complete recovery" from illness or injury), the spiritual response from above is expressed in the words (from Song of Songs), "surround me with fires...for I am love-sick" [in the symbolism of Chassidut, one who pines for Godly revelation but is unable to attain it is said to be "love-sick"]. And our request for physical income and sustenance (*birchat hashanim*) is comparable to *ha'alat ma'n*, or "stimulation from below" [for the purpose of bringing down Godly influence from Above, as already explained]. [In order to achieve these aims], we need, during the *shemonah esreh*, to maintain focus on the name of God that corresponds to illumination from each of the appropriate *sephirot*. For example, during the blessing *atah chonen leadam da'at* ("You bless man with knowledge..." we focus on the name of God vowellized with a *patach*, and during the blessing *vehashiveinu*, we focus on His name vowellized with a *tzeiri*, and during the blessing *refaeinu*, we focus upon His name vowellized with a *cholem*.

There is yet another explanation of "to focus upon His Name," and that is, to bring down additional illumination from the very essence of the One above to within His name. Now, this occurs as we preface the *shmonah esreh* with true devotion (*mesirat nephesh*) during the *kriat shema*. At that time, we pray "to Him," may He be blessed. This, then is the meaning of the ladder [Jacob's ladder, that he perceived in his dream while sleeping on the Temple Mount], with "God (*Havaya*) standing over it." In kabalistic terms, this is an allusion to the inner unity of *av'a* ("father and mother," or *chochma* and *bina* – insight and intellectual analysis), which elicits influx from the inner essence of the Infinite one. It takes place as we call "to Him," with intense devotion during the *kriat shema*. This is what is meant by the "ladder of ascent," from below to above. And in this manner we elicit a descent from Above to below during the *shemonah esreh*.

In truth, both dynamics occur during the *shemonah esreh*, There is both elevation, and descent. Prayer was established corresponding to the constant burnt offerings [that were brought to the temple in the mornings and afternoons]. The offerings themselves represented both elevation and descent, as alluded to in the phrase *re'ach nicho'ach leHashem* ("a pleasant aroma for God") – the "aroma" alludes to elevation, while the word "pleasant" alludes to descent. Similarly, within prayer, there is our silent prayers, followed by the repetition of the *shemonah esreh*, recited aloud.

Our verse says, "The voice is the voice of Yakov." The first time that the word "voice" (*kol*) occurs in the verse, it lacks the middle letter, which is a *vov*. The *vov* indicates descent, and [since it is lacking], the first "voice" [represents the dynamic] from below to Above. This is demonstrated in the episode of Chana, who prayed and "her voice was not heard." That is, she prayed inaudibly. This is also called the "prayer of a poor person." It is associated with the *sephira* of *malchut*, which the Zohar compares to the moon, saying that "it has nothing of its own." For, this level of prayer is about elevation from below to above...

...The second time that the verse mentions "voice," it is spelled with the middle letter *vov*. It symbolizes that repetition of the *shemonah esreh* that is repeated out loud, representing descent from Above to below. And that is why it is repeated in a loud voice, as the sages said regarding the verse, "And the Levites answered, saying in a loud voice (*kol rom*)" – with a voice that is *rom*, "elevated" – meaning that the voice descended from a great elevation, from the infinite light Above...

And this is what is meant by, "A prayer for Moshe..." This indicates a prayer of wealth and riches, alluding to descent of Godliness from above. The wealthy person lacks nothing, and has no connection whatsoever to anything that is deficient. The verse from the Torah that instructs us to give *tzedako* says, *dai m'chasoro* – "enough to make up for whatever he is lacking" – and this refers to a poor person, to whom we must provide whatever he is lacking. But, the wealthy person lacks nothing, and so it is not appropriate at all to speak of "meeting his deficiencies"...In regard to prayer, this refers only to prayer during which Godly influx descends to us, as written in the *Yalkut* regarding Moshe's prayers, "God said to Moshe, 'what do you desire?' Moshe answered, "I desire nothing for myself, but this country is devastated and it is Yours, decree that it should be rebuilt." "This country" refers to the *sephira* of *malchut*, and it is "devastated" [following the destruction of the Temple and the subsequent exile] meaning that it is lacking and deficient. So, Moshe requested from God, "decree that it be rebuilt," as an everlasting edifice...this is what is meant by descent of Godliness from Above to below.

And that is what is alluded to by the *sulam*, or "ladder." The *gematria* (numerical value) of *sulam* is the same as *kol*, or "voice." The word *sulam* may be written either with a *vov* or without a *vov*, just as the word *kol*, or "voice" mentioned above that may be written with or without a *vov*, indicating either ascent or descent. Now, the level of *bitul*, or self nullification associated with prayer is very high, as in the verse *v'atem tacharishun* – "you be utterly still" – because there are no words on our tongue, aside from the phrase, "Lord, please open my lips." Nevertheless, our request stimulates a descent from the very essence of the infinite One. And that is what is meant by, "And behold he dreamt and there was a ladder..." The general theme of the ladder is the joining of creation with the infinite light above, which occurs when creation is nullified. And, therefore the ladder alludes to the *sephira* of *malchut*, and the descent to within it [occurs as the holy light first enters] and is enclothed in *z'a*, which are the six emotional *sephirot* that precede *malchut*. But, the principal descent, that takes place from the very essence of the infinite illumination, brings down a "new light" via of the inner unity of *av'a*, which are the higher intellectual *sephirot* of *chochma* and *bina*. This takes place as we devote ourselves with ultimate dedication (*mesirat nephesh*) during the *kriat shema*, "to Him and not to His attributes," to the essential infinite One above. And this then elicits a descent from His essence, of "additional light" to within the spiritual confines of creation (*seder hishtalshelut*), over and beyond the constant illumination that is always present.

From *Sefer Maamorim 5679* (1919) of the Rebbe Rashab, page 114-116

Songs of Angels and Souls

We find that angels sing a song, but we do not find that souls sing. And the truth is that souls also sing their song, for souls are in a state of perpetual ascent, in a state of "running and returning" (*ratzoh v'shuv*). And every ascent is accompanied by song, as in the statement of the Mishnah, "All the masters of song go out with a song and are led by song." However, we do not find this written in the Torah. And this is because the song of angels is heard in the ears of the prophets, as written (in the prayer, *uvah letzion*), "And I heard the sound of a great noise behind me." And the song was actually a voice, as written, "And I heard the voice of their wings...and sounding off in fear, together in one voice....and the *ofanim* and the holy *chayot* with a great noise..."

And this is because the angels possess bodies, as written, "He created His angels as spirits, serving with flames of fire," referring to their bodies. Their souls are composed of intellect and intellectual grasp, about which it is not appropriate to say "fiery flames." This can only apply to their bodies, as the Ramban *z'l* writes, that their bodies come from the fundamental basic element of wind and from the basic element of fire. The camp of the angel Michael is composed of angels whose bodies are from the spiritual element of wind, and the camp of the angel Gabriel is composed of angels whose bodies come from the spiritual element of fire. And that is why they are connected to space, for there are angels who travel the distance normally covered in "five hundred years," and there are those whose "size" is "one third of the universe," while Michael traverses the universe in one leap, and Gabriel in two...All this is because they possess bodies and therefore they are connected to space. And it is for this reason that their song takes place with a voice, for the voice is a garment...and since they are enclothed in bodies, therefore their song takes place within the garment of a voice, which is heard in the ears of the prophets.

However, the song of souls is not heard by the prophets, for souls above do not possess bodies, as known. And therefore, their song does not occur as a voice. And if so, we can say that their [song] is the *kol demama daka* – the "still small voice." Wind, noise and fire represent the three worlds of BY"A, and the "still small voice" is in the world of Atzilut. That is why it is written, "And Havaya was not in the wind," And, "*Havaya* was not in the noise..." since the main expression of *Havaya* takes place in the world of Atzilut, which is characterized by absolute nullification of the self (*bitul b'mtziut*), devoid of any feeling whatsoever. As in the *shemonah esreh*, which is the quiet prayer. For, the *pesukei dezimra* and the blessings preceding the *kriat shema* and the *kriat shema* all take place with excitement and arousal while the *shemonah esreh* is a still, small voice, "there is where the King is." It is known that the *shemonah esreh* is associated with Atzilut, where the level of nullification is *bitul b'metziut*. And souls above are in Atzilut and therefore their song is of the same category as the *kol demama daka*, the "still small voice."

Although this is within the essence of the soul, for the wind, noise and fire is associated with the *nefesh ruach* and *neshama* of the soul, while the *kol demama daka* is in the essence of the soul. The soul as it exists in Atzilut is the essence of the soul, about which we say, "The soul that You placed within me is pure..." referring to the essence of the soul, and afterward we say, 'You created, Your formed, You made..." But, it is possible to say that the *nefesh ruach* and *neshama* as they exist in Atzilut are also on the level of the *kol demama daka*, for in the *Tikunei Zohar* it says, "There is noise, and there is noise...there is noise that is not the noise of *Havyaya* and there is noise that is the noise of *Havaya*." That is, *nefesh, ruach* and *neshama* in Atzilut, where everything is absolutely nullified. In particular, the four letters of *Havaya* occur in the *kol demama daka*; the *yud* of the name *Havaya* is *chochma, aba ilaa mekanena* in Atzilut, and in general the *bitul* of *chochma* permeates Atzilut...

From *Sefer Maamorim 5679* (1919) of the Rebbe Rashab, pp. 399-400

Prayer as a struggle to join

On the words (uttered by our fore-mother Leah as she named her newborn son, Naftali), "Struggles (*B'naftulei*) with *Elokim*, I have wrestled (*naftalti*)..." there are four explanations. The Targum Onkelos explains that the word is related to "prayer" (*tefila*), as in the verse, "*Elokim* accepted my request..." Rashi mentions in the name of R' Menachem ben Saruk that it is from the word *petil*, meaning "joined," as in "close-fitting (*tzamid petil*), which also implies joining, since Leah said, "And I joined with my sister." Rashi himself explains that the word indicates dogged determination and clever persistence, as in the phrase, *ikeish u'phtaltel* ("stubborn and persistent"). He further explains that this means, "I stood my ground and persisted, with a lot of repeated requests, and wrestled with the One above." Thus, it indicates stubbornness, including repeated declarations and requests. And the Midrash Raba explains that it is from the phrase, *nofet li* ("sweet to me") referring to the Torah, about which we say that it is "sweeter than honey, even from the comb." This was said in regard to the portion of the tribe of Naftali in the holy Land, while the word *li* has the numerical value of forty, alluding to the Torah which was given in a period of forty days.

In truth, "prayer" and "joining" are one concept. For, prayer (*tefila*) also indicates joining, as in the phrase "one who joins (*tofel*) the pieces of a ceramic utensil." And if so, the two definitions are really one and the same. In fact, we might say that all four definitions are one. Prayer and joining are one, and as Rashi explains that the word means dogged determination, this also occurs during *tefila*, which includes repetition of many words and requests. Nevertheless, this matter of repeated requests implies a yet deeper meaning, as will be explained...

Now, to understand the "joining" that takes place during prayer (*tefila*). The purpose of prayer is to join the infinite light above with the emanations (*sephirot*) and the creations. This is why we say, "Pray to the Living God..." "Living God" (*Kel Chai*) corresponds to the *sephira* of *yesod*, which is nicknamed *chai haolamot* ("life of the worlds"), denoting the spiritual vitality of creation. And it is written, "You enliven them all," wherein "You" (*attah: aleph-tav-hey*) refers to the letters from aleph to *tav*, including the five organs of enunciation [hinted in the letter *hey*, of gematria five, in the word *attah*]...this, however is a mere ray [that descends to the world], and it does not include the essential illumination of the world of *Atzilut*, but rather a superficial reflection alone...that is, it descends from the *sephirot* of *netzach* and *hod*, which are the "organs of counsel," which channel the light of *Atzilut* to lower levels, but do not include the illumination as it exists in *Atzilut* itself, but rather only as it descends to the lower worlds of BY"A. This is the influx flowing through *yesod*....

And this illumination becomes less and less as it descends from one level to the next. On the higher levels, it shines as a revealed level of light, and the more that it descends downward it becomes minimized, until ultimately it does not shine in a revealed manner. This is what is meant by "To the Living God," meaning that we desire to bring down additional illumination, *Kel Chai*, through our *tefila*.

Now, it is written, "A ladder standing upon the ground, with its head reaching into the heavens." This refers to *makifim*, or "transcendent spiritual levels." These are the highest of all transcendent levels, preceding the *kav* ("ray of light" that descends to create the universe). From this level (*igul hagadol*), additional light descends to within the *kav*, and from there it bcomes revealed illumination in the lower worlds as well...and this takes place when Jews pray below. For, in general, prayer is inseparable from meditation, as the sages said, "If man directs his heart, then his prayer is acceptable." That is, prayer is dependent upon the intention of our heart, which in turn is dependent upon meditation upon Godly topics. And the main point of prayer is to cleave our souls and unite them with Godliness. For this reason, a main component of prayer is *da'at* (visceral knowledge, or recognition), as written, "Know the God of your father, and serve Him...' For, *da'at* is focus during meditation, to the extent that the concept under consideration becomes a Godly concept. And with this "recognition," we cleave and unite ourselves with a very strong bond. This is similar to how an infant recognizes his father, and clings to him, drawn after him with great longing; in fact he is unable to separate from him. This is the manner in which Avraham, at three years old, recognized his Creator. And in this manner he cleaved to Godliness and was drawn after Him with total devotion. So it is during prayer – our *da'at* and recognition of Godliness should cause us to cleave and unite our soul with Godliness in such a manner that we are inseparable. And then, *k'mayim hapanim el hapanim* ("like a reflection in water, face to face..."), so the heart of supernal man collects with man below, joining Godliness with the creation. That is, from the infinite light Above, additional illumination is drawn down into the *kav*, in order to cause joining and revelation of Godliness in the world. For the *kav* itself, as it descends, contains concealed light which does not shine in a revealed manner. And revelation takes place only when additional illumination shines within the *kav*. And that occurs when Jewish souls cleave with cleave with and unite with Godliness...

...Now, meditation on how all creation is nothing more than a mere ray alone, and is out of range of the essence of Godliness, also includes the desire for the very essence of the infinite One. Yet, this desire does not occur spontaneously. Rather, it is the result of meditation. And this meditation is focused only upon the ray and revelation of how they ("creation") are "out of range." And therefore it produces a strong desire [within us] to become subsumed and included [in Godliness above], and thus the desire does not arise of its own.

However, the essential will is not a desire at all, but rather wells up and occurs without any desire or direction whatsoever. This will is an expression of the supernal will that is granted from Above, since it is not within the power of man to achieve this with his own power. It is given to him from above. And that occurs only after we have first developed the lower will that occurs according to logic and intellect. We belabor ourselves in meditation and arousal of love and fear of God, and then from Above we are granted a revelation of divine will that is beyond logic and intellect. And this revelation occurs during prayer. It is for this reason that prayer is called a *sulam,* or ladder. A ladder has four rungs, which symbolize the four levels of prayer, corresponding to the soul levels of *nephesh, ruach, neshama* and *neshama* of *neshama* (*chaya* and *yechida*). Up until the prayer *Baruch she'amar,* we pray with our *nephesh,* corresponding to *hoda'ah* ("acknowledgment," or thankfulness). The prayer *Baruch she'amar* and *pesukei dezimra* correspond to *ruach,* the *birchot kriat shema* and *the kriat shema* itself correspond to *neshama,* after which we arrive to the essential will mentioned above.

And on this level, we call "to Him," and not to His attributes, for with this level of prayer, we reach the very essence of the infinite One. And we might say that this is what Rashi means when he explains the word *tefila* ("prayer") as "much prayer, with repeated requests..." Normal prayer implies cleaving and unity of the soul, as described above, while the essential will is expressed as "much prayer" (*ribui tefila*), implying intense effort and repetition within our prayers. This is what is meant by "I was stubborn and persistent."

From *Sefer Maamorim 5619* (1919) of the Rebbe Rashab, pages 169-174

ENDNOTES to CHASSIDIC EXCERPTS

1. The Chasidic exposition, *Kuntres inyana shel Torat haChasidus* (*Kehos*) is dedicated to this statement of the sages, and explains it on all four levels of *Pardess*.

2. It is general because it lacks details of intellect or emotion, as it comes from the essence of the soul before it takes on any intellectual or emotional form.

3. Nusach of prayers in the morning, prior to morning blessings

4. Psalms 119:62

5. Deut. 30:15

6. Deut. 23:10

7. For explication, see *Sefer Hamaamorim Kuntresim* 1, of the Previous Rebbe (HaRav Yoseph Yitzhak), Page 328 (the discourse entitled *Na'aseh na aliyas* of the year 5691, which is also printed in *Sefer Maamorim 5691*, Page 204)

8. Ex. 12:12

9. In the text of the Passover Hagada

10. Deut. 26:8

11. Ex. 15:19

12. There are three levels described here; the first is G-dliness prior to creation, in which there was only the potential for creation. The second level is G-d as He lowered Himself to create and to relate to His creation. And the third refers to the future, when the same exalted level of G-dliness that preceded creation will then permeate the creation.

13. The "left side" corresponds to *gevura* ("judgment"), with which we critique ourselves, becoming aware of our own failings and therefore nullifying our egos in order to rectify and improve ourselves. Thus, the left side "repels" the ego, minimizing it.

14. Lev 6:3

15. Ibid, verse 4

16. Numbers 28:2

17. Targum Onkelos.

18. Deut. 4:24

19. Kings 1, 19:12

20. *Ezekiel* 1:26

21. Intro, *P'tach Eliyahu*, in reference to the *sephirot*.

22. Samuel 1, 15:29

23. *Tikunei Zohar*, Introduction 2

24. *Midrash Zuta Shir haShirim* 1:13

25. Deut. 28:1-8

26. *Vayikra Raba* 4:8, as well as *Talmud Berachot* 10A
27. Job 19:26
28. Representing the *sefira* of *malchut* of the World of *Atzilut*. The altar was located out in the courtyard to indicate that *malchut* descends to the lower worlds of *Bria, Yetzira* and *Asiya* in order to elevate sparks of holiness.
29. Lev. 1:7
30. Lev. 1:2. The simple meaning of the verse is "when a man from among you brings a sacrifice." An important Chasidic interpretation is that "from among you" refers to from within man himself – when man wishes to bring an offering from within himself – and sacrifice his "animal soul."
31. The laws of Shabbat preclude any process of refinement (*borer*) in which we remove what is unwanted ("bad") from what is desired ("good"). This physical process has its spiritual corollary in the refinement of our *midot*, in which we seek to uproot our bad qualities while preserving and amplifying our positive traits. Thus, Shabbat is not dedicated to this form of refinement and self-improvement, but rather to a higher process of work upon ourselves...
32. Isaiah 58:14
33. Psalms 150
34. Gen. 48:22
35. Num. 28:2
36. Gen. 2:7
37. Psalms 139:16
38. Psalms 90:10
39. First Book of Chronicles 4:23.
40. Yehezkel 1:26
41. Eccl. 3:22
42. Isaiah 66:1
43. *Taanit* 27
44. *Taanit* 26A
45. Psalms 100:2
46. In *Ofan* 239.
47. *Taanit* 27A
48. Since the purpose of the offering was to bring the person closer to G-d, it was incumbent on the person to be present at the time of the offering.
49. This short paragraph is the very end of the discourse, on page 57
50. *Yirmiyahu* 15:1
51. The Chasidic exposition, *Kuntres inyana shel Torat haChasidus* (*Kehos*) is dedicated to this statement of the sages, and explains it on all four levels of *Pardess*.
52. Talmud *Berachot* 59B
53. Although this verse does not appear in Psalm 113 (it is in Psalm 96:12), nevertheless it is applicable to *pesukei dezimra* in general (associated with the world of *Yetzira*), which begin with this section.
54. Psalms 96:12.
55. Psalms 104:31.
56. Genesis 1:11.
57. *Breishit Raba* 10:6
58. In the blessings preceding the recitation of the *Shema*.
59. Psalms 104:14

60. *Ohr Hachaim* 101 and 582

61. One is encouraged to pray out loud (but not loud enough to disturb others) during the rest of the prayers. Only during *shemonah esreh* is it required to pray quietly.

62. Psalms 100:5

63. Talmud Yerushalmi *Berachot* 12A

64. Mishna, Talmud Babli *Berachot* 5

65. Talmud Babli *Yevamot* 105B

66. *Divrei Hayamim* (Chronicles) 1, 28:9

67. *Divrei Hayamim* (Chronicles)1, 22:9

68. *Zohar*, Sect 1, pp. 223A,

69. Isaiah 2:2

70. Psalms 84:3

71. Kings 1, 19:11-12

72. *Zohar*, Sect. 2, 185A; *Raya Mehemna*, Sect 3, 123B and 127B; Intro to *Tikunei Zohar* 3B

73. Psalms 33:6

74. Psalms 149:6

75. Continuation of Psalms 149:6

76. Genesis 1:1

77. Psalms 145:8

78. From Psalms 33:9

79. The term *radla* is an acronym for *reisha d'lo ityada* meaning literally, "the origin which is unknown."

80. Psalms 148:5

81. Psalms 145:5

82. "Reflected illumination" is as much a part of creation as the "direct illumination" that descends to the world via the *kav*, in order to create the universe as *orot bekelim* ("lights in vessels," or contained G-dly illumination). The best way to explain "reflected light" is with a *mashal*, or parable; in this case, of sunlight. As the light of the sun reaches the earth, we would expect it to become colder and colder, as it becomes more and more distant from the sun. However, what we actually find is that the temperature is greater next to the earth than at higher altitudes. This illustrates the concept of "reflected light"; when the rays of sunlight strike the earth, they reflect or "bounce" off the ground with great intensity, resulting in generation of more heat near the earth than higher up. As a matter of fact, the greater the altitude, the colder it gets, once more illustrating that where the light reflects off the earth is where there is the greatest energy level. In *Baruch She'Amar*, then, as the creative light descends from above to below, there is a corresponding, but opposite illumination of light from below to above, of "reflected light." But, reflected light, while intense, is also diffuse. It is not as directed and predictable as is the light of direct illumination that shines from above to below, *orot bekelim*. It has more of the character of *makif*, or transcendent illumination, that does not shine as illumination within vessels, but "surrounds" and "envelopes," rather than permeates within. So, the beginning phrases of the prayer, according to the Mitteler Rebbe, deal with the holy light of "direct illumination," while the subsequent phrases allude to various levels of "reflected illumination."

83. Genesis 1:1

84. Genesis 2:4

85. The subject of *ohr yosher* and *ohr chozer* receives detailed treatment in *Sefer*

Maamorim 5649 of the Rebbe Rashab, Pp. 233-261 (esp. 254-258). On page 254, "In general, *igulim* and *yosher* ("spherical and linear") are equivalent to *ratzoh ve'shuv* ("running and returning"). And as explained earlier at length, *igulim* occurs when the vessel is too small to contain the G-dly light, and [as a consequence] the light is a general light that does not settle into the vessel, so it automatically "runs" (ascends) above...and *yosher* occurs when the vessel is expansive, and provides a settled location [for the light], corresponding to *shuv*, since the light settles into the vessel. And this is the concept of *ohr yashar* and *ohr chozer*, since the *shuv* of *yosher* corresponds to *ohr yosher* that descends to be enclothed in a vessel, while the *ratzoh* of *igulim* is in general called *ohr chozer*, since it "returns" [ascends] to its original position to be included in its source..." Hence, *ohr yashar* is associated with the ordered, intellectual service of G-d, based upon meditation (known as *yosher*, or "linear"). And *ohr chozer* is mainly associated with the uncontrollable desire of the soul to abandon the body and cleave to G-d, also known as *igulim* ("spherical").

However, on closer examination, we find that *ohr chozer* may be associated with *yosher*, as well as with *igulim*. On page 257, "The difference between *ohr chozer* of *igulim* and *ohr chozer* of *yosher*, is that *ohr chozer* of *igulim* is mainly the desire for spiritual ascent but not for descent below. So, automatically the ascent takes place without limitations, with expiry of the soul to be included in the very essence of G-dliness, in totality. And the *ohr chozer* of *yosher* places emphasis upon the *shuv*, "return" [to meaningful life in the physical world], and the "run" (spiritual ascent) is in order to achieve the *shuv*. And for this reason, the ascent itself, with expiry of the soul, is [nevertheless] limited and measured..."

See also *Torah Chaim* of the Mitteler Rebbe, in the discourse, *Vayitein lecha*, section 2, and the discourse *Samchuni b'Ashishut 5660* of the Rebbe Rashab.

86. Genesis 1:11.

87. Yonah 4:11

88. Psalms 33:6

89. Genesis 2:15.

90. Chasidic literature distinguishes between what we might call "applied vitality" ("life that enlivens") and "essential vitality" ("life in essence"). "Essential vitality" (*chai be'etzem*) is the essence of life itself. It needs no reason or purpose for its existence, it simply is – it corresponds to the internal dimension of the *sephira* of *chochma*. It serves as the origin of "applied vitality" (*chai lehachayot*) which is the life-energy that flows like an extension of the soul into the body in order to enliven it.

91. Rabbi Eliezer ben Durdaya in the Talmud expired while crying with regret over his negative past.

92. Jeremiah 3:22

93. The details were of course known to G-d, but they were not evident from within this specific level of His pure, undifferentiated will.

94. Genesis 1:1

95. Proverbs 9:1

96. Psalms 89:3

97. As is written in *Yom Tov shel Rosh Hashana, 5666.*

98. Nehemia 9:6

99. Genesis 2:20

100. Chronicles 1, 29:11

101. Zecharia 3:7

102. Psalms 145:12.

103. Nusach of *Baruch She'amar*
104. Nusach of *Baruch She'amar*
105. Ex. 15:11
106. Psalms 65:2
107. Talmud *Berachot* 17A
108. *Musaf* of Shabbat and Yom Tov
109. The light of *memalle kol olamim* expresses itself in our intellectual and emotional awareness. When our intellect and emotions predominate, we are less aware of the G-dliness (*sovev kol olamim*) that transcends us.
110. In the future, our intellectual and emotional awareness will function on a higher level, one that includes awareness of transcendent factors. This is because the levels of the soul that are now transcendent (the *chaya* and *yechida*) will become en-clothed in the body in the future. Thus, our present awareness will be subsumed in a higher spiritual awareness – one that includes the transcendent soul-levels of *sovev kol olamim*.
111. Psalms 2:9
112. Samuel 1, 2:3
113. Intro to the *Zohar*, Sect 1, 11B
114. Psalms 84:3.
115. Job 37:22.
116. Song of Songs 3:10.
117. *Zohar* Sect. 1, 199A
118. There is, of course intellect and emotion involved as we meditate and pray during the *pesukei dezimra*. However, they are of a lesser level than during the *shema* and *shemonah esreh*, when we place emphasis upon the "inner mindfulness" associated with the more advanced stages of prayer.
119. Song of Songs 1:15, 4:1
120. *Chulin* 60a.
121. Exodus 23:21
122. Exodus 23:22
123. See Rashi on these verses.
124. Isaiah 25:5
125. Psalm 149
126. Exodus 25:8.
127. Deuteronomy 20:19.
128. Psalms 84:5-6.
129. Psalms 145.
130. Job 29:3.
131. *Berachot* 4.
132. Ezekiel 17:13.
133. Psalms 145:13.
134. Psalms 145:12
135. *Eruvin* 65A
136. Deut. 6:7
137. Psalms 73:25.
138. *Pesachim* 3B, *Chulin* 63B
139. Talmud *Avoda Zarah* 5B
140. Psalms 145:14-15.
141. Psalms 145:17.

142. Zohar, Section 1, 35A
143. Genesis 1:5
144. Eccl. 2:14
145. Psalms 18:12
146. End of parshat Noach
147. Isaiah 6:2
148. Ezekiel 3:12
149. Isaiah 26:9
150. Lamentations 3:6
151. The written Torah is the source of inspiration, thus it is comparable to *chochma*, which is the flash of inspiration within the soul. The oral Torah analyzes and explains the written Torah; therefore it is comparable to *bina*, which is the analytic faculty of the intellect.
152. From the *nusach* of the evening prayers, following *Barchu*.
153. Deut 33:21 *Chochma* is the "beginning," since it is the first of the ten *sephirot*. The verse associates this "beginning" with vision.
154. Amos 3:8
155. Exodus 20:2
156. Kings 1, 5:12
157. Parshat *Terumah*
158. Psalms 96:12
159. Deut. 20:19
160. Genesis 22:17
161. Genesis 16:13
162. Samuel 1, 24:13
163. Talmud Babli, Tractate *Baba Metzia*, Mishna on page 100A
164. Job 29:3,
165. Psalms 5:5
166. Psalms 145:14
167. Talmud *Tamid* 32A
168. Psalms 113:9.
169. *Rosh Hashana* 16A
170. *Zohar* Sect 1, 219A, *Idra Raba parshat Nasa,* Sect. 3, 133B
171. Psalms 104:2
172. Daniel 7:9, *Tikunei Zohar* 21:55A, 69:112B, 69:118B, 70:122A
173. See the *Zohar* regarding the statement, "and he came to the southern corner of the altar" (Mishna *Zevachim Perek* 5)
174. Deut. 32:0
175. Genesis 15:5.
176. Psalms 148:14
177. Mishna, *Shabbat* 51b.
178. Genesis 36:31.
179. In Talmud *Succot* 50b, there is a dispute as to whether the man expression of song takes place with musical instruments or with the human voice.
180. Amos 3:6.
181. Exodus 19:19
182. Psalms 29:4
183. Introduction to *Tikunei Zohar* 3B
184. Psalms 81:3

185. Talmud *Eruvin* 21A, on Kings 1, 5:12, See also *Torah Oh*r and *Likutei Torah* of the Alter Rebbe

186. Talmud *Sanhedrin* 38B, see also *Torah Ohr* and *Likutei Torah* of the Alter Rebbe

187. Deut. 20:16

188. Genesis 36:31-39.

189. Isaiah 3:11

190. Talmud *Gittin* 57B

191. Talmud *Gittin* 56A

192. Talmud *Chullin* 127A

193. *Igeret Hakodesh* (*Ihu vechiyuhi chad...*)

194. *Nusach hatefila, birchot kriat shema*

195. Although the common terminology is the "Red Sea," in all probability this was meant to refer to the "Reed Sea."

196. Malachi 3:6

197. Deuteronomy 26:17.

198. Malachi 3:6

199. Chronicles 1, 29:23

200. Chronicles 1, 29:11

201. Isaiah 45:7.

202. Text of the prayers, immediately following Barchu

203. Lamentations 3:23

204. Job 7:28

205. Genesis 1:5.

206. Isaiah 65:17

207. Psalms 119:89

208. Genesis 1:6.

209. *Nusach hatefila* following *Barchu* (*Birchot kriat shema*)

210. Job 28:12

211. The text of the *maamor* actually says, "water," but this is apparently a typographical error

212. Isaiah 6:2

213. Psalms 104:14

214. *Etz Chaim*, the work by Rabbi Chaim Vital summarizing the kabbalistic teachings of the Ari.

215. One of the names of G-d, first mentioned by Chana in her prayers in Shilo. According to Chassidut, it is this name which brings G-dliness down to the world of *Bria* from Atzilut.

216. Proverbs 15:30

217. Tractate *Yoma* 21B

218. Genesis 16:13

219. Genesis 18:10

220. Eccl. 2:14

221. Deut. 14:1

222. Cf Talmud *Eruvin* 70B

223. Ethics of the Fathers 2:4

224. Introduction to the *Tikunei Zohar* 3B

225. Talmud *Baba Metzia* 84A

226. Psalms 148:1-2

227. Ezekiel 1:14

228. Psalms 73:25
229. See *Likutei Torah* of the Alter Rebbe, parshat Shelach, p. 48B
230. *Midrash Raba Bereishit* Ch. 8, *Siman 7*
231. Words of the *Tzemach Tzedek, Shoresh Mitzvat Tefila* in *Derech Mitzvotecha*, p. 124A
232. Cf statement of R' Yirmiya in *Berachot* 13B
233. Tractate *Berachot* 13B
234. Exodus 33:21
235. The First Book of Chronicles 29:11.
236. Psalms 33:6
237. Psalms 104:24
238. According to Kabbalah, letters of the Hebrew alphabet may be interchanged with other letters, as long as both sets of letters are formed by the same means of speech, whether by the tongue, the lips, the teeth, the palate or the throat.
239. Num. 11:17, 11:25
240. Isaiah 41:8, Talmud *Sota* 31A
241. *Likutei Amarim Tanya*, Ch. 43
242. Psalms 36:10.
243. Psalms 42:9
244. *Likutei Amarim Tanya,* Ch. 50
245. Psalms 83:2
246. Deut. 6:5
247. Psalms 31:6
248. Psalms 86:4
249. Genesis 26:20-22
250. For more elaboration, see the excerpts at the end of the *sefer*, page 399
251. Mishnah in *Berachot* 30B
252. Psalms 33:6
253. Kings 2, 5:16
254. Deut. 11:15
255. *Pirkei Avot* 4:11
256. This and the following translated excerpt will be better understood after the following introduction. Kaballah lists four ways of spelling the holy name of G-d, *Havaya*. All four methods utilize the same initial letters of *yud* followed by *hey*, followed by a vov and another *hey*. However, they differ in the way that they "fill out" the name of each letter. For example, the letter *hey* may be written as *hey-aleph*, or *hey-yud*. And the letter *vov* may be written *vov-vov*, or *vov-aleph-vov*. When all possible combinations are considered, there are four different ways of writing the full name of G-d, "filling out" each of the four letters. Those four resulting names carry the gematrias of 72, of 63, or 52 and of 45. The latter two gematrias "happen" to coincide with the Hebrew words *behama* ("animal," with gematria 52) and *adam* ("man," gematria 45). Accordingly, the name *ma'h* (45 – adam) has a higher, more elevated status than the name *ba'n* (52 – *behama*), and it has the task of uplifting and refining the name *ba'n*. The corollary in divine service of G-d is that we must shine the light of Torah and the divine soul (45 – *adam*) upon the animal soul (52 – *behama*) in order to uplift and refine it.

Additionally, each name (*ba'n* and *ma'h*) has a spiritual source; *ma'h* comes from the name of gematria 72 mentioned above, and *ba'n* comes from the name 63 mentioned above. Both of the latter names (72 and 63) are aloof from the actual purification process, but have an affect upon it, lending "strength" from above.

257. Psalms 104:14
258. Talmud *Berachot* 61B
259. Talmud *Berachot* 61B
260. Jeremiah 15:1
261. See the *Tanya*, ch. 20 and 21.
262. Talmud *Berachot* 13B
263. *Zohar, Parshat Toldot*, 142b, and *Parshat Lech Lecha* 87a.
264. Psalms 121:1.
265. Parshat *Emor* 32A, *Parshat Teitzei* 41B
266. Psalms 103:20
267. In Tractate *Shabbat* 88a.
268. Psalms 84:3
269. From the song *Azamer B'shvachin*, by the Ari, that we sing on Shabbat night
270. Daniel 6:13
271. Text of *Azamra b'shvachin*, by the Ari z'l
272. *Zohar (Raya Mehemna)* Sect 2, page 116B. And elsewhere in the *Zohar*.
273. Proverbs 31:23.
274. "Other" intro to the *Tikunei Zohar (Rosh Hodesh)* 17A, also *Tikunei Zohar* 70, Page 123A
275. *Zohar, Vayakhel*, pp. 216-217.
276. Micha 7:15
277. Exodus 6:3.
278. Exodus 6:6
279. Psalms 117:2
280. Exodus 6:6
281. Deuteronomy 4:7.
282. Cf. *Pesikta Rabbati* 22:12.
283. Exodus 6:6-7.
284. Psalms 117:2.
285. Exodus 6:3.
286. Ecclesiastes 5:7
287. Job 28:27, *Midrash Raba Bereishit* 24:5
288. Talmud *Tamid* 32A
289. Psalms 115:3
290. Zecharia 14:9
291. Talmud *Pesachim* 50A, *Kidushin* 71A
292. Psalms 11:4
293. Isaiah 30:20
294. Kings 2, 20:3, Isaiah 38:3
295. Yeshayahu 3:10
296. Mishlei 10:25
297. Genesis 42:6
298. Genesis 41:49
299. Ruth 3:13.
300. As discussed in *Torah Ohr, Va'ereh*.
301. Genesis 1:4
302. See *Likutei Torah* at the end of the *Biur tze'ena ure'ena*, second discourse.
303. In the second chapter of *Berachot* p. 16.

304. See the first chapter of *Berachot*, p. 6.

305. As is known from the *Zohar* and *Gemara Berachot* p. 28b.

306. These are counted in the Mishna at the end of the first chapter of *Ohalot*.

307. See Code of Jewish Law, *Orach Chaim, siman* 60, sif 4 *(Shulchan Aruch HaRav, siman* 60, sif 5), and
Talmud *Berachot* 12B. See also *Orach Chaim, siman* 101, sif 1 and Talmud *Berachot* 34

308. Deut. 33:21

309. Exodus 2:10

310. Deut. 3:25

311. Malachi 3:12

312. Deut. 4:39

313. Chronicles 1, 28:9

314. In *Sefer Maamorim* 5666 of the Rebbe Rashab, *Parshat Ki Tisa*, starting Page 172

315. Micha 7:18

316. *Zohar* Sect. 1, Page 15 (see *Mikdash Melech*)

317. *Tikunei Zohar, Tikun* 55, Page 88B

318. Talmud *Avoda Zarah* 44A

319. As it is written in Proverbs 8:15: "Through Me, kings obtain advice and reign..."

320. Kings 1, 1:21

321. Exodus 6:3

322. Genesis 15:7 and many other places

323. Exodus 6:10 and other places

324. Chronicles 1, 29:11

325. Samuel 1, 2:2

326. Deut. 6:5

327. Psalms 27:8

328. Numbers 6:25

329. Ex. 20:2

330. In the citations and notes to *Derech Mitzvotecha* (page 454), no precise source in the *Sifri* is mentioned. Instead, there is the following; "In *Ohr HaTorah* (of the *Tzemach Tzedek), parshat Ve'etchanan*, page 376, is found, 'And so the *Pardess, Sha'ar* 32, Ch. 2, writes in the name of the *Sifri* and all of the kaballists, and they bring proof from this that the main emphasis of tefila and of [*kriat shema*] must be upon the essence of the Emanator and not to His attributes..."

331. Deuteronomy 4:7.

332. Talmud *Sota* 14A

333. Isaiah 10:15

334. *Midrash Bereishit* 1, *Siman* 7

335. Genesis 2:10.

336. Proverbs 31:26

337. Numbers 5:7.

338. As written in *Igeret HaTshuva* (of the Alter Rebbe), ch. 1 in the name of the Rambam and *Sma'g (Sefer Mitzvot Hagadol)*.

339. This includes regret over the past, as the Rambam wrote in ch. 2 of *Hilchot Tshuva, halacha* 2.

340. As described in the Rambam, ch. 1.

341. *Petach Eliyahu*, introduction to the *Zohar*

342. Intro to *Tikunei Zohar*, Page 14B

343. Talmud Babli *Baba Metzia* 84A
344. *Zohar*, Section 3, Page 175B
345. Deut. 18:13
346. In *Igeret Hatshuva*, epistle on *Tshuva*, Tanya, sec. 3, ch. 7.
347. Song of Songs 7:6.
348. Leviticus 24:16.
349. Cf. Talmud Babli *Avoda Zarah* 30B
350. Psalms 51:5.
351. Jeremiah 2:19.
352. Job 34:11.
353. Isaiah 44:22.
354. Rashi on Deut. 11:13
355. The text reads *lema'alah*, or "above," but from the context it is clear that the meaning is "from above to below."
356. Deut. 6:21 and 26:8, *Nusach* of the *Hagada* of Pesach
357. Tractate *Chulin* 91b.
358. Malachi 3:6
359. Isaiah 44:6
360. Lev. 22:32
361. Psalms 84:3
362. Genesis 27:22
363. Samuel 1, 1:13
364. Psalms 145:18
365. Song of Songs 5:2
366. Psalms 25:15
367. Deuteronomy 11:12
368. Chronicles 2, 7:16
369. Genesis 28:16
370. Ex. 34:23, 34:24
371. Psalms 126:1
372. Job 12:11
373. Talmud *Hagiga* 13B
374. Psalms 73:28
375. Deuteronomy 4:39
376. The concepts of "breadth, depth and length" take on specific meaning in relation to *hitbonenut* ("meditation") – see the beginning of *Sha'ar Hayichud* of the Mitteler Rebbe
377. Here, the reference is to a song or piece of music that has holy Torah associations.
378. Proverbs 20:27
379. Talmud *Kiddushin* 30B
380. *Zohar* Section 1, 217A, explained in *Likutei Amarim, Tanya,* end of Ch. 4 and Ch. 42 (P. 61A)
381. *Zohar* Section 1, 241A
382. Psalms 115:6, Psalms 135:16
383. Talmud *Tamid* 32A
384. Vol. 2, 247B, Vol. 1, 199A, 38B, Vol. 3, 13A
385. Psalms 32:15, Psalms 37:27
386. Lev. 18:5
387. *Mishlei* 4:19

388. Talmud *Shabbat* 14A
389. Genesis 3:1.
390. This detail is found in the versions of the *Ri'f* (*Berachot Perek* 3), the *Rosh* (*Berachot Perek* 3) and the *Tur* (*Orach Chayim* 56)
391. *Shabbat* 119B
392. See *Shulchan Aruch Harav, Orech Chaim* 60:5. The exception is the first line of the *kriat shema*, which does require our conscious awareness.
393. Psalms 37:23
394. Psalms 62:13
395. Talmud *Kiddushin* 30B
396. Talmud *Hagiga* 15A
397. *Zohar*, Intro, *Petach Eliyahu*
398. Ecclesiastes 2:14
399. Talmud *Berachot* 31A
400. Deuteronomy 28:47-48
401. Talmud *Berachot* 31A
402. Exodus 30:12
403. As cryptic as this piece is, it explains a simple difference in the *nusach* of *tefila* that occurs between the prayer *Baruch Sheamar*, which opens the *pesukei dezimra*, and the prayer *Yishtabach*, which closes the *pesukei dezimra*. Toward the end of *Baruch Sheamar*, we say *yachid chay haolamim melech* ("Singular One, Life of the worlds is King"), while at the end of *Yishtabach* we reverse the order and say *melech yachid chay haolamim* ("King, the Singular One, life of the worlds"). According to this excerpt, the word *melech* ("king") in both cases refers to *malchut* of the world of *Atzilut*, which creates and enlivens the universe from nothing to something. However, the creative process starts by first bringing down infinite light from above during *Baruch Sheamar*. It is necessary to first draw down this light in order to impart to *malchut* the ability to create from nothing to something. That is why during *Baruch Sheamar*, we say *chay haolamim* ("life of the worlds"), followed by *melech,* since the point is to bring the infinite light down into the *sephira* of *malchut*, or "kingship." Only at the end of the *pesukei dezimra* do we manage to draw that power down from *malchut* to the lower worlds to create them. At that point, the creative process continues from *malchut* of *Atzilut* to the lower worlds. Thus, in *Yishtabach*, we say *melech yachid chay haolamim*, because at that point we are referring to the light that descends from *malchut* of *Atzilut* into the lower worlds to create and enliven them.
404. Talmud Babli *Hagiga* 15A
405. Samuel 2, 14:14
406. Psalms 145:13
407. Text of prayers for Shabbat morning, preceding *Barchu*
408. From the text of prayers for Rosh Hashana/Yom Kippur, repetition of the *hazan*
409. *Sh'ar Kriat shema sh'al hamitah*
410. From *Derech Mitzvotecha* of the *Tzemach Tzedek*, page 59 (*nun-tet*): "For in the lower worlds of *BY"A*, there is no need to subdivide the influx to portions as much as in our low world [of *asiya*]. It emerges then that one "portion" of time of *BY"A* includes many portions of the lower world, which is why in "one glance" it was possible to "take in" ten or fifteen years. And from this we may understand the story of the Baal Shem Tov, who foresaw and grasped on Rosh Hashana what would occur afterward, as known regarding the episode with his brother in law, R' Gershon Kitover and a sage in the holy Land. The

Baal Shem Tov wrote to him foretelling the entire episode before it actually occurred. And even though he did not undergo an "elevation" of his soul to the level of *A'K*, but rather to the *heichalot* of *yetzira*, nevertheless there as well it was possible to see fifteen years in one "glance." Therefore, [this occurred on] Rosh Hashana when the entire life force for the year was brought down, which is why it is called *rosh* ("head"). Just as the head of man includes the energy of the entire body, so the energy brought down on Rosh Hashana includes all of time in one "glance."

411. Nusach of *tefilat Musaf* (Shabbat, Rosh Hodesh, Festivals)

412. Exodus 15:17

413. Exodus 25:8.

414. *Berachot* 8A

415. Psalms 119:10

416. Gen. 5:22

417. Psalms 148:6

418. Isaiah 30:20

419. Genesis 29:35

420. "Another" Intro to *Tikunei Zohar*, First day Rosh Chodesh, 17A

421. Malachi 3:6

422. Job 41:8

423. Genesis 28:13.

424. Sifri (see *Derech Mitzvotecha, Shoresh Mitzvah Tefila*, Ch. 7, p. 117)

425. cf *Pirkei Heichalot Raba* 23:1, *Otzar Midrashim Heichalot*, section 32

426. Daniel 7:10

427. Psalms 96:12, Chronicles 1, 16:33

428. Song of Songs 1:15, 4:1

429. Ex 33:20

430. *Shir hashirim* 5:1

431. Genesis 28:12

432. Isaiah 43:7

433. The concept of the *merkava*, or "chariot" is that just as the chariot transports the one who rides in it, so the supernal *merkava* transports G-dliness, conducting it from the higher spiritual worlds on downward. And just as the "horses" of the chariot have no will of their own, but simply fulfill the will of the driver, so the angels of the *merkava* are *butel*, or nullified to the One above.

434. Psalms 148:5

435. Daniel 7:10

436. Ezekiel 1:26

437. Tractate *Berachot*, end of the first chapter.

438. *Zohar* Section 1, 45B

439. Deut. 4:39

440. *Igeret Hakodesh, Siman* 18

441. Amos 3:3.

442. The Hebrew text actually reads, "lower creatures," referring to souls in bodies, etc, but judging from the context, this may be an error and perhaps should read as translated, "spiritual creatures."

443. *Eitz Chaim, Shaar* 42, *Drash* 1, and *Shaar* 18 (there, the text says, "in *machshava* - "thought" - all is refined, however in Igeret Hakodesh, ch. 28, the term *bechochma itbariru* is found).

444. Exodus 34:6.

445. Psalms 48:2.

446. *Shmuel* 1, 23:8

447. *Midrash Raba Bereishit* 10:6

448. Psalms 33:15

449. Intro to *Zohar*, Section 1, 11B

450. *Zohar*, Section 2, 135A

451. See the *Tanya*, ch. 20 and 21.

452. *Berachot* 13B

453. *Malchut* has two modes; one, as it exists in the world of *Atzilut*, receiving influx from the upper nine *sephirot* and two, as it descends to the lower worlds of *BY"A*, to both create and to refine them. Since it is in the higher mode while in *Atzilut*, the letter *dalet* in this instance is large.

454. *Tanya, Igeret Hakodesh*, 5.

455. *Tanya*, ch. 48.

456. As written in *Sefer Maamorim 5672*, regarding the blessings preceding the *Shema*, *Adon uzaeinu, Tzur misgaveinu*, etc.

457. Talmud *Berachot* 17A

458. *Sefer Yetzira*

459. *Midrash Tehilim*, Psalm 91, Siman 8

460. The *Tzemach Tzedek* continues in parentheses in *Derech Mitzvotecha*, forewarning an apparent difficulty, that in the *siddur*, the Alter Rebbe apparently says the opposite; the first paragraph, with forty-two words, represents the *keli* of *gevura* (forty-two words), with the light of *chesed* (*ve'ahavta*), while the second paragraph corresponds to the *keli* of *chesed* (seventy-two words) with the light of *gevura* (*charon af...*). As the *Tzemach Tzedek* says there, "Both of these opinions are the living words of G-d," and that what he wrote is what he himself heard from his grandfather the Alter Rebbe, on Shabbat Noach of the year *5565* (1805).

And in the *sefer Maamorim 5650* (p. 371), the Rebbe Rashab writes that the names *mem-beit* and *eyn-beit* apply to the *kelim* alone of the *sephirot*, but when the infinite light from Above shines into them, then the illumination becomes "inter-included," and the lights "exchange places," so that the infinite light of *chesed* shines into the *keli* of *gevura* (in the first paragraph) and the infinite light of *gevura* shines into the *keli* of *chesed* (in the second paragraph).

461. *Zohar, Raya Mehemna*, Section 3, *Ki Teitzei* 281A

462. Isaiah 59:2

463. *Sifrei Kaballah*

464. Deuteronomy 5:4

465. Ex. 20:2

466. Ex. 14:5

467. Genesis 32:1

468. As it is written in *Torah Ohr* of the Alter Rebbe.

469. Isaiah 59:2

470. From *Azamer b'shvachin*, by the *Ari z'l*, sung on Shabbat nights

471. Ex. 38:28

472. Chronicles 1, 29:11

473. Genesis 2:4.

474. Deut. 20:19

475. While man, with his well-developed intellect is distinct from the animal kingdom, it is not his intellect alone that sets him apart. Rather, it is the influence that his intellect has upon his emotions that sets him apart. Man is at his best when he achieves his potential by "growing" and maturing as he exercises his intellect to "grow" his emotions. In this sense, the emotions are more prominent than the intellect, since they, and not the intellect alone, are the goal. Thus, man's emotions may be said to be more important than his mind, and therefore he is comparable to a tree, since the vegetable world corresponds to the world of emotions (which "grow," as do vegetables). And both correspond to the letter *vov* of the name *Havaya*, which is a straight-up vertical line, as is the trunk of the tree and the upstanding person. (See *Likutei Sichot* of the Lubavitcher Rebbe, *ztz'l*, vol. 6, parshat *Yitro*, for more explanation).

476. Daniel 7:10, *Zohar* Sect 3, 106B

477. Talmud *Chagiga* 12A

478. Genesis 28:12.

479. As mentioned in the commentary of Rabbi Menachem Rekanati as well.

480. Isaiah 43:7

481. *Midrash Raba Bereishit* Ch. 10, *siman* 6

482. Genesis 28:13.

483. *Midrash Raba Vayikra*, Ch. 8, *siman* 1

484. Psalms 75:8

485. Deut. 13:5

486. Talmud *Sota* 14A

487. Zecharia 13:9

488. Mentioned in the encyclopedic work of kaballah, *Pardes Rimonim* of the Ramak (R' Moshe Cordabero, Zefat, ~1560)

489. *Petach Eliyahu*, in the introduction to the *Zohar*

490. From Shacharit prayers, before the *kriat shema* (in *nusach* Ashkenaz) – there the words are "Shine a new light over Tzion"

491. *Midrash Rabba Breishit* 68, Ch. 12

492. This is the language of the *Zohar*, which associates the 248 positive mitzvoth with G-dly attributes, or "limbs of the King" and all of the 365 negative commandments with "nerves" and "connective tissue."

493. Leviticus 18:5

494. Deut. 34:10

495. *Midrash Raba Bamidbar* 14:19

496. Job 35:7

497. Jeremiah 49:16

APPENDIX

The Ladder of Prayer

From *Besha'ah Shehikdimu* 5672 (1912) of the Rebbe Rashab, ch. 382

The spiritual ascent of prayer is an orderly process, corresponding to the verse, "A ladder placed on the earth, with its head reaching into the heavens..."[1] It begins with acknowledgment of G-d, and thereafter proceeds to the psalms of *Pesukei DeZimra*, which are an expression of *ruach*, or "emotional consciousness" in the soul. *Ruach* involves emotional excitement as the result of meditation on the creation from nothing to something. The arousal is more emotional than intellectual, since our main intention is to arouse feelings. Consequently, even though we meditate [intellectually] upon the praise [of G-d expressed in *Pesukei DeZimra*], our emotions become more involved than our intellect. The main goal is to arouse amazement and wonderment over the process of creation, since in essence it is beyond understanding and is subject to mental extrapolation alone ... As a result of our extrapolation to reach the essence of the process [of creation], while ever-deepening our knowledge, we develop fear, as in the verse, "Fear G-d, since He spoke and the universe came into existence..."[2] That is, as a result of experiencing the greatness of the Creator who brought the universe into being, we develop deep reverence for Him, as described elsewhere. [While this is happening,] our animal soul becomes nullified, as it undergoes [the process called] "engraving from without," which induces us to forsake evil. This is also called "pruning the thorns," a process which prepares the soul to become

---

1. Genesis 28:10.
2. Psalms 33:9

a receptacle for G-dliness; [this is necessary because] while the animal soul remains in its coarse physical condition, it is not at all receptive to spirituality...

The initial stage of our service of G-d is summed up by the words, "forget your nation and your father's house."[3] This is a forced exit, wherein we feel compelled to flee from our negative physical inclinations. [At this stage], there is no spiritual light or illumination in our soul. [The escape] comes solely at the initiative of the [G-dly] soul, which has the potential and strength to coerce us, even in regard to habitual and deeply engraved matters, persuading us to forsake our habits and customs. However, during *Pesukei DeZimra* we achieve this via meditation, which fills our soul with divine illumination, which in turn persuades the spiritual powers of the animal soul to detach from physical matters and rise above them. In truth, we do not transform ourselves to the extent that we no longer desire physical matters, since this takes place only later, during [the stage called] "engraving from within." [The later stage] works wonders on the soul, inducing it to desire G-dliness and to reject physical matters (even then, we do not completely transform our physical desires, but merely coerce them. Nevertheless, we no longer feel as much desire for physicality). The "engraving from without" is mere detachment, upon which we ascend to a higher level that is not as associated with physicality).

Then, we move on to the blessings preceding the reading of the *Shema*, as well as the *Shema* itself. Here, the meditation is deeply intellectual, as we attempt to grasp [the words we speak in prayer] how "G-d is one" and "Blessed be the Name of the glory of His Kingdom forever and ever." The emphasis is upon intellect, utilizing our mind, but, nevertheless, the ultimate intention here as well is to arouse our heart. [More precisely], here the goal is to arouse the emotions within intellect [the tendency in our mind, as we meditate, toward love and fear], which is why we say during the recitation of the *Shema*, "And you shall love the Lord, your G-d," since the ultimate goal is love borne of intellect and understanding. Additionally, the meditation and arousal of love produces nullification of our animal soul, inducing the animal soul as well to love G-d. That is why the very first verse of the first paragraph contains the words *bekol levavcha* ("with all your heart(s)") meaning with both inclinations [the G-dly and the animal]. Within this arousal are to be found several soul levels ... as will be explained.

---

3. Psalms 45:11.

In any case, it is necessary to proceed in step-by-step fashion, as we ascend from one level to the next. The entire process of prayer involves elevation from below to Above, ascending toward G-d and cleaving to Him. In order for this process to be real, it must be orderly. First, we must achieve the lowest level, and then ascend to the next rung of the ladder, reaching a higher spiritual power of the soul and achieving higher levels of G-dliness. It is impossible to exceed our authentic level in prayer ... When serving G-d with prayer, it is not possible to jump to a level beyond what the soul has already managed to achieve.[4] Quite the opposite, such an attempt may damage us and cause us to err in our estimation of what we have achieved. This is because prayer involves elevation from below to Above and, therefore, may only take place in an orderly manner.

As we ascend through our prayers, we become receptacles for G-dliness, since by way of intellectual understanding and honest meditation, we firmly internalize spirituality in our minds. And as we arouse love and fear of G-d within, the faculties of our soul become holy receptacles for the spiritual illumination shining within us. (The revelation may be intellectual, as we achieve greater understanding of G-dliness, or it may occur as revealed G-dliness in the soul, as we become aware of G-dliness in the world as well. [That is], we detect revealed G-dliness in the creation and we have it within our power to affect the world using the revealed G-dliness within ourselves). By refining ourselves, our animal soul becomes a vessel for revealed G-dliness. All of this requires an orderly approach, [and then] the process involving logic and analysis provides elevation and desire [for G-dliness]. This is the approach that characterizes *pnimiyut bina* ("inner understanding"), which allows us to [strip away the "packaging" of the spiritual concept and] grasp the essence of G-dliness as it becomes revealed in our minds, which is the very definition of the level known as *neshama*.

The goal of prayer is not merely to achieve understanding, but to cleave to G-d using intellect and to experience G-dliness in our hearts as well. This is what is meant by, "The heart is *bina* [not only analytic understanding but also intuition], and with it the heart understands."[5] This approach is called the *avoda d'pnimiyut hamochin*

---

4. Since G-d is unlimited, He may reveal spirituality from above in any way that He so chooses. However, when man seeks spiritual elevation from below, he is limited, and he may ascend from one spiritual level to the next only in a pre-prescribed order. Any pretense of attaining a spiritual level before man has truly understood and integrated it will ultimately meet with failure – the person will "fall" down to his true spiritual level or lower.

5. Zohar, Introduction 17A

("service of the inner dimensions of the mind") and *avoda d'pnimiyut hamidot* ("service of the inner dimensions of the emotions"). On its highest levels, these emotions are expressed spontaneously without being consciously experienced. [Beyond this], the main intention is cleaving to G-d, which corresponds to the yet-higher faculty of *chochma*. It is known that the highest level of cleaving is associated with *reiah* – "seeing" G-dliness. Just as we stare at a beautiful object and find ourselves totally absorbed in it with full devotion, unable to detach ourselves, so we should succeed in cleaving to G-d from our heart, as the verse says, "My heart saw much *chochma*."[6]

In essence, *chochma* corresponds to *ahava beta'anugim* ("love with delight"), while *bina* corresponds to *ahava raba* ("great love"). Alternatively, the two correspond to *pnimiyut halev* ("inner dimensions of the heart") and *ta'alumot halev* ("hidden recesses of the heart"), as written elsewhere. In any case, the entire process of prayer involves the elevation of the soul and its cleaving to G-dliness, each person according to his level and spiritual status, as he ascends from level to level.

And afterward, as we stand in the *Shemonah Esreh* (the highest point of prayer, wherein we are nullified to G-d), we submit our personal requests during the twelve middle blessings. [At that time], we experience a descent of G-dly influx in response to our previous ascent, as well as an injection of revealed light into our soul; this occurs as a result of our ascent and transformation of ourselves into vessels capable of containing and expressing G-dliness. This appearance of illumination comes as a result of our work and refinement, and we all draw down G-dly illumination in proportion to the ascent and cleaving of our soul, as well as according to our level of spiritual refinement...

From *Sefer Ma'amorim Te'arav* (5672), of the Rebbe Rashab, vol. 2, pp. 812 (Ch. 394)

The act of prayer involves joining the soul en-clothed within the body with its source and origin. Prior to prayers, the "soul is in the nostrils,"[7] meaning that the [part of the] soul en-clothed in the body is neither conscious nor evident. If so, the source of the soul is also not revealed, and by way of prayer, the soul within the body becomes revealed and rises to the level of its source and origin,

---

6. Eccl. 1:16
7. Talmud *Berachot* 14A, *Sota* 4B

uniting with it. It was already explained that this unity is not a simple matter of ascent and inclusion of the lower soul-powers within the source of the soul, which is the spiritual path of *reuta deliba* ("arousal of the heart"). Rather, this unity involves revelation of the source of the soul within the [portion of the] soul en-clothed in the body. As a result of this revelation, the inner soul-powers are rejuvenated by illumination of their origin within them. This is what is meant by the "*makif* ('transcendent illumination') lends strength to the *p'nimi* ('inner soul powers')." The result is a far higher level of intellectual grasp of the soul, on account of the essential illumination that shines within it...

(394) Now, in order to understand this in our *avoda* ("spiritual path" of connection with G-d), all souls are comprised of the five levels, *naranchai* (an acrostic for *nefesh-ruach-neshama-chaya-yechida*). The order of the service of the soul is to first begin with *nefesh*, and afterward to proceed to *ruach*, etc. This is true whether referring to our overall *avoda* (during the entire course of our life), wherein the beginning of *avoda* (from the perspective of the soul as well) must be *nefesh*, or to our particular *avoda* during daily prayers. Then as well we must start with *nefesh* and afterward progress to *ruach*, etc. Now, it is known that *nefesh* consists of self-effacement and nullification associated with acknowledgment [of G-d's existence and presence]. This self-nullification is a component of every person's temperament, including those who feel distant from G-d, and who do not consider themselves among those who attempt to serve Him with intellect and meditation upon G-dly topics and arousal of love and fear of G-d. Even if there is no revelation of divine illumination in our soul, nevertheless, we all possesses the ability to acknowledge the truth, just as we say, *modim anachnu lach*...("We acknowledge You, as G-d, our Lord").[8]

Now, there are several different levels of acknowledgment. There are those who acknowledge G-d without any conscious awareness of doing so, such as the proverbial thief who prays for success in his endeavor. Although he believes in G-d and that G-d watches over everything, nonetheless he behaves in a manner that is totally contrary to G-d's will. And there are those who acknowledge Him with much feeling, implying that they are quite nullified to Him (to the extent that [their awareness] has an effect upon their nature,

---

8. From the text of the *shemonah esreh*

leading them to coerce themselves to resist their animal nature on account of their awareness that, "...You are the Lord our G-d."[9] This is [motivated by] a general awareness of G-dliness, and that there is a Master and Lord, which leads such people to resist their own nature. Now, although it is true that this is mere coercion – performed under duress and by force alone – nevertheless because of this nullification and acknowledgment, the coercion occurs more easily. It is not so difficult for such people to restrain themselves and it is not so against their own will).

In general, acknowledgement is of necessity part of every one's "constitution," and "He who fails to bow during *modim* ("we acknowledge") will not arise for the resurrection of the dead."[10] And if even the attribute of acknowledgment is lacking, there is no good present [within him] whatsoever. It is sometimes mentioned that "his backbone becomes a snake,"[11] alluding to the primordial snake [who seduced Hava in *gan eden*].

In any case, the *avoda* of everyone, even of the highest souls, begins with acknowledgement (during the morning prayers). [And] at the dawn of every day, as we awaken in the morning [we begin the day with acknowledgment], saying *modeh ani* - "I acknowledge." This may take place with a high level of awareness in the soul, and with much honest nullification. In any case, it is acknowledgment, meaning that as yet, there is no intellectual activity combined with it, but only admission alone.

Subsequently, [we arrive to] *ruach*, which is emotional excitement in our heart. It comes to expression during the *pesukei dezimra* ("songs of praise"). And in order to attain emotional excitement, we must meditate (since emotional excitement without meditation results only in false illusions). The meditation, though, must involve intellect that is appropriate for developing the emotions. It may be "external" intellect, meaning intellect that gives rise to feelings, leading to emotions of the heart. Although in our mind, we may also experience a degree of mental stimulation from the concept that we grasp, nevertheless our main objective is to develop the emotional excitement that emerges from the concept.

In general, the meditation that leads to emotional excitement is associated with the ray of G-dliness that is enclothed in the worlds.

---

9. Jeremiah 3:22
10. Talmud *Baba Kama* 16A, *Berachot* 34B
11. *Talmud Baba Kama* 16A

[The meditation is upon such topics as] creation from nothing to something, and "You enliven them all..."[12] since within these topics are to be found lofty concepts, beginning with the necessity of creation from nothing into something, since no object can create itself. As we become aware of the limitations of physical reality, we conclude that [the universe] must have been created, since anything whose existence emerges from its own essence does not "exist" in a form that we might grasp, but is unlimited. (For if it "exists," how can it invent itself? If it were born of its own existence, it could not "exist" as we know it), for who could limit it? Therefore, if it exists as a limited object, it must have been created.

Furthermore, its existence is compound [comprised of various elements], and therefore it cannot owe its existence to its own self. We see that creations decay, and if so, they exist. And we are also forced to say that the creation emerges from *ayn* ("spiritual void," or "nothingness"), since it is impossible for one thing to create something else, without *ayn* as an intermediary. Just as it is impossible for grain to germinate unless the seed first rots, so it is impossible for one object to create another object. The main argument for this [process] is that it is impossible for one object to "give birth" to other objects without limit (since the initial object itself is limited). Of necessity there must be a starting point, and that is its creation from *ayn*, from where it previously did not exist at all. This is what is meant by the creation of the physical from the spiritual, which takes place only from "nothing" into something.

Now, meditation upon and investigation of the subject - of how the G-dly void (*ayn*) creates something (*yesh*), and remains within it constantly, creating it (as written, "Forever Hashem, Your word is maintained in the heavens,"[13] and "He Who renews the universe in His goodness every day"[14]) - produces great excitement within the soul. It also draws the soul into general proximity with G-dliness. In fact, this is a general principle of meditation; there must be a feeling for G-dliness embedded in every aspect of our meditation. The hour during which we are involved in learning and grasping the topic, in order to internalize it and integrate it, is devoted to intellect alone. But, during the period of meditation upon the concept, which of necessity involves the intellect, there must also be G-dly feeling. That is, we must also experience an overall awareness that our meditation is upon divine topics. We must surround ourselves with a general

---

12. Nehemia 9:6
13. Psalms 119:89
14. From the prayer text during the blessings preceding kriat shema

awareness of G-liness at the time of meditation. In particular, we must experience the G-dly element within our meditation, such as the divine illumination that creates from nothing to something. For there are several levels of G-dliness, among them levels that are not a source of created existence. But, the ray and reflection of G-dliness [that descends to this world] is a source of created reality. And therefore it is necessary to meditate in depth. We must delve into each and every topic in order to understand its nature. This is like observing the essence of the concept and its quality. Only in this way are we able to absorb and integrate the matter in our mind, and experience it in our intellect. And upon doing so, we encounter the inner kernel of the concept, which is the G-dliness within it (this is what is meant by the *chush hachasidut* within the intellect, which is explained in *Kuntres Hahitpa'alut*). We meditate and delve in depth to become acquainted with the matter as explained above, and this creates excitement and arousal in our soul, bringing it generally closer to G-dliness.

Overall, this [process also] draws the physical object closer to G-dliness. With true grasp and honest meditation on the subject - how no physical object is an independent entity on its own, but a creation from the G-dly *ayn* that brings it into existence - physical objects no longer seem to be so corporeal. We begin to become subtly aware of the G-dly element within them. A priori, the coarser physical elements within us then [undergo elevation] – all this regarding meditation on general matters of creation from nothing to something.

Summary: By way of explanation regarding the G-dly soul, the beginning of everyone's *avoda* is *nefesh*, which is acknowledgment of G-d's existence and presence. This is a trait possessed by each and every Jew. There are those for whom the trait is far from their consciousness, such as the thief who prays for success as he prepares to break into a house. And for that reason, they will find it necessary to work upon themselves, going against their own nature. And there are those who are consciously acknowledge G-d. Following *nefesh*, there is *ruach*, which is excitement of the emotions as a result of meditation. However, this involves the intellect as it is associated with the emotions. The meditation occurs during the *pesukei dezimra*, on the topic of creation from nothing to something. That is, on how all existence must of necessity have something that creates it (since if its existence is from itself, it doesn't truly exist). Furthermore, the creation is compound, and decays away, and therefore it is necessary to conclude that it comes from *ayn*, since no object can come from another object, especially since one object from another cannot exist as an infinite chain. And all this meditation must proceed with a divine feeling, as the result of *da'at*, until he feels this inside and becomes excited over G-dliness. Simultaneously, this uplifts the physical objects, so that they no longer seem so physical, and all the moreso that coarse physical things should not matter to him at all...

(395) Thereafter, we must meditate on the nature of creation. Creation is the result of a divine ray that descends from one level to the next, passing through a multitude of stages until it is within range of becoming the source of created reality. Within the details of this meditation, we must consider the spiritual chain of ten *sephirot* in the world of Atzilut; *chabad*, *chagat*, etc...and how even from them the creation of the worlds became possible. For although this level (Atzilut) also descended from the infinite light of the Emanator – and emanation is what characterizes the world of Atzilut, as it is written, "And I came down and emanated..."[15] (as written in paragraph 385) - nonetheless, Atzilut still contains revelation of divine light, coming from close proximity. (That is, the *sephirot* of Atzilut receive revelation of G-d's infinite illumination, may He be blessed, from nearby, like something that was hidden and becomes revealed. And their influence [upon us] is also close and intimate).

Now, the proximity of this divine emanated light expresses itself in two ways; one, the emanation is from nearby. The illumination arrives by a process of cause and effect, as if from concealment to revelation. And two, the descent of the infinite light to within the *sephirot* is direct and obvious. As written in the *Eitz Chaim*, "The infinite light illuminates in *keter* and *chochma* from nearby, and in *bina* from afar, and in *z'a* through a window..." It is described as "nearby," because the divine illumination shines clearly within the *sephirot* (and the influence emanating from the [*sephirot* to us] is also close and intimate, with revealed illumination). But, when this illumination descends from level to level to emanate the [tenth and final] *sephira* of *malchut*, "from afar" (both in the manner in which it receives divine light and in how it emanates it), the emanation of *malchut* no longer occurs as if by "cause and effect." Rather, it occurs as if *malchut* is a detached entity, as explained in chapter 388. And so, the reception of the infinite light in *malchut* does not occur from "nearby," even though it states in the *Eitz Chaim* that the descent of illumination into *malchut* is by way of a "hole," implying that it was merely minimized [not that it came "from afar"].

---

15. Numbers 11:17

But, since *malchut* was emanated from "afar," even the [minimal] light that descends to it is not totally revealed. And that is the difference between *malchut* and the higher *sephirot*, such as *bina*. The descent of divine light into *bina* comes from "afar" [according to the *Eitz Chaim* quoted above], and yet it is still considered "nearby," meaning that the light illuminating within *bina* shines in a revealed fashion. And so is the case in *z'a*, as well. That is, since their very emanation took place from "nearby," therefore the illumination within them shines in a revealed fashion. This is not the case, however, with *malchut*, whose emanation is from "afar" and therefore the descent of holy light to within *malchut* is not truly revealed. Rather, it is hidden within *malchut*, and its influence is also felt from a distance – and this is what enables creation to take place.

(The details of this contemplation, insofar that they are applicable to meditation on the creation of the worlds, are regarding the spiritual chain of events leading to the creation of *malchut*. Specifically, [the creation of *malchut*] must be prefaced by [the emanation of] *chochma* and *bina*, and *z'a*, etc. For example, when man speaks, opening himself up to another person, he becomes conscious of the letters of his speech and minimizes the illumination within them. So, in order to produce speech and for him to illuminate his speech with meaning, a progression of events must take place from his intellect and emotions. For, it is impossible to express the will directly in speech (it would emerge as a simple voice), until it is en-clothed in intellect. And it must become expressed in detail; that is, the intellect must be en-clothed in the details. And afterward it must be en-clothed in the emotions, as known that the purpose of speech is to express emotions. That is, the speaker must have an interest in the subject of his speech and want to speak about it, and then it comes into expression as speech. Similarly, the process from Above leading to the creation of *malchut*, must be preceded by the emanation of *chochma* and *bina*. In essence, the quality of *malchut* is exalted and "removed," involving its own separate ray of illumination. And the development (lit: "construction") of *malchut* comes from all of the other *malchiyut* (aspects of sovereignty) of the nine [higher] *sephirot*, as explained in Ch. 388).

But there is something else that needs to be explained here, and that is; why does *malchut* possess additional supernal powers from the essence of G-dliness, that enable it to create from nothing to something? The source of *malchut* is the very essence of the infinite light of the holy One. The power of the infinite One is drawn down into *malchut*, granting *malchut* alone the power to create from nothing to something. And the infinite power of G-d within *malchut* also descends from level to level until it rests in proximity to created existence (at that point, the created entity "occupies space" – possesses significance - [because it] is the fulfillment of His will in the very creation of existence).

About this, we might say that His will from Above, from beyond Atzilut – from the level known as *keter ila'ah,* or "supernal crown" - is also His will to create existence (*yesh*). But, from this perspective (*keter ila'ah*), emanated existence [Atzilut] also "exists" (*yesh*), though not necessarily in the same manner as created existence. From the standpoint of this will, created reality (*yesh*) does not "occupy space" (carry any significance). From this perspective, only the emanated reality of Atzilut has any significance, since it is from this level that His will applies to emanation. From this standpoint, created reality is not significant, since [created reality] necessitates a conscious and revealed G-dly desire, in which exist various different levels. But, within the concealed will of G-d, such as the "supernal will of *A"K*," above the revealed divine will mentioned above (*keter ila'ah*), all is equal [there are no divisions – all levels are equal], whether emanated existence or created existence. From this standpoint, His will encompasses all of existence. From here, everything was initially created, and everything is equal. But, from the [lower] perspective of *keter ila'ah* of Atzilut, as a specific will [relating to the world of Atzilut], there is to be found a distinction between emanated reality, which "occupies space" (carries significance) and created existence which "occupies no space" (carries no significance). In order to establish the will to create [the lower physical worlds], [the One above emanated the *sephira* of] *malchut*. This occurred upon the descent of His will from level to level until it became a will for the creation of existence, as above, by way of a contracted and separate ray of G-dly light).

Precisely here, though (within *malchut*) is found the power of infinite illumination from above (and even more-so), the power that enables the creation of existence, as something "new" [hitherto non-existent]. The greatest expression of *chidush* ("novelty") takes place precisely in the creation of *yesh* ("existence"), as explained above at length, and within *yesh* is to be found the greatest expression of the power of the infinite One (this is the reason for the simultaneous proximity and distance of *malchut,* and its loftiness. What is meant here by "proximity" is not the immediate influence that emerges from *malchut*, but its nearness to created existence. That is, creation "occupies space" – carries significance - regarding *malchut,* since within creation resides G-d's will. Yet, *malchut* is exalted and lofty, so how is it possible for created existence to hold any significance [in relation to *malchut*]? But, this is [a consequence of] the power of the infinite One within *malchut* as it descends from level to level until it comes "nearby." Therefore, from the perspective of the infinite light within *malchut*, it is high and lofty, while because of its descent and decline from level to level, it is "nearby." Similarly, the king is close to his nation, since they are important to him as he is their king, and nevertheless he remains lofty and beyond them).

Kitzur: And we should meditate on the creation, how it derives from *malchut* alone, since the other *sephirot* are emanated and the infinite illumination of G-d within them is from "nearby." And their influence as well is from "nearby," which is why creation cannot derive from them. Only from *malchut*, whose emanation and influence is from "afar," and also the descent of infinite light that shines in it is by way of a "hole," so to speak, so that infinite light becomes concealed in *malchut*. But, the progression and development of the other *sephirot* – *chochma* and *bina* and the emotions – must preface the building of *malchut*. And within *malchut* is found a greater power from Above, from the will of the infinite One to create. In regard to His essential will, created reality (*yesh*) carries no significance (only the emanated reality carries significance). Only by way of the chain of spiritual hierarchy of the ten *sephirot* within *malchut* does the *yesh* take on significance, so that there is a will to create (and this is on account of the descent through the hierarchy of spiritual levels, whereupon *malchut* comes into "proximity" and carries significance, on account of the infinite One in essence within *malchut*, which is removed and exalted).

(396) We should meditate further on the nature of creation. In order for created existence (*yesh*) to become a reality, there must be something [acting upon] the creation in even greater proximity than the divine Will mentioned above [*keter ila'ah* acting through *malchut*]. And that is the en-clothment of the "power of the Actor within the acted upon" (*koach hapoel ba'niphal*), acting, so to speak, to facilitate creation. This [embedding] forms a closer relationship with the *yesh* than does His will, which is nothing more than a divine desire for the creation. But, "en-clothment" in the creation is far more intimate. For the purpose of creation of *yesh*, that is, in order for the creation to truly come into existence, there must be a process of engagement in which en-clothing takes place. In order for the *yesh* to exist, [it must be] completely out of range of the Creator, meaning that it is of a different essence altogether. And this can only take place by means of "en-clothing" within it to act upon and create it. For, how else may a distinct essence be created, if not by way of "en-clothing" in order to enable the new essence? (unless it takes place by way of

an indirect cause – *sibah* – alone. This occurs on higher spiritual levels, such as that corresponding to the saying, "All that HaShem desires, He does..."[16] But regarding *malchut*, which is "nearby" the *yesh*, because within *malchut* resides the divine will to create *yesh*, as mentioned above, the process cannot occur merely by way of indirect cause...).

Now, creation that takes place spontaneously (*memeila* – without any apparent involvement between Creator and created) does not produce creation that "exists" as independent *yesh*. We know this from the concept of *barah* ("creates") versus *venivra'u* ("were created"); *nivra'u* ("were created") indicates entities that were created automatically (spontaneously) and therefore do not truly "exist." [For example], among created beings themselves, regarding the heavenly hosts, it is written, "Since He commanded and they came into being..."[17] and it is also written, "And they established them (the heavenly hosts) forever and ever, as an immutable law, not to be altered,"[18] meaning that the [heavenly hosts] exist in accordance with the will of the Creator, without any distinction whatsoever. This is because they are not truly *yesh* (in possession of their own independent existence). And in order to become truly *yesh*, as a distinct entity, en-clothment is necessary. That is, the divine power that creates the *yesh* must penetrate it by way of "en-clothment, so to speak (in Yiddish, "getting involved") in this creation. Nevertheless, this divine power remains [simultaneously] distinct from the *yesh*, hidden and concealed, as the Creator from His creation.

It must be noted that this topic of concealment of the Creator from the creation implies not merely concealment within "garments" that hide Him, but apparent separation from the creation. Concealment within garments, whatever garments they might be, whether "masks" or "curtains," allows some small amount of illumination to pass through. And since here we are speaking of divine power that is separate and out of range of the physical world, and there is no connection between them whatsoever. If some small amount of revelation does seep through, it does not result in the creation of true *yesh*. And therefore, creation of the physical from the spiritual cannot take place within a framework of concealment such as this, wherein the Creator is "concealed" within "garments." (This type of concealment is appropriate regarding the *chayut*, or energy,

---

16. Psalms 115:3
17. Psalms 148:5
18. Psalms 148:6

that is en-clothed within creation to vitalize it, since in truth this is an energy that is felt and experienced within the creation. But it is not involved in the actual act of creation).

Therefore, creation may take place only when there is separation of the spiritual from the physical. This is why creation takes place "out of range," via a process of "renewal" (hitchadshut) [from afar]. The process is "new" even regarding the "power of the Actor within the acted upon," as explained in paragraph 323. So, it emerges that even though creation takes place in proximity and intimacy with the yesh, in order to create it, as in Breishit barah Elokim – "In the beginning, G-d created"[19] – via en-clothing of the power of the Actor within the acted upon, nevertheless it is removed and aloof from it. (And this is similar to ihu tafis bekulhu olamein ve'leit man detafis bei – "He grasps all worlds, and there is no-one who grasps Him."[20] As explained in paragraph 52, this applies to the divine will that impinges upon all of the powers of creation with a supernal force that impels all of them. And yet they do not grasp Him, meaning that He is not grasped by them even though "He grasps them." And this is because He "acts," so to speak, from a distance, being aloof. And similarly regarding the "power that acts within the acted upon" – its modus operandi is also by way of command and compelling influence. And [this is true regarding] all of the ten creative utterances, wherein is written, "And G-d said, let there be light,"[21] or "Let there by a firmament,"[22] as a king decrees and declares (this is action that takes place forcefully). And as written, "Because He said and it came to pass, He commanded and it was created."[23] He is not "grasped" by this since He is separate…and it is understood that this is not comparable to the divine will that stands alone, completely separate, not embedded at all (and creation takes place from His will, as written, "All that G-d wants, He does – this is by way of sibah – "indirect cause" alone).

This is not true of the "power of the Actor" from within malchut, which acts via en-clothement, as in, "Forever Hashem, Your speech is established in the heavens" to create them. Yet, this power is "separate" and aloof. And this is what is so amazing regarding creation – although it involves "en-clothing" within the "acted upon" in order to create the yesh, and it is impossible for the yesh to truly

---

19. Genesis 1:1
20. Zohar Raya Mehemna (Section 3, Page 225A)
21. Genesis 1:3
22. Genesis 1:6
23. Psalms 33:9

exist except specifically by way of this en-clothment, as mentioned above regarding *barah* and *nivrahu* – nevertheless, creation takes place from a distance, with separation between the Creator and created. This is also for the sake of the creation, so that it remains in its state of created existence (*yesh*), for if the Creator were "fully en-clothed" [without any distance] in the creation, it would not exist at all.

And furthermore, on this we should meditate; "You [G-d] enliven everything,"[24] by way of en-clothment in all of the worlds and the creations in order to vitalize them. In truth, the power to create and the *chayut* [energy within creation, continuously enlivening it] are two distinct levels within *malchut*. The *chayut* or enlivening energy is the influence that is experienced "up close" and in proximity from *malchut*. It is the separate ray of illumination that descends, contracted to en-clothe itself in the worlds and creations to be their *chayut* in a revealed fashion. It is experienced within the creations (and within this light and revelation it is appropriate to speak of en-clothing within the garments that hide and conceal the G-dly light. In general, the concealment acts to produce awareness of the existence of His light, but not its essence). And within this are to be found many levels of the nature of revelation and the nature of the G-dly feeling within the details of the worlds and creations...

Kitzur: And one should meditate on the creation. Regarding "cause and effect," creation takes place automatically and spontaneously, as the effect is within range of the cause. And so it is regarding *venivrahu* – but the creation of *yesh* – true existence – there must be enclothement of the power of the Actor within the acted upon – which is the topic of *barah*. And nonetheless, it is hidden and concealed, the Creation from the Creator, meaning that He hides and conceals Himself by way of separation, and not merely by hiding in "garments." (this is similar to "He grasps all, but nothing graps Him", but in that case there is totlal separation while here "his word is established in the heavens"). And these are two opposites, being the amazing loftiness in the matter of creation...and as well one should meditate upon the light and inner energy of the worlds and the manner of light and revelation.

(CH. 397) All of the above concerns the external aspects of intellect (*chitzoniyut hamochin*), which bear a relationship to the emotions. With the external aspects, we achieve complete intellectual grasp, but nevertheless our grasp is [limited to] the spiritual illumination en-clothed in the worlds. By meditating at length while

24. Nehemiah 9:6

plumbing the depths of knowledge of the concept, we arouse emotions in our heart. Now, the deeper internal elements of intellect (*pnimiyut hamochin*), which result from meditation and grasp of the essential, infinite G-dly light that transcends the worlds, such as the holiness of G-d's infinite illumination and how it is exalted and removed from the worlds – are the outcome of meditation that is associated with *yotzar ohr* ("He Who forms light" - the blessings preceding the *kriat shema*), when the angels utter the word *kadosh*. Although this constitutes the "song" of the angels (as explained above in chapter 369), nevertheless it is a meditation for souls to perform as well, since the soul also gains excitement from it. (For the animal soul, the meditation is limited to contemplation of its source and origin and how it is nullified as it utters the words *kadosh* and *baruch* (and this must also include meditation on the grasp of the angels regarding the subject of *kadosh*. Nevertheless, the main awareness of the animal soul is how its source and origin are subjugated [to G-d], and this creates a spiritual tendency within the animal soul, as explained in ch. 392). And when the G-dly soul focuses on the subject of how its [source] is holy and exalted, it becomes aroused with a desire for G-d's infinite essential light, may He be blessed. We might postulate that in general, the meditation of the soul during the reciting of *kadosh* is upon the topic that "there is nothing as holy as *Havaya*."[25] This meditation corresponds to the immanent illumination coming from the *kav* [ray of G-dly light] as it becomes en-clothed (within the *kelim* of Atzilut. Similarly, [the soul] must consider G-dly illumination as it becomes en-clothed within creation. This meditation is also concerned with the vitality (*chayut*) of the G-dly illumination which is a reflection of a ray of a glimmer of the *kav*, as written elsewhere[26]...)

And nevertheless, G-d is exalted and removed, as written in *Likutei Torah*.[27] Possibly, the *kadosh* of the angels comes from their perception of a ray and reflection of His supernal holiness, known as *kodesh*, which is transcendent G-dliness (*sovev kol olamim*), while the *kadosh* of souls is associated with immanent spirituality (*memalle kol olamim*). This [meditation] requires greater intellectual acumen, and the *bitul* ("humility") associated with it is more internal and essential. As for what is written there, that transcendent G-dliness (*sovev kol olamim*) constitutes the main vitality of the worlds, perhaps

---

25. Samuel 1, 2:2
26. See the discourse, "To understand the matter of His infinite light, in Becoachecha hagadol"
27. See the first discourse Tze'ena ure'ena, where it is recounted that this is the basis for why the angels utter the word kadosh.

this is according to the opinion that creation and its maintenance stem from the infinite light of the holy One, even though He Himself is exalted and removed. But, this also applies to souls. In general, the soul is capable of considering two opposing concepts (such as [how G-d is holy and removed, yet descends to create the universe]). And it is possible that what the angels grasp is the simultaneous proximity and yet distance of *malchut* [from the creation], as explained above in paragraph 396).

In particular, meditation on the topic of *HaShem echad* ("G-d is one") requires use of the inner faculties of the intellect which transcend the emotions, while meditation on the ray of G-dliness en-clothed in the worlds requires only the external aspects of intellect, which are associated with the emotions. Now, the latter is the main focus during the *pesukei dezimra*, corresponding to *ruach* within the soul; that is, to emotional excitement. (Above, in paragraph 392, it was explained that the *pesukei dezimra* constitute an "engraving from without" upon the animal soul, while arousal of the emotions occurs within the G-dly soul. And although it is explained earlier (in the discourse *katonti*) that meditation upon the creation from nothing to something serves the needs of the animal soul alone, elsewhere it is explained that since the [G-dly] soul passes through the realm of the angels, something akin to *ra'ash* ("noise"), meaning to the external elements of intellect and its resulting emotions, of necessity also impinges upon the G-dly soul. Moreover, in order to influence the animal soul, the G-dly soul must express some sort of emotion, since pure intellect bears no relation whatsoever to the animal soul, as written elsewhere. So, in order to refine and rectify the animal soul, there must be some revelation of the emotions. It is just that the emotional revelation takes place within the framework of external intellect (which "nullifies" the emotions, at least outwardly), in order to prevent the attachment of extraneous forces that have no place.

But, the defining characteristic of the "external elements of the intellect" (*hitzoniut hamochin*) is that it utilizes the "garments" of intellectual grasp. That is, our meditation upon a G-dly concept utilizes examples and parables that we grasp with our natural senses, enabling us to grasp G-dly matters. For example, [the prophet said], "...and from my flesh I grasp G-dliness,"[28] indicating grasp of G-dly matters using the natural soul powers of *chochma* and *bina* as well as the emotions with which we understand G-dliness. Because in truth, what we are conscious of and detect within ourselves as the existence

---

28. Job 19:26

and essence of our own abilities, are the native abilities of our natural soul (here, we are referring to souls of the "lower worlds" of BY"A, which are "embedded" in physical reality, since the G-dly soul enters the body only by becoming en-clothed in the natural, enlivening soul), and not the grasp of our G-dly soul. Rather our perception takes place mainly with the powers of our natural soul.[29] From this, we may extrapolate to the G-dly spiritual realm, and conclude that our intellect alone does not enable us to grasp the very essence of G-dliness, since our understanding arrives only through natural and physical matters. Although we grasp G-dly matters in this fashion, and we also experience the G-dliness within them, we do not grasp the essence of such matters, but only their outer manifestations alone.

Now, the inner elements of intellect (*pnimiyut hamochin*), which involve direct grasp of G-dly concepts, do not utilize the "garments" of intellect. This is because the soul has the potential to grasp G-dly matters without "garments" (here, we are referring to those who operate on the soul-level of *neshama*). That is, the soul is able to grasp and integrate the very essence of a G-dly topic, via the inner essence of intellect that is beyond emotions. The elements of external intellect, which do not grasp the essence of G-dly concepts, are in general attuned to what is beneath them, meaning to lower spiritual levels such as the emotions. But, the elements of internal intellect, that do grasp the essence of G-dliness, are not attuned to what is lower (although this intellect is experienced in the heart as well, as known, but this is not because the intellect descends. That is, it is not lower [when in the heart] than in its essence, since as the emotions exist in the mind so they are experienced in the heart, as known. Rather, what is felt in the heart is not a descent but rather lack of limitation, so that the essence of the inner intellect is felt and experienced everywhere. Since it is the very inner kernel and essence of the intellect (*mochin*) that grasps the core of G-dly matters, it is not limited specifically to the mind, but is felt as well in the heart). In their very essence, the [inner elements of intellect] are quite the opposite; they tend to ascend and cleave to levels that are beyond them,[30] and therefore they extend beyond the emotions. Although there are also emotions present, they exist in an entirely different manner than with the "outer" elements of intellect.

Kitzur: All of this is regarding the outer manifestation of spiritual

---

29. See Tanya, Ch. 29; in the beinoni the natural soul is "the person"...

30. This is similar to what is written elsewhere, that the "first three" sephirot of every partzuf (structure of ten sephirot) cleave to what is above them.

intellect, which is associated with the emotions. For, the "inner" manifestations of intellect result from meditation upon the holiness and exaltedness of the infinite One, and since from this we develop a *ratzoh* or "strong desire" for the infinite light of G-d, may He be blessed. And it might be said that within this category is included meditation upon the topic of "there is none as holy as *Havaya*," which is a meditation upon the "inner illumination" which is accompanied by greater intellectual grasp, as well as more internal *bitul* (and also that the creation comes from *sovev kol olamim*, is a concept that is mainly asswociated with souls). But, the aforementioned meditation is upon the outer manifestations of *mochin* in order to create excitement of the emotions of the G-dly soul (and since it passes through the world of the angels, there must be also some excitement of the emotions). The main manifestation of the "outer *mochin*" comes by way of the "garments of logic" which do not grasp G-dly topics, and therefore it is directed "downward" toward the emotions, while the inner grasp of the *mochin* is not limited as are the "garments' of intellect that grasp the essence of the G-dly matter (and that they are felt in the heart is not a matter of descent from their essence but because they are not limited therefore they are not only grasped intellectually but also felt in the heart). And they ascend by way of elevation and cleaving, and there are also emotions involved, but they are present in an entirely different manner.

Chapter 398, Page 819

The subject is as follows; whether we are speaking of external or internal mindfulness (*chitzoniyut* or *pnimiyut hamochin*) - which in general correspond to the external and the internal elements of the heart - both are associated with the entire process of prayer, [beginning] with the *pesukei dezimra* ("songs of praise"), [and progressing through] the blessings before the *kriat shema* and the *kriat shema* itself (which correspond to [the soul-levels of] *ruach* and *neshama*). The only difference is in their spiritual level. For it is known that the three sections of prayer mentioned above correspond to *ruach* ("wind"), *ra'ash* ("noise, commotion") and *aish* ("fire"), all of which are components of the *midot*, or spiritual emotions. *Ruach* applies to the *pesukei dezimra*, during which we arouse our emotions with great excitement through meditation upon the creation from nothing to something. In essence this is a process that goes beyond intellectual grasp, but the lofty origins of this process arouse exhilaration in the heart. In general, this is but a transcendent excitement that does not penetrate the inner core of the soul, but remains external alone. For that reason, there is no goal ascribed to it, aside from spiritual ascent alone (just as the animal soul rises to a higher level, as explained in Ch. 382 and 392, so for the G-dly soul, there is only elevation and ascent, as the soul rises to a higher level).

And *ra'ash* applies to the blessings that we say before the *kriat shema*, as the *ofanim* (lower angels) and the holy *chayot* (higher angels) create a great commotion. This corresponds to our meditation on the subject of *kadosh* ("holiness").[31] The commotion is the result of [meditation upon] the amazing loftiness of the subject. It emerges as a result of the apparent novelty of the concept under investigation. When we detect something new that we never before imagined, we become greatly excited, generating much commotion. That to which we were already accustomed or which was already within our normal range of experience fails to stimulate us. Only that which is outside of our ordinary experience and is new to us is capable of greatly exciting us. Like *istarei belegina kish kish kariah* – "coins in the leg pocket make noise"[32] (they are usually in a purse where they are not heard) - which occurs as the result of the novelty of the situation. Similarly in the realm of spirituality, any intellectual grasp of holiness within creation [generates excitement]. This is because the inner vitality and experience of any created being comes from a mere ray and reflection of G-dliness, while the infinite essence of G-d, may He be blessed, is holy and exalted. And therefore, [intellectual grasp] among created beings is a rarity, and causes much excitement and commotion. Part of the wonder is because our perception is not accompanied by full intellectual grasp, since no thought can truly grasp Him. And this is further cause for excitement, since that which we grasp, we internalize and accept in a calm manner, while that which we do not totally grasp, meaning that we understand, but not completely, produces "noise" and tumult (and this as well is new and novel, since that which is not entirely understood is novel).

And therefore, the noise and commotion of the *ofanim* is greater than that of the *seraphim*, since their grasp is on a lesser level. They know of holiness, but they do not know what it is, and this is what produces a great amount of commotion. And nonetheless, this is a more internal feeling than is *ruach*, since at least the *ofanim* grasp how the infinite light is holy and removed from the worlds. In particular, as they grasp the nature of the loftiness of G-d's infinite light, the resulting excitement, while noisy, nevertheless contains an element

---

31. See Likutei Torah in the second discourse beginning with the words Ani HaShem Elokeichem ("I am the Lord your G-d")
32. Talmud Baba Metzia 85B

of inner vitality since it arrives via the intellect. And therefore the excitement includes a goal and endpoint – the desire to becomes subsumed and included in G-d's infinite light – all this because their excitement is internalized within.

And later, with the second blessing of the *kriat shema*, we arrive to [the stage of] *aish* ("fire"), meaning to the flames of fire of love associated with the *sephira* of *bina*. This corresponds to the world of *bria*, where "the supernal mother nestles in her nest."[33] (In particular regarding angels, this is the level of *seraphim*, whose "place" is in the world of *bria* and who are called *seraphim* because of the flames of fire. But the main theme here is souls, which "arose in His thought," and which are associated with the world of *bria*).[34] As known, *bina* contains elements of *gevura*, since the intellect of *chochma* is cold and moist, while that of *bina* is hot and dry.[35] It is the source of heat that enters the blood from the left ventricle of the heart – and this is why the name *Ekeyeh* bears the same *gematria* ("numerical value" *beribuah*) as *dahm* – "blood."

The topic is as follows; the two intellects – *chochma* and *bina* – illuminate and extend down to the heart by way of the esophagus and the gullet [one for food and the other for drink], known in the Torah as the "butler" and the "baker" [Pharoah's servants]. The intellect of *chochma* illuminates the right ventricle of the heart, as written, "The heart of the wise man is to the right."[36] The right ventricle is full of "spirit of life;" it is devoid of blood. That is, there is no commotion and excitement present; quite the opposite, there is ultimate nullification. Even the emotions within *chochma* cleave to the object of perception until they have no existence whatsoever. And this occurs without any fanfare and flames of fire whatsoever, but rather with silence and total nullification.

And the intellect of *bina* extends into the left ventricle of the heart, which is full of blood, which in spiritual terms denotes great excitement with flames of fire that result from intellectual activity alone. The result of intellectual grasp is excitement over G-dliness with flames of fire and desire. This occurs only when our intellectual

---

33. Tikunei Zohar, Tikun 6, Page 23A

34. See Tanya, Ch. 50; love like flames of fire emerges from the supernal gevurot of bina above.

35. Since chochma is the interface between the infinite light above and the sephirot below, it first of all "receives" from G-d's infinite light. In this sense it is passive, hence "cold and moist." Bina, though demands the use of active intellect powers. The outgoing activity produces "heat," hence, bina is "hot and dry."

36. Ecclesiastes 10:2

grasp is complete and total, since then we experience the concept in our heart, where it turns into flames of fire. That is, with meditation on the greatness of G-d, how He permeates the world and transcends the world – including complete knowledge and grasp of these topics, as written in Tanya at the end of the fourth chapter - [we achieve] what the Zohar calls, *bagin d'ishtamodin beh* - "In order that we get to know Him."[37] When this process occurs accompanied by total grasp and depth of knowledge of the quality of [G-dly] illumination and revelation, we then grasp and become acquainted with the preciousness and glory of the greatness of G-d. And furthermore, when our meditation focuses on how everything is as if naught before Him[38] the result is that our soul becomes aroused with flames of fire and desire for the glory and harmony of G-d's greatness.[39] And from this, we develop thirst (which begins as desire and afterward becomes thirst), lovesickness and expiry of the soul, which is equivalent to the "self sacrifice" of the *kriat shema*. That is, via the introduction of love like fire into the blessing *ahavat olam*, we achieve *mesirat nefesh* (total self-sacrifice) at the word *echad* in the *kriat shema*. All of this is love of a very internal nature, in which all of our ego and "self' become incinerated in this fire. (Like the *seraphim*, whose entire essence is fire) – and with this fire, our animal soul is [also] incinerated, as written, *bekol levavcha* – with "both *yetzers*" – both the good and evil inclinations. This constitutes the "engraving from within" in which we also become a "receptacle" [for G-dliness].

Ch. 399 – Now, regarding the three levels of *ruach* ("spirit" or "wind"), *ra'ash* ("noise" or "commotion") and *aish* ("fire"), the scripture says that they are not the *ruach* of *Havaya*, nor the *ra'ash* of *Havaya*, etc... This means the following; *ruach* ("spirit" or "wind") is associated with the *pesukei dezimra*, and involves meditation upon the creation of the worlds, which came into being from the *ruach* or breath of His mouth, may He be blessed. Now, this is not the *ruach* of *Havaya*, but the *ruach* of *Elokim*, as known that from the name *Havaya* it was not possible to create. The creation took place using the name *Elokim*, as we see in the first verse of the Torah, "In the beginning, *Elokim* created."[40] Only the final *'hey'* [of the four letters of the name] *Havaya* is associated with creation, as we see from the word, *behibaram* ("when they were creation,"[41]) – which may be

---

37. Zohar Raya Mehemna, Section 2, Page 42B
38. This occurs within the intellect of souls, as written in Torah Ohr, in the discourse starting "On the 25 of Kislev"
39. As written in Tanya ch. 50
40. Genesis 1:1
41. Genesis 2:4

re-written, *be Hey baram* ("with the *hey* they were created"). The final *hey*, described as a "light letter that has no substance,"[42] is nothing more than a breath of external *ruach*.

And *ruach* is followed by *ra'ash* ("noise" or "commotion") corresponding to the *yotzar ohr* – [the blessings preceding the *kriat shema*], which involves nullification of the angels and souls in the higher spiritual worlds. [This occurs] as we meditate upon the concept of *kadosh* ("holy"). This word *kadosh* (Hebrew letters *kuf-dalet-vav-shin*) contains the letter *vav*, indicating descent of a ray of spirituality from a higher transcendent level called *kodesh elyon* ("supernal holiness"), in order to bring together both immanent (*memalle*) spirituality and transcendent (*sovev*) G-dliness. The meditation is upon the holiness of the infinite light of G-d may He be blessed, how there is nothing as holy as *Havaya*.[43] And yet, this [meditation] does not lead to the *ra'ash* of *Havaya*, since it involves only the *vov-hey*, or final two letters of His name, and not the first two (*yud-hey*). And also, the G-dliness that descends with the *vov* remains *makif* [beyond us, not internalized], which is what is meant by *kadosh vov* – transcendent holiness that descends.

And *ra'ash* is followed by *aish* ("fire"), corresponding to love of G-d like flames of fire, associated with the second of the blessings preceding the *kriat shema* [*ahavat olam*], as well as with the *shema* itself. Yet, again, this is not the *aish* of *Havaya*, since [*aish* is associated with the letter *hey*, which is only the second of the four letters, while] the most important element of the name *Havaya* is the first letter *yud*, as known. There are those who say that the *yud* of *Havaya* is indicative of constancy, in the present tense, as in the verse from Job, "And so *ya'aseh* ("does") Job,"[44] wherein the word *ya'aseh* means "does continually" and begins with a *yud*. This is the main characteristic of the name *Havaya* – which means "was, is, and will be," simultaneously – it is characterized by constancy, which transcends time. And the present tense is indicative of constancy, as the Ramban wrote in explanation of the verse, "And they said to me, 'what is your name,"[45] – that the past and the future, from the perspective of the Creator, are both in the present. The word *haya* ("was") is in the past, and the word *yiheyeh* ("will be") is in the future, referring to categories within time. But, the present is not in the past, while the future transcends time altogether, and therefore

---

42. From the beginning of Akdamot
43. See Likutei Torah, in the second discourse entitled Tze'ena Ure'ena.
44. Job 1:5
45. Genesis 32:25

the *yud* [representing the ongoing present] is the dominant characteristic of the name *Havaya*.

Now, the inner dimension of the topic is as follows. The name *Havaya* is associated with Atzilut, where the main emphasis is upon its first letter *yud*, representing Atzilut [within Atzilut]. And the love like flames of fire that is associated with *bina*, the first letter *hey* of *Havaya*, does not draw upon the *yud* of the name *Havaya*. However, in the *Tikunei Zohar*, we are told, "There is *ra'ash*, and there is *ra'ash*."[46] There is *ra'ash* that is not the "noise and commotion" of *Havaya*, and there is *ra'ash* ("noise") that is associated with *Havaya*. The words of the verse, "not with the *ruach* and *ra'ash* and *aish* of *Havaya*"[47] refers to the wind, noise and fire of the lower worlds *BY"A* – *bria*, *yetzira* and *asiya*. But, all of these levels exist as well in Atzilut, as *BY"A* within Atzilut, and there all of them are associated with the name *Havaya*.

It is possible that because *chochma* "nestles" in Atzilut, meaning that it permeates all levels of Atzilut, [therefore] all levels of Atzilut are illuminated by the *yud* of *Havaya*, causing Atzilut to be entirely nullified and united. This is the distinction between *BY"A* and Atzilut; in *BY"A*, all spiritual levels are felt and experienced. Whether the excitement is of *ruach* or of *ra'ash*, it is a conscious experience, as one who is aware of his own existence (*yesh*). [Even] the love like flames of fire associated with the *kriat shema* is "felt."

It is known that the love and fear associated with the *kriat shema* correspond to [the kabalistic level known as] *chesed u'gevurah hamegulim* – "conscious kindness and strictness." This is the difference between the *kriat shema* and the *shemonah esreh* – the *shmonah esreh* is called the "tree of life," which is *chesed u'gevurah hamechusim b'aima* – "kindness and strictness that are concealed within *bina* (intellect)," while the *kriat shema* is associated with conscious kindness and strictness, which are the love and fear that we feel in our heart. In Atzilut, everything is nullified and devoid of feeling [of "ego"].[48] But, in *bria* and below, there exists separation. This is because within Atzilut, the *yud* of the name *Havaya* shines, and therefore everything is *batel*, or nullified. This applies to all levels of Atzilut, all of which are associated with the name *Havaya*.

---

46. Tikunei Zohar, Tikun 18, Page 35B

47. Kings 1 19:12 The full text of the verse, "And after the noise, fire, but not the fire of Havaya, and after the fire, a still, small voice"

48. See Likutei Torah in the discourse beginning shishim hamah malachot ("There are sixty queens") regarding the "river that emerged from eden." [There, it states] that in Atzilut, bina is united with chochma.

Now, these two levels are also called *chitzoniyut hamochin* ("external dimensions of the intellect") and *pnimiyut hamochin* ("internal dimensions of the intellect"). The path of G-dly service involving the external dimensions of intellect (which is the path of souls of the worlds of *BY"A*) is entirely permeated with experience of self and ego. However, the path of the internal dimensions of the intellect involves *bitul* – nullification - since the path of the internal intellect is reserved for souls of the world of Atzilut. (Possibly, it could be said that this path is for souls of Atzilut within *BY"A*, since in truth, Atzilut is above and beyond the intellect.[49] Even the intellect of Atzilut transcends the inner dimensions of mind, as will be explained. And the path of the inner dimensions of the intellect is associated with the essence of the soul-level known as *neshama* – and perhaps it could be said that this corresponds to Atzilut in *bria*...) And these souls of Atzilut are totally and absolutely nullified.

Now, we know that there are various types of *kolot*, or "voices." There are voices that are audible, and there is an inner voice that is inaudible. But, regarding the inaudible voice; why do we call it a "voice," when it is internal and unheard by anyone else?

By way of explanation, we know that the voice is composed of three elements; fire, water and wind. And just as the voice that emerges audibly is compounded of fire, water and wind, so the inaudible breath of the inner recesses of the heart is also compounded of fire, water and wind. However, it is internal fire, water and wind that is unnoticeable to anybody else[50]...And this is what we mean by a "cry" and a "scream" from the inner recesses of the heart, as written, "And their heart cried out to G-d..."[51] And we are aware of the distinction between a voice crying out and the heart crying out. The cry of the voice emerges with a simple sound, audible and clear (which is of a higher level than the voice of speech; it is called an "internal voice," but nevertheless both he and others feel and experience this voice). But, the cry of the heart emerges as the heart itself cries out from within, from the ultimate depths which

---

49. See Tanya, Chapter 39

50. See the previous chapters, number 335 and 336 within the discourse in 5672. This corresponds with what is written in the Zohar regarding the verse, ayn omer v'ayn devarim, ("there is no-one who says and there are no words" – Psalms 19:4), which refers back to the verse, yom leyom yabia omer ("each and every day expresses and says" – Psalms 19:3), about which the Zohar says, "These [expressions] are not like the common expressions of the universe that are audible; this utterance is inaudible," as written in the siddur [with Chasidut from the Alter Rebbe, ztz'l] regarding the berachot that we say on Shabbat on this verse.

51. Eicha 2:18

never become audible. It is a voice that is not heard by anyone, not by him and not by others. And nevertheless, it is called a "voice" and a "cry" because it is an expression that is compounded of fire, water and wind (and it must be noted that in any case this happens when there is some inner stimulus, such as intellectual grasp as in the inner dimension of intellect. But, the cry of the heart in true *tshuva* from the very depths – this is completely simple, not compounded at all...).

Ch. 400 – And since the internal voice that comes from within the point of the heart emerges with an inner cry, and it is compounded of inner fire, water and wind, it is understood that within it as well we can find the three above-mentioned levels of *ruach*, *ra'ash* and *aish*. But, there within, all emerges from the internal recesses of the heart, comparable to a kindling of flames from the inner point of the heart, ascending from a deep internal fire that is not visible or recognizable because it is so deep within. By way of explanation; the external layers of the heart are *yesh*, or seemingly independent entities, and so essentially, they are also self-conscious and aware. The two factors are inter-dependent; since they "exist", therefore [the external layers] are conscious and aware. And therefore also, their fire is evident and apparent. However, the internal layers of the heart are not *yesh*, and therefore the fire of the inner core of the heart is neither evident nor conscious. Even though its fire is far more intense than that of the outer layers of the heart, it is concealed and hidden within, so that it is not recognizable.

The same is true regarding the stimulation and *ra'ash* that comes from perception of anything new and novel. (It is explained in chapter 398, that *ra'ash* is stimulated upon detecting something new, and this applies to the internal layers of the intellect, as well. One could possibly argue regarding high souls, that they apprehend essential G-dly holiness as 'something new,' totally beyond their intellectual grasp, since no thought whatsoever grasps Him. And in particular, since the internal elements of intellect are abstract, transcending the garments of the mind [in which we clad concepts in order to understand them], therefore the amazing nature of G-dliness becomes all the more evident. And although within the internal elements of our intellect, our basic pre-suppositions exist in an entirely different manner, and therefore the nature of our amazement must also be different, nevertheless, even here, it is appropriate to speak of *ra'ash* over the novelty of the concept. Possibly, as part of our grasp and meditation upon the subject of

HaShem echad ("G-d is one"), the novelty of our awareness is the following; it is the diametric opposite of what is apparent and evident in the world.

Here, though, it may be necessary to distinguish between whether our meditation is upon the unity of G-d from the perspective of His infinite light that illuminates the world, or from the perspective of creation. All of this falls into the category of G-dly unity from the perspective of the worlds (*echad*) - rather than from the perspective of His singular uniqueness (*yachid*) - but there is a distinction between the awareness generated by meditation on how the infinite light of G-d is united even as it creates (and nothing else exists, G-d forbid), and the awareness generated by meditation on how the worlds are nullified and united in ultimate unity after they were created, just as before they were created. Because when our awareness [of unity] emerges from the worlds, then we experience tremendous novelty since our consciousness is the opposite of what appears to be the reality of the world. So, when the awareness of *HaShem echad* ("G-d's oneness") emerges from the perspective of the infinite light of G-d, it is expressed as flames of fire (*aish*), but when it emerges from the worlds themselves, it is expressed as noise and commotion (*ra'ash*).

But, [these processes] occur within the depths and innermost recesses of our mind (in the realm of inner dimensions of intellect), as well as within the innermost recesses of our heart. And there, the inner point of our heart is stimulated without anybody else able to recognize it – only we know deep inside ourselves.

(This is similar to inner fear or dread, during which one experiences terror and fear in the inner point of the heart. It stops beating and we withdraw inside of ourselves, showing no outward sign whatsoever. For example, during the giving of the Torah, the scripture tells us, "And the entire nation trembled in the camp."[52] This describes their inner fear and trembling. Another verse says, "And the entire nation shook and stood afar,"[53] referring to their outer manifestation of fear. Therefore, "the nation trembled" must refer to their internal fear and trembling). Similarly, the arousal of *ruach* within the vital spirit of the inner recesses of our heart indicates G-dly life, associated with divine concepts exuding great energy, with which we "live." This energy does not express itself as [external] excitement, [but] as [the essence] of an *ish chai* – a "living person" - who lives from his very essence, meaning that his life is

---

52. Exodus 19:16
53. Exodus 20:15

expressed in every detail of his being, and not as external excitement alone. So it is with the *ruach chaim* - "spirit of life" - that indicates that we live with G-dlliness and G-dly precepts.

All this encapsulates *ruach*, *ra'ash* and *aish*, as they exist in the inner depths and recesses of our heart. And here as well, there are various levels, since *ra'ash* is more internal the *ruach*, and *aish* is more internal than *ra'ash*. But in general all are internal. That is, the internal dimensions of intellect, resulting from meditation and intellectual grasp of essential G-dliness, devoid of the shrouds and garments of intellect of whatever subject the person meditates upon, whether the *pesukei dezimra* or the meditation during the blessings preceding *kriat shema* or the *kriat shema* - all of this touches upon and grasps the essence that shines in the very depths of the inner mind and heart. And therefore, all is internal with ultimate nullification, lacking any feeling [of self and ego].

Kitzur - Here, there is *ruach* ("spirit"), *ra'ash* ("noise" or "commotion") and *aish* ("fire"), all of which are internal. The flames of fire, although extremely intense, are hidden and concealed in the heart, not recognizable at all, and the "noise" results from the novelty of perception of G-dly essence. And from the nullification of the worlds, which is the topic of "G-d is one" - the opposite of what appears in the worlds - (and if the consciousness is of the unity of the infinite illumination, even though it creates, the result is fire. And if the consciousness is of the unity of the worlds, the result is noise and commotion) - the person is moved and excited inside, in the recesses of his mind and heart, similar to internal trembling. And *ruach* is the vitality in the heart, with which the person lives with G-dly precepts, as *an ish chai b'etzem* - "one who lives in essence."

(401) Now, there is a spiritual level even beyond this, that is called the inner intention (*kavana*) of the mind. We may describe it as the excitement of the soul over the kernel of intellectual grasp even before it emerges into conscious awareness. It is the abstract source of the divine concept within which the G-dly essence is found. Now, the internal dimensions of the intellect (*p'nimiyut hamochin*) described above, become apparent within the framework of true logic, even though they are not clad in the garments of logic. They convey the essence, as it becomes apparent in the realm of logic. And if so, the expression pertains only to the details of the concept, and not to its very essence. That is, it does not convey the true essence of the point, since all logic pertains only to the particulars of the concept and not to its essence. Since this is so, the expression conveys

only the details of the concept. And therefore, the G-dliness of the concept that we grasp is not the essence of its G-dly illumination, but only the concept as it comes into intellectual expression. Thus, it is called a "divine concept," because it is the articulation of a G-dly matter in the realm of intellect. It is far higher than the external dimensions of intellect (*chitzoniyut hamochin*), which constitute grasp of a topic using "garments and screens" (the explanations and examples that allow us to grasp the topic), ensuring that whatever G-dly awareness we do attain is by way of a "filter." (This is exemplified by *aimah ila'ah* – supernal *bina*, which "nestles in her nest" - after passing through the screen that separates Atzilut from the world of *bria*). But, [this] does not apply to the inner dimensions of intellect (*pnimiyut hamochin*), which grasp the essential kernel of G-dliness within the concept without recourse to "garments." Nevertheless, since our grasp is intellectual and our logic applies only to the details, therefore our entire intellectual endeavor is in the realm of *yesh* [not nullified to G-d], and fails to apprehend true G-dly essence.

However, it is known that within the kernel of intellect that yet transcends grasp, are illuminated the most subtle nuances of the concept, as well as its very essence. (Later, as the concept comes into full grasp, these nuances do not remain so illuminated, even if all the details are explained and elucidated. And that is why, in truth, after much intellectual activity, [our grasp of] the concept may drift far from the essential point – meaning that the essential kernel [of the concept] becomes hidden – and we may err or deviate, G-d forbid, and fail to grasp the details in a manner that corresponds to the essence of the concept. And therefore it is necessary to remain focused upon the essential kernel of the concept at all times in order to avoid going astray, as written elsewhere and mentioned above in Ch. 191. This is the result of the concealment of the essence of the concept within intellect. All this applies all the more-so regarding that the subtleties of the subject, which then become hidden in the course of intellectual grasp).

Similarly in the G-dly realm, the essential G-dliness of the concept becomes revealed within the kernel of divine intellect. Just as the essence of intellect shines within the point of intellectual conception, so the essence of G-dly illumination becomes revealed within the divine concept. That is, within the kernel of intellectual conception, we internalize the concept well and accurately, and then we experience the G-dly essence within it. Now, the intellectual grasp of *bina* provides elaboration upon the point of conception of *chochma*.

Within the point of conception [of *chochma*], we do not yet fully grasp the concept, nor do we recognize its nature – just how and what it is. Since it is still in the form of a general point, therefore even though the essence of the concept shines within, illuminating the matter in all of its subtlety, it remains amorphous alone. But within the grasp of *bina*, the matter becomes explained and detailed, enabling us to grasp the concept well and clearly, just how and what it is. And also, the point of conception of *chochma* becomes clarified in *bina*, since it is possible that our conception contains hidden fallacies that are inaccurate and only by way of intellectual analysis do we clarify the matter. For example, a new idea may occur to us and we think it to be a good idea, but upon further reflection, we come to grasp it accurately, and we see that it is not so. Similarly within the point of conception [of *chochma*], false tendencies may influence our thoughts, that later become clarified in *bina*. And as known that the analytic stage of *bina* is called the *makom habirur* – the "site of clarification."[54]

Now, the process described above takes place within the [confines of the] spiritual chain of creation (*seder hishtalshelut*). There, the origins of intellectual revelation occur [first] within the general point of conception (*chochma*), yet remain obscure, for the time being. The clarification, along with full-blown knowledge and understanding of the topic, occurs within the framework of *bina*. But, one who operates on the level of the point of conception of *chochma*, meaning that he is in touch with the inner intention (*kavana*) of the mind within the point of conception (before it comes to actual intellectual grasp), gets to know the concept in its true pristine form. It does not exist in his mind as a simple, amorphous point alone, but as a concept about which he becomes aware of the details. He does not know them as concrete particulars, like the details of an intellectual concept, but as one who knows the details from their essence. They are illuminated for him spontaneously and automatically. This does not mean that he actively delves into the details (since if he did so, he would lose the thread of the essence of the matter). Rather, he grasps the matter in all of its details by grasping its overall theme. And then, rather than directly experiencing the details, they become revealed and known to him merely because he grasps the concept as it truly is. This is similar to one who grasps the overall theme that emerges from a synopsis after he has truly internalized [the topic]. What he knows is the depth of the concept as it expresses itself in the details (this is the abstract *ayn*

---

54. See Torat Chaim (of the Mitteler Rebbe) in the discourse beginning Eleh toldot Noach.

of the concrete *yesh* of intellect, and it is the stage in which the concrete intellect becomes like abstract *ayn*. Now, within this process there are no details, since this is the theme that emerges upon creation of a summary or synopsis. [This overall theme] negates the presence of details and goes straight to the heart of the matter – the point of conception of the subject and how it may be grasped from its details – and this is the depth of the concept (*omek hamusag*). And it is known that here shines the very essence of the concept). Similarly, within the point of conception of intellect before it emerges as intellectual grasp, one first grasps the subject, not only in general but with all of its details laid out before him (but not as conscious details).

Chapter 402) This process is best understood by way of example of one who grasps a concept when it is presented to him in a concise form. For, "one should always teach his student in a concise manner,"[55] meaning that in the transmission of knowledge from teacher to student, the teacher must first present the general topic in a succinct form. [He should present] an abridged version that nonetheless includes all of its details. As known, this technique of teaching in a concise manner does not withhold information in order to shorten or conceal it. Rather, the teaching includes all that the teacher wishes to convey to the student, but in concise form, so that the brief words contain all of the length and breadth of the details of that particular subject. As the Rambam writes, "One's words should be few and their content maximal,"[56] similar to the language of the Mishna (oral Torah), whose words are few, but which nevertheless encompasses the entire length of the detailed discussions of the Talmud. And as the Talmudic sage, Ilpa said, "Is there anything in a *braita* [extraneous teaching not included in the main body of the oral Torah, but nevertheless cited by Talmudic sages as evidence for their arguments] that we are unable to learn from our Mishna?"[57] It is true that from these few words, we are unable to glean the precise details of the topic, and only via the long discussions of the Talmud are we able to uncover the details that are concealed within the Mishna. Still, one who is quite wise and who possesses an analytic flair, absorbs the concept while understanding and grasping it immediately. That is, when he hears an intellectual concept via these few words, he immediately grasps the true intent behind it from within the brief words, and fully appreciates the intellectual point

---

55. Talmud Pesachim 3B, Chulin 63B
56. Hilchot Deyot 2:4
57. Talmud Ta'anit 21A

underlying it. To achieve this, he needs no lengthy explanation whatsoever, since the length will not add anything new for him. He already knows the subject and is able to grasp all of its dimensions on his own. And utilizing this grasp and knowledge, he also uncovers the hidden details that are within the short words. For, if he is able to put together a concise synopsis of the topic as it becomes revealed from a few short words and yet he does not know the details, then he does not truly grasp the concept. But, when he [is able to] detect the great amount of information that is contained in those few words, then he has true knowledge of the topic. This does not mean, though, that he is fully conscious of the entire length of the subject. He merely grasps the details as they are included within the general overall idea. That is, he grasps the sum total of all of the details, but only as they become manifest [in intellect], not as they exist in essence.

[In our case, though], we grasp the essence, and our grasp is not merely general, devoid of true knowledge and grasp of the topic. Rather we know the details as well, as they are concealed in the brief words, which nonetheless illuminate for us in a revealed fashion. And what exactly is this revelation? It is the essence of the intellectual concept. Within the point of intellect that is still amorphous, dwells the essence of the concept, without us being aware yet of its exact nature. At this stage, it is not conscious, and the revelation is only of the intellectual manifestation of the topic, of which we are aware. But, our awareness is only of the manifestation of the concept and not its essence. However, when within the concise words [of the teaching], we detect what is concealed and only hinted at, without entering into the details but simply grasping the entire idea via a few words, we then become fully aware of the matter, and it is totally revealed to us. We then know the matter as it is, as it becomes revealed to us in its essential form.

Similarly, when all of the details are experienced from within the point of intellect, this constitutes true knowledge of the topic (more-so than when we experience the overall theme alone, as mentioned above). And then, we know and experience its true nature, and our knowledge is of the very body and essence of the topic, more-so than from the example of concise words described above. The words are only a summary following a lengthy explanation (from the perspective of the teacher, his original words were at length but he teaches them to his student in a concise manner. Now the brief words are not comparable to the point of intellect that appeared to him at the moment that he grasped the subject, when illumination of the very essence of the concept was revealed to him. Afterward, as he went into the details, the essential point of intellect became concealed, and if so, when he later expressed the subject in concise words, it lacked the essential revelation that was originally present in the point of intellect. In regard to the student, the concise words are what he receives from his teacher and then grasps with his own sense of intellect and understanding. The subject is not one that he himself conceived). But, within the point of intellect, which is the original flash and revelation of wisdom, the essence shines much more than within the concise words. And then we know the very essence as it truly exists...

Chapter 403) Based on the above, we may grasp what is meant by "inner intention of the mind" (kavana pnimi shebamoach). And that is, if we possess a talent for G-dliness, and are capable of internalizing a G-dly concept including the point of insight within it, with its details, we need not grasp the concept by way of its details (not even by abstracting the details, which is the path of "internal mindfulness" – pnimiyut hamochin). [Rather], we already know the concept from the [inner] point of inception, in its pristine essence. In that case, we grasp the essential G-dly light – that is, we feel and experience the essential point of illumination within, truly revealed. And this awareness provides our soul with essential excitement, far exceeding the excitement of emotions, even in their inner essence, as they result directly from the inner dimensions of the intellect (pnimiyut hamochin). This occurs when the intrinsic point of our mind and our heart is aroused over the essence of the G-dly concept as we know and grasp it, with our "point of intellect."

This level of excitement is described as the "voice of Moshe," and it transcends the "voice of the Levites." (By "voice" is meant revelation of excitement from within the soul, as expressed by song and melody which are the result of stimulation and arousal of the soul. As the Mishna[58] says, "All those animals who possess a shir ("song," but here meaning "collar") go out with their shir" [Since not only the Jews but also their animals must rest on Shabbat, domesticated animals are not permitted to carry anything on Shabbat in a way that might be construed as "labor." But, those animals that wear a collar (shir) during the course of the week are permitted to wear it on Shabbat as well. That is the halachic meaning of the mishna. But since shir also means "song," the Chassidic interpretation of the mishna is that all those who "sing" in prayer

---

58. Talmud Shabbat 51B

during the week, will "sing" on a much higher spiritual level on Shabbat, going "out" of their previous level, because of greater stimulation of the soul]. This is the meaning behind *mizmor shir leyom haShabbat* – "Let us sing a song for the day of Shabbat,"[59] as the *Ari z'l* says that the main expression of song is during Shabbat, when there occurs an elevation of the worlds. And this ascent and inclusion within higher spiritual levels is accompanied by song and melody. Similarly, all arousal and elevation of the soul takes place accompanied by music, emerging from our inner intention and arousal.

As we see, there are inner dynamics of the soul that cannot be revealed in words, but express themselves in song, accompanied by internal enjoyment or love within...(much as a kiss expresses love within, so do songs and melodies). And that is why we have *Shir hashirim* – the "Song of songs" - that reveals the inner love and essential yearning of G-d for the Jews, and of the Jews for G-d as well, that can only be expressed in song and melody alone. And so it is with the inner intention of the mind – it is expressed in song and melody. And there are various different levels, in accordance with the particular inner intention, etc).

The "song of the Levites"[60] emerges from the inner intention of the mind (as known, the Levites are associated with *bina* – "analytic thinking"), as expressed in an orderly melody arranged according to the specific intention. This is what we mean by one who "knows how to sing." That is, he knows how to arrange a melody to fit his intention (*kavana*). This ability is associated with the inner dimensions of *bina* (*pnimiyut bina*). For, we "sing over wine"[61] (*omer shira al hayain*) since wine reveals the inner core of the soul, as in the saying, "when wine enters, the secrets emerge."[62] (And, it is written elsewhere that "wine reddens the face," which is an indication of inner life and vitality). This is an expression of the inner dimensions of the mind (*p'nimiyut hamochin*), as they reveal the essential point of G-dliness without any of the shrouds of intellect. And nevertheless, the "inner point" emerges as an organized melody since in any case it is a product of intellectual grasp. As mentioned above in Ch. 401, even the inner dimensions of mind (*p'nimiyut hamochin*) grasp the details of the subject, though in an internal [abstract] manner. And

---

59. Psalms 92
60. Rashi in Talmud Eruvin 102B
61. Talmud Berachot 35A
62. Talmud Eruvin 65A, Sanhedrin 38A

therefore, the song and melody also emerge in orderly musical dynamics.

But, the "song of Moshe"[63] is a melody that emerges from the inner intention of our mind (*kavana p'nimi sh'bamoach*), from the very essence of the point of intellect. And although we also experience the presence of details, they occur within the essential point itself. The resulting excitement emerges upon stimulation of the essential point of the mind and the heart, as they become aroused over the essence of G-dly light. This excitement is expressed as disorderly song and melody, accompanied by spontaneous movement alone, which is un-premeditated. Since it is not orderly, there are no details [expressed], but rather only the very essence of the spiritual point [itself]. By way of example, the Zohar tells us that "*Raya Mehemna* (Moshe Rabeinu) would sing all kinds of melodies during prayer,"[64] singing without any order or organization. By "all kinds of melodies," the Zohar means that the *Raya Mehemna* prayed with one overall dynamic that included all kinds of specific melodies, just as the inner intention of the mind is expressed in details that exist within the very essence of the point. Similarly, song is one overall movement that is all-inclusive.

Here, the inner intention corresponds to *chochma*, which in turn corresponds to the soul-level of *chaya*, as known. But, it is not on the level of *reiah* – "vision" – within *chochma* that completely transcends intellectual grasp. [*Chochma* is divided into two levels, *koach* and *mah*. The lower level (*koach*, "power") is intellectual, and provides the intellectual substance that descends for further analysis and deliberation in *bina*. The higher level [*mah*, "nullification") is associated with "seeing," beyond intellect]. Rather, this is the point of inception of intellect, the inner dimensions of which express the hidden details within.

And there is a yet higher level. It is the *yechida* of the soul, the very essence of the soul that ascends in song, in utter ecstasy that totally transcends intellect. It is unlike the "inner intention" (*kavana p'nimi*) mentioned above, which at any rate involves G-dly knowledge. The "inner intention" also requires knowledge, similar to intellectual grasp, since it involves perception of the topic and its details (still, it is unlike the grasp of the internal dimensions of the mind (*p'nimiyut hamochin*), wherein the details emerge totally

63. Midrash Tanhuma Parshat Bo Ch. 9, Mechilta Parshat Bo Ch. 14, Zohar Section 3, Page 7A, Ohr Hachaim on the Torah, Exodus ch. 19 and 20

64. Zohar Raya Mehemna Section 2, Page 114B, Tosefet leZohar, Section 3, Page 306B and Section 3 Page 230B

revealed, in a true intellectual picture, and in which we grasp the G-dly concept [but] fail to grasp its very essence. Here, this inner intention (*kavana pnimi*) does not come into full and true grasp, but only becomes evident through its details, in the manner that they existed prior to their emergence into conscious knowledge. At this stage, they are still illuminated by essence, as mentioned above. Nevertheless, even this knowledge bears a resemblance to intellectual grasp).

However, the *yechida* is the ultimate enjoyment of the essence of the soul in the very essence of the infinite One. Like the *Rashbi* (R' Shimon bar Yochai, author of the Zohar), who said, "With one knot I am tied,"[65] and as written, "In G-d, my soul is praised,"[66] referring to the very essence of *Havaya*. (And that this level – *yechida* - exists in everyone is explained in *Kuntres Hahitpaalut* [of the Mitteler Rebbe, R' Dov Ber of Lubavitch]. There it is explained that the *yechida* is revealed when one hears a divine concept that causes his soul to cleave to G-dliness and be drawn to it, automatically and spontaneously, even though he may not understand the concept at all. This is only because the person experiences essential enjoyment of G-dliness through the *yechida* of his soul, and this is why he clings, cleaving his soul to G-d even though he may not understand the concept. Nevertheless, this occurs only when he hears something G-dly, since that is when the *yechida* permeates his intellect. This is because essential enjoyment of G-dliness resides in our mind, which is why our soul is attracted and cleaves...).

Chapter 404) From all of this explanation, we can now grasp what is meant by the "joining of the source of the soul with the soul in the body." For the soul en-clothed in the body refers to the *nefesh, ruach* and *neshama* (three lower levels of the soul), with *neshama* corresponding to intellect. However, the inner dimensions of intellect (*pnimiyut hamochin*), and all the more-so the inner intention of the intellect (*kavana hapnimi shebamochin*) are the source and origin of the *neshama* [the soul-level, not to be confused with the overall soul]. For, all of these levels apply to souls of the world of Atzilut, as explained earlier in Chapter 399. There, it was explained that the "inner dimensions of the intellect" applies to souls of Atzilut as they descend to the lower worlds of *BY"A*, and the "inner intention" mentioned above in Ch. 403 applies to souls of the world of Atzilut as they "reside" in Atzilut itself.

---

65. Idra Zuta, Parshat Ha'azinu Page 285A
66. Psalms 34:3

And so, within every soul, the Atzilut within is the transcendent level known as *chaya*, which nevertheless "makes an incursion" according to the sense of that particular soul within the body. That is, it appears within the theme of intellect, and not as *reiya* ("vision") of *chochma*, but as the intellectual component of *chochma*. And also the nature of perception as well, as it emerges from the details of the concept, is similar to intellectual grasp. It is the arousal of the soul over the very kernel of intellect, which occurs only when the kernel of intellect within does not exist as an amorphous point alone, but when we are conscious of its details. That is, we possess knowledge of the matter from the details before they emerge into intellectual grasp (and this occurs when the kernel itself exists within, with all of its broad details). For, when the kernel of intellect exists as a general point, we may only meditate in a general fashion, and as known this is not true meditation. But, when the inner intention of the mind transcends the meditation on the details, and we are not dependent upon the details within the kernel of intellect, then we [automatically and spontaneously] come to know the details. This, then is similar to intellectual grasp and beyond it (it applies as well to the *yechida*, during which we appear to be cleaving to the G-dly topic as we hear it, even though we may not even understand it).

This, then is what is meant by the source and origin of the soul as it illuminates within the body. Now, it is possible to postulate that this occurs after arrival to the source and origin of the soul. That is, when on the ladder of prayer whose head reaches into the heavens, we arrive to *reuta deliba*, we then have it within our power to worship with the inner dimensions of our mind - *pnimiyut hamochin* - (by way of essential, inner *ruach*, *ra'ash* and *aish* of which we are not conscious, nor is it recognizable upon us) and also with the inner intention of the mind - *kavana pnimi shebamoach*. At the same time, we will experience essential enjoyment of G-dliness, even though we neither understand nor grasp it at all.

And this is what is meant by Adam – *aleph-dahm*. The letter *aleph* is the infinite One, the Master of the world, being the infinity that is within the soul. It is the source and origin of the soul, and it is revealed within the *dahm* (blood), which is the soul enclothed in the body. *Dahm* corresponds to *bina*, (the name *aleph-hey-yud-hey b'ribuah*). It was explained earlier (in Chapter 398) that the intellectual power of *bina* extends into the left ventricle of the heart.[67]

---

67. See Likutei Torah in the first discourse beginning with the words Lesusati berichvi; by "blood" is meant orot becoming en-clothed in kelim – this occurs in bina, as written elsewhere that *chochma* is above the *kelim*, and it is the fourth level within *ohr* – G-dly illumination

All of this refers to the soul as it is enclothed in the body, and *aleph-dahm* is the joining of the source of the soul as it illuminates with immanent spirituality (*ohr pnimi*) in the soul en-clothed in the body. What this means is that the inner soul-powers become transformed to a higher level as revelation of essential G-dliness takes place within them, as in the inner intention of the intellect and essential enjoyment of the mind, and this is what is meant by *Adam...*

Driving away evil
From *Sefer Maamorim 5659* (1899) of the Rebbe Rashab, Page 151

Tanu Rabonen ("The Rabbis taught in a *mishna...*") that we should place the *chanukiya* ("Chanuka menorah") in the doorway of our house, just outside..."[68] [The medieval commentary], *Tosfot* [who were the grandchildren and descendents of Rashi throughout Europe] explained that by "outside" is meant "the public arena." This applies when our house opens out to the public space. And if the house opens to a courtyard, then the *chanukiya* should be placed at the opening of the courtyard so that from there it will illuminate the public arena. Our question is, why must the Chanukah lights illuminate specifically into the public arena? We find no other mitzvah that must be fulfilled in the public arena, aside from the red heifer, whose performance takes place "outside" [of the Temple]. And also, in the days of Ezra, the Torah was read outside, for specific reasons. But, aside from these, we find no mitzvah whose fulfillment took place outside, aside from the Chanuka candles.

The simple explanation is that the principle of *pirsumei nisa*, or "publicizing the miracle" applies to the Chanuka lights. But, in truth that is not enough to explain [the requirement to light outside], for there are other mitzvoth that we fulfill as a reminder of miracles that took place, such as reading the *megila* on Purim, for example – and nonetheless they do not take place in the public arena. So, what then is different about the Chanuka lights that they must be lit in the public space?

In addition, we need to understand; *Chanuka* is derived from the word *chinuch*, meaning "inauguration." The re-inauguration of the Temple, as well as the altar within it both occurred on Chanuka. That is the reason we read the Torah portion about the inauguration of the altar on Chanuka. What, though is the connection between the [two events], and the kindling of Chanuka lights? For, it would

---

68. Talmud *Shabbat* 21B

appear from the blessing that we recite over the Chanuka lights that they are all related, since we say the words, "...to kindle the Chanuka candles." This implies that the candles are associated with the concept of "inauguration," which is difficult to understand. There are offerings involved in the inauguration; the "princes" of the tribes brought many such offerings, and it was their sacrifices that inaugurated the altar. But regarding the [role played by the candles] during the inauguration, at first glance it is not understood – what is the [connection between the candles and the inauguration?]

In order to comprehend all of the above, it is necessary to preface with the verse, "And I established peace in the land,"[69] about which it has already been explained that "peace" implies "joining." Here, this means that Jewish souls draw down and cause the infinite light of G-d to join with the *sephira* of *malchut*...

Now, the Talmud[70] juxtaposes the beginning of the verse, "And I established peace in the land,"[71] against the remainder of the verse, "And no sword will pass through your land," and interprets, "This means that not even a sword of peace will pass through the land." It may be suggested that the "sword of peace" applies to prayer, since Yakov Avinu in the Torah said, "...that I took from the Emorites with my sword and with by bow,"[72] which Onkelos translates as "with my prayers and with my supplications." Now, "sword" refers to the *kriat shema*. This is what the Zohar explains regarding the verse, "And he took a spear in his hand"[73] – this refers to the 248 words of the *shema*. [Moreover], both "sword" and "spear" refer to the same thing. And "bow" refers to the *shemonah esreh*, as will be explained.

On the verse, "The majesty of G-d is in their throats, and a two-edged sword in their hands,"[74] the sages said, "All who read the *shema* before going to sleep are comparable to one who grasps a two-edged sword in his hands."[75] We have to understand what is meant here by "sword," as well as what is meant by a "two-edged" sword, specifically. Now from the Zohar,[76] we know that the name *Havaya* is called a "sword." The *yud* of His name is the point of the

---

69. Leviticus 26:6

70. Talmud *Ta'anit* 22A-22B

71. Leviticus 26:6

72. Genesis 48:22

73. Numbers 25:7

74. Psalms 149:6

75. Talmud *Berachot* 5A

76. *Raya Mehemna, parshat Eikev*, page 272A

sword, the *vov* is the sword itself, while the two *hey's* are the two edges of the sword." So, we need to understand the association of the name *Havaya* with a "sword."

However, the matter is as follows; the "nourishment" of negative, extraneous forces [opposed to holiness] may take place in one of two ways. One, it may occur as the result of myriad contractions [of G-d's holy light]; as a holy ray of [His infinite] light takes on limitations, undergoing myriad contractions and becoming quite concealed and hidden. And then, even extraneous forces are able to leech energy from it. This is what is meant by "leeching from the back side of the 'skin' of *malchut*," meaning from the exterior of the skin, between the "hairs"...When His infinite light is revealed, the extraneous negative forces are unable to receive any nourishment whatsoever, since His infinite light dwells nowhere that is not nullified to it. But, where there is "ego" and experience of "self," there can be no revelation of His infinite light, since "Myself and he are unable to dwell together..."[77] And therefore the extraneous forces, which experience themselves as *yesh* and "something totally separate," since they divorce themselves from His unity, may He be blessed, are unable to receive from His holy revelation. But, when that light is hidden in a myriad number of contractions, then even the [extraneous forces] are able to receive extra "nourishment." This is because they possess a minimal amount of nullification, to the extent that they refer to Him as the "G-d of gods."[78] About this state of affairs, it is written, "Like a sheep before its shearer, rendered dumb..."[79] The "shearer" alludes to its hairs, and when G-d's holy light is drawn down by way of "hairs" (myriad contractions), then the extraneous forces as well may leech energy. And that is why Pharoah announced, "If he is a son, kill him, and if a daughter, let her live."[80] The "son" is *z'a*, or the lower seven *sephirot* of *Atzilut*, which illuminate with much light, as known that *z'a* contains much *chesed*, which shines in a revealed manner, preventing extraneous forces from leeching there. And that is why Pharoah sought to "kill" them, in order to remove the illumination [of G-dliness]. "And if a daughter, let her live," for the "daughter is *malchut*, and the construction (lit. "building") of *malchut* is from *gevurot* ("stringencies"), or contractions. And from these many contractions, that is, from "the back side of the skin of *malchut*," the extraneous forces are also able to leech.

---

77. Talmud *Sota* 5A
78. Talmud *Menachot* 110A
79. Isaiah 53:7
80. Exodus 1:22

And the second way in which the negative forces may "siphon off" nourishment is by receiving it from very high revelation of G-dliness, from the *makif,* or transcendent spirituality that is beyond the spiritual hierarchy of creation (*seder hishtalshelut*). As written, "The spider crawls on the hands, even while in the palace of the king."[81] The "spider" represents the *malchut* ("reign") of the *klipa,* or negative extraneous forces that conceal G-dliness. The *malchut* on the side of holiness is called *shem* ("name"), as known, while the *malchut* of *klipa* is called *shemeimit* ("spider"), with an additional *mem.* [There is a Torah concept which tells that anything additional] minimizes the concept, since whenever something extra [the second *mem*] is added, it lessens the overall effect. "Even while in the palace of the king," since from the perspective of the king, light and darkness are equal, and therefore even the *klipa* can siphon off G-dly energy.

Now, both of these methods of siphoning energy are dependent upon Jewish souls, as written, "Yakov is the rope of his inheritance."[82] As, by way of example, a rope whose one head is tied above and the other below, and when we shake the lower end, the upper also shakes, so the Jews; in whatever manner we act down here, so it is reflected above. The soul down here has a very high source, as known that its origin is in the ten *sephirot* of Atzilut, in *chochma* and even higher. And man is all-inclusive, containing the entire hierarchy of spiritual and physical creation, from the highest of all levels down to the lowest. As written in *Midrash Raba,* man was created from the higher worlds and the lowest, and since he includes everything, therefore whatever he does below arouses a corresponding response above, as well. And so, when man draws down upon himself the innermost will of G-d by learning Torah and praying, so a similar will is drawn down above as well, from the inner core of His will. And then a revelation of the infinite light shines down upon him, specifically in a holy place, and the *sitra achra* is unable to receive any nourishment from it at all. This corresponds to what was written above, that from the revelation of infinite light, the *klipot* are unable to receive any nourishment. However, when man lowers himself to the level of lust and animalistic spirit, descending below, he causes a corresponding descent above, G-d forbid. At that point, the illumination from Above descends in a series of contractions, facilitating "nourishment" of the extraneous forces opposed to *kedusha.* As written, "When *adam* talks below [about idle, unnecessary topics, or slanders another human being],

---

81. Proverbs 30:28
82. Deut. 32:9

then *ish* is lowered,"[83] meaning that when physical man "talks," succumbing to physical temptation, then [his counterpart above] - spiritual "man" -descends via multiple contractions, providing... additional "nourishment" for the *klipot*.

Although in any case, a certain amount of holy energy is diverted to the extraneous forces for the sake of their "maintenance,"[84] nevertheless when man descends, he draws down additional energy [to the *klipot*]. And it is possible that what he brings down comes from a higher level, descending via many contractions, gives the *klipot* additional energy. Moreover, the phrase, "a sheep before its shearer is rendered dumb," refers to the siphoning of energy via the "hairs," of the female [of *klipah*, mentioned above], which provides even more "nourishment." For, what was meted out to them, for their own maintenance, came from "between the hairs," but not from the hair itself. And if so, the nourishment that they gained from the hairs themselves is additional ["illicit"] energy.

In any case, the universe was created such that the holy worlds were located "above" the *klipot* and extraneous forces, and the holy energy that was meted out to the *klipot* maintained them in their appointed location under the worlds of holiness. But, the sin of the tree of knowledge caused the holy worlds to descend and become en-clothed within the *klippot* and extraneous forces. [Furthermore], every sin and transgression causes a reinforcement of the *klipot*, so that they permeate more of the realm of holiness.[85] Moreover, when man "puffs himself up," with pride and arrogance, this indicates the presence of ego as he expresses his pride, even in regard to G-dliness. For, if he were appropriately subdued and nullified to G-dliness, he would automatically express modesty and exude lowliness in his relationships with every man. [He would be similar to] Moshe, about whom it is written, "And the man Moshe was very modest from among all people on the face of the earth."[86] And this is because he was truly nullified to G-dliness, and therefore he was automatically low in his own eyes, more-so than were others [in his eyes]. The very opposite is true of arrogance in regard to others, which is also an indication of arrogance regarding G-dliness. This is all caused by the physical material of the body, as man "puffs up" his heart as a result of wealth and honor, even though he is aware

---

83. Isaiah 2:9, 5:15
84. See the *Remez* – R' Moshe Zacuto – on *parshat Bo* in the Zohar, p. 40B
85. See *Likutei Torah* of the *Ari z'l*, *parshat Breishit* and in the *Sha'ar maamorei harashibi*, *z'l* on the saying of the Zohar, *parshat Kedoshim* page 83
86. Numbers 12:3

of his real lowliness within. Nevertheless, he elevates himself without any reason or logic, and in this manner he generates *chutzpa* and arrogance from the extraneous forces, which raise themselves up to receive from Above, from very high places.

All of this occurs because the universe is within the heart of man, as the verse says, "...and also the universe is placed in their heart,"[87] which is why both types of "siphoning" of energy are the result of man's actions. That is what is meant by the word *Pharoah*, which contains the Hebrew letters, *haoref* ("the neck"). [The level of *klipah* represented by *Pharoah*, sometimes described as the "neck"], receives G-dliness from the "nape of *Arich anpin*," a very elevated spiritual level. And this takes place when the *avoda* of the Jews is [so deficient that it is as if] "they turned the back of their necks to me, and not their faces." This means that to the extent that they (the Jews) "turned to Me," from within their *avoda* in Torah and prayer and fulfilling the mitzvoth, it was with the "back of their neck" alone. This means that it was restricted to their superficial and extraneous faculties alone. This is [equivalent to the *avoda* of] "learned men," who fulfill mitzvoth by rote. Their *avoda* is cold, because they have gotten used to it, and they lack any inner desire to fulfill the will of G-d and to serve Him happily. And this is what leads to *Pharoah*, who siphons off G-dly energy from the neck of *Arich*, where "darkness is like light..."[88]

Now, even though it was explained above that it is due to arrogance that the *klipot* gain nourishment from the *makif*, or transcendent light, it should be clarified that siphoning [energy] from the *makif* may occur in two different ways. One such way is when the siphoning occurs at the superficial and extraneous levels - the external aspects of *arich* - as opposed to from within the internal faculties of *chochma* and the *midot* ("emotions"). [When the process occurs at the external, superficial level], the *klipot* are able to receive energy even in the absence of pride and arrogance. Since [from the perspective of] *makif*, "darkness is like light," when G-dly illumination descends without becoming en-clothed in our inner, permeating faculties, the *klipot* can also gain vitality. This then becomes the source of their pride and arrogance. Since the illumination is from a very elevated place, it produces arrogance within them, as well, in this manner.

---

87. Ecclesiastes 3:11
88. Zohar Section 1, Page 31A; Section 2 Page 38A, and *Tikunei Zohar* Tikun 30, Page 75A

From a holy perspective, when [G-dly illumination] descends from a very high place, it produces [the personal qualities of] *bitul* and nullification to the extreme, as written (regarding Yakov), *katonti mikol hachasadim* ("I am made small from all of this kindness...").[89] It was precisely because of G-d's kindness to Yakov that he [experienced himself as] "small," since "all is as nought before Him." And whatever is more "before Him" is more "nought," as written in *Igeret Hakodesh* (section four of Tanya) on this verse. This is not true, though of the "other side" (the forces opposed to *kedusha*), which when receiving illumination from a high place, become increasingly arrogant. This is what is meant then by, "Pharoah leeched from the exterior of *arich anipin*." Since the spiritual illumination of *arich anpin* does not descend via channels of immanent G-dliness,[90] [Pharoah was enabled to leech from it]. It was from this that he gained his arrogance, as he said, "Me, and noone else, the river is mine, and I made it..."[91]

The cause of this [in our personal *avoda*] is that, "they turned the nape of their neck to me..."[92] When our *avoda* occurs in an internal, meaningful fashion, then the transcendent illumination descends to imbue the inner, permeating light [with G-dliness], and automatically there can be no nourishment from the descent of the *makif*. But, when "they turned the nape of their neck to Me," then the extraneous forces are able to leech from the descent of the *makif*. Arrogance, though results in the elevation of the *klipot* and "other side," opposed to holiness. This occurs because, even when [the holy illumination] does not descend from the external aspects of the *makif*, as opposed to the internal, nonetheless, [the *klipot*] raise them selves up to receive from the *makif*, and this causes pride and arrogance below...

(Accordingly, even when the *makif* descends via channels of immanent illumination, making it is impossible for the *klipah* of *Pharoah* to gain nourishment,[93] nonetheless the arrogant *klipot* raise themselves to nourish from the external elements of the *makif*, as it

---

89. Genesis 32:11
90. Whatever G-dliness flows down to us from above, enters our soul by permeating our faculties of intellect and emotion – this is what is called "immanent G-dliness." But, the forces of *klipa* descend in a transcendent fashion, without truly permeating us.
91. Ezekiel 29:9
92. Jeremiah 2:27
93. As written in the writings of the *Ari z'l* on the words (in the Pesach *hagada*), *avadim haynu...and HaShem Elokeinu* ("We were slaves to Pharoah in Egypt, and G-d our Lord took us out..."), meaning that *av v'aim* (*chochma* and *bina*) enclothed the "arms" of *arich...*

is above the *pnimi*. And this is why G-d said to Moshe (after the sin of the golden calf), "I will separate Myself and your nation..."[94] That is, G-d suggested to Moshe that the *shechina* should not dwell upon the Jews. [More specifically] it meant that the *shechina* should not descend of its own accord, which would have been as the *makif* within the *pnimi*, permeating *chochma* and the *midot*.

It is arrogance that causes all of this, and accordingly, we can grasp the seriousness of excess pride. Even when we fulfill Torah and mitzvoth in a dedicated manner, nevertheless pride may cause the *klipah* to siphon off extra energy to the extraneous forces from the higher *makif*, as it exists above the inner, *p'nimi* light. (Now, all this is stated in regard to the external levels of the *makif*), which is why we were given 365 negative commandments, to distance the evil from us so that the negative forces cannot bloat themselves...).

Now, in order to sever the connection that provides nourishment in the two processes mentioned above, a "two-edged" sword is needed. This is what is meant by, "The greatness of G-d is in their throats, while the two-edged sword is in their hands." Since the "greatness of G-d is in their throats," the Jews receive a "sword of two edges in their hands." This means the following; within the throat are three elements – the *kaneh* ("windpipe"), the *veshet* ("esophagus") and the *vridim* ("vein"). For, the throat is a site of limitations, containing the straits of the gullet, and within it the three "ministers" of Pharoah; the *sar hamashkim* ("butler"), the *sar haophim* ("baker"), and the *sar hatabachim* ("butcher"), corresponding to the windpipe, esophagus and vein mentioned above. Now, just as these elements exist in *klipah* (forces opposed to holiness), so they exist in the realm of *kedusha* ("holiness") as well. Just as there are three "ministers" of Pharoah, so there are three "ministers" in the realm of holiness. The butler corresponds to the windpipe [through which fluids pass, as does the air that we breathe], and through the windpipe pass the nerve-endings of the brain, which transport moisture from the brain to the lungs and the heart, as the sages said: "There are three passages. One leads to the heart, one to the liver, and one to the lungs."[95] And [this minister] is called the "butler" since he channels the moisture of the brain into the heart and the lungs. Just as moisture gives rise to many different kinds of pleasure, so the windpipe generates many kinds of enjoyment of G-dliness, associated with the "greatness of G-d."

---

94. Exodus 33:16
95. Talmud *Chulin* 45B

This takes place as we meditate on the amazing exaltedness of the infinite light of G-d. [We consider] how this light is far above and elevated from the entire category of creation, and how even the highest worlds are not within range of the infinite One at all. And therefore, "I am *Havaya*, I have not changed;"[96] that is, there is no variation at all from before the world was created until after it was created, since [He and His world] are totally out of range of one another. And when we contemplate this in lengthy meditation, the light illuminates our brain and we very much enjoy the wondrous, exalted nature of the infinite One...this meditative [enjoyment] is conducted through the windpipe, which draws it down to the heart, as well. For, the main objective is for the meditation to be experienced precisely there, in the heart. As is written, "Her husband is known in the gates,"[97] about which the Zohar elaborates, "Each and every person according to his abilities, according to what is measured out in his heart."[98] It is also written, "You should know this today and place it upon your heart"[99] – the heart specifically, since it is the most important of our internal organs. This means that our heart should also experience the wonderful exalted greatness of the infinite One...In this manner, we experience *ahava beta'anugim* – "love with great pleasure" - in which we experience great enjoyment of G-dliness. We experience great cleaving and clinging to G-d...like the verse says, "remember the father, to be drawn after Him like water."[100] The nature of water is to cling, and the pleasure that we enjoy in G-dliness arouses us to cleave to Him with tremendous love. In this manner, we sever the connection of the extraneous forces, which were nourishing from on High. This is because our enjoyment occurs on a level that is beyond *seder hishtalshelut* ("the spiritual hierarchy" of creation), [as a result of our meditation] upon the infinite light of G-d that is removed and exalted over the worlds. And it descends to our mind and heart, [via] the *kaneh* ("windpipe"). [About the *kaneh*], the verse says, *kaneh chochma kaneh bina*[101] – "...acquire *chochma*, acquire *bina*..." This implies that first the pleasure of meditation shines in the mind and then afterward, by way of the *kaneh*, it descends to be experienced as pleasure in the heart, to be felt there as well, until the heart is aroused with love with great pleasure (*ahava beta'anugim*).

---

96. Malachi 3:6
97. Proverbs 31:23
98. Zohar Section 1, 103B
99. Deut. 4:39
100. From *Tefilat Geshem* (the prayer for rain recited by the *chazzan* on *Simchat Torah*)
101. Proverbs 4:5

Now, this [pleasure below] has an effect above, as well, arousing a descent of the infinite light from above *seder hishtalshelut* (the spiritual hierarchy of the chain of creation) to descend to the *sephira* of *chochma* and the supernal *midot* (seven "emotional *sephirot*"), from where the extraneous forces are unable to siphon off energy. For, only from the transcendent light are they able to siphon off energy, since from there, "darkness is like light." But when this transcendent light is drawn down into immanent light, then *bitul* and self-nullification is required [in order to receive energy from this level], and the *klipot*, which are egotistical, are unable to receive any energy from there.

Additionally, the great love (*ahava beta'anugim*) mentioned above motivates us to fulfill the 248 positive commands, as written in Tanya,[102] "For the one who truly fulfills them is the one who loves *Havaya* and truly desires to cling to Him…" By fulfilling the positive mitzvoth, we bring down transcendent light [to unite with] immanent spirituality. And them, automatically, the extraneous forces are unable to receive "nourishment."

Now, the "butcher" corresponds to the *vridim* ("veins"). These are the "veins" through which the blood flows from the heart to ascend to the brain in the skull, and also to branch out to all of the limbs. This is what is alluded to by "hot-bloodedness" within the realm of *kedusha*, which corresponds to love of G-d like "flames of fire." For, the *kaneh* (the "butler") corresponds to love like water (*ahavah beta'anugim*, mentioned above), while the *vridim* ("butcher") corresponds to love like fire. Now, this fire of holiness [initiates a process in which] "fire devours fire;"[103] that is, it consumes the "fire" of the "other side" - incinerating foreign lusts and external desires [of the animal soul]. That is why the Targum *Onkelos* [the primary Aramaic translation of the Torah] translates "butcher" as *rav katolaya* ("the master of slaughtering"), since [in the realm of *kedusha*] he incinerates and consumes the foreign lusts and desires, etc. And in this manner, the siphoning of the first category - that occurs as the result of many contractions of His holy light - is severed and disconnected. The multitude of contractions occur as the result of the "spirit of the animal, which descends," lowering itself into physical lusts. But, the "butcher" incinerates and consumes all of the lusts and foreign desires, and automatically they are unable to siphon off any energy and nourishment. Furthermore, love like fire results in *sur marah* ("turning away from evil" - since this love eradicates anything

---

102. Likutei amarim, chapter 4,
103. Talmud *Yoma* 21B

associated with temptation and lust, it is understood that it leads to "turning away from evil"), which motivates our fulfillment of the 365 negative commandments. Now, the 365 negative commandments facilitate the separation and distancing of evil from holiness, so that evil forces are unable to raise themselves up to siphon off [holy energy] from supernal transcendent spirituality (as it exists above the immanent light).

In general, the "butler" and the "butcher" in the realm of *kedusha* are associated with nullification (*bitul*), which is the diametric opposite of pride and arrogance. Automatically, then they lack the self-elevation and arrogance to siphon off from "high" spiritual levels. Now, the [third minister], the "baker," corresponds to the verse, "And ten women will bake their bread in one oven..."[104] wherein "bread" symbolizes the Torah, as written, "Come, eat of my bread..."[105] This [bread] is baked in one oven, which symbolizes the heat generated from love like fire, resulting from our meditation on "One," the "Unique one of the universe." For, as mentioned above, in order for our Torah learning to be acceptable and appropriate, proper prayer is necessary.

And in general, the "baker" alludes to speech, since the "baker" is associated with the esophagus (*veshet*), which is the intermediary between the windpipe (*kaneh*) and the veins (*vridim*), and includes both of them. The veins are blood vessels, and the blood is composed of the food that passes through the esophagus. Water as well passes through the esophagus. [The two together contribute to] speech, which includes water and fire, that descends from the mind to the heart, as mentioned above. And this is what is meant by the nation of *Emori*; the name *Emorites* comes from the word *amira*, meaning "speech." And there is *emori* of the "other side" (opposed to holiness) – this is speech that is associated with the *klipot* which conceal holiness. In fact, speech is the main component of the *klipot*, (since the shattering of the vessels took place in the letters and the vessels of the world of *Tohu*). And as the saying goes, "Words are a sign of nonsense..."[106] It is known that speech of the "the other side" is very low and disgraceful, and it has a [negative] influence on the very inner point of the soul...[This applies not only to] forbidden speech, but even to idle talk, which has a very powerful [negative] effect, as known regarding the many "foreign thoughts" and negative ruminations that occur to us as a result of idle talk. All of this is

---

104. Leviticus 26:26
105. Proverbs 9:5
106. Zohar Section 3, Page 193B

associated with the "baker" of "the other side" [who hides and conceals G-dliness]. Now, it is possible that he is called the "baker" for yet another reason - because speech may create more fiery excitement and arousal. For example, when we speak about matters of lust and temptations of the heart this produces more fire than when these matters remain in thought alone.

Now, in the realm of holiness, the *Emorites* refers to speech of Torah, which in this case is called the "baker" as well, because by speaking words of Torah, we generate an extra amount of "fire." Clearly, when we learn Torah, expressing ourselves verbally, we learn with greater excitement of the heart, and with additional energy, as a result of the heat [that we generate] like flames of fire. And as mentioned, he is called the "baker" because of the theme of "Ten women...in one oven," mentioned above.

[And this brings us back to] the original theme, "The majesty of G-d is in their throats, while a two-edged sword is in their hands." This means that while the majesty of G-d is in their throats – in the three ministers mentioned above (the "butler, the butcher and the baker") - a "two-edged sword" is [in their hands] to sever the connection that nourishes the extraneous forces in both of the ways mentioned.

Now, in general, this [occurs during] the recital of the *shema*, which requires meditation on G-dliness in order to achieve the two different types of love of G-d mentioned above. Possibly, we might say that meditation on [the meaning of] *Havaya Elokeinu, Havaya echad* ("*Havaya* is our Lord, *Havaya* is one") ultimately leads to *ahava beta'anugim* ("love with great pleasure"), since the main pleasure that we derive [during this meditation] is from beyond logic and intellect. That is, the meditation of *Havaya echad*, on how the infinite light of G-d is unique and singular even from the perspective of the created worlds, is a theme that in essence is beyond grasp. Our [limited] grasp of this concept consists of understanding how, even after their creation, the myriad worlds and multitudinous creations, are one simple unity, and are truly united, as written elsewhere. That is, we only grasp that this is the truth, but exactly how it is true is beyond our grasp. And therefore, this brings us to "love with pleasure" (*ahava b'taanugim*), or revelation of light that in essence is above intellect and logic.

And while meditating upon [the second verse of the *shema*], *baruch shem kevod malchuto leolam vaed* ("Blessed be His holy name forever and ever"), we focus upon the ray and reflection of G-dliness that enlivens and maintains the worlds via *memalle kol olamim* (immanent spirituality). This is a meditation that requires us to apply intellect and logic, and the result is that we achieve love of G-d like flames of fire. As known, love with pleasure (*ahava beta'anugim*) is associated with *chochma*, while love like flames of fire is associated with *bina*, as written elsewhere. And this is how the "two-edged sword" is created in order to sever the nourishment of the extraneous forces in both ways mentioned above, so that they no longer siphon off energy from the realm of holiness.

This also implies that the name *Havaya* is like a sword, so that if the *klipa* raises itself like an eagle, "from there I will take you down, says *Havaya*."[107] That is, when the divine illumination descends by way of the name *Havaya*, then the external forces that are opposed to G-liness are unable to receive any nourishment from the *makif*, or transcendent G-dliness. This is because the illumination comes from *Havaya*, which illuminates internally, as immanent G-dliness. Furthermore, the extraneous forces are unable to siphon off energy from G-dliness that descends via many contractions, because the name *Havaya* illuminates [throughout the contractions] in a revealed fashion. And this is what the Zohar means when it says that the two letters *hey* of the name *Havaya* are the two "edges of the sword." The first *hey*, or *hey ilaah* is the "upper edge," through which the light illuminates within *bina*. *Bina* is *aim habanim* – the "mother of the children" [the source of our G-dly emotions] – whose light descends to *z'a* [the emotions] as well. In this way [by channeling the light to the G-dly emotions, *bina*] prevents the siphoning off of energy from the *makif*, or transcendent light.

And the *hey tata'ah*, or second *hey* of the name *Havaya*, is associated with *malchut* [the last of the ten *sephirot*]. When the holy light illuminates in *malchut*, the extraneous forces are unable to "nurse" from the multiple contractions, either.

Now, *kashti* – "my bow" – refers to the *shemonah esreh*, or the "eighteen benedictions" that we recite during the *amida*. The majority of the blessings that we recite – the twelve "middle" blessings, during which we issue our private wishes – are requests. This refers to the twelve "middle" blessings of the *amida*, when we issue our private requests. Now, a request is inappropriate unless we are deficient in something, whereupon we make a request to fulfill our needs. But, if we are not lacking anything, then requests are inappropriate. However, it is known that the requests that we make during the *shemonah esreh* are not only for our physical needs, in

---

107. Jeremiah 49:16

order fulfill whatever we are lacking physically. Rather, we request from G-d to fulfill our spiritual needs as well. For the fact that G-dliness is not revealed and does not illuminate our souls or the universe [results in a "deficiency"]. And this causes a physical deficiency as well, since if G-dliness would be revealed, then automatically, all would be "good" for us physically as well. For example, during the time that the Temple stood, and there was revealed G-dliness illuminating the world, there was abundant influx filling the world as well, including physical abundance, as every man "dwelt under his own vine and his own fig tree."[108] So, when there is a physical deficiency, it is the result of a spiritual lacking. And that is precisely what we request during the *shemonah esreh* - that revealed G-dliness should descend to us. This is what is meant by the words, *Baruh Atah Havaya* – "Blessed are You, Lord" – which means that we hope that His blessing will descend in a revealed manner.

Now, this occurs as we meditate upon the exalted majesty of G-dliness, and how nothing is within range of it at all, and how we are very distant from G-d. As a result, we become bitter within and request, from the depths of our heart for revelation of G-dliness down here in this world. Now, our requests create a "bow" to kill the extraneous forces. The difference between a sword and a bow is that the sword kills the enemy who is standing nearby, close to us. But, the enemy who stands at a distance cannot be killed by a sword. He can, though be eliminated by a bow, with which it is possible to kill the enemy even when he stands at a distance. Moreover, the further that we draw the bow, and in proportion to our extra pull, the greater is the distance over which it is effective. And so it is with prayer; our requests become like a bow to eliminate the more refined evil within ourselves. And what more that we draw the bow; that is, what more that we are embittered over our distance from G-d, the more effective are our prayers in eliminating the evil that is very refined within, that we may not even be aware of. The verse that says, "They are fools – because of the way of their transgressions..."[109] refers to those who do not even experience the refined evil that is inside of themselves. It seems to them that there is no evil inside since they pay not attention to it...or they may not consider it to be evil. And because they are unconscious of the evil within, it manages to "take them down," G-d forbid, slowly [because they are not aware of it]. But, by praying the *shemonah esreh*, we succeed in severing the connection of even the most refined evil.

---

108. Kings 1, 5:5
109. Psalms 107:17

And that is the reason why it is after the *shemonah esreh* that we say *vidui* ("confession"), reciting *ashamnu, bagadnu*...for at first glance we should ask for forgiveness before *shemonah esreh* [rather than after]. However, prior to the *shemonah esreh*, we think of ourselves as innocent, as if we have not done any transgressions, and quite the opposite; if we did a mitzvah or learned some Torah, we therefore think that we are close to G-dliness, and we are unaware of the evil inside of us. However, after the purifying process of *shemonah esreh*, "...as silver is purified..."[110] each person [is purified and elevated] "according to his own praises;"[111] that is, according to the praises and the glorification that we recite during *tefila*, as we seek to approach G-d. And precisely at that time is when we encounter the dregs and waste products (*sigim* and *pesolet*) within, that prevent and block revelation.

Now, during the *pesukei dezimra* and the *kriat shema*, we encounter only the most obvious and coarse evil within ourselves, and not the more subtle and refined evil. This is because subtle and refined evil does not prevent revelation of lower levels of spirituality. Only in regard to higher levels does the more subtle evil inside of us manage to hide and conceal...And therefore, it is precisely when we arrive to the *shemonah esreh*, and we desire closeness and proximity to the infinite light above - from which we are completely out of range - precisely then is when we experience the subtle evil within ourselves and we are become very bitter about it. And that is what enables us to excise the subtle evil within. That is the reason why we recite various confessions after the *shemonah esreh*, since in that way we repel the evil...

Now, in particular, there are five weapons of war counted in the Mishna;[112] the dagger, the bow, the shield, the club and the spear. The dagger is equivalent to the sword, mentioned above regarding the verse, "The greatness of G-d is in their throats, and a two-edged sword in their hands." The bow symbolizes the personal requests that we make during the *shemonah esreh* (as mentioned above). The Talmud, though calls the bow a *gulpa*, which is a club with which to beat the enemy, "because with words [alone] the servant [i.e. the animal soul] will not leave,"[113] and so it is necessary to chase it with a staff. Now, this topic corresponds to what is taught in *Midrash Raba* on the verse [that G-d said to Moshe], "Take the staff..." The

---

110. Proverbs 27:21
111. End of the verse in Proverbs 27:21
112. *Shabbat* 63A
113. Proverbs 29:19

Midrash[114] says, "This corresponds to the verse, 'the staff of your strength will be sent by *HaShem* from *Zion*'[115] - G-d does not beat the wicked except with a staff. Why? Because they are like dogs, as it says, 'They return in the evening, howling like dogs.'[116] Just as we strike dogs with a staff, so [the wicked] need to be struck by a staff, which is why it is referred to as "the staff of your strength." Now, that the wicked are called "dogs" is understood from *Midrash Rabba*,[117] which says that the wicked are ruled by their own hearts, as written, "And Esau said in his heart..."[118] as well as "And Haman said in his heart."[119] The righteous, however rule over their hearts, as we see in the verses, "And David said to his heart,"[120] and, "Chana was speaking to her heart,"[121] as well as "And Daniel directed his heart."[122] In this, they are similar to their Creator, about Whom the Torah says, "And G-d said to His heart."[123]

The concept is as follows; the saying that the righteous, "rule over their heart," means that they govern their heart with their minds, just as in the verse regarding G-d, "And G-d said to His heart..." This verse indicates that His divine will descends, bypassing the emotions, similar to [Yom Kippur, when we supplicate], "So may Your mercy conquer your anger..."[124] This occurs as, "And G-d smelled the aroma [of the offerings]..."[125] [The offerings] draw down a new divine Will, so to speak, to change and to transform the emotions, from *gevura* to *chesed*. Regarding the righteous, they are described in the saying of the sages, "Who is strong? He who conquers his evil inclination..."[126] This saying alludes to the governing power of the mind over the emotions. The mind subdues the emotions so that they act according to the [dictates of the] intellect alone. For, the intellect infuses the emotions with *bitul*, or self- nullification.

Now, this is actually what occurred when Aharon kindled the

---

114. Shemot, Ch.9, siman 3
115. Psalms 110:2
116. Psalms 59:7 and 59:15
117. Noach, Ch.34 and *Toldos*, Ch. 67
118. Genesis 27:41
119. Esther 6:6
120. Samuel 1 27:1
121. Samuel 1 1:13
122. Daniel 1:8
123. End of verse Genesis 8:21
124. Text of Yom Kippur prayers
125. Beginning of verse Genesis 8:21
126. Ethics of the Fathers 4:1

menorah in the holy Temple. By lighting the *menorah*, he drew down G-dly influx to the *sephira* of *chochma* ("wisdom", born of self-nullification) into the *midot*, or holy emotions, so that they became refined and purified, as they became permeated with *bitul*, or nullification.[127] The wicked, however, are ruled by their own hearts, since their intellect fails to hold sway over their emotions. Quite the opposite, they place emphasis is upon the heart, which is why they are compared to dogs, as the sages said, "the *kelev* ('dog') is *kol-lev* ('entirely heart')." The root of this matter, as it stems from the difference between the world of *tohu* and the world of *tikun*, is a known topic. In *Tohu*, the emotions exist as separate entities, distinct from the intellect, and therefore the intellect has no effect upon them. And that is the reason why there is intense revelation of [divine] light, refracting in diverse directions [in the world of *Tohu*]. For, [genuine] revelation of intellect produces nullification of the *midot*, or emotions. [G-dly] illumination weakens the light of the emotions so that they are not so intense. For example, love born of the intellect must be limited. It is limited to the boundaries imposed by the mind, which obligates the emotions to exist in one form or another. And since the emotion is limited, it automatically allows room for an opposite emotion to exist as well. That is, after our love ceases to increase, it allows room for *gevura*. And since the two co-exist with one another, spontaneous inter-inclusion occurs between the two, so that both of them co-exist regarding to the same matters. Furthermore, their co-existence occurs according to the dictates of the intellect, since the intellect dictates that love [which is an outgrowth of *chesed*] should also be laced with *gevura*.

Now, all of this occurs when love is born of intellect. However, when emotions are aroused of their own volition, the arousal occurs with great intensity. This is like an animal that possesses strong feelings, since it lacks the intellect with which to temper its emotions. Its emotions emerge from within, which is why they are powerful, and of course they do not tolerate or include one another. Similarly by way of example, the world of *tohu*, which contains a great amount of illumination of intense light, is not *butel* ("nullified") or tempered whatsoever, but is rather very intense. That is why it is expressed as "separate branches" or diverse directions, which are not inclusive of one another at all. In the world of *tikun*, though, the illumination is minimized, and [the *sephirot*] coexist inter-included with one another. Now, this minimization, or weakening of the lights was produced by

---

127. See *Torah Ohr*, in the discourse beginning with "On the 25th of *Kislev*," and in *Heichaltzu* of the year *5659*

what the kaballists call the *shem Mah* (the name of *Havaya* spelled with *aleph's*, producing a numerical value of 45, or *Mah* – which in Hebrew means "what"), which illuminates within the *sephira* of *chochma*. It is the main component of *tikun*, which occurs when the catalyst of *shem Mah* emerges from the "forehead of A"K." Regarding this level, the Zohar says,[128] "*shem Mah* within, as it is the path of *Atzilut*," since it is en-clothed in the *sephira* of *chochma*. And therefore, *chochma* is also portrayed as *koach mah* – the "power of *Mah*" – [the "power of nullification"] which is equivalent to "nothingness" and nullification. And the *bitul* of *Mah* catalyzes nullification in the emotions as well. [The nullification] is their "weakness," which ensures that they become inter-included.

This, then is the general distinction between the emotions of the divine soul, and those of the animal soul. The emotions of the divine soul emerge from the intellect alone, which is why the divine soul is also called *adam* ("man"), as written, "You are Adam."[129] For, man, for the most part, is composed of intellect, and all human matters – all of them – are motivated by intellect alone.[130] This is not true of the emotions of the animal soul, which are not motivated by intellect. For, as we see, the natural emotions arise of their own volition, either to like something that is attractive to us or similarly to detest that which damages us. Even here, it may seem as if intellect is involved, and it may appear as though arousal of the emotions occurred via the intellect. However, in truth the main development of emotion does not stem from the intellect alone. The proof of this is that the emotion is much more intense than the intellect. The intellect does not demand anything close to the level of intensity of the emotion, and this is proof that the emotion arouses of its own volition.

Thus, the entire basis of the animal soul is emotions alone. In fact, that is why it is called the "animal soul" – it is comparable to an animal that has no intellect, but only emotions. And therefore, wicked people as well as the negative emotions of the animal soul are called "dogs," since they are "entirely heart" – at core, they are emotional. Although they possess intellect as well, it does not rule over their heart in a way that would persuade the emotions to

---

128. In *Petach Eliyahu*
129. Ezekiel 28:2
130. See *Likutei Torah*, in the discourse, *Mashachni acharecha venarutza* – "Draw me after You and we will run" – where it says that even *reuta d'liba* (the "will" of the heart to cling to G-d) is motivated by intellect, but for unconscious reasons, and therefore the principle of "mind over emotions" may also apply to the inner, concealed recesses of the heart as well, as written elsewhere.

operate according to the intellect. Quite the opposite, the emotions overwhelm the intellect. At the point of emotional arousal, the person loses his intellect, as if it never existed, and then he acts like a fool, lacking knowledge. When this occurs, he imagines that nobody sees him, and that nobody knows of his acts, because if he thought that anyone was aware of his behavior, he would cease acting this way at all – thus, he thinks that nobody knows. One with healthy intellect does not think like this. In truth, everybody knows what is going on with him, and [the fact that he thinks that nobody knows] is a sign that he has "lost" his intellect due to his overwhelming emotions. And therefore, we see that he may act in a farcical fashion until he achieves the goal of his lust. And yet, his intellect does not require him to act this way at all, and he does so only because he has "lost his mind."

And that is why the phrase, "with words [alone] the servant will not leave," refers to the animal soul, for which words of rebuke – that is, words of *chochma* and *da'at* - will not achieve the goal of nullifying and overcoming. [The animal soul] emerges mainly on account of his emotions, and since they are intensely overwhelming, they overcome his intellect, and he acts as if it does not exist. That being the case, what will words of rebuke help, since he cannot accept them at all? And also if he hears and accepts these words to a certain extent (before the full strength of his emotions has overwhelmed his intellect) they have no effect upon his emotions, since at that point his mind does not govern over his heart. In such a case, there is no choice but to chase after him with a "club." And about this we say, "Just as one beats a dog with a staff, so G-d beats the wicked..." who are entirely heart, and they are governed by their heart...

Within each and every one of us, this "drama" between the divine soul and the animal soul plays itself out. In order to subdue the negative emotions of the animal soul, the divine soul must chase after and "beat" [the animal soul], specifically with a staff. Even so, it is explained elsewhere that the animal soul is also affected by meditation of the divine soul during prayer, which persuades it to achieve *ve'ahavta* [love of G-d], so that it should also love G-d. And there it is explained that this is because the intellect of the divine soul is en-clothed in that of the animal soul, and by meditating on the divine soul, the animal soul comes to understand G-dly concepts, leading to love of G-d.[131] Nevertheless, possibly this is because the

---

131. See the discourse beginning with *vehinei Rivka yotzait* – within the discourse, *vayatzag et hamakelot* of the year *5659*

process [of meditation] occurs after the animal soul receives its "beating," since then the animal soul in general is crushed.

Now, it is mentioned in *Perek Shira* that the song of the dog is the verse, *Bo'u nishtachaveh venivrechah* ("come, let us prostrate ourselves and bow..."). And the *Yalkut*,[132] says that R' Yishayahu, the student of R' Hanina ben Dosa, fasted 88 fasts and then said, "Dogs, about whom is written that 'dogs, who have *chutzpa* will merit to sing this song..." We may explain this by citing what the sages said in *Midrash Raba*[133] on the verse, *Vayetzavum el Pharoah* ("and issue this command to Pharoah"[134]): "Consider the parable of a king, who had an orchard in which he planted...shade trees and fruit trees. His servants said to him, "What pleasure do you have from shade trees...just as praise of G-d uttered by the righteous ascends to *Gan eden,* so praise uttered by the wicked ascends...they say "You have judged properly, you have appropriately found us guilty." [From this Midrash], it emerges, then, that the wicked utter these praises only after they have already been struck and received their punishment. And similarly, the dogs [in *Perek Shira*] say, "come let us prostrate and bow," after they have been struck.

This process is understood within the soul, as well. The effect that the intellect and meditation have upon on our animal soul, occurs after it has been "struck" and whipped by the G-dly soul. This produces an overall nullification of the animal soul, so that the mind rules over the emotions...(And it is also explained above that the main arousal of the emotions of the animal soul comes from the emotions of the G-dly soul).

Now, the theme of "striking" in *avodat HaShem* refers to the anger that we project from our G-dly soul onto our animal soul, as in the saying of the sages, "One should always arouse the fury of his good inclination over his evil inclination."[135] And as written in Tanya,[136] "man should thunder over the evil inclination in a loud voice and anger in his thought, saying, 'You are evil, wicked and disgusting and loathsome and lowly...how long will you conceal..." and with the anger that he projects upon it, the [evil inclination] is subdued and held in check.

Now, it is possible that this is equivalent to the [process occurring during prayer, called] "engraving from without." One who wants to

132. *parshat Bo, remez* 187
133. *Vaera*, Ch. 7
134. Exodus 6:13
135. Talmud *Berachot* 5A
136. Ch. 29

turn a piece of wood into a tool, first cuts the wood externally and then smoothes it. And afterward, he creates a hollow within it, so that it becomes a vessel that is capable of containing something. Similarly, perhaps we could say that the anger that we project upon the evil inclination has the effect of producing within it nullification and subjugation in general, so that it will be possible to turn it into a proper tool afterward, by way of *avoda* (meditation) of the mind and the heart of the G-dly soul, as mentioned. And the explanation of, "One should always arouse..." is that there is always a bit of anger inside of us, from our faculty of strictness within, since there is no person who does not include both good and bad. And the bad is the "anger" and the fury, all of which is from the "evil side." The anger and the fury should be turned against the bad inside, so that we lose our temper and flare in anger over the evil inside of ourself. This is the *alah*, or "club" with which we "beat" the animal soul within man.

And the spear is the *kriat shema*, as written in the Zohar on the verse, "...and he took a spear in his hand."[137] The spear [*romeach* in Hebrew, bearing the numerical value of 248] represents the 248 words of the *kriat shema* (in more detail, the sword represents the *pesukei dezimra*, which speak of the "majesty of G-d..." while the spear symbolizes the *kriat shema*). For just as with the spear, one is able to totally eliminate, so with the *kriat shema*, we totally and absolutely nullify and eradicate the evil, that was imposed by the "wicked one who ruled over the good man" [the evil inclination that attempts to dominate the good inside of us] and completely eliminate its vitality.

Now, possibly we could say that the difference between the club and the spear, is that within the emotions of the animal soul, there exist two elements. One is lust for permitted objects, and the second is lust for forbidden objects, which comes from the evil of *klipat nogah* [where good and bad are mixed]. Regarding the first, it is sufficient to strike and hit it with a staff, or club, and in this way it becomes subdued and then one is able afterward to transform it into a G-dly force, as mentioned above. But, the second element demands complete and total eradication by way of the sword and spear.

Now, the shield is what we use to protect ourselves from arrows that are shot at us by the enemy. In service of G-d, this occurs during the time of prayer, which [the Zohar tells us] is the "time of battle," when we don our *talit* and *tefillin*. [The latter] are capable of protecting us and offering shelter from the enemy who stands before

---

137. Numbers 25:7

us to knock us down, G-d forbid, with lusts and evil thoughts...And it is specifically at the time of *kriat shema* and *shemonah esreh* that it attempts to overwhelm us, just as do those who fight with each other, as written in Tanya, Ch. 28. And therefore, we don the *talit* and *tefillin* at that time, since as known the performance of mitzvoth produces "garments for the soul." And the mitzvoth then also produce "garments" to protect us from the arrows and hurtling rocks of the enemy, so that they will not touch us...

Now, in general the theme of the "sword" of prayer is equivalent to the "sword of peace." For, it says in the Zohar that, "bread is eaten by the edge of the sword."[138] This means that the time of eating is also a time of "war," as known that the entire topic of eating takes place in order to refine the sparks of the world of *Tohu* that fell into our food. These sparks, when refined, add to our energy level. And this is what the sages meant when they said that, "In the time of the Temple, the altar would atone for us, and now it is the meal table that atones for us."[139]

And at first glance, it is not understood, for how is it possible for the table to take the place of the altar? But the topic is as follows: The altar atoned for man when physical animals were sacrificed upon it. This is because the spiritual source of the animal came from the world of *Tohu* that was higher than *Tikun*, but it "fell" below. And the offering of the animal elevates it back to its source and origin in the world of *Tohu*, which in turn brings down divine illumination from *Tohu* into the *kelim*, or vessels of *Tikun*. Now, since the illumination of *Tohu* far surpasses that of *Tikun*, [when it descends], it is capable of repairing and re-filling the blemishes and leaks that were caused in the world of *Tikun* by our transgressions. As known, re-filling the leak requires that the illumination comes from a higher level of revelation. That is why the revelation of the illumination from *Tohu* was able to rectify the deficiencies [created by our transgressions]. This is what is meant by "the altar atoned."

Similarly, man's meal table atones for him. At first glance it is not understood; how can man receive life energy from plant and animals? Man is of the category of *medaber* – "he who speaks" – which is far above the level of vegetable and animal, so how can he receive his life energy and vitality from a lower category of creation? However, this occurs because the source and root of the vegetable and animal worlds surpass the level of man. Man is from the world of *Tikun*, while the plant and animal worlds are from *Tohu*, which

---

138. Zohar Section 3, Page 185B
139. Talmud *Berachot*, page 55A

transcends the level of *Tikun*, but they "fell" below. They are uplifted and refined by man, so that when man eats his food "for the sake of Heaven," blessing before and afterward, the sparks from the world of *Tohu* within the food become included in the soul of man, adding to his strength and vitality. This is what is meant by ""man's table atones for him" – as a result of the revelation of the lights of *Tohu* that illuminate...

And for this reason, we must be very careful when eating, to keep in mind the elevation of the sparks of *Tohu* within our food. That is, we must eat for the sake of Heaven in order to learn Torah and to pray, and not merely to fulfill our own lusts. And if not, when we eat only to satisfy our own lusts, then we do not merely descend from our spiritual level, which is the category of *medaber*, to the level of vegetable and animal and even lower since we receive our vitality from them. At that moment, we descend even further, to the level of the three totally impure *klipot* [in which there is no good, and only bad, and no redeeming value]. This condition then lasts until we do *tshuva* and return to proper *avodat HaShem*, as written in Tanya.[140] Furthermore, even if we do not eat to simply fulfill our own lusts, but rather we fail to eat for the "sake of Heaven," and we therefore fail to refine the holy spark within the food, then the food pulls us down into *noga*, which is the *klipah* composed of mixed good and bad (it seems that this is what is meant above by "he becomes like the vegetable and animal categories"). And as a result, we become more coarse and physical.

And this is the reason that *amei ha'aretz* (unlearned Jews) are forbidden to eat meat. Since they are unable to refine and elevate the meat, it pulls their spiritual level down.[141] This, then is what is meant by, "We eat bread by the edge of the sword;" within every *avoda* and in particular within the *avoda* of refinement, the animal soul stands against us to challenge, and we must wage war with him and struggle to overwhelm him.

Now, the *avoda* that takes place during eating is called the "sword of war." For, during prayer, the *avoda* is to refine our animal soul. This occurs when divine illumination shines into our soul through meditation on G-dliness. At that time, the emotions of our G-dly soul are awakened. Therefore, the *avoda* becomes easier, since in any case the animal soul is nullified to G-d as a result of the illumination that shines...and in this manner, the "war" is made easier. This is not the case, though regarding eating, when meditation is not appropriate,

---

140. Likutei Amarim, ch. 7
141. See the *siddur* of the *Ariz'l* (from *R' Shabtai*) regarding our intentions during eating

since we cannot remain all day long in a state of meditation. Furthermore, the emotional arousal of the G-dly soul which occurs during *tefila* dissipates afterward, leaving nothing more than a mere impression. Moreover, [while eating] we are involved and enmeshed in the physical world. As we pray though, we are separate and removed from the physical world, although we are nonetheless en-clothed in the animal soul that is also from *noga*. But, nevertheless the [animal] soul is [involved in] spirituality. This is not the case at the time of eating, when we are involved and en-clothed in physical objects, and the revelation of light is concealed. And for this reason the "war" at such times is more difficult (and that is why the advice to make the "war" easier is that during *tefila*, we should make a firm resolution regarding our conduct for the rest of the day. For, during *tefila*, G-dly illumination shines in our soul, and we separate ourselves from all physical matters. Therefore, it is easier to make resolutions regarding how we will act later, while involved in eating, drinking and the rest of our matters. This firm resolution comes from the faculty of *netzach* in our soul. It helps, so that when we encounter physical matters, we actually perform according to our previous resolution). And for this reason, our *avoda* during eating is truly called a "sword of war."

This is not true though during *tefila*. Since there is revealed illumination shining [during prayer], it is called a "sword of peace." And the verse, "And I placed peace in the land," applies to Torah, about which it is said, "And a sword will not pass through your land," not even a "sword of peace." For, it is known that the act of refining the holy sparks may take place in one of two different ways. The first is by way of "war." This occurs when the one who purifies en-clothes himself in the garment of the one who needs purification. He becomes close to him, working and involving himself with him, in order to persuade and refine him. For example, when two people wrestle with one another, they grasp and grapple with each other, as each one struggles to overwhelm and subdue the other. And whoever has more strength is the one who overwhelms and "wins" the match, subduing the other. The corresponding example of this in *avoda* is the war between the G-dly and the animal soul (especially at the time of eating). The G-dly soul is en-clothed in the animal soul, and wrestles with it in *avoda* and labor of the mind and heart, with intellectual grasp and meditation and arousal of love and fear of G-d, in order to overwhelm and subdue the animal soul and to subjugate the *sitra achra* ("other side," opposed to holiness). And then, at moment the animal soul gropes and struggles with its enemy is precisely when foreign thoughts enter our minds every day. This is because the animal soul fights during its war with the G-dly soul, trying to bring it down, G-d forbid, as written in Tanya. However, the G-dly soul in essence has more power than does the animal soul. As is known, its true source and origin is above the source of the animal soul. And from its source, it derives the power to overwhelm the animal soul. This is what is meant by [the Talmudic saying], "Have [the embryo in the womb] swear that it will be a *tzadik...*"[142] This refers to the power that the oath brings down from its source and origin, as written elsewhere.[143] This process is likened to a "war," since the [G-dly soul] is esconced in the [animal soul] and involved with it in order to refine it. Automatically, then, the refinement takes place through labor and work.

However, the second path [of refinement] occurs when the process takes place "in peace," because there is no en-clothement at all in the "garments" of the object of refinement, and the refiner is not involved with the object of refinement whatsoever. Then, the process of refinement takes place automatically, as the result of revelation of light that illuminates the one in need. For example, a great king, to whom everyone is subjugated, need not wage war at all because he is very renowned. He is known from a distance, even on faraway islands, and all nations are nullified and attracted to him. An example would be King Shlomo, about whom it is written that he was a "man of rest,"[144] and "and I will grant peace in his days."[145] No wars were necessary [in his days] because everyone was subjugated to him and they all streamed to him. They were subjugated to him because of his majestic greatness. And so it will be in the days of *meshiach* (the Jewish messiah) as written, "And they will flow to him, all of the nations of the world,"[146] since in the future, everyone will be attracted to *meshiach*. This will enable the *meshiach* to refine the more positive aspects from within all people, so that they [their souls] will be included within him, without any labor or effort at all.

And this, as well is the difference between the *avoda* of the weekdays and the *avoda* of Shabbat. During the six days of the week, it is written, "Six days shall you work,"[147] referring to the work and

---

142. Talmud *Nida* 30B
143. See the discourse, *U'beyom habikurim, 5654* of the Rebbe Rashab
144. Chronicles 1, 22:9
145. Chronicles 1, 22:9
146. Isaiah 2:2, Micah 4:1
147. Exodus 20:9, 23:12

labor of refinement. However, on Shabbat, purification [of bad from good] is forbidden. Nonetheless the *avoda* of refinement takes place on Shabbat as well. But, it is refinement that takes place spontaneously and automatically, as a result of the spiritual illumination that shines on Shabbat, which refines the holy sparks automatically, without any need for labor whatsoever...

Now, the root of the refinement that takes place "in peace" is from the spiritual level of *Atik*, as written in the Zohar[148] – "Your eyes will see Yerushalayim in peace"[149] – referring to the future, since regarding the present, it is written that "G-d is a man of war."[150] The latter is an allusion to the name *Havaya* as it is enclothed in *z'a* – the six lower emotional attributes of Atzilut (and *malchut*)...since it is in *z"a* that the "war" [of refinement above takes place] because there we find the existence of one party in opposition to another – the evil attributes and emotions in justaposition to the holy emotions, and the way to overwhelm them is by war...However, in *Atik* there is no conflict whatsoever, and therefore, a revelation of a ray from this level, spontaneously subdues...

And this, then is what is meant when we say that the six days of the week are [associated with] "war" – the six days correspond to the six *sephirot* of *z'a*, associated with the "six days that *Havaya*" (of *z'a*) [created the universe].[151] But, about the Shabbat, it is written *vayishbot bayom hashvi'i ki bo Shabbat vayinafash*[152]– "He ceased working on the seventh day because the Shabbat arrived and it was the time of rest." This alludes to the elevation of [the spiritual level of] *z'a* to *atik*, to the place of the transcendent name *Havaya*. And from there, G-dliness descends to the ten *sephirot* above [in *Atzilut*], and similarly to the worlds below. From it emerges the *neshama yeteira*, or "added soul" that descends on Shabbat, and therefore Shabbat is a time of rest, as written, "Shabbat comes, rest arrives."[153] And then we are illuminated with the aspect of *naveh sha'anan* ("peaceful place"), the same level as *Atik*. And for that reason, work and labor are unnecessary, and the holy sparks are refined of their own volition.

In our *avoda*, this occurs as we learn Torah. As we know the Torah descends from Above. The origin of the Torah is also in *Atik*,

---

148. *Parshat Nasa* in the *Idra Rabba* page 136A
149. Isaiah 33:20
150. Exodus 15:3
151. Exodus 20:11
152. Genesis 2:2
153. Rashi on Genesis 2:2

as mentioned in the name of the *Remez*,[154] that *tzadikim*, with the power of their Torah, elevate *z'a* to *Atik*. This is similar to what happens on Shabbat when *z'a* ascends to *Atik*, as mentioned above. And this ascent takes place following a descent that precedes it, as the *Remez* writes that we "draw down the influx"…All the more-so, then, when an elevation occurs, a corresponding descent takes place as well. (The main spiritual elevation and descent mentioned above will occur in the future, but nevertheless something of the sort occurs now as well). This means that with the Torah, we draw down a revelation of the level of *Atik*. This is what is meant by, "And the words that I put into your mouth…"[155] – Here, the *Remez* explains that this is an allusion to *malchut* of A"K as it descends to become *keter* and *Atik* of *Atzilut* – this is what is drawn down into the mouth of man who learns Torah down here in this world.

Now, these are the two "orifices" [the word *pi* may also be translated as "edge" in relation to a sword, as above] of Torah – the higher, supernal "orifice" that is *malchut* of A"K descends to the physical mouth of man in this world. [This takes place when we learn] Torah, [and the resulting process] is also a path of refinement. Here, however, the refining process occurs spontaneously and of its own volition, as does "rest." It does not truly enclothe itself in the "body" of the object of refinement, nor does it get involved with it.[156] But it draws down the light, and thereby, the refinement takes place spontaneously.

However, the light must be drawn down to the "place" that needs refinement. We might say that is why the Torah becomes invested in physical objects…[This is] so that the light will descend to the place that needs elevation, because in so doing the place becomes refined. Nevertheless, it needn't become truly embedded in the body of the objective that requires refinement. For that reason, the power of refinement of Torah extends further than the power of refinement of prayer, since the Torah becomes invested in physical objects as well. [It even becomes invested in] objects that are forbidden and articles that are totally impure, and refines them as well. This is not true of prayer, which only operates on the animal soul…which is from *klipat noga*…This is because the refinement process of *tefila* requires en-clothement within the object, like "two who are wrestling," as mentioned above. And this en-clothement

---

154. R' Moshe Zacutto, important 18th century commentator on the Zohar
155. Isaiah 59:21
156. See the discourse *Vecol ha'am roim*, of the year *5655*, regarding the two types of refining of "direct light" and "reflected light."

takes place only in *klipat noga* – which is not true of Torah, which refines automatically. And for that reason the Torah is able to elevate and refine matters that are totally evil, coming from the three totally impure *klipot*, because the descent of light causes them to be nullified and refined.

And this is what is meant by "I established *shalom* in the land...and no sword will pass through..." – not even a sword of peace, since *tefila* is a sword of peace. It refers to the *avoda* that takes place by a process of "war." However, the *avoda* of Torah is not an *avoda* of the "sword" at all, and it does not require war at all, but rather refinement that takes place by way of *menucha* – rest.

According to the above, we may now understand the theme of the Chanuka candles, including the sages' statement, "The mitzvah is to place the Chanuka candles at the entrance of the house, just outside." And the *Tosfot* explained that this means "at the opening, near the public arena."[157] The Chanuka lights represent the descent of the light of Torah, since *Torah Ohr* – "Torah is light." As is known, the war of the Greeks was a spiritual war, in which they sought to make the Jews "forget Your Torah and turn away from the laws of Your divine will." And when the kingship of the House of Hasmoneans overcame and vanquished the Greeks, they decreed that we should light the Chanukah candles. In other words, they drew down the illumination of Torah as it exists in its source and origin, into *chochma* of *Atik*. And this also alluded to by the finding of a single jar of oil, sealed with the seal of the High priest. It is known that the High Priest represents the spiritual level known as *rav chesed* ("great kindness"), which is among the "thirteen strands of the beard" associated with the high spiritual level of *arich anpin*, whose source is in *mochin stima*. And, we know that *mochin stima* is the inner dimension of *keter*, as written elsewhere regarding the difference between *mochin stima* and the *gulgulta*, whose source is in *Atik*. And this level is equivalent to *shemen* ("oil"), which alludes to *chochma* of *Atik*, whose origin is the primordial *chochma* of A"K.[158] And with this oil, they kindled the Chanukah lights, meaning that they brought down the light of Torah as it exists in its source and origin.

Now, this is also what is meant by the phrase, "The Chanukah lights are eight"[159] – specifically eight – because they represent eight times the name *Havaya*, corresponding to the supernal name *Havaya*

157. *Mesechet Sofrim*, Ch. 20.
158. See the discourse, *Hinei Rivka Yotzait, 5659*, regarding *shemen tov*
159. Talmud Shabbat 21B

[that transcends the worlds completely]. We know that seven times *Havaya* corresponds to the name *Havaya* associated with *z'a* [of *Atizlut*], corresponding to the seven emotional attributes. But, eight times *Havaya* alludes to the supernal name *Havaya* [that transcends the entire *seder hishtalshelut*, or "hierarchy of spiritual creation"].

And that is why the sages decreed to place the Chanukah lights at the entrance to the house, toward the public arena. For, it is specifically the public arena that represents the *klipa*, or *sitra achra* ("forces of concealment," "other side," opposed to holiness). It symbolizes the total evil of the "three completely impure *klipot*" that are totally separate from the unity of G-d, and the Chanukah lights are intended to illuminate within this public arena as well. [This is] similar to Torah, which has the power to purify from Above to below, even in places that are totally evil. Similarly, the Chanukah lights draw down illumination even to light up the public arena, as written, "And *Havaya* will erase my darkness."[160] That is, the supernal name *Havaya* from Above repels even the coarse darkness of the three totally impure *klipot*, since it facilitates purification there as well. This means that [the *klipot*] become totally nullified as a result of the great revelation of light, and this then also purifies the small amount of good that was within them, so that it ascends to *kedusha*.

Possibly, we might say that this is similar to what happened in the days of Ezra, when the Torah was read outside – purposely – because at that time there was a predominance of *klipa*, as known, and therefore they read the Torah outside in the street, in order to crush and subdue the total evil of three impure *klipot*.

And regarding the [mitzvah of] the *parah adumah* ("red heifer"), which was performed outside [of the Temple], the most important element was the burning of the heifer. This was equivalent to incinerating the very embodiment of evil, which is totally bad, as known and written elsewhere. The mitzvah of the red heifer originates in *mochin stima* [the concealed source of *chochma*], as [King Shlomo said], "I said, I seek wisdom, but it is far from me,"[161] which is an oblique reference to *chochma stima* [concealed *chochma*], as written elsewhere. And therefore, the red heifer purifies even the impurity that is associated with death.[162] But, the ashes of the [red heifer] represent the remains of *talah bededulcha* [an unspeakably high spiritual level, beyond the source of concealed *chochma*, descending

---

160. Psalms 18:29
161. Ecclesiastes 7:23
162. See *Igeret Hakodesh* in *Tanya*, *siman* 28, in the discourse beginning *lamah nismecha*

from *Atik*, the internal dimension of *keter*], as written elsewhere, and within Torah we find the *tal Torah*, which is the *talah* ("dew") that "drips" from *Atik*.

And consequently, we may also understand why Chanukah commemorates the inauguration of the Temple – the *Beit Hamikdash* – as well as of the altar. Both are associated with Chanukah, from the word – *chinuch* – meaning "inauguration" (and also "education"). And therefore, on Chanukah, we read about the inauguration of the altar. Nevertheless, what is their connection with the kindling of the candles?

The answer is as follows; it was King Shlomo who constructed the Temple. That was a precise choice (from Above), as written, "And not you...but your son, who emerged from your loins, he will build the Temple in My Name." [163] And in Chronicles, it is written, "Shlomo will be his name, and I will establish peace in his days..." [164]

This indicates that during the time of the Temple, there was revelation of the infinite light of G-d from above *seder hishtalshelut*. The revelation was of the very essence of His infinite light, and it occurred mainly in the holy of holies, the place where the *aron* ("holy ark") was located. That was the precise location and the main site of revelation of the essential light of the infinite One. This is because in the *aron* were placed the tablets, which were the main manifestation of the Torah. And for that reason, the *aron* was also capable of inducing nullification of the *klipot* and *sitra achra*. For example, the *aron* preceded the Jews during their journeys in the "great and terrible desert, wherein were the snakes and scorpions..." [165] and it eliminated the snakes and scorpions. (Within the *aron* were the shards of the shattered tablets, as Rashi writes in *parshat Beha'alotcha* regarding the verse, "And the *aron*, covenant of HaShem proceeded before them..." [166] But the main refinement, it would seem, that took place through the *aron* was a result of the second set of tablets within them. [167])

This, then is the refinement process that takes place via the Torah; as a result of the revelation of infinite light from G-d that illuminates from the Torah, all [the *klipot* and extraneous forces] become

---

163. Chronicles 1, 17:4
164. Chronicles 1, 22:9
165. Deut. 8:15
166. Numbers 10:33
167. See *Likutei Torah* (of the *Ba'al HaTanya*), *parshat Masei* in the discourses about the "journeys," and see elsewhere regarding *kaiflyaim letoshia*.

spontaneously nullified. This comes from the revelation of the light of Torah that once shone in the holy of holies. And therefore the Temple was built specifically by Shlomo, since he was the "king who the peace was his."[168] The source of his soul was from the very essence of the infinite light from above *seder hishtalshelut*. And for this reason, he was a "man of rest," and everyone was nullified to him, as discussed above. And therefore it was he who built the temple.

Similarly, it is now understood why the inauguration of the Temple took place by lighting the Chanuka candles. As explained above, the candles represent the light of Torah in its source, in *chochma* of *Atik*. And therefore, the inauguration of the Temple took place via revelation of the infinite light of G-d in the Temple (in particular in the second Temple, where there was no *aron*). [The inauguration] occurred with the candles, which represent a descent of infinite light from the essence of G-dliness. And the inauguration of the altar in particular had to take place through this descent of infinite light from the very essence, since as known the altar represents *malchut*, and the refining process of *malchut* takes place from below to Above, requiring labor and effort. And in order to inaugurate the altar, there had to be a high revelation of light, as known from the parable regarding education of children. When we want to see them off to school for the first time, we give them gifts that are worth more than the event calls for, and similarly the inauguration of the altar took place with a descent of G-dliness from above, with the light of the Torah, which is equivalent to the theme of kindling the lights of Chanukah.

And that is why, when the princes of the tribes brought offerings for the inauguration of the altar, they lit incense on the outer altar. This was an act that otherwise always took place on the inner altar. Yet, at the time, there was a temporary command to burn the incense on the outer altar. It is known that the burning of incense brings down the very essence of G-dliness that transcends *seder hishtalshelut*, for the purpose of inaugurating the altar.[169] ...And in our case, the inauguration took place with the kindling of the Chanuka lights, bringing down revelation of *Keter*, which is the same as *Torah ohr* – the "light of the Torah."

(It is possible to explain this as a refinement process coming from the name *Ma'h* [the name *Havaya* spelled with *aleph's*, with gematria

168. Talmud *Shavuot* 35B
169. See *Likutei Torah*, in the discourse *Zot Chanukat Hamizbeach*

45], corresponding to the saying, "In *chochma*, all is purified,"[170] since *chochma* possesses the unique quality of *koach ma'h* – the "power of *ma'h* (*bitul*)." But, the main ingredient is the *ohr*, the light of *keter* (perhaps *chochma* is the infinite light within it)[171] ...and the purification process of *malchut* involves refinement with the name *Ba'n* [the name *Havaya* spelled with *hey's*, with gematria 52]. And within [that process] there must also be influx from the name *Ma'h*, and that is what occurs upon the revelation of the Torah).

And this, as well, explains why Chanukah is *chanu* – *kah*, wherein the word *kah* ("like" or "as") is associated with *malchut*, and Chanukah alludes to its descent and encampment within *kah*. This indicates that the infinite light from Above is drawn down into *malchut* so that *malchut* as well is in a state of *menucha* ("rest"), which is equivalent to the theme of encampment, being rest. That is, the *avoda* of *malchut* involves labor and effort, and there as well, the extraneous forces may siphon off energy. As in war, when the parties are wrestling with each other, and sometimes the "other side" appears victorious...since at any rate it "touches" [the side of holiness]...[This is] as written in Tanya, that anyone who wrestles...and this is also equivalent to the verse in the Torah [regarding the angel who wrestled with Yakov], "And he touched the socket of his thigh..."[172] However, when the revelation of infinite light descends to illuminate within *malchut*, it provides "protection" so that there can be no siphoning off [of energy] by the extraneous forces. Quite the opposite; they are nullified and the purification takes place restfully, "in peace."

This, then is what is meant by "And I established peace in the land." The verse is referring to the "land" of *malchut*, and implies that even there, all should take place in peace, restfully. And this is also the theme of *padah beshalom nafshi* – "I redeemed my soul in peace"[173] – wherein "my soul" is the soul of David, representing *malchut*. This occurs because *berabim hayu imadi* – "since many were with me"[174] – alluding to *verav shalom banayich* ("much peace to your

---

170. Tanya, *Igeret Hakodesh* Ch. 28 cites the Zohar. See also *Eitz Chaim, Sha'ar* 18 Ch. 5; and *Sha'ar* 42, *Drash* 1, where the language of the text is *b'machshava itbariru* – "In thought, all is purified."

171. See *Likutei Torah* in the explanation, *Mi manah*, regarding *keshot atzmecha*

172. Genesis 32:26

173. Psalms 55:19

174. End of the verse, Psalms 55:19

children"[175]), through learning Torah, and in this way, "I redeemed my soul in peace," in *menucha* ("rest")...

175. Isaiah 54:13